WHISPERS AT DUSK

The National Library of Poetry

Diana Zeiger, Editor

Whispers at Dusk

Library of Congress
Cataloging in Publication Data

ISBN 1-57553-161-5

Proudly manufactured in The United States of America by
Watermark Press
One Poetry Plaza
Owings Mills, MD 21117

Editor's Note

When one thinks of poetry, one's first thoughts are often of flowery declarations of love, filled with sentimental feelings and warm memories. Many a suitor has wooed — and won — his lady fair with recitations of romantic verse; countless poetic tributes have been paid to loved ones and fallen heroes alike. A poet labors to create art, to craft language into graceful forms; at the same time, the poet must use that language to communicate emotions, thoughts, and ideas. Beautiful language most naturally expresses beautiful thoughts — they flow together in a glorious harmony.

What happens, then, when a poet chooses as a subject something that is less than aesthetically pleasing? Is it possible to make art from the unpalatable? Indeed, such a task would be a great challenge to a poet's skills.

For example, "Lilacs Blooming Above the Backyard Grave" (p. 190) by Peter Rojcewicz is about a boy's recollections of his grandfather, which at first might seem a straightforward, sentimental subject. But there are few sweet memories here: the grandfather is dying, and his presence in the boy's home has created tension between the child's parents:

> *Why father turned away, his face tightening like rope*
> *when the old man entered a room, I didn't know. Why*
> *mother wept, speaking softly to herself behind the bedroom door.*

The boy senses that there is something wrong, but is unable to define what it is.

The grandfather is portrayed as someone who is not quite real to the boy: "...I knew him as footfalls against boards of the attic floor, / crystal radio voices fading and returning through the night." The more specific memories he has are not pleasant:

> *He became the wizened dwarf of dreams, drawing*
> *breath from my lungs while we slept. At eighty-five,*
> *he coughed up blood, warming his prosthetic leg by the fire.*

The old man seems to make both a nuisance and an embarrassment of himself, having "[cursed] / shadows from his pine chair on the porch"; he then dances clumsily — even drunkenly — in the garden.

i

In spite of the problems the grandfather causes, the family perseveres until the end, knowing they are doing "the right thing" by caring for him in his waning years. At the close of the poem, although the old man has died, his essence remains with the family:

> *...the man died at home*
> *laid below the bush behind the house where*
> *he can rise nightly through our blood.*

It is implied that even after the old man's death, the unhappiness that his presence created in the household remains.

"Lilacs Blooming Above the Backyard Grave" is a skillfully-crafted poem that features a good descriptive style and well-developed characters. It is moving without being melodramatic; it elevates an unpleasant situation into art through poetic language.

Steven Bromley's "The Beauty Of A Bruise" (p. 292) not only elevates the unpleasant through poetic language, it seeks to find and display the beauty in the unpleasantness itself. This poem sets forth the notion that we are all artists creating great works simply by experiencing our lives:

> *Continuous projections of color appear*
> *on a canvas made by birth;*
> *resolutions in patterns*
> *describe each artist as a painting -*
> *a masterpiece in constant motion.*
> ....
> *The cells of the body, like notes of a symphony,*
> *play aloud the rhythms of life.*

In such a context, a bruise (traditionally, an unsightly symbol of pain) can be considered a vibrant display of colors which occurred while living life. It is nothing short of beautiful.

"Purge" (p. 1), by Alena Smith, takes an unflinching look at another less-than-pleasant subject. This work is a harsh portrait of bulimia painted through the eyes of a woman who suffers from this disorder. "Purge" also notes how society has made the pursuit of physical beauty, especially thinness, into a virtual religion. Eating and enjoying food is a sin; one must either avoid this altogether or purge oneself of the food in order to be "holy." The poem condemns society for this practice, for reducing women to such horrifying rituals in order to be made "clean."

The bathroom in which the poem is set becomes a confessional, wherein the persona feels "guilty." Not only is she ashamed for having sinned (eaten), but perhaps she is also feeling guilt over the act she is about to perform, which, after all, is viewed with disgust by most of society. The bathroom is a cold, unwelcoming place; it seems indifferent to her suffering:

> *it is brutally sanitized and painfully tiled*
> *with bleak white linoleum that smells*
> *like nothing earthborn; alien to roughness,*
> *chemically rendered numb.*

In this setting, the toilet becomes the priest to whom the persona "confesses" her sins: it "is like the porcine, bleached face of a / priest; fleshy arrogance squeezed into a plain black ruff."

The persona is fearful and nervous as she prepares to rid herself of her sins; in addition, she seems fragile despite her determination:

> *...eyes glazed and*
> *breaths frighteningly hurried, each one catching up*
> *with the next like a chaotic race of dandelion seeds,*
> *grey, wistful, and long dead, blown*
> *into a dry, airy, intricate stream of vortices.*

Ultimately, her "confession" is painful, both in a physically and emotionally:

> *...She is at once*
> *ashamed and convulsing. Her sobs embarrass her:*
> *each gagging cry is a declaration of her weakness.*

The persona appears to feel as shamed by the penance she must perform as by the sin itself.

The fact that this suffering is self-inflicted, in addition to the fact that its purpose is to achieve a goal that seems terribly superficial, lends a certain bitterness to the final line of the poem: "Sins disgorged and flushed, she is frail, but she is holy." In sum, the poem is a commentary on the futility of pursuing the grail of ideal feminine beauty, and it questions the worth of such beauty when one must use such agonizing means to achieve it.

With "Purge," Alena Smith has created a vivid portrait of a woman who is suffering extreme torment, yet bears it alone. The well-chosen language of this poem brings this persona to life and allows the reader to empathize with her pain. For these reasons, the judges and I have awarded Alena Smith the Grand Prize in the contest held in association with **Whispers at Dusk**.

There are many other notable poems in this anthology, and these are a few that I recommend you read with special attention: "Transmission Torment" by Dianne Brooks (p. 178), "Time Through A Pepper Shaker" by Matia Burnett (p. 429), Jeffrey Dassel's untitled poem (p. 164), "Jellyfish" by Bill Kress (p. 138), "Sonnet #8" by Stephanie Larson (p. 185), "Demobilization" by Wendy Rondette (p. 196), "Nights Under The Roundtable" by Dave Swanson (p. 169), and "Beer" by G. C. Thomas. I wish that time and space permitted me to provide an individual critique for every poem in *Whispers at Dusk*, but as they do not, I would just like to commend every poet featured herein.

I would also like to thank all the editors, assistant editors, and customer service, administrative, and general services staff who have brought to bear their considerable talents during the publication of *Whispers at Dusk*. My heartfelt gratitude goes out to them all.

Diana Zeiger
Editor

Cover Art: Tracy Hetzel

iv

Grand Prize Winner

Alena Smith / Millbrook, NY

Second Prize

Steven Bromley / Haddonfield, NJ
Dianne Brooks / Pueblo, CO
Matia Burnett / Ferndale, WA
Jeffrey Dassel / Hockessin, DE
Bill Kress / Minnetonka, MN

Stephanie Larson / Falls Church, VA
Peter Rojcewicz / New York, NY
Wendy Rondette / Saint Louis, MO
Dave Swanson / Deerfield, IL
G. C. Thomas / North Haven, CT

Third Prize

Mia Albright / Bronx, NY
Nancy Anderson / Keizer, OR
Margaret Askey / Sherman Oaks, CA
Laura Baber / Sturgis, MI
Rabbi Karen Bender / Douglaston, NY
Larissa Biggers / Atlanta, GA
E. A. Book / Beaufort, NC
Dave Buracker / Harrisonburg, VA
Robert Collins / DeKalb, IL
Scott Craig / Wyckoff, NJ
Rhonda Crews / Warrensburg, MO
Dorothy De Spain / Barrington, IL
Caroline Driggs / Darien, CT
Ethel Engnath / Kingston, NY
Rachael Falber / Wallkill, NY
Kathy Fontenot / Chattanooga, TN
Janet Gardner / Rocky Hill, NJ
Kathleen Gibbons / Lutz, FL
Frances Gorman / San Francisco, CA
Heather Green / Crystal Lake, IL
Lou Guttman / Rochester, NY
Antony Haynes / Champaign, IL
Anneliese Heimburg / Sacramento, CA
Colin Higgins / Chicago, IL
L. Virginia Holland / Clayton, MO
Ralph Jerles / Nappanee, IN
Robert Kluever / Westminster, CA
Danita Kolb / Brookhaven, PA
Christian Kuznia / Rochester, NY
Suzanne LaMarre / New York, NY

Henry Lash / Mobile, AL
Robert Leider / Plainview, NY
Julie Madnick / New York, NY
R. C. Miller / Davenport, IA
Joanne Monte / Bloomfield, NJ
E. J. Netzel / Portage, WI
Susan Peck / Clifton Park, NY
Sonya Petroff / East Missoula, MT
Rick Pope / Atlanta, GA
Patrick Preston / Webbville, KY
Alan Pyeatt / West Hollywood, CA
Margaret Radzilowski / Richmond, MI
Tiller Russell / Dallas, TX
Marjorie Russin / Silver Spring, MD
Heather St. John / Saint Louis, MO
Victoria Sebanz / Claremont, CA
M. Seton / New York, NY
Cassandra Shook / Morrison, CO
Janet Skingor / Glastonbury, CT
Frank Stiffel / Flushing, NY
Richard Thomas / Charlotte, NC
Luis Tijerina / Brattleboro, VT
David Vail / Farmington, NY
K. A. Wandlass / Kew Gardens, NY
Clarence Washington / Boston, MA
Craig Watson / Cardiff, CA
Mike Weltz / Washington, DC
Gus Wilhelmy / Chicago, IL
Grover Wilson III / Blacksburg, VA

Congratulations also to our Editor's Choice Winners!

Purge
She feels guilty in the bathroom:
it is brutally sanitized and painfully tiled
with bleak white linoleum that smells
like nothing earthborn; alien to roughness,
chemically rendered numb. The bathroom's
scent, unnatural and frigid, slashes its stainless
blade down her tautly strained spine.
The bloodless bowl condescends to notice her
nervously determined stare; eyes glazed and
breaths frighteningly hurried, each one catching up
with the next like a chaotic race of dandelion seeds.
grey, wistful, and long dead, blown
into a dry, airy, intricate stream of vortices.
The toilet is like the porcine, bleached face of a
priest; fleshy arrogance squeezed into a plain black ruff.
Tears like wounded, grieving prisms irritate the surface
of the calm depths of morality. She is at once
ashamed and convulsing. Her sobs embarrass her:
each gagging cry is a declaration of her weakness.

Sins disgorged and flushed, she is frail, but she is holy.
Alena Smith

First Kiss

In tender touch
that didn't ask a thing,
two lips met in cautious mingling.
Then the world exploded
and filled the sky with stars,
and lightning flashed and thunder crashed
and all that was... was ours.
And when the pandemonium was stilled
I reveled in the joy of this...
no other moment could surpass
the marvel of my first kiss.

Connie Hess

The Rubber Band, Mundane Eternity

A rubber band, forever?
You must have slipped your rocker.

Round, like the mother egg,
with no beginning and no end,
the rubber band whispers its eternity.

The egg cracked up to be, isn't!
But the rubber band, harmonious with the world,
flexibly flushing stresses and vicissitudes,
returns to its ovality.

Mary, my paper lady,
embraces my copy with a band,
so it won't festoon the bushes,
as she unerringly aims at my doorstep,
for another bull's-eye triumphant.

I treasure these bands for Mary,
tho' we have never met.
When over their box they flood,
at Mary's ground zero it is placed,
and the inevitable cycle takes off again.

Charles N. Bernstein

My Ghost And I

It seems that wherever I go and whatever I do my friend is always there. I can't make a move without a hullabaloo because my friend will laugh and stare. In my sleep at night I am comforted down, by my friend who is anxious and funny. For she only knows what a beautiful rose, she makes my life so sunny. I have played to her, sang to her, and worked myself to a frazzle. But only to find that she is not mine, because she isn't there in the hassle. And when I awake for goodness sake, she's standing there with a smile on her face, encouragement on her lips for me to get up and start my earing. I have fun with her out the day and she finds me quite amusing. For you know down right that she's out of sight and it's of my own choosing. I'd rather have a friend like her watching over me with eyes like an owl. whenever I find my luck runs out she's always there to wipe off my scowl. I know she's only a shadow in thought but don't have another to follow. She has saved my life over again, when she only knew there was only a ghost of a chance, but I love her and she loves me because we only have each other to follow.

Raymond A. Hannes

Unnecessary Trash

Wherever you live you might say or think that there is nothing to do.

Unfortunately, there is unnecessary trash on the ground and if you leave it there, that's up to you.

This unnecessary trash shouldn't be there.

All people can be smart enough or taught to use trash cans. These people do care.

I've seen the need for trash pick-up in Philipsburg, PA and I do. It just takes a few more helpers where ever you live, what about you?

Robert Scott Shoff

Firefly

Golden firefly twinkle for me
while I reach out my hand to catch you
and gently imprison you one little while
as I study your signals;
then let you rejoin your answering mate
who flutters and waits.
Your glow in the darkness is cheerful
and though you're devoid of song
your twinklings fill me with wonder
as I watch you the whole night long.
Firefly, firefly, what is your message?
If only we knew what you say
as you lull us to deep contemplation
and chase away cares of the day.

Sara E. Blundin

Alone At Oak Run

Sitting alone out at Oak Run.
Watching another sitting sun.
With a heavy heart that aches within.
Thinking thoughts of what might have been.
Whisper I love you, I feel a breeze.
Perhaps it's your soul, I am at ease.
I hear you call me far away.
I shall be with you dear one day.
So long we've been kept apart.
Left here alone, with half a heart.
I feel your kisses touch my hair.
I know you and I will eternity share.
I know you still are far away.
but we'll be together again one day.
Love will bring us together, it's our fate.
I'll join you in Heaven, but now you must wait.
I'm walking alone, thinking of you.
Wondering if you perhaps join me too.
Each time I come alone to this lake.
I think of the day God chose you to take.

Karen A. Pierson

Redemption

When summer comes
And lushes earth with green bouquets
To shelter creatures deep within,

The heart remembers times
When glee took flight on wings
Of simple things,

Brown children,
Barefoot slipping through earth's ecstasy,
Eyes worshipping the sky,

Overflowing wonder
Like water from a dipper
Baptizing future sins.

James Hartsell

Damned To Winter's Fate

The forest is tainted with the pungent colors of fall.
Rebellious green trees resist the inevitable autumn's grasp.
They are nonetheless damned to winter's fate.
Strong, proud trees... their trunks shattered by a storm's wrath—
in their broken state, they continue to spawn and nurture their brother moss.
The forest strives as one.
Nature is but a symbiote, bonding and possessing the earth, defying the desolation of man.
It is not damned to the fate of man.

David Moats

'Al'

"Al" is so good it is hard to believe
A young boy could be as good as he
I pray he always stays that way
As he goes though life day by day
I sure do love this boy named "Al"
Who is really my old pal
It breaks my heart, that I can't do
To play the games he wants me to
He loves to run and loves to play ball
But I'm too old and can't see at all
When Al gets old he will understand
You can't do things young people can
I won't be around to hear "Al" say
Now I know why gramma wouldn't play
I'll always be watching in the sky above
Over my number one grandson, whom I really love

Donna Cattoi

The Perfect World

The perfect world that I can see
Is a place where flowers dance happily
In the sky while sunshine brightens smiles
Birds will sing for many miles
On the ground where trees sway in the breeze
Children play outside with ease.

Jackie Gunther

Valleys Of Hurt

There is a peak in which I can stand,
Where I can see for miles, the very rich land.
Most times I'm angry, others I'm not-
There are times free of worry, when I wish I'd forgot-
The pain that lies below, for it's too far to see-
From up here, all I want is to be free.
I rarely go there anymore,
Because when I come down, I'm hurt to the core.
The hurt lasts longer than the joy I've felt-
I often wonder why, these cards I've been dealt.
Why can it be, that my luck has run dry-
When the experiences I've had, have led me to fly,
Fly far away, to a world of being alone-
Where thoughts always linger, on why I condone-
This behavior I have, of letting my life be taken astray-
By people I forgive, but have hurt me anyway.
I often wonder, how these situations start-
And I am left to ponder the lost piece of my heart.

C. Patrick Jordan

Listen To The Quiet

I must find a quiet time:
Away from the press, the hurry,
Away from the fret, the worry;
A time for introspection,
A time to seek direction,
A time to be alone with God.

I must find a quiet place:
Where man has lightly trod,
To see on every hand the handiwork of God;
To pause in awe and wonder.
To meditate and ponder... and
To listen to the quiet.

Willette Caudle McGuire
Be still, and know that I am God:
Psalm 46:10

Times - Past, Present And Future

Like birds that sing and birds that fly
we built our house high in the sky.
As years go by thing change - gone are the mournful
sounds of the fog horn and the whistle of the train
going into the station miles to the West.
Fox with her babies live in the woodpile, mountain
lions visit us now and then, red tailed hawk screams
from the canyon, native birds greet us each day
with mocking birds serenading us from tree tops.
Gone are the Condors that used to circle and soar
in air currents high above the mountain.
Yuccas bloom and stand on hillside like army
dressed in white, mariposas, gold and orchid bloom
at roadside. Toyan with red berries and manzanita
with cinna colored trunks and small ivory apples
are everywhere.
The bright round, full moon comes from behind
the mountain as the colorful sun sinks into the pacific ocean.
This place is so peaceful I will never be ready to leave
this land of the Indians that is now our home.

Peggy Gonzalez

Time

Yesterday's tomorrow is tomorrow's yesterday,
Tomorrow's yesterday is today,
Today and tomorrow were the same yesterday,
Since yesterday's tomorrow is today,

All of our tomorrows and all our yesterdays,
Exist not but for today,
All we've ever been and all we'll ever be,
Exist in us in what we are this day,

We can't wait until tomorrow to live our lives and love,
And yesterday's romance never dies.
Unless the past and future present themselves today,
There'll be no change despite our ardent tries,

Yesterday's tomorrow is tomorrow's yesterday.
Tomorrow's yesterday is today,
Today and tomorrow were the same yesterday,
Since yesterday's tomorrow is today.

Steven C. Heaton

Love Lives On

A pillow rests upon the overstuffed chair,
my long legged boyfriend used to sit there,
he has passed on the heaven now and my heart is bare,
he only told me of the pain in his back and sat on a cushion,
when I could not believe he was dying he called me "unfeeling,"
had I known he had cancer I would have been reeling!
He had asked me to marry him but we didn't know then,
how very sick he would be and would be taken so soon from me,
From his home to the hospital he was taken for special care,
he couldn't stop staring at me when I came there,
coming from behind him as he lay there
I had kissed his forehead with a silent prayer,
This dearest man of my heart and love of my life,
my close and only sweet heart for ever ten years
was now facing death and I was close to tears,
His suffering would be over soon
but now our love filled the room!
Our boundless love will live on and forever on.

Lorena Barrett

"As Though Descended From A Guardian-Kind Of Planet"

Far away and long ago-and as though perhaps predestined-
There was sent, as a slave and a gift from important Christians
A one of their own, a teen-aged youth named Patrick.
To the Druids in old Ireland, young Patrick was delivered
As though to serve a sentence! But, Nobility tends to sire
Nobility...and soon young Patrick had come to seem
More like son than slave to themselves, the very ancient
And somewhat mysterious tribe of Priests and Judges-the
Druids, of old Ireland in the so-called 'Misty Isles'.

Nobility tends to sire Nobility, even when adopted!-
And, pretty soon or by and by the early Christian Church
Of Patrick (and the benevolent little Druids) had been extended
Throughout the fabled 'Misty Isles' and into Northern Europe.

For, the small-boned Druids of all the shapely heads and
often reddish hair, had recognized young Patrick as, being,
Like themselves from his earliest and previous teachings!
Even if not directly from ancient Egypt, the Church of Christian
Patrick would be blessed, by way of all the poetically mysterious
Ancestors, of those firstly pre-evolved and finest things, the
Small-boned and shapely-headed, 'migratorative' Druids.

Canadia Collins

Mother Earth

Oh Mother Earth! Oh Miracle! Oh Heaven that's alive,
your heart's beat I hear everywhere in species all alive.
Whether is the birds that sing, the people or the soil,
whether are animals alive or life which is being spoiled.
I hear your heart beat at the tide each time I go by,
and always reminds me how much you are alive.
Your speed which goes around each time, a symbol all so great,
oh mother Earth you give us life around the clock each day.
You spin in circles always as to wish to say,
that nothing dies when you're alive but it recirculates,
when we are alive we are one with you through your atmosphere,
and when we pass away again we are one with your body and
heart so dear.

Sophia Demas

Dear Friends

She's passed away,
  But not to linger in the ground;
A happier life she's found
  In Heaven, with God!

When Christ shall come
  And take our hand to lead the way
To our new home, some happy day,
  We'll tread the path she's trod!

We'll feel no pain — our minds will be alert,
  No way again, can we ever be hurt;
Friends old and new we'll see — relatives, too,
  I'm looking forward to that day — aren't you?

Marilyn Ruth Dahlgren

The Big Island

Oozing lava is flowing along making the Big Island bigger than all
of the other islands around. Hawaii is growing bigger. The lava
is creating more ground. The new flow of lava is covering black
sand beaches, forest and homes. Even the road has been shortened
as the lava flows over the ground. Red hot lava is changing the
landscape as it slowly flows on. Who knows what the future
dimensions of the Big Island will be as the slow moving lava
continues to flow into the sea.

Alyce M. Nielson

What Is Reality?

Is life a hallucination, a figment of ones imagination?
Is the innate desire to create so strong, in humans, that he
must imagine reality?
Is what we see really so, or is there room for doubt?
Do you really see the stars at night, but intelligently realize
that millions of those stars are "burnt out", just holes in space.
What is reality?
That which we imagine we see, or that which we know?
Vivid imagination creates reality.
Do we imagine a brilliant sun moving across the sky or do we
know there is nothing but a small star in the galaxy and the
earth is revolving around it?
Are we real or is some strong need of others, on the same
crowded plane as we, making us real.
Is life real or do we imagine it to be so?

LuJuan Bartlett

Education

What is Education? It is the knowledge of knowing.

Education provides instruction to your life which can be cherished
for the rest of your life.

Everyone needs to have the vision to complete their education for a
higher standard of living.

Education will allow you to achieve, encourage, influence, and
teach others who will follow after you.

Education keeps the mind ticking like a clock, and provides
self-empowerment.

Education is for everyone who so desires to enrich their minds.

Through education the brain consumes positive information for
growth, reasoning, and understanding.

Education will allow you to command and demand your expectations
for self.

Education will keep you cultivated, motivated, and stimulated.

Rita Marks

Time Enough

If time is a road leading to infinity,
Why must life be progressive?
Why can't I sit beside the road,
Watch for a while, then go on?
Or walk beside the road and look over at time passing?
Or move obliquely at a different rate?
Or retrace my steps? Or turn left or right?
If the road was a spiral
Could I jump from track to track?
I can see back on the road, why can't I see forward?
What of our individual perceptions of time:
A man, a tortoise, a humming bird, or a butterfly?
Would time inversion cause storms,
Ripples in the fabric of time,
As does temperature inversion?
If I travel in time, could I meet myself?
Would this cause and explosion or an implosion,
Two bodies occupying the same place at the same time?
Then I become an anachronism to myself.
Time enough to think of time.

Philip A. Eckerle

What Answer Do We Give — ?

How can we, the world's richest nation,
Turn our backs on mass starvation,
Pretending that we just don't see
The needs of a suffering humanity?

Are we not, after all, our brother's keeper?
Should we not dig a little deeper,
And share some portion of our plenty
With all of those who have not any?

That we inhabit the richest land on earth
Is not because of our own special worth,
But because we've been blessed from above
By our Lord's great mercy and abundant love.

So when we lie beneath the sod,
I wonder what we say to almighty God,
When He asks us to explain why
We stood by, as so many of His children died?

C. N. Wesson

Mouse Trap

Dark House on a tall, tall hill,
Everything is quiet, everything is still.
I'm alone in the middle of the room,
I'm all alone with my thoughts of you.

The mouse in the corner is staring at me,
Trapped in my trap he wants to be free.
I just might free him, you never know,
I just might free him, but what would it show?

He might just wander until he dropped dead,
Maybe go crazy, go out of his head.
No, I don't think I'll set him free,
I'll keep him trapped, like you keep me.

Spencer L. Willardson

Turn Of The Century

At the turn of the century everything was good.
Prosper prosper was the word, no boys in the hood.
Then came along the first world war life as we know ended
Blood and guts and peace no more things never to be mended.

Then came along the second one more vicious than the first.
Whole nations organized to kill and quench a bloody thirst
Korea, Nam and Desert Storm the carnage has not abated
Kennedy King and Kennedy all assassinated.

Civil rights and women's lib and riots in the street.
An evil presence plays the tune and we march to the beat.
War, hunger, Aids and poverty, little kids with guns.
Murders, rapes and suicides, tarnished priests and nuns.

Shattered lives, twisted metal, blood and broken glass
The dead and crying innocent victims of a terrorist's blast.
Cancer eats a friend I've loved wish I could bear her hurt.
We turn our heads and count our change while man pollutes the earth.

If I could travel in back time I'd change these hundred years
I'd use the knowledge that I had to minimize the tears.
But since I can't I'll do my best to sow good seed I vow.
The past is gone let's learn from it the future starts right now.

P. H. Medina

In The Wind

I know I'm always on the outside of your heart,
you just wouldn't open your heart's door to me.
And I just cry and I cry, even tho I wonder why.
It seems our love is out there somewhere, in the wind.
I'm like an eagle coasting in the wind; when I'm with you,
you make my spirits soar.
You lift me up, where I just seem to fly, so high,
in the wind.
You lift me up, where, I just seem to fly so high.
I'm like a stone from the street, without any destiny.
I just seem to roll and roll, I just seem to roll and roll.
But God knows the plan, he has for me, only for now,
it's in the wind.
I'm like an eagle coasting in the wind, when I'm with you.
You make my spirit soar, you lift me up. I just seem to fly so high
in the wind.

John W. Newman

Bird Dog

He was born on a Texas ranch in the middle of the night.
The north wind blew, it rained and it was awful cold,
A pure bred bird dog pup that was bound to be sold,
Perhaps he would be bought by a bird hunter, so bold.

With any luck his master will make his future so bright,
By training him well to be an outstanding bird dog,
He has all the traits to hunt in the bright day or fog,
When he points to the birds he always as still as a log.

Well his master turns out to be a bird hunting giant,
And the dog was just perfect during his training phase,
He found the birds and could work study for days,
He became a champion dog in the bird hunting craze.

During the off season the bird dog's duty was light,
Laid around the house all summer and got lazy and fat,
He had a good temper and made friends with the cat,
When the new season started he had his duties down pat.

William J. Morgan

Friendship Of Harmony

Our friendship was forged by the hand of God and put together
as a unique package, a very special gift, that keeps on giving down
through the years.

As friends we walk side by side or lend a listening ear, open
heart, and a mind not lending to judgement, but giving into the moral
support and words of encouragement.

For our life is like a river filled with rapids and rough spots,
but it smooths out when the faith is felt and God's hand intercedes.

For us, Jesus stands at the helm of our lives and we walk that path
every day holding in our hearts one prayer of peace, one of hope which
is harmony for one and all, and in nature, and the other is a dream of
understanding for all of mankind.

Far greater than the gifts, we receive and will be placing beneath
the tree. Is the gift Jesus gave to both of us, our friendship of
caring and a warmth of understanding.

Sandra Allen

Mother

You've always known the way I feel.
I know you want my pain to heal.

I will be strong, I will get by.
But, it's so hard to say good-bye.

If... what we believe is true, a better
Place awaits for you.

And those we've known, who've gone before.
Will meet you there at heaven's door.

I'd gladly walk this path for you,
But I know you wouldn't want me to.

So, I search my heart for what to say
Before you have to go away.

Bonnie K. Hills

Juliet Roams The Earth

You've allowed yourself to carry that torch
For the rest of your life you'll bear that cross

Juliet roams the earth
insatiable being, unquenchable thirst
Thousands of years in unrest on a never-ending search
Now we must all beware her touch
lest we fall victim to her vengeful curse

Just when you thought it was safe to die
the winds grew wild and tormented the tides
Waters raged and waves grew high
as spiteful spirit turned rain into fire

Juliet moves the earth
How does she touch us and what is it worth
Thousands of years in unrest seeking potion for her thirst
Now we raise our empty vessels
Toast temptations, timeless vengeful curse

K. A. Wandlass

Virginia

I'll never see the aleppo's reaching for the sky
And the skinny eucalyptus rising up high
But I'll think of my darling caring for her trees
With her golden hair tangled by the breeze

And when I hear the turtle doves cooing away
Searching for their mates at the end of the day
I'll think of my Ginny and our 38 years
Now all in the past and blurred by my tears

And when I see the lilacs bloom in early spring
And hear the mocking birds as they merrily sing
I'll remember the days on our rock covered hill
And wish that time had then stood still

John L. Floyd

Love Again

If I say I love you would you run away, or would you stay
that's what I ask my self over and over again, I think I am
falling in love with you again.
If you stay and love me I will give you in return my heart forever.....
Many times you heard my words that I cared for you and
wanted you as my man but silly me I just didn't see
my friends say I am stupid to love you and you don't even care
I gave you my heart and you gave it away that's when I promised
myself to never love you again, but when I heard you liked
her my heart just fell and to this day that's where it's at
I could cry, I could be sad but what's the use I will just end up mad.
Many times I thought it would change and my love for you
would not cause me pain and maybe one day we could be friends
But will I ever love again.....

Megan West

War No More

Warrior, Warrior, do you hear the battle's cry?
Does it lure you to leave hearth and home?
To postpone dreams, plans and love for life?
Will you heed the call for destruction and death?
Must You Go?

Warrior, Warrior, look around you,
See the fear in your loved ones' eyes,
They dread the return of a broken body, or no return at all.
Must You Go?

Warrior, Warrior, whose command do you obey?
Whose hatred and greed do you honor?
Which nation needs to be extinguished?
Which mother's child to be destroyed?
Must You Go?

Warrior, Warrior, for the love of God and self,
No more hate, and above all, no more wars,
Turn guns into plowshares,
Or is our world and life to be destroyed?
To the powers with greed, we plead...
Don't Make Them Go!—War No More!

Janet C. Blechner

Like Father Like Son

A young black male joins in a gang.
Didn't have a father so him he blames.
Look up to his OGs, called them his uncles and his daddies.
Them young Gs he called them his brothers and his rels.
Didn't get jumped in cause he was raised in the set.
The ones we know as pimps, killers, and hustlers he gives them respect.
His momma tried her hardest to keep him away,
But she knew he was bound to do it cause look where they stay.
She knew he was bound to fall in the gang,
Cause all the youngsters in the neighborhood did the same.
She even saw their mothers trying to hold on tight,
But they all gave up because their kids was wrapped up
    by the street light.
She even prayed to God to let her son be strong,
But only thing he saw was people doing wrong.
She even tried to send him to away out school.
The mothers in her neighborhood tried the same thing too,
But it didn't do no good.
Their kids were away for a little while then back to the hood.
His momma where tried but the trouble was done.
So only thing she thinks like father like son.

Damon Rx Colbert

Musings

Watching Gamble Quails is a lot of fun
They never walk, they always run.
I think the devil must be on their tails,
Could they ever slow down?
Those hurrying Gamble quails!

Estella M. Provencher

The Undefined

A life of death, undaunted, unbroken, undefined.
The will to die by my own hand was overwhelming
The world had left me standing on the precipice of life
alone in a vacuum.
I must face the truth of my convictions,
Self destruction is not the answer.
I need strength and courage to hold my life together
and release the bonds that have strapped my mind.
As set trails in the sky dissipate and die.
So will I.
Another bell has rung, another song unsung
We know not why.

Betty Derby

Trees, Rain, Wind

The pine and the maple stood side by side
They talked about the weather
They talked about the fall,
The maple tree said, "Woe is me, I hate to lose my leaves"
The pine tree replied, "Poor maple you look as if you'd freeze",

The wind heard them talking
and that he would help a lot.
So he took the maple leaves
and placed them on the pine tree
Now he thought, "I must get them to stay".

Then the rain came tumbling down
like a bad boy
more like a clown.
He crushed the leaves on the pine needles
and threw them on the ground!

The wind was sad but he didn't get mad,
He grabbed the rain and froze it up tight;
and covered the tree with the glitter so bright,
The maple was happy and warm you see?
and everyone said, "What a Beautiful Tree".

Florence E. Maxwell

Shoreline

The sea breathed with a sigh
As gulls soared treetops high
  And white golden sun was shining;

White pebbles on the beach
Beyond arm's length to reach
  Lovers stroll, and families are dining.

No longer can this scene be true
The population exploded and quickly grew,
  Now more high rises dot the skyline;

Tourists in cabanas jut along the shore
Where once white sand was an empty floor,
  Tomorrow the lights of a city will shine.

Carol Newport

Memorable 2nd Chance Love

This 2nd chance love that answered their dreams,
on loan from the Lord, his glory of schemes;
met them head-on, gladdened their days,
with sharing and caring in numerous ways.

Lifted two hearts, their spirits did soar;
in toil and in sparks their lives did explore.
A wondrous passage in days and in years
for two lovely people their neighbors find dear.

We count just the moments when such lives entwined
for memories most precious of a couple so kind.
As one life is re-claimed, our Lord sends his love;
good memories remain as His strength from above.

To comfort and nurture the ones who must grieve,
we recall a full picture for all to retrieve!
This 2nd chance love left us the seeds
for planting a garden of memories sweet dreams.

Patricia L. Purrett

Song Of Moderation

Sing the song of moderation
Harmonize in realm of reason
Polish the sheen of common sense
Mellow note lived in modest manner.

New sound in tones of temperance
Humble music for our true worth
Keyed for behavior and conduct
Unlock the silken strands of virtue.

Play on the chords of courtesy
Tranquil pleasures linger longer
Pluck harp strings to psalms of patience
Be a good companion to wisdom.

Great action with grace is charming
Worthy praise of friends is a hymn
Cover your talents with a veil
Trust the giver of gifts from above.

Myrl Newhouse

Untitled

I know how little cares the world for grief
How little mercy comes when needed most —
For I have heard the hollow trumpetings proclaim
Affected Christian virtues of a yet barbaric host.

Long have I seen the way of greed,
The selfish pulse that pounds in every blood,
Triumphant o'er the ones who bleed —
As might, in mass, perverts the bad to good.

While man pretends and basks behind the law
That he creates to meet his minute needs,
The greater forces, still beyond his grasp,
Sweep on the natheless current he but feeds!

And, thus, the ageless serial pursues
The ending of the tale that's never told!
While I? The nearest Christian rite embrace
And, Pagan-like, preserve my most Un-Christian mold!

Joel Wright

The Trees In All Their Splendor

The mighty oak from a little acorn grew
Lifting its branches towards the sky so blue.
It watches over the shrubs and other trees
As it bends and sways in the warm summer breeze.

Of the maples, the best are the sugar maple trees
Besides shade, it gives sap to the birds and bees.
From the sap, we make syrup and sugar and candy
When we have pancakes, that syrup comes in handy.

There are the orchard trees, all covered with fruit
Apples, pears, peaches, cherries, and plums to boot.
Of the citrus, we have lime, lemon, oranges and more
Also many kinds of berries and nuts galore.

The beautiful evergreens stand so tall with pride
Giving pleasure all over the world at Yuletide.
Dressed in tinsel, ornaments and boxes of cheer
To welcome Kriss Kringle, with his sleigh and reindeer.

Some trees look happy with blossoms so white
The poplar, magnolia and dogwood so bright.
But we see the sad weeping cherry tree, too
And the weeping willow, shedding tears of dew.

Florence C. Sheaffer

Ode To Fay

She is like an ocean wave
Which ebbs and flows with the tide
At first gently still and calm
While gathering strength in the undertow

The momentum of steady growth
Builds its image to a dynamic force
Appearing as a crested and glorious form
Upon the vast world ocean surf

Continuing to gather the surrounding waters
With promise of greater motion to bind
An unending blending of caring and sharing
Overflowing love for all mankind

Each drop of water, each person touched
Some measure of human suffering eased
Boundless replenishing waters encourage
And create a future of fulfilling need.

Mable T. Hawkins

Angel Of Light

A man came before me; a comely man was he,
Clad in robes white as whitest wool.
His eyes sparkled, and his hair was long and neat.
Upon his handsome and gentle face was a smile,
Yes, a smile most becoming of him;
For a long pause I beheld his visage;
He gazed upon me benevolently and opened his arms slowly,
As though silently to say, come, my son, come to me.
I am the way; I am your protector.
Come to me, and I will care for you.
Accept me, and your worries will leave you forever.
At this, I promptly approached.
But as soon as I was within his reach,
Between his arms and in his grasp,
His countenance grew dark as night, black and heinous.
His eyes glowed red, and his hands became talons.
His laugh was shrill;
He would not let go of me.

Nathan Daniel

Class

America boasts of a classless society
But reality refutes the statement.
In schools we have the top class,
The slower class and those in between.
Even on airplanes, you are put into a class;
The first class and the regular class.
Fashion dictates to those who aspire,
Relegating no insignias for the poor.
Judge's robes, uniforms, designer clothes
Clarion call with a voice louder than a roar.
The view, the Bayshore, the Seashore, or Belair
Speaks volumes to those upward bound.
All this is wonderful only if you keep in mind the end
When allotted an urn, a sprinkling on earth, or a small plot,
And donated a fork or a crown in eternity,
God, housing, clothing and insignias
Not spoken for the rich or poor.

Margaret Mae Woltering

An Ideal "Career" Position

An Ideal Career........
A Position where quality is the rule and not the exception,
   Where there are no office politics or deception.
A place conducive to productivity,
   Where one can use their creativity.
A place to learn, grow, and prosper intellectually,
   as well as financially.
An atmosphere of friendliness, open-mindedness, and
   tolerance, not pretense and jealousy.
A Position where integrity, team spirit, and a sense
   of humour are valued.
A place where people cooperate, respect one another,
   and are given due credit.
A Position offering versatility, exploration, use of
   imagination;
And, an opportunity to make a significant difference.
   Where the world is made a little bit better by one living in it.

Sarahann Marie Funke

Late Date

Trucks and cars and busses and cycles.
Most all contribute in sharing the roads.
Many accidents are just waiting to happen.
It's almost impossible to avoid such action.
Too many drivers going much too fast.
All are usually in a very big hurry!
Why do they continue to drive recklessly?
Could it be they have no conscience?
Or is it that they don't care?
Thoughtless drivers doing this must be "Sick".
Our loved ones are ruthlessly being killed!
How much heartaches can all of us take?
Can these drivers be taught a lesson?
Is it possible to let them see?
Perhaps viewing themselves speeding, captured of film.
Maybe then they'd realize what they've done.
What will it take to awaken them?
Must "their" loved ones be killed?
Surely they're "sorry", but much too late!
Sorry doesn't count at this late date.

Eve Westaby

Understanding Love

She sits in silence, and tears, and wonder.
Day by day, she awaits, with hunger.
His place in her heart is full, yet her soul feels alone.
Love has no other, but to fulfill its own.

The hopeful longing for the man she loves,
Who she believes came blissful, from above.
Again to feel the comfort of his warm embrace.
To look once more upon his beautiful face.

For she knows faithfulness is as permanent as the sky.
Her heart flutters for him, as though it had wings to fly.
Darkness and light are the same.
As she awaits for him with, no shame.

Her soul thirst for him like, no other man.
Most happily describe in her life's plan.
Always remembering his charms.
When he welcome her with open arms.

Her love for him will never subside.
Somewhere she awaits, strong in belief.
Through the woes of understanding love, she abide.

Janice Brooks

Downward Upward

'Tis ever so kind ole gent,
To lend me your last one dollar, and ten cent.

Will it be soon, when
you come this way again?
Clouds look like we are in for rain.

I do not wish to take your last one dollar, and dime.
However, I must take the cross town trolley, in order to be on time.

Where employment for me awaits, early in the morn.
My pocketbook is empty, weather-beaten and worn.

Much gratitude I owe, I must say.
Will gladly give back your one dollar and dime, from my very first pay.

May God ever bless, for being indeed a friend.
To one whose life downward spill,
is looking upward, and greatly on the mend.

Elvera Story

Descending

Passing over the sleeping city, I see it shine like glistening drops of dew on a web woven by some great, iron spider. I feel the heat released like pent up emotion from the miles of asphalt and tarmac and deep steel canyons that drank so, so much of it this past day, the pleasure of it suddenly cut off by a cool northern wind that flaps my clothing and wraps me in gauzy clouds that glow grey in the moonlight. Lower, smell of gasoline and sweat and mixes of things I can't imagine, the night folk going about their business, weaving around each other in a social dance underneath the fluorescent yellow cones of light. A bus passes into view, turns the corner and moves on. They will never look up, not one will watch the glaring moon or the grey sky above them, or have the precious box they call reality ripped open by the sight of me, what I represent. This is to my advantage. The corner is lifeless once again, the street rises to meet me, the street light flickers as I descend, I hear its high buzz just before my shoes touch the sidewalk. Just another face in the crowd.

Kenneth Rapp

M e

I loved you, more than I even thought possible.
I tried to make you happy,
    even at the expense of my own happiness.
I was there for you,
    even if there was somewhere else I should have been.
I would have given you my all, but you didn't want it;
    yet still I tried.
I've tried and now I'm tired.
I'm tired of trying to convince you about me.
I was so worried about the things you might not like,
    the things that might make you love me;
That I forgot about me.
Me.....that's who I am and proud to be.
I'm not perfect, and if you don't love me or want me,
    well.....I'm sorry.
I'm not sorry for me, because that's who I am.
And if I tried to change, I wouldn't be me;
    and that's just who I want to be!

Andrea Turner

The Superior Posterior

Though some may consider my motives ulterior,
It has come to my mind that a lady's posterior,
To her male counterpart seems vastly superior,
Some folks may consider this thought most inferior,
But of what others think I grow increasingly wearier,
Gay rights, equal rights, nothing could be drearier,
Though a woman's charm some say is interior,
My eyes can't help wandering over the exterior.

Leonard G. Elliot

My Philosophy Of Life

To leave a feeling of endearment behind
    treat people with respect and dignity.
Weave humor in your discourse,
    and watch them respond to your litany.
Be ever honest in what you say
    or you will be found out which causes decay.
So love all mankind, be they good or bad,
    and watch them respond in turn,
For love is in the core of each heart,
    like a beacon waiting to burn.

Gilda Messina

Mother's Hands

Her hands once soft and wrinkled free
Lightly touched my head as I knelt beside her knee,
And as a child, they oft caressed my face
When helping me with my shoes to lace.

When ill, on hot and feverish brow
They gently rested as her head did bow.
So many things those hands could do
With loving care... for others too.

They were strong upon the garden hoe—
Making straight each long long row.
Always they were quick and sure—
Letting us feel safe and secure.

But her hands today, wrinkled and worn
Telling the tales of cares she has borne.
Are not soft, but gentle still,
As she strives to do the Father's will.

I'm so proud to take her hand
And walk beside her on this land.
Then shouting, for all the world to hear,
"This is my mother! To me she's most dear".

Isabelle J. Hanson

Providers

They are always here at my command
and serve me well in all I do.
    Throughout all time they give me food
and serve me well my whole life through.

    Without their help all work would fail.
No farms would be or cities rise.
    No ship, nor car, nor whistling train,
nor plane ascend in azure skies.

    Computers store and print at their command:
The daily news, prepared and given:
    The holy word preserved for all
who seek the only way to heaven.

    One is right and one is left:
The Father's precious gift to all,
    and with each hand, each one is blessed:
Hold to the rod, avoid the fall.

Wallace B. Pingree

Messengers

Wise
men are
learned souls
who ponder their
thoughts at length then speak
with brevity: and with
understanding hearts, they pour
forth (with fervor) faith, hope and love.
These are the messengers of God who
bring ethereal peace to all mankind.

Jean Ewing Kuhn

My Love Is True

I woke this morning with a gleam in my eye
As I thought of the last few days gone by.
I can't remember ever feeling this good.
You gave me your love like only you could.
I wish I could show you just how much I care.
But it's that much harder when you're not there.
But today is the beginning of a wonderful start
For two people to share with love in their heart.
Today is the day we become as one
As we make our commitments in front of everyone.
I promise I'll love you forever and ever.
I won't let you go, I want us together.
I'll make you so happy as long as I live.
It won't be hard with all the love that you give.
I need you beside me every step of the way,
Holding me close from day to day.
And if you are wondering what I'm leading to,
I want you to know that my love is true.

Thomas E. Hawkingberry

I Thirst For You

I thirst for You in the green, regal glade of the darkest forest,
in the musky scent of pines and moss, amid the dew-kissed ferns
that caress the ground like a featherbed of lace.

I thirst for You in the mountain with its changing face
and majestic peaks, capped in a crown of snow and clouds and ice
beautiful to behold, treacherous to traverse.

I thirst for You by the waters of the singing brook
as it sparkles on its way;
by the waters of the pounding surf
as I feel it spray fierce against my face;
by the waiting waves of the languid lake
with depths of blue unknown.

I thirst for You in the brilliance of the sunset
as it throws forth intense fragments of light and dark,
hue and form, calling...
a divine pallet stretching, yearning to touch me,
to embrace my spirit in the glow of its glory
so that we might become one;
and then I'll thirst no more.

Suzanne Bielec

Our Life

I look to the light of a new morning sun
And know that our lives are coming undone
We never look at life
As each day may be our last
Instead we look to the future
And try to leave the past
We throw life away,
We let it go by
We should soar like an eagle,
Not lay down and die
So, do not throw life away,
Don't let it be spent
Live all your life as your very last moment.

Tammy Males

Set Me Free

Set me free, so my heart can soar toward
heaven on the wings of an eagle.
Set me free, so my spirit can run through
trees, like the wind on a warm summer's day.
Set me free, so I can laugh like the babbling
brook, skipping over rocks coursing down a hill.
Set me free, so when I return, I can be completely
yours; because you had the courage to -
Set me free, and that allowed me to grow.

Janet Burton

You Are The One

You are the one I run to when I'm happy.
You are the one I ask for when I'm hurt.
You are the one who holds me tight and
tells me everything will be alright.
You are the one who sets me straight when
I have taken the wrong leap of faith.
You are the one who is there to meet my date.
You are the one who tells me who will make a good mate.
To sum it all up I'm very lucky because you
are my mother and you are the one.

Jaime Thornton

Deception

Beware the snake, who never sleeps,
Lurking, cautiously, he is waiting,
Within the grass, temptation creeps,
A decision in need of contemplating,
Risk the game, timing to him a must,
Uncertain his illusion of lust,
Beware the fruit, said to be forbidden,
Sweet to the lips, but bitter the taste,
Behind his smile danger is hidden,
Gentle eyes, with contempt, his thoughts are laced,
And his twisted tongue, will only seem to make sense,
While thriving on deceitful suspense.
Beware wounds, that tend to deepen,
Baited by the devil in disguise,
Virtue the prey prone to weaken,
In this garden of truth and lies,
The serpent lies scheming, with his hand held out,
Confusing all who have suspicion of doubt.

Barbara McCormick

The Dark Place

The dark place seeps in stillness
Like the ones who quietly go there
To complete a work of art
Ready for unveiling.
Quiet acquiescence pervades and surrounds
All who enter
With a calm and vital longing.
Kingdom of Power, Jewel of thine eye,
Equipped to see through mountains
As though mist, venturing further
Than the valleys below the sea.
A secret place, a quiet place -
An empire surrounded with tranquil beauty,
Permeating all who dare to enter.
The dream -
The sanctum of souls who,
Having flowed through the chasm,
Never elude the silent visions
On the other side.

Emily Richardson

Oh, They Are All Wonderful, You Know... Grandchildren!

And my ten-year-old Morgan,
With her wide open, delighted eyes
And the little freckles on her nose.
How can you help but wonder about her accomplishments,
So intelligent already!
And a smile that is open and oh, so completely happy!
And my eight-year-old Erin,
With her slow little smile, and her dark eyes,
Already hiding a bit away you know, to her own counsel.
But sharing too her joys, her jokes, her artistry.
Two little girls so different and yet sisters...
On the threshold of life!

Evelyn Winston

"Man's Best Friend"

I think each time I mow the yard
you sure must love that dog
as I pick up all those piles
that dog must be a hog!

Then there's all those big ole holes
where she's buried balls or bones
and bare spots all over the lawn
where once the grass had grown!

I walk out of the bedroom
in the middle of the night
step right in the middle of that ole dog
and nearly die of fright!

But every night when I get home
she meets me at the door
wags her tail and gives me a kiss
it more than evens the score!
"morewood"

Daniel L. Rice

With Reluctant Regrets

Dear Ones,
What an honor to be a part in the Induction meeting!
The ultimate thrill of a lifetime.
To meet you and listen to your poetry or prose
What a happy and meaningful greeting.
A joyful time goodness knows.
Words cannot express my deep regret
I will not be able to be there
An experience you will never forget,
It fills me with deep despair.
I just had a total knee replacement
My shoulder has a nasty rip.
Rheumatoid arthritis just won't relent
Now I need a total replacement hip.
Best wishes to everyone of you.
That is why I won't be able to go
Even though I really truly would love to,
Cheerio,

Eunice Abby Reding

Pele's Tears

Conceived in the pyre of Pele's tears
Beneath the great blue sea
The islands grew ten million years
A paradise for bird and bee
Days of steam and nights of fire
Continue to this day
Mark the rocks where Pele's lips
Kiss the ocean's waves
But Pele dreamed of higher things
Above the island shore
She fed the fire to raise the land
Far beyond the sea
The islands now tickle the clouds
They take away the rain
Sprouting the seeds the trade winds bring
That make Hawaii green
Man has come and scarred the land
Pele cries, tears of flame
From these tears, Loihi comes
Tomorrow's paradise, born again

Patrick A. Younger

Eternal Circles

She consumed me with nurturing care,
unconditional, constant, was her vigil of love.

Ever watchful, always helpful, ready to protect,
as a lion with her cubs.

My care giver, for more years than I care to admit, yet she
was unselfish with time, unfeigned in love for her little one.

It was never work that I beheld in her eyes through the years
but joy...and her face beamed pleasure, pure and proud.

Now that my time has arrived...she will lend me the mantel
of care giver and place that yolk on my shoulders,
her chosen heir...molded to her perfection.

I accept and embrace this worthy yoke of privilege and
honor that will assist me in teaching that which is good and
right to my little ones.

And when my time comes and my right of passage is spent I
will gladly pass the mantle on to my heirs so that out eternal
circles will join complete in a never ending chain so strong in
links of love...that it will go on forever.

Shirley Fugate-Hopper

"Happiness"

Is a state of ups or downs
Either moments of smiles or frowns
As flowers bloom, finally do wilt
Unlike a fine lasting, sewn quilt
Many mood swings, quickly spent
On going, going, going, gone, went
Words, books have been written
Frivolous loves, joy now smitten
Happiness, a state of ups and downs
Either moments of smiles or frowns
Faith, once attained, never fails
On life's rough seas, set sails
Faith stands within, on its own merit
Pit falls challenge, not to inherit
Life's temptations, spent, hell-bent
Trying always, to reach the inner-content
Faith is not borrowed, leased or lent
Loves merits, proven, ever to be content
Where as happiness, a state of mind
Contentment, as faith, always sublime.

George Zartner

Long Term Illness

I wasn't sure what I was suffering of.
I feel things often, and in various ways,
And the greatest of these is Love.

A glance, a touch, the slightest word
Would set me a shakin' all of the day,
And I wasn't sure what I was suffering of.

Love is sickness, from the poets I heard.
But the things I felt I could not even say.
And the greatest of these was Love.

My lover said Love is not a noun, but is a verb,
And love is not a mere game that children play.
But I wasn't sure what I was suffering of.

My lover said Love is the Gift that is offered,
So I said that Love would not lead astray,
The greatest of Gifts being Love.

Why lovers feel pain I always wondered,
And I also saw their pain would not go away.
I wasn't sure what I was suffering of,
But the greatest of Gifts was Love.

David Panagotis

Sonnet To The Queen Of May

O Mary, Thou who Queen of Angels are,
And Queen of Men, to whom we daily pray,
How oft we hail Thee as the Morning Star;
But now we'd fain salute Thee, Queen of May.
Come reign within our hearts O Mighty Queen,
And bring to us the graces that we need.
Thou art the only Mediatrix between us,
And Our Saviour, Christ the Lord indeed.
Although we find Thee joyous on this date,
We'll not forget Thy Sorrows and Thy Tears.
Thy Mysteries we'll often meditate,
And bring to Thee our troubles and our fears.
   Though Anti-Christ would steal this Feast so fair,
   Thou art crowned Queen on May Day everywhere.

   Marjorie Perry Russin

Full Sea

Many orphans at sea. That's where they end-
up after no one's watching where they go.

They drift aimlessly around in oceans
trying to touch the sun. The only warmth

freely given to a child born without
parents. Sailing safe at sea on wave-tips

that remember memories that weren't
Days of comfort without comparison.

There are no judgments if there are no eyes
And the waves are arms if you imagine.

   Celeste Garrow

Paradox

I know you can't understand my love, how can you?
For me to crush a thorny leaf in my hand and by the
same miracle see God in a furtive, trembling tear.

The long narrow rows of vigilant magnolias bowing
at my knew, know, will know appearance, complied with a deep sigh.

I glanced at the sky and there were whole and broken stars.
The moon pulled her shade down not even saying, "Good Night."

I begged of your eyes and a puzzle formed and broke in your face.
You grabbed for the word, you grabbed for the fact
as it poked the tortured reason.

I then turned to the night,
She thus embracing me, murmured,
"Please don't try to understand."

   Delia M. Longworth

The End

Amidst all of this confusion and chaos that is me
My one and only harbor has, at last,
Abandoned me as I knew it would,
As all come to do eventually
While burning bridges, brings fleeting relief,
There's abundant guilt. And if one plays with fire
Indeterminately, one shall always get burned eventually.
So I drift a little listlessly, a little
Endlessly, a tad triumphantly. A great deal
Painfully, and extremely broken,
Seared beyond recognition, questing for what
Was once right. That is now suddenly so wrong.
Playing with sparks upon my tinder of a soul,
Searching for rest, with my feelings eternal
Death.

   Kimberly A. De Freese

Forge Forward

Many things do not come easy in life
There is sometimes struggle and strife
And many times it is best not to fight
But first of all we should remove the blight
If we do not twist things about
We should always try to remain stout
It's best that we take things with less doubt
In the long run it's best to stay afloat
For when we sink - we alone are on the brink
And this is not the way we wish to think
To pull ourselves out of a hole
It certainly requires us to be bold
We can overcome by getting a new hold
Sometimes it's best to look away
And the problem could be solved in another way
What we propose could be the beginning of a new day
Sometimes it's difficult not to bray
But we should always look forward to a new day
And let yesterday's problems fade away
With little or no delay.

   Edward T. Philpitt

Earth Awakens

As the bright sun rises in the morning sky,
All earth is awakened.

Specks of dew drops melt away,
Adding life into nature that cries for a touch of help.
Meadows of flowers open once again,
To reveal their colorful secrets.
A waterfall quietly slides toward a clear, cool brook
Whispering words of peace through its wondrous presence.

And as the bright sun rises in the morning sky,
All earth is respectfully greeted.

Blue birds sing in harmony with the wind,
Carrying their tune of praise for all to cherish.
Trees add everlasting beauty to the land,
And offer a comforting home for all creation,
While the clouds just painted across the heavens,
Shelter nature from the unknown world above.

And as the bright sun rises in the morning sky,
All earth replies with pleasure.

   Stephanie Steele

Day To Day

Let it be said that future reality
lies solely in the unpredictable
hands of chaos theory and in that
a fruitful inexhaustible realm

But this does not guide us
in day to day routine complacency

Consider the impossibility to
express the universal wave function
which carries inside itself the
foundation for all physical law

Or perhaps priest de chardin's
omega point and the theory that
followed predicting the eventual
collapse and condensation of the
universe into a single omega point

But when we lay wakeful in our beds
at night it is not these that occupy us
it is always the gum stuck to the bottom
of our shoes.

   Mike Weltz

The Last One Home?

The World, we called it from way over there,
when we found out that life, really wasn't fair.

Honor, respect, acknowledging our elders,
but the love left behind, someone else held her.

The dreams they still haunt me, and so would they you,
the lost comrades, some I never knew.

A nation divided in more ways than one,
college students, it was said; "Shot just for fun."

Guns all around us, some new cannon fodder,
the youth of our country, that would never father.

Limbs all around me, hurled in pain,
our government held back, it all seemed insane.

Madness at home, we were called; "Baby Killer!"
The strange wave of hate, made us all very bitter.

The people we stood for, at home fast asleep,
so ashamed, that they wished, we were all six feet deep.

The grave that they dug me, over here is quite spare,
if only because, my remains you left there.

But the God that I pray to, finally took me away,
and said, I was <u>Welcome</u>, in his USA

John S. Keller

The Little Angel

She lay there sleeping.
So still and for his keeping.
Her skin was pure, and rosy.
Hair to her shoulders gold, and curly.
Lips of rosebuds, teeth like pearls.
A perfect child in beauty.

The sleeping beauty oh, so sick,
No treatment could help, or lick.
Our loving care and devoted duty,
Our hearts, and hands couldn't pick
A miracle to change, or kick
The fate of this child in beauty.

Too short a time this world you stayed,
Your innocence too pure relayed.
For the sins you found
Made life too roughly bound
For such a precious Angel.
A perfect child in beauty.

Ruth Dyson Hadfield

Daybreak

I wake to see the morning light as the moon caresses my shoulder
On the edge of my bed and throughout the room
The first light that I will see today
Day breaks the evening darkness as I wake from my deep slumber
I start the day anew with not a thought in my mind
The first trace of heat seeps through the cracks
The door left ajar and the fire roars
Coaxing me to exit my warm sunny place
Daybreak reminds me of everything new
The day starts fresh each morning
Making with it what we wish, molding the daylight with our hands
The warmth permeates the blanket that surrounds me
As I breathe new life on a new day
Taking a deep breath and beginning to wake
I remember just how hard it was yesterday at daybreak
Each day seems easier these days
As the sun grows stronger so do I
As each day grows longer, each day feels better
I can climb any mountain, swim any sea
As I wake, at daybreak.

John Gonski

Ryan's Rhymes And Reasons

I had a boy who was self-reliant
Some might say he was unruly or defiant.
He looked at the dandelions instead of the game,
He watched the rocks, whirlwinds and the bumblebees,
His dreams floated like clouds through the trees.

The bat and the ball came flying through the air,
Over his head, came the balls and the screams,
"Three strikes and you're out, now get and run!"
And the little boy didn't hear a word that had begun!
He was watching a dragonfly with his buzzing, blue-black wings,
Catching the fluttering rainbow of the sun reflecting in his eyes.

Some say he did not play the game that day,
But that dragonfly knew something in that May,
He caught the magic within that little boy's eye,
And I already knew, as I did sigh,
He's not defiant but self-reliant,
Creative and true,
His thoughts venture a different flight from you.

He will play that game on a different day again,
And when he's ready, he'll tell you when to begin!

Marlene Groth

Christmas Joy

Christmas joy we find ever year giving
And caring and spreading good cheer.
We look for this day as Mary and Joseph did then.
Great miracle on this day the greatest ever been.
Mary gave birth the Mother of the little one.
Our Father in Heaven it was his baby son.
The greatest story that has ever been told.
It happen so many years ago. The night of his birth
Oh what a sight the heavenly heaven open up so bright.
The heavenly star guided the people through the night.
They knew God's baby son would be born on that night.
The star was so bright as if it was day.
The star lead the people to the place where God's baby
Son lay. The people gave their gifts then on their way.
Every year we have a Merry Christmas giving gifts love
and care we think you Mary and Joseph and our Father
we hold so dear.

Genevia Bell Beard

Savior

He gave his life
That we might see
The love he felt for you and me
His path was lonely
He had no home
Like all of us, he felt alone
Heart heavy with so much love
A mission for him from God above
How can I help to make them see
The love I bring will set them free
Rejected, abused, turned away
Broken hearted till his dying day
If you love some one to day
And some times feel you've turned away
remember jesus loved not only you and me
But all of us
That only through love
Can we ever be free

Mabel E. Lodge

This Old Mean World

Don't let this old mean world get you down
Always walking around with such a big frown

There's nothing you can do to change
This old wicked human race

But, you do have the power to change yourself
So, hold your head high no matter what you face

For life is not designed to be kind
To the lowly "Under Dog"

Its purpose is to pick the flesh until it is "Raw"
But, if you have a little faith I know you will cope
And you'll make it as long as you keep the hope

Phyllis Talbott

When Friendship Fails

There are few things in life so consoling
When life's problems so heavily weigh
As the knowledge that someone who knows us.
With empathy, comfort conveys.

There are few things in life so fulfilling
When one thinks he has something to say
Than to seek out the company of that one
Who so obviously thinks we're "okay".

But there's nothing so tragic and lonely
In the course of life's turbulent change
As to learn that that one once so loyal
Has begun to regard us as strange.

We would that we all might be constant
Available, loyal and true,
But alas, human nature is fickle
And influenced by current milieu.

Barbara Olsen

Summer Afternoon

I sit on the weathered, wooden porch, surrounded by tall trees,
The intense blue of the sky peers through the leafy branches,
Making lacy patterns against the sky.
I listen to the sounds around me, of children laughing and playing
In the summer sunshine. And the breeze, rustling the leaves
Of the softly, swaying trees.
I feel the coolness of the breeze as it blows through my hair,
And my curls tickle my sensitive skin. The warmth of the sun
Contrasts nicely with the breeze, as it soothes each muscle.
The fragrant fruit blossoms drift toward me, tickling my nostrils.
The rich, brown earth mingles with the clean, fresh air,
Filling my lungs with life.
The taste of the beauty of nature lingers through the evening.
I close my eyes and let myself succumb to a world
Of magical beauty.

Jo Jaimeson

Child Of God

It's such a revelation, to feel the sure salvation,
That comes with the joy, of being a child of God

It eliminates damnation to every one in every nation,
If they turn to the great Jehovah and become His own.

It is a wonderful pleasure to receive love in abundant
Measure, even tho we are sinners in every way.

We should all have condemnation, instead He brings salvation
To the wretchedness of all, who will receive?

In the abundance of all His love for us, we oft
forget to say - Thank you Lord, Get down on your knees, Pray.

Bette Brodhagen Ziakin

What Is A Father

What is a father? I asked one day, then searched my head to see what I could say. A father is rugged with shoulders quite wide to give children and grandchildren a fine place to hide. All snuggled up close to father's chest, a place quite secure that kids like the best.

A father should listen when his children speak; be understanding and gentle as guidance they seek. He's dictator, pal, counselor, and peacemaker see; straightening squabbles 'tween siblings. A fair judge is he. His children all love him as does his wife, to provide for and nurture his family's life.

A man who's like this has friends that abound, always neighborhood kids and parents around. He's fun and he's crazy; his eyes flash and smile. He bubbles through troubles and laughs all the while. God fearing, patient, and sensitive too; He's easy to love for me and for you.

Where can an example of this father be found? I've searched through the heavens and over the ground. There are many I've met who're fathers they say, but fall short of the mold I've set here this day. There's one this mold fit like a lock to a key; My Brother, My Friend, was the father that's He.

Jerry L. Earl

Fifty Years Together

To my wife on our 50th Wedding Anniversary
When I first saw you across the room
I never thought that it would be soon
That I fell in love with all my heart
Never to leave you or to depart

From that day on you were in my thoughts
Your smile and your pigtails had me caught
We laughed and we loved as we were together
Praying to God that it would be forever

We were married in December one fine day
Honeymooned in the mountains and wanted to stay
But God had plans for our future life
With you beside me as my wife

In time four sons came to fill our home
We were now a houseful and never alone
Grandchildren now number the figure of ten
Oh what a joy our full life has been

I praise God who has kept us together
With his love we have loved each other
Fifty years is nothing as we look ahead
To be with Jesus, by whom we are led

Lee Stuck

True Feelings

The look in his eyes,
lets me know of his love,
he must be sent from heaven above.

The softness of his touch,
can take away the tears,
and give me comfort in the golden years.

The warmth of his arms,
as they hold me in an embrace,
let me know I will always be safe.

The sound of his voice, soft and low,
can bring a blush to my face,
a girlish glow.

And as for the beat of his heart,
it lets me know we will always be together,
and will never part.

You see I have found heaven on earth,
he's my partner, lover, and friend,
  he's Lyn...

Nikki Goodman

The International Poet's Convention

It had been my intention
To attend the International Poets Convention.

However, when I tried to walk
My legs would balk.

There were supposed to be surprises
And that I had won some prizes.
Contemplating the anticipated enjoyment.
Does not compensate for the disappointment
I am determined to solve this problem
With my rehabilitation program

Irving Kaufman

Thankful

The good Lord gave us the chance to have a good and productive life
What we make of our opportunities may include struggle and strife.
Without trials and tribulations along life's path to help us grow strong.
We could drift aimlessly and end up useless and going wrong.

To have the world laid at our feet without working to earn our way
Has no merit in my book, for in a productive life you can have a say.
Thank you dear Lord for my loving family, husband and friends dear
Life is not always full of happiness, sunshine and cheer, but Lord
you are always near.

So many little blessings daily easily can come our way
The traffic light changing to green when we're running late can
   make our day.
Being able to get out of bed each morning even if we groan
Certainly deserves our thanks, being able to greet the day and you,
knowing we are never alone.

Nadine M. Bushong

Move The Walls

Along life's journey, so many times we're being stopped
Allow our inner spirit to move these stumbling blocks
Father in our weakness make us strong
Give us courage to make right out of wrong
from each corner of the earth we are met with Satan's temptation
but we're children of the heavenly family, nothing can cut short
   our destination
The heavenly Father will supply his children with grace from above
To move all these walls of hate and replace them with love
let us go forth and prove to the world reaching our goal is our
main determination.

Elsie Wilson

A Christmas Tribute

When we were growing up....
Parents made Christmas special.
By showing their love and buying
gifts that you wanted.
When the golden years came, it became
   more difficult for them to do
      these things for you.
But now....
You become the parent.
And they become your children.
Now it's your turn to make their Christmas.
Merry Christmas!

Bert Teraoka

My Sister

You go on errands, take care of their needs,
only the beginning of all your good deeds.

You brighten the homes of persons with your visits to share,
the news and the hopes, the words that "you care"!

You give rides to those who walk on the street,
mindful just maybe, you lighten their tired feet.

And you give to the Outreach with food and clothes,
is there any wonder you should have no foes!

You still make time to feed God's hungry birds each day,

May God and Our Lady watch over you always, I pray!

Eileen J. Donlon

Big Brothers

I'd always been told that big brothers always watched out for their
little sisters. If that is so, why did he hurt me so?

I'd always been told that big brothers were there to protect their
little sisters. If that is so, did it mean that he had the right to
cause the harm himself?

I'd always been told that big brothers could be trusted with
anything. If that is so, did that give him the right to smash
my innocence beneath his toes?

I'd always been told that big brothers were there to help their
little sisters with problems. If that is so, was he supposed to
be the source of the problems to be solved?

I'd always been told that big brothers should be loving and
caring of their little sisters. If that is so, did that give him
the license to violate my body so?

I'd always been told a big brother was all of these things a friend,
a protector, and champion too.
If that is so, why was he none of those things for me?
Please tell me why he abused me so, I'd like to know!

Debra L. McCombs

Little Millers

I can't remember very far back,
but I do remember my Ma's warm lap;
Whenever my sister and I felt insecure,
we knew our Ma was in her rocking chair.

We had a good childhood even though poor,
and our Pa worked hard for sure.
"Eight is Enough," five boys and three girls
which one we were the neighbors were never sure!

People couldn't ever tell us apart,
they'd always ask, "Are you Dick, John, Ed, Bob or Art?
We three girls were not alike either,
they'd always ask, "Are you Helen or Mary?" And I'd giggle
"Neither!"

I remember gallivanting a lot with my Ma
to downtown, the beach or rides at Sea Breeze;
These are some of my cherished memories
as well as romping in the piles of fall leaves.

Irene Miller Holleran

I Want Money!

I want money
to buy me that Easter Bunny!
If someone gives money to me,
I will buy a great big T.V.!
I want to buy something funny,
but first I need some money!
If I had money that would give me
great big thrills.
I would pay off all of my parents' bills!
Now aren't I a sweet child?
Don't get too wild!
I want Money!!!!

Katie Hughes

Defeat

The room was filled with listening spaces,
    Watching were the living chairs;
A thousand eyes with missing faces
    Sat and whispered on the stairs.

Exciting in a hushed exertion,
    Boiling hot the bodies' saps;
But something blocked; the live assertion
    Wilted to a dead collapse.

Because desire hung defeated,
    Back into a mental heap
The eyes and living chairs retreated.
    Yawning doors stretched out to sleep.

In haunting failure love lay flaccid;
    Horrors clawed in crazy twists
As if the brain were sunk in acid
    Screaming through the clench of fists.

Lou Guttman

December Winds

The winds of December blow colder this year
    I'm alone, and all on my own
Lonely and I, are intimate friends
    and the cold goes straight to the bone

Friends, and warm memories, come calling at times
    but I turn them away at the door
I've filled my life, with memories of you
    and the life we shared,—before

I'm not the same, as I was with you
    life is distant, and cold
I once was young and happy
    now I'm suddenly, gray and old

The days pass by at a dreary pace
    and from habit, I eat and sleep
We planted the seeds of happiness
    but sadness and tears, is the crop I reap

I'll join you soon, for I can't go on
    your love was my guiding light
I close my eyes at the end of day
    with a prayer that God, will our souls reunite.

Frank E. Konieska

Summer Eve

Woodbine spices are wafted through air.
Butterflies flit through the trees.
Fragrant are zephyrs that gently blow.
Soft is the warm summer breeze.

Hear the chorus of blackbirds.
Over your head they fly.
Soaring into a roseate cloud
Of lavender sunset sky.

High are the rushes and reeds that grow
Beside the lily pond.
Deep is the joy every child knows,
Though summer will soon be gone.

Tiptoe through a sylvan glade,
Feel God's Holy Peace.
(Try to count the stars that shine
On the Shores of Infinity.)

Marian Hallet

The Wind

What is this powerful, invisible thing called the wind?
We can't see it, we can't touch it, we can't smell it, we can only
    feel and hear it.

It can blow wet or it can blow dry - it can be sweet, soothing,
    and cool.
It can freeze you, warm you, blow you off your feet-or kiss you
    gently on the cheek.

What is this powerful invisible thing called the wind?
Where does it come from, where does it go? What in the world makes
    it blow.

What is this invisible, strong, powerful, twisting fury with a force
    that can't be matched?

It covers the earth from side to side - some days we love it, some
    days we hate it.
Nothing can live without it.

I would really like to know where it comes from, and where does it go?
What is this invisible, powerful thing called the wind?

Reba E. Rainwater

Ghetto Teacher

    The Wizard of Bristol Street was his name,
Art teacher was his game,
With hands of gold,
He made, with children, artwork brassy and bold.
    In this place of blood and tears,
With its innumerable fears,
There is no opus for Mr. Holland,
There is no goodbye for Mr. Chips,
There is only survival for those with a somber face,
And stiff upper lips.
    For every push and every shove,
There was a mitigating dose of love,
However, no matter how many paintings,
No matter how many sculptures or sketches,
The stomach always wrenches and wretches,
For there is always, in you, a hole,
It is the great emptiness in your soul,
For you know, no matter how high the toll,
You could not make things whole.

Joel H. Finkel

A Baby Sleeps

Though earth erupts in cataclysmic fury, spitting forth a blazing heat,
And seas, with rampant waves, ravage a silent shore that can't retreat;
When every man-made terror, holocaust of war, where evil creeps,
At peace and with a trusting heart, a baby sleeps.
Untouched by life, protected by its innocence, free of guile,
With arms outstretched, safe in slumber, upon its lips a smile;
One with God, whose will is still unquestioned, love given love received,
Simple untried love, uncomplicated by life cynical age half believed,
With little faith and trust; half forgotten memories dim.
As more and more we separate ourselves from Him,
No more the child whose simple prayer uttered before sleep's descent,
Though whispered, filled the room with peace and rare content.
The simple prayer was heard by God who blessed the child.
And sent soft dreams, not nightmares wild,
That haunt our grown-up world both day and night.
Dreams should end yet these are ever in our sight.
Is all the fear and pain that fills our world our due?
For getting too complex, letting worldly things cloud our view.
I pray one day with aged wisdom, hard learned,
We utter simple prayers, Love given, Love returned.

Patricia V. Leonard

Just Hold My Hand

Hold my hand, sweet love, to calm my fears
As we go wandering through our twilight years.

Come stroll with me along the trail when the sun is on the land.
And though I'm old, I will not tire if you just hold my hand.

Hold my hand, sweet love, while I remember
Our wedding day that bright September.

Such a wondrous day so long ago!
You held my hand and I loved you so.

Hold my hand, sweet love, while we wait for the sunset.
Just hold my hand and I'll not fret.

As twilight becomes night, I'll not despair
If you hold my hand so I know you're there.
Just hold my hand so I know you're there.

Dorris M. Botts

My Mother's Tears

I left my mother this morning to take a plane to my home
Memories of my mother's tears linger in my memory
99 years she has been with me here
So many miles and so many memories linger in my mind
I hated to leave her as she stood and waved at the door
Into a car that would take me far away
Spring had come another year for her to spend
But Dad in her heart—why doesn't it end
floating in the clouds-I sing a song of hope
God why don't you take her up to heaven soon
She's lonely as she sits there everyday
My sister and I if we could only stay
But our home and family bring us back this day
And have to leave my mother with tears in her eyes
Just me

Margaret D. Brueske

My Dreams

Sometimes I dream of impossible things, no one else can imagine.
I hope... or wish for them to come true. I dream to dance on clouds,
sing to the ocean and fly to the heavens. I imagine leaving the earth
to look down at once used to be my home.

Now I sit on the deserted beach watching the sunset, the waves
bounce against the shore, and the day roll throughout my mind.

If I would compare my mind to something it would be a... jungle.
For many reasons why because, I'm wild and exciting. You never know
what lies around the next corner. Or, are you always wondering what
is happening inside me. That is the one thing nobody knows.

Another dream is I picture the wind dancing, as the rain sings,
the thunder chants in harmony. I stand and watch a miracle as the sun
breaks through the clouds and brings forth good and evil to join
together as one. Not for all to go to one side but, to meet together
in the middle. There is a hand of good and for evil. The two have
held together so, you cannot tell the difference. Everyone from each
world joins to be side by side. Not till the end but, to the
beginning. To start over and do things right for a change. Let our
bring us together once again... let us unite.

Allison Nicole Fontenot

Hummingbird

Hummingbird, hummingbird, where have you gone?
You came for a visit, but you didn't stay long!
We all love to watch you, and listen to your wings;
The music they make, is like an angel that sings.
We watch as you flitter and dance to and fro,
You even fly backwards, as you put on a show.
Your movements so graceful, as you feed on the nectar,
Then you dive in the air, we don't know what you're after!
So tiny a bird, with courage of a lion;
Defending your territory, almost all of the time.
So fast and so quick, you fly up and fly down,
From flower to feeder, and sometimes to the ground.
You visit us in August, and leave in October.
We are always so sad, when your visit is over.
But you always seem happy, tell me what is the reason?
Are you on your way home, at the end of the season!
So please little hummingbird, come and visit again,
It makes us so happy to feed you, when we can.
Migrating to your home is your nature they say,
But I surely am glad you stopped here on the way!

Wilda Winder

Pink Pagoda Moon

With mind of before we met
The core of which recoils to confess
I cared not for love but for comfort and caress

With eyes of before we met
Hastens blessings blushed
Pride swells twice justified in approval of my longing

Even though, thoughtless rushing of you to my bed
Inconsequence of reason risked your heart's retreat
There is great holiness in hope

Like a prayer, defiant of chance
Invokes the self into a whispered chant: "want me - need me"
From inside my secret, a fire still rages

Indigent of reason, gentleness incompetent
It burns through time and task/no mood can mask
The equal part of lust in my love for you, gentle man
Belies my walls of pink and carpet bluer than the sky

For underneath our pink pagoda moon
I am a Savage for you
Within this pink pagoda room

Eileen Malaspina

If I Had My Way

If I but had my way there'd be a-going back in time
  I'm sure it's not the way you'd think, this passive plan of mine
It wouldn't be the good old days of cotton, corn, and hay
  When sun was beaming down so hot, and all by first of May,
It wouldn't be the days of yore when life was labor-filled
  With nothing else to do but work 'til sun went past the hill.

But it would be when Moms and Dads still ruled their house by law,
  And kids could find security behind those guarded walls;
Not TV shows so full of smut, their minds to feed upon—
  But things created by their hands, good things to make them strong.
And it would be when kids were made to honor those in love
  With, "Yes, Ma'am," "No, sir, Papa dear," all prompted from above.

And it would be when Moms and Dads again at close of day
  Would call the children to come in, "It's time to kneel and pray,"
With giving thanks to God above for every bird that sings,
  For flowers, trees, and fish that swim, well, yes, for everything.
These things I'd choose for peace of mind to bring back pleasant days,
  I bare my heart, this would I do, if I but had my way.

    Irene Armstrong

To A Mourning Dove

Sounds of a city wakening,
Muffled raspings of commuting tires.
Not welcome to my ears
In the dim light of morning,
As I rouse my slumbering mind
To its daytime tasks.

A soft and gentle voice comes through my window,
From a mourning dove.
You, of a graceful, warm lovely gray,
With your greeting midst urban's dreary morn.
Sounds of your tender cooing, and blessed presence
Lift my spirits, and with grateful mind
Have thoughts of you, one of nature's own,
Steadfast in your trust, still living, still giving.

Quite true, the voice I heard
Came from just a little bird,
Like asking if we can also learn
To give and to share alike,
When in nature's trust, it becomes our turn.

    John Hanna

Steps

I hesitate each languid step toward death,
But yearn to be alone with God and fright.
Unworthy to see The Light,
Though in life, God's strength I claim,
For 'twas He who gave me thought and breath.

Silent storms burst forth within my soul
From sanguine thoughts that fail to sound,
And petty enemies imagined 'round.
My hollow boastful righteousness
Echoes lust for the heavenly goal.

I ran. I walked. I tripped. I fell.
Sometimes in life alone for God,
But knowing I must go alone to God.
Thank you, His earth-bound angels.
You surround and lift me well.

    Derry D. Sparlin

A Widow Weeps

There weeps a lady so sad and forlorn.
There weeps a lady in silence all alone.

She speaks into the silence but no one hears.
There is sorrow, sadness, anger and remorse
Confusion, loneliness and fears.

She feels them all like the stab of a knife.
She tries to reason... Why-why
For now she is void of love, purpose and life.

There weeps a widow so sad and forlorn.
There weeps a widow in silence all alone.

    Mary Lee Gaier

The Bonding

As he embraced her gently
And wiped a tear from her cheek
The bonding was happening
As all emotions peaked
The lost past
Had caught up with the present
Becoming one and the same
As she held her infant son to her breast
And explained the choosing of the name
With a peaceful feeling within
It was very plain to see
She was now, her Daddy's girl
That she had always wanted to be

    Vera Thompson

Scotland Of Old

My daytime thoughts and nighttime dreams wander through Scotland
of Old.
As I remember the glens, the lochs and the perfume of heather
so strong, I yearn to see you again.

I will walk on the path to ages past
pink, purple and green mountains, crowned in mist that take
my breath away.
Unforgiving enemies wanted from you, I know not what.
But you survived with dignity and pride that is admired.
My heart weeps for all the cruelty and harshness you endured.
Looking down upon Glencoe, sensing ghosts that roam and claim
the land as home.
Walking the field of Culloden I hear swords rattle and anguished
tears of death.
Hard to forget you Scotland of Old, castles in ruins, mysterious
carvings on stone.
Because it was once forbidden, you wear your tartans proudly,
as you should.
Your bagpipes call to me and I will come.
Wait for me Scotland of Old for now, I am content with the Scotland
of today.

    Frankie Augustine

Listen

Can you hear the children cry?
Why you ask, oh why?
Hunger, bruises, suffering from land to land
Abuse, wars, fear-no-one there to extend a hand
Tears, broken hearts and broken bones
Do you care enough to let them know they are not alone -
Do you pray that man's cruelty to man will cease
Or has the world grown callous to the voices for peace
Can you hear the children cry?
Need you ask why, oh why!

    Shirley Campbell Horton

Guardian Of My Life

I picture you, a beautiful lady dressed in white
Soft face emerald eyes loving smile a majestic sight

Long shiny auburn hair resting at your waist
I say a prayer that you come to me in haste

God whispered and placed an angelic being over me
And I thank God for just allowing you to be

Guardian of my life with love for all of creation
Pathways burdensome, Lord give me strength of dedication

Twilight moonlit sky my companion, be my hope
To see my angel, oh starry sky through a telescope

Burning desire to know your ways in a loving way
God allows my angel to watch me day after day

Martha Warden Chainey

"Angels" Surround Them

A child's cry pierces the silent night...
    innocence with hope and souls of light...
        those precious ones with spirits bright...
            May the "Angels" surround them

Mankind's wickedness strolls our earth...
    and entices our guiltless ones from birth...
        a nation comes together in search...
            As the "Angels" surround them

A family's tears are touched by all....
    even strangers heed their anguished call...
        concern themselves and get involved...
            While the "Angels" surround them

Divine intervention sometimes is required...
    our prayers ascend—even the sky heard...
        our hope and faith is much admired...
            By the "Angels" that surround them

Thanks be to the beings that inhabit the heavens...
    may more little ones return to family and friends...
        because of prayers, wishes and hopes that ascend...
            To the "Angels" that surround them

Linda Lennington

Freedom

I am like a butterfly, shining so brightly.
Everyone wants to catch me, my freedom to steal away.

The world is mine to explore and love,
that is what I am envied of.
Gliding so gracefully,
trusting in what I can't see.
My life is made of peace and beauty,
covered in serenity.
Just when they think they have caught me,
I take flight and the wind rescues me.

Anna Redwine

My Mother

When I was a child I thought;
She's like a blankey that warms me in the night,
kissing all the boo-boo's and making everything all right.
Now I'm a mother, too, and know
how profound and hard to measure,
the love that I've been given, the love that I treasure.
She's lived her life for God above,
thus gave her greatest blessing.
She gave the gift of greatest love with the Light she was reflecting.
My mother, who God chose especially to be,
a living inspiration of His wonderful love for me.

Marie H. Dawson

The Dark And The Light

There have been days of sorrow and grief.
There have been nights, long, without relief.
There have been times, I felt so alone.
When in reality, I was so wrong.

For you have always been near,
To comfort and soothe.
To relieve the pain of my fear,
To show me hands-on proof.

That no matter how hard,
Life may seem,
You at night, are my stars,
And in sleep, peaceful dreams.

And at daybreak,
When the light shines through,
You are still holding me tight,
To greet the day that is new.

Together we'll forge,
The dark and the light.
And revel in the knowledge,
That all will be made right.

Regina Keene Hines

When Things Look Hopeless

When things look hopeless, smile,
    And turn to find the sun
Or look upon a distant star—
    Then stop and think a while,
And when your thought is done,
    You'll know how small your troubles are.

When things look hopeless, smile,
    And pluck a small, green leaf
And watch a thousand others fall—
    Then stop and think a while,
The others showed no grief,
    They didn't miss the leaf at all.

When things look hopeless, a smile,
    And don't despair, my friend,
Solution can be found—
    Then stop and think a while,
For troubles have no end
    When fools just carry them around.

Louis F. Conca Jr.

"Prophecy I"

With his coming man shall know death.
No man, woman nor child shall be untouched,
Cities shall fall, nations tumble.
The very earth shall quake from his touch.
The seas shall rise, mightiest of mountains shall tumble.

Hunger, death and pain shall rain upon the earth,
Plaques shall run rampant, the undead dying.
Man shall kill man for morsels of unclean food.
Man will forsake others, even woman and child.
He will be like the beast surviving only to kill.

His power shall grow, stronger than any before him.
He shall sweep the land with the eternal fires,
Leaving a barren world in his wake,
All who stand before him shall perish,
All who stand with him condemned.

He shall bring upon the world the extinction of man.
Nature shall replenish, heal itself.
One day man shall walk again, a newer man.
A man knowledgeable in the sciences of peace.
A man ignorant in the sciences of war.

Dennis J. Keenan

Promises

Promises are meant to be kept, not broken.
You promised not to hurt me, but you lied.
You promised not to hit me, you lied again.
Then you said "you'll never cheat on me."
But you lied again and again.

You never kept your promises.
Why should I trust you again?
Your promises don't mean a thing to me now.
Promise, all you want.
I'll never believe in you again.
I've gotten a wall that keeps all the pain away.
Promise, all you want, cause you've blown it all away.

Sheila Denney

Ex Lebris Vitae: A Sonnet

Hail! Neophyte transient of the library of life,
born of passion pain and strife,
permanence earned, when you have learned
borrowed youth must be promptly returned.
Does heart and blood run cold at thoughts of growing old?
Browse, sanguine savant, peruse rare volumes you can't use.
It is the end for you, life has done all it meant to do
Tempus pugilist, it was no great dishonor to lose, forsooth,
Heracles fought bravely for, and had lost his youth.
The mighty Pluto personally, with a latin bite,
will remind you of your lost fight,
and as a reward, in your name, to ease the sorrow,
issued a lifetime membership card dated yesterday,
That will expire tomorrow.

William Mendelson

Contentment At Last

In my innermost being I am composed.
Once there was turmoil-peace was opposed,
Frantic I was- not tranquil at all.
My chance for rest was very small.

Long I had endured pain and stress.
My life was unraveled- A real mess.
All of sudden- strong I became
Absolutely nothing remained the same.

Be gone those things that bother me.
In my life I will not have you be.
Only misery - and hurt - you ever bring
You silence the song my heart wants to sing!

Fight we must to rid our life
Of negative forces that cause us strife.
Surprised you'll be how quickly they go.
This is a truth that I well know.

How quiet it is- Can you not feel?
Healing has begun- what a thrill!
It came to me- it can come to you.
Embrace it quickly whatever you do!

Helene Treadway

My Baby

The heart beats from my baby within,
What a wondrous feeling this is,
Knowing she is stretching and growing within.
I can hardly wait until that day,
That God's Blessing will be in my arms,
And then as she lays upon my breast,
Our hearts will still beat as one.

Joanne E. Wellman

My Husband, My Best Friend

You're everything I wanted and hoped you would be
You're the very best thing that's ever happened to me
Because of you I know who I am
I know where I'm going
And know where I've been
I'm sure it was meant for me to love you
And just as sure it was meant for you too
My greatest wish is to always be together
To find each other all over again
And know that this is forever
So thank you for choosing me to share your life
And even more for being your wife

Bonnie Dues

The Calm Center Of The Tornado

My soul has learned where to go
to find the calm center of the tornado.
For above the wind-torn sky,
far below the crashing sea;
I find the safety that I need,
and the courage to strip off camouflage
and just become me.
I am learning to discover,
I can walk on open ground without cover.
I have become my own medicine woman,
stumbling through hell, but never losing sight of heaven;
learning to mend myself and slowly heal
from deep wounds that are still festering
and nightmares that are real.
But no matter where I go from here,
I will walk my true path without fear;
no matter who discourages and disparages me,
I never have and never will let go of my hope and dignity.

Candyce King

Black And Gold

The curling fingers slowly close the galaxy.
The outward reach of stars have reached their apogee.
The whirling worlds, receding, soon will turn to black
The final pages of its space-time history.

Ten billion years, or more, this darkness will remain.
No spark will light a dream in this deep-sleep domain.
Since all created must traverse this rounded universe,
The galaxies will re-unite again.

Such speed occurs when two huge galaxies collide,
That atoms loosen, leaving naked their inside!
Their passing through each other leaves an endless cloud of fire
That parts in half as they reluctantly divide.

Electron's golden threads rewind the scattered tears
For suns and satellites that fall within their spheres.
And then at last it hangs the dome-shaped diamond veil
Protecting secrets that the mystery might prevail!

Leland Embert Andrews

My Tombstone Last Will

On the glory Day of Resurrection,
when Lord your face will lighten more than Sol,
when raised from graves and lived must go as whole
to Hell or Heaven - ever justice pole,
on the fearful, glory Day of Judgement,
O God of Mercy love me, save my soul.

Stefan Lukacik

What If A Flaming Candle Goes Out

You set a goal and you strive for years
Success or failure, you say with tears
It matters not, you refuse to care
What the heck! If you do go nowhere.

But still you struggle with all your might
Insisting upon keeping your goal in sight
Then Glory be! Recognition you get
Those challenges were there, and they were met.

One step, then two, upon a ladder you climb
You await with patience, one day at a time
You add up the score, then confusion sets in
Gosh! you've only started to just begin.

But amid all this joy and instant elation
There is something missing and it's jubilation
A lonely Star - falls upon this scene
But otherwise a void dips in between.

But still the struggle must never wane
In climbing the ladder to success or fame
Never have fear, uncertainty or doubt
For If You Do, The Flaming Candle Goes Out!

Elma M. Rasor

To All Fallen Veterans

On the crest of a fall horizon
With a cool crisp breeze all 'round,
While the darkness has yet not disappeared
Yet a radiant glow abounds;
I can see "Old Glory" flying
Unfurled within the wind
Reminding me of my freedom
Bought by brave young men.

The flag takes on new meaning
As darkness fades away.
As I think of all the men who died
This great land of ours to save.
For they made our lives worth living
In a land so free and brave,
These gallant men before us
Whose lives they proudly gave.

Brenda Johnson

"The Ride"

You see the awesome beauty and, then when you feel the power
It makes that ride around the block turn into several hours
I never mean to do it. Every time I say "I'm sorry"
But honey, you would do the same
If you'd just ride my Harley

There's magic in the moment while that engine's keeping time
Then I'm lured out to the highway chasing double yellow lines
Only gone I thought for minutes. But now "home" is with the dog
You wouldn't be so mad at me
If you'd just ride my hog

The weekend fast arriving, I was thinking of a ride
On that masterpiece of metal: In my garage there sits my pride
He went out all dressed in leather to find a note stuck on a spike
"Don't be mad at me, I'll be back soon."
"I just had to ride that bike."

Michaeline Crooks

The Battle In Lafayette Square

It's January, and Lafayette Square looks bare.
The French General faithfully rides on his horse,
several inches of snow blankets his stony majestic bearing.
The benches are used in their full capacity,
layers of covers, pathetic bags of worldly belongings,
twisted minds groaning, dirty faces peeking,
matted hair protruding, hands rearranging,
a futile effort to stay warm in the freezing air.
But, this is the only home they know,
Lafayette Square and the raging, boundless sky.

How long has it been since there was an anchor they called home?
Homelessness is such an indecent vocabulary.
How could one believe in hell after death, I challenge myself,
after all that they have had to go through in this temporary visit.
Could it be that there is only paradise on the hereafter,
where God extends His arms on the outer door,
His sigh of relief loud, His smile most loving,
welcoming long lost children finally home.
Lafayette the General faithfully gallops on his horse,
life is a battle after all.

Anna Maria Siti Kawuryan

"The Maker Of Peace"

Every person carries forth with them, a thread
Never seeing, that which is being woven
The purpose known only to Father Time
For he is the maker, the one chosen

Taking each thread from every person
A delicate task, and tedious as well
Those who do evil, or create war
Will never find grace, for they have fell

When time has ended, and all has been done
It will be presented, for all to see
Showing everyone, past and present
What peace has made, or could be

All have a choice to be peaceful or chaotic
That is well known, to the maker of the quilt
He knows in his heart that peace will prevail
Chaos will father, and eventually, wilt

Joseph D. Osborne

The Professional

Black shaven beard, with a mole on his cheek-
Angle of his hat, debonair and chic.
An enchanting smile, on a handsome face-
Appealing, charming, to the female chase.
A renaissance male, so virile, so meek-
Is often forgiven when indiscreet.
Each female feels that for sure she's the one-
Who will inspire loyalty in Don Juan.
From black hair, to red hair, to golden blonde-
His interests are many-but not for long.
Girls shamelessly vie, for time by his side-
And openly strive, to engage his pride.
He usually leaves, the same as he came-
Enjoys the conquest-but won't play the game.
He's the greatest catch to ever hit town-
And parents are hoping, for miles around.

Mirtha G. Moreno

Tomorrow

He said he was going to alter his ways—tomorrow!
And that he would do something worthy of praise—tomorrow!
But this time was so taken with things to be done,
   With loafing and laughing and pleasure and fun,
But he said that he'd finish the things he'd begun—tomorrow!

He said he'd be kind, and gentle, and good—tomorrow!
   He'd start helping travelers along life's rough road—tomorrow!
   But today he must play and be a good fellow,
If he tried to reform they would say he was yellow,
But surely he'd do something worthy to tell—oh—tomorrow!

   He certainly would have been a great man—tomorrow!
   But he never seemed to quite understand, that tomorrow
Is the day which we hope for, but it never arrives;
   Today is the day we are living our lives.
No plan or ambition will be realized—tomorrow!

Raymond W. O. Knowles

I Looked For You

I looked for you today at Harper's Grill
Hoping we could have a cheese on rye
Or something light for lunch and talk a while
But you weren't there and so I wandered home

At five our daughter came, just dropping by
Looking in on me on her way home
I was staring blankly at your photograph
Waiting for my supper I suppose

She told me Harper's has been gone for years
Perhaps I had a dream I'd find you there
The way we used to do when we were young
The mice are making scratchy sounds upstairs

She fixed a meal for me and we had coffee
Cleared days of clutter from the crowded kitchen
Brought in all the mail and several papers
Watered plants and things I just forgot

She put your picture back inside the Bible
Knowing I could find it there again
The Company's retiring me next month
Is it really twenty years ago you left me

Gordon Dean Schlundt

Song Of Sisterhood

Oh, sister dear, your music play,
My lonesome fears will it allay.
Where would I be if not for you?
At my beginning you heard the clue.

Oh, sister dear, your music play,
I am made of spirit and of clay.
There was a reason why I was born,
Though Dad was old and Mom forlorn.

Oh, sister dear, your music play,
My life's pattern you began to lay.
As a mere child you took care of me.
You carried me and heard my plea.

Oh, sister dear, your music play,
My memories of you will ever stay.
My flame is lit; my candle will burn.
The secrets I learn shall I intern?

Oh, sister dear, your music play,
Let it take the separating curtain away.
Time and space now keep us apart,
But I still love you with all my heart.

Ramona Welch

What's New

Today is not new, not even to you.
It is filled with days of yore.
Look all around and nothing is new.
It is older than ever before.
There are birds in the trees
And the quaint honey bees.
There is robin, eagle and lark,
Whale in the waters all over the seas;
Still sunrise, high noon and dark.
So when you say something is new
Remember the things you've been told
And from all the things that we do.
It all started from something quite old.

Virginia Null Miles

Sandra

Has compassion that branches out like a seed,
To all the children who have a need;
Her work takes her to and fro by day and by night,
To whatever child's plight — she'll make it right.

The same phrases she uses again and again,
At ease these children realize she is a true friend;
The work is hard at times with an air of sadness,
But the end result will be nothing short of gladness.

She has that goal by seconds to teach,
The human kindness and trust she must reach;
Inside each child they will one day see,
Why the angels in heaven smile down on she...

Wynter Bryte

"Amber Wake"

In the amber wake,
of the crescent dawn,
the souls and sprits of,
poet, author,
king, ruffian,
fly together,
over creamy silver mounds,
and effulgent gold foliage.

Lapping sapphire waves caress the beaches
where,
the sands of time,
run their course.

Paths of brazen moonlight,
lead into the stars,
of day,
there,
the wishes of men run through space,
like water,
through a sieve.

Alicia Alvarez

To Daddy

My father to me is the greatest man around. He's there when I
need him, and he never lets me down. I count on him for help
when I need some good advice. He's always willing to lend a
hand, because he is so nice! I'll always love you Daddy,
please don't ever forget, because I know you love me too, sure
glad you and mama met! I'm proud to be your daughter, and you
to be my Dad. To think I have a father like you, makes me
awfully glad! I hope your birthday is special in all things
that you do! May many more birthdays come your way, and I hope
they're happy ones too!

Sandra M. Barthlein

The Night Before

Whispering winds flow through her auburn hair,
As she strolls down a long winding road.
Daydreaming of the night before,
Longing for it to never have ended,
Only wishing for it to be real; not a fantasy.
As the light begins to fade,
And the night embraces her,
She stumbles upon a stranger.
A man with eyes as blue as the ocean,
And long locks of golden blond hair.
The man in her dream
Just as she dreamt,
The night before;
Only so much more,
For this time it felt so real.
Love at first sight,
Knowing he was the one.
Only to wake up to another dream,
More vivid;
Than the night before.

Melissa A. Bifano

Untitled

Shadows of Flowers: In the dark forest of the soul all shadows
menace and mimic demons. Sounds return and echo back our
fears, beliefs coronated to kings of our realms. Boundaries kept
by chimerical beasts, issuing forth their opiates, numbing all
who traipse here. Beleaguered knights, we're drawn as silence
rings loud the welcome bell enticing weary, worn and battle
scarred. Eyes look out from pools of war for spells of sleep;
respites from the blooded stage. A whispering... silent... pierces
through the darkened sky; cuts sharp into my weary sleep.
"There is a land of beauties unparalleled, where wisdoms flow
like wine from open casks into the goblets of the brave who grip
Excaliburs, mount glistening steeds and ride into the battle of
the night unfurling hearts bearing colors of the soul." The
dragon stirs; white heat fire spews out; reflects a wasted image
who we are. In gallant fight our labored heavy heaves resound
with weariness, stretching time like strands of web. Death's
handshake brushes our fingers and splitting open numb. Burning
pain mounts fire to strike a final blow and slays this dragon of
our night. Jubilant, we crown a new king to our land as our
soul throws flowers across our conquering path.

Bonnie Cannon

"My House By The Sea"

I can picture myself in a
 House by the sea,
Where calmness and serenity
 Always surround me
Quiet walks along the shore
 Are just what I
 Am longing for.
No worries or cares to
 Burden me
In my cozy little house
 By the sea
The tides will come and go
And storms will surely blow
But my house and I
 Content will be
Weathering any storms that come to the sea,
Gulls fly overhead,
In the lonely sort of way that they do.
But I know they are, as happy as me,
In their cozy little house by the sea.

Melinda W. Chance

Animal Limericks

There once was a great horned rhinoceros
Who fell into a pool of phosphorus.
Said a tick bird bemused,
"It's a glow worm diffused!"
Said the rhino, "That's quite preposterous."

There once was a comely young louse
Who lived in an elegant house,
Which was made of fine hair;
And the floor of this lair
Was skin soft as a cashmere blouse.

There was once an impatient young worm
Whose mother with him was quite firm,
"Wait 'til you're taller
To be a nightcrawler;
You're too little to do more than squirm."

Once a Portuguese man-of-war
Fell in love with a balloon offshore.
Reaching tentacles out,
He had ardor devout;
But alas, his dreams burst evermore.

Henry M. Ditman

Be Strong In The Lord

In the Lord be ye strong
A time will come to right wrong
I will shake the sky above
Earth, too, for there is no love

The world is in turmoil and pain
Awaiting peace - 'tis not in vain
Earthly people turn to me
You have no fruit for me to see

There is no hope for those who hear
Come quickly, get release from fear
Keep faith strong in the Lord
Learn how to serve Him in one accord

Joy will be everlasting in each life
As they walk in obedience free from strife
Seek earnestly God's word! His promise sure
Forever his righteousness will endure

In Kingdom under royal direction
All beings will grow into perfection
Tranquility and Happiness with pure love
Blessings from God showered from above.

Susan Essler

The Farm

On Prairie Road near Junction City,
As road name suggests area country-pretty,
Home where Derelle and John live and pray,
And generations of kids come to stay,
Hugs the brown ground,
Low and high green hues surround.
In winter all white on white,
Even wisp of smoke from chimney is white.
In summer quite a different sight,
Soft pink and deep crimson glads accent delight.
Choo-choo signal, not of era late,
Welcomes one at the gate.
Most creatures native, not of heritage afar,
But Brahma cattle in pasture are.
Horses in another pasture have nothing to say,
If they did, would always end in Nay and Neigh.
Contrast to wind-stirred splash on lake shore,
A melody not far from the kitchen door.

Joseph Rutkowski

Dark-Horse Gambler

I never knew the old man or where-ever he came from.
He wasn't there to lend a hand, though we met once or twice.
Yet, by the way that he lived, I picked-up this advice:

There's a dark horse with no rider coming out of the sun.
So, run with the wind, kid, don't quit till you've won.

Life's like a mustang, a wild, untamed thing.
It will bite you, and kick you, and throw you out of the ring.

So, grab hold of the reins, and spur-on your wild dreams.
Just spur your dreams on kid, spur-on your wild dreams.

Don't look to your back, don't make any deals.
Your life is a race with luck at your heels.

Just take what you're dealt, and deal what you can.
Don't look for a promise, there's no magic plan.

The joy is in loving, the pain is in loss.
Your birth was the ticket, your life is the cost.

There's no trophy, no ribbon, no win, place, or show;
But that everyone finishes, God only knows...

Love's a dark horse with no rider running easy as pie.
So, go fly with the wind, kid, don't let love pass you by.
Go, catch that dark horse before it kicks mud in your eye.

   m. l. farahay

Thankful

I'm thankful to be in this world
I'm thankful to see our flag unfurl
I'm thankful for all the mistakes made
I'm thankful for the foundation it laid

I'm thankful to see the beautiful sky
I'm thankful as the day go by
I'm thankful you are my friend
I'm thankful for all you send.

I'm thankful for the littlest of things
I'm thankful for the freedom that rings
I'm thankful for Mothers and Dads who care
I'm thankful for people that share

I'm thankful for those who have less
I'm thankful because they are blessed
I'm thankful for people who love
I'm thankful most of all, for "God" above

I'm thankful that children exist
I'm thankful for soldiers that take a risk
I'm thankful that my life was made full
I'm thankful because I'm thankful

   Louis Freeland Green

To The Wind

O mighty messenger of God,
Against whose pow'r man dares not lift his hand,
Whose forcefulness brings giants to the sod,
Who sings from vale to mountain o'er the land,
Your mood respects no rule of place or time;
Your strength possesses day and claims the night,
But through the ages you have been sublime
In nature. Yet thou'rt hid from human sight.
Our lives, less strong but visible, retire
And leave no legacy of lasting fame.
Our tireless efforts fail to fan the fire
That sparks a state of greatness or acclaim.
We've toiled, like you, but left behind but aught
To show the work our hands and minds have wrought.

   Owen Everett Humphrey

Shedding

Dedicated to Eleanor Julig

I heard this morning that it's illegal to own certain bird's feathers.
Federal Government should concentrate on serious issues,
   not the weather.
Each animal, even we humans, have the ability to shed their outer skin.
They even become more colorful and beautiful when we are allowed
   to see in.
I watched a friend so tenderly help her Iguana's itchy flakes as
   they fell.
The Iguana became MORE colorful once its old skin became an
   empty shell.
Writing poems is one way that I began to change my own clothes.
It enabled me to trust the others that God above has chose
to assist me in my shedding process which can be hard to do alone.
It can be extremely painful for me. It felt like I was hitting bone.
Shedding is a part of life. Feathers do fall off of birds.
I know not if they grow another one but I am still full of words.
So shedding is an eternal process that we all need to recognize
because at the end, skin or none, we are able to win First Prize!

   Lisa Lindstrom

Sierra Stylings

Caring,
Oscar Sierra,
Empathizing with people,
Listening to idiosyncratic personalities,
Understanding.

Understanding,
Individual needs,
Styling each curl,
Sniping here and there,
Longevity.

Longevity,
Customer loyalty,
Befriending like family,
Believing everyone is special,
Caring.

   Betty Luddington

Peace

In the days and years of my life
Peace has come to me in various ways,
It speaks a language all its own
And quiets and comforts many of my days.

Seeing a stream that flows along
In its lazy tranquil role,
To me, it sings a joyful song,
And peace abides within my soul.

Walking in the wooded hills
Such existence of beauty I see,
All nature is awake and bringing
Calmness and soothing peace to me.

Years ago when my children's bedtime arrived,
Hearing their prayer was such a sweet part,
All of the wonderful love we shared
Brought peace that dwelled within my heart.

When wars have ceased, and hatred ended
As well as anger and pain,
When justice for all is won
Only then, will lasting peace reign.

   Jean Nabhan

Chaos

Emerging like a charging locomotive
From dense darkness of misty mornings
It shatters all delightful day dreams
With the actuality against which I pray.

Its whistle sounds ominously close
Heralding my deftly declining existence
Which with relinquished relish has soured
To meager motions in a dubious domain.

Why has life been rent from my grasp?
A fertile future now dimmed by death
Through an agonizing anticipation
Of understood utterly unknown lands.

Eugenia A. Nero

Love's Journey

Along Love's Journey, pain occurs.
Above all, that of separation.
Through this pain, one is able.
To open, the door to understanding.

That in love, one is not abandoned.
But only, the other has gone ahead.

The human way, only understands,
The here and now.
Look beyond the door to tomorrow.
For when one looks, one sees.

The final perfection of Love's Journey.
Which, when again together, is forever.

What then is the purpose of the pain?
The answer being, impart to those,
Who surround the one waiting to be one again,
The strength and understanding,

To continue, in kind,
Love's Journey.

John Nevshemal

Amber's Smile

I know a young lady named Amber.
She's the daughter of my dearest friend.
Be warned, to those boys whom come calling,
For young hearts which are broke may not mend.

She walks with the grace of a princess.
Her manners are always at best.
You could spot her in a crowd of millions,
Cause her beauty divides all the rest.

Her eyes, they shine as bright as the sun.
Her dark tresses are worn straight and long.
Red roses embrace each side of her cheek,
So perfect, I can find nothing wrong.

Yet, it's her smile that captures her prey.
So brilliant, it is seen from afar.
It compares to nothing I've ever known,
More stunning than the moon and the stars.

Yes, I know a young lady named Amber.
And as she grows, each day I will pray,
That this beauty she wears on the outside,
Shall also be worn inside, as it is today.

Karen Shahidi

Just Love Me

I love you, she said impulsively; a planted seed.
I love you, I love you, I love you,
The words echo through my mind unstilled!
No other words could arouse this anguish unfulfilled.
I love you, I love you, I love you,
Unfettered in my memory, as said appealingly at the start;
From a murmur to a shriek as it repeats relentlessly,
Long smoldering desires explode into being in my heart!
Let there be an end to this benign complacency,
Ere it turns into a farce of futility.
Tormented with twinges of agony for desperate meeting,
A joining of our very inner senses in deed,
The ecstasy of our mating bodies completing
By union so long delayed, a satisfaction to my need.
Oh, was there a tone of dalliance that I have failed to heed?
Could this be guile or a faithless myth proposed to me?
Were these words, so firmly planted, only said in vanity?
Have a modicum of pity, please leave me at least my sanity.
Just love me, just love me!
Oh please my dear one, just love me, just love me.

Robert J. M. Unger

God

Is there any way I can prove there is a God, I asked myself day in and
day out - And finally it came to me within, almost as in a shout

Yes there is a God - but - you have to open your soul so you can see
So I closed my eyes - said okay - my soul is open - show me thee

I opened my eyes and to my amazement for which I had been blind
God opened my soul to see He is real and that He is extremely kind

With a voice within my soul said look to the sky and you will see
So I stood in amazement and asked, who but God could have made all
the heavens/galaxies/planets/moons/stars/earth and me

Then I opened my soul to look again to see God's wonderful
works on earth
Who but God could have made nature the way it is,
trees/plants/bushes/grass/fruits/vegetables/all on this turf

One more time I was told to open my soul to see all God's handiwork
for man to marvel at - Fish of every kind/animals of all sizes/birds
of every color and beauty/and even the dogs and cats

And lastly the voice within said to go look in a mirror to see the
last of God's wonders He put on this planet which He made from dust
So I looked in amazement to see me in that mirror - and - I no longer
asked to be proven if there was a God - He proved it all too well -
I looked no further - it's Him I now trust.

Gary Vochatzer

"At Heaven's Gate"

I will be there at Heaven's Gate, waiting for you my son
So continue to be faithful and pray, 'til your earthly life is done
Because later you will meet the Master in His Golden chair
And oh, the Glory then you will also share
I have heard you singing each morning you see
And oh, I am so happy for thee
I tell the other angels about you too
So they all gather around when they hear you
I also tell them you were given the great talent to write
And all of your poems are always right
You write about the Master and His great love
And about the beautiful Golden Mansions here above
You always pray for the ones that have fallen away
And ask the Blessed Lord to help them return to Him someday
So you see my son is a believer and prays every day
And some day we will be reunited, when the Master calls him away
So I will be waiting for him to come you see
And then he can sing the beautiful songs with me.

Eugene Ward

The Awakening

This morning as I lay sleeping, the sounds of dawn came creeping.
A tiny bird awakened me... when he started his lovely symphony.
Determined was that little bird, to sing his song till he was heard.
"Wake up earth- each one of you,
Time to get started - there is work to do."
Don't form your opinion by what you see,
Although I am small, each one must hear me.
Time to get going with his songs of mirth,
Empowered to awaken inhabitants of earth.
Crying softly to creatures- have no fear,
To face the day, your Father is near.
What a wonderful way to begin the day,
With a lovely song in a special way.
This music was sweetest I ever heard,
From the gentle chirp of that little bird.

Betty M. Waugh

Rodney Kruse

I have a chiropractic doctor, his name is Rodney Kruse.
I go to him for visits, the pain in my body won't refuse!

He is a very happy person,
He's been so good to me!

He gives my body treatments,
From my head to toes and knee.

He is a very good man, he makes my pain is own...
He doesn't want his patients to suffer, "if you have any pain,
   just phone."

Thanks be to this dear doctor, from the bottom of my heart..
For if I didn't have this man in my life,
My body would fall apart!

Ellen Kaye Webb

"Grafting"

As in the "GRAFTING" of a rose bush
with the buds from others grown,
we all could live united...
greater beauty never known!

We all can live on common turf
and grow in harmony!
With the diversity of cultures,
enriched our lives would be.

If we traced our family tree,
we'd find we're all related;
as the One inside the greenhouse,
each seed... He equally created.

Just like the "GRAFTING" of the rose bush
creates a blend of radiance!
Protect each seed... nurture the soil,
inspire peace rose continuance!

In this world... a flower bed,
a mixture of such crafting!
Each bud a beauty by itself...
greater beauty when there's "GRAFTING"!

Patricia A. Wessel

An-Pta-Ni-Ya - Dawn Coming

In the profound stillness I wait. Darkness. Night
as the nether-world without a dawn; tenebrous obscurity on and on.
Interminable the wait, without starlight or ray of
sister Moon. Benign, the constellation of Great Warrior
sun o'er the Long Yellow Road; so subtle — the pristine alpha.
Evanesce the night tide Spirit's acquiescence with
Great Warrior Sun; interminable and infinite the
iridescence in the chaste Father Sky on this untouched new-day-dawn...

Owen R. Britton

A Daughter-Father In Baffling Teens

Through memory's album tonight I skim
In haste but find no more than painful times
When draining hours of nouns and verbs and French
Made our struggle so much dreaded nonsense;
Or sitting in a car by school to wait
For teachers whom you begged that I refrain
From asking questions that embarrassed you;
Or when the cold-cracked ice entrapped your skate
And snapped your leg and left you all alone
Outstretched on snow in throbbing fibril pain;
Or on return from German lands, you deplaned,
A peacock in teutonic clothes, while I stood,
Bouquet in hand, and you held back your glance
From me and I troubled, "Will memories
Of pleasant past and happy sparks of yore
Remove from present times these hurts
That penetrate the moments now longer
Than forever and wipe out always pain
Around your face until you swim in star-dust
Streams that flow like golden floating rainbows?"

Gus Wilhelmy

A Purpose For Prayer

In life when there is no meaning,
And our work feels real demeaning,
Dreams we have dreamt have no key,
Our eyes are blind for good to see,
Our ears hear joyful thoughts fly away,
That's when we need to stop and pray:

Dear God:

Send us some hope today,
Keep us out of sin and harm's way,
Make us feel your work will be done,
Keep us in faith, believing in your son,
Let us know of the love he gives,
Remind our souls that he still lives,
Help us appreciate an eternity we'll see,
By believing in you and the Holy Trinity.

Karen M. Wilson

Dusk To Dawn

Tis neither dark nor yet is light
Tis not day, nor yet tis night,
But merely dawn, or is it dusk.
It is a time which in God we must trust
To see us through just as we do the rest of the day

Be not frightened as shadows draw nigh,
But trust in God on high.
We will make it through the night,
Till morning comes, the shadows flee and the sun shines bright.

Our loved ones have gone on before
They are gathered on that other shore.
With God they now reside,
Till we join them on the other side.

Glenda A. E. Zimmerman

If I Could Wish a Wish Tonight

If I could wish a wish tonight,
My wish for you would be so bright.

Days of joy and days of love,
My wish to you comes from the Lord above.

If I could wish a wish tonight,
You are my wish; you are my light.

A Rainy Day Poem by
Raymond John Valentine Koerner

Childhoodless

Everyone was treated the same
Except for their names.
The same amount of money
So we could live with
A pretend happy family.
I suddenly became the adult
After receiving his paid sexual assaults.
When the secret was told
I went to a home where
Everyone was treated the same
Except for their names.
The same amount of money with paid care.
I was young among the old
Waiting for my life to unfold
With yearning for a love that I didn't have to share.
Gradually, I gained partial freedom
Where everyone is treated the same except for their names.
Different amounts of money and I'm still the young among the old
Still wanting to feel that body hold.
I wish someone had enough tenderness not to let me die
childhoodless.

Whitney Lyons

The Tables Of Time

When fate decides to turn its tables, dear
When time and all its little tricks are done
And when my last breath finally draws near
You still shall be my one and only one....

Through all the dark eternities of death
In caverns of the winds, in shadows deep
I'll play a part in everything you do
Until you join me in my lasting sleep....

I'll follow you down each long road you wonder
Through all the quiet times of each new day
And I'll make you remember of a love
Not meant to be, but happened anyway....

Upon the pages of your heart and soul
I shall inscribe each vivid memory
I'll always be a dream away from you
You'll always be a thought away from me....

Helen Dodge

Innate Perception

Millions of Lights are shining on our Hill
For people who work long and stop to think.
There is a fire which can destroy the Earth.
It is the will of man against his Kin-
Against his own God who created him.
Power unlimited we do resent.
A child needs to grow in security,
With those who see the Lights upon the Hill;
No mandates, embargoes and grief by law
To vex Public Schools. They need time to think.

Lucretius said long ago in Rome: "Men
Lead on and none to hold us back",
The aftermath of war and sin and hate.
Our health is ours to build and stay alive.
Our minds are charts to rate technology.
Self control builds character, love and peace.
Children are aware of security.
They learn to help and serve the cause of Peace,
Against the centuries of war and woe,
They can work quietly for days to come.

Mary K. Dissinger

Mind Mime

The rhythm of words conveys a secret
Which only the heart can hear.
Pythagoras taught the music of spheres
And poetry paints it most clear.

A subtle drumbeat inherently throbs
Within every phrase, every breath,
A chorus bearing the soul songster's meter
'Neath a harmonic whispering near.

A poem is a waterfall fluting soul's tinkling
When wind chimes come shuddering still.
A gallant attempt to communicate depth
Without speaking or hearing at all.

A zephyr in tempo with riplet unspoken
In pace with Summer's last gasp.
That breeze so benign blows the cloud from the mind
Revealing the poet's word gift.

Craig Watson

The Heirloom Teapot

The delicate china teapot that sits on the dining room table
is very impressive to look upon with its exquisite decorative
scenes, depicting days of long ago which to the eye is a delight
and to own a heart's dream.

An heirloom passed down from mother to daughter, a gift to
forever treasure. Enjoyed by all 'round the table where tidbits
of gossip are shared as they sip their afternoon tea.

The teapot is handled with tender loving care as if a priceless gem,
to be admired, held dear to the heart and preserved for generations
to come.

Many wonderful memories are attached to this teapot with its brightly
colored scenes. (If only it could talk what amazing stories it could
tell, so it seems).

We thank God for this precious keepsake, the likes of which we have
never seen as we lovingly gaze upon it. For the caring and handing
down of this teapot to a daughter who will love it and do the same.

May time grant that more wonderful memories will be added to its
store and continue to flow to this heirloom legend which will be
cherished by each daughter evermore.

Marolyn E. Baker

Veritia

I sought nothing and that is all now found,
Here, there, and everywhere for no reason.
My left eye burns; the other right one drowned,
Amid colors and tears for each season.

Listen: the sky has wept and wailed once more,
Waxed and waned, then shudderingly is sad.
Veritia, always true, is a sore
That lingers and festers, then becomes bad.

She was so unfaithful, like all the rest,
The one that my blind eye knew very well.
Once I thought of her truthfulness was best,
Then learned nothing else as down I did fall.

I have discovered that words are but words,
And their meanings may be something not heard.

Ashton John Fischer Jr.

The Joy Of Poetry

Poems should be ever so joyful
   filling your heart with glee
Picturing something perfect
   setting your imagination free.

Try, if you will, in your mind's eye
   can you clearly and truly see
Laughing and giggling children
   that were once you and me?

Or lovers on a dance floor
   lost in blissful reverie
Whispering words of love
   that were once you and me?

Can you close your eyes and see
   a bride in a gown so lovely
With a tuxedoed smiling groom
   that were once you and me?

Yes, poems should be ever so joyful
   capturing enrapturing thoughts perfectly
So enjoyed by those with imagination
   that nostalgically - were once you and me.

   William Henry Jones

Based On Right... A...Shining Knight...

Words from a pixie... not a rogue... inspiration gathered from vogue...
To the plant kingdom and the animal kingdom... too...
   came an eggplant's ultimatum... Just like that...
I'm crowning myself King of Easter in my pixie hat...
   an eggplant's ultimatum... Just like that...
   and there will be a change in the pastel hue...
   were the words that followed from a visional view...
   then... Operation Sage... just grew and grew...
Yes... It started with a veggie... that shining eggplant...
   then came the noise and the shouting you can't...
   your reason being... you're an eggplant...
   you're capitalizing on your name and you can't...
   admittedly tho'... you are an eggplant...
Then came affirmative action in his voice...
You be the judge and make the choice...
I'm crowned... in my pixie hat...
   the one I was christened in... it's as simple as that...
   the deliberation proceeded... no that hat's not a crown...
   admittedly tho'... it's the most authentic around...
   and based on right... that eggplant was christened to be a
   shining knight...

   C. Jeannette Myers

To Dance

I want to dance among the moonbeams
   while the angels are at play ——
I want to hear their joyful singing,
   "Wasn't this the greatest day?"
I want to hear those happy voices,
   and the true sounds of their harps.
Their praises are so heavenly,
   they sing from such loving hearts.
Sweet sounds abound, and love surrounds,
   as I dance among the moonbeams —
And the angels play around.

   Delight Melaragño

Midnight Calling

Awoken by your presence in the middle of the night,
A haunting, sickening feeling of unmistaken fright.
By the hand you took me, as if it was your deed,
A never-ending journey, I followed in your lead.
Winding turns and narrow roads, a most confusing path,
Consumed by your gentility, despite your evil wrath.
Glimpses of the sun I caught, as you unlatched the gate,
To a world I had not seen before, a world conquered by fate.
I continued in your footsteps, for now I was your slave,
Motionless we stood when we came upon your grave.
Illuminated by the dawn, with a devilish sort of glow,
The graveyard home to ghosts and spirits who now rest down below.
A rose was set upon your tomb with a faded, unclear name,
My cheeks were stained with tears while I wondered why you came.
As my hands clutched yours tighter, I felt you slip away,
Back into the earth you went, without a word to say.
An enchanting sound of silence, the willows did not weep,
I was bewildered by the reason that you took me from my sleep.
Never did I visit, you were nowhere to be found,
I gathered up my sense and pride, and simply turned around.

   Julie Leventhal

Endless Bond

Years of love... Of trust... And caring
Our lives together... Ever sharing

Deeply aware... My love for you
How right... For us... To say, "I do."

How meaningless... Without you... My life would be
Me without you... You without me
We without Yuki... For we are three

Our love abiding... Makes for ease of this writing
Words of love from my heart do spill
For you, my love... For your heart to fill

Like a river rushing... In continuous motion
Our love flows like a sunlit ocean
Swirls of glistening light... Reflections of present and past
Of by-gone times... And now... How they last
Thinking back on then... And then now
How we have loved and kept our vow

Your strength and laughter... Ever there for me
Like an ever-constant river... Flowing endless to the sea

Beyond that... Which is love... There is... Not a thing
If life without you... You without me

   Eunice Ann Gearhart

Dayspring!

I don't like to miss the morning,
I love the earth before the 'world' begins...
I test old sayings...
Does rain before seven really stop before eleven?
Usually. (I've been there to know.)
Does the early bird Really catch the worm?
Yes. (When the ground is damp, but firm.)
I listen and watch...
On the road, the neighbor's cat aims for Home,
Anxious for breakfast and a good day's rest.
From the north, a cheerful rooster crows!
At dawn, the birds sing in celestial chorus!
The sky reflects the glory of the unrisen sun!

I Love The Earth before the 'world' begins!
I Dare Not Miss The Morning!

   Virginia Pease Ewersen

When You Say Goodbye

Unto this Earth a child was born
To live and learn and die.
To love and hate then love again
Before it closed its eye.

What lessons did it learn when
Its life touched yours and mine?
Did it put a smile upon your lips
Or bring only tears to your loving eyes?

And now that the child is grown old
And its life is slipping away,
Can you say goodbye with love in your heart
And wish it peace in its last days?

It lived its life upon this Earth
Without following a perfect pattern.
And of all the riches it acquired,
Your love is the only one that mattered.

So say "I love you" when you say goodbye
You'll feel better for it.
And the soul that passed this way today
Will keep that love forever.

Doris Upchurch

Join Our Cruise

I'm sailing on the seas of peace and forgiveness,
Won't you come along with me?
Jesus is the pilot.
He's chartered the course carefully.
When storms come along,
He calms the sea.
No need to be frightened,
He's at the helm.
He's the only one
Who can lead us home.
  This vessel is headed to the New Jerusalem.
  With Jesus at the helm
  It won't take long.
  With the Holy Spirit for our crew
  We'll make the trip comfortably.
  He'll see to our needs
  All day long.
  So come along and join
  This cruise of tranquility
  The price is believing in Him.

Lorraine Kay

My Mother's Heartbeat

The heart of a Mother, I am told,
Is made of the purest kind of gold.
The constant rhythm of its beating plea,
Telling all who taunt me, they'll have to flee.
While laying against my mother's breast,
Her talking and heartbeat gave dreamy rest.
Sometimes now that I am old with age,
If I listen very quietly, these faint beats will engage.
Soothing and peaceful her heartbeats return,
Preserving forever, linking heartbeat and me, I yearn.
My Mother is eighty-eight, I am twenty years less,
But I'll always remember her heartbeat,
  as I lay against her breasts.

Royce D. Wellman

I Promise You

One day God reached down, from heaven above,
And touched our hearts, with the miracle of love.
Since that amazing day, we have walked assure,
That our wonderful love, shall forever endure.

Upon our wedding day, we shall stand, side by side,
Heart to heart, in faith and love, we shall abide.
And face to face, we shall see mutual love reflected,
As by the invisible embrace of love, we are protected.

Hand in hand, we shall declare our love, heart to heart,
And vow to honor an cherish, until in death we part.
Then soul to soul, we shall pray as husband and wife,
A prayer for guidance, upon the journey of married life.

And arm in arm, we shall face the world entwined,
As if one, which neither angels nor demons can unbind.
Two souls joined together as one, heart to heart forever.
I promise you, that bond of love shall not be severed.

From this day forward, we shall walk, side by side.
My beloved, I promise you, we shall always abide,
Hand in hand, together forever, as if one not two.
I promise you my perfect love. I promise you.

Patricia Stone Guynn

When Under Our Care

It's hard to deny what clearly we see
But yet there are those who just won't admit
That the violence displayed on T.V.
Motivates notions for crimes to commit

Granted...violence has always been here
Way before we had so much to review
But why encourage what year after year
Has been a national tragic issue?

With more and more youth clashing with the law,
I have to wonder about role models
Was it their parents, or T.V. they saw
...Who was home developing their idols?

Children are the seeds our future grows from...
When under our care...their conduct, we own
In place of rage, let's cultivate wisdom
They don't know the way...don't leave them alone

If you don't raise them, the media will,
And their eyes and ears are willing to learn
As parents, this is our task to fulfill
...Don't throw it away...it's your Divine turn

Bob G. Martinez

Pollen's Prelude

Mulberry, Sycamore, Maple and Oak
All scatter so freely their gifts of pollen,
The outcome for many brings eyes which are swollen.
We'd rather not have this April fool's joke.
Another "side-benefit" starts-us sneezing.
Have you a cold or some obscure allergy?
"No," you may say, "I've just too much energy."

In time our trees will be clothed with green.
Song-birds will build, - then start to sing,
Welcome shade will defeat heat's sting.
Instead of pollen, life then is serene.

For ev'ry single complaining negative
There's a glorious, glowing exciting positive.

Carl Hackman

Grandpa And Three Visiting Canadian Sisters

Grandpa entered the U.S.A. in 1887
With his parents and most of his seven siblings.
All lived near Sioux Falls, South Dakota, deprived
For many years, pursuing their goal: homestead living.

My great grandparents became impatient and moved
To Winnipeg where they settled down in Canada
With all but three of their children who endured
A fruitless nineteen years of searching for homesteads in America.

In 1921 three of grandpa's sisters
Boarded a train for Temvik, North Dakota
To visit three elder siblings
For a few days of enlightening and frolicking.

During 1918-1923 my father was farming the homestead, proudly.
Grandpa now lived in Temvik near his livery stable.
He hitched up his team of horses to meet the train, eagerly
Where he picked up his sisters in a buggy, neat and capable.

Grandpa hauled his ladies out to his homestead post haste.
What a scene that was as I, age six,
Watched him showing them his successful ventures with such grace.
At last I recognized my grandpa's truly noble characteristics!

Theodore R. Reich

Rainbows

I live in a rainbow place
where the world puts on its rainbow face.

Sometimes they arch majestically.
Sometimes they're just little bits for me.

I see them dance upon the mountains.
I see them hover o'er the sea,
I see them shining in the valleys,
shimmering beauty for all to see.

I see them in the morning mist,
I see them in the rain.
No matter where I see them,
I'm blessed again and again.

So I live my life in this rainbow place;
I love my world with its rainbow face.

My soul soars as they arch majestically;
I cherish the peek-a-boo bits for me.

Edna Pakele

Life's Tapestry

Life can be compared to a tapestry
Woven each day at a time
The pattern fashioned by our doing
Of things, either negative, helpful, needed or fine.

I hope that my tapestry be woven
With thoughtful loving care
So when I come to the finish
"A worthy one", people shall declare,

And may I in the weaving
Find the challenges of daily life
Not too great to be taken in stride
And each day's efforts seem just right.

Then shall the work be joyous
Though some days brighter by far
But the fact that I still can be weaving
Should make me most grateful to God.

May I show gratitude by continuing
To design a pattern that flowers
And may that which still lies ahead
Be woven in peace and understanding in happy hours.

Helen Shagrin

A Place In My Heart

There's a place in my heart where your love used to live
and it aches from the pain since you've gone.
And you think what you want is a world without me,
but too soon you will see you are wrong!

For I paid all my dues, walked away from the world
just to come here and be by your side.
And some day, all too soon, you'll be old and alone
and have nothing left but your pride.

You broke all your promises and shattered my life
and I'll have to go on without you.
I sadly remind you that because of your choice
our dreams will never come true!

There's a place in your heart....
where my love used to live...

Jo Tucker

I Am Here And I Don't Sleep

In our hearts your memory lingers.
Always tender, fond and true.
there's not a day, dear Mother.
We don't think of you.

It was 6 years ago today.
That God took you home.
You will never be forgotten.
You are always in our hearts.

I think about the happy times.
That we had shared.
I think about your special love.
And the way you always cared.

And with each thought my heart is filled.
With gratitude and pride.
Because it meant so much to me.
to have you by my side.
I am the swift up rush of birds arching in flight.
I am the soft shine at night.
We did not stand by a grave and cry.
I am not there, I did not die.

Evelyn T. Tallman

"Who's Pushing Who?"

As I toss here in bed - a thought rings through my head,
    I wonder, if this could possibly be.
It'll stay on my mind, - 'til an answer I find,
    Am I pushing eighty - or is eighty pushing me?

I suppose it could be said - he's "teched' in the head.
    With this, I don't quite agree.
A below the belt blow, don't really let me know;
    Am I pushing eighty, or is eighty pushing me?

It's been rattlin' my brain - like a rushing freight train,
    It really has me up a tree.
This puzzling doubt - I can't figure out,
    Am I pushing eighty, or is eighty pushing me?

There's still time left - to get many things done.
    With time set aside - for some good, honest fun.
But, now you know son, why I'm on the run,
    It's old "Father Time" that's pushing me!

Richard E. Nickel

The Blue Sky Club

In Memory of Dick Olney
Lying in an open field, half hidden by the grass,
Immersed in green, I gazed into a clear blue sky.
I listened to the sounds around; the sounds of birds;
Trees whispering in the wind;
The distant sound of people far away;
The sound of my own breathing.
Washed over a by a myriad of perfumed breezes
I felt myself become as one with earth and sky,
And then dark clouds began to gather overhead.
All about was dark and I began to fear the darkness
Had become my life and I began to doubt the light.
Just then from the murky sea of doubt,
Because my prayer of fear was heard,
My soul was lifted up above the clouds.
I floated in the clear blue sky suspended by the light.
It's then I learned I always have the light of life,
It's always there within me and without.
Because of this I know my life is not the gathered clouds
But ever more a clear blue sky of endless possibility.

LeRoy Douglas Taylor

The Stranger

Panic Disorder is something I have, which took a toll on me.
But I had to learn to deal with it, or it would never let me be.
It's put restrictions on my life, and I can only go certain places.
Where I can only be around, very familiar faces.
Until my husband met this stranger, who had suffered the same
  problems as me.
And showed him a medal, and explained to him, how it helped
  to set her free.
This stranger gave this medal, to him to give to me.
She wanted me to have it, to help me to foresee.
Our Lady of Knock was the name of the saint, a name I never
  heard before.
But when you get to know her, she's a saint you will adore.
She's helped me through some rough times, and I swear by this saint.
And if she wasn't there to pray to, I would become really faint.
I want to meet this stranger, she changed my life around.
Just so I can let her know, how my life is not so bound.

Laurie Oddo

Ocean Side View

Racing down the oceanside road of
past life follies, I see a beauty in nature
that I've never seen before
consciousness and innocence are mine again
you gave me this new life, this new joy which
before I had never felt, but when I looked into
your eyes the trees were green, the sky was blue,
and the sun was a golden yellow like the color of your hair
your plainness was extravagant to me and your extravagance
was blinding, but never had I beheld such a beautiful
blinding sight. I can only say what I mean in
this medium that is always unseen and every time
I see you again you only feed my new vision to
maybe try and crawl out of this hole they threw
me into. You gave me a hope, a vision and a light.
You gave me the chance to once again question
right and wrong and to see God again, not as
fiction but as something I can believe in.
You gave me something that I can never repay you back for
you gave me back my life and you gave me back my love.

Stewart Schuster

The Two Of Us

What to me is a beginning
To you may be an end.
What to me is everlasting
To you may be the opposite my friend.
What does life hold in store for the two of us?
It's a waiting game based on mutual trust.
Time alone will tell us which way we're destined to go.
Then and only then will we understand and know
If it's together, forever, just you and me,
Remember, in this life, what will be, will be

Janice Schultz

The River Of Life

The river of life flows swiftly, turbid and deep, never still.
It rushes on, cutting its course through sorrow's valley over joy's
  high hill.
It sighs, it sings, it murmurs; it roars a hearty protest,
As it meets each newly found challenge and rises to the test.
Each of us has a restless wave, whose variant crest we must ride,
To face each day to its predestined end, to sink or float with the tide.
The river tumbles on, rushing each bend over rapids of turmoil,
  waking whitecaps of pain.
'Til at last it reaches the delta of peace to sink into the earth,
  to seek once again
A new mouth, a well-spring, a source of release.
Forcing its way with the current, seeking what fate will ordain.

Grethe G. Bichel

A Little Star

I saw a little star on high
It shone so very bright.
I closed my eyes and whispered low,
And made a wish that night.

I wished that I was not so old, that it didn't hurt to walk,
For times when I would run so hard that I could barely talk.
I wished for sounds that I could hear when I was younger too,
The whippoorwill, the babbling brook, the footsteps in a shoe.

I wished for things I could not have, yes, I know that it's a dream,
For I will die in a moments time and know what life can mean.
It means to dream and wish aloud on all the stars above
And know that God will give to you His precious, precious love.

I saw a little star on high
It shone so very bright.
I closed my eyes and whispered low,
And told the Lord, "Good Night."

Nanette Taylor

Wyoming's Palette

Hot summer wind, quivering green grass, scarlet Indian Paintbrush
  Silver streams flashing with rainbow trout, quench parched
  brown earth
Great Blue Herons glide across the water
  White, black, yellow, brown—complexions of frontier adventurers.

Vast amber plains ripple on cool autumn morns
  Shimmering gold aspen leaves cascade—evicting summer tenants
Harvest moon, trails of blue-green pine and juniper
  Red-blooded laborers seek harmony with subtle hues of nature.

Frigid white blizzards sweep through mountains
  Lustrous tan herds migrate, gray-coated coyotes hunt
Ranchers, farmers, sun-browned stewards of the land
  Withstand winter's iridescent sparkle of merciless cold.

Rambling wild pink rose, swarming yellow bumblebees
  Rusty marmots, golden eagles, birds of purple, cinnamon, teal
Vermilion cliffs, sagebrush prairies, white-capped peaks,
  cornflower skies
Myriad colors of man and nature paint tomorrow's landscape.

Catherine Hefferan

A Child's Prayer

As in my room I lie abed,
A small voice reached me and it said,
"God! Bless Mommy and Daddy, too.
I know they're special to me and you!
Bless all of us, this I pray.
From thy righteous route, let us not stray.
Bless our leaders, may they understand
Peace is to reign throughout all the land.
Thank you God! Now I will sleep,
Knowing my soul you'll safely keep."
'Twas my voice I heard from days gone by.
And I repeat the words, as here I lie.

John W. Kauffman

Love's Infancy

Love is hard to disperse, to separate, to take apart
Even that of the mind, from that of the heart
Because one grows from the other and both can start
The feelings, of a brightened day, an awakened sense of new
Of blue days that now hold fast a favorable hue
And why it is this way, most do not have a clue
For, the infancy of love disguises what one knows
Like a shadow cast by moonlight on new snow
Clear and distinct but void of details though
But Oh! The image is so vivid, so easy to see
Look! It's in black and white, how plain can it be
It's not. For it's the heart not the mind in love's infancy
For it is the passionate, infatuation kind
Seeing only what it wants to see, it's blind
Influenced by the heart and not the mind

Larry D. Wallace

Remembering My Love For You Gerald

Straight into my life you walked that night; that old brown hat on head and a gleam in your beautiful blue eyes.

God answered my prayers, I said day after day to guide you to my house that way, with the beat of my heart and the change in your voice I knew that I loved you right there at the start. The first time you kissed me was a breathtaking dream, as my prayers went to heaven always let it be me, as your arms held me in comfort and you loved me with joy, I knew that forever I would want to be yours. So the day that you left me you had no choice for the pains that was dealt us weighed heavy on our hearts, with God in his heaven and you in your state, I am alone and feel out of place.

As days may come and days may go, we may meet again in a soft fallen snow, and with the beat of my heart and the change in your voice, we will have once again the love we had at the start and vow to each other we will never more part.

Love Forever,
Roni Lane Skaggs

Wrought Iron

The muted, metallic sound of
  sheet metal flapping in the wind
The night is blackish - grey like wrought iron
I see things that aren't there
Flashing visions out of the corner of my eye
They appear and are gone in a second
I tell myself they aren't there, but
  I'm not sure I believe it
Was that a scream, a cry?
Voices on the breeze
A far off sound perhaps only in my mind.

Troy Young

The Visitor

Rapping on the door came to me,
It was late, who could it be.
Cautiously the door was opened,
Surprised at who I seen,
Tear faced, she stood before me.

Gently I took her in
Not knowing what I could do.
A lot of emotion came tumbling out,
Pain and hurt seemed to swell and mount.
Why was she here and so late out?

Many hours we talked in the night,
Things I felt uncomfortable about.
Soon her problems seemed smaller, to our delight.
Comfortable and yawning, we were a sight,
As the hours seemed to pass us by in the night.

After a while a smile appeared upon her face,
A good listener was what I had been.
Feeling relieved of all pressure, she left my place.
A mother-in-law but now a friend in this case,
For Wisdom she had came to me in my place.

Marcia Vandervort

Little Golden Band

The sparkle in her eye was just a twinkle.
Her wizened old face bore many a wrinkle,
But on her tiny third finger, left hand
She still wore her treasured little golden band.

Many years ago her true love placed it there.
Though her step was slow and she had gray in her hair,
She carried in her mind memories in store
As she remembered those long sweet days of yore.

Now the little golden circle of a band
Reminded her how he held her heart in his hand.
His presence no longer there to be her guide,
But in her aged heart, he'll always abide.

Their love was pure and sweet, a treasure to relish.
Some children she bore, their lives to embellish.
Memories of yesterday have come and gone,
But one of her memories will always belong.

Nothing from the present could ever erase
The thoughts she had in her heart of his dear face.
Smiling, she gazed at her third finger, left hand
And her very own treasured little golden band.

Alice Myers Allgood

Prelude To The Sea

The ocean's rough and choppy, the sky is black with night,
The breakers ripple steadily against the sands of white;
'Tis peaceful now, 'tis tranquil, like an opera written well,
By Nature, the same Author of Heaven and of Hell.

That night I saw a cruise ship lighting up the sea,
Sailing over waters, deep as deep could be;
Wishing I were on that boat, yearning to be free,
Yet now I have to turn back to my poetry.

The waves roll together in gentle harmony,
Slashing on the jetties as soft as they could be;
There must be Chopin out there as the waves reach rhythmic heights,
And this opera is continuous for many, many nights.

Lawrence Rothman

What Of Time

Time it comes, time it goes
Sometimes fast, sometimes slow

A second here, a minute there
Time just seems to be everywhere

Time tells all, time never lies
Time never stops, time never dies

Time fills our hearts with hope and fear
Time gives us life from year to year

What is time we often say
Time is eternity a heartbeat away

David C. Shoenfelt

A Pastor, A Friend

I know a man not very old, who serves the Lord.
He has touched so many hearts young and old.

He has brought Jesus into so many hearts;
Changed so many lives, by his generosity.

Over the years he has been there with a helping hand,
Guiding the lost to the Lord.

We all have been blessed with
A helping hand guiding the lost to the Lord.

We all have been blessed with his words and praise.
We all have seen his faith on bended knee.

I know a man not very old,
Who has opened his heart to all those in need.

We thank God for blessing us with you.

Lora Albright

Respect And Love A Woman

Always respect a woman regardless of the cause
God created them for a purpose and it should never be at a loss.

They may not be in the same category
and have a different face but she must be respected
each and every day of grace.

Remember the early years when you were just a child,
who was there to embrace you and taught you how to smile?

As time progressed and you were off to school
who was that person that taught you the golden rule?
If you become broken hearted as you begin to date
remember that person who said "Sometimes It Pays To Wait"

Through life so far, you've been separated - discriminated -
irritated and at times duplicated, but remember
she told you to meditate.

As life proceed to fulfill our needs,
let it be an omen - respect a woman

A woman is, mother, wife, girlfriend, companion and God's gift
to man to help. Because if God made anything better than a woman
I'm sure He kept it for himself - peace and understanding equals love.

Azel R. Brown

The Artist

The Artist rests His brush on the pallette
To stand back for an over-view of His subject.

A demon child rushes in, takes the brush
And mixes the paints into a melange of dark colors.

Now Artist knows His purpose must be served,
So, with infinite patience, once again He sorts the hues,
Picks up His brush, and with timeless mercy,
Continues the pattern of life.

Lois M. Stevenson

A World Of Hope

Lord, take my heart and replace it with your own,
So I may follow the path that you've shown.
Lord, Give me your eyes so I may see,
All of your people who really need me.
Lord, give me your ears so I may hear,
Your heavenly angels singing to our king with such cheer.
Lord, give me your feet so I can walk that extra mile,
To get to your crying children and leave them with a smile.
Lord, give me your hands so I may help more,
All of your children who are tattered and torn.
Lord, give me your wisdom to always know what to do,
If we all helped our neighbor we'd be living like you.
If only I could make everyone see,
Loving each other is the way it should be.
Jesus is throwing us a big golden rope,
Lets climb up with the angels,
To a new world of hope.

Sheila Sumrall

December's Rose

On a cold and windy December day.
I could not believe my eyes.
Out under a lonely dogwood tree
A crimson rose had survived.

I gazed upon its beauty.
This rose I had never seen.
To wonder why it did not bloom
In the warm summer's breeze.

One has to wonder about this rose.
That bloomed around Christmas day.
To see its blossoms in December.
Only to die and fade away.

Everyday in cold December
I look for the crimson rose.
It has never come back and bloomed.
From under the winter snows.

The rose that blooms in the winter time.
Will never see the spring.
It has no warmth from the winter sun.
Will die from December's winds.

Margaret V. De Hart

Silence Of The Sunrise

I scream words of shattered dreams and ending days,
Yet no one listens, for the sun has not yet touched the horizon.
I stand drowning in the pounding raindrops and endless tears of fate,
And cannot run for it is time to face the truth.
I know the sun will soon rise and find me standing here,
Paralyzed by hidden emotion held locked with the key of true destiny.
I wait to hear the song of the pure dove,
For maybe then all will be still and solemn.
I still stand screaming, drowning in the silence of my heart,
And yet the sun is growing bigger, ever bigger,
In the untouchable corners of the horizon.
My dreams echo through me like the whispering winds
of a raging storm,
Furiously blowing, endlessly ceasing.
I am caught, and my pulse ceases,
For the sun has now reached the everlasting light of heaven.
This new day has brought tomorrow's fate,
With the wish that my dreams can now be touched
Through the never ending glass of time, seen only in the
Silence of the sunrise.

Lacy Ann Mills

Awakening Dreams

Lost in thoughts of you and me
  Strolling on the beach alone and free
When all of a sudden an image appears
  A little girl face streaming with tears
She whispered... "Mommy... Daddy"
  The vision fades
And once again I realize the choice I made.

A little girl that could've been mine
  Whispered so softly from the sky
A little voice only I could hear
  Promised me that she would always be near
First, she said, you must forgive yourself
  Then you must place the past on a shelf.
Look up above into the night
  And know you'll meet me when the time is right.

    Denise Kadach

My Grandfather Was Cremated

Every little speck which sparkles through the wind
and combines with the sparkle upon the water
Was my grandfather.
How I wish I could glue them all together and have
him before me again.
To watch him do the things he loved to do,
To ask him the questions I have to ask,
Just to see him once more.
But I'm afraid that is too selfish a notion for God to entertain,
because if I was to see him again
once would not be enough,
and I'd want to see him just once more,
and once more,
and just once more,
Please?
So,
instead,
though he feels missed to me on this earth
I must try to be satisfied with my memory,
in my heart, where he now Lives.

    Michele Nosal

Grandmom

How come your back is bent and
Your hair's so grey.
How did you get that way.
How come your steps are short and a stick
Leads your way, and when I stand beside you
I'm bigger than before
How did you get this way
The other day you called my name and it
wasn't the same, I feel so bad
Why is it you forgot my name
I asked you to remember the games we
played, the times we laughed.
I liked it the way it used to be
Instead you sit at the window eyes
fixed on nowhere, or are you just
trying to remember, the way it used to be.

    Martin F. Whalen

Love Is Like A Rose

Love is like a rose as long as you give
it nourishment it will grow.
But as soon as you stop it they both will die.
And love just like a rose as long as
it is growing it will become more
beautiful everyday.

    Norma Jean Floyd

Ode To Zachary

I have a little grandson that means the world to me.
He is just two years old and his name is Zachary.

He is big for his age, he never was a runt.
His favorite animal is the elephant.

He plays me out when he spends the night with me.
But, as soon as he goes home I am lonesome as can be.

If you have a grandson regardless of his name
I'm quite sure that you feel the same.

    Paulette G. Flowers

Roads

The roads to life are neverending
I have finally stopped pretending
There's hills and mountains, roads to cross
And none save God is quite the boss
You'll walk in darkness, through the night
An endless battle you must fight

Understanding is the key, some wise old man once said to me
But I locked the wisdom in a cage
Forgot that wisdom comes with age
And walked along the endless roads
To fight without a friend untold

Then one day a small light shown
Along the path a bird had flown
A flicker here a shimmer there, an old man's voice made me aware
Of pointless battles I had fought
Betrayed by youthful lack of thought

I staggered half berought my soul, tired of wandering, frozen cold
And saw the flames within the night, wisdom's fiery, cozy plight
And knew I had to fight no more
To thoughtless dreams, I closed the door.

    Christina Holmes Sanchez

No More Brain Wash! An Outcry!

Stop putting the bug in our head
You will get cancer and poisoned by lead

Stop taking away all of our pleasure
Instead of telling us "use but with measure"

Stop predicting our future in dying
If we don't "check up," You call it denying

Stop telling us all the bad food we eat
Don't wag your finger, give us a treat

Stop creating new measures of testing
In the name of prevention I am protesting!

Give us hope, say life can be wholesome
Let us enjoy it. You don't know the outcome.

Tell us, that if by chance we fall to the ill
We can get well again, if we have the will

Don't just credit MRI X-ray and CAT scan
Let us have the power "Yes I can, Yes I can"

Than you will see, the next generation
Growing up healthier, for a better nation.

    Eva A. Schiff

What Love Is

Love is strength, sweet, pure and true,
Something to always bring along with you,
Friendly, sharing, perfect caring.
And there will always be an open door,
For love is the happiest kingdom forevermore.

    Isaac Durand

Sonnet

If when you left me, I might yet exhume
The brittle bones of what was once myself
And knead with flesh again, there might be room
For comfort. Now, no sorcery-cogent elf,
Nor all the Gods, could Lazarus-fashion wake
What you with Merlin-touch have stretched in sleep
Forever. The peace of line-scored pages take
Their leave of me. Nor can I longer keep
The hounds of Loneliness at bay with Bach
And Brahms. And taunting neigh, and swan arched head
That challenge bold behind the paddock's lock
Find me colder than the fresh laid dead.
And yet, as trance days spell Infinity
A phantom hunts a lost identity.

L. Virginia Holland

The Scroll Of Secrets

Around every corner, behind every wall, there are secrets,
Secrets known by none at all,

In a flowery garden, by a magnificent wall,
How many promises were kept?

At a window overlooking a city, how many dreams were dreamt,
So long forgotten- even from within those walls?

In a wooded park, not far from home,
How many hopes were buried as somebody wept?

Around every corner, behind every wall, there are secrets,
Secrets known by none at all,

Perched on a pile of clouds, surrounded by mists of all colors,
Looms the silver and gold of a library of old,

Through marble halls and a lifetime's learnings,
Searching for something no mortal's eyes were meant to behold,

A page in a book, in a dream dreamt by most,
The secrets of life are hidden from all,

Around every corner, behind every wall, there are secrets,
Secrets known by none at all...

Brittany Rohrer

Embracement Of Love

Grasping that special someone in an
Embracement of one's heart, mind and
soul places them in an everlasting circle of love.

An embrace like holding a newborn child
which expresses a feeling to remember
and cherish eternally.

With open arms, one could receive the
love of their life holding their heart in
their hands that would relieve that special
Love one from everyday in every way that
they can with an embracement of love.

When someone has that special person
as the love of their life, a million tears
would not change the way they feel inside
where it does not matter what one does cause
they will be right there waiting for them
with an open mind, heart, spirit and
embracement of eternal unconditional love.

Roger F. Fisher

On The Edge

It's very scary being on the edge,
You feel so sad and all alone.
The days are dark, the nights are long,
And it seems so long since the sun has shone.

You try, but you can't concentrate,
Thoughts go racing through your mind so fast.
You weep, then you pray for rest.
And you long for a peace that will last.

You feel like you're losing control,
And about to slip over the edge.
But you hold on for dear life,
Grasping at people and things on the ledge.

Painful memories wash over you,
You feel like you're being swept out to sea.
But, down deep, you realize strength must come from inside,
And that nothing in this life is ever free.

Anita R. Hursh

Life

Welcome my little lady to our realm.
After clean up your yacht with hot sweats, then
Look at the tears for morning of Kingdom.
For mourning many tears make tears for each sin;
One picks flower's filaments of Goddess,
One attaches to apples' pollens of God,
One longs for the black lily on wild grass,
One wishes leaving summer stay with for good.
Mine! Now on a fine field, on a new leaf,
Please rejoice in our Eden forever.
Mine! Leave the hurts, made at the gate of life.
Leave the strain of the test for being here.
    Let us wake up, what our life is for...
    None of all of us remember...what for...

Yayoi Saito

Not Alone

As he lay by her side caressing her hand
He knew in his heart, that this was the end
She was going off to heaven, to be with the Lord
Going off to heaven, to a better world

They had been together, for oh so long
Sharing their life, their love, their song
There would never be another, to take her place
Never be another, to hold his embrace

They had been in love, for oh so long
With the kind of love, that never goes wrong
Now it was time, to say goodbye
As he held her hand, and began to cry

As he leaned over and kissed her on the cheek
She closed her eyes, she was very weak
So he told the lord, she must not go alone
So he closed his eyes
Now they will never be alone

Thomas Jackson

What Happens

What happens after all wars stop
What happens after population too large for our world
What happens when we take too long to populate other planets
What happens
    You think about what happens

Donald C. DePalma II

"Pictures On The Wall"

Pictures on the wall. Flashes of one's past. It makes one wonder what they all mean. Drawings and photos hung like a gallery gazing about in their splendor. A picture of you; a sketch of me. What do these all mean, these scraps of memories, hung on the wall?

Is it, maybe, to remind us that the happiest times are the simple ones with the people you love? What about the scenery pictures, why should we have them? To remind us of the beauty of Nature and glorious splendor?

Then it all comes to me; these are pictures of my past, present and hopefully, future, the ones I lost among my misery, "never forget the pictures on the wall." I thought to myself.

Karen Richards

Home For Christmas

Summer is past and winter is here.
Christmas comes but once a year.
People have come for dinner from far and near.
There's only one dinner like this but once a year.

The wind will blow the snow hard and fierce.
The snow will dance upon the ground.
We will have snow cream for dinner.
When clean snow is at last found.

Prayer will be lead by the head of the house.
It will be said, "Bless all throughout the year.
Those that came to eat from near and far.
Those that come by plane, train, and car.

Bless the turkey, pies, cake, dressing
and snow cream and all
for who answer the call
God bless all with Love and care. Amen"

All will sit down to dinner.
Those that came so near and far.
All came home for Christmas dinner this year.

J. A. Y. Randall

Back In Time

The years rolled back in time
as I sat in a Restaurant at the
counter, though the chairs were
different. There was the laughter,
the comradeship between people.

Their different tastes in the food
that they ordered, and a smile crosses
my face. I listened to their conversations,
and they were a mixture of the personal and
the news in Newspapers which many were reading.

The Restaurant was small, so people were close
but not cramped, many knew each other from
times before when this Restaurant was at
another place on another street but now
they are here reunited again happily.

Suddenly there was loud laughter again,
and I felt warm inside, the people were friendly,
as I drank my iced tea slowly, waiting for my
companion to return, I smiled again to myself
as I saw these years rolling back in time.

E. P. Frasure

"Love At The First Sight"

I met her in May.
She smiled, and took the second look.
I can't remember just what day.
She wrote her number in my book.

My mind was in a whirl.
I ask her, "How can I make you mine"
You are such a pretty girl.
She said, "You can take me out to dine."

I said, "My name is Bob."
She said, "My name is Rose."
Bob said, "I have a good job."
Rose ask, "Do you live here close"

Bob ask, "What do you like to eat"
There is a steak house in this block.
An Angel helped us meet.
This makes me as proud as Peacock.

Bob said, "I know, I am in love with you."
Rose said, "I am sure, I love you too."
What shall we do?
I want to marry you.

Victor S. Wallace

My Memories Of "Hurricane Marilyn"

"Marilyn" came to St. Thomas on September 15, 1995
I thank the Good Lord that we are alive
The winds howled, the house shook and other roofs flew by
We could not sleep that night, the strange noise made me cry.

As daylight came the next morning, the winds ceased to blow
Many folks were suffering and had no place to go
Their roofs were gone and such a loss was hard to bear
When they searched through their closets, they found nothing to wear.

My home had less damage then we had feared
So my son who I had stayed with will have it repaired
Our once beautiful Island had no telephone or light
And our hope of obtaining them seemed nowhere in sight.

My wonderful children came up with this plan
"Mom, go to the mainland as fast as you can!"
I was sad when I left, but I want them to know
I can never forget "Marilyn", but I'm glad to see snow.

As I visit with my family, I am very much aware
Whatever is in store for me, I have my children's love and care
In my heart I believe God does things for a reason
He wanted me to come here this Holiday Season!!

Juliana Gumbs

Independence Day

As the flags fly, high on the hill
We have remembered it, still

The small gathering in a hall, at town square
to sign a document, that the colonies declared

That from this day forward,
   we are a nation free
to be separate from English sovereignty
To govern ourselves as we see fit
So through the years,
   we have kept the torches lit

A democracy was born, that will not,
   cannot die
that started in 1776 on the 4th of July

Brenda McCaslin

"I'll Be Right Here"

I sit here on the East River Drive
and for the first time in my life I feel alive.
I pass here almost every day
but never before have I seen it this way.

Nature is all around me it's singing our song
as I start very slowly to walk along.
Here at my side you always will be
Sharing the love you have awaken in me.

Like the treasure of life which we are given at birth
I now know what it means to live on this earth.
And each and every day we are given is another chance
to move with the rhythm of the music we dance.

I watch people jogging and rowing along
and in silence I hear the words to our song
"Live life to the fullest - make each minute count
the secret is in how you spend it - not the amount.

I want to thank you for your honesty
and for the support and the love you have shown to me
For it has made it so clear to see
that my life is what I'll let it be.

Kathleen Waerig

Old Friends

They were just two old and lonely men, comforted in their age by a
    friendship as old as they were.
They played checkers in the park on one of those stone tables
    chased clouds from a park bench and fed popcorn to the squirrels
    every day.
As they sat together, or walked in the park, they relived the days
    of their youth...
        And smiled (with a tear) at the memories brought back.
Children sat at their feet to hear the tales, and brought them
    ice cream cones
that melted down their weathered hands.
Where there was one, so was the other
    to help across busy streets,
    to listen and to share,
    to be ALIVE with,
        and to love as only old friends can love.

Jenni Walcher

Clouds Making Faces

I laid one day on the cool green grass
Waiting for a cloud to cross my path

When as quiet as a bubble in fight
A cloud softy drifted into sight

I was entranced as its softness took shape
At first it looked like a big white cape

Then it spread its wings like a bird
Swooping down so close I thought, I'd heard

The whisper of winds softly reminding me
Of shapes imagined how clearly I see

So if you're looking into blue skies
And within a cloud your imagination flies

Taking mind to magical places
Whispering clouds making faces

Cliffton Clay Cromberg

Untitled

They bring a person to his knees
They make you pay some heavy fees
They make you see things the wrong way
And with your life they'll make you pay
At first they're just a fun experiment
They'll start to take your every cent
There's nothing you won't do or say
You'll give the things you love away
Money is the golden key
For your first priority
Without cash, there is no deal
And you know how that makes you feel
You're looking bad, you're feeling low
Can't stop them now, you can't say no
They're in you now, they're part of you
It seems they're all you want to do
They take your health, they start to feed
That's what they want, that's what they need
You love them so, you'll be their slave
Until the tears fall on your grave

Alan Stahl Beneventi

"I Wonder"

I wonder about things I don't understand
Creation, and how God made man.
Seems it would take more than a day
A lot more than a chunk of clay.
I wonder about nature and how animals get by
Some creatures walk, others fly.
Some crawl on their belly no legs at all
An ant won't get hurt even when it falls.
I wonder how we have turned things upside down
Polluted the air and poisoned the ground.
Stealing and killing, as if life meant nothing at all
A world like this is sure to fall.
I wonder if we're so smart then how can it be
We can't walk on water nor drain the sea.
We can't make heaven, can't make earth
We're still amazed at the miracle of birth.
I wonder how much longer God will let us stand
Just tiny creatures, made by His own hand.
He put us here, He can take us away
There surely must be a final judgement day. I wonder.

David A. Dellinger

"Rose"

Love grows up and breaks through a
crack-in the ground.
Growing stronger with every tear dropped
from the angels in the sky.
Growing more and more with each tender
stroke of the sun.
Love grows and blossoms into something
beautiful and bold.
Love starts to wither and turn ugly as
things turn gray and cold.
A soft white blanket comes down and
wraps around love.
Love lies down on the blanket and
peacefully dies.

Tami Michelle Thomas

My Little Box

Up under my bed where dust balls grow,
There is a box lying low.

In this box lies my treasures,
My memories and my pleasures.

My box is blue and gold you see
And is known to no one else but me.

In this box lives pictures and notes,
Notes from friends and pictures of my relatives.

And as I grow up through the years,
My box will be filled with happiness and tears.

My box will be shut, and put away.
Up in the attic where no one can play.

Someday, I will find my box,
Find the keys and unlock the locks.
Then show my children the fun I had
All locked up in that little blue box.

Lindsey Barwick

First Love

Time and life are too precious
Like the love we once shared
You taught me how to cry, to laugh, to love
And how once in our lives
For each other we so much cared
My love, my life, my everything for I live
My hopes, my dreams
For you I would so willingly give
From the time we had to so painfully part
You held the most loving part of my heart
Until the day we share love again
I mean it now
I meant it then
You will forever be
A very special part of me

Donna Lynn Sudol

"Rainbow Colors And Emotions"

Red represents the anger I feel when I'm troubled.
Orange gives me a warm feeling and I'm relaxed.
Yellow lets me know that I possess fear.
Green shows that I have a love for nature.
Blue represents my feeling of sadness.
Violet gives me a sense of royalty.
Whenever I see a rainbow,
  it reminds me of myself.

Brian Boyle

"The Faded Rose"

I saw a rose within the garden down by the riverside.
Its leaves seemed to have lost their glow, its petals tried to hide.
It stood within the shadow of a beauty I could see.
A drop of dew fell from the rose, it seemed to cry to me.

I lifted the rose from out of the shadow and planted it in the sun.
I trimmed back its limbs so carefully from where the place they hung.
I gave it water to quench its thirst and gave it food to eat.
Then I watched my faded rose begin to blossom for me.

Take the one within the shadow of this world of sin.
Take the time to give them kindness, show to be a friend.
Put forth the love of "GOD" inside you and it will begin to grow.
Many in this world beside you is like "The Faded Rose."

Chrystal Plotts

The Answer

A young man stood in the middle of the lane
Calling for his Father again and again
He heard in the distance a sweet sounding tone
Fear not my son, for you are not alone

I gave you a world full of what you need
All that I ask is that you plant My seed
Your time is short, and your mission essential
I'm giving you a chance to show your potential

I'm leaving you these words to hold in your heart
From My grace ye shall never part
Mine eyes are on you always, My shoulder at your side
Behold! God comes, with his arms open wide!

Charles S. Trull

Sweet Jesus

How do I know you are here?
Because you are the light that I see by.
Because I can hear your beloved words in my head.
I can smell your precious scent.
And I speak only through your voice.
I breathe in your beloved light.
I can feel you.
You are the love at work in my life.
And even though I could not find you,
You did find me.
And even though my faith in you was doubtful,
Your faith in me never wavered.
Because you love me.
You have always been here.
I love you and thank you.
Sweet Jesus

Mary Ann Martinez

My Personal Physician

My daughter is my legacy,
She has always been there for me.
She has seen good things and bad,
For this I hope she is not to sad.
She is my companion and my friend,
I hope through the years this will never end.
Though times were rough and we had great sorrow,
Through this I hope will give her strength for tomorrow.
I know she has a bright future ahead,
With all her good qualities, abilities, I've said.
There will be greatness for this daughter of mine,
Her intelligence and compassion will all show in time.
She is like a beacon shinning through the night,
On her travels through life, she must not lose sight.
She has always been there helping and sharing,
People that really know her, recognize this caring.
She has the power to heal mankind,
Through her studies and schooling this will show on her sign.
To be a doctor is her destiny,
This poem is dedicated to my legacy.

Kathleen Dzurka

Untitled

Racist comments are like painful marks
They're painful and hurt like the bite of sharks

Could it or will it ever go away?
"It may," I say "if we all say okay."
We've had enough of prejudism
Now, let's stop the racism

Black, white, brown, yellow or tan,
We should all be good to our fellow man.

Ryan Lance

Color Blind

What's in a color or shade of skin that
can make one hate from within?
Does the color of one's skin determine
whether we are kind or mean or is that
just a screen? Can your color make you
say or do things that you wouldn't if
say you were green? Does our color
change the person inside or is that just
how we choose to hide? If everyone's
color was the same as mine then would
everything be divine? Or would I begin
to hate you because your eyes are
blue and mine are hue. I just don't
see what difference it all makes
because everyone will just find
something else to hate, so if all
you see is the outward appearance then
you will miss out on a great experience.

Jennifer Anthony

A Mocking Bird's Story

I, the mocking bird fly up in the sky,
It is so beautiful way up here,
Near the waterfall, I feel the spray of
water on my wing,
Once, I was on my way back home
when it began to thunder,
My heart was pounding and I flew faster,
When I reached home, lighting struck
The tree fell, my wings were broken
and I was Wounded,
I lay there cold and scared and crying,
A little girl found me and fixed my wings,
That's how I fly here through the sky and
over the waterfall.

Lia Kalliath

A Sunray Of Decision

There's daisies by the walk, and there's petals by the path
And as the sun shines bright; baby robins take their bath
God looks down upon us, from way high up above
And we know that He will care for us, with His tender love.

There's shadows from the clouds, that make designs below
And we know that the Angels, have pretty wings that glow
From the windows of our thoughts; our minds are not at ease
It's not so easy, as when the wind blows through the trees.

While birds and many airplanes, fly over this land of ours
We sometimes wonder, just how God made all the different flowers
So at times, when we don't know just what decisions we must make
We'll pray and do our best, as we watch the ripples on the lake.

Marion M. Welker

Home Sick

The thunder I hear reminds me of Texas days,
The rainy days of April...in the month before May.
A place where they sing "Home on the Range",
Where outlaws were men like Frank and Jesse James.
There are ranches and pastures as far as the eye can see
And good ol' boys can wild cat to find Texas Tea.
It's a place that has a certain Spanish flair,
Yet the scent of southern home cookin' fills the air.
I love that place...that wide open space.
I hear the thunder, it's April, it's warm...
I wish I were home...in Texas.

Laura Upton-Bell

Come Back

Watching you leave out the lane to the road
Brings relief yet sadness to a heart so low.
How I wish life could be different for the three of you
The miracles I prayed for to see you through.
But the road you have taken is the only way out,
Desolate and lonely I have no doubt.
Two men and a boy so far away,
Why couldn't love be enough for you to stay?
Wolves at the door, giants on the job,
No way to pay Peter when Paul can't be robbed.
"Come Back" I cry! Words echoing deep in my soul.
My arms limp and empty without you to hold.
The ocean will cradle you with its warm, foamy waves
The seagulls sing lull-a-byes on breezy days.
Please come back to the flock, we'll try again,
No giants on the job, just family and friends.
I will make life better than ever before
How I long to see your faces looking through my door.
Little boyish grins, bright glistening eyes,
Like the little fellow with you who only asks, "Why."

Marla L. McMillan-Griffith

Another Sound Of Silence!

The rain falls hard and fast,
yet, so very gentle.

I hear the silence!

Drop, by drop,
the earth's ground gets wetter, and wetter.

I hear the silence!

Strike,
a bolt of lightening, flares the sky.

I hear the silence!

Drip, by drip, by drip,
and the sound of our hearts, beating as one.

I hear the silence!

Dawn, arises.

and the smell, flows so near.

The flowers and trees,
are glad to still be here.

I hear the silence!

So peacefully clear,
and I feel like I'm, the only one who can hear,

The Silence?

Shirley Bowers

The Merciful Heart Of Jesus

The Merciful Heart of Jesus,
died for each and everyone of us.
He died for all your sins,
and in each and everyone of us He lives within.
His love for us is never blind,
for He is always forgiving and kind.
So if you are burdened with trouble and strife,
turn to Jesus for a change in your life.
You'll be amazed what that change will do for you,
you will feel love and kindness for others too.
So if you want the world to be a better place,
pray to Jesus for His Mercy and Grace.

Linda M. Hartranft

On The Passing Of A Friend

Perched atop its metal altar.
The television tells its tale for the third time tonight.
So many hours and people have passed.
Stone faces all around me!
   In them - glazed marble questioning eyes.
   Behind them - cold dumfounded minds that
Know but refuse to accept the horror that
lies behind electric double doors.
The pain of a loved one.
The passing of a friend
Slowly and sweetly sleep slips
The paper lids
over marble eyes
And loved ones
And lovers
Await the mourning sun
The tolling bell
And the phrase
"Ashes to ashes, dust to dust"
(It is 2:30 AM - on a Tuesday)

Charles Robinson Wheeler

A Message For My Sister From Heart To Heart

I often say, "Oh Lord hear me pray."
He will always say do not stray.

Come to me, I will comfort your heart.
For, remember your sister will do her part.

There are days when I am so terribly low.
I look for her smile, but see a glow.

She has been there for me, no matter what.
With a cheerful word and scripture,
That always means so much.

At times she is my ears, for I can not hear,
Your spoken words, Oh Lord, which are always so clear.

My God, My God, so keep her near.
Because your children truly need her,
RIGHT HERE.

She was sent to me, by my God above,
To Praise Him, to Thank Him, and to Give Him her love.

So Dear Lord, please keep her safe, and in your tender care,
For she is so close and very dear.

Erline Dennis

The Embrace Of Night

Embrace me, oh ye who are affectionate;
Thee; to the touch of one to one
So two alone, in the midst of summer's night,
Spend an evening full raptured to the
Rise of dawn's newborn light upon
Your loving youthful face.

And thus embrace me to thyself
When each new night dost fall;
Through blue and velvet midnight skies;
And silvered golden stars above do
Watch over love's embrace;
To crown upon us sweet content,
As silence our love keeps.

Cindy Lee Strand

Chef Shilo

He is a wonderful inventive cook.
His recipes aren't to be found in any book.

Gummy bear pie is deliciously good,
You'd try a piece if only you could.

Cookie soup is the best delight,
Simmered to perfection, seasoned just right.

Its delicate aroma fills the air,
It's hot, so handle your bowl with care.

He fusses over even small details,
You won't leave hungry, he never fails.

Hot cocoa is your after dinner treat,
The cook beams proudly, his smile so sweet.

He may be only a young chef, age six,
But he'll tell you there's nothing he can't fix.

Oh the magic he fed me that day !
His special magic, may it never go away.

Elizabeth L. Thomason

Healing

Beside the shimmering, mirrored surface
Of the backdoor pond, the gentle breeze stirred
And swept the skin like the touch of cooling
Salve to the sun's warm healing rays. Her face,
Reflected, revealed the tensions interred.
Leaves fell and tree trunks whined in the dueling
Pitch of April's high winds. Streaks of misty
Clouds, interlaced with a fading jet stream,
Raced over the basin's hollowed shelter.
Chimes reverberated in the lusty
Echoes of the cliff's green arms. Building dreams,
Catching my breath for life's go round; I felt the
Tautness of my baited line
Release the same in my spine.

Carolyn Webb

All I Ever Want

All I ever want,
In the gentle cool night,
With not a care of the world,
Or of the morrow;

To hold your lovely hands,
Gaze into those beautiful eyes,
Soothing deep black pools,
Of compassion and kindness.

Why should I take a walk,
In the lovely Central Park,
Up and down the majestic Fifth Avenue,
Or the glittering Grand Central Station?

Why should I drive a Mercedes or Rolls Royce,
Have property on the Riveria,
Own a castle in the countryside,
Or on a moonlight night be on a gondola?

What need have I,
For any of these?
When all the feast I ever want,
Is right before my eyes.

A. V. Rao

One At Heart

Putting on the lipstick, shadowing the eyes
Mirroring her mother's image
What for...these tears she cries?

Pieces of yesterdays falling apart
Ashamed of his silence, can't open his heart...

The words he's not spoken ring clear through her mind
Why's this happened to them?
She's determined to find...

What she has done, to cause them this grief
The message unclear - it's so hard to believe...

That it's all really happened, that her mother is gone
To forgive, not forget
With the coming of dawn.

As she drifts off to sleep, slipping into the night
An angel appears through a warm peaceful light

"I love you", it whispers - her mind is at ease
For her heart hears the message,
And it truly believes...

Though her mom is in Heaven, she's still by her side
Wiping each tear that her daughter has cried.

Karin Leigh Didinger

The Distance

A solitary robin
perched in a bare tree
speaks to me
of immortality.

The late December sun
briefly touches the branches
before sinking swiftly
to the distant horizon.
Why is the robin still here?
Has it been injured...
Knows it can not make the distance
to a warmer climate?
Does it fear the coming cold?
Or is it poised in quietness...
waiting to be released to peace.
Somehow I am reassured for it, for myself
Know that I need not be afraid
but can peacefully look to my Maker
when I know that I too
can not make the Distance.

Leona Enns Hepburn

"Waiting For News"

Anyone who's ever written one,
anyone who's every dared,
it is very hard to wait!

You've toiled over thoughts and words
You've lined them up just right
You've crossed your t's and dotted the i's
and now you'll just have to wait and see.

The eyes who read them what will they see?
What will they think? What will they say?

Does the value of you or I, rest on a yes or no? Heavens No!
But still we wait and hope and pray that today might be
the very day.
That news arrives and does not disappoint
that someone will see themselves and me in a poem
written by me.

Jeanne Brewer

Love

Love is one of the strangest things
That in this old world exist,
It can make the day seem bright and gay
And then turn to blur and mist.

Love can increase the best traits you have
Make you live up to your code -
Sometimes it has quite a different effect
When you start down life's crooked road.

There are people of all kinds on this earth
And it isn't for us to say
Who are living as the Father of all intends
And the one's who have drifted astray.

It seems we lose all our faith sometimes,
Conclude that everything's wrong
But when the heart is filled with love,
You can turn troubles into a song.

It is truth, sincerity, and doubtlessness
That wins the right kind of friends
But just try hate, deceit, and lies
And see how your happiness ends.

Marlene M. Naylor

Gidget

Poodles I love and always will
No other pet can fit the bill
Wagging tails and twinkling eyes
Waiting for a big surprise

Some are white and some are black
Some have spots upon their back
But, my choice would not compare
Because I picked one with silver hair

She was faithful and true as could be
Always sitting near my knee
Tricks she would do quick as a wink
Faster even than you could think

Ready to please at the drop of a hat
My little Gidget was smart like that
Little silver poodle with heart of gold
Even more precious as she grew old

Now my dear pet is laid to rest
In a pet cemetery; one of the best
Peaceful, with the song of birds all around
A rainbow of flowers blooming on the ground

Ruth Rucker

"I Am"

I am that which I am.
I am here, there and everywhere.
I have been, I will be, and I am.
I am from inside and from outside,
I am from where time and matter do not exist.

I am from an infinite dimension,
A dimension of infinite possibilities;
All possibilities can, and do exist.
I am multidimensional;
I exist on all planes at all times,
As separate and as one.

I do not think,
Yet, I am all thoughts;
I am all thoughts, and I am no thought,
I am within and without,
I am also that which is not within or without.
I am all things to all, and I am no-thing to all,
I am all that exists,
All that exists I am.

Lena Weinstein

Your Lies

I need to rest my eyes another night is out,
tears have run for days and sleep, I've done without.
But I have nothing nice to reminisce about,
for it was only lies what spoke your mouth.
And when it's dark and late, and I can't fall asleep,
my heart starts to ache for the wound is deep.
Your lies were just like knives,
no, they were like tools,
that work their way inside,
to hurt the hearts of fools.
Having been your fool is bad,
it brings out all my fury,
'cause I never stood a chance,
how could I resist your beauty.
And it's late and God it's cold!
and my eyes open in the dark,
search for a spot on the wall,
as if that could send me back,
to before I met your love,
to before you broke my heart.

Ramiro Sierra

The Lunch Pail

I remember a black metal lunch pail, with hinges attached at the back, with two metal clips on each side of the front, that clicked when they closed with a snap. The handle was made from an old leather belt, buckled snugly on the top where it laid, the edges were worn at the place near the end, where the leather was cracked and frayed.

I wanted to feel closer to who carried that pail, sometimes working all night as I slept, a stranger who came and went at all hours, a guardian that I'll never forget. When I'd see that black pail on the counter, I thought if I just looked inside, I would find a piece of him somewhere, a scrap that the crumbs couldn't hide.

The person, not really a stranger, but a father I hardly knew, who slept when I played and worked while I slept, over the years as I grew. A strong tall figure in the doorway, who made me feel with a word, a man who sang songs and bought ice-cream and candy, and told the best stories I'd heard.

I hoped that day I would know him better and I waited for years for that day, then finally I found him at the end of my youth, but the years slipped to swiftly away. There wasn't enough time to fill up the void, no time for my childhood to replay, I'll have to wait for another chance, when we meet in heaven one day.

Until then I'll remember the years he worked and provided a safe place for me, a home that was filled with love and respect, a place I was happy to be. I'll remember him in the light of a campfire, and when I see the Big Dipper in the sky, the echo of footsteps on an old back porch, feeling safe without knowing why.

Linda Irwin

Feelings Within

The feelings that are flowing from within
change more than I can stand.
First love then hate then the confusion invades.
Anxiety bursts from inside
Bouncing off the barriers I have built!
Nothing can contain them or slow them down
They keep getting stronger and stronger as they go!
A fire is raging and can't be put out.
The more water that's used to quench it-
The stronger-more out of control it becomes!
I keep grasping for air
It feels like the only thing that keeps insanity and me apart.
But it grows and grows without a doubt
And nothing has worked to put it out.

Stacy Wright

Don't Fly Away

Like two birds, side by side, on a wire
Just being with him set her heart on fire

He touched her soul like a gentle breeze
That carried time softly through the trees

They began to sing love songs together
She thought they would survive any weather

But then one day
He just flew away

Maybe to sing a different song
She was left to wonder what went wrong

And hoped it was all just another dream
But tears of truth from her eyes did stream

Down her face and into the air
She cried for him but he wasn't there

As her world filled with clouds and the sun wouldn't shine
It was hard to pretend everything was just fine

Reluctant to fly away and spread her wings
Constantly reminded of how her heart stings

She remained alone and abandoned on that cold wire
With only her despair and forsaken desire

Tracie Tunison

Space We Share

Fighting for my place in time I stood
listening as they spoke their line.
Broken words fill the air, pushed
back by the space we share.

Striking back one in midair.
Blinded by the strikes they paired.
Two more took to the air warning of
The Space that was there.

Picked by one thrown in the air.
Faster than he ten more were there.
Catching myself I tried to prepare.
For he arose and broke hold the strength,
That would have been his nightmare.

Down again nothing could compare.
For he would have lost if I wasn't just lying there.
(Now understand a "good stand" beats a run all to hell)
Grandpa's words came slow, but I remember them well.

Freddie E. Wade

Blizzard Of '96

The new year came in very quiet
Everything peaceful and still
We thought what a wonderful new year
We would have in the year '96
Then all of a sudden out of nowhere
A snowstorm fell on the eighth
Blanketing the earth with this white stuff
We shoveled snow until we ached.

Then morning arrives and more snowfall
So it's out with the shovel again
Just have to get the mailbox
Seed catalogs should be coming in.
We'll have loads to think of for springtime
New flowers and veggies to grow
And the tulips and flowers we planted in fall,
Will be peeking their heads through the snow.

Then all of a sudden it's springtime,
And showers to make the things grow.
With the sun and the showers, the earth comes alive,
Again, nature puts on quite a show!

Dorothy M. Zamoroeze

Jessica's View

Dad? Can I sleep with you tonight?
Ok, Dad. I'll reach for heaven and fly on a cloud,
 Far from the crash of thunder and away from
the lightning flash.
Okay, Dad. But where am I with that rain
rattle noise?
...Dad, don't go. I can't see.
I'm afraid to be lost.
I know, Dad. Tell me what to dream again.
That fairy tale. Oh, yeah.
Before? Yes, we have.
Before? Yes, big brother did.
 With my eyes closed? That's silly, Dad.
 Daddy? I'm scared of that flash.
 Is it lightning again?
 Do you hear that big thunder?
I can't see　　Why does the fairy's tailspin?
I'm cold　　My thumb's (burnt) up
Father, are you in heaven with me?
 Father, I did like I was told.

   Kenneth Bono

You Are Appreciated

Dear Mom, lovely one, I want to say,
You're the joy of my life in every way,
You are kind and gentle and know what to say,
Even when things can't go your way.

I appreciate you more and more each day,
You lead me and guide me, so I won't go astray.

You're a very good listener and me you understand,
You're the backbone of our family,
The greatest in all this land.

Dear Mom I must tell you, I appreciate you so,
More than you ever, ever will know,
Continue to be the woman you are,
My love for you will never go far.

   Karen Gaines

Something Of Myself

Over and over, isolated by day, sadness comes when one thought
   returns.
For those I love, what can I do to leave...
Something Of Myself

Not just photos, the fading copies of my face,
but a gift for their tomorrows. I want so much to leave them...
Something Of Myself.

Reminders of their dreams, our memories,
things there may not come the chance to say.
Maybe I can put it on paper so they can keep, their own...
Something Of Myself.

Time to do this is uncertain, so none can go to waste.
For those I love I must have recorded, if but a few pages, a little...
Something Of Myself.

So the days after I've gone and they miss me, wanting to hear my
voice, a book containing my words can be taken from the shelf
bringing back their smiles with the remembering...
Written on the pages of their special...
Something Of Myself.

   Consiwella R. Ray

Stalking The Hunter

Hiding in the bushes, climbing in the trees.
Work by day and hunt by night, killing enemies.
Stalking the hunter, revenge of the prey
Death to the masters, and freedom the slaves!
One by one a revolution shall purge this land of ours.
Let's brand *their* beaten bodies, and throw *them* in the towers.
Centuries of oppression are ended here today
The stalking of the hunter, revenge of the prey!
Chains and shackles disappear but scars will still remain
To serve as grim reminders of the countless tears and pain.
Souls are now uplifted, generations are reborn
Life has newfound meaning that sprang from souls forlorn.
We shall raise our heads in triumph, and proudly we shall say,
"This is the stalking of the hunter, and the vengeance of the prey!"

   Ron Fields

Mountain Top Experience

We took a trip to a mountain top,
The roads were narrow... you couldn't stop!
People were impatient but that was okay,
As we chugged along in our ole Chevrolet.
We traveled the distance at our rate of speed
And, after a few hours we arrived, indeed!

The mountain was high and the roads were rough,
That is what it takes to make a man tough!
We spent the day working, 'til it was late,
Then dinner was ready so we filled our plate.

The air was brisk, a lovely night,
The moon was half out so it gave some light.
As we stared into the sky at the wonders of God,
We knew He created the stars with a simple nod!
They looked so majestic, high in the sky,
He must have made them with a twinkle in His eye!

Out trips to the outhouse reminds us of the past,
When the darkness and strange sound made us run so fast!
Even so, it was enjoyed by all
So we're thinking now of a trip in the Fall.

   Paul Smith

Wisdom Come Out To Play

Their thoughts to me as gentle teachers
I dart from woman, to woman, to woman, to woman,
Learning forgetting envying searching trying to be wise.
My head where a brain should be great hollow chambers,
Thought steps echo, echo, echo... and aimless.
My heart..... void chambers, empty, hard, small.
Wisdom come out to play
I'm waiting... waiting... waiting... waiting... waiting... waiting...
waiting...
Be still and listen sister
Memories, future, past, tumble from my senses making a din in
my body
Be still and listen, sister
Wisdom come out to play
Rest in my friends for solace, for guide, for mind holding
Warrior friend teach me the way of woman
Wisdom friend teach me the knowing of women
Joy friend teach me the way of happy
Bible friend teach me the way of the book
Be still and listen sister
Wisdom, come out to play

   Regina M. Duggan Moritz

My Dad Henry O'Neill

He wasn't much to a lot of folks, in my mind you will see,
A Tender Loving Father, The Good Lord chose for me.

He wasn't big or handsome, an Irish Temper he had.
When I was wrong, he scolded, as a Tender Loving Dad.
He mended my shoes and polished them after working nights.
He took my side and defended, this little girl in a fight,

You see, we had no Mother: she died when I was five.
My Dad was there with his loving care, defending his kids,
   day and night.

He really was a special Dad, the one God chose for me.
He liked strong tea and coffee, "His Baby" he always called me.
I was the youngest of the five my Father had to raise.

The best years of the life I have had was in those early days,
Now He is gone, fond memories of my Tender Loving Dad;
That "Special Man" who raised me, the best a girl could have.

   Peggy O'Neill Sproat

"Without A Friend"

"Without a friend" we find the road,
too long a trip, too wide a load...

"Without a friend" we stand alone,
to face those things that are unknown...

"Without a friend" we could not hear,
the ringing joy, the silent tear...

"Without a friend" we would not see,
the bluest skies, the greenest tree...

"Without a friend" we could not touch,
the tender heart, that means so much...

Our memories will keep you near,
for in our hearts we hold you dear...
Please know that even in the end,
you'll never be "Without a friend"...

   Lynne M. Chase

God's Country

I step back and with reverence take a look at the land I love,
the beautiful sandhills of Nebraska.

It is spring and the valleys are dressed in shades of green.
White cotton clouds decorate an azure sky.
The call of the Meadowlark is music, sweet to the ear.

A windmill, an abandoned relic of long ago, is immobile yet
the wind ripples the tall grass on which it stands.

This land, the sandhills ... the sandhills of Nebraska could
only have been painted by the hand of God.

   B. W. Ray

Thundersnow

In the midst of white mountains of winter's flow
is a seldom seen phenomenon of electric snow.
Cold lightning ghosts, of faint white-blue light;
where real thunder echoes, but it's not quite right.
Confusion reigns, in these wet-thick storms,
but our senses are focused by the unusual forms.
Gently falling snow, with searing-hot flashes,
and short, hollow booms-when we're expecting crashes.
It leaves a puzzling worry, just the slightest fear-
but surrounded by softness, our inner voices jeer.
These are Ol' Man Winter's perplexing epistles;
gruff rumble-ruffles through his crystalline bristles.
One of many weird storms out of Mother Nature's show,
it has the dramatic cartoon-name of thunder snow.

   E. J. Netzel

Growing Old

They say I'm growing old
I hear it times untold
In plain and bold English
I'm not growing old

What if my hair is turning gray
Gray hair is horrible they say
So what if my eyesight's dim,
I can still see Jesus when I follow Him.

Upon the Cross, he sacrificed his life for me
Time's old plow has left its furrows on my brow
A mission not made with hands
Awaits me in glory land
If a falter in my walk, and my tongue refuse to talk
I can still tread the narrow way, and I can still watch and pray

My hearing may not be as keen
But I can still hear my Saviour
He whispers softly "This way my child"
This robe of flesh I'll drop and rise
To seek the "Everlasting Life" I'll meet you on the street of gold
And prove that I'm not growing old.

   Linda Raines

This Song I Sing For You

This sunlight splashing through the curtain I see
This steam wreathing the shower I breathe
This entwined laughing woman, this world, is me

A glance of grace, of blooming roses, falls from her face
into a furrow of my soul, taking root, making me whole

That starling streaking away from the alley I understand
That song weeping music through my hands
That entranced laughing woman, this world, my land

I, under our spell, am owned by and own as well
A life, a love, a universe only we can tell

   Mark H. Gillespie-Dipinto

True Companion

A person to cherish, someone who is there,
Through sorrow and laughter, just knowing you care.
You're by my side even when we are apart,
A special place for you, I have in my heart.
You are the one I trust most to tell my secrets to;
Sharing my thoughts and everything that I do.
You're there for my highs and even my lows,
You are the one, my friend....my foe.
We grow closer and closer each passing day of the year,
If ever you need me, just know I am here.
Friendship like ours is so rare to find.
Especially in today's world where so many are unkind.
So now and forever and each passing day,
Know we are Friends... Companions, in every way.

   Ruth Hoover

A Helping Hand

Our friendship means so much to those,
   Whose memories are of days of yore;
When one's thirsting for a drink of life's
   Eternal fountains of delights.

We cannot hope to understand,
   Mysteries from God's loving hands;
But we can keep our visions bright,
   With help from God's eternal light.

Our friendship means so much to those,
   Whose memories are of days of yore.
We're doing God's work here on earth,
   And reaping blessings by the score.

   Jasmine M. Schoeny

Symbiosis

We had started life together and we never were apart,
I for him and he for me our life it was,
It had seemed that we were destined to be fast and steady mates,
Then Kismet exercised the hand it often does.

He went there and I went here so that no one could have guessed
That our selves had been connected once before,
But the season had kept pace with the content of our lives,
Made apparent by the judgments that I wore.

It had been a half a score since we last had shaken hands,
For he had shot a different sun than apparently had I,
But we were brought again together when the time was right for both
And discovered what had lasted was our homemade, binding tie.

More diametrically opposed we couldn't ever be,
His right's my left, his nay's my yea, so here we'll always be,
A reflection in a mirror where opposite's the same
And what's the same is different within that binding frame.

Duke Potter

Life

As I look into times past,
    Wondering how long things will last.
I try to find a shred hope,
    to give me a reason just to cope.
For life deals dreadful hands,
    and you gotta just change your plans.
You gotta live with what you got,
    and not ask for a heck of a lot.
Some people are rich, some are poor,
    some never stop asking for more.
I know what has to be done,
    and stop thinking just of fun.
Stop being so damn curious,
    and be a little more serious.
Not look for the easy way out,
    not so quick to fight and shout.
So what I'm trying to say I guess,
    is just try to do your best,
    and not worry about the rest.

Nicholas D. Baron

"Where Did All The Butterflies Go?"

Years ago when I was young
I never missed a setting sun

We lived in "God's" green wonder land
With babbling brooks and golden sand

A woods so dense filled with pine scent

With star sprinkled skies and pink
Tinged sunrise

Time flies. I still remember the fields
Of wild flowers and all the butterflies

Their beautiful colors rimmed in black
I promised one day I would come back

Today, I returned to recapture my youth
And had to face an awful truth

The woods became a shopping center
Cars parked fender to fender

Stores, parking areas and people galore
There weren't any butterflies anymore

Now I will never know!
"Where did all the butterflies go?"

Anita Y. Natoli

Untitled

I still hear the words, once spoken to me,
Though silent to others, sweet memories they be.

We were both much younger, though ages apart,
Never getting along, but much love in our hearts.

As now I look back and wonder; Did I do wrong?
Making her worry; would I safely return home?

Knowing if I were sad, surely she was too,
But somehow, she always knew exactly what to say or do.

Many happy times I remember through these years,
She shares all my joys, laughter and tears.

Although some friends seem to come and go,
She was forever there, the right path she'd show.

After all those years, I'd really just begun to know her,
Too quickly it ended, with tears and flowers.

I'm really proud to say, even though I cry,
I knew my MOTHER loved me, when she died!

Andrew Philip Lindsay

The Petals Of Nana

Her color was beautiful that changed
with the seasons,
Her stem drank from the water of life,
Her fragrance was sweet and fragile
to the touch.
At full bloom in her life, she spread the
seeds of her souls to flourish upon loved
ones for all to carry on.
She was indeed the flower of our lives.
And although now she has gone to her own
special garden,
We will always see her in every living
thing that the earth tenderly produces.
That was our Nana.

Christine Bellino

"Roses By Gordie"

In memory of Gordy Reitz

   Let me take a nap in the roses, which labels me the
greatest grandpa in the world. I know that while I was leaving,
their minds were being swirled.

   They tossed the roses to my grave, as they cried and said
"goodbye". I was saddened at their faces, looking, standing where
I lie. But I know that I was the best grandpa, the time I was alive.

   For me, being the greatest, was that I had made them cry.
Although their hearts were saddened, their tears were full of joy,
for I have gone to a higher place, I think I will enjoy.

   Yet, to my family back on Earth, I know this caused you
hurt, but if you wish to see me. Smell the roses in the dirt.

   I nap, there, in the roses, which labels me the greatest
grandpa in the world. So smell the roses, roses by Gordie.

Brooks Reitz

AIDS

Anguish; Isolation; Desolation Severe
Moonlit nights are hazy; sunny days austere
Please know you're not alone, my friend
I'll be here to embrace and comfort you
Give solace; support, the journey through
To hold your hand; to weep with you
And finally dry your tears
Contrary to all the bally-hoo
I know the world still cares.

Gerdine Newsome

Sweet Memory

I thought of you today - I do not know why
Amidst my busy day - your memory came like a sigh

You whispered into my mind like an old song
I had not thought of you for way too long

Your presence felt so real - closed eyes revealed your face
I tasted your warm breath - I felt a fleeting embrace

I felt so loved, protected and warm
Like a baby cradled in a mother's loving arm

Like the unexpected visit of a long, lost friend
I did not want your memory to end

It brought joy and pleasant reprieve
I was rested and filled with such peace

But alas! A few brief seconds and you disappeared
If I could have held you longer - I would have kept you here

It was a moment beyond my control
An unexpected welcome console

I crave another silent siege of my mind
You may capture it again - any time

Sweet memory - please call again soon
Sweet memory - please call again soon
Frances G. Browning

Make Your Father Proud

May God keep you safe and healthy
May his love be with you too.
May your wants and needs always be filled
May all your dreams come true.
May your voice be heard by others when you have spoke aloud
If you live a life that's righteous, you'll make your father proud!

May your heart be filled with love and hope
and compassion for others too.
May you always find the strength you need
to do what's asked of you.
May you always know the answers, never to be left in doubt.
May you always live "your life," but make your father proud!

May you always wish upon the stars
you see falling from the sky
May your words always be honest
never hide behind a lie.
May you always keep within your heart the things that you
have vowed
If you live your life this way you'll make your father proud!
DeWayne H. Legge

United

How special is this relationship, why the most important of all.
You are Husband and Wife, Father and Mother and head of a family.

God created this relationship to withstand everything, for better
or worse, till death do you part. Why else would you marry if
not for the rest of your life?

You are two different people who have operated as one.
You have Loved, Respected, and Worshipped one another.
You had to Forgive and Forget and Apologized for getting upset.

It's the beauty of God in your life that has brought
you through the rough times and kept your heart opened wide.
He has filled your life with enough Love, Patience and
Understanding to weather all storms.

So continue to begin each day with your mate in mind,
And thanking GOD for your marriage divine.
Karen Royster

Tomorrow

It's the little pebbles along the path, that makes you stub your toes.
If you're the one who gets picked by the thorn, when you lean to
smell a rose.
If the bee is still waiting in the hive, when you reach in for honey;
Or you get to the beach to get a tan- and the day ceases to be sunny.

You hook up the hose to water the lawn, the rain comes pelting down
Your toast doesn't pop up—(it's charred and black) instead of
golden brown.
Getting dressed in a hurry you discover a run, in your very last
pair of hose.
The warmest week of the year and you get a cold in your nose.

You're the one who has the car, when it runs out of gas.
In the muddiest puddle there is around, the driver behind will pass.
When it seems like you are "Destiny's Tot" just sit back and say
"Ah tomorrow-tomorrow, I wait for you—this too shall pass away!!!"
Shirley J. Mackey

Anniversary

I've been through so many relationships
Heartbreaks, aches, and pain
I wanted to find something different
A love that would always remain.

I remember when I met you
I looked into your eyes
I wondered what was in store for me
And boy was I surprised!

The more time I spent with you
I knew that it was love
The laughing, caring, holding hands
There is a God above.

I often wonder why I'm so lucky
What is it that I have done
I found that special someone
Who's definitely number one.

It's that time of year again
When I'm reminded of just what it is I have
I'm so thankful for the love we've shared
In the present and the past.   Happy Anniversary!
Wendy Nichols

Symphony

Life is an unceasing masterpiece, perpetual as the years of
time. The tempo of its seasons all consuming, yet elusive as
the haunting refrain of a symphony.

Spring is a lilting tune, light and quick, softly running
from one measure to another carrying with it the promise of a
fuller melody.

As Summer appears, the strain becomes broad and warm; captures
the passion of the heart, fulfills itself, and flees quickly into
Autumn on staccato feet.

The theme builds in fervent colors and the march of maturity
blares forth from golden trumpets with a steady beat, beat, beat
of constant drums.

Now the days grow short, the ballad of life fades to a
whisper of a new sonnet about to bloom in the Spring of
Eternity.
Marilyn Sines Allman

Beauty Is Life

Beauty is life, when life unveils her holy face.
It shall rise up with the sun from the East
Beauty is kind and gentle, it is a thing of might and dread
With its soft whisperings, she speaks in our spirit.

A garden in bloom forever.
A flock of angels forever in flight.
We have seen her leaning over the earth
from the window of sunset.

The winter snow bound shall come
Covering the earth with her diamond studded blanket
Like a bride with all her fineries.
Beauty comes with the spring, leaping upon the hills
With all her vibrant colors.

Beauty is not a need, but ecstasy.
Not mouth thirsting, nor a hand stretched out
But rather a heart inflamed and a soul enchanted
Beauty is eternity gazing at itself in a mirror.

Percilla G. Nader

Dads Summer Seasonings

Summer.
Under the hollow hull of your Cris Craft
I found my private hide-away, amongst beach towels and blankets
Still warm from the day. An echo chamber of wet wood
   cradled inside the sound of water
   lapping up around me
   I am protected, I am dry.
My small body balanced between pain and sheer delight
as the bow smacks the waves, lurching forward rhythmically
racing an oncoming storm
   rocking me to sleep
   the song of an outboard
   my lullaby.

Adrienne Winters

Moments Of Pleasure In The Rain

Moments of splendor, moments of pain,
The surprise of pleasure in the rain.

Moments of darkness, shrouding the light,
Then faith and wisdom conquer night.

Moments of courage, coping with fear,
Comfort whelms as love draws near.

Confounding moments of the shrinking soul,
Repelling the doubting flows,
We unchained the ebbs we knew consoled
The incipient glows.

We rode the crestless rising tides -
The waves of surging hope-
Buoyed by your essence at my side-
Sweet fragrance of heliotrope.

Oh moments of grandeur, limp moments of pain,
We nurtured pleasure in the rain.

Richard J. Ward

Love

A warm, happy feeling that tingles inside.
A skip of a heartbeat, a sparkle of pride.
You're walking on air, on top of a cloud.
You can't hear a sound, no matter how loud.
A wonderful gift from someone above.
A magical gift, the gift of love.

Julie Ginsberg

Doomsday

Gods of metal sleeping so silent
Poised and pointing they stay
The engines and silos are quietly manned
And ready to blow off someday

These weapons were built by rational men
Destruction only in mind
If and when they leave their pad
These rational men they will find

They will find a world sent back in time
Ruled only by demons of shame
Only to wish they could set the clock back
And knowing they will go insane

Insane with no reason insane with no rhyme
Zombies will come out and play
All of this because rational men
Set a clock on a bright sunny day

Now the problem with this clock that ticks
It will always keep ticking away
To a time and place of unsettling grace
When we blow up the earth on doomsday

James Foscaldo

Despair

This night I've shed buckets of tears. I was all alone with nothing
but my fears. I cried and I cried, wishing I had died because I was
hurting so deep down inside.

I cried out to God, "Won't you help me? I feel so bad and I want
to be free."

I feel my life is going nowhere, but you told me you would always
be there.

These tears that I shed come from deep inside because I want to do
something that will fill me with pride.

I'm sinking fast and I don't think I'll last; these tears are all I've had.

Please hurry up and answer my prayers because right now I'm so
full of despair and there is no one around who even cares.

I don't want to live, but I'm afraid to die and I would like to
give life another try, so these tears in my eyes I then can dry.

Queen Shalom

Dad: I'm Fighting For You

You make me so angry
high on your horse.
You'll fall one day,
with my helpful force.
You will never know
what it's like to be him
because you'll never look
past your nose, so straight and thin.
You don't know what you're causing
with this calamity,
But you're making this a harder battle
for my family.
You'll see one day
when you need a friend and a chance.
Being who he is,
Bad will give you more than an unearned glance.
So remember that someday
You may be the one who is hurt.
Hey, twice shy,
Once burnt.

Jennifer Johnston

Natures Gifts

Let us think of many other thing
that nature brings flowers, Birds
we enjoy these gift make us proud
when everything can be very sad
they sure cannot be all that bad

Many such things come and go we find
their beauty always come and go we find
their beauty always leaves memories behind
but nature's gifts we should treasure well
because they have a lasting bright spell
one that lifts your hearts with pride
sending joy of every kind

Philip Arthur Burton

Look Inside

Where can I run to - where can I hide?
Who's going to listen - who'll take my side?
With all this pain, I just can't cope.
I've lost all my dreams and I've lost all my hope.

Everyone seems to forget about me.
I'm always neglected - why can't they see?
They never say what I want them to say.
They just turn their backs and they just walk away.

I asked God up in heaven to give me a sign.
I'm tired of hurting - I just want to shine.
I heard someone's voice say, "Look Inside".
I went to the mirror and sat there and cried.

I realized for once that nobody's to blame.
Like the moth that flies to the deadly flame.
I must help myself - on me I must depend.
I must be my own, very best friend.

Thank God in the heavens above - He showed me that it's me
I should love
It's me I should run to - my heart's where I can hide
It's me that should listen
Now I'll always "Look Inside"

Merla-Lynne Pollitt

My Sweet Midnight Dreamer

When you're around you take my blues away
My sweet midnight dreamer
Just thinking about you
Brings back my piece of mind
Your arms around me sets my soul free
My sweet midnight dreamer - I love you.
Your ship may sail far away
But your heart it stays here with me
I have no inhibitions when your eyes look at me
I feel free like a warm breeze blowing
It don't matter where we're going
As long as we're going there together
Don't let the U.S. Navy separate us baby
Let's flip a quarter
Tails we go home; heads we stay
Let's be rebels together
It don't matter about the money
I just want to love you forever
My Sweet Midnight dreamer

Patti Kostiou

Eternal Slumber

Everyday I pray for my own death
To leave this life of hell on earth.
I live a life of hate, not love,
And now I'm bleeding because of you.
I loved by chance and lost
-Love does not conquer all-
And not even time can heal these open wounds.
For my heart bleeds to feel you close to me once more.
To feel your lips pressed firmly against mine,
And your breath hot on my neck.
I see your face as my reflection in the mirror,
And in the flames from the cross that doomed me
To this eternal fate.
For I am not alive, and I am not dead.
In our quest for happiness our sins cannot be freed.
For the devil is the evil that condemned me to this hell,
This blood lust that drags me to forever.
My endless life cannot be stopped, only prolonged.
And so to you, my love, I offer freedom.
I free you of my fate, a victim to evil's hatred,
And grant you a mortal's life of pain and suffering.
To you I grant the chance to live,
And the comfort of a grave...

Rebecca Shoemaker

Peace On Earth

Most strifes in life are created by man
And adversities have existed since earth began
Man must try to survive together
Then enjoyment of life could be so much better

It's hard for man to control his feelings
But he must employ restraint in his dealings
His relations with fellow-men must be with respect
He should treat others as they would expect

Man must strive to control his temper
And never to speak with a tone of anger
When man manifests an emotional outburst
It's a display of character at its worst

Man must endeavor to heed these considerations
Perhaps then there would be truce between nations
If man could resolve that hostilities must cease
It's possible for the earth to be at peace

William Rin Ishii

The Dove - A Masterpiece Of Heaven

During Creation...you became the symbol of peace.
The smooth beautiful entity of tranquility and gentle ease.

After the cleansing affect of the flood...Noah set you free to explore.
Time and time again...to find land...there had been no score.

And then one day...you against the sky...did not return.
It had been good...after the thought of undying concern.

For then the flooding water began to slowly-subsequently subside.
After many days of the sea meeting the sky...when for us to freshen
    the earth...to once again reside.

We were blessed once again...later to be on this Dot of Blue.
As the reflection of the sky in the water...made the earth into an
    interesting colored hue.

It had been shown..the Spirit of the Holy Ghost prevailed for mankind.
In you gentle dove of peace and tranquility...it is Grace...to
    remain in the spirited human mind.

Weston W. Rudel

"A Tribute To Grandpa"

Yes, today is a sad day;
For you went to heaven to stay.
You were always there for us,
Whenever we would stray.
Your warm smiles and hugs never faltered;
And our lives you never tried to alter.
We'll miss the holidays without you
For you made each day bright and new.
It saddens us now that you're gone,
But God only knows you're in heaven, where you belong.
Our hearts hurt, hoping - But God only called you
For it was time to say our good-byes
And remembering "Grandpa" with tears in our eyes.

Patricia Jean Justice

My Brother

You were my older brother and you died, now there is no
other way to describe, about these feelings I have deep inside.
I saw the hurt and the pain, it showed on your face, this
was a feeling I didn't know how to embrace.
You were brave when you reached your journey's end. Now you
can only hear the prayers that we send.
I hope you are happy and in very good health, and I know
you are blessed in God's house of goodness and wealth.
So when my time comes dear Brother, I hope you will be there
to meet me with our sweet Mother.

Sharon H. Day

Midwestern Spring

A welcomed aroma permeates the air
Another winter has passed on by
Wild morels burgeon everywhere
In safe cover, newborn fawns lie

Flowers blossom in the sun's rays
From the south birds promptly return
Outdoor recreation no longer delays
And for this season I truly yearn

To cabin fever, we bid farewell
Fishing lines soon will be cast
Boats near the lake await to set sail
Warm weather is finally here at last

Fertile soil, the farmers tediously sow;
Abundant crops they hope to reap
With plentiful rain, God sends His bow
And the fields become quite replete

Randal M. Weston

Reality

I drifted in the soft clouds
wandered through the chambers of my mind
touched with the reality I find
secluded within the unwantedness
that crawls around
burnt into the ashes
that lay along the ground
blown up with the wind
and never but back down
hidden in the darkened hell,
that shadows over me
marked with a symbol to tell
I will never truly be free
etched within the beauty that I see
shook with the fear of reality

Crystal Moenius

A Part Of Us

A part of us has gone away
Because out mother died today
She loved us all so very dear
She wouldn't want to see a tear
We can cry and cry and cry
But we know her love will never die
We can cry and cry and cry some more
But we know our mom's at heaven's door
So what is there for us to do
You be there for me and I'll be there for you
Let's live our lives and make Mom glad
She wouldn't want to see us sad
A part of us has gone away
But we'll be with her again someday

Larry S. Young

Precious Moments

Of all the grandchildren in the world life could have given me
Anyone you might have been
Jessica my sweetie, I got lucky because it was you
A tremendous love I felt within
A Love so new and it's just for you
You have a beautiful heart and soul
You have brought great joy to my life
For you give me such endless delight when you are with me
I'm as proud and happy as can be
Your personality is like a precious diamond in the rough
Beautiful, priceless, sparkling
The makings of the best stuff
With your addictive magnetism
And your wonderful smile
It's no wonder I love you so much.

Norma Norris

"Functioning Dysfunctional"

My dad got mad when my teacher called.
I saw stars when he hit my head.
The blood poured out of my broken nose.
Then I was sent to bed.

I didn't tell mom what dad had done.
I was afraid of what she might do.
She would probably yell and scream.
Then he would haul off and belt her too.

I was strong just like I was told.
I didn't shed a tear.
The day after when I went to school.
I called this kid a queer.

The kid got mad so I beat him bad.
When I hit him he yelled real loud.
Then he took the blame for my broken nose.
I made my father proud.

Isn't it strange how things work out?
No one ever knew.
Now it's my son with a broken nose.
He said, son I am proud of you.

Dean Waterfield

For Jim, my son —

The crimson sun sets in the west
And throws its rays o'er the water's breast,
And as it sinks in rainbow hue
It whispers softly to me and you,
"I've gathered the clouds of snow white fleece
And all is peace, and all is peace".

Kathleen G. Davis

"Daddy's Little Girl"

Maybe I haven't been the father that
I should be, but I want you to know
My Little Girl you're always with me.

You are the Greatest Daughter in the world
and you'll always be Daddy's Little Girl.
With your eyes so bright and your smile
so sweet you'll always make Daddy's
Heart skip a little beat.

I Love you so much and I want
you to know that you'll always be
with me where ever I may go.

So I end my sign of Love with
only one thing to say Daddy Loves
his Little Girl more than he'll
ever be able to say.

Tawyna Thompson

A Step In Time

It is a cool crisp October night,
the harvest moon is shining bright.

Autumn leaves of red, gold and brown,
come tumbling quietly to the ground.

Jack Frost will soon be at the windowsill,
pristine white snow, up on the hill.

We will miss the warm summer sunshine,
as we now step into wintertime.

Mary Trout

Love's Swallowed Thirst

The words are there at the tip of my tongue.
Who? What could possibly stop me from saying them?
So easily spoken they could be sung.
Outrageously loud I could yell these words at him!

Decide who, what I am? When I have right?
You push me, threaten me. I have to push you back!
So with words you throw you hurt out of spite.
Only you keep score, pretend points I can not track.

Very easily I could break the strings.
I only wish for your affection, attention.
But you fight my wish, striking out to sting.
Natural order of things never to mention.

For you believe I am always up one.
Why fight me? Why not accept me? Love me.
I can take the blame, the shame. Simply done.
Constantly you beg me to forgive. You hug me.

And yet your nearness could have stopped the fate.
If only we had tried that at the very first.
No more scores would we keep with which to bait.
Silent sit my words. Yet again love's swallowed thirst.

Katrina Lee Payne

A Child's Silent Tear

What happens to those children whose tears we can not see?
Whose cries are louder than words can express.
Could we call this courage?
Or do we want to know what causes these tearless faces?
These children are crying and no one cares.
They carry their load on the inside and not out.
Their pain is strong and their sorrow tells all.
But, still no one hears their voices, or can see their silent tears.

Michele Lankford

Wail Of The City

Dark fairies, where the eyes cannot see them.
Storming down from a front of screaming balloons.
Rank and abuse so the children are frightened.
Coarse like a God from a starving baboon.
Trees are falling down on the day of the light and
wish for a kiss that takes you off to the moon.
We've killed for days like this and would settle for grand.
So the seat of the crown has got a lot to get down.
the simples hear the sound, they've got their witness inbound.
Tickled they want-ease, and shroud the fertile ground.
Raising some whirling, the fires a burnt sea...
My mommy don't want me...

Grazing boys without claim to their seed.
Pushy, so snoopy, got a big mouth to feed.
We trapped a vulture and an angel, which will it be?
Waiting for answers while beating a-greed.
Once a lone sand piece and this love that I need.
Let the man go please, he's trying to lead.
Frail little earth under the whale of the city.
We are the glass through which one can see.

Bryan D. Raaz

I Am

I am a confused teenager trying to survive on this roller coaster
    called life
I am confused as to whether there really is a thing called love,
    and if there is how are we to know
when we've found it if we are forever searching for it?
I am confused as to whether I am doing anything right in this life
I am confused as to what the schools are trying to teach us
I am confused as to what our generation is supposed to be;
    or do, will we blow up the world or save it?
I am curious as to what there is waiting out there in the real world
I am curious as to what I will be doing in ten years, or will I even
    be alive?
I am curious as to whether I will ever not be so confused.

Wendy Gibson

Life

The moment
Catch it
Before it is whispered away.
The talent
Catch it
Before it is thrown away.
The pleasure
Catch it
Before it is taken away.
The memory
Remember it,
For it is all that is left of the everyday.

Joshua Joseph Tuttle

I Wish I Could Fly

I wish I could fly high in the sky to see what the future holds
If I could see into the unknown, what would it hold
What could I learn, would I change, could I change,
I will never know

If I could fly, would I be free from pain and fear of the unknown
Could it be the past holds the key to what lies ahead
But the past is dead, how can that be

We bear the scars of pain and fear, all of those we loved so dear
If only we could open our eyes to our minds and hearts
See things as they are and not as they appear

Are we blind to the truth that is right there in our grasp
Right there for all to see
I wish I could fly high in the sky to see what the future holds

Barbara Campbell

Everlasting Life

To leave this world,
To go so cold,
To live forever,
To never grow old.
I'm stupid,
Yet smart,
It hard to explain,
I always had fears,
Yet, never had pain.
Something's inside of me pounding to get out,
Telling me I'm stupid,
And walking about.
I open my eyes,
I've gotten too deep,
It's too late,
Life is cheap.

Courtney Hurst

Lessons...

I know much learning comes from pain,
And flowers can't grow without rain.
Such wisdom to be gained through strife,
Great untold mysteries...this life.

But, Lord, you know how hard I've tried,
And rarely for my pain have cried,
I have no doubt I shall endure,
But why pile on so much manure??

Perhaps I will become much wiser...

Manure being fertilizer!

Ellen Damian

The Fisherman

I did go fishing this fine wonderful day
Some would call it a lake, I call it a bay.
As I baited my hook and threw it over the side,
I wondered what creatures the sea did hide.

Then the winds from the North they did blow
But a voice from the deep said "don't worry - don't go."
The voice was so sweet, like music to my ear,
That it calmed all the animals, even the deer.

As the voice spoke, I could feel its beauty and charm
So that I had no reason for fear, or alarm.
She told of herself, so witty and cute
That I could do nothing, except listen and stay mute.

All at once she took form, this I did see
Then I realized that she was only meant for me,
Now many years have gone by, since we did wed
And our love still grows, yet nothing be said.

Soon the children will grow up and move away
And I shall always remember fishing, that fine wonderful day.
Many times I've told this story, for which it is true
First to my children, and now unto you.

Glenn Bagby

A Senior's Christmas

On one Christmas Eve in the cold,
There I stood all wrinkled and old.
The pills were all lined up on the table with care,
In hope they would help me for another year.
I in my flannels, my cat with his scat,
Had settled ourselves for a long winter's nap
At dawn came a thought from above.
Happy Birthday Lord Jesus,
It's you that I love
A different version of the night before Christmas

Shirley Crowley

Grandmother

For seven years, I slept in your four-poster bed
while Gramps snored on the back porch.

I sat in the dirt in your garden patch
with salt for onions from the ground.

I watched you cook and bake.
You fed me well.

I rocked in the hammock
and played my uke,
wearing a silly straw hat.

I read every Tarzan book,
played piano in the parlor,
and dressed-up in the attic.

I can still taste your chocolate cake
and hot mince pies.
I loved you so...

I sat with you the night you died
and held your hand in mine.
I wrote the poems to honor you
and voiced them for all to hear.

What a grand mother you were to me.

Patricia Woodring

Unspoken Love

Painful truths were spoken today...
A piece of my heart was torn away.

A love that was buried away forever
Was blindly awakened to a stolen treasure.

Emotions reached out to no one there...
For my choice is my strength to know that it's fair.

I live with the love I know is mine...
For our love was never clearly defined.

My blessing I give you without a trace...
Of the pain I felt in our last embrace.

Envisioned fantasy was a beautiful affair...
As whispers of reality are secretly spared.

Ilene Sue Haskin-Colovas

From A Wife To Her Soldier

I hurt; to the point I think I just can't hurt anymore;
But one tear left uncried soon eases past the door
of my broken heart.

I cry; until I'm so numb I just don't know what I cry for.
But then one more crack—and another fragment lay on the floor.
It's my broken heart.

I'm depressed; that strong hand of loneliness has pressed me
then left me
deflated.

But just as I fear that I've gone as low as I can
sinks again
my broken heart.

I'm dying; the hope of your return only delays it.
But as soon as you go again
I will die some more...

Kimberly Moore

Connected

Are we connected you ask or want to know?
I say we must be connected
heart, mind and soul.
Yes your heart may be in the
right place but your mind and
soul may be on a different road.
For example: When you can't
forgive; that's your soul.
You might say I wasn't thinking
when I did that; that's your
mind. Then the love in your
heart declines.
Connecting is nothing new, rather
old, like diamond, silver and gold.
So before you say your vows
and wear a ring,
Ask yourself are we connected
all three of these things?

Sharlene Cobin

My Weary Mind

I'm very creative with a lot of ideas
but can't do anything
for the money and fear

My mind won't stop turning
it whines and it squeaks
they put me on Prozac
that made me say "Uh Duh" for weeks

I haven't been able to work
for a year
maybe the rust has drained into my ears

Although having a problem now-a-days
is seemingly quite sporty
maybe all I really need is a little WD-40

Wanda Cunningham Thurston

Survival

On this earth, is where we thrive
in life's struggle to be alive.
The problems we have here, we all must face
not just one person, the whole human race.

The kids are victims of rape and abduction
the parent lives are, bound for destruction.
The lovely forest, that was so sweet
is now gone, the condo's complete.

The people that, are cutting down trees
leave us some air, so we can breath, please.
The precious air, that's full of pollution
the water we drink, with its dilution.

A couple things, I don't think I'd miss
living without them, would be total bliss.
If we don't stop, while we are ahead
it won't really matter, we'll already be dead.

Certain things, like acid rain
make the plant life, go through pain.
A pain that they, would never survive
and without them, where would we thrive.

Matt Warhover

A Fool's Pledge

I live for today not tomorrow, Tomorrow will solve its own joys
    or sorrow
I live for today not tomorrow.
I eat drink and forget my worries because I live for today not tomorrow.

Cyrenaicism is my philosophy I will satisfy all my immediate needs
I will revel in greed
I will copulate, masturbate, intoxicate because I live for today
    not tomorrow.
I will flirt, I will splurge, I will maximize my pleasurable
    sensations because,
Hedonism is my game and I play it with no shame. I live for today
    not tomorrow

What! Where! When! Why! It is! It is tomorrow hey! Hey!
    Somebody please can I have a dollar to borrow....
Don't leave me in my mess and sorrow, I will pay you back
Tomorrow.

Andrew Hall

Until Love Came Along

They had liked each other for many a day,
And no matter what happened, their friendship would stay,
When they first met, they liked each other from the start,
Neither thinking that one day, they would be sweethearts.

They were just friends, until love came along,
And then they both heard the same sweet song,
Calling to them, as it made their romance strong,
They were just friends, until love came along.

They protected their love both night and day,
They wanted each other, and didn't want love to fade away,
They hoped in their life they would never part,
Because they both had the same love in their heart.

They were just good friends, until love came along,
And then, they both heard the same sweet song,
Calling to them as it made their romance strong,
They were just good friends, until love came along.

Charles V. Anthony

Chains

For you, I'll turn the axis of the world, until every direction
turns back upon itself.
I'll fill the night sky with the living seas and place the planets
at your doorstep.
For you, I'll capture scorn, and string it on a silver chain, that
you can wear it always at your throat.
I'll beckon down the sun, so that you can taste its light, and I'll
entrap the fair moon, so that you can caress her silver bones.
I'll bring you blossoms that smell of summer rain, and fruits that
taste of autumn wind.
I'll paint a canvas of thunder, so that you may see it.
For you, I'll ask the stars to sleep, that you can know the darkness
as I know it.
For you I'll seek out a dream, and lock it tight with golden chains
to the window by your bedside
So that it may sit and watch the night circle past,
And so that it will be yours.
And for you I will do the impossible.
I will exist.

Kyle Treiber

Midnight: The Third Of October

Shards of fragmented diamonds
frost will soon limn the last of the impatiens
and roses
Skies of ebony velvet
ice crystals bearing and early death
for grasses not quite ready.

Gently, I love the dog
and wash my hands
in the dew from giant leaves
of the moonflower vine
that cover
and shelter the shed.

I shiver and go in;
ready for the warmth
of the duvet
and the man sleeping;
waiting
with a warmth of his own.

Barbara W. Quinn

Today

Fallen
from the Grandmother branches of the Oak
floating to the ground, listless—waiting

Lifted
by the wave of the wind
singing on the breeze through the Meadow
traveling on air

Watching as the World passes by
now swirling faster and faster

Creation lost to the cunning Typhoon
blown into the echoes of Relentless Day
slamming hard into Reality—missing.

Now twilight.
Sky slows to a crawl

Searching
for what's missing, miles away
gone now
as the Sun goes down....

Over again?
Maybe tomorrow.

Amanda Murphy

I Go On

I go on.
I no longer look forward in time.
I fear what lies ahead.
I tremble thinking I'll never
be what I'd like to.
On a forgotten island,
I'll watch the sunrise, alone.
Tranquil... yet forever in the eye of the storm.
Full of power I stand, in the
face of fear I cower.
Wishing to see where I'll be someday.

   What is real? Why do I wish for things to be
   Real that never will be?
      Why do I dance as a puppet on a string?
     I sense the gleam of Passion
      within my soul,
       Yet... I feel
        Nothing

Christina Nelson

You, The Funny Man

You the funny man,
who often lent me a hand,
I refuse to believe must leave this land.

You, a father, husband, and brother be,
one I've known since we were wee,
will be missed by many, not just me.

You, the rebel, who soared through life like a gull,
seem to have acquiesced to the coming lull.

You, the great debater, spoke load with a lion's roar
asking only to be heard, nothing more.

You, our very own Huck,
never, never, seemed to get stuck,
but sprinkled laughter in our lives when things went amuck.

You, the exitor,
having honored life and others, now concur,
you have seen your best and must now defer.

You, the second in line, leave three behind,
to convince our Mother that things will be fine.

You, our Mother's son, who made our get-togethers fun,
leave me helpless with a heart weighing a ton.

Bonnie Allen Briggs

"Stagnant Waters Of Life"

The stagnant waters, like time standing still,
Days, months and years go by,
But like stagnant waters time stands still,
The sun rise and set, yet we wish it away,
And to live the next day is our only will,
Go to bed late and rise early to find,
Us wishing to exist only body not mind,
To take up space and only physically be,
But we need to live, if only people could see,
Yes it will surely come, that judgement day,
And no time will be left to live and to play,
So, you should freeze time now, and have
  your own will,
To make time, like stagnant waters,
  stand still.

Mandi Tatman

On A Drive Through Catskill Park In Autumn

The trees, postured as color guard, welcomed me to the court

The sky, folded like the delicate white silk
of her majesty's finest gown, surrounded me

The air, chilled like bubbling champagne, tingled my lips
and quenched my thirst

The mountains, standing like great monuments, paid tribute
to the long-lived kingdom below

The waterfalls sparkled in the sunlight like the brilliant jewels
adorning her lady's crown

The cliffs revealed beneath the spectacular fallen leaves
arranged, like a banquet table prepared for a feast

The road wound like the regal purple ribbon weaved through
the hair and robe of her most graciousness

The wind echoed like the soft sweet melodies of a flute
falling gently upon the ears

Oh, what beauty at hand!

A celebration of your autumn, your highness, Mother Nature.

Antoinette Valiante-Wagnerman

A Thought

Are we real or are we paint
Or are we just a thought we think?
We wake up here a babe in arms
We live a life (we hope) with charm

But we play a role with borrowed tools
For they aren't ours, we wise fools
Our sons, our daughters, our mothers and dads
Are also borrowed like passing fads

So what do you think just might be
A classroom perhaps for you and me?
We hold so dearly the things we own
Never quite realizing they are just a loan

So perhaps if we learn of the things we can
but keep in control of our fleshy sham
Though this world of matter does stir our zeal
We'll find we are put here to test our steel!

Barbara Farrow

Mother

My Mother who I love so much
Cared for me with her gentle touch
Took care of me when I was ill
Through bad times she's with me still

Promised me she'll be there till the end
Due to that she's my very best friend
Always taught me what's wrong and right
I thank God for you every night

You did a good job bringing as all up
In your future I wish you good luck
This I had to tell you, this couldn't wait, I had to tell
how I feel, before it's too late.

Samantha Blackford

A Troubled Youth

I have known the death of my father
and so left to the mercy of
an unstable matriarch

I have known the sting of mothers
cruel words
and the swelling of defensive anger

I have known smoldering guilt, so black
if seen by others
they would recoil with fear and dread

I have known living anger
running full speed towards calamity

I have known the suffocating grasp
of too many sorrows holding fast

I have known a troubled youth

Greg Bauman

Emma

She's two years old and very bold.
And has a funny face.
She thinks she's four and acts like me.
I love her more then anything!

She's special as you can see.
She's the best from near to far.
She has this face that is cuter then anything!
She's my sister and I love her more then anything!

Amanda Schisler

My Third Child

God has created you completely.
From Him you are sacred and unique.
He has entrusted you to me for care.
You, child, are a gift to cherish.

I look forward to your talents, emotions,
Intelligence, creativity, and love.
My family, that you're a part of,
Will protect, guide, and teach you.

I will try not to mold and shape you,
For God has already done so.
I shall seek, learn, and accept
Who you are to be.

Please try to understand my faults,
Weaknesses and mistakes.
There will be times of fear, confusion,
Disappointment, and sadness.

Mostly, I will give you joy, hope,
Gladness, and unconditional love...
For you are perfect, wonderful, and special.
You are a precious gift...My Third Child.

Dana M. Davis

Free Throw

I feel the seams
I grip the air hole
Form is key
Pressure is on
How do you react
Does your stomach drop
Do you say it's going down
What kind of man are you
Can you handle it
Do you choke
Do you bury it
Everyone's relying on you
A parallel to life
What kind of person are you
Do you come through when people need you
Sometimes a free throw
Can be all it boils down to

Bradley Scott Burnett

True Love

Say that you love me and hold me so tight
Comfort these tears that fall,
I don't know what to do
All I know is I need you

I remember when we used to laugh
We'd both feel so complete inside,
We were two loving people basking in our love

Now my lover's gone
and I don't know where to start,
I feel so lost inside
I guess it was your time, but I still want you with me.

I remember when you called on me
and your blue eyes sparkled with delight
I'm still looking for you,
but you'll never come back to me

Lover you are gone, and I don't know what to do
as these tears fall down my face
I feel so lonely, half of me died with you
All I know baby, is that I still need you
Don't you know that I'd give my life for you?

Amy L. Zajac

I Am Not Dead

Don't mourn for me or grieve or sigh, for I live on, I did not die.
If you miss me—that I understand; I wish you, too, could share this
    land.
It's you I have sympathy for, 'cause life is hard 'till you pass that door.
Now I am in the world beyond, where sin and pain and sorrow's gone.
Where love abounds, all is beauty and truth, in a brand new life of
    everlasting youth.
I miss you too, my family and friends, but fear not, we will meet again
Here, where I am with our Lord, living the promises of His Word.
Go on with life with love and mirth, we'll be close while you're on earth.
Miss me not for I'm always there; sharing joy and sorrow, to love
    and care.
With friends and family before me gone, you're in our prayers
    as your lives move on.
And when the Lord calls you home we will greet you, you won't
    be alone.
Then, my dear, you'll plainly see why I've asked you not to grieve
    for me.

Suzanne M. Schaeffer

"My Best Friend"

I open my eyes to a very strange place ... thankful to see the love
    in her face,
She embraces me filled with hope and delight, knowing the love she
    has shared has made things so right.
Through diapers and fevers and tantrums I threw ... she was always
    there guiding me as I grew.
Mistakes I have made through the years come and gone ... yet without
    hesitation her love and support carry on.
She never expects anything of me, but to be true to myself and be
    all I can be.
A special closeness has developed through love and respect ...
    one as a child I never would expect.
A bond between two - never to be broken ... even when the words are
    left unspoken.
She's been there from the start, and she'll be there to the end,
You know who it is ...?

My mother ... my best friend.

Brenda Ragazzo

Thicker

A pane of glass, separating your world from mine
You look towards the sun, but it doesn't shine
It is as pale as the moon, you no longer see light
Tomorrow is an eternity away, years until night
All that's left now is the memories of years long past
The greatest of those years, went much too fast
Days in the sun, watching your children grow
And then they went their separate ways, and you had nowhere to go
When they put you here, you never objected
Knowing all the time how you would be neglected
Now your hours are spent praying you soon will die
And every day you awake, screaming why, why?

A pill is shoved down your throat, and your thoughts cease
Your only escape, an artificial peace
We lock them up, to set the young free
It's all around, but no one seems to see
Our selfish needs are satisfied
At the cost of the elderly's pride
I want to help, but I don't know how
A pane of glass is thicker than my attention will allow.

Kevin Haller

The Unforgotten

She was to be the first to go up there,
But little did they know they were going nowhere.
I can see it as though it were yesterday,
For no one among us can forget it today.

We all watched in excitement and joy as it left the ground.
We all watched unknowingly as it took its last flight, heaven-bound.
It flew through the air headed for the stars,
But unfortunately, they did not make it that far.

They are role models for us all.
They showed us how fast we could fall.
They are the angels in our lives.
We could never forget them or how they died.

We will never forget you or all that you've done.
You are the crew of the Challenger, the astronauts that are gone.

Nathan Noertker

Granddaddy

(Dedicated to Wilbur B. Owens)

I was sure the world would end when you took your last breath,
    but today went on, tomorrow too, and for us there is no rest.

I was sure that you'd awaken when I reached and took your hand,
    but you knew all along in a way we couldn't understand.

All the loved ones you've left behind still yearn to have you near,
    we'll never again be complete and for this we shed a tear.

Our hearts will break, we'll crave your smile and the tenderness in
    your touch,
    Granddaddy, we all loved you so very, very much.

You've left your mark upon our lives as bright as the rising sun,
    and all of us have regrets of things we wish we'd done.

In our hearts and in our souls, you'll be with us everyday,
    and in gratitude and remembrance, this is what we want to say:

Thank you for the guidance when we didn't know where to turn.
    Thank you for the lessons that you've helped us to learn.

Thank you for your humor that made us laugh so hard with you.
Thank you for being honest with each of us when it wasn't easy to do.

Thank you for your simple way that gave us new insight.
    Thank you Granddaddy, for being our guiding light.

Thank you for your wisdom that you were always willing to share.
    But most of all, thank you for always being there.

Deborah R. Cremer, David L. Ray, II

Seer

The desert comes alive
Mornings are hot.
I anticipate the day.
No clouds. No wind. No sound.
Heat waves. Thermal currents.

I am the mermaid of the desert.
Swimming through its liquid heat.
Sea salt flows in my veins.
Ocotillo move gently like seaweed in thickened water.
Yuccas branch and divide as giant tuberous anemones.
Dust devils swirl, whirlpools across the sand.

Once this was the bottom of an inland sea.
Ancient sea shells embedded in alluvium.
Seer tones of color: brown, ochre, sage, saffron.
One floats on the silence.

The land is thirsty for water.
I hunger for the flow of human contact.
Burnt on the surface, we are seared shadows of ancient tides.

Melinda Hamlett

Quisemodo

I may have a hunch on my back,
My face can be disturbing,
But I wish you would treat me like
every other human being.
I sit in my tower all day long wondering if there is something wrong.
I may be deaf,
But I know what you say,
"There goes that monster, take the children away!"
The looks on your faces tells me where my place is.

I can't roam the streets without getting beat.
I sit in my tower,
Thinking of sorrow.
The sorrow you caused me.

I may be different on the inside, I know.
That's because my heart is filled
with sorrow.
There's nothing you can do to fill my shoes,
Because we're just too different,
Me and You.

Kari Reedy

Yesterday...Today...Forever

Eight long years since I've seen your face
neither time or distance can erase.
The memories we shared, ever so clear.
The strength of your presence, still lingers here.
I feel for you now as I felt for you then,
a love much deeper than that for a friend.

I adore you

Yesterday...today...forever!

Like the sun, you are warm and bright.
Full of fun...and witty insight.
Your qualities so great, you never cease to amaze.
I need you so much, I can not count the ways.
Thoughts of you, make my days much more complete
Dreams of you, make my nights ever so sweet.

I love you

yesterday...today...forever!

Larry Donell Edwards

Blooming Buds

Blooming buds sprouting fast,
Butterflies land on everyone they pass.
Many kinds, many colors,
Many glorious springtime wonders!
There's roses, carnations, and tulips, too,
In colors of red, purple, yellow, green, and blue.
When the seasons change, so do the flowers,
It also matters how much it showers.
In the winter the flowers die,
But luckily in the summer they come back alive.
You can give flowers to someone sweet,
Because it's a present you just can't beat!

Nicole Bednara

You

You started off life so sweet and small.
You grew like a weed so straight and so tall.
We gave you the best that money could buy.
But life took a turn as the years went by.
Now death stares at us, and we wonder why.
When we knew in our heart there was nothing left to try.

Deborah Spragling

Night Dreams

Dreams have come to what of a place
With dolphins of white never to trace
Thoughts of being prolonged of the day
Simple as time, though harder than clay
Actions of Me, all about You
Hush as Wintermen follow us through

Remember the day of sadness in me
Put off the flowers and turn the key
Life is what meant for hours to go
Hum to the song that we all know
Forget the time of drowning complaints
Remember what's Hell and who are the Saints

Sharks in the dusk, too wild in the sky
Grizzly as might, wild and Rie
She drifts unto you as cold as the cave
Her sole is gone, gigantic wave
To the dead moon, and seals in the sky
Wild fire hell, then we'll all die.

Clinton E. Currie

Could It Be?

Why do I feel this way?
Thinking of you everyday.

I remember the day we first met,
wasn't quite sure what to make of you yet.

Something strange stirred inside of me,
and I asked myself "could it be?"

Are you the one in my dreams?
For nothing is the same as it seems.

I prayed for someone to love,
And when you came my prayers were answered from above.

You took the pain of loneliness away,
Will you always be here to stay?

You've shared a new meaning to my living,
and have given me the joy and pleasure in giving.

And everyday the good things I do,
are because my thoughts are of you.

Why do I feel this way?
Thinking of you everyday.

Are you the one for me?
Tell me, could it be?

Geraldine Silverio

Doubts About Time

At some past instant in the dark void, a point of light explodes afar.
Eons later, wobbling, cooling debris circles a burning star.

On one turning, congealing cinder, hardening crust shudders and drifts,
water forms then follows the moon's pull, while starlight shifts.

Feeling change, now darkness then light, cold then heat, flowing,
    ebbing,
each life awakens to effects and notes their passing; some time thus
    beginning.

Each lifeform clings to its cycle: some to the moondrawn tide
some to the suncast light. In passing, a time for each is
    separately prescribed.

Could time be more? Will it stop when this one cinder is gone?
Will 'where and how each life is moving' measure time after life is done?

Hopefully, time is more than noting shifting, transitory effects.
Suppose time were the intervals between bursts of light as God directs?

Could we accept on faith that God plans on a scale so great,
a time exists with God that we can't grasp in our limited state.

Gerald W. Dyer

"I Remember"

I remember many things, all of them not good,
I remember being tired from which the line I stood.
Some people went left; some people went right,
Whichever line you went, you were overcome with fright.
I remember people crying, thinking could this be the end?
I remember finding comfort in the arms of a welcome friend.
The days and nights went on, as if to never stop,
I felt my body giving up, and my faith began to drop.
Sometimes I wished it were a dream, and eventually I'd wake up,
But I knew deep, down inside, I was there, and I was stuck.

Nicole Coselli

SonneTNT

Bomb Squad got a threat about five o'clock:
Thirteen lines left to defuse the device.
Called on Timmy the demolitions doc,
He goes through plastic doom with veins of ice.
Ten lines until the charge will detonate.
Tim's kevlar vest would keep his chest concealed.
Better hurry, no time to litigate;
Don't think about ransom demands or deals.
Watch is ticking, trigger's set to ignite.
Five lines to snip the mercury switch wires;
Can't borrow courage to shield dynamite,
Bomb will explode, so wield steady pliers.
    The sonnet's couplet blows—what will Tim do?
    I guess be thankful it's not a haiku.

Scott Craig

I Thought It Was Spring

I thought it was spring, but not anymore,
because the weather got sore.
The wind tossed and turned,
but what really got me burned,
was the snow.
Now I want to see the robin, not the crow.
Just to let you know,
I want to see flowers,
in about two hours.
I want the sun to be warm,
so there is no more snow storm.
I want there to be leaves on the trees,
and to see birds and bees.
I want the weather to be like spring,
then everyone will sing.
Streams will seem to be talking,
and birds will be mocking.
Oh, I want it to be spring!

Denise Rockwell

Hope Unmended

My heart bleeds
The tears fall
Hatching a sea that ebbs and flows
A current commencing from the pain of unjustified repercussions
Jealousy oozes from she who has it all,
Yet has nothing.
A hermit in a fortress of righteousness and self pity
A friend to only those who forsake life in favor of death
A long and lonely waiting game,
Pointing the finger of sin,
When wasting life is the great sin.
How futile.
My heart bleeds

Margaret Furlong

Trees Change

Trees sustain amid the life, and they are ok

Fragrances are sexy; care are beautiful; the clothes make the man,
    dress compliments the woman
The building makes the city
In the cement we find the security of the known and never-changing
    life that presents no challenge; in the cement we find the safety.
    Trees change

Trees keep the sanity and insanity inside for the others to take for
    granted, that is how they stay sane, and it is ok.
Others cut them, others climb them, others burn them, others pollute
    them and yet are still themselves
Trees eat our sounds, feel our sins, manage our winds and still hold
    the ground beneath our feet

Trees aren't afraid to change; instead of trees seeing color, they
    become that color
Trees die. Trees live. Don't you see they aren't afraid to change?

Amid the cement they find the beauty in themselves; amid the
unchange
    the change for the better
Would a city be beautiful without trees? Would our ground be solid
    without trees?
Would others breathe without trees?

They branch out, they come in different shapes and sizes, they come
    in different colors
They all serve the same purpose: Trees live to support others, and
    it's ok

Trees guide the misguided toward acceptance, yet the followers are
    too blind to see
Trees change
Can't you see?

Seth Walker

Nature Knew

The sky whispered you were my fate
But I didn't hear it then
And when the trees said it was true
My heart tried to pretend

The mountains majestic, and the water sparkling
Agreed you were the one
And I would've believed it, had I known it was true
Something told me to be alone

The years passed, and the flowers bloomed
Telling my future bliss
But I didn't see it, you were not there
Looking back, you were missed

But with the sunrise, there you stood
My soul mate, my love forever
And if someone would've told me
I would've been here sooner!

Denise Valadez

Goodbye My Love

Alzheimer's is your name.
Destruction is your game.
You sneak in unheard and unseen
to rob a beautiful and loving lady of her
ability to reason and destroy the memories of her
family, friends, and loved ones.
Try as I might I couldn't stop you.
Would that I could kiss her goodbye,
Hold her gently, and help her, with dignity,
glide slowly into the silent night.
Life is great, Life is good, but a nursing
home shouldn't be its goal.

George E. McCord

To A Friend

I look at a picture of you
It really means a lot to me
Hope all your dreams come true
And all the world will see
You've worked so hard for all you've got
Enjoying what you have - forgetting what is not
Making sure it's there to stay
Never looking in the past
For fear of missing something new
Knowing this won't be the last
Of the many things you do
I respect all the courage and truth
Of your determination and gain
The complicated is your move
The hardest to get - the one you claim
This is why I often look to you
If I fear the road ahead
Because you always come through
Without a word being said.

Leslie Cooke

Shadow Of The Star

While I moved along in the darkness
I pulled my wrap about me, shivering...
It was cold and clear,
the stars twinkling brightly in the dark sky...
"Such a quiet night," I thought, "silent...is more the word."
Near the inn, I passed a stable...
I heard the movement of cattle against the straw,
and the cry of a new born baby.
"funny," I thought, "a baby in a stable."
As I hurried on, I heard voices singing...
the melody haunting...
the words unforgettable...
"Glory to God...!"
Then suddenly I was bathed in a great light...
I looked up to see a beautiful star...
it sparkled and shone,
piercing the darkness,
sending its loving rays to forgive and cleanse...
it even had a shadow...
a cross...

Jo Williams

The Victory

A father once said to his son,
There is a task that must be done,
In the land there is evil you see,
The people must have a chance to be free.
The work won't be easy, the load won't be light,
But you my son are up to the fight.

And so the son went softly at night,
And brought with him a shining light,
And touched all the troubled, and told all the host,
That their greatest treasure, need not be lost.

The people were sullen, unbelieving,
No faith that this son could help with their grieving,
So they arrested him and gave him a trial,
And doomed him to walk the rugged mile.
And not by chance or the father's whim,
He wore the darkness for all of them.

From "take this cup" in Gethsemane,
To the cry—"have You forsaken Me?"
While standing lonely on that tree,
He passed love's victory on to thee.

Ruth Faulkner Grubbs

A Bridge To Cross

Whenever you wonder whether you are ahead
you may want to take a stab at
anything traveling faster than light
you may not fall as you would think much far behind

Whenever you think you are way behind
you may want to take a shot at
anything running faster than life
you may already be heels over head

There are things in life that may seem unfair
but when you think of the story of a grizzly bear
whose paws were well on its prey
but it was shot instead

Starting the day our parents let ourselves grow
we should expect from time to time rain on our parade
if there were no expectation of silver lining
we would not be able to see ourselves being great

Chihoi Duong

The Telephone

It's a unique little thing;
Although if we're not careful, it will constantly ring.
We all use it every single day,
Whether it be in business or in play.
Some find it to be quite useful;
While others, the plug they want to pull.

The telephone can help us, though,
When you're in danger, it can let someone know.
To a family, it can bring such joy.
A child might have one as a toy.
It can be a wonderful thing...
Gladness or sadness the phone will bring.

Although it can be annoying; sometimes a pain,
Through a telephone there's a lot to lose or gain.
Use it carefully; use it wise.
By a telephone someone can spread lies.
Good or bad, we all need a telephone.

Roxanne Shiveley

Purification

It thunders, lightning flashes.
The rain, how it pours.
As I watch, my body wet, my senses numbed,
Yet, my soul, in awe, how it soars.

I watch the jagged streaks,
As they chase across the sky.
The bright flashes, followed by thunder.
Oh, how it rolls, and slowly dies.

All too quickly, the storm pushes on,
Held back by no man; it fades into the distance, and is gone.
In its wake, the grateful Earth soaks up the water,
The plants replenish, and the air is pure and clean.

Oh, that such a storm could sweep
Through my body and soul,
And to them, the same promises keep.
To remove the sin and corruption, that be the goal.

Paul Rector

A Piece Of Land Just For Me

A piece of land just for me is all I wanted, so I could feel free.
I asked the Lord to lend me the need,
so my family and more are able to feed.
A small plot of land is all that was needed,
I asked the Lord, again I pleaded.
He said work my soil and you shall see
How easy it is for you to feel free.
This may be to much for me to grow, but what a feeling, learning to sow.
My soil was clay, rocky and dry, how saddened I was wanted to cry.
Fertilizers were needed, my test would show
That phosphorus was needed, it was way too low.
Sulfur also was called by the test, this was used for the good root
    strength.
Organic matter was all that was left,
I brought enough bags to complete my test.
I tilled my soil high and low
And when I was done-Lo and behold, rich looking soil, all ready to sow.
I planted my seeds neatly apart, patiently waiting for them to sprout.
I thank you Lord for giving the need,
I promise you now my family and more will able to feed.
This feeling I have deep inside is warm all over because I have tried.
If I had not the need to ever feel free, I wouldn't need land,
JUST FOR ME!

        Kenneth A. Meyer

Lonely

Loneliness, a term that I fully comprehend,
    It reaches for me at night when I dream;
Creatures creep, and I attempt to pretend,
    Try to relieve myself without a scream.
They enter my mind in the days always;
    Demons who tell me what I really need.
To them, I just simply say my mind stays,
    No desire to conform on what they heed.
They will seep in at any rate this day.
    My mind is an open portal for them.
Cretins tell me I'm alone and pray,
    For deliverance and a precious gem.
        So here I am with my education,
        No friends, no hope, no life, no relation.

        Brian Boundy

The Time Bandit

When I was a boy, I spun a toy one day,
And saw it whine its way through time.
The sound got lower, the top got slower and fell over,
yet still a friend of mine.

You stole my top and other toys and all those things that boys
    hold dear,
The Earth was spinning and you kept winning,
but I did not shed a tear.

Morning light turned to day. I knew that top would not stay,
your appetite which feeds on fear:
That the top would stop its spinning,
that I would cry for Mother—Oh, the world was ending!

You see, there is always a beginning and an end,
to everything that spins:
We are born and we shall die and we have loved and we have cried,

And, that's the most important thing to me: to keep this victory alive,
For all to say when we are gone: He did not leave alone,
His love keeps on spinning.

        C. Michael Bradshaw

Aurora Borealis

Forever dark are the nights up north
Marred only by the diamonds of nature.
When, out of nowhere, beauty comes forth
Whose brilliance shall always endure
    the emptiness.

Song of beauty, gift of love
Filling the nothing of the void,
Glimmer of hope from above
Shall always and forever be devoid
    of darkness.

My heart follows after the light of lights
And eternally it shall always be.
Illuminating the darkest of nights
By brightness as if it shall never see
    the blackness.

Haze of glory, shower of truth
Always within my sight.
Intensity that shall always soothe
My infinite struggle to fight
    the nothingness.

        Ezekiel Nono

Justice

Is Justice dead? It must be!
Control hides conspiracy.
Corruption hangs in the depth of
law enforcers, morally tainted.

Cover it up, who will be wiser?
If they just keep it locked in files; Tell more lies,
just don't look in the victim's eyes!

"Tell the truth; Not today"
If they find out, we'll have to pay".

Justice is gone, Citizen,
Please believe what I say.
I know, for I am a victim,
of the corrupted Justice way!

Justice is dead and so is my love.
Both buried and covered in innocent Blood!

        Irene T. Douglas

Heaven's Rain

Heaven's rain takes place of my tears.
Sadness overwhelms my whole being.
Thunder roars out my frustration
I stand alone in the field.
Grief, desolate, and wilting away.

Oh Lord, how long must I suffer?

Why have you not taken me off the Land?

How long must I endure these pain?

I am ancient and futile. Yet Death
leaves me alone.
My branches bear no life, they're hangin'
on, just as I.
Friends no longer visit.
The fields, they mock me.
But my eyes will shed no tear, for
Rain takes my place.

        Som Chaleunvong

As The Sun Rises...

As the sun rises, the mountains steam;
With clouds so low, that they blanket the hills;
Purples and Oranges fill the ancient blue beyond;
Gorgeous you say? I think so too.

With the wind to our backs we run;
Along the stream of eternity;
Into the cool, crisp, clear as the horizon awkwardness;
Islands so close you could walk, not really.

A kiss and a hug for everything and nothing;
Thanks.

The world is spinning, time to catch up;
Beautiful, ravishing, a dream;
Picture perfect.

Only once in a lifetime do we get to
    see something so desirable;
Heaven, only a touch away.

Steven E. Fritz

Imagine

There was a time in days of old,
When instead of movies, stories were told.
There wasn't the glamour and lights of the screen,
Only clever minds that were filled full of dreams.
The appealing portion was not in violence or crime,
But of peaceful surroundings, and life sublime.
Nor was the interest found in passionate lust.
But of the purest romance, with innocence. And trust.
Adventure came from the unanswered questions.
Of lands unexplored, with fortune suggestions.
Story tellers of old had a priceless treasure,
Of giving their audience unblemished pleasure.
Imagine.

Jennifer Huffaker

THE ESSENCE OF THERESA

Like the boom of thunder
Like the crack of lightening
So this was THERESA

Like springtime rain she formed eight blossoms
Like warm sunshine for their constant growth
So this was THERESA

There was the voice of harshness
To hide her softness
So this was THERESA

There was the frown
To disguise her smile
So this was THERESA

Proud and Strong but invisibly Vulnerable
Outspoken and Determined
Kindhearted and Giving
Hard working and Dependable
Wife and Mother
Who believed in the glory of God

So this too was THERESA.

Patricia Hill

Mother

We thank the powers that be for woman, for all that you do
When you look at us, do you ever wonder, why we make you cry
From a husbands embrace, to a child's sad face
Everything, Everything comes back to you
WE THANK YOU, WE PRAISE YOU, WE LOVE YOU
FOR BEING MOTHER, FOR BEING MOTHER
For that strong hand, for being there when no one
else would stand
When all else is gone, and there is no place to go
WE THANK YOU, WE PRAISE YOU, WE LOVE YOU
FOR BEING MOTHER, FOR BEING MOTHER

Frederick D. Perkins III

Can I Spot Jesus?

He a troubled, downtrodden man,
    approached

He of unkempt clothes,
    smelled

He of unsightly way,
    in mine

He of slow deliberation,
    unpaced me

He wearing life's havoc,
    mumbled

He asked for meal money;
    I passed.

A liquored charlatan,
    I all too quick discerned.

It is much later now,
    on pause, I was judge.

I passed Jesus,
    again.

Encourage me not to judge hastily. Amen

Robert Lanphar

When The Moon Comes Out

When the moon comes out from behind a thick cloud,
The stars rejoice and bathe in its vast gleaming light.
The wolves cry out for love for the darkness
Envelopes them from all sides.
The birds are quiet as if holding their breath
And they sat snugly in their nest
Knowing the ball of glowing beauty is watching them

All through the night.
The owl's piercing cry shatters the silence
That is cuddling the forest
Waiting for the dawn to come.

So the moon goes to sleep
And the sun comes out to warm the earth
From the chilling night.
And sometimes I wake up in the middle of the night
I look out of my window.
I can see the moon staring at me
I know it is up there watching over me
And when I think about it being stuck in the big, black sky
Saddens me greatly.

Jennifer Dainard

Fear Is...

Fear is the creature hiding under the bed
Fear is the nightmares in your head
Terrors coming from everywhere
It's you they're coming to scare.

The terrors of the night are near
This is a good time to fear
Fear watches us constantly
Watches you, watches me.

Sleep if you dare
You're in for a scare
No one can help you now
No one knows how.

Scream, yell, and shout
And try to get out
Of this nightmare you've gotten into
The choices are up to you.

Get out and be fearless
Or, stay in the nightmare and be afraid.
That is what fear is...

Ashley Firth

"Maturity"

Maturity is an interesting concept,
Apparently a lot of people have trouble with it.
Growing up and maturing go hand and hand,
Then again - someone can grow up and not mature.
Maturity, is a very important part of life,
If you do not have it then you will not succeed.
Success and accomplishments,
Are how we measure ourselves.
Decisions play a big part in what we call "Fate,"
Fate is in essence what we call "destiny."
Destiny is how we are all going to end up,
Reach the end and find out you have nothing.
Reaching the end and having nothing,
Will show you that you never did anything right.
When you never succeed or accomplish anything,
People label you as a failure.
No matter what you do in life,
You are judged by someone.
If you refuse it,
It will destroy you.

Raymond D. Choiniere II

Life & Death In Abuse Shelter

It's like I and my child have died. No longer
among the living. We have been placed in a waiting
room, just waiting our turn. We have been told of
our new life and what we must do. Now in this limbo
of souls, a voice has instructed, "It's almost your
turn to go". Labour is coming, prepare ourselves.
For soon you will be re-birthed and sent on a new
journey with one big push. Your life will be as
a new-born; at first you won't see clearly, at
first you will be motionless. Time will move on.
Your vision will clear. And soon you will be
walking and running. You will have new dreams
and new goals. And sometimes you will even
remember that time before. And it will
seem as if remembering a past life. Because
it is one.

Carole McLaren

I'm Not Me Anymore

I guess I'll have to stop dreaming, 'Cause when I do I plan
Of things I want to do someday, When there's more time at hand.

Then some stranger says "Hello Pops", Or helps me with a door;
And once again I'm made to see, That I'm not me anymore.

Still in my mind I'm young and dashing; Romantic as can be.
Though all devoted to my wife, Young girls must dream of me.

Till some real cutie smiles so nice, My heart yells out for more.
She says "You look like my grand dad", Then I'm not me anymore.

My son wanders through our garage, An old ball comes in view.
Surely he's no challenge for me, But says, "let's shoot a few".

I soon see him running and jumping, While I sweat from every pore.
I think as I stoop, hand on knees, I'm just not me anymore.

I drive through a familiar town; A thing I often do.
I look for all the old landmarks, And people I once knew.

But something's wrong, it's changed. They're strangers at each door.
I realize, it's been forty years, And I'm not me anymore.
Someday I guess I'll be too old, To dream what I should be.
I'll probably give up travelling, And girls won't notice me.

Perhaps I'll think of times like now, For who knows what's in store.
I only know one thing for sure; I won't be me anymore.

Marion Kyzer

And Again

My Thoughts, I must constantly rearrange
To accept the things I can not change
To live through all which comes my way
With the passing, of each new day
To leave my yesterdays behind
My questions, answer with a clear mind
With the hope, that peace and happiness I'll find

Reflections of my past, and all I thought I knew
Seeing now, just how much I grew
To learn to act with more reserve
And receive the respect, I deserve
Being always positive, about every situation
Having confidence, in each decision
To attain whatever goal, I envision.

And when the problems have you beat
Remember, there's always one exit on a dead street
And remain ever constantly persevering
Soon you'll find the problems disappearing
Just take another deep breath, and carry on
Until the arrival of a brighter dawn.

Deborah Hansen

Infestation

Rebecca bugs me like a buzzing pest
When she, the wildcat trapped, begs to be freed.
I open up the cage called "carelessness,"
But bites me she and shuts it with much speed.
When she complains she screeches like a bat;
She strews her things about just like a dog.
She bathes as much as would befit a cat;
Such hours spent show'ring—what a water hog!
Yet I should not judge harshly on her since
Undisciplined, we both are prone to mess;
She soothes her ailing neck in heated rinse,
And I feed fuel to gripes with tardiness.
  And though she seldom heeds my wise advice,
  Hence I shall call her escargot, not lice.

Marcus Andrew Arreguin

62

Casper

To my baby—whose life was short and sweet;
who had tiny paws that I call feet;
who was as white as snow
and almost as bright as me;
who was as quick as a bullet
and who was as sensitive as the leaves on a tree.

I feel your presence when you are near.
It feels as soft as when you were here.
I see your face run down with tears.
It's in a place that all kitties fear.
I feel your touch as soft as cotton.
It is a touch I will never have forgotten.

I know your life was as rough as mine.
The pain was all I could see sometimes.
It was in your eyes saying "Mom please don't go."
But as soon as I knew it, we reached the end of the road.

The tears began, and never ended.
And the pain of love was never mended.
To a child of mine "'til death do us part"
you will always be here in a special place in my heart.

Nancy Coates

Reminiscent Of Whitman

Up around the curve she flow'd with great vengeance
Her body form'd by the earth, rock, sand, leaves, limbs
She comes from nowhere having no idea where she goes
Enjoying her unit one in the whole

And outlining her intentions from whence they understood
Someone will follow her and rest upon her bosoms
The feeling amongst the follower will be harmonious and one
Leaning upon her whole-they will be apart of her

For suddenly from the sky comes a light bright as day
To lead the follower on his path to nowhere understood
What is there is bound together for eternity
The love for them together shows who Nature is meant to be

Birds fly naked above this willing union
What shall blanket these creatures of the sky?
Am I the one who so justly sees the joining of the two?
Soon the sun will allow this bird to cover her body

My lips meet hers and together we end
The bird has covered us both and protected us from others
All parts joined together to make the one whole
Can the savage not comprehend how the next curve will unfold?

Kathy Fontenot

Little Round Top

A sight so enchanting can only be found,
In a place so preserved and made to astound.

Where a significant hill is a mountain of lives,
Where the nation's greatest dreams are on two sides.

The wonder, the glory, this hill has endured,
It has earned its protection which shall be ensured.

Where a great mist of magic falls over the crescent,
That promotes a sense that the brave men are present.

So little and innocent, who could suspect,
Its inspiring history not one could detect.

The summit of gravestones, so grandly it is crowned,
Oh, oh, the sight I have found!

William Dowd

"Me Now"

I see you enter
but ignore your presence,
hooded eyes piercing heavy lash.

I stir slightly
reminding you I wait.

You reach for me hands trembling,
fingers gently touching lanate limbs.

I roll over
stretching legs, reaching high, body supine.

My belly welcomes soft caresses
curling 'round legs reclining next to mine.

Your stroke sends shivers down my spine -
a lightning bolt of warm anticipation.

I lick your ear,
my breath across your neck,
our tousled hair as one.

You're home at last.
I purr.

Sue Hendricks

Nocturnal Awakenings

Greens, Yellows, Reds suspended in air,
Silent mist adorns her hair
Where Evening's halo shies from sight

A clean, crisp smell,
A quiet world,
Night descends terse and sure—an Artisan
at moulding minds
Painter of Light, Sculptor of Sound, Creator of Questions
on a merry-go-round
Senses awaken! Imagination revive! Inquiry
relive last night's ride!

Mourning's insomnia brings subtle light
As she quietly replaces mind with sight

Kira Russo Bauer

Love's Lost

My heart aches with vacancy.
Emptiness and loss have overcome.
Where, my love, did we go wrong?

We had a love that seemed so strong...
Dreams, hopes, our lives to live
What was it, my love, that we didn't give?

Could we go back in time?
To retrieve our lost love that was divine.
Could we go back in time?
To retrieve the love that was yours and mine.

I look into your eyes to see
What used to be my hopes and dreams.
All I see is vacancy,
From love's lost gleam.

Where, my love, did we go wrong?
To lose our love, once so strong.

Jill Talley Hynes

A Girl's Opinion Of Chris In 1492

In fourteen hundred, ninety-two
Columbus sailed the ocean blue
On this trip he was lost at sea
A fact some thought never to be.

He said he had found
This wild ground
And claimed for the queen
"Something never before seen."

He said that he would not kill
If it was his majesty's will
This was a promise he never did keep
When he caught natives sneaking a peek.

And never once did he think
The natives thought him a terrible fink
For he raped many of the women
And shamed them in the eyes of the men.

Now, it is said in a history book
That upon this land, Chris was first to look
With this statement I disagree
For Chris was not the first to cross the sea.

Amanda Ricketson

Untitled

There's hope up there in the sky
There's hope up there, yet I wonder why.
The sky is sad, gloomy, and gray
Although there's hope in a funny way.
The clouds will pass over, oh so fast
The gloom is gone, now in the past
There's hope up there in the sky
There's hope up there, yet I wonder why.
The sky is now blue and bright;
Some how filled with a magical light.
I look up now and what do I see?
A rainbow stretched from sea to sea...
There is hope up there in the sky
And with God's promise we all know why!

Angela P. Wheeler

The Forest Of Thought

To hear nothing but the rustle of your thoughts,
The soft beatings of ideas flying around in your head,
To walk through the trees of your mind,
and remember the good times and bad,
The sun is shining,
The moon is alight,
Love is in blossom,
As the flowers grow bright;
The canopy of the mind protects you,
Allows you to roam free,
Whenever you please,
In the Forest of Thought.

Brian David Huard

We All Must Pay The Cost

As the lost look above,
The Lord's love is as a dove.
They plead and cry with all their might,
As the Lord can't stand that sight
The Lord puts us on earth for his will
As some of us turn around and kill.
When we disobey the Lord's laws
The devil has us in his claws
It is sad to see the lost
But we all must pay the cost.

Sarah J. Dennis

Tears

I hear the sound of a woman crying.
She sounds like there is someone dying.
I look for her, but I cannot see.
I hear the sounds but she is hidden from me.

The trees turn brown as they are pushed down.
Bare earth turns a stripped face 'round.
Again, I hear the moaning sounds of someone crying.
But all I see is the bush and tree dying.

I feel a tug at my heart, as though a part of me is dying.
How faint the sound as it drifts by, the crying.
I see her there on the earth so bare, knelt down and crying.
What is your name and who is to blame?
I am Mother Nature, and my world is dying.

Keith Monti

Pale

Walking through the city's veins
Neon,
flashes of despair
Regardless of the chaos
of the smoke
of the news

Walking through the naked body of this town
beaten by empties eyes
denying many words
    many names
    many faces

Walking through the city's veins
Unknowing myself
drinking this tequila
while you come as always
pale

J. A. Ale

Letting Go

The body of a man with the tears of a child looks and speaks not.
The mother of the son sits with tears in her heart, deep and searing
    tears, filling the already deep cracks in that heart.
She wonders when her little boy left, or, did he ever.

Is this indecision his leap into manhood or a leap into the unknown
    fantasy of his unwelcome independence?
The mother is not to go along-she must let him venture alone. No
    longer can she protect or kiss it and make it better- no longer
    can she tuck him in and kiss him good night. He must do all
    things himself though unsure how or when or if or...
"He'll be just fine, this too shall pass," they all say, but pass
    to where or what?
Letting go and letting him try was far easier when this mother could
    take away the hurt when he fell and cut his knee- letting go into
    the world of unknown is scary at best and so very painful as the
    day draws near.
I will let go for I must, yet, my heart weeps silently and will never
    ever be quite the same.
Someone should have warned me of this day- maybe I would have
    better prepared myself? Yet, how could they, for only I, my son, can
    ever be your mother and your departure as my baby boy is mine alone
    to bear.

Janet Pope

Planets Peril

There was a time, not long ago, when clean water did flow.
From the mountain to the brook, a long journey the water took.
Animals and fish all swam and drank, through long days and nights
    of fun and prank.
Now all that is left is pollution and death for all God's
creatures, no matter what their rank.

Edward Earl Schlotterback

Five Senses

God gave us Five Senses
Hearing, Sight, Touch, Taste, and Smell.
Each does its part.
And serves us well.

The Five Senses are a means
  of security.
They protect the shy,
  as well as the bold;
They protect the young;
  as well as the old;
They protect us from heat
  As well as the cold;
They protect us from danger
  that is untold.

  Merle C. Johnson

"Gone With The Wind"

He's like the wind,
Soft and gentle, slowly sweeping through the sky.
He's like the wind,
Blowing white rose petals upon the heavens.
He's like the wind,
Sweeping the gentle scent of wild white roses into the air.
He sweeps his love gently through me like an angel singing
a sweet heavenly song.
His breath soft as the gentle breeze sweeps onto my lips.
And as the wind sweeps through the sky
His love for me has gone with the wind.......

  Lisa Lhotan

Just One More Day

Just one more day to grieve
Just one more day to cry.
If you wanted to hurt me, I ask myself why?
The tears of death have fallen on my shoulder.
When I smell the fragrant aroma that you so often wore
It puts a tear in my eye and an ache in my heart
Just one more day to grieve
Just one more day to cry.

  Dustin Hanson

Revelations

There's no way to stop a child from growing old before her time.
Her innocence fading slowly from her eyes.
Her mouth firm with quiet determination,
stemming from all of Her stiff-necked pride.
There's no way to stop that child from growing older.
Her strong voice fading softly into sighs,
though still with quiet emphases and courage,
Her dreams are made known far and wide.
There's no way to stop that child from growing flowers.
Nurturing them with all the tears she cries.
Walking through the sands of time and life and war,
watching with weary eyes the coming tide.
There's no way to stop that child from growing too old...
Until one sad day she slowly dies.
Knowing finally the truth about who she is.
A truth in everyone we all try to hide.

  Kasha McDonald

Saturday Night

The sparkle in her brown eyes
made me forget Jamie's lies.
Her straight brown hair
made me think she really cared.
When she gave me that innocent look
she read my mind like it was a book.
I tried to give her a friendly hug,
but I couldn't help my feeling's tug.
During the hug our feelings were together,
after the hug our lips came together.
I guess me and Michelle just couldn't resist,
we both needed a good-night kiss.
I know this poem may cause a fight,
but I'll never forget that Saturday night.

  Dennis Prater II

Love

Again my thoughts are with you (As they always are)
Just as the frost comes with the falling eve,
Or as in the summer, falls the dew
I keep wishing to be near you.

These long winter nights I spend
Listening to those beautiful love songs;
Which over the ether waves, weave their way
Making me wish you would come my way.

Those songs are our love songs.
The songs you and I hear together.
Tho' in different cities we shall, ere long
Keeping up our love, be again together.

The happy moments we have spent together
Keep me wishing you were here at present
To help me spend my time with you; together
We'd have the most wondrous time,
There wouldn't be anything I wouldn't do
To make you happy
One who loves in hope and lives in love
Far from his loved one.

  Walter G. Richter

I Am Not Any Less Than You

Just because I am poor,
I am not any less than you.
You may have more,
But I have something too.

Just because I live in a slum,
I am not any less than you.
You may think I look like a bum,
If only you knew.

Just because I was not born here,
I am not any less than you.
You may think I can not cry a tear,
But I do.

Just because you do not understand what I say,
I am not any less than you.
Treat me as you may,
But I will still start my life anew.

Just because I come from across the sea,
I am not any less than you.
You are no different from me,
Yes-it is true!

  Lisa Pratt

True Love

Love ... That's what life is all about.
People fall in and out of Love,
Some are hurt and some are glad.
But this hurt I'm feeling has me mad.
I thought you were the type that
Never believed the rumors that were said.
I guess I was wrong.
I'm not done crying, but now I know
That you must go.
It's for the best.

Jennifer L. McCullough

The Old Wooden Cross

The old wooden cross,
If people would listen;
they could still hear;
the sounds of the nails that were driven.
The old wooden cross,
is the light in my Life.
It took me from darkness,
And gave me new sight.
The old wooden cross.
Can light your way.
Through darkness, or sadness,
Our even at death one day.
The old wooden cross
Is a symbol of peace, if,
people would only, get on their knees,
And pray to the man, whom died on that cross,
They would feel all of his love,
And, all of his wrought.

Ronald Nelson Pipes Jr.

Five Olympic Rings

Dedicated to Kokayi Tankersley
Her hidden force invited the winged
men into her castle, carrying an
attitude that slaved their destructive minds.
An orgasmic knowledge.

Smiling cutely, she stripped and controlled
their roar, they climbed on her and
sparked her soft inner walls, with neptune,
jupiter, and saturn tying her hands
and knees to the ground.

Her taste for the crime of nature
could not be stopped this day.
Her dreams are the truth, her lusty
savagery is brutal and stimulating to
watch, her cannibalism experienced by each titan.

The crazed angel men, masculine,
vulgar hustlers, rip her apart, leaving
nothing but blood stains, and teeth marked
bones completely sucked dry
of its marrow.
Winged whores left to rot.

Efrain S. Hernandez

Come Home

I was in the meadow sleeping,
When I heard the willow weeping.
The daisies hung their heads in sorrow,
The clover waited for tomorrow.

The grayish clouds blocked out the light,
The lilacs all sank low in fright.
Pansies sang a dreadful tune,
Come home my friend, come home soon.

Kelli Jean Huber

Dances

Dances at dawn in fields of joy.
Wind through the soul, lifting me up.
I carry the beat; the rhythm of my heart.
Light as a feather, it shall be my dance, lost in the
Oneness of you.
No other could teach me this dance,
   No other but you.
Moving through the air, I am connected to nothing,
Putting my joy into gestures for you.
Calming and peaceful for we are together.
Dances of joy; my dance is for you.
Feelings that can not be contained spring forth from my being,
To be captured in the wind.
   Captured by you in the wind.
Reaching for the light; the joy surrounds me.
Higher I reach for the infinite
   Oneness of you.
You are my light and my fields of joy.
   My dances are for you.

Dianne Guay

Get Away

Every day my life is filled with sorrow,
I always hope the day will be better tomorrow.

I wish the arguing would stop in any way,
Because I can't take the hurt and pain every single day.

I feel my warm tears run down my face,
And I wonder how long will I suffer in this place.

My body aches and my feelings are down so low,
I just can't take it anymore, I have to go.

So if you wake up one day and I'm gone,
I hope I come back, I hope I won't be that long.

I have to get away and sort things through,
I have to get away, away from you.

Candace Freer

To Be Free

Everyone has been asked this one question;
If you could be anything in the world what would it be?
Not a movie star, not a billionaire, None of this for me I would
be a BIRD.
It may seem a simple request.
A common average everyday bird,
Never to know boundaries or limits,
Never to know time or a schedule, Never to be captured,
or seen by the same person twice.

To go here or there as I please
To sit and sing with others or just merely fly as a loner.
To land in the lush greens, or to fly amongst the bluest of skies.
My wish may seem as a way of escape, to you,
But for me a bird is what I would be.
TO BE FREE!!!

Sonia A. Adame

Yellow

Yellow is the color of the sun
the scent of a daisy
the color of a lemon.
Yellow resembles my family tree
it also resembles the heart in me.
You can see yellow wherever you may go.
You can see yellow where the wind blows.
But if you really try you can see yellow
or it may pass you by.

Chris Brown

Remem'bring River

That time will come for voyages unknown
For a norseman toward Valhalla's shores
And a gaelic man to purgatory sent
Their souls to sail on remem'bring river

With youth's ethereal memories spent
One fair maned, the other ebonied
From whitened and deep furrowed brow
Come manhood's sigh of never cry

Their souls to travel down that final stream
Under suppressed rules of manhood bent
And vermilion shadow'd skies that light
That final darkn'd bend of remem'bring river

William Daniels

Christmas Pryer

Bitter cold winter morn
families praise God's child is born,
Together through life we stand,
rejoicing, singing, hand in hand.

Life separates us one from the other.
a bond never broken, child to mother.
Her prayers to God are given,
bring Lord each one to your good heaven.

Even in times we are not there,
in our hearts, these times we always share.
True Christmas meaning, to the world is lost,
his birth, his resurrection, God's greatest cost.

For some small few have learned,
what God's grace has given, not we have earned.
Came from his birth God's greatest gift,
with all his love our souls to heaven lift.

Roger W. Oxford

Questions And Answers

If you look at yourself in the eye,
Can you see the sky?
It's like a flower in the perfect bloom,
Do you see it like you assume?
Look up at the clouds and hum 'a song,
Do you think it's really wrong?
If you don't care,
Is it bare?
You don't talk nor speak like a bird,
Is it unheard?
You try, and try; and try all day,
Is it really your way?
If you say you don't like it but you really do,
Are you fooling everyone or just you?
If you sit and stare,
Is it because you care?
So look at yourself,
Do you like what you see?

Nicole Tranquillo

Love

Love is like a butterfly
With the wind underneath its wing
It flutters around so freely in the sky
And with the rush of a new feeling
It can scare you that you fell so fast
It may confuse the hell out of you
And make you wonder if these feelings will last
Because so many others have been untrue
But give it a chance and it will prove itself to you

Jennifer Henry

Death

Death is a curtain of dark sadness,
A melancholy veil that closes over your heart.
A piece of you that was there before
Is separate, missing, forever apart.
The agony of never knowing
Where their eternity may lie
Until your own day of reckoning comes,
You'll know when it's your turn to die.
You cry every day in gut-wrenching agony.
Cry and sob until there is nothing left inside.
You shut yourself away from the rest of the world
And contain the peace of knowing you can hide.
Because when you hide you have the solace of dreams,
Once again you see their dear shining face.
The happiness they have, the pain they don't feel,
And your heart can now rest, they're in a better place.
Even though you still long to see them,
Your heart still cries out for their love,
You can feel peace and know when you look to the sky,
That they are living in happiness in heaven above.

Dalicia LaFleur

The Springs Of Life

We rode the twin stallions of fear and hope
and we breached the valleys of the ocean
and we rose above the clouds to the hills of the gods
and we ate their bread and drank their wine,
and we held each the other's soul
and we danced upon the flames of the sun, rise and set,
and we dandled each the other's feathers of joy
until our wounds bled honey from our fingers and mouths
and the springs of life ran sweet salt
upon the hills and hollows
of our breasts and bellies,
and our breath was wet and hot and ragged
until at last our eyes were drawn from the heavens
to the fires on the plains of man,
and we survived our death and slept
until again we waked and burned for the bitter kiss
that steals blood and breath
so that heart and soul might again fly free.

Susan C. Peck

The Night Will Never Stay

The night will never stay,
The night will still go by.
Though with a million stars
you pin it to the sky.
Though you bind it with the blowing wind
and buckle it with the moon, the night will slip away
like a sorrow or a tune.

Kate Gould

"Shoshone Trail"

Afternoon shadows hasten to lay
a soft veil, on the open spaces
of a Shoshone trail.
Moccasined feet ride safely toward home.
And eyes are lifted to gaze upon
Crystal fingers, that explore the sky.
With the mountains all splashed
with gold, rose, and blue,
by an "Infinite Artist" whose
brush strokes so true; apply
with Majesty and purpose,
To give each creature large and small
God's blessing, and prayer to all

Mildred Dempster Schmidtman

Alone

The Time I spend alone I find
Is some of the most precious kind

When I can chase the blues away
And dream those dreams of yesterday

And for a very little while
Those thoughts can cause my heart to smile

I push the dark and dreary away
And spend some time in yesterday

Back when worries were quite small
And the future held it all

I pause and think about my life
And though I've had my share of strife

I feel that I've been truly blessed
But, when I take some time to rest

I drift away to a place
That puts a smile upon my face

And there alone, I float away
And remember dreams of yesterday

Eleanor A. Burns

The Quest

Once upon a night of old,
There was a man who many foretold.
Many a stories glistened with Gold
of this man foretold.
Into the night he ventured on a quest
    Wandering through the tangled nest.
To where no one could guess?
Around and round he would go,
    through the blackened night's glow.
For what reason no-one would ever know.
Did he roam to do something right?
    Or just drift through the sullen night,
Aimlessly on one plight.

Kerry L. Tracey

Things That I Miss

Long walks in the rain...
Short walks in the evening...
Walks...anytime...anywhere...

No lurching or stumbling,
just long easy strides carrying me forward...
to wherever I wanted to be.

Once I walked everywhere. I lived just a short walk
from life...restaurants...shopping...dancing...
ahhh...dancing!

Times change. Now I watch in awe
as someone skips lightly down the stairs...
not even touching the rail!

It wasn't easy, but I've learned to let go.
I don't cry anymore when, not knowing,
someone suggests a long walk in the park.

Now, I just smile...
and suggest a movie.
But, still...I dream of long ago days...

Jana Clark

The Thunderbird

Each and every night upon drunkenness I'd lay to sleep.
    Only to rise each morning, hung over, I leave to earn my keep.
So miserable had I become, barren of purpose and happiness,
    I prayed it was not true of me: "That which is cursed cannot
    be blessed."

A curse it was that morning when mother nature sent a wake-up call.
    Who's the culprit of this prank, what child is pounding on my wall?
The drumming at the window created quakes inside my head.
    Through bloodshot eyes I squinted, disbelieving what I saw instead.

The thunderbird was feasting on the bugs inside the window frame.
    His furious rhythm and red crown I knew as his claim to fame.
He looked at me for a moment — the longest moment I ever knew.
    Then twice he tapped upon the pane; then one more bug
    and off he flew.

In the several months that followed, as winter yielded to spring,
    I changed some lifetime patterns through discipline and opportunity
My course was hammered out by summer, the drunk became a man.
    I found a rhythm with a purpose; happiness was mine again.

Of all the creatures on this earth to come that morning to visit me,
    Appropriately 'twas the woodpecker, a foreshadowing, a prophecy.
This wondrous bird, Circe's love denied, foretold of love divine:
    The Almighty smiled upon my life; my darkened heart was
    made to shine.

Eric L. Mueller

Burning Crime

No emotions are shown as it rages,
Unfeeling it murders and steals,
It brings forth hot burning fear,
Sweeping across a nation.
Scorching, it takes.
Lapping up peace,
Dancing freely, getting away,
Escaping the anguish it bestows upon others.
Scars left behind do not heal,
Burns throb at a touch.
Raging it destroys our homes, our friends,
    our family,
Causing them to hide and mourn.
Unable to be extinguished,
Ongoing no shame shown.
Left behind are the ashes
    The remains
      The sorrows
    Victims left to suffer.

Holli King

"Keepsake"

As I look out across your vast ocean of life,
I find I'm looking down through velvet crystal waters.

I see your Spanish galleons heaped with treasures,
and the depth of you almost takes my breath away and
sometimes I cry.

I wonder if others see you as I do?

For, the friendship we share reaches far beyond
mere thoughts of man into an endless spectrum of light.

And if I am to dwell here with you,
A vigil I will keep of your treasures so heaped.
As surely I should.
For, there is no greater pleasure than to sail
your waters of friendship.

Sunny Kershaw

Which Christmas

Colored lights twinkle bright
People pack the stores each night
To buy some toys and then some more
To purchase for Tomi a game of lore.

The days draw on it's ever so near
You almost forgot that case of beer
That morning arrives with hope it seems
"I didn't get that doll" she screams.

A lone star shown ever bright
Guiding its followers that very first night
To a stable of animals lowly and poor
The kings first house had no door.

The night drew on bringing them ever so near
To present their gifts to a child so dear
Until morning arrived with hope and dreams
To fill a world with love's bright beams.

Is Christmas truly gone from sight
Has Christ's one star gone out tonight
Can CHRISTmas truly be once more
Or have we forever shut the door?

David L. Wilson

Expectation

In a bowling alley west of town
He parked his Harley at the door.
The ball was unlocked from its storage place
And he went inside to bowl once more.
Frame after frame he threw the ball
And strike after strike the pins did fall.
Then in the ninth with tension high,
He approached the lane with hope in his eyes.
But, this time his arm, had lost control.
And after the ball had hit the pins.
There stood the four, seven, eight and ten.
He shook his head.
How could this be?
A perfect game he would not see.
But, he took heart, for in the end,
He did help his team to win.
And when it was over, he strode out.
Straddled his Harley and rode off once more.
He knew that soon he would be back.
To try once more for that perfect score.

Anita K. Hecker

My Loves

My days are like the tides that rule the sea
   And cause the endless boundaries to withdraw
To open arms, or so it seems to me.
   They swell with love and then they retrogress
To skeletons without the flesh and blood
   That passion brings in all its ecstasy.
My days are filled with oh, so many loves;
   My boundaries are increased as the edge
Of sea. As tides recede from where they kiss
   The earth, my loves ebb and leave the space
An open void until another love
   Moves in to swell the tide once more.

Barbara Rogers

Untitled

Across the pale parabola of joy
Love on the wings of a humming bird
Comes siding gently down the curve
And whisks away into the excruciating twilight
Of a day whose life is spent,
Never to return again.

Stephen H. Childs

Celebrate Life

What is Life?
Life is living each day we have left
Learning new things with vigor and zest.
Giving a smile and a happy "Hello"
To each person we meet as we go.
Spreading cheer even while in pain
So that others may comfort gain.
Come, with brush and palette, my dear
Paint a picture of beautiful things near,
Read a book that gives you great joy,
Play a game and laugh and enjoy.
Do a puzzle to keep your mind sharp,
Ever ready to do your part,
Make each day worthwhile to the end,
Hoping to help others find love, not revenge.

Mae Gilmour

"Wind"

The wind is blowing
gently though the open doors of my mind
Bringing words of hope and wisdom
Far beyond my time
They're possessing and caressing me
The softly blowing breeze
gently stirs my restless mind
and brings memories
drifting through my open mind
It brings back tears of sorrow
mixing with the summer rains
The sea of memories brings
back ocean waves of joy
washing the shores of time
The breeze brings back tears of joy
like stars that softly shine
It's bringing back the memories almost lost in time
Then softly the dusky twilight
weaves its spell on me
Bringing floods of memories almost lost to me.

Aimee Frank

Prayer Of Thanks

You take care of sinking ships
and its passengers Lord.

So what ever might trouble me
or this household today

May we put it all
in your hands Dear Lord.

We've already prayed
so we won't faint.

Now we're looking up to you Lord
to pull us safely through.

Lord, work a miracle in our lives today.
We will forever give your Holy Name the praise.

It's through your grace, your love
your mercy Lord that we're able to carry on.

Thank you Lord for the times we've
shared in prayer.

We can come to you knowing that you
truly do care for you're always there

To hear and answer
our every prayer.

Ruby Noel

Untitled

Your love's lost light is as black as night,
Even the bluest of skies seems gray.
The aching of my broken heart has started to physically hurt.
Memories aren't enough to wipe away the tears.
Wishing with all of my heart doesn't mean I'm in your arms again.
Longing for the past doesn't turn back time,
And just because I love you doesn't mean you feel the same.
What seems wrong is the only sensible thing to do.
To settle for second best is never the way to go.
It won't make you happy.
It won't erase the pain.
With love it has to be all or nothing,
Otherwise it can't really be love, can it?
Nothing can ever be totally perfect,
But everything can be wrong.
The trick is to find even just a little good in everything we do
    and see and feel.
Beyond the gray clouds there is always blue sky where the sun
    shines bright,
And love is the only thing that matters.

Carrie Anne Knapp

"Waiting"

Waiting has never been my favorite thing
The stopping to see what life would bring

I've always had to wait and wait
Not realizing the Divine One holds my fate

I waited for a bike until I was nine
At last, blue and shiny, it was mine

I waited a whole year for Christmas - every year
Filled with anticipation as it drew near

I had to wait until I was sixteen to date
And then for someone to ask me out, I had to wait

I waited nine long months to meet my little girl
And then she was here and life became a whirl

Of caring and sharing and hoping for her
And as each year passes, I become ever sure

That the waiting is preparing, preparing us for more
More than we could handle if into our lives they'd pour

Without the waiting, the learning, the waiting
The forever anticipating

We'd just be hurrying life along our way
And maybe missing the best of what we have today

Kimberly Garroutte

Flower

Like a flower printed on rock
By the long kiss of time,
We have pressed upon each other something
Of ourselves indelible and fine.
And were they to unearth my heart
Some million years into the starry future
And try to gauge the tenderness
That left that stone a jewel to the eye,
They would need to know who you were
And something of the human touch and cry:
The nerves; the palest shadow of the blood;
The skin of our bodies sliding together;
The words in breath barely our own,
I love you, I love you,
Washing the gullies of the smallest bone.
And how when separated hour by hour,
The dull rock aches
For that green and petaled moment of a flower.

Gregory Polakow

Like So Many Strangers

I sit, staring as the seconds tick away
Oblivious to the strangers who pass me by
I am lost in the face of the clock and wonder how long I've been
sitting here.
Has it just been minutes as the clock seems to think or has it really
been years.
It seems that just earlier this
morning I was dreaming of how my life would be
But now it's almost noon and those dreams are fading memories like
    a nightmare after waking
I wonder, as I sit staring at the clock, if I spent too much time
dreaming of what is to become
And not enough time becoming of what I dreamed
As I leave the morning of my life, I still sit and wonder and dream
of what is to become
But the time for dreaming is over, the time for becoming is here
But I have spent so much time dreaming, I do not know how to become
So I still sit and wonder and dream of what noontime will bring
With it, will there be more dreaming or will there be learning and
understanding of how to become
And in the evening, will I be able to sit and wonder and remember
the dreams that became reality
Or will there still just be the emptiness of time ticking away
I fear that I am stuck dreaming, and as the clock strikes midnight
my days will have passed me by, like so many strangers

Christopher Todd

The Cure

Smile through the pain,
laugh though the tears.
And when the smiles fade,
and the laughter is gone,
and your heart forsakes you,
turn to a friend
and cry on their shoulder.
Explain to a stranger
the heaviness that pulls your gaze to the street.
Curse the man in the moon for your heartache.
And then smile,
and laugh
and continue to live for the rest of the tomorrows
(when the todays fail you)
— for one of them will bring you peace,
comfort, and one day...
Love.

Beverly Simek

The Blind Man In The Bottle

There was a young woman who loved her man so.
But there came a day she had to let him go.
She stood by him through thick and thin.
Even though the blind man in the bottle sinned and sinned.
There was a time the blind man was strong.
But then somewhere in life something went wrong.
Blind at one time, he was not.
Something happened and he became distraught.
His love for his family and God meant all.
But somehow in life he began to fall.
The man became blind from the bottle he held.
For the devil made a pact that held like a weld.
Now is the time for the blind man in the bottle to see.
Now is the time for the blind man in the bottle to be set free.
May God be with this man of sorrow.
For only He can help him with tomorrow.
The past is gone forever, and tomorrow has not come.
Today is the day, the day to be done.

Richard J. Kuebler

Of My Choice

As I live my life,
I find that some doors close,
Only, so that, other doors may open.
It is my choice, as to which doors stay closed,
And, of the open ones, which I'll
pass through.
Expectations and anticipation may be held high,
Only to find that passing through open doors;
Is to be, as that of fighting a losing battle.
Keeping expectations close to myself,
And anticipating, only what I know;
I'll pass through the open doors,
Sometimes quickly, sometimes slowly,
But...
    always, of my choice.
    Janette Conger

Daddy

Somewhere between sunshine and rain you drifted
away. And in your place stands an empty space. You
left a trace as you drifted away for each passing
day you can see the trace you left in your place
in the heart of a child still searching to fill the
empty space. Somewhere between sunshine and
rain the child grew up still saving the place for
daddy in the empty space. Do not despair the
child has gone home. And in the place somewhere
between sunshine and rain the search goes on and
in your place stands an empty space now left
in the heart of a grandchild as she stares at an
empty picture frame that marks the trace of an
empty space for granddaddy.

    Joyce McKay

The True You

Unspoken pain with secrets never to be told
Hiding something from the world
Keeping all your feelings inside
All the hurt, all the guilt, all the sorrow
An empty face
With a head full of thoughts
Thoughts that won't be expressed to me
Nor anyone else
A fake smile appears once in a blue moon
But that's all it is... fake
Tell me your troubles, I beg you
In reality I know I'll never know
The true you.

    Jennifer Franks

The Last Goodbye

You shall be the last to see me.
Me, your friend like none other to see.
See and think what you will as I close the door and leave.
Leaving forever the burden of life.
Life has been good and fair and sweet, but it has come to an end.
Ending my own life is needed for the survival of others, you know.
Know that others need to see that it can be done.
Done with peace and calm, not with hate and fear.
Fear has driven too many away from this task before.
Before I go, I must say that you are the greatest man I've ever known.
Known to me as a great man, but only as a man by all.
All is not needed for me, though, all that I have now is enough.
Enough has been said my friend, I must go now, goodbye.
Goodbye, my friend.

    Brian Rice

The Light

A scholar came upon the broken man, whose arms were reaching high.
The scholar gathered up his robe, turned his head and walked off
    with a sigh.

A warrior walked right up to the man, whose head was bowed in shame.
He kicked at Him, he pushed and spat at the man he left bruised
    and lame.

A child tumbled down the road, and looked right into His eyes.
She picked Him up and helped Him walk. He was weightless,
    much to her surprise.

She clothed the man, and fed Him too. She washed His feet
    and His hands.
When the man asked why she had helped, she simply said,
    "It's what God commands!"

Upon her head He laid His pierced hands, when at once there appeared
    a small flame.
God's angels sang, the trumpets blared as the Master began
    to proclaim.

"The scholar is dead in his mind and heart. The warrior does not
    have his might.
But you, my child I bless with true wisdom and give you this very
    special light."

"Go forth and share your kind gentle way and tell of the things yet
    to be.
For I shall save all those who come and give up their lives for me."

"You are a light to the world, my dear. Now then my work here is done."
When suddenly the angels appeared and took to heaven
    God's only Son.

    Denise Coletta Neuschwander

To My Grandma

When life seems gray, you're always there
to let me know you care.
And when I become grumpy and grouching so,
you always know what cheers me so.
The things you do and the things you say,
help guide me through each passing day.
While other grandmas are busy knitting,
you're full of livelihood and kidding.
So thank you grandma of mine,
for being there all the time.

    Beverly Anderson

Spring Fever

Spring fever is an annual condition that descends on people unawares
It comes upon you with no warning and it just adds to your cares.
It makes you want to do things that you know you cannot do
But that doesn't keep it from putting its grip on you.
You know you can't go fishing, though the sun is shining bright
And you've already heard that the fish have begun to bite.
You get the urge to get out the ol' boat and water skis
But common sense tells you that you would surely freeze.
You know you don't have time to play, but to find the time
    you'll try
As you look longingly at the golf course and slowly pass it by.
The birds sing to remind you that spring is here again
And you know you're going to respond, you just don't know when.
The flowers bloom in profusion, by the millions it seems
And only serve to add to your other springtime dreams.
There is no known cure for spring fever except to go on and do
The things that caused the fever to come upon you.

    Randal L. Baldwin

To Dad

My eyes open
   to the wonders of the universe;
My ears listen
   for the whispers on the breeze;
My fingers touch
   the rain of many storms
   renewing their blessings,
   gathering brooks into ponds
   that reflect the sparkling joy
   of God dancing
To the music of the lessons of your love.

Cessily Wotring-Burke Thalacker

At First Sight

I see you, I want you,
You want me too.
I wish for you, I wish for us,
But it just wouldn't do,
Someone like you, people like us,
Lust just wasn't made for us,
Something like that, something so true,
It just wasn't made for me and you,
Yes it's true, there is someone new,
But when I'm with him I think of you,
Do you think it's there, something true,
Or do you think I'm crazy too?
Do you feel the same? Do you think I'm sane?
I hope it's true, I hope for you,
But if it can't if it's not
My love will always be in this spot,
But if one day it is not,
Keep it hot keep it sweep,
Then come sweep me off my feet..

Melissa Tidwell

I Am You

It seems as if in all I do...
I remind myself a lot of you.
I see your smile upon my face,
I see your eyes in my eyes' place.
I hear your voice within my mind....
I think it's you and then I find,
the words I speak have come from you,
the way I think, you've taught me too.
The values I have you instilled in me,
the way I am you caused me to be.
You could never leave my heart,
we could never be apart,
for every time I look at me...
It's really you that I see.
I know that it will take awhile,
to replace my tears with a smile,
so when I'm sad all I have to do...
is look at myself and I'll be looking at you.
I Love You Dad.

Sharon M. White

Her Mama's On Drugs

Her mama's on drugs ain't that sad
Her mama's on drugs and it hurt her real bad
She smokes marijuana and sniffs coke through straw
She sticks a needles in her arm 'til her veins
start to draw
She goes to the dopeman and tells him lies
Bang! He shot her, and there she dies
Her mama's on drugs, ain't that sad
Her mama's on drugs and it hurt her real bad

Qiana Towns

Untitled

As I sit here,
gazing into space,
upon my cheek, a tear,
my love, he had to race.
I wonder why
why did he go?
I'm not ready to say goodbye,
I loved him so.
Now he's gone forever,
there's nothing that will bring him back.
We can't be together,
my world has turned black.
Never again will I
see the light of day,
and never again will I
be able to lay
in my love's arms again.

Jennifer Allen

I Want The Sun

*I want the sun in the palm of my hand,
and to have the stars and the moon.
I want the clover I see on the path,
and I want the showers of June.*

*I want the dawn AFTER the dusk,
and to tame the angry sea.
I want the snow to be crystal clear,
and the Heavens to smile for me.*

*I want the trees to breathe and sigh,
and a rainbow at my door.
I want my thoughts to come to life,
with silver doves, and more!!*

*I want to know the true meaning of life,
and in clouds, for the sun to shine through.
I could have all these things and more,
if I could have you.*

Linda S. Stout-Barletta

Brennon

I bore a child,
A special gift,
The one whom I adore,
Perhaps I've pampered, spoiled, indulged him
But his smile makes my heart soar.

In my arms he lies,
So silently asleep,
His warmth against my breast.
His shallow breathing, flaxen hair, his quiet peacefulness
Are fleeting moments so soon passed.

Too soon will time destroy the child to bring about the man;
And then a mother's heart shall have but memories at hand.

Sandra W. Callaghan

War

Booming,
Banging,
Burning,
Crying,
Yelling,
Screaming,

After the treacherous fight is over a serene calm crawls over the land,
And it is quiet as a sleeping baby,

The brave crawl from their homes,
Only to be shot down by the few remaining gunmen.

Danielle Stubbendeck

'Self Discovery'

Criminally insane or am I just in pain
For I don't know do my tears show
Everyone asks why don't you do your tasks
But I really can't say and all the
Heartache stays
My head is confused
My body's been used
My heart is in pain but do I scream
In vain
No
I hold it all inside I'm just afraid
To cry
No one understands the love I must
Demand therefore I do not receive the
Love and care I need
And so I must continue to dwell upon
This issue
Until I have uncovered
The self I must discover

Alaina DeHart

Princeton Lane

Do you remember the time, my love?
 The time we strolled in the driving rain?
'Twas a cold winter's day, that day
 The day we walked down Princeton Lane.
You laughed, I cried, we kissed, and you tried
 To resurrect my soul; no matter it was in vain.

You lived in Heaven, I dwelt in hell
 Still, I tried to feign
A semblance of the life I once held (though you could tell)
 That day on Princeton Lane.

For my eyes still see only she
 How do I stay sane?
Her chilled heart unbeating in her breast
Where so oft my head did rest.
Her hair of gold where my hands would fold
Her scent of jasmine I could never hold
 So how can the gods blame
My crime of soullessness
 That day we walked in the driving rain;
 The day we strolled down Princeton Lane.

Christian M. Corp

Happiness

Happiness oh, happiness where did you go?
Happiness oh, happiness where is my glow?
We use to walk hand in hand.
Oh boy! all over this land.
We would walk east, we would walk west,
You would give me the very best!
We would stroll north, we would stroll south,
Laugher sure came from my mouth!
Happiness oh, happiness where art
Thou?
Happiness oh, happiness my
life's gone sour.

Corinne Hall

Untitled

 The angels will be waiting in the sky
to greet the beautiful saints while they are
passing by; that is why it is good to live
righteous on this earth before we die.

 Because the angels will be waiting in
the sky to greet the saints as they are passing by.

Esau Moore

12/26/95

A crescent moon hangs in the sky,
on its belly.
The ground
a frozen, glossy glaze,
reflecting the light on this clearest of cold nights.

December 26, 1995

Bereavement
for this self-imposed exile.
A lover
who doesn't call-
and one who does
(he doesn't know, it was over years ago).
So excuse me
if I choose to laugh
at something benign and stupid.
I left my pizza box on the roof of the car.

Therese Smith

Untitled

As a lay hidden here
People in fancy cars zoom by
Not giving a damn for me
Their cars much like them are full of exhaust
As they flick out their butts
Ever so often a jogger drops his spare change
As to give charity to one
One who was once just like him
Except now he feels superior and I inferior
Why can't one just realize that I didn't ask for this?
Why can't one just realize that it can happen to anyone?
Why can't they blow out the exhaust and see me?
One who was just like them.

Christina Bennett

Watching Him Sleep

 On his stomach he lies, hands
tucked under the pillow, his face
becomes visible when headlights
pass through the window, even
in the dark I see his silhouette
Wedged against the night. His breathing
Alters first loud, then soft. When
I move he wraps himself around
me tighter, needing me even in sleep.
I resist sleep, I refuse to lose the
perfect stillness of this moment,
feeling so close to him that his
breath could be my own

Cheryl Sewell

The Day She Left Me

I'm sad and lonely today - she left me
My girlfriend died today, I just must say,
good-bye and get on with my life, you see.
I am depressed for the rest of my days.
When I find someone new, I will be brand new
She may not fit my ex's place, cute like her,
as long as she gives me space and likes Sue.
She has to cook like Sue. Sue's my daughter,
the only one I have. I may commit
suicide, but I don't want to die now.
At her funeral I didn't even sit
down. In two weeks I'm going out of town.
I will someday rejoice with my girlfriend
Until then, I will love her 'til the end.

James C. Brown

Untitled

My sister who was carrying a child of God to God was no foe,
But God still called that child of hers and he had to go.
We all knew at this time my sister would feel a lot of hurt,
Because she would really miss this child she could have given birth.
My sister needed love and support from her family,
I know she was given lots of it from both God and me.
My sister also knew that God did not mean any harm,
In fact right now he's probably holding that child in his arms.
I know we will all miss that child and think about it day to day,
We'll think of God and that child every time we pray.

After God the father realized how my sister felt,
He wanted to do something, for he knew he could help.
He knew this child was joyful and always wanted to play,
So he sent my sister back this child in 8 months and some day.
This child is adorable, it's as cute as can be,
My sister said the nickname for this child is raki.
My sister takes care of this child, has no time to be bored,
Thanks to God our savior, Jesus Christ Our Lord.

Mary Elizabeth Williams

Sometimes The Knight Doesn't Get The Girl

What would the audience think if after the knight
In shining armor rescued the damsel from her plight
He didn't get a kiss?
Confusion, disappointment amiss.

But there's always two sides to every story.

Sometimes in the tower of life the maiden in distress
Doesn't wish to be rescued or delivered from duress.
But still the knight comes,
No matter what becomes.

And so does every story relate to life.

So in confusion, frustration, desperation he
Devotes himself to love and honor she,
For he is a man of honor.
But still he loves her.

But he is a knight.

He is the Knight, the ever-steadfast Knight,
Whose armor shines despite the absence of light.

Travis Cale Self

Beauty Slipslides

Oh how beautiful this world could be, if there only could be peace.
We could sit in the night and look at the moon's bright light
    without worrying about a fight.
We could make love on the beach without worrying about some drunk
coming to preach.
We wouldn't have to lock our doors, so we could sing out
    glorious roars.
We would praise the world in which we live and give and give.
If everyone could be just friends, oh what a life we could live again
Oh why does beauty have to slip away?
Why do we look at a sunset as just another day?
Why do we always look at what we don't have, instead of looking at
the wonderful things we do have?
Love, friends and family are what life should be, not possessions and
obsession of what we could be; but what are and let the rest be free.
And love and love and love thee.

Kathy Grome

Railroad My Heart

Don't derail my train... after you build my track,
Ruin my surface and then expect slack.

Mold my parts and build me from scratch,
break down the motor and repair it with a patch.

Patches unseal to reveal what's beneath;
imperfections come forth and the motor overheats.

Railroad My Heart and side track my mind.
Dress up the train, but what happened to inside?

You colored the cars as it suits you.
Mirage the image to make it seem true.

I know the image of this train,
the tracks are now flooded - my heart is filled with rain.

The train moves on, people collected and packed.
Railroad My Heart, but it gets back on track.

Continue to run your railroad the way you do.
Someone will turn the switch
To avoid crashing with you...

Mary Brooks

Broken Arrow

A rose of the night was given to me
To find me a way, to set me free
It unlocked my jail and showed me the world
I am free as a bird, my wings uncurled
The sparkle of heaven is my reach
My soul is a new, cleaned with bleach
A shot of an arrow made me fall
The petals of life crumbled my wall
I was back where I belong, locked in a cell.
The opposite of heaven, now living in hell

Angie Riese

Little Golden Angel

Little golden angel on the Christmas tree
Little golden angel a smiling down at me
How my mother loved her and held her tenderly
Whene'er she told the story of the angel to me.

Little golden angel on the Christmas tree
Little golden angel that means so much to me
How I loved the story my mother had to tell
All about the angel and I know it well.

For long ago when grandma was a little girl
A goldsmith made her with her golden curls
Wings and dress so lacy, made of filigree
Prettiest little angel on the Christmas tree

In her hand she holds a tiny golden horn
Heralding the message that the Christ was born.
Now every year at Christmas hanging on the tree
Is the golden angel for everyone to see.

Little golden angel with a halo round her head
Little golden angel I have heard it said
That the goldsmith made you with all his love and skill
So you would last forever and I know you will.

Evelyn V. Briscoe

There Is Hope

Here I stand alone, just a man.
The world's come against me once again.
It left me hurt and bleeding
and wondering if I had a friend.
The wounds, they grow deeper;
the salt stings as it's poured in.
The punishment doesn't seem to fit the crime of my sin.
Blank-stare-irrationality as my deeds question my intent.
The outcome of my pain is in search of what I really meant.
Can anyone help? Can anyone relate?
I feel so numb I can't even feel hate.
It seems hopeless
to try and cope with this.
Rain falls slowly around me,
quietly.
Can't hear a sound 'cause my mind is behind me—
thinking of past pain:
Resurrecting hurt feelings to torture myself in vain.
Darkness, you call me but I won't answer.
You'd like me to embrace you as my tragic dancer.

L. C. Edward Vaughn

Roads Beyond

In the cool fall air as dusk drew near,
A young boy listened with careful ear,
To the luring sounds of approaching night,
His soul set free on a special flight.

Off in the distance, he saw it still,
A mighty mountain looming till,
He found a way to scan its height,
As he would again in his dreams tonight.

He had done it many times before,
But each new path would prod him more,
For on the other side he knew,
There lived a world just out of view.

He'd climb again to the mountain top,
But there his quest could never stop,
Because it led to worlds beyond,
New paths, new roads to travel on.

Pat Grunden

The Lonely Little Classroom

The lonely little classroom was as lonely as
    could be,
    Not a child, not a teacher, not a
    picture could it see.

Desks and chairs were piled high and walls
were empty too,
It was dark and shades were drawn
preventing any view.

Absent were the living creatures—kids and
plants galore,
All that remained were a few
paper scraps sitting on the floor.

The little room was filled with stillness—not a
single sound,
How it missed the children frolicking on the
playground.

"It won't be long," the lonely classroom
thought, "when summer will finally end,
Then I will be filled with drawings,
books, and children once again."

Barbara J. Ruggiero

The Wedding Ring

It sits abandoned and lonely in a recessed corner of a drawer,
A tarnished symbol of an old love that is no more.
The worn remains of an earlier relationship in life,
A mere reminder of deep feelings that ended in anger, grief and strife.
A pathetic object that with time has lost its beauty
But can still speak longingly of passion, caring and duty.
A cold metal circle that evokes memories of laughing,
    loving and birth,
It's only a piece of jewelry that no longer has any worth.

Jackie Biltoft

All Nite Diner

there are no prisoners here (save a
waitress and her cook and even they are
paid), but we stay late sipping wisdom from
coffee cups some lipstick-stained, others
cracked or discolored. it is no matter
though, because what we learn from each
other is more important than the fountains
from which we drink (and that is only the
first lesson). early hours bring laughter
    especially knowing that sam's meat loaf
    could be on the way at one a.m. so
we'll invite them to sit at our table until the
next customer comes. share a joke or
some fresh brew, a story about you or
maybe find the answers. why do we live
long into this night and hide beyond? how
do eyes stay open during the hours of
dream and darkness? stay a while, drink
some joe, and feel the unspoken need to
help us know.

Christopher Cummins

The Gentle Woman And Gentle Man

There's a gentle woman and a gentle man,
Whose joy they bring to all they can.

Everyone whose lives they have touched,
Their lives have been brightened so very much.

They have reached out and touched
everyone they have known,
Without any expectations of their own.

Their wisdom and hope they bring to us all,
So we won't give in to life's trivial falls.

Their pain and suffering they keep to themselves,
So we don't have to carry the burden of their hell.

But if they would let me take their pain,
I would gladly take it, and it wouldn't be in vain.

They forget the pain that's in their hearts,
To help us heal our wounds and scars.

It is both a privilege and an honor,
To have a friend in this gentle woman and gentle man.

P. J. Lopez Sr.

Rape My Soul

Through pleasure,
        aggression, or
                forced curiosity

The Soul is ripped from its womb, and
lain on the stomach,
            exposed for the touch of Humans.

never to be inside again, safe.

Janis Hopkins

Mother

My mother's a special person, who means a lot to me.
She care's about everyone, especially family.

When I have a problem, she let's me know she cares
Whenever I need anything, she's always ready to share.

We have a special bond, that no one can deny.
It's a thing called love, that money cannot buy.

She holds a special place for me, down inside her heart.
And I know she worries, whenever we're apart.

As kind as she can be, as gentle as a flower.
But if her family's hurt, my mother will not cower.

When I need to talk, she does not digress.
With sticky situations, she has great finesse.

She always cheers me up, whenever I am down.
Around my wonderful mother, it's very hard to frown.

She loves me a lot, that is very clear.
She would never hurt me, that I do not fear.

Sometimes she complains, and becomes a pest.
But that's just because, mother does know best.

There are many things she's taught me, and some I've taught her.
But that's the way it goes, with mothers and their daughters.

Misti Dawn Stegall

Untitled

What is the purpose, the why of all things?
What is the purpose of a porpoise as in the oceans it swims?
Why is there a tree to shade the ground below?
Why do we have eyes to see the sunset's golden glow?
Why are there seasons to change the face of Mother Earth?
What are the reasons for the old to be replaced by new birth?
Why do we have emotions ranging from love to hate?
What are the true notions of being early or late?

Whatever you may think of near or far,
A purpose for being they all have to share.
For the greatest purpose for existence of all,
Mankind must the greatest burden bare!

Eugene J. Strasser

One Petal Falls

Blue skies, bright sunshine
  I gaze at a single red rose
Insignificant to most, yet it holds truth in each petal
The wind blows steady and cool
  One petal falls
A drop of dew slithers down the rose, like a tear
  It cries for what is now lost, what may be lost forever
The rose is still as wonderful as before, but no!
  It still has great beauty, yet now it's so different
Part of its meaning and existence has drifted away
  Leaving it tearful and sad, never again whole
It does not know what is next to be lost,
  or if happiness shall ever return
Just as any other life, it expected it to be there forever
A tear now falls down my cheek
  As I try to shake it away, my gaze drifts to a daisy
  For it is not crying
And as I watch, the wind blows, and...
  One petal falls

Rebecca Twa

Sons Grow And Go

Relaxing upon my bed, drifting in and out of sleep
my mind peeks back into yester-times
when baby smelled good, breath of pure mother's milk
curls of soft ribboning swirled atop his head
clinging to my neck for safety

Time allowed for another to follow
bouncy and full of cuteness and devil dealings...
"Adventure," be this small one's name

And grow we together
those two and me...
the basics of life did feed us well

But, now dreams slip into brightness of day
and caught in my head is the squeaking of chairs
as we three, away from the table must push

The breast and the milk, a thought for one's head,
The dealing of devils, a whip for the other
and watch as we part, do I with my heart
for I shall dream of two babies and me no more
but of two men I do now give my thoughts

Vikki J. Raniolo

The Solution

Just give me a truck...
There will be no more thievery.
Just give me a truck...
There will be no more deceivery.

Just give me a truck...
The stupidity will end.
Just give me a truck...
And minds will bend.

Just give me a truck...
The past will return.
Just give me a truck...
The foolish will learn.

An era of problems quelled in a minute.
Those who thought they had lost will be able to win it.
Scourges, disease, riots, and death.
Deprivation, trickery, loss of wealth.

One solution, one answer.
A simple end to this cancer.

Just give me a truck

Todd Schuble

Untitled

Deal me a hand
I'll put it all on the line
I thought it could only get better with time

This isn't the luck of the draw
You took my cards away
Now I'm empty-handed
Now I can't play

You aren't playing fair
You had some tricks up your sleeve
You think this is obsession
You think that I can't leave

I'd advise you to check the deck
It just might be stacked
You aren't so untouchable
Respect is what you lack

I won't be there to tell you everything is fine
I'm sick of being the healer
I'd just watch your back this time
Now I'm playing the dealer

Alison Wayland

Babysitting

As 7:00 pm comes around
I want to run out of town
They pull my hair
'Cause they really don't care
They hit my face
All I say is you're a disgrace
They run all around
Jumping up and down
Throwing all their toys
And hitting all the boys
Going wherever they please,
Eating chocolate, cookies, and cheese
When the parents come home, I fall to my knees
And say "Thank God", I can finally leave!

Danielle Blotkamp

Take My Hand

Take my hand and walk with me,
Take me where I want to be.

A garden path strewn with flowers,
Fragrances that fill my thoughts for hours.

A river bank on a sunny day,
As the breeze so gently plays.

Childhood memories come back to me,
As I lay beneath that tree.

Time stands still but for awhile,
Wanting to stay a little child.

So take my hand and walk with me,
Take me back to where I must be.

Mary J. Craft

Haunted

Run, child run, they're coming for you
They follow you everywhere, there's nothing you can do.
They stay in your dreams and haunt you each night
They won't go away no matter how hard you fight.

Their faces are blank and their skin is all pale
You can't win them over, they rate you on their scale.
Once you're on their list, you're there forever
You'll feel all alone but they will leave you never.

But wait, what about the dream you had last night?
They weren't there when you turned out the light.
Someone is there but who can it be
Someone has arrived to come and protect me.

Tina Westmoreland

A Flower Or A Dandelion

A flower or a dandelion what will it be,
  Both are found in the garden you see.
A rose beautiful and fair,
  Its fragrance permeates the air.

The lowly dandelion is found everywhere,
  Multiplies quickly without any care.
Its flower soon turns to an umbrella of seeds,
  Soon to become many more weeds.

A rose is something to be desired and given,
  The dandelion a weed to be got ridden.
Let us take the Rose of Sharon into our hearts,
  And let His beauty and fragrance our lives impart.

Joyce Moore

Home In The Snow

Silent calm covers the earth.
In a mantle of white.
Soft flakes fall in profusion.
Caught in tranquil confusion.
Each seeking a special place.
Frosted prisms caught in space.

Laced in a line a row of moonlight jewels
A cosmos of color and transparent pools.
Washed by a tiny tear.
Icy pinnacles tapered and clear.

An opalescent pond of shimmering light
Dances neath trees in the pale moonlight
Where no footsteps cut a line,
This mantle so divine,
Shrouds and entwines, the silence of this space.

Yet a vision of a tiny place
With a light of warmth and homely grace,
Stream from a window like a candle glow.
A sparkling jewel set deep in the snow.

C. Arata

Humbled Heart Of Winter

Winter's grip has tugged at us like a stubborn child,
The chill hold of its icy winds pervades our very bones.
Whenever will the season once again turn oh, so mild,
That the sprouts of new grass peak from 'neath the weathered stones?

Frosty flower-patterns etch, each day, the window panes,
And flurries float down from the sky, now a steely gray.
Ice, snow, and slush still crowd the roads and country lanes,
Warning that spring's warming hues had better stay away.

Weary faces press the glass, wishing winter gone,
Sentinels of anticipation willing warmth to break
The cold that holds tenaciously to every tree and frond,
And causes hearts both young and old, longingly to ache.

Yet then a glow streaks through the clouds - oh, is it sunshine now?
The trickling noise of melting snow the sun sends on the run,
Tickles the nose of an early bud sprouting through the snow...
Spring's waking from its lengthy slumber - winter's nearly done.

Swathes of green, ever widening through the dwindling snow,
Melt our winter-hardened hearts and bring the earth alive.
No, more shall we take spring for granted - this now, is our vow:
Remember the lessons etched in our hearts by the winter of
  ninety-five!

Carole L. Parisi

Rainbows

Without the clouds and crystal raindrops,
Without the sun — that blazing sphere,
Without God's love and nature's talents
Those beautiful rainbows could never appear.

But nature, in all her splendor,
Has yet to create in the heavens
A rainbow whose beauty surpasses
That of the magnificent rainbow
Which arcs across my thoughts,
Visible only to my mind's eye.

Oh! How I wish
I could share with you
The beauty of
My own private rainbow.

Without my tears which keep on flowing,
Without the heartache deep inside me,
Without the love that keeps on growing,
My beautiful rainbow I'd never see!

Joseph P. Dembski

In This Life

My mind wonders back to childhood days
Carefree moments and foolish ways
Precious memories of yesterday
Some of them just a haze.

Those that were so special to me
Wondering why some things had to be
All the places I didn't see
Of times I prayed on bended knees.

So much sorrow, trouble, and strife
Guess it's just a part of this life
Wondering what's wrong, what right
Spending a lot of sleepless nights,

But through it all, I now see
You were always there with me
For all my help, I thank thee
Please guide me through what's yet to be.

Leslie McCuiston

Toy Soldier

He went to war with a staccato walk,
Face a grim mask no whispered talk.
He left so bravely, with head held high,
Listen heart the wind softly cry?
Back straight and proud, eyes so clear,
Like a toy soldier he showed no fear.
I'll go to battle for my country spirit cried.
I'll free the people, silent yell with pride.
But scared he became when it was so near,
No toy soldier every felt such fear.
And each man alone made his stand,
And cried (coward take my coward's hand:)
For no preparation made this an easy task,
Now slipped away, the toy soldier's mask,
Words tumbled forth from the silent lips,
And life was felt through all finger tips,
Against background of sun rays blended,
Lay all the toy soldiers, mission ended.........

Barbara Kizzar

Mother Missed

My Mother, my friend, you left me too soon
No one to talk to, to listen, I don't know what to do
I'm like a child again, crying, I miss you
I know you were hurting and wanted to die
Sweet Mother of mine but not for long, I will say goodbye
Mother I love you wherever you are
In the sky, in Heaven among the stars
Now we are apart but soon you will see
Hi Mother! It's me
Dear Mother how I miss you so
In my heart I will always know
In the end we will be together again
God above to you, I he will send.

Brenda Laleman

Wind Is Silent

The wind is silent, the wind is soft. Its breeze blows by you like the flap of an eagle's wings.
The wind can be warm, and the wind can be cold. It can be soft when it sings in the trees, and can be reassuring like a firm hand to hold.

It can speak to you, it can teach you. If you listen to it, it can show you things that you've never known. The wind is silent in the trees, but loud in my heart.

Alyssa White

Don't Explain

A co-worker and I were working on a project.
Those things happen. It doesn't mean anything.
Please realize that I have other friends.
It's not what you think at all.
I'm sorry I missed your call.
I'm sorry you called when you did.
Don't start.
I will call you.
I love you. Nothing has changed.
I will call you when you can be civil.
We haven't learned how to resolve our problems yet, have we?
A friend of mine was using the cottage.
Why are you so upset?
I love you but I am only human.
What did you think I was doing?
I am sorry you had to find out this way.
She reminds me of you.
You would like her.
I have been trying to tell you, but I just couldn't.
What do you want to do?

Jeri A. Hill

Jenna

Born on May 9, 1993, our grand niece Jenna became a big
part of me.

This precious child stole my heart the first time I saw her,
right from the start.

What a joy she is to my wife and me...we can't get enough of her...
can't you see?

Everyday we want to see her and make excuses by going to her
home bearing her favorite juices.

Yes we spoil her but so what? She is a special treasure that we've got.

As each day goes by she gets sweeter and sweeter...you would
certainly agree if you could meet her.

My wife and I have been so blessed with our dear little Jenna,
the very best.

God please guide her and lead her and give her your best and
she'll return the same to you when she finishes life's test.

Gene C. Hurt

14818

To My Sister
My beloved sister is growing old
She thinks her life is about to fold
I don't think she fits the aging mold
There is still excitement in her soul
Only God has her life in his control
I am getting older too, so I am told
My sister wanted a house on a knoll
There she will live and then it will be sold
In her life she has certainly met the goal
When life is no longer and everything is cold
She will be forever in that magnificent mansion with streets of gold.

Mildred H. Sartain

Untitled

There once was a boy of two
with hair that was fair and eyes that were blue.
To him each night his mother would say
Alex, Mommy loves you.

She'd give him a kiss,
tuck him in tight,
stroke his cheek
and wish him good night.

Lakin Crane

"Wisdom's Advice"

(A poem for Lawrence #2)
Outside my window I watch the snow drop I think about my son who I
love a lot, but he knows me "not". Too far and too long I've been
away I've missed him grow and I've missed him play and today is yet
another day another week another month another year that I won't be
next to him to whisper in his ear, words of wisdom from a father who
want's make the path of understanding clear-for a son who is
unprepared to run full speed ahead in a world filled with the pit-falls
of life ready to devour anyone who doesn't think twice for in life it
is a father who must give a son "wisdom's advice"

Lawrence J. Peavey Jr.

Crazed

The walls are closing in on me,
keeping me from the truth.
It stares me in the face,
yet I can't quite understand it.
Why do I feel this way I want to know,
but no answer comes to me.
Stop the feelings, grasp the pain,
turn the tide of thoughts away from you.
Never to think of you again I tell myself,
but it never works.
Always below my thoughts you are there.
How to rid myself of you I wish I knew.
Maybe tomorrow you will disappear,
I pray, before I go under the tide of memories again.

Jacqueline Marcus

Who Is This Man?

*Dedicated to Timothy J. Rearick (Daddy), from Jennifer M. Rearick
(14 months old); Written by Deanna L. Rearick*
Who is this man that stands so tall,
Yet makes me feel big, tho' I am so small?
He is my Dad, for which I am glad,
You make me so happy, when I feel sad.
When you look down at me from above,
I can see in your eyes so much caring and love.

So I wrote this poem, it's just for you,
Mommy helped me, cause she feels it too!
Thank you for my life you see, for
Without you - "Daddy" - there would be
No me!
Please be my valentine
Daddy, I love you!

Deanna L. Rearick

"Love Without Anatomy, But Mind And Soul"

They say, Love is a strong potion of cure or hate
But what price is there that a man should pay for it?
What is Love that a price be placed against it?
What Love is there that there be a price to acclaim it?

But as the fool I am you make me to perceive
    the wisdom of the wise heart
That lodged so deeply betwixt thy breasts.

Now I see, says The Blind Man
The things far beyond his horizon
So entitled Agapé.

My Limbs say, The Cripple - The Lame
Haste hurriedly unto his Beloved without legs
On His prompt arrival He hears many words of
    consolation that speaketh Love from
The Heart of the Heartless.
So says, The Deaf who hears His own testimony -
That testifies, "This is I that Loves".

David A. Edwards

I Am A Girl Who Dreams

I am a girl who dreams.
I wonder what my life will be like a year from now.
I hear the silence of my life screaming.
I see the lost city of Atlantis.
I want to have all the experiences and adventures of life.
I am a girl who dreams.

I pretend I am sitting on the moon laughing at the world.
I feel the curiosity of man kind.
I touch Jupiter without getting burned.
I worry about all the poverty and pollution in the world.
I cry for the lonely.
I am a girl who dreams.

I understand that there is good in everyone.
I say believe in love and the power unknown.
I dream of traveling all over the world and discovering things
    that no one else has discovered.
I hope that peace will never die.
I am a girl who dreams.

Tiffany Sadergaski

Who Am I

You are the ray of sunshine that brightens up my day.
The warm feeling I get from your embrace.
The flowing waters that fill my emptiness.
The April showers in winter
that drench me with happiness.

You are my dream, my thoughts,
my reality.
The reason to live forever
and into the eternities.
The raging storm that sweeps me
off my feet.
The summer breeze that
puts me to sleep.

You are my rainbow, my ray of hope.
The stars in the heavens that lead
my feet where to go.
The angel that watches over me
day and night.
The echo of the thunder
that reassures me everything is alright.

Janette Chambers

Common Love

He stirs deep down inside of me
Like the unknown of the deep blue sea
And every time I hear his name
I burn inside like a wild flame.

He has touched the inner part of me
A part no one else could ever see.
For so long it was hidden, the hurt and blame
But then he entered and lifted my pain.

He brought joy and happiness back to my life
And honored me by asking "Would I be his wife?"
An honor so cherished, he'll give me his name,
A treasured inheritance I will never shame.

And so together, this day we become one
Hand in hand, I will marry your son.
Forever and always, an eternity of we,
For ours is a love that was meant to be.

I am to him, as he is to me,
Two hearts bound together, as love should be.

Linda L. Zupancic

Sweet, Sweet...Yesterday

I was looking through all my treasures one day,
Wondering what I would find.
A purse, a dress in which I would play,
"Cinderella's slippers"-They were one of a kind.

My reasons for all this searching,
Was to move on from my past.
For I hadn't a choice, but to move on,
These memories would always last.

I past by my old games,
Like "Topple", "Dominos", and "Monopoly".
I remember playing with "Barbie",
And some drawings made by me!

The Rocking Horse, that I road upon,
Or the story I called "Mothers",
Would soon become another's.

I don't want to get rid of; My "dressy" jewels of gold.
As I remember the make believe "solos that I've sung".
Or all the mystery books- that always left me cold.
For I realized that there is so much to life-And I've only just
Begun!!!

Dana Kaplan

Fallen Leaves Within Filtered Light

What I see with my eyes and
feel with my senses is unique
in each living moment. Gracefully
floating down either one at a time
or gathered bunches. The variety
of colors mesmerizes my movement
I glance at each stage as perfect
as the seasons. Wondering in times span
how long it will take. I don't want
to move afraid I'm going to miss
each scene. I know I will see this
again although time and space
will be different. The eyes relish
in beautiful colors bathed by the
flickering sunlight. Do I dare turn
away now and lose that one single
moment treasured by sight. ·As I
draw the drapes and say goodnight
to another day. Tomorrow will come
and with it a new sight.

Sherry Anaya

Winter Time

Someday the skies are dark and gray;
While other days we are warmed by the sun's ray.
There are other days that the winds howl and blow,
As we bundle up with our faces all aglow.

When the night falls as the temperature reaches the zero mark;
Everyone huddles together by the fire in the park.
As the dawn breaks bright and fair
The wind is still chilled in the air.

For those of us who labor at night;
We all turn the darkness into the light.
As the morning breaks and the sun beams bright
It is our cue that we can sleep the night.

Each morning the air is icy and cold;
While heat is needed for those who are old.
When skies are cloudy and snowflakes fall;
Children all want to play and have a ball.

In winter time the days seem shorter;
And that allows us to sleep a little more longer.
While days go by and ice and snow are all on the ground;
We know that spring time one day will soon come around.

Eddy Dorris McLocklin

As Darkness Falls

The day is done and the darkness falls,
from the wings of night. A feather is wafted downward,
from an eagle in his flight.
I see the lights of the village gleam through the
rain and the mist, and a feeling of happiness
comes o'er me that my soul cannot resist.
And though my heart may break, my eyes may dull
But my mind will always be able to recall the memory
all through the night, till the sun shines no more.
I will Love thee all the more.

George E. Davis

Just Between Us Girls

All dressed up and lady like,
    Just between us girls

Conversing, telling secrets only a woman knows,
    Just between us girls.

Bridal showers, Baby showers, time out,
    Just between us girls

Now bring in this lonely male stripper
    taunting and teasing our inner desires,
    and only heaven knows.
Watch Out!!!
    Just between us girls.

Bettie Jean Nelson-Lowhar

Precious Rainfall

Our prayers were calling, now raindrops are falling
    We have been so awfully dry.
With sunshine glistening, if you were listening
    You could almost hear the trees cry;
They so wanted a drink. Now blessed drops sink
    To bring them relief with a sigh.

If we were out where, there was dry desert air
    And no water was to be found
The sunlight's glare, the water hole bare
    Hot sifting sand all around
Then sudden clouds appear, rain falling clear
    To fill that dry hole in the ground.

Then we would know, how rain could bestow
    Such a blessing upon our earth.
The trees wouldn't cry, we wouldn't be dry
    We'd know what a rainfall was worth.
Here comes the rain! If you listen again
You'll hear the trees shouting in mirth!
    "Precious rainfall"!

Myrtle Dyer

Unspoken Truth

The soul feels love perceptively as a warm chill of pleasure,
I can see it around you glowing like treasure.
Welcoming my soul in addictively the beauty can't compare.
Now everything fades out and you are still standing there.
The connection was felt for a second,
The joining of our minds
Just think deep and see a thought
and maybe it was mine
'Cause what you felt and heard inside
is simply the soul trying to guide.
So open your thoughts to the vastness of space
and there you can see anyone's face.
Smiling and staring you in your eyes
Your soul's message never lies.

Bryan Munoz

Tree Of Hope

A lonely tree on a hillside
A hill bare and rocky
Granite erupting from an endless desert
What could grow here
What a seed that once was planted
Now a tree stands proudly
A strong root it must have
Yet it seemed to appear overnight
It was not here when I last past
Or was it just not noticed by me
I have seen but few travelers on my road
Yet they have made no mention of a tree
Could the tree have been inside me all the while
Waiting for that one ray of light
No matter it is here for me now
Was I so hard and rough it could not grow
Could it be that this tree brings new life to me
This tree with its many flowers in bud
I shall protect my new found tree
For someday I may wish to plant another with thee

Steven W. Meyers

The Thirsty Flower

I am drowning in my tears.
I can feel the stream trickle down the mountain
into the lake of sorrow.

Every day I bear water
and light to nourish you.

Your stem is a green satin stalk
with sharp shiny leaves
and your petals are as blue as the sky
and as silky as a dove's feather-

You are the most beautiful
and august flower on the earth.

Every day I give you rain to feed on,
but when I need nurture
I must pierce your shallow heart
with a lonesome look fixed upon you from my eyes,
for it seems that reality's harshness
is all that lets your youthful mind cry.

Bethany Sheeler

"My World"

My world isn't built around a Fortress as you
say. But my world is built around peace and
happiness. The world I have is the one you
built for me, therefore, that is not my world.

All the pain I've endured was caused by your
world. You say nothing can break you, but look
at what you have broke. My love, my
trust, my being as a human.

If my world is different from your world, why
can't you see my world for a change.
Because in your world, and by your world, there
is revenge (for what), hate (who), cruelty, coldness, and
abuse. If this is "Love" then I don't want
to live in your world.

I only count in life living my own. I cannot
control you nor your world. But I think
we should be grateful that "God" has let
us live in this world.

Cassandra A. Curtis

The Canary

I stare at the bars others have placed around me;
day after day waiting, planning, dreaming.
Self proclaimed masters taunt me to perform.
Their hearts lifted by the rapture of the melody
which emulates from my heart and my soul.
Yet, my song is not for gaiety, but a dirge
rising deep from within. An expression
of bondage, a desire to be free.
My appendages cleave to my side in despair.
What once took me to heights beyond human reach
now have become disgusting to my sight.
A constant reminder of my lot and bondage.
Of what once was, but will never be again.
Of what I wish, but will never obtain.
How can they callously place me in this cage;
an ornament to their dreary lives.
My design and purpose have been altered
and my freedom removed for their folly.

Gary W. Jeter

Time

A rose is beautiful, until, time changes its future.
It wilts, crumbles, and then- is lying in its ashes.
Then all that is left, is the blackened core. Until
nature spits it into the wind. Nobody cares!
Why should we?! It is insignificant.
   Just as we are to Earth.

We long to be wanted, we dare to feel the human touch
of hope- when there is none. We want to be loved.
Then we are used to our last breath.
We are the lost sheep- but are lost forever.
We are the black death- that is never to be reborn.

And sometimes when I am alone, I believe there won't
be another tomorrow. Another day of hope, no other
way out. Then I think of you, and how you've helped
me through the times I've needed someone to care. You
have always been there. There is hope beyond my
sadness, there is love beyond my darkness- and you
light the way. I need not worry of how I'll make my
way. I now believe, no matter how far away we both
are- I'll always have you to light my soul.

Anne Frances Mastellone

Remembrance Of A Tragedy

It was a annihilation of the peace
a jagged line through consummate sand.
It stirred our minds
with piteous thoughts
that would not cease but swept the land.

Corruption in a tainted world,
a nation's face eroded now.
The dwelling virtue
disguised from us,
our sovereign eyes are blind somehow.

Like a drop of blood on shattered glass,
a splintered plank of hardwood floor.
Was white as snow,
now speckled black,
a placid scene serene no more.

Joshua L. Free

Elegy For Dad

The days of old
When you'd laugh and joke,
The times you kept your nose in your book-
Dead to the world:
Those times have ended,
An utterly sad ending;
Yet now comes a new beginning,
A time where remembrance takes hold,
And you shine from the lights of our hearts.
Brightly you shine and will shine
Forever with my memories and those passed on.
Your books now gather dust,
But i see them;
And I smile for I know
That your last page has been written,
And you will be read for ever,
And on your memory dust shall not gather.

Jeremy Daniel Perrin

Untitled

I watched her through the window as she danced upon her toes.
She moved so lithely, gracefully, and effortlessly posed.
Her arms, like wings were bending around her lovely face.
She floated lightly here and there, like wind through curtain lace.

To dance that way has been my dream since I was very small.
I've wanted nothing more from life; to dance - that has been all.
To hear the strains of music and feel my feet reply,
To watch as my legs lift me through the air and let me fly.

But here I sit and always will, trapped in my hateful chair.
My legs lie shriveled and useless, as though they're not even there.
I'll never dance upon a stage, never leap and spin and twirl.
I'll never fulfill the dream I've had since I was a little girl.

But dreaming is better than nothing, and sometimes the hurt lets go,
When I watch her through the window as she dances on her toes.

Carol M. Robb

Reflections

First day of school
Little girls dancing in party dresses,
shoes of patent leather.

Little boys standing tall, some copies
of older ones.
Some just brave young men.

Excitement, apprehension, fear, joy
and wonderment.

What lies ahead for you?
Who knows, who knows.

Last day of school
Round and round go the yellow
school buses,

Teachers waving, good by, good luck.
Some children sad, some sing fare-wells.
Happiness and laughter blow in
the warm summer breeze,
What lies ahead for you?
Who knows, who knows.

Margaret J. Gundal

What Do I Want?

I want Gods help in everything I do.
I don't want wealth, just a bit of gold
to provide for more than two.
A small square of the good Earth,
A firm foundation that will be worth
A small house built upon it new.
A shady lane with flowers along a leafy path.
To twine among some orchard trees,
All glorified by blossoms in the warm Spring sun
My family beside me there
To share with me this contentment rare.

Frank C. Eberly

Lullabies

I fill the emptiness with lullabies.
The room is gray from night not yet complete.
The chair rocks slowly, rhythms under songs,
And I sit, moving with it, keeping beat,
My heart beats fast under the drone of peace.
Where is he? Late again, that's no surprise.
His bedtime long ago, he's not asleep
But doesn't wake me up to close his eyes.
He used to cry from dreams, and I would come
Rescue him from his crib. Then snuggled tight
In blankets, he would breathe and I would sing
In whispered strains all through my sleepless night.
He is not here, no cries break through the dark.
He doesn't seek my comfort anymore.
I have the chance to rest, but I'll stay up.
He's gone, and now I need the rocking more.

Emily Card

Punishment

Confused thoughts fly through my mind.
I closed the windows of my imagination
And trapped inside the knowledge of the world.
I am the lonely wise man,
Wondering on the dusty ways of life,
Looking the ground in the eyes
Careful and afraid not to step on
The Hope that still exists
In the dark corner of my soul.

Mandy Gheorghiu

Ode To A Horse

You are running fleetly swiftly,
Are you trying to raise the wind?

You are gentle and you're savage,
Changing at the slightest whim.

Remembering those who mistreat you,
Remembering too, those who love you.

Ever beautiful, loving, trying,
Oh, dear horse I do love you!

Remember when you were a colt?
Running, jumping with carefree bliss.

And now you've grown and you are working,
How'd it ever come to this?

You see the life of your comrades,
Wish to do the things they do?

Some things may be better,
Some things maybe worse.

But won't you please tell me, tell me,
Won't you stay and be my horse?

Joy Wiedenbeck

War

War is a clash of evil on the innocent's turf,
    a raging hound programmed to kill.
War is a nest of sparks flaming when controversy strikes,
    a desperate struggle for survival, the best man not always
    the victor.
War belittles family and friends,
    the proud destroying relations for principles.
War is the eleventh plague, concerning everyone's lives,
    a lethal tornado, crushing anything on which it lands.
War is a game where the winnings never equal the losses,
    a suicide mission which only faith in God will save.
War is a rendezvous with the devil,
    a force greater than all mankind.
War is as vast as the skies,
    an enemy too immense to defeat.
War is a crimson rain falling on the stricken areas,
    a color darker than black which only a few wish to view.
War is a gift of evil, sent only to devour,
    an unneeded pain, powerless to heal itself.
War is a lottery,
    "the only way to win is not to play."

Scott Ginn

Passings

The blinds are level, framed by the glass.
The harvest sun slowly slips into the past.
Only a piece of the colored orb remains.
Providing light and color in my domain
Shining on the wall like a movie screen
Telling a story in color and light
Slowly dimming, brilliant colors are seen
Eventually slipping out of sight
Leaving only the beauty of the completed day
etched in the soul of all who stay.
The memories enrich our lives and allow us
to cast beautiful hues of our own
and embrace the colors of everyone
who touch our lives and enter our home.

Thomas F. Wieland

My Searching Soul

I looked for Jesus everywhere
In meadows filled with spring
In mountains with majestic flare
In songs the bluebirds sing.

I looked for Him upon the shore
Of the glistening, salty sea.
He 'twas not there. I must search more.
Oh, where could my Jesus be?

I looked for Him where roses lie
In sparkling, silver frost they rest.
I looked for Him where eagles fly
From high and lofty, hidden nest.

I searched for Him in all I cherished
In all that I held dear.
I'll search for Him 'till sunlight perish
And twilight draweth near.

I looked for Jesus everywhere
'Till I was at a loss.
And then I found Him dying there—
I found Him at the cross.

Jennifer Lee Daugherty

"Within Me"

There is a place that I know,
where only I can go.
    My place keeps away bad spirits and vibes,
ones only I can describe.
    In this place is where I release,
all these feelings and peace.
    This place contains,
emotions of my past, present, and future.
    My secret place is within me stronghold,
beneath me, in my soul.
    See, my special place is in my imagination,
which leads me through life and my creation.

Courtney Stehlin

The Mask

I am so lost and so all alone, not a soul to call my own.
Surrounded by people each and every day, not a single one in the
right way.

My mask has crumbled upon the floor, I stand betrayed, knowing it will
never be restored.
My very soul weak and frail, I hide within like a dog without a tail.

Layer by layer, my skin stripped away, so naked and full of shame,
each and every day.
The bitter cold that runs within my veins is not enough to keep me sane.

I stand alone as they strip my branches, like a tree in the forest
afraid of matches.
I reach for my mask in all its little pieces, my shaking hand just freezes.

The warm secretion flowing down my cheek, becomes my
realization of the bleak.
The shattered pieces weakly stand, with a little help from my hands.

Hold them, help them, don't let go, or all will see what I can't show.
One more pain I cannot take, hold on tight for sanity's sake.

Pretend for all who come around, don't expose the pain that is
so abound.
Mask, oh mask, you're my best friend, I know you will be there
in the end.

We will continue to walk alone, and you will hold me when I moan.
And when we lay ther without life, we will know it was not death
by knife.

For we had died long before,
when you fell and broke upon that floor.

Sandra Williams

I Am A Flower

I have pink petals and shiny green leaves
Honeybees visit and sunshine interweaves
Rain keeps me watered, roots keep me fed
Soil provides my nourishment and a comfortable bed

To keep on growing and sowing my seeds,
I must be kept free of weeds

Delicate and beautiful, straight and strong,
Trees provide me shade and birds sing my song

Do not stamp upon me and I'll bring you much pleasure
With visions of me you will always treasure

I am but one flower

Xuchitl L. Leith

Litter Box Blues

I'll tell you a job not to do in your socks,
is cleaning out the litter box.

It's an awful job, a smelly task,
I wish I owned a gas mask.

I may sound angry, I may sound bitter,
but you try working with kitty litter.

You'll know that I mean when I tell you that,
It's not always a joy owning a cat.

It will make you cough, it will make you choke.
I remember the time the bag broke.

There was kitty litter everywhere,
A foul smell filled the air.

I had to clean up every last bit,
I'd rather smell someone's arm pit.

The cat walked by, all snubby I guess,
As if he had nothing to do with this mess.

It's grosser than gross it's true I swear it,
I knew we should have gotten a parrot.
If you don't want this disgusting job,
I'd advise you to buy a dog.

Ashley Phillips

Dark Shadow

I feel a dark shadow come over me,
When I'm alone in my deepest thoughts.
  The dark shadow is my past,
  Past I wish would return,
  But if it were to return,
  How would I deal with it.

The arrival of the new is long.
It scares in so many ways.
I only wish the past were back.
I know how to deal with the hurt,
  But shall I put forth
  The new that may arrive,
Know stay in the shadow of the old,
Only to be once again hurt upon its arrival.

Michelle M. Sovay

With Open Hands

She's a kindly soul from a far-off land
Who now makes her home on a foreign strand.
I'm a simple man and a native here
Who has made a friend whom I hold so dear.
We don't share so much as a common speech,
But we both are able somehow to reach
Out beyond the boundaries that come between
What we want to say and to feel and mean.
It is not on differences that we dwell,
But on things we share that we both can tell
That the other has a major part
Like an active mind and a caring heart.
With these qualities we can both transcend
All the barriers that the world can send.
We share open minds, open hearts and hands.
Does it matter if we're from different lands?
Not at all! The message our friendship sends
Is that any people can be good friends.

Donald Delmar

Autumn Song

October evenings always play the saddest song,
an overture of falling amber leaves.
Looking up in heaven's eye, music's carried from the sky
and delivered by the smoke-torn breeze.

Once again it's time for all the lonely trees
to shed their tears along the winding streams,
and as the years decay they belong to yesterday
and they are forgotten like our dreams.

And so I sing this song of autumn
and though I never meant to cry
still the season makes me sad
when I think of times I've had
and I just can't stop the mist that's in my eyes,
beneath the autumn skies.

October's sunset has left the sky a blaze.
It dwindles to a dark and fragrant night.
In our wilderness of mind, sometimes we are so blind.
While in slumber we can not see the light.

Henry E. Celentano

Untitled

Your hair reminds me of a darkened moon,
As I stand here and at it I loom.

Your elegant face,
More prettier than a reliant lace.

Here we're like a child.
Beneath you I vile.

Soft is your skin's Meadow,
Silk, scented as a thousand rose petals.

Deep dark brown eyes,
So full of a beauty, that'll never run dry.

I am one that does not posses,
And you are one that can never be assessed,

Like a deer panteths for the waters,
So my heart longeths after thee,

You alone are my souls desire,
And I pray to be with you.

Like a soaring white Dove,
All I offer is Love.

My mind, heart and soul are all a Bliss,
But you can say your love with a Kiss.

Bruce W. Goodrich

I'll Love You - Forever

Just yesterday it seemed you were a little girl,
Running bare-footed through a field of golden sunflowers
Playing, care-free.

As you grew older, you loved me,
I loved you.

But today, you are gone.
But you, I will never forget.
Your smile, your touch, your laughter,
Are remembered by many.

You are gone - but not lost
You are always in my heart.

And someday, we will meet again
Among the clouds, so soft, so white,
But 'til then, I'll love you in my heart.
For Great Grandma

Tiffany Nelson

84

A Life Without Her

Lost, alone, forgotten, rejected,
A life without her, still unaccepted.

A heart of black, beaten and bruised,
A life without her, one born to lose.

Endless pain, seen through broken dreams,
A life without her, is hell it seems.

Hopeless days, followed by restless nights,
A life without her, no hope in sight.

I'm always thinking of the time we had,
A life without her, to be forever sad.

What happens now, where do I turn,
A life without her, while my soul burns.

I've been scarred, for all to see,
A life without her, means nothing to me.

And to look back, over where I've been
A life without her, is a life I can't win.

Jonathan Coulston

Reach Up And Pull Love From The Sky

Summer time a time for humming birds, Butter flies
rainbow colors and tender words that harmonize.
A time for holding hands a time for principles and
pride, Reach up and pull love from the sky.

Warm sun light sun light in the spring life is beginning
worth living for a time for hope a time for faith,
A time for love in our heart give a little take a little
Be true to yourself, Reach up and pull love from the sky.

Flowers bloom a garden of colors a blanket of green
spread over the land and the fields.
Beautiful are the trees that stand so tall so near to the
sky. Reach up and pull love from the sky.

In winter spring or fall up a hill down a hill, you just
might come tumbling to the ground, just pick yourself up
and try it again, it's all a part of living there is beauty
somewhere in sight, Reach up and pull love from the sky.

Dorothy Fyfe

Much More Than An Example Of Mother's Loving Ways

I can hear her in the kitchen, sometimes as early as 5 a.m.
And I realize she is ready to tackle this adventure once again.
I lay there thinking about each year with all the lovely dinners
    she prepares without fail,
Doing everything in harmony, and precise lovingly detail.

As the turkey is nibbled down absolutely to the very bone,
She'll be lucky if she's not left again to clean the kitchen all alone.
It was a wonderful dinner and we rejoiced with gayety in the yuletide,
With peaks of soft meringue that look like heavenly clouds on every
    piece of pie.

But please don't get the notion, her love stops at pleasing
    everyone's palate.
There's nothing she wouldn't do for you, with her gifted ways and
    enormous talents.

Some might call this a love note, Lord knows she deserves one
    everyday.
I'm hoping all will understand the message I want to convey.
I know the hours are long and quite exhausting but honestly with
    every good deed and morsel we do savor.

When God made you Mom, he did our family and all the rest
    of the world
A wonderful and beautiful favor.

Linda Kay Good

"Sach Mo"

A stubby little tail,
Furry hair of silk and shine

Deep, dark brown eyes
That never aged with time

Five years have passed since you've been gone,
To somewhere better where you belong

Forever are the memories
Of the thirteen years you spent with me

No more meeting me at the gate
Playing fetch or keeping me up late

Gone are the days we'd play in the rain
Old age and arthritis had filled them with pain

I'll never forget the day we said our good-byes
Your merry little soul still shone through your eyes

Now I must touch you only in my mind
And remember my best friend,
Always so gentle and so kind.

Kristina Marie Johnson

Zachary

As I look across the empty yard
I see you run when you were nine
Freckled, wild haired, playing too hard
Your looks and actions were mine
I look to the oak tree you climbed when young
Carving love eternal in hearts
The limb still sags where your tire swing hung
Memories... where loneliness starts
We remodeled your room, that den I desired
Left your posters on two of the walls
I still feel your presence, your youth and fire
Almost hear you in the hall
From dah-dah, to daddy, to dad, you grew strong
All the years on the door jamb in ink
Love you forever, good or bad, right or wrong
Tho' sometimes I don't know what you think
Our lives intermingled, by blood and by time
Just remember son, whatever you do
All the sentiment I've put down in these lines
As you changed, you changed me, too...

Jim Weber

Two Old Men

Two old men standing in the wind
Two men out in the cold
They have seen the world change before them
Their surroundings have changed as well
A home was built before them
They were there long before the house was
The valley before them is now a field
It was once filled with their friends
But now their friends are all gone
They have stood together through storms
The wind has bent them but they
always reach toward heaven
Their arms hang low and they touch in the breeze
They have weathered through rain
They have been covered with snow
Their friendship is timeless
Someday they will fall but for now
They are two old men standing the test of time.

Scott Moeck

Creating Creations

I am completely involved
In what I think, and say, and do.
I feel the knowing
I can't seem to express or make known.
I try anyway,
Only to find,
I have created a new image,
And new unknowns.
On and on and on
Into eternity.

I want to be an engineer, a writer, a nurse —
Or something.
So I become involved
In the problems and difficulties encountered
In the who or what I have chosen to be.
On and on and on
Into eternity.
Or until I choose to be someone or something else —
On and on and on
Into eternity.

Kenneth L. Orris

Nature

You see the sun in the woods. You feel the wind
that blinds with your skin. You see the little bees fly
around the trees. No trucks no smoke that could choke you.
You see birds that are trying to say words. You see a monkey
that swings with grace and skill. You see the wild. You see
a bear chase a bear. You see a eagle flying over a seagull.
You see the squirrels, that twirl around their trees. You see
a lion. You feel the chill, he feels the thrill. You see a
wolf howling as he hungers for his prey.
You see a deer run. The tiger his a new game
Which he is untamed. You see a snake that hungers
for steak. You see all the creatures. Who are showing
all their features. You see an elephant stand old, but
bold. You see your eyes look at the sky. You
see the ocean that has a lot of motion.

Kevin McNeil

Nature's Images

A smile, a laugh, a tear, a sigh,
we often stop to wonder why;
the grass blades green, and the tree leaves too,
how you see me and I see you.

A splitting image to fill the soul,
reflections in nature - that makes us whole;
one life in the middle and one life just begun,
but like the leaves and the grass - we blend as one.

Was it luck, stroke of fate, or maybe just love,
that you stand beside me, sent from above;
or were we simply suppose to see,
reflections of you, seeing reflections of me.

Like the beauty of nature which cannot hide,
together we'll nurture our spirits inside;
rooting together an unbreakable tie,
creating a love that never can die.

Nature's images, reflections of God,
a genuine beauty that cannot be fraud;
a picture of life - the way it should be,
a picture of you, and a picture of me.

Janet Winslow Kelchner

The Well

In yonder wood some paces in
A well was dug in forest dim
Its water tasted sweet I'm told
For weary travelers refreshing and cold

The decades came the decades went
The well's old frame grew old and spent
From time to time it was repaired
To service those who for it cared

It's now been years since it's been used
The water is poisoned from man's abuse
So...in yonder wood some paces in
A well decays...in forest dim

Lillian Chabot

Purification Through Pain

Formidable
Exciting fear
Incessant awe
Streets of madness
An' men dealing with it.

Amorphous
Distort
Shapeless creature of the desert
In love with everything
In love with everyone.

Taking in
An extension of ego
An extension of living
Pure indulgence
Yet, strangely and continuously deferred.

Purification through pain.

Steve Martin

The Wave

As the chain of waves swell,
They move closer to the awaiting shore.
Gliding across the open sea
Reaching the sandy beaches.
The warm, silky land
Becomes overwhelmed with the crash of the
strengthened waves.
One after another they pound upon the shore.
The sands shifts under their power.
Coming to the end of this surge,
A last frothy swell hits the weary beach
Leaving behind a foamy, exhausted shore.

Kimberly J. Greene

Mother Nature

I'm your biggest fan.
I enjoy being entranced by your beauty.

But, it disturbs me when buildings
Block my view.

I adore all creatures.

But, it kills me to see them
Sacrificed for our own progress.

I sometimes wish that I lived when times
Were simpler.

But, I'm afraid that I have fallen
Dependent on the present.

And that scars me.

Edward L. Nowak

86

Memories And Dreams

The old year is over, the new one is here.
It's a time for reflection, perhaps for a tear.

It's a time to remember the good things I've had.
A time to forget all the things that were bad.

It's a time to forgive all the world and me,
to let go of the old hurts and set myself free.

As the peaceful night lightens into dawn,
it's a time to remember loved ones here and gone.

I'll embrace the new year, say goodbye to the old
and never forget time's more precious than gold.

Ruthann Koenig

To Mother And Dad

Today is your day
It's 65 years since you first said
"I Love You"
These are "living words" that show,
In your Children, in your Grandchildren,
In your Great Grandchildren,
And in all the people, whose lives you have touched.
Your memories are beautiful!
What are memories?
The good times, the bad times,
The happy times, the sad times,
But the good times,
Seem to surface in your sea, of Love.
What the world needs more of
Is your kind of Love.
Today, We all wish you many tomorrows
Filled with Love with good health,
With smiling faces with happy tears,
And many more beautiful memories.
Don't ever forget to say, "I Love You".

Evelyn M. Meyer

Resilience

There are times in life when, try as we might,
It's a difficult task to keep our goals in sight.
Fate steps in and gives us a whack—
Then it's one step forward and two steps back.

Time and again we are challenged anew.
And we ask the question, "What did I do
To deserve this big thump?
Am I strong enough to once more climb over the hump?"

We humans are resilient, though.
And always after we suffer a blow
At the whim of Fortune, whenever she pleases,
We're right back at life, on our feet, not our kneeses.

Somehow we manage to hang on to Hope.
Somehow we overcome, and don't stop to grope
For answers to questions that begin with "Why"
We just forge onward... "Here's mud in your eye."

It's great to be living, to learn every day.
Life is what happens when we just glance away
From our plans or our goals, our pre-scheduled aims,
We live life as it happens, even with its salt grains.

Darlene Smitley

Music - Music

The sound of it puts me to sleep
And sometimes it makes me weep

It's a part of everyday life
With us through sorrow and strife

It can be about love
Or about the sky above

It can be about feelings inside
Or just about the way a kite glides

Music makes entertainment fun
This is true for all, most, and some

No matter what it's about or how you use it
It's all one thing - music - music

Quiana Brown

Winter

Winter is so magical, a world of snowy white,
Sledding and snowmen, a wonderfully joyful sight.

Children preparing snowballs to throw,
Others making angels in the snow.

Snow on the ground and in the air,
Mittens and a hat for you to wear.

Winter brings Hanukkah and Christmas too,
Lots of holiday fun just for you.

Sipping hot cocoa with cream,
I stare out my window into a dream.

Snow and frost everywhere,
A lovely scene too hard to compare.

The world is glittering with frost and snow,
The earth around us is aglow.

Rebecca L. DeCillis

What Kind Of Friend?

Did you ever have a friend who was here today and gone tomorrow?
One who broke your trust, and filled your heart with sorrow?
That kind of friend is easy to get, but who wants such a friend?
You want the kind of friend who's loving and faithful to the end -
One who makes you feel free to be just who you are,
One who lifts you up and helps "hitch your wagon to a star"!

But in order to have this kind of friend, you need to also be one,
For who wants the other kind, you can get them by the ton!
So always be helpful, loving, considerate, and kind:
In other words, practice the Golden Rule - keep it in mind,
And you will surely be blessed with friends - the very best,
As those you do not wish to have "hang out" with all the rest!

Henrietta Finch

Struggles Of A Modern Day Teenager

Struggles of a modern day teenager go far and wide.
They are problems that a teenager can never seem to hide.
Struggles of a modern day teenager seem to come from both
   Heaven and Hell,
Hitting you from everywhere, even the place you dwell.
Some problems that teenagers now face,
Are fighting, drugs, and being disgraced.
Other problems that teenagers now look at,
Are hanging out, drinking, shooting a gat.
Problems are dating and finding a girl with whom to go out.
Which eventually leads to arguments and many a shout.
A girl, a gun, money, and a tear,
These are the problems that always appear...

Trelane Martinez

The Neighborhood

This neighborhood is known for violence,
Sometimes I wish for silence,
A car goes by, once in a while,
As do people of every style.
Gunshots, screams, and dogs are barking,
The cars going by are steadily parking.
People are sleeping in their bed.
Yes, someone could get hit in the head,
If on the streets this time of night,
Walking or running or maybe in sight.
Once you're accepted, it isn't too bad,
Except watching these people is sometimes sad.
Ragged and poor but they seem content.
A man falls down and his face is skint.
Drinking and drugs are always present,
I wish from this area, I could be absent.

Sybil Grisham

To My Son

Then you dwell within me and I within you -
   How this was I still can't realize -
Yet we are not one.
   From your first here I close around
You who were within me are now without.
   I hold you close because — we need each
other and so I lock you in my mind's corridor -
   Forever

Now - must go to - build your castle at 21 -
   There is a Season for everything, a Reason
You know
   Severance - always to live out life gainfully.
I know
   But can no longer see to dwell through you
And not myself.
   Who will record all this -
My Son to none at my last vestige
   of here and gone?

"Renee" Maureen Sheffield

Bay Window

I see you there
on the window sill
placid content.
Resigned to the edifices around you.
Creating into magma
black and crusty with the sun
Heat.
Burdening the concrete walls melting your ice.
And you sit still happy content with life
the surroundings you lay yourself in
once crystal, the azure water reflects your face
in the cool viscous liquid
the wavering image of crystal like eyes
sparkling bits of broken glass light into the depthless space
around
a kaleidoscope of stars against black.
Breathing a sigh of spring upon the infinite winter.
I'll wait forever.

Paul Trimmer

The Power Within

My life has gained a power within
A power that saves my soul from sin
A power that relieves me from the chains of sin
"Jesus Blood Sacrifice"
-In-
Holy Spirit Power within
To create in me anew
a new attitude - a new lifestyle
a new way to think - a new way to act
a new way to be grateful and to be a genuine person,
To love - to give
Thank you Heavenly Father for this gift of power,
to change myself and to be an example for other men -
God's Power Within
Jesus - without a doubt - It's Him
The Power Within.

Joe Hendrickson

To The Irishman Paul On His Birthday

We think he's a saint, but an angel he ain't, his Irish demeanor shows through and here we are hoping on his special day, that all of his wishes come true.

We once heard him croon and old Irish tune, it's clear he's a very good singer but his talents are many, 'cause along with his voice, he's a pretty good golf club swinger.

His fashions are clever with colorful fabric, he really stands out on the tee You can spot from afar, it's Paul up ahead, 'cause his plaid pants are easy to see.

Not older but better, he's one of a kind, as we read our poetic verbiage While he might prefer cranking up the old cart, that sits charging in the garage.

But he'll have to sit still while we joyfully speak of his merits that come from our heart those of smiles, cheer and laughter that must be applauded before he gets back to his cart.

Let's raise up our tribute in Paul's recognition, and wish him the best through the years.
Happy birthday to him from the Hurleys and all, to this gem of a man and a dear.

Deborah Hurley

Star Voyage

I gaze upon the stars,
   wondering when we might visit them.
It seems like such a simple task,
   to go to the stars.
As easy as going to the local store,
   or to a friends house.
For are they not our neighbors, friends,
   these other worlds that circle their own suns.
I know we can reach the stars and beyond,
   and I know that it is both dangerous and exciting.
But would it not be a great voyage,
   if we were to travel to these other stars,
      and visit with those who live there.
Would it not be a great triumph for us,
   to prove all the doubters and nay-sayers wrong.
That in the end,
We as a people are better than we give ourselves credit,
   and that We as a people can achieve great accomplishments.
So I wonder when we shall go to the stars,
   and if I will see that day......

Chris R. Mullicane

Walk In The Serenity Of The Morn And Eve

Take a walk deep in the woods
When the crisp night air lingers no more;
When a magnificent display of dewdrops glisten
Before evaporating from foliage-covered floors.

Take a walk deep in the woods
When the day has grown old;
When the sun's brilliant rays
Turn to hazy red from dazzling gold.

Take a walk deep in the woods
In the serenity of the morn and eve;
See how explicit this creation is,
That no other mind—except God's—could conceive.

Stephanie L. Weber

Untitled

The human spirit is like the eagle...
    born to be free,
    to fly where it may,
    to seek new truth,
    to be free from anything which
      might bind it
    or confine it to a small space.
For it is only beautiful when it is free...
    unbound by chains,
    to soar to new heights,
    to survey all that is in nature,
    to rejoice in its life,
    and to go where it pleases.

Pamela Ardrey Dickerman

Summertime

Thrashing, nakedly, drunkenly in the pool, helping fingers
are crushed.

Working, arranging, rearranging,
monotonously, the boring job
will end soon.

Lights blaring flashing sirens in the night, the speeding chariot
overturned, "the japanese boy was lucky."

Calmly contemplating robotics,
in chelmsford, this pleasant activity,
can't last forever.

Chasing madly down the street, "floor the cab," lucky for us she
won't be seeing california today.

Walking, slowly, cheerfully,
drunkenly, stumbling to the show,
fun times afoot.

Running, crazily to nowhere, stopping for nothing and no one,
gotta get away.

Talking jive in the corner
with physicians from Harlem
summer's great.

Herb Blackman

Who Is He?

This world that we live in is so full of strife
But the peace that awaits us is brought by the Bread of Life
(John 6:35)

Some remember Him today and forget Him tomorrow
I know in my heart, He's A Man Of Sorrows (Isaiah 53:3)

Some say He's a myth or just a simple man
But the Word tells me, He is The Lamb (Rev. 5:8)

We are told by Him to let our light shine
To grow in His presence, for He is the True Vine (John 15:1)

In Acts 1:8, we receive great power
From the man who is known as the Wonderful Counselor (Isaiah 9:6)

Some say His word changes, but if you were clever
You'd read that in Hebrews, He's The Same Forever (Heb. 13:8)

Do you need a close friend, are you feeling alone
Call upon the name of the Lord, The Living Stone (1 Peter 2:4)

He'll keep all your secrets, never leaving your side
Be one with Him, the Word Of Life (1 John 1:1)

He loves you because He's no respecter of persons
Let Him lead the way, The Chief Of 10 thousand (Song of Solomon 5:10)

For some it's too late because they never asked
Is the Lord in your Life, have you gone to the Axe? (Matthew 3:10)

Darla Berry

Strong Woman

She's willful as a bond of steel, yet loving like a valentine,
She's beautiful like a flower, yet caring like a friendship.
Strong woman with pride, strong woman with beauty.
Men were attracted, they didn't know why...
She's rough, she's tough, she's honestly a handful.
In her attitude there lies femininity,
In her self image there lies confidence.
Family appreciates, history respects.
Strong woman with pride, strong woman with pride.
Admiration, emulation, I want to be...
strong like her, beautiful like her, wonderful like her.
She taught my mother,
radiant like her, beautiful like her, strong like her.
Stories of the past,
tell of strength, tell of strife, tell of preen.
Strong woman with pride, strong woman with beauty.
Society ashamed, I am proud,
She is my grandmother, always and forever
Her essence guides me, her lessons teach me.
I love you, thank you.

Jennifer Muir Hemminger

Down By The Sea

As I crunch my feet across the hot, brisk sand,
The sun sparkles into my hazel eyes.
I peer across a vast, endless, strip of glistening blue water,
So rich in salt,
With enormous waves that crash on the sea's shore as
    it churns unforgivingly.
I look at the peaceful horizon and hear the gentle breeze,
While the sea gulls chime their soothing sounds of harmony.
Smelling the crisp air,
I can just taste the plump, juicy hotdogs the vendor's selling.
Waiting until late at night,
When the moon is brightly lit, sitting in the breathlessly still sky,
I say to myself -
I wish I were a rumbling wave in the giant waters -
    Down by the sea.

Lisa Taub

Morning Song

At morning time, when all is still
There comes upon my window sill
Our most delightful feathered friend,
The golden throated little Wren.

He gives a nervous flick of his little tail,
Throws back his head - then runs the scale.
Such glorious melody now outpours,
That to Heaven those shrill notes seem to soar.

No instrument of man has e'er come near
To those dulcet tones so wondrous clear.
"Make a joyful noise," he seems to say,
"To our Lord in Heaven on this - His day."

Lovelier, even higher his notes seem to bound,
From a creature so small, such magnificent sound.
Now quietly, how sweetly, he tells of his love
For the Source of his talent in Heaven above.

Now if this tiny, simple, plain, little thing
Makes the woods resound and the hillside sing,
Why can't we humans our voices employ
In acclamation to God in praise and in joy?

George M. Pearce Jr.

The Plane

Deep rumbles of anticipation -
As a timpani
Urged on by the conductor.
Prepared for duty, the assistants demonstrate.
The rumbling intensifies,
Filling every being with its energy,
Its anticipation.
It rolls.
Then, with a great shudder,
lifts.
Light as a feather,
seems this monster
Slipping effortlessly through the white -
It greets the blue...
Flashes of sunlight bounce brilliantly off of
            The Plane.

Lindsey Strauch

His Last Ride

In Loving Memory of my Grandfather, Joseph E. Springer
There are people that dream
Some that hope
Others who wish

There is a man who we all know
That might have done these things

But for the most part
He took life as it came
And played the hand he was dealt

With this we give him his last ride,
His last ride in the snow

To one he was a lover
To others he was a father
To some he was a grandfather
To many he was a friend

From what I've learned he loved to hunt
Not for food, not for sport
But for snow

With this we give him his last ride,
His last ride in the snow

Shannan K. Watkinson

Reverence To The Creator, Earth, And Nature

Let Us Culminate Our Spirit

Give thanks to the sky, water, winds, and the earth,
For they are part of creation.
Thanks to the trees, animals, roots and herbs,
For without all this we could, not survive.

Let us culminate our spirit, as the Eagle flies high,
In reverence to the beauty of nature.
When the land is destroyed.
The trees are ripped from the earth's heart.
Humans will suffer the consequences, when on this earth,
they cannot survive.

Let us not forget that the trees, roots, and herbs,
Let us breathe and our bodies live.
The earth and nature are our mother,
Without it we would be in a state if necrosis.

The Indian people thought of the earth as their mother.
They know the wisdom of the earth and nature in respect for it.
The Creator put the earth here, put humans upon it to protect it,
For the earth is their home, not a necropolis.

Gloria J. Abel

Honeymoon

Capture me
Carry me
Whisper softly gently quietly
Laughing with me
Talking with me
Feel me, need me
Touches
Tingle my toes
Butterfly my body
Understand
I
Am
Here
Love me every minute of every hour of every day
Play tickle, grow, hold my hand, kiss me
Romance me in candle's reflection
Love me
A lifelong friendship
I am
I am in love

Diane Michelle Hart

A Fire House Prayer!

Lord, we inside these hallowed halls, are but mere shadows along
    its walls!
We travel to such places that have not been foretold, in search of
    the little ones, and some of old!

Be it a scrape on their knee or a broken bone, be with us oh Lord,
    as we enter their homes!

We enter not knowing who might be there, in need of thine tender care.
Grant us the wisdom to handle such cases, which sometimes belong
    to such young tender faces.

And help us to honor thy fallen comrade, who gave his life
    to help his fellow man!

Please take him to heaven to that Fire House in the sky,
    to ride the apparatus above us so high!

Lord, guide us back home in your loving hand,
    to hold us while waiting till the alarm sounds again! Amen!!!

Delbert Patrick Wait

God's Little Angel

She was just a little angel,
Sent to earth from God above.
A special gift from God himself,
An extension of your love.

And with every breath you take,
You know how precious life can be.
One day she's here and then she's gone,
But she's always in your memories.

For to lose a child is the hardest thing,
A parent must ever face.
But you must believe God has taken her,
Into his loving embrace.

She will always live inside your heart,
And in heaven now she sings.
She is an angel of God,
And with your love,
She has now received her wings!

Mari H. Diana

Old Anger

My Grandpa said this for his very last time,
Now I'm inspired to write this rhyme.
On his deathbed he said it, he was always sore,
"You won't have this ole dog to kick around no more!"

I took it to heart and never forgot,
It helps me out when my temper gets hot.
For women don't understand the ways of a man,
and will take all the money he has in his hand,
and most come back wanting more, but one day,
"You won't have this ole dog to kick around no more!"

I remember the time I was to go fishing,
I'd finished the laundry, the ironing, and the dishes.
But no, the kids must play in the park,
We didn't get home until way after dark.
My pride was hurt and my new fishing shirt tore,
"One day you won't have this ole dog to kick around no more!"

Grandpa would be proud, the way I've turned out,
when angry I always stomp around and shout,
"One day you'll be sorry, keeping me broke and poor,
cause, you won't have this ole dog to kick around no more!"

Monroe Nivens

What Might Have Been

The way it happened was hard to explain;
it gave me joy; yet exposed my pain.
I tried to say it was different this time;
My eyes would believe it but my mind was blind
I thought this was the place to make my new start;
to fade my memories and unleash my heart.
But my solemn heart had strings attached;
From many times being broken and patched.
I tried to smile to start again;
Still remembering what might have been.

Sara Mau

Horizon

Twilight and Moon
Stars bright and marvelously out in outer space
Clouds bellow
Winds swoon
Sun shines brilliantly on the Horizon
I am a tear drop of the Messiah
I am a thought of Elohim before he spoke
Faith into existence light be and it
glowed triumphantly.

Muneerah Roberts

"Oklahoma City"

Oklahoma City a good fair town,
Until it was visited by some evil clowns,
Destroying the Federal Building,
Not knowing what love ones were in that building.
Many innocent lives were lost,
And the terrorist not knowing the cost.
Many workers and volunteers hurried to the scene,
Looking for any surviving being.
As days went by,
The death rate went high.
But I know God will take it in his hands,
And I will pray and do what ever I can.

Jamie Saldivar

Dream Person

I begin to dream, a dream about you
I don't know who you are but I would like to know you better
You appear in my dreams ever so slightly
Causing me to feel the pain of loneliness even more.
To me you're my inspiration, my guide through my troubles
Even though people forget their dreams I remember mine clearly
Always remembering your dark hair and your dark eyes
That showed love every time I look into them
You listen to my problems so matter how boring they may seem
You comfort me and make me forget about my fears and my troubles
When I wake up I find that it is nothing more than a dream
It causes me to shed a tear because you're not here by my side
Like a silent film you never tell me your name when I ask you
I would like to know who you are in real life
To me I have you all by myself in my dreams and you'll always be
there when I need you.

Duane Fish

Cee Cee's Song

Cee Cee Miff sailed away one night,
On a dandelion bloom.
The next morning "Lindsay" awoke,
In what was once Cee Cee's room.
Her tongue no longer was a slipping spool,
Where words were knots of cross stitches.
After the dream weavers needled and unlaced her tongue bows,
Her words spilled forth swimming like fishes.
The weavers three then joined hands,
and with the ribbons tied themselves together.
A left to right and right to left,
The strongest hand hooked the tail of the dandelion balloon.

The toddler awoke from a runaway dream,
As a comet raced past a midnight moon.

Myra Wise

Untitled

Hot August sun
Beats down on the marker of the grave
Where my father lies.
Six years have passed, and it is never any easier to come here.
Each time feels like the funeral day
And all of his pain and suffering come back
All of my pain and suffering floods back
And i blink back briny tears
And try to swallow over the aching lump in my throat.
I recall my childhood when my dad would bring me to visit
His father's grave,
And here I stand, on the other side of the same stone
Sorely missing that man, wishing I didn't have to come here
Holding only memories for comfort when I really need his hand.

Lynne H. Simon

Catch That School Bus To The Farm

Today is so special for girls and boys, finish your breakfast and clean-up your toys
Give good bye hugs to everyone and soon a yellow school bus will come.

When you want the bus to stop wave your hand or hold it up
Doors will open, bus will wait, climb inside and don't be late.

In the bus you must sit down, don't be running all around
Find an empty seat inside and get ready for a ride.

The driver will drive to the place that's fun. Where? Driver please
tell everyone Not to school and not to show, to the farm is where this bus will go.

You can ride the horses and milk the cows, you can see a farm cat chase a field mouse
you can pet the puppies and feed the dogs, you can go to the swamp to catch a few frogs.

If you see any snakes or spiders there, you can jump on a cow or climb on a chair
You can swim in the lake or swing on a tire and for lunch make hot dogs over a campfire.

But soon it will be the end of the day, all the children and animals will get tired of play
then the sun will go down and the stars will get bright, and evening time slowly will turn into night.

The school bus will open its doors to all kids and tired they'll slowly sit back in their seats
and soon, when at home children go to sleep they'll dream of the farm and this beautiful trip.

   Jimmy Vadim Grinzaid

The River Of Love

In the mystical land of Heart and Soul— the River of Love ever onward flows
   first just as a trickle, then in a stream — then in a torrent of passion it goes,
As a sacred gift — from Mystic Sky born — high up in the tall Mountains of Romance,
   Plunging to the Valley of Work and Play — so that there all lives it can thus enhance.

The sacred waters — sweeping across the landscape - bring beauty to the land they've built,
   Washing Heart and Soul clean of selfishness — and melting mountains into liquid silt,
Molding — forming — shaping — changing our lives — forever anew and never the same,
   Feeding the spirit with sweetness of joy — and thus all the harshness of life to tame.

The River of Love is sometimes wild and restless — sometimes deep in silence going
   Onward across the Plains of Reality — in a ceaseless and unending flowing
Pulsing, caressing — bathing and enriching — all of the lives it touches on the way
   Surging, urging — ever urging — a melding unity of oneness toward the bay.

Flowing thru both sorrows and mirth — borrowing deeply from both the Sky and the Earth —
   So blending earth and sky together on — the new Delta Flats of Rebirth
The magic melding river creates anew — Lifeland that never was before to be
Then it gently tends the new life's growing — ere it returns to the Eternal Sea.

From there it begins once again the ceaseless —
                   — And unending — Cycle of Rebirth—
Rising up to Heaven to replenish itself —
                   — As the River of Love on Earth.

   Richard S. Clarke, April 1996

Life's Little Nasties

Life has got its good points and its bad, some things in life can make a person sad.
If I could bottle up all of life's little nasties in a jar, more people in life could get very far.
First I would bottle up all of the hate on this earth, people would be born with love at birth.
Earth is very precious to me, the land, the sky, and even the sea.
So you'll understand why I want to get rid of these nasties right away, it would be great if I could bottle them up today.

Life is so short because of sickness and stress, so I just want to get rid of everything that is not best.
I would get rid of AIDS, Cancer, Diabetes, and Lyme, I think this would give life a little more time.
The racism next would have to go, everyone would be treated the same as they grow.
The stress in life is a little too great, so this would be next to wipe off the slate.
Little by little the world would unite in peace and love, and the symbol of the world would truly be the peace dove.
Even though this list sounds small, it is very hard to accomplish it all.

Next and probably last, I would have respect for the earth, and treat it for what it is really worth.
As long as the pollution and garbage stops coming, we can stop the world from what it's becoming.
So to fix up the earth I would jar up pollution, to me this is important to find a solution.
To me tomorrow should be better than today, and for this I often pray.
I would love to jar up everyone's pain, gone and forgotten would be a world gain.
Earth is a special place to be, so why not make the best of it, you and me.
So let's bottle up these problems one by one, and enjoy all of what we have done.

   Amy Lynn Newhoff

Answer To "Empty Arms"

He came to our house one day
Tear-stained, and torn, and sad;
He was looking for a home,
He had no Mom nor Dad.

He was looking for some hugs
To make him come alive,
Some kisses to heal the hurts,
For he was only five.

We opened our arms to him
And he walked in so close,
As though he had known he was
The one that our hearts chose.

Day by day he grew more dear,
And latched on to our love;
He was the answer to our prayers
We had sent up above.

Mary L. Shelton

Beauty

Beauty is like a flower
with perfection by the hour

Colors by the rainbow
glistening from the suns glow

Caressed by the wind
who's the carrier of beauties end.

Gene Spraggins

untitled

I saw you walking
towards me
I caught your eye

(So never to be born your pain child
from your own poison vine of hate
the sky's all raven-echoes and mist
the wind whispers of imaginary truth
and you are caught in the scarlet ivy again)

I passed you by.

Elizabeth Kelly

Wonders Of Spring

Each year as spring appears,
everything is in arrears.

Daylight hours increase in length,
sun rays develop strength.

Rising temperatures become mild,
winter's chill gone with winds wild.

Climate changes bring April showers,
nectar to awaken early flowers.

Grass sheds the winter coat of brown,
a carpet of green covers the ground.

Buds erupt on shrubs and trees,
soon we hear the hum of bees.

Birds fill the air with song,
happy after a winter so long.

Smell of air, a fragrance of spring,
encouragement for hearts to sing.

Mother nature performing her duty,
a classic act, showing off her beauty.

Giving us fuel to proceed in life,
inspiring us to escape strife.

Robert M. Rampani

Caritas Volventibus Annis (Love Going Through The Years)

Now That I've found you in person
I could love you more than anyone,
If you would let me see you soon.
I know there's none who really can.

I cannot promise you riches
Nor jewels that corrode and fade,
But I'll hand you all bits and pieces
That make me solely to your spread.

Both of us have some kind of past,
Which is best kept blown in the wind.
We'll have a New Start without fuzz;
As one, do things that don't offend.

What matters most is happiness
No wealth on earth can truly buy.
True constancy with earnestness
In loving is what I will vie.

Going the years on loyalty,
I'd love you more than anyone
When I can be with you shortly
And lavish on you all I can.

Allan Magallano

Fantasy Child

Michael Magill, angel child
A fantasy, to delight and make smile
Lively, vivacious, with dancing feet
Brings happiness, makes life complete
Lovely, cunning child, so fair
With gray, twinkling, laughing eyes
And soft, golden-brown curly hair
Too sweet and beautiful, for a boy
More like a precious, priceless toy
Always happy, merry, and gay
Gladdens my heart, through the day
An imaginary angel, in disguise
To cheer, to brighten cloudy skies
Romps, plays, frolics, having fun
Like a little wood nymph, in the sun
A myth that will never be a reality
Is and always a dream child, to me
Yet, in this vision, you are so real
Fantasy child, Michael Magill

Monettia Phillips

Quest For Truth

How I lost you to eternity,
Sunrise and the day begin;
My heart weeps for sorrow,
My life cease for tomorrow.

Destroyed by the shadow of dark,
You ascended to his throne;
Mocked by the laughter of evil,
Stood for the virtue of dawn.

Searching for eternal truth.
You rest on restless quest;
Cease the flame of ceaseless,
End the story of endless.

The story of noble knight,
Echoes on timeless space;
Greater than the greatest,
Adored by a lonely heart.

Emi K. Obenhaus

Remember Yesterday

Dream about tomorrow
and you will remember
yesterday.

Promises, desires, riches,
Love, devotion all
Come on gossamer wings

Caught in the wind, Lingering
for just a little while
But giving joys untold

Then, all too soon
Sometimes too late,
We say, "Oh, yes, I
Remember yesterday"

Bernadette Harris

My Beloved

It came to me
Like a bolt from the blue
The things I buy
Are to keep me here
When I'd rather be with you.
But, I have promises to keep
And pets that need me too
And friends and family
Who don't understand
I'd much rather be with you.

I wonder where you have gone
Do you still remember me?
Do you ask the angels
And can they tell
Life without you isn't going so well

The days are lonely
The nights are long
It's a game of "let's pretend"
Till, again, I can be with you.

Ruth E. Merrill

My Inspiration Box

I have an "Inspiration Box"
High on a closet shelf.
So when I'm feeling kind of low,
And sorry for myself,
I take a journey through the box
And search until I find
A thought, a poem, or scripture,
To ease my troubled mind.
I often send a poem or thought,
To help a worried friend.
Today I searched but could not find
The words I wished to send.
I must content myself and say,
Remember, I'm your friend.

Nancy L. Goode

"Pillsbury's Best"

Mother made my clothes when I
was just a child, feed sack
dresses with pretty prints of
flowers growing wild.
I felt so very special even tho'
my feet were bare, I didn't mind
"Pillsbury's best" across my underwear.

Kathryn Bailey

Untitled

I stand here, poised,
Ready to step into tomorrow.
But am I ready?
Today is comfortable,
Warm, known.
Tomorrow is full of uncertainty,
Unknown.
It would be easier, perhaps,
To stay with all that's familiar
And known,
But then I'd never know
What's around the corner,
Down the road.
I'll take one step,
That's a beginning.
After that, each step
Will be easier,
And my tomorrows
Will begin.

Joanne Zumpe

Seasonal

Like a bud the light flowers.
Watered roots, spring bloom.
Winter causes dormancy.
Summer springs expectancy
Drink - in all seasonal.
Attitude is longitudinal.
Enjoy, for life is seasonal.
All is cyclic.
Bloom and gloom.

Donald Lawrence

Ode To A Black Woman

There you are,
Like an African star,
Twinkling in the black velvet night.
Is it not right,
To see you totally free?
Perhaps some ancestor of mine
Is wrapped up in thee,
And all through your heart
My brothers and sisters
Ah, thou art.

Maybe I will never
See you again.
Tomorrow, maybe the end.
But today, and tomorrow true
My heart is full,
Is full of you.

Charles Rathbun

Night Flyers

Some people
blinded by adulation
seldom to taste defeat
are like the insects
who circle lights
webs await.

E. Ruth Van Appledorn

Mother

Her life is a beautiful memory
Her absence a silent grief,
She sleeps in God's green garden
In the sunshine of Perfect piece.

Henry E. Jacobsen

Fear Of The Day

The cry of a lonely child echoing
  through the night.
The sounds of two fists colliding in a fight.
The calling of my name from the man I love.
Diving into a pool of cool watery mist.
Listening to the sound of wolf baying
  at the new full moon.
Watching tiny little bees working to
  fill the comb with honey
A father yelling at his son to pick-up
  his bedroom.
A girl collapsing on the floor cause
  she was so drunk.
Someone dying far away from all the
  disease and fear of the day.

Katie Stebbins

Love

I am the snow
  falling through the air.
I am a snow leopard
  catch me if you dare.
I am as white
  as a polar bear.
I am in all the world.
  I am everywhere.
I am love
  please handle me with care.

Regina Lawson

Untitled

You have dreamed
of me
in your dreams.
I am here
for you now.
I am
every woman
you have ever loved
and every woman
who has ever loved you.
I am here now
in flesh
and willing.
You know me
for I have been
your fantasy.

I am here.
Come to me.

Cheri Walter

Dream Trip

Flying above the billowy clouds
  Up in the sky so blue
Off to some enchanted land
  To make all your dreams come true
Through all the hustle and bustle
  Of preparing to depart
May God graciously grant to you
  His peace within your heart
In all of your excitement
  Please take time to pause
And know that you are wished
  A very happy bon voyage.

June E. Farrington

Victims

There was a time in days gone by,
When love was all they needed.
Their silent shouts, of who am I?
Were neither heard nor heeded.

Perhaps they should have cried aloud,
To have their story told;
See each child in a shroud,
Alas their graves grow cold.

Victims of war laid to rest,
By humanity gone insane;
They who tackled every test,
Had come to terms with pain.

For those of you come to mourn,
And keep vigil with each ghost,
Know they're no longer burden borne,
They've left to meet "The Host."

We'll wonder as the years fly by,
While time keeps marching on,
Is there time left to cry
Or ask where have the children gone.

Thomasina E. Jordan

First Day Of School

It was early in the morning
on a bright September day
That Johnny was awakened
when he heard his mother say
Hurry and get dressed, you know,
you to go school today.
Johnny thought it over
and decided to obey
Mothers they know best, you know
Or so he'd heard her say
Altho' he knew he'd rather
Just stay home and play
He had a gentle teacher
He loved right from the start
But when she did get married
It almost broke his heart

M. Edward Nielson

The Twinkling Of An Eye

I saw a bolt of lightning
streak across the sky
In a moment I was changed
in the twinkling of an eye.
I wore a robe of righteousness
for the Lord of Lords was here
Tis the trumpet of the King
whispering gently in my ear.
He dressed my corruptible mortal soul
and crowned me as a saint
Incorruptible and immortal because
I did not faint.
Oh grave you have no victory
Oh death I will not die,
The King is here to raise me
In the twinkling of an eye.

Walter M. Horton

The Image In The Mirror

The image in the mirror
stares back at me,
doing whatever I do.
The image is me,
or is it only the image that
my mind creates?

Sara Brines

I Am Fire

I leap with uncontrolled delight!
My tongues lash out; I dance and swirl.
I ravish forests; life takes flight.
I gorge myself on deer and squirrel!

I soar into the heavens blue,
And tall trees whet my appetite.
I light the night in splendid hue,
and see tall men quiver with fright!

I race the wind o'er field and plain;
I creep, I pounce! Consuming flame
Envelopes all; leaves but a stain
To mark my path. I am to blame!

Untethered, Devil's kin am I.
Relentless foe with shameless greed!
Corralled, a strong, enslaved ally.
I serve you well, whate'er the need!

Mary Eileen Drake

Hands Touching Wood

Baby hands
Reach out and touch
The crib side
The rough wood scratches
And leaves
Small stains of blood.

Young hands
Hold and shape
A new beam
The tool slips
And pierces flesh
The cut oozes
And heals over.

Man hands
Nailed to a crossbar
Marks that will never heal
Blood flowing out
To heal the world.

Carolyn Shafer

Ms. Schreiner

I have a teacher
Who's afraid of mice.
Even though
She's very nice.

The sight of mice,
Makes Ms. Schreiner sick.
So her fellow teachers,
Decided to play a trick.

They put a fake mouse,
Where she gets her mail.
And when she saw that mouse
Her face turned pale.

They also put a mouse,
Under her car handle.
When she saw that mouse,
She flipped out her sandals.

But now she's back to normal,
Or so we think.
But what nobody knows is,
Ms. Schreiner now visits a shrink.

Dusty Shannon

Pathways Of Life

So quickly I am off and gone.
Down that magic pathway.
My heart alive and free.

Which road should I follow?
The choice was soon made.
Searching for the streets paved in gold
and the rainbow at the end.

After traveling that long road with
it's many bends and turns, I pause
to look back and wondered,
did I take the right one?

Some will want for nothing.
They are rich and famous, having seen
the wonders of the world.
Others have nothing but there dreams.

As we near the end of that
long journey, we wonder. Did it
really make a difference which
pathway was followed?

Margaret Roy

A Timely Reminder

What judgment lies in store
for the nation
that ignores God
and refuses to heed
His commandments?

When people misuse the gift of life
so freely bestowed by the Creator,
and wantonly produce life,
and just as wantonly destroy it—
to appease the gods
of lust and convenience—
what judgment is appropriate?
Tell me, if you know.

Yet God the Eternal Sovereign
remains upon His throne,
invincible, and in full control
of His universe,
and will bring to heel
the insolence of Man
one way or another.

Elvira Van Orman

A List Of Wishes

If I had just one wish to make,
    what would that wish be?

Would it be to have world peace?
Or maybe to save the ozone layer?

Could it be to feed the hungry
    and to clothe the poor?
How about a cure for cancer and more?

What about the rainforest?
Could one little wish protect all of that?

But after all, a wish is nothing
    more than just a wish,
Until people, like you and me
    believe and do our part to make
    the wish come true.

Janell Adaway

Entranced

So softly, tenderly
With a rare sweetness
He touched my heart.
I fell in love.

Silently he embraced me.
His eyes, full of delight
Spoke of his love for me.
I was thrilled.

His world of stillness
Oh, those wonderful eyes
Moved over my total being.
I was in love.

Never to feel those arms
Or to hear those words
Yet his love was complete.
I was entranced

Sheri S. Whitfield

The Thought

There comes a thought
    that just won't go away.

Sometimes it's so bad
    what it is, I can't say,

What it comes in my mind
    it seems it's there for good,

If only I could take it out
    trust me, that I would.

I often wonder
    how long it's been there.

For it to be constant
    doesn't seem fair.

Who can make it leave
    could it be you,

Or is there anything
    I can do?

Just to make it go and not come back.
Is what I honestly in me lack.

Debbie Higgins

At Your Age

At your age the clock
is ticking away.
Somewhere between 60 and 70
you say?
That accounts for gray hair,
the slack in your back,
the hitch in your get along,
your bones that crack,
your head in the clouds,
your mind out to lunch,
your eyes that don't see well
and wrinkles that crunch.
But don't feel bad.
You're not alone.
Age has its rewards
unless you can't reach the phone.

Ruth Ann Myers

Why

There is the word why
It asks many a question
Some answers elude me.
Time is but a measure
Of from here to there.
The meaning of time
Is as nebulous as fate.
For fate is naught but destiny.
One plans the life he lives
But time has no plan at all.
What does tomorrow bring?
Only that which yesterday foresaw.
Tomorrow seems forever
That is why it takes so long.
To synchronize the events of all
Requires many moments of today
For each must think that he thot
That he did as he did say.

Jenifer V. M. Wilcox

Untitled

Who do you see when you look at me?
Do you see the woman who is together
    and in control?
That is who I show you.
Do you see the smile, the confidence,
    the peace?
That is what I show you.
Who do you see when you look at me?
Do you see fear, the uncertainly,
    the tears I long to cry?
That is what I cannot show you.
Do you see the loneliness I feel,
    the insecurity, the need...
That is what I am afraid to show you.
Who do you see when you look at me?
A woman or a child...
One I will show you...
The other I am...

Tracie L. Dye

Untitled

The iris stands a beacon
In the cold and wet and gray
A bloom and a reminder
of summer yet to come
other hours and other times
Moments flow in passing
And same ethereal clock chimes
The flower blooms and is a reminder
Of other times and other hours

Jeanne Cooper

The Kraken

The Kraken stirs within the deep.
Awakening from his mid-night sleep.
Eons pass as he slowly stirs
Tentacles huge as conifers.
Twitching his great hypnotic eye
Hiding a force we can't defy.
I dread the day the eye will ope
For then I know there'll be no hope.
    The Kraken stirs—
      and I'm afraid.

Daniel Holquin

Happy Mother's Day

A teacher is a mother
Of a very different sort.
She helps them learn their lessons
And participate in sports.

She hugs them when it's needed,
Or scolds them when they're bad,
She helps them solve their problems,
Sympathizes when they're sad.

These things are the qualities
Of a mother, I am told.
You surely fit that pattern,
Happy Mother's Day, Rose.

Marjorie Hutchison Weber

See The Light

Why is it I am so sad
When you are always right?
Shouldn't I be most glad
Because you help me see the light?
I don't want to always be mad,
It isn't reason to pick a fight.
Since my love for you is not a fad,
Nor is it a tail on a kite
To twist and soar or make me out a cad,
But to let you know how I might
Show that I'm not so bad,
Only concerned that I stay in sight
Of the dreams for me that you had,
Which are much more than slight.

Tep Lint

Nature's Symphony

Conductor's cue- wind chimes sing.
Then the wishing of the trees.

Mountains caress the winded horn,
playing so violently.

Softly, with conductor's cue-
a quiet moment comes.

When triumphantly! the winded horn,
wakes up a nodding head.

Conductor's cue- with vibrant sounds,
of natures symphony.

With gently strokes our minds unwind,
in peace with tranquility.

Retha Waddell

Oh Boy, What A Life It's Been

I've seen life's precious jewels
From urban to rural
I've seen the mountains, the valleys
I've walked through many alleys
And, oh boy, what a life it's been

I've travelled across the nation
I've travelled to faraway lands
I've enjoyed the various cultures
From food to marching bands
And, oh boy, what a life it's been

There was something about the people
I met on the street
They were friendly and heartwarming
My heart never skipped a bet
And, oh boy, what a life it's been.

Juanita Bratcher

Blue Eyes

If good things come to those who wait,
Then I will wait forever.
If destiny is a reality,
We shall one day we together.
If love will always conquer all,
Then I can win every war.
And if my heart doesn't give enough,
My soul will give much more.
If your blue eyes don't lock to mine,
At their first glance my way,
I won't give up, won't love you less,
For my love grows each day.
And when another questions
How I could love so blind?
I always find my answer,
In the depths of your blue eyes.

Kelly Mason

Healing Is A Mirror Shattering

If yesterdays are
like today's...
lose the grit...
sacrifice the power...
abandon the protest...
allow today to slide into
tomorrow...
unencumbered...
without a trace...
lest today...
remains yesterday.

Joanna Ayers

Life's Journey

A babe is born. He knows nothing
but what he learns; a tender touch
through bathing, the babble of
language, the strange texture
of food on the tongue. He
grows—
    walking;
leg and crutch
in a hunchback
sway upon a marble
precipice— tendons,
tight as guitar strings
    groping
for knowledge—
love, honor, truth,
compassion purpose...

Anthony C. Winegar

Bath Time

Bubbles in the bathtub,
Water underneath,
Washcloth helmet on my head,
My sword of soap is sheathed.

I'm now on the battlefield
Fighting germs and dirt.
My water gun hangs by my side,
The enemy to squirt.

I have won the battle,
At least for today.
Next time I have to take a bath
I think I'll run away!

Ananda Fuller

Temptation!

The garden in the park
has many shades of red.
They are beautiful roses
in their flowery bed.

Once merely little seeds
planted in many rows.
Now, each beauty
takes an alluring pose.

I could not turn my eyes
away from one red rose.
While its sweet smell
filled my sensitive nose.

It sways back and forth
as the gusty wind blows.
Tempting me to take
this delightful red rose.

Joseph M. Snyder

Twilight

Reflections of reflections,
Dreams within dreams.
Do we see the world as it is
Or only as it seems?
Is what we see reality
Or are we deep asleep,
Dreaming of what might have been
And wishing we could keep
That warm soft sense of safety
That's ours as we slip into night,
Drifting between sleep and slumber
Under the covers, tucked in tight.

John Krajeski

Beyond The Gate

Beyond the gate
Our love ones wait
For us to meet them there
The path may seem long
But wrapped in God's love
We'll be strong
Our memories as our guide
Until we reach the other side
And go with them
   Beyond the gate

Kathleen A. McMillan

On Materials For Construction

Steel is real.
Wood is Good.
Brick is thick.
Stone adds tone.

Mohair is fair.
Glass has class.
Clay is okay,
But, sand is grand.

Glue will do,
Still, remember this to be true:
Sometimes mastic is elastic,
And plastic...is always
Spastic.

Richard N. Roberts

Please Find Time

You were there
   When your children born...
They needed you then...
   They need you now.

Please find time for them...
   For time is swiftly passing by
And we can not retrieve
   A single day
   Nor turn back
   The hands of time...

Please remember this
   And spend some time each day
Getting to know and understand
   Those who are entrusted
   to your care
And in Heaven with our Creator
   May you one day share
An eternity of bliss beyond compare.

Priscilla Davenport

Bless The Healers

Bless the Healers
Who walk by our sides
through our darkest days
and our longest nights.

Bless the Healers
who give of themselves
to all who are suffering
in pain and despair.

Bless the Healers
that they may continue
to teach and heal with
their compassion and love.

May Healers themselves
be blessed with strength and commitment
to educate us who cry out
to be healed and taught.

May the true Healers
be filled with the spirit
so they may continue
to heal and teach us all.

Judy Barner

Winter's Night Wonderland

How relaxing it is on a winter night,
   to watch the falling snow.
Powdery flakes waft through the air,
   as a chilling wind does blow.
The lingering silence following,
   when the snow ceases to fall.
Then cracking sounds of weighted trees.
   echo nature's call.
Bright golden moon's radiant glow,
   casts shadows all around.
Dancing softly in ballet.
   they silhouette the ground.
Steadily trickling water,
   from a winding silver stream.
Ice crystals upon its narrow banks,
   create hypnotic gleam.
A winter's night so peaceful,
   it's beauty one must see;
Presentation of God's wonderland,
   a gift to all that's free.

Edward.A. Nicholson

Tell Mother

Rose realized that she never knew
How much she loved her mother
Until they had taken her
To church for the last time.

Rose gazed upon her mother,
Who was so still and so silent.
O Lord, she had been so active.

Rose agonized, "Why did I not tell her
How dear and precious she was to me?
Why is my heart so tender
When her ears can no longer hear?"

Rose prayed fervently
For an unspoken bond between them
Which told her mother all the things
That she wanted to say.

Will others learn from this poem
And tell their mothers
While yet there is time?
What a blessing it would be.

Ava L. Russell-Benn

Transforming A Dream

A dream of loss,
A dream of tragedy,
A dream of darkness,
A touch of pain.
A blanket of healing,
A touch from God,
A dream of greatness,
A march of truth.

Therese M. Wheaton-Harkins

Mercy

It didn't take long
For us figure out
What my father meant, when
Due to illness
He ate his gun
And the note just said
"They shoot horses, don't they?"
He was a proud and gutsy man.

Henry A. Sarkissian

The Journey

Life starts out like a river.
When you're a baby very small,
A little brook becomes a stream.
The baby soon turns into a boy,
A stream in time is then a creek.
The boy matures into a man,
The creek inches into a raging river.
A man in years followed by old-age,
The roaring river is slowed by lakes.
The elderly man is slowed by sickness
and meets with death,
Through slowing lakes the river soon
finds its death into the ocean.

William R. McLemore Jr.

Memories

Let's find a nook by a tinkling brook,
And stop there just you and I.
Let's live again for a little while,
In the life that used to be.
And I'll paint memories for you,
While you weave dreams of me.

Tony Costa

Terminal Disease

It is almost twelve years later
But for him I still mourn
For the day he left me
A heartache was born.
A permanent heartache
That will never cease
And there is no cure
For this terminal disease.
He is forever in my mind
And not a day can go by
That I don't think of him
And try not to cry.
It is almost twelve years later
But that doesn't even matter
For time heals nothing
It only makes me sadder.
When will the pain fade?
Oh God won't you help me please?
I am so tired of suffering
From this terminal disease.

Dena Leichnitz-Amos

The Devil Is In The Corner

The devil is in the corner
  Wearing a white shirt and tie
With a grimace of a smile
  And a dented, tarnished crown.

Taunting and jesting, antagonizing
  Exchanging the truth for a lie
The hell, you say no wonder
  The devil is in the corner.

Should you dance with the devil
  You'd better be careful
'cause he'll stomp your feet
  With his hooves
If you run with him
  May not stay apace
As he runs fast and hard
  In the dark.

Behold the King of Hades
  And the root of all disorder
For a glimpse, look inside
  The devil is in the corner.

Edward Easterling

Some Day

Sunday is almost over
And I'd like to hear your voice.
The silence is unbroken
But I do not have a choice.

The sun still is shining
Even though we had some snow.
Your face in the warm photo
Does no emotional change show.

You were a warm loving man
Who wanted to fill a need.
Many times I saw you pause
And then do a helpful deed.

If only you could come back
And sit beside me as before.
It would be so very happy
To talk as in days of yore.

Someday I'll see you, honey,
In a heaven where there's no pain.
Then we will talk and laugh
And be together again.

Frances E. Tolson

Mountain

Be thankful for the mad ones
Who climb the mountain.
Each foothold, each grasp
Will be a haven
For the rest of us
Who follow.
If all of us were cowed
By our fears,
Who would challenge
The unchangeable?
Who would walk the Darkness,
—And who would harness our Terrors?

So climb you grimy bastards!
Climb the Mountain—
Covered with sweat and grit
And scared witless...
Climb... Climb!
Climb your Mountain...
Climb!
And soon perhaps we will follow!

David Glaser

Brief Encounter

Can you spare a dollar?
  I need some food
  I need a home
  I need some shoes

A dollar's enough?
  A small price
  It's better than nothing
  I can buy some rice

Where do you sleep?
  I have a box
  To lay my head
  With worn out socks

Can I do more?
  You've done enough
  You've helped the poor
  Enjoy your lunch

Can you work?
  Yes, I've tried
  I have no home
  I don't qualify.

Patricia Johnson

"Change Of Heart"

There was a time
  when every minute felt
    like hours spent apart
But how things have
  changed between us—
    a change of heart

Now absence has no meaning
  you spend quality time
    with your friends
My presence is
  a strain at best—
    I can no longer pretend

You feel the way you used to
  back when there was a time
    you loved me more than anything
But that was then
  and this is now—
    my lonely heart is aching

Sue Chesak

If I Weren't Me

What would I be, If I weren't me
Cut earthly shackles, set me free
To soar on high as eagles fly
To unbound limits in the sky.

To travel far to distant shore
To jungles deep where lions roar,
And climb the highest mountain peak
No wondrous things I would not seek.

The sights I'll see would fill my head
And softly lull me back to bed
To dream of all that I could see
What I could be, if I weren't me.

Clark S. Beardslee

Night Lights

Night lights are slowly budding
  Multiplying one by one,
Soon the streets will be dotted
  Countless, since setting of the sun.
Though I searched to count the lights
  But I could find nowhere to start.
So, in my imagination
  I hid them all inside my heart.

Then with morning came the dawn
  As all the lights began to fade,
And bringing out of hiding
  From the secret place I'd made.
Now the town will keep its lights
  While I stand by and adore,
And just enjoy the beauty of
  That, which I started with before.

Pauline Day

The Poet

Writers leads
pen's at easy
what does rhyme
pen-tameter find
freelance style
meter in line
a writer dream
what does it mean?
Cross the "T"s
a few dotted "I"s
is it true
the poet is "I"!

Robert J. DiGennaro

Guide Me

Today I ask you Dear Lord
To walk and guide me through
The burdens are so heavy,
I feel, I won't make it through
The trials I face are so tiring and
Trying but, with your help
I know that I can make it
Each day as I began afresh
I ask for your love and guidance
I seek you out to guide my ways
Sometimes less, and, sometimes more
And sometimes in various ways
Many a question you haven't answered
And you may never show me
For reasons only known by you
But, Dear Lord Jesus, you are my
Staff and stay for without you
I could never make another day.

Iva L. Foor

The Different Facets Of War's Faceless Lifestyle

Many's needs are diamond mines or rue
De Oro! - - - promissory, of course!
    Necessity's child, is politically
Feasible only when we need
    our own salvation; as waning...
Means of light, or vacuum tests
    of life-standards...versus quality!!

    Mechanical-rote is a dual
test of crusts of brittle
Cracks; as life begins,
it wanes as a sliver of
moonglow!
If knowledge breeds
Contempt, wheat and Barley Chaff
make — perhaps the meal
of Christ — without gravity!

    R. C. Miller

"Spring Tidings"

"Today we feel so happy,
Everything's going right-
The weather is clear and balmy,
The sun is shining bright."

"Spring is with us once again,
For everyone to enjoy -
We'll visit America's Playground,
We know it's the real McCoy."

"We have so many choices,
As to how we'll spend our time -
To take a stroll on the boardwalk,
It won't cost at dime."

"An ocean swim is refreshing,
And to spend time on the beach -
Do we hear the Casinos calling,
So near, and within our reach?."

"I tried my luck on this slot machine,
One special, I wanted to play -
I hit the dollar jackpot,
This big hit made my day."

    Marty Rollin

Requiem

Do come, the invitation read...
We'll meet at eight to break some bread
And greet again our long-time friend
Whose stay on earth will shortly end.

Will shortly end? But he's not old!
He's in his prime!
Can Death be bold
Enough to reap before it's time?

It cannot be! He is so young!
With melody still on his tongue.
What grim decree says life is spent
And must begin its swift descent?

We meet at eight to break our bread,
We greet our friend.
We see, instead
Of youth we thought would never end,

A sea of strangers gathered, all
With faces we can scarce recall,
Who once were young and bold. Like he
We face our own mortality!

    Shan Shipp

Political Quicksand

Rhythmic flutterings
    Sophisticated utterings
Unearthly stuttering
    Abnormal muttering
Clammy shuddering
    Political buttering
Congressional puttering
    Presidential cuttering
World falling
    Into itself.

    Giula S. Wiggs

My Terrible Life

Mourning and weeping
Crying and seeping;
These are all signs
of dying, but dangerous minds.

Parents try
friends shut you out,
You have tried
so die without a doubt.

Live long and prosper
Live everyday to its full,
for tomorrow you might be gone
But for today, just live and pray.

    Christian J. Williams

Small World

Yes, I know you
Though we never crossed paths before
You're the people we live among
But never get the chance to meet
You're the people we hear about
Everyday on the news
You're the statistics we read about
Throughout our textbooks
You're the face we see
On the cover of a magazine
I know you're out there
Living, breathing, surviving
The day to day struggles that await you
I know this
Because I'm out there too
Just like you
Waiting for the next battle
In which to overcome

    Lisa Arnone

One Can — Pass — The Guards

If he knows the parts,
One can go in
    with a grin.
If he knows where to go
    and in what door.
Or if he could wait at the right gate.
If he knew where to run
    in case a guard come,
If he knew he was strong
    even in doing wrong,
Or he can sneak in the dark
    and make a dog bark!
One can pass a guard with care
    and end up in the electric chair?

    Lois Wilson

Full Circle

He plowed the fields when only seven
Amazingly—so young was he

Stayed in school, earned his degree
Scholarly—so smart felt he

He took a bride in '65
Devotedly—so pledged was he

Became a Soldier 'til '67
Honorably—how tall felt he

Accepted work in a factory
Methodically—so wise was he

The plant closed down in '95
Inwardly—so scared was he

Searched for work to no avail
Tragically—"Too Old" was he

He plowed the fields at fifty three
Finally—at peace was he

    Carole S. Schulz

Farewell To Zora

For a lady so warm,
    In a day for the cold.
For a lady so caring,
    With that she will hold.
For a lady so loving,
    Ever willing, ever able.
For a being so rare,
    And Zora is her label.
Farewell.

    John Gatchell Jr.

Heritage

Why did we have to grow
I'm not saying physically
But expanding our minds
And killing our heritage

My heritage is not the best
But the way I was taught
I was not to steal or take
Without my asking permission.

So why did the soldiers
Decide to take and steal
All the land the Indians owned
And never kept their deal.

They've destroyed a heritage
That could have grown and taught us
How to live a simple life
That would have grown and shown us.

That heritage is now gone
You can't find that again
The days that were so simple
Have painfully come to an end.

    Julie Pope

A Summer Storm

The clouds turn dark gray
The rain falls quick and hard.
The wind gets very fast
I hope the storm won't last.
The summer air is warm and sweat,
The grass is wet beneath my feet.
The summer storms are very short,
Helping flowers grow of every sort.

    Dominic Bombace

Names

Names what are they?
Names what do they mean?
Names what are they for?

Names are to identify you.
Names mean many things.
Names are for you to know yourself.
If we didn't have a name no one would
Know who they were talking to.
Names

Heather A. Schuchhardt

Sometimes

Sometimes.....
I like to sit alone in the
silence and think.
Then I can make up rhymes,
And give water for my soul
to drink.

I feel a certain freedom,
A warmth from the Holy Spirit.
Accomplishment that comes,
No other feeling can come near it.

And when the night grows long,
And sleep is not at hand;
All the worries are gone.
I am touched by God's hand.
And I am caught up in
Heaven's song;
Now we all can understand.
It's a world where we all belong;
God's perfect plan.

Bill Fleming

Love They Lack

Love your enemy,
Like he is your brother.
Love your foe,
Like she is your Mother.

Love a rebel,
Like your closest kin.
Love every man,
No matter what his sin.

Love the dictator,
Who scars your back.
They aren't wicked,
It's love they lack.

It's love they crave,
And attention they want.
And when they don't have it,
They tease and taunt.

Give them attention,
Give them love.
And you'll be rewarded,
In Heaven above.

Trisha Famisaran

"In Memory Of
The Oklahoma City Tragedy"

For those who are lost,
  we mourn you
For those who are left,
  we are here for you.

Brian P. Nichols

Dusk

Above the water and the wave,
The time of night the sun does pave,
Moving further to touch the lake,
The end of day this scene does make.

A gentle wind flows through the air,
Removing one from all his care,
Twilight comes to the beach,
Placing stars within one's reach.

A feeling pervades the inner soul,
A calm speaks of the greater whole,
All is now within our sight,
Stars and sun forever bright.

Frank K. Kovac

Peace

Confusion.
That's what the world unveils.
Fights, bickering, judgment calls,
Prejudice and betrayals.
All this hatred in the world-
What does it bring?
More hate, more confusion
Why can't we see equals
Instead of inferior and superior?

No one is forcing you.
Do what is right, not always popular.
You can make a difference
As a single person,
A single thought,
A single voice.
Everything starts with someone,
Why not let peace start with you?

McKensy Gruelle

The Golfer's Prayer

Lord, please make the day a golden one,
  Balmy, bright and still.
No rain upon the fairways fall,
  No snow upon the hill.

Help my old bones move
  In fluid continuity
And help me groove the perfect swing
  In perpetuity.

Help me remember all the rules,
  And keep my muscles strong
To hit the ball a "country mile"
  Through fairways wide and long.

And when I hit those irons
  So clean and crisp and true,
To chip close on the green,
  Lord, I'll give praise to you.

When I sink that long, long putt,
  I'll really be in clover...
Happiness is a good golf game,
  My cup runneth over!

Virginia Cremens

Untitled

Lips salted from tears
Kissed in trembling fear.
Love lost, passing or near.

Ken Davis

Reminisce

I remember mother well
And the story she would tell
Of little Red Riding Hood,
And that children must be good.

Three in bed, quite at home,
We were never left alone;
There was also Granny,
Looking just as merry.

The next story was the Beggar Girl,
The saddest soul in the world;
Her tresses were matted
And her clothes tattered.

"Tell us another!"
Cried us to Mother,
But she look her head
And said that it was late.

We then began to pray,
Thanking God for a perfect day;
And hugging Mother and Granny tight,
We kissed them good-night.

Irene T. Xavier

List To The Sound

List to the sound of yesterday
  Oh heed its becoming call
For footsteps have passed before you
  And lamented their young men's fall.

Why say ye this I ask you
  Why look to portals past
For life is full with songs to sing
  The revelry of youth will last.

You age old drones, your time is gone
  Your ageless wisdom withered
Think, listen I in bud of youth
  Nay, never say I never.

Tis time to sing and frolic
  In light of moon I'll bask
For I am full of life's embrace
  My time on earth is cast.

Oh, list I pray thee listen
  I was you so long ago
Learn from mistakes of yesteryear
  And peace our world will know.

Patricia Martens

Untitled

A magistrate knocked at my door,
Forwarding questions.
There are none, was my reply:
Except a lad, a teacher,
Those documents on the wall;
And of course the deeds...
And who are you, to ask me why?
Well a magistrate
Then knock.

Michele M. Mena

"The 'Nam Wall"

If you could see what I hear
if you could hear what I see
you discovered LSD
  a Lonely
   Soldier
    Dead...on the Wall

Donna Gabusi

Beetles

Beetles alight,
   Scan the view;
      Mandibles set,
         Start to chew.

Palps to help them
   Hold on tight,
      They devour the fruit.
         Then they take flight.

Coleen Potter

Milo Seed And Millet Grain

I kept the feeder high
Filled against the wintry sky
When sleet or snow sought to dwell
I brushed it off so well.

Milo seed and millet grain
All to hear a song again

On my lips sweet words to say,
Chick-a-dee and Blue Jay -
Yes, I know every name
Of those found at feeder frame.

Well I know every song
That was still the winter long
And how well I know that I
Must feed the birds that fly

And give to my winged friends
Every succor that sends
Spirits strong into spring
With numinous songs to sing.

Milo seed and millet grain
All to hear a song again

Francine Madeleine Tyler

To Mother

Where is the end
My oldest friend
inside you and her I grew
Is it true
there is no end
Life is but made anew
Is life not love
and love be old
preceding all that is
I must believe
mine began again
When you
through her
met His.

P. Gundunas

Some Time

Some warm moonlit night
We will walk hand in hand -
On the beach in the sand
With you by my side -
We will listen to the tide
And as the waves roll in -
And hug the shore
They still come back -
For more and more
So will we sometime.

Catherine V. Holahan

I'm Strong

Don't get me wrong when I say
I'm strong. You see I'm a
Cradle Mother, African black,
made, shaped, and molded out
of the muddy Nile River bed.

I'm a challenge. I'm a wind.
I'm a whirlwind. I face the
east and the sun rises to new
creations and new life. I turn
toward the west. The sun sets
bringing rest and sometimes death!

Don't get me wrong when I say
I'm strong. My African red blood
runs through your veins, too. The
color red is the same. Do you
really care if we share this
planet earth?

Lucille R. Willis

Sudden Changes

Looks maybe deceiving.
I once heard,
I didn't believe
Most people don't.
But it happens.
Dreams turned into nightmares.
Love turned to hate.
Wishes don't come true,
Though we'd like to believe.
Everything's a fantasy
Or not.
Nothing is real
Nothing's the truth.
But we love to believe.
Hope keeps us alive
But it's not even there.
We want everything
But when we go,
We take up six feet and a stone.

Eleni Andreou

That Winter

When Aunt Harriet taught me
How to bake
Oatmeal cookies for Valentine's day
She advised:
   Avoid Churchmen
   They brag, they boast
   But can't wonder
   about life in an orphanage
   'cause they've never known
   a disadvantaged life

   These Holy Men
   Can't dream, either
   For their hearts
   Are within white Mercedes
   in some parking lot
Don't have any other anchor

D. A. Dawn Stegenga

Icicles

Gleaming with great pride
Drip, drip, drip, melting away
in the blazing sun.

Jennifer Jia

Friend

Squirry, Squirry come out to play
It's the start of a brand new day
Move closer, stay awhile
Pretty soon you'll see me smile
Wag that tail, sit a spell
You sure are looking well.
Don't be afraid, I don't bite
I'll try to pet you with all my might
Ah! Stop that running!
You really are cunning!
So long for now;
I'll see you tomorrow
When you'll take away my sorrow.

Barbara A. Nichols

Being Alone

It's like the crying of a child...
   The dying of a friend...
It's like a child without a friend...
   The gangs and all the violence...
It's like the divorce of a family...
   The beating sound of sadness...
It's like the racism in the world...
   The hate and the crime...
   Being Alone

Jacqui Ashley Sheehan

Alone

The day he died
He was filled with gloom
He walked the floor from room to room
No one came and no one called
Friends were scarce
But he stood tall
I'll take one pill and try to sleep
But all he did was weep and weep
Oh what the heck
I'll take one more
He never made it to the door
Darkness came so quick that day
No one cares much anyway.

Sandra White

My Heart

My heart aches
every time I look
at you. Every time
you look at some
one new. My heart
aches for you.
When I look at
you I feel so
blue. Oh my heart
aches for you.

Amber Lynn McClintock

"Take Time"

Take time to speak a loving word,
where loving words are seldom heard.
It will linger in the mind
   And gather others of its kind

Till loving words will always echo
while the heart is poor and bare
somewhere on the heavenward track
their music come echoing back.

Lisa Carpenter

Sun Set

I set on the sandy beach
I hear the waves splash
Against the rock.
I smell the fresh air.
I watch the flickering stars above.
I feel the wind blowing my hair.
I set and watch the sun set.
Again I smell the fresh air.
I hear the wind.
I hear the waves splashing.
The sun set is gone.
The stars aren't flickering.
I don't smell the fresh air.
I wonder was it just a dream.

Kristy Linda Monize

A College Student's Summer

Summer, a time, a season
When childhood reappears
And I am home doing what
I did long ago.

Summer, a time, a season
When I stop to examine the
changing essence of my life
And the beauty of my definition,
My home,
my parents,
my town,
my old friends,
myself.

I need this time, this season
For it helps me to step
forward, into the other seasons
of my life.

Lyuba Sesay

One Night Stand

You desire an answer -
And I care not to respond.
For today will never be yesterday.

I should have said no -
Yet the feelings were so right.
What we had is now a memory.

Don't just stand there -
And ask for another yesterday.
Just let me gather my things and leave.

Jeffrey A. Hall

ON HAVING MET YOU

Crucified by the pain of existence
    on this tree of time
  we gush out our lives joyfully
    TOUCH
      MINGLE
          AND PASS ON
    taking each with the other
      our separate way
        till in eternity
    we are **BOUND**!

William J. Louis

Jesus's Return

Jesus is coming back someday,
In all God's glory and power;
   So we must all be ready,
For we do not know the hour,

And all of those that know Him,
They will be so surprised;
   When they behold their Savior,
Ascending from the heavenly skies.

Every tongue it will confess,
And every knee will bow;
   When Jesus tells His children,
"Your redemption day is now."

He's coming down from heaven,
From His Father's home above;
   To rule the New Jerusalem,
With his light and with His love.

Kathleen A. Vigue

Three Cinquains For A Friend

Cinquain 1

Editor,
Inventive, creative;
Designing, redacting, rewriting.
Fills one with admiration!
Expert.

Cinquain 2

Gleams white,
Angled for speed.
Zigging, zagging, zipping.
My friend making a break for it?
Fast car.

Cinquain 3

White car,
Truncated trunk.
I see this car everywhere.
My heart leaps up — is it my friend's?
Wrong car.

Alice D. Firgau

Baby Brother

You followed me everywhere
when you were small
and made me laugh
as you grew tall

Then one day
you went out fishing
How could you
end up missing?

Sister called to tell me
that you had drowned
Sorrow fell
over our hometown

I always thought
that you'd be near
I can't believe
you're no longer here

Eileen Stone

A World For Two

Love is this sharing

A world for two,
Awake,
Or sleeping,
Together renewed each moment,
Infinite in proof,
Truth's diurnal presence
Of word, smile, touch,
Equal need,
And equal giving,
Ambiance of nurturing desire,
Feast of mind,
Remembered music,
Beloved books,
Names,
Tremulous with beauty,
And haunting sensuality
Of intimate joy

Love is this sharing.

Bill West

Friendship

Friendship is a lovely thing
And makes my heart
   joyfully sing.

Friendship is golden as the sunrise,
That adorns our glorious azure skies.

Friendship is a state of bliss
and precious as a lover's kiss.

Friendship is always inspiring
and never will be tiring
Oh, Friendship is a lovely thing
Like dew on a flower in spring.

Mildred E. Stacey

An Angel

I look upon the faces
Of everyone I see,
And wonder if one could be
The angel meant for me.

An angel's right beside us
With His protection to bestow,
To help us and to guide us
On a path that we should go.

You cannot see an angel
On just an ordinary day,
But trust that he is with you
As you journey on your way.
An angel cannot help you
If you do wrong and sin,
Ask God to fill your heart with love
Your angel's favor you will win.

If ever there is someone
In need that you should see,
Give a helping hand without question
To them an angel you will be.

Kathryn Marnell

Untitled

Eyespoken she tells me,
Roselips unfolding,
She breathes of summers past
in winter's presence

(you know,
there's April in my glaciers
and the storm blows fierce outside
and the clouds obscure my Vision
and the trellis grows Inside
It feeds upon my skin
and wishes to bury me in a winter's
blanket of snow
But although it welcomes me I can't let go
And there is April in my glaciers
and I want the melting snow
to drench and quench my garden
and drink my roses grow)

Victoria Sebanz

Beauty On The Beach

As I sit here on the beach,
The waves rush to the shore,
The sun is warm upon the sand,
The sea shouts her mighty roar.

The birds are sailin' through the air,
So peacefully, so free,
It seems they have stilled themselves,
To take a look at me.

I know they cannot read my words,
Nor, know what's on my mind,
It seems they are showing me,
All is good and kind.

This is the perfect place for me,
To let my spirit run,
To absorb all the beauty,
Beneath the glistenin' sun.

Now the sun is setting,
The moon soon takes its place,
The stars are dancin' freely,
To God's amazing grace.

Charlene J. Hatton

The Beast Of Nature

Fifty pounds of iron
Found twenty feet wide
Spread across the beach
Brought in by the tide
But try to get people
To come forward, maybe change
Stop pollution of our waters,
The mountains and our plains
For I crossed this great nation
From mountains west to the cities east
Been far north and traveled south
And found humans the true beast

Michael D. Wilson

Pressed Flower

I have fenced in my heart
I don't feel the pain and hurt.
You mowed down my ideas
I have closed the gate.
There isn't a future
No room to grow
I am wilted
Crushed

Linda Harju

A Tragic Play

I think of Shakespeare
Love that is but cannot be,
I think of Shakespeare
When I think of you and me.

Inflamed with passion
Unquenching thirst
Separated by life
As if by birth.

Our hearts cry out.
To this soundless void,
How can sweet love
Be so unrejoiced.

I think of Shakespeare
Sweet love that cannot be,
I think of Shakespeare
Sweet tragedy.

Rohan Hall

The Essence Of Life

Look into my eyes and see
A world that's forever changing.
Watch as the night blankets the sun,
Its light slowly dwindling.

Feel the very pulse of life
Thrumming through your veins in awe
Of the moon rising above the darkness
With stars at its beck and call.

Hear the music of the wind
Whispering among the trees
Its songs gently touching your heart,
And calming the raging seas

Taste the sweet breath of God
Washing the world anew.
Its waters softly cleansing your soul
As morning's rays fall upon you.

Neil Daniell

"Random Haiku's"

The sun rose today
As it has done everyday
For all of my life

I hear that music
Notes floating through the air
Patterns on the wind

Their music changed
My life forever, them never
Knowing how it changed

I loved the way
He took the pain, bit his lip
And went on with life

Running ever from it
Man cannot stand in its way
Fear, Anger, Defeat, Death

Arwen LeQuieu

Rabbits

The rabbits have long ears
and in them there are little pink dots.

I like rabbits very much.
I am never going to shoot one.
I love them.

Matthew Krom

House Call

Feelings
flushed down
form a
clogged drain
foul-smelling
functionless
awaiting the
plumber's
plunger
performing physical
therapy on the
paralyzed
debris turning
turbid but
alive!

Benita Rose

I Feel

Love, hate, happiness,
sadness, pain and sorrow,
these feelings can't describe
how I feel for you

When I'm with you the clouds
smile does my heart
Good is what I feel when I'm
with you

The Gods of the sky and air
don't understand how it feels
to make love to you here and
there

What I feel is total bliss when
I'm with you and I know you feel it

Donte Williams

The Greatest Gift

The greatest gift of all
Won't be found in a store
If you're lucky enough to find it
You'll appreciate life more

People have searched for it
Since the dawn of recorded time
But the ones who seem to find it
Are the ones who are always kind

Some people think they've found it
And that may or may not be true
I think that when you're ready
The greatest gift finds you

If you find the greatest gift
You'll want to dance and sing
Take extra special care of it
For it's a very wondrous thing

You may wonder what it is
So I'll tell you the honest truth
The greatest gift of all is love
And I'd like to share it with you

Jeffrey Glenn Ayers

Love

Love is the color white for purity.
Love smells like a precious rose.
Love tastes like a sweet ice cream.
Love sounds like sweet poetry.
Love feels like a gentle kiss.

Rachael Zebrowski

Imagination Land

Reach out and take my hand
and come with me into a place
where people seldom go today,
Imagination Land.
Where ideas grow upon the trees
instead of leaves,
and thoughts plucked from a branch
turn into story tapestries,
woven thread by thread from
the material of one's mind,
whose endless depths we probe
to see what we might find.
You'll find no T.V. sets, computers,
or other forms
of man's communication.
All that exists
in this vast land
is one's imagination.

Audrey Robinson

Deadly Night

An owner, yet a proloner
As dark as the night,
swift as an eagle's flight.
It creeps up on you,
as quiet as can be.
Just let it in,
and you will see.

Prolonging for the ways
you left it there before.
Now it wants back in,
and is clawing at the door.

You sit crouched tight,
in the corner silently despair.
Try to ignore the pain, which is
so much more than you can bear.

And through the night,
everyone hears you scream.
Then you wake up and realize,
that it was only a dream.

Erica Moorhouse

Just A Kiss

Oh yes, this young man from Camden
Liked to kiss girls with abandon,
She said "this isn't fair,
You messed my hair,
Just do not take me at random!"

The next night he came without fail
Saw her sister, an adorable frail.
And so just in spite
The following night
The naughty "Mr. Kstr Sistr".

Irving I. Verter

"Betrayed"

Pain running down my face
Sorrow in the sound of my voice
Anger shining through my eyes
Confusion in my heart
Doubt in my mind
Yet I hold my head up high
As I stride with grace
Stunned by grief
Scorned by a love lost

Nefertiti Mimmitt

A Pet's Prayer

I cannot let you grieve for me
For those who love must let us go.
In comfort, please believe I'm free
From all the pain life can bestow.

As I begin my world anew,
Consider not what used to be.
I'm sending happy smiles to you
While I enjoy eternity.

Lord, bless the home from which I came
Yet brush each lonely hour away
With fond remembrance of my name
And sunshine for a newer day.

Rosann York

Since The First Time I Saw You...

Since the first time I saw you
I knew you were the one
I'd want to spend my life with
Until the end of time.
You always make me smile
You always make me laugh
You are always there for me
In the good times and the bad.
I'm giving you my heart
So don't treat it like a toy
Take care of it and love it
And give it lots of joy.

Susanna Coronel

The Littlest Angel

Into the world came
    sweet Becky D.,
Looking as cute as
    she ever could be.
Lots of black hair and
    big eyes so dark,
No doubt about it
    she'll make her mark.
At 6 lbs and 10, she's the
    smallest one yet.
Tho' little, she's feisty,
    like her mother? you bet!
And Steve, he's so proud
    his buttons are bursting.
For this moment he's been
    a long time rehearsing.
And Grandpa and I are
    as pleased as can be
To welcome Rebecca
    to our family.

Kathleen C. Wendowski

Soldier

A soldier marches on in war
Never fearing what is ahead
Facing rain and storm with his
Fellowmen leading the way
On to victory they soar with hope
In their hearts for a safer world
Tomorrow will be a better day
When the flag to victory sways
May God bless all our soldiers
Who made our country what it is
Today

Charlotte Burke

On Observing Comet Hyakutake

In the evening when it's dark,
Look up into the sky - -
When you find the larger dipper,
You will note a comet is nearby.

In order to observe it well,
Keep away from shining light
For you'll find this distant comet,
Isn't really very bright.

For this celestial heavenly body
With its fuzzy-looking head,
Looks more and more just like
A dull, hazy mass instead.

They say this comet first was seen
By an astrologer from Japan.
So thus it was named Hyakutake
After this observant man.

I'm glad for all great wonders
God placed up in the sky.
We may observe their beauty,
If we only look on high.

Geraldine Borger

Quiet Rain

The sound of a quiet rain
in the midst of a hot summer's day.
So pleasant to hear
a song to the ear
like sweet music, coming your way.

A cloudburst releases
tiny droplets today.
Blossoms appear,
renewed life is clear,
to all that had wilted away.

The sun now is shining,
the day crisp and bright.
Things seem refreshed,
as tho they'd been blessed.
A few remaining dewdrops delight.

N. Loy Higgins

Fearless

A ball of fire
That zigzags through the night
Rounding, winding to the last fight
Faster and faster
It turns around
Again and again
Like it knows no fear

Soundless, quietness
It flies through the night
No worries to conquer
No hatred to fight
It scatters faraway
As it only has one flame
To guide it the rest of the way
Fear is its prey

Paula Cary

The Squirrel And The Nut

The squirrel scampers about
Gazing in and gazing out,
Hollows in the trees
Hark! A sudden breeze,

Sees the nut break free
Falling from the tree,
Wisp of wind whirls it high
Squirrel sees his dinner fly.

The nut falls upon the road
Sitting silent as a toad,
Squirrel moves in for the kill
Soon to eat his tasty meal.

Speeding car squeals to brake
But, alas, it is too late;
Nothing left but squish and bone.
Squirrel and nut both are gone.

Wanda Atkins Almodova

Love Is A Gamble

Love is a gamble
Love is a game
Boys do the nasty
Girls take the blame.
9 months of pain
Sitting in the hospital
With a baby to name
Boys say you're cute
Boys say you're fine
But when the baby
Comes they say it's
Not mine.

Marian Mariani

Best Friends

We've been best friends
As the years have slipped by.
There for each other
Whether clear or stormy sky.

We've been through a lot,
A lifetime I'd say.
Sharing and caring
Day after day.

We've had our share of rough times,
Troubles with a capital "T"
But I was always there for you
And you've been there for me.

We made lots of memories,
Some better than others.
But they're all part of this life
That we've shared with one another.

I'm glad that you're my buddy
As we journey through the years.
"Forever Friends" we'll always be
Through all our smiles and tears.

Fay L. Willis

Sea Of Life

As we sail down
   The Sea of Life
Storms and gales
   May arrive
But with God's Help
   We'll Survive
And reach the
   BRIGHT HORIZON

Dianne Modglin

Hope Springs Eternal

What is this time -
   when hints of new life
   haunt the emotion?
Vague pastels flow among
   stilled branches.
And formerly inert brooks
   bubble warm with
   suppressed excitement?
How is it that -
   the sky now contains
   undiscovered shades of blue?
And newly released birds will
   soon give birth to
   an explosion of color?
Is this the answer to the
   perennial riddle of the
   pathos to eros transformation?
And what could revive man's
   essence of perception more than
   the gentle hand of spring?

Brendan B.

Little Girl

Little girl so very new,
With shining eyes,
And face so clear,
Our love is yours you little maid.

Of hope and peace,
Your name shall speak,
Our joy is yours to keep,
Now doors of love will open here.

Little soul, little heart,
With love and tender care,
Your angel guards you every day,
And guides you on your way.

Nadine E. Moonje Pleil

The Twins

Two pretty little girls,
Who are only five years old.
One with soft brown hair,
The other with hair of gold.

One has pretty blue eyes.
The other softest brown.
And two happy smiling faces,
That seldom wear a frown.

With skin as brown as berries
From playing in the sun -
They look like little Indians,
And they're always having fun.

There's never a dull moment
With these two imps around.
But mommy wouldn't trade them
For any other girls in town.

So give them plenty of love each day,
For too soon they leave the fold.
There are many things money can buy,
But love is more precious than gold.

Kathy Gordon

The Flowers

Await with nosegay in hand
for life to enter
and death to depart
The Flowers
line our path with wedding blooms
and bow to Spring's return;
rain droplets fall into cupped petals
and nurture the woodland.
The Flowers
give the feeling of pleasure
and fill senses with the
symphony of sway.
The Flowers
color the land,
color the spirit,
color the soul.

Carol Polacek

"Tears Of Pride"

If I should find
A love that be so true
I would only pray
That it be with you

I never wanted, in my life
To be single again
My life was my love for you
God has punished my sins.

It came softly to me
While I watched the water
She was the one
The only one I'd love forever

Together as one soul
Was how we started
Now it seems as though
I'm the only one broken hearted.

I wish I could have said
"I love you" then, "goodbye"
Yet I was too proud to let her see
The tears fall from my eyes.

Sylvia M. Pohlot

My Phantom Lover

I have a phantom lover, who lives
within my heart. No one else can see
him, but we two shall never part.

He creates a lovely rainbow and
makes dark clouds fade from sight,
then caresses me in a special way
and lights the darkest night.

He is always in my wildest
dreams, and with my passions he does
abide. Oh, foolish one, he often says
but stays close by my side.

Unbelievers say he is just a
phantom, but he brings me joy when
I am blue, so I'll go on loving him,
be honest wouldn't you?

Nadine Sharpe

Ode To Nature

When the sun is shining
And the sky is blue,
When the clouds are puffy
And the world looks new.

It's time to look up
To the heavens above,
And know it has been done
All in the name of love.

The rivers and valleys
The clear mountains streams,
All have their place
In His great scheme.

The oceans, the forest,
The mountains and trees,
The flowers and grass,
The butterflies and bees,

The worm, the snake,
The alligator and fleas,
There's always some beauty
In all the eye sees.

Ruth Arentina Schofield

Whisper

She whispers to you, but
still you cannot hear, every word she utters.
She whispers again, but this time
in your ear.
To let you know how much
she really cares.
The whispers of the mellow sea.
The gentle kisses in the breeze.
Scented petal roses that smell so pretty.
So soft and so airy.
She whispers all that she feels in her heart.
The whispers of her endless feelings,
to last you an eternity...

Cindy Toy

"Children Beyond"

Children beyond its reaches, peaces
it its laughter. It lost between.
Understanding of its faith, of reasons
why. Hope within the eyes of sight
in views of the crosses of roads
within its own time, children beyond.
Of its deepest light. Hoping with the
knowledge of wisdom truth and trust
of whom they are beyond.

Mitchell Brockington

Tornado!

Roaring!
Twisting!
Garbage can powerhouse!
Originator of nightmare phantasms!
Creation holocaust!
Blasting obliviator
Of humid afternoons!
Get out!
Get out!
Seek shelter elsewhere!
Nature's sickle
An impartial harvester.
Howl —
Hossana!
Hossana!

Madeline F. Weaver

Going Home

I'm going home
The world has kept me
At her feet too long
Shut me out
Only to let me look in
From the outside
To see
But not to touch
So I'm going home
Where the teacups are cracked
And the floor boards are warped
Where I can feel the imperfections
Instead of idly standing by.
Watching others overlook them

Christian Piccolo

Music

I am a mysterious language;
I am mastered by only a few;
I know of no places
Where I may proclaim
My thoughts and my feelings
And fail to gain people's acclaim.
I please young and old
Who are willing to listen
To that which I offer
From the depth of my heart.
I am Magic. I am Labor.
I am Hope and a Promise.
I will be yours,
If you try and never give up.
I am Love.
I am endless Endeavor.
Let me in,
To be part of your ultimate Being.
I want to, for ever,
Be yours from the start.

Norman Kertzman

Fireflies

Fireflies know not
The arbitrary measure
Of moments, nor
The concept of days
That are numbered
They jewel the night
Like stars in miniature
Luminous invitations
To couple, likewise to fall
In glowing arcs and spirals
Across the ink
They dance designs.

We were silent watching
Our eyes like moons at midnight
As I held you, a clock
With broken hands
Ticked each soft second
You were mine.

Elisabeth Marren

Clouds

Clouds come in wisps
In the baby blue sky
Talking softly with the wind
Floating by.

Singing to the ground far below
In a gentle voice
That you must know.

Morgan Asher

Recreation

In a room not my own
looked in the glass
saw not me— you
Okay once more
looked in the glass
saw not you—her
Certainly not
expected

Through the kaleidoscope
expecting a rainbow
found clay instead
Creating
not a dutiful adobe pot
not a beautiful marl urn
not you
not her
me
certainly
Not expected

Cynthia Valdivia

"The Hatred Of Man"

From yonder comes the hatred of man
With death at its hand
spreading hatred across the land.

As it stroll
glitters the sword to smite the soul
all of hatred it shall moll
to a configuration
lasting generations.

A task it shall seek
to devour the strong and the weak.

To bring about change
but only to suit the lame.

Billy E. Harris

Dying

Your soul flies up in Heaven
Softly lies down.
It's not bad.
It is good.
You see a bird
You see a plane.
Then you lie down
On your big white pillow.
So soft, so cozy
And so white.
Dying is not bad.
Sometimes a little sad
But don't be mad.

Jennifer Comblo

The Heart

The most predominate symbol of love
The dark raven and the blue-white dove

It is the sponge of the human soul
And the life of you as a whole

It is as fragile as an angel's wing
It is as strong as the devil's sting

Through its veins runs an evil juice
The devil is near when it's cut loose

You need one for your heavenly start
It....is the beautiful heart

Clay Wosnuk

Moment

Inside her eyes...time stood still.
How long did we stare?
Was it mine...or combined will?
Did we really share?

I know we share...if only that moment
....Eternity stood still.
In radiant glory...she magnificent
Did all my desire fulfill.

Ron Orr

Jealous Sun

Through half drawn blinds
Its light touches my cheek
Time scoots the moon along
Soon it must retreat
Then I rise
To face a new day
A jealous sun
Has chased the moon away.

Keith Brown

The Reticulated Giraffe

I have a very awesome height,
Which means I am not very light.
My legs are like 6-foot stilts,
Which help me from having tilts
My neck is even longer than my legs,
So you better watch out for my head.
With my long neck I can feed on leaves,
Beyond the reach of leaf thieves.

Urooj Jawed

Pine Knoll Shores

So calm, so sunny
so unhurried
such hot day for May

Sandy beach, wet from lapping waters
Filled with footprints
birds and humans passing this way

Sea shells, various sizes
covered and uncovered
by the tides on this day

Older adults, mid-lifers too
surrounded by children
parents alert as they play

Fishermen — on the pier
Surfers catching the swell
riding the waves without delay

Suntan lotion, the magic potion
rubbed into the skin
safe browning, hurray hurray

Relaxation, with no demands
what else need one say!

Lila Gilbert Kuehnert

Mother (My Audience)

A light directs itself towards me-
It penetrates me.
I find that it follows my movements.
It's solid loyalty somehow justified.

I realized it's engagement-
And in the end-
I know I am not alone.

Jayson Westfall

Awakening

A rose is such a lovely flow'r
Its petals when they spread
Give artists what they need to paint
In gold and white and red.

So love itself when truly seen
Can be expressed in ways
That magnify as does the rose
Exposing splendid rays.

Christ's love is even more empow'rd
Because of Calvary
Where giving all was meant to show
God's love for you and me

Anne M. Nymann

Untitled

If moms were yellow, mine would be
As golden as the sun.
So full of light and fun and joy
To shine on everyone.

If moms were red, then mine would be
As scarlet as a rose;
But twice as sweet and petal soft
To everyone she knows.

If moms were white, then mine would be
like snowflakes in the night
That come down soft and gentle
Close to earth and feather light.

If moms were blue, then mine would be
As bright as summer sky;
Clear and true and cheerful
To each one that passes by.

But if I could draw the perfect mom
And choose from any hue,
I'd paint her with a rainbow
And the color would be you.

Kathy Tayon

"Horton"

To anyone who might ever care
I hope one day maybe I can share
The ship in the bottle locked so tight
That sails the same seas every night

The destination always the same
Back into the bottle from which it came
Anchor dropped ever so harshly
To let it bother I try it partially

Time passes to rot the ships wood
In every way anon it should
To escape the window which enclosed
Another page of time will unfold

To anyone who might ever care
That of which I can never share

Nathan Slater

Karma And Reincarnation

You were
Here
"Yesterday"
You are here
"Today"
What will you
Become
"Tomorrow"?

John Clifford Welch

The Death Bell

Death camps and killing,
no people were willing,
silently the death bell rings.

Children crying,
people dying,
silently the death bell rings.

Angry shouts from behind iron bars,
men transported away in cars,
silently the death bell rings.

It called Jews and Poles to the grave,
mothers and children tried to be brave,
silently the death bell rings.

People hung on gallows like sacks,
Deep marks on a bare prisoners backs,
silently the death bell rings.

Why such a brutal Holocaust,
men, women and children lost,
silently the death bell rings.

Jessica Moore

Ship In A Bottle

I feel weighed down,
trapped and frustrated,
with no direction,
or identity.

I am surrounded by glass,
Only to be looked at.

I have no individuality.
I am just a clone, that was patiently
thought of.

Andrea Sharby

Deception

Sweet lover, disclose
the moments of heresy
as dreams fade
into malignant hopes.
There's no forerunner
to expose desire.
Live in darkness
as the sagging moon
plummets the past
waning wanton wishes.
Starlight slips slowly
into casual castration.
Daylight penetrates
a betrayed horizon
embracing a day
that dawns immobile.
Desolation looms
over the morning.

Carol M. Ludovissy

Can You See Me?

Can you see me, do you know?
Will you see me in a show.
Lights around me, none to share,
Times of greatness in the air.

I'm an actress, yes, I am.
And you've got to understand
That an actress isn't free!
But your presence is the key.

Cassandra Lind

Snow Snow

Snow snow
Blows and blows
I don't care if
it bites my nose.

Grandpa's out
catching racoons
Under the bright
and distant moon.

Grandma's out side
feeding Mitsey
looks around and
can't find Fritsey.

Grandma's itchen
To be in the kitchen
She's making bread
that nobody dreads.

Justin Lohmann

Through Death's Dark Door

My heart is sad, I can feel the pain
Of the map faced beggar, shedding
Rain.
With cupped hands round a
Borrowed smoke, a never ending
Rawness constricts his throat.
A mind befuddled by last night's
Wine, half forgotten memories of
Better times.
The fear of living in the streets,
The longing of sleeping on tide
Smelling sheets -
The memories of feeling soft
Round curves
The shudder of his pain wracked Nerves.
He drops the butt between his feet
And staggers blindly into the street.
The rain and memories he will feel no
More - as he is hurled forever
Thru deaths dark door

Waynard Ridge Jr.

Slalom Race

Uphill
  Downhill
Small thrill
  Big thrill

Left turn
  Right turn
Windburn
  Legs Burn

Black skiis
  Two skiis
White Trees
  Pine Trees

Tuck down
  Look down
Ski race
  First place!

MacKenzie E. Hanna

The Pain Of Glass

The window:
a pain of glass,
a barrier separating me
From the outside world.
Holding me back,
containing my freedom.
The sight of blue skies
and a flaming sun
tortures me,
for I cannot breathe the air
or feel the golden warmth
waiting just outside.
If only I could get past that pain.
A rickety frame of metal
allows me to watch
the sights of nature and life.
Then- the shade goes down.
I know the pain is behind it,
but the sights outside the window
can torture me no longer.

Rebecca Ostman

Ode To Life

Children of Pain
Voices of Innocence
Little ones who weep
Abandon your cry
Lords of my conscience
Gate keepers of the Earth
Life's second chance
Rewrite the music
And Dance

Tina Belstad

Enchanted Effort

When the night falls
she is glowing like a flame
dancing romancing
as if to tame
my restless soul

Never stealing more
than she gives
I'm only trying to live
another night
blessed by the light
of her love

She hopes some day
she'll find a way
to tame
my restless soul

M. Michael Downing

The Ant

An ant who passes
through a forest
of grass,
pauses to drink
from a miniature
sea.
To him a rock is
a hill tip-top,
and a fern is a
monster tree.

Nelva K. Grossnickle

Thoughts Of Him

The trees are green - the road is long,
I can't help but cry at this song.
I've lost him now, it seems that way,
I'll never see another day.

Without thinking of his name,
The hurt it seems is all the same.
I won't make it through the night,
I don't know what is right.

So I will cry all my tears,
And try to make it through the years,
Knowing only one true thing,
I'll never wear another ring.

'Til death do us part is all he said,
What happens now that he is dead?

Sandra Lynn Christiansen

Untitled

What connection
have we here?
Are we all alone,
in our worry and fear?
Are we helplessly
searching for love
at great cost
or will we be certain
our dreams will be lost?
Will we touch the face of God,
as we amble forth slowly
this earthen sod?
Will we reach destinations
not previously seen,
Will we realize the wonder
and truth in our dreams?
The questions are many,
the hope still survives
that the truths will be found
and expressed in our lives.

Karen Lindquist

Faith

Faith can move a mountain
Just the worth of a seed
It can part a sea for crossing
It can fill a hungry need

Aches and pains can pass away
The lame can even walk
Deaf ears opened and hearing
Tongues once silent can talk

These things a few of many
Miracles faith has done
Faith in our Lord and Master
Faith in the Holy One

Through God all things are possible
There is nothing He can't do
Only our lack of faith
Keeps us from getting through

Let us put our faith in action
Let us waste no more time
For the end is getting nearer
Time is short yours and mine

Mary Ann Corbell

Homeless

No sleep at night, don't have a bed.
No steady home to rest my head.
No love to call my own.
No steady job to buy some bread.
No family on special days
No life, I'm all alone.
No friends on days when I'm in need
No one even dare smile at me
No face, I'm on my own.

Brenda Lou Vargas

Vision

Looking out my window at nothing,
I see something...

It is so dreamy,
It is real.

My mind scape drifts,
This vision is a gift.

Now!
I see it!

Out of black comes beauty.
My vision has a duty.

It wants me.
It owns my every thought.

I pledge my eternal love to
my vision... of you.

Madeline Michelle Parrish

Beyond The Stars

As the years get older
And my mind is bolder
It dares to investigate
The future of mortal fate

When my mind was younger
It could often wonder
There is a heaven
When I am only seven

Why do I need
My soul do feed
On the mere thought
That destiny is bought

If I soar past the stars
When my soul ajars
My life here on earth
Gave a meaning to its birth

Mary Ann Marlow

The Wink

I imagine the way you smile at me,
I am never again to receive,
The touch of your hand,
The deep timbre of your voice,
The way you always care.
The day that you let go...
You don't need me now,
I know.
These tears that stain my cheeks,
The salt that sadness wreaks,
This pain within my heart,
Because you're no longer there.
Memory makes me think
Your love was like a wink.

Jessy Marie Bird

Dearest Sweet Daughter Of Mine!

Dearest sweet daughter of mine,
We had some very happy times.

With your flowing brown hair so fine,
To the child you left behind.

The task God gave to you,
You must have carried through.

For he took you Oh! So young,
To help him with things that are wrong.

If you hear me speak your name,
Or feel my tears of pain,

Just whisper in my ear,
The all things will become clear.

So spread your wings and fly!
Fly high above the sky.

And when it's time for me to go,
Swoop low and take my soul.

To your gentler place in time.
Dearest Sweet Daughter of Mine!

Roger Lambright

Accepting Help

Often we find that it is
very difficult to accept
things from other people.
We don't want to be obligated
to them for loving us, giving
us money, or helping in anyway.
We feel that we may have to do
or be things in return for
their help. But let us remember
that all of their help comes from
God, and God works through people.
As long as we remain true to
Our God, all things are right.
God loves us and will provide
all things if we remain true to
His purpose. "Lord, I want to
accept all gifts from Thee,
by they mental, emotional or material.

Jesse C. Braley IV

Looks

I look at you with eyes of fire
To make your heart beat with desire
You look back with a sensual peer
To hypnotize me and bring me near.

I grasp your tender hand in mine
To gently lay your palm across my chest
And softly whispering the rest

Feel my heart, it beats so sweet
It flutters and throbs for thee
Our bodies now shaking with ecstasy
The desires are there to see

Sophia Gardias

Memory Of You

I am thinking
As time wanders by
I am thinking of you
And your bright bluish eyes

How beautiful you are
How beautiful you'll stay
In my memory

Christopher J. Easlick

"A Lost Breed"

A cowboy
A western, rugged girl toy

Not to play with his emotions,
But to sit back and admire
His manly devotions

Rough, calloused hands
Experienced from traveling
The lands

Dry chapped lips
From the harsh blowing winter winds
Yet still knowing how to gently kiss

Squinting eyes
From the sunset and rise

An intelligent man
Not so hard to understand

I yearn for him
So passionate
So rare

Where are you cowboy?
Let met care -

Mandy Heiner

Grandmother's Silence

I wonder in her silence
What she's thinking today
I wonder if she dreams
or promises or prays
No murmur, No whisper
No noise as she lay
something destroyed her
through Silence she say.
Her teardrops they fall
And perfectly stay, I wonder
if they're tears of tomorrow
or today, I wonder what she
Wonders in her silence today.

Veronica Blackman

I Walked

I walked into the garden
In the stillness of the night.
I walked into the forest
Of eternal light.

The flowers bedded 'round me
As nestled as can be.
When I walk into the garden,
Hope is there for me.

I walked into the danger
To find what is in store.
Hope is pouring down,
A wild raining pour.

In the danger of the forest
You do not have to fear.
For there you can remember,
That hope is very near.

Hope is always waiting,
Just waiting there for me.
The magic door of hope -
Just turn the magic key.

Megan Mitchell

Love Of A Child

The love of a child, has no rules,
the love you have for a child, can
only be brought by the pain of
delivery, the pain you feel can only
bring you closer, the love you have
for a child will never die, it will
stay with you until you die, the
love of a child, will live forever
it will last until you find them in
Heaven the love of a child will live
in your heart until the day you live
in a cloud, the love of a child will
never die.

Thelma Montoya

Diversity

We stood apart, both lonely;
pride had won our souls.
No communication...
in silence so complete
someone could hear a heart break
in words neither one could speak.

We stood apart in silence,
our thoughts...our path...our own.
A look...A glance...A wary smile-
In tears we stood our ground.
The pain we made was ours.
Then alone we walked our separate ways.

Dora Stallworth

The Dark Closet

The past resembles a dark closet
Open it, and it scares you
Leave it closed, and it haunts you
Forget it, and it corrodes you

The closet is full, the closet is fear
It leaves you empty, it leaves you sad
The darkness is deep and thick
The sound is loud and irritating

It never leaves you alone
It never lets you breathe
You bow to its power
Never bending to its reminder

The closet contains those things
Most horrid and true
Most happy and satisfying
Most shameful and demeaning

It cries out to your soul
Remember those things that are hidden
Remember those things that are you.

Curtis A. Childs

Dreams

When the sun falls
I fall with it
into my warm bed
I dream about dreams
dreams that come true
waiting hoping
that one day
my dream
will too

Kattie Gonzalez

Keep The Faith

I awoke this morning,
With tears in my eyes,
From all the pain,
I held deep inside.
I went to the window,
Hoping sunshine I'd find,
But all I saw,
Were cloudy skies.
Deep in my sorrow,
I started to cry.
Tears fell on my cheeks,
As the rain fell from the skies.

And just as I thought,
I could sink no lower,
There came a voice,
From over my shoulder.
"You are not alone,
I'll be by your side,
Give your Heart to God,
And warmth of sunshine you'll find..."

Shirley Ann (Dyer) Muncey

Untitled

Sometimes I get to wondering
Had I lived in Jesus' day
If I'd known He was Messiah,
Or just shrugged and turned away.

It's true I am conservative
And often shrink from change;
Would I have rejected Him
Whose teachings seemed so strange?

Might I have been so pious
And certain of God's will
That I couldn't even recognize
His prophesy fulfilled?

Could I have been among those
At that mockery of a trial
Demanding He be crucified,
Self-righteous all the while?

But, Oh - His Resurrection!!
Then surely I would see
He truly is Messiah,
That Man from Galilee!

Elaine W. Johnson

Seasons Of New England

Spring is finally here.
And summer must be near.
With it comes outdoor fun.
Playing games in the sun.

Autumn is not far behind.
With colors brought to mind.
Then winter takes its toll.
As indoor games unfold.

Evan Piacente

Signs

As we travel along
Life's highway
Through coldest night
And sunlit day.
Would it not be divine
To have a sign
Emblazoned red
That boldly said,
"WRONG WAY."

Barbara W. Rule

Just A Joker

I'm just a joker
Not a jack or an ace
I try to keep up to you
At your fast pace
The two reminds me
Of the both of us
Just seeing you
Is really a must
Even though I joke around
I wish we could spend
Many nights on the town
Then when I hold you
I think of one thing
Then I'm no longer a joker
But now I'm a king
Then when you hold me
I think of one thing
You're no longer my woman
But now my queen

Rod Sutter

Untitled

We were there for such a
short time,
But it was a beautiful time.
A time when you felt at peace,
At peace from everything around you.
A time to think,
A time to love.
It seemed you could see forever,
Felt like you could touch the sky.
The moon shone brightly,
The stars danced with pure delightment.
It was a magical place,
Filled with wind blown music.

Shannon Smith

I Don't Know Why

I was eating cotton candy, I
Got stung by a bee; I don't know
Why.
I was eating a candy apple, I
Got stung by a bee; I don't know
Why.
I was eating a lollipop, I
Got stung by a bee; I don't know
Why.
I was eating jello, I
Got stung by a bee; I don't know
Why.
I called the doctor and said,
I got stung by a bee; I don't know
Why.
And he replied, it was only a
Fly.

Madeline Murray

The Loss

I always laughed at anger
And cried when I met hope.
I hid behind courageousness
And told seriousness a joke.
I rushed and hurried patience
But I made anxious wait.
I teased and taunted kindness
But then I cuddled hate.
I energized depression
Then dared and challenged fear.
I bored excitement
Then brought isolation near.
I mocked and tortured love
And lied to honesty.
I disregarded faith
And embarrassed modesty.
I overcame all emotions
Now I question at what cost.
I never felt true joy or sorrow
This was my tragic loss.

Michelle Marie McCombs

I'm Glad You Came To Live With Me

I'm glad you came to live with me
I hope you feel the same
You've made my heart so happy
Since the day you came

I'm glad you came to live with me
I didn't know just how much
That I could love a little girl
Until I felt your touch

I'm glad you came to live with me
You've brought me bright sunshine
And when someone asks, "Who Is She?"
I'm proud to say, "she's mine!"

I'm glad you came to live with me
I thank the Lord above
He chose me to be your mother
And gave you to me, to love.

Gerldene Elmore Stewart

Anxiety

Humming telephone lines
tied up in boy scout knots
So close to the edge
shiny, razor sharp
One false move
and I might slice
  Spilling
    Desire
    Hate
    Passion
  Love
  Fear
    Anger
    Pride
Cascading down into
The dark abyss of my soul.

Micheal Fraley

The Storm (To Victims Of The Liberian Civil War)

I bent down,
stooping.
Stepped aside.
Crawled,
like a crab.
I shrunk.
I curled in
like a snail
into a shell.
I hid, a leech,
under a green leaf.
I quit breathing
quit laughing
quit talking.
Only with a deep sigh
I waited;
giving up
so the storm would pass.
But the storm lingers still.

Patricia Jabbeh Wesley

The Epitome Of Beauty

Millions of diamonds
dancing on glass.

Forever and beyond
before you,
face to face.

The beginning and end
come together in time.

Empty solitude
strengthens the soul.
But its power
weakens your every desire.

Shining brightness
blinds the way.
Though the path the eyes see,
clear as crystal can be.

Gail LaRosa

Have You Ever Seen A World...?

Have you ever seen a world
filled with rainbow streams
that was made
from rainbow beams?

Have you ever seen a world
that had a lot of bees
which loved to play on
the peppermint trees?

Have you ever seen a world
filled with peace
and all that fought
were the big white geese?

Have you ever seen a world
with streets of gold
and it shined so bright
that it was bold?

Have you ever seen a world
just like mine
where everybody can play
all the time?

James McAlister

Untitled

Large dark Clouds hovering
sweet rain drops on my lips
soothing breeze whistles a sigh
rain coming from the sky
smiles from the deep,
pounding in my heart
Willow trees asleep
Crisp and round
each drop rides down
she breaks through the watery vapor
bursting out
her suns beauty has come about
She shines her glisten in all...
....for all who will listen.

Heidi Neal

Longing

Forever lonely is she
Who clings so closely to Thee
Will her longing end today
Or is death still far away
Her heart full of anxiety
Will peace come from the Deity
Once happiness was on its way
But then again it slipped away
Surely someone's yet to come
To bring again a shining sun
Will her wishing make it so
That he will come and never go
And yet her agony lingers on
With no one there to share the dawn.

Ramoella Sianipar

Wanna Be My Friend?

Smiles that lie
Hiding faces of disgust,
Headless chickens
Wearing masks of gold.
It is not possible to sit
In the corner and escape.
They are hunters
With social butterfly nets.
Very nice people,
I'd rather hang out with
The dude who punched me in the
                    face.

Patrick Keaney

My Best Friend

A friend so true,
A friend so dear...
Close to my side
And always near.

One who listens, but
May not understand.
Only to cherish a pat
Of the hand.

Your gentle eyes - the
Playful things you do.
I'll never forget these
Memories of You.

A friend whose love
Will never end...
That's why you're
"My Best Friend."

Diana L. Frey

I Would Know You Anywhere

I would know you anywhere
With my eyes closed
I would know the touch of your hand,
the feel of your kiss,
the scent of your skin.

I would know you anywhere.
In a crowd of people,
I can feel your presence,
Find your face and
feel our love when our eyes meet.

When our time on earth has passed,
and we soar to another place
or hasten to another time,
we will never be apart because
I would know you anywhere.

Shirley J. McLean

People

Some people are mean
Some are nice
But they all seem to
have the same meaning in life

Some people lose their tempers
Some people get rough
But they usually don't mean
that kind of stuff

Some people are black
Some are white
But we live on the same world
and have the same rights

Some people are smart
Some are not
But if we work together
We will accomplish a lot

Danielle Perham

Gary

The demons-they fight against me
with their spears and stones
But I fear not
for I am a star

I am a warrior
A warrior from the light
fighting against the dark
I will overcome and prevail

When I am in battle
You will not hear me cry out
You will not see my flesh tear
You will not feel me against you

But you will hear me in your heart
and you will see me in the sky
Shining bright
and fighting the fight for the Lord

Stephanie J. Kraus

Untitled

Deep crevices of the mind
Come out - shed light
At weird times.
In absence
And at the lowest points,
Important questions become
Unimportant
And my insides sleep
While I do.

Jessica Kosman

"Empty Shell"

Emptiness is his robe
Cloaked by despair
Sadness that encompasses him
Untouched by human care

For emptiness follows him
To plague him by his side
It stands to mock him of his pain
It's stolen all his pride

For pride was all he bore inside
This hollow man to be
A loneliness has grasped his heart
To never set it free

His heart a shrine of endless hope
A wondrous sacred place
The image which now appears
So tainted with disgrace

And clouded in his reflection
Hazed by disbelief
A once proud man to stand no more
An empty shell to be

Brian Stroup

Escaped With You

I used to escape by music
I'd hear it and there I'd be,
an angel flying above
tending to all of one's needs.

I used to escape into the ocean
I would lie upon the sandy beach,
pretending I was one with the world
my heart perfected by peace.

I used to escape through the sky
I called the stars my home,
the sun evaporated all worries
the clouds allowed me to roam.

I can choose to escape by moonlight
or into a sea of blue,
but nothing truly escapes me
then being escaped with you.

Katie Fitchie

Reawakened

After twenty years
I thought they were gone
All of those feelings,
I've hidden so long.
But you called last week
And I learned I was wrong.
I cannot go back
To that long ago place
I've watched you for years,
Your image is on our daughter's face.
All the love that I had.
I've given to her.
How I feel about you
I'm not really sure.
We've both made new lives
It's better that way.
I don't have to worry
When we meet again someday.
You know I still care,
So our daughter, I'll share.

Rebecka Ann Vigus

Car Payments Don't Matter

4 A.M.
Outside early April's
thin warm breeze,
crescent moon's mock, green smile
hangs low over the city's
blinking lights like dying stars
one above and not below.
Reflect through obscure clouds,
the pale light of a distant fire
burning half a world away
on the other side of life.
Orion slays the beast.
Love is lost.
Love is lost.
Planets collide and
worlds die and
somewhere something suffers.
Car payments don't matter.

J. Struzzi

The Battle

The battle rages on,
the fight never won.
The shield - glinting in the glare
of the rising sun.
Blinding... blinding...
The knight rides away,
defeated, but will
return again.
Someday, to bring another
hopeful soul to light,
or rather, another light
to a hopeful soul.

Elizabeth Sprinkle

Precious

A product of our love
Miraculous, incredible

We watch your every move
Investigating, observing

Each wondrous milestone recorded
Proudly, diligently

We offer freedom of experiences
Controlled, uncontrolled

We ask - be true to yourself
Emotionally, physically

Our bond will remain
Securely, lovingly

We are your parents.

Donna M. Militello

Echoes

To feel so lonely and so scared
One tries to find the strength inside
But with so many questions dared
The answers never there
One needs to have an eternal flame
The one to set you a glow
To feel the feelings
The need to grow
The echoes that the wind blows
If only the wind could take the
    beauty that love bestow.

Vicky A. Turcotte

Help Us Understand

Help us Understand destruction,
As did happen that sad day,
When Oklahoma City,
Was bombed in sad array.

How the building stood devastated,
And the floors were snapped into,
Taking with them falling shambles,
Many families broken into.

How brigades of men assembled,
Lowered debris piece by piece,
Did evacuate the victims,
From their captor, to release.

How the lives of little children,
And adults were snatched in death,
How firemen and rescue workers,
Worked in fear of their last breath.

How the strength of all the nation,
Who lent a helping hand, and -
All the prayers helps to revive them,
As God gently heals the land.

Annabelle Isaacs

"A Broken Vase"

Our friendship is like
A rose in a vase.
When it falls
And the vase shatters
Then nothing matters.

I'm the rose
And you're the vase
Holding the water
That keeps me alive,
But when the vase shatters
Then nothing matters.

I'd rather have died
From thirst and hunger;
By wilting in the sun,
But you weren't strong enough
And the vase shattered.
Now nothing matters.

Rosie

Dance Forever

Once in a lifetime
Does one have that chance
To sit in a circle
and make up a dance
Depending on a partner
and what you decide to do
The ability to start
a wonderful, a new
Creating a theme
that will often be seen
The color and size
will most likely be wise
As time progresses
a new dance will begin
Never to be said
the first is a sin

Kasey Grado

Positive Insight

When days are filled with tears and heartache
I remember three words that are music
    to my ears
With hope anything is possible
Courage gives us the way to make it happen
Strength we need and comes from the God
Faith makes the other three come true
Happiness will fill our days
and the future look brighter

Celeste Strazziere

My Little Boy

My little boy came into my life
    On a Thursday night.
Never had I ever
    Beheld such a wondrous sight.
I knew when I held him that
    I had lost my heart forever.
I also knew that molding him
    Into a fine young man would
    Be my greatest endeavor.
Now that he is three,
    I see all the possibilities
    There will be.
Particularly, because it is really he
    Who is teaching me.

Pamela A. Sprott

Pondering

Looking back upon your past,
Dreaming, musing, aching
of things gone wrong.

A futile trip of memories
charged with guilt and
some remorse.

A wasteland better left
uncharted;
A tour without a guide.

Better to recharge the mind,
pump up your heart,
begin each day as new.

Create fresh memories;
Start today, think forward -
Forge a path for future dreams
and hope will spring anew.

Janet Stikeleather

True Love Of A Friend

To love with one's heart and soul,
Goes deeper than the outward man.
To give as much love as taken,
Is giving all one can.

To love with deep divinity,
Shows divineness and loving grace.
To comfort as much as needs comfort,
Applies a smile to a tearful face.

To know serenity is bountiful,
Shows strength and faithful soul.
To be enduring as much as endured.
Mends a broken heart—whole.

To know true love is forever,
And will never know an end,
Is surely to know, however,
The true love of a friend.

Myra L. Davis

"Liar's Heart"

This sin is my love,
And this love is my life.
It's so unfair,
This liar's heart.

Is this my fate,
This calling,
This cry,
This hurt, I feel inside.

Now it's done.
Can't be undone.
This love,
This pain,
A lonely loss,
Never to gain.

"This" beginning love,
Is the ending Love.

Donna Tisdale Evans

Life In The Fast Lane

Life in the fast lane
To work, to school
Don't be late
Aerobics at ten.

Life in the fast lane
Do laundry, vacuum
Make dinner
Drive the kids to soccer.

Life in the fast lane
Homework, bath time
Do the dishes
Tuck in the children.

Life in the fast lane
Make calls, pay bills
Kiss the kids while they sleep
Make promises you won't keep.

Life in the fast lane
Try for bed at ten, make it twelve
So you can begin again,
Life in the fast lane.

Stacy Trierweiler

A Fresh Start

In times of despair
when you don't seem to care
and your life is falling apart

When you just can't cope
and you've given up hope
take time to look into your heart

By searching your soul
and finding a goal
that gives meaning to who you are

You can turn your life around
hold your head up high, not down
and reach for that shining star

For it is God's intention
that we take every dimension
to be the best that we could be

Through his loving grace
our pains will be erased
and a new beginning you will see

Julie Stammer-Edling

The Cello's Sound

I hear the bells of sadness
like cellos
tuning the cells of my body

I hear the violins of longing
like the wind of a gallop
on a horse's back

I hear the swans rising
to meet the seagulls
motionless in mid air

Like the flute alone
above a sea
of swollen instruments

I am the spirit of love and war
I am the flute calling the drums
entwined in a mad song

Now I can rest in the music
the torn colors of my solitude
the falling leaves of the cello's sound

Raina Paris

Untitled

An ache
deep down
Not unhappy
I can smile
or laugh
and mean it.

And yet
this Ache
has made me numb.
So many
seem so
trivial.

So much
has changed
inside of me
how Dare you think
I am
the same
as Yesterday.

Vanessa Oliver

Forced Mistrust

Hurt and pain
pierced
life regained?
Denied
fallen, bruised, and crying
smiles stolen away
insides shriveled and dying
wanting to believe
truths broken, tempted and lying
wanting to dream again

Grasping, gasping
a pale blue wisp
fading, falling
hope gone amiss
folded hands, yet doubting knees
grey thoughts deep within
confusion and conflict of the mind
heart and soul of din
faith yet doubt intertwined
good will always win?

Joy Liang

My Twin The Angel

This is the happiest day on earth,
  It's the day that I gave birth.
It was special, like no other,
  It's the day I became a mother.

I was proud and full of joy,
  I knew it would be a boy.
His hair of blond and eyes of blue,
  I didn't know that there were two.

As your life on earth begins,
  I'm glad I was blessed with twins.
You were sent from God above,
  He gave me two of you to love.

As years passed by I hate to say,
  He took one of you away.
I still have one, but not the other,
  God has taken your twin brother.

I think of him and I still cry,
  I never got to say goodbye.
Then comes a smile and then a sigh,
  Now he's an angel in the sky.

Brenda Whitten

The Anonymous Letter

I see you in the distance,
but yet my heart races.
I don't want you to notice
so I hide among the faces.

You never would imagine
all the joy you give me.
Just seeing your smile
I imagine what could be.

I do not have the courage
to ask you out just yet,
but for the chance to hold your hand
I would go forever into debt.

Soon I will let you know
the name behind these words,
but until that point in time
I will be flying with the birds.

For when I am near you
I feel like I can fly.

Daniel J. Colsch

Kansas

I go home now, waiting
for chiseled brick streets
to soar away from Santa Fe tracks
in angles and dips; breathing
sword fights and musty spies
in secretive stacks of an
abandoned Carnegie; watching
lemonade buses carry my
reflection to teachers
behind the big desk barricade; smiling
at ancient, pickled drugstores
selling sanity in small
over-the-counter doses; dancing
with myself around swing sets
and soccer fields; echoing
assurance off twin spires
of gold-plated religion; competing
with ATM domes and the corner Italian
spinning a mean pizza in the crisp sky.

Kathleen Davis

Time

Time, what a wonderful thing.
Time, what a horrible thing.

We rely on time to live,
We rely on time to die,
We rely on time to ask questions,
We rely on time to reply.

We rely on time to be strong,
We rely on time to be weak,
We rely on time to find,
We rely on time to seek.

We rely on time to be nervous,
We rely on time to be content,
We rely on time to sin,
We rely on time to repent.

We rely on time to be born,
We rely on time to grow,
We rely on time to reap,
We rely on time to sow.

Without time, where would we be?
The question is, would we be?

Trevor Brunsink

"My Love"

My Love for you is
Deeper than the Oceans
Broader than the Skies
I melt in your Arms, and
Quiver from the look in your eyes
Your heart is warm and
Tender as spring.
I Love you dearly because
you're everything.

Scott R. McLean

The Mockingbird

I listened to the mockingbird
As slow the evening came,
No nicer sound have I yet heard
No song is quite the same

I listened long there on the hill
Above the valley floor,
Then darkness fell and all got still
I heard the bird no more,

But from the river far below
A sweeter song came near
Reminding me of long ago
My sweetheart's song so dear.

Jack T. Graf

Delicate Love

Love is like a flower,
Sweet and undecayed,
If it is kept lovingly,
It will shine in splendid array.

If you treated your love right,
It will blossom and stay,
But if it is kept unattended,
It will wither away.

Love, delicate and fragile,
A challenge until the end,
Will bring you comfort and joy,
If this is where it is led.

Kimberly Wapp

My Future

I can look out of the window
And see heaven in the sky.
I can hear the angels' wings
When the birds sail by.

I can sense the beauty
Of our human lives
Every time the sun sets
And when each day arrives.

I hate to leave this Earth,
Familiar, beloved, and dear,
To take upon myself
Transit from this sphere.

Perhaps I'll live again
To work, to dream, to strive,
To build, to love, to suffer,
And so to be alive.

Lucile Hutton

My Pain

My pain,
doubles,
triples,
quadruples even,
each time, I see her.
Each time, she sees me—
nothing.
Now I feel lost,
unwanted, empty,
but still
I want to be acknowledged.
So there I wait...
and wait...
and wait...
until the day she does.

Ricky Deleguardia

Sunshine

My life is an eclipse
  and you the first light I see
Like dawn through the night
  you brighten my day.
Your warmth penetrates my soul
  like the sun on my skin
You are a ray of sunshine
  radiating love
In my darkest hour
  I am enlightened
Knowing the sun will shine on me
  once again.

Lori Johnson

"Now The Rain Is Falling"

Now
the rain
is falling
falling down
on me. I hear
myself calling out
to an endless sea. Like
a wilted rose that cries out
for the rain, I long for the warmth
of an eternal flame. Now the rain
is falling and I hear my heart
sigh. Only the silence is
calling for the river
runs dry.

Brandy M. Byard

Tall Timbers

Tall Timbers
Bending,
Swaying,
Sometimes still.
Stalwart,
Enduring,
Winter's chill.

Pine needles,
Cones,
Falling to the ground.
Silently,
Nature sighs—

Spring is coming.
Gentle breezes,
Raindrops dancing,
without a sound.
Slanted Evergreens,
Rugged,
Strong,
Unwavering.

Naomi J. Hall

Blast Off

As we rocketed
into the sky,
like lightning striking a tree
we glanced out
the glistening window
of the spacecraft
and saw
the crystal like stars
as questionable as cat's eyes
under the night's sky.

Brian Donatelli

Trinkets From A Childhood

A familiar yellow bowl
All plain and ordinary
Holding hot cozy soup
In the middle of January

A golden locket
Given at birth
With love from a grandmother
Only the heart knows the worth

A smelly ole sock
That won the game
Which created a memory
Of little boy fame

A half filled diary
With passionate scenes
Of little girl hopes
And little girl dreams

All those ordinary things
In our memory trunk of goods
We store our testimonial
Trinkets from a childhood

Patricia N. Hildebrand

The Owl Is Wise

The owl is smart.
The owl is wise.
He sees with his very big eyes.
He sees a mouse.
He licks his beak.
He swoops down and eats his prey.

Gregory D. Parks

Always There, Always Will Be

I think of him in the early morning
I think of him at night

He always was here for me,
When I needed support and guidance

He always was here for me,
When I just needed a love

He always gave of himself,
More than he had

I think of him in the early morning
I think of him at night

I miss my Dad

Rudy Kalas

Ode To My Dog

My dog is fat,
his face is thin.
Not a lot of brains within.

His best friend is the cat next-door.
The cat's a stray, she's very poor.
She sometimes steals my dog's dog food,
Which sets my dog in a bad mood.

He died on a Friday afternoon.
I for one, think he died too soon.
Dad ran him over with his truck,
and now he has to clean the muck.

Good-bye old friend,
I'll miss you heaps.
But when I die,
come back to me.

Anna Almendrala

A Mother's Pain

I awaken at the early dawn
Another day has just begun
I wonder what today will bring
If this the day I'll reach my dreams.
A single parent is what I am
For only his mother is here at hand
The questions do get asked at times
And sometimes the answers I cannot find.

Janice A. Cooper

I Don't

I don't need you.
I don't want your pity
or sorrow; I don't want
to let you close.
You laugh at me,
at my expense.
Why should I
share myself
with you?
When I don't need you;
I don't love you...
I only want you,
to be close to me,
from now till forever can fly.
But my lock must remain locked;
My dreams must remain unknown;
as I must remain unloved.

Robyn Futterman

Across Two Octobers

Across these two Octobers, my heart has
never felt so much.
In all my life, I've never loved this much.
It's time to call it quits though,
    time to wash my hands
Will I ever love like this again?
    There is just too much confusion,
      too much pain.
Everyone is trying to pawn off the blame.
I'm tired of this spider web,
    You must release me!
My eyes have been opened to your empty
promises and false securities
    I was the only one trying.
The whole time inside, I was dying.
    It became a contest we all wanted to win,
But I'm not a playing piece, Just someone
who, to easily could forgive.

Shelley Jessup

Gifts From The Dying

Sitting by your side, I hold your hand,
Giving you comfort, peace, and love
As you die.

You have taught me the value of each day,
Each precious moment,
And how quickly it is gone.

Now I know the absolute need to tell all in my life
How much I love them
TODAY
Because I am not promised tomorrow.

Seeing the light that surrounds you,
I feel the very Presence of God in this room.
We are filled with the Peace that passes understanding;
As it blankets your doubt, fear and pain,
It goes with me into my life
And each life that I touch.

Lying by my side, you hold my hand,
Giving me comfort, peace, and love
As you die.

Debra Anthony

The Day And I

The day was despondent and dark and drear
My mood was just the same.
The rain drizzled down upon the ground.
My tears fell without shame.

I knew not why the day was sad,
Its sorrows, troubles or woes,
I only knew it matched my mood,
As only one can who knows.

We two, together passed into the night,
Not knowing what was to come,
But knew there would be another dawn
When we would not be so glum.

Ramona Seeley

My Life, My Love

When life no longer flows forth from this husk of a body
and my soul has found its rest in Heaven, Nirvana or the darkness
    of space
When our memories of youth are found in the albums of yesteryear
and the joy of having lived is but a whisper on the wind
My love for you will carry its song till the end of all creation

James G. Lang

There Was A Man

Ever since I was a child I knew there was a man
A man who God intended to have and hold my hand

A man whose strength of character inspired and lifted me
Who stood as an example of his high integrity

Whose warmth and loving nature touches everyone he sees
Whose giving, caring attitude shows generosity

A man of lyric thinking with poetry in his soul
Who fills my every emptiness and makes me know I'm whole

A man whose touch is fire, Who makes my spirit sing
Whose passion captivates me with all the love he brings

My heart did know there was a man and now I know it's true
For God has filled my fondest dreams and I know that man is You.

Carol Cormier

And It Happens

And it happens, the feelings grow cold.
Conversations are lifeless and old.
Dreams and desires no longer are told.
Nights are lonely, there's no one to hold.

And it happens, as time passes by.
No more love no more reason to try.
Neither one of you really knows why.
Hurt feelings, too numb now to cry.

And it happens, you head for the door.
From him you no longer adore.
You know you can't take anymore.
You wonder what it all was for?

And it happens, you feel you could die.
From the hurt and the pain and the lie.
But it's over now no need to cry.
There's a new life, you've just got to try.

Nancy Loeffler-Root

Fragile

Heart of glass O'crystalle glass this tragedy can not be.
Shattered Heart Broken Heart, your fate has captured me.
You found a love that was your love, and things began to be.
In your heart is face O'heart; That is happy and carefree.
Things have happened that should have happened.
For this love was meant to be.
But time dealt you a dirty blow
That tore your heart apart.
Now tears roll down the face, that's captured in your heart.
Words were said that knocked you down
though they weren't really mean.
And as you fell down to the ground; No one heard you scream.
Now half your heart has fallen, the pieces lay on the floor
And you weep from the thought, "You can love nevermore."
As I look at your broken pieces, Whose face is it that I see?
In this story of broken hearts
That face is actually me...

Leslie Alexander Jr.

Alone

She sits with her head folded between her knees
Her tears rolling down her face
Thinking of a loved one that has gone away
Her heart is broken from the sadness she has inside
While her loved one's soul is taken in the tide
She thinks of the past and how close they were
But everything now is a total blur
She'll never forget the old times
She sits with her head folded between her knees
And she is the one alone and lost in the breeze......

Jason Vena

Enlightenment

Madness haunts the enlightened mind
For darkness lost an ancient grip regained so long ago
An altered forest stands before it
Concealing its members behind an unbreached wall
That exists unto it.

A shrill echoes through its blended mass
Reaching deaf eyes that conceive of its truth
Which must lie beyond.

One by one its members vanish by unnatural foes
Each revealing portions of truth
Until the puzzle is complete.

A vast wasteland mirrors its work
Above the empty soars the eagle whose pleas
Were in vain
Abandoning his world long since destroyed
And the enlightened mind stands, alone.

Andy Nichols

Thoughts Unknown

When you speak to me your words sound
  genuine and ideal for my ears.

But when you gaze at me the entire world
  changes like Black Magic.

I distinguish your motions and they tamper
  with the questions in my mind.

For you to answer what I inquire is immoral
  and inappropriate on my part for I know
  you will not state the truth

As I strive to grasp everything you say
  and do,

I will never understand you.
  "Thoughts Unknown"

Alaina M. Septak

Untitled

Shadowed memories
of dreams and wishes
Conflicting ideas
causing heartache and pain
Angry and relieved
by the pointing of fingers
Sharp felt words
followed by meaningless affection
Desires of more or less
out of a passion that used to be
Changes in the soul
making attitudes flare
Not knowing whether to care about the change
not really caring to bother
Lies that begin to cloud the mind
and eyes telling no secrets at all
Gestures explaining the reasons
while actuality slips away.

Jennifer Roeser

You

Your kiss is like a touch of satin. Your eyes are like a deep
  healing passion.
Your touch sends fire racing through my veins.
I never thought I could feel this way again, my pain wouldn't let
  it through.
But now I know my heart had started to heal when it fell out of
  my chest unto you.
Your words hurt me, but also soothed my dying heart.

Andrea McChesney

His Majesty

Far out into the black night;
Your face appears to shine.
A voice felt within the soul;
And inner peace divine.

When in darkness you invade,
The stars do light your trail.
A sweeping presence in the night;
Where peace and love prevails.

There is no mortal to compare;
No greater love anywhere.
The moon is your pillow; the stars your bed.
And love of light always follow
On the paths you have lead.

Linda Annette Lickteig

A Bird's Life

Birds fly so high,
Like specks of dust in the sky.
Making a nest in the tree,
They spread their wings and fly free.
See the birds by the sea,
Looking up, there are birds for you to see.
Birds eat insects, worms, and fish,
To them this is a gourmet dish.
Some birds fly high and some fly low,
Some birds fly fast and some fly slow.
You might find birds in a tree or at the dock,
Birds fly alone or in a flock.

Andrew Balasbas

Masculine, Feminine

Lying scattered are the wounded
  an ego, the heart
    ....her intuition

She's integrated the ideals of love and passion,
Are they one entity on this spiritual plane? Or perhaps they
wither in all the blame

Overwhelmed and confused by two emotions
I will disguise the fears and still they worsen,
  I've known no other than severing
And despise the references of myself in third person.

Is it masculine? Is it feminine?
  Though as a man......
    I'm still hidden

As action to male, I survive great disappointment

As emotion to female I miss living

It is here understanding begins I learn
to live and begin forgiving.............

Richard A. Thomas

The Seasons

 Spring has come, the trees have grown their leaves back.
As I climb the trees I scrape my knees and watch the flowers grow.

 Spring has ended Summer has come. It's time for a fun filled trip
to where you get sun chapped lips.

 I think to myself as Fall begins that will the green grass grow tall?
I look in my mind and I see the crisp blue sky and what do you see?
I hope you see it too. As Fall has a beginning we all know it has to
have another thing—it has an end.

 Fall has ended Winter has come it's time for snowball fun.
I think about skiing, boy what a big joy!

Laura A. A. Vergez

My Pilot

My pilot hails from Washington,
He's a very true American son-
He flies by night and through the day,
In his carefree, but assured way.

He walks up with his manly stride,
And boards the plane with a childish pride-
Of him we all are very proud,
When he opens the throttles and heads for a cloud.

When he comes in to land, oh so fast,
We relive our lives-things of the past-
But when he hits the deck with ease,
We realize then, he just likes to tease.

As we say Good night to the stars,
And to this man, with Silver bars-
We look up to the Angel that sings,
And praise this Flyer, with Golden Wings.

Bill Cox

Gardens

Garden you swayed with colors very bright.
You brought our day with soft, lovely light.
Smiles were brought out on our walking mission,
Holding hands and kissing future visions.
Gently we caressed that what love beholds,
As he brought me gardens, to my key folds.
Smiles were exchanged and hardship forgotten.
For blossom is vivid, with past markings.
Garden you helped to liven my lost days,
However, no more sights, for suitor lays.
So sweet garden, I call once, not for me,
But for my lost love, to lay at his feet.

Elisa Guerra

The One

I want to be the one,
    The one who gets the attention, the one who gets the girl.

I want to be the one,
    The one who has the answers, the one with a lot of friends.

I want to be the one,
    The one who is loved, the one who can laugh at himself.

I want to be the one,
    The one that doesn't cry, the one who can be happy.

I want to be the one,
    The one who doesn't have to worry, the one with great faith.

I want to be the one,
    The one people go to, the one who makes them laugh.

But I'm not the one
I'm not the one who has the answers, I'm not the one who can
    be happy, and I'm not the one who gets the girl.

I am the one,
The one who is seldom happy, the one who hardly ever has
    the answers, and the one who still wants to get the girl.

Joshua Biller

Dark Snow

The snow covering the little branches began to melt.
All was quiet on the front porch. It was cold and dream-like.
The young grass washed its face in the melting snow.
The trees bent down, yielding in silence.
Dawn came hesitantly. A man bowed his head,
Finding no reprieve in the coming day. The pale light
Suffused his eyes with grief. Beyond the birdless sky,
Dark clouds hung heavily with remembrance like dull pain.

Nhac Nguyen

Kevin's Heaven

There once was a man named Kevin
When he died he went to heaven
What he saw we do not know
Maybe a sky as white as snow
Maybe he grew great wings of silk
as white and lush as cow's milk
Maybe his hair turned to gold
for all the secrets he never told
but we know he is in the sky
for not once in his life did he tell a lie
He may have turned into a dove
for all his days full of care and love
What really happened we do not know
but our love for him will only grow

Rebecca Lynn Williamson

Angel's Wings

You are my everything,
You are my angel's wings.
We soar so high, way up in the sky,
with the stars so bright.
You are my heart's delight.
For together we will be, for all eternity.
If by chance we're torn apart,
remember you always hold my heart.
For nothing in this world so right
should be separated every night.
Sweet dreams for you my love.
For I'll be thinking of you from above
with whispers every night
and soft kisses in the sunlight.
Now I must say goodbye
and beg you please don't cry.

Nancy J. Welman

Colors Of The Day

First pink blush of dawn
growing stronger with the rising sun
what shall be the colors of the day?
A clear blue sky or clouds of gray?
A pause in time, we'll wait and see
if yellow sunshine is what will be
white puffy clouds sail by
cotton candy in the sky
black clouds will not be seen today
nor leaden rain will have its way
the day grows long and shadows grow
in shades of purple and pink rose
look up to the sky as twilight shadows fall
and watch the blackness embrace us all
so what shall be the colors of the day?
It is a mystery of life that goes its own way

Jean C. DeBoer

Long Island

The earth here is for growing silent brown
Rich earth pale green the leaves
And all subdued to quiet earnest living
Seasons here belong to earth and by the earth renewed.
The unpoetic leaves of a dirt crop
The rutted fields and early autumn day
The scraps of pine the deeply rooted oak
Sing out the land but of the land betray
No secret of its source the same that moved
Walt Whitman living here who on his walks
Saw all and in reflective mood wrote to himself
And God - like were his thoughts.

Andre Hubbard

Special Memories

Fifty years ago on this special day,
A miracle occurred on the first day of May.
Memories and laughter will always ring loud,
Mother you make us all feel so proud.
Our childhood years we cherish with memories so dear,
With you by our side we never could fear.
We had moments of sadness where tears did fall,
But you never gave in, you stood by us all.
I hope to raise my children as you raised me,
In a home filled with love and laughter for all to see.
So on today, your special day,
I send you my love in so many ways.

Sherri L. Caruso+

To Fly

Did you ever look up at the sky and wonder what it would be like
to fly...?
To fly is to glide and feel your body being lifted into the sky.
The feel on a good day, of the gentle winds hit your face body
and hands-all at the same time.
To go beyond where nobody is able find...
Being able to see the billowy, white, soft blankets of clouds.
If we could fly it could be the most beautiful experience in all
of our lives.

Imagine feeling the warm sun hit your spine.
As we fly into the night from day, the moon and the stars go by.
Feel the beauty carry our minds up, up, into the sky so high.
At one time or another we have all wished we could fly-this you
cannot deny.

We envy the very beauty of the precious bird in flight.
We all wish to conquer the beauty of the sky by learning to fly.
To reach the unlimited height... reaching through all the skies
into the eternal light.

Mary E. Clark

Twelve Giant Steps

I'm home again; alone again
    just as the days before.
I search my soul for the power it takes
    not to do it anymore.

I promise myself. I demand my self
    not to reach for the refrigerator door.
But my control is nil. I have no will
    not to do it anymore.

If I were a drug addict or alcoholic,
    I could check into Charter By The Sea.
But there is no place to run and hide,
    because food is always with me.

I curse God, then admit to God,
    "I'm weak. I have no control."
I cry to God, then pray to God,
    "Please, God, help my soul."

My heart does ache as I struggle
    to find happiness for me.
Do I take twelve steps to the refrigerator,
    or twelve steps to recovery?

Dolores J. Wilson

Ode To Youth

There was a light once burned so bright that now is just an ember.
I searched my heart to find the cause and faintly I remember.
The fire that burned was fueled by youth and hopeful innocence.
Time past on, hope grew dim, and youth could not then recompense.
So none was left but just the coals fueled now by age and
forgotten goals.
I pray that God give me the wood to build a fire where embers stood.
A fire that God alone can start, time or youth not now
apart, an eternal flame within my heart.

Nancy Crain

If I Could Wish For Anything

If I could wish for anything
I don't know what it would be,
but I'd sure like a great, big money tree.

Maybe I'd build a tall, long wall
that would keep war away and over
on the other side there would be peace everyday.

Perhaps I'd grab the moon and stars
so they would never again be blurred away
by the pollution from cars.

I might bring back extinct animals every one
I'd provide them with clean water
in a world without guns.

Maybe I could make all blind people see
so that they would know
what a beautiful place the world can be.

Now that I think about it
I don't think I'd want a money tree,
I just want all people to be happy
people like you and me.

Rebecca Hafner

All Things Need Something

Prayers can't be answered unless they are prayed,
Games can't be won unless they are played,
Songs can't be heard until they are sung,
Bell can't resound until they are rung;
Kites cannot fly without any breeze,
Locks will not open without any keys,
All Nature's creatures and man need a mate,
God gave us power ourselves to re-create;
Life deals out bitter along with the sweet,
All things need something to make them complete.

Ethel T. Jacks

Galactile Eclipse

The Earth shines bright in the Day night Sky
Look to the around and be blinded by the Sunland's Rays.
Read a paper in the Noon night
It says, "Earth orbits Sun
    Sun orbits Moon"
Look up, reach up, grab a Blanket of Asteroids,
Pull Them close to warm Yourself
It's cold
It's so cold
It's so unbearably cold

Julie Mitchell

Life

Sometimes I wonder,
If God will sit down and say,
What have I done that was so great,
I created man and a great world too,
But they insist on destroying it,
Because I gave him a free will,

The things that go on in their minds,
As they murder and prosecute their own kind,
Does this show I am a failure,
For what I have done,
Or is it just man one on one,

I gave them a great love,
All the love I had,
A love that is so great,
It would last for all eternity,

Man has to learn,
Their heart can be pure,
But their mind will remember,
What they where.

  Terrence J. Roese

The Mirror Sings A Different Song

I rise in the morning now with bones that creak,
I'm getting frail - I'm getting weak.

My thoughts however stay youthful and young.
The mirror sings a different song.

I can see the gray hair instead of the blonde,
I see all the wrinkles - the youth it is gone.

Though my thoughts however stay youthful and young.
The mirror sings a different song.

I remember running and jumping in play,
I remember life in a different way.

Though my thoughts however stay youthful and young.
The mirror sings a different song.

The mirror shows a stranger - who is it that I see,
Yes, I'm almost positive this cannot be me.

My thoughts however stay youthful and young.
The mirror sings a different song.

I yearn the life that used to be,
The one when I still looked like me.
My thoughts however stay youthful and young.
The mirror sings a different song.

  Carrie Ross

Veiled Truth

Mirage of friends, having fun
They see my smile, my work being done
Hollowed smiles greet my Concavity obscured
Hidden depression not so observed
They all hear my words of delight
They do not listen to my offered plight
A make up artist, my masks well made
And when they're all gone, my smile fades
Alone in a crowd
Wanting to cry out loud
Why hide my pain
My smiles hold only vain
I want for all to know
But do I really want to show
All this affliction growing inside
Why do I run, why do I hide
There is no way out, my pit too deep
All I can do is sit, and weep

  Bradley A. Kopp

You Are, I Am

You, my love, are the sunshine that breaks through on a cloudy day,
And I am the flower that buds forth from your warm ray.

You are a brook that flows free,
And I am the rock that moves slowly along so happy with
  all the world to see.

You are a novel with only love to tell,
And I am the fingers that turns the pages entranced by your spell.

You are the sword that wins every fight,
And I am the hilt that is so proud of your might.

You are the summer rain that falls slowly through the night,
And I am the parched earth that looks anew come first light.

Together, we are One.

  Carol McCulloch

Untitled

It's all too beyond me
too far away to hold
the dark man and all the lost girls
striving, pleading for a life denied.
(For how long?)

For a quarter she offers me
A lifetime of jaded wisdom and
old fortune-cookie sayings.

I could be one of the Magi
at the top of the mountain,
giving away my knowledge to the single-stone warrior

I could hold you in
the palm of my hand,
caressing you with
Ambrosia fingertips.

So I drink her milk and honey
and fish the quarter out of my pocket.

  Brianne Bolstetter

A Cry In The Night

Lost, confused by his Paradox, man starts his search.
At first he is not sure, but in the looking glass he sees nothing.
his inspiration, his motivation, his soul is no longer visible.
Oh, the things he tries!
He vows, he breaks - he takes and takes.
Oh, the times he cries...
He shoots, he bombs - he's alive then dies.
Living, ah, the answer to the enigma of life.
To not do so is to quench the Fire.
Leaving the endless, everlasting, embers of the soul
  to smolder forever more.
To do so, to live and love for another,
To answer his question of himself is
To be of Nature again, whole -
unFallen and unSpoiled.

  Doug Frazier

Morning Call

Leaves are dancing toward the ground,
Grasshoppers are flying all around,
Raindrops are falling off a rose,
Fireflies etch disappearing prose.
Night descends into a pinkish mist,
That fairies catch when they close their fists.
Cicadas then begin to hum,
While inch worms beat a silent drum.
You know that morning's drawing near,
And this night time magic will soon disappear.

  Valarie Kobrovsky

Untimely Love

Untimely love, you have been planted many years too long;
yet you have blossom in an untimely season upon the
heart of one that refuses to let you flourish to beautify his world.

Untimely love, why did you have to be so eager to burst
through the soil, and reach out tenderly to one that refuses
to let you grow fully into the strong love that
you really desire to be?

Untimely love, please return again to your secret place,
so deep into the soil; that you will never surface again
to touch or be felt by anyone.

Untimely love, you are beyond any human understanding or
imagination, but yet so true and yielding.

Oh, oh untimely love no one will ever believe you are
genuine, because you are so different than any love that
has ever existed, so please return to your secret place,
never, never, never to surface again; then I will not have to
cry or hurt anymore.

Letitia Vania Villines

Hope Is The Only Sound

Come and see this battle!
Come and see this fight!
Come and see how challenger's chances are dim,
But how his hopes burn hot and bright!

See how he keeps on trying.
See how he holds his ground.
See how that in his ears,
Hope is the only sound.

Also how that in his eyes,
Winning is all he sees.
Also that in his lungs,
Victory is all he breathes.

He may get hit and beaten.
He may get thrashed and tossed.
But once it's over, and the dust has cleared,
He will not be the one that lost!

Phillip Seibel Jr.

Lauren

I see wonder and amazement in your blue eyes
As you tiptoe and stretch to reach the stars in the skies.
A shy, sweet smile automatically lights up your pretty face
Even when you struggle to keep up in the world at your own pace.

Sometimes you reach up for a big helping hand
To keep you steady or to help you stand.
What is it like to look up at others who are so tall
As you stand there so fragile and so very small?

You laugh while you try to learn to kick a ball
Like a colt, your legs become tangled, and you fall.
I watch as you chase an elusive butterfly for awhile
Or reach down to touch or smell a flower, then sweetly smile.

Will you look back on your childhood with fond memories
And remember the startling sunshine peeping through the trees?
Will you remember the rainbows, moonbeams, and the stars in the sky
And forget those times something broke your heart and made you cry?

I hope you challenge life like a ship in a storm at sea
And you struggle and strive to be the best you can possibly be.
I hope you hold life dearly, and sweetly as a petal on a flower
Living life to its fullest every day, every minute, and every hour.

Evelyn B. Williams

My Worst Regret (Is There Still Time?)

Spoiled views unbowed,
    then paved over by hard times.
On my own too soon,
    mistaking paths and signs.

Lot of things I should have done:
Played more with my kids, having fun.
Hug their young bodies,
    tossing them to the sky,
    kiss their red cheeks,
    baring a tenderness before I die.

Too, looking back over the years,
I'd be unmanly, showing them my tears.

Now they're all gone, living their own lives;
I save this conscience by telling myself lies.
A better mind would have opened that door
    by telling them I loved them more.

Allen E. Brogan

Clandestine Prison

I am an inmate of a clandestine prison, my bars you cannot behold,
The transparent walls are a mighty fortress standing lofty and bold.
My jovial appearance is quite illusive for there are none who know,
Of the confinement that I am trapped within and how it pierces my soul.
Fear and anxiety snare me, it is these that make up my cell,
With perpetual misery they put me in torment making this life a hell.
A depressive state of mind hinders as that of a ball and chain,
hopelessness gouges the soars and compels me to go insane.
Weakening hearts are like shackles, they allow no way to run,
Flesh will grow exhausted as it swelters in the sun.
In languishment I am withering as I'm hemmed on every side,
From this latent penitentiary, there is nowhere I can hide.
Freedom I am yearning for you with an intensifying zeal,
Please lend an ear to my cause and harken to my appeal.
Let me vanquish these arduous bonds, give me victory over my foe,
Release me from the clutches of pain and permit my mind to grow.
Clandestine prison, you can't last forever, you'll surely meet your day,
And when this bird breaks from its cage, with grace it will fly away.

Robert Calhoun

The Dog's The Host Of The Flea Party Tonight

The dog's the host of the flea party tonight.
He fights those fleas with all his might.
Scratch, scratch.
Sniff, sniff.
He fights,
Till those fleas are out of sight.
Take off my collar, he whines,
As he sits under the pines.
Scratch, scratch.
Sniff, sniff.
He fights,
Till those fleas are out of sight.
The dog's the host of the flea party tonight.
He fights those fleas with all his might.
Scratch, scratch.
Sniff, sniff.
Oh that dog's got to be sick.

Erin Gorsich

The Lock The Key

The lock has a certain key
The key is made of something you can only feel
You can't feel the key with your hands
You can only feel the key with your soul
Many have the lock, but few have the key
Many search for the key, but never find it
The lock is your heart
The key is true love

Erin Joyce Anderson

Dreams

At Five, I could be anything I dreamed.
Cinderella, a Princess, or even a Queen,
the world was a giant playground to me.

At Eighteen, I was ready to pursue my dreams.
A diploma, plans for college, I was ready for anything,
the world was brand new with limitless options for me.

At Twenty-three, I got the education to pursue my dream.
Dorm life, some parties, and a bachelor's degree,
the world should watch out, there's no stopping me.

At Thirty, I had everything I dreamed.
A house, a good job, and loving family,
the world not my oyster, but a struggle everyday.

At Forty, I could not imagine this in my worst dreams.
No house, or good job, I lost almost everything,
the world is now different and cruel to me.

Now if you see me on the street, do not look down on me.
Just know, that just like you, I had and still have many dreams.

Alison Watt

There Is A Tree That Stands Outside My Window

There is a tree that stands outside my window.
It is small, it is young, but its spirit is of ages old.
Through the months I watch it live.
Its leaves flutter in greeting to the winds, its branches sway and
bend, yielding.
Every fiber reaching for the sun, its breath of joy at the loving rain.

Every year it bursts into leaf, resplendent and giving.
It grows, straining to reach new heights.
It rests.
And it dies a little death.
But always, it awakens from its slumber, and it grows ever more.

Are our green friends not reflections of what we are?
In youth, the flamboyance of life.
In maturity, the peak of living.
In older years, sedateness and vibrant pride.
In wizened age, the beauty of truth without adornment.

Spring, Summer, Autumn, Winter.
The four sisters of the life cycle,
each bearing four daughters, each who in turn bear four more.
The cycle is eternal, so be the way.
And the tree is my guide.

L. May Kee

How

The rain drops descend from the sky up above;
Lovers run wild in the streets of love.
Children play in the sandboxes of care;
While feelings are floating everywhere.
I look up and feel the wetness upon my face;
As I feel as though I'm caught in some race.
I keep trying to win a battle of thoughts,
But all of my thoughts seem to be lost.
As my search continues and the race goes on;
I look long and hard for the memories gone.
I noticed a picture upon which was your face;
Then suddenly I hung my head low in disgrace.
What could have I done to change in your eyes?
It hurt so much when we said our good-byes.
The one thing I cared about is nothing now,
And I'm left with the continuing question of
"How"

Johnie M. Doyle

namecalling

when i was born, *they* called me colored
i thought it meant i had a choice
so i chose brown 'cause it looked like me
and then when i was ten *they* starting calling me black
somehow i must have looked different to *them*
'cause to me i still looked brown and everybody i knew
still looked brown, but now they were black too
except sometimes we were called n****r
and I didn't know what color that was

i don't think that color thing worked out too well
'cause around the time I turned twenty *they* starting calling me
african-american, hyphenated just like that, like a woman
strugglin' to preserve her identity after marriage, and
it made sense a little 'cause i always felt like i was struggling
strugglin' to be all the things *they* wanted me to be —
colored, black, african, american
strugglin' to figure out what else i was
other than what *they* kept calling me, and
after years of strugglin' and figurin', I finally knew who i was
i was all the things *they* had called me after all,
only not the way `thought
i had become a wonderful, colorful woman of african heritage,
filled with american pride

Iris Stevenson

Summer Nights

Summer nights take me away into a peaceful place
Like a sponge I release the stress absorbed from the world
So then I float with the wind that pushes through me
I am alone with my thoughts and a silent melody
Without a care or worry
I am pure...
I close my eyes as visions pass through the back of my mind
I do not see but I care not to
I feel safe in the darkness
I feel as if I could disappear along with my mind
I am without emotions...
I unfold to become a waterfall
I settle between the rocks and become the summer night

Bridgett Wines

Goldfield

Under the shadow of the mystical Superstitions,
Sits the old mining town of Goldfield.
Beneath the majestic spires that rise up to Flat Iron,
The ghosts can be seen and heard at their work.
There are horses tied to the hitching post, metal these days.
Music rings out from the saloon, guitar and not piano.
Landscape that use to be beautiful and unmarred,
Now is dotted with modern houses, ugly with them.
Gunfire can still be heard on main street,
Entertaining the tourists who flock to get a taste of the old west.
The players dress their parts, even down to wearing pistols.
Trying to bring the old west alive, but it's dead and gone.
The train whistle can still be heard on occasion,
But the train doesn't pass through anymore, it just carries
    tourists around.
The beer still flows in the old saloon and whisky too,
But it's out of aluminum cans and bottles with screw tops.
The only constant thing is the mountain with its mysticism.
Goldfield is alive, but it's dead and the wild west with it.

Dina M. Dean

Sorry

Sorry about your wedding day,
The one you had the first of May.
Sorry your dog got out of the yard,
It must have been pretty hard.

He ruined your dress,
And made it a mess.
But that's O.K.
It didn't look good anyway.

He ate your cake,
The one you had to bake.
It was disgusting and crusty;
It made the room all musty.

So next time you try to plan a wedding,
You might want to get some help with the setting.
You might want to check the lock on your gate,
Otherwise, you might lose your mate.

Vickie Huntsman

A Walk In The Woods

The trees, so pretty covered in snow,
We went for a walk in the woods you know.
The air was fresh, the snow was bright,
The snowflakes sparkled in the light.
The stumps wore a lovely cap of snow,
When we went for a walk in the woods you know.
I caught a snowflake on my tongue,
And over my head some branches hung.
A blanket of snow covered the ground,
And lots of sticks were broken I found.
A beautiful day with lots of snow,
We went for a walk in the woods you know.

Justine Pinskey

Heroes

The Angels came down from heaven,
On the day all my heroes died,
I saw the end of Brenner's Seven,
And I saw the kryptonite bring the big Man from the skies.

The Angels surrounded me that day,
When Mr. Wayne took his last breath of air,
And we heard the last song by the little Runaway.
It was a day when other people passed on without a care.

The Angels could not hide my tears,
On the day my greatest hero died.
My pain has still not rested after all these years,
Because Grandpa, I never did get to say goodbye.

That same day, the Angels flew back into the sky.
They placed the heroes inside my heart,
And that's when I knew none of them could die,
Because we will never be apart.

Brandon M. Detwiler

"True Love"

I love you from the bottom of my heart
To the depths of my soul.
I come to you freely, willingly, and clear of thought.
You have captured my heart, my mind, and my soul,
And I am here today to commit my pledge to our union.
Before, my strength was the strength of one;
Today my strength is much more than two.
Drawing on the strength that comes from true love,
We will rejoice in the power of our new partnership.
This I pledge to you from this day forward,
With everlasting love.

Chester L. Smith

Lies

You said you loved me, was that a lie?...
You said we made love, was that a lie?...
You said nothing would come between us, was that a lie?...

As I sat and heard the hurt in your voice when you said
good-bye I wonder was it really there or was it a lie?...

When you told me you might come back some day did you
mean it or was it a lie?...

It seems lies and love are connected somehow, how you
ask... Some people may say the truth hurts more is that true or
just a lie?...

You said people change and grow and can't find time for
love is that true or just a lie?...

As I stood and confronted you and said love comes once,
and only once, and I found it in you and couldn't love another,
was that true... or just a lie...

Jennifer Wampler

Marked With Love

Jealous and isolated, but free and divine.
Why does one feel?

Irrational and impatient, but tolerant and collect.
Why does one act?

Listen and sigh, but agree and nurture.
Why does one do?

Contradiction reveals...
This one in love.

Rebecca Movall

Hearts Of Darkness

Hearts of darkness
a dark black heart
like a sharp broken knife
it can stab you like a dart
taking away your life
and it hurts
like the teeth of a dog
taking away your words
it feels like you're being crushed like a dog
there's no way out
not a way you should try
it makes you want to shout
and just start to cry
but stand up put your face straight ahead
don't let them hurt you
and be glad that you're not dead
you'll know when you break threw
you're free now
cause you found out what to do

Sara Sever

Summer Smell

Summer rain hot side walk pain
sweet smell summer mist sustained
drenched love rain
drowned her love pain
quenching fire first time desired
clouded souls roll maverick colors blame havoc
wake up shower rhyme fired color of time
sleepy eyed night stand candle flames
a young wife and the keys to the beamer
are gone again.

Joe Cantalamessa

The World Today

I lay in bed on this cold, dreary night
Knowing that all in the world is not right.
The hope of the youth has been blown from my mind
By the thunder and lightning that has made my eyes blind.

Blind to the terror all over the earth.
For every three deaths there is only one birth.
Why must we live in this world full of fear?
To cry a cry, just one single tear.

I walk outside into the dark, dreary night
knowing that all in the world is not right.
I stand in the rain, my mind is washed clear
of the rage and the terror and all of the fear.

As I walk back inside, I think to myself
of the terror and hatred inside of itself.
So I lay in bed on this cold, dreary night
knowing that all in the world is not right.

Kasey Williams

To Those—

To those who claim to hold stature,
And to those who proclaim power,
Who believe their word is a Foreseer's,
And their equals stand only their mirrors,
Who question if their thrones are too low,
Laugh and label the ones below,
Exist no higher then the ground at their feet
Or the people they once believed to defeat
Who possess no majesty in which to seize
Their purity ravaged with disease
And their crowns are plated with pure ignorance
Their equals only mirror their own indifference
And the pedestal in which they rule upon,
Is nothing more than the crate that we stand on.

Michelle Kinnaird

A Special Friend

Life has many pitfalls
To test how well we've learned
The lessons we encounter
Around life's every turn
I've had my share of setbacks
And I'm sure you've had yours too
But through it all one thing remained
To help me make it through
Some may call it friendship
Tho' to me it's so much more
It's a special link between two souls
That lets the spirit soar
A friend is one you talk to
At a party or the fair
But a special friend knows when you're hurt
And shows you that they care
It doesn't happen every time
In fact, the times are few
And I consider myself fortunate
That I share that link with you

Rebecca Dye

Endurance

I've had to live for several years,
    With such bad pain it's hard to bear.
But with God's help and faith and prayer,
    Please give me one or two more years.
I am not old, I am not young,
    But in the heart and body stung.
I have good family and good friends,
    But tell them little and pretend.
Most people do not want to hear,
    Bad news which is so hard to bear.
I only ask one thing of God,
    Please make this pain just not so hard.
I can not do too many things,
    But when I can- to God I'll sing.
So God and I will be best friends,
    Through life and death until no end.

Georgine S. Gunn

Spellbound

As I stand at the ocean's door
    and gaze across the crashing waves,
I am hypnotized....
My senses are stunned
The trail of the blazing sun with
    the caress of the trade winds kiss my face.
The embracing of the sand by the surf
    plays at my feet.
The gentle roar of the waves rushing to the shore
    greet my ears.
The mingling of the sweet essence of the hibiscus
    and the tangy salt air
    Fill my lungs.
All harmonize into one blissful moment.
As time stills
    and the amber globe sinks into the horizon
I am captured....
But as the sun drops from the sky
    and dusk turns to darkness
    The spell is broken.

Michelle Park

My Friend And I

My friend and I walked down the street.
In 1960, they said: "There goes a man and a n****r."
And my friend and I kept walking.

My friend and I walked down the street.
In 1970, they said: "There goes a man and a Negro."
And my friend and I kept walking.

My friend and I walked down the street.
In 1980, they said: "There goes a white man and a Negro man."
And my friend and I kept walking.

My friend and I walked down the street.
In 1990, they said: "There goes a white man and a black man."
And my friend and I kept walking.

My friend and I walked down the street.
In that year, they said: "There go two men."
And my friend and I turned and smiled.

Duane Smith

Unbearably Bare

Wouldn't it be terrible and oh so unbearable
to have been born a bear with no hair
a bare bear
Without his little self all wrapped up in fur
brrrrrrr
He would have to find a warmer clime
And lie around in the sun
fun!!!
But to be a bare bear is very rare
Other bears would surely
stare!!!
He must find a fur skin just his shape and size
wise!!!
Then zip it up tight wear it day and night
surprise!!!
No more bare any where
totally bear

Linda Johnson

A Different Face Of Pain

Sleep, come forth,
deliver my tortured soul
from the bondage of the devil's wrath.

To close my eyes and see nothing,
to feel or hear nothing, would be a blessed reward.

My soul feels the madness of a thousand raving lunatics!
A pardon from this prison of ignorance...
A gift...
Far better than any I have ever known.

My sadness engulfs me like a dark green tidal wave on a raging sea!
A coldness that I alone know at its darkest depths.

I envy the heavens so vast,
the wind so free,
the night so quiet.

Someday...
My total body...
Mind and soul will finally be at peace.

David E. Gower

Sadly Missed And Always Loved By Everyone

Two years ago, we lost our beloved grandmother, mother and friend.
Her lifelong companion, our beloved grandfather, father and friend,
Recently joined with her and the Lord in the heavens above.

We saw their suffering and their pain, that part of life left unexplained.
The Lord looked down upon them and, then touched them with his
   gentle hand.
He embraced them with his loving arms, and freed them from all
   worldly harms.
We all have said from time to time, "I wish the pain you feel were mine."

He calls us in gentle way, not promising another day.
He is the one who must decide, from all of us who lives and dies.
Stay prepared your whole life long, there comes a time we must
   move on.
We often find our chances gone, to say "I loved you all along"
For those of you still left today, I have but one thing left to say:
Give all the love you have today,
Tomorrow soon may slip away.

Theresa A. Roberts

I Never Cry....

I never cry, why?
Those years I saw so many pass,
I could not cry, my soul locked with wrath,
They say a man should never cry,
Now I see, it's an honest lie,
Who would tell who would believe,
Tears are weak to men of steel,
Angels cry, dressed in black,
no love from heaven, no getting back,
Willows weep without any emotion,
not tears of strife, a devil's potion?
A crack in the air, a flash in the sky,
Rain comes falling, and God starts to cry,
That's when I stumble through the rain,
There I know you won't see my pain,
What must I say, what do I mean?
Instead of cry I'd rather dream,
There tears can fall;
For it's a shadow of reality, a hollow ball,
Now do you see why, I never cry???

Sheldon Gatewood

Child

The boys marching off to war
Some had left cause their town's a bore
In the sand, in the sun and rain
They have yet to feel the pain
They want to make something of themselves
But if they will only time will tell
Some will live while others will die
In husbands arms some mothers will cry
Soon these men will be obsolete
No more sound of their marching feet
Progress can be so unfair
Our demise reduced to one quick flare
He'll press a button that no one hears
Where they land all just disappears
All the people still busy loving
All the animals who had done nothing
All the children robbed of their start
In this tragedy they had no part
All the trees all the life and land
Accomplished all by one man's hand

Laurence Bajbek

Along The Road

It seems like years ago when I started out to find
what I thought I needed, so:
I searched the land, I searched the sea
The only place I didn't search...was me.
It's a funny thing to meet yourself Along The Road

It seems so long ago when I started out to change
what I thought needed changing, so:
I changed my name and my image for the world to see
The only part I didn't change...was me.
It's a fright'ning thing to meet yourself Along The Road

Ah, the road, ah the road, it goes on and on and on.
If we seek ourselves, it gives us what we need.
Ah, the road, ah the road, it goes on and on and on.
If we seek ourselves, it gives us a way to be.

It's not so long ago when I began to understand
What I needed to know.
I looked at my life, it left me cold
So I searched for my spirit and I found...my soul
And it's a wondrous thing to meet yourself Along The Road

Mona Marshall

Cubicles

Hurry-Hurry-Hurry!! Observe beyond, the world of strangeness!!
If you can, visualize the conjectures of your conceptions,
And enter the unknown with curiosity and unsureness,
See the implications of the many and form your own interpretations.

Beyond the temporary curtains of endless boundaries-
Are thoughts of strange visions transformed by necessity.
Be sure to witness the succession of contradicting definitions-
Of how one thinks in different realms of great perplexities.

Observe the surrealistic images of someone's living nightmare,
And touch the swirling depths of all those distorted realities.
Conclude with strange realizations the obsessions of the
    confused insane-
As each cubicle reveals the inner thoughts of one's mind in disarray!!

Be receptive of one's inquisitive eye as you attempt to decipher-
For one's own sanity eludes us at times-so, please, Beware!
To few it's undeniable comprehension for they are captious interpreters.
Be Cautious, for it maybe you, not they, whose reasoning that
    has been betrayed!!!

Linda M. McGarry

Strength On Turbulent Seas

When anger and desperation take hold upon you, and tides of
an angry storm are making you blue.
When all that is heard is invective yatter from souls who
just cannot begin to know.
Those pretentious ones who abhor and make you feel so low.
For this, I have but a few kind words to speak.

Be thou versant, be valiant, and refuse in thyself to be weak.
Do not remain idle and alone.
For there will soon come a day when all thy seeds shall be sown.
Refuse all petty and frivolous talk; but rather be thou
diligent in thy walk.
Always remember never be in great or sudden fear; for help is
certainly at all times very near.

Kimberly A. Lewis

If You Wear A Crown

If you will start each day with a prayer,
If you will take time to show that you care,
If you will not be afraid to shed a tear,
You will help others their crosses to bear.

God speaks. If you will listen to hear
His messages—coming from everywhere—
You will know that He is always near
And you have nothing at all to fear.

When you know you are right, then you must dare
To conquer all evils as they appear
As you journey through life from here to there
And reach Heaven's portals your crown to wear.

Fern K. Ulmer

Untitled

Through the trees the soft winds blow,
The wings on a bird flow within the breeze
The petals on a flower are whisked
Away by the wind
Children in fields playing
Families gathered in harmony
The world together in peace
The day love conquers evil.

Melanie Wright

Untitled

A little boy goes to a straw hut no bigger than a large outhouse.
He eats whatever is under the rock outside of his hut.
His teeth are rotted to the core, and he has a cold, a fever,
chicken pox.
All his bones are visible and he is hurting all over
On the other side of the world,
A little girl complains that her chicken doesn't taste good.
She complains that her hair doesn't look good.
The little boy doesn't have a choice, or a chance.
He is there,
He doesn't deserve to be there, but he is.
The little girl should try living like the little boy for a day.
Then, she would never complain again,
Or she still would, and it is hopeless.
She never will change her ways.
She won't change.
Don't worry about her,
It's her problem if she doesn't like anyone or anything.

Allison Allen

Years Ago

Years ago there wasn't crime and stealing in the street;
There wasn't people bumming money from everyone they meet.
There wasn't people suing for falling in the yard;
There wasn't people quitting because the work got too hard.
There wasn't people lying to try to get more;
There wasn't people selling drugs just so they can score.
There wasn't all the sex on T.V. every night;
There wasn't all the kids always looking for a fight.
There wasn't all the diseases killing people everyday;
There wasn't all the problems that never go away.
There wasn't people dying for a jacket or pair of shoes;
There wasn't all the killing they tell you on the news.
No one ever locked their doors, it never crossed their mind;
They never worried that their neighbors would come and rob
    them blind.
If the world keeps on changing, the way that is has been;
There isn't going to be a world for our kids to grow up in.

Susan Amburgey Stevens

"Me And My Creature"

As the rain comes down
While the air is still warm,
Everything slimy comes up from the ground.
Crawling and slipping into the nearest place,
There I was sitting as we came face to face.
Smiling and wondering what that creature could do,
Did it have any friends, would it land on my shoe?

You could hear the birds chirping
And a far church bell ring,
Just me and my creature,
Not doing a thing.

An odd looking fellow,
It didn't say much.
Just sitting so still,
I was afraid to touch.

Very content, my new friend and I,
We sat there just letting the time fly by.
The rain had stopped falling, now a bright, sunny day,
In the prettiest month, the month of May!

Susan J. Phelps

Angels We Are One

For the apocalypses straight from the mouth of an Angel Lord!
"Angels We are one!"
With word of procrastination we are going to make this war a lot
  of fun!

Arm yourselves with virtue and the amour of undone justice
Attack the America V I P with legal tender and make his mind on OPUS
The Adversary is strong no matter which way you see it
Oppose and take no stuff

This is democracy and a wee bit
All in favor of Christ the I con the enemy is you State...
Fill old glory with Love and Honor
that she may have good Fate.

When the American dream gets back to family living
We'll execute our laws of Love and giving! And make
all creation one again!
Angels We Are One.

Tony Anthony Walker

The Puzzle

I've lived my life in stolen moments
wedged between "I must do's".
I've watched and I've waited, and bided my time
'till reality's what I could choose.

The child in the photos - that isn't quite me
reminds me of someone I knew.
Is it mother or father or sister or self
that fires the flame flicking through?

I want to live cries a voice from inside.
To feel joy and sorrow I'll sacrifice pride.
My pocketbook's full. I'll pay the price.
The cost is too high to keep numbing with ice.

A tentative venture. A trial to endure.
An eggshell that's starting to crack.
Do we all know at the start of the line
this new life's just the old one come back?

I've gathered around me the mortar and stone.
I'm groping about for the key.
I've assembled the puzzle, the pieces are fit...
and I'm climbing the stairway to me.

Cheri' Erdman Adesi

Rebirth Of The Soul

In the past loves are lost,
  In the present loves are gained.
Until I gazed upon your beauty,
  The future merely waned.

Your smile more potent than a spring day,
  Stolen when an angel turned her back.
Did raise me to the heights of heaven,
  When all seemed dark and black.

The brilliance that is you,
  Warmed the gloom into a joyous heat.
The flame burst into a blaze,
  That no one else could beat.

Now that your heart flows within me,
  I see a long future filled with life.
Without you I see many unfilled dreams,
  Dying and slipping away into a world of strife.

Kevin Henderson

Chicago Canvas — Personal

Chicago, I shall paint you as I feel,
Your image in my mind from start to end,
With opposites galore like cold and zeal,
Or beauty and the beast she had to tend.

A face of steadfast mother, fickle girl
With dodging taxis screaming at your feet,
Sleek high-rise condos and Victorian swirl,
And elevateds pounding out the beat.

Steel bridges bobbing o'er a river green,
While busy barges glide and launches rest,
And ethnic booths dispense the best cuisine
As friendly folks stream toward Chicagofest.

The Pope and stage stars plus the tourist boons,
Arts of Picasso, Calder, and Matisse,
High opera, disco, rock, and country tunes,
Fresh sights and sounds 'til sleep and a surcease.

Chicago, when my picture is complete,
Your image in my soul forevermore,
My spirit singing lauds in one fine fete,
Will join two famous lions with due roar.

Dorothy Shields De Spain

Dad

Dad, although I never knew you my heart still feels the pain,
  you're a missing link in my love chain.

Although this link is missing Father, I still love you,
  a distant love you might call it, but a love oh so true.

When others talk about their fathers over and over again,
  all I could say is my Dad died before I turned ten.

If it weren't for God almighty in Heaven above,
  I wouldn't know the meaning of a fatherly love.

We may not have shared the father-son routine,
  but for nine years long it was a beautiful dream.

A dream I call it because I can't remember it all,
  but I'll carry your name "Felix"! and always stand tall.

Stand tall, Dad, I said with pride,
  but you being gone really does hurt inside.

So as I close this note I know just what to do,
  I will dedicate this poem, Dad, to you.

Ronald R. Felix

Chasing The Wind

Solitude is a dangerous thing, bearing from its difficult womb
that there must be something to live for
something to die for
something more than a white picket fence and a two car garage
something more than a college degree and financial security
something more than feeling good.

This why and what after is killing me
will it lead to the rainbow's end
or Oz
or Heaven
or somewhere with the authority and wisdom
to answer, to satisfy my rage
and wonder to challenge
the blasphemous notion that all things are as they ought to be.

It's not the idea of existence which so bothers me
but existence itself
dividing the pair a vast chasm
of could've been's
should've been's
and never will be's.

Jeffrey Bryan Littner

"Let Me Show You"

"Let me Show You"
Why the love I embrace, cherish, and feel overwhelm my soul as
it patiently waits as the flowers do the rain that showers them
with joy and intimate feelings of security and love, love that we
once knew that seems like a sweet dream as time past through as the
world slowly begs to be untrue, but not me and you.

"Let Me Show You"
Why birds fly so high and free and descend in a tree and sing
a love song for you and me.

"Let Me Show You"
Why as the sun shines the birds and trees are at
peace and down below we act of beast, but I know Love is
true and one day will find you.

"Let Me Show You"
As the sun fades away and we see less and less, light
then the night appears to rest and you and I caress, and share
of things to come, remember I showed you once upon a time,
And for the moment maybe you'll be mine.

Junious Samuels III

Reflections Of A Lover Past

I reflect upon the day we met
Remembering well the touch of your heart
How we knew each other's smell
In those moments when we were never apart

I reflect how your sweet voice calmed my soul
The mention of you thrilling me so
How warm you made the coldest of days
You redefined my very path
In your kiss I knew life,
and in your kiss
...I also knew death.

I reflect on how I fight to stay afloat
Your words still threaten to dissolve
all of the pride and anger lurking strongly about.
I put behind old friends for you
yet peacefully you say we're through
And though I fight to not give in
I know forever my heart you'll win.

Ivette Aviles

Untitled

As you sit still,
You listen to the clock pass the seconds away,
and softly praise yourself,
for making it through another day.
You think to yourself,
Why everyone expects you to go far,
When to you everything seems so hard.
All the goals you once had seem so faraway.
and all your dreams seem to vanish
more each passing day.
Everyone has lost touch with reality,
and nothing anyone says is true.
You smile thinking nothing will happen to you.
But that smile won't last long
because soon you will see,
no one's life will be spared from the evil that will be.
And no one can protect you,
from the mistakes that you will make.
and no one else can save you,
from the falls that you will take.

Sabrina Chapman

The Eyes Of My Father

I looked through the eyes of my father
And wept.

He saw the world more as a bother
And wept.

I looked through the eyes of my mother
And wept.

She saw the world like no other
And wept.

I looked through the eyes of my sister
And wept.

She thought the world wouldn't miss her
And wept.

I looked through the eyes of my brother
And wept.

He wished the world he could smother
And wept.

But then I looked through my eyes
And saw the world as a prize
And wept.

Josh Galicinao

Full Moon Serenade

At the full moon sweethearts
stroll hand and hand down lovers lane
You could almost hear the man in the moon
singing them a serenade
with an orchestra of crickets
playing from afar

The two danced under a
spotlight shining from a star
As they headed home and
nestled on the front porch swing
Both saddened at what the
light of day might bring
when up in the sky the man in the moon
caught their attention with a wink
of his eye
Then he said, do not be sad the
magic doesn't have to end
Because in a month as always
before, I will be back again.

Susan Marie Farrell

Lost Love

Sailing rough waters loosing all sense of direction
nothing but stormy clouds ahead obstructing my view.
Rain drops pounding on my head darkness engulfs me
my head hangs low haunted with thoughts of you.
Longing for your arms wrapped tightly around me
holding me safely why did you let go?
Absorbed in my loneliness I can't stop thinking of you
two people tried by emotions how was I to know?
Those kisses that greeted me gone forever.
The arms that sheltered me hold someone new.
If you had only turned around and looked into my eyes
you would have seen my heart reaching out fervently for you.

Edda Elid Elias

In My Heart

My heart beats really fast or completely stops around this
certain guy. I think this is love, but I don't understand why.
How can I love him if I don't know why he lives and breathes.

But when all I want is to reach out and touch him as he walks
my way. I've thought about confessing my love, but don't know
what to say. When I think I'll die because I haven't seen him in days.

Sometimes I walk the long way just to see him one last time.
It could be that I melt when I make contact with his gorgeous
eyes. And every little glimpse of him sends chills up my spine.

His voice sounds like a symphony playing sweet music, his laugh
brightens my whole day. A frown upon his face makes the sunshine
seem light years away.

When someone is talking about him my heart begins to dance.
Can this really be love I have to ask.

I write my first name with his last and add Mrs. and imagine
all the sweet words he may whisper. When I think of heaven I
see myself embraced in his arms, and that's how I know I'm in love.

Vanessa Sophy

My Love Like The Dew

Does the dew ask the morn
Can I kiss blades at dawn,
With my tears from the evenin' now gone?

Can I glisten and shine
On honey suckle vines,
And hang weightless on humming bird wings?

May I linger and cling to the time that is mine,
Till the sun makes me one with the air?

And will you miss me at noon
Or at dusk when you rest,
While stars float upon the night breezes?

But you know I'll be there
Where fireflies tease me and taste me
In the cool air.

Then I will turn golden
When your light I am holding
And once again morning we share.

Crystal Liberatore

Questions To God

Why did you have to put me in this life?
Why do I have to live this life?
Why couldn't I have been someone's princess?
Why couldn't I have been someone's spoiled child?

Why did you make my daddy go away?
How come mommy has to be sad all the time?
Is it necessary for my family to argue all the time?
Will all of this make me fit for heaven?

Did my eyes have to see the things they saw?
What good will that do for me?
Make me stronger?
I'm already strong, I've carried the weight of ten men.

Why was my load heavier than my friends?
Is it fair to see the world through scarred eyes?
How will I see its beauty for its worth?
For my pain will my future be brighter?

If by chance I have no reward,
what will become of me?
After I lived such a dreadful existence,
Will you at least save a spot for me in heaven?

Melissa Berger

Scarlet The Brave Cat

Scarlet rescued her litter of kitties
From a burning building.
Brought them out one by one
Never stopping until every one
Was there safe in her care
They were named Misty Blackey and Tan
Whitey and Brown
This story was heard all over town
with patches and blotches all over her face
The last I heard they were on the mend
With offers to take them in
I hope Scarlet and her kitties
are not in that situation again

Josie Maxton

Civil War Poem

Our destination is just over that hill,
the smoke is thick; the air is still,
the damp grey shrouds of this dark day;
concealed the bodies where they lay.

But as we stood and mourned our dead,
shots rang out and blood ran red,
and suddenly we charged again
against the black stone batteries.

The brave legions press on, but still I can see-
some terror stricken cowards who turn and flee,
oh moment terrible; moment grim,
I fall to the earth with a shattered limb,

but I would not retreat; to stubborn and proud,
I rose to my feet screaming my country's name loud,
and in a last glorious rush as I fell with my pride, I yelled;
"Long live freedom, for this I have died."

Margot LeClair

My Little Child

My little child is asleep in his bed, safe and sound there he's lying.
Across the town on the cold hard ground another child lies dying.
He's a throw-away child left to make it alone,
The ground is his bed and the street is his home.
My little child has hugs and kisses and holds his teddy bears,
The throw-away child knows little of love or anyone who cares.
There's no warm cooked meal when his stomach is aching,
No gentle support when his young heart is breaking.
In his struggle to live he'll fall victim to many who'll take
advantage of him,
He'll eat trash, steal, push drugs, and sell his body to them.
This child is hungry, sick, and cold and no one cares that he's dying.
He knows he won't make it and he's angry inside but no one hears
    him crying.
What chance does he have left all alone in a world so cruel and insane?
Why must a child, an innocent child, experience so much pain?
We must reach out with the love of Christ and help children meek
    and mild.
We do to Him what we do to these - yes to him the throw-away child.

Stacy Hamer

Spring

Fresh morning dew enveloping the earth,
Robins singing mellow tunes,
Sunshine brilliantly warming your face,
Trees swiftly swaying in the breeze,
Flowers exploding from underground,
Grass bursting with shades of vivid greens,
Butterflies fluttering in fields and meadows,
Kites jumping and leaping above,
Children laughing and playing with joy,
Cool nights refreshing you after a long day.

Jennifer Przydzial

"Give Me A Chance To Live"

We walk together, and breath the same air,
I eat the same foods and drink the same liquids,
I can't make choices for myself.

Your eyes are my eyes, and I can't see without them.
even though I have a mouth, I can't speak for myself.
and the only thing in the whole world, that I am asking you,
!please mother! give me a chance to live.

But I know it's impossible, because I have to submit to your
decisions. Even if I don't agree with you, but you are my mother,
and I feel sad because I can't tell you that I am a
human being, that I have a life just like yours, and I wish, to live.

I know that it's hard for you to understand, because of your
personal problems. I know that you don't have someone to help
you raise me with when I am born, but if it's like that you can,
give me away to someone who loves, me and cares for me.
After everything there's one more thing I want to say...,
Mother please don't kill me.

Jose W. Negron

Let's Face It

It's election time again and everybody's in a line.
They're watching the candidates, looking for a sign.
We don't want any more taxes, or new laws on the book;
We need more money, and some rights they already took.
If the "Signs Of The Times" is what I'm seeing in the street,
Then actually it seems that my future's not too sweet.

What we need in the White House is someone from our side.
To stand up and let them know that freedom hasn't died.
Drop half the legislative branch, and all the lobbyists too;
We don't need that many people telling us what we can do.
Stop solving world problems, letting us fall on the way.
There's problems here to solve, ones we're facing everyday.

Businesses leaving the country for cheaper labor over there.
Americans are loosing jobs here, and nobody seems to care.
Let's tell them we want a change, everyone yell it out loud;
Let them know we're still Americans, standing tall and proud.
We're tired of seeing the line between the rich poor expand,
Soon, just like the Indians they'll push the poor off the land.

Anthony Saunders

Snow Angels

The kitchen window is an orchestra seat as I watch
the snowflakes parade to the ground; left...right...left.

Then, the day-long storm heightens causing flakes to snow up,
and then down, changing as quickly as you can blink an eye.

Changes that challenge my usual comfort level with these
unique art forms. To my dismay, they are behaving much more
like confused tourists, making U-turns on the Interstate.

Finally, the storm abates and only the blue-white softness
on the ground is available for the wind to spoof into tiny whirlwinds.
The sun emerges causing shadows to appear in sharp relief.

Now they pour from their homes; men, women, children,
their cats and dogs. Some, armed with sleds, shovels and snow
blowers prepare to conquer all 25 inches of the silence.

How many consider that it was deposited to cover the stains
and refresh our over-used planet? How many re-discovered the
joy of halted traffic, home-cooked meals, a higher power?

Just then one, small, laughing boy completes his 12th and final
Snow Angel. While I watch him clap his mittened hands in delight,
they obey his signal....and rise up to fly away Home.

Pauli Joyce Magargal

Stricken

Sadness swept upon us,
Though the night draws near,
To many the moon is not happy tonight,
That seems quite clear,
But he wouldn't want unhappiness,
Not even a slight tear,
For He is much happier there than he ever could be here.

Darkness has now fallen,
Yet still the night's not becoming.
For quite a while,
A simple smile,
Will not easily be returning,

Pools of tears,
Are unfortunately clear,
The only way to explain,
How inside, with any loss,
We can show our pain.

Ashley Matson

Forgotten Trust

Being able to trust is a wonderful thing.
Knowing you have one to share with is more than can be seen.
But after your confidant, your lover, your friend,
Turns and betrays you, the pain never ends.
The feelings of hurt, of disbelief, of revenge,
Go through your mind and become your best friend.
No one else can you trust, you feel so deprived,
Knowing that now in your life you have nothing to hide.
Your secrets, your life, all out in the open.
Paranoid and confused, you can go on no longer.
Not a piece of information, a tid-bit of your soul,
Will ever be mended because of such a big hole.
The trust can't be replaced,
The past pushed in your face,
The times you'll never forget,
Thanks to people you regret.
Opening your feelings will never happen again,
For,
Never will you trust even the most
Loyal, loving friend.

Diana Calo

Vader

The red glowing tip of an energy blade,
The hilt of gleaming steel,
The crisp, clean movements like a sunbeam in shade,
An extension of the arm it feels.

A figure in onyx.
A black cloak hangs behind.
An evil from comics,
With a dark twisted mind.

He breaths through a mask,
His voice resonates fear.
He kills with a blow of his mind,
Those too near.

He serves his one master.
He's the Emperor's clone.
His son will show him the light side,
But can it save his soul?

Russell Miner

Untitled

White is for purity it is said
Red because Love is deeper than Red
Black because I'll love you until I'm dead

These Roses say a lot
Hearing by ear I am not
Rather it is felt in my heart
I'll love you until God calls us apart

Even then
I know I'll see you in heaven
For one who has brought so much
joy to husband and sons
Surely shall not be parted long
from her loved ones.

Ronnie Pinnix

Enraptured

Last night I dreamed of walking down
A well worn road, that came to a hairpin
Curve and to my surprise ended, I looked
Across the road, and was captivated by
The view of the valley, it was breathless!

Untouched by time, I saw a peaceful
Village, streets of cobblestone, lantern
Lamp posts and lovely old buildings.

I gazed upward to a high volcanic rock,
Where stood an ancient medieval cathedral,
Its towers reached skyward, bathed in
Hues of golden rays from the setting sun.

I woke from my dream and the remembrance
Brought tears of joy to my eyes, warmth to
My heart and the flow of peace into my soul.

Eugenia C. Eyerman

Life

Life is very special
It's in all God's things
We all have the gift
We all breath the same air
We all see the same sun
It's the green maple leaves
It's the red ladybugs
It's the white daisy petals that bloom so bright
It's the baby animals like the young fawn
It's the plants and us
We are all brothers and sisters through life

Carissa Joiner

I Remember....

I sit and hide and think all day.
When I get back to school (If I make it) I'll have so much to say.
First the nazis came and took away my teddy bear,
Then they yelled at me because I had straight hair.

I sit and hide and think.
I hear so much the shouts the screams
I am so young and I have so many dreams.

I sit and hide and think.
I touch the roughness of my skin,
All these bad things happened to me, did I sin?

I sit and hide and think.
I smell the gas from the chambers,
suddenly everything becomes a blur.

I sit and hide and think.
I see the nazis coming to me.
I might not survive, and there is so much to see....

Tiphanie Rosenblatt

Vaulting Ambition

The glowing sun was rising in the east,
first rays of fire glistened on the sea;
a thundering forewarned a coming beast,
It galloped in and headed straight for me.
The salty wind whipped through its tangled mane,
few flecks of foam had splattered on his hide,
his flaring nostrils proved it was not sane,
a crying gull screeched and away He shied.
the pounding surf flowed in, then pulled away,
while sucking sand squelched underneath his weight;
old Horse Shoes left to perish and decay,
he pawed the scrub, oblivious to his fate.
then suddenly his head jerked up in fright,
He wheeled away forgetting all his might.

Vicki Tseng

What Is This?

What is this?
It falls from dark clouds;
It smells clean;
It holds within.....life;
How I long for this life;
How the world longs for it;
See the dust jump up for it;
See the plants lift their heads;
Extend their limbs;
But, greater than this moisture,
The well of life, springing within me;
Giving me hope;
Reason for facing this dry desert, we call life.

What is this? He comes from above;
He cleanses; he holds within.....life;
I hold this life; how the world longs for it;
See the inhabitants lift their eyes
Extend their voices; how great thou art;
This well of life, living within me; giving me hope;
Reason for living, looking ahead to heaven!

Joyce Tyler

Untitled

to speak to the deceased and ask them of Life,
reaching for the fingers of my teddy bear tree
i kiss the cheeks of Eternity.

the answer awakens the pitched sky at its peak,
when i smell the breath of Death
and it's not bitter nor sweet at dark when the dim disappears.

my Mind slips off,

i feel the damp open arms of the rain, yet nothing gets wet
and mother whispers I Love you.

i want my moon to speak again
it spoke when i was three.

i still don't know the answer, yet
beads of Blood cascade like velvet slowly drying out.
and i ask you - who've Lived before,
do you live in a cotton candy cloud?
i always wanted to live in a cotton candy cloud,
i always wished i could fly.

And i was young and innocent
i looked up at my mother's rose petal face.
i never wanted to Die.

Brooke Emery

131

Life Is.....

Joy, sadness, a trip, a happening, an experience, a miracle.
Who can define it, or explain it.
Does a house, clothes, wealth bring tranquility.
What does it for you, for me.
I hear a voice within say, 'Just be glad to see the day.'

We don't choose the beginning or the end,
But the in-between is for us to tend

The road at times may seem smooth and straight ahead.
Be on guard, there may be bumps in the road, and
    remember what I said.
I hear the voice within say, 'Just be glad to see the day.'

When we think that life has let us down and feel that we
    are getting a raw deal,
Remember we are tested, one and all.
Do we rally or do we fall.
I hear the voice within say, 'Just be glad to see the day.'

Grace Pascocello

A-46

A-46? What is this thing?
Is it alive? Is it dead?
Does it belong to a king?

A-46, What do you contain?
Are you good? Are you bad?
Are you totally insane?

A-46, What is your soul?
Is it light? Is it dark?
Is it black as coal?

A-46, Whatever you may be,
Is not in my mind,
But the reader, you see,

A-46, is a part of you,
Believe it or not,
It's all very true,

A-46, Is your secret, you see,
While you cling to and hold it,
You can never be free,

A-46, Will haunt you this night,·
It will come to your dreams, and there's no way to fight.

Jared G. P. Morris

It's All True

   A tear holds so many thoughts, sorrows, pain. I must be hurt a lot because so many tears fall from my eyes which see so much distress, fighting cold hate. It rolls down my cheeks that used to turn red with joy. Past my ears once hearing laughter and happy stories. On by my mouth which used to form a smile. And drop to the ground below into a pile of grief.

   The sun no longer shines in my mind but is clouded away by hate, unhappy thoughts, and confusion.

   I want to be where I used to be, in a place of happiness. But now it seems that world is gone, far away as the stars and the only way to get there is in my dreams. And it's true, my dreams are filled with the memory of there where everything and everyone was joyous and filled with laughter. The sun rose to smiling faces and the stars lit the way for happy memories.

   But now the cloud of darkness has brought me here to this lonesome desert filled with fear. A fear of never returning to the world we knew. Can this fear be overcome? Why is it here? All because, All because.......

Rebecca McCue

Faith

I was groping through a storm with no let-up in sight,
my future looked dim and lonely as night.
No relief I could find nor shelter to hide,
My tears overflowed, the storm raged inside.

My heart had been thrown carelessly at life,
my emotions were seared by a two-edged knife.
Echoes of laughter sung through my mind,
as my thoughts reversed to previous times.

Gone were the days that I walked in peace,
gone is the joy, my happiness has ceased.
For now I'm on this lonesome road
No one understanding my weary load.

So I lift up my hands for spiritual relief,
I find I have strayed from my soulful belief.
God, if you're here, please help me now,
I beg for your mercy as I humbly bow.

Judy T. Wrenn

Woman On The Hunt

You sure are a beautiful African American woman, by far
Yes, Black Pearl, you look real good in that expensive white car
You're styling in your Auto to be seen
Girl, the way you have driving ain't cool nor keen

Slow down— Foxy one— and survive
It takes a real live woman
To catch a man's roving eye
When you go cruising by, at the speed of Ten
His heart will pound, as his eyes take you in

Now GIRL-Stop- swing that door open wide
Unfold your TALL, LEAN, TEASE and TAN body
Now step outside— pause a minute-SMILE- then STROLL away
Man will yearn to know you in every way
Cause Black Pearl, no man can deny
You're something special to a man with a roving eye

L. Edythe DeLaine

Return From Cythera

Louis's dead
let's decorate the house
we'll invite all our beautiful friends
Playfully plaster the salon with shells of glitter and gold
hang ornaments from the banister
sing songs holding hands, dancing circles around Aphrodite
spitting diamonds into our wine
And as the outside foliage nudges the windows with jealousy
I'll brush your hair
and you can lick your lips for another lover
We can whisper frivolous lies and tantalizing secrets
into everyone's pink, dainty ears
while bursting bottles of champagne spray bubbles
leaving patterns of flowers on our powdered faces
- a drop on my lash, a mist in the air?
It will be a festival of erotic, pushed up curves
walls and bodies, hills alike, all burning in youth
And while I will be dressed in love
you can be the centerpiece, poised, in control

Matthew Perrin Henry

132

Raging Waters

Though I see a flashing light
and the skies are blue and clear
The calm waters are no longer in sight
and all creatures have disappeared.

The ocean currents begin to sway
as the night starts to grow
The tides are moving faraway
and so they're raging waters I know

Raging waters of the seven seas
Which are crashing from side to side
Its violent waters come to be
Over and over on the tide

As the light of the sun starts to set
the waves begin to lose the current
the ocean seems to show respect
and the raging waters are no longer for certain.

Karen Garcia

Reflection Of The Mind

The images in mirrors we see,
show only shells of what we be.
the actual essence of the soul,
shall be what all men come to know.

The beauty of a shell you see,
can be the darkest hell to thee.
while lack of loveliness makes one shy,
aesthetic values of souls shall cry.

What age old concepts meld man's mind,
that shells be factors of man's design.
why not the soul direct the ways,
The wisdom shown in future days.

The mirror you see reflects the vain,
for good or evil, it looks the same.
no judgments of the mirror can stand,
if souls of man should raise their hand.

What men have wrought upon themselves,
where vain and vile prosper and swell.
why not the mirror reflect the soul,
to reveal the beauty or the ghoul.

Michael L. Ricklefs

Coming Together

From two different worlds,
Yet not so far away;
Coming together absolute,
Not listening to what others say.

Sharing the pleasant times,
And some not so good;
Sometimes staring back,
At the shadows where we stood

Holding each other close,
Protected from any malign;
No harm, hazard, or evil,
Shall ever cross our line.

Forget the past, it means nothing now;
Errors I know we've all made.
Think of the present, and things to come,
And we'll build a bygone barricade.

I see our differences fade away,
like shadows into the night.
Not a thing can bring the shadows back,
As long as we hold each other tight.

Jeremy Weber

River Road

Though it's hilly, rough, and curvy, and I've got a heavy load,
I still look forward to my drive down the winding river road.

It's fun to watch the birds as they take their fleeting bath,
or see the streaking ground squirrel as he darts across my path.

A touch upon the water in the early morning lull.
another fish for breakfast by the slanting, swooping gull.

A large majestic heron like a statue made of stone,
moving not a feather as he stands there all alone.

On the road I see a gopher looking toward the sky.
A hawk is out to get him, at least he's gonna try.

Out upon the gravel in a somewhat hungry mood
sits a lonely little ground hog in a frantic search for food.

A snake had tried to cross the road, I knew just where he sat.
Looked like he was really big and very, very, flat.

The casting out of fish lines, while many boats they share,
some who want the big ones and some who do not care.

My journey nearly over I slip into high gear,
but have to slow way down for a little baby deer.

Though it's hilly, rough and curvy and I've got a heavy load,
I really like the things I see down the winding river road.

Albert E. Patchin

Sunrise

The bright ball of fire ascends slowly,
To station itself in the vast universe.
A new song is sung fit only for holy,
They sing one slight verse, for need to rehearse.

Precise in categories voiced A to Z.
A song is sung to inform of the new day,
Or sung purposely to pleasantly greet me.
I switch sides somewhat roughly in dismay.

A sudden clatter quickly notifies
The nighthawks, crickets, rats, raccoons, and all,
That nearby giants are beginning to rise.
They surrender to the light; the park where they sprawl.

We rise to bid the world a final farewell,
And to take flight to heaven or hell.

Adrea Anise Simmons

Untitled

Many will challenge your convictions few will try your faith
Some will tempt your heart others will lie in wait
They'll try to test your courage and even curse your God
But remember this my son how your feet must be shod
Fight the good fight lay hold on eternal life
Put on his whole armour stand upon his word
Draw nigh unto God resist and satan will flee
Some will call his name and deny with their deed
Others will laugh and say you must live by some man's creed
A few will try to tell you that you must go here or there
But listen to this warning son they don't really care
So be careful my son when you live in this worldly land
Have no fellowship with darkness but tell them where you stand
Don't ever take your armour off till you make it to that land
Fight the good fight lay hold on eternal life
Put on his whole armour stand upon his word
Draw nigh unto God resist and satan will flee
Fight the good fight lay hold on eternal right

Larry N. Williams

Untitled

Lives that we touch —
fragile, broken
fragmented human beings in transition.

Lives that we touch
coming and going
communications that say we care...
fleeting, momentary, or weeks on end.

Lives that we touch
in darkness and light
in crisis and joy —
seeing wishes granted and answers to prayers;
watching dreams dashed
and hope running out;
giving permission to pick up the pieces
and start over.

Lives that we touch
day in and day out —
they cannot help but touch us.

    Hoskins

"An Ode To A Floor"

People always go around walking
Preoccupied and always talking

People's minds are so far gone
They don't even realize what they
are stepping on

The floor is helpful when you're on the go
it supports your feet through rain or snow

If you're walking down the hall
The floor will be there if you fall

So when you're walking with no time to spend
The floor will be there till the end.

    Jeffrey Marshall

The Joys Of Life

Ah, the joys and wonders of life, around each corner I see.
It ever changes and moves about, intriguing the mind as it goes.
This is the song I have come to sing, the melody in my heart.
That life is grand, a wonderful thing, and I am an intricate part.
Ah, sing with me now of the laughter and sadness, let each note
a story be.
And I'll join in the chorus and sing 'long with you, in a
melodious rhapsody.
Come drink with me now of the fruit of life's splendor, we'll
dance in the field so tall.
And when the day's done we'll say it's been good, and we'll
meet with our friends at the mall.

    Larry D. Steadman

Trying Something New

Two dead bodies,
On the river floor

Their lips and faces blue
Limbs only motion from the river current

Their free-floating hair pulsing back and forth
With a rhythmic motion like a beating drum

They thought it would be cool to try something new
Guess doing drugs and swimming wasn't the thing to do

They had their thrills
But now, their life is gone to the river

    Conrad Rogers

Sombra

I see my shadow on the wall.
It's me it wants, after all.
It'll eat me when it's all said and done.
No escape, it keeps pace when you run.
If you'll look close, you will see.
Our shadows have a purpose to be.
Always one side of us is in the light,
The other ever withheld in the night.
You can be righteous and you can be good,
But always near us, our shadow has stood.
It's wise to understand this, the better you will be.
For when you're in the darkness, it's easier to see.
You can ignore me and make my love shoo.
But I can see the shadow behind you.
Think you're so big with your wonderful figure?
Astuteness will show that your shadow's even bigger.
You think that you're so much better than me.
Lift your weights, do your Trigonometry.
But I can see, straight through your thick skull,
And I know that your soul is very dull.

    Matthew W. Stewart

A Night Off The Streets

As if it had been heaven sent
a fifty for a transient

Twirled from a high-rise window, to land
face up in his calloused hand.

As General Grant stared up at him
he thought of a fine stratagem:

Staying in the Vagabond off Third Street
would be a long overdue retreat:

Its manager was greatly shocked
when that old bum proudly walked

Into his office toting cash
for a king-sized bed and a nice, hot bath;

But money's money so he gave him the key
to spend one night in luxury;

And that hobo slept all night long
with the T.V. going and lights on.

    Todd Clary

Photographs

Standing so proudly, his stick, a gun.
Later he would help in a war to be won.
Photographs
Picking up another, he looks like me.
It appears I am more like him than the other three.
Photographs
Who was this man whose life came to an end
From some sinister ill that destroyed from within?
Photographs
The light of the Lamb shown in his room that day.
Joyfully he took His hand and was led away.
Photographs
He was not me; I was not him.
Wait, maybe I should rethink that again.
Photographs
Life's cycle continues, as you can see,
We are adding to the family tree.
New Photographs

    Kevin E. Schindlbeck

A Letter To A Friend

What gives meaning and value to life?
Is it what we take with us when we go?
Is it what we leave behind?
Is it our capacity for giving to others,
Our ability to experience joy and share it with those around us?
My heart is filled with joy,
It is my time to reflect on people, memories and simple pleasures
held dear in my heart which have enhanced my life.
Memories of bright, sunny days; cool, gentle breezes;
songs; smiles; tears; laughter; hugs.
You have shown me the way to capture the joy of the simple pleasures
we seem to lose sight of.
You unselfishly and lovingly have given me
the gift of a magical and irreplaceable friendship,
and I thank you,
and I love you.

Sean P. Hunter

Under Sea World

The Under Sea World is a mystifying place. The seas
make our planet a very unique and interesting place. The
sea is a challenge and mystery to all.

It is source of unexplained Mythology. Of strange and
dangerous sea monsters, to beautiful, elegant mermaids and
mysteriously drowned cities never found.

Sunken treasure ships in the deep depths of the sea might
hold unknown priceless jewels or maybe precious pirate gold.

Cures to diseases may lie in the hands of the sea to unfold.
The ocean provides a fountain of life to sea animals minute
size to the unbelievable sized giants.

The sea is still a vast body of knowledge waiting to be
revealed by future generations of man kind.

Courtney Becker

Untitled

He wakes in the middle of the night,
Not from a nightmare, or restless sleep,
But from the sensation of someone else there
With him.

He turns to look at her, so quiet and peaceful,
With her long locks of dark blonde hair
And a nose that curls up ever so slightly.
Her eyes closed and at rest, as she softly breathes in her
slumber.
He gazes at her mouth, soft and slightly smiling,
Crinkling at the edges in a way that is so beautiful
And so calming.

He rests his head on the pillow, watching her sleep
And dreams of one day rocking his grandchild
In that old wooden rocking chair.

Jason Wade Farb

The Old Arm Chair

Come hither, come hence, my blue eyed boy,
Please do not stop to play.
The sun is setting in the West,
And there is no time for delay.

So along we hurried, this boy and I
Till we came to a great broad stair,
Up we hurried for to find
Our Mother in her old arm chair.

What would we do without a Mother
To wait at the top of the stairs
For us to come with love for her
Up to that old arm chair?

Lillian L. Gallagher

Farewell

Your mom, truly one of a kind,
Remains imbedded in our mind.
Chatting with the dogs-as she loved to do,
An exciting yapping would ensue.
Fond memories of many years
Has helped us in our tears.
"Reach out and touch someone"
That's what the Lord has done.
Using his heavenly clout,
He's picked a winner-
There's no doubt.
Where serenity and humor abound
That's what "Bert" has found,
Be happy she's made her way
To her maker this very day.
Through the golden gate
She will go,
Waving to us below.

Isobel Mitchell

A Warrior's Mind

He was seasoned well in the fires of hell,
   but was it evening, night or morn,
when the light in his eyes suddenly died
   and a warrior's glare was born?
Or when a mournful sigh become a battle cry
   and lips begin to thirst for blood,
or when the gentle hands of a caring man
   caressed cold steel with love?

When his heart inside begin to die
   and his tears turned to dust,
he filled an empty space as he took his place
   in the ranks with the rest of us.

He's still his mother's son, but not the one
   for whom she cried when he left,
cause his heart and soul is now black as coal,
   his remains an empty shell.
Yet the records tell, he did his duties well,
   he numbered among the best,
but now he waits in line with a tortured mind
   for his turn to kiss the lips of death.

John C. Colyer

Dark Miasma

It started with a night of understanding
Holding, comforting, banishing the hurt
And then, swifter than a flash of foreboding
The emotional stream did it assert

Sullen, somber, and with sluggish reluctance
The cloak of responsibility you did don
Heavy was the burden you carried at once
To have it slip and fall away with the dawn

Children, children, wake up and tell Mommy
What were the night-terrors all about?
Tell me, tell me, you should have told Mommy
With such pain, packing he went, the lout!

Escape is the goal to be sought with fervor
Run, run till you believe the past is left behind
With no sanctioned recourse for which I favor
Imprisoned in darkness, You find you were blind

Deception, Deceit, Decrepitude hidden for long
No longer! We will pick up and piece together
Shattered pieces of the puzzle and move long
With our new cloak, so close-knitted to treasure

Sharon L. De Remer

Life

LORD I know you have a reason
 And some day I'll see it too
 But for now I'm full of questions
 I need to learn the rules.

IS the game always played this rough?
 Is there ever a break in the score?
 Does a winner really win?
 What am I striving for?

FIGHTING to keep ahead in the race
 Wondering if I'll make it through
 It's a challenge I intend to take
 One I will not lose.

EVENTUALLY the game will end
 As quick as it began
 I know I will win in this game called LIFE
 Because I fought and kept my stand.

Deanne T. Sharpe

I Wonder Why?

Women and men who long to feel and be accepted. And for what?
I wonder why. Mothers who struggle to achieve the ultimate in
motherhood. And for what? I wonder Why. Babies born addicted
to drugs, and no-one understands it. And for what? I wonder why.
America is going to war for more land, money, and power, when we
as a whole have enough. And for what? I wonder why. Everyone
wants a piece of Americas apple pie, when were too full off of the
meal we had from yester years destruction. And for what? I wonder
why. Children want to go outside and play under a beautiful sun
filled sky, only to get caught up in the middle of a war that we create
within us. And for what? I wonder why. People hating themselves
for the things they have or have not done. And for what? I wonder
why. Only to die at the setting of the sun and the start of a new one.
And for what? I wonder why

Tonya C. Davis

Untitled

Ten thousand pounds of love, with the main ingredients of pure
passion and radiant romance. In creating this dish, we have to have
the perfect amount of measurements in this exquisite ensemble. With
the decorative colors of red radiance and passion pink, we threw
together this most scrumptious and desirable meal to enlighten
anyone's dull evening. Using only the best of what we have to offer
in this affair leaving out dishonesty, and hurt, but with the pinch
of trust which will surely top off this envious plate. And for
dessert only the finest touch of pale peach passion lifted by the
fairy tale of Cinderella, with a cherry on top.

With all our deepest respects, we hope you will enjoy this special
which is rarely offered and given only once in a life time. So don't
throw any away and share what you don't eat, for this will not be a
cheap thing to waste.

Laura Hess

A Star's Destiny

In the glowing Heavens, where our destinies await,
A star sighs its last breath, and fulfills its fate,
It slowly dies, and falls to the earth,
In the womb of a mother, ready to give birth.

In the petite hands of a child, the star's loving caress,
Opens his eyes in wonder, laying all fears to rest.
The innocence of this child, lies in the dying star,
While the Gods give their approval, from the lands afar.

And then the child is born, and all is as should be.
Peace is once again restored, because of a
Star's Destiny

Heather Knight

It Will Never Amount To Nothing

Is the world coming to an end or is it just me?
Is my life being destroyed or burned in hell's
fire to succeed. Is this another diminution
that can not be handle. One-by-One another life
is taken like a lit candle. One by the
moment a child is born, By another child whose
life has been torn. Young as myself trying to
survive; Trying to accomplish something in life.
I look around and see other life styles. Then I have
to focus on mine for a while. When complain
I stop and think, Wonder about the things I can't
see. I know it's hard but someone has to do.
What the Lord expects me to do. Now while I
speak wise like the old; Some one's out there stealing
silver and gold. As you grow you have accomplish, things
you never even notice. The wrong that you have
done in life, and never even tried to make them right
My words to you are just a little something,
You will never amount to nothing.
A broken heart, A shattered mind, an unhealed body Another Life

Jihan Morris

"Behind The Mask"

Sometimes in life we're afraid to ask;
who is the man behind the mask;
Hidden inside we all keep our fears;
why is it so hard to share our tears;
If we open ourselves we can understand;
It's o.k. if we need a helping hand;
We don't have to live in a world apart;
Share with others the love in your heart;
For peace and comfort come from with-in;
When we get truly honest we find the way to win;
if we let a little love come inside;
we find out there's nothing we need to fear or hide;
So take off your mask and be yourself;
Look around, there's always a way to help.

Ross Wollschlager

Questions

Are Mommy and Daddy happy, Lord?
I ask 'cause I don't think they are.
Except maybe on the holidays
And when they happen to be apart.

I know some people don't believe in divorce,
And I didn't either, used to.
But, I can't help but think if they can't love each other,
There're two others out there who could.

And when they're asleep, Lord—in their separate beds—
Do you let them be happy then?
Do you send them sweet dreams from above
To make up for the way things have been?

Or, are you afraid that when they'd awake
Arising from pleasant dreams,
That things would be worse 'cause they'd mourn for the past
Or for things that might have been?

Sherie Nicolle Parker

Serenity

Burden follows me wherever I go
Causing me to run, to fall, to go no more
Inept words seize expressive joy
It harps on past love I no longer know
Where will I find the answers I need
To fill my body and soul with please
I reach outward in hope of ease
Realizing home is my only serenity

Cathy Sims-Coney

Warland

I look into the vast wasteland of nomads land.
The ground all ripped up from the barrage of bombs,
And the stamp of many booted feet.
Looking out I am alone with only the whistling wind,
And my gun to keep me company.
Black darkness cannot altogether hide the slumped forms of my friends.
Comrades, lying still and cold on that unforgiving ground.
I wonder when we attack next or defend next.
Will I live through it or will I die never again to feel the heat of
the sun on my back.
Only God will know.
I think of this,
And nothing else as the sun rises over the horizon,
And the bombs begin anew.

Aaron Quilling

For Some Strange Reason

For some strange reason, You have been on my mind everyday...
Wanting to see your face more and more...
When I don't hear your soft spoken voice I feel like something
   is missing...
Why?
I think it's because I feel very relaxed around you...
Or it's just your touch...
The way you hold me in your arms...
Maybe it's your kiss...The way your lips feel so soft touching mine...
I really don't know the reason...
But I do know...

I like the way it makes me feel!!!

Michelle Hendrickson

Seasonal Moods

In the South the sun yet shines;
all green trees, and tall grows pine.
Where nights are short, and days are long.
Where wind is weak, and warmth is strong.

In the North the wind blows cold;
thick lay mist, and clouds seem old.
Where air is cold, and wind can freeze.
Where green is all gone, just snow covered trees.

In the East it is cool like a nice fall day;
the leaves are brown, and children play.
Where air is fresh, and chill is the night.
Where trees are all bare, and the wind has a bite.

In the West it is warm and life is just starting;
green things grow, and the cold is departing.
Where trees stand tall, and flowers grow fair.
Where birds are all singing, and up wakes the bear.

Thomas C. Townsend

Man

What is a man if he has no love
He is like a withered plant
That has no chance to survive

What is a man if he has no hope
For hope is the unseen you want so bad you could die
What is a man if he has no dreams
He is like a pilgrim in a desert land

So my friends, don't be like this man
Please love your fellow man and have hopes and dreams
And fill your life with all the good things that life
Has to offer and when you are old you can look back and
Say I have lived a full life...

Donna Kerr

In This Time Of Sorrow

When we were young and we were urged
To "join in prayer," our voices merged

With others in the psalms and airs-
Sometimes memorizing prayers,

Never guessing that the morrow
Could bring to us such depths of sorrow;

And words which were just pleasant sound
Now brim with meaning, deep, profound.

Now I bring a few of these
Hoping they will give some ease.

"In my Father's house are many mansions. I go before you
Prepare a place that where I am, Ye may be also.
- If it Were not so, I would have told you."

Diana Behrens Swann

Burnings

I can't understand
The way people treat me,
But I am glad you can't eat me.

The way I am blown out and lit up again,
The way people shape me with their knives,
Cutting and thrashing, Cutting and thrashing.

I am stuffed in boxes,
Like Christmas tree ornaments.
I am lit up and blown out,
Like at old people's retirement.

My smooth waxy figure
Is burned to a puddle.
The wick that is in me
Acts as a funnel,
Inside and out, Inside and out.

Why am I like this?

Joseph John Rana

The Oak

I'd seen the oak before
but I never wanted to climb it-
it looked too jagged and rough.
As I walked on, I saw different kinds of trees-
some with lots of thick branches,
some with only a few wimpy ones-
wondering if they were worth climbing.

I tried to climb the pine,
but it was too difficult and uncaring.
The weeping willow made me cry,
Its bark was sharp and biting.
Weary then of all trees,
my mind believed they were all as rough.

As I walked on,
I came across the familiar oak.
I stood, and stared,
until finally I decided to climb.
I haven't fallen,
nor have I gotten any cuts and scrapes.
The oak tree holds me firmly.

Jocelynne E. Broderick

"Heaven's Grocery Store"

I was walking down life's highway a long time ago.
I saw a sign that read; "Heaven's Grocery Store!"
As I came closer, the door opened wide. When I came to
myself. I was standing inside.
I saw a host of Angels standing everywhere; one handed me
a basket saying; "My child shop with care!" Everything a
christian needed was in that store; What you couldn't
carry, you could come the next day for more!

First, I got patience, Love, was in the same row.
Next was, Understanding, you need that wherever you go.
I picked a box or two of Wisdom. Then a bag or two of Faith.
I couldn't miss the Holy Ghost, He was all over the place.
I stopped for some strength and courage. To help me run this race.
I didn't forget Salvation... Salvation there was free.
I tried to get enough to save both you and me.
Then, I said to the Angel; "Now how much do I owe?"
He just smiled and said; "Just take them everywhere you go."
Again I smiled and said; "How much do I really owe?"
He smiled once more saying: "My child, Jesus paid your
bill a long time ago!"

Kenneth Delaney

On The Horizon Of Valor

From footstool to throne,
United we must travel.
Endowed, on the eve of creation,
With full provision for this venture.

Clad in the armor of God,
The map of knowledge secure in our vesture,
Backed by the Light which leads us;
That Torch is our Life and our Way.

With valor and diligence, led by the rod,
We march in this royal pursuit.
And slaying serpent hosts,
We climb the steps to perfection.

At the dawn which ends these last days,
Upon the pinnacle of glory and peace,
May we be worthy to stand
And receive the privilege of life eternal.

Eileen DeStasio Clark

"Jellyfish"

Saltwater blue jellyfish swims in my head
  A steal gray rail becomes horizon towards dead
Twisters and unicorns dance out of sight
  Pussycat acrobat come out tonight

Taciturn shadows asleep on the floor
  They understand what tomorrow is for
Blood trespasses through me as rust turns to new
  Blackness engulfs all between me and you

Molasses love was so sweet to the taste
  It dripped from my eyes then it stuck to my face
Crackerjack vices and harsh winter nights
  I pull the stars 'round me to protect me from sight

Blood red candy and cold staring eyes
  Time travel backwards release me from wise
Apricot monkeys and demons beware
  Licorice and teddy bear memories live there

Orion watched over me all through the years
  The jellyfish grew and the salt turned to tears
River cuts through the land down to the sea
  Bubble jet memory what will I be

Bill Kress

"Winter"

The beginning of the end? A time for rest,
and a time for renewal. All is quiet, and at
peace, for a long winters sleep. Everything
looks so barren, and foreboding. A feeling of
overwhelming death is in the air. The sights,
and sounds, are like a cold and distant
uninhabited planet. Only the warmth of the
sun is a welcome feeling. A blue sky; a soft
billowy cloud; the distant call of a bird, are
all but a glimmer of better days to come.
Winter, a time to reflect the spring, summer,
and fall of our lives. It all continues at a
pace unequal to life and being. It does not
stop; it does not end. Life depends on it,
and death is so close to it. Winter, a time
only designated by man.

Edward S. Powers

Dreams

As he carefully dimmed the lights in our room the night was so perfect,
My new love laying there in the dark beside me,
He stirred in his sleep,
and I thought to myself is he dreaming of another?
That couldn't have been possible he promised to love me,
and only me or did he.
As I then thought to myself do I know the person,
I was careful not to awake the sleeping stranger next to me.
I got out of the bed easily and walked to the window,
I looked out into the peaceful nights as if all was well.
The animals in the woods didn't even wake as I opened my
bedroom window,
I gazed out of the opened shutters and inhaled the crisp clean air,
I decided to return to my bed next to the stranger,
As I drifted off to sleep, my alarm startled me.
I looked over at the stranger and he wasn't there.
I had then realized it was nothing but a dream.
I seem to always enjoy
Dreams
But not, Nightmares.

Racheal Carney

Untitled

So....you have a baby on the way,
And it's a boy, or so they say.
You've a lot of joy ahead, but there will also be a tear or two,
When you'll wonder what on earth to do.
Babies don't ask for very much you know,
A lot of love and room to grow.

So....here's wishing you luck and heartfelt congratulations
On your new-found situation.
Store each memory .. for all too soon
He'll be grown and gone and you'll have an empty room.
But you'll look back with fond reflection
On the first word; the first step in your direction.

As you guide him so he'll grow.
Teach him well and he will know,
That home means mom and dad, and warm loving family,
That will always be there when he's in need.
That with your help and that from above,
He'll always know that he is loved.
He'll be secure and feel so safe
In the loving home that you have made.

Betty Jackson

Dear Grandpa

Hold my hand like you did way back when;
Can you swing me once again, like an airplane in the wind;
Can you teach me how to flick the lid of your tobacco can;

Can you teach me how to bait the hook;
To give it the right amount of tug,
So you wouldn't loose the catch at the end of my hook;

Can you take me to the snow, or to our favorite picture show;
Can you and I just sit and watch all the weird people go by;

Can you teach me how to make a garden grow,
You've always had the right ingredients to do just so;
Tell me, is it the love that makes it grow;

Can you teach me to smell the sweetness in the air;
The beauty that grows through each passing year;

The rising of the sun when a new day has begun;
To listen when the day is done;

Can you hear me Grandpa, I am whispering softly in the wind;
I am telling you I Love You Till my time too has come to an end.

Robin Boy

"Once A Man, Twice A Child"

Once a man, twice a child I'd Say-
Cause daddy's Alzheimer's had him that way.
With eight children to support and Carpentry only as a trade,
he never went a week without getting paid.
As a man in his younger days, he belonged to many clubs and
Organizations he'd say: with his Masonic Bible he kept on a stand,
Forbidding us to touch with our hands.
The weekend ritual he had with the lot, On Saturday mornings we'd
grocery shop. On Sunday mornings he cooked breakfast for all,
to eat after church, the fish he had boiled. This is the daddy I
thought he'd stay, but no; Alzheimer's said he had to go.
As years went by he changed in many ways,
it became evident he would have to stay,
with us of course in good old L.A.
A child returned within my Dad
For he began to play child games at long last,
He tore paper and often threw it on the floor and continued to regress
as never before. Near the end he would play with his Teddy Bear
just like a child, kissing and touching it so tender and mild,
therefore, I say to one and all, remember,
Once a Man, Twice a Child, we might have to endure.

Jean E. Brown

Seasons

White with blossoms brims the tree,
Lusty lips lull I Love But Thee,
And time moves on.

Windkissed wheat winks golden,
The braided maid is him beholden,
And time moves on.

Apples redden, in green seas swell,
The fruit springs forth from her body's well,
And time moves on.

Snow sinks softly, covers the ground,
Leaves bare the spot where he was found,
And time moves on.

Blossoms bloom barely, bashful, still.
Son, oh my son, I live, I will -
Yes, time moves on !

Anneliese Heimburg

Soul Mate

Agitating permeating waves of despair
Engulf my once strong self
Weaving twisting lobbing plunging
Tales of old that kept me firmly footed
Unravel in the coldness of awakening
No new days to celebrate and keep
Only wind and rain pummelling me
As if I were a tuft of dandelion
Fearful and nervous I tread
Hating this me that I do not know but am growing used to
The other soul is made of different substance
Perhaps no substance at all
Perhaps no soul
No, put it to rest and be assured there is something there
Only the coupling was so intense
Blissful moving cogent cries
That as many walls were built as came down
Faith is all that can recover them
Open wounds everywhere

Debra Franklin

A Long Winding Road

The journey of Love is unpredictable,
  like driving in a foreign place.
No signs or maps to follow,
  just files of open space.
The comfort-zone is smooth,
  and doesn't seem to end,
Suddenly turns rocky
  as this road seems to bend.

The path somehow unsteady,
  with rocks and bums alike,
the vision now is hazy,
  as the dusk descends to night.
With happiness arrives the sun,
  as this road bends even more.
To life's unanswered question-
  What does Love have in store?

If there's a lesson to be learned by Love,
  like the scorpion taught the toad.
"It's in my nature", Love said
  to be a long and winding road.

Crystal L. Hayes

Gram

The Angels were called upon this day
To take a special soul away
To heaven
A smile always cheery and bright
Gave us all a guiding light
Through life's bitter storms
A spirit that will be greatly missed
And memories to be always kissed
Like upon her tender cheek
For many years she stayed
Making sure her children did not stray
From the path of right
Now knowing her life's complete
She closes her eyes in gentle sleep
Memories of wedding rings and a bright bouquet
She chose this day
To join the one that holds her heart
And walk with him now, forever.

Amanda M. Hale

Stars

Stars, they are not just in the sky.
They are in us.
Stars guide us into the Future.
Stars bring us from the past.
Stars pave the way to eternity.
Stars are like childhood friends,
they stick with you through thick and thin.
They laugh with you, and cry with you.
Stars embrace the child in you.
They make your heart twinkle.
They sprinkle stardust in your eyes.
Each individuals star, has its own
unique quality.
Stars take us on adventure that
mesmerize the mind.
Stars are with you at birth, and in death.
A shooting star means we have
earned our place in the universe.

Faye Wright

Memories Of A Man

Remembering back to the days of past
I know now the good times, they never last
Missing the feel of your loving presence
God, I wish I could capture that essence
Again.....
Hold it dearly, here within
But, tragedy came to be
Grandpa, you're not here for me
Now my life just ain't the same
Catch myself murmuring your name
Wondering why that angel came
To take you away from where you're needed the most
To hear again how you would boast
About your Baby Doll or your lil' Trace
Damn, it hurts not to be able to see your face
Closest thing I had to a father
Thank you for taking those extra steps, to even bother
Knowing you can't return again
I'll hold you here, DEEP WITHIN......
Close to my heart, never to part.

Adam Gomolinski

Baseball Dreams

As I walk through the hall,
I dream about playing baseball.
Hitting so many homeruns,
Would fill my heart with pride and fun.
As I stare up into the sun,
My dreams add up one by one.

As I stand up to the plate,
I know this pitch could make my fate.
As I grip the bat in my hand,
No one knows where it might land.
As the pitcher does his wind up thing,
It makes me wonder if I can get a World Series ring.

As I hit the ball with a 6-6 tie.
I admire the ball as it flies through the sky.
As the ball hits upper deck,
I realize that I've been working like heck.

As I round third base,
I can see my manager's face.
He finally saw what I could do.
Now all my dreams have finally come true!

Shawn Fitzsimmons

Written Love

I look at you with the love I feel
Then write just what I see,
With promises and hopefulness
That you'll be loving me.
With replies you honor us
Will show that while loving you,
I do not love alone.

My written love is
Sweetly chosen words of promise;
Desire the written love,
and I will feed your hungry fires;
Allow me to and I will warm your stricken heart to life.

If poetry is artistry,
Then imagine so is truth,
For poetry is true of lies
honest through and through.
With promises to hold
I'll give you all my written love,
and promise to be loving still
When all my ink is spent.

Carrie White

An Empty Page

My life is like an empty page in the book of life.
The hopes and dreams we shared so long were cut so short-so deep
    I cannot sleep at night.
The anger I feel inside overwhelms the love and life we shared.
Are memories enough to sustain me, to ease the ache, the emptiness?
I cry, I laugh, I remember how it feels to love you, miss you,
    want you, touch you.
My life totally revolved around your presence, your being.
Like two right hands or two left feet I do not match with anything
    right now.
We were two, but we were one - inseparable.
There is a reason for this pain - I know there is.
Is it that the empty page you left me with can now be filled with
    shared moments, hugs, kisses, warmth, tenderness,
    forgiveness and compassion?
I will go on and fill that page, because I have loved and been
    loved and can now accept and deal with the loneliness.

Carolyn T. Vivas

A Parent's Dream (Or Reality?)

Another day, another dollar.
    If I hear it again, I'm gonna holler!
Overworked and underpaid,
    Oh, dear God is there another way?
A job, two kids, cook and clean,
    And then they wonder why you're mean.
"How do you do it?" they say with a sigh.
    "I have my dreams." Is my reply.
"I win a million dollars, and never work again,
    and lay around in bed till quarter after ten."
"I buy a mansion with a maid and butler too,
    and don't forget the Mustang and big ol' swimming pool."
Once my dream has ended, I give a little sigh
    for tomorrow when the boss says "jump"
    I know I'll ask "how high?"

Karla Erdman

Ode To My Dogs

I hear them breathe as they sleep.
And they sleep. Content to know that I will protect them.
And their world is still.
With only my heart beat can they hear.

They hear my heart beat as I sleep.
And I sleep. With them by me still.
My world is content. And they will protect me.
Their heart beat I can still feel.
They choose to protect me-with their lives.

I hear them breathe no more as they sleep.
And they sleep. Content to know that I will protect them.
And their world is still.

I am content they feel my heart beat -
Through their shallow graves.
And I breathe slowly as I lay across, in an open field
and our breath becomes as one.

Peggy M. McQueary

Killing The Inconsiderate

To kill the inconsiderate isn't hard to do
you simply get tired of biting your tongue 'til it's black and blue.
Just reach down underneath your racing heart
gather all your anger; this is where you'll start.
No need to pussyfoot around it like it's a priceless piece of art;
the inconsiderate throws rudeness as if you're the board and
they're the dart.

The less tactful will never apologize for being hours late,
of all the faults of the inconsiderate, this is the main one I hate!
If you know what I speak of get in line
we'll set the 'hit' up good (you know so it won't look like a crime).

Killing the inconsiderate won't be difficult to do...
Just don't tell a soul, THEY may be inconsiderate
and tell the boys in blue.

Amisha Sanise Guinn

Winter Morning

Lazy morning sun, pushing away the gray dawn,
Shines through the upper window pane,
Striking the back wall,
Bathing the logs in melted-honey hues.
Pristine snow clings to each bush and tree...
Complacently hiding yesterday.

Heat from the fireplace
Has not yet permeated the room
And I snuggled deeper into my fuzzy old robe.
My steaming cup warms my hands...
Sunshine warms my back...
The love in your eyes
Warms my heart.

Beth Y. Shurtleff

The River Runs Deep While My Soul Cries

The river runs deep while my soul cries.
  It's not an ache or a pain or a sweet lullaby,
    it's something I feel deeply inside.
      My heart starts to wonder why?
      Is it love or a broken heart.
        Is it fear to know myself or pain to see,
          or is listening my worse enemy.
            In time I will know if it's just the icing
              on the cake, or the sweet sound of a melody.
                Tip toeing nearer and nearer, fear of the unknown.
                To find out,
                  The River Runs Deep... While My Soul Cries

Kalisha Rousseau

My Mother

My Mother is a special lady
Who has always been there for me,
No matter what my problem
She found the answer it seemed.

She's been a Mother who did Mother things
And was there when I needed a friend,
She always knew the difference
Of what to be - and when.

She shared in joys and sorrows
And listened to tales of woe,
And after her patience and sharing
Her true caring I would know.

I've loved her for everything she did
And some things she knew not to do,
But somehow she always did what was right
And guided me to where I should be, too.

May God make me the kind of Mother
That my sons will love and cherish,
With a love as deep as mine for her
One that will never perish.

Elizabeth A. Kent

"A Poet's Dream"

To describe in detail the fragility of life
The perseverance of love between a man and his wife.
Seeking and searching for the soul of man,
The quest for wisdom, knowledge, and peace from within.
To create, capture, or record with a pen.
The dreams of a poet, and hope for fellow men.

To escape a broken heart's prison — secure without bars,
Or describe with passion the brilliance of stars,
And the coolness of a ride on distant moonbeams.
For there are a few dreams, that a poet might dream
To unlock emotions and rediscover hopes
Or scale castle walls beyond the deepest of moats.

To feed all the children, destroy all the drugs.
And shatter the violence with kisses and hugs.
Yet, in a world such as ours — impossible it seems.
To accomplish even the smallest of these things.
I ask you, "Must they all become just dreams?"
That a poet might dream.

Howard Lee Kitchen

Where Is The Love To Be Found

Love is for a man who loses control
Love is for a woman whose heart is cold
Only love for colors of skin
Only love for those who win
Love for the soldiers who fight the war
Love for a country who thinks it's poor
A mother had love but could not love back
A father had love but could only smack
No love cause they're macho, none cause they're brave
None so at school, they misbehave
Love for those who have all the wealth
Love for the person who only loves themselves
Love is a drug some will say
Drugs then love is some people's way
Love always gives, but never takes
This is where many make mistakes
To fall in love, gives power to others
Let us stand and love, so we can all be lovers

Stephen A. Sisson Jr.

My Love Has Gone

On warm summer nights, I take a stroll down the beach.
I listen to the waves crashing on the shore,
I feel the soft wind blowing through my hair.
I look down at the changing colors of the sand as the water
    washes it away.

I see you and all of our wonderful times,
But then, you drift away just like the sea.
Oh, how I long to see you again,
How I long for you to hold me in your arms.

My heart is empty and crying for you.
The tears fall fast soon there is nothing to cry.
Without you, my life means nothing.
I feel I have nothing to live for.

Oh, please come back to me!
I need your love, I need you.
All our dreams, all our plans,
I can not leave that behind me.

But still, waves crash and trees sway
Just like the day you faded away from me.
So here I sit next to your cold grave.
My love has gone.

Alicia R. Pendergrass

Night Tide

Sweeping across a midnight plain,
Racing the wind on an endless terrain,
The echo of day is seen not here,
All sunshine fades and disappears.

Stretches of sky in unending blackness,
Dusty with diamonds, small bits of brightness,
Seeming quiet, but not so quiet,
A current sweeps under, under the night.

Turning, a whisper, an unseen small breeze,
Few understand the mystery of these,
The echoes of cries succumbed by the tide,
Swept by a force some seek to hide.

Moving apart from the hands of time,
Hands that will try the strongest of ties,
Immortal and forever the spiral of this,
Destruction breaks way to Night Tide and bliss.

Laura Ellis

The Son Will Shine Again

As the green meadows sway in the westward wind,
We see the Son rising over the hills of Judah.
In all of its radiance, disregard the Glory
And give way to the dark of night.

The blackened hue of darkness envelopes the sky,
And conceals the twinkling eye with its wrath.
The ebony empyrean flows over the land,
And reveals a new sight to man.

Death has vanquished the mind of the lost,
Bringing with it torment and pain.
Why are so many trusting a blind man's sight,
And being led to Sheol without a second thought?

When all is said, and when all has come to an end,
The firmament will open wide, and the sky will remain.
And the glory will be restored to the Son,
And He will shine again.

John S. Ambro Jr.

Driving By Night

The rain washes the ground,
the sky is dark with flashes of brightness.
The beads pelt the windshield and the wipers chase the drops
from my sight. The road is deserted,
my lone headlights beam across the misty covered blacktop.
Make way for the space cadet driver.
I'm not watching the road,
I'm watching the dream playing out in my head.
The beat of the music hypnotizes.
I think of everything and nothing. My mind is full and empty.
The car runs on auto pilot.
Pictures of the past mesh with dreams of the future.
I don't want to think of the present.
I don't want to live at this moment in time.
I want to fast forward my life until it gets to the good parts.
Skip the worry, anxiety and frustration of today.
I'll dream of tomorrow when the present goes away.
I'm driving by night on a voyage to tomorrow.
I hope I make it straight through
without getting stopped at the lights.

Valerie Becker

"Promises"

You said you were going away,
Far away
But you said you would not stay

Days have turned to weeks
And weeks to months
But you said you would not stay

My heart grows weak from anticipation
Waiting, hoping, yearning for you
For you left me, but you said you would not stay

Now I'm old and death is at my door
I must obey my calling
Away I go, far away

But I promise you I will not stay.

Marvalet Donald

"A Comfort Within"

Oh what a foolish man I'd be,
If all I use is my eyes to see.
For the truth I seek is very near,
If I use not my ears to hear.

All my life I searched for a key,
When all along it was inside of me.
For we should wait more patiently,
For him to teach us spiritually.

Love God with all thy soul both day and night,
And he shall be your guiding light.
There is no difference between new and old,
They are both the same, so I am told.

To believe and be baptized I know is the way,
But thy mercy is greater than that I pray.
Thy will be done in Heaven and on Earth,
In the death of a sinner and then his rebirth.

Hope, faith, and charity,
To have these things is wise you see.
But of these three I do believe,
The greatest one is charity!

Charles E. Myers Jr.

Love

Love, everybody wants love,
And some people, don't seem
To find its pleasure at all,
Yet it's somewhere, you can
Find when you want.

Love is so deep, love is so
High, yet you can find it any
Time you try, love is a baby,
It is something inside.

You should never give up when
It's on your side, love is a dream
Even the stupid will find,
You can make it work,
When you give some time.

Oh love, yes love, give it to
Someone, or your heart will cry,
You should never stay aside and watch
Love die, open your heart and let it fly.

Leroy Carthy

The Rose Of Spring

Just as the rose of spring withers away,
    So fades love's first love.
Ever so gradually it falls away that suddenly there is nothing left
    to grasp.
Every passing moment seems to intensify the loss until it becomes
    unbearable.
Memories of the rose grow sweeter in its absence until truth cannot
    be told from fiction.
You reach out in search of what you cannot find—
    The pain of uninhabited air seems to be too much.
At times you wander aimlessly and blindly longing for what seems
    will never be.
You console yourself, softly, with the memories of the rose and
    the thought that maybe, someday, its likeness will return.

Cheryl Armour

A Child Once Like Me

Often I gaze into the eyes of the young, realizing that they are
a child once like me. I look into their souls, watching as they
perform as adults, when they should be skipping rope, riding
bicycles, and sharing secrets with their bestest friend, instead
they are carrying the burden of lost childhood because their
parents choose not to take on the role of responsibility. These
children suffer, as a child once like me. It is often I see them
pretending to be bold and not be afraid, pretending not to cry
and be brave only because their hearts ache to be loved and for
once to be a kid. The love of another they may never know
because they are a child once like me. A tender kiss or a warm
hug is something never heard of, eyes of praise or special days
is something these children will never see, only because they are
a child once like me!

Dionne S. Gray

The Path

On the winding path of life that always bends.
On the indestructible road that never ends.
Hold your head up high, every day be more proud.
Everyday shout, shout for your views, shout them loud.
Shout for your beliefs, shout for the right.
Be proud of your accomplishments, be proud of the light.
Do not look too far into the future road.
Take every step with caution and never drop your load.
When you must leave your path.
It will continue through the ages of happiness and wrath.

Shauna Duffy

Heart Source

It's like a siren's song
That calls you home.
This place where your beginnings are.
Nowhere else has that feeling of connection.
The sense of all things are possible.
The expanding of your center;
You feel nurtured like a seed planted
And tenderly cared for.
You flower and reach your purpose in life.
When away, the energy withers
And the connectedness scatters.
You try to focus but it's like grasping at straws.
Too far from your source - - -
But realize that it is within our heart
That keeps us connected to all.

Beverly Kane

Glimpse Of Hell

Insanity's face, an ugly sight,
Far worse when it strikes a friend.
The bitter struggle to overcome its hold,
A struggle that will never end.
Eyes that burn like glowing coals,
Burning up her very soul.
Sweetest perfume turns to sulphur,
A mind going out of control.
Years of memories turning rotten,
Stories I could never tell.
Memories doubtless best forgotten,
For I have seen a glimpse of Hell

Kent Crouse

Family

I can still see yesterday, when I close my eyes...
The gentle touch of summer's breeze, the cool blue morning skies.
Daddy's in his easy chair, reading the morning news
Mom is going crazy, helping to find our shoes!
The smell of bacon frying, fills the kitchen door.
Sourdough biscuits rising, another stray upon the floor.

When I remember days of youth, that helped to mold my life;
I think of all the people, that share a common light.
For each of us are different, but still we are the same;
We share the same beginnings, if not a common name!
We all grow up and move away, our lives no longer touch;
But no matter how far away, you'll always mean so much.

You see, even though we live apart, And our lives go different ways
You can still look out into the world and find a kindred face.
A thread that runs strong and true, that links my life to each of you
In thought can make me smile out loud, and make me oh, so very proud
We all share a special bond, A common thread you see;
That links us all together..that makes us family!

Vella Meador

The Eyepatch

I can not tell another lie
It wasn't a bug that hit my eye
I was at the park when I heard a whistle
It sounded like a nuclear missile
So I looked way up into the sun
And turned around to start to run
And then, oh yeah, it started to rain
And I thought I heard a choo-choo train
The sky grew dark and the winds did blow
Now the rain had turned to snow
I could not see but I ran and ran
I ran into a portly man
I bumped into his buckle latch
And that is why I wear this patch

Kelley Murphy

143

I Love, I Hurt, I Grieve, I Feel!

Inside I weep for little ones never to "be".
How can one miss what's never been known,
  or held or seen?
Not even a complete dream of who or what
  they might have been.

I grieve the loss of "knowing".
  Of knowing their giggles and smiles.
Of knowing their hopes and dreams.
  I grieve the loss of not rocking each
  one to sleep.

I love, I hurt,
  I grieve, I feel!

It was my loss, too,
  My tears are real.

  Linda E. Johnson

Frank And Scents And Fur

Francis Joseph Xavier Mudd
Is trudging through the snow.
He spies some tracks and follows them
To find out where they go.

Into a hollow log he peers
And much to his surprise.
A startled family of skunks
Glares back with frightened eyes.

In an instant war begins.
And Frank becomes alarmed.
With wits he may have fought the foe,
With scents Frank came unarmed.

Now here stands Frank on his front porch.
His mother wears a grin.
She's very glad to see him but,
Why won't she let him in?

  Janine Curtiss

Ofei

A very good looking, married lady, whom I
enjoyed having as a friend
Ofei came to the United States Mint, thus
finding additions to her job, she had to attend.
Ofei, with her I love joking,
especially when she is in the break room,
and I'm still working.
When I see her in the break room,
there's a shipment to be processed, she is told.
Then Ofei thinks my heart is very cold.
I walk away laughing, then she knows I'm just joking.
Ofei, while you are here at the United States Mint,
for your efforts in tasks performed on the job,
may you receive your just rewards.

  Sauls DeSuzzs Suezs

Faces Of Stone

strip off your mask
  break away from your facade
faces of stone eventually crumble
  leaving you naked, like a new-born babe
vulnerable to the world around
  not knowing how to act, or feel
not knowing what is, or isn't real
  wanting to scream in anger
wanting to weep in sorrow
  emotions never seen in faces of stone
  emotions never penetrate faces of stone

  C. Tyler Jarnagin

I Want To Live Again...

I want to live again, but how do I go about it?
I want to feel the wind hitting me against my skin giving me a sense
  of freedom.
I want to smell like a rose, so the gentleness of me comes out.
I want to shine like a star, so the inner beauty of me comes through.
I want to live again, I want to wake up each morning and say
  good morning world.
I want to live each day as a day to remember, not as if it was my last.
I want to live again. But how do I go about it? How do I get back
  to the sense of being?
  I Want To Live Again!!!!

  Kevin Butler

"Darkness"

I walk in the night and sleep by day,
Many have questioned my strange ways,
But I am nocturnal and day is poison to me,
The sun is too bright, my eyes can not see,
Black is my favorite color, because it expresses me,
My spirit and my creativity,
But I am not evil, my heart is full of love,
People criticize all the things I think of,
My perspective on life may not be the same,
But I'm proud of myself, and proud of my name,
I am more like you then it may seem,
The only difference is the morning is when I dream.

  Keyon Bounds

To A Cow

What am I to say about an animal that gives us milk,
she can be one of the most mule-headed creatures that
  God ever custom-built!

This cow that I'm referring to, if you will let her,
can kick you all over 'til you are black and blue.

So be very careful as you try to milk her today,
as she will try everything in her power to try to get away.

So let's give her the benefit of the doubt,
as you go to try to turn her on out.

A salute to the men and women that have to milk these cows,
trying to make a living by putting up with them somehow.

  Nancy Ball "A Country Belle"

Life Line

God is life all around
Now you stop just to frown
A frown for what? You don't know,
But I know it will surely show.
Now and then as you go,
But what you don't know is bound to
Fall way down below.
That's because life is just a line in our time.
Now and then this is the way we will surely know how to stay.
In between we will beam as a light in its means.
God is life in between, as the light from the beam.
It is a shine in our time.
Before we see the last line.

  Betty Davis

144

Couplet

On the eve before the holidays,
Alice was excited in many ways.
She would have a celebration,
That would be a great sensation.

What Alice didn't know,
Was that it wasn't going to snow.
She waited and waited and waited some more,
But the chances of snow were less than poor.

It was five o'clock when the doorbell rang,
Alice opened the door with a bang.
Her frown was gone in a flash,
She was ready to have a bash.

Outside the door was an ice-cream truck,
Selling snow cones for a buck.
Now was their chance to have some fun,
They will party till the day is done.

When the day came to an end,
Alice said goodbye to every friend.
As the ice-cream man went on his way,
She told him that he made her day.

Korinne Chiu

Dear God,

Although I think of You each and every day,
  This is different, in a special kind of way.
On this certain day, a most precious gift You gave.
  For someone like me, You wanted to save.

Sometimes I become so very sad and often I even cry.
  How sad You must have been when Your son had to die!
Then You sent an angel who gave a very gentle wave;
  Away the stone rolled from my Saviour's grave!

I think of Your sweet love when I see the birds fly,
  Or as I watch the puffy clouds go rolling gently by.
A simple thank you is not enough; for He was Your only Son.
  So I give to You my heart for the wonderful things You've done.

Your loving servant,
  Chauntey Wages

Flowers

Two flowers,
born of the same root,
spend all their time and energy
to push through the earth,
to reach the air, to feel the wind,
to see the light.
After seeing the light and feeling the warmth,
these flowers continue to grow,
trying to get closer to the light,
stretch a stem and spread a leaf,
they strain on.
Each reaching for the light,
trying to outdo the other.
But the sun soon sets,
and the wind turns biting,
and the flowers must
turn to each
other or face
the winter
alone.

Matthew Toht

Our Mother

Our Mother is very special, as you can see
Because God blessed her with not one or two but three

From our cries in the night
To breaking up our fights

She has been a patient Mother throughout the years
Even through the shedding of some tears

She has always been there for us day in and day out
We know we could always come to her without a doubt

Though the years pass by fast
We realize now at last

That God gave us a mommy then
Now she is our best friend
  Paula Vickery Hilton

"The Darling Girl From Clare"

Mary Davoren was her name
From the shores of Ireland, she once come
She settled here in good Ol' New York
A real hard worker, she never believed in too much talk.
She had twin sisters, Betty and Sue
Mary being the oldest, often told them what to do
She was strict, yet kind and far
They knew if they were ever in need, she'd always be there
That's Mary, "The Darling Girl from Clare."
All in all, Mary raised ten, five women and five men
Mary was very proud of her fine clan
To be sure, she ruled them with a firm Irish hand.
Marie, Daniel, Catherine, Joseph, and Pat
George, Theresa, Helen, Thomas, and Ann after that
some of them dance and some of them sing
Some are quite funny, they can do almost anything.
"The Darling Girl from Clare" was the best cook around
John Cudmore was lucky, when Mary he found
He knew in his heart that no woman could compare
With Mary, "His Darling Girl from Clare"
  Ann Cudmore Martinez

The Rose Bud

How is a woman like a rose?
  It is through the many years that she grows.
These words of wisdom were spoken long ago to
  a very young man.
Yes, he was told, your wife is like a rose bud in your
  hand, and if you hold it too tight it will never grow.
The young man didn't listen, so he lost the rose bud from his hand.
Every petal developed and grew into a beautiful rose,
  that the young man never saw or could ever know.
Now that the young man is old, he asked, where did
  his young wife go, and why wasn't she there for him to hold?
It was because he wasn't much of a man, and he
  wanted to hold the rose bud too tight in his hand.
How do I know, because I am the rose that grows.
  JoAnn P. Jones

The Pledge

There's a path that leads to the heavens
  a road traveled by many
and if we follow a few golden rules
  then heaven awaits.

Caring, Sharing, Sincerity, Honesty
  Compassion, Understanding, Strength
  Loyalty, Commitment, Dedication
  Respect and Love
    Unconditional Love.

This to you I pledge.
  Ellery M. Liburd

Ibiza

Swimming around the boat at 7:00 a.m.
With the smell of coffee
Rippling over morning waves,

I watch the old men
In their black berets
And brown lunch bags
Walking slowly
Down the side of the hill
To their row boats:

The fishermen have come
To take fish from the sea
For tonight's town feast.

Listening to the click click click
Of silver to glass at the seaside cafe
Readying for the morning lovers,

I, dripping wet
Climb to deck
And shiver the crystalline salt off my body

As the boat rocks on the top of the swells
Tipping from side to side, my cradle, my lullaby.

Karen Devonshire

If I Never Pass This Way Again

If I should never pass this way again. I have lived a full life.
Sometimes up and more times down. But I shall never have to
Worry about these things any more because I will never pass
This way again.

Life can be sweet and life can also be very cruel. Many times
we wonder how could this happen to me. Then we look around
and see that something happening to others only worse, in
some way. But we all know there is a God up there, and only
he can control the universe.

So no matter how bad things maybe in this life. We have the
assurance that if we live right and do God's will, we will
make it over to the other side. So we don't have to worry
or be afraid. Because we shall never pass this way again.

Be very strong my black sisters because we hold the keys
of the future in our hands. We have come a very long way
in our lifetime, and there will be many to follow in our footsteps.
There are many more paths and roads we must travel
down. Each one may be a little harder than the last, so we
strive make to things better for the next generation. For we
surely know that we shall never pass this way again.

Geraldine Taylor

Indigo

There is nothing like emptiness
To fill a broken heart
Or the chains of cold silence
That bind vacant arms
The flowers that were given her
Lie forgotten in the back of her mind
They sit and die in a black corner
With memories of our shared time
The rooms bright once are now pained in sorrow
Without the glow of her pilgrim soul
I have no longer the need to replace her
There was no one else I want to know
The walks we had through the park are not the same
I wander and cry under indigo skies and shudder autumn's chill
I curse the gods for telling me to forget her name
And try hard not to love her, but know I forever will.

Joseph P. Grant

Special Bouquet

God picks the flowers, at different times and seasons,
he doesn't have to have a reason.
God created us in his special time,
he doesn't make us wait in line.

God loves, "rose buds" in his bouquet;
So every now and then,
"He picks one along the way".

God loves each and every flower,
they mature in different ways.

The "rose buds", are young and tender.

Some are older and wiser;
Others have a special talent.
Many are fully grown, some are about to fade,
So before they fade and fall apart,
He cuddles them to his heart.

And picks the "precious ones" for,
"His Special Bouquet"

Lou F. Harrington

Dreams

Those wonderful encounters that you have
at night. They take you places of sheer delight.

Fantasy and make believe, show you all that
you can't see.

Feeling found there can not be compared,
But with you my dear and the love we now share

For in your heart you know it is so, for
where those dreams take you. You are willing to go.

And when I look, The sun I see. It is
then I know I have been set free.

You see my love I am not asleep. And
this is a dream that I plan to keep.

Because you are here, and I have found
that special meaning that makes life go around

I Love You

Tom Richardson

Pretty

Some place right now somebody is being beaten.
Some place else somebody is about to get theirs off.
And I'm here, in my chair writing;
you're there doing whatever it is you do.
And God's asking an angel how many humans it takes to change
a light bulb.
Two countries are on the brink of war.
A dog's barking, the mail's late:
A baby was just born.
A grandmother is dying.
A flower is in full bloom.
Someone is being betrayed,
and loved,
and it's all very pretty.

Brandon Cox

146

Untitled

In the morning as the sun shines down
and the earth gives her dew
the Lord smiles on all His creation
Everything that has breath should praise the Lord
For he is the Maker of Heaven and earth
It is right and good to sing praises
to His holy name
Now is the time of Salvation
which should bring joy to everyone's
innermost being because of His love for mankind
Reach your hands to the precious Lord
who lifts you up on high
where perfect love casts out all fear
and makes your feet like hinds feet
so you can leap like a deer away from the enemy's snare
and into the arms of the Lord

Michele Peterman

White Tigers

White tigers are black and white,
their eyes are like a neon-light,
especially at midnight.

White tigers are very vicious,
a moving bush makes them suspicious.
While attacking prey, they are malicious.

White tigers are courageous and swift.
When they hide in the bushes spying on prey,
they peek through a rift.

The white tiger gets an enemy in his sight,
then plunges out with an appetite,
it sometimes attacks one twice its height.
The white tiger will leap up and the enemy will fight,
but after awhile he'll be out like a light.

Leeann Lara

Birth

Green is the new born life,
How precious it can be,
To see your loving wife
Having your newborn baby.

Who knows what could ever happen,
When a woman is in birth?
Oh, doctor what is wrong?
Oh my God! What on Earth?

Doctors and nurses running 'round,
One yelling "Hey where's the OB?"
Something falls and hits the ground,
My Lord, what's going on around me?

A smile crosses my face
When I hear my baby boy cry.
But then a nurse, white as lace,
Said, "Doctor, look she's going to die."

I'm taken out of the room,
My skin as thin as twine,
The doctor comes out shaking like a groom,
Then smiles at me and says, "Don't worry, she's fine."

Tony Blackmon

Nike's Shadow

Though siege is broken,
Fear-wrought night still clings.
Among hopeless houses,
A sharp death-wind sings.
Memories speed on-coming darkness,
And torch light only shadow brings.

The city while besieged was stronger,
Then fear fed blazing anger.
Now wraiths in shadow creep,
Nightmares displaced from sleep.
Sensed by all but seen by none,
They slowly shatter all we've done.
By deeds regretted are shadows bred,
Each walks toward sleep with growing dread.

Mary Kemmerer

Nannie

I don't know why I feel this way
I felt that everything would be OK.

I love you both, you and Pappy
We're keeping high hopes and staying happy.

It's hard without you, here, right now
I wish I could see you but do not know how.

In my words, love is more powerful than a sword
But you are in good hands with our dear Lord.

I will miss you very, very much,
But you are within our great God's touch.

So I wrote this to you, my Great-grandmother,
You were a great person - I would pick no other.

Chris Villaronga

"Lost Beauty"

She lay trembling in the cold
Thinking of when her life seemed meaningful.
She shared with me her every thoughts
Her husband and children all deceased.
She had often wished for the exact same peace
All she has are memories and pictures.
Though still maintains faith in the scriptures.
A photograph reveals the beauty she once had
How age has robbed that from her makes me sad.
She asks not for much and seems easy to please
If only there were a cure for this mortal disease.
I sat and held her fragile hand
She thanked me for being a nice young man.
Of all the love and beauty she had to share
Seems a shame that few should care.
She expressed her gratitude that I was there
Struggling to get her last few breaths of air.
She left this world fast and sudden
Her special beauty will not be forgotten.

David M. Cushman

Hope

(In loving memory of Greg)
What I wouldn't give to turn back the hands of time,
and change our past so you could still be mine.
I never got the chance to say "I love you",
even though there wasn't a time I didn't love to be around you.
And now you've gone away,
taking with you my light of day.
When you weren't around my thoughts of you were in my heart,
I only wish I was the one who had to depart.
I hope there comes a time when we can be together,
side by side, you and I, always and forever.

Azure Fern

Reflections

It all began not so long ago
We both decided to take it slow
You said you knew from the very start
That I would be the one to steal your heart
We talked every day on the telephone
You said you couldn't stand to be alone
I looked forward to the time we'd share
Just doing nothing or going here and there
When you told me you loved me, I knew it was true
'Cause no man could show it the way that you do
You've been there for me in good times and bad
You've cried with me through happy and sad
We've prayed together to our Lord above
And asked Him to dearly bless our love
We know He will 'cause we both believe
That our love was truly meant to be
Some time has passed since that all began
You are now my husband and my best friend

Karen L. Barnes Swan

"Where's My Baby?"

Where'd the light go? I stare out the window,
and wonder will I ever see it again. All I see is
colors red, and yellow, and blue can't you see them too?
Red here Yellow there and blue everywhere.

The moon shines brightly like the sun, and I wonder
if I'm the only one who travels through the night
searching for the light. The light is gone from my life now
so I sit by the shore and watch my life fall like the sun.

Another day has come and gone and I still can't
find my baby, she left me for another, so I'll never
ever find another baby, to love like the one I had before,
so maybe I'll just collapse on the floor.

Joel M. Siano

The Last Words Of Love

The day begins with a child,
Feverish but feeling fine,
Joyful of a day at home and the attentiveness of both.

A phone call later that day,
"How are you, baby?" "Feeling fine, daddy."
The last words of love.

Later, he's late.
Burnt roast, still roasting.
Waiting, watching at the window.
A car approaches, but drives on by.
Blue lights.

Moments later, a knock at the door.
The mother already knows, but the child can't comprehend.
The last words of love.

Andrea L. Kaye

The Pierce Wounds

Do you see them? They are the pierce wounds,
where your loss has ripped through me
like a thousand needles from the pine.
You sent them falling, falling slowly,
like ebony flakes of snow before the storm.
Do you recall? or shall I remind you
of your villainous smile, Cousin to the starfish.
How it laughed at my defenses
and invaded the innocent temple of my soul.
Now nothing is left
but this sun-bleached shell,
and my lonely memories
of a painful trip to Hell.

Nunzio Calce

A Daughter's Father

To be a daughter's father
You must be loving and wise
For the first ten years she's with you
You're a hero in her eyes.

The next eight years she's with you
You become a doddering old fool
Her time is spent teasing boys
The rest is spent in school.

One night I went to sleep
My little girl asleep in her room
When daylight came I realized
The years had passed to soon.

When I sit in the house in the evening
When it's quiet and the fire burns low
I still can hear her dancing and singing
In her room, it seems so long ago.

To be a father's daughter
She must come home now and then
And let me look into her eyes
To see my little girl again.

Jim Hale

Choices

I'm doing today
    What I should've always done
    And will continue to do;

Learning and accepting
    Who I am, What I want,
    Understanding why.

... I now make my own Choices...
No longer suppressed or dominated by
The pressures and demands from others;
    Free to pursue my dream.

I approach the future with confidence;
And hope that the results of my decisions..

Prove to have been
    The right
        Choices.

F. Eileen Mock

The Four Seasons

What is a season anyway?
A jar of pepper? A stack of hay?
"You are mistaken", I must say.

Some seasons make you shovel snow,
Some seasons birds are on the go.
You may count there are just four,
Winter, Spring, Summer, Fall.
"I love them all!"

Yes indeed that's what I said,
Although the Winter you may dread.
Winter brings out mother's quilt,
In Spring the birds are chirping loud.
Summer shines with golden gilt,
While Fall may come out with a cloud.

It is quite simple can't you see?
One after the other they keep coming,
As slow as a snail or like a hummingbird humming.

Some seasons excite you, others are dreary.
Others bring joy, or may make you weary.
The point is, "Enjoy and be cheery!"

Michael Katsap

How Excellent

How excellent is God's name. He is all together
  lovely and he always remains the same.
God has brought me out of darkness into the light
  and this is truly a beautiful sight. I'm
So glad that he sent his son Jesus for our
  Salvation because Hell is definitely
too hot and eternity is truly too long. Go to
  God and not the devil because my
redeemer is so mighty and strong. Whenever
  I was down, God picked me up,
turned me around, and set my feet on solid ground.
  My God is King of Kings and Lord of
Lords. He brought me victory with His mighty
  sword. God has brought me a long
way and it is a true fact that in my heart I
  know there's no turning back. And so,
how excellent is thy name oh Lord. How excellent
  is thy name.

    Tania La Fosse

Proud American

The United States of America has sired many valiant men,
Who fought the fight to victory, because they fought to win.

Not just win the battle, but win the hearts of men,
To be loyal to their country, for storms will rise again.

The flag still flies in the USA, but somehow we've forgot,
Just why it was those valiant men courageously have fought.

They carried the flag to remind them, in each battle they engaged,
To defend its strength and honor, their blood they freely gave.

Our nation's been blessed down through the years,
Because God knew we cared;
The love and mercy God proclaimed, these valiant men have shared.

So when you see the flag unfurl with its red, white and blue,
Stand straight and tall and be real proud;
For ole glory flies for you.

    Lee Cowfer

I'm Your Gift

Sitting under this tree, awaiting your arrival.
You come, pick me up,
admiring my shape and dress -
the red ribbon, floral coverings...

You untie my ribbon, tenderly, gently,
telling me how you love me - willingly I believe

You unwrap my floral coverings, fold by fold, slowly,
admiring my beauty yet eager to get inside -
all along making me feel special.

You dispose of all my dressings,
fondling the plain shape before you,
saying how you're thankful for receiving me,
and how much you appreciate me - I am vulnerable.

You open my lid, exposing my beating heart,
becoming aware of my emotions.
Ripping my heart from its casing,
you hold it in your hand - my life, my love.

You toy with my heart, get bored,
and discard it like a child's old toy.
I can no longer live on.

    Teresa Masotto

"Things We Should Know" (The Saga Continues)

I was a man of the world
and that wasn't all
but when you are doing wrong
there comes a rise and fall

Even when there's no folks around
I suffer no sorrow
Cause once you know Jesus
he's same yesterday, today, and tomorrow

You see friends come and go
like the lands riches and wealth
but there comes a time
when we must humble ourself

We want this, and want that
Continuously trying to pass the test
take your problems to the Lord and prayer
Trust him, he knows best

God doesn't go back on his word
folks just give up on their faith
believe in him with all your heart
he'll deliver you, learn to wait...

    James Davis

Emerging On A Lifetime

What if you knew that I loved you?
Or the extent to which I care?
Would you hold it against me?
Would you walk away?
Or would you hold me near and ask me to stay?

If my heart had a window,
Could you ever really know?
The excitement in your eyes
The pleasure in your touch
Never having loved anyone so much!

Why can't I stop shaking?
Be proud of What I feel.
Communicate a love you have made so real.

Lay with me tonight.
Keep me safe and warm.
And when the light breaks thru,
illuminating the place where we lay,
let me wake to find,
You are happy to have stayed
Not just one night But a lifetime and more.

    Melissa Greco

My Wife

The one who bares this sheet of view
To conceive the thoughts of I and you

A tender kiss to conclude the night,
sends purest emotions of delight!

And with this kiss to exchange the soul
Someday to be, our body's whole

In sickness and health to death due part
a union forever pined in the heart

No fight no quarrel no death will end
forever she's mine to love and defend

To love to cherish intertwine in life
I give this sheet to my dear wife

    James A. Bomenka Jr.

A Story Told

Let stories be told of when your days were filled with flowers
and bows.
Happy hours it would be as you played underneath the big
umbrella tree
Sometimes you played alone or with your cousins and friends as
they came to your home

The earths floor baked by the sun always provided everyone
withy plenty of fun

The vast blue sky, along with the sun shinning way up high
Created plenty of smiles that would go for miles and miles

The wispy wind that would always blow left little cheeks with a
chapped red glow

The essence of a child's presence filled these days up in ways that
made them extraordinarily very pleasant
There was always such a solitude that brought with it a great gratitude
To experience such play one could only wish that here one could
always stay.

Joni Calvano

Naturally

Understand now ignorant one, when it is said no one is
more beautiful than that of the young.

The young are not always what meets the eye, there's much
more to them deep down inside.

The ignorant are taught what already had begun, where the
young only know to look past the clouds into the sun.

So now ignorant one we try to mend the values held by
our fellow friend, in hopes the young will lend a hand in
understanding all of man.

Kristen Gerth

Eschenheimer Tur

A brick garden wall,
surrounds my peace.

Four benches, for all of us,
to sit and rest our feet.

A huge tree, a small one,
some flowers.

A fountain, gurgling waters,
calming my spirit.

My friends and I can sit here,
high, for hours.

It's a secret garden,
where only we can play.

Games of fun and laughter,
Why did those days go away?

This place is where I met my best friend,
my true love and my soul mate.

Now this place is a memory,
a dream, a stargate.

Stephanie J. Dixon

Promise

I am the prism of light that sparkles like a diamond in the drop of
dew on a rose petal in the early morning...
I am the warmth you feel in your palm when you hold a small,
sleeping kitten...
I am the quiet sound of snow falling in the forests of your mind...
I am the shouts of triumph and the salty tears of defeat...
I am the raging storm at sea and the whisper of the wind caressing
the swaying pine boughs...
I am the ripples on the tidal marshes and the sandpiper's cry...
I am the quiet moment of complete solitude and peace you feel just
before you fall asleep...
I am the quiet moonlit night that forms the backdrop of your hopes
and dreams...
I am the relentless sun that parches your throat as you cross the
burning deserts of man's inhumanity...
I am your succor in an inhospitable world filled with confusion and
consternation...
I am the cosmic map by which you make your way from the womb
to the edge of eternity...
I am that I am...
You are...because of me...
My precious child of light.

Rob Reynolds

You've Danced

My dearest,
To the beautiful spirit, I have come to known
The one I speak of, the wind blows
You've danced in my mind, so many times...
Each time the wind blows

Where did you come from, where have you been
I long to feel your breeze again
You're soft and gentle, just like a dream
Kind and spirited, an angel, you must be

A love that comes, so complete
Love that honors each word you speak
You've danced in my mind so many times...
Each time the wind blows

The old country, we have been
I stood at your door, you let me in
You didn't deny, you knew me then
Oh, I long to feel your breeze again
come walk this world with me
God bless the inspiration you have set free.

Jeffery James McClintock

Seals

Seals are funny when they play.
Actually they are funny in every way.
Gray seals are big, gray seals are small.
Gray seals have a fin like paw.
Seals eat meat. Seals are neat.
Sometimes seals eat penguin feet.
Seal don't sleep in a bed.
All seal pups sleep after they're fed.
Elephant seals are big and ugly.
Fur seal pups are soft and cuddly.
I hope one day when swimming in the sea
A cute little seal comes up to me!

Joseph Workman

All God's Gifts

Sunny skies, tall green trees
  glistening water, cool spring breeze
Fresh cut grass, blossoming flowers
  soft sound of thunder during spring showers
Baby birds in trees do hatch
  playful bunnies in the flower patch
Squirrels jumping from tree to tree
  everything new from bear cub to bee
Children run and play and sing
  All creatures gay, it's finally spring
Thanking the Lord for all things true
  but none compare to my love for you

  Margaret K. Nelson

My Friend, Imagination

Reality is my enemy, and Imagination is my confidant.
Ambitions, dreams, goals all seem accessible with her.
She believes with her heart, and does not underestimate the impossible.
Freely, she gives unselfish advice.
Impatience is far from her gentle spirit.
Encouragement is abundant on her lips.
Never does Imagination question my thoughts or motives.
Fervently she listens and stimulates my spirit, no aspiration is
unrealistic to her.
Motivation is her trade.
Everything is achievable; nothing is immeasurable in her
thoughtful eyes.
A true solace is she,
My unrivaled friend, Imagination.

  Lindsay Funkhouser

The Perfect Happiness

By love our souls will always be free,
Our love is as innocent as innocent can be.

The happiness that you have given to me,
Opened my heart and that's where you'll be.

Thy beauty is so great, you make a stand,
You're an angel floating in the Holy Land.

Twas your inner beauty that shone so great,
For many a moon I would sit here and wait.

It was you, your happiness, and your internal grace,
Which opened my life, my soul, a smile upon my face.

But time passed and so did we.
This world is without you and me.
Our love for each other people can not see.
But our souls are together eternally.

  Fred Nagle Jr.

Who?

Who will...be the mentor of my inspiration,
...stay awake with me for late night conversations,
...kiss away the fears that cause all my frustrations?
Who will love me?

Who can...help me question all I have to fear,
...climb the wall I've built from bricks of wasted tears,
...swim the sea of doubt just to tell me that it's clear?
Who can save me?

Who is...always willing to sacrifice their time for me,
...wise enough to make a land of pure simplicity,
...the other lost soul that was sent to fill my destiny?
Who is the one?

  Amy Loseth

You Are Not Alone

  Left alone and willing to do it all on your own. Things
once understood are now not known. You were once against the
world and showed nothing but hate, all you have to blame is what
brought you there which is fate. Bring it up before you bring
yourself down by no one will you be found. Trying to understand
all of the things that went wrong while singing and crying over
and over to the same sad song.
  The things you are doing to yourself are destroying your
mind and in your thoughts you didn't think you were really that
kind. There's no excitement and a whisper of a cold silence as
you only become confused. Thinking of innocent fun gets you too
amused. You walk on past the bloody man of filth as with his
whiskey bottle he drinks, all you can do is look back and
remember that all that needs to happen is for someone to think.
You walk on past the little girl of salty tears that fall to her
dress of pink and still you know that someone should think. You
walk on past the lonely man, you look into his eyes and fear is
shown and now you know where ever you go; when you think you are
not alone.

  Labriska Ligon

Taste Of Heaven

You stood there before me
Time was not our friend
Crystalline droplets caressed your face
Consoling stature arms open wide.
Welcoming you to a long life of bliss
So there we were our final embrace
Scorched by your love
Your soul forged to mine
My departure inevitable I left with hope.
For my appetite was not diminished
By that taste of heaven

  Dorian Alexis Santiago

Untitled

With grateful heart
This resting spirit soars on wind song,
Breezes cooling on sunning bodies
Time for thoughts to flow so clear and certain.
With eye gazing across white capped waves
To horizon beyond
Sense of the Eternal's awesome peace and power
Bring cleansing tears,
Sounds of Ravel 'mid the chattering gulls here congregating
Lift one to swell with joy
With the feet wishing to dance
The voice to sing.
Amen to a blessed day.

  Kathleen L. McDowell

Ashes Of Rose

Wispy fingers reach out from the grave.
Fingers of fire and smoke.
Her essence, trying now in its last hour
To atone for her sins, drifts over her loved ones,
Shatters, and falls among them with a peaceful sigh.
Will they ever know, will they ever care?
The fire burns hotter and brighter.
Her essence, gathering itself together,
Cries out, though none will hear, "Forgive me for not
Being all you wanted me to be."
Then, returns to that darkness that comes but once.

  Arlette Dudley Green

Jason's Eyes

Jason's eyes hide a lot inside
Behind the blue and green
There has been much that has been seen
What have the eyes seen?
Why does it have to seem like such a mystery?
Give me time and maybe I'll find what they have hidden behind
When his eyes look into yours, it's like they hypnotize
They're so powerful it makes me dream and fantasize
I've been with him for four months now
And I think I've found what he's got hidden
inside and behind.
It's all the caring, loving, and feelings he has to be mine
And there is more to that you see
There's sense of humor, a personality, and an
all around nice guy.
He's told me day to day, but I've never seen it in
him 'til that special day when I saw it in
his eyes.

April R. Maust

Is There Any Hope?

Kids in the streets at night
Walking with a piece at their side.
Their profit from a little line, sitting in a bag.
A shot rings out, they crossed the line,
Now one of them must pay.

Two young girls outside
Playing hopscotch near the street.
The chalk to draw the game, laying in the grass.
A car drives by, the innocent hurt,
The victims have no hope.

Young women on a campus
Coming home late from a lecture.
Their books in a bag, hanging on a shoulder.
A stranger walks, following behind,
The girls never make it home.

Do we have any hope
In a place full of violence.
The future of our children grows darker.
The world sinking deeper each day.
There is hope, if you believe.

Tracie D. Rollins

Fate

A candle flickers against and envelope of darkness
A flame with hope, squelched with hurt and unfulfilled dreams-
Crying out for the kiss of a breeze to bring it to life-
To accept the fading glow of its essence as it truly is
It burns bright once more with new found love
Only to have its flame extinguished unexpectedly:
Standing alone against winds and rain
Never to die - holding fast to a dream to be loved

In a nearby place, another candle flickers
with the same soul as the first
waiting for the freedom to express its inner glow;
The flame is dull, barely alive
"Is there another like me?"
A power way up high - could no longer ignore
the fate of the two which stood alone
side by side they touched; sparked a glow so bright
That even the strongest wind couldn't threaten them
souls enmeshed with mutual giving and taking
Making each other radiant, brighter than ever before
Deserving of each other to love, cherish forevermore...

Donna Forman

"I Am"

I am sensitive and fearful.
I wonder how the world will end up.
I hear people crying.
I want abortion and crime to stop.
I am sensitive and fearful.

I pretend I could rule the world.
I feel for the homeless people.
I touch the hearts of the aborted babies.
I worry how the world will become.
I cry to think how good we have it.
I am sensitive and fearful.

I understand how the world is today.
I say what goes around comes around.
I dream for peace.
I try to believe the world will be a safe place.
I hope everyone will be happy.
I am sensitive and fearful.

Kelly Bonin

For My Sweetheart

I wish I may, I wish I might
be in love with you tonight.

However near, however far
close in heart, you always are.

Hold you in my arms, hold you oh so tight
hold you in my heart, keep you in my life.

Love be near, love be dear
without any fear - let love be here.

To share with you, let our dreams come true
no matter what - always with you.

We have this day, we have this life
we have each other to make it right.

Love be near, love be dear
love be always - love be here.

I wish I may, I wish I might
keep you in my heart and always in my life.

Bobbie Lynn Chandler

Heart Song

My heart is lonely and unfulfilled, searching for the
perfect tune that will play eternally sweet and tenderly soft
flowing down my spin, settling in my soul and soothe my
mind of its reckless play. I close my eyes tune into my
heart only to find it's truly lonely.
The days go on still searching for the beauty of the heart
song, so I'll open my heart to the flying emotions in the
air-reaching up to pull them in. Sort them out and
continue to find my heart still empty.
United my heart through my own soul with my mind to
create my own song that fulfilled me. I finally found
my own heart song.

Tina-Jo Mitchell

God's Artistry

The "Rose," so dainty, fragile, fragrant,
In hues of red, yellow, white and pink,
What breathtaking beauty, aroma too,
However delicate it may look-
Rain, winds, sometimes storms, it withstands.
We, too, are somewhat like a rose,
Created in races of Yellow, Red, Black and White
God's greatest masterpieces of art,
Our life develops, unfolds, blossoms, withers, dies-
A life we pray, as beautiful as a "Rose".

Mildred B. Tynes

A Lotus In Burma

Aung San Suu Kyi
Would like to see the Myanmar Regime die
She is a wife and a mother
But knows that there is no difference between self and other

Her Bodhisattva way
May result in a democratic Burma some day
She has had many a test
Such as her years of house arrest

Her suffering would be great
Had she attachment to her fate
Cruelty and oppression are government tools to keep the people silent
Yet she persists in her quest for freedom without ever becoming violent

As she ceaselessly practices the dharma
She works through her karma
Her future is not clear
But to the free world she is dear

Out of the political quagmire she arose
Just like the lotus grows
Having the same attributes as Avalokiteshvara
She too should escape samsara

Albert G. Duffy

"A True Friend"

All my life I've been rather quiet
I've sit alone many a day and night,
When times were getting ruff
I thought I had to act tuff,
All those guys I thought were my friends
Didn't stand by me in the end,
Sometimes I would bump into a real nice guy
He wouldn't have much to say because I was high,
When he gave me good advice, I would get mad
He would look at me very sad,
Now that I'm older and look back at life
I thank my friend for my life tonight,
I'm looking forward to bumping into my friend
I know he's the guy that will stand by me in the end.

LaDonne Argo

Wishful Thinking

On a rainy, dull day when I'm down and feeling blue,
    these are some things that I wish could come true.
An entire day filled with hope, where no sorrows interrupt.
A society working together, where no one is corrupt.
A news broadcast cancelled due to the lack of tragic stories.
A special report aired showing only people's glories.
A city not in crisis; a country not in alarm.
A day where innocent children are safe from any harm.
An hour without minutes so no one can rush the time.
A school filled with knowledge not with guns, knives, and crime.
A world without races, a job without ranks.
A navy without missiles, an army without tanks.
A night filled with warmth because the sun always stays.
Never a repeat of these rainy, dull days.

Megan Trombley

Chasing Shadows

The wind warped boards long bleached by heat,
Birch after grass, protected wheat
And oats and sheltered mares from rain;
Now scorn a furrowed facial plane
Of gray-grooved planks disjoined yet stern,
(Surrounding fields now slowly burn)
From narrow bands of glinting rays
That bake the boards like stone hard clay
And bleed between their rippled joints;
Chasing shadows with slivered points.

David L. Aeschbacher

A Castle Garden

I close my hand upon a knob to turn wisdom's door
Closing my eyes I feel overwhelmed to peek into my soul
Not scared to pass a foot upon a plank of its floor

In a dreams wake my eyes fell upon a surreal serenity
With a lake of emotions reflecting a castled garden
Glass walls hold the beauty and to keep there my entity

As now one door has been opened to a world I never knew
Realizing that was only fear in itself that had locked this door
Until now I never knew of the keys I have had all this time to
    unlock these doors I now can go through

Anthony D. Jones

I Wish

I wish that you could realize how I really feel,
I wish that you could take my heart and see my love is real.
I wish that you could see the thoughts that I forever see,
    and know our love together was always meant to be.
I wish that I could taste the tears of sorrow that I cry,
    and taste the bittersweetness with a love you can't deny.
I wish that you could hear the song that day by day I sing,
    of all the joy and happiness that you will always bring.
I wish that I could tell you my dreams of you at night,
    of when you kissed and touched me and always held me tight.
I wish that you could only know that I believe in you,
    and everything you tell me is somehow always true.
I wish that you could take these wings, these wings that made me fly,
    and together we will always be, our love will never die.

Megan Given

Pam's Dream

In my dream my prayers came true,
That God would send someone like you.

And in my prayer to God above,
I prayed He'd send my precious love

To be consumed by a heart's desire,
To share this lover's ember of fire.

With the one I love, I'll court awhile.
Just holding hands can make me smile.

A love so rare, our flower of desire
Has bloomed in full and lifts us higher.

Now we come to declare our love
To joyous heaven and God above.

And the world will shine brand new
For our entwined heart, once two.

God's love shall hold us in his hand
Until the day we leave this land.

Debbie Ciminero

She

As I held her little hand in mine,
How would I know how our destinies would entwine.
How I was programmed to pursue certain dreams,
And spend my energies toward completing these schemes.
Yet the tale that was to be told,
Would be somehow deficient in the single mold.
For before all our combined time, hers and mine, was gone.
Many of her thoughts and dreams would be,
Evolved and honed versions spawned by me.
Much like the apple is to the tree, falling to the ground,
To become the seed of herself and also me.

Helen Struck

African Queen

You are an African Princess
bound to be a Queen
you stand dutifully welcomed
to meet Christ, Your Savior, Your King.

All through the wilderness you submitted
to be so proud
But then when you cried out, you was
not lead astray.

Christ the King was there to meet you
he even lead the way...
He carried you through the wilderness
He shut the Lion's Den, he told you
that you were, His African Queen...

He stood by you in darkness so that
you could see the light...

He gave you the Holy Spirit to
testify of His Love,
One day he's going to ascend upon
you like a Dove...

Barbara Bailey

Heart Full Of Feelings

The power of living is to look ahead,
keep your feelings locked inside you.
Follow your goals.
Let them reach your soul.
Maybe you can find ways to fly
if you just give it a try.
Take your chance
at any glance.
Look around you,
see the new you.
Touch your heart.
Feel that it won't fall apart.
The reason we stay on life is to try
    and make things turn out right.
The power in your eyes
is the first beautiful skies.
The day is new
with lots of things to do.
Don't look back, stay on the right track.
The power is the way to a brand new day

Stacy Schwendinger

New York, New York

New York City is a very special place,
It brings a big smile to my face!
There are many things to see and do,
Like shopping at Bloomingdale's and Saks on 5th Avenue.
It's exciting to take a ferry boat ride
To view the majestic Statute of Liberty,
To experience the memories of Ellis Island,
With a bull-horn touting tour guide.
Riding in a horse-drawn carriage
Around Central Park,
Is very exciting in the daylight
But even better in the dark!
New York! New York!!
It was a Ten.
Someday.....
I want to go back again!!!!!!

Tracey Black

Indian Trading Post

The sign hangs over the old log building,
deep brown as the woods that surround it.
Standing against the granite hills of Danbury.
At the Post entrance, a concrete deer greets us,
the paint on its face chipped, antlers falling off.

Beside the Post,
the remains of a teepee,
its frame exposed and filling up with snow.
Before the super highway was built,
did the children come to play in the teepee
in the days when the deer had all its antlers?

Now in the yard are frail wooden shacks,
their paint wearing off, red and green, with chimneys.
Does anyone live there still?
One by one, they'll surrender themselves to these hills.

Timeless oak trees, clay brown branches, rich green firs
create winter's pattern against white blanketed granite.
Someday, they will finish the super highway.
No more the concrete deer, the Post.
Only the hills remember.

Diane M. Waterman

Learning To Live Again

The sun fights to be seen
The curtains allow only a tiny amount to show through.
The rocking chair still squeaks the same as it always did.
Boxes scattered about the floor.
Broken pictures
Broken dreams
One broken heart,
Share the loneliness of the dark.

Picking up the pieces is what she does in the back of the room
And in the back of her heart.
Ghosts echo through the walls
Only to be heard
Never seen.

The mail is overflowing outside the door
The paper boy stopped coming.
Finally in the window
Is a flower clinging to life,
And she's learning to live again.

Melissa Berry

Nothing In This World

Nothing in this world can compare to the way you smile at me!
Nothing in this world can compare to your lovely face
And nothing in this world could ever take your place!

No evening star ever shined as bright
And the moon glow never filled the night,
the way you do!

Sweeter than the honey from the bees
You are the very dearest thing to me!

All of my life I will pray,
That I might see and hold you everyday!

When I hold you in my arms, in my heart I know
That I will always love you so!

Just to say I love you could not possibly reveal
Just how much you mean to me or how I really feel!

For words have never been written and there is no song to sing
To tell you how I love you or to me the joy you bring!

Nothing in this world can compare to the way you smile at me!
Nothing in this world can compare to your lovely face
And nothing in this world could ever take your place.

Dennis J. Petty

Can't You See Fool

The feeling of wanting it.
The feeling of Debit.
Not knowing which way to turn,
Alone fools, alone fools;
Don't you know you're alone.
Keep it coming, I don't want to fade,
Yet you're dying all the way
My heart racing
My mind flying
My body lay still
Alone fools, alone fools.
Keep it coming, I don't want to fade.
Can't you realize fools,
You're dying all the way.
The more it comes,
The more you fade
Yet you can't see, your eyes are full of white clouds.
Keep fading fool and you will see,
The white clouds, turn to black ashes.
My fool you're dying all the way.

Nancy Elizbeth Helganz

Leaves Of Life

The rustling leaves of life
Do they whisper of joy or strife?
Our lives are like the seasons
Ever changing for a different reason.

Our souls longing for the not yet -
Our hearts echoing it is God we should get.
Sometimes our heart may slumber and hope may run away
But then a voice will whisper - I'm here with you to stay.

Like the leaves we will tumble and need help along the way
It is then in our journey that faithfully we must pray.
And so with patient eagerness we wait and yearn
In quietly listening His plan for our lives we will learn.

So as we drift along life's way
He'll hold our hand and beside us stay.
A peaceful heart He'll give to us -
When on His Love we always trust.

Linda H. Callaway

Stand Back And Watch Me Fly

You clipped my wings and kept me imprisoned in a glass bubble
Rationalizing my sentence by your sad attempts to recreate heaven
Filling my cage with a soft cloud to cushion the pain
And further distort my vision of the real world
But you are not a God, you're not even an angle
And your heaven was no Shangri-La
I felt weak and helpless so I crawled inside and let you wrap the
   cloud around me, tuck me in and I fell asleep like a good girl
But I couldn't sleep forever, I woke from the dream
Not the kind of dream you wish for,
The nightmare you wake from in a cold sweat
But my wings have grown out now and I have grown up
I have rested and regained my strength
It's time to burst your bubble, shatter the make believe world
you created for me, time to create a world of my own
I want to discover people and places I could never reach before
Hold the world in my hands, feel it, touch it with my finger tips,
read it like Braille,
There are no longer boundaries, no longer limits
Nothing I can't see and no where I can not go
Now that I am free stand back and watch me fly

Leslie Monique Soule

Ma Ma's Kitchen

A double decker baked in two
Smells like hungry sweet,
Ma Ma is baking again.

Powdered sugar, flour, and salt,
Looks like cake to me.
Ma Ma's apron tells the tale.

Slam! Bang! Clang! in the kitchen.
Measuring spoons dangle the counter.
Ma Ma's bowls soon will sparkle.

The spatula filled with frosting
Tastes like almond to me.
Yum.. Ma Ma gives me a squeeze.

Sitting down to have a chat,
Mouth full of cake and frosting,
Ma Ma says, "Let me cut you another slice."
   Feels like home to me!

Ann L. Dummert

The Helmsman

When the stormy seas of life they rage,
And through them you must sail.
When the enemy whispers,
"Don't go! Turn back! For surely you will fail."

Don't listen to the cry of one,
Who know's only failure and defeat,
But give the helm to Christ the Lord,
Who can every challenge meet.

For He can make the wind be still,
And the troubled sea be calm,
Because He is the Prince of Peace,
He is the Healing Balm.

For Jesus is the light,
The light that shows the way,
A beacon you can follow,
That will never let you stray.
He is the one to stay your course,
And keep it ever true,
If you abide and trust in Him,
He will take you through.

Jack Brumley

She The Heated Anger

Peerless, you felt about me
She, the heater anger. ShhhSh... ShhhSh... ShhhSh...
Quick...! Quick...! Hide within me.
I'm safe... I'm safe...
In my special place.

Affronted, holding my ears...
I cry, I cry of silent tears.
Oh God! the fear...
As she, the heated anger, appears.

Upon her face, furrows of hate.
Each stroke she takes and takes.
I dare not fluctuate.
For she, the heated anger, makes no mistakes.

I, the little one, so benign.
Lost in the heat, the heart of time.
Through all this, I made it through.
She, the heated anger, could not subdue.

Time is the healer...
For I am a success...
I beat she, the heated anger, at her best!!

Debbie Butler

That's When I Cried

I have rehearsed this day in my mind a thousand times and each time I still end up at a lost for words. It is so difficult, at his moment, to fully express to you how much I love you and how much I want us to be together forever. Although my lips have forgotten how to work, and although my thoughts seem to be all used up, I have found within me a way to coordinate the two.

As my mind races through memories that we have formed together, I abruptly stop to recall a time when I was holding you, as I have done so many times before, I had just rustled your hair and stirred the sweet fragrance of you when all of a sudden I became overwhelmed. —At first I was afraid. I was afraid of loving so much that I would lose control, thus I would be controlled. But that never happened. —After the fear subsided, I became anxious. Wanting everything yesterday, and not willing to be patient for tomorrow. -Next I was grateful. I had been given the most precious gift I could ever pray for, or could ever imagine. My gratitude lifted way above the ceiling, above the clouds, above the stratosphere, and soared passed our galaxy until it stopped at the foot of God. Once it reached its destiny, God took it, blew on it, and it floated back to me in a soft breeze that gently caressed my whole body. I shuttered because it was then that I knew that what we have is real and that God has blessed it. That's when I cried.......

Latonia D. Staten

"Friends"

A friend is one who will always care
And has a heart to listen
With faith in everything that you do
And trust that is strong like a tornado
A friend is not always cherry
And will definitely have a different opinion
But a friend can always look through that
And find beauty in who you are
A friend is someone God sends down
To help mend our broken hearts
To laugh, cry, and grow together
And learn from one another too
A friend is someone who is on your side
When the rest of the world is against you
A friend is one you can always look up to
For something that they hold
And you I will always look up to
Because you are a true friend!

Shelby Jackson

Hello

The light peers from the edge of the curtain,
like two hands and an eye of a timid child.
The yellow-white barely enhances the texture of the vase
clutching the window sill like an ivory cat.

I once had a dream that I could float
like that light through everyone's window.
I would boldly throw aside the curtains of each new stage
and let myself in, like a familiar visitor.

I'd mold myself to each face
causing browns, blues, and greens to sparkle,
like all vases should, like a lost memory
hidden inside a diamond falling from the sun.

Then I would say hello with my photon voice,
and as they replied to the empty rush of curtains,
to the invisible auditory shine, I would ride
their tongues, a slide of light all the way down.

Krista Watson

In My Mind

It seems that lately we've had to think too much,
about living and loving and what it means to us.
How it eats one's soul, when forced to betray,
in order to get what we long for each day.

Ideally, in this world there is black and white,
good and evil, wrong and right.
But in our world of secrets, so much gets in the way,
transforming our color to a passionate gray.

With much help and guidance, there is something divine,
constructing two puzzles, yours and mine.
Many lessons remain to be set in place,
each lesson learned, creating a base.

I can only hope, in the puzzle of you,
the color of me dots all that is true.
And that yet to come, will be much the same,
ensuring that I, forever remain ..... In Your Mind.

And I know that in the puzzle of me,
the color of you tints the periphery.
And that yet to come, will be much the same,
ensuring that you, forever remain ..... In My Mind.

Pamela J. Taunton

Solicitude

The seed never falls far from the tree
It lands, it's planted, it grows
It learns from all around
Learns to live
Learns to think
It becomes what it learns
It becomes a tree
....still needs to grow....

I saw a flower in a field
I wanted to pick it
Make it my own
But decided to care for it instead
Help it grow
The most beautiful flower
Its thorns were sharp
And her petals soft....

Grow tall and wise
Learn wisdom and emotion
Reach a point when love and life are one
Then, then we can create a life of our own....

J. M. Mulholland

Today And Always

For today I fell in Love with you,
I melted with a single touch it's true,
Your smile and strength just pulled me in,
And captured my heart, a great victory to win.

With such gentle hands, and loving arms you held me,
Through what seemed my roughest hour, you made me see,
How a love between two hearts could bring someone such bliss,
And those words "I Love You," you sealed with a kiss.

I want to tell the whole world, how you make me feel,
All breathless and fiery, yes, it's very, very real,
When we're apart, an emptiness surrounds me; you're always
  on my mind,
You've treated me as an equal, something I rarely find.

A friend, a Lover, romance and passion, you'll always have with me,
I want you and I need you, you must surely see,
Apart or together, this I say is true:
For today and always, "I Love You!"

Allison D. Pleva

Half Wrought Truths

Beginning in the beginning, I remember sand, and warmth grew
from this. And separate but unitary things, like painting and plays,
PTA and pottery, festivals and friendly gatherings.

Grandma came... Who is she... Tornado is what he called me.

An accident, with permanent recognitions. It changed it all
forever. I saw by living with diversity, that truth is what you
make it to be.

What actually happened in the greenery, and why me out in the rain
Sacrificed to the Sky God for fun or Tom foolery.
What really kept me from the funeral or make me refuse to call.

Torn again... A horse, the promise of trees. None of it really
mattered to me. I was left behind, let go to gain understanding and
learning...Alone.

Gone, Gone, She's gone... Success and money... Cool things, but
No Real time. Cook, Clean, Domestication... Food fill the need, gap
left to bleed and bleed and breed... Bent helpless...down bitch on
your knees.

Excuse Me...Tell me now, what I have done to deserve all that you
have given me. Show me now, boy... what I have done, boy...to
require you to service me.

Perri A. Doutre

There's Music In My Heart

There's music in my heart,
Keeping time to the tempo of the day,
Playing the medley of the changing pace,
Echoing life's events along the way.
Did I hear a waltz in my heart
As love tapped my shoulder
And gave my life a new direction?
Or was it the softness of a quiet lullaby
As a sleeping child's head
Lay nestled against my shoulder?
Maybe it's the even tempo of a patriotic march that I hear,
and the passing of the honor guard at a patriotic celebration.
There are times that I listen anxiously as the music plays
A composition not of my selection,
Reminding me of my role as instrument and not conductor.
Or perhaps this is all an overture,
A prelude rehearsed today,
Tomorrow's dreams sleeping in my imagination.

Sandra Johnson Barker

His Gentle Touch

A gentle touch on the shoulder with a comforting word
Startles her senses with such compassion and warmth
So unexpected the stirrings of emotions unearthed
That rush to the surface responding to his gentle touch.

Years of control learned from countless hurts
Secret longings buried beneath her fragile surface
Suddenly become released flooding her senses completely
Aching to respond to his gentle touch and comforting word.

Hurriedly the mind sends signals, the pulse quickens
As each awakened fiber strains against the repairs of defense.
These fragile tender emotions must be protected
Never revealing the purest delight of his gentle touch.

A facade of calm returns to her flushed surface
Emphatically denying the brief emotional storm
Leaving an unseen scar on a heart forever longing
Never once forgetting, his gentle touch and comforting word.

Kaye Meaker

Red Revolt (1991)

The Red Star ebbs before the freeing Thunder,
the cracks in the Kremlin wall sprout vine.
What was the boot the common folk lived under
cast aside before the Tide of this new wine.

No nineteen-seventeen or -05 of Bloody Sunday,
no tread of tank to grind the will of State;
instead in heaving breasts the people say
what we shall be, we'll choose the fate.

Unto the dust of the ages the idols fall,
as those the Maya saw the jungle crest.
To the Attic go the Bolshevik heirlooms all.
The names join those of Ozymandias.

The lights are dimmed in "the City of Yes and the City of No"...
The Bolshoi will come and pirouette as before.
The epoch many names in the list of its lusty bravissimo
become part of the record the future should not ignore

Might and impact are not the same enduring,
nor steel, Time shows, beneath the spirited word
which, thriving in the mind so alluring,
thrusts a whole people forward like a freed bird.

E. A. Book

Through Out Eternity

To say I love you is such a general expression,
It has been used since the beginning of time,
Until the present as we know it.
To be as simple and common as all the others before our time,
Seems such a lack of truth in the strength in which I gather from you.
For what I feel for you,
Is like looking on a shoreline with its never ending beauty.
And as the stars run one with the ocean,
Our souls run one with the other.
You are my world in which time is infinite with the stars,
You are my life in which every beat is a breath I take from you,
And my soul reflects the twinkle and glistening from which I
  absorb from you.
So that's why my love,
I simply cannot say I love you.
For it doesn't hold the deepness of forever,
Which fate has laid out among the stars in heaven above.

Raquel Welch

I Remember

I remember love
  fun and laughter
  grief and despair

I remember old friends
  in faraway places

I remember first snows of winter
  tulips in the spring
  asters in the fall

I remember all the words
  to nursery rhymes
  and Christmas carols

I remember sounds of music
  of children puppies kittens
  and voices now stilled

I remember church bells on a Sunday morn
  easter hats and black patent slippers

I remember being young and sure
  long hikes mountain tops

I remember love
  but where did I put my glasses?

Alice Powell

Staring At The Wall

Sitting, watching, wondering.
The night air flows over your bare legs.
The darkness of night calls to you.
Your mind swirls with thoughts.
As you stare at the wall, you leave your body,
soaring through time and space,
learning the answers to all of your questions.
A low humming noise rings in your ear, as if someone
were calling to you.
You plummet through the clouds towards the ground.
Your eyes flash open and you realize
you're back.
Where were you, what happened to you?
Do you dare to dream again or do you
sit and wonder...
Staring at the wall

Stanford James Bryant

The Faces Of Travel

Often times it occurs to me, to look into the faces I see
Driving in the cars that pass by me
The faces of travel

I wonder what's going on inside the minds of millions, as they pass by
I get a short glimpse into their lives
In their faces of travel

A Mercedes Benz cruises by, the rich old woman has
her head held high,
But all her make-up cannot hide, the sadness that she feels inside
You need only look into her eyes, to know there's things money just
can't buy
And the pain you see could make you cry
In the faces of travel

Some seem happy as can be, like the couple with the new baby,
Or the teenagers driving to some party
With their faces of travel

But most of the time what I see is sad, like the man who's angry
cause the traffic's bad
Or the couple that's arguing like mad
With their faces of travel

There's so much suffering in this world, people are lonely,
frustrated and hurt
And their cries for help can sometimes be heard
In their faces of travel.

Londa Isosaki

Infinite Love

Amazingly wonderful is what you are.
If God meant for two to pair,
I feel he meant for you and me.
Being without you is unimaginable.
Words cannot fully define my feelings for you.
In this strange and unfamiliar place we call Earth,
to find someone as loving and as kind as you,
is indeed a miracle and a blessing.
Perhaps it is chemistry, or perhaps it is destiny,
but it is definitely what we call love.
You add such sweet meaning to my life.
If I knew reincarnation to be certain, I would choose you to
accompany me in all of my other lives.
As obscure as this may sound, it is said with the utmost truth.
For you I have infinite love engraved in the depths of my heart
and the soul of my being.
I thank God for your presence and your love in this harsh and
bitter world.

Verna Thomas

Wild Rose

The dew has set on its back and limbs,
The smell of perfume has entered in.
The scent of morning; scent of care,
Scent of wild rose is in the air.

The touch is soft, as soft as wool mittens,
They flow delicately as diminutive kittens.

It starts to rain as the sun flourishes through,
As it washes off all of the mornings sweet dew.

The rain falls onto the lacy petals,
As it helps the flower bloom, and then settles.
The snow comes down and freezes its statute,
When during Fall petals blew right past you.
They blew afar and land in large bends,
Until spring comes and they bloom again.

Spring is here and they start to rise,
They grow strait up till they meet the skies.

The patches of roses are marvelous and sweet,
The petals are soft as they brush against your cheek.

The smell is carried over valleys and hills,
Large white cranes feel petals against their bills.

Kiana Lynn Garcia

Homeless

When the cold winds blow, I think of you and weep,
for the moon that lights your way,
has no time for little boys that dream,
walk softly child of sleeping heart,
for the trees have ears,
and a voice to mock your very soul,
even now as you wander the streets alone,
amidst the mothers call to young,
you peer into each waiting glass,
to see the warmth of a caring embrace,
and a love you will never know,
the ache that swells inside you,
grows hot like the fire of the hell you call home,
each shaking head that looks upon you,
shamed to offer a dime, and quick to cross the street,
will never know your name, or know the reasons why,
when the cold winds blow, you think of us and weep,
for in the end, when backs are turned,
we are truly the homeless, and you have gone to a better place...

Karl Richards

Untitled

Spring is faith
  Spring is hope
    Spring is love

Have faith in spring, it will always come
  Have hope in spring, may it appear very soon
    Have love in spring, to make flowers bloom

The skunks are out
  The robins are nesting
    The geese are pairing and the bats are singing
      All good signs of spring, they have faith

The lake is still frozen and there's snow in the air
  Faith turns to hope for warm sunshine tomorrow
    Love of the land and the shifting seasons
      Keeps us here, it's home

Faith,
  Hope,
    and love

It's springtime in Minnesota

Mary Jane DeVaan

Dreams

Dreams are not for eyes that are closed
Nor eyes that have weakened to sleep
For the will's possibilities can only intrigue
Those eyes which stay open to seek

Dreams, never will they be attained
If illusions are their only feed
Achievements are the vines over the castle wall
And encouragement upon what they shall seed

Goals lay a path through life's wilderness
With failures as detours that teach
And like stepping stones, our triumphs are
The limbs which will lengthen our reach

True faith keeps the vision aloft
When desires unleash the balloon
If each try were a rung in a ladder
Persistence could reach for the moon

Colleen VanHout

The Death Penalty

Murderers kill other people,
when they're caught they're sentenced to die.
Their sentences are carried out by
the judge, jury, you and I.

We believe we have justly served his wrath
by righteously sending him to his death,
but who will accept the blame for this deed
the judge, jury, you or me?

You see we haven't the right
to determine one's fate
no matter how much we like, love or hate,
instead we should make him work for his sin
and let only God determine his end.

Niya F. H. Parks

Ode To Ladybug

Today they tell me that you may die
    and I sit here crying, wondering "Why?"

This day of autumn is bright and clear
    and I sit here wishing that you were here.

Remembering your favorite spot on the rug
    and I sit here wishing you here to hug.
Your favorite spot by the chair is cold
    and I sit here wishing you weren't old.

Your bed is empty, waiting for you
    and I sit here crying; waiting too.

The doctor is trying as hard as he can
    and I sit here waiting for my old friend.

The house is empty, cold and dark
    and I sit here, yearning to hear your bark.

Your paw on my knee meant so much to me
    and I sit here wishing you running free.

I know you're alone, with tubes and needles,
    and I sit here wondering how you got old and feeble.
The years together have been so few,
    and my little buddy, I love you!

Nicolle C. Woodward

Five Seconds Of Cerebral Static

I woke up in bed with Minnie Mouse. Mickey looks angry with that
shot gun in his hand.
I dial 911 to find there's a blue light special on adult diapers.
Why does my breakfast insult me before it crawls away?
I was dead on the night of the fifth. The Beave is the Uni Bomber.
I dropped a dime and it didn't fall. Case dismissed.
You can't stab me with a gun. Micheal fly your boat ashore.
The harmonica claws at my eyes as Satan prays for forgiveness.
I vomit a cuckoo bird and he steals my lucky charms. He unplugs
my door and runs away to Mexico in my ten gallon hat named Forest.
I seem to be in the wrong country. If trees had legs would they
help me to write a country song?
I am so cold that I just burnt my tongue.
Who was that masked man? Oh it's just Satan looking for a job as
a real estate salesman.
The darkness
    fades
        to plaid.

Jerry B. Leineke

Butterflies

Tiny little butterflies flitting in the sun
Flying high in the sky, down they come one by one!
Then, they fly "to and fro"—"up and down" in twos they go,
Joining others on their way in their flight, and in their play.

Many butterflies flit by, some fly low, others high.
Soon they'll flutter on their way, hunting food for the day.
Again, and again, they'll come in several groups
"Back and forth", and away they'll swoop!

Chasing and playing as they fly, many butterflies fluttering past,
The bigger ones come first the tiny ones come last.
Attired in love's apparel, each one shimmering in the hot sun.
Bowing so gracefully as they pass each one,
Dressed in yellows, orange, whites and golden browns
They'll swoop, flit and flutter all around.
They shimmer, glitter, chasing one by one as they pass,
In twos they'll flit lad and lass
Along the flowery road, the path of weedy grass -
Joining others as they fly
Waving their little wings GOODBYE.

Johanna M. Wolt

Daring To Discover Your Inner Being

When I look at him what do I see
When he looks at me what does he see
Do I see him? Does he see me?
To an alien what would I be.
Would I be an alien just like he.

When I'm walking down the street does he watch me.
Do I watch him and turn and laugh at everything I'm looking at,

Is this what humans like you and I do
Is all of this really true

Does he fear me like I fear him
Do we both feel the same deep down within
Do we really know if aliens have three toes
We all wonder about UFOs...

Was this all an illusion or was it true
I don't really know... do you...

So deep within us we all have an unknown place
Is it real? Should we believe?

Am I an alien..or..is he
Dare to discover your inner being.

Jovan Nicole Freeman

"Our Country When She Calls"

There is a voice few people hear
For those that do it rings loud and clear
And when they hear it they rise and stand tall
They're the people who answer our country when she calls

They come from all places from all walks of life
Some are sisters or brothers some are husbands or wives
Their race is not an issue it doesn't matter at all
To the people who answer our country when she calls

They sail across oceans they fly through the air
Traverse mountains and valleys they go anywhere
They give of themselves and ask nothing at all
They're the people who answer our country when she calls

They pledge their allegiance to the flag and their God
They're the ones who stand firm when the going gets hard
When the world needs a hero they rise above all
They're the people who answer our country when she calls

They sail across oceans they fly through the air
Traverse mountains and valleys they go anywhere
They give of themselves and ask nothing at all
They're the people who answer our country when she calls

Jonathan T. Morey

Your Friend

Every flower has a thorn
Every thorn has a flower...
This doesn't mean that your life;
Can't be the best you ever had...
When you feel lonely or depressed
Look back I'll be there;
to cheer you up...
When you feel that everyone
has turned their back on you;
look around I'll be there with you...
In good times or bad times
look I'll be there no matter what;
A friend is a present you give yourself...
And most of all I'm glad you're my Friend...
Thanks for your Friendship...

Carmen Robles

A Nation's Sorrow

- The Bombing of Oklahoma City -
Thunder rolled and the Earth shook
But a storm was nowhere near,
In a flash many lives were changed
With the loss of someone so dear.

Many of us looked helplessly on
As the shock rocked through our souls,
As the dazed survivors emerged
And Death began its toll.

Who can begin to imagine
The sorrow they must feel?
How many more sleepless nights
Till their hearts begin to heal?

If only we could have seen
The Angels leading the way,
To take with them all the souls
Who would be in Heaven that day.

If a person's heart can be healed
By the hopes and prayers of another,
Then this Nation will heal its sorrow
With the prayers of its sisters and brothers.

Deborah Pilmaier

The Search

Obscure as a great sunken treasure.
The mysteries of myself begin to unfold.
Immaturity of the mind - as I think that my skin is my sin.
As I continue to shift the weight of defeat in the lap of others,
I learned the real struggle is within me.
Trapped - mentally and spiritually.
Prophecies of destruction!!!
They push me to great opposition of such.
As I rise to offer to myself what was never offered
I begin to unlock the Peace which Passes all of my understanding.
As it guides my heart and mind, only then will
I find freedom.
Often confused. Confusion all around!!!
The search. The struggle. It leads me again to myself.
The Me. The I. The learning.
The search for victory
It continues to lead me back to the perfection of Myself.

Shaurice E. Lee

Untitled

I'm like an old coat hangin' in your closet
that you'll never throw away.
You take me out, and try me on
Do I feel the same old way?
You look in the mirror to see what's missin'
The pocket's torn and a button's gone
Have all the colors faded since you last put me on?
Last time I saw you I noticed a change
You didn't feel the same old way.
It wasn't warm - and you didn't seem to care.
Maybe now you can throw me away.
Remember when you brought me home?
I never left your side
But now my home's your closet -
Do you sometimes wish coats could die?

Karel Hecker

Night Fires

The explosion of lights and sound,
Echoing across the night sky.
Feel its awesome power,
Thundering through your soul.
You stop.

You stare in awe and anticipation,
For the next streak of light.
Climbing higher and higher into the night.
Ever exploding into a ball of color,
Just like you knew it would.

It draws you in.
You become part of the music,
Power and light.
Your heart has cried,
and danced with delight.

Karrie L. White

Confusion

Light and dark, black and white, what does it all mean?
High times and low times contained in a dream.
Swirling emptiness in a sea of black
Nothing to go to, nothing to go back.
Constantly running, always a place to be
We sometimes never open our eyes to see.
Connecting lives, connecting ties,
Everywhere, running circles inside one another
Never say a word nor mutter.
Just running in silence, amidst the confusion.

Joe Cavanaugh

Eternity

To live a thousand lifetimes
See all that can be seen
I would do almost anything
To live all eternity

Living beyond the pain, and suffering
Where the body and soul are free
An eternal land of enchantment and beauty
Is where, I do now seek

Enraptured in soothing beauty
Caressed in the sweet spring air
A land where every dream comes true
Will truly quench this thirst

Where the power of the universe
is at your command
And everything you want to know
Is within your grasp

Eternity, Eternity.....

Paul Sherfey

The Contemplative Lover

Utter contemplation;
plagues my wearying mind.

Fighting to maintain the belief;
that a sane man is the only one who fears the madness.

Patience;
as days fade into weeks; then months; then...

Faltering confidence in my "enlightenment";
boundless faith in her.

All the while, waiting;
painfully loyal to my memories;
aggravatedly steadfast;
to a breathless promise.

As I struggle;
to grasp thy ever-fading image...

Brent Koenes

The Eyes Of The World

There are four eyes in the world
that guide our thoughts and actions.
One for evil, the injustice in this land.
One that is good, the justice served well done.
One that stands for hope and another that is despair
Hope for the future, a bright one full of goodness,
Despair, when all you fight for comes undone
and evil takes over your soul,
then eats your heart, and pollutes your mind.

These four eyes see all things,
and exist together in blissful harmony.
They rule with an iron fist,
and soothe with a gentle touch.
Four eyes, one world, one universe,
Chaos, Destruction, Healing, and Repair
Heed them well, for to battle one you must use another,
To conquer one you must conquer all.

Mark Partridge

"I Believe In Unicorns. I Believe In Dreams"

I believe in Unicorns
I believe in dreams
I believe nothing is as it seems

I believe everybody needs something to believe in
I believe in nature, flower-fairies gnomes
But most of all I believe in unicorns- I believe in dreams.

Rhonda Waitkins

Happiness Is...

Happiness is,
Walking hand in hand with a loved one,
Seeing the sky turn pink during a spring sunset,
The smell of flowers blooming in the month of May,
It's the greatest feeling in the world.
Happiness is,
Cuddling with that someone special,
Watching children play in an open field,
The sounds of laughter filling the air,
It's the best natural high around.
Happiness is,
Spending special moments with the one you love,
Looking into the horizon while the sun sets behind the mountains,
The aroma given off from a field a roses,
An incredible inner peace which won't subside.
Happiness is,
Being with that special someone every minute of every day,
For the rest of time to come.

William Oden

As I Stare...

As I stare, I see a cipher,
for when you go day to day without being noticed you feel nothing,
you are treated as nothing

As I stare, I feel disappointment creep upon me.
I feel my heart breaking as I shed a tear.

As I stare into my mirror,
I decide that I will make a change.
I will no longer be a cipher.

Kelly Rainwater

The Rain Of Past Pain

Sometimes we are so lonely because of love departed
All the dreams have shattered and have left you broken hearted
Good times seem impossible to ever grasp again
You try to look ahead but everything seems so grim
Only time can take vivid pain away
For the wounds of a heart are not healed in one day
Time will go by and somehow you will muddle through
Slowly, you will realize that your heart feels good as new
Then one day when you are standing tall
You will realize your strength from it all
On that day, when you look inside yourself
You will be able to take those old wounds down from the shelf
Maybe you will dust them off, recalling the pain from the past
Though now you will know, that the rain will not last

Hannah Wright

Missing You

My heart aches when we are apart
I miss you dearly sweetheart.
I miss your smile, I miss your touch,
When you're not here. I miss you so much.
I miss your arms as they hold me tight,
This love we share just feels so right.
I miss falling asleep at night in your arms,
The sound of your heart beat keeps me safe and warm.
I miss your sweet lips caressing mine,
As we build in rhythm, a love divine.
You've taken me to heights as never before,
Your gentle touch excites me once more.
I'll never regret you coming back for me,
This love of ours will last to eternity.
I miss you so much my sweet lover,
For me there will be no other.

Margaret A. Troyer

"Him"

I see it, I feel it.
Curled in the fetal position, grasping my stomach,
but I know it's my heart.
I delve into it as it deepens,
forming as a black hole,
poking and digging into the hollowness
probing for the ache and numbness.
He says embrace it and let it go-
the empty pit.
How?
My breath occupies this space
allowing me to view its desolate passage through me.
How deep can it run-run as I do from it.
Only to find it chasing me
with beautiful memories which paralyze me.
How I long to fill it like a grave,
to kill the comforts that have long been destroyed,
to forget the nightmares that were once reality,
to know the peace and laughter of a child.

Samantha Dunbar

Life And Happiness

Dismal, oh, how dismal
Is a street blanketed with fog
The thickness is as stages in ones life.

We sometime feel life's trials will choke us,
But as the fog lifts slowly
With rays of sunlight drifting through
So does happiness seep into each life.

Penetrate and pierce into my heart
You intangible thing
Make me feel your warmth
Enclose me, smother me.
Take hold, do not lose me.

Realization contains me
Fog come and goes
Happiness enters and departs.

Catherine A. Hannah-Lesko

Infinite Journey

We began this journey of the unknown with hopefulness
Our journey unplanned held many surprises for us all
We held on tight for the ride of our life

The wounds are deep and almost unbearable at times
Our journey is frightening with uncertainly
Our friendship held dear to our hearts
through all the pain we share
Our journey continues with uncertainty and hopefulness
The hopefulness that our love will with stand it all

May our friendship deepen with every step we take
For our friendship is most important
in completing this journey
Our openness is helping us dissolve the uncertainty

Can our hearts endure the pain to finish the journey
Can we look beyond our fear with understanding
Will our friendship dissolve if the journey is incomplete
Will our friendship dissolve if the journey is completed

Our friendship has been put to the test on this journey
Time is all we have now to wait it out alone or together

Diane Thomas

Love What Is Love

Love can make your heart fly
Love can make you want to die
Love can take your heart
When it's over you fall apart
Who knew Love was kind
Who knew Love makes you blind
Love is like a soft breeze on a warm summer day
Or like a storm that takes it all away
One moment you feel life is great
Then it's gone and feels like a big mistake
How could I be so blind thinking he was mine
Forever and ever is what Love is
Then why is it ending the way it is.
My heart is aching, my heart is breaking
I'll get over him I guess
But right now my Life's a mess
We can work it out, you'll see
He will come back to be with me
If our Love is meant to be
We'll be back together again you'll see.

Christine Guenther

To My Husband, My Love

When one loses a love who has been your confidant, your
friend and lover, there is no greater loss.

In our many good years together, the most dreaded thing
happened, you became ill, you were so brave, you fought
very hard to keep your spirits up and face each agonizing
day with new hope.

A lesser man would have given up, or become bitter, but
you kept on trying.

Not long ago we talked at length about our parents,
and our families, how fortunate we had always been to
have their love and support.

Of all the many long days and nights you were in the
hospital, I always knew you were coming back home to me.

The last several years of your illness seemed to run
together, with no beginning and no ending, now your
suffering has an ending.

A person cannot watch a loved one die and not be changed,
I shall be forever changed.

I will remember you always with love, therefore you will
never be gone, only out of sight.

Ena Audora Orindgreff

Where Were You?

I looked for you for support.
    Where were you?
I wanted and needed love.
    Where were you?
I was oh, so very lonely and depressed.
    Where were you?
I needed your hand upon my shoulder to help
    me through the day.
    Where were you?
I needed and longed for a friend just to talk to.
    Where were you?
Now, my friend, just look into the mirror.
    There I am. I am you.

Kathleen Ann Linskens

Faith

When all else has failed
  Have faith
When your house can no longer
be called your home
  Faith will find a way
When your parents are no longer
around to say, You'll - be - just - fine
Don't worry
Faith will embrace you
In time of need and there's no
one to lend you a hand
  Faith will lend you a hand or two
When you think you're at the end
of your rope
  Faith will add 2 inches more
To have faith is to know there is a
higher being.
Keep the faith

    Karen Jones

The Reaper (A Villanelle)

I did not see him standing there at all
And yet, I felt a presence near my bed
I did not hear the Reaper's urgent call.

I raised my trembling hand and let it fall
"Who's there?" Confusion burned inside my head
I did not see him standing there at all.

My soul rebelled against the bitter gall
Of helplessness before some nameless dread
I did not hear the Reaper's urgent call.

My hopes and dreams were lost beyond recall
There were no thoughts, no words left to be said
I did not see him standing there at all.

Soft voices murmured sadly in the hall
My room was cold and silent as the dead
I did not hear the Reaper's urgent call.

Surrendering I turned to face the wall
At last all trace of consciousness had fled
I did not see him standing there at all
I did not hear the Reaper's urgent call.

    Adrienne Marchmann

A Ballad For Betty

I open my eyes to a cotton candy sunrise, life is bittersweet,
full of goodbyes.
The coffee smells strong in the air, no surprise.
I wash the sleep off my face, as I get ready for the race, I get
no ribbon, I don't even place.
Today I'll walk, I won't run, I'll savor the day that's begun.
I look at the tranquil mountains, I think of the gray city strife,
how it has no heart, and gives little life.
I see even in the winter air a weed pokes through the dirty
sidewalk bare.
I did dance once for a little while, perhaps I'll dance again
before I go.

    Christina J. Morrison

Baby Girl

She's a brindle, flop eared, and hairy;
  To some she's even scary.

This is because of her unusual size;
  If you come to my house you'll get a surprise.

She's pushy, demanding, and wants to be boss;
  Her path you shouldn't dare to cross.

All seven foot six of her fits on my bed;
  When she steps on my toe I really see red.

She is one hundred sixty pounds and still growing;
  Looks especially fierce when her eyes are glowing.

Don't knock on my door or ring my bell;
  Or you will surely think that you're in .... well

She loves and protects me like an oyster to a pearl;
  She is my dog and I named her Baby Girl.

    Heather Wiland

Nightmare

When the demon comes to get me
Under the covers I go to hide

Another day alive he will not let me
For more time I try to bide

A baseball bat a caliber forty-five
Is all I need to last the night

Now I know I cannot survive
And into my heart he does put fright

He leaps upon me
And I gasp for air

Tightly his strong hands are wrapped around me
And in my head I say a silent prayer

I wake up dripping in sweat
My poor little heart doing about one o five

I now find out that what I did fret
Was all a dream in disguise

    Matt Gabriel

What A World

We live in a crazy mixed-up world all right
And Satan is waging his last bitter fight.
Men have become just so fierce and berserk
That some explode at the least little quirk.
There are nations killing nations for no sound reason
Women and children who are cold, naked and freezing.
A seven year old child, given permission to pilot a plane
All for the cause of pride, pomp, and fame.
With all the food in this world and plenty to spare
Yet millions starve to death or are living in despair.

A world filled with hatred, violence and greed
We have strayed so far from God and cannot succeed.
A universe spinning on a sure collision course
And the devil himself is the true deceptive boss.
What a shame, what a pity, we lack that pure love
Which Christ died to give to us from his Father above.

    Natalie Rutledge Lewis

Daydream

As I walked along the sandy beach,
  the wind whipped through my hair.
I noticed the sun had turned the sky peach,
  and the clouds that weren't really there.
I thought about how lucky I was
  to be alive right then to see...
The beautiful sun,
The sandy beach,
And the pretty peach sky
  as the wind whipped through my hair.

Heather Rowe

Untitled

Dressed in your red, you blush the rose
stripped
you consecrate with the backseat priest
with absence, you're inferior
as he forces his reign

Eye for eye, you only cry
as the saints leer from above
sodom and gomorrah
chastity stolen
you turn to sour rock

His fish like it wet, your tears excite them
with raccoon eyes
mascara hides your soul
hide it, lock it, burn it with incense
but don't unveil it in this perverse wedding

Crawl home
wash your face, your hair ...your soul?
Sister, you know john can't cleanse you

Shave your wrists, play the leech doctor
let yourself flow as he did.

Jeffrey Dassel

Pigeons

The lightning strikes the pigeon's anxious crowd
who spoke about the judgment they avowed:
"It is the time; we will be coming home
for we have passed throughout the finest comb,
as if the camel fit the needle's eye".
But then their congregation, by and by
transfigure into doves, emerging from
the fire erupted by the lightning. Some
reach far above their limits, yet the clouds
place barriers, enmeshing them, like shrouds
encasing heaven, as they rebound back.
And then their feathers turn from white to black
as they descend back to the earth as crows;
they plunge into the soil, and stick their toes
up in the air like charred and brittle twigs.
Their hopeless carcasses, like fallen figs,
split open to reveal their futile seeds.
The cardinals, who frowned at these rash deeds,
turn to the wise old owl, who spoke down low,
"And there they went, again! I told you so!"

J. P. Anderson

Shifting Sands

The masses live their lives like shifting sands in the desert night
And when the morning comes very few see the changes done
But those that do will rise above these dusted dunes and desert shrubs
To leave their mark on humanity but you and I will never see
These shifting sands will bury us turning our dreams back to dust
And all the things that we possessed are empty shells of a tattered past

Aaron McCall

Looking Through A Window

Looking through a window, there's a whole world to see.
One point of view shows nothing but beauty, another shows misery.
Looking through a window, things are not always as they seem.
Sometimes they look like a nightmare, and sometimes like a dream.
Is the sky clear and blue? Or is it dismal gray?
Are the birds out singing? Or have they flown away?
Looking through a window, everything is bright.
But only if you choose to view things in their best light.
Do the flowers wake to the glow of the sun?
Or do they look as if their blooming days are done?
Looking through a window, may make you feel depressed.
But only if you don't see things when they are at their best.
Is the world being blessed by Mother Nature and her powers?
Or does the day seem to drag on for just too many hours?
Looking through a window, all of your views can change.
Things can seem so beautiful or they can look deranged.
Are the clouds out dancing? Or running away?
Is the light breeze whispering? Or has it run out of things to say?
Looking through a window, there is so much to see.
Which way will I view it? That is up to me.

Nicole Lee

Luminous Shadow

Leaves fell into the pond
  creating delicate wrinkles
    against the listless surface

Two eyes gazed upon the distorted figures
  through the crimson haze
    as it descended
      beyond the blackening trees

One figure formed from two
  as the ripples disappeared
    into the moon

The cool, damp grass stealthily slipped
  between the beads of water

Dancing with the breeze and the waves
  as they caressed the shore

Secured by the luminous beams

Wrapped by the eternal
  shadows of night

Megan Lawson

Such A Longing For You

Lately, I miss the warmth of your arms
I remember the spring, beautiful things
If you only knew
I have such a longing for you

Lately, I long to wear exotic perfume
Dance in our favorite room
Surround myself in beautiful things
I still wear your ring
Such a longing for you

Lately, I'm listening to musical choirs
Remembering our nights by candlelight
Oh, remembering the fire
Such a longing for you

Lately, I long for one tender kiss
It's something I miss
Miss oh, so much
I still feel your touch
Such a longing for you, such a longing for you

Julia E. Leyba

The Story Of You And Me

I hear music in the air,
Birds are singing everywhere,
They're telling the story of you and me,
And how our love has come to be.

You have taught me, the art of love,
That God has sent from up above,
You showed me sunshine, you showed me rain;
You showed me laughter, love and pain.

When we are together we are one,
Two people who's life has just begun,
And never to leave you, I'll always stay,
Right beside you, to guide you, along the way.

So just remember deep in your heart,
That nothing will ever tear us apart,
Because I love you and you love me,
And that is the way, it will always be.

Cynthia M. Tyler

Miracle

An angel a promise did proclaim
To an earthly maiden Mary, her name,
Of a gift from God, sent from heaven above
To folk on earth to show God's love.

Lo the promise was fulfilled.
The babe was born on a Christmas, still.
His coming was heralded by angel's song.
He was the love for which troubled hearts longed.

The wonder and joy of his blessed birth
Can rekindle again in man's heart on earth.
Blest spirit of Christmas, envelop our days.
Temper our spirit and show us the way.

Barbara Kefauver

A Shadow From The Door

Open your eyes from a long night's rest;
What do you see?

Not your dog,
Not your cat,
Not your mother,
But a shadow, yes, a shadow.
Why is it there?
Who is it?
What does it want?

Well, it can be anything, anyone,
And it can want anything and everything.

The main reason that the dark, tall shadow is there is that
It wants to let you know, not only in your dreams,
But in real life, that there's help right behind you,
Through the ups and downs.
And, never to worry—
This shadow will be with you all your lifetime.
Even when you die that shadow will always be at your door
To guide you all the way.

Kristie Lynn Masuda

A Moment A Place

Swish,
  Swish,
    Swish,
      Against the beach the gray green water slaps the clear
      brown and white pebbles on the shore.
        They glisten with the water and the sun.

Bunny K. Schall

"I Am"

I am the healer of the world
I wonder about the wildlife
I hear the hate
I see the violence
I want peace
I am the healer of the world

I pretend nothing is happening
I feel the pain
I touch the wounded
I worry about the pollution
I cry about the extinctions
I am the healer of the world

I understand the waters
I say to human kind "Why don't you stop this"
I dream of peace
I try to make the world better
I hope this will come to an end
I am the healer of the world.

Shannon Hubbs

"How Mite Makes Might"

We were just a tiny trickle as we rippled down the rill
pressed from her breast at our Mother Earth's will;
We circled and danced and tumbled in glee,
we gave our cool nectar so seedlets could be.
We wet the green pastures, heavy with grass
and shot through the rapids, down through the pass.

The sun, high in Heaven, was warm and was bright
but now chill of Winter is shadowing the night.
The Jaws of Jack Frost are frightening to see,
he's clutching with ice my sisters and me.
No longer will we wander through thirsty field
and count the blessings of the crops it will yield.

Hail Mary! this morning I saw a crack in the ice!
It looks like the sun and breeze will be nice;
We can shake our North shivers and swirl to the South,
Let's aim our champaign at Mississippi's mouth.

F. Satterfield

Heaven Let Me In

Hell is only a short breath away
I want to be with you for eternity but first I'll have to pay
Our love is strong but my spirit is weak
We've been through a lot and you, I want to keep
My soul is tired, I hurt inside
I only need your heart, It keeps me alive
Deep down I want to cry, I hold back the tears
You seem to never know why

Earth, heaven, hell
I'm leaving this world wish me well
Your soul is good and clean, even though I love you
Mine is cruel and mean
I've let you inside my cold black world
Forgive me for I have sinned, I love you forever
Heaven let me in

The fallen angels have come for me, I can already feel the pain
You don't want me to suffer, but I have nothing left to gain
I'm burning in this terrible dark place and
All I want is you
I've always thought about death, now this prophecy is true

Lisa A. Raines

165

Inspiration

Screaming sometimes comes
Before the dawn of an awakening
The occurrence is quasi-dimensional
To the soul as a river
Flowing over the earth in a thunderstorm
Its requirements is an action or non-action
That stimulates the thought process
Into disseminating the disposition
Toward a viewpoint
Is it beneficial for growth?
One wonders what one thinks
Contemplation and restfulness many times
Bring closure to the screaming
It delineates the worth of a thought
In such a sense
We often find the answer
To why we scream

Annette M. Smith

Old Shoes

Why are you so comfortable Old Shoes?
Is It because of the miles we shared, or because of the life we shared;
Or is it because you were always there during good and bad times?

Old Shoes, you were around when my children were born;
    You were there in a house of joy and a house of sad.
Old Shoes, we walked in the rain, we walked in the sunshine;
    We walked in the mountains and we walked on the beaches.
Old Shoes, we went many places, Some good ...,
    Some we can't even talk about.

But Old Shoes, we stayed together for so long, we became as
one — Old Shoes.
Today I was about to throw you out. But, Old Shoes, I can't,
    Your heels are a little rounded and we both show the scars of time.
So, Old Shoes, your place there in my closet of life is safe.
    I put you beside new shoes.
But our time in life will always be a comfort to look back on...
THANK YOU, "OLD SHOES".

Gary Reno

I Weep In The Night

He enters this world on a cloud of pain and love.
So warm and soft, this child of mine. He looks to me with love.
My heart so big, I weep in the night.
I feel him leaving this child of mine. I feel sadness and pain.
I weep in the night.
Home again this child of mine, so tall and strong. He smiles at me
    with love.
My heart so big I weep in the night.
This child of mine A father to be. I am filled with so much happiness.
I weep in the night.
The end has come, God has chosen my child.
He leaves this world on a cloud of pain and sorrow.
I weep in the night.
She enters this world on a cloud of pain and love this child of
    my child.
Her daddy's look. I am filled with happiness.
I am filled with love.
I am filled with sorrow.
I weep in the night, I weep in the night.

Mary Rutz

Through Magic Windows

My magic window-lakeside-view
Sparkles like clustered diamonds
In the midst of a shining lake.

Vibrating waters leap and dance,
Like sequins
Moving on a fine silk-robed blue dress.

Sprigs and Trees stand still, tall and firm
On the brown brown lifeless grass banks, at my
magic window lakeside view.

Sun rays shine brightly through
White clouds and clear blue skies,
Bouncing on the moving lake,
Near my Magical window lakeside view.

Mariette Robinson Greene

Love

Love is something that will always be.
It's something you cant taste, touch, or see.

Love can last for many years.
Love can break you down to tears.

Love can make you feel so high,
but love can make you want to die.

If you feel that love is gone
pick up your heart and carry on.

Finally one day you will find
love comes from the heart and not from the mind.

If she breaks your heart, hold on to it tight,
it will mend it self together though she's in
your dreams at night.

Then some day another heart you will find,
you will know it's love in your heart and not
in your mind.

Roger M. Wilson

"Weeza"

Black with a little white on her chest,
Never was ever a little pest.

Barely eats food out of her dish,
But loves to eat fresh live goldfish.

Inside she holds a lot of care,
Outside she holds a ton of hair.

She is not a dog who takes commands like heel,
But watches the store to see if anyone will steal.

It is really neat to feel her purr,
And the pet shop really loves her.

She likes to get petted near her head,
She always rests in one favorite bed.

She loves to go with someone outside,
In the store she would never hide.

Soft and friendly with all that fur,
Unforgettable that is her.

Elizabeth Cerven

The Dead Young Soldiers

The dead young soldiers do not speak.
Nevertheless, they are heard in the still house:
  who has not heard them?
They have a silence that speaks for them at
  night and when the clock counts.
They say: We were young. We have died. Remember us.
They say: We have done what we could but
  until it is finished it is not done.
They say: We have given our lives but until it is
  finished no one can know what our lives gave.
They say: Our deaths are not ours; they are yours;
  they will mean what you make them.
They say: Whether our lives and our deaths were
  for peace and a new hope or for nothing we
  cannot say; it is you who must say this.
They say: We leave you our deaths. Give them
  their meaning.
We were young, they say. We have died. Remember us.

    Alicia Hammons

Where I Live

Where I live it's cozy, peaceful, and quiet, you
  could feel the warm food in your mouth
Where I live it's so quiet,
  you can hear the snow falling from the sky
Where I live,
  you could smell the cologne the boys wear
Where I live,
  you could watch t.v all day long especially MTV
Where I live,
  you can taste the chocolate melting in your mouth
Well I live,
  in Throggs Neck.

    Natalia Montes

Sibling Rivalry

The angry voices, deep within;
shouting aloud, sources of sin.
Words so harsh, verbal pain;
days of toil, hours in vain.

Those feelings crumble to the floor,
when left waiting for an open door.
To feel and breathe the pure clean air,
the wind blowing through your hair.

Darkness overrides your beautiful dreams,
to be free of all your sibling screams.
The long days of feeling so low,
when we the weak will weep and woe.

A tear glistens down the cheek,
sorrow fills the heart, so weak.
Marks unburied, the silent cry;
today, tomorrow, it will die.

All in time, this could bring,
a deeper depth where darkness clings.
Can a warmth of greater love show?
All who will see, all will know.

    Tammy Vititoe

Unexpected

You came into my life,
At a time when I could not care for you.
You were unexpected,
But not unwanted.
It wasn't easy,
But I had to let you go.
Not just for me, but also for you.
While you were with me for just a short time,
My life will forever change because of your presence.

You may not have noticed,
But deep down inside I did care for you.
If I held on to you,
We would not be as happy as we should.
That's why I had to do what I did.

I acquired a symbol of you,
As I watch it grow and give it love,
It's the love that was meant for you.

Today I ask God to hold you tight,
And give you the love I could not.
Please forgive me for I feel I made the best decision for us.

    Maria Butera

Memories Of You

Another weekend is over, it's come to an end.
You've just driven your car out of sight.
How can it be that you just drove away,
When only hours before you arrived.

I can still see your smile,
Smell your scent in the air,
Turn quickly around and imagine you there.
But alas, I am here all alone

Impressions on my pillows,
Notes scribbled by your hand,
You were here, you must have been,
But still I am here all alone.

Something's missing in this home,
Could it be your laughter, so bold and strong,
Laughter that turns my house to a home,
But I'm here, I am here all alone.

What's that light coming forth from the dark,
Like a candle illuminating the night.
Memories of you, your warmth and your love,
You are here, I am no longer alone.

    Jacqueline M. Carfi

When I'm Old

What will I remember?
Commercials - I think!
I will remember the Oscar Meyer wiener song.
I will remember that today is the first day of the
rest of my life - Start it right with Total.
I will remember the Cadbury bunny at Easter.
Generations of commercials that have guided my life,
and been prominent in my thoughts whenever I shopped.
I won't remember all the details of daily life, just major events - clearly.
And as time goes by, to remember Birthdays - vaguely.
My last thoughts will probably be - to let Hertz put
me in the driver's seat today, or that Chevrolet is
hot dogs and apple pie.

    Alexis Ann Station-Gest

Dreams And Screams And Moonbeams

Dreams with screams and cars crashing in the moonbeams.
Jaws of life, mangled body, robbed of speech.
Would anybody visit? Would they care?

Guns and punks shot up with heavy junk.
The junk aims the punk who aims the gun that aims at me.
Is it a good shot, bringing peaceful sleep?
Or incapacitating? but my life to keep?

Dream with screams, my cries lost in the moonbeams.
Reaching for the help that nobody knows I need.
Does anybody listen? Do you care?
Disfiguring the face, crushed 'tween the cars.
Scars and scars upon more scars.
Pain sweet pain at least you are real.
Tell me please why I can't feel?

Dreams with screams, I'm fading in the moonbeams.
out of touch, isolation, alone with my dreams.
I'm still on the outside, looking in.
I can't take it no more. Time to end.

All alone

Goodbye
Chelle Benson

Husband

You are a loyal friend
A grateful son
A fulfilling husband
A true servant of God

You are strong, yet you handle things so delicately
You are sensitive, unafraid to show your feelings
You are a giver, always being there and helping when needed
never asking for anything in return
You are a rock to which my foundation is built upon

The Lord has blessed my life with your presence
just as he has blessed your family and friends
There are so many more lives you have yet to touch

You are a very special person that I am proud to call "husband"
just as your parents are to call you "son"
and your friends to call you "friend"
Trisha Marincin-Walker

The Past Repeats

As a girl growing up, I never understood why
my mothers Need to cheat and lie
She always got Caught, Then would cry
This fervor she'd plea, She just can't fight.
Knowing full well that it's not right.
Father would stay and forgive her adultery
Even though it confused me
Daddy promised someday I'd see the Love for her from he
Now I'm married and have 3 Boys
I struggle to fill this strange void
With my stomach in knots I approach thee
as this feverous Lust consumes me
I suddenly stop and Realize, as a child I did cry
as tears of shame sting my eyes
In my husband's arms I now cry
I understand the past as such
how a patient Love from a man
Can conquer fervor and Lust
Now I am forgiven
Rena Harrod

Oh Black Rose Awaken

Black awareness is poetic - compare
it to a lovely rose bud; given the
proper amount of sun, love, the
bud will unfold unto a beauteous
rose giving off effervescent adore.

This is Black Womanhood. Oh to be
aware of the love, kindness and inner
depth that she possesses - to peer into
the very core of her passion. Only
a responsive mind can visualize this beauty.

To savor the redolence she emits in just
one gentle touch - or partake of the
kindness in a glance - oh so oblique.
World behold! the Black bud has
burst into brilliant illumination.

Oh don't you see, this rose of beauty,
it is beyond the conjecture of mere
platitudes.
Frances L. Fox

Flower Petals And Pocket Watch Tributes

First I define what I am and then I define you.
And as I just barely finish the substance of the world dissolves.
It melts like fired lead and runs through my fingers.
Now the definitions are meaningless like the dissipated world.
For that substance was what I based my definitions on.
How am I to establish a starting with no ground to found on?
I can not form order when I am stumbling through phantasm.
Illusions surround me all around yet I know solidity is there.
If only I could cut to the real or at least form a tangible imaginary.
Then I could finally make a start at figuring out what's going on.
My hands could grasp the sphere of power hovering before me.
The locked door would swing open, revealing what it has hid.
David S. Atkinson

Respect

This is my space.
I am the Boss.
You may love me
If you like.
When I say.

This is my space.
I want to spread my arms
touching nothing.
I want to spread my arms
touching you.
When I say.

This is my space.
I will share me with you.
Pleased to be a friend.
When you have room too.

This is my space. Don't crowd me.
Don't press on my mind.
My thoughts are my self.
Don't bring me your bad, bring your good.
Please knock first.
Sharon Schumacher

The Old Woman

A woman sits in the afternoon sun
    perhaps someone's mother once.
The shadows that were once held at bay
    now have colored her hair grey.

The sadness lurks within her eyes
    as she sings a lullaby.
When the sun shines on her wrinkled skin,
    it seems to tell a story within.

Her mind is gone, but yet it seems
    to remember little things.
The little things that she recalls
    mean nothing now at all.
            Elizabeth Anderson

The Rose

Love is a rose, everyday it bloom,
but one day the rose will die,
it hurts me more to watch the pedals fall
before I can tell you goodbye.

I sit here alone thinking of you,
Hoping and dreaming that my wishes
would come true.

When all the pedals from the rose
fall to the ground
My heart will stop, it will not make a sound.

I love thee so much, you're the rose in
my heart
With the love that I have for you
I hope we shall never part.
            Carrie Palmeter

Untitled

You are so young and innocent
Smiles are all you should know
No worries is what you will eventually control
I look in your eyes and I see a future
that is far more wondrous than you thought it
would ever be
You love people for who they are not what
they own this is a gift you should never let go
Always be yourself and you will be fine and
never worry as time goes by
Live each day to the nearest near and we
will hope that we don't take for granted what
we hold dear
You are the keeper of your soul therefore
Never let it go and always know that you
will not grow old
If your heart is young than you will be
too forever you are in my heart and always near
            Kelly Pinkerton

Untitled

In the mornings I wake up and wonder: Why
you're not here beside me, with our sleepy bodies
nestled together lovingly, I miss you... I miss us
being together, talking laughing, and loving. Now that
you're gone I see all the happiness you brought into
my life, and now I feel sad and alone, lost without
you. The loneliness crawls over me, covering me like
a blanket, and as I lie here with my heart aching,
longing for you, another day without notice quietly
slips away...
            Margaret C. Schultz

Nights Under The Roundtable

Vague vice whispering anonymous words
        No gossamer goes gliding on an informed myth here
It's hovering spirits without a mist,
        legends languishing into shadows
            wisps

Inner journeys
hammered into sparks on the dreamanvil
        Failed, the bright hope of out fathers' fathers ideal
    The strains of this chieftain harp, only shadows
        Cringing simulations
        Out of the loop
            The impending oblivion sitting downstairs on the stoop

    Boyfathers not taught—caught, abandoned; esteem
        perverted, seared into violent loyalties
    Girlmothers not instructed—discounted, discarded;
        Fatherboys carry the curse—shamed, named;
            alibis kicking dreams
            down the alley
    Mothergirls follow the hearse—stunned, shunned;
        left only to look out dirty windows
        Dave Swanson

In Pursuit Of Happiness

What is Happiness, where can it be found?
Can it be seen or held? Can it be heard or smelled?

I don't know the exact description of happiness.
It is very elusive, yet everyone seeks it.
It can be described as sunshine after a rain,
a child's laughter, or a lover's embrace.

Serenity can be happiness after a long period of despair.
Desire can be happiness when one has been lost and needs care.

Chocolate, sweets, desserts and other such decadence galore is
happiness for some, while for others the quiet buzzing of a bee
around a garden of fragrant blooming flowers is fun.

I have had fleeting moments of this evasive feeling.
But that was long ago and long forgotten.
The pain that overshadows my happiness
grows denser with the years.

Perhaps the time has come for me to begin my search.
Like many lost warriors, I shall arm myself
with the weapons of hope, desire, warmth and strength,
on my journey to battle despair, ambiguity and disgust.
I shall succeed or die!!!
        Lynda Wexelbaum

Do You Ever Wonder?

Do you ever wonder if your dreams are true?
If they are happy ones you would be glad
they came to you.
What about the sad ones, would you want to
know of them too?
Do you believe that our dreams can reveal
the future or past?
Can you remember what kind of dream you
had last?
Was it a monster that scared you, or an
Angel that took you up high?
Either way you wake up and wonder why.
Would you change anything because of a dream
that you had or let the future bring what
it will, good or bad?
I say dream your dream and let it come
as it may,
You can only live day by day.
But, that's my belief, you probably don't care.
We all must pay our own kind of fare.
        Debra Stanley

Upon This Wood

I looked upon this piece of wood
Blood-stained and worn away
I heard the crushing strokes
I saw the thrashing of flesh

The agony that rips the mind
The tears that open the wounds
The loss of One whose love was golden
Now hangs in the midst of all that was forgotten

I looked again, His arms outstretched
Shedding His life for you and for me
I wept for He was all I had
He was love and life and all that was good

Come and follow were His words to me
Through suffering and death to everlasting life
Pick up your cross and bear My world
For the truth lies in My thoughts left behind

    Joseph C. Kissner

The Tree Handed Me A Flower

Yesterday
I wasn't feeling too good.
I really wanted to, And I knew I should.
I got in a fight With my best friend. Last night I
thought it was the end. But then, The tree handed
me a flower. It was my favorite hour. The flower
was so pretty; quite a sight to see. Then, happiness from
head to toe Just happened, suddenly. Today I
made up with my friend and shared
my joy with her.
Now we are
best friends
again.
And
the
mystical
flower
Remains.

    Ariel Sundel

Wisdom Of A Child

A newly born child
Asleep in his bed
Never an unkind word has he said

Sweet and innocent as a small lamb
Beautiful miracle, tiny and soft
Graceful as an eagle aloft.

Delighted child, so small, so sweet
Stands and wavers on unsteady feet
His mother to guide him, his father the prize.

Sweet, innocent child... tiny but wise.

    Rainey Howarth

As A Child

When I was a child I was nice and funny
My mother thought that I was as sweet as honey.
My sister did not like this at all.
She wanted to grow three feet tall.
When I was learning to ride my bike
Down the hill to have a freight.
When I went to school for the very first time
I wanted to find a very good friend of mine
Now I'm in fourth grade, and having fun
I wish I could remember when I was one

    Krista L. Keen

Together

Together we have inspired each other to do
Things we would have never dared
And we have helped each other get through
When we didn't think we cared

Together we have spent a lot of time
Which we will always and forever cherish
And all of our "rhythm and rhyme"
In our hearts will never perish

Together forever and side by side
That's the way we thought it would always be
But the time has come for us not to hide
But to find our own key

Together we felt that the end was near
But life had only just begun
And as we shed that one last tear
We know we will always be under the sun
together

    Amy Lemna

Music Of The Night

A brilliant orange sky is all that's left of a day that's fading,
Colors of red and yellow mesh with a midnight blue that slowly
takes over the sky

Night falls across the land.

For most, it is time to sleep,
But the greatest conductor of all orchestras is awake,
Mother Nature

Crickets chirp like a thousand violins tuning for their parts,
Leaves rustle like tambourines in the night air,
A stream trickles its course down the land like a harp setting
the mood of the night.
A light rain falls, playing the leaves like drums,
and locust sing their choruses,
All this combines to orchestrate a symphony of the night,
A music of nature.

The beautiful music is broken by a lone wolf's mournful song,
As the howls echo through the night, they are joined by other
howls, all singing the feral music of nature,
All part of the orchestra of life,
And the music of the night.

    Trevor Barrett

I Reach Out

I reach out to hold your hand,
To feel the whisper of your breath.
But instead I feel a touch of smoke
Where love turned from life to death.
And still I reach out, never to know
The clock of time ticking on...
For I never took time to pick you a rose
Before the day you were gone.

I reach out so I can be a friend.
I reach out to grasp the light.
I reach out to feel the warmth of summer,
Not the bitterness of winter nights.
And I know someday we'll see all the good things.
I know those moments might be few.
But I do know that good things live and evil things die
As I reach out for you...

    Rick J. Espinosa

Birth Of The World

The clouds blow in. The light soon flees
Cool winds blow fierce, whipping through the trees
Thunder growls vehemently, lightning illuminates the sky
Rain begins falling on the ground nearby
I sit and watch calmly as day turns to night
The storm hits strong; what a beautiful sight!
Rain scents the night air, so cool on my skin
Putting words in my mind, giving meaning to my pen
Then it gradually begins to slow down
The rain is more gentle as it falls to the ground
The air grows cooler as the storm blows on
Enveloping my body until the clouds are gone
The silence amplifies as the storm passes by
The thunder and lightning no longer fill the sky
Now comes the time to walk outside, smell the fresh earth
And witness the world in its new birth

Stephanie Murray

"Never"

Ninety-six and things have not changed
Black Folks are still working on the chain gang.
It's hard surviving in this white world
It's about long stringy hair - no world of curls.
Our culture's being beat into the ground
Pretty soon there be no blacks around.
Black history month should have been everyday
Cause racism we face day to day.
Trying to teach my girl the right way,
Teach her what's right, and what not to say.
To many our color is just no good
They say there's always trouble in our neighborhoods
Our ancestors have had it rough
and our people have finally had enough.
Never will the white man just let us be
Never will free be really free
Never will they ever just treat us equal.
Never-ending story - A never ending sequel.
Following tradition, following our ancestor's courses
Continue to work, working hard like horses. "Never"

Felicia R. Hendrix

In Memory of Lt. KBM

No use in counting weeks or months,
Full fifty years are gone.
There was no need for you to die,
A sacrificial pawn.
But war, who slays both young and old,
Had chosen you that day.
Conspiring with his brother, death,
He stole your life away.
You're still a lad, though fifty springs
Have tempered winter's cold.
A sorry trade - to lose your life
To keep from growing old.
But angels wrote beneath your name
Upon the sacred scroll:
Though death has claimed his flesh and blood,
God gathered up his soul.

H. J. Adams

The Banks Of Frog Creek

When the moon comes out and there is a gleam
On the shores and the waters of the swift-moving stream,
The frogs of the creek come out of hiding,
Hopping and jumping and bounding and gliding.
They croak their glad songs all the night through
On the Banks of Frog Creek and the waters of blue.

Lauren L. Hawley

"Autobiography"

The times I stand behind are dying fast-
A river flowing swift, the seasons fade;
One moment to reflect my cradled past
And wonder, to remorse my everyday.

These dreams are but a page within a book
Without a steady hand to play them true;
Eternal life, a studied hasted look
Across my life - those times I come unto.

A halting glance, a passing memory,
Remains to satisfy this empty soul.
A taste to thirst this curiosity,
And bind this heart with memories untold.

This volume holds my blood and life within;
And with these words my soul may live again.

Nicholas Pry

I'm Mad

Do you know how long it's been
Since you and I have been like friends?
How long have I wished for you
To be the way you used to.
You used to laugh; you used to smile;
Now all that's between us are miles.
The gulf is widening. Oh, how wide.
How we let important things slide.

It was different long time ago, but this is now,
I want happy coexistence, but don't know how.
With you or without you, I got to go on
Hope for the best and tackle trouble 'til dawn.
I go to work and eat the food;
I want more out of life than to brood.

It can be better; this I know.
I don't want to be just for show.
I want to be wife, honey and all;
and can't stand a man with too much gall.
All I've said may not matter to you.
But I've said it; now I'm through.

Barbara W. Harrell

The Butterfly And The Turtle

As I walked through the desert feeling no pain
I felt something hitting my face, it felt like rain
As I looked around I noticed not a cloud in the sky
It was then I noticed they were tears from a passing butterfly
As I followed I asked why are you crying and carrying this mud
Not paying attention I tripped over a cactus and broke its bud
It was then a butterfly landed on my shoulder and said
People like you is why we are helping a turtle that's almost dead
I felt so terrible and said please tell me where
Dropping precious tiny tears I followed her over there
As I approached I saw the turtle, butterflies were coming and leaving
When I got closer for a look I couldn't believe what I was seeing
The butterflies were putting mud in a hole in his shell
the turtle said please stay away I can't stand your smell
Please in God's name how can I help you I said
Tears flooding my own eyes, it was too late the turtle was dead
Thank God when butterflies cry they don't make a sound
If you even notice only their tiny tears hit the ground
Now as I walk through this desert land
I pray for the respect for it from all man

Andrew Costa

Held The Day

The thin black girl
  Not out of her 'teens
Came through the hospital door
  in New Orleans,
Her body shivered
  beneath her skimpy vest
She clutched her baby to her chest
  Against the Mississippi wind.
I loaned her my coat
Our glances met
  Laughing eyes, sweetly, neatly
With gentle smiles
  That caress the feel of life,
I moved to help,
  Then saw her anxious look
Her body stiffened, her vest grew tighter
  She hurried away.
Two humans, reaching at creation
  But centuries of hurt
Held the Day.

Samuel Adams Darcy

Granite

I have ridden through the storms.
I have cried many tears.
More in darkness than in light,
I have fumbled through the night.
At times, I have felt weary and beaten by the rain.
Alone, I keep on fighting, never succumbing to the pain.

Each new challenge in my life,
I will meet with strength and power.
Never yielding to my woes,
Until my final hour.

I will survive.
I will succeed.

Paris Jason Fealy

The Generation Before

We both sit back and watch our lives be drained by the generation
  before
The generation before sits in her recliner repeating every word she hears
Her white streaked hair holds the many stories we will never hear
The lines below her eyes are·the never ending tales of her life
We wipe her mouth, fix her diaper, and fold her walker
Slowly we exhale, hold each others hands, and see our reflection
  in her dead blue eyes
The generation before has no other choice but to gently smile
She shakes her head, and closes her eyes
We then realize that our present problems will soon be nothing but
  creases on a recliner

Lucia Rivera

The Insomniac Dreams....

To search for sense
In necessary Madness
For the loss of good,
I deserve something equally pure
"Don't worry, You'll get there"
(she stroked him softly)
Inspired by the meaningless of wrong or right
Infinity will lead me on to Paradise
Who else would long to know all that could have been?
And lose all that would be gained?
If I succeed in falling out of time
Then my salvation will of the true mind

Jason McKee

Your Son

He was with you all too briefly,
He had so much more to do,
Why did it have to happen?
Why couldn't it be you?
We may ask a thousand questions,
We may never know the reasons.
But I think there may be comfort,
When we realize the seasons:
The time to reap,
The time to sow,
The time to embrace.
And of letting go.
He is doing his Father's business,
He's been called to a higher place,
And some day you will see him again,
And kiss his adorable face.
Then we all can rejoice together,
And the pain will be washed away,
It's a plan that no man can fully understand,
But just pray for the state of grace.

Ken Bieschke

Untitled

Never mind your instrument—
I could listen to you talk for hours.
How your voice would play in all twelve keys
And jump two octaves as you take another chorus.

There was that time we were in the room
And you played only five notes on your horn—
Like a tease.
Those five notes race through my
Body like hot cappuchino on a cold New York morning.

That is what I remember the most—
Those notes that you played as if
You'd been born a hero.
It happens every time.

Angie Adee

Fearful Love

The fear that I have is greater...greater than life and more
powerful than the heavens.

Tears fall from my shattered cries and lighting strikes my heart.
What cause can I have for my fears? The fear of loving someone
so much that you drown in the pain of the hidden words.

The fear of you vanishing from my life as does goodness into evil.
The fear of losing someone who I never even had.
The fear of never kissing those lips that gave me sweet dreams,
ever again.

The fear of feeling hopelessness and danger without those arms
that protect me.

The fear of having to miss that smile that can make the devil fall
in a trance.

The fear of living in dead silence without hearing those words or
that voice that can make the dead laugh.

The fear of looking deep into your eyes and opening the door to
your heart, causing me to fall, fall so deep in love and not being
able to be ventured out.

The fear, the fear of falling in love....

Maria A. Abud

You

When I think of you I want to cry
But I lock the feelings deep inside
Wishing you knew how I truly feel
But then I think it's all in my head.
I wish I could be with you every day,
But I know inside there could be no way.
I wish I was with you, I wish I was there.
I wish you knew how much I care,
I sit in front of your picture for hours,
I would just stare
Into your soul capturing eyes I would look.
My heart you have stolen, a moment it only took.
From the first time I saw you
I knew you were it.
Till this moment
I haven't stopped loving you one bit.

Robyn Svenningsen

The Boston Marathon

35,000 runners standing belly to back
patiently waiting for the gun to signal their attack.
At first they will only be shuffling their feet
but within miles hearts will race as they move down the street.
Months of training to be tested this day
the strong willed shall let nothing get in their way.
Then comes Heartbreak Hill an old friend named pain
that's when the mind tells the heart it must be insane.
Soon enough the city comes into sight
six miles to go and now starts the fight.
Emotionally and physically drained from the run
even a day at the dentist now seems like more fun.
Next comes Fenway Park then Hereford Street
one last turn onto Boylston and this journey is complete.
As you round the last corner and see the crowds on each side
the pain disappears and is replaced by pride.
The journey now over as you will know
just look at the runner's face and you'll tell by the glow.

Richard Robichaud

Myself

I have to live with myself and so,
I want to be fit for myself to know,
I want to be able, as days go by,
Always to look myself straight in the eye;
I don't want to stand with the setting sun,
And hate myself for things I have done.

I don't want to keep on a closet shelf.
A lot of secrets about myself, and fool myself, as I come and go,
Into thinking nobody else will know
The kind of person I really am.

I want to go out with my head erect,
I want to deserve all peoples respect;
But here in the struggle for fame and self
I want to be able to like myself.

I can never hide myself from me;
I see what others may never see;
I know what others may never know,
I can never fool myself, and so,
Whatever happens I want to be
Self respecting and conscience free!

Tammy Gonzalez

Hometown: D'Hanis

Take me back to my little home town
Where I can move freely and look around
Tasting the goodness of the country fare
While breathing in the good clean air.

Watching the home team score a glorious win
Taking me back to the old school days again:
Meeting good friends at the local stops
Hoping that all good feelings never leave off.

Farmers going down the road to their fields
To harvest their crops that the good earth yields
Driving their tractors from dawn to dusk
Turning the dirt over and raising the dust.

From Monday through Friday from seven to five
The road to the brickyard comes wildly alive
Traveled on by the hard working men
That are on their way to make their daily living.

As night time falls on this little ole town
Everything is shut with the crickets the only sound.
As I bring this poem to its reluctant finish
I want you to know the town is D'Hanis!

Donna Louise McGraw Schlueter

Falling Stars

The patience of perception pervades on the sky;
a great artistry grown by millions of years,
sought in the canvas of astronomy's eye,
and brought to light by the moon's dusty tears.

An evening unfolds to exhibit its show
as the artist looks on toward his master;
and the depths seem to warm with iridescent glow,
so much the stars twinkle but faster.

And tonight, the painter with his deep desire,
can be seen on some drawn constellation,
streaking cross stars in such a great fire
with his acrobatic coalition.

And we, full of wonder, watch them all prance
about this one wistful moment of magic delight,
still holding hands as they boastfully dance
coloring the plain oceans of night.

And, tiring from the evening work at hand,
Beauty washes its brushes in the sea,
and dazedly drifts closer to land...
for, its art is always and only for we.

Joey Sdono

Thinking Of You

Thinking of you is all I do,
wishing so hard for the dream to come true,
Love to see,
Love to care,
Love to comfort your despair
Coupled love in passionate grace,
Beautiful smile I want to taste...
Don't let this end,
Don't let it be over,
Your beauty so rare,
Like a four leaf clover,
Think of love that has been missed.
I look in your eyes, a feeling of bliss.
The love in your heart starts to shine through,
The kiss of life I give to you!

Merideth W. Foard

Autumn's Last Dance

Today the sky is blue with white clouds sailing by.
There's a chill in the air to tell you that Winter is nigh.
But before the first snow and all becomes barren,
the event of the year is ready to happen.

The trees are twisting and shaking around
dropping their leaves upon the ground.
The oaks have donned their browns and bright reds,
and the maples are sporting their beautiful yellow "threads".
The dogwood has added a crimson glow
and every tree is putting on a show.

Now they are ready for their big dance.
Just watch how they twirl and spin and prance.
The wind is their symphony; now it's a jazz band,
and it plays slow or fast as they swirl about the land.
They dance with abandon and then sail high and free.
This is Autumn's last dance, dedicated to you and me.

Keep the memory of their colors for a dreary winter day,
when you are sad or nothing has gone your way.
They brightened our thoughts and our souls were enhanced;
as we saw, once more, Autumn's last dance.

Betty J. Walden

The Pain Just Never Goes Away

Sometimes the pain never goes away.
The tears and the memories prolong
Locked in your heart they stay.
Nostalgic thoughts are rooted deep.
Letting go is too hard.
The anguish you will keep.
Looking for tomorrow, trying to forget
You struggle for your happiness,
Your sanity and yet ....
    The pain never goes away.

You ask yourself when will these sentiments cease?
But the recollection of the past
Just makes the agony increase.
Trying to adjust, hoping for relief
You alter your way of life,
·But your success and comfort are only brief.
Wondering how long you can go on like this
When the contentment you once possessed
Is what you truly miss ....
    And the pain just never goes away.

Nicole Devlin

The Last Drink

As you grabbed the keys,
And looked at me,
My mind went astray.

Oh, the price you would pay,
For drinking and driving, all in one breath,
You would have to pay the consequence of death.
The last drink shouldn't feel good,

Then again maybe it should.
You've led me on a wild chase,
All to have death hit you in the face.

What will your family think?
You've killed yourself and another all
because of one last drink.

Erin T. Laik

Secret Place

San Antonio Heights up Mountain Ave thru curling road
when i was a child where daddy show'd me & touch'd me
pretend'd to talk to a family of beavers
this place this sacred holy place
i uncover'd only to the kindred spirits
found a rope & swung into the water with her
with them i collect'd cans & papers the Philistines left
& lament'd the paint'd trees
but mostly alone
bruis'd limbs & bloody'd face a drunk lover
or when mother accus'd me of desir'd rape
soothing balm of running water & birds & trees & solitude
but i grew afraid
saw eyes black eyes panther eyes dead eyes
everywhere
knowledge of comfort lost
the hideousness of dissipat'd fantasy & innocence
tears at the throat

Jill Mayuko Naponelli

There He Lay...

There he lay...
on a field of dead and dying.
My teacher...
My knight...
My liege...
Broken now,
as on a field of trampled flowers.
Bravely fought...
and Bravely fallen.
His honor will live on.
For with countless hours of practice and study,
Mine now,
are his honor...
his Duty...
and his Chivalry.
And soon also to be mine, the taste of Victory
as I right the wrong
that has been done to my Lord.
But now,
we shall honor his memory as he passes on...

Dan Naponiello

All Former Things

Pollution and smoke
Things in the air that surely can choke
People on crack cocaine
Humans not acting sane.

Death is all around
Bodies that are found.
Sickness that is bad
Serial killers that are mad.
Sorrow which is very much
Bodies in funeral homes that we are afraid to touch.
Pain that people have to feel
Older and young ones in chairs with wheels.

Crime which is all around the place
People have to resort to use a gun or mace.
Ones that are being hurt
Children that can't look at Sesame Street and see Bert.

All of these former things will pass away
This is not up to any Parliament or Congress to say yea or nay
But God will cure the world from its problems
The Bible is the clue.

Steven L. Hawkins

Southern Splendor

Time to rest in the old porch swing
And listen to a chorus of crickets sing.
Iced tea cools the warm Georgia night
As faint shadows dance in pale moonlight.
A firefly entertains on his silent flight
Bravely blinking his magic light.
Scents of gardenias and the magnolia tree
Mingle to make southern potpourri.

A sleepy spider guards her web on the sly
And a distant freight train rumbles by.
The lonesome whistle moans long and low
Time ticks by, a little lazy and slow.
A gentle breeze through the lofty pines
Whispers the splendor of summertime.
My bare feet touch the tracked in sand
And my heart is home in my Dixieland.

Lawanna Malcom

The City Of The Damned

The sun rose over the city of the damned,
and the people had things to do.
They had the whole day planned.
The sun was bright, the sky blue.

The people raced over the ground
and had to stop to catch their breath.
They suddenly heard a buzzing sound,
no one knew it was the sound of death.

The bomb fell through a cloud
and some began to cry,
some prayed, and some cursed aloud,
for not all were ready to die.

The bomb exploded with a boom,
the buildings burned like paper reams,
and among the wreckage of the doomed
lay the victims' hopes and dreams.

Nicholas Dietz

A Child

A child is a ball - a bat and a glove
A bike to ride and a dog to love
A stick of candy or bubble gum
And dirty shoes where mud comes from

They're full of pep and energy
Usually a band-aid on one knee
A dirty face and uncombed hair
They inevitably sit with their feet in the air

They can make a mess without a plan
When they take out the trash and miss the can
They never make beds or hang up clothes
And can use twenty tissues on one runny nose

Yet - through all this - God only knows
They're as true as the petals on a rose
God made them ours to have and hold
And they'll only be as good as they come from the mold

Ronald L. Narad

The Student's Voice

I came to this country five years ago.
I didn't know any English what trouble, oh!
I decided to come to school to learn and grow.
My uncle told me, "that's a good decision. Don't stop. Go."

Everyday I come to school I learn new words.
English is important to succeed in this advanced world.
I know if I learn it I will be successful in any work.
If I stay at home and do not learn the language it will be worse.

When we are making a decision, it is better to stop and think.
Now I don't write only in pencil. I also do it in ink.
My teacher teaches me grammar and a lot of things.
If we learn the language, we will progress as human beings.

Hector Salinas

Friends

On a dark, wintery night a little girl stares through a window
  from outdoors.
Her clothes are old and mutilated.
Her hands are like ice, and her lips like a berry.
She wanders around the town, nowhere to go and no one to go to.
She licks her lips at the sight of warm food.
With her face plastered to the window,
her hands reach out, but she cannot feel it.
Her heart is heavy, and her eyes are tired.
How she longs to sit by a fire, hearing stories,
and laughing amongst the group. If only she had a companion.
Someone to keep her warm at night, and make her happy.
She can't even remember the last time she smiled.
With her head hung low, she wonders why,
then crawls into a corner and falls fast asleep.
That same night, a little dog meanders around town.
His fur is cold and wet, and he whimpers for the pleasure of food.
After hours of searching, he finds a pile of rags containing a little
girl, and snuggles up to her.
Little do they know that they will become the best of friends.

Julia Romstadt

"When The Light Goes Out"

As another day draws to a close,
The sun falls behind the pines
That stand along the horizon.

The sky is God's canvas.
Strokes of luminescent pastels
Surround the orange hue,
Of the brightest star in the sky.

Light dances on the water,
Making wonderful waves of diamonds.
I sit back and wonder,
Could anything be brighter than her eyes?

The sun has vanished.
Warm waves of color remain in the sky.
The light above may be gone,
But your eyes are shining brighter than ever.

Many sunsets have come and gone.
I cannot remember when they were so wonderful.
When I watch the sunset with you,
I realize how great nature is,
And how great you are.

Eric R. Smith

"For The Children At Dunblane, Scotland"

"Can anyone out there hear me?..."
"I was just going to school on an ordinary day...
I just wanted to laugh, and have some fun... and
I laughed and giggled...
Until a...man? Came in with a...what?...A gun???
Now I am gone, and most of me class-mates too...
Wee little tykes, little lads and ladies...
Just hop, skipping and jumping along...
Then he came in with a gun???...
Now most of us are gone...
He "shots us"...what means that???...
It means we cannot go out and play...like we did yesterday...
We will be in a place that is very new to us...
But, Mom and Dad, be happy... for the dear Lord Jesus
Is with us...and we have become his angels...
And, you know, Mom and Dad, we get to go out and play...
Every hour of every day...
Mom and Dad, be at rest, for he is a sweet Lord Jesus...
And, above all, he was here waiting for us..."
With love from your children...

Carolyn S. Sax

Amanda Mary Karas

Amanda Mary Karas, a child God
    Sent my way to touch my life,
Only ten years old, how could she
    Mean anything to me and my wife.

We have no children of our own
    Never close to a child you see.
Amanda shared the day with us
    So much fun we had what did it mean to me?

My heart was touched by
    Her sweet and kind ways,
I found care and love in
    My heart for her through the days.

She showed me what a child
    Could mean to me in my life and heart,
I hope our friendship will last a
    Lifetime and never grow apart.

God bless Amanda and show
    Her how much I care,
And let my life and love
    Influence her is my prayer.

Myron Leggett

The Call

Drifting away, like leaves in the fall,
forever awaiting her Creator to call.
He called her to heaven, and ended her pain,
But here on earth, comes the falling of the rain.
She's in heaven, living in a world without sin,
Given a second chance, her new life begins.
Even though it's better, there's a deep ache in our hearts,
Why does it hurt, when someone we love gets a brand new start?
Just like the leaves drift away with the breeze
The reason for death is so hard to see.
Her suffering was ended, late one night,
Waiting so long, she left without a fight.
She's gone now, just like leaves in the fall,
God, our Creator finally gave her the call.

Edna Parker

The Voters Lament

The time has come the voter said to talk of many things
Of Medicare and Medicaid and getting rid of kings.
    Why polytricksters fly away just spending all our money
When we're in debt up to our butts and I don't think it is funny
    With other countries taking all the jobs and we pay them to do so
GATT and NAFTA passed at night without the voters say so,
    It seems we have lost control of our beloved land
When we are down and out who'll give us a helping hand?
So when you go to the polls this year study hard and long
The country could go down the drain this time if we are wrong
Remember how they voted when they sneaked out in the night
and passed a law that they knew wasn't really right.
So throw the beggars out this year and hope that we are right
We might get some one good in there yes, we, just, might.

Robert J. Culp

A Surfer Missed

They look over the edge of the cliff
to take a whiff of the ocean
A boy and his long board
Oh, with such devotion
To ride the waves in slow motion
you had such a love for the ocean

Like a dolphin you would glide
in the hollow of the waves
But they misbehaved
they couldn't save
and they sent a shock wave
like thunder crashing on the shore
oh, how sad, dear brother

Your long board will stand still
like the waves that will remain hollow and empty
you shall be missed
Farewell... till we meet again
to surf the perfect waves in paradise.

Joshua Brandon Parsons

My Aunts

Some aunts are smaller than others.
Some aunts are bigger than others.

    Ya! They're Aunts
Some aunts are fat, others are thin.
    You could name one Aunt skinny bones, if thin. You
could name the other pig, if fat. But, of course that
won't be polite.

    Ya! They're Aunts
Some are kind, others are greedy.
Some are grouchy, others cool.

    Ya! They're Aunts.
Some are generous, others cruel.
Some are beautiful, others ugly.
Of course it won't be polite, so don't say it!

    Ya! They're Aunts
Some of them love you, others don't.
Some you like, others you don't.

    Ya! They're Aunts
They are yours, they are mine. They are aunts, and
That's all!

Sunita Ashok

"Ode To the Street"

Find any corner on most any night
People are huddled and cursing their plight
Living in boxes all stacked in a row
Wandering alleys with no place to go

The scream of a siren the clap of a gun
One lies there bleeding and one's on the run
A trading of life for a handful of change
A modern Dodge City no home on the range

You'll see a cruel circus performed on the street
Kids turning tricks just for something to eat
Or rolling a stranger and selling his clothes
To buy snowy candy to put up their nose

A tenement hallway a lost part of town
Addicts all gather their troubles to drown
They're sharing their pain and needles as well
One leads to misery the other to hell

Greg Simpson

So We May Survive

The earth is warmed by the sun,
Like a newborn baby warmed by its mother.
The plants and animals are nurtured,
By the earth and sky together.
With the earth and sun working together hand in hand.
All living things upon our world shall survive,
And live and thrive.
We too must work together to keep our earth alive.
To live and grow and thrive.

SO THAT WE MAY SURVIVE!

Sara J. Crago

The Cookies Due

A spiced aroma filled the air,
    Those small round morsels baking there,
All golden brown, so plump to see,
    Such luscious eating for us three.

She made some crispy, others soft,
    As bars or balls, though circles oft,
Were sweetest bits our mouths could hold,
    Washed down with lots of milk, ice cold.

Holidays came at given time,
    Cookies were made; that favored kind.
With colored icing we could see
    Them grace the family Christmas tree.

I learned to make what I liked best,
    They tasted better than the rest,
I baked a batch late in the fall,
    To the contest, I took them all.

They're best of all the cookies there,
    Won first prize at the County Fair,
Were crisp and munchy spicy too,
    My favorite cookie won its due.

Vione Schow

Fate

As fate awaits an unborn child,
the question of life is pounding
She's a girl not wanting to be a mom
To the clinic to solve the twisted tale
The child now taken life would not prevail
Ten years pass as memories blossom
Now a wife to be a mom
The brother one will never know
Just because mom didn't want the world to know

Lisa Miller

Atlantic City

Lone footsteps like taps on tile
    clatter over rough planks of boardwalk,
    forte, then fade into dampened darkness,
    blend with the slapping of waves
    against a deserted pier.

From pizza stands, neon lights flicker,
    then dim, until all is empty and black -
    empty save for day old papers stirring
    listlessly whene'er sea breezes nudge them-
    black but for a sailor's moon blazing
    a path from sky, to sea, to sand...
    Silence yields to the sea's staccato.

From afar, from out of the mystic darkness
    wails the lonesome warning of
    a buoy, its bell clanging ceaselessly
    as it churns against the roiling waves.

Eleanor Marshall-White

The Best Things In Life Are Free

The taste of spring water from a bubbly brook...
To curl up in the winter with a wonderful book.
The feeling of a cool breeze on my face...
The beauty of satin, pearls, and lace.
Beautiful flowers that bloom in the Spring...
The happiness a loving family brings.
A loving hug, a smiling face...
These all make the world a sunnier place.
The sound of rain on a tin roof...
The foods that Mom and Grandma cook.
Memories that bring a smile to our face...
The beautiful song, "Amazing Grace".
The best things in life are truly free...
All there for only the asking from you and me.

Phyllis Alexander

"Allen"

It's been years since we parted.
Yet it seems only yesterday, I last saw your smile.
Memories of you come from out of the blue.
My heart fills with an overpowering love.
Without you my life has been so bleak.
I have the moon but no light.
I walk in the sun but not the shine.
I see the stars that are no longer mine.
Often I sit alone and weep for the friend and love
I have lost.
Yet I still hold on to the hope that someday we will
once again be joined.
Then never again will our hearts be apart.

Nancy A. Jones

Growing Up

When I was a child and very small,
I looked up at my mother who seemed so tall.

When I was in my teens and wanted to be the boss,
my mother always seemed so cross.

As I have grown through the years,
I understand my mother's pain and tears

Now that we are both old and gray,
I see how wise my mother is today.

In the future, I know in death we must part,
but I'm thankful to my mother for such a loving start.

Shirley Robitaille

177

Woman Of True Love

True Love is honest and constant, not deceptive and sporadic.
Therefore, unswervingly, she comes forth—with open arms, a clear
mind, and with special features that are well defined.

This woman is a new breed—new in content, new in form,
and new in the wealth of information she has to offer.

She comes with a deep sense of responsibility
as the custodian of True Love.
As she ages, intimacy takes on new meaning.
The days of unconscious love may be filled with memories of
  her youth. . .
Maturity searches for that oh-so-delicate balance of real intimacy.

She takes pleasure in knowing who she is
and in allowing herself the time to experience others.

The pursuit of romance is far more gentle
as she can see the renewed wonder of its beauty. . .

True Love, perhaps a bit faded,
but nothing could be sweeter than to say,
"Do you remember, True Love?"

Gloria J. Fluker

A Mystery To All

There is an odd vehemence, surrounded by awe and wonder.
All can possess it, but few have grasped its hold.
It may be abstractly harnessed to free one from servitude
Or abused and cruelly manipulated to obliterate another.

This is an odd sentiment, encompassed by mystery.
The more it is used, the more it is felt, ... the more pain it can bring.
You ask the meaning, the answer is vague.
At times it feels God-sent, at others, Satan's work.

It is an odd sensation that has been alive for all time.
Amazing is the process by which such a complex ideal
Can be so simple, easily understood, with the clarity of crystal
Then become so dense, extraordinary, and brought back to its
  confused light.

I do not believe there are rules or regulations,
Nor an explanation or measure
For this wonderful, mysterious emotion:
Love.

Robert Gilbert

Because Of Her

When I think of you my tears just want to fall
I think of all the times you said you would call;
We were once friends but that's in the past
When you got your new girlfriend I knew our friendship wouldn't last;
You said things between us would always stay the same
But you have changed drastically and it's her I have to blame;
I miss the way we confided in each other every single day
Why did things have to change between us it's just not fair that way;
We were once so close I wish that didn't have to end
But I know as long as she's in the picture we just can't be friends;
I'm gonna miss all the talks we used to have on the telephone
Until I find someone else to confide in I'll have to get through
  it all alone

Jenny Hamilton

Transmission Torment

Most malignant male dominion, abode of ominous enmity
And mumbled muddled phrases that deliberately disguise
The mysterious inner workings of the engine of my car:
Of the motor, the brake linings, and the pistons, points, and plugs.
One part, though, I know and don't-know:
Terrible tyrannous transmission,
Mystery maze of oily metal,
Thousand dollar devil disk.
Mechanics, mealy-mouthed, malevolent,
Labeling females feeble-minded,
Whisper warnings of disaster wanting hundred-dollar bills.
Point to shiny grease-soaked sections and reiterate the re-words
Re-place, re-pair, re-build reverberate, repelling all my reason
Reinforcing male opinion of dim-witted woman-person
Spilling coins and buying hope that the grunting, grumbling, grimy
Guru of machinery bent and broken
Might tame the money-gulping voracious vulture-vehicle
So its torturing transmission will finally cease to torment me.

Dianne Brooks

Lost Child

My distressed soul anxiously awaits the soothing breeze...
The tantalizing dance of the autumn flowers
Amongst the swaying trees...
Stronger still is my yearning for your effervescence,
The soothing warmth of your youthful presence
  and yet...
I know you must find your own way...
Sing your song, dance your dance...start your own new day!
My days shorten and my season enters winter...
Your days are before you and beckon you enter.
I love you, my child!
As you conquer this earth...
Climb new mountains and offer your mirth...
You will be saddened someday too and mourn things past...
But you will still brighten my world, though you've left much too fast.
Good-bye my child!

Nancy S. Cole

Black Medicine

Black medicine, the last liquid animal,
primal intellect, fire in the belly of my brain.
Food for brown people dancing around the flames
in primary colors like wild birds, racing to and fro,
naked flesh and feathers flashing in the light.

An anaconda, marked in coffee-bean patterns,
carries the word of God down the river.
Steam rises from the jungle in my cup,
grinders tear the mahogany nuggets,
slaughtering and ripping them asunder,
gushing forth fragrant, dirty, masculine,
floral blood-smell into the air.

Unspeakable urges obliterate me to a vapor
inhaled into the soul of another writhing junkie,
tattooed by scalding euphoria,
steeped in the passion of the ritual letting of the black blood.

Drink it and curse everything civilized.
Brandishing, stained fangs at the cowards drinking
their decaf - a perversion that needs liberation
like a Siamese twin.

Tracy Faucher

"Name"

Stay close to me, just for awhile.
Tell me what went wrong.
Every time I saw you...
Pain was all around you.
Help me understand your hurt...your anger.
Endless before we really ever began.
Nothing spoken, now it's really gone.
Go quickly before my heart cries.
Let's pretend that we've never known today.
Even though we did, now we must go.
Nothing will ever bring us back.
Still my heart breaks with every beating moment.
Now I only see you in my dreams...
Your face remains unchanged, your eyes drenched with pain.
Distance is all that I can feel.
Even though you are still very near.
Right down the road or so it appears.

Ellen Derting

We, The Children

They are our pride and joy, their laughter reminds us of our good times.

Children are so innocent, yet born in this hard and tragic world.

Our mistakes cannot be fixed with a handshake
and a smile. We considered them mild and
now we take our advantages when we can.

We have to have the strength to carry on and
one day, hopefully not too far away, the country
which is average now, will be one we can only dream of.

We, the children have to do well, because
before you know it the future will be in our
hands, and we should know what to do with it,
if we don't our country might not expand.

Valerie Mathiesen

"With All My Love"

I don't feel the joy that I once felt with every beat of my heart,
 I can't explain the emptiness since I read your words, "we must part".
I don't notice the colors in the rainbows anymore,
 I can't get dressed without it being a major chore.
I don't hear the crickets singing late at night,
 I can't hear the birds chirping at dawns early light.
I don't hear the tap dancers dance across the floor,
 I can't hear the crackling of thunder anymore.
I don't hear the rattle snakes rattle when he's in a coil,
 I can't hear the whistle on the steam kettle when the
 water is about to boil.
I don't see the stars flickering in the heavens above,
 and it hurts beyond words not receiving your letters
signed.... "with all my love".

Nicholas J. Giammarinaro

The Bird In The Sky

I am a bird flying so high,
in the mist of the blue sky.

Flying so lonely in sorrow,
wondering will there be a tomorrow.

Looking for a mate to soothe my pain,
but knowing that my heart will be forever lame.

I know I will find my mate someday,
but until then it might be too late.

Arrita Oler

Portrait of Insanity

You and I are not the same - you are whole and I'm insane.
You see lightness in the air, I see darkness everywhere.

I'm alone and I'm afraid - there's no comfort, only pain.
Visions come to me at night - voices crying, horror, fright.
I reach out - it's in vain - no one's there, no one cares
and laughter echoes in my brain shattering what mind remained.

Emptiness, loss of self, my humanity torn to shreds.
I look at you, you look through me - as if I no longer do exist.
I am deemed to be insane - so I stand here and I wait, clothed
with what dignity remains. Waiting...

Waiting for you to notice me, to look into my eyes and see -
the person that could have been - had lightness filled my air.
And, if it doesn't frighten you, take an even closer look -
and you will notice that you'll see - a mirror image - that is thee.

Marcia P. McNeely-Jimenez

A Dim Light Shines On A Bright Night

The dark night and her bright stars smile.
Her voice whispers to my ear like a melody that plays alone in a
forest of pines. The old stitches in my lonely dreams begin to
unravel in front of her.
She gives a moment of time that only two lovers can share.

Her sweet fragrance is a reminder that she was once here on a night
like this. I want to hold her like a child again, reassure her that
the world is what is should be.
Her touch, so warm and slow, never has she touched a dim soul before.
In the darkness and thunder, a hand will reach out.
It will be met by empty air that desires to apologize

A burning coldness fills this room.
Her fragrance is no more, her voice is screaming mute sounds.
The thunder is still here, each bang is a stab in my chest.
 Do you plan to be an immortal forever?
Dreams of a warm smile are now filled with shadows and passing words.
 "Mi amor, no puedo estar aqui."
I want to marry her divorce her in one day.
It seems proper that the circle should be complete.

This will be an empty room soon. The stars try to sing a moonlight
serenade in hopes that sleep will seduce me. A hand reaches out
and it is greeted.

Rene Chavez

Life Has Many Gifts

Looking back on the past brings back
memories that will last, Some are happy
some are sad some can even make you mad.
You live life as you see fit in hopes
that you did your bit, and look
towards the future's light, and know
God will help in all that's right.
It takes time to see a picture
but if you look you can see a future.
Happiness is what we strive for,
we are lucky if it falls upon us.
Remember a secret of life is to find
peace within, that's half the battle
 You Can Win
It may take your whole life through
but what the heck you have nothing
more precious to do.

Maxine Lumicisi and Karen Becker

"Shadows And Light"

Why do you tempt me, in the shadows,
with passion in your eyes?
Why do you seduce me, in the darkness,
with hunger in your voice?
Why do you enchant me, in the emptiness,
with desire in your touch?

Does she know the dark side of you?

Why do I understand, with the dawn,
the mendacity in your eyes?
Why do I discover, with the sun,
the mockery in your voice?
Why do I feel, with the light,
nothing...

Because she knows only the bright side of you.

Barbara Pickle

Spring

Spring, it's coming, it's very near, I can sense it. By the smell in
the air. Dogwood trees blooming in the backyard and just below them
along the cement wall that separates the yard from the sidewalk are
some Jonquils. The honeysuckles narrowly spaced on my neighbors
fence, and a yellowbell bush, on the other side of the yard, careless
of what the summer will bring. A Sparrows melodious song lingers
through the air, hoping to find a mate for nesting. As the diligent
squirrels return to their tampered oaks and senile maple trees. The
mischievous kids playing in the street waiting for their mothers to
call them in for supper. Robins and Cardinals soaring in the cool
spring air impatiently looking for a place nest before it rains. Oh
yes, "Spring is almost here."

Jeremy Sexton

Carolina Beach, 7:00 A.M.

Out of the mists, a child comes walking
Along the lonely beach,
Sea grass bowing before her,
As to a young goddess new-born of mist and water.
She skips among the shells to the water's edge
And hunkers down, and gazes out over the ocean
That looms, vast as the mind of God.
Then she begins to dance.
Leaping and twirling above the waves,
Her long hair streaming out behind.
At one with the mists, the breakers and the gulls,
She throws back her head with joyous abandon
And sings a song of joy to the rising sun.

Oh, to be a child again!
To sing... to dance... without fear.
To throw back my head with joyous abandon
And sing my song of joy to the rising sun.

Audrey E. Nickel

Life

Life, like nature starts microscopic small.
As an infant, you're dependent on all.

The child full of wonder in their eyes.
Trusting hand, in a world full of lies.

Time is like a rock in the adolescent hand.
But the elements will soon turn it to sand.

With unyielding grasp, grains still slip away.
The body now a journal of your short stay.

Life than is viewed through a fading light,
But, can't see stars, with everything bright.
Raw

Richard A. Welk

The Woman Was A Rose

Hair of white and silver, neatly intertwined...
Little fragile bones, filled with such grace...
So strong, and envied by others...
Compared mostly to a red rose because of her lively spirit...
And a warm heart filled with love and beauty...
Her stem was her strength and will...
Her delicate leaves resembled her caring for others...
Thorns that protected her from all that could harm her were as
sharp as a knife...
She brought happiness to all... until the day she began to wilt...
This little rose's delicate leaves began to droop...
Her strong stem was limp and her bright color was fading...
The thorns were now too dull to protect her...
She was suffering and little by little she was slipping away...
Sorrow filled the air as tears flowed like a river...
Love was keeping her here...
Until the day heaven opened its gates to her...
In a moment she was gone...
As if someone had come along and picked her from a garden...
And with that the rains came and washed a part of me away...

Stephanie Delgrosso

The Beach

Wonderfully warm
Wild and wet with waves
Cracking, crabs crawling,
And countless shell-clad creatures
Covering the floor of the
Fantastic and sometimes
Frighteningly furious ocean...
Where more than one ominous
And agile animal approaches,
Apparently curious
Concerning the countless pairs of appendages
Appearing and passing precariously
Through their treasured terrain,
And with willful determination demands
Their departure back to the beautiful,
Beckoning sands called
The Beach.

Carolynn Vogel O'Dell

"Just Open Your Eyes And See . ."

When I open my eyes and see,
I see the world around me and the days ahead of me.

As I blink my eyes and see,
I see the homeless asking for different kinds of money.

As I open my eyes and see,
I see how love, peace, hope and joy have enjoyed living in
many people's lives like you.

As I open my eyes and see,
I see the little boys and girls the same as you and me play happily.

As I blink my last before leaving town,
I see the youth gangs producing more violence and how
pollution have made a big impact in the world.
JUST OPEN YOUR EYES AND SEE
How the world can change with just you and me!

Jenese Fuller

Seven Deer

Do you remember the night we saw seven deer?
Granite-grounded they stood in golden beams
as if frozen transfixed in time.

Breathing man scent and machine fume all turned as one.
Wet brown wide orbs glass-glared umbrage not fear;
snow-flash blazes blurred as stone leaped free.

Barbara M. Dickinson

"One Day"

One day he came from out of the cold.
At a time my life seemed out of control.
He makes me feel good, head to toe.
And makes me feel special, heart and soul.
Yet it seems wrong with someone I've known.
Yet it feels right for reasons unknown.

Could this be love? Or could this be lust?
Or maybe the soul-mate that fate deals to us!

I feel totally his from head to toe,
then suddenly feel, that I must go.
For being hurt by some other guy,
I guess has made me an little "gun shy."

We all have a soul mate, so I've been told.
One day he'll come from out of the cold.

Patti DenBesten

REFLECTIONS ON SCHIZOPHRENIA

Genius in the Spring...
A Virgin in the Fall...
Why, she hardly had the wherewithal!

Lily of the Field in Summer,
Fool in motley in the Winter,
Did ever one see such a sinful splinter?

A boon, a bourse, her nature demanded,
Yet that which her God commanded
Is all in due course, all in due course.

Mary Joyner Henry

Me, I Am

Me, I am
Me, I am the unborn soul of tomorrow's youth.
Me, I am what God and my parents created.
Me, I am an original from my birth.
Me, I am a weaved basket from the hands of an African.
Me, I am a watcher over the menaces of society.
Me, I am the ideas of Dr. Seuss.
Me, I am the Tooth Fairy's redeemer.
Me, I am the watcher in the woods.
Me, I am all the materials of Willy Wonka's everlasting gobstoppers.
Me, I am Albert Einstein's greatest creation.
ME, I am.

Stephanie Galvin

A Precious Gift

People don't appreciate the beautiful joy
Of giving birth to a baby girl or boy
A baby is a joy a baby is a gift.
When you're down they give you a lift
If you can't handle all the strain
  Don't think with you body
Just think with your brain
People who hurt babies should be in jail
No ifs, ands, or buts that's the deal
Don't let them out put them away
Throw away the key that's where they should stay
Babies can't talk so they have to cry
But that's no reason for a baby to die
Babies are helpless they don't know better
That is why I am writing this letter.
They have to stop the people who hurt
They have to stop them from giving birth

Susan Jackson

Untitled

Lord, let me not be free
  From stormy skies and rain.
But let me see the billowy clouds
  And the wind gusting o'er the plains.
Let me see the bending trees,
  The ripple of golden grain,
The black clouds falling from the skies
  As they bring the welcome showers
To restore the bounty of your hand
  The grass, the trees, the flowers.

Let me not take for granted
  Sunny skies of blue.
For I know the storms are there, Lord
  To lift my eyes to You.
Lord, let me be a blessing
  To the ones I love so dear
And hold onto Your promise
  That You are always near.

Marie Brady Borchers

Together

Longing for that special touch,
  And that warm feeling it leaves within me.
Hoping for a gentle kiss,
  Telling me, he will always love me.
Wishing for a life together,
  In which we will live happily.
Rejoicing for that special news,
  Of the miracle we will bring into the world.
Enjoying watching, side-by-side, that child,
  As they grow and mature.
Living life to its fullest,
  Doing all of it together.
Relaxing in the end,
  Never feeling closer.
Passing away together,
  Never feeling more alive.
Moving on to heaven,
  To spend eternity, together.

Michelle Tuffield

Life

Life is the edge of a ravine.
Feared and respected, mostly hated.
We lose people to the darkness at the bottom
  again and again.
It gathers all into itself eventually,
But we must risk all and walk the edge to achieve
TRUE GLORY.

Erik Koster

Desmodontidae

Ashes drift into a crimson haze.
An inferno-like ocean,
Rife with the motion
Of bats, living things, oblivious of the ways
Of the winds. The sun's garnet rays
Paint an angry emotion,
An amorous notion,
As anonymous flying things dance in the blaze.

They dance, and they dance, and they dance
In the night,
Awaiting the banishing of the sun.
They exist by the will and whim of chance,
Not knowing what awaits them in the next night.
They retire to the music of the morning to come.

Robert Kluever

Until We're Together Again

Oh death on tiptoe feet, so quietly you come.
Leaving behind grieving hearts, mourning our precious one.

Oh death your gray foggy hand has snatched life away.
And now cold and empty my dearest lay.

Loving eyes closed to the world that we know,
to another life my beloved's spirit must go.

And death, no longer can you have claim to this offensive deed,
out of your hand and to life everlasting my loved one is freed.

Even so my heart is filled with such pain,
so lonely without you, void I'll remain.

But shhhh, do I hear a whisper ever so faint in my ear?
"I'm with Jesus, I'm happy, I'll wait for you here."

And then for a moment I feel your presence with me,
in my mind and in my heart you will always be.

Until the day that we will be together again,
I'll miss you my darling, goodbye until then.

Penelope Edwards

A Letter Of Apology

To My Baby...
Whose eyes I will never see,
Whose hands I will never hold,
Whose Mother I could never be.

To my precious baby,
I realize I made a horrible mistake,
You deserved at least a chance,
And the guilt is something I now face.

I can't turn back the clock,
And I can't change what I did,
I'm asking you to forgive me baby,
I was only a kid.

You are in God's loving arms now,
And you are always in my heart...
There is not a day that goes by,
That your memory doesn't tear me apart.

We will meet again, I know
And I will look in those eyes and smile,
And hold those hands I never held,
And be a Mother to my first child.

Nicole Renee Haymon

Untitled

People say that when the world is going to end,
that there will be terrible earthquakes,
and that there will be giant fires covering the Earth.
But what if God makes some people go mad,
where they create bombs to blow up their assigned sections of Earth.
What if he goes by the same rules but different actions by
destroying the people, person by person, ruining their lives.
Where their lives deconstruct right front of them,
where they have no more, and no more to lose.
So they commit suicide, by blowing their heads off,
slitting their wrists and dying a slow and painful death,
or take the easy way out by carbon monoxide poisoning sitting
in their cars in the garage,
and simply going to sleep, and not waking up.
And that is how he will destroy the human race,
and save the planet!

Christine Hansel

From Our Hearts

In our minds of truth we sometimes stay,
Suddenly the end of our lives begin to fray

When guilt and fears start to grow.
We find out things we have never know.

Our true friends and family begin to appear,
And with their hearts they lift our fears.

With their love and guidance so true,
We see the fraying ends and start our life new.

To thank them seems so subtle,
In the midst of all our troubles.
But love them deeply in our hearts,
Seems the place we should start.

From your little hugs and your helping hands,
From a warm smile and talks you spoke in such grace and style.

We can only say we thank you and love you,
In the deepest way!

Lori Rockwell

"Youth On The Run"

We hung out all summer, and we had some fun
We were friends together, we were youth on the run
We could be seen together, just about all the time
We shared everything, what's mine was yours, what's yours was mine
We'd drive to the woods and stop by the lake
We'd sit and share our secrets for each other's sake
Then the sun would set and the evening came
I'd tell you how I felt, we were one in the same
Then you'd smile and laugh and wrap your arms around my back
And our lips would move closer together
Slower and slower until they met, our kisses were long and slow
    and wet
And the time would fly cause we were having fun
And we'd lose the last rays of light from the sun
Driving you home at night, I could see the beautiful sight
Of your face by the shine of the dashboard light
We'd pull onto your street and our lips would meet and our kisses
    were long and slow and deep
Then we'd say our goodbyes and I'd get lost in your eyes and you'd
    give me one of those great smiles
Then I'd watch you walk away and I'd go home and pray
That we'd be together forever, until the day that we died
Because when we were together, we always had fun, we were friends
    together, we were youth on the run.

Todd Marren

Night Fairy

As the stars twinkle in the night,
I see the water sparkling bright.
I lay in the cooling sand,
My toes and fingers hidden from the dark scary land.

My hair is flowing,
My skin is cold from the winds blowing.
I run toward the cold glimmering sea,
Diving in I think, how silly can I be?

All the fish look and stare,
The ocean floors feel my feet that are bare.
I emerge to the top,
My body moving away from the waves that drop.

I'm trembling.
My heart is beating fast.
The sun is eagerly popping up from behind the trees.
It is time for me to disappear into the sky.
For if I stay, there will be nothing left for me, to be.

Laura Parquette

The Zebra

Have you ever looked closely at the Zebra?
A coexistence of both black and white
Embossed upon the back of a usually
Stately and graceful animal.

Its build is common
Yet the coloring is odd.
No exact stripe pattern,
But each one has a signature of its own.

If only our lives could coexist like the Zebra.
Both black and white; light and dark
Living in harmony with each other.
No conflict or controversy.

Perchance we could take out some time
And re-evaluate the content of the inside;
Eliminating what the exterior looks like.
Then we could all be like the Zebra.
Zebra: An African mammal of the horse family
having black or brown stripes upon a white body.

Karen Wilson

Gone

Gone, gone into the cold,
  gray mist that hovers over my heart,
    into the depths of my black soul.

It has gone into the deepest, blackest
  depths of my being, to hide away,
    away from the prying eyes that
      seek it.

There in the black part of me
  it can hide, hide and fester
    into a burning, towering inferno
      of rage and evil,
        to come forth and find revenge.

Revenge upon those prying eyes
  that would not let it go.

Michelle L. Burwell

Family And Friends Are Forever

Each day we cherish the joy, the pain
Each day we cherish the beauty, the rain

Stop and smell the roses that bloom,
Give yourself to be well groomed

Because family and friends are forever.

Lord grant us a peace of mind,
Remember each other as we unwind

We are centered in divine clarity and understanding
We are strong peaceful powerful people

Because family and friends are forever.

We are the center of abundance and the magnet of prosperity
We are facing the challenge with courage and faith
As we run this race

We must be in perfect harmony with all people and things
We must not run this life in vain

Because family and friends are forever.

Protect us, guide us, assist us
And all members of our family, living and dead
Still our hearts and minds with perfect peace as we tread
Because family and friends are forever.

Easter I. Miller

Corvettes

Corvettes are my favorite car
Can't believe how much they are
Driving down the roads so fast
Hit the town with a blast
When I get my own Corvette
I will make a lot of bets

Black or blue or even white
You can drive one day or night
Leather seats and a black dashboard
Big tires, pedal to the metal, they can beat any Ford
Even now with no money
I still ride round with my honey

Hope the prices soon get slashed
So I can get one in a flash
Corvettes are so very cool
Anyone who thinks otherwise is a fool
Circle taillights are very famous
Corvette's my dream car, they're the best you ignoramus

Raymond T. Marcum

"Don't Wait Too Long"

You think about a person for a long time but, you wait too long
You try to be nice to a person but, you wait too long
You try to be a gentleman but, you wait too long
You try to be helpful but, you wait too long
You try to be a good friend but, you wait too long
You try to be a good son but, you wait too long
You try to be good daughter but, you wait too long
You try to be a good husband but, you wait too long
You try to be good parent but, you wait too long
You try to be a good person but, you wait too long
You want to be on time but, you waited too long
You want to worship the Lord but, you thought you waited too long
But, remember the Lord will always wait for you!

Devery W. Freeman

Focus On Me

I am looking for a man to be my friend.
One that is truthful until the end.

I am looking for a man who can achieve.
Who can set a goal and expect to receive.

I am looking for humor and a big warm smile
Someone stable and can stay a while.

He can wine me, dine me and pamper me too.
A selfish man just won't do.

You must me willing and able to please,
Don't come knocking with a disease.

So if you have the body, the mind and soul,
Focus on me as your ultimate goal.

Clara M. Hampton

Racism

Racism lies on everyone's shoulders,
like two large two ton boulders.
Some don't know the real meaning of race,
It's not just the color of someone's face,
It is what makes everyone unique,
like the scales of a snake or the fur of a mink.
Racism is a hateful act,
It just shows the education racist people lack.

Kelley Ann Marler

"Pendant"

A candle is it
a breeze enters the room
I watch in silence
as the flame flickers
like the decadent land of an artist over her canvas
the candle itself is lowering
most of its substance dripping
forming as it falls.
Thereafter a beauteous pendant of wax
twisting on a golden chain about my throat
delicate, vulnerable and irony
this token is a constant reminder of
the laws of the universe,
this charm so easy to disturb its stature.

Bobby Brown

For Love Is All I've Got

I wish that every star would fall
because if I could make your dreams come true
I'd gladly give them all.
If I could be the moon
I'd watch over you every night.
If I could be the sun
I'd fill your days with light.
If I could be the ocean
when you walk along the beach,
I'd bring you ocean treasures
and lay them at your feet.
If I could be the earth
I'd bring you flowers all the time.
If I were the rain I'd give you rainbows
and pots of gold to find.
But I am only me and all those things I'm not
So I give to you my heart
for love is all I've got.

Lisa Chanley

Ringmaster

I was born with a lion in a cage.
I'll balance the ball on my nose.
The greatest one man show.
Put my head in the mouth of the beast,
It's the crowd I aim to please.
I'll swing like a monkey on the trapeze,
Roar like a tiger, dance the high wire,
Wrestle with the likes of which you've never seen,
Strength beyond your wildest dreams.
Grace in the hands of disaster,
The ringmaster.
I'll juggle a dozen cleavers,
And be the real crowd pleaser
In the middle of this three ring fling
While all the clowns will wait in the wings.

Daniel Miller

A Journey To The Sunset

A journey to the seashore I know I could make,
A journey to the sunset... that I'd have to create.
Where it gently shines upon me,
As I chase it from sea to sea.
And when I make it there... for if I do,
I shall feel the greatness inside me through and through.
For God has put all of his glory into the sunset,
And if you try and get there... He'll help you I bet.
And when we get there... we hope to see,
That God lives there... and there He'll be,
Waiting for you and me,
Patiently.

Gretchen Dobsch

Firing Missiles

They say it's only a military exercise,
    Others say it's a threat.

They say Chinese people won't fight each other,
    Others say it's a plan to conquer Taiwan.

They say Taiwan should not be independent,
    Others say they are afraid of Taiwan's Democracy.

No one can deny Democracy,
    No one can contradict History.

For the first time in 5,000 years,
    The Chinese people have elected their first president.

For the first time in history,
    The Chinese people have become their own president's boss.

This historical moment took place in Taiwan,
    It will also happen all over China.

Firing missiles cannot stop the Chinese people's dream,
    The dream of having a free and democratic... ONE China.

Anita C. Co

Never Ending Wall

The roll of a thunder, a flash of light,
This is our day, our life, our fight.
We seek to understand and be understood,
What we would give if only they could.
Night darkens on the horizon each day,
As our hopes and dreams are dashed the same way.
Yet, each morning at dawn a new horizon opens its eye,
To a new day and a new way to try,
To love, live, work and play, giving all our all,
Life is like a ladder on a never ending wall.
But we climb and climb, higher and higher,
And little things happen that help to inspire,
Us to trudge on and give 150 percent,
We try to lead our lives the way God meant.
Then in the eve when our day is through,
And we have taken off our coat and thrown off our last shoe,
We can look back over the day and reflect,
On whom our actions have had a positive effect.
As satisfaction fills our souls and creeps into our heart,
Lay down your head and rest my friend, a new day soon will start.

Heather MacKenzie Waddell

My Momma Said

My Momma said there would be days like this.
When birds would crawl and the cows would hiss.
When people would turn one against the other;
when men and women would slay their brother.
When the clouds in the sky would look
down on a world filled with sadness.

My Momma said in spite of it all, God
would fill the world with gladness.
In spite of it all, we will learn to love
one another; in spite of it all, we will
learn to love ourselves; in spite of it all,
there will come a day when races will learn
to be proud of their heritages and stand tall.

When African faces will become a visage of
pride for us all - my Momma said the time
will come for us for God to judge us - one by one.
My Momma said these days will come.
The moment nor the hour we know not.
Only to love the life we've got - My Momma said.

Lisa L. Wells

Consequence Of Labor

Oh, the pain of work
Strenuous and drudging
Meeting demand
A finished product of your efforts
Yet, toil only so arduously
Ponder only so perplexively
Forget not, your fruition shall stand alone,
When your sound conscience is left in a wake.

Scott Kaplan Belsky

Untitled

You've stood by me through thick and thin
And you've let me lean on you
Without you by my side
I don't know what I would do

There were times when I was unsure of myself
And my life was very dark
But you always reassured me
And kept me from falling apart

You've walked me down the road of life
And you've helped me see the light
You've taught me about life and love
And to fight for what is right

You're always understanding
And you know just what to say
I can't believe I was willing
To throw it all away

I just want you to know Mom
You are my whole world
And no matter how big I get
I'll always be your little girl!

Jaime Mueller

Hell

The smoke lightly caresses my neck and face
The fire tickles my feet
The screams are whispers in my ears
The laughter echoes through my brain
The taste of sulfur numbs my tongue with a vengeance
The stench of burning flesh irritates my nose
  I have always wondered what it would be like to live in hell
  Now as I open my eyes and the house burns around me,
  I know.

Beth Stoudt

S.O.S

I go round and round
And find myself in a vicious circle
I try to come near you
To understand you, to love you
To share my fears with you
To fill up the vacuum that tries to swallow me
Why do you look at me as though you are a stranger?
I get disillusioned by beaten hopes
I try to come closer to you
To your heart, with my soul
Why do you make the rift wider and wider?
Come close to me, give me your warmth,
Why do you remain silent?
Please answer my questions, I am restless
Help me understand myself
Help me to break this spell
I am sinking and I am tired
Please - rescue me
Relax me
Rejoice me

Monica Shekar

Untitled

When I woke up this morning, I felt the cold.
I saw no sunset, I heard no morning birds.
The sky was dark, the lightning and thunder rolled.
I know you cried for help, but no one heard.
Staring at this empty space, I remember
your smile, it was just yesterday we passed.
In your eyes, I thought you had found your cure
But today I discovered it was a mask.
It struck me hard when it was announced,
I tried not to cry, not to let it show.
My head was a mess, the world just spun 'round,
I didn't know what to say, or where to go.
  So now that you're gone, I don't know what to do,
  I can't comprehend how much I'll miss you.

Stacey E. Jensen

Sonnet #8

To you whose perfect petals flaunt,
Beware: Whose pink curled curtains part,
False blush will fade and never haunt
Your frame again. Soon dried death's smart
Will wither and pierce, pluck you barren.
Cut off from wealth's well, you will mourn
The days when striped fellows would hum,
Buzz over your perfect elegance.
From valley lilies you bid those come
Far, drawn tight by dew jewels and fragrance
Seductive. Your passion's fire will drown
By tears; a new Rose of Shar'n they've found.
Your mortal savior disappears
As boasting locks maturing shears.

Stephanie Larson

Loving You

When the sun stops burning, and all the days are black as the night
is when I will stop loving you.

When the sea dries, and turns to hard cracked mud,
is when I will stop loving you.

When all the trees have withered from old age, and exist no more,
is when I will stop loving you.

But when Jesus has arisen all souls in their Spiritual body,
and today's world becomes the new world of peace and plenty,
is when I will never stop loving you.

Walter Nelson Bivens

Ode To The Spirit Warrior

Here's to the unknown soldier, the living and dead.
Here's to those brave men the world has unknowingly led.

Regardless of race, creed, or color or the essence of their battle cry,
Their spirits will live forever in God's own given sky.

They fought in the days of Alexander in conflicts fought in vain.
They perished in the fields of Europe - in snow, sleet, and rain.

Deep on the waters of Midway they met the vanquished foe
  while their fathers rest in Flanders where the poppies grow.

Of all the books ever written - of all the songs ever
  sung - no greater praise has the world so nobly rung.

Yet I know in the solar system, it must somewhere keep
  in space an award for these courageous men - a credit
  to the human race.

For God's plan would not seem perfect unless it held
  in some sphere an award for the toil and talent and
  love that was wasted here.

Joseph A. Vanier

"That Dancer"

Her love for dance is ever so clear as she glides across the stage.
Her auburn hair flowing like a feather on air.
Her cat like grace is hypnotic, every eye is on her.

I watch the faces of those nearby, not one can look away.
Her presence is spell binding as she comes closer.
Hearts begin to race, the young grow old, the old lose age.

Her eyes, her lips, her touch, that angelic face.
She looks into your eyes, your only thoughts are of her.

The music stops and silence is short lived.
Applause and cheers fill the air.
The dancer fatigued and half spent,
withdraws from the spotlight

The experience is never long enough.
But time after time she brings me Joy.

She's the best I've ever seen.
That blue eyed beauty.
That dancer!
That dancer, Coleen!!
  James R. Moore

To One Lost

You go now.
Let my narrowness grow tight.
Let oneness choke my heart with lonely mist,
Let darkness make my head swim in its light,
Let quietness thunder out the words I missed,
You go...

I knew you, but my chance is passed.
I waited, but the time is gone to wait.
I thought, but thinking times can never last.
I should have said it then; it is too late.

I would have loved you, had you only known,
You might have been, not close, but not so lost...
I loved you, but my words have died unknown
Even our gazes dropped before they crossed.
Now, I sit alone, and solitary sing,
The metaphysics of a broken thing.
  Ernestine Messer Linn

Untitled

The way I look, the way I talk
The people I hang with, the music I listen to
The grades I get
The front people think I put up
The way I'm treated
The crap I don't take
It all makes people think I'm something I'm not
Most of the time they see something that isn't even there
Everyone sees a mean bad ass, brute or rebel
When I'm really someone who cares
I'm the kind of person who if you don't step on my toes I won't step
  on yours
I have a very strong personality
It's mainly who I am
I'm myself, my own person
Everyone should be that way
If you're like everyone else
What are you going to do when they're not there?
Be yourself, You'll be on top of the world
If you're not yourself don't ask for a hand up when you get
  knocked down
It's a shame people put a tag on you and it stays even when
  it's not true.
  Harmony Wilson

Learn Where Life Shows You

Little black spider in my bathroom sink
Tell me now, just how do you think
You're going to get out of there, climbing like that?
When you get to the top you always fall back.

This porcelain prison will become your grave
It's rendered you helpless your own life to save
But nobody told you and you do not know
So again and again up the side you go.

Your failures mean nothing, you'll just try again
You'll stop when death claims you and not before then
Futility, fear; you know nothing of those
And logic won't tell you the secrets she knows.

Undaunted you plod, though driven to dying
By a spirit that doesn't know how to stop trying
You never will conquer this smooth shiny slope
But little black spider I envy your hope.
  Lorie K. Bjorkman

"Party Night"

The band is playing the top 10 hits
The 9-to-5ers are calling it quits.
Turn the radio off, you're all alone.
The party is over, it's time to go home.

Confetti on the floor and streamers everywhere
Bottles overturned, kitchen cabinets bare.
Headaches in the morning and pills to see you through
Questions come to mind, "Oh my, what did I do?"

The jokes are passed around and laughter fills the air.
You walk through the corridor and everyone seems to stare.
You check in the mirror and come to the conclusion.
The confetti in your hair, it's just an illusion.
  Wanda S. Smith

The Mountains

Lords of the land the mountains are,
They almost touch the stars,
The mountain's tops survive the floods,
Their sturdy roots stay planted firmly.

The mountains guard the hidden valleys,
With crystal lakes and flowers overflowing,
Rich lush grasses and tall pines are their subjects,
The mountains rule gentle and kind,
They keep watch o'er all the land.

The winds may blow and the waters may rush,
The mountains never leave their spot,
Look down from above and see the view,
All the colors crisp and bright,
Look at their majesty in wonder,
The mountains,
Lords of the land.
  Desiree Corbett

Return

Winter comes, a flower dies.
Snow falls, tears from an angel's eyes.
The ground is tough, hard, and cold.
Could one little flower be so bold?
Spring shall one day come and boom,
And this flower will one day again bloom.
Then summer shall come and forever play,
And this flower shall forever stay.
  Kelly L. Johnson

"The Book - The Bible"

The book was laying where it had been all day.
I'd been meaning to read it since morn.
Things kept getting in the way.

So many things to be done:
Cook the food, make the beds, tend the baby dear,
Wash the clothes, iron some shirts, then I had to do my hair.

Pick up the children, then the Dad, sweep the car-port and walk.
Finished with these, I was glad I could call my Mother and talk.

Then I passed the book on my way to bed.
"Maybe I'll get time to read you tomorrow," I said.

Then a thought came to me, it seemed to shake me through:
Suppose God said to me, "Maybe tomorrow, I'll think of you.?"

I took the Bible in my arms and held it close to me.
"Forgive me, Father," I whispered inside. "Now I finally see."

This isn't just a book for me to read whenever observed,
But this is you, for you have said, "I am the word."

Louise Ward

Innocence Forever Lost

Yesterday, an innocent babe
lay cradled like an angel, carefree

Today, a deviled soul smothers her spirit
while she watches from afar

Tomorrow, alone, she searches
for what was lost,
Forever, she searches...

Deborah S. Richardson

"Papa I Miss You"

God has taken you away from me too soon, I'll never know the sound
of my voice calling out your name.
My daughter will never call you Grandpa. You will not be able
to see her become a woman.
You'll always be with us in your own special way, and you'll
be in our hearts where you are safe.
How I wish life could last forever but like time life too must
pass that's how we know we are adults.
Papa, the little girl you left behind is now a woman with a child
of her own. She loves you as much as I do and always will.
Papa, although your life was short God knows when where, why and
how we all should pass, and soon we will meet again.
I will always have the memories that I will cherish forever, until
we meet again in heaven where we were before time on earth began.
God's will, will be done when it's our time to meet our maker in
heaven again.
Papa I miss you, in Heaven we will meet, I love you.

Dora Wilson

The Workaholic (Father Unknown)

He awakes in the morning a whiff of cologne and then he's gone,
like a shadow of a stranger we've never known.
In the middle of the day as the children want to play
he's alone, and sits not a feeling of his shown,
in the evening he comes home another whiff of his
cologne and then to bed he goes, we don't know him
he's a phantom he hopes to when they're grown but
until then he's content to be known by a whiff of his cologne.

Sherry Curtis

Chilito Chick

The woman in the Taco Bell was middle aged and blonde.
She was as tan as a shipwreck victim.

Hold the sour cream!
She doesn't need it.
What hangs below her shorts projects that across the orange seat
of the booth when she sits down.

A preteen boy stares at the pink bikini strap that protrudes from
the back of her T-shirt collar.
A vision of her tanning in her backyard reels through his mind,
and then passes with a bite of his taco

Her boyfriend sits across the table,
wishing he had sex as often as she does.

Her chilito had no beef,
but she didn't mind.
She just poured two hot sauce packets over the cheese and
tomatoes and began to eat.

John Ingle

"First The Stars Are Gone"

Fire tears from the starlit sky fall slowly,
Extinguishing on the cold icy floor,
The stars cry no more.
Fading from the forgotten tears,
The stars turn black and disappear.
Now salted tears hit the dead brown grass,
From children's faces there's no more smiles nor laughs.
Some how connected there are no more dreams,
No more thoughts, only silent screams.
The world forgets the stars, children and now themselves.
The world is now dead, who started it all?

Misty McDonald

The Torn Beholder

The wind swirls through the gallows of the mind
With it comes the night of a spring blossom in the morning sun
Thoughts of the love ever wanted to share with her
Opening passages to bring into view
Hair the color of a wild stallion of the night
Flowing with the length and beauty of an Ozark spring
Eyes which speak with the sensitivity of the heart itself
Sparkling with the grace of the heavens up close
Lips which shine from the crack of dawn
Parting sweetly as the song of the meadow lark
Body of perfection derived straight from Helen of Troy
Sure to draw a clash from the warriors and gods themselves
Spirit as strong and fierce as the pride of a lion
Personality as clear as the parting of daylight fog
Wishing to grasp till the fall of the ages
Unable for claims set on not letting go
Swelling of the chest wishing to burst
Forced to give the heart to the soul of another
Reasoning fades unsure into the howls of the night

J. Dale Prater

On The Jungfrau

Scalded by the deep frozen ice fire
She patiently lets us track up her side,
Though it burns the eyes too much to stare.
Some glide down gently, others in bright costume,
(How unSwisslike) race madly,
Laughing as they dare to escape her white folds.
The Jungfrau, however, prefers a comfortable cloud,
Settling softly within her sharp-scarred stone,
As in a passing misty veil, when we leave.

Bruce Ganem

"Angels"

Angels exist in very many ways.
They give people happiness, days after days.
When you're in trouble, they're right by your side;
If you don't see them, it's not 'cause they hide.
It's cause they're very, very deep in your heart.
But don't worry, you and your angel are not far apart.
Your love is great, and your trust is true.
Remember your angel is always right beside you.
Your angel never leaves, it never goes away.
It always understands every single thing you say.
Your angel is with you, even when you sleep;
So when bad dreams happen, there's no need to weep.
Trust your angel even when everything you own is gone.
'Cause if you really believe in him, he'll help you move on.

Eric N. Salazar

Loneliness

Feeling as if there is no one to talk to,
wanting to run as far as you can away,
wanting to end your life forever because
you think that you will never be happy again.
Feeling left out,
not wanted,
feeling hurt.
Loneliness is like having your heart ripped out
of you, and stomped on by all the people
who you thought like you.
You cry your eyes out every second of the day.
Staring off to space and wishing
you were there.

Liz Lemmerman

Colors Of Life

Death is but a love
   of a sweet smelling rose
Death is pushing life
   as this poetry, it flows
And death is a magenta
   which is one more shade of red
Red is but a color of a rose
   lying atop a death bed
Death is but cyan
   just another shade of blue
This color stands so high above our heads
   and looks down on me and you
And death is but a yellow
   the color of the sun
This color makes me shiver
   as I mouth the barrel of this gun
And as I think of all the colors
   that stir within my head
It makes a black so deep and dark
   I weep upon my bed

Jessica Erin Bierman

Christian Findings

As having the wealth of the Lord Jesus Christ in our heart.
For knowing that; he is the almighty...
But being weak and of the flesh.
We sometimes lose our ways in life of spirituality.
For patience of the unknown is sometimes scary.
For His purpose for Us for tomorrow is a mystery to us.
So fulfilling is his timing of our life.
That as being of the flesh, we lose our wisdom, temporarily
in this fleshly world.
But by His grace and His workmanship in us.
Can we find His peace again by His spiritual blessings of His grace.

Steve Hunt

Rejoicing

I see you smiling, halo gleaming gold, sparkling
above your fiery hair. You know me where
it is darkest and not settling for it, you
reach out your hand and invite me to put on
my sequined shoes and to dance. We trip
over blades of grass and copper leaves
to the sound of the wind whispering like a
senile widow. I get a glimpse of fireflies
captured in your eyes and I laugh out loud.
I sing a silly song while you pull a spider's
web, perfect and silver with dew, from a
tree branch. It falls like a silk cloth as
you drape it over my hair. "There," you say,
"now, pretend you are a princess." We spin,
Bend into the marbled colors, my laughter
with the pink sun, spills into the night.
In the purple-tinted dark I spin and spin.
Night drapes me in a gown, velvet and flowing
glittering with bits of the moon. Then, I run
and I leap, and finally, it is you who laughs.

Gina V. Dell

Why

Why is there hatred of different things
Why is there no peace after winning a war
Why is there no one to hold all the children
Why do you not see me as beautiful

Why is there a calmness in weapons
Why is it easier to get high then to get happiness
Why are there diseases that exist with intense pain
Why am I not perfect to you, no matter what I do

Why is suicide tranquil
Why are words used to demean
Why can't all animals live safely in this world
Why can't you give yourself fully to me

There are no answers to this why
Because malignancy is here, can't you hear the cry
And it does not matter how hard I try
Because at this rate, the world (like our love) will die

Kathy Skelding

How Big Is Your God

The Lord protects me when I'm weak,
He warms me when I'm cold;
By grace, heals those who are in pain,
And His love doesn't ever grow old.

The Lord would never cheat on me,
He's faithful to the end;
Even during my sinful acts,
Guardian angels He will send.

The Lord I worship is always there,
He will always be here to stay;
Where is your God when you need him most,
My God will never stray.

Brenda F. Smith

Misty Woods

Where trees with long branches spread
and on the ground leaves make a bed.
I lie on nature's padded ground in silence deep.
There is no sound.
I think of the beauty nature provides
and tears well up within my eyes.
Standing up and looking around, I found from where I stood
why it's called Misty Woods.

Grant A. C. Dunn

Friends Forever

She sits lifeless in the corner
with star gazed eyes and hair in knots.
Rags for clothes and hugged by sheets
of dirt. Does she have feelings?

Those days when she was used as
a comforter, a friend, a shoulder to
cry on. Many days of playing outside, and
once used as a dog's toy.

Now she sits rugged next to a
beautiful, sophisticated competitor.
I hope she knows she is still my best friend.

Tiffany Wilson

Free With A Friend

The horse runs wild and free,
And I on its back just me.
Him knowing all his sores I will mend,
As my hair flies free in the wind.
Up on his back I am mounted,
The butterflies that have passed I have counted.
The flowers are full of bees,
As I ride I feel a nice breeze.
His color is such a sight,
He is as black as the darkest night.
His hair is the color of fire,
That raises higher and higher.
My hair is the color of the sun,
With sun rays that fly with fun.
On the ground I can hear his feet patter,
Where we go really doesn't matter.

Britany L. Turner

The Meaning Of Moonbeams

Those silver white spectra dancing just beyond my reach,
In the land of nonsense, and make believe, and truth,
Are the stuff of dreams, and illusion, and nocturnal longings,
Of Saturnian rumination into the mysteries of our being.

Soft, subtle, gentle, with secrets more piercing
Than the sharpest spear,
These messengers from Luna sprinkle rapture in my heart,
Illuminate the crevices of my soul,
Yet never, never stand to be caught or caressed by mortal touch.

Sent from the numinous realm of reflected light,
They forage the dark within-ness of my existence,
Felicitously connecting through unspoken song,
The subterranean impulses of my open heart.

Sally Palmer Thomason

A Happier Time

Why are there tears falling down your face?
You are almost through with life's little race.

Many others have gone before you.
You are not the first to say you're through.

Don't worry you will go to a much happier time.
You know how you always wished that drinks were a dime.

I will miss you, I hope you know that's so.
But there are things you must do and you must go.

I will say goodbye to all your friends.
So you just go and wait for my race to end.

And when it does I hope you're there.
Please wait for me on the golden stair.

Terri P. Lisenby

Just To Let You Know

Just to let you know how much I love you,
And how much I care,
Nobody will ever, ever know,
Exactly how much I feel about you.

Just to let you know how much you mean to me,
And how much I adore you,
Nobody will ever, ever know,
Exactly how much I miss you.

Just to let you know how much the years get shorter,
And the days get longer,
Nobody will ever, ever know,
Exactly how much I enjoyed you.

Just to let you know that you are mine,
And I am all yours,
Nobody will ever, ever know,
Exactly what life would be without you.

Violet A. Samonte

Older And Wiser

Her parents were always on her
Case about her little brother
Her brother didn't have to do
Anything. He was younger.
If she replied "It isn't fair."
They would answer: You're

Older and wiser

When her brother would break
Something, he would blame her.
If she said she didn't do it, her parents
Would tell her not to lie. She was

Older and wiser

If her brother cried, her parents would
Blame her. Don't pick on your
Brother; You should know better. You are

Older and wiser

But she did get to stay up later
Than her brother. She was

Older and wiser

Leslie Dupuy

Untitled

Pain is poison to a heart made of tears
Mirrors reflect memories of past years
Loneliness sweeps up like a call from the grave
Of living grace one can never save

I seek happiness I'll never find
Burning alters into my mind
Even the blind can see life's pain
Tears washed away by the falling rain

I can hear as your soul cries
Burning through a million lies
Love is a legend in my mind
Something to see though never find

Feel the chill of the wolf's cry
Mourning sobs of those who will die
Silver shadows cast by the moon
Of fallen angels returning soon

Janee Houston

Lilacs Blooming Above the Backyard Grave

As a boy, I knew him as footfalls against boards of the attic floor,
crystal radio voices fading and returning through the night.
Why father turned away, his face tightening like rope
when the old man entered a room, I didn't know. Why
mother wept, speaking softly to herself behind the bedroom door.
He became the wizened dwarf of dreams, drawing
breath from my lungs while we slept. At eighty-five,
he coughed up blood, warming his prosthetic leg by the fire.
Mother insists the lilac has grown thick since
he stopped taking meals at home. He wanders
in a pale light from the house, no longer cursing
shadows from his pine chair on the porch. He chews
tobacco, rehearsing the rib-bone of a dance on loose stone
in the garden, his good leg mocked by wood
alcohol and falls twisted beneath cabbage leaf.
Father bites his lip hard, sucking the sweetness up
through his teeth, knowing the man died at home,
laid below the bush behind the house where
he can rise nightly through our blood.

    Peter M. Rojcewicz

That's My Son!

The year was 1965. My prayers were answered.
  My beautiful baby boy did finally arrive.

I'll always be thankful for not only was I there to see
  But those first steps of his, they were to me.

Going to school just wasn't part of his plan.
  So that first day we went together, hand in hand.

Now a body builder he wants to be,
  I'm his photographer, his biggest fan.
  That's him there with the trophy in his hand.

Then came the drag racing.
  I'm there praying before each run.
  So very proud when he gave me the first trophy he won.

His rides on his Harley are included in our prayers.
  And repeated by him when his Mom and Dad ride theirs.

The year is now 1995
  Someone very special has been sent to share his life.
  Therefore on this their wedding day,
  His Dad and I stand together,
  Each of us giving thanks and proudly say

THAT'S MY SON AND THAT'S HIS WIFE!

    Mary Hobbs

True Love

If there were words to express how I feel...
  I would say them to you.
If there was a song whose melody carried my thoughts...
  I would sing it to you.
If there was a book whose chapters told the story I need to tell...
  I would read it to you.
If there was a picture that could demonstrate the way I feel...
  I would show it to you.
The words won't come,
The song can't be sung,
The book isn't written; and
The picture hasn't been taken.

    Tracy Sadowsky

"The Heart Of Friendship"

Within the heart, all thoughts acknowledged
rejected by the world, accepted with friendship.

Within the heart, all pain obliviated
heartbreak and heartache, soothed with friendship.

Within the heart, all love expressed
no words spoken, understood with friendship.

Within the heart, all failures destroyed
no excuses needed, forgotten with friendship.

Within the heart, all success rejoiced
parties unnecessary, celebrated with friendship.

Within the heart, all fear subsided
no reason to hide, protected with friendship.

Within the heart, all emotions experienced
trapped by the world, freed with friendship.

    William Q. McCormick

Urbanic Poetry

Their prose etched upon walls
liquids, aerosol ink
A writer's tools are these
tell of inner city life
Saga's of murder, hate and strife

Superscriptions speak on buses, subways and trains
Billboards utter stories of pain
As we travel through each block, a page is turned

Verses of love, and racial rage
Modern proverbs, most fail to comprehend
That city nomads grasp with childlike ease
Poverty, oppression, crime that stalks
Upon 5th Ave and the walk of stars
Sonnets of youth in lust, packing cold steel

The most read literary work of all
Are not found in halls of great thought
Nor in the colleges of the Ivy League
But upon street corners in urban life
Words of contemporary reality which need to
sink, deep within our ears, the poetry of urban life

    Tom Wilmas

Colors Of The Wind

As the wind whispers through the trees,
It turns into the sweet red colors of the cardinals.
As it dashes across the ground
And leaps off the small ledges,
It turns into the slender grey body of a deer jumping through
  the forest.
As it passes through the tall grass in the pastures,
It turns into the shades of the black and white cattle.
As it winds through the wooden stables,
It becomes the hues of the painted horses.
And as it swirls gently around me,
It paints these pictures before my eyes.
Ever blowing,
Ever changing.
The colors of the wind.

    D. Brennen Noble

Death Cannot Sever

There's a link in life's chain that death cannot sever,
Love and remembrance live forever.
Remember the good times, let go of the bad
Your loved one is in Heaven so rejoice and be glad
Keep your spirit elated, don't let it sink low
Open wide your heart's door to God's sonshine and let his love in
    you grow
As his love lifts you higher and your spirit does soar
When God's love surrounds you, you will never be poor
For all of heaven's treasures he holds out to you
Let go of your negativity and learn to live positively anew.
The sonshine of his love your dark cobwebbed corners will
    sweep clean
As you learn on his promises and his love to lean
Hold fast to his hand as from that dark valley you climb
For he will sweep away the darkness and give you a sunny clime
For there is a link in life's chain that even death cannot sever
Love and remembrance live forever.

   Dessie E. Hancock

Bye, Bye, Daddy

Bye, bye, Daddy I hate to see you go,
I love you very much, just thought you should know.
Things have changed since you have gone
Why did things have to go so wrong?

You hurt us all so very much,
You're like a stranger by your touch.
Where did my Daddy go,
I need to tell him I love him so.

Soon after you left we were all depressed.
But we'll just start again and do our best
I hope you find what you're looking for,
Maybe you'll find it behind some door.

I'm not going to let it get me down
Or be seen everyday with a frown
I wish you would come back home with us
And be a family with no fuss.

Your mind is made up,
And you're giving us up
Bye, bye Daddy you've made me cry for the very last time
So give us a call when you have a spare dime.

   Tracie J. Speckman

Caleb

Caleb is a baby not very old,
who has big feet and little toes.
He can walk, talk, and crawl really fast,
he likes to do the perfect cast.

Sometimes he'll let out a yell,
when he stinks you know you can smell.
Funny jokes make him smile,
getting used to him may take awhile.
Because, he's my nephew I can't give him away,
there's lots more stuff but, that's all I've got to say.

   Clint Powell

Forever Friends

True friends are like birds that fly in the sky,
singing their greetings as they soar by.
True friends are like flowers that bloom from the earth,
making you feel welcome at home and at hearth.
True friends are like diamonds so shiny and hard,
their strength guiding you like a personal guard.
Forever may seem far off - like eternity,
but forever friends are as true as can be.

   Patrick Cecil

"Thoughts"

Like two little birds that fly through
the sky, so does our love grow as the years
go on by. Deeper and deeper into our hearts,
our minds get together on the same kind
of thoughts.

So we both know how much we mean
to each other. She loves me so or shall
I say we love one another, because we
walk together, we walk by and by with
that easy feeling that God's on our side.

I'll always love you until eternity
you will always be happy, because my
love for you will always be.

   Robert Moreno Sr.

Shared Hearts

A warm August evening
Her brown eyes, rich and soft like spring's freshly tilled earth,
Meet mine and draw me closer to see inside.
Slowly our hearts become entwined
As wild vines weave in the branches of a tree.
Our love is as gentle as dandelion seeds caressing the air
On a lazy summer's day.
Yet strong and true as the tiny acorn grows to a mighty oak.
We pass blissfully and wordlessly through the passing seasons
Enjoying and savoring each shared moment.

Without warning tragedy strikes.
Panic! Chaos! Hurry! Faster! Faster!
But time runs out and her heart beats its last beat.

Grief, heavier than an anchor that steadies a ship
Weighs my mind and body down to a silence, dark and lonely place.
As the first ray of sunshine finally emerges from menacing clouds
So do the happy memories of times shared.
She is not gone and will live forever tucked in the safety of my heart.

Just a dog.
Perhaps, for those who can see only with their eyes.

   Kathryn Christie

Alone

Each night I sit in a corner and softly start to weep
Very mildly and gently, crying me to sleep

A tear rolls down my cheek
I stutter when I speak

I'm all alone in this corner, everyone else outside
I can not face the world, I must stay in and hide

I see no more beauty
I have no more fun
I think my life is ending
Though it had not yet begun

No sun shines
No moon glistens
When I speak
No one listens

Oh, how I miss those flowers that in the springtime grow
And those beautiful rivers that always kept their flow

But everything is still, nothing moves no more
And I'm in the corner, weeping, like before.

   Theresa Christopher

Just Passing Through

I'm just a stranger here, I didn't come to stay
I'm only here for a season, then I'll go my destined way

Just as the rose in spring do bloom
My very presence bought joy, not gloom
As each petal does have its place
I also have my special space
I am in the place where love first start, for
I'm planted deep in your heart and where
I am I'll always be, even when eyes no longer see

When time has come and time has gone and my
Footprints no longer shown
Don't be sad and don't be blue, just remember
We're just passing through.

Charleen Davenport

A Sonnet

They will say I was born a lucky kid,
One with intelligence and good luck. Gee,
I wish it hadn't ended when it did.
Only eighteen, I hit that big oak tree.

We were having fun, someone brought some beer.
I always knew I shouldn't be drinking
But when around my friends, I had no fear.
I'd still be alive had I been thinking.

My body mangled, I screamed in agony.
The cops and doctors came as I cried—but
I thought only of my parents when I died,
What will they say, will cops tell them for me?
  The cop turned away, a tear in his eye.
  How many of us children has he seen die?

Becky Gard

The Race Of Life

We see you running like the wind
We see you as you stride
We see all your potential
Something you must never hide.

You possess a miracle
You possess a gift
You possess all that we want
And gives us all a lift.

Do you know of all your greatness?
Do you know what this world will gain?
Do you know all you may do?
But we all know it took some pain.

You have always been so humble
You have always been so kind
You have always been so happy
And this will bring you what you'll find.

The world it may be cruel
But you they will embrace
You'll show them skill and honesty
And this will win your race.

Katrina Siefert

Analects Of Thought

Sustenance of body and mind, nourishment to fill unfeigned
desire and to feed many folds. Knowledge to allay the appetite
of the spirit and the hunger of the soul.

Seeds of infinitive consciousness sown in fertile fields
and harvested by gatherers to reap the bountiful yields.

Tables set for inspiration and sapid wisdom to share with
those who quest the reward and accept its priceless fare.

John Alexander Malone

"Carry On My Love"

Darling, you must carry on as if I was there
Just lay your problems down to rest
And put all bad times behind you Dear
Always strive to do your very best
Carry on with confidence, Darling
Because your hands now hold the reins
Don't think your talents don't compare
For my love runs through your veins
Carry on with honesty and pride
You know what is right and fair
Just call on me when problems strike
You know that I will be there
Carry on our dream my Love
Let your conscience be your guide
And remember when you feel alone
I'm standing right by your side
For awhile you must carry on without me
But pretend that I am there
For I will never be far away
And you know that I will always care

Charles G. Neel

So Free

Why must they die so young?
Why are lives pushed aside?
Why must they not have any more fun?
What will we say to those who have died?
"I'm sorry you never got to see
All of the many beautiful things yet to be?"
"Sorry you never fell in love."
But what will they say to us?
"Sorry you never knew to be as a dove.
To fly so free from this world's cares
and to go beyond where
all of the lightning flares
and to have peace unknown
and to have a place where only angels have flown."
They may even lament for us as we strive
those who are dead but still alive.
For they now know life's greatest mystery
and how it is to be so very free.

Benj Clark

"Reflections"

On this last night of the year '95
I'm amazed that I'm reasonable sane and alive
So much pain, anger conflict and strife
Made this year one of the worst of my life
Supposedly confession is good for the soul
I must confess that I don't feel whole
Gone is the joy that filled my heart
At what moment did the peace depart
Seemly life has gone astray
Taking the happiness from each new day
Missing is the swing from my walk
Stress and tension color my talk
Most of the glow is gone from my eyes
Black has erased the blue from the skies
The sun doesn't seem as bright
My thoughts are darker than the blackest night
Love and laughter has been replaced
With time lost, looking off into empty space
One can only stand so much pain
I'm sure I don't want to ever pass this way again

Dianna M. Buckrem

"My Heart"

Instantaneously, you become my friend,
I loved you from the start
But more than that, you become my love.
Then I gave you my heart.
My heart, you held so very close.
That's one reason, I loved you most.
You seemed to know, my heart could break
The pain of life, it couldn't take.
Then from nowhere - our life changed.
Death came and called your name.
My heart so quickly, broke in two-
No healing now, will make it new.

Edna Rogers

Earth Spins

The fragile ice cracks.
Heart stops beating and for a brief moment —
A lifetime—can't breathe.
Eyes tearing
Don't touch my soul.
Who is inside my head turning me away?
Chance meeting
Thunder roars within my being, numb to the core.
Muscles tremble weak and sore; smile fleeting...
Girl no more.
Mind's broiling
Body's recoiling from the touch of things unseen.

Regina Wright

I Am

...The brilliance of rainbowed sky; inspiration
   the freedom of spirit.
...The beaming ray of golden sunlight,
   warmed with pride by every accomplishment.
...The lush caress of fresh green grass;
   a blanket to uncover dreams.
...The ever flowing contentment of a peaceful brook;
   that trickles away all of life's fears.
...The lofty winds of ambition,
   soaring on the gentle breeze of guidance.
...The piercing crackle of a lightning bolt;
   a spark to set imaginations ablaze.
...The billowy emotion of precipitous clouds,
   who shed their tears in failure.
...The dancing tide, on the seasons of change;
   unwavering gifts of love.
...The tree of new life, with outstretched arms;
   hearth and home, forever sheltering the generations.

I am nature's child,
   Mother

Roberta C. Green-Rich

Alone

Down a dark winter road I walk,
A single, solitary street that never ends;
An emptiness, immeasurably immense, engulfs my aura.
My clothes are of no comfort from the cold,
For it is the fabric of my soul which no longer warms me.
Exhalations of frigid smoke exit my lungs,
Evidence of an enraged fire within me.
Every passing breath is more purposeless than the previous one,
An infinitesimally small reminder of my existence.
My one true love has prematurely ascended,
And all I want is to be with her;
To be with the only one who fuels my eternal flame.
There is nothing left for me here;
All I can do is wait to die.

Casey Guillot

True Love

She sits idly thinking,
but thinking not of me.

She sits there carefully watching
but not watching for me.

She sits there whispering,
whispering not of me.

I think of her in every thought of my thoughts,
I whisper of her every time I whisper a whisper,
I see her every time I use these eyes to see,
I wait for her every second that passes by.

Idly I wait for words to be uttered from her lips,
When she does, I hold these words dear to my heart,
Wishing with every breath,
That these words are meant for me.

Thinking of her, waiting for her, wishing of her.

Jonathon Temblador

My Secret Place

There is a place I run to inside
   When I need a place to hide.
In my secret place I never cry
   Eagle's sore and rainbows fill the sky!

There is so much I want to be
   There is so much I want to see.
But I can't, my hands are tied,
   So I run to this place inside.

I want to run barefoot thru the sand!
   I want to dance to the band!
      I want to sit and talk with old friends...
Until then, I'll keep running as fast as I can
   To the place inside,
To the place where I hide.

Sandra M. Fish (12/28/48-5/17/96)

Tropical Cocktail

I want to live on an island with neon trees and chalice
shells. I want to wade into calypso nights where King
Humidity rules with a wet fist, and only spit cools the
skin. Drums will rumble over thunder clouds: funnels of
cream that taste of molasses and precipitation.

I want to drink from your soul so that I might taste
sweetness unspoiled, and find courage to continue my
velvet journey. I want to wander at will, dining on goat
and crab while creativity bubbles from my ears, the snare
drum beat of a rough-and-tumble-billy-back-shack shelters us
as a storm approaches.

Firecrackers erupt over my shoulder; sandal toes curl into
ash that is licked by Neptune's tongue. Promises roll forth
like pennies upon the hot bones of this edifice.

I will stay and listen forever.

Laura Baber

Eyes

Eyes are wonders which will never cease,
You control them and they do what you please.
Some are big, and ever so bright,
While others are small and ever so light.

Some show gladness and others good cheer,
While others show sadness from things which they fear.
But no matter how big, no matter how small,
Whether they glisten or don't shine at all,

Be thankful you've got them for some haven't at all.

Shirley Colino

Night Sky

Send a flash of lightning
Through my sky
Of new clip
Make the prints run down the wallpaper
And form clouds
In my room
Of meaninglessness
And let the clouds rain the tears
I've saved
From the times you weren't here
Dry my face with your flashlight sun
And fill my life with blue violets made of plastic
To remind me of your eyes
On a night sky

Elin Johansson

'What Do You Want Me To Do?'

I love you and always will
It just doesn't seem enough for you
"What do you want me to do?"

While our family was growing
I stayed home
It was what you wanted
"What do you want me to do?"

We don't talk or hold hands
You don't even want hugs
and kisses anymore
"What do you want me to do?"

There's a wall built between us
Regrets and badly learned traits
"What do you want me to do?"

It's our silver year and for reasons untold
You walked out the door
and broke my heart
"What do you want me to do?"

Cheryl Allen

Love

Love
I never knew what it was, until I met her
Love was brought us close
And yet it will bring us closer
I always though love was a waste
That was until I met her
Whenever she said she loved me
It sent shivers down my spine
I hope we can spend a lot of our lives together
That way we both can say I love you
Time after time
I love her and she loves me
It should never change
Love

Kyle Kloster

Untitled

O bleed my precious soul
The winds of cold and bitterness blow
For not a thing cast down on thee
Shall ever replace that sparkling glow
When once you did shine ever so bright
That beauty was stole away
By cruel and thoughtlessness prevailing North
Everlast, ne'er without passes a day
Through life, an eternity
   Pain clothed in blood.

Lindsay E. Crain

Untitled

This may be the last thing i write.
   Could be the last breath i breathe,
      The last note i hear,
         The last poem i read.
So if i never see you again in life,
   If i never look into your eyes,
      If i never touch your soft skin again,
         i'd like to say goodbye.
But there will be another chance for us -
   i know that this is true,
      Because every time a new night falls,
         The day begins anew.
So if i never speak another word -
   If i never again sin,
      And if i can't say goodbye.
         You'll know we'll meet again.

Adam Emery

Hanging In The Balance

Our hopes and aspirations for tomorrow
Hang delicately from the cliffs of our dreams
Each one rooted in the side walls of our determination
Waiting for us to make the leap
To reach out
To grab hold
And not let go
For to fall would be to fall into everyday obscurity
And to have never been known for making a difference
in this world
To have never been lauded for attempting such dreams of
huge proportion.

Diane L. St. Cyr Janelle

Gunshots

Anything quieter than a gunshot we don't hear,
And even then we don't listen for long.
We should try to improve the methods of equality in society,
It has caused some of humanity to leave this world with bullets in
   their heads.
The world is ours,
Still, we continue to live with color.
We are blind, we refuse to look for the truth,
No one actually appears to comprehend.
Some wonder why others would rather leave this world,
Than to keep the constant struggle alive.
Those who wonder why, are sure the end of the struggle is near.
Some still don't realize what we are fighting for,
Blood is a terrible thing to waste.
Surviving each and every day,
To make sure they aren't labeled murderer because of the color of
   their skin.
Everyone says accept racism, it won't change,
But we can't, we haven't struggled for equality and survived to see
   tomorrow for getting no justice.
Sometimes I think there's nothing left to live for,
Except for the out lines of chalk and the smell of death.

Rose Ferrari

Red

Red is roses and cherries, and getting hit on the head.
Red is the taste of strawberries.
Red sprinkles and a red pepper smell red.
True love and candy hearts make me feel red.
Red is the sound of thunder and drums.
Red is a cherry field, a raspberry field, and a lovely rose garden
blowing in the wind.
Sharing friendship with one another is red.
Ice cream cones with cherries on top are also red.
Red is all around your eyes.

Sherry Ann Griffis

"Xmas Is Coming"

Xmas is coming and Santa's on his way,
to give a bike or a doll to Donald or to Fay.
While Santa is a working to find the
good and bad.
Children are shopping for mother and
for dad.
12 days till Xmas. How can we ever
wait, to see the snow on chimney tops
and on the front door gate.
And sleighing down the hill tops, we
laugh and shout with joy.
While dad and mom just wonder when they
were that girl and boy.
At night we hear Carolers sing songs
like Silent Night.
While were are all around the tree, where
ornaments so bright to see.
The clock strikes nine to sleep we go.
Until we wake and then to know, that
Santa came through ice and snow.

Betty Raffele

Untitled

I see a cardinal and it sees me. I see a bluebird and it sees me.
I see a black cat and it sees me. I see a Great View and it is named
Mount Greylock.
I see some plants and they smell great. Today is nice out.
I see a blackcapped chickadee and it is eating.
Outside I am sitting on a bench. The bench is sitting too.
Outside I see a bunch of trees and they are pretty. Outside I
see some kids playing in the sun.
Outside I see a robin getting chased by my cat Sweetie!!!!
Outside I see an orange cat named Marty soaking up the sun!
Outside I see woodpeckers. A male and a female eating suet.
Outside I see a head of deers in my backyard. And now the day
    has ended.
Night creatures come out at night. Outside at night owls come out.
The stars come out at night with the moon. Rabbits come out at night
plus bats, worms and raccoons. It is morning again. The rooster
is calling.
The sun is rising, time to start a new day. Good bye!

Charlene Emily Michon

Snow Wolves

The night is cold and black.
The snow is falling down.
This is when the snow wolves,
come across the ground.
They guide the dogs through darkened woods,
the racer on the sled.
The blizzard harshens to the point,
they wish that they were dead.
The woods are still;
the woods are quiet.
Still the snow wolves lead.
Not until they reach the light,
do the snow wolves leave.
As they go there is no sound,
as if their feet were off the ground.
Never to be seen again,
these saviors of the man.
Until another stranger
is lost upon this land.

Kristie Matter

Indian Summer

Patchwork shadows on the ground softly lie
As white cotton clouds drift slowly by.
A soaring hawk swerves, mounting high
Against the burning, azure sky.

Pink, purple, and gold flowers blaze
Gaudy and gay in the shimmering haze.
A silver stream winds its wandering way,
A green velvet ribbon in the glimmering rays.

In the drowsy heat, cicadas sing.
A bee bumbles by on a honey fling!
The sun glints gold on a butterfly wing,
Glowing with vivid, iridescent sheen.

The Earth bears the print of a mighty hand,
Stirring to life at unheard command.
Burdened with fruit, the orchards stand,
The corn grows green across the land.

Under the molten sun's pulsating light,
The life-force surges with unseen might.
Blazing crimson and gold, it sinks from sight:
The land breathes deep in the cooling night.

Anne Twete

Face To Face

Looking in the mirror, Face to face,
Lies another world, one without boundaries.
An imagination running wild,
Like horses galloping through an open field.
Underneath this face is freedom.
Freedom to be anyone, Freedom to follow any path.
Choices are within.
This world is built with dreams,
Dreams to achieve, Dreams never fulfilled,
Dreams just worth dreaming.
Without "inner-self", there is no self.
Unique ways of thinking,
Unique ways of getting things done.
Thoughts, dreams, and actions,
Begin within,
Hit the surface,
And shine.
Never quit.
The outcome,
One Beautiful, Unique, Individual.

Teresa Bell

What Is The Light?

What is the light at the end of the tunnel
that has guided us for so long?
What has given it so much power
that we can always come back strong?
It could not have been a candle
because as the winds of question came about
the flames of our candle would flicker and go out.
Could it be a lighthouse? No, I'm sure it's not.
The beacon of a lighthouse is either off or on
where the light we've seen has been constant and is strong.
It's not a lightning bolt, powerful and bright.
Lightning as we see it lasts for only a second or two
and since our journey would take more time, that would never do.
Where does the power then come from that can emit such light?
What can cause something so constant and so bright?
It's not found on the outside, but within two hearts entwined.
The hearts of which I talk about is yours and mine.
It is the love that we have found, the flames it has ignited
and guided us throughout our journey and kept the end in sight.

David E. Tallant

The Spirit Of My Heart

Life is a marvel...a true work of art,
There's so much to discover, but what intrigues me is my heart.

It beats in a steady and continual motion,
As it sifts through my life and every emotion.

In moments of ecstasy, it soars to the moon!
And at times of deep passion, it dances and swoons.

When I'm in despair, it genuinely aches,
Sometimes so intensely, I can feel it break.

Whether I'm elated, unhappy or tense,
My heart is in control in every sense...

My heart bears my sorrows and celebrates my joys,
It nurses burdens inside while to the world appears poised...

I'm in awe by the magic and I still fascinate
At the intensity and beauty this heart captivates.

When I think about my heart I get sentimental,
For, in forming my Spirit, its force was monumental.

How shallow I would be without its inspiration, and
I am forever humble with beholden appreciation.

Connie Saccomanno

Demobilization

Ah, but we had an audience
when we came back from war, us girls.
Two rows of notable officialdom,
high-up muck-a-mucks of corporate control
sat scrutinizing, studying, speculating on our wounds.
Us worn-out shattered cast-offs the military grabbed from them
to pinch-hit, proxy, spell, defend the land of liberty.
Our scrawny mass of hurts that moneybags
had held by slavish wage in dire subjection
in a land of milk and honey.
Us brave ones, who escaped the petty protocol
and pecking order of typing drudge
that builds up paper litter for triumphal whoop
when lads and laddies all return
to front page bacchanal.
Us brave ones who dared,
only to be battered by the boys in uniform
with rank, abuse, smear, sex and law, and with
identical coercion corporate servility employs.
Yeah. We had an audience, us girls.

Wendy Rondette

Final Dance

When it's time to die
you need to decide.
Think about how your life turned out
and think what your life was about.

Some people will weep
and want to be put to sleep.
Others will fill with laughter
and want to stay away from the hereafter.

Do you have a last request?
you better make it the best.
Remember it's your last chance
so you better have your final dance.

Karen E. Boucher

Mothers Day

One time a year the calendar marks,
a day to make moms proud
when you tell your mom, and your children tell you.
For their love and caring out loud.
When the fact of the matter each day and each night.
With every breath you take in and out
the love and the caring, giving, and sharing
is what every minutes about.
When you're apart for an hour or maybe more.
And you spend each second of time,
hoping and praying, worrying and saying.
"I'm sure that everything is just fine"
I hurry to see him, hug him and hold him
each morning when he shouts my name
when I look in the eyes of my little man,
I know that he feels the same.
When the last thing I hear each night is his voice
"Night, night mommy, loves you", he'll say
I know by the feeling beating in my heart
that everyday is Mothers Day

Holly J. Colbert

Happy Anniversary

On this our anniversary, I am reminded of years past.
Years filled with uncertainty.
Years of pain and growth that challenged us.
We stumbled, we fell...we stood united.
Those years belong to us forever.
And for that I cherish you.

On this our anniversary, I am living in the present.
Never tempted to look back.
I rejoice in how far we have come, and have no regrets.
You are the deepest part of me...and I, you.
My heart and my life are yours.

On this our anniversary, I await our future.
Never sure of what lies ahead,
I am only positive that we will face each day together.
In that thought there is serenity.
We have committed ourselves in blind faith, for that is what love is.
You are my world, and I adore you.

Karen Porter-Mendez

Here Kitty, Kitty!

Here kitty kitty! Come here and see me!
Here kitty kitty! Come down from that tree!
Come join me in fun. Come play for a while!
My, aren't you so cool. Ain't you got style!
Here's a feather to toss. Won't you come play.
Here's a big ball of yarn you can chase for the day.
You're always aloof. And you never will come
When I call you by name, to come and have fun.
You're so independent. Most cats are that way.
But, dog gone it cat, why don't you come play?
Here kitty kitty, oh, where are you hiding?
Here kitty kitty! Do you want to go riding?
Am I hearing a purr? It's getting so loud!
Come here silly cat, we are drawing a crowd.
Ya know what I think? What I really should do?
I should get me a dog. He'd always be true!
He'd always be faithful, and come when I call.
He'd come and play fetch with his own rubber ball.
But, I'm a cat kind of people. I must be a sap!
Oh, you finally came! Must be time for your nap?

Jan Harrison

Breaking Into Heaven

He sits at the keyboard while the city sleeps
He watches the screen of numbers roll by
Waiting patiently for the entry he is looking for
There it is! The passwords he has been waiting for
He mumbles to himself, "I'm in"

He is a Hacker
A group of people who seek information, for good or evil
Information: millions of bits of data
Hackers seek the information the is held back from us

Hackers: These people are separated not by race or sex
Nor are they separated by age or physical appearance
These select few are judged on what they say and do,
    the perfect society

Still they are condemned for their actions
These pioneers of the Cyber Frontier are becoming extinct
Killed by the people who own the information, and want to keep it
    from us

We are moving into a new generation
One where bits are appraised above atoms
Who will lead us into this new realm?
Who can provide us with the information we seek?
Hackers will

David Lazo

Harvest

A wintery sky gives way to rays of warmth and luminescence
To find its home on ice-cracked flesh, of barren stricken essence
A breath, a sigh, a golden hue A wounded one now healing
A rainy sky to cleanse and quench We all must share the feeling

Gather all both chaff and grain
The harvest time has come; 'tis the season of the sifting
Kingdom here Thy Will be done

A gentle wind combs fields anew A dance in celebration
The winged farmers buzzing brew Await the pollination
A mountain song sung high with praise A harmony unwavered
This time of joy alive with life A honeysuckle savored

Gather all both chaff and grain
The harvest time has come; 'tis the season of the sifting
Kingdom here
Thy Will be done

Gather all both chaff and grain
A miracle lies waiting
The time has come
The pain undone
In Love We're now creating

Anthony Miele

Hangover Horrors

I woke up one morning not too long ago
Hanging on tight to the bed
I drank too much liquor the night before
And had demons hard at work in my head

And right there beside me with a smile on her face
Lay a woman in a flimsy nightgown
She looked like she had fallen from an ugly tree
And hit every limb going down

She could have starred in a Frankenstein movie
Or won the world's ugly contest
I have never since looked at a bottle
But I will... when these demons rest.

Don R. Duganich

"Just Because"

Just because I'm a Girl
I'm not stupid
I might have better grades than you.
I'm not only worried about how I look.

Just because I'm a Girl
It doesn't mean that you are stronger
It doesn't mean that you are better at sports
It doesn't mean that you can boss me around.

Just because I'm a Girl
Who cares?
It doesn't matter if you are a girl or a boy.
It matters what is inside.

Barbara Bow

Dreams Or Memories

Blue sky, light fully clouds reflect in a river
    winding down from a mountain regal and tall
Rimmed by trees adorned with the colors of Fall

In my dreams, my soul alights once again
    to gaze at the wonderful sight
Wearing a long dress, crisp and bright

Holding a basket in one hand and a
    child with the other.
We stroll along on a shimmering sand
    loving the day and each other.

I raise my head and smile,
    looking towards that mountain high,
Knowing I will meet someone
    after a while.

Dreams or memories of things
    that used to be?
I will have to wait and see.

Norma Florence Gilbert

Stormy

It was stormy outside and the lightning was incredible.
I stood and listened as thunder rolled.
I could imagine how all things in nature must be watching.
The trees were bent and bowing graciously.
The birds found safe havens in their branches;
They were secure near the sturdy trunks.
Insects were clinging underneath leaves and blades of grass.
Cows were lowing in their pens, knowing it would pass.
All creatures waited. As did I
Knowing in all of life, storms do come, but they also pass
Leaving in their wake freshness, cleanliness,
and a newness felt once again.

Mauline Barker

Tigers

I come in two sets of colors,
Many other colors I do lack,
In zoos you can see both color sets of me;
My most natural set of colors are orange and black.

I'm covered in fur from head to tail.
Whiskers, a pink nose, a mouth, two little ears, and two eyes,
Are the main features of my face.
Four legs and paws, and I don't wave, even for goodbyes.

Many people believe that I'm mean,
It's not my fault other animals happen to be my prey;
I hunt them down for my meals,
But humans hunt me down, for no reason, every day.

David Richter

Nature's Bounty

As the waves broke and rippled onto the shore
I could feel the strength
the strength of an everlasting tug of war
Not brought upon by man
but solely by nature itself
destined to be conquered
and won
a war harmless to those around
Solely a breath of beauty to be taken in by a picture
and enjoyed for those to view season to season
year to year
from century back to century forth
nature's war of endless fury
battling upon the sands of time
telling a story, to each his own

Karen Thibeault

An End To Life

We take a walk through the grave yard.
The smell of moldy grass fill the air.
We view the martyr with tombstones broken and cracked.
The fog seems to rise as we proceed.
We can no longer see our feet.
Fallen limbs seem to grab our feet.
The old man statue guides our way.
A stillness fills the air.
Pain swells in my leg.
I tumble to the ground.
The stroke of pain causes me to scream.
As I rise up, I find myself alone.
My companion fled in horror of my scream.
I face the statue alone.

Mary A. Robinson

"An Allhallows Cheer"

Now comes All Saint's Day, Samhaine's fiery breath.
The season rolls over, and cold blows its breath.
So eyes to the dark-side of the reaper's slick scythe;
All who rot in their coffin were once surely alive.

They once drank with greed of life's wine and its song.
They thought the draught endless. Like us, they were wrong.
The laughter and fury now gone from cold throat,
They lend fetid feast to the worm and the stoat.

Then why celebration? What for not to grieve
This triumph of the worm on this Allhallows Eve?
We toast not our ultimate loss in death's heather.
We cheer consolation; we face it together.

A cheer to the fear! We shall pass through death's door!
Raise a tankard of ale to those gone before!
Then raise it again to those at your side!
Now drain it to those who will drink when you've died.

That is the cycle, and such is the season.
To laugh at the terror is just enough reason.
Fear now the coffin no more than your bed.
It is none but the living who raise toast to the dead.

Hugh Evan Gorman

Look Up

Don't be sad,
Don't be blue
A whole new life is waiting for you.

When your heart feels empty,
When your soul feels alone.
Look up to the heavens and the sun will shine
   And you will feel your home.

Life can bring heartache,
Life can bring pain.
But when you look back you realized it was wisdom
   That was gained.

We all have a spirit,
We all have a soul.
If you look to God for all the answers,
   He will show you your goal.

Regina Young

Footprints In Time

Where do they lead? I wonder!
Those footprints in the endless sands.
They have spanned seas and touched ancient lands;
Begun, perhaps, amid the fire and thunder.
When chaos reigned and hills were torn asunder.
They inched from the sea with kindred minds and hands,
Desperation formed the mass brigands;
To awkward plod, mid fallacy and plunder.

The campsites where they rested know their treasure.
The pyramids, their wisdom can but speak.
The legacies they left are without measure,
And knowledge they forgot, today we seek!
Led by Pharaohs, Chieftains, Kings and Tsars,
Marching from the sea to reach ... The Stars!

Ellen B. Garcia

"Revelations"

Someone, at sometime, somewhere, somehow,
Once thought that she was on the outside looking in.
Until she came to realize,
She was on the inside looking out.
At the revelry and debauchery going on,
Never thinking to join in;
But wondering if she's missing anything.
As wondrous thoughts of glorious things happening,
Sadness sometimes envelopes her,
Thinking that she is missing out.
Alas one day she came to realize,
Nothing. Oh but nothing, has she missed.
Her soul remained pure and pristine,
Preserved like a child's.
Though no place in the world can she really fit in,
Except to stand on the inside looking out.

Annette Kisling

Earth

The beauty fades away as each second passes.
She constantly struggles . . . a struggle to survive.
She doesn't want to die,
but her life approaches its end as each day passes.

Still . . . she holds on to love,
For the love of life is greater.
She knows the end is near,
But the triumph of life makes her stronger.

The end appears near . . . but the battle is not over
It goes on forever.

Aristeo Rubio

Fishing In Fall

Leaves, leaves in the brook.
Here come those spotted crooks.

Now they have taken the bait
There is no more,
So I walked a mile
To the nearest store.

Upon my return I had not a bite.
But then, all of a sudden
The line became tight.

As I reeled the fish in again, it got away.
So I packed up my gear for a better day.

When I got home, to a cooked bowl of Sauerkraut
I thought how much better it would have tasted
with one of those ol' speckled trout.

Robert Craig Corrington

Last Will

What can I leave you, my children?
What can I give you, kids of my kids,
to soothe your hurt, to heal your pain,
to cushion the blows when the moonlight wanes?

The ring that I leave you with dazzling stones
is cold as a bone picked clean.
The coat, velvet collared, is sleek and soft.
Can it nourish your dream?

Items of value, bought and sold,
traded, paraded, can never hold
the joy of a birdsong, the roses you plant,
a kiss or a tickle. They can't.

Better to hear the music of the stars,
feel the sun on your face, than run a race.

The fun of your giggle,
the warmth of your kiss, I'll miss.

What can I leave you, my children?
There is only love.

Elaine Denholtz

Untitled

The seed catalogs were stacked haphazardly, leading my mind
backwards.
The freshly turned soil, rich and black under the windows.
Catalogues and seed packets ordered by the back door,
And the garden trowel leaning against the wall.

Giggles and cries of laughter echoing around and around
Chasing the shadows from forgotten places of my mind,
Driving each memory to bound and break before my eyes
Returning me to a simpler time.

Watching lean hands turn and work the soil, guiding my smaller ones.
The sun blocked from my sight when he stands and smiles
Before bending down to work the ground once more
In a time past remembering.

Now I am the gardener, blocking the sun and turning the soil,
Guiding another child in the art of growing plants.
The original hands are stilled now, but on the memories grow.
As I work the ground with my father's trowel.

Dianna Short

Life As I See It

Though we see the prophecies of what's foretold, we still go on with
our so called incurable ways. And still we know that tomorrow is
never promised. We live for what could be, not what is.

You see the lowly homeless, a starving child and only pause for a
second and then keep walking. Never stopping to think that one day
we could be the ones that everyone's passing by, taunting saying
get a job: but who knows what lie's behind the eyes of someone.

Any one can carry the torch to victory, so who are we to judge, we're
only men. When the day comes for ourselves to be judged, will we
have a clear past? Will our record be untouched, no red mark on the
diary of our soul?

Follow the path which was laid long ago. For one man gave his life
so we could live. Keep the heart pure the tongue laid at rest. Harsh
words not spoken are like undrawn swords.

Bob Nolan Coward

Emotions

I can see the sunset over the ocean.
The sky is a bright golden red,
and the sun seems to touch the sea.
I feel the warmth of the sun on my face
as the sun becomes one with the ocean.

The waves crashing on the rocks below,
the wind talking to me.
I can understand what it said to me,
and the song of the sea gulls as they fly above the splendor of
   the evening.

The salt air as it cleanses my breath.
It refreshes me and brings me to a tranquil state of emotion.
A state in which I can express myself to the world and myself.

The freedom of my words and actions
as I release myself from the chains that keep me silent.

I can feel the sand beneath my feet as I walk across the sandy desert
   of my life
smooth and gentle, able to be molded,
or drift away in the wind that passes me by.

I am the keeper of my heart, emotions, and sorrows
and shall decide what happens to me now and forever.

Hector M. Rosa III

Untitled

Dear Lord when I die,
please take me above,
for I shall see the ones that I love.

Lord hold me in your beautiful kingdom
where there are so many wonderful things,
and I can hear all the birds' pretty songs.

Lord fill me with your greatful amounts of
laughter, and assure me that my hopes and
dreams will come faster.

Lord
I give my life, my love, and my spirit to you.

Alicia Smith

Untitled

God has placed his hands on you;
You are his chosen one;

There is a time and place for everything;
Everything under the sun;

God has called you to do his blessed will;
No matter what anyone thinks or how bad others may feel;

You try to run and sometimes hide;
But by his rules we have to abide;

Where he leads me I will go;
No matter what rain or snow;

There is but one and only one;
That we his children are trying to please;

So my dear, dear friend stay steadfast,
Unmovable and always on your knees;

Because God give ear to the righteous
And hear you when you pray;

Hang on, Hang on, Hang on dear friend,
Because your help is on the way;

Naomi Barnes

Snowflakes

See the fairy-like shower of white
Floating, swirling bits of cloud
Whitening the forests and earth below
Joy to the kids playing snow games
Nightmare to stranded mountain climbers
Delight to skiers, sledders and snow shoers
Fright to foraging, hungry animals
Inspiration firing the mind of painters
Walkers' fear of ice beneath its coat
A melting snow swelling rivers over-night
Overflowing and covering the countryside
Flooding roadways, farms and homes
This fluffy shower of crystal snowflakes
Piles up by wind, burying all in its wake

Steven J. Shaw

Guard My Angel

Angel watching over, don't let this be the end.
You reached out to protect before,
please try to help again.

Her trust lies in your wings that soar.
Her faith lies in his might.
Her trust will never waiver, her faith will not deplore.

Guardian Angel, cradle her this night,
hold her in the darkness;
help her win her second fight.

Angel in your highness,
lift her up for him to bless;
grant her the embrace of our Lord's caress.

Janna Tomecsek

Six Week Love

You were the spark
that ignited my fire,

You fanned the flames
until I came to life.

Like a wildfire we were,
burning out of control.

Suddenly the wind changed,
and so did you.

You doused me with the water of your fears
and left me a slow dying ember.

Now all that remains
are the ashes of my heart.

Cathy M. Thompson

Lessons Of A Lifetime

The prairies are empty, Fields covered with dust
Where eagles once roamed the land like the stars in the sky
I sit and watch the sun fade away to nothingness
Nothingness

As the moon draws to the center of a starless sky, I sit
So many things they teach us
And so many stay untaught
Emotions in my heart are fireworks in the midnight sky

The mist encloses me and I see her
With skin like soft roses blooming in the springtime air
Her hair like silk blowing in the summertime wind
Thoughts of seasons long past, and a heart as cold as ice

It is then that I realize that to every creature there is a pattern
To the fish, it is the current of the streams
To the birds, it is the freedom of the skies
To life, it is a puzzle of mist

I'm reminded of the task that lays at hand, the unplaced pieces
    of the puzzle
So guided by the moonlight, the memories fade away

Benjamin J. Wolf

Ellis Island

Thick, thick
musty with tobacco and sweat and old linen

Feel the press of hope

See weary eyes with deep lines
tired crying infants' smell of urine
ragged huddled families with bundled belongings

Feel the press of hope

Get in line
Wait your turn
Process through
The haggard raw clay that shaped America

Feel the press of hope

But this building is empty
high ceilings - worn walls - vacant benches
No use - no use now!
High dirty windows let in warm light

Oh yes! Feel still the press of hope

Margaret Radzilowski

What Is Happening In Our World?

Round and round the world goes.
What has happened do you suppose?
Why the Hate, Why the Sorrow?
Don't put it off, and wait for tomorrow.

Too bad most people don't care.
It is the truth they really cannot bare.
Out there, there's a continuous war.
It doesn't stop, there is always more.

Happy are the people who do the good.
They hope for the best, everyone should.
What ever happened to them, I don't know.
Those kind of people are starting to go.

Now, this is the right time,
To go and speak what's on your mind.
You, yourself, can be the voice,
To help people make the right choice.

Emily Christine Gilles

Tracks

You only pass over them once
Each time being careful not to fall
on the tracks

Taking each step one at a time, as it comes
balancing and looking
before crossing the next rail

Some might be bumpy
Some might be smooth
Some might be that had
never been expected

You may fall off the tracks
and lose your way
but in time you will find the right track
and get right back on it

All the while struggling each time
to get to the next rail
that each step further taken
the closer you get to reaching the next rail
Then find yourself
in your longing destination

Heena Lakhani

First Dream

It seems so far away,
But it was only yesterday
That I had my first dream:
  I was in a creature war
  Which took place in an apple core.

  It was a war of worms and of bees,
  And of ants and of fleas.

  What could I do to protect myself
    from these creatures,
  For they will soon be upon me to
    partake of my features...

I'll never know how this dream ended
Or if the creatures ate me: "the apple seed."

For suddenly I was awakened by a hen,
Which sat outside my den.

Robert Key Poundstone

Hidden Meaning

Windows to the soul, they say
But I don't see a thing.
Two dark orbs latch to mine;
But what does it really mean?

By themselves they don't do much
But rather need those close at hand.
Those who open and close, rise and furrow,
Or crinkle merrily on command.

For that, I understand.
I don't see daggers, ice, or flames;
And nothing sparkles or shines
Like noonday rays.

So, windows?
Maybe; but not to me.
For when I look at them,
Only stained-glass I do see.

Elizabeth R. Carson

Deep Within

Although you are so far away
In a place I dare not say.
Thoughts of you are deep within,
For me to hold again and again.

So memories I will hold
Through summer's heat and winter's cold,
And boldly will I stand in place
Until the day I see your face.

When times seem hard and you cannot bare,
Remember us who really care.
There's always a place to begin,
That place of course is deep within

James Avery

Everyday

Homeless people in the street
old worn shoes around their feet.
Deadly emissions are released in the air
smog shrouds the sky the day is called fair.
Soldiers in foreign countries awaiting a war
patiently sitting not knowing what for.
Trash being tossed here, everywhere
a mountain of refuse we all add our share.
Gang-member juvenile you see him frown
innocent people being shot down.
Mistreated children and battered wives
abusive fathers shattering their lives.
Through it all
I think of you
behind the smog the sky is blue.

Fernando Centeno

My Honey

My honey is a girl who is very pretty
When she gets home she likes to pet her kitty.

Krissy Meuer's her name, but I call her honey
When I don't have any she loans me money.

I love it when she gives me a kiss
that is something I never want to miss.

I love her greatly with all of my heart
I don't think we will ever be apart

This was a poem, not very funny
It's more about love I call it my Honey.

Derek Sullivan

Out Of The Night

Out of the night, a vibrant dawn;
Death's darkest hour is now long gone.
In dawn, time and space can't intrude
The interior plight,
The exterior mood.

No longer lost, searching for sight,
Floundering through an endless night.
I now stand tall, head off the ground;
Supported by past dreams,
Searched for, but never found.

Still people with their varied schemes,
Try to destroy those star-crossed dreams.
But in the dawn I fin'lly see,
My dreams alone are true;
Only they set me free.

Andrew Hoying

Untitled

Walking hand in hand across the ocean's sand
Watching the tide rise high, then fall low
Our love is like a wave that never stops to grow
And when our love comes crashing down
We pick up the pieces spread all around
We got a love that will keep us together
And it's gonna last forever
With that love that will never end
We'll pass it down to our children
As tears go by and it's time for them to go
We'll know in our hearts their love will flow
We passed down a love that will keep them together
And it's gonna last forever

Amanda Hudson

Letter To Heloise

I know many a washday hint,
how to soften water, get rid of lint.
But one thing no book has ever unravelled,
what happens to the one sock that has travelled?

The holes in the drum are so tiny, so small,
a sock, be it short, medium or tall
cannot glide through; be the water lower or higher.
But the sock gets lost, so call me a liar!

In the laundry I think of Noah
who at Ararat counted two sheep, two boa.
I hold up one Argyle, one Tartan.
Neither one can I wear with my Doc Marten.

My feet are not protected from my shoes,
You might well laugh, 'till one sock you lose.
The loners lie in a bag which weekly grows bigger.
How do their lost mates return? You go figure!

I'm only accepting foolproof solutions.
Or hence there'll be no more ablutions
Of clothes worn below the knees,
So, make it soon please, dear Heloise.

Tanya Hochschild

The Devil's Hour

It is midnight once more and I am alone
Amongst shadows that haunt me
To the very depth of my soul.
I am kept awake by these beauteous apparitions
Who appear to be messengers from hell,
Fallen angels whose visages I cannot perceive,
Crying out my name with voices echoing in the darkness.
"Stay away!" I should say but I cannot
For they have me trapped in an embrace
So sweet it would be death to break free from it.
I force my eyes shut only to be tormented
By their persistent clamor calling to me
Like the sirens that they are
Tempting me like the devil does with lavish gifts,
Promise they cannot keep, but most of all,
Offering themselves to be mine for all eternity.

And when the devil's hour ends,
The imps return to the deep dark hole
From whence they came and silence lulls me to sleep.
Sweet, sweet sleep.

Franz R. Tempongko

Dreams Of Sanity?

Turbulent water
Thunderstorm crashing down
I struggle
Keeping my head barely above
Murky waters pulling me down
Black spiraling nightmare
Unavoidably caught in the whirlpool
I fight, to no avail
I concede, only to become engulfed
Dragged further under
Losing myself I learn
Heading out, I swim through
Till once again head is above water
Light shines down from a crack in the sky
I discover the wings I had all along
Stretching them out
I soar above
Leaving the waters of normality forever below
Vowing never to return to its madness.

Jodi Schneider

"Freedom"

Born here in this wretched place,
With tortured expressions upon our face.
I am but a weakened rose
Thirsting for the water and love not giv'n.
And [they] are the thorns
Which were borne in my side.
But I will have the strength to surpass
The whips and chains — the stormy blast.
For the Lord will hold me in the palm of His hand;
He will carry me through and through.
An I will one day be as free as the eagle,
Which flies o'er the peaceful earth.

Now, as I think back to those days,
I know the true meaning of freedom — remembering it always.
The thirst for water and love has at last been filled;
This once weakened rose is now full and strong-willed.
Those wasted years have come to pass;
For now I sing a song of joy...

Freedom At Last!

Janet Buford

Buried In Pain

From the depths of my heart,
My mind began to start,
My soul lay buried deep,
Beneath pain too much to keep.

The wounds I tried to hide,
With food and walls of pride,
But when my heart bled out,
Ugliness began to shout.

After years of harm untold,
My spirit had no mold,
Submerged inside of me,
Pleading to burst free.

My precious Lord delivered me,
From the den of iniquity,
My spirit was finally free,
For eternal life in glory!

Peggy Brigman Hearne

Life

Calm and peaceful is my soul.
No wind can stir this part of me.
No quarrel or worry will enter.
My sleep, calm and peaceful

Hurrying all around
wiping the sweat from my brow
Time flutters by.

A speck of dust,
Finding nowhere to land,
is swept around.

We all return to dust.

Sandra A. Silvia

Boil Evil

Under your body I struggle;
I writhe and scream beneath.

You've violated my trust,
Violated any remaining love.

Making me hate you.
Making me violent.
Making the rage inside burn with hate;

Bubbling over, exploding.
Spilling its violent, hateful contents
All over your body,
Scalding you and your violations.

Rebecca Clark

Sunset

And again the sun kisses
the Great Salt Lake bay,
Seemingly saying "I hope
all had a nice day."
There are beautiful color rays
that filter through a single cloud,
A big bright orange fire,
So bold, so proud.
The darkening mountains
get a fore warning,
I'll be hovering over you
come tomorrow morning.
Where else in all the
universe, could you get,
Such a mood moving God's
creation, we call a sunset?

R. Joel Bright

Who?

Who can stand in evil's face
And help mankind run its race?
His name is Grace.
Who reigns in majesty
Yet stoops to hear the human plea?
His name is Humility.
Who helps the struggling soul to cope
Holds the anchor, steadies the rope?
His name is Hope.
Who gives us daily breath
Leads us through chilling death?
His name is Faith.
Who reigns supreme above?
Who has power we know not of?
Emmanuel! His name is Love.

Beverly Joyce

Hollow

Hear the winds
Blowing through my empty heart
Feel the push of the pins
Splitting me apart

No blood to spill
Too hollow to feel
No hopes to fill
No need to heal

So hollow am I
Without any feeling
Tears used up, can't cry

I lost myself to this girl
Beautiful like a pearl
But she stole my heart
Like jewelers would a clam
So hollow I am

Ron Cheng

The Playing Of Hearts

I use to think that love
Was just a game
I swore I wouldn't do it
But it's always the same

There is no meaning
To the words I say
And with your emotions
Is just something I play

I say I love you
But tear you in two
And there is nothing left
When I am through

I take everything you own
Including your heart and soul
I'm a whirlwind of fantasies
But soon you will feel the toll

I've been called names
In all different parts
But most of all
I'm called the "Queen of Hearts"

Melissa Dyal

Limerick Called, "Kayak Zach"

The once was a man named Zach
Who bought a brand new kayak.
So he left from Nebraska,
and went to Alaska,
but his paddle he forgot to pack.

Robert J. Fitzpatrick

J.T.T.

J -is for the jolt I feel
when I awake from dreaming of you.

T -is for the terror I'd
feel if you weren't in this world.

T -is also for the temptations
for your beautiful, sparkling,
blue eyes, and blondish, brown hair.

Alice Odom

He Did It Once

He did it once
We didn't tell her
He did it again
This time we told her

She cried, but
She kept him.
He lied, but
She let him.

He broke her heart once,
But she took him back.
We told her the truth,
But she turned her back.

What can we do
To make her see
His love is only
Imaginary.

We are her best friends,
Better than he
And unlike him we'll
Love her unendingly.

Kelly S. Jaeger

Sometimes

Sometimes in my mind
I reach out.
To the past,
to the future,
to places I'm not.

And I wonder why I'm not there.
And what it is that makes me
want to be there.

Sometimes I wonder,
"Why can't I be somewhere else,
someone else?"
"Why am I where I am
and not where I wish I was?"

Maybe sometimes
people see me and wish they were
where I was.

Maybe I should want to be
where I am.

Martin A. Shepherd

What Is?

What is blue? The water is blue,
When you put it in a shoe.
What is green? Slime is green,
When it's in your sister's spleen.
What is white? Mold is white,
When it is not polite.
What is red? Blood is red,
When it's spewing out your head.

Eric Koenigsknecht

Twilight Green

When the grass grows greener
and the night sets in
You're in my heart
and my soul gives in

My mind longs for you -
for us - and then
I fall into myself
and thoughts of back when

Before I let us be
more than only friends
How empty life appeared
now emotion transcends

Far beyond the transparent
to the twilight green
That can't be reproduced
and is so rarely seen

Vikki W. Thresher

Too Soon

Too soon the time just slips away.
The seasons come and go.
Our lives are spent in such a hurry.
Where did they go?
We flitter here and flitter there with
    thoughts of fulfillment in mind.
Instead, stop and look around
    to see what you find.
Enjoy what you see, for time waits
    for no man.
Our lives are set to flee.
We are here for a reason just stop!
    And think what for.
A little kindness to our fellow
man, will make our lives and
stay here worth more.

Mary Ann Farmer

I Hear

In the quiet of my mind
I hear nothing
But the beating of my heart

In the quiet of my mind
I hear nothing
But my thoughts.

Sometimes one or many
Sometimes good and bad
Sometimes satisfaction and contentment
Sometimes guilt and remorse.

Could it be the voice of my soul,
The voice of a higher power?
In the quiet of my mind
I hear something.

Donna Reed

My Journey Discovering Christ

I never knew who Christ was
Until I asked my mother
She said he was the Son of God
I thought he was my brother

Until one day I started to pray
I saw a light that shined.
That solemn day, I'm proud to say
That Christ had entered my mind.

Stephanie V. Brown

The Soldier

Then the man stumbled
    And the thorned crown
They had placed on him
    Made blood gush from his forehead
To cover our sins.

When they nailed him to the cross
    A soldier sank to his knees
This man he thought was evil
    Now became his king!

Then the shaking lips
    High upon the cross,
Forgave them of what they'd done
    Until that life was gone.

Then the soldier fought the tears
    That threatened to come down
Then he raised his arms up to the sky
    And said, "Surely, this man was God."

Rebekah Dement

Epitaph Of A Lost Soldier

I'm sorry I died...
Leaving you empty inside,
But that will not hide
My love for thee.

Keep on keeping on.
Do not keep weeping on,
For one day we will meet again.

In your heart, strong and warm
My love for you will be...
Protecting you from all the harm;
Staying safe 'till you meet me.

Keep on keeping on.
Do not keep weeping on,
For one day we will meet again.

Mary L. Kaliszewski

Come To Me

O Jesus, my treasure, come to me,
Transport my heart in ecstasy
Come Jesus, and teach my soul
The knowledge of sweet docility.

Come to me, O Divine Guest
And your holy gifts impart.
There is always room for you
In the shelter of my heart.

Come to me, O Divine Light
Shine in my intellect, my memory.
Purify my sorry thoughts
That I may love you more worthily.

Come into my heart Sweet Jesus,
Keep my gaze fixed on you.
Strengthen me, O Divine Heart,
Come and lift me up to you.

Celina C. Oakes

Fondly For Family

I wish I could write a poem
That would say all I want it to say
It would speak of my on-going love
And my thoughts of you every day
But alas! I am tongue-tied
And pen-dried
Too deep are the roots to convey.

Betty Jane McClain

Think Before You Think...

To behold a beauty
is to know the woman,
To show the woman
You know the woman.
Yet knowing is knowing,
True love she's showing,
As together you're growing;
Kisses he's blowing.
Poetry he's flowing,
or better yet going
out to the show
or walking nice and slow.
As time gets to know,
Unique even though,
She looks up and oh,
He looks down below...

The Comforter...
Lenzell M. Rhodes

"Picking Daisies"

Hello there.
I couldn't help but notice
you flaunting yourself.
I think you're very beautiful,
but answer me one question:
How can something so radiant
survive in a world so dim?
Something tells me there's more...
More than the delicate shell
in which you hide.
Allow me to see the inner strength
that permits you to reach for the sun.
With your feet planted firmly,
and your head wandering,
you establish an impeccable balance.
However, do you not become curious
as to what lies beyond?
Go. Free yourself and explore,
but please, do not forget
to take me with you.

Christopher Pellicciaro

Remember The Day

Remember the day we first
met? I'll never forget, the
warmth in the color of your
eyes, as beads of sweat dance
about your nose.

Remember the day your
smile made my heart stand
still? I sometimes hear the
whispers of your voice say
I love you, with eyes
closed I feel your touch.

Remember the day we
kissed? What passion it was
I watched the look on your
face while we embrace.
The motion of our bodies
Make fluid flow like the
River Niger; remember the day

Bernadeen Cole

Praise God!

Let us praise our Lord in the morning
When everything goes tip top;
As "busy bees", let us praise Him,
As we find a moment to stop-
To commune with Him, in silence,
Or to sing His praise in the soul;
Let us pray that others may know Him,
Let us make winning souls our goal:

Let us praise our Lord for salvation,
Through His blood shed at Calvary;
Belief brought us into His family,
And by His redemption we're free!
Let us praise Him when trial cometh,
And march with His banner unfurled,
Praise Him in every circumstance,
He has overcome the world!

Grace A. Bunt

Love Mother And Father

I love my mother dearly, she's
sweet as she can be; I think many
hours she worries over me.

But what about my daddy, I love
him just as well; the love I
have for both of them no
human tongue can tell.

Some people speak of mother and
never speak of dad, but take
it to yourself and think it hurts
him mighty bad.

Who works the very hardest to do
his best for you; who sets the
food upon the table, it's left
for dad to do.

Oh yes! I love my daddy
and I can truly say; if there
ever was a Christian my
daddy's one to-day.

Helen R. Moody

Destiny

Thus the last beauty
   laid in my arms

I felt the wind
   gently blowing
into my ear

As I laid
   my first
my last
   and only love
to rest.

A white rose
   the only existing
one of its kind

Until a war had come
   between
this lovely soul's
   eternity

But somehow
   it's destiny
for all of us.

Krista Singh

Kittens

Kitties are kind
and oh so sweet
they love to cuddle
and make you warm
when there is no heat

They are so playful
and so fun
they love to sleep
especially in the sun

I love my cat
Pebbles is her name
she is the best in the world
In my heart she came

Carissa Mann

The End

The end is coming.
The end is near.
Scattered minds,
Are troubled with fear.
Have fear not,
For the world will fall,
And leave you with nothing,
Nothing at all.
Blinding lights,
Forces so strong.
There's nothing you can do,
For it won't be long.

Josh Swindell

Penguins

Deep in dark
Antarctica
They waddle away
In their tuxedos,
Black ties and tails.
These little butlers
Who wait patiently
For a month
Of sun days.
Taking dips,
Dripping,
Flipping
Flippers,
Flopping,
Belly whoppers
Keeping cool
At 40 below
Keeping everything
On ice.

Nicole Ann Haverland

Why?

The moon rises
And sets in
A dark blue sky.
Tell me why.
He listens, but
He does not
Hear the lie.
Tell me why.
You and I flock
Together like
The bird and the fly
And I know why!

Kaite Duff

Untitled

How much I seek,
Yet rarely find
Answers to questions
Which fill my mind.

How close I come
It always seems,
The vaguest whispers
Of bygone dreams.

Still I go on
The truth can't hide
From what I feel,
So deep inside.

How sweet it is,
When Light shines through,
And darkness fades
From answers true.

James Steimling

The Architect

Inspiring thoughts are eternal.
The insight is magnified through time,
Driven by a passion unseen,
Committed to a purpose uncontested.
Perfection is attainable.
The design must be without flaw,
As eyes perceive lacking knowledge.
The cast is broke,
Production reveals the concept.
Thought and mass are one.

David B. Post

Snake's Eye View

Do you ever wonder why,
Are there even snakes that fly,
I will tell you this is true,
the snakes that fly are even Blue.

I went for a walk last night,
eat a frog a mouse, I might,
but I wanted something new,
something blue, not a shoe, silly you.

Even then and even now,
I get stepped on by a cow,
I must go and eat some frogs,
and try to keep away from dogs.

John R. Groh Jr.

"For Love Of Mary"

I love you more
   Than you'll ever know
More than a kiss
   Could ever show
There are no words
   That could ever express
I give you all my love
   And nothing less
Emotions set free
   By your loving touch
I never knew love
   Could offer so much
With your gentle kiss
   My heart beats anew
All as reminders
   Of how much I love you

Edward L. Aronson

Untitled

When dangerous minds are flying high
You never know who will die.
Drugs are killing by the million,
Kids are dying without even trying.
Hopeless are the dreams
That always seemed
To keep us going
Without us knowing
Who we are
But we are far,
Far from all hope
Of knowing how to cope.
They could kill us all
Without us knowing we are going to fall
The pit is so wide,
How will we all hide?
When the light turns to dark
We cannot mark
The love that was felt
On such a glorious day.

Samantha Elenbaas

Almond Eyes

She was small and pure
With eyes like almonds
Her very soul was love
   Deep and tender

She touched me
And I touched her
Then I cried eternally
This world was not for her

She fell suddenly
And fear was on her face
I touched her then
And security took its place

The child was innocence
Too soon would it fade
The laughter of a child
Upon the bleeding earth was laid

She was small and pure
With eyes of almonds
Her very soul was love
   Deep and tender

Martin R. Higley

Palette Of Wind

Gales whistle cobalt and slate-grey
   between bare branches.
I observe sap beneath the bark.

Zephyrs, chartreuse and citrine, puff
   among fresh leaves.
I discern swelter under the foliage.

Breezes waft azure and ivory
   through sultry arbors.
I perceive harvest behind the blossoms.

Gusts, auric and burnt orange, bluster
   amid sparsely clad boughs.
I behold slumber below the roots.

Winds inhale onyx and alabaster
   exhale claret and verdant
   wind afflate life full circle.
We cycle without end.

Grover C. Wilson III

Untitled

Love is like the springtime.
New and old in many ways
Love is like the sunshine,
Peeking through on rainy days
Love is like a mountain top,
Looking out across the land
Love is like the Lord,
Always near to lend his hand
Love is like a mother's arms,
When your heart is full of fright
Love is like a candle's flame,
On a dark and weary night
Love is like a feeling
Between a father and a son
Love is like today
When two shall become one.

Don Crosby

Scent Of An Angel

I prayed to God this morning
Help me make it through this day;
Give me tolerance and patience
In whatever comes my way.

Without you Lord I'm helpless
Just can't make it on my own;
" Could you send me down an angel?"
Lord I feel so all alone.

No sooner had these words been said
A peace came over me;
My prayers had just been answered,
" Was my angel here with me?"

In turning very quickly
I saw no one was there;
But a sweet unknown aroma
Very briefly filled the air.

Someone definitely was present
Though I didn't see her then;
Lord, I know that was the angel
I had prayed for you to send.

Gary Buchanan

Happiness

In a quiet, dark room
I am listening,
but nothing around me
is whispering.

In this quiet, dark room
I sit without light.
I strike a match,
for a glimpse of sight.

The flame from the match
has begun to dance,
and my surroundings
have become enhanced.

The match it burns,
but only for a minute,
and the quiet, dark room,
I'm back in it.

Christopher J. Ledford

Like A Rose

Like a Rose I want to
grow into a beautiful person
I want the world to take
notice and say there's a
young lady with beauty
written all over her

For you see I want my
personality to shine out bright
before everyone so they will
know that I'm like a city
that sit upon a hill shinning
ever so bright

Like a Rose I want to be
notice that everyone will
see the God in me the
glow of his beauty will
forever shine in me.

Vanderlyn Hawkins

"What Are The Effects Of Abuse?"

What are the effects of abuse?
Would they be told outright?
Are they echoing through the streets,
Or being displayed at night?

What is the proper season?
Could winter be the right mood?
Or spring, when souls are vulnerable,
Searching for their inner food!

Maybe loneliness is a big issue,
That all could be wrapped around,
Or satisfying that outer man,
Where creativity can be found.

What are the effects of abuse?
Only the ones that know can identify,
Where one may lose their self-worth,
Or their inner self being crucified.

To leave you a memory of the effects,
Where love and passion is no more,
Maybe you can make the difference,
To reopen that inner door!

Riva L. Green

Loneliness

Like the darkness
loneliness falls all around
Water to life
We must grow
For ever alone
I don't want to die alone
never looking at thou
heart grows old
time grows slow
My life is short
Love is gone
Alone alas on to part
The shadow of death grows near
I think time and time again
Still with out a friend
Time comes to a stop
I breath my last breath
My heart is alone
Alas I die alone
Alone Alone Alas

Aaron Lee Gardner

Clouds

Let me join you in the journey
  to fly high in the limitless sky
    to see the enchanting beauty
    which takes my breath away.

Let me join you in the journey
  to hear no crime
    to feel no time
    to see no boundaries
    to play with moon and stars
    to touch the purity
    and to get the serenity.
     Ramani S. Pilla

The Calming Of Will

The events of becoming
Day and night fall,

The heart and mind contend
The tender winds do call.

The love swelling in my heart
Shocks thy own stern will,

The destiny unknown
Of my gift to feel.

Striving for the utmost
A balance of both worlds,

Heaven and earth emotions
So intensely inside they swirl.

The art of the flowers
And the spirit of the sun,

Can't seem to ignore the beauty
I'm trying to run from.

The eyes they are seeing
So many hearts beating,

The truth is unfolding
And with God comes a meeting.
    Karen Miller

My Sea Slug

(Little Billy Bob:)
My sea slug isn't snugly
But I don't think it's ugly
Because it's just a sea slugly!
I keep him in a pan
I feed him when I can.
And when he dies,
oh, I won't cry,
I'll just fry him in a frying pan.
But soon he'll be too big
to be fed a tiny fig
I don't know what he will eat.
Maybe a piece of pizza for a treat,
or just a...
AHHHH!!
(sea slug:)
Slurp!! BURP!!
    Ashley Vigneaux

Untitled

The fluidity of the body
the fluidity of the mind
love in a caress
whispered to the flesh
to the but a man
and know the divine
  Brinton Smith

Him

Forlorn strays wander my way
Searching for a hint of companionship
Yet, his image haunts my memory.
I look into the face of strangers
and know the eyes are not his.
A part of him dwells inside me
as if I've known him before.
Our minds have connected-
Though our bodies have never met.
Someday,
his eyes will be more than an image,
they will be reality.
I will hold him and know he is the one.
    Amy Strong

The Dream Man

I am the dream man. You
can find me in sleep land.
When you close your eyes
you bring me out. I don't
get high. Drugs is not my
thing. I'm the work man.
I get into your head. Every
night at 5. Working on your
mind. Boys and girls. Don't
get high. Getting high will
not make you a big guy
or a big girl. It will pull
you down to the ground.
And no one will give a damn.
When you're down and out. No
one gives a damn. So let's
get real. Please keep me. In
your dream and you
will be cool. Good night boys
and girls. I have to leave
you.
    Edith McGee

Rapunzel

Fear, the faithful, fickle thread;
bound upon our childish dread:
Rapunzel! Rapunzel!
No fortune thou to bear.

Nigh, the hour of truth approaches;
Chill, the night forsooth encroaches:
Rapunzel! Rapunzel!
Thy parting wreaks despair!

To pine for thee;
To weep for thee!
What yonder story springs?
From twixt thine lips an epitaph
for days thy fancy brings!

Rapunzel, Rapunzel?
Is't merely thou hast flown?
Do eastern sunsets fill thine dreams,
or none save mine alone?
    Rocco A. D'Andrea

I Love My Mom

I love my mom.
I love my mom.
I love my mom
Because she loves me.
That is why
I love my mom.
    T. J. Wheeler

The Beginning - The End

In the far, far reach of infinity,
beyond our vaulted heaven's dome,
dwell the ones we call the Trinity...
it's where the Masters make their home.

And amid that blazing splendor
lies the womb where life begins,
spreading 'crost all space to render
life on earth, with all its sins..

The intelligence that we're given
is like a tiny hidden seed
that will flourish when we're driven
to develop... to succeed.

But intelligence and morality
can sometimes be a world apart
and be the cause of our brutality...
just a brain without a heart.

So this earth we take for granted -
that we keep in disarray,
and the good life that we wanted
the Masters, yet, may take away!
    R. L. Davis

Cornered

I look out my window
  to anger and shame.
I stare in the mirror
  and know who to blame
My past is beclouded
  by shadows and black
Afraid to look forward
  ashamed to look back
Deep within my soul are
  secrets that I hide.
Confessions, emotions
  forever locked inside.
Living life in darkness
  always looking for a light
Needing hands to guide me
  through this cruel, endless night.
The savage whip of rejection
  butchers and beats my soul.
Now this battle for survival-
  is all about control.
    Roger Fawcett

The Storm

The bruised clouds weep in despair-
Hesitating to start again.
The drums roll and the chimes ring:
Waiting for the signal.
The black dress of night bends
The sky, as the carriage awaits.
    Haley Bone

The Angel

The angel smiles and the heavens are
aglow with her beauty.
She sings and the breeze is
Softened by her voice.
She laughs and all my cares
Fade into the night.
Her bright eyes show me the love
That I could not live without
She asks "Do you love me?" and
My heart pounds with the joy
of the love of one girl and one boy.
    Michael Mills

April

It was a rainy month of April,
April showers, bring May flowers
I know this month like a drill,
For my love flows like a shower.
For it's not only the Holidays
It's the Birthday of my soul mate
Holidays are only Special days
But a birthday, is to celebrate.
Not too fancy, not too plain
For the memory, is the joy
There's nothing he won't gain
Knowing all he sees is his toy
To brighten his day, I will
For the world is at his feet
Just the thought gives me a chill
For the momentum, my heart beats.

Sue Carrillo

Junking

Man's history, just inside the door,
in bits and pieces: buttons, books,
portraits fading at the edges —
eyes gazing out unblinkingly
with hope, with promise.

Fragments of disintegration,
no use to the present, no use to
the future — unclaimed — except
the frame around that face.
"Perfect above the sofa."

Lu Reese

"Alone"

Tears of pain out loud I cry
to tired to live, to scared to die
Expectations to be met, and still
myself to find
Struggling to get ahead to only fall
behind.
Afraid to be alone, wont try
to be accepted
I'd rather be alone than to
be rejected
I'm now use to the taste of tears
and not being part
I just can't deal with the
pain in my heart.

Susan Beckham

Elegy For Childhood

Once, sorrow was
a dead bird in the street;
worry was
stolen candy from the pantry;
fear was only in the dark.
Once, future was unreal.

But, once, happiness was
a nightly snowfall;
longing was
for Christmas morning;
love was
a white bunny named Puff.
Once, future was unreachable.

Fredrik Westin

Everything Lives On Me (Time)

I control when or where things happen.

The stars in the universe,
the stars and clouds,
the rising and setting sun.
All in their place because of ME.

My grandfathers,
tick and tock,
in the houses of mortals,
They LIVE.

Like my grandfathers,

I am not a God.
Though,
People think of me as such.

What I am,
people have so little.
Before I
RUN OUT.

Leo Malkin

'Lizzie Borden'

Lizzie Borden used an axe,
To kill her mom and pop,
But first a little cyanide
In hopes that they would drop.
   "DEAD!
      DEAD!
         DEAD!" she cried.
"Poison is so neat!
But if at first you don't succeed,
An axe just can't be beat!"

Kelly Muckleroy

The Cage

No matter how gilded the cage,
It's still naught but a cage;
And I, how could I willingly
Submit to captivity?
I refuse to be your magnificent beast
Hidden away in your den.
Does a lion not lose its eminence
When taken away from its pride?
And is a little band of gold
Supposed to buy my soul?
If my heart is a trophy
That you feel you can win,
Then you've already lost the game
Before it even begins.
If you try to force my love,
I will disappear
And you will be left to wonder:
Was she ever really here?

Kandace Blevin

Untitled

Together
You and I
We know each other inside out
I can finish your sentences
We communicate on an intuitive level
hardly talking
breathing
Together

Sarah Smith

Today

Today,
is our day
to make a difference.
We have to break down the fences
of hatred and racism.
We have to live in a world of equality.
Listen to me we have to be
FREE!
If we work together,
we can make it happen.
Make each other your brother or sister.
Take the pen
and sign the peace treaty.
Make it happen today.

Joshua Poeta

A Dream

As I awoke from my sleep
and reminisced of a dream,
as clear as the sun that
reflect on my window pain.
Increased by the pure white
brilliance of the sun, the
glistening of the snow, a
beautiful red bird as he sung.
Even more to my surprise,
as the wind blew like a thief

A vision of you lying next to
me, I pinch myself, I know
I'm not sleep.
Your body's right here next to
me, so calm so still so
soft so sweet,
I hoped it was real, I close
my eyes again. I say a
quick prayer and when I
opened them you were really here.

Glen Snow

Kindness

Be kind to Sue who broke her leg
Don't tease little Sally
And be nice to Benny who threw up

Have as many friends as you want
And there's always room for more

Friends are caring
And fun too
So keep your friends
And hope for more

Jessica Joiner

Death Wish

I dream I shall die in Ireland.
As the mist around me curls.
My spirit will hear the dirges
Softly sung by sad-eyed girls.

To have strong men bear my brier
Over hills of rolling green,
To be laid to rest on a mountaintop
Where the sunrise first is seen,

To hear the sea birds cry for me,
To hear the priest say Holy Words,
To know the mourners soon return
To the Master whom they serve.

Cheryl L. Kennicott

"N. Y."

I have been in the
Clogged nostrils of
Long island city
At 4 A. M.
Watch how the empty streets
Sing the tale of even time.

Along comes a footstep,
Tapping out a history
Of useless labor,
Heavy breathing
Beyond mouthfuls
Of sauerkraut,
Shuffling under the
streetlight
Bright as eyes,
Clicking
Of eternity's Last End

Joel Orzack

"The Power Of Love"

Love is like a volcanic candle,
That burns in your heart,
Making you feel so hot,
The blood runs through the veins,
It feels like lava,
Melting inside your hot body.
Feels it's going to explode,
As the body starts to erupt,
And suddenly lava emerges.
Your body starts cooling down...
Relaxing...Satisfying...
And so cool.

Nicolo A. Ingrasciotta

Sleepy Head

Go to sleep, my sleepy head,
and tomorrow will come fast.
With the sun so high and bright,
and the birds singing light.
Go to sleep, for me tonight, and
tomorrow will come.

Go to sleep, my sleepy head,
and tomorrow will come fast.
But for now it's late, and the
moon is high and bright, and
the stars are twinkling light.
Go to sleep for me tonight and
tomorrow will come.

God blesses your sweet soul
God blesses you sweet dreams,
God blesses you good night.
Go to sleep for me now.

Janice K. Hayes

Laundry Day

My lipstick's worn a path
across your face and neck
and left stains on collars
only to be washed away
in a load of laundry overdue
and I've found my affections
following example
until nothing remains
but a faint outline
of what once was.

Alison K. Topham

"Your Future Dreams"

Going for your goals,
Looking for your destiny,
Having friends and family,
Will help you find your way.

Buying toys and games,
Wasting all your money,
Thinking only of yourself,
Won't get you anywhere.

Studying, working, doing
what you can,
Helping other people,
Give a helping hand.

Doing this will get you far,
So keep reaching for the sky,
You never know but someday,
You just may touch a star.

Nora Marchetto-Ryan

Believe In Him

His flowers bloom,
Maybe we forgot him,
Maybe we don't believe,
We should believe -
For God our Father,
We should run away from evil,
For our majesty's
Newborn sheep.

Marcie K. Wilson

"Our Dreams"

I dream about faerie tales.
U dream about killing and death,
Y must it be this way?

U have to be free!
U have to be bold and daring!
U have to C the ways of life!

Live your life and dream your dreams,
but not like this.

Lisa Peel

The Free Life

The waves are very strong,
they can take you down
The wind plays a song,
all the way to town.
The sky is very clear,
The water is very far
You can almost hear,
the sound of beating hearts.
There's seagulls everywhere,
flying in the air
They're swooping in the water,
near the little otter.
Then they fly away and come
some other day.
The dolphins and whales
swimming in the sea,
are very far away from me,
I would love to be as free
As the animals I cannot see.

Wendy Patterson

Save Me

From the Earth I come.
What am I?

The Earth is my heart.
What am I?

I am everywhere, yet some times
stand alone.
What am I?

From me, comes life.
From me, life is given.
What am I?

When cut I Bleed.
I have a soul,
oh God.
To the Earth I fall.
What am I?
A Tree.

Egbert H. Chandler Jr.

My Wish

Sometimes I wish
I could fly
Up to the clouds
In the blue sky
I would watch the birds
Sing and play
And then watch them
Fly away
Then I would drop down
to the ground
And pretend I was a pirate
nice and proud
I would sail the rivers
and the oceans blue
Until I could find a
treasure chest
Just for you!

Nicolle Davis

Elegy

For myself do I dare grieve,
My earthly sentence foretold,
I pray for Heaven's reprieve,
To be spared death's infinite cold.

Sweet life so swiftly blown,
God's greatest gift yet given,
But be it then well known —
Death is the gate to Heaven.

How should I enter Paradise
Yet haunt this lofty goal —
By bargaining with the very skies
And the Maker of my soul?

To feel the warmth of Thine embrace,
Oh joy, eternal bliss,
To gaze upon Thy loving Face,
My all was made for this.

To feel Thy love, my Lord and God,
What more could I dearly crave?
My bones will rest in earthly sod,
My soul will cheat the grave.

Albert R. Carcieri

209

Untitled

Fall, winter, summer and spring,
They all have their special thing.
But I can't choose who will lose
I guarantee you I will choose,

Fall, winter, summer, and spring,
I just realized they have
EVERYTHING!

Erin Chastney

My Love...

You see me
True with all my fears
Laid to rest.
You understand me
In all my actions
That sometimes do
Not make sense...
All the days gone by...
Only to get better
And better.
We stand still
In time...
We are 'You and Me'
Forever...
True to form
Real with
Our selves...
You are my only true love...

May Keene

You Are

You
   Are:
Beauty to my eyes
Peace to my mind
Melody to my ears
Joy to my heart
Excitement for my body
Gentle touch to my hands
Pep in my step
Pride and confidence within side
Calm when I'm upset
Smile on my face
Glow in my eyes
You
   Are:
The love in my heart.

Leonora L. Graves

Write

What is this
An empty page
I must fill it up
With poetic rage

Writing, writing
When will I be pleased
Reciting, reciting
When will it be ceased

Rushing, rushing
Rattling my head
Gushing, gushing
No more to be bled

An empty page
A sorry sight
Fill it with what
Who cares, just write

Nathan J. Blackwelder

Untitled

"Wherever is your treasure,
   there also is your heart..."
God's Message to His children
   through His actions did impart.
Look not first at outward beauty;
   Hold not high amounts of gold.
The treasures God intended
   cannot be bought or sold.
Hugs from caring people
   smiles, kind words, good deeds;
Petting puppies, holding babies...
   God provides to fill our needs.
Sandy beaches, golden sunsets,
   dew on roses at sunrise;
Slowing pace to wait for others,
   love reflected in soft eyes.
Beauty is as beauty does...
   the soul the place to start.
"Wherever is your treasure
   there also is your heart..."

Pat Yongue

To The Daddy-In-Waiting

A family is growing -
It started in our minds.
And now it's coming true-
A you-and-me combined.

A family is coming -
Each day draws it near.
And one day least expected,
Our baby will be here.

You should be the first
To hold our new little one;
Whether it is a daughter,
Or whether it is a son.

I want you to be the one
So my little darling will know -
That Daddy has so much love,
And dreams and tenderness to show.

You will be the perfect Daddy
To share your love and time.
So our child will love her Daddy
Like I love mine.

Angie R. Robertson

The Sun

The sun peeks o'er the horizon
Shining, shimmering, bright.
Filling all things near it
with a soft, pallid light.

The sun continues upward,
Calm, subtle, smooth.
To meet its destination;
The top of the sky, high noon.

The sun falls down its pathway
The sky turns pink and blue.
Clouds tinted with color;
Their white to pastel hue.

The sun continues falling,
Continues on its way.
But just to come around again
and begin another day.

Jennifer Lynn Salamone

My Mother's Flower Basket

There once was a little bird
Can you guess,
Where she built herself a nest?
She built her nest in my,
Mother's flower basket.
She laid five eggs in my,
Mother's flower basket.
She took good care of my,
Mother's flower basket,
And the five babies that grew in there.
Can you guess what happen next -
In that flower basket nest?
They all flew away from my
Mother's flower basket.
It was a sad day for my
Mother's flower basket.
But - wait 'til spring, I'm sure
She'll be seen, building another
Nest in my -
Mother's flower basket.

Inez Marie Rissman

Just Let Me Be

The epitome of originality
Is letting the individual be
The person he or she wishes
Whether through poverty or riches.

I am who I am -
There's no mistake about it -
That's no accident, no miss or hit.

God made me to be the way I am
Sweet and humble as a little lamb.
I am glad to be one of a kind
There's no better friend you will find.

I accept my differences from others
Including cousins and brothers.
So accept me and let me be
All that God wanted for me.

Donald Wayne Chavis Jr.

Darklight

Figure in the moonlight
Standing still with pride,
No one will ever know
The secrets that you hide.

Staring across the valley
With your shining emerald eyes,
Trying to distinguish
The truth from all the lies.

The river in the canyon,
Twisting here and there
Winding through the high stone walls
Without a single care.

As the silver moon is rising,
And the daylight, fading fast,
The memories of old remind
That nothing good can last.

And as the blackness closes in
The shrieks of tortured souls abound,
Those condemned to roam the night,
Part of the lonely background.

Jennifer Watts

What Is Color?

What is blue?
The pools
are blue,
heating in the summer weather.

What is white?
The snow
is white,
in all its winter splendor.

What is gold?
The leaves
are gold,
when fall finally comes around.

What is green?
The grass
is green,
when spring birds make their sound.

Callan Green

Mother's Masterpiece

She paints a little every day,
Teaching me along the way.
With each stroke she does guide,
Through the valleys deep and wide.
Many colors so bright,
Which ones are right?
Picking and choosing,
It's all so confusing!
From a rainbow of hues,
She will help me to choose.
With palette in one hand,
Her brush in the other,
She's quite an artist,
My dearest mother!
After many years of painting,
Always ready, never fainting,
There will come a day,
She'll be able to say,
"It is finished, come and see."
For it's her masterpiece, and it's me!

Maryrose Harrington

Thank You

You took the time
To hear me through.
Gave me guidance
On what I should do.

"Turn it over to God"
I heard you say.
That is the reason
I am here today.

Never said thanks
For the wisdom you had.
Went about living
Life instead.

Moments alone,
Gave time to reflect
About all the people
I did not mean to neglect.

Now is the time,
The debt is past due.
I offer my sincere
"Thank You".

Chris L. Thorne

Broken Diamond

The perfect diamond I could give you
Was the one you could not wear
It brought the biggest smile
When you were the only one to share

All the brilliance and the dazzle
It shone brighter than the stars
And we all know that diamonds
Are the hardest rock of all

Yet the diamond that I gave you
Was gentle, strong, yet soft
It was broken and shattered
Because I gave you - my heart

Broken diamond in the dust
Left to tumble, left to rust
All the pieces have turned gray
This broken diamond tumbles astray

Steve Kudart

Hands

If our love was only hands
we would be much happier.
We wouldn't curse each other
for holding on too long.

If our love was only hands
it would be natural not to let go.

Andrei Ridgeway

Sunrise

Come, listen to the sunrise,
    With your eyes, you can hear it.
The sky sounds gold, and pink and red;
    Spools of sounds to thread and knit.

Do you hear the trees growing?
    They shout and sing clear and plain-
Stretching, yawning, touching sky,
    Green tears to cry, when it rains.

He said, he couldn't hear trees,
    or the sun like me, "Goodbye."
You can only hear birds sing,
    While I'm hearing them all fly!

Diane B. Procaccini

A Quality Life

What blessings I have
at this time of my life,
Even though at times
it is filled with such strife.

I have a family—
my spouse and 3 boys,
My share of hurts
as well as joys.

I have wonderful friends,
supportive and true.
they all let me know
"we're there for you".

But what makes my life
the most worthwhile,
is spending time with God
and feeling His smile.

Mae Nix

Summer

Summer is coming,
Jump in the pool.
Feel the water.
It is nice and cool.
See your friends.
School will be out.
Go fishing with dad.
Catch him some trout.

Melissa Leach

What Is A Warrior

A warrior is the protector of
His family. Clan and his tribe

A warrior is the guardian of the
Old ways so that they are not
Forgotten

A warrior is not motivated by
greed. Political ambition or fame

A warrior will not put himself
Above others in need

And above all
A warrior is the living spirit of
Our grandfathers

Mike Baker

A Path

Two special people
A path is worn.
A path of friendship
That cannot be torn.
The path is always open
Never over grown.
The secrets that are shared
Will never be known.
But one thing is for certain
The path of friendship
Will always be worn.

Martha Flournoy

Untitled

Are you afraid to die?
I sure am.
Everyone checking me out
poking and pinching
looking for the problem.
All the while gossiping
about some sport or T.V. show
like I'm not even there.

Michelle Horstman

Untitled

A smile that illuminates the
prewritten sorrows of my heart,
Lips that moistens the insanity's
that tear me apart,
Fingertips as gentle as doves that
dangerously approach premonitions of love,
Innocent eyes that blindly see
truth in every word,
This a spectacular demonstration
of a being unheard.

Karma Duke

O Bold Warrior

O bold warrior
Mine! All you sit here,
By your sewing machine,
Mouth full of pins
And thread to weave
Your magic dreams.

I cannot help but think
And wonder why?

Of secrets heard!

Years you have labored
With me as with
Those many others

Dear mender of Hearts
Mother of mine!

Eugene Zaia

Bouquets

Too often
In this hurried life,
We fail to pause
To give a word of praise or thanks
To those who've given to our lives
A thing of beauty.

Perhaps it was a sermon preached,
A word of hope,
A loving deed,
A tender smile or gentle touch,
A song well sung,
But still we go about our busy ways—
No time to give bouquets!

And then, some day,
When eyes are stony cold—unseeing,
Ears are closed—unhearing,
Lips are sealed—unspeaking,
Finger tips—unfeeling,
Then, we send bouquets.

Lois Jackson

The Poet's Sacrifice

A pen to express my heart
A poet's gift for words...
But for what purpose, this,
If it will not console one I love?

My heart is heavy with her grief
Black and thick as ink...
I long to end the sorrow
With a word, a verse, a song.

I want to find the answers
In a rhyme to ease her pain...
But the words escape me
The pen falters in my hand.

Sweet Muse, where is your comfort now?
I hold only ink and paper...
They have no arms that embrace
Nor eyes from which tears flow.

I would gladly trade the rhymes
To fulfill a single wish...
The power to take away the pain
To put happiness in her heart again.

Angela Marie Lloyd

Reality

Sometimes dreams are lost
Knowledge is often gained
Maybe that's the cost
Of growing up with pain

Life goes by fast
People tend to forget
Because it seems so vast
You can't out run it

Things keep changing
Mistakes are made
We finally end up dying
Life's dues are paid.

Logan Polk

A Promise

I was ten when you were born.
The day you were brought home
You were so small and cute.
I held you close in my arms
Making you a promise that never
could be broken.
My promise to you was to never
let anyone touch you in any way
you shouldn't be touched.
I kept my promise to you my little sister.
Now you are grown, married, and have
a beautiful daughter of your own.
I'm glad I made you a promise.

Virginia D. Robertson

Raymond's Place

Death's gateway opened up today
You didn't turn or look away
I held your hand, so close, so tight
And then I felt your soul take flight
A dim light rose, it made no sound
And I could feel you looking down
"Be Not Afraid, I'll Be Okay"
"I'll Wait For You," I heard him say
I know he's with our Father
I know this is his plan
Please God take good care of him
Til once again I can
When I look up into the heavens
I'm special now, you see
I have my own sweet angel
Who's watching over me
One day we'll be together
It will be God's grace
That our next life will be lived
In a new and better place.

Debbie Holladay Rauch

Untitled

Upon this poem and you shall see
that all my dreams stand beneath me
for my heart is filled with joy
people play like it's a toy
for I know that in my heart
my dreams will not be pulled apart
succeed in your dreams and you will see
that you can be what you want to be.

Rachel Harper

"The Final Goodbye"

He's gone
He's gone forever
I'll never see his face,
Feel his touch,
hear his voice,
I'll never hear him whisper my name
He's gone for good this time.
He's never coming back.
It's time for the final goodbye.
The one that's meant forever.
The one you can't take back.
I'll c-ya around
I'll c-ya later.
The things you wish you could say.
But it's the time for the goodbye
The Final Goodbye.
Never to speak again!

Amy Dolph

Untitled

I gaze out
over the night.
Twinkle, twinkle
little star.
You can see the ocean
they say.
Of course,
only on a clear day
but after all,
this is L. A.
It seems so black.
I look for your light.
Where are you
in the darkness?
My longing extends
as far as the night.
Star light, star bright.
You are my wish,
my wish tonight.

Debra A. Shinn

Veterans Day

Veterans day I looked around
Crowd was small, what a shame,
With all the promises that abound
I wondered who's to blame.

They went, Did the job
Even in mud and rain.
Some a grenade to lob,
Then came home in pain.

The years pass by
Now too old to serve.
Have we the right to deny
The respect that they deserve?

Boys came home, unable to walk.
After all they went through
Even now, don't care to talk,
They did it, just for you.

Is it to much to ask
As we go on our way,
That we make our respect last
As we set aside this Day.

Harold R. Smith

Dreamer

Someone left
this morning
without saying
goodbye You
chase them out to see
them off
but they're gone
You go back in
thinking your
life has gone from you
But nothing has changed
You're in your
bed
with the one you Love
She asks you
how you slept
but all you
can say is
I love
you

Amy Bradbury

He Is

He is a good
basketball player
He is on the Honor Roll
He is in the
Pace Class
He is very
very cute
He has
a lot of
intelligence
and he is
all of these
nice things

Keith Adams

"Our Grandpa"

I see the American flag,
I see the power,
hear the joy, feel the pride,
understand the triumph;
I see the fighting, hear the screams,
Feel the shaking,
understand the will;
I see the past, hear the crying,
feel the nightmares,
understand the cause;
I see his face, hear his words,
feel his pain,
understand his sorrow.
All these years,
he's lived with the pain.
So please don't take
the Flag in vain.

Vicki L. Olson

"Waves In My Heart"

Where ever my travels
take me
Around the world's
globe
The stars and stripes
waves in my
heart

Jamie June Barber

True Love

Can you know
Can you tell

What he does
What he does without

Kindness felt by a touch
Honesty heard by a word

Trapped in his eyes,
hidden

A man's
A man's

Love
Few only know

Karen K. Campbell

Girl

You need my loving
As I need yours
I write these humble words
As fast as you can right them.

Your eyes so clear, so true...so blue
Shimmering with might so fierce
That my heart, those eyes might pierce.

A voice so sweet, so angelic...so you
Echoing with spite so cruel
That my heart, that spite did fool.

You need my loving
As I need yours
I lose myself in your undeserved beauty
And you...
you
just lose
me.

Nicholas Tapazoglou

"Pictures"

Windows in time, that's
    what it seems
Remembering our past
    looking back on our
dreams.
    Memories of good
times, of scenes from
    long ago;
moments frozen forever
    like an Arctic Snow.

Carolyn Langston

Primordial Soup

The water shimmers with light.
Its wetness invites me in
Its coolness surrounds me
I am transported to the origins of
    our beginning.
My head clears as I descend
Altered perceptions hint of
    a secret world.
Below the surface, the light dances
To ancient rhythms of our
    planet's song
    Primordial Soup
    Our beginnings.

Megan Lowder

Jesus Is My Hero

Jesus is my hero,
    He saved my soul
And my hide from hell
    So I wouldn't burn
There he gave me
    Light that I might
See the beauty of
    This world he made
And the garden of
Eden for me-and oh
The birds that fly
in the air how hard
they try -
He feeds us by the
Word - tells us not to
Fear - that God is
Near - so we must trust
Him and hold him near
To our hearts
so dear

Rev. Linda G. Wilson

Smiles

If worth in life were reconciled
by times a day a person smiled,
then most I fear, or half at best
would fail to pass that simple test.

And on who's shoulders lay the blame,
I sought the answer and his name.
A smile seems simple, but alas
I see no smiles as people pass.

I prayed to God, allow me know
one word that makes these others so
uncaring that in all that while
I saw them and they did not smile.

And then in prayer, God spoke to me,
"One single word thy culprit be."
"Contagious, is the word you seek."
I wept a tear, I could not speak.

For with that word my soul was healed.
The one at fault, at last revealed.
For then, my pride allowed me see
that FIRST smile had to come from Me.

William H. Millette

Furless

My child legs
were wet in the summer.
Dandelion fur broke in my hands.
I climbed trees into the sky
I sat on recliners like a princess.
My mother was queen
wearing pigtails and jeans.
I came for magical kisses
for dirty feet.
I came from her star
and hatched in the galaxy womb.

Bite me and I'm alive.
I wear sewn butterfly wings
I hold onto the bellies
of daphne and kittens.

Wings break.
Genies bottle corrupting me.
I shatter and float on bad air
swindled and skinned. I shed
triumphant in my furless flight.

Sonya Petroff

The Arctic

The Arctic is dark in every way
With the creaking of ice breaking away
Being on land
Guarded by snow
makes it conventional to walk slow
The light of dawn
Aids our way
Makes it practical
For us to stay
The secrets to endure
Fading away
If we preserve our environment
This land will be okay

Marc Brandon Frenkel

Immortal

Immortal, me? I wonder
However, tonight I feel I am
But this is no time for sham
For I am traveling on
As best I can...

Sorrow, I've known it
Trouble, I've shared it
Fear, I've fought it
Joy, I've felt it
Hope, I've kept it

Now I return
To the everyday cares of life
The everyday stress and strife
And I'm homeward bound
Feeling my way through the crowd

How my days I'll spend
How it will end
Is a mystery
Only time will solve
For I am traveling on.

Margaret M. Tindall

Firefly

Tiny flash of light
in the sky at night.
I love to sit
and watch you blink,
In the dark as black as ink.
You make me think of
tales and poems,
About fairies and gnomes.
You make me wonder
how short our life must be
Compared to God's eternity.

Kathleen A. Miller

Earth

A place where,
in good times and bad,
human creativity begins to dare.
Through good and bad,
happy and sad,
this globe, this world, is our home.

Justin Larson

Baseball

The crowd stands
high, when they hear
the crack of the bat.
As the ball sails
high in the air!
The smell of the
popcorn, and the
sight of ball
sailing over the
fence as the crowd
is shouting "Home run!
Home run"!
As the man is walking
around selling
popcorn and pop to the
crowd he looks with
the crowd and shouts
with the crowd as
they see their
favorite team winning!

David Beemer

God Is On Your Side

God is with you
So don't you fear
He'll answer your prayer
Your voice He'll hear.

He'll keep your mind
He'll see you through
There is nothing at all
That the Lord won't do.

So don't give up
Because you can cope
With God on your side
There is hope.

Carol Owens Ford

Beloved Father

When I am gone,
and laid down to rest

Don't cry for me,
for I have been blessed

I am in heaven,
where I feel no pain

Just peace and love,
is what I have gained

So don't weep for me,
when I have gone

There has to be you,
to carry on

I had to leave you,
but not all alone

God will be with you,
to keep you strong

We'll meet again in heaven above,
for I am saving a place,
for the ones that I love.

Carol Crawford

"For A Believer"

With outstretched wings they hover,
Silent, kind and glorious;
For those who know their presence,
Death is made victorious.

Why are you here, we ask?
Their answer is but a whisper;
We have a joyful task,
to comfort an ailing sister.

Angels, angels we implore
Do your duties strong and sure;
Gently, lovingly, forever more,
Until you take us through the door
To your home and ours — in Heaven!

Margaret J. Fry

Death By Consciousness

Here lies
A woman, now wise
Beyond her lofty dreams

She holds no truth
Her soul is bare
Of scavengers and schemes

She died a death
Of shallow breath

Awakened to behold
A life of riches
Fruitful bear, adventures
Strong and bold

Lucinda K. Fienhage

"Passing By Alone"

I've been all over this land,
    and touched everyone's hand.
I've brought relief to some,
    as I cooled the blazing sun.
Pain to others as I passed by,
    bringing darkness across the sky.
Though you may never see me,
    for I have no shape to see.
I often bring fragrance with me,
    as I'm passing through the trees.
Though I pass by always alone,
    myself I've never shown.
For I am known as the wind,
    blowing freely around each bend.

Robert Carmody Jr.

"Changes"

Change! Change! Change!
How effective is change?
Motivational, operational change
Impositional activational change
How easy is it to really change?

Life as it may be is
a continual change,
Informational, organizational change
Implementing, educational change
Can you cope with the change

Positive and negative redefines change
Learning to be receptive and
accommodating helps us to handle change
Sometimes emotional and
irrational one must change
What would we do without change?

Alma K. Pratt

Beauty

Beauty is...
an unborn child
anything wild
the setting sun
children having fun
Beauty is...
a droplet of rain
killers in pain
a child in love
everything above
Beauty is...
whatever your heart desires
droplets of water or wild fires

Shelly Hobson

Dreams

A dream remains forever,
unattainable....
Forever ruled by one's heart....

Being dealt the winning hand,
Securing the missing puzzle piece,
Fulfilling one's dreams,

Left merely to open the door....

Instills a deep rooted fear,
in finding merely a fallacy....

Shattered dreams....
Are they repairable?

A true dreamer forever believes,
Never tastes of said dreams....

Sad.

Yet, true in heart....
believes still....

Amber Dawn

"Silence Speaks"

Silence speaks a thousand words
And time stands still
No sounds are heard
But hearts shatter like glass
Silence speaks a thousand words
Words that heal or kill
Nothing is said, everything is said
Someone is left alive or dead

Heather D. Amos

The Agony In Victory

The stealthy breeze scents out despair
Whirls about in shapeless search
Quick as a bee becomes the wind
Stings the nudity of flesh picked bare

Lash and splinter pierce the sponge
Draws the blood dries up the plunge
Fractured eyes in marbled thought
Broken slag on crashing seas

Ice floes slant the frosted sight
Iron jaw in sculptured head
Feathery fingers lift the blight
Still the breeze and kill the wind

Margaret Askey

"He"

He is our savior from heaven above
Though we're not worthy
He still gives us love.
He stands beside us
When things seem so wrong
He gives us courage
That helps us along.
He sits beside us
When we're sick in bed
A smile on his face
Means there's nothing to dread
He will always be faithful
Whenever we pray
He will never stop listening
At night time or day.
Don't ever give up on our savior above
Just give him your faith and your love.
"He" is Jesus our Lord

Eleanor M. Lohr

When A Tree Cries

From a seed growing tall;
Spread the shade, seen by all
Something inside, always dies,
To hear of this; when a tree cries.

Mourning loss, as mother's shows;
Life of love, comes to know,
Broken limbs sever ties;
Caring always, when a tree cries.

Pain is felt, strike the blow;
Again and again, no longer grow.
Distant echoes rings the sound,
Forest gone, trees cut down.

Hearing a tree cry, seems to me,
Always seeing, not wanting to see,
What we have done; not to deny
Darkness hurt when a tree cries.

Jon Golden

"What Would I Do?"

What would I do,
If I didn't have you?
I would go on with life
Not being your wife.

Not being fulfilled,
Not being complete,
Not sharing our love
So deep and so sweet.

Not having our dreams,
Not having our desires,
No hare-brained schemes,
No emotional fires.

You are the answer
To all my hopes and plans,
To all my fantasies and wishes,
To me, my perfect man.

Judy Turocy

"Out My Window"

Out my window I see the sky
I see the birds that fly so high
Out my window I see the trees
I see the grass and the leaves
Out my window I see the sun
And everyone having lots of fun!!!

Lauren Marchetti

Nothing Is Forever

Flowers bloom in the spring,
Look what water can bring,
They die to the change of weather,
Nothing is forever.

The sun rises each morning,
As the day intends to be boring,
Though the nights seem better,
Nothing is forever.

People have their ups and downs,
When love turns us around,
Two lovers are together,
But...Nothing is forever.

Terra Renee Atherton

Afternoon Story

A cloud bursts
A bird flies
The feather drops
The raindrop falls
The two collide
Mingle as one
Merged they descend
Landing in beauty.

William D. Woodard

Break The Hate

Ugly smiles
dirty faces
All because of
different races.
People hate
because of color
Losing faith
in one another.
We have to unite
and form a team
Peace will shine
and love will gleam.
Just because
some people hate
doesn't mean
that it's too late
We can stop
racist people
by being proud
to love all people.

Tara Guerriero

Miracles

Children are miracles,
Precious treasures from God.
Each one to be valued,
In his own right,
Each one to be needed,
To be just who they were made.
Each one with their own,
Separate window to Christ.
Each one to be who,
God wanted you to see.
Each one with her own.
Beam of Christ's light.

Ann Carnicle

It's Not Really There

"Such is life".
Said, the man,
With the pink balloon.
Flying high,
On his fabricated wings.
"Don't call on me
To be what...
You want me to be.
For not even I
Can build with that which...
I do not have".
The air, evaporates quickly,
And all of our dreams,
Fall to the Earth,
And die.
"Then you and I
Have to admit
To that which,
We have lied".

Laura J. Raaz

"I Am A Black Man"

You cannot see the suffering and pain
You cannot feel my shame,
Every wrong I'm to blame
I am a black man.

You say I will never succeed.
You put a bullet through my heart,
You make me quit before I start.
I am a black man.

Sometimes I feel that I'm alone
I have no friends—I have no one,
All my friends shot by a gun
I am a black man.

I am a person.
Black, poor, and trying to be
an educated person, a somebody.
But according to what statistics say,
I won't live to see many more days
Unless I change my wrong ways.
I am a black man.

Maurice Williams

A Poem Of Hands

One man stands
mouth foaming malice
a two-by-four in his hands,
hands that murder
hands that hate
hands that love the smell of blood
war-worshipping
killing hands.....

Another sits silently
serenading the sun
lightened, enlightened
dough between his cuticles
hands with eyes
hands sculpting symphonies
raw clay made magic
artist inspired hands.....

Ours to choose
hell or nirvana
Hitler or healer...
with the same hands.....

Beverly Frank

A Reason To Wish

Look! at the stars above us;
And they all may grant a wish.
Yet we argue and we fuss,
When a star deems us selfish.

But if a star's wish could wish,
Would it wish not to be used?
Would it choose its existence,
To serve us and be abused?

Would it choose an existence,
In which it needed to wish?
Or wish itself everything,
That others have want to wish?

Well, a wish has not a choice.
Only your wish can come true.
Just use your own voice,
And wish to be you.

Matthew Connelly

"Passing"

The sun shines
And the wind blows
The clouds drift
And the moon glows

The rains descend
And the water flows
The seeds sprout
And the wheat grows

The trees sway
And the birds sing
The deer play
And the insects cling

The eagles soar
And the children sleep
The lions roar
And the willows weep

We see and hear
And smell and taste
Our lives are dear
With no time to waste

George Schreiner

"Christmas Eve"

Snow flakes danced in cold night air
Soft and clean upon the square
Carollers singing Holy Night
Stores long closed and shoppers flight

I heard the Santa's ringing bell
And church bells offering their peal
I wiped the frozen tears aside
Remembering that my family died

And so this night I volunteered
To help the shelter to bring cheer
The doors were opened to these souls
They could not stay out in the cold

I set the tables full of food
And opened cots in comfort mood
I lit the small bright christmas tree
And played "Nearer My Lord To Thee"

When morning comes there will be toys
For all these little girls and boys
And me, the greatest gift of all
Giving comfort when God calls

Dottie Egan

For You

I think of you constantly,
care about you, worry about you,
wondering if you're o.k.
You will always be in my heart,
you have taken a big part of
my life into your arms,
for you to hold, for you to love.
My life is so new because
you have changed it so much.
Now that you are gone,
I have to replace everything that
you have taken and start all over again.
I just wanted you to know
that this is FOR YOU.

Colleen Reavley

Just In Case

When I see you each day,
A smile crosses my face
You're the one who makes me happy,
You're the one who decides my place.
You're the only one I want,
I mean that with all of my heart
I pray each night,
That we will never part.
When I first came here,
And saw you look at me
I fell in love with you -
It's true love... Can't you see?
Sometimes when I'm sad
You pay attention to why,
I feel comfortable with you
You'd never hate me if I cried.
I guess I'll let you go now
I don't want to take up space
But here's a little "I Love You,"
To take with you - just in case.

Michelle Guinnee

Whatif

Last night while I lay thinking here,
Some Whatifs crawled inside my ear
and pranced and partied all night long
and sang their same old Whatif song:
Whatif my father turned smart?
Whatif my name was Bart?
Whatif I turned dumb?
Whatif my dog was a bum?
Whatif my fish dies?
Whatif the sun doesn't rise
Whatif the plants don't grow?
Whatif the wind doesn't blow?
Whatif the TV doesn't work?
Whatif my friends call me a jerk?
Whatif I don't pass my test?
Whatif I get no rest?
Whatif my Sega broke?
Whatif I couldn't tell a joke?
Everything seems swell, and then
The nighttime Whatifs strike again?

Alexandra Mondrala

Never Know

I look to the sky above
in wonder of the road I've taken.
Could this be a dream of shadows
from which I'll soon awaken?
I cannot see far ahead
for darkness clouds my eyes.
If I should follow the path I lead
will it end in my demise?

As I remember all that has been
I crumble to the ground.
What a heavy heart I carry
as it beats without a sound.
Within myself I must decide
the direction which I will go.
It has to be now or never
or about life I will never know.

Cynthia S. Thayer

In The Eyes Of A Mosquito

Infliction of pain
Is the name of my game
I come in the night
When you turn off the lights
When your eyes are shut
I make my move
Hearing no sound
I fly by your head
Sticking my stinger
Into your skin
My dangerous poison
Now is within
You feel my pain
And turn on the lights
   SWAT
I'm dead... It's all over.
Good Night!

Richard Lemonie

"The Stag"

The graceful moving mammal
Is now drooping down its head.
The sorrow is unbearable,
A fellow stag is dead.

The hunter now can see,
The pain that he has caused
The graceful moving mammal
And the dead one; now Above.

He cried out, "Oh my dear Father,
How could I be so wrong
To kill one of your creatures
Just 'cause of the lack of fun?"

In later years to come,
We can all go and view,
The gravesite of that dear old stag,
And learn God can forgive you.

Laura Grimes

"The Daydream"

If I could sit writing
words of beauty,

and gaze across a field
of freshly fallen snow,

Looking towards the sun,
reflecting on a cool crisp lake,

I would see the you I Know.

Patrick Joseph Mahoney

Mother Earth And Father Sky

Mother Earth
and Father Sky
Do not quite
see eye to eye
Mother Earth
is kind and caring
Father Sky
is bold and daring
Mother Earth
says, "Save the trees!"
Father Sky
pretends to wheeze
Mother Earth
pleads,"Try to care!"
Father Sky
adds, "Save the air!"
But one thing on which
they both agree
They love their child
Daughter Sea

Kimberly Demuth

"The Rose"

I pressed a rose inside a book, so
that it could stay!
   The perfect way it looked, when
given to me that day.
   It was so red and lovely, and
smelled so fragrantly.
   I put it there inside the book,
so I could always see.
   Something from someone, that
meant so much to me.
   It was so many years ago,
you'd think I would forget,
   Every time I pass it, the memory's
still there, yet,
   A beautiful spring day goes
through my mind,
   Wind blowing through my hair,
Thank you for the rose, time
   hasn't changed it yet.

Harriette Browning McElroy

The Thinker

There he sits, stone cold,
With his fist upon his chin,
On a tree stump he always sits,
On his face, never a grin;

As people stroll by they gaze
While he attempts to concentrate
On what lies before him:
His future, his destiny, his fate;

The imminent facts of life itself
He discusses within his mind,
He contemplates many concepts
And ponders views of every kind;

He'll speculate many theories,
And his wisdom may always linger,
But due to his concrete capacity
He's limited, for he's only the Thinker.

Chris Sigler

Dare-Devil

The ruffest hair
The keenest eyes
And the growl of the angry
I fear what I see
but it is I who urged this creature
To its defense
And not its trust and respect
It is I who chose to fight
And now I shall, until my death or his
Because I am the Dare-Devil

Marquita Dorsey

The Shore

Moonlight, glistening
on the water.
Faint music, drifting,
from the cars beside us.
The skyline in the distance.
The breeze, in the night.
Our ritualistic dance,
as the evening grows late.
The scent of the ocean,
as we,
move to the beat.
The Fury...
The Warmth,
as we collapse.
Leaves rustling,
Calmness all around.
Daybreak coming.
Freshness in the air.

Gloria Darling

The Dream

The dream came again tonight
(and may return another time?)-
"I dreamt I dwelt in marble halls?"
Oh, no——
Rather in a secret place,
among the flowers I love so well.
Is there a way that I can tell-

   What is dream?
   What is real?

Or does it happen only in
my mind -
And sometimes break the seal
where dreams become reality.

Frances Weber

A Game Called "Love"

For it never seems fair,
when one plays the game of love.
Though cupids arrow may have pierced,
blood is all that runs.
The potion, is just a potion
on a time schedule.
Soon the blissful effects
turns ill residual.
It is never expected, and all
are blind to see.
That when playing the game of love.
It was never meant to be.

Shawn Ruttman

Untitled

Saint Patrick's day has come again,
bringing along its fun
"You must wear green cause otherwise,
The Preaching will never be done!"

I don't believe in fairy tales,
or even crooked tales.
So the character St. Patrick
Sounds like crazy whales!

Christina Brooks

Made With Love

I've been made with love
Fashioned by the potter's hand
Hand crafted in the molder's plan
Shaped in every detail
Cleansed from every flaw
Glazed with his righteousness
And painted with his blood
Yes, I've gone through the fire
Seven times in fact I have,
But it makes me more beautiful
For you see, I've been made with love
For the master's use
A vessel for honor,
Fit only for his table
To be used only by his hand

Sandy Waltman

Toward The Sky

Good morning my Grandpa
Way up in the sky
I'm thinking about you
Don't mind if I cry

Not one day goes by
That you're not with me
All the years with such pain
Now you're finally free

Sometimes I find comfort
I still feel you there
As if you just hugged me
When the wind blows my hair

Some days I look upward
I talk toward the sky
I find myself wishing
For old days gone by

But rather than wishing
For things I can't touch
I'll just say I love you
I miss you so much

Dana Paige Vail

The Universe

The Universe is full of mystery
and secrets.
It has an endless history
which only the past has witnessed.
Its wonders give us curiosity,
that later lead us to discovery.

What clues we have
and what clues we find,
are only up to humankind.
The stars prove that
there's life out in space,
the universe is a continual place.

Adrienn Szilagyi

Untitled

Frost appears outside your window
Barren trees stand all around
Adaptation leads to solitude
White blankets cover the ground

High in the alpine meadows
Ice slowly begins to thaw
Cascading down the mountainside
Awaking rivers from their crawl

Morning dew forms all around
Life starts blooming far and wide
Venturing beyond their secluded den
Spring warms the newborn's hide

As the leaves turn full of color
And the lakes become crisp and clear
You can hear the distant echoes
Winds of change blow through your ears

Michael J. King

Thoughts

The painting
on the artist's brush,
the rhyme
of the poet.
The reasoning
of the analyst,
the music
they dance to.
The imagination
of the creative,
the value
of the wealthy.
The reason
that I love you,
The meaning
of my dreams.

Lisa Marie May

Prison

I've never been in prison
And I sure don't want to go
It's a place of retribution
A place to shun, you know

There are bars on all the windows
Locks and bars on every door
A tall fence topped with barbed wire
Coils of razor-wire galore

The guards are big and burly
You seldom see one smile
Some of them are pleasant
Others are as bitter as bile

The inmates come in all colors
All sizes and shapes, as well
Some of them look real good
Others look like hell

There are inmates who are industrious
They learn as much as they can
Others spend their time finagling
Trying hard to trick "The Man"

Athalone H. Brailford

Untitled

You are the sun in my morn
without you in my life
I would be torn

God allowed me to keep you
for what purpose He's in mind
I can not view

Whatever your purpose be
you have helped me to grow
for the world to see

Aeriell, always know you have my love
as unconditional as God's
from above.

Julia Joiner-Tidd

Strength

Muscles bulging,
Eyes burning,
A fiery fierceness inside.
Hardcore strong.

"Outta my way" attitude,
"If you aren't running,
You're not fast enough!"
Livin' on the edge.

You have to be the strongest,
The fastest, the best
Before you're good enough.
Can you prove it?

But, I've turned my back
And walked away
From the challenges
Thrown to me.
I've found out that
Strong isn't one thing.
Strong isn't the old oak in the storm;
It's the new flower in the snow.

Jana Jacobs

Secrets

The Secret's out,
You've gone away,
What's left?
What is there to say?

You went out
and told everyone,
now look,
look what you've done.

You've ruined my life,
my hopes and dreams,
and now this nightmare will never end,
as though it seems.

About my pain,
you cannot know,
from what I think,
and what I show.

Eventually, I know
it will be okay,
somehow,
someway.

Jessica Matthews

218

Asylum

I spend my life in complacency
Letting them get the best of me
Drawing every last drop of my blood
Still they try to feed
The more I do
The more they expect
It's getting to the point
That this dam is going to break
Daddy don't commit me
Can't you see it'll be my death
Just because you can't rule me
Don't let them take my life's breath
I'm well past a sane man's domain
Creeping down these dark streets again
No one will ever find me here
Back beyond accountability
You blame my sickness on the T.V.
Afraid to face the stark reality
When I cried out in madness
You weren't there for me

Kevin McDonald

The Beast Within

There lives a Beast within us
Our bodies have no control,
But our minds they can free us
If we simply just let go.

Many will deny it,
Some will only see it,
A few will ever grasp it
For they know they can defeat it.

But when we fight this Beast within
We find we're not alone,
For some believe that we can win
That battle with the Beast within.

We find there's only one way to win,
To take one day at a time;
For if we give in
The Beast will win
And we will be gone in time.

Susan Elaine Toy

Untitled

The day, today
Ways are found
    paths are arising
from times just past,
    And direction is chosen
The tomorrows' future
    the right way, says left
Now is the present
    a strait circle is centered
And mind's eye moves

    My spine aches, I feel it;
growing in childhood is pleasure
    end to beginning it stretches
but the void time is change
    and head to head are one
innocence becomes aware
    love must see to be;
who are you

David Orth

Angels

If you want to see an angel
Look in a baby's face.
They can take a nothing day
And make it a heavenly place

They have such sparkling eyes
And a smile from above
Those precious little bundles
Can fill your heart with love

When they hold your finger
And they talk and coo
It's their special angel touch
That means so much to you.

They may be very small
In this big world they are in
But they give adults a certain glow
With just one little grin.

We should thank the Lord above
For sending those small angels to earth

For they truly are a priceless gift
From the moment of their birth.

Linda McKinney

No One

No one seems to notice
how much I hurt

No one seems to notice
how much I need
a hug
a touch
someone to listen

No one really seems
to care

I only can speak
when I can

There is no one
I can talk to

My heart aches and
my chest feels the pain

Catrina Rockwell

Slave Girl

    There's this man who I've met, he said he
was the glory of my soul, time went on and on.
    Then this man reappeared once more, and
this time he told me that if I should die, let my
soul go on to heaven to be free with the Lord.

Brandi Leigh Golden

The Hat

The hat is worn
to hide my faults,
to disguise my person.
But the Lord sees through all.

The hat is worn
to enhance my beauty,
to change my person.
But the Lord sees through all.

The hat is worn
to protect my appearance,
to keep me sheltered.
Just like the Lord.

Mary Huston

You Have My Sympathy

Someone killed your song today,
Pulling the last breath of note.

It died as you slept.
I don't know what to say...

It was your favorite.

I love you.
Even in your grief.
You are beautiful.

Michele Ross-Douglas

Equality

Black and white join the fight!
Make the world a place that's right.
Children hear me
Open your minds in freedom,
Towards equality.
We all have our liberty,
Why not fight for equality?
Freedom is not free,
You have to fight for it!
And so equality,
Make the world a place that's right.

Thomas Kovalenko

William

Big bear hugs like no other
A wonderful one-of-a-kind smile
A Loving but strong father
Takes his family to heart
That laugh, Oh, you'd have
Thought it came straight from
his toes!
His anger was fierce but his
love was fiercer!
Fishing and hunting and time
with his family made him
a happy man

Adrianna Mendenhall

A Child's Face

May the sun
shine
on your child's face
every day, every year,
and feel no tear
roll
    down
into space.

Laughter and joy, yes;
a smile is a thousand words
glitter of the soul,
sparkle of the lips,
chatter of the brain.

God bless you and
your child's face.

Paola Stone

Untitled

Splendid flowers bloom
Colors feast over the earth
Old sun welcomes them
(Haiku)

Janelle Ross

The Silver Stream

I walked alone
through the deepest forest
In search of my life time dreams
Always worrying about tomorrow
kept on walking
I found this silver stream.
The sun shined brightly, and
the birds did sing
But, in my hurting heart
it didn't mean a thing.
I thought your love had left me
my tears fell like rain
Then the skies opened up to me
I heard him call my name
Lift up your head my Child,
you're not to blame
The world is so different now
So believe in my name

Katina Kriegsmann

Feathers

Floating in the wind
all alone
Not anything like a
real small stone
Reaching out to grasp
something that's not there
Just floating along
on a breath of air
It flutters down begins
to fall
Then settles on some old
brick wall
A gust of wind begins
to blow
And sends it up again
so very slow
I wonder if life for
a feather ever gets boring

Angie Gill

The Water....

Like a bird, and like a flower,
I can not ignore the water....
In a world I am killing,
The sun will give me power.
I will rise, like the flower.
And when a feather falls, so will I.
Unto the ground, I will die.
And still, remains the water....

Patrik Walton

Let's Hear The Storm

Let's hear the thunder,
Like a mother rocking her
  child from its fuss.

Please no lightning,
Like a father starting to cuss.

Let's hear the rain,
Like a mother singing her song.

Please no hail,
Like a father's voice not at low tone.

Let's hear the storm,
  Peaceful and calm,
Now child at rest with
  motherly bond.

Tara Gentry

The Wait

Have I waited so long...
  So long it takes,
To reason why,
  Have I waited so long?
  Found no other direction to turn.

Discovering a light in the sky,
  So bright it causes my eyes to burn.

And I've waited so long,
  So long it takes.
To reason why
  And I've waited so long.
To walk a path that's true,
  Knowing that I'll be there with you.

Now the waiting is done,
  Found a light in the sky,
So bright it caused my eyes to burn,
  Only to find it is the Son.

Gary A. Pierce

"You"

Often times you've asked
What do you see in me?
My answer was always vague
It lacked coherency
Your gift, what was it?
I, myself did not know
Your hair, your lips, your eyes
Superficials, my heart told me so
One day I came to you
Poured out my secrets within
You calmed, you eased, you soothed
Gave peace where chaos had been
As I drank your words of comfort
Your eyes their secret now told
They filled with the beauty of you
The beauty of an understanding soul

Julie Masters

To Paula

It was the morning
of my life
that saw the sun eclipsed
become too dark to see
too cold to feel
alone and afraid.

Awake, and the sun dispels
the darkness - love and renewal,
she still sleeps
so soft, and warm, and sweet
my love, my wife, my life.

Leo Gorelkin

Online

I never met him
Yet my soul is bound
To the words he writes
And the love he shares.

We have been secretive
Exchanging hidden wants
Unknown desires
We have yet to pursue.

Perhaps in the future
The miles will not be
A means of denying
What words used to say.

Sybille Watson-Jones

Death Of A Cloud

The angry cloud came fast
And furious overhead.
Lightning flashed,
Thunder crashed,
Rain fell.
Then silence.
The cloud had spent its fury
And quietly died.

Brett Waite

Submission

Relentless train of sorrow
Pulling its obsidian caboose
Unfeeling juggernaut of doom
Beating the spirit down
The depleted will crumbles
Under foot of bitter past
Dark tyranny victorious
Life's meek cause surrendered

Ryan Tei

Mankind

Why is the world so blind to see
That all men are men, and men are men
What ever is hue may be.

Why is the world so blind to see
That eyes are eyes
And minds are minds
And men should see
That men are men
What ever is hue may be.

And if men cannot see
That men are men
Then death shall be
To all mankind
What ever is hue maybe.

Ronald B. Hurlock

Silence

Like a sad song
with dreary stories
cast upon her life
had to make the same sacrifice
more than once or twice.
Sitting in her shadow
reaching for the light
looking it all over
trying to make it right.
Like a penny down a well
all her wishes fell
all the feelings locked inside
not a soul to tell.

Brianna C. Leaver

Summer

The sky is blue and clear.
The sun is bright and overhead.
The only cloud I see,
  Is far off in the distance.
There has been no rain
  Nor will be soon.
For this is summer
  And nothing else.

Layne Dylla

Sleepy

I am tired.
I'm falling back
into tingling comfort.

Away from you...
Away from you...

Prying questions
like pins and needles
irritating my sleep.

I can't sleep...
Let me sleep...

Angela Boomer

The Mountain

I'm climbing up a mountain,
Aiming for the top,
But every time that I advance,
It seems like I just drop.

I try to get my footing,
On the rocky wall,
But when I think I have it,
I begin to fall.

Plunging for the ground,
I'm caught up by the rope,
And then I realize once again,
That there is still a hope.

Joshua Collison

Butterfly

Tranquility in motion,
The stained glass butterfly.
It hasn't any notion
That some day it will die.
A truly innocent creature
Whose only thought's to fly.
It missed out on the feature
That makes us wonder "why."
It hasn't any worries.
Its mind is happily free.
It is its own judge and jury.
It's happy just to be.

Elizabeth Doubles

Conscience

The right thing feels...
Rusted metal into my flesh
Memory at a time
Send me to hell
Sake of the right thing

The right thing feels...
Darkness of my nightmare
Flowers lay upon me
Space without air
Sake of the right thing

The right thing feels...
What have I done right?
Lightning strike me
Fly away, o soul
Sake of the right thing

The right thing feels...
Brown leaves tossed by wind
Look down upon me
Nothing matters
Sake of the right thing

Marcia Roberts

For Chris-tena

Sun shining on green grass
Dew resting on damp leaves
Dew falling down my cheek
It's cool and sweet

Sun shining on a big tree
Branches reaching for the sky
I am reaching for the sky
Reaching and reaching

My fingertips just scrape eternity
I have touched Love
Even more
Love has touched me

Sun shining on my feet
my head is in the shade
Under a big tree
And dew is falling
Down my cheek

Lisa Laguna

Lost Without Love

The footsteps I take,
seem to lead me to pain.
Without your love,
I'll only know your name.

The footsteps I take
are sinking in the sand.
Let me kiss your lips.
Let me hold your hand.

The footsteps I take,
so many, yet, so few.
Help me find a path
that will lead me to you.

Let me find the way,
the way to your heart.
Footsteps come together,
my love shall never part.

John Scheffel

Reflections

Prisons and castles
    the places are the same.
One is the world I live in;
    the other is where we've lain.

Thoughts of you can be painful
    in the absence of your touch.
I want to press you close to me...
    I love you very much.

My hours are filled with happiness,
    when you are on my mind.
Reflecting... remembering...
    as the fantasies unwind.

You're that special ray of sunlight,
    on a dark and dreary day.
You're a rainbow, after showers,
    in all your loving ways.

I'll lead two lives, my darling,
    and wait to hold you longer.
My love for you is here to stay...
    and every day just gets stronger!!

Pencie L. Williams

Spring And Summer

The newness of Spring and Summer
Always in a unique way
Excites me to this very day,
No matter how fast the days go.
Year after year blades of new grass
Like tiny green spikes pierce through
    the ground where a mass
Of snow had been. New clouds appear,
    soft baby chicks
Come out of their brown speckled
Wrappings after weeks of
Warmth under the sitting hen.
They, too, have a yen to welcome
A new life, a new world, a new season!

Harriet Ahmels

A Picture Outside

I looked out the window
to see what I could see
I saw a chestnut tree
and I knew it was time
for me to look for chestnuts
before the squirrels got ahead of me
but a few moments later
I saw as many as three
they were running away
from the tree with nuts
in their mouths as fast as
they could be,
I did not know they
had a home close by
they crossed the road
and ran into a hole
but came out to run to
get more nuts at the
big old chestnut tree
I thought how smart they could be.

Jessie Day

Truth Matters

I'm being crucified
on a self-made cross.
I built it with my hands,
bitterly caressed the smooth wood.
I splintered my finger
and allowed it to fester and infect.
The tree soon began to take shape
as did my self destruction.
My deteriorated life...
it's all I have, to cling to, to love.
I am the great pretender,
always going along with what
I'm told to believe.
I try too hard-and I know it.
But I keep trying
and persevering,
hoping someone will
stop me from
hammering in the nails
myself.

Tiffany Puryear

Untitled

High priestess of my distress,
Goddess of my loneliness,
Oh, ephemeral body of mine
doomed to decline with time,
I beg of you to set me free
that I may join the eternal three.

Caroline Bucquoy-Brown

Need

I need someone to hold me,
  I need someone who cares,
I need someone who'll love me,
  and always be right there.

I need someone to hug me,
  to make me feel secure,
I need someone to kiss my lips,
  to feel tenderness there.

I need someone to walk with me,
  to be with me every step of the way,
I need someone to be beside me,
  to always be my friend.

I need someone to dry my tears,
  to be there when I fall,
I need a shoulder to lean on,
  will you be there till the end?

Dawn Marie-Ann Balders

Hello

Everyone's on the world wide web
So we're led to believe,
Nobody's inaccessible
There's nothing, we can't achieve
A hundred ways to say hello,
To millions of people,
We do not know.
And as we roam the world,
Play the games
And surf the net.
Perhaps we'll find the man next door,
The man we've never met.

Barry J. Porritt

Wishes

Sometimes I wish the world was perfect,
I wish the sun would always shine.
Sometimes I wish the trees would grow,
I wish my wounds healed with time.
Sometimes I wish the pain would leave,
I wish the scars weren't so deep.
Sometimes I wish I wasn't born,
I wish I could be born again.
Sometimes I wish I knew myself,
I wish that I could find the answers.
Sometimes I wish I was someone else,
I wish the memories would go away.
Sometimes I wish for happiness,
I wish I could find a smile.
Sometimes I wish to be in love,
I wish I had someone to hold.
Sometimes I wish I could be loved;
Sometimes I wish that you were mine.

Brad Leagle

My Solemn Soul

A turbulent tear stained my heart;
And contradiction played the part.

Fast pace morale, conscience astray;
Your goals, my dreams drifted away.

With solemn soul I bowed in pain;
With dignity, yet much do strain.

My heart was posed in solid stance,
No second guess, no second chance.

Nancy S. Gipson

Life

Planet earth is the place for me
with its mountains, trees,
and beautiful sea.

It's the only place
for the whole human race
why can't you people see.

That it takes a part
of everyone's heart
to live and breathe and be free.

So take some pride
next time you step outside
and feel what you can't see.

For it will grab your heart
and that's a start
to the way it was meant to be.

Mark R. Viets

Bald Eagle

Soaring, gliding, wild and free
Over an ocean or a sea.
When Many were wiped out,
And almost all were gone,
A few had the strength to live on.
Because of that they still fly high
And call out their screeching cry.
It would be an honor for me
To be that eagle flying high and free.

Kelly Wassel

Months

January is bitter sweet
February is freezing love
March is clover green
April is eggs-tra rainy
May is Mother's Days
June is Father's Days
July is firework hot
August is sweet corn days
September is leaves jumping
October is spooky red and orange
November is turkey great
December is a merry month
All the months put together
Will make a year Forever and Ever!

Jessica Looft

Ann

If I did have a sister named Ann
I think she would understand
She wouldn't judge me, or you, or us
She'd be our friend
I do wish I had a sister Ann
  I wish I was your wife
  I could give you my life
If only your wife wasn't a better wife
Than I could ever be...
And if I had a sister named Ann
She would love you too.

Kathleen Cantrall

The River

Light rain creeps in
  unscheduled, with ease
Kissing the soul
  familiar, bittersweet
Soaking the conscience
  burdened, passion and guilt
Stirs the myriad of emotions
  merging, intimate horizons

The road is bathed in shadow
  dangerous, ideals
Tearful laughter disturbs the journey
  welcoming, intrusions
Each step reveals the morning dew
  arousing, rapture
Guided by a hesitant heart
  transcending, adrift

Linda Grace Boon

The Moose And The Mouse

The moose and the mouse
Both lived in a house
Out in the far far west
But moose got so big
That he looked like a pig
So he had to find a new nest.

Soon moose found a mate
After making a date
And asked her to share his new home
But she had a pet peeve
And wanted to leave
So the two of them set off for Nome.

Now mouse was alone
Without even a phone
And he didn't know what he would do.
So he ate a small tart
Then hitched up his cart
And ran away to the zoo.

Alice K. Pierret

The Flower's Day

As our bodies sway through the air,
Our bright petals gleam with delight.
We have many friends,
With beautiful delightful smells.
Some of us are blue in color,
The rest of us are mixed in color.
We rejoice everyday
Until the final day comes,
Then we say goodbye to each other
Until another year comes.

Martine Roe

Goodnight

The wind has gone away,
  Away with its whistle.
The grass is asleep,
  So is the thistle.
The barn door is closing,
  The cows soon will be dozing.
The animals are all asleep,
  Even the geese, even the sheep.
They are all asleep in the house,
  Including the mouse.
The day is done, the day is through.
  It is time for bed, for me and you.

Nathanael Rodda

When Will You Free Me?

I am Mona, I patiently await to
see when master will set me free.
When he will let me go I don't know.
I worked and worked on his big
plantation for so many years.
I've seem many slaves that were
tortured, burned, and beaten to tears.
I in my room at night with my candle
as the only light. Master burst in my
room to lay upon me as his whence
for the night. He says to me strongly
shuck down for me, which means
undress. If I do's what master wants
he makes my work chores less.
I often ask Master, Sir when can
I have's my freedom? Master says
as he holds me tight, I'll free
you one day. I'm, now seventy-eight,
yet I still wait.

Leamona Scott

"The Light I See"

I have known that special
feeling and the beauty of the
smile on her face
And it shows what she's feeling,
her eyes express the love that
words can't say
I want you to know that you
mean so much to me
I want you to know that you're
the light I see
I've been down and so weary
with nothing all around but
silent hate
And I've looked up to see you
near me, time and time again
I've seen your faith
I want you to know that you're
so beautiful to me. I want you
to know that you're the light
I see

Billy Hearwin Junes

At This Moment

The deafening sound of silence
Pounds upon my ears.
I utter a muted scream...
No one hears.

Immobilized by the pain of loneliness,
I cannot break away.
Unable to swim in the sea of life,
Upon the shore, I stay.

Invisible on the stage of the living,
Without a speaking part
An extra whose cue to leave
Is when the other actors start.

The deafening sound of silence
Is pounding upon my ears.
I utter a muted scream
But no one hears.

A. Perry Adams

Where Do I Belong

Alone, alone, alone,
no place to call home.
Like ice cream without a cone,
Oh, where do I belong?

Friends? I have none,
I have not a day of fun.
I feel my life is done,
like I'm dried out by the sun.

Sometimes I wanna moan,
for I feel like a cold hard stone.
Oh, how I long for a home,

Alone, alone, alone,
no place to call home!

Stephanie Hill

I Was Left Alone

And in my final hour, I was
left alone.
No one there for comfort, I was
left alone.
Not a single soul saw my pain,
I was left alone.
No chance of recovery, none
wanted to be near, I was left alone.
The hole was dug where I would
go, but I was left alone.
Dead, not yet, but soon will be, I
was left alone.
Then in my grave, silently I
went, while a few stood 'round.
And when they left, there I was,
I was left alone.
For I had died a lonely death,
cause all the time, I was left alone.

Sarah Keyes

Deaderina
(Something Else To Ignore)

I would walk on water
but it would only get hotter.
In my messy room blues
I twirl on my toes
and avoid knowing the use,
like a ballerina in a noose
washing the stage
with blood on the cage
but the stain left a sty
changing my baked salmon eye.
It's just a fishing line failure.
If I was ten pounds lighter
my anorexia could get better
because I like dancing
to your acceptance
but where's your security
here's my resistance.

Gregory Steven Rogers

Way Down Deep

Way down deep
Underneath the pond
Way down deep
In the wet ground
Frogs leap
Leaves decay
Minnows sleep
Underneath the pond
Way down deep

Joey Hobbs

Shadow Souls

Walk down the bloody alleyway
Wearing darkness like a coat
Singing silence through my veins
Crumpled bodies by the dumpster
Reeking alcohol and vomit
Creeping shadows seeking light
Spinning dreams with echoed sight
Here lies the poet yearning to forget
Here lies the athlete soaked in regret
Forgotten by kin
Marinated in gin
Suns coming up
The lightsiders going to their jobs
Stumbling in the blinding white
Sucking from the bottle
One last drop
Crippled eyes
Looking from a pile
Of filthy rags
"Can you spare a quarter, mister?"

Anthony Glenn

"The Arena"

To all who may challenge,
Please..enter the game.
My gates are forever wide open.

But be you warned,
All faint of heart.
You reside in the rule maker's castle.

And I am the king..

Richard T. Odom

Pink Dreams

I am awake in the night,
meditating our love,
like a beautiful love of innocence
it irradiates fervor.

Suddenly...your face,
overcomes my mind,
in a serene image,
soft, tender and refulgent.

Now...I am asleep,
with you and our love;
I am living a divine world
of pleasure and illusion.

Olman A. Madrigal-Ledezma

Untitled

My friendship with you
means most in this world,
I'd never give it up
not for my boy...
or your girl.
We've been through a lot
in these past few years,
had a lot of laughs
shed a few tears.
We are very close
as close as two can be.
And sometimes that's scary
you truly mean the world to me.
So whenever you have doubts
that my feelings are true
look back on these words
and remember...
my heart is with you.

Reyne Arbuckle

Tiger

Tigers are running after
their prey.

In the wilderness with
exotic flowers and trees
watching.

Growing vines swing past them.

They are a blur.

Each one watching.

Watching as they fly
past them.

Revealing danger in the
wilderness.

Alixandre Alter

Feelings

Lithe, limp, devoid of life
A zombie moving through
the animation reel
Fixed like clock numbers
Watching hands move
As a door dependent
Upon the winds of nature
to show some change

Distant, no passion, no soul
Unable to hear, to feel, to live
Tossed by the waves of time
into a rock crumbling
from the claws of the enraged Ocean
The reel advances rapidly
Zombie proceeds most listlessly
Sin ganas...sans desire...
into a soulless underworld

Monique Anthony

I Saw Me Die

I turned around and saw me die
I wondered why these people cried
I went to them and asked them why
What reason do you have to cry
I asked and asked but no reply
I sat down where my body lied
I pondered until I realized
They could not hear my woeful cries
I was here but was not alive
Another sad and wasted life was I

Aaron Willmon

From Far Beyond

Although we've never met
I feel as though we have
We are connected in some spiritual way
Family stories passed on
Painting vivid portraits of you
I feel your warm presence
Are you watching over me?

From far beyond the white puffy clouds
From far beyond the rich blue sky
Will we meet one day?
Of course we will
And I will know it is You!

Mary Kate McNamara

Cacophony

Crash of thunder
    As skies darken
Clouds thicken
    And winds roar

Energy levels build
    Power immeasurable
Life anticipates possibility
    Destruction inherent

Torrential rains drowning
    Volcanic eruptions
Swirling winds ripping
    Chaotic interruptions

Waves crash reverberates
    Windblown sands reshape
Natural transition approaches
    Sun hesitantly appears

Deaths meaningless summons
    Steadfastly refused
Positive growth resumes
    Life prevails

Keith N. Gantz

Winding Through Time

The sun will rise, the sun will set.
The year will have its own quartet.
Winter, summer, spring, and fall,
Forever stays the flaming ball.

But my own life is held by time,
All the joy, all the grime.
A candle burns, dripping wax.
Time slips through the myriad cracks.

A winding path walled up in stone.
Labyrinth knocks a tone.
From mahogany clocks that swing free,
Pendulum rides over me.

Hypnotic tick-tock it makes in phase,
As I slump through this chilled maze.
Auspicious hours just rampage through,
And time is spent like morning dew.

Michael Luc

Never Ending

Your hair flows like a flower
    Blowing in the breeze.
Your eyes shine like a beam of light
    Glowing through the trees.
Your skin is like the finest silk
    Woven perfectly.
My love for you is like a river
    Flowing downstream.
My love for you is never ending.

Ryan Lantis

Melancholy

Have you ever just wanted
to lay down and die
open your eyes
and look up to the sky
see what you want to
get what you get
see what you see through
and pay off the debt
if you have, don't cry
as a friend, so have I

Lindsay James

Where Is My Dad?

Little one listen close
The one you love the most
Is nothing more than a ghost

The stories and memories you hold
By a fool were they told

The one you hold so dear
Will never be near

He is far away
Never to stay

He will never come for you
No matter what you do

You may often think of him
But his memories of you are dim

Little one please let go
Make room to grow

Monique Bocock

Mr. Pheasant

Good morning, Mr Pheasant,
    it's good to hear your call
As you wander through our dooryard
    shouting greetings to us all.
We look forward to your visit
    each and every morn
Searching with our sleepy eyes
    'til we see you in the corn.
The vivid green and spot of red
    that grace your regal head
Your presence is a welcome sight
    as you reach the flower bed.
We love to watch you strut your stuff
    when you make your daily rounds.
You're a most important part
    of the joyful morning sounds.
Good morning, Mr. Pheasant,
    you help to make our day
Another of God's treasures
    may it always be this way.

Virginia S. Kemp

Lonely

This pain inside, which is so strong,
No one should ever feel.
This pain that is forever long,
It's a dream, and yet it's real.
All my dreams are grand and new,
They're goals that seem so clear.
And yet I know they can't come true.
For they go to other peers.
I need a friend in times of need
To help me find my way.
To touch my heart and plant a seed,
To drive this hurt away.
Please come find, and rescue me,
Take me from this agony.
Away from pain no one can see,
From this world of misery.

Naomie Barnes

The Sun

So soft and bright
as it holds me in warmth,
shining in the cool breeze light,
reminds me of home.

Kim Drobac

Who I Am Is....

Who I am is a flower beginning to bloom. A rose that is basking
in the sun, soaking in its rays, obtaining nourishment from the soil
beneath. Absorbing the gentle raindrops that are softly falling around me.
This is a new spot for me in the garden of life. Mostly I have
felt like a weed, just growing wildly, multiplying, wandering in all
directions. Never having any specific destination, just moving
without restrictions. Covering as much territory as I could,
smothering the flowers, always just wanting to be accepted as one.
My dreams weren't too high. To have just been accepted as a
flower would have been enough perhaps a pansy, a violet or maybe
a carnation. But never did I dream of becoming a Rose, that was beyond my wildest expectations.
Today is different; dreams can come true. Anything and everything
is possible. However, you have to be willing to dream the dream.
I can make a difference, a Red Rose, the ultimate symbol of Love.
Who is to say that as my petals unfold a new color in the garden of life will emerge.
It's possible my colors could become the ultimate symbol for Love...

Shirley J. Clarkson

Spring Time

Spring time is the time of year when the flowers wake up and stretch their petals to the sky.
The birds come back and sing their beautiful tunes while the trees' leaves are about to bloom.
In the mornings the grass looks like a spring shower has passed by, instead of Jack Frost.
Mid-day the world seems to come to life with the sounds of frogs croaking, birds chirping, and people yelling.
Yet at night, things quiet down a bit. But if you listen hard, you may hear crickets chirping softly to each other,
    and a far off wolf howling to the moon to say good-night.
Spring time is the time of year when everything comes alive.

Jessica Elaine Estes

Baby Boy

What scar is this? Placed there by a surgeon's scalpel.
He cut from side to side to protect the life of an unborn child.
And as she laid there awaiting the birth a resilient
    baby boy was born on earth.

She held her breath like a windless day for no cry had come her way.
It seemed as hours had slipped away until she heard her son that day.

Her tears filled the room with joy as her arms held her baby boy.
Her heart was dancing like a grand ballet cause her love had blossomed on that day.

Her pain was like a throbbing heart when the nurse took him from her arms.
This would only last four days for home they went on Wednesday.

Their life together began that day for two years he had grown each day. The scar she had faded away
But the memory will last always. Brett

Ruie Simon Jones

As Death Awaits

The skies darken and the thunder rolls throughout the valley as the sweat pours from my hot face.
Darkness slowly begins to envelop my head. Death comes but not soon enough.
The pain that I suffer is so intense that my heart beats against my chest.
My eyes water, sending floods of tears down my hot cheeks.

My mother's gentle hand against mine leaves imprints against my fingers.
My father, I can hear, paces back and forth across the bedroom floor.

As I lie waiting for the darkness to engulf me,
I can see the white swiftly-moving horses galloping toward me through the heavens.
The King of Death is pulling at the reins, coming to call for me.

Now it is my turn to see the God Almighty and to sit upon his knee,
and to have him whisper to me a soft luscious lullaby as he tells me that I am safe.

He is finally here now lifting me up into his arms.
He places me upon his horse-drawn carriage as he drives me to heaven,
where I know that there will be angels waiting for me, and all of Death's beauty.
As my soul parts my body and I breathe my last breath my mother weeps.

Donna Erquhart

Let Me...

Let me be the one you love, the one who stands apart;
Allow me in, behind the wall you've built around your heart.
Let me be the one whose touch allays your inner fears,
The one whose tender kisses can evaporate your tears.
Let me be the one you want to tell about your day,
The one whose smile and voice you miss whenever I'm away.
Let me be the one on whom you lean when you're fatigued.
Let me, and I'll lovingly fulfill your every need.
Let me be the one to whom, in trouble, you can turn
And when, at night, you reach for warmth, for me I hope you'll yearn.
Come with me outside your wall, where love is not confined
Where everything that life can give is there for us to find.
Share with me what's out there, both the sorrows and the mirth
And let the love within us be the measure of our worth.
Let's take this walk together — a couple — side by side
Let me make my love for you a compass and a guide.
Let me be the one with whom "forever" yields no fear.
Take my heart and make it yours, hold it ever near;
Join me on life's journey, one that's poised to start
Let me be the one you love — entrust me with your heart.

John W. Chierichella

"The Rosebud"

A strong healthy rose bush of excellent quality was growing in a
    garden of rich soil.
Someone dug up the sturdy bush and transplanted it into a
much finer
    and more desirable location.
He fertilized and nurtured the bush until a vibrant bud appeared.
Just as the newly formed rosebud had turned her slender neck to
    the sun...
    trembling in ecstasy.....
    glimmering with hopeful expectations.....
    stretching her petals.....
    shining with the dew of life itself.....
The man plucked her from her bush!
He withdrew from her the essence for sustaining life, and placed her
    on a table.
She slowly began to wilt and fade as her desire to live ebbed away.
    Her petals turned inward.....
    Her dew kissed leaves withered.....
Just as she had almost slipped into oblivion, in one harsh sweep
    she was cast upon the floor.
A heavy boot crushed the remaining flicker of her life from existence.
The potential of her blossoming glory was forever lost.
He never witnessed her flower.
                    I was your rosebud.

Joanie Lassiter

Belligerent Believers

When we were wee, wavering, wholly wet waifs,
Worshipping one wise welfare warden was worthwhile.
Who wouldn't want worrisome wrongs whipped worldwide?

Whereas what went wildly wayward were...
Wily, whimsical, word-wielding, warped warmongers.
Wicked, wand-waving wizards, warts withstanding,
Willfully woo weak well-wishers while...
Widely waging wretched, wrath wreaking witchery.
Whirling winds will whistle with...
War weapons' whanging, wanton wails.

Where we witness witless, worthless waste...
Why won't we warily watch warnings?
When will we welcome wisdom's wistful whisper?

Robert Leider

Silence

Nature is a silent orchestra
The cries and calls of birds rise in a constant chorus,
The sounds of a babbling brook, a rushing stream, a
lapping lake, provide the string instruments,
The vibration of a snapping twig, a rustling leaf, or a
swaying branch, give way to the brass section,
The wind blowing through the trees and across the fields
make the wind instruments sing,
The growl of a bear, the chatter of a racoon and squirrel,
the howling of a wolf, the cry of a bobcat, intermix in a
wild array as the brass section.
Even as the first spirit of the morning light meets the
final glow of the moon and the stars, with a pallet's
blend of colors, the silence never ends..

MeriBeth Moon

Dance (For One Night)

All these faces blur
People act so strange
Heading out to dance
Play this masquerade
Hide the hurt inside
Make it go away...
Sometimes I dream and
See her smiling face

Strobe light flash
Strangers move and sway
Still feel her close to me, now so far away
Her skin so pale and soft
The warmth of her embrace
Thought we had inertia
But night turns into day

I still think of "Charlotte" sometimes
Pictures of her linger in my mind
Remembering her...
Dream a wall around myself
And the night just fades away...

Teresa Rorstrom

Shadows

I lie in bed at night curiously watching the shadows
Dance across my wall to music they can only hear

Listening to the wind blow gently against the leaves,
I finally hear the music they're dancing to

I rise from my bed like a magical force bringing me to
Dance with the shadows in the pale moonlight

Jeremy Smith

My Father's Father

The back forties are separated
by Grandfather's wooden bridge.
Like Grandpa weather beaten by years,
needs more attention now.
The boards are aged even my pony cannot cross.
And for Grandpa he left us years ago,
but not before he taught us a bond for family love.
A greatness his children knew,
a specialty the grandchildren would learn.
And now, no one can ever replace
the boards of Grandfather's wooden bridge.

Donald James Crosby

Heart Warming

Mom, I know that you are not here-
But in my heart you're always Dear-
The Love and kindness that you shared-
Showed the world how much you cared.
Your image is fused within my mind-
Your Love will always remain behind-
Thank you for all the years of love-
I've missed you so, since you went above...

Barbara L. Collins

Awakening

Wandering through the Forest - Deathly Dark,
searching for the lake's cool waters of sleep and rest - Eternal
Sleep, God in his wisdom smiles - perfect harmony.

Knowing that I once lost my way - stumbling silently,
as leaves slowly float and fall - endlessly sentenced to Fall!
Remembrance floods my soul, an ancient eclipse darkened the sky as
thickening thorns pierced his flesh. Nails bleed three times on
the lightless hill, screaming in pain
endlessly.

Terribly, the moon's crimson light glares revealing the anguish,
the love, the ecstasy of my heart.
It begins, the sparrow sings her final note - so sweet - so clear -
so final - as the music fades into twilights gloom - echoing silence.
It begins, a quiet so still, daunting me, haunting me, ringing in my
ears with the roar of a thousand bells on a blessed morning.
It begins!

The lamb cries no more and His suffering has ended as I am allowed
to live no more.
The Blackened Sunless Dawn Approaches - for its final time-
Endlessly!!!

Andrew L. Cazier

"Summer Sun"

The welcome glow of your first light
Erodes the edges of the night.

God's feathered creatures start their song
Excited by another dawn.

The silent darkness pushed away
By the promise of the brand new day.

Both hi-tech world and nature's grace
Are marveled by your brilliant face.

Morning glories, clad in sparkling dew
Begin to turn their heads toward you.

You climb up to your lofty station
And fill our hearts with inspiration.
Beneath you children laugh and play
While grown-ups toil for their pay.

We've learned to love these summer days
Accented by the warming rays-

You radiate with bursts of glee
On simmering land and shining sea.

Robert J. Darnick

Goodbye My Beloved One

I didn't even know him,
I didn't even see him,
I only saw the wonderful pictures of him,
I heard stories of him.
But now he is gone,
a caring person,
who I hope to see in the future.
Rest in peace my loved one.

Susanna Hong

Where Are You?

Where are you, I wake up, get
dressed and leave.
The only sound, my footsteps.
I sign in, where Are you, get
undressed and wait.
The only sound, my silence.
I get dressed, become frightened,
where are You, and cry.
I am not dressed, scream in pain, and give birth.
Where Are You?
The only sound, our baby's tears.

Katherine Johnson

The Road to Home

The road to home
Marked by two white lines
Two souls not far apart
Two souls yet so alone

A storm descends upon each soul
a thundering rain, a misty fog
The eye now strains
For two white lines
on the road to home.

The road now winds
The hill goes steep
Two faltering hearts search for the lead
of two white lines
For the road to home.

The mystic lines of love and truth
They never lose their glow
They show the path, they open up
The only road to home.

Hedwig Kempf

Battle Rhyme

Here I stand
With sword in hand

Ready for war
With enemies of fabled lore

These trolls and ogres are truly ugly
But our dwarf allies are very smugly

The battle was gruesome and gory
Few lived to tell of our glory

We saved our land from destruction
Not only at the kings instruction

Our homes and family were also at stake
We destroyed our enemies like a mighty earthquake

Back to the king's palace we go
Trying to forget our fearsome foe

To where a well deserved celebration has started
For those of us who are heavy hearted
A toast I make with goblet high
To lost friends and family a last goodbye

Rick Gray

Dolphins

Dolphins are beautiful, elegant and free,
They dive in and out of the water so gracefully,
They play water games with all their friends,
They swim in and out of all the coral reef bends,
Dolphins are beautiful, elegant and free.
I guess that's why they amaze me.

Richal Rudnick

Rainbow

Screaming red-kissed blossom
Floating down a lavender stream
To die a bloody passion
Hinted in a shade of green
Blue glistening in the sun
Sparkling shade of gold
Light to dark: once new made old;
To die a thousand dances
And lie naked in the sun
Cherish violet moments
And linger in black fun
To kiss what once was orange
Turning it grey-green
Lemon-yellow stars
That never hear the screams
Pink-stained tears
That fall from hazel eyes
Boiling crimson pain that shuts out all the lies
Shades of midnight lust blanket cold bodies in shine
That forever glows silver; chaotic moments in time

Kari Skagen

The Desolate Old Man

A thunderous rapping
at the window or the door?
Not really sure; for I see no more.
The winds they are howling,
they come from every direction,
the demons they are prowling
I know no resurrection!
for I begin to realize it is death
beating at my door
to take my very last breath
to leave nothing ever more!
I have no fight left in me
and it's easy to understand why
I have created doom and misery.
And now it's time for my demise.
I begin a long and tiresome journey
down into an abyss of despair
I don't dare beg for forgiveness
it's not even considered for men like me
and I do not even care.

Stephanie A. McDaniel

"As She Laid There"

As she laid there peacefully and calm,
Tears ran down my face.
Feeling her face upon my palms,
She was now living with grace.

She had left a lot behind,
Taking a piece of my heart.
As thing went through my mind,
I, not knowing how to restart.

She laid there with nothing left to say,
But the tears they shed was to be seen.
She became an angel that flew away.
She is now forever a teen.

Good or bad, the memories will always be with me.

Maiwa Lor

Man Of Many Skills

Crippled in the eyes
His fingers feel rose petals and give him a surprise
He can not see the Earth
The blind man knows the great amount it's worth
This man of wonder sees with his hands and heart
He knows every animal together or apart
This kind soul understands why people stare
He does not blame them for they are true and care
The blind man does not weep
His eyes are able to sleep
The man plays the harp with ease
He travels the many seas
He is just a man with no sight
A man who has won the ultimate fight.

Jessica L. Corrie

A 50's Porch

I remember so well that old porch of ours,
There's no way to count the many hours I spent there,
Curled up in the oversized swing,
Thinking about things I'd do in the spring,
Sometimes I'd eat supper there, do homework too,
The world seemed to go by within my full view,
It was my place to meet friends, both girls and boys,
In the corner Mom always stacked the grand kids toys,
It was the place I sat; with the love of my life,
Shyly planning our bright future as husband and wife,
Screened, so bugs didn't bite, and painted battleship gray,
The air had the hint of cigar on any given day,
I still see my Dad, sitting almost perfectly still,
Relaxing from his long hard day...
        At the Mill

Linda T. Sanders

Preservation Of Mankind

Victory upon victory in battle-wars nefarious rewarder
by decimating and desolating our beautiful planet
reaped at expense of human fodder!

When will basic moral ethics behaviour kick-in,
or must contemporary humanity be so kinked
by persisting this assault on fellow brethren.

Surely an unyielding altruistic effort by all
is obligatory in over-coming this soluble dilemma
for man's perpetual survival.

Max G. Cherney

New Experience

The door slams. I am locked in a new world. I wish to go back but I have no choice. This is all new to me. I am moved from a world of darkness to one of color. Freedom of movement in all directions, and sounds. I hear sounds, voices of other people, and it bothers me. In the other world I was alone now I am surrounded by people in masks. They sound very excited and happy. I am handed to one person who is laying down, she holds me and makes me warm. And as I drift off to sleep I realize that I am with my mommy. I am just a newborn.

Mike Waters

Just Another Interpretation

The sounds you hear are coming from your headaches,
And the sights you see are just illusions from my imagination;
But it's these sounds and illusions that drive you insane,
An it's the softness of the walls that caved you in,
And it's the darkness of those halls that brought you back again.

The moonlight guides you to a place of desolation
Where you let your heart explode creating a windstorm
where your soul blows across this barren and dry atmosphere,
As hail pours through a gaping wounded revelation;
Which is the only way you can battle your fears.
I know you want to run - just hideaway
From this anticipated sense of wisdomatic stupidhood;
And the blood red stains in the heart of a Shadow
Where dreamers die trying to find the other side,
Trying to find the lost civilization of the unconfused.

The insanity that drives you to the edge,
Tripping on lifelines, falling off the side of illusions,
Back into the reality in which your imagination dwells;
In the world that you know of the revelations,
In the dwelling in the coffin, in the grave.

Robert A. Wirick

The Song Of The Rain

The tiny raindrops fall softly to earth,
each drop with its majestic mirth.
The little fairies dance around,
as each little drop touches the ground.

The grass reaches out for a taste,
as the worms and bugs weave a pattern of lace.
The flowers seem to glisten and glow,
as the birds shake and shudder from below.

The children love the tingling of the rain drops.
They run and play in hope that it never stops.
Adults run for cover as they do,
They don't remember to say thank you.

Soon the rain will go away,
and leave us to play.
But while she is here,
let us enjoy instead of tear.

Alice E. Spence

"The Ocean"

The ocean relaxes you,
Swimming, snorkeling and watching seagulls.
If you're angry, just go to the ocean.

Crashing waves on the shore,
Washing up colorful shells, even fish!

Storms release the ocean's fury.
Waves pounding,
Crashing,
Dragging whatever's in its path.
Eroding beaches, strong undertows, claiming lives.

Suddenly, it calms.
The beach returns and beautiful shells appear.
The fish are back
The ocean again is a pleasant place.
Boy, how I love the ocean!

Kevin Beach

He Is There

Once my life was filled with fear,
As I walked through each day.
I didn't know what to do,
I didn't know what to say.
   You see,
I didn't know He was there.

One day as I started walking through my day,
As I was going along my way.
I looked up into the sky,
I looked way, way up high.
   Right then,
I found He was there.

As you walk through your day,
When you don't know what to do.
When you don't know what to say,
Look up into the sky,
Look way, way up high.
   You'll find,
He is there.

Edith F. Gosnell

For Brendan...

You've seen the world through your enlightened eyes. Met people in many places, you've touched many hearts. People will remember you! Your life tells a fascinating story of caring, love and helpfulness. It saddens me to see you gone.

But now, you shall see the world again! Visit places you've loved in your nineteen years of living. But now, you will see them in a far more beautiful way than you've ever seen them before. You shall see them from a bird's eye view. It saddens me to see you gone.

But, flutter your wings! Embrace the world, for one life has ended, another just begun! For many people loved you, they will remember your love of them. And though I hardly knew you, my life will never be the same again. There is a special place in everyone's heart that you touched. It saddens them to see you gone.

Ryan Fissel

Pain

I see it there deep down below,
Something burning long and slow.

I see the flames growing strong in your heart.
Please, dear friend, tell me how this fire did start.

You think no one notices the tears in your eyes.
You say it's the sun, but I see through these lies.

If you give me a chance, I'll help extinguish the flames.
Together we'll stop your heart's painful games.

Keep in mind that happiness is just around the bend.
As hard as it seems, your heart will soon mend.

Just remember one thing before you leave.
Pain again you will receive.

But if you are ever again in deep despair,
Remember for you I will always be there.

Angeline Restrepo

The Battle

The warship glides over each wave
Meeting her enemy in full gaze
Coming up her port most side
With the rising of the tide
With cannon loaded and with trimmed sail
Turned to meet the approaching gale
Fifty feet from ship to ship
As the sea rises and then she dipped
Then the enemy fired their cannons' bores
Emptying her weapons store
The warship matches her enemy blow for blow
As they both hang in the water dangerously low
Then it quieted and came their chance
To take a more aggressive stance
Forty-nine cannons emptying in a single scream
Her broadsides power breaking every beam
Destruction from the bottom of the hull to her enemy's topmost mast
Bits of debris here and there are cast
Then the enemy sank into the locker of Davey Jones
Their crew still there, but nothing left but bones.

Flory Frank Toto IV

The Butcher Of Bagdad

The Butcher of Bagdad, oh where does he live?
In Iraq or D.C., which one of them hid?
A killer of babies-how smart we've become.
A new world order starts with missiles and bombs.

Propaganda, the media did eat,
Regurgitating it back while in our seats.
Thanks to the Arnets who monitored our views
Did everyone loose sight or forget their cues?

I still ponder the "Butcher" who struck in the night.
Who is to say, was he wrong or right?
His motives outrageous, the ribbons so yellow
The Halcion drug such a neurotic fellow.

Human dignity caught in flight,
Remember the Kurds, we will help you fight
We'll support your quest for freedom and land,
But then in essence it's only sand

What happened to compassion and the intelligent mind?
It was lost on a people whose tears are blind.
Goodbye to the dead that were buried and blown,
And the flags were waved when they all came home.

Lauren V. MacGregor

Southern Comfort

I wiggled my toes in the warm sand
as the lambent waves nuzzled the shore in soft caress.
Verdant palm foliage whispered soft harmonies of a
never ending summer with the promise of forever porcelain skies.

On the horizon triangles of white sail seemed to flitter
precariously tempting the edge of an eternal sapphire sea.

From down the beach, cries of sheer delight mixed with shrills of
the gulls when the walls of golden sand castles were tumbled over by
the taunting paws of a younger brother.

I breathed the scene like air.

Time retarded for that moment, framing the scene like a picture.

"I want you guys to remember that in four hours from now, we will be
back in Chicago where it is fourteen below and the sun isn't shining
and Mr. Winter is still holding court. Savor this moment and let it
be a spark that you can take back to Chicago with you to rekindle
flames of memory that will warm you in the winter months ahead."

I looked at my mother and realized for perhaps the first time ever
that she wasn't talking goofy, as I had thought before, or perhaps
the first time I felt the words.

Rebecca Schlachter

Summer's End

Leaves rustle gently under unnatural light,
due to false breezes; as darkness continues to overpower
an ever stirring population.
Reflections of a luminous sphere above as seen
seven time at mere glance become non-existent with
the pull of a chain and only quiet murmurs from
nocturnal inhabitants of the marsh echo unaltered
as reminders of reality through the still night.
While the mind, never-ceasing, contemplates questions
which still puzzle individuals this eve as they have
since the beginning of time.

H. L. Roberts Jr.

I Remember

As I hear your voice I remember the feel of your touch.
Your smooth, dark skin.
The look in your eye, the smile on your face.
I remember.
So many thoughts have I held inside.
Buried deep under the hurt that I once felt.
As time passes by I wonder, but I'm scared.
I take a deep breath and I let go.

As I hear your voice I remember the feel of your fist.
The anger I still feel.
The darkness that I tried to hold inside.
The silence that became deep and penetrating from within.
I remember.
So many thoughts have I held inside.
Thoughts that were too strong so I let go.

Sara L. Davidson

My Mother Is...

My mother is like a flower who gives
me life to live.
She's like a sunshine that shines
right through my heart and the hearts
of my family.

My mother is as wonderful as the
morning light,
as delicate as a petal on a rose,
as sweet as honey,
and loving caring.

My mother is like an angel from above;
she watches over me,
she makes sure that I'm well tucked in
when she turns off the light, and
she never complains or fights with anyone.

Instead she tries to make peace with
her enemies and gives them a friendly smile...

My mother will always be my sunshine.

Maria Arreola

Success

The years come with change
And why not the diversity?
A river without fresh water becomes lifeless and still
Producing only the quiet of emptiness.

I'd rather the change that comes with the cleaning rain
That makes the Rivers swell and alive again
Producing the fresh water of new ideas
And hear the noise of Success
Rippling free

A Smile By Angel

Cynthia Cole

Daylight Dreamers

Perpetual dawn, the innocence of morning is do.
Daylight Dreamers, dreaming up glorious illusions
for a new day has now presented itself.
Through the kaleidoscope eyes, ravishing mist upon
a mountain top, in this distance there are miles
between me and my destiny, yet the confusion of your
voice seems so near, the scent of your perfume surrounds
me, I thought I heard you call my name, then a figment
of reality interrupted as I stand staring into the empty sky,
dreaming, daydreaming.
a vision of you, I feel the warm touch of your fingertips
descend into my heart, softly a spring breeze smashes my face
so beautifully appearing the gift of your lips, also revealing
the presence of your body. I'm holding you, I'm loving you
I'm missing you, No! No! Please, don't go.
Back to reality, our conscience is a precious thing we can
ponder up any thought, any dream, and make it seem real,
Hold firm to your dreams. Dreams are something no one can steal.

Robert Slater

Thinking Days

Thinking days, dreary days. I sit and think, thoughts
falling through my mind as the rain falls through the air.
My mind is dark and cloudy as a front moves through. Thunder
rolls through consciousness, and lightning zaps through me,
electrifying my feelings. Slowly, the incessant precipitation picks
up its tempo, as the mind grows darker, cloudier. In this
darkness, lightning flashes, as strobes of conscious overflow
begin to grow and breed distortion. I begin to lose all light
as false night envelops my little corner of reality. I try to
recall my sunny, warm days of past, but it is much too dark, dreary.
Now, outside, the wind is howling, lightning crashes, rain plummets
down in sheets, and thunder rolling is the only thing I can hear.
Where am I? Where is anyone? I give up, and begin to look ahead,
into, and through the rain. It has to end, the sun has to shine
again. The storm grows, and rages on. Stop! Too much rain is
falling through my darkness. I am scared; worried. It will stop
eventually, but will the clouds ever roll away from my mind?
    I welcome the sun.

Jeremy Parratt

Dawn's Rise

As a soft beating rain quietly dies,
A faint mist sadly drifts on.
The morning sun peeks shyly over the horizon,
And begins to transform the dark night into dawn.

The Earth slowly comes to life,
As a gentle swirl of colors fall from the sky.
The last of the stars fade away,
And the moon waves a silent good-bye.

A salty sea breeze dances with the wind,
And beautiful flowers bask in the pale light.
The prairie grass sways to an unknown tune,
As midnight black starlings take to flight.

A fresh mountain spring wanders aimlessly among the rocks,
As a cool gust of wind contentedly sighs.
The Earth awakens from a deep sleep,
During dawn's mystical rise.

Megan Dixon

"My Cage"

I stand on the inside looking out
Where I say I seek to be
But no sooner do I attain it
That I begin to ask , why me?
I run and hide, then once on the outside,
In circles I travel,
From here to there,
And still, I'm nowhere.....
Where is my place?
What do you see in my face?
I'm locked in or is it out?
I reach and then I pull away.
I arrive, but not to stay.
I'm mortal—a mere of a man
Created by God,
Striving to understand me.....

Barbara Lewis Eckles

Cassandra

Amid the burning flames I stand
A tall proud figure with knife in hand
And strike with this weapon if I must
To protect faith and trust
But though I find in raging fear my unfaithful heart
And my eyes turn to tear

And as I watch my home burn down
the ones who did not believe
now see
That I was right and they were wrong
But it doesn't matter now
All is gone
Lost like a bluebird's song

A poor lost soul am I
Who finds herself within a burden's eye
And as fools must surely die
So must I be cast aside
But though I ask why
all hope of an answer is left, far behind
And with that I go

Iris Dickhoff

My Prayer

Oh heavenly father, full of grace
Create in me a clean heart, and let it show on my face.

Not wanting this just for a show,
But I want your love in me to glow.
And to help love between others to grow.

I also want your love to show in my words and deeds.
Like in helping someone's material or spiritual needs.

I know that a Christian is not
Just a holy name to wear,
But it's a deep concern for our fellow brothers
And sisters that we must share.

Lord, help the people that are hungry, sick,
Or in pain, and shelter the ones from the cold and rain.
I pray for the courage to undo all the wrong I've ever done,
Because I feel bad if I've caused some angry thoughts in anyone.

This is more than I should ask of you Lord,
Except to help me live free from sin.
Good night heavenly father,
Thank you. Amen

Mary Vessie ("Shakey")

My Sadness

Peace and Harmony
Something I wish we owned.

With wars and the fighting and killing
I stand not afraid all alone.
For God will protect me and keep me safe.

If you believe and you have faith,
you shall learn not to be afraid.

The sadness though is still inside
and salty tears want to fall,
although I keep them locked up with my pride.

I know I will be happy one day,
but for right now I stand alone with myself
Not Afraid
Not Afraid

Pamela Daniels

Christmas Is For Children

The world's an inconsistent place and there are times we ponder;
Will our children be prepared as into the world they wander?
Armed only with their wits and the values we've imparted
We pray they love and learn and laugh and don't become dark-hearted.

We fill their packs with self-respect, with pride and honesty,
And leave behind intolerance, it's made of lead you see.
We pass along our maps of trails that we have walked before
And hope they heed the warnings that we've left at danger's door.

But if they choose to blaze a trail and leave footprints of their own,
It's memories and traditions that won't let them feel alone.
These are the gifts, more dear than gems, we pack with diligent care,
And secure them for our children who can take them anywhere.

So this is why, at Christmas time, we try so very hard
To decorate as best we can and send out Christmas cards.
We bake delights, wrap our gifts and fill our homes with cheer,
As we treasure up these sights and sounds and scents
    from year to year.

And, for our loved ones every where, our wish for you is clear,
We send the message of the season that comes this time of year.
So guild your homes with gladness, as in holidays of past,
And fill your hearts with memories that will always last.

Camera C. Bartolotta

"Our Friendship"

Our friendship is like the ocean
    it goes on and on forever
And even though the ocean is spread out
    it always stays together
Our friendship is like the ocean it has
    its ups and downs
And through it all and in the end it always
    comes around
No matter how long and deep the ocean is
    we all must try to cross it
Just like no matter how far away you are from
    here we keep our friendship lit.
Our friendship will keep on burning forever
    like the stars
Even if you lived as far away as Mars
Our friendship is like the ocean's waves
So powerful and strong it will never fade
You and I are the greatest friends
And no matter how many oceans are between
    us our friendship will never end!

Danah Cordeira

"Belong"

Warm is the sun that shines on your hair,
so light that it matches the clothes that you wear.

Smooth and silky is your skin, which tempts
me to create a move from within.

Subtle yet sexy is your body, closest to
mine as we embrace.

Awesome is your charm which causes some alarm.
Tight in your arms, which all so strong,
right where I know I belong!

Annette Gingles

She Lives

Beyond the Wind,
She lives.
Beyond the meadowlark's call,
She lives.
Beyond the hearts of those who loved her,
She lives.

Cricket Cat lives
And we who knew her Beauty,
Rejoice.
She lives
And we are glad.
We remember her, for in our hearts
She Lives.

Clinta B. Ingraham

Love

Love is a flower that blossoms in every heart
Love makes people do their part
Love makes the little bird start to sing
Love makes the wedding bells start to ring
Love gives the colors to a small rainbow
Love makes a friendship start to grow
Love makes the crystal white snow fall
Love brings joyfulness to one and all
Love makes the still waters blue
Love takes the old and makes it new
Love is a baby being born
Love is something we all mourn
Love is something you give away
And I shall give it everyday

Kathryn Cooper

The Little Bird

Look how the little bird soars through the sky.
It makes you wonder how he got up so high
It makes you wish that you could go to such a place
Where you could meet the bird face to face
He asks you how you got up here so high
I have my imagination by my side
He asked you where are you going to go
And as you were about to answer him you woke up
And you said, I did really fly in the sky
And only I will ever know

Erin Walczykowski

The Move

One too many glasses of wine,
one too many miles apart,
Mom, do you remember how I held you there?
And you, me.

Together we searched for comfort
child holding child
your face filling the crux of my arm,
and you saying,
  I understand,
  I understand,
  I always understand how everyone else feels, what everyone
    else needs.

And me, finally comprehending your sacrifice for him, for us.
If only he were here,
if only change weren't so fast approaching.

Joslyn Matthews

Untitled

Soft in my youth, unblistered
You called me out of the shabby world of the word
And drenched me in the wet universe of your love
I tied my sleepy heart to your mad star and together
We abandoned the future for our own rare possibility
You were the genius madwoman, the liquid mind
I saw more in your electric eyes than I could ever dream
I lay humble in their sight long after they stopped looking
  through me.

Those magnified lives died in our youth
The unfired memories melt with my manhood, warmed
I reach for you again
No longer heart to eccentric heart
But fingertip to fingertip, stiff with age, my crazy love
Remember for me the world your wild eyes see.

Gary E. Blackburn

To Fall In Your Hands

Like a leaf upon a tree...secure I was.
Vital, alive and strong...in love I was.
Swaying with the swirls of air, not yielding to wind's destruction
  for I loved...I cared.

Oh, how the sweet sap through my veins did flow,
Brought to me by that tree so steady...making me ever keen and ready,
  enabling me to live, to grow,
'Til brown with spots I began to turn; suddenly the sap was for
  what I yearned.
Holding on with each thread of hope that the lack was just a brief
  delay...that soon my veins would throb again with renewed
  strength for another day,
It never came to my disbelief and there I was...a dying leaf.

The bough no longer held me close or called me its own,
I felt myself get weak and then...I saw how pale I had grown.
The wind who never I did fear...I dreaded its breezes drawing near.
Before me I could see the fall...and I could not save myself at all.

Rosemary O. Robinson

Fear

To fear the unknown is to Fear
the ordinary. To quiver at the mysterious
is to shake at the sight of the
common place. For how can you fear
what you know nothing of unless you
fear what you already understand.

Nathan Godwin

Four South

Twisted, turning
your mind careens and catapults out of orbit.
Contact lost,
you howl in havens beyond the known globe.
Stoned pilots soar and sing
toneless tunes. Dark spreading wings
softly suffocate sight.
Some sprawl dazed, wearing caps for the current,
while locked in the Quiet Room, Gertrude,
(now gyrating, gaunt Gwenevere)
parries and pummels the Great God of reason.
Weeps "Where is my child? Gone, oh gone!" Weary seasons;
No map and failed charts...Can they halt the wild flights?
Please come back to this Earth To...
peace?
balance?
light?

Jena Smith

Distance Talk

Far apart we talk each day.
The words roll endlessly like baby babble.
With little meaning and little understood.
Nothing urgent.

Women called the radio today to reveal their secrets
of how they persuaded U.P.S. men to come inside, seduced them.
It's Valentine's Day, 7 a.m. People are getting married at
What A Burger. Can't wait to see that scrapbook of Polaroids.

It's August. Went to brush the horses down today. It was warm
so I hung the laundry out on the line. Picked ripe, red apples.
Baked an apple cake. Picked some wild flowers-
purple, violet, and blue. Small and frail. They'll die soon.

Chatter lingers long each evening. The sound of the voice
on the other end. That's what we're listening for.
Hear the pitch go up and down to vision her sitting there, here.
No noise. The dread of hanging up, being alone.
Tomorrow is so far away from the loneliness of now. Say
good-byes and wait again till the night of the next lone day.

Kara Hastings

Dreamer

Life is full of different people and different minds
I am a dreamer
A person who looks for an outlet of fears
I escape through the windows of imagination
I go to a world yet unknown, in which I let my dreams take over
  my fears
I become the dominatrix of threats
I can be myself and there is no one to criticize me for being unique
I love the dream world
Everyone has no one of these worlds
A world where they can escape the traumas of reality
But no one will ever understand how in depth the thoughts in mine go.

Tricia VanderGroef

Mourning Dove

Mourning dove, O mourning dove
Why do you call so sadly
your plaintive call cries out to me
like a puppy who's lost its way
or a lover who is longing for someone to love
Mourning dove, O mourning dove
Why do you call so sadly

Heather Cowan

Thoughts And Listeners

My mouth has been shut for so long,
My feelings seem so wrong.

I'll share with you the secret of my life,
The pain cuts at my heart like a knife,
Let me tell you what I have to say,
The pain will lessen and some will go away.

It's so sad,
It's all about my dad,
Let me tell you,
Don't cut me off even if you have to.

Listen with an open heart,
Forgive me if what I say isn't that smart,
None of it is a lie,
Forgive me if I start to cry.

All the memories that went by,
It seemed as if time really flies,
Please don't leave,
I need to cry on your sleeve.

Forgive me if I'm not that strong,
I held it in my heart for too long.

Suzi Langston

The Rolling Tides

She sits alone in an empty room,
the lamplight shattered, the atmosphere gloom.
She quivers with fright, a tear in her eye.
She blinks aimlessly and musters a sigh.
Her once shinny hair hangs limp and dull.
She shrinks, and she whimpers at the shadows on the wall.
The thin sunlight streams across her beaten face;
it streams across the door - she is trapped, encased
She wonders if he'll be back today.
She dreams of hiding, of running away.
Suddenly, the doorknob turns, and light parades inside.
She drops her head, and shuts her eyes,
and dreams of the rolling tides.

Dawn Sturgill

Untitled

In the darkness of the night,
  the luminescence of moonlight,
    your face is the only one I see.

Through the suffering of souls,
  In the thundering of silence,
    your words and voice are the only sounds I hear.

Through the fear of feeling numb,
  like the pounding of a drum,
    your touch is the only thing I know.

When the stench of death is all about,
  And the screams of victims fill the air,
    your scent is the only thing I smell.

In the violence of the world
  with the coldness of blood stained in my mouth,
    your lips are the only thing I taste.

With confusion of hate and rage running through my brain,
And the wondering of how life can be so cruel,
  The only thing I think is how much
    I love you.

Jessica Grattan

Priorities

One morning I woke up to a sound and
I cocked my head to listen and there it was
again. A rooster crowing! Here in the city - how
wonderful. It transported me to a farm in the
country and I would fall into a deep sleep
hearing the horses whinny, the cows a-mooing,
the chickens clucking and the rooster crowing.

And then one day I realized the rooster
wasn't crowing any longer because the city
is not zoned for such.

Instead it's zoned for cars a-starting, motors
running, police sirens wailing, dogs a-barking,
boom-boxes blaring, guns a-shooting, and motorcycles
zooming, while the poor roosters' crowing
and my dreams are silenced.

Mercedes Otero

"A Prayer"

Lord, we pray to you each and everyday,
  to stand by us and show us the way.
Please grant us thy blessings and peace of mind,
  for a love like yours is hard to find.
Lord, please replenish our souls that we maybe worthy
  to receive thy grace, for in you we've found a resting place.
Please bless us Lord and make us whole, that we
  may make heaven our goal.
Lord, help us to be steadfast in thee in every way,
  for we surely know you'll brighten our day.
And Lord, protect us from evil and sin, for
  the battle ahead we know we'll win.
We give you dear Lord, all the praise and glory,
  for one day real soon will be the end of this life's story.
Lord again, we pray to you each day, to stand
  by us and show us the way.

Wynemia O. Thompson

My Heart

My heart is like an eggshell be careful or it will break.
If that should happen what a mess that would make.
Telling all the mysteries of me.
What a horrible sight for anyone to see.
Please do not break my veil so delicate and light.
Underneath my veil are all my fears and delights.
Please do not throw stones.
My shell is now broken and my secrets shone.
My shell is all I truly own.
If it is broken I will be forgotten and all alone.
So please be careful of what you say.
Because hearts are not made of clay.

Regina Jones

Sun block

When the summer sun burns really hot,
Causing stinging every spot
We'd like to stay outside and enjoy our vacation.
But how can we with this warm circulation?
So here is my solution,
To cure all of this confusion.
We can use a magic potion,
A special oil or sun block lotion.
This lotion will protect our skin,
So the sun's rays cannot get in.
Then we can be safe and have fun too.
As salamanders and lizards do.

Vanessa Washington

The End

Darkness seeps into my day
Pointing a sharp finger through my sunlit window
I try to run,
Hide,
But the Darkness finds me
Slowly clenching its hands round my neck
I try to scream away this bad dream
But the clinging digits tighten, tighten
I gasp
Sucking the air through the last straw of life
No avail, I fail to catch my breath
Death appears at my door, quietly
Laughing
Icy, cold pellets spray my face
As He slowly erases the memory of...
Who am I?

June Rachelson-Ospa

To Be Dishonored Is To Lose

There is no dishonor in being defeated,
Only in losing.

For to be defeated is to succumb to the strengths,
Of a superior opponent.

To lose is to give up!
And I will never lose!

Jeffrey J. Farah

"Spring"

Spring has just begun;
The park is as a graveyard;
Filled with skeletons;
Standing erect and picked clean as left over turkey,

But the man in the moon does not worry,

The trees appear barren,
Yet soon they will bare daughters and sons,

Their arms stretch out to the sun,
To the spring awakening;
stretching,

These mothers-to-be look so hard,
But spring has just begun.

Cheryl Drake

Shimmering Shell

As you walk along the beach
and the waves wash over your feet,
do you ever feel like you just can't be beat?
The cool breeze is sweet as it blows across your face
and you feel like you would rather be in no other place,
but here... at the beach.
With sand under your feet as you walk right along
you get to feeling like singing a song, 'cause your spirit is high
and you feel like you're soaring way up in the sky.
You bend down and pick up a shimmering shell
and you throw it and make a wish,
thinking of the fisherman with his fairy-tale fish.
And then...so suddenly, you're back on the beach.
And while you head for home you know, there are lessons to teach.
Just like you when you're on the beach,
or the shell you just recently hurled,
you can't stay on the beach for the rest of your life,
you have to come out and face the world!!!

Allyson Melton

Forever Has Finally Come

After failing so many times at what I thought was love, I swore I would never promise anyone else forever. Then I met you. I was skeptical at first, but you made me open up my heart and let you in.

You've taught me to love and trust again without doubts. You have made me believe that the prince in my dreams exists and has come alive in you. You swept me off of my feet and made it so easy for me to fall in love.

Please don't feel as if you've done anything wrong if my doubts periodically come back. It's just that everything is so right, it scares me. You have made me realize that I am finally ready to promise my forever to you.

Heather H. Meecha

At One

The cold pale dark,
a trickle in your skin from the morning dew,
that sudden light that appears,
when the day begins,
I sit and watch,
As my thoughts go by,
The world as a whole,
stumbles through my mind.
How could this be?
but it's true.
false imaginary of myself,
is all that is,
Not but a single truth,
Somehow I must be.
bring out myself in me,
then I can go in peace,
and be one with me

Nick Tieman

Hopeless

I lay awake,
wishing the night would end
and a new day could begin.
Wishing there was a way,
wishing there was some hopeful thing to say.

Praying for the sun,
knowing you're the only one.
Smiling my fake smile,
pretending all the while
you sit there and cry,
asking me why.
If only you knew,
I'm just as lost as you.

Katherine Marie Holbrook

Your Fertile Earth

Look forward to the day for all it's worth,
Till your mind, your fertile earth.

Depend on yourself, your feelings are true,
If you can't look to yourself, then to who?

Follow your spirit, wherever it flies,
Kiss your restraining straps goodbye.

Make use of the day for all it's worth,
Free your spirit, let it fly off this earth.

Sarah Saint John

Time Lost

I look beyond and see, no past, life is lost.
A momentary thing, fleeing so fast.

Gather your dreams, love, hopes of morrow,
remembrance of yesterday and hold no sorrow.

Rays of sunshine, on a smiling face, to be gathered
as yarn, woven into beautiful lace.

Yesterdays are lost, a fallen leaf, soaring in
the wind, to be seen not again.

Time is Lost, life goes on, a bud on a rose,
opening to a new dawn.

Carrie Elizabeth Bowman Hensley

Love Please Stay Away

I've tried and tried
But, the love just died
you told me that you wanted me too,
And the deal with the other girl wouldn't last,
So, of course I believed you and went ahead and feel in love.
Not regretting what happened...before
But, now I'm starting to regret everything
You hurt me when you died.
Now, I know I tried too hard.
I want to understand,
But, it hurts to even try,
So love please stay away from this heart,
If it's gonna cause more pain,
I can't handle any more pain!

Jennifer Michelle Amyx

Beer

Down the paths of ages, before pyramids were built,
'Ere Stonehenge was envisioned, the ancients used to drink -
A heady brew, a steady brew, a brew from far and near,
From hops and malted barley, our forebears brewed their beer.

And now across this Earth of ours, from Europe to Japan,
Long live this mighty beverage, from England to Siam,
A malty brew, a salty brew, a brew for every season -
Enjoy your beer, embrace your beer, you never need a reason.

To be the biggest drunkard I never did aspire,
But to quaff my ale upon an eve I frequently desire,
A frosty brew, a frothy brew, a brew to make you cool,
Drink enough, but not too much - you know the golden rule.

Lager beers from Germany are models for the rest,
And stout that comes from Ireland whose flavor I'll attest,
Colder brews, and bolder brews, that sparkle in the light,
Add balance to the palate and make a meal feel right.

And now within the USA, the microbrews are here,
To bring us more variety, add choices to our beer,
Hearty brews, and party brews, and brews for all who think
That beer is best, the very best - the ancient, modern drink.

G. C. Thomas

Black And Blue

My soul is black-
My mind is blue-
My body is usurped by the shackles that possess it;
My love is choking on mine chains, that cannot see-
My fear is me

My forced breath suffocates the life that is but a wink-
My anguish that enraptures my head is prison endured-
And I have felt without feeling, yet that appreciation cannot see.
My fear is me.

Dana Buono

Hope Of The Poet

Oh, come my restless pen to trace
With gossamer and silvery lace
The wordless language of the heart.
Oh! stir in some breast a fervent prayer!
Be the sword that sunders truth from error.
And cleave atwain benighted thought
To let in the wonders God Hath wrought.
Weave with threads of understanding
On the hallowed loom of love
A glorious mantle,
For the simple poet, who
Paints the bow that spans the firmament
From God to you.

Anne T. House

Earth-Rise

I am the mountain.
Owned by none yet named by many,
I was here before then. Before them.
I have been here - ever.

Contoured crags and cadenced waters, I am
Keeper of the spirits, of the boulders, trees,
The creatures, hold them land-bound
With my body - I contain

Through seasoned cycles, weathered rhythms, primal
Patterns as I shift, re-birthed eternal,
Into who I was, who I am,
Who I will be - again.

I remember, you who come with weighted footfalls,
Bearing burdens, dreams and sorrows,
Sheltered shadows of the soul.
I bear witness - always.

I am the mountain.
I endure, sounding ancient echoes,
Archetypal earth-scape rising.
I will be here - ever.

Valerie H. Mantecon

Post Script

Everyday, without fail
I go to my computer for E-mail
Hearing from friends and family on-line
Makes my life feel divine
Letter writings was a lost art,
Until the E-mail solution did start.
I wait for the mail-lady no more.
I just open my computers door.
In the big world my children have moved away
To jobs and marriage and just to play
But with my E-mail going strong
We're still in touch all day long

William F. Wray Jr.

Hungry Souls

I have become hungry, hungry and cold,
scared and restless
I'm hungry for food, for company,
for sweetness.
The woods do not shelter.
The winds howl by.
It strips me of my being and I cling to my soul.
Without my soul I will not rest.
I'd search forever,
to the world's end,
until my soul and I were once again,
One.

Allison Perry

My Daughter

Today my heart was full of pride!
My little girl is growing,
Although she's not a woman yet-
Her love and grace are flowing.

Her body's changing, this is true.
But it's her soul that has impressed me.
She shows a wisdom beyond her years.
I'm catching glimpses of the "Woman" she can be.

Her compassion for her friends and family
Has shown me a great deal,
Her patience and understanding
I know that they all feel.

And so my daughter, I want you to know,
That I love you with all of my heart!
To watch you grow has been a joy-
and has been from the very start!

    Heidi Ellefsen

A Piece Of Clay

Oh Mighty Sculptor mold me and shape me
Take your loving hands to the task
I wait to be reshaped in your Son's likeness
Blessed are the hands that do a good work in me

Misshapen and seemingly forgotten all these years
Suddenly came face-to-face with your Son
Our friendship grew in love and grace
Behind the scenes the Master Sculptor had begun

Ah! Now I have been formed and shaped in His likeness
His return drives me to do a good work
Servant to all is His command
Soon to stand before the Master Sculptor

Loving hands covered with clay
Another creation that now will obey
He reshaped me in his Son's image
All this from a battered old piece of clay

    Russell E. Pohronezny

"My Wedding Gift And Vow"

Riches such as silver and gold on thee I cannot bestow.
Nor precious stones, land or wealth. All I have
  and to thee I give is love and myself.
My two hands to help you
  through each day,
To love and caress and try to smooth
  your cares and pain away.
My eyes to look upon you each day
  with love and compassion,
My body each night to give you
  warmth and passion.
My lips to show how much
  I love and care;
That God made it possible
  the rest of our lives to share.
On this our wedding day
  My darling believe me when I say,
I'll love you always, till the end of time;
Even when the sun and stars cease to shine.
May God grant us happiness until the end of time.

    Mary Sallie Dunfee

Spring Is Near

Spring is near. I could smell it in the air.
Trees are growing. Flowers are blooming.
Spring is near. I could feel it on my skin.

Spring, Spring, please come now.
Spring, feel the grass. Feel the air.
Spring is near. It fills my soul.
It brightens my days.
Spring, I could hear the songs of your love.
Spring is here now.

Spring, Spring, Oh wonderful Spring.
The birds are singing. The sun is shining.
Oh wonderful Spring.
Spring, babies are here.
Deer are running.
Joy has filled the air.

    Robert Cline

"My Heart Is Not Dead"

She came into my life quite by surprise,
A smile on her face and love in her eyes.
My intentions were good yet my desire grew strong,
Was falling in love with her so wrong?

I've never told her just how I feel,
Yet this love in my heart I know is real.
What do I do, how do I say it,
How in the world do I try and relate it?

I've got a million questions running through my mind,
How do I answer them do I even have time?
I'd like to think that someday I can.
Just open my heart and make my stand.

As it stands we're still so many worlds apart,
So tell me Lord, where would I start?
I'm just a man with dreams in his head,
Yet as strange as those dreams may be... My Heart is Not Dead...

    Monty Lee Johnston

Dreamer

Dreamer seeks for a love long lost
Dreamer sings his song of agony
Dreamer travels through the fated night
Feeling the loneliness of pain

Lost without home or heart
Lost within the sorrow's hearth
Lost to the world of life
Bring the eternal tears of red

Cast away from peace
A cast away in an ocean of purest black
Cast out life
To embrace the cold unforgiving death

Brought to justice four days ago
Brought to darkness of suicide
Brought before a judge of life
His executioner the blooded knife

Dreamer forced to travel the plane of pain
Lost of all his glory in life
Cast out of societies hole
Brought him to his final confrontation of life

    Peter J. Wilson

Let Us Sing - Ode To The Earth

Once upon a time, the air was clean
The oceans blue and the grass so green,
Now smog blocks the sun
And being outside is no longer fun.

The roadside's littered with heaps of trash
An oily film blocks water's flash,
Acid rain and dirty skies
Make the past impossible lies.

Let us sing together
All who believe,
The Earth can be forever
If only we could see.

A lonely, dying bird
A cry that won't be heard,
Their pain falls upon deaf ears
We won't believe the end is near.

If only we would look at our slowly dying earth
The animals and plants we have so cruelly hurt,
So let us sing, for all that we believe
What we have to make the others see.

Valerie Jordan

The Quest

That night, I couldn't sleep, for
  the moon had stolen my dreams and
    written them on her face.

So I wandered to the beach, finding there
  a moonbeam like a staircase.
    I danced upon it,
      ascending,
        to demand my dreams of the moon.

They found me near dawn,
  curled on the sand,
    staring into the tide,
      with fading starlight in my hair.

Julie West

Kismet

Calling out to a vague silhouette, I become the voice of an unheard
whisper: silent shadows frisk the earth, for no one seeks this
  missing sister.

Tender sands don my feet, hot rain drops scourge my eyes; I throw
myself against the waves as no one hails good-bye.

Starfish fill my pockets as water empties out my soul, endlessly
drowning, as cunning peace is revolving coins for the relic toll.

Ascending in rapture to the arctic sky, I leave raw bones behind, a
benevolent spirit led by the wind, chastened by contemptuous crime.

I remain the voice of an unheard whisper that bends to the gale of
rage; a fleshless heart of fervid covet released from my throe
  soaked cage.

Shannon Wood

Racism

Racism lurks in the dark sky,
Through the shadows of one's eye,
It cannot be seen, heard, or felt.
Too hot to contain too cold to melt,
The only thing that will give it a scare,
Is the love from everyone of us, and the will to care,
Till that day Racism will fly,
Through the shadows of one's eye,

Harishkumar Nandagopal

Untitled

How do you learn to love yourself,
When only hate runs through your veins?

How do you learn to love yourself,
When you can't put aside the pain?

How do you learn to accept your faults,
When there are too many to count?

How do you learn to accept your faults,
that no one else seems to forget about?

How do you learn to get past your failures
When you can't get past your own face?

How do you learn to get past your failures,
When you realize you're going no place?

How do you know when to give up,
When you just can't put up the fight?
Is it when you realize you've accomplished nothing,
Or when you have no friends in sight?

Or is it when you're pushed to the point
You twist and squirm and bend
Or is it when you find the comfort,
in knowing you can make it all end?

Amanda Beegle

The Master Within

Will there ever come a day that I will be set free?
To go on my own way and not follow the Master in me.

He comes from behind when I least expect
So I must no be blind to this kind of attack.

The Master has guile and tries to lead me astray
From a life worthwhile, but I will not obey.

It is worse than death - not to do right
So to my last breath the Master I must fight.

No matter what the cost I cannot give in
Or the battle I have lost to the Master within.

The Master I can beat - If I am strong enough
But he will try to cheat - I have to be tough.

I must go deep inside where my thoughts begin
To a peace the Master cannot hide
Only there, I can win.

Carl Whitehouse

A Stormy Night's Rain

My life as a girl was very rough-
Hatred followed me, made me tough-
I'd look for new, all I'd find was old-
Neglected as a girl I was thrown in the cold.
I began to freeze so I shut life down.
Rebelled against all, a new life I found.
I looked in my heart, it was not clear-
my hatred and pain had risen to fear.
I needed to let go, I needed to release.
I needed to find true lasting peace.
Cigarettes didn't do it-
Drugs didn't give me the chance.
I needed out of this deathly trance.
Then I found after my rough life-
I needed to make one last sacrifice.
I let go my anger-
I let go my pain-
My life has been through a stormy night's rain.

Karen Zellmer

238

The Ghost

The wind blows through the golden fields,
It carries a magnificent sound,
The sound of pulsating drums,
The cries of warriors preparing for combat,
An unknown combat.
The wind blows over the dying land,
It carries a ghostly sound,
The sound of faded drums,
The cries of a confused people,
No tradition, custom, or laws guide them.
The wind blows through the city streets
It carries the sound of empty dreams,
The cries of the lost child,
The cries of the lost tradition,
Now all that can be heard is the cry;
The cry of a dying race.

Heidi Mayhew

Untitled

Their lives have always been linked to value,
not a value of self-love but one of the hate and hurt

They may have a variation of that of my own
but where it counts they are the same

They have a heart that beats
a mind that thinks, lungs that breathe

They have a soul that lets them live
live a life of feelings,
of hurt, happiness, of love

They are people
people made from the same as me

But with a small touch of the earth
this should make them special

not considered an amount
of value

Amie Danielle Marie Kirn

My World

My world is special place, a place where
I could walk outside with my niece.
And every where I go people would want to make peace.
Now don't get me wrong we all get in fights,
but if we were really mature we'd settle them right.
My world is going to be a beautiful place, cause
everyone is different colors but still the same race.
My world is fair, you wouldn't be judged by the
color of your skin or the way you did your hair.
But this my world, it probably won't come
true, but if you want it to be real you can only
start with you.

Andrea McKnight, Age 13

Untitled

As I lie in the grass, in an uncut field.
I slowly drift off to where nothing is real.
Shortly I find I am on a beach in the sand.
With a beautiful girl with a drink in her hand.
With the breeze gently whispering a song that I know
And the sun softly setting with a crimson glow
Then I turned and asked her where I am
Why the place of your dreams, as she sifted the sand
Then I reached out to touch her—this had to be real,
But I awoke lying in the grassy field,
To the sound of children as they play,
I thought to myself—I'll go back someday.

Steven J. Kent

Life Reminds Me Of A Busy Street

Life reminds me of a busy street,
along its path so many people you meet!
As one travels down the busy road,
one must stop to inspect what's being sold.
The house on that street that is one's destiny,
many linger on in one's mind a mystery!

Life reminds me of a busy street,
strangers along with friends you must greet!
Check out the many bumps as you travel.
Take care that you don't slide on the loose gravel!
Ups and downs and potholes are there,
To add to the hazards of life everywhere!

Life reminds me of a busy street,
some of the scenery seems to repeat.
There are hospitals on that road,
and churches for your burdens to unload.
There are courthouses and many schools,
One must avoid the trials and not break the rules.

Janice S. Burton

Dreams, Goals, And Life

Names-
    Names, they're all the same.
Faces-
    Faces, floating through places.
Eyes-
    Eyes, disembodied and searching for the way.
        Where are they going? But why?
Hands-
    Hands, reaching out for the nothing the eyes see,
        only to grasp themselves with the lifeless hold.
Legs-
    Legs, on feet on toes silently, lightly wander through
        the fog in search of the light of day as it gets
        darker. To their disappointment they find it is
        not what the eyes thought.
We-
    We, write, make, produce, and change our dreams into
        our goals and as soon as they are ours they are not.
        For like our lives, they are easily removed.

Christoph Obrecht

"Linger"

Whirling winds and falling snow
I think of your pale skin.
Cold biting hungrily at the bones
I think of all that we had been

Starry nights and summer's gold
Fiery sunsets and warm water wishes
Sweet summer rain carving the road
To distant lonely places yearning for kisses

Everything seems to be of you
Even this room remembers when
You entered it upon the wind
And the sweet words you had spoken

Making love to all you had touched
Leaving your scent on everything
Leaving your mark in everything
Making love to all that was

You are not here, yet I am still yearning
Like you, the wind enters me
Like you, the rain kisses me
Like you, the sun makes me burn

Mara Melina Bjornstad

Bright Morning Star

Distress has fallen upon the land
They have stolen our beautiful prince
Salty tears fall as all the land cries out
They have imprisoned our beautiful prince

Stop, wait a minute, before you tear him from our embrace
Stop, wait a minute, before you take him from our sight
Stop, wait a minute, let us look upon his face
Stop, wait a minute, they cried out day and night

Wailing and lamenting, as they beat our prince repeatedly
Wailing and lamenting, as they paraded him through the streets
Wailing and lamenting, as they nailed him to a tree
Wailing and lamenting, as he took his last breath

Many years have gone by since Mary came running with glee
She shouted, "Our Prince has risen from the grave"
and till this day we look to the north and see
that the bright morning star still shines today

Prince of peace, bright morning star
Because of you we shall live forever
Prince of peace, bright morning star
We shall dwell in paradise with you

Luana F. Qualman

"Time To Think"

I heard the music under the darkness of a clear night.
   The figure of a person stood alone playing with vigor, with might.
I could barely tell where he was, but that didn't matter,
   I could hear, I could sense, the music play on, sadder and sadder.
I saw the burning hills by people trying to forget what happened
   in their land.
With the smell of burning grass and wood, I was at ease,
   peaceful music was at hand.
The Scottish knew what could comfort many.
   Low tones, mixing with treble and a texture that could mystify any.
Alongside the rolling fog and darkness of night,
   the shadows danced in circles and the stars took flight.
Too dark for the spring flowers to be seen
   but with peace in my mind and love in my heart, I can't imagine
   anything being more keen.

Timothy Wayne Stebens

Albert Eclipse

That now one knows,
emanating on the prism of golden rays.
Go, do not go, go,
eyes fading in a blue haze.
My Prince of Precious Past days.

World that was young
shuns to have graces die.
That the moon was hung
in heavens where no man abide.
There is nowhere to hide.

The Prince of my youth,
to look thee in the face once more.
Glimpse the moment of truth.
Hurry before the sound of the shut door,
before time totals the score.

Time has come, time to part,
gallant times, days radiant and fair.
Take away the beating heart,
brief of a life, did we share.
Ordinary fate of one so rare.

Alberta Waddell Rutter

Must We Murder Our Mother

Must we murder our mother
Slowly killing her where she stands?
She cannot run from us
She cannot hide from us
Must we murder our Mother
By putting our Metropolitan poisons on her skin?
We take her for granted
And we push her away
Must we murder our Mother
As she cries to us for mercy
She eternally screams
Calling for us to stop
Though we've turned our ears deaf
How much longer can we continue like this
Before our Mother takes us away to end her pain?

Bryan S. Robertson

Rainbow

What is a rainbow, that ribbon in the sky?
All those different colors, so pleasing to the eye.
There's something very special about the way the colors blend,
And the solemn, peaceful message those blending colors send.

Each color alone holds its own trait,
One single color is uncertain of its fate.
But when blended with others, they share but one duty,
To blanket the world with lasting peace and beauty.

No color would be superior, there would be no minority,
And the one thing that kept them together would be equality.
These color combinations would restore what Mother Nature made,
And undo all the hatred that Father Time forbade.

We are each a color painted in that sky,
All together we'd be so pleasing to the eye.
There's something very special about the way we'd all blend,
And the solemn, peaceful message that, together, we'd send.

We could be a rainbow, together, we hold the key,
We could be that rainbow, just open your eyes and see.
So forget all our hatred as we stand hand in hand,
A barrier against racial tension, a rainbow across the land.

Rachel Joy Ingel

Alone

Sitting in a room all alone
No lights are on, just a candle burning
Wondering if this is how it will be
Wanting to care for someone, but only yearning

Trying to find that special someone
Always looking, but always wrong
Why put myself through all of this
It's too depressing and takes too long

She's out there somewhere
We'll meet someday
I'll have to ask her
If she ever felt the same way

So I'll wait until tomorrow
The days and nights go so fast
Not knowing what will happen
Or if I can last.

Brice A. Milligan

The Kid On The Street

I'm just an orphan kid out on the street
with rags on my back, worn shoes on my feet.
Nobody cares if I sleep, or I eat
I am just "the kid on the street".

I keep my eyes open for the cop or the beat
He's always my friend, when we chance to meet.
He knows of my problems, he's heard them before
sometimes we discuss them, in front of the store.

Some people are lucky with plenty to eat
nice clothes on their backs, shoes on their feet.
I sleep in the alley, stay out in the rain
for the Kids on the street, just heartaches and pain.

This story is true of kids that I know
out in the street with nowhere to go.
For them there's no future, nothing to show
for all of their troubles, with their faces aglow.

God up in heaven, will take us someday
to a home in the sky, that is far far away.
for us "kids on the street" we'll never more roam
finally in heaven, we'll have a permanent home.

Thomas A. Brooks

What Is The Area Code For Heaven?

I need to call you tonight
You are the only one who understands
The pain and the emptiness.

Tonight you envelope me like a warm mist
Rising from a tropical sea
I feel a helpless rage at not being able to reach you.

I can't remember your worldly telephone number
If I could, some one else would answer.

Lady Day is singing a lament of lost love, I know how she feels.
Is she singing in heaven?
Have you been to hear her?

Can you get good reefer where you are?
If you can, cop me some sensemilla
We'll get wacked and go to a concert.
And after we'll stay up all night
And listen to Janis and laugh and cry.

Do you miss me as much as I miss you?
Have you made new friends?
I have a hunch that I will be joining you soon
It will be like old times.

Mark Bready

Homecoming

The lights are dim
  The music is slow
She just might win
  She walks down the row
The drumroll's played
  The names are read
She's wearing the dress her mom had made
  She turned to me and said
I won I won

The flowers came
  And the crown was placed on her head
As we danced everyone did the same
  I ran my hands up her silk dress of red
I couldn't refrain
  I slid the ring upon her hand
As we danced the night away
  We thought about together forever we'd stay

Ben Balduin

To My Daughter

There is so much pain
It's hard to try to fight it
I want her to have it all
But she only tries to deny it
if there are powers that be
Help her to see the reality
make her strong in this angry world
There is much that would make her hair curl
God I love her yes I do
I may not show it but it's true
She may feel like we're against her.
All she's doing is building up fences.
Lord hear a mother's prayer
Keep her, Love her, Let her know you are there.

Fernande Joy Odery

The Cabin Builder

In the mist I saw a cabin at the
  silent crest of a green and grassy knoll;
And the workman who had built it
  as the bell of the chapel softly tolled.
I saw his face so clearly captured
  brightly in the new morning's sun.
His charm and laughter softly expressed
  the pride of knowing God's cabin was done.
His strong hands and simple tools echoed
  faint sweet voices down the corridors
Contented where loving hearts will meet
  In the early light on God's distant shore.
"Come and join me in my cabin my friend."
  Said his accommodating host.
"Live forever with me, take the hands
  of your Father, the Son and Holy Ghost."
"I had you build this cabin for
  night shadow's escape early mornings rain.
You'll have this simple home of love
  to be with your family once again."

Johanna L. Honaker

Choices

How do you choose what's right from wrong
When the choices to be made have been there so long
It seems as though to make the right one, with results that would last
You'd have to change so much from your past
Often choices are made in order to avoid the pain
Even though deep inside you'd like to make a choice that will last
Even after the pain has passed
How do you choose what's right from wrong
When you know, in order to make the right one
When it's all said and done those you love may be gone
And how do you find the courage to stand alone
When you're so afraid of the unknown
How do you choose what's right from wrong
When you're afraid to be alone
It's at that time that you need to recall
He has been there with you through it all

Ruth Anne Ristow

Contemplation

I walk sometimes among the graves to ponder long dead bones....
  To read the dear departed dates that are chiseled in the stones.

And I wonder if these dead ones somehow see me as I stand,
  Contemplating this old mystery that befalls all earthly man.

And do these dead ones whisper as their spirits ride the wind,
  And as they ride, I wonder if they speak of living friends.

Fred M. Moody

A Prison With Gold Bars

The three Mexican gardeners laugh together before they
mow the lawn, trim the bushes and water the plants.
Meanwhile I, the lonely, white college graduate
with no friends and nothing to do
sit on my bed in my room
of my mother's nice house
in an affluent neighborhood
while she is on vacation in Louisiana.
I watch her house, feed the dogs
and listen to John Coltrane and Dizzy Gillespie.
I wonder what would happen
if I asked the Latino workers
if they would take me on for a day
even though I've never used a lawn mower
because I once met a guy with a glass eye
who, while mowing the lawn,
ran over a stone with his lawn mower
which knocked out his real eye.
The Mexican gardeners would probably say,
no, go back in your house.

Scott Struman

A Special Someone

For everyone there is someone,
For me it is a friend.
He is talented, and kind
He smiles and frowns
He's quite average in everyone else's eyes
But to me he special, extremely special
He's my sunshine on a rainy day,
He can make each and every dark cloud roll away
We laugh together and dream together,
With no one to stand in our way.
Another of my friends tells me he's not right for me.
But how could she know,
Even though this is a first
The first time I've talked with a guy,
About things that I wouldn't
Even with my best friend.
Some people call it love,
I call it deep friendship.

Denise Villarreal

Childhood Home

Shimmering on the rocks like
a rainbow studded with diamonds is her house.
That is where first grew the roots of her childhood dreams,
dreams that she just started to paint,
Stealing the colors from the
glorious flowers, the rainbow and the sunset.
She got carried away by the tide of time,
Forgetting that life had its share of ups and downs.
In a pensive mood in shades of blue
and positive pain which tears her through,
she stands to view her past.
She has not regrets,
for she has had her share of happiness.
She grasps those memories, dear and strong.
She is thankful for the sound of music,
the break of dawn, the moon and stars shining bright.
Her heart and soul is in that house
where she grew day and night...

Anjali Udoshi

The Eye Of The Devil

I have seen the eye of the devil
In the faces of my childhood
I have reached out my hand for a savior
To save me from being sucked into an eternal pit of pain
Each time, I found myself in a house of mirrors
Grasping at shadows
Repeatedly crashing into myself in the endless maze of glass
Alone, unlovable, frightened
And, each time, in the end.....
I was face to face with myself
I have seen the eye of the devil

Robin Dee Brown

April Storm

Palm trees dipping and swirling,
Twisting and hurling
Their arms into the air
In shocked dismay,
As sand and debris race past
Just steps ahead of rain
Intent on drenching all.

Then the eery storm-wind
Whirring, whining through the palm fronds,
Driving rain against the earth's face,
Washes all —
Grass, flowers, trees,
Small shops, and buildings tall.

Then winds are gone
As tiring of this caper,
Storm moves on.

Esther Ferrell Seadeek

Taking A Ride With My Son

It was a beautiful Spring afternoon -
My son took me for a ride through the countryside.

Being a stroke victim, I began to realize
the things I had taken for granted over the years -

It made me want to sing because I felt so happy inside -

The green grass looked like velvet and the flowers were
in full bloom -

My young son so handsome made me feel somewhat young again -
He talked and he listened -
What a patient young man.

Oh, I'll never forget that ride in the country with my son,
the handsome young man.

Pat Single

She Makes Me Feel

The sun glows through the morning
mist... Making my heart feel the same
whenever I think of her.

When the mist cleared and the sun
warmed... I thought of how I feel with
her arms around me.

Later in the day there was the scent
of rain in the air.. It finally came cooling
everything.. I was reminded of the many ways
she uses to calm me and to make me feel so content.

My day is done and I'm on my way home
to her. Knowing that when I get there I
will see her beautiful smiling face that
will tell me again how much I am loved

J. R. Clarke

The Ideal Woman

The ideal woman with light brown hair
The ideal woman who could share
The ideal woman in his life
The ideal woman he found his wife
The ideal woman who let him see
Everything in life there would ever be
The sun the moon the sky above
There they found unbeatable love
The kiss the hug, the push once more
The love that was felt right to the core
The walk, the talk, the very look was like a woman in a story book
The spy, the fiend, the bitter end
Now the man could not fend
For life, for death not even a breath
Because without his ideal, he saw no deal at all
So he decided to take a fall
A dreaded leap a fall to the ground
But to every one else, he made no sound
He fell, he fell, he felt fiery hell
For the ideal woman could only ring his bell

Jacob Fistes

How Wonderful Is The Heights

The Heights is a school full of love and joy;
You get to choose your own classes,
No matter if you're a girl or a boy.

When wonderful things happen at the Heights,
The students and teachers just shine so bright;
If you show these teachers what you're made of,
Your grade might just go average or above.

If you try your best to do your work,
Of all the other students you might just be the biggest expert;
The teachers will give you lots of attention,
But to the teachers you will have to listen.

The activities at our school are great;
but when something goes wrong,
That's the part I hate.

Some things can go wrong after a while;
But when they come out good,
You'll put on a smile.

On this poem I have spent many of nights;
Now you know,
How Wonderful Is The Heights.

Charles Moorehead

Siren Song

Allow the seas to breathe again,
Cut loose from the bounty of your noble ship.
For let lie here your countenance,
Let the wheel penetrate your mighty grip.

The masts of the wise would sooner dip down
So as to be of the effect,
Of the Godly powers thriving here.
Let loose of mortal defects.

A quintessence of the human race,
The merit of King Zeus,
The almighty power granted here,
Abandon your ship. Let loose!

What a foolish beings do not know,
Simply put your fears aside.
So long as it is understood-
may your trust, in us, here abide.

Aileen Valencia

Love...

Love needs compassion and care for many others,
Sincere smiles and comforting mutters.

Love shows kind souls and generous hearts,
Forever togetherness that must not part.

Love requires mercy and pity for the hungry and poor,
The tired, unfortunate, homeless and more.

Love represents sorrow and sympathy for those in need,
And helpful hands doing good deeds.

Love could last from here to there.
Love could be kept and love could be shared.

Love can be found on land and sea,
Love can come from you and me.

Christine Ma

Those Disappointments

In my haste and greed to be free
  I have made my self a jail
In my selfishness to be happy
  I surely found my hell
I thought making others happy
  Would make my life so grand
Instead I'm cursed and blamed
  And in God's name, I'm damned
Friends? They tell me I'm too easy
  So I try to be strong
And even when I know I'm right
  They convince me that I'm wrong
Why can't I be bad?
  For it says, "The Good Die Young"
I turn the other cheek
  I've learned to bite my tongue
I close my eyes to things
  That I choose not to see
And those things are "those disappointments"
  In that's right...me!

Mary Ann Wrigley Jones

Falling Grain

The fields of grain are yellow
The heads are bending down.
Unless the harvester comes quickly,
The grain will be falling on the ground.

Everything must be in readiness;
Everything must be done in haste;
because a strong wind or rain storm,
Would cause the grain to waste.

Our harvest field is the world.
The grain is the souls of men.
the field is white; the grain is ripe
So, let us work quickly to gather them in.

Now, is the time of reaping!
Tomorrow may be too late!
for the grain is falling,
What will be their fate?

Maple Curtis

Vision

What I see with my eyes is not always valid;
but
what I see within my heart is always true....

Cherie Y. Smith

The Willow Tree

There in a clearing by a little stream is a Willow Tree.
It has nooks and crannies where Squirrels play,
Mysterious mushrooms mushed together,
Loving Robins care for their screaming young.
Twenty-four caterpillars climb at ease,
In the built in halls made of wood.
Red ants squirm up the giant mass.
But the tree itself is tall and graceful
With fluttered dainty leaves still in bloom.
This tree is a home where creatures big and small,
Live and love together.

JennyLynne Johnson

Kaleidoscope

Morning dawns amid smoke filled skies
As its people rise to face each day.
So much to do.....so little time
To feed the family, then hurry down the dusty path
That leads to a long day's labor in the sun.
Tote the water...lay the stones, one by one.
Keep the coal fires burning to quickly cook the rice.
Beat the laundry to a clip-clop rhythm on the stone.
Drive the lorries, rickshaws and bikes at breakneck speed,
Never mind the chickens, cows or goats!
Haggle in the market place! Peanut vendors and
Tea sellers cry out to sell....Chai!....Chai!
Saari and cloth merchants spread their wares.
Loaded busses hurry along their routes
As the mournful whistles of overcrowded trains sound nearby.
The "holy man" sits motionless under the spreading fig tree.
The day wears on,.....sweep, sweep, sweep....
There seems to be no end in sight to it all,
But suddenly, the curtain of night falls, first pink, then dark,
Candles and fires burn low, and India sleeps again.

Arlis Jamerson

My Gem

My love for you is like platinum but it's worth its weight in gold,

Your love is like a rare gem, so unique and very distinct.

On a dark and cloudy day it only takes for you to stay
hey, and all of sudden it's a clear and beautiful day.

I want the world to know how much I love thee
and what you mean to me, my precious gem,
my found treasure, oh what a wonderful pleasure
my gem is to me.

Brenda Scott

Insignificance

'Tis autumn and the trees are bare
The barren bleak ground bursts forth in solemn splendor
It seems as if God doesn't care
But the ruddy red leaves are rich with Nature's candor

Ah Winter! Your coldness and chill
The icy wind and the rain
The sun slowly sinking o'er the hill
The mounds of snow in the lane

The bushes bending in the breeze
The green grass growing ever
When one takes time he sees
The extent of the Lord's endeavor

The wondrous wending of Wintertime
Through the street and lane and field
The magnificent mountains—None are mine
For Man to God must yield.

Gene G. Gould

Graduation

Your accomplishment can be
Likened to climbing a mountain.
In the beginning, an exciting challenge
With only gentle hills to follow.
Your steps are sure and light.

With time, progress becomes more difficult.
Every foothold becomes labored.
Midway, you sit to rest
Gathering your strength;
Doubtful of your success.

In the end, you set your mind
And heart on the summit.
Continuing your tedious progression upward,
With renewed hope
For victory over the mountain.

At last, with your final reserve of strength,
You hoist yourself over the top and are rewarded
With the caress of the limitless blue sky
As it meets the humble earth.
Here, in this place, the world is yours...

Kathleen Wynands

Take Time

Walking through an open field,
a warm summer day, gently flowing breeze,
Sun on my face, the wind in my hair,
sprays of wildflower, tickle at my feet,
their smell, so intoxicatingly sweet,

A small running creek, I now stand by,
submerging my feet, eyes toward the sky.
The water runs cool and crystal clear,
insects play their music, it hums in my ear.

The sky, the land, the flowers and sea,
often times we pass these things,
and still we do not see,
that the greatest things in life are free.

Take the time to smell the flowers,
to embrace the warmth of summer day.
See the beauty God has given,
to help you on your way!

Renee Le Claire

Winds Through The Seasons

When the wind whistles its sweet song through the leaves I'm awed.
At the sound of the hum I want to go right along with the song.
I'm awed as the sight of the winds at night.
In summer the wind plays with the leaves of the trees as they dance
to and fro.
Wouldn't you know in the fall when the leaves turn bright red and
orange fall to the ground then children run and spread them all around.
Then on comes winter with the sky so bright blue and the winds
full of chill.
Then just as soon there's spring when the winds start to cease and we
go to the mill to watch the breeze spin, spin, spin the wheel.
A while later the wind starts whistling its sweet song once again.
I'm awed.

Erin Stensrud

Anger

Anger is a well that's bottled deep down inside.
The anger won't go and you can't hide it.
You can't run away.
And you can't fight it.

Jamie Robtoy

The Glass Graveyard

I have a secret, a little graveyard
And every day I visit my patch of ground.
To this small monument, I am the guard
And I create a garden from this mound.

I plant new life in my graveyard
And every flower is a treasure found
For every serpent I plan to discard,
Is one less chain by which my flowers are bound.

With every fossil in this excavation,
Today brings forth a part of my history;
With every relic, an intense fascination,
For all the broken pieces, somehow a mystery.

In every fragment, there is a seed of light,
rising and growing like offspring in the night.

Bonnie Pratt

To The Poor Children In My Neighborhood

I like to see children play.
I like to hear them laugh.
A rope or a ball brings them such joy.
Sometimes they push or shove or roll on the ground,
But malice is nowhere in sight.
The line between self and others
Is not yet clearly drawn.
They do not know that
Some kids will go to good schools
And then on to good jobs,
That society is a huge sifting machine,
Forever separating wheat from chaff,
That some will have everything
But others none.
So play on, you children,
Laugh all you can,
Run and shout till stars stud the midnight sky.
There will be ample time later
To learn that life is not fair
And the playing field not level.

Isabelle Wald

Persimmons

On Sundays past, we would be loaded
into a metallic green Chevy.
Jostled and bumped out back
on dried heated gravel roads.
Radio played Roy Acuff and Kitty Wells
while we pursued the elusive persimmon trees.

Mama and Dad in the front seat
Granma Hall between directed the quest.
Jack and me in the back seat,
with great-granma Hall redirected.
The green sedan started and stopped,
through arguments of where the best trees were.

Great-granma took a broom handle
hurled up to the branches. Sending showers
of persimmons, golden nuggets of treasure
To be gathered in grailed brown crocks.
Each toss yielded more of the coppery pirates booty,
for past white hot Sunday afternoons.

Glenn Black

Love

Love is a four letter word. It can be words
written by heart, or said with hatred. Love can
be misunderstood. Love is a word with no
meaning. Love is another four letter word.

Sarah Brocato

Purge

She feels guilty in the bathroom:
it is brutally sanitized and painfully tiled
with bleak white linoleum that smells
like nothing earthborn; alien to roughness,
chemically rendered numb. The bathroom's
scent, unnatural and frigid, slashes its stainless
blade down her tautly strained spine.
The bloodless bowl condescends to notice her
nervously determined stare; eyes glazed and
breaths frighteningly hurried, each one catching up
with the next like a chaotic race of dandelion seeds.
grey, wistful, and long dead, blown
into a dry, airy, intricate stream of vortices.
The toilet is like the porcine, bleached face of a
priest; fleshy arrogance squeezed into a plain black ruff.
Tears like wounded, grieving prisms irritate the surface
of the calm depths of morality. She is at once
ashamed and convulsing. Her sobs embarrass her:
each gagging cry is a declaration of her weakness.

Sins disgorged and flushed, she is frail, but she is holy.

Alena Smith

My Love I Am Near

My love do you hear the whistle of the wind?
My love do you see the sun that shines the sky?
My love do you see the ocean that divides you and I?
My love do you feel the night that seems so long?
My love do you see the stars that guide you along?

Remember it my love for I am near.
It is my voice that whispers in your ear.
It is my passion that calms your fears.

It is my love that fills the oceans so wide.
At night it is I who lays by your side.
It is my kisses that fill the dark sky.

My love I am Near with each beat of your heart.
No time or distance can break us apart.

My love I am Near if my memory you hold.
My love come to me and let our embrace enfold!

Michelle Bermudez

"Pinned To The Ground"

Pinned to the ground, sharp spears through my arms, legs
Holding me down, down
Arms around me pretending to love, but really trapping me
Can't you let me go free?

Lost in a swamp, dark, cold
But I can see the sun
You say everyone else is lost with us, and they're happy
Blindly happy, but I'm not-you've trapped me

But there's a hole in your cage
A rhyme to your rage
And I'm breaking free, running towards beauty
Running, running, closer to the light

Almost warm, almost home
Can't you be happy for me? Can't you let me go?
How do you know it's wrong for me to be different from you?

You can't see, it's not me that is blind
I'm in the light, its beauty surrounds me
You pull me back into the shadows
You strike me down, you kill me
I'm pinned to the ground.

Elaina Wilkinson

The Sea

Eternal rhythm of sound and movement
the waves gently kiss the shore.
The white and frothy embrace of an elusive, mysterious bride.

It's the music of yesteryear, today and tomorrow!
The soothing melody, so familiar, yet never growing old.
What keeps the allure alive
in spite of being so often repeated.

The sound that graces our ear, the movement that holds the eye
like a music and a dance so carefully choreographed.
It is a beginning and an end
of something that shaped our first awareness of being
and will go on beyond our limited existence.

Maybe the mystery is enshrined in its very eternity.
We came and it was there, we heard its message
while at the same time it paced our so many heartbeats.
And when we're no more the same splash goes on without us.

The sea, always the same
across the continents, across the world,
always playing the same song, the same dance,
and never growing old.

Ernest A. Braun

"Reflections On The Stages Of Life"

As a painting increases in value with age,
Life's Winter of Wisdom, gains the respect of a sage.
Every moment we're here, has great value and worth,
Each one's story unique, from the instant of birth.

Every history is shaded, with dark hues and bright,
As memories replay past sad times, or delight.
Such events etch the picture, that's unfinished as yet,
T'won't reach its completion, till life's span is met.

Now's time for hope, anticipation, wonder expectation,
For growth, and expansion, self enrichment, education.
For gaiety, spontaneity, and a new flair for living,
Free from deadlines and schedules, and more time for self giving.

Time for travel, or research, in pursuit of the arts,
or to Plumb the Very spiritual depths of the heart,
perspectives change, viewpoints vary, open up and let go,
Of old ideas and assumptions, regarding things that "we know".

The future's exciting and replete with surprise,
Of fulfillment of dreams; hereto unrealized.
Be aware, and awake, and alert and alive,
Since God's Gifts appear in the strangest of guise.

Gertrude Caton

Brave Soldier

Stern and upright, rising high above the clouds
You stand so sharp and secure.
Ancient to the floor which now you bend to see.
The sun relinquishes your immense.
Yet you stand humble and right holding on the fort.
You sway to stray a bullet
You dodge an old time friend, and in harmony
with the rest of the cadets
you carry on the night, and the morning, and the noon.
Primitive and fragile are your arms, yet
not a cell in you hastens from a fight.
a mighty toss, whip whorled around, and still
you keep your composure.
Cloth transforms into thick skin, like armament
and your leaves are perched as shields
Beauty, elegance is eternal
dotted on you as gracious is not forgotten
You, the beneficiary of all life.
Come now a vibrance from within your sacred rings.

Susan Bolich

Memories Of A Friend

Softer than a wild rose and gentle as the wind,
there isn't anything more comforting than your very best friend.
They've been there since you were small,
laughing and playing and that's not all.
You've told them of a secret love or hatred form the past,
why and how have the many years gone so very fast.
Just yesterday it seems we were sledding in the blissful snow,
now all we do is fight; for reasons I doubt we even know.
As we come near toil and strife,
I wish you were back in my life,
So I could tell you the trouble I'm going through,
If only I knew why we grew apart.
yet it's important to find friendships new with a fresh start,
but hear me now my greatest friend,
If I could, our friendship I'd mend,
If that cannot be ever done,
I'll continue to remember the greatness of fun,
and I'll continue to see your smiling face
with all those happy memories locked in place.

Jill Hamilton

Untitled

I wonder at the brevity of youth,
And contemplation costs me precious time
From that I seek to keep; and yet, the crime
Of wasting days is hard to charge, in truth.
Society demands I earn my wage
With constant repetition of its tasks,
While Education of me often asks
A precious span with every turning page.
Then dreary passage of long Summer's day,
And the brisk flight of Winter's chilly night,
Both pain me equally, just as they might,
And leave me pond'ring still just what to say
But this, of certain pertinence: "What else
Could I have done while I was writing this?"

Jason Curtis

The Foster Child

It all started out when a little boy
needed a place to live.
He needed a bed, some clothes, and toys
and parents with love to give.
He thrived on good food, structure, and limits
and a chance to make a new start.
He wanted a family, someone to love
and let him into their heart.
We had the room, the bed, and the food
the rest would be there for the take.
And letting him into our hearts, of course,
would be a piece of cake!
Now, if this time, it should all work out
we would be happier than ever.
If we can give him the chance he needs
maybe we'll always be together.

Donna M. Brock

AIDS

I thought it would never happen to me, but now
I have a certain disease

I guess I was wrong, but now is the time in life
to be really strong

It only started as a kiss, it went on from there,
then he ran his fingers through my silky hair

He was suppose to use protection, but he lied to me,
Now from the holds of my parents, I'll never be free

I cried and I cried, all because he had lied

Things are now the way they are, and I will soon
be very far

I have now paid my dues, and he will never care
what I've been through

Lisa Patton

The Factory

Cold, bare walls, and murky window panes -
No time to view the outside world -
Strip lighting all above the lanes
Of benches, where the metals hurled
And piled in boxes, the intricate designs
Drawing the eye, with steely sheen.
It waits, the human hand to grime
And nick the flesh, with edges keen.
Cold concrete floor, where workers' feet have paced
Between the monsters of machines, that wait
To roar and thump, all iron cased -
Like beasts that crouch, their appetites to sate -
The hands work on, the toilsome hours away,
The mind spins dreams, amid the noise and grime
Toward another destiny, another time -
Only the heart flies free, bearing the dreams away.

Brenda Orndorf

The Passion For Life

The passion for life is it found
within our souls. Who knows this great
knowledge that can be for told.

It is I that know's the secret
for the passion for life the passion is
in us it's in us from first light it's there
when we are born it's there till death.

To find your passion your
passion for life look deep within
yourself until you feel confident and
bright guilt is no more the pain is
gone love fills your life and can not
be withdrawn now you've found your
passion your passion for life.

Rochelle Cornelius

Take Care

When a seed opens a child is born, take care.
Taking a can, water them well.
When chilling frost is in the air, take care.
Fertilize with love, let the roots grow deep.
When weeds crowd around, take care,
Let the sun shine down, feed the soul.
When a young lady blossoms, take care.
for some day an admirer will pick her
When a seed opens a child is born, take care

Karen Kimes

Journey

On a journey I've embarked, of detours
and side roads, I'll have no part.
Straight the course I will keep, my
destination only, I'll seek.
The despair that's lurching in my heart,
the grief and sorrow too, these burdens
being to heavy, leaving them behind, I'll do.
I'm searching for love and joy, things
that know no tears. The one that promises
these things, eradicates all earthly
fears. He'll receive my soul and free
my heart, and from his side I'll never depart.
I'll find him at my journey's end, upon
my earthly demise. He'll welcome me home
with love and joy, my heavenly father so wise.

Nancy Milligan

The Decision Of Hope

He could hear everything they all had to say
While on the white sheeted bed in the hospital he lay
They told him they loved him but amongst no reply
He heard all their sorrow he heard all them cry
He wanted to get up and dance all around
He wanted to talk or just make a sound
But because of the accident his life was taken away
He would no longer walk, he would no longer play
He felt pain for his mother she had a decision to make
It was a pain in his side he just couldn't shake
She sat next to his bed and was mournfully crying
Because she knew that her son was now slowly dying
So the decision she made was not without hope
That one day his body would learn how to cope
Then the last thing he heard was the buzz in his head
As the machine was unplugged and they considered him dead

Robert Thompson

Tribute To Mom

I could search the world and those beyond
But there could never be anyone
More precious to me than Mom, dearest of all.
Whatever treasures infinity could hold
There are none so dear or more adored
Since you are loved far more
Than any mother ever.
You alone could nourish such seed of devotion
Simply for being you, dear Mom.
Unlike and above any mother God has graced
This earth before, now or ever.
Tears fall freely from such feeling so great
This love for you
My heart, the love of my soul belongs to
This darling mother, mine.
Giving thanks this day to have
Been so blessed.
For being granted... being part of you.

Katina Richardson

Pain And Laughter

There is not enough laughter in the world
To make up for all the injustice and inhumanity.
Still I will,
With rolling, belly shaking guffaws
And giggles,
Peal away at every opportunity to celebrate,
Knowing full well all humor, except the pun,
Is based on pain.

Twana Sparks, M.D.

Dream Not

Somewhere between dark and dawn, it creeps upon you
And you become the pawn in just another wisp of a dream.

Just enough remembered to bring the cold sweats;
A chill steals over you, and the breathing quickens
As the fingers of fear push back the dawning of rational thought.

Held fast in the realm of unadulterated terror... you scream!
The rush of sanity returns,
To make a mockery of all that held you fast.

What if... the vision that hovers just beyond your sphere,
Is that which you choose not to accept?
Alas, your belief may not be reality.

Dream not tonight, for what you see may be the reality;
And that reality may be death!

Deborah D. Cruthis

My Search Is Over

I walk this earth, both night and day,
Searching for a soul mate, along the way.

I have this emptiness, that my heart needs to fill,
Life without a partner, seems all up hill.

My search brings me places, I dare not to think,
My soul cries out, for that missing link.

Searching is tiresome, but I must see it through,
Cause at the end of the rainbow, it might lead me to you.

Fate has a way, to make things right,
But life has a way to give love flight.

The clock is ticking, is it getting too late,
Will fate treat me good, and find me a mate?

The search is relentless, my soul won't rest,
Will destiny deliver me, from east to west?

I thought love eluded me, I felt so blue,
Then unexpectedly, along came you.

My journey has ended, my soul has found rest,
Fate introduced us, God gave me the best!

Rocco Mastermonico

"Sonnet: To My Little Aborigine"

Once I thought that you could not permit
yourself to hurt someone for whom you care.
Now the cinders of my soul you've lovingly lit,
or is this flame your ever fearèd flare?
At times your deep-soul comes rupturing out
yet you hasten from these sensitivities
your conscious mind makes your soul to doubt
let free your soul and set your mind at ease!
I believe sometimes if only I could express
this yearning, earnest desire to be with you,
you'd find that in your heart you'd acquiesce
"yes - your love is what I'm lacking too!"
I can't restrain and give you half my love,
you are for me the one - my sole beloved.

Charles Keith Lea

Hunger For A Father

It's that time of year when fathers are praised
For the children they've helped, loved, and raised

But what of the children whose fathers are gone
And see no man that is good and strong

Sadness in their eyes, tears in their hearts
For that bit of life, they've held no part

For a father is a gift of strength and love
Given by the true Father from above

To guide them and protect them with a gentle strong hand
To know that his voice is their loving command

It's so hard for the many that have truly lost out
They grow with no wisdom, only hurt and doubt

They hunger for a father to show them the way
To help them not to wander or go astray

For not only is his presence a true strong touch
It's his love and his image that's needed as much

So as you envy this day and the man that it's for
Think of the many that can share it no more

Alicia R. Feigt

Untitled

I truly believe deep down in my heart,
that each baby girl born is a mother in part.
The instincts are there, from very young on,
to give love and compassion when something goes wrong.
Just watch a young girl nurse her doll back to health,
a pattern is formed, there's no price on such wealth.
God gave them this gift, do the best that you can,
to make it, "all better," for girl, boy, and man.
It's her mother she calls when she has a bad dream,
and it's to her that he turns, when he's cut from the team.
It's a rare talent to have, to kiss a boo-boo away,
or to find the right words to teach a child how to pray.
But for reasons, God knows, some can not have a child,
but that compassion is there, so strong, yet so mild.
That's why....
I truly believe deep down in my heart,
That each baby girl born, is a mother in part.

Donna Marose

The Night Is For Those Who Sleep

The night is for those who sleep.
But what about the prostitute selling her body to make ends meet?
Where is her refuge?
Where does she sleep?

The night is for those who sleep.
As the young children wander without direction.
Without guidance in the street.
Killing and serving a community that should love them.
Instead, deserts them.

The night is for those who sleep.
The mother strung out on crack.
Selling her daughter, so she can be whacked.

The night is for those who sleep.
How do you sleep?
Knowing you have closed your eyes to me.

Sylvia Brown

Flying High

When the eagle is flying high
I'll represent, and throw my sign,
While the bright colors gleam all around
I can hear the screaming,
While I'm still on the ground.

As I sit, or maybe lay
The eagle that is flying, is so far away,
I spin in circles, trying to go astray
but nothing happens so I just stay.

Think about the eagle
Think about it please,
Try to determine, why, the trees are at ease
Why are the leaves so green
I don't understand
Soaring high, looking down, at a distant, blurry land

Like the eagle flying high
It preys on little things, just before they die,
Looking up so deep into the sky,
I can feel a drop
Coming from my eye.

Michael Avilla

Color

Glorious colorful sunsets, brilliant skies of blue,
    flowers of every color, in many different shades and hues.
The trees and grass that are growing, in magnificent tones of green,
    a majesty of color, everywhere I look, I see.
For God our great creator, took His artist's palette when He began,
    and blessed us with all His splendid color,
        even when He created man.
Not one is more important than the other don't you see?
If only people believe this, maybe we could live in peace and harmony.
For it takes all the different colors to make a rainbow shine so bright,
Not one by itself, would make a such wondrous sight.
So thank you God for color, especially my sisters and brothers
    who share the earth,
For we are all your children, and should recognize each one is special,
and value each one's worth.

Angie Yoakum

Sister, Sister So Long Of A Time

Sister, Sister
Who would know us any better than us.
How is it out there sis
It's been too long within
But within time things will change.

Sis,
Things are going find here
Long and sweet
Enjoying the cold north wind blowing
Working day and night
Enjoying life as it comes.

Sister, Sister
I'm glad to hear the good news.
don't know when the chance
will come again for us to be together again
But sis not worry it won't be long.

Shele Vallario Jenkins

Waiting For A New Day

I'm waiting.
Waiting for my change to come,
waiting for this part of my life to be over to be done.
This part that seems so gloomy, this part that seems so dark,
I patiently wait for something new in my life to start.

When this part comes to an end, I will rejoice, I will dance,
    I will shout.
I will lift up my voice in triumph for the breaking of a new day
    will have come about.

But as I wait, I rest in the divine presence of the one who knows
    me best.
He knows the tears I shed in the darkness of the night.
He knows how much I dread every step that I must fight.
He knows my days seem dark to me yet soon he'll set me free.

I'll keep on waiting, I'll wait until it comes, that day when
    The Lord will say no more waiting, no more tears, for this part
    is over, it's done.
You see, it's a new day and for me it's just begun.

Maureen D. Shaw

Sunlight Of Love

Believe me when I say
When I look in your eyes,
Grace soars forever in aqua blue skies.

Your presence has come into my life
around me is the warmth of loving sunlight.
Your touch, so gentle, as a summer rain
a cleansing mist washing past pain.

The universe has blessed us with new stars to discover
A chance to rejoice
To feel things only courage and faith can uncover.

We can voyage together
adventuring our knowledge on how to grow,
where the sunlight of love
melts cold ice and snow.

We will hold on to this wave of love we share
A place where few people never dare.

We have been
and always shall be,
...One!

Jeffrey Lawrence Benjamin

Seeing The Cross

Life, it seems, goes on and on.
Becomes more complicated as days are gone.
People and time pass by each day,
Each only concerned in going their way.

So many become lost on the pathways of life.
They become prisoners of confusion, slaves of strife.
They just can't "hang in there" one more day;
They believe nothing positive will come their way.

It is times like these, when hope is lost,
That people fail to see the cross.
They forget that Christ wants to enter in.
They forget that He can save from sin.

Laura M. Stephens

Decadence Of Death

Whiteness descends to the jingles of Christmas
Shrouding her in a veil of forgiveness.
Forgiveness turned dawn red
For her last labored breath gave birth to the dead.

Diphtheria eggs dipped in sunshine,
Bestowed to the bunnies of the earth,
Have raped her offsprings
Of Mogadishu.

Among her lily-white fields
Guerrilla attacks flower,
Coloring the black and white blossoms
With the spirit of apartheid.

Fairy wine entombs her rainbows,
Upon their deliverance of existence
For wickedness of the sire
Dwells in the colorful veins of the virginal dead.

Phantom children flirt with the whispering snake
Slaying her maiden owl from the great oak,
With the science of the metal fire ball
Empowering the soiled hand of the youthful Cain.

Cassandra Ann Shook

Darkness

As I sit here in the darkness a hollow feeling creeps upon me.
Like the way the moon's beam takes over the sun's light.
There is no one here to share the pain; No one to tell
the sorrow's of a day's belonging.
Yet only a smile would bring this helpless soul to life
An only way to build a staircase to help her climb out of the darkness.
At the highest point of darkness when I feel at my most plunge.
A hand, a smile, cuts through all that is surrounding me.
The voice talks and comforts; the one smile becomes two.
The joy, the laughter, that I thought I'd never see is here.
The darkness might surround me, but the smile permeates my
    atmosphere
And I laugh, I smile, I love once more.

Jacklyn Yacenda

My Hero

In the mystery, of why, I am here.
You bring me courage through my fear.
Though female and with a bonnet
I have to say, that I am thankful, for today.
As the follower way, that in the midst, of self assure.
You're the one, who displayed, one to endure.
With an oath of the sword, how can a man's will be heard?
Lead into battle, we mold your saddle!
Thanks be, to the Maker of all.
The presence, the splendor, the gall!
For what, she embeds, in my mind, winter,
summer, spring and fall.

Ken R. Moss

Family, Friends, And Harmony

On a soft, blue, misty day it happened to occur to me
That deep down inside my lonesome heart, I miss my family.
I know I have good friends and that they seem to care,
And for fun filled occasions they are always there,
But the truest tragedies of youth, given unto me
were presented as terrible times for I and my family.
Sometimes I wonder, to myself: "Where are they all?"
"Did I lose any in death's walls?" "Will they ever call?"
So, as this system progresses, I call out in a harmony;
After all o' sins confesses; "you are still my family!!!"
And to all my so call friends I cry out in truest need:
"Jah has blessed many times, true friends you are indeed!"

William Figueroa

"Inspiration"

My loved ones whom I desire the most,
To my wife and daughter I make this toast.

For my beautiful daughter that has just arrived,
She's a blessing from above.... a miracle in disguise.

An exuberant feeling of joy and care,
To love her always... my wife and I will share.

AS she grows and matures with each passing day,
may the light of God guide her way.

And my lovely spouse for whom I adore,
Many times over I've told her before.

Her love and inspiration that fills me within,
Makes these words of poetry flow from my pen.

A love that is so strong as ours,
Can only be found in the heavenly stars.

These words of wisdom I will keep passing down,
My love for you two will never frown.

David M. AuBuchon

Stanley The Manly

Stanley the Manly collected hockey pucks,
Collected busted carnival ducks.
And old radios that wouldn't play
And clocks that wouldn't tell the day.

Many dollars from times of old
And loafs of bread with green mold.
Old baseball cards worth lots of money
And flashy garters from his honey.

Laundry soap by the boxes
And many pelts from rich red foxes.
Hundreds of marbles by the pound
And a name tag from a bloodhound.

Old wrenches with lots of grease
And hippie stuff with the symbol of peace.
Training wheels from a small bike,
Climbing stuff used to hike.

Many novels made into books
And rubber raincoats on rusty hooks.
Stanley the Manly collected this stuff
He had by far, more than enough.

Greg Boben

The Essence Of Time

Time penetrates the transparent skin and envelops the mind
carrying us along, twisting, turning, as if by the wind
our fate at its whimsy
Time awaits for no one,
ideas continually changing within its flux.
We are but a reflection of time, our existence counted in
    seconds,
        minutes,
            days,
                years....
And as time takes us from conception to imminent destruction
here we are in this present moment
reflecting on our past
contemplating our future
Our praxis measured with time is made orderly by
day and night appearance
yin and yang occurrence
so are we here just marking time
    or
can we transcend its realm into a world of just being.

Kathryn Ackroyd Powell

A Secret

At last a secret that I kept is told.
My heart began to pound as I gave up
the story that had made his heart so cold
began to spill like liquid from a cup.
His name has not been spoken of or said.
I shielded fam'ly from his out-stretched hand.
It was as if this living soul was dead.
I saw him born but now he is a man.
He called to ask me why I would not tell
the others who deserved to truly know
this piercing story of my once-lived hell
had kept me silent of my tale of woe.
I told them with my eyes all full of tears,
they've had an unknown brother forty years.

Emily M. Kolber

Crystal Daydreams

Vivid images dancing in your mind
Going places where only you can find
Worries and troubles seem so far away
Into a world that I'd like to stay
Leaving boring life right where you stand
Maybe deciding to tour with a band
So many places where you could easily go
So many things that the natural world has to show
Seeing people who have already died
The truth is so wonderful you never need to lie
Your daydreams so fragile they seem like glass
In the back of your head where you can never pass
To crystal to hardly be true
And that's in my mind when I think of you

Lindz Bryan

Hate's Pain

As I sit and dream, I can hear Hate's voice
cold and horrid
It drains me away, sending me into oblivion
I once had a smile
now there's a look sculptured into my face
by the hands of Hate
Hate destroys, Hate takes
I try to forget the dismal, stunning
words and voice of Hate
I begin to laugh and smile
but it's fake
How can I let it destroy me?
I must forget I must move on
let love bury the Hate
I hate back at first, then release love
smiling and kindness
heal up my wounds
Hate has to end
It's a must

Ashley Hill

Diary Of A Handicapped Child

I'll never forget the day I was born, and while in my pink
blanket so tightly wrapped;
I could hear my mother crying, because the doctor had just told
her that I was handicapped.

Though mom felt sad, frightened, and oh so all alone;
I was her little girl, and she loved me, and soon took me home.

Daily, with the help and love of my parents, I slowly learned
to play, work and yes, even talk;
But, no matter how hard I tried, I never was able to walk.

I remember when I was ten, I became ill late one night;
My parents rushed me to the hospital, filled with sorrow and fright.

Little did they know, and neither could they see;
That while lying in that hospital bed, the Angels came for me.

I quickly ran up to Jesus, and while I had my arms around Him
tightly wrapped;
I suddenly realized that I was finally Home, and no longer handicapped.

Irene Groulx

Tears Of Love

I try to hide my feelings,
I try to look away;
But I don't think my love for you
will ever fade away.

We are together now,
With love from the heart;
The moon shines softly in the sky
that never parts.

You are the angel in my eyes,
The beating of my heart;
Together we could find
where the rainbow starts.

The love we shared was truly special,
And definitely one of a kind;
But now that you're gone
our love is hard to find.

My love for you will never die,
And the tears that fall will show my pain;
But the words I speak
will be hidden by the rain.

Tara Lee Copp

Hold Me

What do I wish
What do I need
What do I want

I want you to want to hold me. At night,
I lie with my arms crossed over my breasts,
Wishing... wishing.

Then the heavens sing me to sleep with
a lullaby of you, and I dream of you
wanting to hold me, every part,
My body
My heart
My soul

With the morning, I wake, and I pray for
the Lord's blessings, because I want it
to be perfect
to be like my dreams
to be love

Judith Martin

Ode To Unrequited Love

Such sweet agony fills my heart with pain,
Like fields of flowers opened to the sun,
As clouds of grey bring forth a heavy rain,
The petals close as if the day is done.
But, nay! The day is far from over yet!
As hope peeks through with shining rays of light,
The petals open only to get wet,
And close again.... bewildered by their plight.
But then the sun just melts the clouds away,
As flowers burst forth with a gentle dance,
And brilliant colors in the breeze do sway,
As if to thank the sun for their last chance.
The flowers' time to die will surely come,
But they found their happiness in the sun.

Joe Thompson

My Mother's Hands

When I was small, cold and fresh
On my face in the early morn
Softly waking, sweet and gentle
  My mother's hands

Brushed my hair, bandaged my knee
Tied the lace of my dirty shoe
Always found time to fill my needs
  My mother's hands

Dried my eyes and calmed my fears
Lifted my head when I felt ashamed
Never judgmental, always caring
  My mother's hands

They are old now and showing the years
Not as steady as before
Still, they comfort and reassure
  My mother's hands

And just last night as I wiped the tears
From a small and tender face
I saw my hands, my mother's hands,
Soothing my own sweet child

Robin Beckman-Jones

A New Beginning

It was heaven when a voice came to me.
"It's time to leave and go to earth you see."
I left my heavenly home and my heavenly fathers side,
to come to a world so different, spacious and wide.
I came out crying, wondering where I might be.
When all of a sudden I felt strong arms around me.
It was the arms of my daddy who cuddled me near,
kissed my head and said, "we're so glad you're here."
I was given to mommy, such a warm place,
I could feel her tears as they fell on my face.
She said, "You're so precious and special, so clean and pure."
I knew I was loved and felt so secure.
How I thank my father and mother for giving me birth,
And to my heavenly father for sending me to earth.

Angie Carrigan

"Lost"

With the muted scream of death, I express my deepest feeling;
down in the hollows of a cold heart, I search for life's meaning.
If the world is what you make it, what have I concocted?
A memory of an angel gone bad, and a soul too scared to stop it.
Prophet for a cruel world, I recite an ominous phrase,
"of all the terrors of the night, I remain to be truly amazed!"
But a light from heaven's grandeur, touched my weakening heart,
something perished inside me, the hopelessness shattered apart!
A word was softly uttered, the discourse just a mere breath,
and I found my deeper meaning, and searched for heaven instead.

Jennie Roberts

The Protector

Clouds cover shoulders of mountains.
The cloaks of Kings past.
Standing guard over the valley below,
No harm shall befall all who live there.
Stationed throughout the mountain side,
Saguaro stand straight and tall.
Marching through the day,
Battling the molten heat of the sun,
Soldiers stand tall awaiting the night.
Moonlight throws shadows over the valley.
Soft diamonds blanket the majestic range.
A cool desert breeze sings softly, sweetly.
The night drifts quietly by.
Protected by the vigilant omnipresent spires,
The valley pays homage in safe slumber.

Rebecca A. Hoffman

A Mother's Lament

I missed you today my eyes filled with tears;
My heart felt the anguish of unfulfilled years.
I wanted to hold you I cried out your name;
Though surely I knew I had nothing to gain.

If we could live those days again, if I could make things right;
I'd turn back the hands of time and hold you oh so tight.
I'd whisper to you gently and hold your little hand;
We'd sail through life together building castles in the sand.

We'd count the stars at midnight and roam the woods by day;
We'd catch a moonbeam in a jar to help us on our way.
We'd hop aboard a passing cloud and ride it with the wind;
Searching for that pot of gold at the rainbow's end.

But God in all His wisdom gives us just today;
He promises His hope and strength to help us on our way.
And so my precious one, my child though we are world's apart;
You're often on my mind and always in my heart.

Laurie S. Crawford

Untitled

There is a moment at the advent of dawn
As swift as a gasp or a stifled yawn,
When the world lies gripped in an indigo light.
Is this the birth of day, or the dying of the night?
Can this moment be a time to rejoice,
Or an echo of Gaia's grieving voice?
For though the night belongs to land,
Daylight brings the rule of man.
A harsh master is he,
Preferring uniform conformity.
Conqueror of all he knows;
Satisfied with the order upon chaos he imposed.
Never guessing the power of time or its might.
Never seeing this world by an indigo light.

Samantha Erickson

Imperfect

A policeman is lacking nerves;
A thin girl wishes she had curves.
It's a prom with your corsage missing;
A date without ever kissing.
It's too many freckles on your face;
Or coming in second at a race.
It's like a report with one mistake;
A birthday cake you forgot to make.
It's a large house on a small lot;
We wish things were perfect but they're not.

Myranda Pasco

In My Backyard

Off my backyard of long ago,
There was a forest where flowers grow;
A sparkling creek, a winding trail,
Fluffy clouds that seemed to sail.
We'd run through the woods or climb a tree;
It was very fun for my sisters and me.
We'd play in the creek and catch small fish,
Blow a dandelion and make a wish.
We'd walk down the dirt road every day;
We'd see goldenrod, a fat blue jay.

In my new city it's different and strange
No woods, no creek, a whole new range;
But my whole family is all here,
It makes it better to know they're near.

Stephanie Pasco

Mom's Everywhere

When I was little I didn't really see,
Just how special a Mom could be.
She wiped my tears, as well as my nose
Always was there to help smell a rose.

My clothes were handmade; coats, unders and dresses,
Mother's were used, torn apart and pressed.
Patterns were drawn to fit my shape,
Laid on the pressed pieces, cut, and sewn my body to drape.

Three boys and two girls with both parents a hugging,
A family of seven in our car was a snuggling.
Chores, gardening, cooking and eating you see
Was the recreation for a big family.

A ride in the car held an extra treat,
Found all of us sitting up right in a seat.
We didn't bounce or belt in, as jammed we'd be
We sang, tunning up chording on "C."

Mom was the center of everything done,
Keeping us clean, warm and on time really was fun!
Take time you see to enjoy while you should
Every moment of life, God and of course, motherhood!

Dru Hoxie

Us

Hand in hand
as we walked.

You fulfilled my day. My everlasting happiness.

You loved me.
You cared for me.
Why must you leave me?

You left me stranded.
You came back to me
and begged.

Your own world ate you as if you were a roach and they,
the ants.

You loved everyone as you loved me.

They figured out your game.
It does not take a genius,
but an idiot.
When they kicked you out, you crawled back.
Your little baby face begged.

I will not take you back,
you are the deserted baby in the street.

Hayley Norman

Dream Of Heaven

I had a dream of heaven.
It was ever so beautiful there.
There were wonderful garlands of flowers
And I dreamed He was everywhere.

The Lord looked down on me alone
And told me, "Have no fear."
"If you have served me well and good
Come home, I need you here."

I dreamed I went to him and knelt.
He said, "Stand up. You are my child"
I looked at him, what love I felt.
The I bowed my head and said,
"Lord, I have not been good enough."

Wanda Hampton

Real Or Not

Spirits, ghosts, goblins, ghouls.
Are they real or are they fool?
Are they just tall, tall tells,
or from the darkest realms of hell?
Do they want to harm us or to joke around?
Do they want our help or to be left alone?
What do they want does anyone know?
What do we see on the cold, damp night of October 31?
Are they dreams or hallucinations?
Was it a spirit, ghost, goblin, or ghoul?
Are they real or are we all just fools?

Addrean Walker

My Crush

I stood waiting at my front door.
It was such a bore.

I wouldn't move an inch though, I was waiting for you.
Dreaming of the day that we would say, "I do."

My dreams were interrupted when I saw your van.
You're more than just a boy to me, you are a man.

I saw you get out of the van and wave.
I waved back, my soul you were just about to save.

Everyday I took a walk,
Hoping you would come out and talk.

You always came out,
My life was finally working out.

Then your friend butted in,
It was my heart he hoped to win.

My life with you slowly drifted away,
Your friend was the one who called me day after day.

I told him I wasn't interested in him,
The one I loved was his friend.

He knocked me off his shoulder with a slight brush,
And let me be with you, my beloved crush.

Tawniesha Shelton

The Sea

The beautiful sea rushes about, often in a hurry,
Almost always seen dressed in shades of blue and green.
Usually kind and gentle, she creeps up on the seashore and
    falls back again.
But occasionally her violent temper arises and SLAM....she throws
    her large body against the sand.

Etta Jane Pagani

Untitled

Not feeling your pain alas so well hidden so
Recently shared, was surely my loss
A greater loss have I should you echo my unfeeling
Moments remembered with hurt
Toward your progeny in wasted haste
Moving a moment ahead of its time
A child's simpler purer feelings
Are easy to behold in terms beyond their intent
If measured by grown up values they seldom meant
As a parent I wish life better by far
In loving consent you feel their joyous frustrations
And sad little cries deeply felt
With untainted hearts of unsure yearnings
Toddling first steps into our stormy world of
Hate anger fear
And yet love tenderness warmth
We cherish because they were hard earned
Felt step by tottering step
Feel them again with simpler hearts my greatest wish

Denis Bilodeau

To My Son Dusty

What I wasn't, you'll be
What I couldn't do, you will
All that I wanted, you'll have
Things I don't know, you'll learn
Opportunities I lost will be in your grasp
Love I never had is yours, always
All that I am, ever was, ever will be,
Is all wrapped up in you, my son
All that I strive for is so you'll
Never be in need
You are my radiant star of hope and joy
Happy easter son
My total undying love.

Claude E. Reidenbach

Daisies Don't Lie

Daisies are so pretty growing wild just every where
And the perfume of the Daisy as it floats on through the air
And that game we played way back then when you were twelve and
I was ten
The Daisy I held so tenderly and asked it if you loved me
The petals I pulled off one by one underneath the bright hot sun
Saying he loves me he loves me not
I never stopped playing until I knew and the Daisy said you
Loved me true

Many years have passed since way back then when you were twelve
And I was ten
But one thing I found out was true Daisies don't lie
My love is you.

Salome Souza

The Rose

A small, red, rose blooms
in the spring.
Its color looms,
higher and brighter then the other flowers.
Your hand reaches up, the thorn pricks your finger
and you bleed.
You change your mind you do not wish to
linger there, you have fulfilled your need.
But in a friendship you can't back out,
it's your job to care,
Even if things go wrong you can't cry or pout.
It's your duty to be there.
Because the only rose without a thorn is
a friendship.

Kate Brigden

"Friends"

Friends are something special
Friends are always there, when you have something to share.
Friends are really wonderful
Friends love you and they care
Friends are people you can trust
Friends will not betray your trust
Friends will always pick you up, when you are feeling down.
Friends know just how to turn your frown upside down
Friends will always lend you a helping hand.
Friends will always help you to plant a blooming seed
Friends always know what to say when something is wrong
Friends will bring you sunshine to an ordinary day.
Well, all I have to say is that friends are someone
special and everyone needs a friend to make their
life a happy one. So the next time you see
your friend tell them they're a special one.

Julie Newell

Busy People

Busy, Busy, Busy. This world is full of busy people.
I want to slow down and I want to keep up,
Why's the world so confusing?
Talking to faceless phantoms.
is talking to the real people.
Nobody listens, Nobody cares.
The world goes on around me, I just stop, and stare.
I wonder why the people are so busy.
They're not like me, not at all,
They care too much for things that don't really matter.
Where's the grieving, where's the loss,
This world is void of feeling.
Where's the love or what's the cost,
Friends or family, I don't know.
My head is spinning out of control.
Busy, busy, people!

Cheri Eddy

Magic

Is there magic inside of us?
Maybe there is, maybe there was.
Maybe magic makes us special.
Maybe it makes us all different and unique.
Perhaps it is what gives us emotions and personalities.
Was there once magic?
Did it disappear with peace and harmony?
Did we all try to be like one another and end up forgetting
our own personalities and traits?
Is there magic inside of us?
Maybe, there is, maybe there was.

Maria Elgass

Please, Never Forget Me

If my life is to have meant something,
Please never forget me
If all of my trials and tribulations are in vain,
Earth is somewhere I do not wish to remain
But if something I said or did touched you,
Please never forget me
My time on earth is borrowed,
My work here never done,
But if one person can remember me,
Then my life-long battle's won.
So I ask you to remember my love and desire,
Remember my anger, my fury and my fire.
The years, they pass so quickly,
My time here now is through,
Please, never forget me
I know I will never forget you

Lisa G. Osborne

The Day Oklahoma Cried

The U.S.A. was in peace
but all went Boom
for one whole day
some bodies lay
and no one knew
who? Why? How?
It was as if the whole world had come to an end
the trembling and shaking through those endless seconds
and all who heard, the lives of many were taken away
on that sacrificial day
The cries for help, the screams, children too
but all knew there was not much they could do
when a person was found
there was a feel of joy and pride
Some where found alive
but others were less fortunate
and that is the story on April 19
when the bomb did decrease many lives and made many worries
throughout the streets of the heartland, Oklahoma
for there is no longer peace

Jessica Russell

Starting Over

You say that you love me
Then why don't you care
You say that you need me
Then why aren't you here
You'll say they'll never be another
As I watch you walk out the door
Why you keep hurting me I'll never know
Maybe you just need some time to grow
This time you need I cannot give
For the time I have I need to live
Live my days as if they were my last
Stop to think and forget the past
To be happy again and start all new
I need to find a love that's true
Within myself I know I still care
But this time with you I can no longer bear
You say you love me and if that's true
Then maybe you'll realize
That I no longer need you

Jennifer Cooper

Insane

I have a conscience, though not like yours.
I do not ponder on which door.
I don't care if what I did was strange...
Or even just a bit deranged.
Who's to say what's right or wrong?
Not a book or look or song,
Not anyone that we can see
Not you or them or even me
So if there is no right or wrong,
We won't be guilty very long!
We all can now be utterly free!
Unlock your self-created cage, you'll see...
Society is not a law that's made by God or you.
It's made by ideas you think are right.
So you scream your protest to the night
But all your screaming is in vain,
Because your ways are all insane.

Misty Peteraf

When I Sing

When I'm sad, singing tugs at my soul and opens my mouth.

It brings the words through my lips in perfect harmony with
   everything around me.

When I sing, my voice rings out to every darkened corner of the world.

My spirit catches a gust of wind and floats into the air; free
   to do and see whatever it likes.

When I sing, my heart brightens up like a light bulb glowing
   inside me.
When I sing.

Leah Barlow

The Sun's First Glare

As I look at the sun's first glare,
I remember it's for all to share.
A big bright circle of yellow light,
Glimmering in the morning bright.
Over ponds, rivers, oceans and lakes,
Over everything God creates.
Once you see it, it takes your breath away,
From the soft green grass were I lay.
The soft soil brushes my hand,
It feels like I'm in a safe land.
With no guns or violence on the street,
But friendly people you always meet.
But no that's just a fairy tale,
It seems our world just may fail.
But I want to imagine our world full of care,
All because of the sun's first glare.

Crystal Heagerty

Determination

From my doorway I see on my back porch
Two puppies as black as coal,
And to get into my kitchen
Is both these puppies' goal.

First they bark, then they whine, then they whimper
But little do they know
I too have a strong desire
That outside's where they go.

They back up-then tackle the screen door
And I think that they'll break it in.
I cover both ears with my hands
To block out this horrible din.

Then all of a sudden, all's quiet
So I peek to see what's amiss;
There's a method to their madness—
They cover my hands with a kiss.

I get carried away with attention
And beam with a glowing pride,
But in the meantime we've changed places
And they stare at me from inside.

Janet Frantz Hankin

"Flowers"

The sun has shone its brilliance for just another day,
Its warmth and glow abounds us for pleasure here to stay.
The little flowers blooming are young so virgin pure,
Their lives have not yet meaning, too young to be so sure.
The petals that will sprout aside are beauty all within,
The growing buds that you shall see are perfect void of sin.
The rain that falls so dreary may wet their little heart,
It is this rain that fuels them and lifts their soul to start.
So when the petals fall and smiles it cannot send,
I see two flowers rise again and live to life's dear end...

Sergio Parsi Jr.

Grade School

Remember those days my friends
Those ones we wished would never end
How life was always fun and new
The rainy recesses we played right through
That washed out, sticker patched grade school field
No matter the weather our determination would never yield
Remember the wars waged there
Remember the heroes made there
We miss these days this is true
Now the bills keep coming due
Puppy love is done and through
When the clouds come to gloom
   your such few, free days
Don't forget your grade school ways!

   Casey Sadler

Brocade And The Bastille

She walked upon the garden stones
with the press of want on her heart and mind.
Her object of Love was far away
and soon to be out of time.

Taken by force and jailed by the Three,
he is sentenced to pay
a debt he never incurred;
Common in this land on this terror-day.

She remembered the lavender moments
among the roses and thyme;
He remembered days of tenderness,
life, fire, and "She is mine."

He ascends the scaffold, while drums roll
with the soul-stoppage of thunder:
Bound and lain — the death drops —
and head and body are torn asunder.

She walks upon the garden stones
with the pain of loss on her body and soul.
Her object of Love is in the absolution
of eternity as victim of revolution.

   Robert Campbell

Why Me

I am lost at the sight of you.
  Don't know why?
You fell in love with a girl like me.
  I ask myself over and over "Why Me?"
   I don't have anything special.
I have you that's very special...
  but why do I have you?
I don't deserve you, I have not deserved to be happy...
I am just another girl that is lost.
I am glad that we have each other...
  but like I've asked myself before, "why me?"
You deserve better, than me...
  Of course, you could settle for less
   Than best, you can have me, but I'll always ask
   "Why me?"...

   Terri Johnson

My Hatless Spirit

Never kiss my mouth like that, my love
It makes me believe in forever,
and I cannot see past my false eyelashes.

I miss your silk and bleach and gold plated tooth,
brushing and combing my femininity for hours,
did you notice its silky texture?
For you, my hatless spirit.

   Mariana Maddocks

On The Path To A New Day...

I sit on the dirt path
With the hot sun on my cheeks
And feel sad

I long for those days
Before spring came

I should be happy
No more layered clothing
Or shovelling snow or fireplaces to mess with
Yet I wish for those cozy times
When I could build snowmen
And make snow angels in the front yard
Or sitting around the fireplace, telling jokes
Feeling the snow brush against my face
Like quick,light kisses
I miss the reassuring glow of the evergreen
Or the sweet cocoa warming my inside

But then I summon all my strengths
And remember that new memories come
With the sun's golden rays
And I start down that dirt path- without looking back

   Lila Dominguez

Let's Take Advantage Of The Day

Where for art thee summer's day
Poetry is dying?
selfish lust has lost the way,
leaving souls a crying

Many of times shall encounter rough
though life is smooth, much like the roses pedal
we must learn just when it is we've had enough
and fight each task as though each task obtained a medal

Measure your love in what you can give
measure your life by what you have given
pass your time with a will to live
and it is then; that your heart is driven

respond in ways only you could
think of thoughts that come from inside
remember the times you said I would
then show me your passion, I'll show you your pride

It's the little things that get us by
take all the poets and all they have said
stand on Mount Everest and yell out a cry
for so many live; but so many more are already dead!

   Michael Rodriguez

A Child's Love

A child's love isn't guilt, shame or blame.
A child's love should feel no pain.

A child's love isn't a hospital stay, to mend that,
bruised or broken bone, you gave today.

For a child's love, is to surround him, tenderly, and
lovingly, with help along the way.

Love is earned, but love can die. It can slip away
before your hardened eyes.

So don't lose sight along the way, for your child must
have a better day. For your love will see him on his way.

   Vicki Sovern

Distant Ocean, Distant Shore

Walking down the hillside and crunching through the snow,
  the few remaining autumn leaves linger at my feet
  as I walk amongst the shadows of the trees.
The winter sun, peering through the dormant limbs,
  warms the back of my head.
From up on this hillside, I can hear the rush of the ocean.
I can hear the cawing of few, lonely birds and gulls.

It is desolate.

The boughs shimmer with icicles...
The loneliness of the atmosphere penetrates across the blue.
It can be heard all around.

Jenifer Khan

Committed To The Shadows

I hear the mature, and their noble reasons,
The way they laugh in front of spite.
Yet to these beings of tolerous humor,
They strand us in the shadows of long lost dreams.

And there we stand, mute, yet unblind to their horrors.
There to be seen; we speak; never heard.
How can you dream our future to be;
Of the purest, wonderworld, with no desires.

We watch you, we mock your actions, as being;
Our dreams you form from the start.
The day you listen, the night you hear,
We will be in command then on.

Why dream if dreams are planned.
Why speak if the deaf cannot hear,
Yet we will yell, and scream;
Forever being in the midst of ourselves.

April Bentley

Green

Green is the grass
In the summer sunshine
Green is a tart, sour tasting lime
A jungle, a hill
And a one dollar bill
Are all green
Green is a thumb
That makes plants grow
Green is a pine tree
Covered with snow
Green is a feeling full of spite
Green is a cat's eyes glowing in the night
Green is a house
That keeps plants warm
Green is the ocean
During a storm
Green is inexperienced, green is mold
Growing on food that is old
Green is all around us

Jessica Knebel

A Salute To Moms

"In Remembrance"
There is a lady that we know well and often take for granted.
But when we are young we never think of what can really happen.
She shows us love by just a glance, the hugs come free and plenty.
For she's the one that sits up nights when we are feeling gloomy.
She gives us love in many ways that we can never say.
All of this is given freely and no payment is expected.
The only thing that would be nice is sometimes we can say,
I Love You— Thanks; these words mean plenty.
For my friends if you don't know yet, this lady is your MOM.

Steven Z. S. Szerlich

Mother And Dad

What can I say about my mother and dad,
except they were the greatest a girl ever had.

I remember the day, dad, first came into my life
he asked my mother to become his wife.

Mother said yes, on one condition,
he get the approval of her children, by asking our permission.

Mother was widowed when I was two, sister and brother,
  five and seven.
When dad asked to Marry mother, I was ten going on eleven

Mother worked hard, keeping us together, and providing a good home
she did very well, after being left all alone

Dad was a sheep and cattleman then and reflected
"The tall rugged cowboy," honest, kind and well respected.

So...What little girl wouldn't say yes!... And think it was super!
To have a cowboy Dad, like "John Wayne" and "Gary Cooper!"

For over thirty-seven years, they gave us love, security and direction
as parents and grandparents, they really were perfection!

They are both gone now and I miss them so...
I write this poem, so all will know... "Mother and Dad I love you so!"

Maxine Witte Aballi

Demons

There is a little girl that no one sees or hears.
Her hands are reaching out but they can never grab on to anyone.
She pretends.
The tears fall but no one sees them.
If enough fall maybe she'll drown.
People look but they don't see;
People listen but they don't hear.
Someday —
Somewhere —
Put the cork back in the bottle, it's safer that way.
Keep the demons under control
They can find you and still hurt you.
They'll eat at your mind until there is nothing left.
They'll win.
Somebody else is always winning.
    Amen

Helene Zimmerman

Eisenhower

E - Means an Expression, on this man's face
I - Means Intelligence, and that's what politics take,
S - Means a Scholar, who's very refine,
E - Means Education, which fills this man's mind,
N - Is for Neatness, this is what he has,
H - Is for Honor, a capacity everyone should have,
O - Is for the Oath, which he took in Jan.,
W - Is for Wisdom that he had on hand,
E - Is Essential for all his good deeds,
R - Is for Righteousness that all of us need,
  Education, Intelligence, Chastity and Power, put them
  all together they spell Eisenhower

Fayetta Higginbotham Townsend

Old Faces

Glimpses of rooms
All faded to the point of disappearance.
Lace curtains, frail and slight
Pulled aside by trembling hands.
Faces framed in windows,
Watching time slide by.
Thinking of what was.
Vividly clear in a mind's eye
And faintly hearing the ticking clock.

Bette Katz

Road Trip

Wandering birds circle the sky.
The wind carelessly attacks the oncoming brush;
It is though the trees have their own distinct
language swaying to and fro, like deaf people using sign.
Could they be communicating?
It is a question I sometimes ask myself,
but nevertheless, has no merit.
The road ahead always seems neverending.
Boredom is my feeling when time stands still.
Strangers looking in as they pass; each with a
unique disposition, as though they were curious of your thoughts.
Personalities clash when sharing small space with acquaintances.
Daydreaming is inevitable, but overwhelms your being.
You come to and wonder how time stood still.
The destination approaches and a smile precludes.
On the journey back, the cycle repeats itself.

    Todd G. Hoyt

"Cycles"

We came from darkness
Into a world where the sun shines bright.
We brought with us
Countless dreams and notions;
Many a big, new idea,
And accomplished them all with time.
But all too often
Fantasy surrounds reality.
We speak without thinking;
Making a lot of noise,
Yet we say nothing.
We are wise — we're fools,
Young — but old,
Giants — yet so small.
We reach too high;
We expect too much
... We are still in darkness.

    Robert J. Feldman

First Love

Your sweet and ravishing words
teased my naive mind
as did your tender touch,
the warm embrace in which I was held.

Loyal and true— like the undying light
descending from the heavens
you seemed to always be there
as a reassurance of our incessant mutual love.

Like a forsaken and admiring child
I was tethered to you,
your Herculean construction,
your unparalleled beauty.

Awakened was I
by the discordant concept of reality—
you did not love me—
merely a triviality I was to you and nothing more.

Now I comprehend that which I should have grasped before—
my young juvenile mind and soul both needed you
and I believe that you needed me too.

    Lauren Goldsmith

Lonely

As the cold wet sand oozes between my toes,
the frosty ocean brushes my ankles
like a purring cat
and then scurries away.

The muskiness of fresh fish,
seized by the brisk wind,
that flaps through my jacket,
arouses the screaming sea gulls overhead.

Far out on the rocky point,
waves crash idly against the jagged feet
of the unyielding sentinel
guarding, guiding...

Patterns of winter clouds are quilted
across the sky as the soft, bleary grayness
of the damp fog lingers over
the angry white capped waves.

I am the ocean and the shore
with the gray loneliness resting in my soul
alone... as a private friend.

    Joshua Smith

My Little Ghost

One quiet winter's evening as I sat by the fireplace
A little boy came from the shadows, he had a thin sad face.
His hair was long and scraggly; his shoes were scuffed and worn.
His shirt was small and threadbare; his jeans were patched and torn.
He startled my composure when he walked out from the gloom.
He didn't say a single word, just looked sadly around the room.
Then he spoke on how disappointed he was on how I've spent
   my years.
I've amassed a lot of worldly things; their loss would cause no tears.
He looked at my old dusty books. I knew that he was right;
I no longer could read them because of failing sight.
"You always took the easy way, you never even fought.
You could have been an explorer, even an astronaut.
Those are the things I dream of," tears welled in his eyes.
"Shall my dreams just be dreams?" he said, with sobbing sighs.
Suddenly he started fading back into the gloom.
And I sat beside the fireplace in a now empty room.
I thought about the little boy: who's ghost that he might be?
He looked familiar - then I realized that - the little boy was me.

    Joseph P. Racher Sr.

Dreams

Night and day I like to dream,
To make things different than they seem.
At night I sit and lie awake,
And make the day a big retake.
I think about events to come,
To make what I want to get done.
I get the hits and make the plays,
In school I even get straight "A's."
I talk to people who aren't there,
And say the things I would not dare.
The things I say about how I feel,
Can not be trusted to be real.
The things I do to show I care,
Can be misleading about what's there.
This is why I like to dream,
And make things different than they seem.
Unfortunately, when it's time for me to wake,
I'm still the failure I was before my break.

    Kevin Glynn

A Daughter's Memory

It was I who waited for you to return from the darkness
She hurt - You knew
It was I who wondered if you were ever going to be there for her
She hurt - You knew
It was I who hoped you would not disappear without a trace
She hurt - You knew
It was I who feared you'd never look back
She hurt - You knew
It was I who waited, wondered, hoped, feared
It was she you hurt - It was you who knew
It was you who never returned
It was you who wasn't there for her
It was you who disappeared
It was you who never looked back
She hurt - We hurt - You knew

Lisa A. Cassidy

Summer Days

In summer time the clouds are fluffy white.
The trees are painted a palette of green.
Flowers, a beautiful blossoming sight.
Sun shines down creating a peaceful scene.

In rustling grass the children romp and play.
Beneath the powdery, blue sky shimmers.
Blue, soaring kites dance a graceful ballet.
Until the day fades, and light grows dimmer.

The heaven's drumming signifies light showers.
A rainbow arched across the misty sky.
As butterflies soar with tremendous pow'r
Strong breezes rustle leaves as they float by.

Summer days are filled with joy and delight.
When you feast eyes on nature's stunning sight.

Leslie Schultz

The Rain

The rain; marking a course of change, diversity is upon
us as things will no longer be the same. Drenching the land
of good nature, our thoughts will not be shared as the rain
has spoken for all. The water of our earth, pure as love,
whisks us all away to filter our minds and isolate us from
our bothered thoughts of despair. An illuminance of our world
of which without we would die, falls in abundance from the vast
cloudy sky. Today it brought us fortune, I can feel it in my soul,
will we have such luck tomorrow, I'm afraid we have no control.

Darren Olson

I Watch

I watch as my patient's systems fail.
I watch him grow cold, tired, and pale.

I keep him comfortable and his family too.
I reassure them in this time of gloom.

I see the family accept his dying.
I see them sad, and feel like crying.

A bone marrow transplant, these last months he's lived.
He fought long and hard and gave it all he could give.

I do not question this death's manner or time.
I trust in the Lord for He is divine.

I watch as my patient's suffering comes to an end.
I watch the death of another friend.

Vickie Volrath, RN, BSN, OCN

The Passing Years

As I gaze upon the pictures
That I've collected through the years,
I think about the time that has past
As I wipe away my tears.

The times that held such precious moments
Along with sad times too,
The times that in my weakest hours
I thought I never would get through.

I think about my family
And friends that paved my way.
I smile and thank the Lord above
For them each and every day.

And my priceless little treasures
Have grown so quickly through the years,
From blankets bottles and rattles,
To car keys, proms, and peers.

But this is all a part of life
As I remind myself once more,
To make sure you make each passing day,
A memory worth living for.

Linda Laramie

The Making Of A Hero

"Not again", he said quietly
Yet knew he would answer the call
As he had a thousand times before
When darkness began to fall

He sighed as he donned his armor
And pushed away all doubt and fear
He put on a mask of contempt
As the time of his calling drew near

Should he win he would never hear praise
Only silence and muted jeers
And if fated to fall once more
They'd celebrate with laughter and cheers

Although he had won many battles
In the end he would never win the war
Yet still he fought on while believing
In what he was fighting for

For what is a victor without the fallen
And darkness without the light
So when you cheer your hero's victory
Remember the cost to the Black Knight

Danny E. Campbell

"To May"

Of all the months you are most fair;
among the twelve a jewel rare;
your golden days, your fragrant nights,
month of one thousand and one delights.

I like April, June and all the rest
but it's you, dear May, that I like *best*.
You are the very *heart* of Spring
you really make *my* soul to sing.

Would that of days you did have more!
you are like all good things, soon o'er
how nice 'twould be, what wonderful fun
if they were *more* than thirty one!

Kenneth St. Clair

The Mountain's Heights

I look off in the distance and wonder at the sight.
My legs are far too weary to climb the mountain's heights.
I've lived in the valley for seemingly far too long;
the art of climbing mountains requires one to be strong.

I sit in this valley, now so dismal and sad
for I dream of the joy that I might have had.
Oh, the rewarding journey I could have made
if only I had not been so very afraid.

But, wait now! A shepherd's voice I hear,
"To the mountain's heights, do not fear!"
I hurry to him, to take my flight.
"Master, take me to that lovely site".

With that step of faith these cumbersome limbs
are suddenly as light as the wind.
The majestic mountain's heights are sweet,
so easily scaled with hind's feet

You see, it is only when I trust in God,
that I can be uprooted from this sod.
My pleasure is then to taste sweet new wine
from my home up in Heaven, 'tis now mine!

Darlene Robinson

A Small Heart-Shaped Box

A small heart-shaped box
Holding my fears, my loves, my secrets
Locked shut;
Never to be opened;
Never to let the secrets go.
Holding my breath, every day
Wondering if the wind will blow,
if it will blow my life away.
In the small heart-shaped box
A boy's picture, who broke my heart,
A cigarette stub, which hurt my lungs,
The side of a best friend's necklace, which has no meaning,
A gun holding two bullets,
In the small heart-shaped box.
Things never to be used again,
Never to be seen again, unless...
The wind blows
    away my
        precious secrets
        of life.

Lauren M. Gross

To Little Gold Fish

You swim around
Like you don't have a care in the world.
But you always look at me,
Hoping you get fed.
I look at you and think,
Oh what a wonderful little friend.
Then all of a sudden
You turn on me,
I look at your bowl,
And what do I see,
But you lying dead on your back,
Still without a care in the world.

Kelly Schnoor

Out Of Africa

Out of Africa my ancestors came
Most on boats, all in chains
A land unchosen, A world unknown
Leaving behind seeds, still unsewn
Carrying with them, their faith and their pride
Only time would heal the marks on their hide
Across wide oceans, and deep blue seas
America! Land of the brave, home of the free?
Trust in thy God, they had to place
For they were slaves, in a strange new race
Placed on blocks, families sold apart
The pain and torment, that burdened their hearts
The years were slow, as the days were long
Remembrance of home, the freedom to roam
Songs in the fields, passed time away
Bones weary and tired at the end of the day
Now times have changed, we're shackled no more
Our spirits can roam, our souls can soar
A toast to you, with roses and wine
For the heroes of time, were ancestors of mine. Out of Africa

Janice Saunders

Some Say

Where does the Universe end?
Some say infinity.
But if it is then where does it start?
And who decides that?
Some say God.
God is this person who is supposed to forgive people for their sins.
But if he forgives, then why do people end up in Hell?
And if there is a Hell, who is in charge of it?
Some say the devil.
But if he is real, then why would he want to ruin people's eternity?
And if all I have just said is true, then why do so many question it ?

Jennifer Rounds

Smoke And Ash

The house my brother built is gone
erased, extinguished, purified by flame,
nothing left but smoke and ash.
Dialogues of despair can still be heard
now entombed within these walls.
Cinders smoldering in heaps of hurt
hiss, squeal, and crackle.
I can feel the pain, it remains
tortured, tormented, disappointed.
Beams that held this structure scream,
charred black with soot
still feel too hot to touch.
Rummaging through steaming rubble,
broken glass, the scattered pictures
mark the moments captured
that time will no longer tell.
I so loved my brother's house,
one thought helps to comfort me...
in empty rooms "fond" memories
help fill the vacancies.

Wesley Carlton Dennison

Conformity

That wicked and unfeeling beast, whose name shall be conformity
Took, yet another, devastating blow against my ever weakening
heart and soul!
Leaving but a mere shell of who and what I used to be.
Oh conformity, how can you feed on hearts, souls, and dreams
Stealing from them all you see...and yet, be so cold and heartless?
Taking the zest of life from those who dare to live,
leaving behind the living dead...those who simply exist!
Would it not be a kinder death to steal the very breath,
To rob us of our very life in lieu of our very essence?!
Oh, you bastard of all that's shallow and meaningless!!
You demon sent from hell!
Get thee back to the hell from whence you came... and from
where you have put so many!
Leave some life, some dreams, some hope...Oh, please go,
please leave!!
I beg of thee...please leave, oh wicked beast whose name is conformity!!

Cheryl D. Cox

The Prayer Room

There is a place I dearly love
Know as the room of prayer
And oh I find such perfect peace
When I am kneeling there.

And while I'm in this quiet place
Just talking to my Lord
I know that he is with me there
And hears my every word.

I send petitions upward
As I bow my head and pray
For those who are in trouble
As they travel down life's way.

I thank you Lord for all the prayers
That you have answered for me
And for leading me through the dark valleys
As I've sailed life's stormy seas.

And as I leave this room of prayer
My day is so much brighter
As I go about my daily tasks
My burdens seem much lighter.

Nell Cagle

"The Search"

Love is a search
Never to be found,
Our heart awaits
While our eyes probe each crevice up and down.
Our mind draws a blank,
Our bodies feel destitute,
A flower craving water at the end of each dry root.
A grasshopper hopping
From one blade of grass to another,
But eventually it must settle down
And catch its breath there.
The road unwinds
And the dead end appears,
We figure it is the extremity this time
And that is our most majestic fear,
Will we ever learn
To watch each step we take,
Maybe if not
The rock we stumble on
Will prove to be fate.

Carlee White

In The Meantime

Like fireworks being threatened by a match; terrified,
he squeezed the life out of me.
As she took him,
I felt a piece of me drift farther and farther
Away from everything real.
While I grasped desperately for some sort of justification,
intimacy hung in the air like tension.
A voice invaded me,
light killed us,
a touch fueled us.
A virus devoured the moment.

Sara Jean Anderson

Lost Love Found

As children, we grew together
A bond nobody could break
With a smile, a laugh, a holding hand
Something that should have lasted forever
As teenagers, we grew apart
In a fast world, full of problems
Drugs, Alcohol, Everyday pressure
God, how did we survive
Totally Lost and confused
We separated without a trace
Now twelve years later and a letter
I took a chance and sent it
And you took a chance and answered it
As adults, we will grow old together
More mature and responsible
A new smile, a new laugh, a gripping hand
Two hearts filled with love
May you never leave me again
Lost Love Found!

Edward Lodzinski II

The Winds Of Time

Where has the time flown?
I barely can recall
Except for the memories of my childhood I once knew
Words spoken from my dear Mother and others I can relate to
Bringing happy thoughts to mind
I cannot keep up with time
Because time slips away so fast
It passes so quickly by
Before I realize that another month and year has passed.

It seems it was just yesterday when life was
    so simple and pleasant to recall
Then life became complicated adding problems by the score
Alas, the simple life was there no more
Survive I did and much more
I made a new life for myself
I opened up another adventurous door.

Harriette Catherine Lane

Fishing Together

A boy sits with his fishing pole
Near a mountain lake clear and cold
Its waters colored by the setting sun
Peaceful now that the day is almost done
A weeping willow stretches towards the water
And the boy eagerly awaits for his father
Together they will fish for bass that bite
Looking up to see wild geese in flight
The day will darken before long
Soon frogs will begin their croaking song
Father and son sharing a moment together
The memory of which will last them forever

Bonnie Stone

Everlasting Love

Love is a powerful and mystical thing
Bonded by prayer and a golden ring
Sealed with a kiss and warm embrace
Love is something only the heart can trace.

Love is wonderful, love is kind
I hope someday that it will be mine
To have someone so gentle and bold
Someone there to always hold.

Someone warm, someone who cares
Our lives together we shall share
Forever more faithful and true
That are the vows when you say "I do".

Susanne F. Castillo

Careless

Through the blood the fox was hunted.
We searched and tore the cupboard bare.
And, strange, we thought of no disservice
When realized that the dead were there.

Ingrained they strode the empty walls
And empty, they, in turn, were free.
For mercy's sake and mercy only
Left them solemn silently.

Their voices, later, chose to haunt me.
A penance for their time unshared.
And now, alone, I share their silence.
My life a burden mine to bear.

Elijah J. Graves

My Dearest Sweetheart

I can't get you out of my heart,
I can hear you say, that's not very smart
No matter how hard I may try,
You'll be my love until the day I die.

It's odd how things can go around,
Twelve plus years, how crazy that may sound,
but that's how long I've loved you my dear friend,
And I know you will always be there to the end.

When I look into your eyes as we meet
I know that your love for me is oh so sweet,
No matter what happens or where we go,
I can count on you my love, I know,
That you have a love that we can share,
When my heart needs fixing you are there.

My love for you at times has made me sad,
but things are different now and I am glad,
for you are so understanding and kind to me,
it just took a while for me to really see,
that my love for you is so very strong,
I realize that is where I wish to belong.

H. S. Mishoe

The Titanic

A groan and a heave, the ice rips through,
Tearing through the great ship as it moved.
Silvery laughs, the music playing,
Turned into screams and prayers.
Water rushed in, the hold was giving,
The Titanic was no place for the living.
Bodies gliding around the bow,
There are no boats waiting, now.
Down and down and down they plunged,
Fathers after their children lunged.
Then there was nothing but screams and waves
The Titanic had gone to a cold and watery grave.

Sue White

The Time Clicks By

There were really only two times of the day when you ever used
　to call me
I still watch in a state of breathlessness as the probable times pass by
And there is silence

I didn't ask for much from you, and in the end you were only too
　able to comply
I only asked that you keep in touch
Though we were no longer touching
I knew that danger lurked for me in your conspicuous quiet

I don't think I will ever know (I wish that I knew)
Just what it is about me that seems to send you running
Head down, full speed in the opposite direction, Away

I see you on those chance occasions now
Which I know I would elude if I could
I search you so intensely for a sign that you perceive my pain
That you concede your contribution
Intensely, while I fight for nonchalance as if my very heart's
　survival were at stake
It is It is

I seem to repel what I wish to attract
I wonder if I'll ever know (I wish that I knew) why
The time clicks by

Tracy L. Newirth

Losing Our World

As the world turns gray as we lose
another day.

When we could have united as one
underneath God's sun.

But as so many ignore to be kind to
one another.

Out in the streets you're shooting
each other.

Take a hold of your life and reconstruct
the matter to make this world happier
not anymore sadder.

Curtis

A Poem For My Wife

Just to think of your beautiful face,
Puts my emotion back in place.
I go crazy, not able to see you,
In front of me...What am I to do?

When I say "I love you" you see,
I give you every part of me.
My heart, my soul and all the rest,
Of my feelings, you have the best.

You are my life blood...understand,
Even before the wedding band.
And even though it's difficult to show,
My river of love won't cease to flow.

I want us to share our lives together,
There could never be an end to forever.
I know that if there was one,
Our love for each other would not be done

For even in the afterlife,
I'll still want you as my wife.
And we could walk, hand-in-hand,
Through the beautiful, heavenly promised land.

Raymond A. Gohl

Learning To Ski

For me the year begins to November
When all the leaves are in their grave
For it is this time of year, with skis
In hand that I become so brave

With boots buckled and bindings gripping tight
I eye that steep decline with what many would
Say is fright, pushing off on wobbly knees and
Wrongly placed poles, what comes to mind are
The missed lessons which I needed, I was so often told

Traverse that slope avoid that hit, bend those
Knees never allowing those skis to split
Faster and faster the moguls come
Wrongly I approach them one by one. There's the one that
Got me dead, letting me know I'm skiing over my head

Edges grab the blue glare ice
Causing skis to cross and poles to slice
Airborne now no chance to recover take that fall for
I'm sure there will be many another

Ronald Blazejewski

Love's Dream

If this is a dream don't wake me up, just let me
lie here for a while. For when I think of you my
dear all I can do is smile. The happiness you've
give to me can never be compared because
in these times of tenderness the love we have
is shared. These feelings that I have for you
will never go away. That you feel the same
for me is my only wish everyday. My fantasies
are filled with you, and in my dreams you're there
letting me know in your own little ways how much
you really care. You're the dawn of my mornings
and the stars of the midnight skies, and I would forever
be content just to look into your eyes. In your
arms I feel secure when you're holding me so
tight, and when you take my hand in yours I
know we'll be all right. This love that I feel
for you is hard for me to explain, but if I
should ever lose your love I would surely go insane.

Roxanne McGee

Wonders

I wasn't born with all the tools to play
but perhaps with hard work there would come the day
that I could play baseball and have people rant
about the things I can do and not the things that I can't
they'd say "The kid was great, one of the best at the game
why him and the Babe...they're one and the same"
it's always been a dream to go up against the best
but me versus the legends...surely I jest
for they are the grandest the games ever seen
from the hitting of Gehrig to the pitching of Dean
however, I wonder and it seems quite unusual
how do you pitch to the great Stan Musial
what would you throw? A slider or deuce
or maybe a knuckle or just cut one loose
and throw the ball as hard as you can
and pray that it doesn't end up with a fan
I'll just keep my hopes of playing in the pros
and keep working hard then maybe he knows?
I know that I'm good but the part that I hate
for all that I do it's all up to fate.

Stephen Shores

My Homeless Brother

There are things I want to share with you,
They come from deep within,
Spiritual things, my thought, my cares
and the remedy for sin.
We walk through life with blinders on,
and stumble all day long.
We never really realize that in our
weakness were made strong.
When life knocks us to our knees,
and we can run no more,
It does not make us cowardly
to call upon the Lord.
We all need help sometimes my friend
You know this to be true
Call out the name of Jesus now
and let him comfort you.

Billy W. Caldwell

Signs Of The Times

World changing, people re-arranging, signs of failure,
families fighting, not doing the right things, times of failure,
feelings drifting, bonds alifting, sure of failure,
storms aplenty, few with "thee", still signs of failure,
fires burning, rivers churning, warning signs of failure,
no time to worship "thee", take time to worship "thee" then...
Your peace will flow from within, if you only give in...

To everlasting freedom from being free from sin,
good times pass you by, you wonder why?
just slow down the pace, give "God" his grace,
and "He" will show you signs of tomorrow,
slow down the pace, give "God" his grace,
and he will take away your sorrow,
slow down the pace, give "God" his grace,
knowing there will be peace and happiness in "His" place.
AMEN

Gwendolyn Delores McClain

Changes

I gaze at this picture, I feel that I'm old.
This five by seven view of my world, my coffee is cold.
Bare trees, dead grass, an empty basketball court
Icy water, cloudy skies and more snow they report.
Old wood is decaying, the winds they blow fast
My mood is somber, my energy past.
The seasons, they change and so does my view
My spirit replenished, a return of my youth
The photo's not grim, no longer "old" do I see
My grass is now green and there's leaves on the trees.
No more wood decaying, it just doesn't rot
My goodness, I've just noticed my coffee is hot!

Joanne Kramer

Why Is It?

Why is it that I feel this way,
On such a happy day?
I mean I shouldn't,
Most couldn't.
On holidays you're supposed to be happy,
Sitting with mama and pappy.

Why is it that I feel this way,
On such a happy day?
Maybe in my soul,
I know it won't come around this bowl
In my life again.
It will never come again this gain
Of days that have been added.
However, for some, this realization is not padded.

Jennifer Gilman

Depression

In a dark wood wandering.
Quickly moving so as not to get caught unaware by what you may find.

In a dark wood wandering.
Alone.
You go back further, and further, deeper into the abyss.
Finding things you'd thought were long forgotten,
   and didn't want to remember.
You've been here before, this place is vaguely familiar.

In a dark wood wandering.
Looking in all the crevices that you discover.
Searching for an answer.
Wondering...Why me?

In a dark wood wandering.
Aimlessly.
Never knowing what comes next.
Feeling despair so deep, that you know you'll never get out.
It's hopeless, you're lost forever in a black dungeon of mazes
   that lock you in,
with all the things about you, that you never let other people see.

In a dark wood... Inside your mind.

Amanda Reaman

The Devil

As I felt the anger boldly printed across my face,
As the fire burned deeply in my eyes,
I felt the presence of the devil.

He was right there inside of me,
Pressing at every thought I had,
Every happy part of me crushed by the anger of the devil.

As if I was just a toy to play with,
A mind to work,
A soul to torture,
Who worked in side of me?
The devil!

As wind pounded on my face,
I thought of heavenly grace,
Who died?
The devil!

Tina Miscioscia

"Not One Of My Friends"

My life is going to be messed up.
That's what my mom says.
She keeps on blaming it on them.
But it's not one of my friends.

She claims it's all their fault.
But she doesn't quite know how it is.
I'm the one who does what I do.
It's me, not one of my friends.

I'm not quite sure why she don't understand.
That it's them on which I depend.
Still she thinks I need her,
Not one of my friends.

One day she'll get it through her head.
Once I get my revenge.
She never should have blamed it on them,
For it's not one of my friends.

I wouldn't have to do anything,
If she knew a hand is all they lend.
I do everything on my own.
Not one of my friends.

Lynn Trowbridge

Let Me Stand By The Edge Of The Road

Oh, Let me stand by the edge of the road
For, If I stand I can carry my load.

Oh, Let me stand by the edge of the road
For, If I stand, I can see beyond the
fork of my direction in life.

Oh, Let me stand by the edge of the road
For, If I stand, I will avoid the
curve of misfortune, despair and deception.

Oh, Let me stand by the edge of the road
For, It is there I will stamp my footprint
of the past and present.

Oh, Let me stand by the edge of the road
For, In a little while and just a little
while, I shall step in the path road of
death and stand no more.

Phyllis Colclough Smith

I'm Trapped

I'm in a high place I'm a queen
But I'm looked at as though I'm only a scene,
I've been sculpted into something that's not me,
I'm half myself and half something I can't be.
They've turned the King into, I don't know
The people used to bow to us low.
I'm here sitting on my throne,
I'm always bored, always alone.
People come by. They laugh,
They don't realize my long path.
I lived my life to the fullest,
I want to go off and die, I'm depressed.
But I can't live. I'm a sculpture.
I must live my life. I must endure,
But I can't, so good-bye to life.
I want to slit my throat, I need a knife
Now I'm dead. Life goes on forever,
Just like the drifting away of a feather.

Rhonda McDowell

I Asked, You Said

I asked "What will I See?"
But you only said "it's okay, just close your eyes".
So I closed and I saw gypsies and angels
I saw my fate waiting, standing untrue
I felt the warmth spread throughout my
body. But the iciness stayed in my veins.

I said "can I open my eyes?"
You said "No, not just yet!"
But I sneak an unknown peek. What did I see?

I saw your mouth with a bandage I know
Your mouth is like a gash. If I remove the bandage
The words will come out like the infected blood

I closed my eyes and saw fairies with 666
Tattoos. I saw my love, sitting upon hate.
You said "Okay, myself is waiting!"
I opened my eyes to an impatient gape,
Only to see myself pinned down, ready for rape.

This poem is dedicated to rape victims everywhere.
You're not alone, don't forget to survive.

Molly Bean

The Storm

We once swam in a crystal lake of love and peace,
enjoying each other just by being there.

One day, a mighty storm came over the horizons.
This storm was filled with hatred, mistrust, selfishness and denial.

This storm rushed in on us without warning; lasting
several years, eroding the very foundation of our love,
tossing us at each other, pulling our love apart, until we
were too weak to hang on anymore.

As the storm us apart, we tried to reach for each
other, but we couldn't touch.

As I watched you being swept, away, I cried out, "I Love
You", and you were gone.

Now, all I hear are waves of loneliness and despair crashing
on the empty shores of my heart.

Jerry Fouts

Mom

Mom was in her twenties when she married,
All that Mom touched was blessed from up above.
Inside Mom's heart and womb nine children she carried.
We were taught the most important lesson, to love.
When Dad passed away it must have been hard
to raise nine children all on her own.
No time or money to spend except maybe on a card.
Sometimes a hello over the phone.
Yes her hands were full and tied.
Trying to get by and take care of bills
on a low income, Mom had her pride.
No not much for material frills
to boast and brag all about.
Mother was rich with a love
and there is just no doubt
that it all came from up above.
Now that you're gone we love you no matter how far.
You are one of God's Angels
Looking down from up above where you are.

Kathy P. D. Flick

"I Am Afraid"

I am afraid.
I wonder when in time this world will end,
I hear the cries of women and men,
I see people loading guns with shells,
I want to know if I shall go to heaven or hell,
I am afraid.
I pretend that nothing is bothering me,
I feel that I need to get a way, be free,
I've touched the body of a man deathly ill,
I worry if I shall be stabbed, shot, or brutally killed,
I cry for the innocent who are murdered each day,
I am afraid.
I understand that I can be forgiven for my sins,
I say my prayers over and over again,
I dream of a place where life never ends,
I try as I may to live life without sin,
I hope I go to heaven to be amongst friends,
I am afraid.

Adam Edwin Coe

Jim's Love

There was a young boy, who learned how to love.
   A love that was taught from our God above.
He grew and he grew, till a man he became.
   A tall man at that and Jim was his name.
He loved all his family and friends that he knew.
   And many were they, for they loved him too.
He was a hard worker and did his own part.
   A man on the outside, but still a kid at heart.
He could be serious if he needed to be.
   He could be silly for he wanted to be.
There then came a day we were saddened to see.
   A day Jim was taken from you and from me.
He now lives in Glory and it's easy to see,
   The love that he showed can be learned by you and me.

   Shelly Onley

Untitled

In Memory of Greg Mitten
Don't think of me as a winter oak tree
with no leaves upon its branches.
Rather think of me as sunlight on snow
the way it sparkles and dances.

Remember me in my childhood days
carefree and full of hope.
Not as an adult, alone and afraid
totally unable to cope.

Don't picture me in the empty chair
where I was too sad to stay.
But look for me in the eyes of my children
as they run outside to play.

Don't feel as though you've lost me forever
never to see me again.
For I shall be waiting just through the gates
as you enter the Kingdom of Heaven.

   Lisa Chipman

Untitled

In the town of Duluth, down by the bay
The ships enter and leave all through the day
With a ding, ding, ding the bridge begins raising
I've watched it a lot but it's still really amazing.

Ships go under the hi-bridge from Wisconsin to here
They glide through the harbor as I watch from the pier
A blast from their horn is deep and aggressive
Both the ship and the bridge sending a message.

Their motion seems gracious and moves fairly slow
So it won't disturb living, deep down below
The ships are so long with a strong, sturdy build
And many are as long as a football field.

With big decks with the railings that sailors lean on
Some guys smile and wave until the harbor is gone
A blast from the horn says they're all clear
So the bridge lowers down until the next ship is near.

When bedtime has come and I shut off the light
I hear the tug of a ship's horn as it moves through the night
The ships have all left and are gone for the day
But there will be more adventures tomorrow - down by the bay.

   Pat Reed

265

Celebrate Christ This Christmas

Is Christ in your Christmas?

Christmas is Celebrating the birth of Christ,
A Gift from God, not received, no eternal life.
How can you get Christmas from a mall?
Spend, Spend, Spend, nothing left at all.
Pockets empty, Spirits hollow inside and out,
Christmas come and gone, What's it all about?
It's about the bond, the blood and the birth,
That's why Jesus Christ lived on the earth,
His life lived, his blood shed for all mankind,
God's perfect plan, made not hard to find
So keep Christmas the only true reason
For Celebrating Christ this Holiday Season!

Chanda Boone

Untitled

Have you ever talked to the sky
Have you ever answered the call of the wind
Followed a shooting star
Ignored the wisest man
Invested in a fool
Been caught in a duel with greed
Extended a helping hand
Lost in a game you never entered
Won the unexpected
And wanted the opposite
The rules are never right
Unless the game is unbeatable
Only follow your soul
Listen to your heart
Never follow anyone else's dreams
And make your chases count
The rest of the knowledge...
Will find you.

Katherine Stahl

The Impossible Dreams

There is a dream, oh, such a wonderful dream,
That the world is peaceful and we all get along.
And there are no worries of anything,
Because everyone is joining hands as they sing beautiful songs.

Another dream, oh, such a greedy dream,
That we become famous and our names are those of heroes.
And everyone who sees us bows down
Because we have the wealth and power like old King Pharaoh.

These are dreams, oh, such impossible dreams
That peace and glory are mixed together as one.
And the reason for being impossible is clear,
Because you cannot live in two worlds all alone.

Jeffery Brian Young

Mother

If she had nothing she gave us love
There were no looking behind or too high above
Keeping your feet on solid ground is the way it was
Mother always had a listening ear and a pat for
Your back
Mother did not have much schooling but wisdom
She did not lack
Mom I love you and will never forget you
Your life is the foundation for what I choose to do
Your wisdom has caused me to survive through and through
Now you have gone to rest in a much better place
Mom just do me a favor and reserve me a space.

David E. Singleton

Granny's Good-Bye

February 14, 1923
was the date of my birth..
and on February 26, 1996
God took me from this earth.

My pain and suffering is over now
and it's time for my final rest...
Your love and strength helped ease the way
and surpassed God's ultimate test.

My family, know that I love you,
My friends you are so dear...
I'm in a better place now,
please don't shed a tear.

I'm with my husband once again,
Standing by his side...
Hand-in-hand we'll walk together
and God he'll be our guide.

Health and Happiness to each of you
for this I'll always pray,
Keep me close to your heart,
'til we meet again one day.

Michelle B. Cease

What Baby Will Be

Two babies were born one April day,
Each to loving parents with hearts filled with joy,
"We are thankful they're healthy," was all they could say,
As they showered them with love and lots of toys!

One set of parents was strict and determined they say,
To make baby mind in every way,
The other more tolerate, they just talked it all through,
"He just didn't understand...didn't know what to do."

Both babies went to school, the other day,
Now ten years old and quite set in their way,
One got a star and an excellent report,
The other sent home as a last resort.

One mommy laughed, the other cried,
One filled with sorrow and the other pride,
To one set of parents, their child is a delight,
To the other set of parents, their child is a fright.

What is the difference of sorrow or pride?
What will mold, change and turn the bitter tide?
It's discipline...It's discipline...oh, parents, can't you see,
Discipline makes the difference in what baby will be!

Millie Britt

One Woman

A soothsayer cried that Gwenyvere lied
And the archers all pierced their hearts
A lion roared in the dusk till he died
While a basilisk weeps in the dark
King Arthur sullenly sits on his throne
Crestfallen by passion and rage
As Lancelot escorts his despair away
Stripped of legacy and love
The round table spins-entranced with discord
And the knights war for their deaths
The Lady in the Lake extends her hand
For a broken life and sword
Excalibur wails at glancing this hell
And Arthur battles his son
Lancelot comes, without pause, to his side
Loyalty proclaimed, Honor Regained
Camelot Falls
All for A Fair Skinned Maid.

Casandra Kokoska

To A Wandering Daughter

We miss your smile and dark brown eyes,
The happy times we've shared.
We miss your presence around the house,
And we think your heart still cares.

We do not know just why you left,
The bosom of your family.
We pray for your health and happiness,
For inner peace and your souls security.

Please know our hearts are full of love,
No matter what you do.
We cannot seem to do things right
Or to get our message through.

Although our communication may be lacking,
Our love for you is there without asking.
So understand our values are traditional
But parental love is unconditional.

So if you find you cannot cope,
Just pray to God, He will give you hope.
We want you home, no matter what,
Because the door to our heart is never shut.

Mary Nadeja

Looking Out At The Night

Looking out at the night,
I'm lost in a dream.
Thinking of things that will come to be.

The silent night, It seems so sad,
I've no regret of the past
or for the things I've had.

My day begins with the break of dawn
and carries through dusk
till the day is gone.

Without a means I'm all alone,
in a busy world without a place to lay my head
or even call home.

I'll keep following this lonely dream
until the things that come to be.

At the end of the path I'll hold my head high,
knowing it's started;

Looking out at the night.

Donald Johansen

My World

I ran through the grass from which I came
But somehow it is not the same
Dove in the sand, what a great feel
Playing and laughing just doesn't seem real
Climbed that big tree that I never could
Somehow it was better just staring at wood
I miss the kiss that took away all the pain
Nothing new my curiosity slain
Kool-Aid, bologna, a day in the sun
Never settled down, never was done
Scooby-Doo I remember too
Coinciding with nap time, oh what to do
I wanted to grow up way too fast
Now I wish youth would have never passed
Time to move on, what are my plans
So many choices, life in my own hands.

Trent Schultz

Olive Kristense

She saved the roots from her mama's orange blossom bush
Because her mama had loved it so!
Planting it in honor of mama
Praying it would grow
Then another for her grandma
And her aunts, not one, but two
All four grew so beautifully together,
In the lovely morning dew.

The scent of sweet, fragrant, flowers
Wafting through the house for hours
And from the open window screens
Came nostalgia and summer full of bygone dreams!

It was if her mama, grandma and both aunts, too
Were pretty much there with her
And each enjoying the view.

Together once more
As they used to be
Only this time they are flowers
For her to see.

Mary Anne Chipman Jones

In The Night

The whispering winds passes by
Stars ignite our dart-blue skies,
    In the night.

Leaves from trees blowing here and there
As shadows of objects appear everywhere,
    In the night.

Optical-illusions seem to be real,
But attempting to touch you cannot feel,
    In the night.

Noises seem to come and go,
From what strange place you do not know,
    In the night.

Sight of anyone is seemingly far;
You're semi-conscious of where you are;
    In the night.

Nothing seems to be quite alright,
But try not to scream,
Alone in the night.

Jerry Williams

"The Garden Of Life"

When the garden of life is empty
You always seem to plant new seeds;
And when that seed begins to sprout
You provide the living water it needs.

And if the spirit of the sprout hungers
With manna from heaven you daily feed;
And if the garden gets bogged down
You can clear the way of any weeds.

For only you can fill the garden of life
With so many good and special breeds;
And prosper it with your loving care
To overflow with rare beauties indeed.

"For as the soil makes the sprout come up
and a garden causes seeds to grow, so the
Sovereign Lord will make righteousness and
praise spring up." Isaiah 61:11

"Father, I thank you that when my garden
was empty, that you filled it with words
of beauty to pen for your kingdom."

Victoria J. Mozingo

Yearning Autumn

To yearn for your ancient homeland,
is like yearning for Autumn.

To yearn for your rightful birthright,
is like yearning for Autumn.

To yearn for your beloved Nation,
is like yearning for Autumn.

To yearn for your justified fight,
is like yearning for Autumn.

To yearn for your future destination,
is like yearning for Autumn.

To yearn for your forgotten honor,
is like yearning for Autumn.

To yearn for your lost pride,
is like yearning for Autumn.

To yearn for your spiritual guide,
is like yearning for Autumn.

To yearn for your forgotten dignity,
is like yearning for Autumn.

I yearn for you to accept my sorrow and apology.
I Yearn for you to realize reality in Autumn.

Teri Madrigal

More To Come

Now it's cold, wet and dark.
You left here without even leaving your mark,
not even a hint or a vague reminder.
Last thing I heard you say was I'll always stand beside her.
But times have changed, for better or for worse?
I don't know whether to take a bow or to curse.
Merciless time is an unquenchable enemy.
Your beauty fades and your soul is left unhealthy.
But it's not quite over yet.
I still have time to do more things that I will regret.
So I won't give up and just lay down to die.
Sometimes the hardest thing to do is try.

Amber Karen Klassen

The Golden Haired Maiden

Glimpse the lovely maiden fair,
Tawny face, and golden hair.
Locks hanging to her waist,
Wearing finest silk, and lace.
Elegantly poised the lass,
Sipped finest wine, from crystal glass.
Mine eyes feasted the gorgeous sight.
Slithering about the ballroom polite.
The crowd applauded from the floor,
As the golden haired maiden waltzed out the door.
Never before did these eyes see,
A maiden so lovely, and lively as she.

Twyla Beauchamp

It Hurts

It hurts to be at the bottom, an endless pit of nothingness,
   where no one knows just how painful it is to sink, while others
   are swimming.
   It hurts to wake up, to dress, to speak, to ask for help, to laugh,
to weep. The diagnosis clear, the cure impossible...
   Science has yet to give me a chance, to laugh, to enjoy,
to smile, to dance.
   It hurts to study, to read, to write, to eat, to walk.
Every breath must be the last, because for the
   unhappy, death is the only way out.

Susan Goldberg

If I Was A Pirate

If I woke up one morning and I was blind in one eye,
I'd get me one of those eye patches so I'd look like a pirate.
I'd stop brushing my teeth so they'd become rotted by jagged
   black filth,
and I'd walk around all day with a smug look on my face,
like I was a cartoon and had just been shot at,
and I'd look at everyone like they raped my mom.
I'd grunt a lot and would never smile-not even a little bit-
and I'd let dirty whiskers devour my cheeks and neck.
I'd chug whisky like it was water and would never comb my hair,
so it would have that slept-on look.
I'd scowl at the sun and prowl when the moon called,
and when no one could hear me I'd hum my secret sailor song
and dream of the day when I'd get my wooden peg leg.

Scott Siders

Grandmas

   Grandmas are someone who smiles at you and it just warms
your heart.

   Grandmas can give hugs like no one else and it makes you feel
innocent and special.

   Grandmas talk in soft voices and through that voice you can
hear all their years of wisdom.

   Grandma's walk is gentle and maybe a little shaky, but through
it you can see all her years and hard work.

   Grandma's eyes sparkle and through her eyes you can see her
loving soul.

Karen Mori

"The End Of Forever"

   He who was indestructible and led me down
paths, some wrong and unfair, wishing sometimes he'd vanish:
thin air. Not knowing the darkness that's here, would be there.
Caring I must because forgiveness prevailed.

   And time has grown old, pale and weary with age,
and my mind has began to feel not so encaged. Suddenly broken
by a theft in the night, I know all your wrongs have become
all your rights.

   Throwing my wishes in a pond of alone, everybody
is here but nobody is home. Storms, growing, unsettled
peace blows with the wind, and my chances are now but never again.

Amanda Knauff

Winter Fun

Sledding down Suicide Hill
So fast I put one foot on the ground
But the bumps rise up and bounce it back on the sled.
Freezing shards of wind pierce my face.
My fingers, numb inside the wooly mittens,
Pull tightly on the rope
As if my sled were a spirited steed
Who could respond to my command
But it does not react.
Then suddenly there is flat stillness all round.
I'm safe, but...
The tingle of thrilling risk is gone.
I trudge to the top
And begin my reckless ride again.

Marilyn Hayden

The World I Know

The world I know is a cruel and jealous place. Everywhere I look
there's nothing but people in a dark corner with barely any clothes on.
Children beg for food from passing strangers, and they still haven't
found a cure for aids. Although excluded from society the homeless
still search the trash for bottles and cans, and that's the world I know.

Tears running down a mother's face, she's lost a son in the war. A
father's working over time to bring home fifty cents over minimum
wage. Teenagers are dropping out of school to experience what drugs
can't do for you, yet they do it anyway. That's the world I know.

The blind, the poor, the homeless, and those dying of aids, none
have found an answer. All suffering, but still going on. Gangsters,
the prejudice, and the terrorists. What kind of example are they
trying to set for todays generation? But we let it continue, and that's the world I know.

Everybody helping everybody get on their feet. Lending a helping
hand to those in need. No more prejudice or wars against each other.
That's the world I want to know.

   Tiffeny Wilkinson

Mountain Raiders

In the misty haze of the new fallen dew, the Mountain Raiders pressed on.
Outnumbered five to one, they rode like hell, into certain death with the approach of dawn.

With a cry of rage and a clash of steel, the Mountain Raiders flew.
The evil minions of hell's own spawn, the valiant warriors slew.

As one foul demon fell to the blade, two more would take its place.
The Mountain Raiders were holding ground, skill and courage their only saving grace.

They fought with sweat, they fought with blood, they fought amidst the cries of pain.
That precious ground they fought upon, was soon a crimson stain.

As dawn's glorious light shown through the haze, the Mountain Raiders knew,
the fight was won, the vanquished fleeing, peace restored for hope anew.

   Arleigh G. Hamilton

The Two Big M/M's

Marriage is like a well orchestrated game of Monopoly. The goal of
marriage is to make each other the happiest couple among all others.
The game pieces is two people, love, respect, and honesty.

Marriage, like Monopoly, is a game of chance and we have to play hard
to win. But, being that human's are involved, chances are that one of
the two players, will not give, or is not all that honest.

There are many winners and losers in both games. The losers are the
greedy, the snatcher, the clutches. The laying the faults on their
partners; and what's in it for me, me, me; for this reason the losers
are never in harmony with marriage nor monopoly, Thus never knowing what could have been.

While in a stable marriage, couples share and are equal to each other,
sharing in all their material possessions; working towards their mutual
goal without losing prospective of each other's needs, in good times as well as hard times.

As the marriage progresses, the happy couple realize they have all
the game pieces with togetherness and win the game...

   Eva Provencio

Fascination

A flash of coldness...
   and the restless wind lays me upon the water's edge,
   where my only comfort is the filtered, iridescent moon.
The silver water cascades upon my limp body and cleanses me of my sins.
My pulse beats rapidly, and I feel myself falling deeper into the tender sands below me.
I'm kissed gently on my wounds, and your expressed words fill me with delight.
My soul becomes liquid, and I'm dissolved in the pond of ecstasy, as I sink to the depths of tranquility.
The silent flame is lit, and the glistening crimson travels down my body to a puddle of one.
I raise my hands to the started stars and close my eyes to be engulfed in circling swirls of dying love.
The rain has not yet found a way to let up, as it falls to the ocean's security to be blanketed next to my severed body.
I can taste your voice through the wind, the presence of your body is unwillingly comfortable next to my bruised heart.
My journey has been found in the deepest shadows of my burdened life,
as one last eternal kiss is laid upon your plush lips.

   Lari Whittig

Feelings

You look at me
Which feelings run through your mind?
Which words would you use to describe me?
A person, or another kind?

What have I done wrong?
That you look at me with hate
My skin is just a part of me
But feeling we can relate.

We both cry tears
We both have laughter
We both have dreams
We're chasing after.

Racism, they call a sickness
Grows on you with time
The longer you let it linger
The more it ruins your mind.

Latisha Baker

Music Of The Earth

The sweet air of autumn dancing on the awakening rose.
The hum of the bees pollinating the beautiful blooms of the earth.
Even the cry of the wolf howling his song to the moon is a melody
of mother nature.
The dew of the earth on the fresh spring daisy, a sight of mother nature.
The velvet touch of winter snowflakes, a gentle touch of
nature's delicacies.
The sweet taste of summer's cider, a sip of the earth.
All are prizes you are destroying for yourself, preserve them, or
miss them forever.

Aaron J. Haltom

I Will Live Happy

It's all about me,
who I choose to be and how I choose to become.
How I choose my dreams,
in both high and evaluating obstacles.

I will live in peace,
fighting is never an option.
Because I perform to my potential,
complete is never-nothing, halfway is never done.

A smile heals,
It is worth more than all the money in the world.
Give to those in need,
never expect anything in return.

Holly Payne

Out Of Darkness Into Light

A light reaching out of the darkness,
 warm, embracing, encircling lonely souls.
Shining, and reflected in each brilliant face,
 a righteous glow engulfing mortal hearts.
Promises of forever glimmer in their eyes,
 and beauty leaves a shimmering trail behind,
as two torches burn brightly, pushing away the night,
 and fuse as one eternal flame.
Two hearts, two souls brought together in blazing unity,
 forming a single gleaming peace.
Golden moonbeams, stretching out of blackness,
 a sparkling web of dreams and desire.
Loneliness spirited away by radiance,
 as one moves from darkness into light.

Monique Reidhead

"Ode To An Outhouse"

Sitting alone in an outhouse on a cool, dark night-
No words can be thought of to describe the sight.
At your feet, shivering and whining, three dogs huddle-
Hoping against hope you'll invite them to cuddle.

All too soon you spot several flakes of snow-
Filtering down from the cloudy sky amidst a wind that's cold.
Off in the distance the coyotes begin to sing-
Staring at each other, everyone is too cold to think.

The "Streak" suddenly appears in the snowy swirl-
His cold little feet and brain in a whirl.
Killer happily jumps onto your lap- ,
With cold nose in your face, he appears to laugh.

With an audible sigh the "paperwork" is complete-
Back up the trail you plod with chattering teeth.
Reaching the door accompanied by the crew-
Gazing fondly they seem to say "we'll be waiting for you."

Joanne Cara Myers

The Storm

So many things-So little time
Always changing-Never staying the same
Always churning-swirling
Like a storm
Building up strength-Ready to unleash
Never knowing when-Always anticipating
Going with the wind-Rolling with changes
Being tossed like a lost bird-Never knowing how to feel
Where to flee
Going through the motions-Not with a care
Feeling the pressure-Of the wind
Pushing you along
Then the fury is unleashed-Turmoil and chaos
The world has a mind of its own-Uprooting and taking what it wants
Not with a care
The lost bird now has a broken wing-Then suddenly
The calming quiet settles in-Only the rain is left
Quietly falling like a comforting blanket-Surrounding the body
Streaming down your face
Bathing the earth-Cleansing the soul

Abby Hanson

Fugue

The forgotten goals and shattered dreams
Of broken souls leave vengeful screams
That peal like bells from churches' steeples
To warn of hell the evil people
Who break the souls and steal the dreams
Of all of those that heaven deems
Shall come by night to take the breath
From those whose plight is tattered flesh
And broken bone and fearful fight
When faced alone in still of night
With their fate they made, the wage of sin
The pain they gave returned to them
Lo, through dark valleys under distant skies
And o'er the hills will harmonize
Peaceful songs of vindication
With frantic cries and tortured pleas
A fugue of hatred and elation
That hangs like mist upon the trees
Replete with peace in symphony

Mark Walker

If Time Could Seize

The lingering scent of innocence filled the air,
Of a prolonging moment we were about to share.
Memories filled of previous moments when we met,
Bestowed our minds as our loving eyes drew shut.

Our hearts both one as we abundantly embraced,
All the past hardships in love which we both faced,
Seemed to vanish in the dramatic romance we felt,
Our prayers finally answered as if to God we knelt.

Our lips awaiting the exact moment in time,
When thence I should feel I would want you as mine.
The simple caress of both our lips we thence bestowed,
Made everything else dissipate in our present mode.

The symbolic act of kissing creates many complex memories,
To intermode the inner self with anticipate loving restories,
If only time could seize that night our lips first become one,
Just think of all thy memories which have yet to become.

Cheryl Wenner

Untitled

Walking into a field this morning
It began to scream in pain
Bulldozers have torn the land
And the destruction killed the game
Then a bird flew over head
And his squawks sounded like sirens
Warning me of dangers to come
As all of the animals start crying
As the day went on and I walked farther
I noticed some winding trees
There were few left after construction
And they blew wildly in the breeze
By mid day I walked to the stream
Ribbons of waves flowed gently over the rocks
And at a distance I could see a farm
And in the field stood the livestock
Blowing, flowing, and glowing
The wind, the stream, the sun
No one really understands
The destruction that's been done.

Tina M. Delauter

Used To Be

We used to be best friends, but that was long ago
for now I lost a friend, and inherited a foe.
Our friendship was the best, the best that it could be
But now when you see us together, the best is hard to see
I tried my best to save us, in our time of need
But my best was a failure, for I did not succeed
I have already tried, and made my apology clear
But an apology from you is far from what I hear
And I'm not gonna wait, for your apology on the phone
For now I'm giving up, and leaving well enough alone.

Tara Courtney Brown

A Thought Of You

Laying down in an earthly forest bed
While essence of daisies surrounds my head.
Patches of white pass the sun above
You right beside me to hold and love.
Evening enters into the skies
We swim in cool waters with delight in our eyes.
I whisk you towards me on the sandy shore
Looking forward to caressing you more and more.
My arms reach out to hold you tight
Seizing nothing but the empty night.
Suddenly awaken realizing again
I have only been dreaming of you my friend.

Sheri Lynn Wallace

"Unrequited Love"

It was willed that we should meet
Entwine our lives in one great feat
To quench a passion that grips our soul;

The agony replete, the ecstasy sweet,
As mother time holds us in her womb
Nurtures our wish to be complete;

When at last the truth is known
May we together in heaven be born.

Gladys Abbott

Grief

The dead live so much longer than we expect
it's a wonder we mourn at all.
I laugh at loss.
Loss is nothing compared to the eternal present
of your time stopped carcass I keep trying to heave up off my life.
Why won't you be gone?
You are much more heavy dead than alive.
Alive, I hardly noticed you.

Sue Allison

Impressions Left Behind

It was autumn and maple leaves were gold
and crimson against the
darkened sky. The leaves were as bright
as a kaleidoscope,
whirling around me.

As I walk I notice the soles of my shoes
are weaving an impression
on the carpet of leaves behind me, intensifying
the color due to the
rain that had fallen earlier.

As I ponder for a moment, I look at each impression,
noticing how each one of them
is different. And my mind reflects to my own
life, how every breathing moment
is a reflection of impressions I choose to make.

So I pray Lord, for your rain of wisdom to fall
on me so that my array of colors
can be of brilliance for you.

And that my life will not dry up and be
as dust blown in the wind.

Angela Dawn Webb

Choices

Yearning for friends I fell
Sucked into society's depths
Turning to lies, stealing to please
Violence was my playground
Injury my victory
Fight to live, steal to survive
Get stoned to forget the hell that follows
Fear caught up to me
Kicked my butt
Turned me around
A year of deep thought
Aided by frustration
Yearning for friends I stood
Found my path to follow
Answered my questions
Face my fears
Allowed love to penetrate my soul
Now I stand on both feet
Tall and proud
Now I am me.

Brian Dominguez

So Young; Where's Nana?

Only five years old,
Nana's in the hospital,
Daddy flew me to kiss her.

Nana has cancer,
We can't do anything,
Nana's going to die!

I don't know much,
But I know Nana taught me to sew,
I know she loves me.

Nana is gone now, where did she go?
"She's gone to heaven!" Mom says.
But what is heaven?
Heaven's a special place people go after they die.

Why did Nana have to die?
I don't know,
All I know is that she's gone...

Come back Nana, I miss you,
You've been gone so long,
I'm thirteen now and I don't know you or very much about you!

I'm lost without you, Nana...

Michelle Ann Venable

Thank You

You've guided me so gently,
You've been there for so long,
You've trusted me, you've taught me.
but it's time that I move on.

Little One, you called me,
Bright eyes and princess too,
and many, many times you taught
the rules of how to do.

You've kissed away my boo-boo's
you've wiped away my tears,
you've taped up injured, banged-up knees,
you've chased away my fears.

Your loving me and teaching me
has meant so much, it's true,
you always have been there for me,
now I am here for you.

Now we can laugh together
and cry together, too,
and Mom, just so you know,
It's my way to say "Thank You"

Hillary Skaggs

The Journey

Once, while on life's road, a stranger, knowing,
Queried as to our journey of the day.
While then unsure just where we were going
We paused and said we thought we knew our way.

The stranger mused, then starting up anon,
Turned back, to leave with us this last aside:
"Tread lightly down the road that you are on -
It's rough, and makes for quite a restless ride."

We parted then, and took a different way,
Oft wondering 'bout this man we never knew;
'Til, as we neared our Journey's end, one day
We learned his name from one who'd met him, too.

"They call him 'Fate'," said he. But, had we known,
What road would we have taken on our own?

Paul R. Rogner

Images On The Horizon

To create is to give life and bring to breath;
to invent and renew that which was asleep,
or else that which had never slumbered before.

To create is to conjure existence;
to conjure existence onto that which
once only held existence in the mind.

To create is the noblest of aims;
to seek the ultimate of honor
in playing a role in the beginning of another.

To create is to form a branch;
to mirror part of a greater whole,
and in that part, understand the original reflection.

To create is the greatest of quests;
to search for the mold with which to create,
a mold that has existed since the beginning of time.

To create is to see the moment of beginning;
to destine that creation to come to an end,
but in that realization, give creation true life.

Geoffrey Scott Brown

Spring Medication

The birds are singing, there is a gentle breeze
The crocus are awaking, from a cold winter freeze
The trees are dressed in their loveliest green
Spring showers last night have left them so clean
The violets are peeping from their mossy little beds
And their neighbor the robin sings as he lifts his head
This planet Earth is shining through its every vein
Its simple medication was the lovely rain.

Jerrye Cargill Blevins

Untitled

Sand slips through an hourglass
with each grain of sand
a memory of my life.

There's an empty feeling inside
as I try to ignore the pain closing in on me.

What were the words you said?
Why can't I get them out of my head?

As one world grows dark,
Another grows lighter.

Slowly I slip out of sight...Oh so far away
Your world is no longer mine
You'll have to go on without me,
For soon I'll be gone,
A memory you won't be able to find
I guess love is blind.

Jennifer Pierce

School's Out

When school's out I feel free
I think I'm flying like a bee
I go out East and swim in the water
I don't have to pay even a quarter
I love the feeling of the sand in my toes
I hate the tickling when it gets in my nose
Morgan, wake up, no sleeping in school
Oh brother, that's the worst rule!

Morgan L. Brunner

Madame Butterfly - Il Coro Muto

Sheer Magic.
Velvet eve in bloom translucent,
delicate sepals of mellow-pink cherry
and buds of lemon scent of tea and roses.
Il Coro Muto, subdued music river,
in flume of petals flows on peach tree blossoms,
melodious essence in soft evanescence,
so fragrant and tender as a stream of flowers,
light-pink as petals floating on the ether.
In sorcerer's Grove she flutters in despair,
The Butterfly dying on the balmy vapors.
The edelweiss mournful on Butterfly's stupa
pour tears of sorrow with dew fresh from meadow.
Flutes slow, nostalgic, in moon's mournful shadow
in sadness brood the mute sound of Good-Bye,
and chant the tender tale of Butterfly,
and sing of Love so innocent, so tragic,
and of Her ruthless, cruel death.
Sheer Magic.

Frank Stiffel

Sentimentality

What are you?
You linger in spite of the fact that all is gone.
You possess no logic
You are there to suffer for something that does not exist.
You're like the ashes of paper that is left over.
You're like the torn flower whose petals lingers in the wind.
Sentimentality, you are the source of human suffering.
You are the source of all inspiration.
Sentimentality, are you biological or environmental?
Where do you come from?
Are you a magic, an enigma by nature?
Sentimentality, why did you have to exist?
Sentimentality, you are the turmoil of human beings' existence.
You're the biggest killer that ever existed.
Sentimentality: God of Art, inspiration of humankind, killer
of man's heart; isn't that what you are?

Nehla Zikria

My Daughter

Lord I want my daughter to know
That you are with her, where ever she go.
For you are her father, the one who cares
Watching over her, guiding her,
I know you are there.
Lord my daughter is having such a hard time
I want her to know through you,
Everything will be find.
Her trust, she must put in you, knowing
you will bring her through.
The trials of life, we all must fight
When darkness comes there will be light.
My daughter this fight will not last long,
you must not faint, but stand strong.
Build up your faith, don't become weak
Trust in his love and his words you must keep.
Oh my daughter you must stay calm
pick up his book and read the book of psalm.
Oh my daughter I Love You.

Barbara J. Brown

I, Was Older And She, Was Young

I, met a lovely, girl, one day,
While I was traveling in the month of May,
She, was the lovelies girl, I, ever seen,
I, found, out later, she was just, eighteen.

I was older, and, she, was young,
We, could, never, have a song, that, could be sung,
She, could never be, my only one,
I, was older, and she was young.

One day, she, will meet someone,
Sooner, or later, this will be done,
I, know, for sure, she's not for me,
As young, as she is, this, could never be.

I, was older, and she, was young
We, could, never, have, a song, that could be sung,
She, could, never be, my only one,
I was older, and she, was young.

All, a man's got to do, is think of the past,
When, he was a young boy, but, it didn't last,
She was, out of my reach, just like the sun,
Because, I, was older, and she was young.

Debra M. Carrier

Untitled

Like a bird flying freely over a misty ocean at dawn
She fills my world with ambition
Undone with the deeds of her heart
I am able to live life with meaning.

Like a winding road on a mountain pasture
I search for direction
Filled with admiration of her love
I yearn to hold her.

As tears flow freely from my eyes like a river
I will look unto her
And I will feel safe.

In the end
on my final day
In my final hour
It is her I shall think of
It is only her I shall love.

Andrew Biele

Night

Outside it was dark,
With a faint glowing light
The moon didn't shine so bright that night.

The earth was shaking,
With each blow of lightning,
Those loud shrieking cries became quite frightening.

The rain had been falling,
And the windows were wet,
The thunder and lightning had finally met.

With a quick blast of thunder,
That tree was struck down,
Sadness took over that small little town.

Outside it was beautiful,
With a bright shining light,
Her soul has been taken out from the night.

Kathleen Guill

When Love Hits You

Deep down inside I'm dying.
Inside I'm filled with fears,
But, then on the outside I am crying,
I just can't hide my tears.

I didn't think this could be love.
I thought that that took time,
But now I'm seeing signs from up above,
And everything is starting to rhyme.

Someday I know you will be mine.
Until then my heart will continue to burn,
When I can be with you, I'll be fine,
How to cope till then I'll have to learn.

   Julie Hanson

Untitled

Dost thou spill the milk right now
Roosters cry out
The sun rises above the mountain
Slow waves in the distance sparkle.

How far can we carry on this charade.
Sail boats in all colors march along
We try to stay abreast of all that happens
But alas we are only human beings.

I feel the approach of him.
Is it real or imagined
We do not see — we do not feel
Let us just laugh aloud.

   Nancy Jean Parker

An Adult Child

For months my womb cradled you
Anticipating, waiting for the unknown.
The birth day arrived and you are uniquely you.
The first sound, motion, word, step, hug occurred.
The firsts declined and the lasts took their place.
The last book read, the last car ride, the last support
For you are secure.
The letters scarce, the calls sparse, the sharing selective.
My heart resides in longing, my mind in sweet memories
For an adult child.

   Barbara McGould

Reflections

Like a song which soothes the soul
Like a heart, that is of pure gold.
These things be true and true they will be,
But none so more as my feelings towards thee.

The pain in your eyes, I can see quite well,
I know I'm the reason you're going through hell.
But the touch of your hand, or the feel of your skin,
Takes me to a place I've never been.

The fork in the road is coming near,
To the left or to the right, choose well my dear.
And if the path you choose does not include me,
I still want to be your friend, for all eternity.

   Brian Wright

The Promise

The Sun rose last night.
She knelt with Him in the sand.
He kissed the pain from her eyes,
Tied white-laced ribbons in her hair.
He trickled a drop of ocean water onto her lips
And started away from her toward the sea.
She followed Him.

   Jacqueline Hardy

A Short Snow Story

Quiet is a day in the mountains.

Gentle is the wind upon a soft white blanket,
crystallized in form but soft as downy feathers.
Cool crisp air upon my bare face,
nipping my nose and tingling my cheeks.

Oh what a feeling of tranquillity I have
while strolling among the pines
that dwarf me in all their splendor.
Waving their pin - like arms effortlessly
day after day, year after year
time is of no meaning to them or to me.

United with nature for a while,
happy for the moment, and at peace till eternity.

   Diane Goodenough

Strawberry Picking

With head down, cheeks pointing skyward,
we search for ruby treasures.
Our eyes glazed with greed,
mouths watering with hopes of captures.
They try and elude us
by hiding under vegetation.
Only to surrender when discovered.
Boasting of our conquests,
we race each other for the best.
Oftentimes tempted beyond our limits,
the best is sacrificed along the way.
On hands and knees we fulfill our quota,
with red stained lips,
take our captives away.

   Barbara L. Becker

The Search For Love

We search for our love, where it takes us,
Random meetings of strangers on the street,
Courting, friendships, of which may turn to lust
Looking for what so few have when they meet;
The parts of a love are unsettling, true
Life partners soulmates, man, woman, one whole,
Courageous in their plight from more to few
It is within this game we pay our toll.
Even though our hearts break we grow stronger
For it's not to leave experiences,
Knowledge gained may make us survive longer.
We must make the most of our differences.
If not for ourselves in our search for love,
for those we may be holding from their love.

   Roger Douglas

A Love Game

It was dangerous to play.
We knew the rules quite well.
A love game It was; with only you
and I to tell.
without hesitation I began to make
the first move; knowing not who
would win and certainly who
would lose.
In summing up the points; I began
to get the score.
And with much satisfaction, it was
you that I adored.
In astonishment I wondered, in
effort to play the game.
If perhaps you would figure out,
If so would you feel the same.
We were down to the last move I suggested that we stop.
There was no-one at bottom or no-one at top.
The rules were all laid. They didn't seem the same.
I knew these were the results of playing the love game.

Kimberly Pandora Young

Scared

I'm scared of the dark with nighttime shadows.
I'm scared of horror movies with gory scenes.
I'm scared of some costumes on Halloween night.
I'm scared of thunder when it rumbles.
I'm scared of loud, eerie noises like whooo and BANG!
I'm scared of ghosts and fear of death.
I'm scared of flunking sixth grade.
I'm scared of snakes that slither and strike.
I'm scared of spiders that crawl and bite.
I'm scared of people who scream and yell.
I'm scared of earthquakes which split the ground.
I'm scared of hurricanes, tornadoes too.
But when I'm scared or afraid,
I let my mind wonder and the bad things just fade.

Christina Paruthi

"Mother"

Mother, there's only one you.
You make me happy when I feel blue.

Mother, I love the way you cook.
I love the way you look.

When I am in need, you are always there.
Thank you, Mother, for your loving care.

Mother, you are the flower of my heart.
Your love, Mother, makes me happy as a lark.

Like you, there is no other.
I love you, Mother!

Elizabeth J. Psillos

Repressed

Spirit...Repressed through time.
Repressed, depressed, no reason to live.
Broken by man
beaten from twilight to dawn.
In spite of this the fight continues.
No sword or sling,
only strength of limb power of verse.
The spirit is chained, the eternal curse.
Risen to life, risen to glory
hope remains, faith retained.
Repressed, always.

David Lu

"The Dream"

It was a cold, snowy, January day
When the angels took you away.

You were riding with us in the hearse
We could not help but think that by
Life we were thus cursed.

And all the pain we held inside
God, Himself would find hard to override.

God helped us to know that day
That you left this world of pain and strife
And that you would find peace with Him
You didn't have in this earthly life.

We loved you, but all in vain
For the grim reaper, Death, came.

When I became with sorrow heavy laden
And tears just seemed to flow down my face
You came to me in a dream
With a peaceful, smiling face.

And you said, "Rejoice for I'm not dead
My body died instead."

Anna Maria Canillas

Endless

How moments drift slowly into endless years,
How sorrow slowly turns into a stream of tears.
As my mind drifts into an endless thought,
As I smile on all I've got.
For at then I felt how endless love was,
For of course everything like that does.
As surely as no one knows,
As surely as endlessly as the wind blows.

Audra J. Miller

The Mist

They once had a home, but now they emerge
from nowhere, and people say it's because
they were from the mist.

They were the same as you and me, but now
something was different about them, and
people say it's because they were from the mist.

They had smiles across their faces, but now
the faces tell bitter tales, and people say
it's because they were from the mist.

They went as boys, but came back as broken
men, and people say it's because they were from the mist.

"Why have these things changed?"...The mist.

"What mist"...The mist which rises from the ashes of war.

Theresa Ku

Eyes For You

Every time I see you my feelings are true
I want you to look into my eyes
and just realize that I can make you happy
as can be just care and see
the world was full of darkness and my life
was a mess but out of the blue I
found you my heart is racing because it's
you I'm chasing there is no time
to waste just be mine without any haste.

Pamela D. Jackson

Life!

It is not the ability to see,
But the ability to see life.

It is not the ability to hear,
But the ability to hear life.

It is not the ability to feel,
But the ability to feel life.

It is not the ability to accept life,
But the ability to challenge life,
and to appreciate the ability to see,
hear and feel life!- And the ability to accept
this challenge of life!

Kari Thompson

"Big Jim Buddy Brother Of Mine"

You were always known as "Buddy"
From all your family.
But to me you were Big brother
That was just right for me.

You always knew just what to do
That's why my sister set her cap for you.
Not having a brother from the start
She certainly made a perfect choice.

You played it cool, right from the start
and calculatingly won her heart
you even let her think she was boss
which with anyone else was a total loss.

Our mother and grandma was always quite choosey
But even they, thought you were a Doozy
Which goes to show they had great taste
With all of us, you held number "one" place.

Well there are brothers that come and go
But as for me, wouldn't you know
There is no other quite so fine
As you "Big Jim, Buddy, Brother of Mine."

Isedora Wilson

Reverse Control

We need to bring God back to school,
Don't you know you've been made a fool?
When you remove God from our lives,
There is relief, but things don't jive.

To separate the Church and State,
Jeopardizes you on God's slate.
With worldly ways there's no belief,
It gives a false sense of relief.

Just look at children of today,
And see them in their worldly way.
It seems that they will self-destruct,
If things aren't reversed, the system bucked.

We know what's in our hearts and minds,
We must speak up, lay it on the line,
Open the trap at the Dead-End Street,
Bring God back, to control the beat.

Mary Matthews

"Mommy Elf's New Year Blues"

'Twas the month after Christmas and without a doubt,
every card in my wallet was completely maxed out. The
shopping been done with a nary a care with just a vague inkling
of the bill to be there. Nintendo and Reebok and Starter they
say. Your children not seeing the price you must pay. A little
while later... When it's all made the trash. You tell 'em next
Christmas - Santa only takes cash.

Karrie M. Katcher

Spell Maker

The moon is a bronze medallion
Hanging about the neck of heaven
Just above the silhouette cleavage
Of Douglas Fir.
Honeysuckle drifts on the lazy breeze,
While leaves softly applaud the hush.
Midnight's cloak, with its satiny glint
Of butterfly wings,
Is draped across Earth's
Gently curving emerald shoulders
Where he and I rest
Upon the cool August grass
Slowing sipping summer's romantic muscatel
And gazing at the stars
That stare back as curious keepers.

Diana Shilkett Jamison

Awake On The Ground

This place is so noisy
The carpet's design is revolting
And the shadow of the table
It disturbs me

Above where the chandelier is a dangling
The ceiling it is a hanging
An annoying design

We must go to the ceiling
To meet the bee hive's bees
To make peace
And to leave the revolting carpet

But we might get dreary
So let's stay awake on the ground

Louis W. Holsten

The Insignificant Other

She holds near her heart one rose, to remind herself that every
facet of the world she comes into contact with loves her. She keeps
the second rose far from her heart, out in the open for all to see
that come near her; to show that she caresses and embraces each
aspect of this confusing maze she lives in. The final rose she gives
away, to that one special someone in her life. This most significant
rose was to express her undying faith, in the love that she shares
with that other person, even if the love given back is nowhere equal
to the love given away. She has tied her end of the love-knot.
She knows that even though they will wilt and fade away, the Idea of
Love behind each will ascend, living for all eternity. But if she
only knew. At least I made this effort. I tied my end of the
love-knot. But then again, maybe I just want to live in her head,
always being known as the insignificant other.

J. D. Bryan Cardwell

"Baseball Season"

Widows of the baseball season,
ask yourself is there a reason.

Why you should fret for being ignored,
when the ball game is close to being scored.

Truly you should know you are blest,
because your man is at his best.

He's cheering for his favorite team,
to win the trophy it would seem.

But when you are young you feel betrayed,
for the ball game being played that day.

But take my advise from one who knows,
It's just a season and then it goes.

Charlene Cacy

Virginia Virginia

Virginia, Virginia, I don't want to pass through,
Virginia, Virginia, I want to stop and stay with you,
Virginia, Virginia, home I want to go,
Virginia, Virginia, I love you so.

Virginia, Virginia, you're home to me,
Virginia, Virginia, the place I want to be,
Virginia, Virginia, you're a long lost friend,
Virginia, Virginia, hold me again.

Virginia, Virginia, take me to your breast,
Virginia, Virginia, the state I love best,
Virginia, Virginia, I'll always care,
Virginia, Virginia, bury me there.

Virginia, Virginia, Virginia
My own,
Virginia, Virginia
Home sweet sweet home.

Bernice L. Ownbey

Voice Of A Nation

Emotional detachment is the plan this year
Echoing lofty words and shedding phony tears,
Listening with closed ears,
Grasping out, while clutching fear

Empathy is outdated,
Sympathy is over rated,
Stand together, far apart
Avoid unlocking secrets of the heart

Keep caring to a minimum
Empty smiles express chagrin,
Reach out, but do not touch
Don't expose naked souls so much

What happened to "Love thy neighbor?"
or, "That's What Friends Are For?"
or, "Hands Across America"
or, "Let's Gather Together At The Shore?"

So vulnerable in our isolated state
Creating confusion, anger and hate,
Detaching body from soul of man
Like dismembered statue, head without hand

Candi McLester

God's Flower Seeds

God Bless these little flower seeds, I plant today this spring,
Shed Your rain upon them, and flower may they bring.
God Bless these little flower seeds, I plant today for You,
Cast Your Love upon them, and make Your Love show through.

God touch my little flower seeds, and make them grow so fast,
So all the world can see Your beauty and make them really last.
Through the spring summer months make the flowers soar,
Show them all their beauty, I couldn't ask for more.

As I pick the flowers, that You've Blessed with Your own hands,
I will give them all to others, and Your Love, they'll understand.
When they see their beauty, that is way above the rest,
They will know Your Everlasting Love, and they will sure be Blessed.

I thank You for my flower seeds, that grew so beautifully,
And thank You for the honor, of sharing Your Love with me.
I thank You for my family and friends I have so great,
Someday I'll plant Your flower seeds, right at Heavens Gate.

Linda G. Berry

Isn't It A Pity

Just think if all the minds of men quit chanting words of
aggression and all the hearts of mankind were cleansed of hatred
towards their fellow man what a beautiful world it could be, alas
I fear that it may never happen, isn't it a pity.
Just think if all the nuclear testing stopped and there were no
more reports of acid rains, the fighter planes fired no more rockets,
if all nuclear war heads were disassembled, alas I fear it may never
happen, isn't it a pity.
Just think if all the political prisoners were set free and at last
the warmongers of the world sat down to resolve their problems in
peace, what a beautiful world it could be, alas I fear it may never
happen, isn't it a pity.
I look around and I think of all the unfortunate souls who
haven't enough to eat and receive no help at all, yet billions and
billions of dollars are spent each year upon the bloody war machine.
It makes me sick at heart to think that it may never end,
ISN'T IT A PITY.

Daniel N. Cognito

Peace

We stand like rigid solders, gazing but do not speak.
If dust to dust we all go back,
souls un-cloaked and bare.
To show the way we all must be, to trust, accept, and share.

When tools of war are made no more,
and seas and lines can not divide, the love and help
for which we came, we surely must provide.

Not color of the skin, nor language of the tongue,
the song now written for one and all,
and bravely must sung.

Be free, my friends, be free, as you have let me be.
We see all things with different eyes,
as they were meant to be.

Peace I give to you, and you give back to me.
This world and those to come,
will be— will be— will be.

Glenda J. Moseley

Cross Roads Of Life

I have come to the cross roads in my life.
Looking back, I see mistakes - some made twice.
Looking ahead, I do not know where to go.
I do not know what to do.
Who can help me? Can you?
The road ahead of me - will it be the same year after year?
Or will it be filled with mystery, heartache, and fear?
The road to the left - where does it go?
No one can tell me, because no one knows.
The road to the right - where does it end?
Will it be alone, or among friends?
If I were a bird, I could see which way to go.
I would look down, and I would know.
A bird I know I can never be.
Thus, the blind choice is left up to me.

Kathy M. Lowry

"Spring"

The sights and sounds of spring abound.
The feeling of restlessness is all around.

The chill of Winter's quiet has past.
The longer days are warming fast.

The earth is once again reborn
It's time to sow your seeds at morn'.

The birds and bees are now at play.
A continuous cycle forever to stay.

Toni M. Stok

A Dark Soul (Sole)

The darkest of souls has he.
Light penetrates only from the glint of a knife,
Or the arch of a hammer's steel striking the feline's head.
He has no pity.

He cries a tear or laughs a laugh like any other.
The difference is their's are real, his are not,
Woman's carnal duty his only treasure of women.
He needs no morals.

Life is just only if he is correct.
The night has brought many misdeeds,
Laws are cold and unfair when used against him.
He knows no justice.

He's the oldest of many children.
Punishment was severe for him, lacking for the rest,
He learned to cherish hate and lust for revenge.
He wants no love.

Life has turned many a stone.
Incarceration is a permanent arrangement,
In the mind or behind steel, it makes no difference.
He wants only death.

Patrick R. Salokar

Just For You

If I could take back
All the bad things I've
Ever said and all the bad
I've ever done, I would

And if I could ever find
A way to repay you
For all that you've
Ever done, I should

If I could turn back the
Hands of time and change all
Those bad times into good times
Lord knows how hard I'd try

And I wish I could have
Been there for you
Every time a tear
Fell from your eye

If I could I'd stop at nothing to
Make all your wishes and dreams come true
I'd do all this and much much more because
You're my Mom and I love you

Bonita Suzette Clark

Trust In The Lord

Be still, trust in the Lord.
    Step back now and then so that you may hear His Word
    for your life.
    Panic, fear, anger and frustration only block
        His Light from shining upon you.
Be still, calm your soul, listen...
    His Word could be as hushed as a gentle snowfall on
    a new winter's dawn.
    His Word could be as thunderous and flashing as a
        spring rainstorm overhead.
    Will you hear His Word and open your heart to His Love?
Be still, trust in the Lord.
    Allow His Light to wash over you.
    Allow His Light to warm you, heart and soul.
Rejoice, trust in the Lord.
    Allow His Light to overflow from your heart
        with praise and thanksgiving.
    Allow His Light to radiate from you so that others
        may see Him, and follow, in their own way.
Praise and thanksgiving, trust in the Lord.

Lyn Drathring

Granddad

His height is a towering seven feet tall,
His body is twisted steel,
He has the strength of a thousand men,
This is how I feel.

My Granddad was the purest man,
That I will ever know,
I only wish he were here today,
For my respect to show.

The memories that I have of him,
Show him wearing a smile,
I didn't know his greatness,
Because I was just a child.

I regret not being with him,
The whole time that I could
I was young, and foolish,
And I never understood.

That times like those were precious,
And wouldn't last for long,
I never dreamed that I'd wake up,
And Grandpa would be gone.

Zach Walker

Bloodless Coup

Where yellow eyes of crocodiles roll back,
open mouths display an amphitheater of teeth.

Here in rich Thailand, military commanders,
those aspiring capitalist dragons,
keep Vietnamese refugees behind high walls.
Thai commanders, eyes shot with veins
of rubies mined by Khmer Rouge guerrillas,
greenbacks in their tiger teeth -
aspire to sit among pit viper superpowers.

Here in rich Thailand, prime ministers
are arrested, peacocks caged, cobras milked,
adolescent female flesh sold to tourists,
orchid blossoms squashed.

Janet Gardner

Time-Time-Time

It's about time,
It gets one in a bind.
Often said, "Time I can't find,
Not even to eat a watermelon down to the rind."

Yes, it's about time,
One doesn't have time to be kind.
Don't disturb — to tell what's on your mind;
Some people seem to be blind, when it comes to time.

Do I pine for some extra time?
Others hustle and bustle to be on time.
Even on overdue books on your mind;
Better hurry, or you'll get behind.

Can't seem to get the meals on time,
Everyone's at the table and ready to dine.
Everywhere you look, no cook can you find,
Cause she's outside watching the sun shine.

Mary B. Blailock

Seems Too Late

Seems too late to say the words I want to say,
To find myself suffering more as I watch you fade away.
Seems too late to express my most inner feeling,
Only to find tear drops wishing you were healing,
Seems too late as my emotions all at once collides,
If only there were something I could do till that moment arrives.

Charles A. Watson

278

Understand?

I pointed to somebody and I told my sister he was a nobody,
And then I thought of the day when I was a nobody,
I thought of the changes I made to be a somebody,
I thought about how easy it was to be a nobody,
Now I think about how hard it is being a somebody,
And the bull that comes with being a somebody,
I also thought about the good things,
But nobody knows the grief from the foes that goes with being a
    somebody,
I wish I could be a nobody again,
I'd probably be a better nobody than I was,
But then I'd just be somebody,
Understand!?

    Tyree Cole

To A.J., With Love...

My friend, you're bitter, stubborn, unwise,
Willing only to fight.
Not realizing the reign of darkness
Is only overthrown by light.
"Fight fire with fire!" you always say,
"He can't take me!" you think.
Blindly, foolishly rejecting reason,
To a childish level you sink.
I love you too much to silently watch-
You throw your life away.
From the fight he'll be famous, respected, and feared,
While in a coffin you'll lie.
Many dead people could be alive
If they had the sense to be meek.
Don't let the words of uncontrollable anger
Be the last words that you speak.
LISTEN TO WISDOM! REFUSE TO FIGHT!
YOUR GUNS AND KNIVES, RELEASE!
SWALLOW PRIDE! ABANDON HATE!
AND LEARN TO LIVE IN PEACE!

    Erin Swinney

We Are The Many

We silently wait our turn,
Our spirits strong and flowing.
Patiently letting our passion burn,
We are the many, we are the knowing.

The pulse of nations beating
Yet quietly on every shore.
Anxious for the final meeting,
To reclaim this Earth once more.

From within we hear each distant cry
For the Earth that's raped and dying.
Echoing through the universal sky,
Voices united in crying.

We stand together hand in hand
Outraged by political slander.
Silently waiting, together we band
With purpose, not just to meander.

We are the many, we are the knowing.
Patiently awaiting our day
When love is restored, and our souls fly free,
And we end the Earth's decay.

    Dana B. Miller

Bird Seen Walking

Two saying, for the stranger's reaction.
"Our souls pain, we can't go on"

As one with the other strayed
The bird was seen walking

Like ramparts blasting in air
They chose to leap
As the dissident spirit shined

Each pressed an ear to the lips
of the judged destitute figure

The hour glass, the last grain, the answer

Disguised as ignorance
A piercing siren
The divine words
"Rest your feet, and your soles will heal"

At the sound of loose change
the vagrant soul doctor smiled

    Donald F. Crespino Jr.

Eyes

Random signs
and whispers fast,
Undrunk wine,
The grape's last gasp.

Phantom's sing, of un-truth's due,
Sentiments sting, as witches brew;
Callous, relaxed, faxed; with no intent,
Glow lapsed due, in part, to neglected rent.

Swimming aside,
Blue eyes rain,
Wrinkle, dried then pressed to abide,
In sanity's vein.

    Lee S. Lassow

The Rose

A rose in the mist all alone
has only the grass for a home.

No one around to give her love
all she has is the sun up above.

She dreams of happiness, she dreams of joy
longing to be given, to a girl, from a boy.

As she sits there she studies the sky
letting her dreams float way up high.

She dreams about heaven, she thinks about hell
where her best friend went, it is hard to tell.

Some people came and cut her stem
now all her loneliness she owes to them.

Being alone is breaking her heart
for she promised her family, she would never part.

As her soul grasped for passion, and her heart grasped for love
a person to belong to, is what she dreamt of.

While she was sleeping one dark filled night
alone in the moon light was her very first sight.

A boy with some scissors and a smile of joy,
she was now being given to a girl, from a boy.

    Krista L. Moyers

Alive Always

What of life does the clock slay?
Can we tell time by age?
Observe the vicissitude of night and day.

Our visions are in disarray
When spirits execute the calendar gauge.
What of life does the clock slay?

The sun falls throughout the day,
And conceals drama upon the stage.
Observe the vicissitude of night and day.

Within an hour our dreams allay
Rhythm ticking whilst in the cage.
What of life does the clock slay?

The moon rises its enchanted way
With ambulant shadows across the page.
Observe the vicissitude of night and day.

The character of whom we play
Results from the world we engage.
What of life does the clock slay?
Observe the vicissitude of night and day.

Julie Tieman

In The Heart Of The Green

In the heart of the green,
Where the tree branch breaks,
Where life flows to and fro,
Where the cool touch of sap,
Against your silken skin,
Raises goose bumps, and you know,
Where the wind blows softly,
Quietly singing its gentle, sorrowful song,
Is where you'll find the life which flows,
Where the tree branch breaks,
In the heart of the green

Laura Maltz

The Kingdom Of Forever

God... let this generation of hate peddlers pass swiftly,
Like the locust darkened skies;
They ravage the land, but then, they die.
Let the abyss of darkness be but a fleeting moment,
So that the genesis of love and understanding dawns.
Bless the parents that teach their progeny that we're all
Equal: skin, flesh, blood and bones.
Remind everyone that our existence on Earth is ephemeral,
That our bodies that look so different will soon corrupt;
And it's the soul, the spirit, our essence, that will roam,
The kingdom of forever.

Radames Morales

Untitled

Last night watching TV I sat in excellence and thought of you

I thought of you and now I am feeling my stomach roll with pain,
  I was thinking of you

When you turned three I kissed you and you laughed
  Now we can dance

Once we played in the weeds and killed one another for truth.
  Silver was the barrel and it clung to your teeth

When I turned ten you kissed me in my dreams
  (when I woke there was crying)

Once I was an apple and you were the tree, now we are excellent
  (now we are free)

Matthew Moore

Visions

From my standpoint I can see
The craze behind those icy eyes
You realize not the pain to me
Caused by the silence I despise

I feel the breeze's frosty breath
Upon my neck so late at night
He whispers horrid psalms of death
I listen and my face grows white

Emerges from blackness the silver of knife
Then howling echoes through the place
That's drowning in the essence of the absence of life
I do not watch, I hide my face

The pines converse, the moonlight glares
They urge me off their property
I'm flaming with guilt but no one cares
Won't someone come to rescue me?

I cannot cope; I'm in a daze
This wasn't something I could plan
I'm smothered with a mass of haze
I can't believe I've killed a man.

Alyssa Sussman

My Feelings

The hour is late and I am feeling at peace as I have
My sweet Jesus close to me. Where ever I go or where
Ever I have been my dear Jesus is deep within, I have
Only one way to go and that's with the Lord and walking
Slow. You can live a happy and full life if you turn
Your heart to Jesus Christ. Take one day at a time and
walk with Jesus your Lord Divine.

Gordon M. Morse

Sunday

A baby cries, a mother stirs, and rises to the task.
A church bell sounds a morning call, do I have to ask?
It's time to go, to praise our Lord, to pray for peace unbounded,
Raise our voices as one in song, and let our plea be sounded.
Dear God, protect our fighting men, and keep them safe from harm.
End these wars, and give us peace, never more to arm.
Teach us all the path to peace, to understand our brothers,
Once again to see the light, to unity with others.

A baby cries, a mother stirs, and rises to the task.
For she alone will hear the cry, and hide her tears behind a mask.
One that hides a fearful heart, that knows a heavy weight.
She waits alone for his return, the man she loves, her mate.
Will baby ever know her dad, will he hold her in his arms?
Will he watch her grow to womanhood, and keep her safe from harms?
A baby cries, a new day dawns, and prayers are raised to ask.
Hear our pleas, protect us Lord, that we may be equal to our task.

Blanche L. Boylan

It's Love

His eyes have a soft touch,
When he looks, he says he wants you so much.
His caress; it melts.
His kiss is like nothing you've ever felt.
You never dreamed it could be like this,
Moments with him fill your every wish.
You heard love was grand
But this part you thought you'd understand.
It's all so clear now.
It's love; it's wow!

Denise Lipe

Spring Came Early To The Valley

Spring came early to the valley,
heralded by the hardy robin,
waking nature from the slumber
of winter's icy, death-like trance.

Spring brought colors for her palette,
lavender clusters of wisteria,
yellow bells of fresh forsythia,
dogwood blossoms, pink and white.

On the trees the young green leaflets
joined with tender blades of grass
to spread a hue of pale green lustre
o'er the sylvan wonderland.

She brought music of birds singing,
the gentle murmur of the breeze,
the soothing hum of insect wings,
the gleeful sound of children playing.

Spring came early to the valley
with the promise of renewal
of the life we feared was ended,
released from winter's death-like trance.

L. Hubbard Jr.

Whitman's Resting Place

You pass down the narrow, oblong streets,
Making the odd turns that once a lane made,
Past the soup plant with raw cheese scent
    in your nostrils,
Past the rendering plant with dead-horse-scent
    in your nostrils,
Past the radio factory with a canned rattle
    disturbing your ear channels,
You stand beneath the pier of the huge
    concrete link,
And scan the purple oil film,
From the shadow of a mountainous coal supply.
You wipe the grime from your cheeks with a dirty cloth,
And think of a white-bearded man
    doing the same.

Henry J. Lash

Empty Lakes

"I love you", she said, as he drifted away,
her head hung low to the ground.
She simply could no longer hold her tears,
yet, he did not make a sound.

As the distance between them forever grew,
no more of time would they spend.
Together they had passed through the storms,
their voyage had come to an end.

"Don't go", she cried, as he drifted away,
the fog rolled by and by.
A glimmer of light from across the lake,
a glimmer of light from the sky.

For his life had shown a thousand years,
a thousand years and then,
forever, the sun was gone away,
their time had come to an end.

Yet, he never did turn, as he drifted away,
into the dark night sky.
"I love you", he heard her cry through the night,
as the wind whispered good-bye....

William W. Clark Jr.

My Valentine

I could reach beyond the farthest star,
Or sink to the lowest depths of the deep blue sea,
And I could never find anyone more wonderful from afar,
Whose gift of Love is more glorious than anyone can conceive.

On a special day which comes once a year,
Lovers get together, and one thing is perfectly clear.
That Love is not one of many cherished holidays,
But a deep feeling between two people in many ways.

What is the meaning of the phrase, "Be Mine?"
Is it an expression of Love for all time?
Oh yes, it is this and so much more
for my True Love possesses these virtues of which I adore.
Her beauty, affection, love and care,
Comes from her heart and soul which she shares.

And if I should formally ask her "Would you be mine?"
I pray she would affirm my dream, and be my Valentine.

William Clure

Pino

From the pleasures of minds
that come from other destinies,
I lie within the folds of time.

Existence, as you know it,
is but a memory of pasts.
What is prevalent, is the
ingeniousness of mankind to
resolve and abate his disillusionment.
What has been achieved is merely a
drop in the golden pool of tomorrow.

Remember me, as I have been.
Remember me, as I will be.
Recall not past nor misery, but
Dwell in your tomorrows.

What lies ahead is an adventure
of life and love and mists of lives.
I must remain away for now, but
let us now remember, the best of all that was.

Julie H. McKelvy

♀♂

Scars left behind remind them
of all the screaming, fighting, and mayhem
they could not agree on anything
she thought he was him, he thought he was king
the day had come to decide
to stay or catch the next ride
the decision was for the best
their relationship had flunked the test
the love they once did share
did not fade, but hung in the air
they passed each other in town,
and always passed carrying a frown
they could not stand the depart
he called her back and expressed it from the heart
in time they were back together
and they soon realized there was none other
both hearts filled with glee
once again he and she

Abram E. Timmer

Guardian Angels

Parents are a gift you get everyday of the year,
They always make sure you have nothing to fear.

They're there when you need them in good times and in bad,
Especially those times when you're feeling very sad.

They put up with whining and crying all day,
Also changing diapers is a small price to pay.

Later you explored and learned how to drive,
That's when you grew up become more alive.

The day finally came when they let go of your hand,
You walked down the aisle to the music of the band.

They've loved you so much your whole life through,
We need to give credit for all that they do.

So to all you parents who love and care,
Thanks a million for always being here.

Amy Schwarz

Morning Blues

It always happens at the same time.
Early in the morning, time to get up.
Going to school, or is it work, which one this time?
Too early to rise, I lay back down.

It barks out loud, time to get up!
I rise to see, I'll be late this time.
Why get up? I lie back down.
It barks again. I give in this time.

Kevin M. Richardson

When I Die

When I die, I will be
The spirit of the glittering sea
The sparkle in a sparkling star
The fluffiness of the clouds that are afar
I will be the softness of a baby's skin
I will be the glowing soul within
A gentle mother with a soft touch
Who loves her sweet baby so much
I'll be the crystal in the snow
I'll be the proudness of a child starting to grow
I'll be the playfulness in a pup
I'll be the sweet sugar left in a coffee cup
I'll be the song of a child's call
I'll be an angel, protector of all

Angela Theiss

Life's Not Long Enough To See Everything

The siren call of distant ports
An irresistible urge to explore the unknown
Life's next adventure may lie across the border
But life's not long enough to see everything

With jogging shoes and walking shorts
Records kept of mileage flown
Even airline food and rocking boats
Do not deter the stubborn explorer

Life's not long enough to see everything
But therein lies the challenge

Sanford Rothenberg

Oh! But If I Could Give The World To You

Mother, if I could give the world to you,
here are the things that I would do.

I would shower you with diamonds and pearls.
Oh! But if I could give the world to you!

For a mother's love - there is never an end.
No matter where you are, you will always have a friend.

Mother, nothing would be too good for you.
Without mothers like you, the world would be blue.
Oh! But if I could give the world to you!

I'd give you my heart of purest gold,
and for all the world, this is a story to be told:

Mother dear, my love for you is true.
Oh! But if I could give the world to you!

I would write you a song, I love you one thousand times,
Mother. With God and you by my side, the world would be mine.

There is no greater love than a mother's love
sent from the one and only God up above.

Mother, I love you more, than you could ever know;
you're the greatest, my love, and the one whom I adore.

Cynthia Lynch

"Love At First Light"

'Twas a crisp November sunrise whilst atop this very hill
That my admiration became eminent; my heart's motion became still

There you stood by the lake side, your mind yet not aware
I felt as if I'd known you and that fate had put us there

Trying to draw closer, a twig gave me away
And then looking in your eyes, my love I could no longer convey

Your enchanting silence was misleading; yet my inner soul was
beaming and screaming to keep in mind that love does take time...

The kiss we shared was magical, like a fairy tale dream come true
And from that moment forward I completely fell for you

At one time my mind was vacant, a loveless and empty place
But now it's full of blissful thinking and a warmth I can embrace

Michele Marino

Subtle Change

Today I saw the sun dancing for me. The trees were shifting
   without the wind and their souls were laughing, although I
   heard no sound.

Today I saw a rose petal too beautiful to pluck and too tempting
   not to touch. Almost too precious of a thought to put in
   the back of mind, it was; too alarming too keep in
   conscience.

Today I heard the voice of an angel, imagined strumming a harp of
   gold and I, myself, standing with the pitchfork.

Today I said a prayer thanking God for the good and unrighteous I
   have endeavored, but also pled for forgiveness while my mind
   was tempted more.

Today I realized, just as our past was destined, our futures will
   be our destiny, as well as our love, for love is eternal.

Scarlet Maria Simpson

White America

I was bought here against my will. From my homeland to yours.
I've been beaten and killed.
I want to feel the wind across my face.
Let me stand in grace.
Don't look at my color I am just another fellow.
I don't have a dark secret to hide I am just tired.

Make me feel I'm in place not to disappear without a trace.
I am an American, how can you tell me to go.
When being an American is all I know.

Charles I. Rodmon

They Were There, I Never Knew

As I wake up in the night,
I look out my window to see a sight.
Bright white angels passing through,
They were there, I never knew.
To ask a question is too far to go-
For they were putting on a show.
Within my heart, I knew not to be scared,
They were here and I was prepared.
With each new day, they would stay,
In the sun and when I play.
To watch, protect and keep in view,
All the things I say and do.
As I wake up in the night,
I look out my window to see a sight.
Bright white angels passing through,
They were there, I never knew.

Kristine Kunz, Age 11

I Don't Know

I don't know how to act, I don't know what to do
I feel so lonely being here without you
I can't handle this anymore, I just can't take the pain
It started out so simple, without stress or strain

I don't know what to say, I don't know what to feel
But with all the pain that's in my heart,
I know that this is real

I don't know where this will lead,
I don't know that I'll follow
I do know that I need you with me
to save me from my sorrow

Now you're gone and I'm still here
I need you here to save me,
for I'm drowning in my tears

I don't know why this happened,
Indeed I'm rather stunned
I know now why I feel this way
You were my only one

Nikki Lanane

The Wish

I stepped lightly upon the grass, my feet wet from the midsummer's dew.
I gazed longingly at the million tiny lights glistening
in the dark southern sky, and made a wish.
I wished not of love past, nor of love current, but of a love yet to come.
A love without fear, without apprehension, without the
inhibition of a world full of made-up faces and words.
And I Dreamed.
I dreamed of a time when I could walk the street without
the hushed words and judgmental eyes of a prejudiced time.
I dreamed of a time when love could be mine.
Love without torment, anxiety, or misconception.
So, as I stared into a sky so full of wishes and dreams,
I wiped a tear from my eye and waited for my time.

Brian C. Buckles

The Rose

I am the rose.
You are my rain.
As you roll down my red, velvet petals on this warm Spring night,
You fall off an leave me along in the dangerous darkness.
You fall onto the ground and loosen the earth which helps me stand.
The next day, I wish for your return,
But all I feel is the bright, harsh sun throwing its rays at me.
It dries me up until I wither and become old;
My once red, velvet petals are now wrinkled and brown.
They, too, fall to the soil in search for you.
They become one with their ground until the day you return.
Then, I rise again, only to allow you to leave me once more.
I am the rose.
You are my rain.
Without you, I will surely die.

Melissa Combs

"Imagine"

I can't imagine how it'd be
    if through life we could not see.
The grass so green, as if velvet to touch
    the flowers nestled within its clutch.
The streams of water, crisp and clear
    as sun rays dance to those so dear.
I can't imagine how it'd be
    if birds weren't singing in the trees.
The mountains as they stretch so high
    compliment the pale blue sky.
The deep, dark night and starry sky
    the sounds of nature pass us by.
I can't imagine how it'd be
    if God had not made you for me!

Stacie Gates

"Head Injury"

There once was a girl named Narissa, who due to a misfortune,
got lost. She traveled long and far in what seemed to be
darkness to find her way. She searched profusely for
landmarks but could not find anything that was familiar.
She felt scared, alone and slowly sensed her being dying.
She tried not to think of herself as being there because this
was too painful.

As time went by she was totally stripped of her hope of
finding her way and could not understand why she could
not find anyone to help her. It was then that she
realized that she must take a different path. This path would
be unfamiliar, yet eventually will become her way.

Narissa Lipka

A Special Place In My Heart

As I look into your face, with my surprise.
I see a shining light, coming from your eyes.
It makes me think, what a beautiful girl.
You will always be a diamond or my sparkling pearl.
I hope you recognize, What I'm speaking is true.
And if I ever fell in love, It would be with you.
I would never take the word of another man.
As long as we're together, I would understand.
Cause you'll always have a place down deep in my heart.
And I hope that you never try to tear it apart.
Cause I would never play you wrong I would treat you right.
That's why you're always on my mind, when I'm sleeping at night.
Having dreams about us spending time together.
Letting my hands caress your body in the stormy weather.
Cause what I just wrote, I'm saying for real.
That my heart can never break, cause it's harder than steel.

Marcus Daugherty

Sanctum

Alone
Lying awake
Pondering life
So much it means to so many
Yet hell is the path that I see
Mourning only the bad
Seeing none of the good
Frightening myself to sleep
Nightmares stalk me
Fearing only that I will have to open my eyes
To face the next of my horrific life
To add to my mournful thoughts
Only to scorn the day which has passed
Alone
Lying awake
Pondering Life

    Clark H. Scholl II

Untitled

I feel the crashing of the surf in my soul,
The sound of the breakers in my ear.
The vibration in the sands.
The placid waters in my heart.
The raging tempest in my soul.
The calm sea in my mind.
The roots of my existence are with you,
  and my being is locked to your existence.
For I am bound to this Earth, the Earth Being
  and I spin with you...
    through the stars.
I leave my body and look down at you,
  circling tirelessly...
    about the sun, so faithfully...
Locked, as myself, with your design,
Your orbit confines your freedom,
  and provides my home...
As I walk your face, I am only as free as you...
  faithful to your existence is my destiny.
For I am as you, a vibration in the sands.... of the stars.

    Walter Gene Kuhlman

My Life No Longer Belongs To Me

Once, I knew my mind and my thoughts were dear
The things I planned, my course was clear
Now, my mind is cluttered and thoughts strange
My goals in life are rearranged.

Once, life was easy and choices simple
My path laid out, I felt invincible
Now, life is hard and choices terrible
Simple mistakes make life unbearable.

Once, I was young and so full of life
No concerns, no worries and no strife
Now, I am old and my flame burns dimmer
My life ends soon, but my soul still glimmers.

Once, my road to life lay ahead of me
The promise I knew, my soul so free
Now, my life slowly fades away
I would not change a single day.

    Allen MacNeil

Untitled

There is a time for you and I
  to see the dreams we feel have gone by.
To gather them into our hearts and minds.
  To feel again the love that binds.

    Nedra A. Creamer

About My Father

How do I steal your heart away?
Before it joins your soul in the abyss

I look into your empty eyes, my father,
my father I desperately miss.

Brown little man of sinew and skin,
all your knowing, the knowledge within, your mind

What was it that creeping came
and tore your life away, from us,

Will scattered fragments of a memory stay?

Weep bitter tears of sorrow, and cannot make you whole

Did God forget, the body to sleep,
when he took the soul?

Remember me father,
I can be as brave

Remember I love you,
the father that to me, you gave.

How do I steal your heart away?

    Yolanda Saldivar

Dreams

Is life real? Are dreams fantasy? Is life a fantasy? Are dreams real? How do you know if you are in reality or a dream? Could dreams and reality be the same thing only in another dimension of time?

What we hope for in a dream can become reality in broad daylight. Is our whole life only a fantasy passing around us as we observe from another dimension?
Do we really know when we are awake, sleeping, dreaming?
Are we always in some sort of dream state wishing for a reality?

I am in a time tunnel racing toward the end of life. Can I dream my way back, can I dream my way forward? Can I dream an outcome I desire or can I desire an outcome I dream? Is life a Rubik's cube to be solved through dreams? When we dream are we connected to the earth or otherworldly? Should we let our dreams take us past reality or let reality take us to our dreams?

I need to dream, wish, fantasize. I need to be real and make believe at the same time. I need to float out in the sea of dreams and bring back the catch of reality. I want to be a dream maker and a life dreamer. Am I only a figment of others' imaginations? Am I part of everyone's dream or am I my own reality?

Life and dreams can they be separated?

    Michele A. Luna

"A Woman's Love"

I have seen the most beautiful sight
and, I have heard others speak
of this heavenly delight.

It has given birth to life, since the dawn of man.
For, no other creature can turn a fierce
warrior into a man of peace,
with a gentle hand

This creature can put him in
a trance, where he will risk
his life to receive a chance,
just to obtain its honor.

Its internal powers can reach
the soul of any man from any nation.
It has been said, to be the greatest of all
God's creations.

    Robert Douglass

"Early Fall"

In the chill of an early Fall, the world is slowly dying.
The leaves drifting to the ground are tears the trees are crying.
They mourn the loss of Summer gone and dream of might have been;
of bright and happy sunny days blown away by chilly winds.

The sounds of childish laughter echo gently in memory,
Like the sigh of someone dying, going, gone, no more to be.
This year, as every one before, I wonder what will be;
Will I still be on this earth long enough to see?

The gentle warmth of Springtime, the mist of April rain;
Will the searing heat of summer warm my soul again?
Will I see the world renewed, smell the sweet, fragrant flowers?
Will I be here years and years or only for an hour?

I want to live to see the Spring, I don't want to die;
But ones I've loved have gone before, so who's to say "Not I"?
But the golden leaves upon the ground are a blanket warm and deep.
This is not a sign of death, just of peaceful, restful sleep.

And someday when the time is right, the leaves will bud again;
A symbol of eternity, that life will never end.
So should I die before the dawn, please don't cry and mourn.
I'll be back in the Spring, I will be reborn.

Sandra French

Peace Disrupted

As I sit admiring my peaceful garden, I watch the birds
as they flutter and pick the ground for worms and seed.
They test the new bird watcher filled with feed.
The squirrels chase each other around and around in circles
until one decides she's finished with this game.

I am distracted by a tiny dragonfly as he flits to and fro,
back and forth, east to west or would north be best.
He can't decide. Stay or go, own or rent,
buy or sell, home or condo, to and fro.

Life itself becomes a test. An endless series of questions.
This indecision drives me dizzy, like the dragonfly,
I can't decide. So, back and forth, here and there.

Does he, like me, live alone or does he have a mate,
or is his like mine, belated. And goes he mourn
or does he scorn, or back and forth, to and fro.
I think we must be related.

Brenda K. Croom

First Love

Your love is lost,
your love is gone,
You have no love to carry on.
You swore you'd never love again,
When all you feel is pain to the bitter end.
You cry and cry, 'til you have no more tears,
this is how you hide your tears.
He said he'd love you 'til he dies,
but now that's all a hurtful lie.
You remember now he held you close,
Knowing that you will love him most.
He told you that he cares for you,
But now you feel that's all untrue.
You try to hide the pain inside,
When all you feel is the hurt in your eyes.
you remember his fingers stroking your cheek,
and wonder why you've become so weak.

Shima Delkash

L. A.

The beautiful people, all tanned and tonic/ed
Juiced up and hyped up, health fed and fueled,
Jogging or jaunting to smart destinations;
Palm-tree/ed and sun drenched and sparkly pooled.

The trends and the setters, the racy go-getters
Transplanted earthlings, they cling to take hold;
The fancy, the phony, they sing for their money
All laid back while rushing that big pot of gold.

So what will you find at the end of the rainbow?
Smog-lunged and smug-lived, Rolls Royce/ed and arrived,
You'll sit there and ponder: Where's the BIG ONE sir?
And pray you're back east when the FAULT
      shifts
       and
      writhes.

Sedra G. Schiffman

Untitled

Thinking back to yesteryear
When little girls wore pinafores
Plaited braids and ponytails
When the rage of every child
Was saddle oxfords and penny loafers
Many a mother heard it said, Aw Ma!
What's a mother for?
With four pretty girls and two fine sons
I thought it would be swell if I owned a store
Instead I learned to sew a seam
Two or three dresses a week was no big thing
I was just beginning to see
What a mother's for.
One by one they left the nest
Yet today is much the same as was back then
The telephone rings and once again
I thank God for letting me know
What a mother's for.

Katherine Hedgepeth

My Testimony

When I look back over my life thus far.
To see how far I've come. I'm reminded
of God's loving grace and all that He has done.

I now realize what I was experiencing is
preparing me for better things, cause God is
in my plans each day to guide me in my dreams.

When I go to God in my quiet time, I
know that He is there, cause His Spirit
begins to teach me things that lets me know He cares.

As God reveals Himself to me, I experience
Him in many ways. He's been my help,
and hope, and guide during many down or low days.

And when I feel like giving up, He steps
in right on time. He reminds me to have
faith in Him because He's on my side.

Cammie Johnson

"Friends I Hope We'll Always Be"

It breaks my heart to see you in pain,
To see the tears fallin' like rain.
I will always be true to you,
No matter what you say or do.

You're my friend and I'm your friend,
All the way to the end.
You are so dear to me,
Friends I hope we'll always be.

You to be happy is all I wish,
You are the only one I miss.
Whatever will be — will be,
All you need is some TLC.

I wish I could make all your pain go away,
I wish I could show you the way.
I love you as my friend,
That love will never end.

I'll always be there for you,
Call my name is all you have to do.
You're so special to me,
Friends I hope we'll always be.

Guy E. Stubbe

My Grandpa Joncas

My Grandpa Joncas is a very nice man.
In time of need, he sends a helping hand.
I lived with my grandpa for many year.
We shared tons of laughter, even tears.
He has been very close to me all his life,
I did the same for him when he lost his wife.

He worked real hard for everything he had.
He teaches us grandkids between good and bad.
He preaches to me to do good in school,
Hearing that from him is pretty cool.

He fought against Hitler in World War II,
Maybe you had a grandpa that did the same too.
My Grandpa Joncas is a very nice man,
My love for him is really grand.

Chad D. Shoulders

Precious Moments

Come on babe, lay next to me
Let me clothe your body
In soft fresh nicely scented petals
A symbol of my everlasting love

Together on these smooth satin sheets
Bring all our dreams to life
Let everything around us sparkle
Like well polished marble

Allow me to massage your mind
With love that's soft and sweet
Dispense of every doubt or care
For tonight is yours and mine to share

Choose the road; create a place
Where you and I alone will be
Unblemished! Untouchable! Unreachable!
The perfect place for you and me
To spend the night alone...

Cecilia Edghill

Untitled

Listen and they will hear
Watch and you will see
Speak and they will obey
The mountains will kneel
The birds will sing
The mind can make such wonderful things,
Dreams are a gift
Not a prize to be won
Imagining is a private thing for every one.

Courtney Carter

Becky's Lullaby

Go to sleep, my child, go to sleep.
Go to sleep my child don't fear.
Go to sleep my child, go to sleep
for in the morning I will surely be here.

I'm not changing rearranging, I'm not
leaving, dear. And in the morning, when you wake,
I'll be here.
Go to sleep, my child, go to sleep.
for in the morning I will surely be here.

Pamela L. Hackman

Till Death Do Us Part

I sat on the corner of your once used bed.
I gazed into the glass of your once used mirror.
Thinking with the thoughts that filled my head.
Why did you take your life, how come, what for?

I lifted your shirt and brought it to my face.
It smelled like you had smelled before.
You couldn't handle your life having such a fast pace.
Why did you take your life, how come, what for?

I laid down my head and remembered you.
The pillow that rubbed against my damp face made it sore.
I loved your thoughts, emotions, and everything you could do.
Why did you take your life, how come, what for?

My love should have been reason to spare your life.
God itself could not have loved you more
My dream was to someday be your wife.
Why did you take your life, how come, what for?

Robyn Sullivan

Fishing

A sport for the patient type.
Rod 'n' reel in hand
Fishing from boat or pier
Choosing bait and learning to wait
Catching big fish, little fish, and the one in between
Casting and reeling a tedious task
Rewarded with a fish
Knowing where to go and when
Is the area where knowledge is used
A bite, the thrill of the fight
And the satisfaction of a job well done.

Ben Kuo

Anguish

I must live this life over again
In another place, some future time.
The wisdom gained in lives before
Arrived too late, dumped at my door
In grievous bundles of "conscience-smitten",
Of "Roads not taken", and "It might have been".

The timorous gesture, the pleading eyes,
Begging consideration, a little time;
Consideration of overwhelming problems
A suffocating brain could not unriddle.

A mighty brain, oxygen starved,
Cells panting, neurons straining,
Memory pulsating, now strong, now weak,
A panic stricken colossal brain
Weakened by aortic aneurysm—
The hidden sword of Damocles.

But will I remember, in a life beyond
"The road not taken", "The might have been?"
Will I remember this gentle man
If not this time, will it be then?

Marjorie Richmond

"Dreams"

When you're sleeping you think
As your eyes closed very slowly and slowly
What in the world is this!
It is your imagination doing its job!
Well in a way yes!
But it's only a dream.
You can dream just about anything you want
There are good dreams and bad dreams
called nightmares!
Well of course you can only
Make your own dream up!
So good night and dream away!

Robert Saul

"Leaving"

Your going will leave me alone and adrift,
Empty rooms where my heart once soared.
My soul will be filled with sadness and tears,
In place of your wonderful smile.

The days ahead look grey and bleak,
With precious moments fleeting.
Time drifting slowly, without end,
While I still care and love you friend.

Janet Calfee

Of Flowers And Fate

Amid a dark cloud of fear, he has been here before
Under his veiled spectre of tyranny the proud nations slept,
The flowers were crying for a white commodore
But before he was gone the olive branch wept.

When the carnage had ended we said "never again"
These nations united to protect the weak and oppressed,
Like eagles we've soared, a watchful eye on our friend
But were blind when the call to allegiance was expressed.

He now has returned bringing fear but no veil
His delight is the arrogance of the eagle above,
The flowers again cried but were met with betrayal
The nations would only offer a wingless black dove.

No lessons were learned, though we know what's in store,
Amid a dark cloud of fear, he has been here before.

Martin L. Daesch

Untitled

Have you ever looked in the mirror,
Did you look in your eyes,
What did you see,
Were you about to die,
You begin to look around,
And you started to cry,
As you see your soul start to leave,
You look straight up and begin to plead,
Then you think to yourself that this is an error.
And you wish that you never looked in the mirror.

James Willson

Pocket Shoes

Tattered shoes
Have holes and fold up
To go in my pocket
So I can walk on the beach
And feel the waves washing my feet clean
And cold crisp salt air parching my throat.

I stop for a drink and meet an old pale man
Who stares deeply into his beer and speaks of
Faraway beaches
And distant Jew-killing feet that can never be cleansed.

Fear pushes me out of the tavern
While dark locks me in.

I run and I run and
Meet a glitzy outdated lesbian with
A New York accent that talks of beaches near
And feet that need cleansing
But cannot remove their shoes
For fear of getting hurt, killed, or worse.

I run from her
With shoes in my pocket.

Carolyn Bondurant

Polar Signals

Words-
    Are a clever swindler,
    Diametric, shape shifting, two-faced-
        A raging locomotive, the unleashed flood
        The murderer's blade, a strike in the face.
        A quiet rainfall, the waiting lover,
        The sleeper's dream, a savory wine.
They are the vulture picking flesh from the bone-
They are the jazz man playing his soft melodies-
        The dissonance of our frequencies,
    Opaque, befuddling, contradicting
    -words.

Jason Middlekauff

Memories

We are born to create memories.
A priceless gift to be cherished.
And a gift that has no limits.
Each memory is true and unique.
Just like snowflakes, no two are alike.
They earn a special place inside,
And slowly become part of the past.
Memories are untouchable and unchangeable,
Lost and forgotten, or remembered and shared.
But all will linger somewhere in our collection.
A collection which only exists inside.
As we are born to create many such memories,
We sooner or later, leave and become memories

Monica S. Munoz

The Mother In You

Initially when I think of mother's day I become sad,
because my mother is gone and I dearly missed the time we never had.

Then I think about this world and all the wickedness it posses,
my spirits are lifted because I know my mother is truly blessed.

Blessed to have a home on high, a home above the sky,
a joyful home where you will never even hear a sigh.

Blessed to never again have to endure pain,
because she's in the bosom of the one with the holy name (God).

I'm blessed to have had her as my mother,
blessed now to have you to guide to guide me further.

Through your daughter I was led to Christ,
and by the grace of God, like my mother I will have eternal life.

I know my mother is pleased with me, my wife, and you,
I also know she doesn't mind me calling you mother number two.

Arthur Purifoy

Now That You Are Gone

Now that you are gone, I wish I would have kissed you.
If I only knew how much I was going to miss you.

I missed your body and I missed your touch,
And I missed your gentleness that I loved so much.

I missed those days you were nice and tender.
To your wishes and desires didn't I surrender?

Wasn't I always Happy when you were mine?
Didn't I cherish you like the rising shine?

I knew you loved me and I knew that you hated me too.
Your endless anger broke my heart in two.

You hated me my darling because you had loved me.
You picked me up high and then you dropped me.

You have been hurt before and your heart was cold.
To the Lord of disbelief your mind was sold.

I played your game and O how faithful I was.
To your tortuous pain how grateful I was.

Soudabeh Etessami

Crystal Clear

It use to be so clear to me just what I'd grow up to be;
but when I had made up my mind a new career would come to mind.

Well, I've walked some 40 years away and still just not sure today.
As the days quickly pass I have come to know that nothing last.

I looked in the mirror this gray morning and saw there's little hair
left upon my head. I take my teeth from the jar and put them in my
mouth. I bribed my sore limbs to serve me today, because I realize
this could be my last. It rings even louder now more than ever that
nothing last.

I vaguely remember the sickness that overtook me, but today I feel
as young as a babe. My hair is long and snowy white now. My form
is sleek and glows. I spring from place to place with little effort
on the very tips of my toes.

My career is definite now I no longer wax and wane. I'm so glad that
I grew up and figured out who I am and was to be.

You see, I am your guardian angel dear. By your side I will stay
near. Wonder not what your life is to be.

Grow up slowly, enjoy every moment because as I have learned that
nothing ever lasts.

Teresa A. Brown

The Strain Of Words

I speak from one of many wretched heart,
    To triumph o'er a dense melancholy cloud.
Of selfless love and will drifting apart,
    Influencing the muse to cry aloud!

The simple thought of fluent fire,
    Thus inspire, from mountain peaks on high.
Yield not thy thunder of shadowed desire,
    Of thy cramped hand and thy poet's sigh.

My good measure of faith and trust,
    Hath been forgotten for a long time.
So, now the muse begins to rust,
    Reaping few fruits on the branch of rhyme.

Seeking an image to amuse,
    My weary heart of disdain.
Let not thy imagination abuse,
    Leaving thy poetic voice in vain.

Behold! Thy sorrowstruck design,
    Mingles with thy soul's dark embrace.
Hath bent in favor of a blank line,
    Moving my pen with such modest grace.

Michelle Lynne Marcak

Ominous Sunday

Ominous Sunday, why is it that you
always lead into somber Mondays without breaking your quiet solitude
or sharing your secrets with me?

Why do you promote thinking, and why do you bring with you
that special feeling, that creeps deeply into my heart and soul?

A feeling only to Sunday.

Why are you always the poor follow up to Sunday night?
And why is it you, who is always chosen to transition from one week
    to another?

The amazing thing is that your feeling never changes, a dull feeling
holding no significance as to how good or how bad the week has been,
you never change your mood.

Always calm, no matter how turbulent the times may be,
resting peacefully in the midst of constant restlessness.

It is a relief to know that you come only once in seven days,
for you are too totally apathetic for me, ominous rainy Sunday.

Carol Sciannameo

T-Ball

With mighty swing he hit on strike five,
The crowd roared as the ball came alive.

Past the short and into the field.
What a swing, what a hit, what power he wields!

Slinging his bat, he ran for third,
To second and first he sailed like a bird.

He missed home plate by a foot or more.
Said the ump, "now there's a score!"

With pounding heart he walked to the cage.
A little man had come of age.

F. Neil Denton

Thanks-Giving

Did you give "Thanks" this morning, when you opened up your eyes,
To see the sun a shining, and brightening the skies?
Did you give "Thanks" when you sat down, to your toast,
   and eggs, and cup,
And think of those unfortunates, who barely get to sup?
Did you give "Thanks" when traveling, to your daily routine grind,
That you were really on your own, not dependant like some blind?
Did you give "Thanks" returning home, to your children and your wife,
That you are living in a place, where there's very little strife?
Did you give "Thanks" you're healthy, and so seriously do you care,
That you're thankful to be able, to divide your lion's share?

   C. H. Smock

Foot Print In The Snow

With great sorrow I saw the printed snow,
Deep and irregular were the marks to see.
Awful the load of pain making the way so slow,
My loved ones path there never more to be.

Lonely and cold I stood seeing a wonder to behold,
Farther along those tracks began to fade.
Neither burdensome nor nearly as bold,
Yet by and by no mark upon the snow was made.

A thought came, standing there that day,
That neither angels nor those that leave us,
Render marks of burdened anguish in the way,
Free and light and no more fuss.

Thank you, oh thank you Lord for taking care,
To see when the departing time had come.
That the many hurts and pains to bare,
Taken from their shoulders on the journey home.

   Peter B. Page

Sacrificial Mind

   What's inside my box is overtaken by the guilt of innocent tears
of ordinance. The time of listless memories of happiness have now
come to an end and I've destroyed your nidification in my mind. I
am your molding clay of anger and unfinished obstacles. Why have
you not completed me? Locked up in a cage with myself to defend
our enemies of truth. Personality overview of what I should be and
destroy. I lock myself alone, in my box to be of myself without myself.
But the destination to be myself is repelled by your fear of desertion.
What you see as reconformity is the depth at which you threw me.
Demands of a stolen perfect picture, cowering at your every whim.
What you thought was my submission is my everlasting scream
which is muffled by your alacrity. Pushing me back toward the
walls of my cynicism where I unobtrusively, unsuccessfully,
destroy you back. You promised my completion of pain by your
hands, not what I have destroyed by myself. The anger that lingers
restrains you, distorts you. I'm not the tableau of your imagination,
you have made me real. Real enough to conform to your manipulation.
You use my eyes to see the danger, you use my tongue to taste
the fear. Fear of what you've made me, but then again you knew
your destination....

   Lili Franz

The Storm

The waves splash as the wind blows.
The boat floats and churns.
The ocean pressures the water and acts as if it were mad.
Suddenly it comes to an end.
The ocean slows and the water cools.
The storm is gone.
The sun glistens on the water.
The tide rolls in and brushes up against the shore.
Rocks and shells are borne in with the tide and lay along the beach.
Whites ... pinks ... purples ... and blues are their colors
A rainbow is made in the sand.

   Ilana Isaacson

Wind

Wind is the lightning darting around my roof as I dream,
The yellow eyes of a hooting owl,
Wind is a calm before a storm,
A mysterious man on a black horse galloping around at 8,
An ancient greek warrior charging with his gold chariot,
A bloody white wolf, and his howl.
The gangster train flying an inch off the track,
Through darkness it moves
Like the speed of light...
Until it stops...
Everything that is the wind ends,
And disappears.

   Alexi Shaw

In The Waking Hours

Hush, my friend...
Hear the falling rain
On the leaves outside my window.
The sky, she sheds what she cannot hold,
And keeps what makes her currents flow.

Rivers flow, tides recede -
   Never wishing their run to cease.
And merely humans, we share with them
   Renewal of our peace.

Quiet, my love...
The bird outside -
The mourning dove announces Dawn.
Rosy light reveals your face,
And I am no longer sleeping.

   Ann Marie Veca

Son

In my heart there remains a war,
battling as never before.
You are the love and pride of my life
and we have given you so much inner strife.
Please forgive us, for we were only human
and knew not what we had done.
Now it is too late to change our fate.
So we will always live this war,
in consequence of the little heart we tore.
May God help you find peace within,
along with the ability to live life and win.

   Sherri L. Stark

"Earth And The Maiden"

   Dripping with deception, a silvery liquid moon
casts molten shadows of lust and madness
across vast, tepid pools of shallow faith.
Just as the thickening swells
of the deepest sea, at the end of the night
rise as pillars of stone...
boldly jutting forth to caress
the tempting sunrise.
Night then falls like a raven
and the heavens explode with electrical vengeance,
cracking our conscience with a whip.
Once powerful birds of prey
have now become sparrows in the mist,
unable to rise above drenching desires.
We are born,
and we are blanketed,
wrapped warm and wet
in colorful moral fabric.
What is: Is. What shines: Will shine
and only the darkness will keep you awake.

   Brett James Crawford

The Master's Voice

Dogs will respond to the master's voice,
  when trained well, they have no choice.
They love to respond to voice commands,
  then eat out of their master's hands.

If we treat our dogs well each day,
  they will be with us for a long stay.
Dogs love to be well fed,
  then given a spot by your bed.

They love to romp around outside,
  then in your car for a long ride.
Dogs can tell if you are well, or ill,
  being a dog is a hard job to fill.

Dogs have been here for years,
  Man's best friend forever it appears.
Seems you will always have your dog friend,
  a pal to the very end.

We depend on our dog in many ways,
  even outside when he plays.
It is still the dog's only choice,
  to respond to the master's voice.

Kenneth Paul Hlavinka

Brand New Start

I don't know I don't know I've heard these words before I
don't know I don't know will you ever open that door?

Once again a friend stepped in and love went on its way things
are different than before if only you know you'd come back and stay.

I've always been friends with you but now I'm wanting more
this time things will go our way this time it's number four.

Friends may come and friends may go but love has found its way,
its way to you and back again forever more to stay.

Maybe no rhythm maybe no rhyme but for some reason it's all
different this time.

Through thick and thin and back again my love will be brand new,
I know you say you've heard this before but this time
it's all so true.

Things went bad and I got a broken heart now I can finally
open up and love once again it's time to make a new start.

Time and time again I was afraid of commitment and wouldn't
let you in.

My heart has slowly mended and old times have been erased
now it's time to start again and put a smile upon my face.

Lisa Cunningham

The Journey Of A Soldier

Espy the blood that runs from the soldiers hands
  The tears that flow from his eyes
  The fear upon his face as if carved in stone
He must go on yet he doesn't know why

He feels the pain
  Sharp twists of the spawns of the weapons of war in front
  He tastes the bitter, he tastes the dust
He's the target in this senseless hunt

Vision, vision is gone
  Except for the light, what is it?
  No one knows, except for this boy
He beholds a figure and seizes it

This soldier knows not what awaits him later
  Leaving behind the ones that he loved
  Watch his soul rising higher and higher
Joining the river that runs thicker than blood

Sandra S. Lee

Cat

Mine, the silence of ballet shoes on stage
as I slip between the hours,
leap on top of the day's furniture,
and sleep under the twitching tents of my ears
with my dream curled around me.

My tongue is broken glass
on rooftops, at twilight
I turn like the alleys
behind burned-out buildings,
offering strangers old newspapers,
a handful of ivory knives,
going soft as light
on stagnant pools.

This is the hour when my eyes
trap light and go to green,
where I become every shadow
and eat up the night,
drag its bones out of drawers,
break them to get the marrow.

Martha Grant

Thoughts Of Amy

I know a girl named Amy.
When she speaks, a gentle breeze stirs the leaves.
When she smiles, the sun shines through.
When she laughs, chimes sound.

When she moves, it is with the grace of a doe,
Slipping gently through the woods.
When she loves, it is wholeheartedly,
With trust, warmth, and the tender touch of innocence.

Just a few years ago, almost unobserved,
She crept quietly into our lives;
A tall, charming, gentle beauty,
Bright, witty, enchanting.

Four decades ago, a young married couple,
Thought we wanted five children!
Along came one, a boy, and three would do.
Then came a second boy, and that was enough.

Two fine sons filled our lives with joy.
But we never had that third child,
The one that would have been a daughter.

Until now.

Will Adams

Yellow Sensation

In a room full of black they sat,
hardly noticeable, hardly recognizable.

And it was a long night,
but that sweet smell and silky texture were soon to be seen
and they were glorious in all their beauty and innocence,
so pure, and yet to be discovered.

And they were cherished.

But night came upon them once again,
and a cool chill passed over them so swiftly that it touched their
heart and soul,
and the sun no longer shone for them.

Yet with Spring's return, they are here,
with reminders of all that was good.
And they too are caught up in this cycle of life and come and go
with memories past on and dreams yet to have.

So in a blue vase, they now do sit,
my sweet daffodils.

Lisa Montelle

Seasons

"Spring is the time," I gratefully croon
As I leap out of bed and throw off the cocoon
Of Winter's dark days and freezing cold nights
The ice covered steps
The days with no lights.

But Spring soon disappears
And Summer turns on the heat
Then I want cool drinks, fans, ice
and bare feet.

Next comes Fall and all those great leaves
Songs of Thanksgiving and gathering sheaves
Fall is a good time for deep self-reflection.
Preparing to face the almanac's prediction.
For a winter that's coming with cold, snow and sleet
The dark days of winter shout
"Turn up the heat!"

We have completed the cycle in such a short time
Days turn into years.
There is such a fine line
Between seasons and lifetimes.

Mary Lou Ford

Ultimate Conquest

Scales of gold like those of cold
   contain a death from a drawn breath,

Mighty in power land or air
   beautiful as a flower bland or fair,

Dragons' love thieves shove
   gold be found greed their hound,

Battle is willed
   lust be filled,

Blows are traded
   cowards be hated,

Spells are thrown
   kiss of death be blown,

One will lose
   God's favor may chose,

Pain feels like hell
   but dulls after the victory yell,

Silence, Silence, a moment only
   a tribute to the fallen foe by the holy.

Jonathan O'Neill

Friends

People who care
Ones who are always there
Someone to laugh with
Someone to cry with
Someone to share with
Someone to dare with
.....to be yourself.
That's what I see in you; my dear friend
Never leave my side -
For without you - my soul could not live
And my feelings I would hide -
For there was no one for them to give.
In you I see my second self.
Only you can undo my chains and lighten my load -
For it is "you" my friend that has my life to hold -
In your hands.

Carol J. Holleran

The Unicorn

Racing through virgin green Meadows
Tripping through clear clean Streams;
Prancing and pawing the Mother Earth
Dancing across the Sky of Dreams.

Skipping along a Rainbow
Lighthearted with Happiness and Love;
A Soul full of wondrous Magick
Galloping on to the Heavens above.

Forever young and free-spirited
Wind-tousled tail and mane;
Soaring among the Stars
As the Night begins to wane.

Eyes that flash defiance
Possessor of a twisted horn of gold;
A milk-white coat of ghostly sheen
Guardian of Things Untold.

He lives on, unchallenged and undefeated
A wild and untamed beast, the Unicorn.
Believe in him and you will find that
Love, Magick and Dreams can be reborn.

Krista Bratt

Untitled

No one can tell you how I feel
The pain in my heart is deep and real
Here I sit and cry, remembering these memories
And knowing how my love for you will never die
Now these memories that I recall
Will always burn high in my heart and never fall;
You kissed my lips light
And the way you caressed me - with all your might
I had hoped our love would grow and grow
But now we are to part, forever you will remain in my heart
For you will always be the one and only true love for me
Maybe one day you'll feel for me as I feel for you
And I'll be a fool for going back to you
My friends tell me not to worry - but how can I not?
I wonder what you do and think
And try to put these thoughts together in links and knots
My days are long and hard with you always on my mind
I was once really in glee and am now in a lonely misery
I can not put all my feelings into words - but I assure you that
   they will stay close to me,
As close as you are my dear, and that is in my heart

Vivian Rose Rick

In A Wood I Found...

I found some rusty railroad tracks while wandering through a wood,
And a jumbled pile of lumber where a little shack had stood.
The stove was there, a small wood burner, and a pile chimney of stone.
I felt bad for that old shack, abandoned and alone.
The shack that was just might have been some shelter from the weather
Where conductors or other railway men would play cards
   or talk together.
Here laughter swelled and stories shared, dreams and memories
   were made.
But time has caused the laughter silenced, and dreams
   and memories fade.

And then the tracks, those rusty rails of steel and steam and sweat,
Which point the way to destinations I've not dreamed of yet,
Go to the right and to the left as I stand in between
The times that happened in the past and times I've not yet seen.

John A. Morris

The Beauty Of A Bruise

Purple splashed on yellow,
a touch of red, then maybe green -
the explosion of emotion
from delicate vessels of human anatomy.
As artists we have the task
set forth by the mother of our natures
to display from within
the blending of our bodies and our minds -
the racing of our metabolisms with time.

Continuous projections of color appear
on a canvas made by birth;
resolutions in patterns
describe each artist as a painting -
a masterpiece in constant motion.

We work like clocks
for years and years and years
and never realize we are working at all.
The cells of the body, like notes of a symphony,
play aloud the rhythms of life.
And we demonstrate the beauty of a bruise.

Steven M. Bromley

Tragedy

A screech,
A crash,
A bang.

Everything is blurry,
Something happened,
Trying to move but can't.

Straining to see what's happened,
But can't see,
Screaming for help and nothing comes out.

Seeing flames rise,
Can't do anything about it,
Struggling to get out.

Hearing sirens wailing,
Relief at last,
Urging muscles to move,

Seeing a hole,
Crawling over to it,
Getting out!

Worried,
Scared,
Relieved.

Kristin Majewski

Innocence

When a love is lost, so is life. No rainbow is seen, only clouds
not sunlight. When a dream disappears, hope is gone. Love seems
not worth the fight. A fight it is to notice a bird in the sky, the
flowers lose their color and we lose faith in each other as innocence
dwindles away. The price is steep that we pay. Our whole being
changes, everything rearranges to fit a new pattern. Sometimes
stronger love grows, time is the only thing that knows whether
this will happen. When a heart breaks, the earth shakes and looks for
a new foundation. When one is betrayed the skies are grayed,
All joy is gone and hearts can be swayed. In a matter of minutes
someone can change, all is questioned that was known but in time
you will find that you have grown. All of this sorrow makes for
a better tomorrow. When the flowers regain their color, we have
new faith in each other, but innocence is gone forever.

Marilyn Eppenbrock

Saying Good Bye

Say farewell my friends
for today I have gone away
Never far from your thoughts
and always in your hearts
Just slightly beyond the shadows
just barely out of sight.
Say good night one last time
here in this world that was ours
Kiss me, embrace me
so that it shall linger with us
as I long for the time we will share our souls again.
Say good bye for now
and wipe the tears from your eyes my friends.
I will miss you so...
But I will wait
always watching over you
Until at last our Savior
finds a place with me, for you.

Lorrie Reid Votrian

Mount Hebron

No! No! It's the valley of the shadows.
A sea of monuments.
Cold granite, artfully embellished.
An opiate for the living

A patch of earth still barren
Lilliputian by comparison to the vast holy ground,
Mother earth waiting for another
to fill her dark hollow emptiness.

Mother earth?
Who honored you with this title?
I call you nature.
Mothers have arms to hug,
lips to kiss away tears from my beloved son, Philip.

I envy your possession,
I resent your passivity
Your bosom is an arid cold hole.

Be kind! Let his spirit rise
Let him enchant the heavens
With his lovely music.
As he enchanted my life

Luci Gilman

The Ocean

Only by the light of the moon.
Could the rolling waves be seen.
Breaking close to the quiet strip of sand,
Stretching endlessly, it seemed.
Glistening flecks of silver,
Like diamonds floating on each crest,
Crowned every wave as if the ocean
Was an ancient treasure chest.
The warm, salty sea air
Whispered gently across the night.
The gulls that seemed to fly forever
Were still in endless flight.
A star-filled sky watched over
As if it was full of twinkling eyes,
Shining in all their glory
Before the dawning sun would rise.

Nancy Bucko

The Search For Salvation

The children of the earth are lost.
"Help," they cry, "Help!"
But no one is there to listen.
They turn to look in the face of evil.
They search for salvation, but only to find their destruction.
Their new found savior, who was thought to be holy,
    was in fact the devil.
Trust no one who claims they have all of the answers.

Samuel Steele

Autumn

It was autumn.
Leaves carpeting my way to the temple.
I had always pondered over death after dying
and here were these dead leaves
dying again to cushion my walk.

An autumn morning.
I was out for my morning walk.
Thinking about life after death.
The dry leaves shone red
in the virgin rays of the sun,
creaking under my feet.
They were alive once again.

It was an autumn noon.
I walked along the pavement.
Musing what life was exactly all about.
When I saw the old tramp
curled up on the garden bench
In this frosty weather
that's what I guess
life is all about

Dinesh H. Rathi

It Happened To Me And It Could Happen To You

So I sit here all alone
My life has changed
Nowhere to call home
I was warned and begged
But too blind to see
My last chance was the end of me.
I have been forgotten,
So many promises have been broken.
All alone on the streets
A nameless face, you don't see.
Don't you remember who I am?
I used to be your daughter, your sister.
Your best friend.
I used to be just like you.
Why can't you see I'm human too?
You think you could never be like me.
All it takes is one mistake to be free.
Just like me!

Luna Nilo

The Test Of Time

There comes a time in everyone's life,
When we're challenged by God to see a different light.
Obstacles occur throughout the path,
For He wants to see how we will react.
He can test us in ways in which no others can,
But we should know, that this is part of the plan.
It may seem hard, but we know we can do it
It'll take some time for us to get through it.
We ask ourselves why, still we don't understand,
Why we were the ones called by this Man
To be asked to do something that seems way out of line,
For we have just begun The Test of Time.

Beverly Lawrence

Untitled

Where were you when I needed,
    someone to talk to!?
Where were you, when I needed a friend?
Where were you, when I needed help,
    to put all the pieces back together again?
I thought you really cared for me,
I thought we were in love.
I thought we'd always be together,
You know eternal love,
    now we one have become two,
Will it ever be the same between me and you?
    As time goes on,
I guess we'll understand,
    why were no longer hand and hand!!!

Mary C. Starr

My Sister By Blood, My Friend By Choice

There are some who have gone and come
with fair-weather faces and erasable eyes;
others more resilient before betrayal's dull thud
thumped its way into the widening space between.

One with a biblical name
shared her childlike, wise beyond her years soul,
so that even now, the Bible's laughing matriarch,
giggling at God's promise come lately,
stirs something within.

There have even been angels unaware,
those who consecrate the day with fidelity
and spangle the soul's dark night with flickering faith.

But you, my sister by blood and friend by choice—
though you sometimes enter my mystical soul
of art and intuition only obliquely,
and shake a wondering head
at my metaphoric mind,
still, you are the one I turn to when I need to belong
most fully to me,
most finally to God.

Elly Sparks Brown

Skin

Skin of yellow, skin of black, skin of brown, skin of red, skin of white,
All born to be brothers and sisters.

Skin of white, skin of black, skin of yellow, skin of brown, skin of red,
All warmed by the same flaming sun.

Skin of black, skin of yellow, skin of white, skin of brown, skin of red,
All washed by the gentle rains.

Skin of black, skin of yellow, skin of white, skin of brown, skin of red,
All cooled by the chilling winds.

Skin of brown, skin of red, skin of yellow, skin of white, skin of black,
All cover bodies who walk the earth.

Skin of white, skin of black, skin of yellow, skin of red, skin of brown,
Skin all gone,
Only bare, dry white bones.

Nan Wright

My Heart's Desire

My one true love on all the planets,
Stole my soul in a glance,
Her heart's as hard as ice,
Still I love her madly.
Though I don't know the price,
I speak truthfully.
So try I shall with my love burning brightly,
To melt her heart just slightly.

James Crockett

My Brother, My Friend

You're always there, right by my side.
We walk together, you never leave me behind.
Trusting and loving with nothing to hide.
You teach me with patience, for sometimes I doubt.
You always so gentle, always so kind.
When I'm with you my faults have not meaning,
for all that you see is my beauty within.
You never judge me for what I am not,
you only see who I am and except me with love.
You say let go of yesterday, for now it is gone,
to live in this moment with only love in my heart
and tomorrow will come so worry not, to cherish
this moments so I can feel the beauty it has brought.
You say you will be with me always, that I am never alone.
And I know this is true. For I know you are my brother,
you are my friend and you will walk by my side till I reach
home again.
Jannice Giuliani

Beautiful Fish

She hummed a sad song to herself
As she combed her flaxen hair.
The rock she sat on was like a shelf;
But for her, the shore was bare.

Esmeralda was a lonely lass,
The sea was her only friend.
Though she was full of spirited sass;
There was no one to offend.

Gathering seashells at ocean's floor
And braiding seaweed by the hour;
She had moved about from shore to shore,
So she knew each lighthouse tower.

It was not destined for her to mate;
Thus life's cruel plan was laid.
A lonely existence was her fate -
Oh, woe to the poor mermaid.

Doris Kinsfather

Soaring High

I soar through the sky
Enjoying the clouds, water, and land below me
They are so beautiful and breathtaking
I love the sights from up here
Wish you would join me
There is so much up here to share
Sharing is caring
Feels like Heaven
I want to soar up here forever
Would you join me
The water below is so clear and blue
You can see the colorful fish and coral
Beauty is everywhere
Please join me and we'll soar together
Forever

Carla Weiss

Losing It All

Draining of thoughts through the void
My dreams again the doctors have toyed
learning my sleep to be a dreaded need
Having no rest causing my eyes to bleed
Running on low they take more tests
Jabbing long tubes and needles into my chest
Searching and looking for my fate to find
Slowly losing my state of mind
Hanging onto the very last thread
The doctors let it snap, and now I'm dead...

R. C. Michael

Reflex

Too old now to walk the beach,
I watch things from a chrome-framed picture window,
four flights up, that looks out on the sea.

The sand dollars still wash in, no doubt,
for someone else to claim. I have a bowlful, anyway.
Right there, right where the white foam
swirls around your ankles,
that's the place to find them.

Yesterday I watched a dolphin herd,
mothers with their young, shadowing a trawler.
Each baby bowed and bubbled beside the sleek body of its mother,
assuming her artless rhythm.

Through the sea scope in my window I brought him into the room,
one baby, large as life.
I held my breath, arching and diving along with him,
and gasped for air when we broke the surface -
a reflex action, like the spasms in my limbs
when a fullback on TV, somewhere in New York,
is brought to earth so hard my muscles flinch,
and I feel his fall, on a sofa in San Diego.

Lyn Snyder

Living With Love

Living with Love, who would know, helping yourself
    to love and let go,
      superficial people sad and angry
      hating their lives without love

Living with Love is so easy even when you feel things are unfair
    people are rude with bad attitude,
      let it go, you don't care, because
      living with Love will take care of you

Living with Love is everything you do, passionately
    caring, sharing and helping others,
      new life and wonderful feelings,
      come hand 'n' hand living with love

Living with Love empowers you, with a healthy mind
    and body too, I am so glad I found
      living with love would help me through
      the sad times that I knew

Gary Lodemore

Untitled

...And in the shadows she hides
trying to get away from the laughter

Though the pain rarely subsides
a smile dies in order to capture

the little girl,

What is left? Only a light
she blows it out gently

It is a struggle-losing sight
of all the flowers burying me

I began as just another searcher
became a starving puppet
drove to the end
and found myself
in the process I lost a piece of my puzzle

If ever you find it
care for it-never let it die

It is so hard to survive in another body
you drain yourself of complexity
and become anyone - need be...

Velvet A. Silva

Young Love

Young love stroking springtime passion
Young love your presence forever in fashion

Young love rejuvenating my zeal
Young love wooing with sex appeal

Young love my ardent admirer
Young love sets my heart on fire

Young love adorning a new season
Young love please share the reason

Young love you're aging far too fast
Young love is "in love" a thing of the past

Young love no longer burning with desire
Young love are you planning to retire

Young love distant lonely and cold
Young love commitment has grown old

Niya D. Walker

That Last Little Boy

He is growing up, that last little boy
  Just look at him standing there
    With his firm little chin
    The dimple turned in
And his thatch of light brown hair.

Soon he will be gone, that last little boy
  Trudging his manly way
    Up the tree lined street
    To the school so neat
To his pleasant work and play

Mother will send that last little boy
  Cheerily waving her hand
    He must never know
    His going hurts so
For he is starting to be a man.

Paul D. Fouts

Thank You

I lie here, wanting to give myself to you
and make this moment last
But there are things you don't know, things in my past
I love you and want to prove it to you
but you have no idea what I've been through
You feel that it is my love beginning to lack
but that is not what I'm holding back
I love you more than life itself
but I still have bad memories sitting on the shelf
You are what I need in my life right now
You keep me happy and alive somehow
And I fear that if you and I are ever through,
My life would also be through
You are the missing piece to my heart
Before you came along, my heart was like a puzzle torn apart
You have mended my broken heart
and given my life a new start
And before I end this, I just want to say
Thank you, in each and every way.

Melissa Cunnings

What Have We Done?

Begging in a Santa Fe parking lot,
An outcast from society,
Having thrown away his ancient heritage and pride,
Drunk,
His relatives at work in a casino or in a gas station,
What have we done?
What have we done?

D. Hunter Smith

"The Fields Of Home"

Mom, as a child, did work and play in
quiet fields of grain and hay.
Her father said to her one day, "not always
will it stay this way,
The time is coming when these great fields won't be.
I won't see it, but you will for me."
Mom married and raised a family of her own,
Her children also played over these fields of home.
Grandpa was old and then he died, now things
are happening like he prophesied.
Fields where three generations since did
work and play, now man is building a great freeway.
It's not quiet there anymore, for the
gigantic road graders do roar.
Where once the grain and hay did stand,
the plan of progress is made by man.
Living today grandpa would have said,
"The wheels of progress must roll ahead".

Audrey Kittel

My Dare

You swore to me you loved me, you swore to me you cared,
I believed your tainted lies to me, for all of that I dared,

Dared to have a heart for you, dared to face the pain,
I have risked all of myself for you, this hurt I can't contain,

How can I live without you, perpetual pain that never dies,
This is something I am afraid to do, but still I believe
    your useless lies,

Can I be abused anymore, broken and decayed,
It seems all my hate unborn, can never ever save,

My sufferings repeat themselves, each day in my mind,
Will I ever forgive myself, or can I never die,

Is there a way to get you back, to redeem this shattered heart,
Or is this all a just game, and this is how it starts,

You left me with a broken heart, and tears in my eyes,
Now I will not live at all, for eternity I will cry.

Casey Benedict

The Dark Side

Every human being has a dark side
created by Satan himself.
Where there is love he will bring forth hate
by chaos, strife and misery;
all evil he can create-only if allowed to enter
the dark side.

With the swiftness of a bird in flight
The demon doth take over creating darkness
where there once was light...

Be not deceived the devil can take on many
different forms.
He can cloud the mind to the utter extreme
make you do and say things you never dreamed.

Yes, he is a many splendored bird.
This demon in disguise;
So be careful watch out. Don't allow him to
enter your dark side.

Julia O. Bonner

Roadside Candles

Roadside candles, like the moon they glow on borrowed rays
As someone's headlights kindle them to full kinetic blaze.
They mark the ebon roadway with their phosphorescent light,
Then pass behind the car and turn as flameless as the night.

Judith Weintraub

To Miss Jessica Dubroff

When I heard the news of your untimely demise,
It was impossible to stop the tears in my eyes.

Although I didn't know you, I have to say,
Thank you for reminding me to "Live For Today".

In your seven years, you've lived so much more
Than many who have passed seven........years before.

You had a dream and you followed your heart,
Yet people are trying to tear that apart.

I am encouraged and inspired by your spirit and flight.
A special little angel who followed her own guiding light.

In your memory I hope those who are looking to blame,
Will instead find inspiration to live when they bring up your name.

Your story has brought back my Faith and Desire.
Your smile, zest, and courage leave much to admire.

I trust, Miss Jessica, now that you have earned your wings,
That you will share your magic and help others to realize and
accomplish their dreams.

Your spirit has touched me in such a special way.........
Miss Jessica, Thank You for reminding me to "Live For Today".

Katherine Sanchez

"My Endless Love"

This is an endless love indeed,
Because blood was shed on Calvary,
It was the blood that was to cover all our sins,
as well as, bring salvation to all men.

We were guilty and worthy of death,
We weren't worthy to breathe God's breath,
It's the mercy of God that keeps us today,
We should be thankful in every way.

Just keep believing that God is real,
He'll strength you through every ordeal,
Sometimes it seems hard just to stand,
But Jesus stands before you with outstretched hands,

So many things come my way,
I know it comes just to try my faith.
So I stay before you in prayer today,
Just waiting for your endless love to make a way.

Carol Venning

"My Life Is Built Around You"

My life is built around you,
And has been all these years.
You've stayed with me through good and bad,
Through laughter and through tears.

I'll always thank the Lord above
Each day throughout my life
For blessing me the way he did,
And giving me my wife.

The years have passed so rapidly,
Our children now are grown.
I wish for them the happiness
That for 40 years I've known.

I pray that we have many more,
But if that's not the way
My love for you will be the same
As it was from that first day!

Robert Porter

For Them It Is Time Consuming

Few people walk beyond their own backyard,
And go see what their neighbors are doing,
For they feel there is safety in one's yard,
And walking is just too time consuming.
So few even wish to rake their old leaves,
That lie over the suffocating grass,
Who have the burning desire to heave
In unison, in their own little mass.
Even fewer leave their own bedroom door,
But they still keep their radio on loud,
And ignore the need to work, do a chore,
So they lie covered in their own white shroud.
Yet, the fewest even leave their own mind,
Fearing that it is their soul they might find.

Muhamet Alijaj

Spring

Spring,
What a wonderful thing.
Birds chirp and flowers bloom,
and the sweet smell of honeysuckles fill the room
the cheerful bees buzz
and they do it because
they're happy it's finally spring.
The green grass grows
and the blue water flows
and the yellow sun shines bright,
as the sun beats down
on the green, green ground,
Kids play till the end
of the day with a friend,
As they scream and shout
and run all about
So happy that it's finally spring!

Brandie Michelle Luneau

The Dove And The Plane

Certain sounds in life take me home; the familiar sounds of my childhood, not the ever-common laughter of children on the playground.

Or the carnival music of a merry-go-round. For whatever reason which I cannot identify, they make me blue...

The sound of an otherwise quiet day, the lonesome Dove crying somewhere amidst the wind, the flowers and trees... the Dove hasn't a particular preference -

She cries, it seems, when I do. Does the Dove, perhaps, in its respective grey clothing, remind us of our immortality? Our numbered days?

In the heart-racing climax of a day, we can hear her cry if we choose to - I have learned over the years, she is always there... just listen.

The man-made cub airplane - slowly, quietly, gliding its way out of earshot... To where? To whom?

In all my years, I've never seen one - I have only heard them scraping the walls of the sky. Why such a lonely sound? Like the crying of a Dove...

Funny, they both have wings - one made by man, one made by God. Why do I feel blue when I hear them?

Sandra Rothermich

NPC

Church does not work for me anymore.
The incense, the Host, and the conversion of wine.

This is not to say God doesn't.
He still does; only,
I don't need to be in His house to see Him.

When I stand on the steps overlooking Corpus Christi Bay,
I see whitecaps and clouds
Of infinite shape and size.

Or, when Orion rises high behind me,
Ever in pursuit of Seven Sisters,

That's when I feel His presence the most,
and it comforts me.

Roberto I. Ramos

Spirit Waves

The news this eve exceeds mere shock
Your scent your touch I cannot block
I close my heart and bolt its lock
My stare is blank into the clock

The tick of time without you here
To fill my world and ease my fear
Is like a pain that will not clear
Your love I feel in every tear

A moment more with you I crave
A simple glance, a wink, a wave
Yet I am trapped in despair's cave
While some strange man prepares your grave

I wish you here dressed blue and white
Your hair aglow bathed in sun light
The tears come strong to blur my sight
As your eyes say be free of fright

I'll miss your love and perfect rhyme
Your tender touch and purest chime
Within my heart you will stay mine
Thank you my love for our time

Thomas Gamet

The Paintbox Lover

When you went, you took away the sun,
And left me only sepia tint and charcoal shading.
My tears have made the watercolors run,
And all your brightest pictures now are fading.
Those days of crimson lake and cobalt are forgotten,
Burnt ocher lies the landscape of my heart;
Spring green is parched now, dead and rotten,
And love alone is scarlet, torn apart.
Though night is black it will be over;
The colors will return, the paper dry,
And the memories of you, my paintbox lover,
Will, like your picture, fade away and die.

Caroline Driggs

America My Country

America my country shines like the sun in the sky.
In the north it has Alaska and Maine, and on the sides oceans
   spread wide.
Rivers like the Mississippi and Missouri flow through the plains.
Here people of all colors, races, and religions live like brothers
and sisters sharing freedom and happiness.
The future will be bright.
The teachers, parents, and doctors work with all their might!
Friends for the sake of our country we love so much, we must
   spread the message of love and trust.

Sarah Shapiro

Spring Is Here!

It is time we shed our coats
And get out our boats.

The first cutting of the grass has come,
So you better get out your lawnmower and run!

The birds are all back from their winter nests
And building their nests for their future invests.

The flowers have stuck out their heads
And you can smell their perfume as they lay in their beds.

Mother Nature has taken out her paintbrush
And everything looks bright and plush.

There is not enough time in the day to pick all the flowers
Or paint the house and fence today,
Because your wife will be giving out orders you have to obey!

Spring is short and the Summer is hot.
So, don't sit around, get off the pot!

Robert Liedtke

'G'Day! Down Under'

'Down Under' you eagerly chose to go
A third time, to catch, That Great Last Show.

Australia has captured both of your hearts
Seems you aimed at 'Down Under' with all your darts.

So, don't miss a thing, while you are still there.
Soak up its beauty, Plus, some to spare.

Australian Splendor is all around
Great scenery, great people, are sure to be found.

Bad weather here, keeps our spirits low,
Mudslides, floods, - rain, ice, and snow.

Sunshine's been sparse, 'nd at times 'A No Show'.
Grey skies look sad, They've Got To Go!

Have a great time in that wonderland
Be sure to go swimming, and bask in the sand.

You Timed It Just Right, to pack-up and go!
Goody! Goody! For You! I Love You Both, So.

We'll Welcome you back, when you return
From that lovely vacation, So Well-Earned!!!

Josephine Spranzo

Thunderstorm

A faint distant rumble is roving the skies.
The glorious sun ephemerally dies.
Darkness is steadily wending its path.
Preparing the way for a long heavy bath.

Louder and nearer comes that angry discord,
Oh! Avenging element created by the Lord.
It is probable that we, as humans, have erred,
And so His vengeance against us is stirred.

In one flash of lightning the whole world is bright,
Defiantly aiding in this chaotic flight.
We stand at the mercy of its unabated fury,
Just as a prisoner in the hands of his jury.

Great splashes of water are now falling down,
Quenching the earth and flooding the ground,
Thrusting aside all in the way,
Gripping the earth as a hunter his prey.

And now, once again, all is peaceful and calm,
While gentle zephyrs soothe like a balm.
Would that emotions would react so in men,
Then, surely there'd be "peace on earth" again.

Rose Vaupen

297

Spring

Spring, a human realm
The ring of the dinner bell.
A lovely season indeed!
A time to plant the flower seed
And pull out the roots of the bamboo reed.
In the winter you can only read about the fresh
hand picked fruit you eat.
The feel of grass getting squashed by your feet
And every scrumptious tasty treat.
Waking up to the smell of spring
And all the things you can bring your mother
like flowers and plants.
You'll march home like army ants,
You'll wear shorts instead of pants.
Now you've got a taste of spring!
Just listen for the birds to sing.

Justin B. Gordon

A Bat

A bat?
No way!
I could do without them any day.
They're ugly and mean.
They're dirty not clean.
You say they're not good and they're bad.
Well this makes me really mad.
They fly at night, that's just normal.
Birds fly in the day, they're not nocturnal.
So bats are really nice and not mean.
And they're also really clean.
Bats are mammals, like a bear.
Bats don't get caught in people's hair.
So what I'm trying to tell you is that
you should really be friends with the bat.
That's what you should really do,
because bats are really nice to you!

Rhiannon M. Trajlinek

The Story

Look at me, now I'm so lonely
I don't know what to do, I don't know what to say
I can't just live without you, missing your every way
The mind can bring you back, even though you're not with me
How can I react to this pain and grief?
I guess you chose her, there is no doubt
I can beg to differ, but you'd shut me out
Those words, said by certain people
Thought we could lost, all the way to the steeple
So many things, but I'll do all I can
Anything, everything, to get my man
But wait! He's running back
Should it be him I take, or is it just a selfish act
This could only happen in my dreams, this can't be for real
He's calling out to me, yet I found myself turning, him stumbling on
   my heels
What about me now you say? I have wandered on my way
Sometimes things are hard to see, but something deep inside of me
Had a special victory
Only my heart knew,
The whole story....

Heather Seymore

People's View

I am defined by my friends
My strengths, weaknesses, generosity, caring, and soul
Friendship has no boundaries
Other then self-love and preservation

Friends are judged by what they need
From what I have to give
Their potential that I see

When people stop seeing them as others do
They realize the truth and worth of another individual
Estimate their value by how they treat and act toward you

Define in your own mind and actions
What a friend is and who yours are
And be proud to be counted

Everyone in this life needs at least one friend
That if boundaries of trust are broken
That the love still binds no matter what
Lord's goal to us all- To Be Like Him

Janna Lee Hankin

"Christmas"

Christmas! 'Tis a joyous time when children's eyes are gleaming,
   At the brightness of so many gifts with bows and ribbons streaming,
At the tree all lit and shining, at the stockings hung with care;
   The red and yellow bike, standing next to the old grey chair.
The children's hands all busy tearing paper, breaking string;
   While outside the frosted window we could hear the carolers sing;
"Peace on earth, good will toward men", and many, many more.
   When in the midst of the excitement, came a knocking at the door;
And in came many more gifts and grandparents full of joy,
   For they had come to spend the day with their favorite girl and boy.
And later on in the evening as the day draws to a close,
   You'll find around the fireplace, an air of great repose;
For the day is finally over and there's joy in every heart,
   For tomorrow is another day, a new Christmas time to start.

Robert W. Glover

Freedom

I know that I won't live to see
Another Statue of Liberty
In a harbor standing free
That's what freedom means to me
For the young, freedom is just a word
They know no other way
But who's to say what's down the road
Or the price they'll have to pay
Life's road's not easy for most of us
We make do with what's at hand
But unless you have been over there
It's hard to understand
This country, our freedom, built with blood and sweat
So many lost, so high the cost, and it's far from over yet
Our choice of work, those dreams we chase
The things that all seem nice
Remember, friends, let's never forget
This all came with a price
Our rights, our privileges, throw in some blessings, too
Then consider all we've endured, we are the chosen few.

Robert LaPierre

The Seasons Of Love

The Winter of Love gives the warmth of a glowing fire
on a cold December night and the sparkle of a new
fallen snow shining in the moonlight.

The Springtime of Love makes each day feel like a new
life just beginning and a great contentment in each
glorious sunset at the day's end.

The Summer of Love gives a breath of fresh air on the
hottest of days and makes the heart flutter like
butterfly's wings.

The Autumn of Love sets the heart aglow with the
brightness of nature's colors and gives the feeling of
wholeness as complete as the seasons be.

Joyce A. Biedler

4:30 AM

It is as cold as it is calm and still
Perhaps it was the quiet that awoke me
Red and Green LED displays softly whisper their times
(some differ from others, but I can't hear it)
Even the little night bumps are so faint
The entire world, save me, must be asleep

Leaning against the window places radiator heat below
The frigid outdoors has chilled the glass pane
There seems a moon glow, but I don't see the moon
The trees are not disturbed; there's no wind at all
A sudden shock of headlights makes my eyes crack
Then, gone as quickly come - one car traffic

Pressures and anxieties intensify in darkness
Avoid "shouldn't haves" and "need tos"
The night is the time for satisfaction
Soothing thoughts and "way to gos"
Let the day worries be settled in light
They're better faced at full advantage

David G. Moser

FreeDom

His walk moved slowly off to nowhere.
He'd bought a book of matches.
His coat looked warm even with the tear,
Front closed with strings and wire latches.

The back pack refused to set.
Motions looked unsure and virginal.
Shoulders pulled forward without a fret,
Right strap snapped free and terminal.

Never hesitated, or step did he miss.
The stride continued in latitude
as the pack dangled, left shoulder, his,
The whole round world remained a platitude.

C. Allan McGowan

I Am

I am the girl who dreams that she will be someone someday
I am the girl who doesn't chase those dreams

I am the girl who knows where she is going
I am the girl who is always lost

I am the girl who judges by wrongs or rights
I am the girl who judges those other than herself

I am the girl who wants to be in love
I am the girl who feels only hate

I am the girl who wants to be beautiful
I am the girl who sees only ugliness

I am not the girl I think I am

Melissa Bailey

Death

I lie on my hospital bed, the doctor sighs, "Any time now,
she will be dead." My mother's hope strains from her face,
"Mama" I whispered, "I'm going to a better place." Mama
stands up, "she's only a child." I close my eyes, my imagination
runs wild. What will happen, and where will I go? The answer
is, nobody knows. I open my eyes, expecting it to still be night, I
am floating in a place, flooded with light. As I lean back,
where is my bed? I discovered a soft cloud behind my head. As I
looked around, a white pony came near, I am puzzled, how
did I get here? I hopped on the pony's back, it took me for a
ride, as we arrived at a gate, I felt all jittery inside. The gate
was lined with flowers, they were all white, I knew right then
that things would be all right. There, sitting on a cloud
was my Grandma, she died at age 87, it finally dawned on me,
I was in heaven! I looked down and saw my parents crying, I
wanted to yell "Mama, I'm here, don't cry!" She couldn't here
me, I let out a sigh. I hugged my Grandma, she said I could
reach my parents some how, I shook my head, "This is my home now."

Laura Abramson

"The Man"

There's a girl I know who's got it made.
God blessed her with the home He gave.

When things are down and she's feeling low,
she knows there's a place she can always go.
To find the understanding she sometimes desires,
because there he will be, the man she admires.

He's showed her how to live, to laugh, and how to love.
He's taught her there is no sorrow she can't rise above.
he made the difference clear between right and wrong.
And he's always been, the man to keep her strong.

Now she doesn't always listen to everything he says.
But when she falls he picks her up again.
He's always there no matter what she does.
And she knows he cares, for he shows much love.

Now the reason that I tell you about this girl.
Is because she's very happy with this old world.
And she wants that man to know the truth.
See the girl is me Dad, and the man, he's you.....

Joyce A. Young

Autumn With Grandma

Cognizant of my growth
Each day we spent
Anticipating the crackle
Of rainbow leaves
Myself, becoming taller and older
With each passing second
My grandmother, the immortal
age — irrelevant to her essence

Now, at the close of each October
When the smell of freshly fallen leaves
Blends with autumn air
She resumes her memorable form
As I look upon her, I retrace youthful steps
In a pink hooded coat
Through the yellows, reds and browns
Blissful regression
I listen to my own impish giggle
Hand over mouth
To muffle the sound
So no one will find me.

Andra Feiner

Mountain Splendor

The beauty of the mountains is grandeur to behold;
from the snow peaks to the river banks its magic it unfolds.
Mountain flowers everywhere, hues of every shade;
constant reminders of the wondrous world God made.
Barren deserts flaked with sand; fertile valleys laid by hand.
Trees which reach up to the sky, touched by clouds as they roll by.
Tranquil forests standing still, while deep reflections work at will.
Canyon gorges shaping pathways; wildlife wandering for days.
The beauty of the mountains manifests in many ways.

Louise I. Moore

Morning

My thoughts of you sleep sweetly on my pillow o'er the night
and come softly as the morning breeze
to awaken me to a fresh new day.
And on the sweet breath of morning
gently soars my soul to thee,
apparent only in the sensuousness of life
born in the womb of nature new.
The birds aflutter on the early breeze,
The water still, sentient, and nurturing
all it bears in rapturous delight.
As morn creeps o'er the land,
life 'wakes fresh and undefiled by day,
and quietly 'waits the sun to christen its rebirth.
I glad'n at the freshness of the new morn
and wear it serenely upon my brow.
And in all the pureness of the air
I feel your presence there
in sweet accord with all the gifts of nature,
and wonder at the nearness of you,
On this new and precious morn.

Sonja F. Burroughs

Niki

Niki, my daughter you've made me proud. You are the
air I breath, the life of my heart, and the strength of my soul.

I called you "Little Bit" before you were born, now
I see you for the beautiful young woman that you've become.

You give to others with no questions ask, yet others
have hurt you and you forgive and go on.

Niki, be strong, be happy and never give up and always keep God
in your heart. For you are his special gift which he gave to me.

With all my love, Mom.

Beverly J. Canada

You Are

You are the center of my life...
All that I do and feel either comes from you or winds its way
    back to you.
You are the purpose of life's experiences...
the fall of the leaves,
the dark of the night,
the warmth of the sun
and the cold blanket of snow.
You are the meaning of each breath
you are my little girl, a daughter full of tomorrow's promises.
You are the reason to continue to aspire to be more than I am.

Suzi Beeby

My Daughter

I watch her closely
The little affectations of her age were once mine
Flirtatious tossing back of the long, brown mane
Eyelids closed a second too long when the question is dull
The giggle sarcastic, self-conscious, too loud.
Do I like her? I'm not sure.
I miss my chubby-legged little girl
Who is now this long-limbed beauty
With the face of a Flemish madonna
Those rocking gurgles or mirth have gone the way of her Barbie
    dolls and buck teeth
In their place is a perfect smile
The artistry of her orthodontist evident
Hiding yearnings and secrets I fear and recognize.
We have grown up in different worlds
My daughter and I
She must learn to be a woman and I
I must learn to let her do it her own way
And love what she is
And not what I could not be

Vera Buglione

The Navy Wife

As I live each day as a Navy Wife,
I find that I lead a very rich life.
For the friends I make along the way,
Help to brighten even the darkest day.
When the days grow long and time stands still,
My friends help me make it over that hill.
The Good Lord knows how to show us the way,
So he brings us together each and every day.
Friends like mine are so very few
Cause they give with their hearts the way that I do.
Deployments are rough, each and every one,
But my friends make sure that I have some fun.
As our ship deployed on her final West Pac,
We planned and prepared for her return back.
After our loved ones return home from sea,
My friends will always remain special to me.
You see, I truly do have a very rich life,
Cause I live each day as a Navy Wife.

Vicki M. Spaulding

Untitled

Around us it's sunny
The wind is warm as it blows
People laugh, sounding happy
We all lie sometimes,

She says I hope you don't mind
If I'm completely real
Because I think really
We have nothing to lose;

Her arms around me, she cries
for her pain and my pain
And this world neither of us understands

She see's everything as beautiful
Even in its blackness;

She feels always alone, and she smiles,
A smile that lights up her face
but beneath the glimmer in her eyes
is a distance you can't reach
A sadness only she can touch.

And she thinks death is freedom
and life the hell we must conquer first.

Jeannie S. Jeffrey

A Song Of Life

The little house wakes slowly in the pre-light of dawn,
Opening its windows to the rising sun.
Its inhabitants stir themselves in preparation for the unfolding day,
Each to his chosen task of labor.

As the day grows older, the desire to achieve and conquer
Makes the struggle greater.
And that desire sustains them
Through whatever comes their way.

The long shadows of evening bring the weary laborers home
Anxious to rest and relax,
Sharing their victories with loved ones and friends
To forget the fears and frustrations of the day.

So may I, when evening's sun is setting and dusk drifts slowly down,
Have grace and wisdom to lay aside the toils of the day,
And enjoy to the fullest
The beauties of the approaching night.

Chrystal Wamsley

"The Beauty Of Love"

The flowers are blooming.
The rivers are flowing
The birds are singing.
My heart is gay.
I love flowers.
Roaring rivers.
Yes, my heart is full of love.
For the one I love.
The love of my dream, my love flow for
you like an endless stream.
Oh, love of all love, how beautiful it shine.
Like the glitter of priceless gem.
Like the brightest star in the heaven
Like the early morning dew.
My love, my entire being shine out with
all my love for you.
So let your love flow for me, like the
current of the sea.
Come, let us enjoy the beauty of love
Throughout eternity.

Esther Jenkins

Deep Dark Thoughts

With my black mind comes my black face along with my black
lips - I have black hands - I have black feet - and when I
leave here I'll be taking a black on black wall - U. Want to
go - come on - just put on your black coat - Oh! And you can
leave your gats and player hater stands at the door because
we're going to have some black on black fun - you're definitely
gone think beautiful black thoughts and have sweet black
dreams on our black on black trot! - one day with my womanly
strength I'll be able to lay hands on my brothers and sisters
like a healer and stop all this black on black crime black
on black think on brothers and sisters we've thought up on
some things - black on black thoughts - just remember what
your momma's and grandmomma's used to tell U. Hold your head up
high and your shoulders back and always remember this sister
for her sweet black thoughts - I'm out of here - peace -
gotta go take my black on black wall

Overstanding Misunderstood Understanding
Vivian Kincaid

Morning Glory

As morning rises, it's like God
Is giving you, a new canvas, to paint
a new picture.
I love to make, the new painting,
better than, the
previous.
The proud cock, wakes the sun,
the sun rises over the mountain,
bringing glorious light,
to every thing it touches,
awakening life to the land.
I awaken, as the day passes
I conquer a goal!
And make things better,
than yesterday.
I also make mistakes, which gives
tomorrow to improve.
When day is gone, it's beautiful,
better than yesterday but never perfect.
That! gives me reason to live.

Branden Mattox

Posy Smellers On Bike Trips

We bask in all the sunshine, we laugh at all the rain;
We stop at half the bridges - we're thought to be insane.

We smell at all the posies, we poke at all the fun.
We pick at all the berries (we're stuffed when day is done).

We push up half the uphills - coasting down is our reward.
We're tired when day is over - at least we're never bored!

We snap at all the pictures, we shout Go Home to dogs.
We dress for any weather (you'll know us by our togs).

We love to meet the natives; we stand and gab awhile-
Don't cover many miles this way, but how we love each mile!

We take some unplanned detours - it's known as getting lost.
We huddle under trees to wait when we are tempest-tossed.

(By the way, we even have one hardy soul who goes swimming when
it is raining and the rest of us all bundled up in our parkas).

We thank God for His bounty, the scenery that we see,
The friendships that we cherish, -Adventures that will be.

Eyrlis McClish

Rodeo

The pressure is on.
This is it!
The final draw
which boils down to the three
finalists on their way to the Palace.
The run had to be perfect!
Nothing could go wrong.

I came in on the haul
and saw a light that said,
"Go for it".
The wind whipping my face,
sent a sensation through my spine.
As I weave through the
red, white and blue,
pushing, leaning, coaxing,
I knew I had done it.
My heart was ready to burst,
my chest ready to explode!
My companion and I were on our way to the gold!

Emily Burfield

Good

I think every human being
Should do and think good of each other;
and when this love accomplished, What a wonderful
world this would be. "Can't you see"
Let's do this for each other especially for you and for me.

Stop the war, fighting and crimes it is not
necessary. Be thoughtful and considerate in what
you do. I want you to know a lot of love from
your heart. Just show some smart.
    "Just do good"
Like the way you should.

Neville Brown

What Is Love

Love, Love is so strange. It's complex
and uncertain, it can not be explained
Love, one day it's warm, and the next day
it's cold as the wind driven storm.
Oh Love, I'd like to know, does it come
from heaven, like the rain and the snow?
Where does love go?
Love, what does love mean? Is it just an emotion,
a plan or a smoke screen?
We can't see love, so we say Love is blind.
I wonder if it's imagination playing tricks,
on a sullied mind.
Today love made us happy, but tomorrow it
could bring us tears.
Of one thing though, we can be certain.
This thing called love, has been around for years and years.
Love, it can't be defined with no end or
beginning, nor measured by time.
Love, is love really real? Then why can't
we explain it, and the feelings we feel? Just what is love?...

Liz Beaver

Where Was Mine?

When I made my first touchdown...   Where was mine?
When I swished my first basket... Where was mine?
When I got my first 10 Speed... Where was mine?
When a nice girl got to call me for the first time Where was mine?
When I began to steal Where was mine?
When I was in need of that special conversation Where was mine?
When my friend was jumped Where was mine?

I think about that question "Where Was Mine", and when I do I
wonder, Why, Why
Why do I even have to ask.

Where Was Mine? Is a question that isn't the focus of my life.
This is because of She!
She, who wrestled and played with me as a boy
She, who spanked and punished me for my wrong
Even though She is not He
She was mine, She is mine, Always has been, Always will be Mom
The savior, protector and guardian to many.
Mom.

Christopher Gerome Cole-Bailey

"Sounds Of Freedom"

When sonic booms ring loud and clear
My land is safe and free from fear
And roof tops shake and windows rattle
Then I know peace reigns instead of battle.

May these booms I continue to hear
Sounds of freedom, music to my ear
May God guide those who above us fly
Like defenders at Concord, Minutemen of the sky.

Eldon H. White

Untitled

Spring is like a rainbow,
appearing after a rainstorm.
    The bramble bee's buzzing with the wind,
is like a whisper in your ear.
    The ocean waving gently,
is like a joyful, salty tear.
    The moon softly glowing,
is like the child's happy face.
    A predator escaping from its prey,
is like conquering life's hardest race.
    When spring is over everything will go away
but you know it will be back again,
    like waiting for the sun to shine
after a rainy day.

Sarah Sylvestre

In Loving Memory Of Ed U Kation (1880-1996)

Today we celebrate the life of Ed U. Kation;
a man that once prospered in teaching a nation.
Reared by reading, writing and arithmetic;
his early days proved but successful and hectic.
America asked that all, not some, acquire his traits;
movements and legislation opened the gates.
Eventually we became a nation to be reckoned with;
Ed's unselfish love gave us the advantage and wits.
As time went by, Ed progressed in years;
lost, were his ability to reach new peers
He lost his stronghold in many a county and city;
his final days were spent in despair and pity.
Though dying inside, he always appeared happy;
finally succumbing to social breakdown and apathy.
His spirit will never be weighted, not even by rocks;
the door is still open to anyone that knocks.
Though his untimely death overshadowed his birth;
we give him thanks for putting America first.

Jermaine Bruner

The World Goes Round And Round

As the world goes round and round
smiles turn into frowns, and sometimes the
other way round.
    Babies come out crying knowing in the
end they'll be dying.
    Stars she bright as lights as dreams
some to their heights
    With no end and no begging, time flies
by while singing
    With tunes that's heard, some absurd,
Throughout time which is all mine to spend
and mend, until my end,
    As the world goes round and round
with no begging and no end.

Jen Wulwick

Highway Journey

The summer sun beats down on me, on you.
Alone, I sit in my car, hands on the wheel,
Parked unnoticed among all the other cars.

From here, I see the constantly moving highway;
It is a journey of others going anywhere.
I close my eyes in a well rehearsed parody of my own.

My mind travels the road, fast and knowingly,
wishing for you, searching for your eyes your touch.
I search for your warm sun and white clouds.

I miss you, my love, my husband who answers the call
of duty to this country which is our home.
Do you feel my warm breath? No it is only the wind.

Lori Green

Bombing Of Oklahoma

Burning buildings everywhere
Smells of darkness here and there
Horrible for the people who live in this state
They'll never for get this really bad fate
Singing songs so that fears die
And that they go away so they don't just sit here and lie
I hope you're safe
Just stay with the pace.

   Good luck Oklahoma I'll always think about you the people
that had to suffer.

Jonathan Park

Getting It Off My Chest

Isn't it sad what love can do?
It brought us together, me and you.

To a life full of hope and companionship and wishes to fulfill.
Dreams come to light, what was all up now downhill.

Then time and life's trials, losses not counted on made us grow apart.
One of us decided to find another heart.

And now that it's done, we're no longer two,
Not happy not together, lots of regretting it's true.

Isn't it sad what love can do?

Kay Cox

A Savior Is Born

God said, "I want the sky to be swept clean,
I want the stars polished to a brilliant sheen,
I want the angels to be in spotless array,
So the heavens can herald a miraculous day.
The Savior of the World will be born in a manger of hay.
Wise men will travel from afar to adore
And Shepherds will kneel at the stable door".
You come, too, to sing his praise
And stay close to Jesus
The length of your days.
May God always be your guide
And love, joy, and peace in your heart's abide.

Dorothy L. Peek

Untitled

My people must overcome our former
oppressors; now is the proper time more than ever.
They say there's not a shred of decency in us,
Striving for our dignity and self respect is a must.
Our satisfaction is urgent and very much a necessity.
The history of this world has been
resistantly revealed to me
I am very fortunate; for my upbringing will
have not been affected with such injustice and hatred.
As I undergo hardships I shall not ask anyone
for permission to love my youthful life,
I shall not be approached by a situation in
which my self respect is sacrificed.
My ambition as to go on a mission. To grope for
my immortal happiness, and to accomplish all
that I must and wish.
Loving thy self is the true beauty in living.
For happiness shall await you; you shall feel
more forgiving.

Xi'an Glynn

Friend

What is a friend to you? Or, do you even know?
Is it someone you can trust or, just another place to go?
Actually, it's quite simple; at least it is to me
So, keep on reading this poem if you would like to see
A friend is someone you feel comfortable with whenever you're
  together
A friend is someone who is there for you always and forever
Someone who is always there to help when you are in need
Someone who praises you whenever you succeed
Someone who'll share a dry shoulder when you feel the need to cry
Someone who will give good advice when you wonder why
Someone to talk to when you want to clear your mind
Someone to have fun with when you want to unwind
Someone with whom you can share your thoughts and dreams
I know there isn't many like that, or so it seems
When you want to share a secret, that is where a friend comes in
Someone who is on your side whenever you lose or win
I hope you understand what I am trying to make you see
Is that when you're in need, you can find a friend in me!

Karen Byers

Happy Mother's Day

Happy Mother's Day, Mother
Beautiful woman, woman of the fields, you who gave me life
You who sat and watched over me when I slept on my cradle bed
And shed tears of affection and joy
When pain and sickness made me cry, you who gazed up
  on my heavy eyes
And wept for fear that I might die
You who taught my infant lips to pray, to love God's Holy Book
  day and night
And to walk in wisdom and pleasant way
You who is always proud of my achievements, although little
  they may be
When you would become feeble, old and gray, my healthy arms
  shall be your stay
And I will shoot your pains away
Oh! No, the thoughts I cannot bear, but If God shall spare my life
  I hope I shall reward my cares

Chuks L. Iheke

For Seen Reflections

Sights seen in the waters's reflections
Visions of what the earth right become
Do you dare to wonder what they are.
I will just tell you one.
I foresaw the world and the people crying
out in screams of pain.
Is this what happens to earth and all its beautiful plain
There were no trees or no flowers anymore
Is this a punishment from our Lord.
Or is this mankind's greed and wealth.
Is this our fate, I believe it's not
to late the vision here can be changed
I know a paradise can be gained.
We all have a choice.
We all have a voice.
We all can come together
So our children can live on earth forever
If we live in peace
Throw down our guns
A new way of life can come.

Tanya Cashion-Watson

Walk With Me

Travel with me through the sleepless lands,
Feel the dreams of lost souls.
Walk with me hand in hand
Into eternal tales told.

It is here you shall learn of life and death,
See the horrors of the soul,
Live the life of those that can not rest
Deep within the loud.

From this point on I go no more.
You must travel on alone,
For my powers are for merely war
And death has called me home.

Conquer the darkness in your heart,
Feel the power of the land,
Let your spirit loose, for this place to part,
Then please retake my hand.

And guide me through life's trail,
Let the darkness pass beyond,
For together we can not fail,
For true love is an eternal bond.

Robert Hight Jr.

The Ocean

The ocean is blue and calm
The waves crash along the shore
Ripping and tearing everything in its path
The fish wandering around in the ocean
Swimming from here to there in a flash
And the seagulls soar over the ocean
While lighthouses flash around
Here and there
Far and near
As far as the eye can see

White the sunsets over the shore
The ocean
What a thought
Never a thought so beautiful
Would ever be created by man

Eden Dozier

Untitled

The office chills me by its air conditioned frigidity
But outdoors all is warm and filled with beauty.
My mind's eye sees the vibrant green of the dogwood leaves
As I type names and addresses on envelopes.

How long the hours grow if thoughts turn to the lake
Where my four-footed friend walks with me along the shore.
The great blue heron takes flight and pulls my eyes skyward
And striking fish cause bubbles to play on the water's surface.

Hurry, clock! Move on, hands! The lake is waiting
And so is my four-footed friend.

Darolyn M. Weaks

The Only One

For whom this may concern for thee I'll gently stand aside;
With hopes she'll stand besideth me where others can't abide;

Displaying what I've earned I'll give; for thee I shall provide
A way of life that she can live, though I may stand denied;

And all I've ever learned I'll hand to thee and we'll confide;
Our substances impaired will stand renewed as they collide;

For thee I'll always yearn and shall continue in my stride
To see for whom this may concern who's my best friend
  and is my bride.

Brian P. Cluse

A Prayer

Upon a long and muttered breath
Came a pain with sudden death
In a room where she now lays
With hope for life her family prays
A room full of love knelt to their knees
Begging and hoping, asking God please
Let her live, give one last chance
Let her live to finish her dance
She so has loved and praised you humbly
Yet you take her away with a death come suddenly
They all held hands, pleading why
We love her so, don't let her die
In the end she got the chance
To awake and finish her dance
With a pain like a needle, a needle with a sharpness
He took her away, back into the darkness
Then the saviors came to mention
There's now no chance of her redemption
In her bed, she's now passed on
A better place is where she's gone.

Catrina Dick

Roots

Let our love be deep and strong as the roots of the birch.
And like their branches, may we bend with resilience in the storms
  of life.
And sway together in the gentle breezes of joy.
Let our marriage provided the shade and shelter for the product of
  our seed.
As we are united as One, for today, tomorrow, and for life.

Janice Du Bois

If I Could Give The World A Gift I'd Choose Love

If I could give the world a gift,
I'd choose love,
Lots of love.

Picture the world full of people who care,
with everyone treating each other fair.

If I could give the world a gift,
I'd choose love,
Lots of love.

No swearing, no fighting, no guns, no drugs,
just happy people giving lots of hugs.

If I could give the world a gift,
I'd choose love,
Lots of love.

Jennifer Goeddertz

The Wind, The Spirit

The wind you can see,
  you know it's there by how it
  affects things around it.

The holy spirit you can't see,
  but know it's here by how it
  affects the people who have
  been touched by him.

As the wind comes as a gentle breeze,
  or a gale wind its presence becomes known,
  so does the holy spirit like a gentle touch
  or sometimes it comes in a tragedy we experience.

James Burkett

My Little Brother!!

He will fuss
And he will cuss he can knock
But he would rather not
He will stomp on the floor
And kick in your door
He has a lot of fun
Especially when he plays guns
With all the noise he makes
You would think he was grounding in a lake
He likes to be a dog and jump like a frog
He goes fast in his truck
But some times he gets stuck
It is just a power-wheel
But he thinks it's real
He follows me every where
With his fuzzy hair
He likes to rassel
And play in his castle
He likes to shoot me with his toy gun
And dance to third rock from the sun

Nicole Gilpin

Ruthless Heart

In a space devoid of dimension,
they exist in fantastic reality.
Down a path trodden by time,
they pace in ceaseless circles.
With a desire fed by fear,
they embrace the shadow of all things.
And in a voice plagued with pain,
they scream in piercing silence.

In a sea of confusion,
the walls of the mind grow thin
In a wave of emotion
the reason of life drowns.
Muted by unrelenting apathy
and silenced by unattainable peace,
The swells of two hearts rise
uniting the tides and leaving no dry harbor for thoughts.

Krista Ramyead

Untitled

Here Ye, here ye, here ye, welcome, all gather around,
to meet the most wonderful mother in town.
She's got taste, class, personality and yes, eight children to boot,
why she's wise, and some may say, even cute.
A comic, yet, down-to-earth soul she possess
Performing miracles better than Houdini and all the rest.
To know her, is to love her, every one agrees.
Her dedication to her family, co-workers, and friends
are a blessing indeed like a cougar-sleek and smooth,
everyone wants to know her moves.
Powerful and strong like a locomotive she is, twenty-four seven,
Yes, I know she has a special place in heaven.
Her words are gentle, and loving, and spoken to touch one's heart,
for this mother I shall never part,
Rubies, diamonds, and pearls is what she deserves to behold,
because no one match her beauty-not even gold.
So, here to Ms. Frances Trowell Gomillion the best mother of all,
May we congratulate you on a job well done
and may you be happy, successful and loved by all.
So, it is written, so, it shall be done.

Robin Gomillion

Guitar Man

Guitar man you are old
Yet all you sing about is love.

You sing of a maiden whose lips are petals
But the words implore sorrow
As if she should mourn you.

Is it a young girl sing for,
Sweet as the rain of your guitar
Lips swollen at its strings
That your fingers might never grow cold?

Or do they climb the last frets
With a smile of cold distance, slowing
The strings and kissing your fingers-

Until your song is a moan on the ice wind
Begging her to take you with her.

Albert Sigal

Is It Love Or Destiny?

I have a love who lives across the way, I think of him every
        minute of the day.
His eyes, how they sparkle with stars from the sky.
His lips tender like grapes from a vine
Oh, how I wish he were mine
I've told him I felt, his response was to ignore me
Like I was a window, something he could glance through
We're like two that pass each other on a foggy night
with so-sign of hope for a guiding light
They say 'beauty is within', if this is true, why can't people
        except you for you?
Instead of what they want you to be.
But I haven't given up hope because hope, what becomes
        of destiny and the feeling of need?
To be loved, feel passion on that special feeling you hold
        within to go on,
In search of a love that never needs to end.

Kim Celeda Gabor

Rainbow

A full ninety one years, the world has been
her stage and she used it well.
Her strong character and loving strength and
love to her family, her friends and sometimes strangers too.

Dip in the rainbow and color her love.
No task was too great to undertake.
If help was needed she asked God to help her do
what she could not do alone. Yes, she accomplished a lot.

Dip in the rainbow and color her bright.
Her unselfish love she shared with
all from the shores of New Jersey,
to the shores of California.
Nursing the sick feeding the poor and teaching the children too.

Dip in the rainbow and color her good.
To the heavens that innocent souls has fled.
Leaving a christian testimony of her faith that shall never die.
This jewel, that we have lost on this earth,
the heavens her spirit has gained.
We shared her with you, as "Sister Warnick"
We call her "Big Mommie". She was our rainbow.

Nancy Warnick

Once Upon On School Day Dreary...

Once upon a school day dreary,
I fell asleep, tired and weary.
I dreamed a dream of terrific horror
And of a hero who is a magnificent soarer.
I was kidnapped by a big, bad man
Who tied me by a rope, foot and hand.
And as I started to break down and cry
I turned my head up to the sky.
There I saw the most awesome sight;
Superman in his fantastic flight.
He scared my awful kidnapper astray,
Untied my limbs then flew away.
I was left alone staring after my Superman
When I felt something strange upon my hand.
There was Superman's insignia on a gold ring,
He was my Superman, my hero, and my king.
There was where I had suddenly awoke,
Looked upon my hand and began to choke;
For there was Superman's insignia on a gold ring,
He is my Superman, my hero and my King.

Jaime Anne Hassler

Rebirth

Desolate and gray
Seems the winter day
White is the deep snow
Bold is how the ghostly wind will blow
The rising temperature is nice
It melts the cold snow and ice
The sun shines bright
There are longer days than nights
Spring is here!
Warmer days are very near

The earth is wet with rain
As the budding trees are no longer plain
The flowers bloom in pink and white
The warm sun's rays are always bright
The dead brown grass turns a lush green
The bold wind is no longer mean
Birds and butterflies flutter around
As rabbits and foxes scurry on the ground
Spring is here!
There are no more winter colds to fear

Jaimie Just

The Newborn Spring

As you take in your first breath
Mother nature rejoices
For her last was stillborn
New baby, see your world:
Grass the color of dismay and decay
Wind pricking goose bumped skin
Sky the color of lonely hearts
What a world to be born in!
Stars and comets
Are your mobile for
Chubby fingers to feel
Mashed hail, jarred clouds
The elements for your first meal
Butterflies, birds, beetles, and bees:
Sing him your gentle lullabies
While delicate breezes rock him to sleep
Sweet child: Close your tired eyes
Dream your dreams and sigh your sighs
Goodnight little one
Goodnight

Kelly Ann Pearson

Knowing Why

A part of us is gone to never return,
why he is gone we will never know.
Pain, has replaced the hose that was left,
there is no way to describe how we fell and burn.

Only a few understand what we feel,
we hope no one else will have to ever understand.
Long are our days,
and some nights become hell.

We love, like never before,
but we'll never be whole again.
Our trust is still there,
and we'll never understand why.

Fred H. Weeks Jr.

Someone Set Me Free

I'm trapped in a dark dream
    that is full of evil beings.
I wondered if I'll ever be free
    from my never ending dream.
I pretended not to care, if I'm not free
    from my nightmare dream.
I worried that nobody will ever set me free.
I'm trapped in my dark lonely dream.
I thought I say a hand reaching out to me.
I reach out to touch it, but it disappear
    like magic into the dark, cloudy, quiet night air.
It was only hallucination in my mind.
I say it didn't matter, but it did.
I wanted to be as free as the blowing wind.
I wished someone would set me free my dark dream.
But until that someone come along.....
My knight in his shinning armour, to set me free
    from my dark, lonely never ending dream.
I am trapped in my dark, lonely dream!

Kia Moua

Mountain Peaks

  Mountain peaks so high in the sky—
Almost too high to see the top with a human eye.
Beautiful Eagles fly gracefully by the top
Soaring, soaring without taking of stop.
The beautiful Eagles soaring as light as a feather—
Determining, predicting on the peak our future weather.
Glittery snow on the mountain peak -
Too beautiful for words, one is not able to speak.
The peak is now hidden behind a fluffy cloud—
"What a sight!" I exclaim, thinking out loud.
Everyday I come out to enjoy the view—
I bet if you were there with me, you'd enjoy it, too.
The time comes for me to leave, my sadness I can't hide—
But to the rules I must abide.
Looking at the top—
I say, "goodbye"—
Glancing at the peak, so high in the sky.

Alma Cacan

The Beauty Of The World

The beauty of the world, means so much to me.
The beauty of the world seems so much to be.
Beauty, beauty is in the air
I could look at a rabbit or stare at a hare
I could gaze at flowers for hours upon end
But that's only when I'm not driven 'round the bend.

Christopher Hannigan

The Dance

I danced in the morning when the world was begun
I danced in the moon, the stars and the sun
I came down to heaven and danced on the earth
And at Bethlehem I had my birth
So dance wherever you may be
I am the Lord said He
I'll lead you all wherever you may be
I'll lead you all in the dance he said
I danced for the scribes and the Pharisees
But they wouldn't dance, they would not follow me
I danced for the fishermen, for James and John
They came with me and the dance went on
I danced on Friday when the sky turned black
It's hard to dance with the devil on your back
They buried my body and thought I was gone
But I am the dance and I still go on
They cut me down and I leaped up high
I am the life that will never, never die
I live for you, you live for me
I am the Lord of Dance said He

Donald L. Marshall

In The Deep Blue Sky

In the deep blue sky
I see your face.
And always ask why?
Why did you have to leave this place?

I know in my heart it's great up above.
But down here you had so much love.

I miss you so very much.
Night after night, I twist and turn, longing for your touch.

The memories I have are as real as ever.
Oh Nani, I'll forget you never.

Whenever you're ready, I will be waiting.
Hugs and kisses I'll be anticipating.

Until then, I'll look up in the deep blue sky,
Knowing you're that pretty white dove that always flies by.

Michele LaGiusa

Happiness

Can happiness be possessed?
Like property, like inheritress.
Does it control or command?
Does it rule as king or is it a tyrant?

Is it a swagger, that walks through our existence?
Or is it the alms, given to the poor, broken hearted despondence

Can it be legislated?
Can you promise or guarantee it?
Did pharaohs, fuhrers, and presidents,
Esoterically have the intelligence?

Is it pervasive, and we're too blind to see?
Or maybe it vacillates, in the mix of variety.

Some claim to have embraced it.
Several say they were sated by it.
A few have been miffed by it.
But we all dream of it.

Happiness, what is it?
What is it for?
Are we to possess it?
Or is it an open door?

Evelyn Williams

Mother

I'd like to send a bouquet your way
Since this is your special day.
But what flower should I choose?
One kind of flower just wouldn't do for you.

A flower's beauty alone doesn't mean my Ma!
But what the pollen that's found in them all.
For Mother, you're the inner part of life
Before you were my Mother, you were a wife.

Your caring was so strong and needed more to love
So God knew your soul and sent children from above.
Therefore I thank you Lord for my Mother
She is better than any other.

Deanna Doolin

Untitled

I look at the word outside
and it just tears me up inside
I hurt for God's green earth that once was
I hurt for the animals that
roam free, no longer
I hurt for the pain in your eyes
I hurt for my sadness inside
I want so desperately
to live, to feel, to grow
I long to be me
So today I leap with broken wings
trusting that you'll catch me if I fall
I'm committed to being as real
as I can possibly be
no matter how scared or terrified I might be
I dare to be me
totally and completely
To have the strength and courage
to stand alone in my nakedness
and expose my authentic true self

Lori Zimbra

Memories Never Die

Soft foot tapping
rhythmic hand clapping,
on the evening of a long-ago July
"Ah" says grandpa
but, time has gone, time has passed,
but memories never die."
Warm summer's evening,
breeze blows gently.
She leans back and she sighs.
"Ah" says grandma,
"But, time has gone,
time has passed,
but memories never die."
this day I'll remember
when I am old.
What's happening now
will be long ago.
I'll lean back in the breeze, and gently...
I'll sigh...
Because memories never die.

Amanda Begley

Blinded

Angels shy away from your face,
made bashful by the glow of your eyes—
more innocent, more trusting than theirs.

Your soul shines through to people,
giving understanding and shedding new light
on emotions once thought impossible.

The caress of your grin
as your cheeks blush and sparkle
sends thoughts into a frenzy of adoration.

You emulate love.
You exude it from every pore,
giving it so freely
to my other wise empty heart.

And I feel a pulsing through my skin
beating words of love for you.

Joanna B. Capps

Blossom And Explore

And you said that if I kneeled and prayed,
I'd hear the voice of reason say,
That the children have all walked away
And don't know to ask or care to stay

It's a simple world
It's a simple line
It's a simple code
That I must find,
But it's lost
It's gone
It's nowhere near
And I've asked the children
If they could hear
They are in a world
Lost in time do they really care
If versus rhyme?

And you said that if I kneeled and prayed,
I'd hear the voice of reason say
That the children have all walked away
And don't know to ask or care to stay

Eric Schempp

Goddess

Across the event horizons of ten thousand black holes, She waits:
Resplendent, bold, black as the heart of space
  Spirit of woman, celestial Goddess
  Alpha and omega of this quiet, desperate plane
And I—I the humble son of beaten—do want her.

O! To know the lips of paradise, and live among Gods,
  A mortal man star-blessed
To ride the flaming sail up, up to the stars!
To build resplendent castle so gorgeous
  She extols my work, and even dwells a pace—
And I—I the humble son of beaten slaves—do want her.

To explore!—more than all who've seen the hazy edge of space—
And leap the event horizon
  Where time and apace slows down, and reality falls apart
And there, in the firmament of nature's ti light, find her—
  Spirit of woman
  Celestial Goddess
  Queen of quasars
  Alpha and omega of this desperate plane.
And I—I the humble son of beaten slaves—do want her.

Antony K. Haynes

God's Musical Dance Of Nature

I hear a bird in song
Singing opera to its own kind
Seeking the next wonder what will we find?

The wind us humming a breezy tune
from the top of the hill
Persuading the largest tree to movement even the daffodils

The clouds are in abundance all grey and blue
A modern dance of expression for you
Here comes the tender singing the blues
Rain falls tap dancing in twos

As the sunshine awakens
to embrace this canvas of a sky
God paints a rainbow that comes from up high

For this production is in its final stage
The mountains echo songs of praise
As our loving saviour speaks through the purple haze
Remember that you have a choice
Walk in faith then hear my voice
Follow the pathway of God's musical dance of nature

Wanda Ann Dillard

"The Mirror"

She leans into the mirror and she dabs her puffy eyes.
The that's reflected only makes her realize
That fifty years of living is a justified excuse
For feeling tired of giving and feeling very used.

Her daughter's grown so distant and her son is now aware
Of other ways of comfort and her husband doesn't care.
They all seem not to need her now, but it wasn't long ago,
She was the center of their and they often told her so.

She wonders where the time has gone that robbed her of her youth.
She now is painfully aware that she's staring at the truth.
The mirror does not tell the lie—she justs looks the other way.
She stares into it blindly—and remembers—yesterday.

Wil Raynor

The Vision

I once looked in a looking glass
and saw lovely fields of plush green grass.

The flowers too, were bright and gay
with a gentle breeze to make them sway.

Then a gentle voice spoke from a cloud
it was so soft and yet so loud.

It said this world was made for thee
but you have forgotten me.

I am the one whose on his way
and if you're smart you'll prepare today.

To receive me in your home tonight
Where I will shine an undiming light.

Peter C. Sjoberg

Human Contact

A hug, a touch
These mean so much.
The human warmth thus transferred
Is always to mere words preferred.
The human contact calms the soul,
Makes us all feel one, feel whole.
Extend a hand to touch another,
To soothe your child, to greet your brother.
Can any phrase say quite as much
As a kind and gentle, loving touch?

Greg Cote

Our Prayer

Dear Lord keep her sweet in thy tenderest care
For we know she patiently awaits us there
Keep her smiling and happy in her hoe above
Where there is no more hatred but all is love.

Dear lord for her our tear drops fail
For she no more doth answer our call.
But help us to see and to understand
She is happy now in a better land.

It seems to us we can hear say
"Grieve not dear ones, I am just away
I've gone to heaven with Jesus to be
Till you dear ones, all come to me."

So dear Lord, please guide feet
Till in that beautiful city, we soon shall meet
And when our toils on earth are o'er
Let us rejoice with thee evermore.

Caryl Anderson Toedter

My Soul Aches

Son, you are my son, my first born, my name sake. And, when I think
of all the memories, my heart cries... My soul aches.

How did you get so mixed up? Was it the pressure of being a man?
I did my best to explain things to you, I thought of all people you
would understand.

But you went on, you did your own thing. You lost all self-control.
Yeah! Son, you got so high and might you didn't try to see the
picture as a whole. You got mixed up. Got with the wrong kind of
crowd, out there; acting like you had no upbringing, out there;
Talking bad, out there—talking loud.

Son, I tried to love you but you got grown; didn't want me around
But I'm the one starting while you're six feet underground.

It just don't make no kind of sense, but I'm trying to understand.
Son was what you did in your short life your meaning of a man?

I know I taught you better. I know I did my best. And, I hope
and try pray that maybe, one day your soul will finally rest.

Son, you are my son, my first born—my name sake.
And, when I think of all that could have been,
My heart cries...my soul still aches.

Kimberlee A. Lucas

And God Wept

Arched doors beckoned towards the candlelit altar,
Jeweled angelic madonnas danced crucifixes, heavy with gold,
Candles bought for a sucre,
The poor came to worship.

"Oh, Hail Mary, Mother of Our Lord,
A piece of crust to give us strength," echoed the footfalls of peasants
Who trod, piling stone on stone,
To build the altar of rock, and gold.

The rich swept in, smiling on godly gold,
Worship the altar mankind has built to worship the Lord and Master.

The peasant, broken from the day's load,
Trudged to mud and thatch.
"Lord Our Lord Thy Kingdom come,
Why doesn't man love his own kind?"

"Beggar, vayas! Go, wretched one!"
The rich, tightening their collars, struck the peasant from the path.
"Oh, Hail Mary, the Lord is Good,
Look upon our Altar and Bless us."
And God, looking upon what man had wrought wept.

Barbara Fitch Haumann

Masked

It's a mask
   you see that hides me.
It's just a shallow image
   of what's really me —
      hidden deep—buried
      still.
That's where the
   real me dwells.
      Frightened and alone
      I seek solace there alone
Only daring and wishing someone
   would reach deep and find the real me.
Hovering in the past, a sea
   of great despair,
      lost vision, hope—just despair.
   Oh, the pain that comes from the deep—
      Oh, the joy to know, to believe someone
      would seek me there.
Dig deep my friend, rescue me from within
   past the shallow mask I wear.

Roslyn Havertape

The Killer Of Us All

Shots ring through my ears, like fire crackers,
Only quicker, faster, sharper,...deadlier.
The whimpers of babies death calls from the wounded.
Violence controls.
Children crying, people dying.
Crime at its highest, outsiders biased.
Rapes and killings police help unwilling.
Violence controls. The blood flows everywhere.
All are wounded even those who are not hurt, but too, are aching and
enduring the agonizing pain.
They are onlookers, the ones spared for now at least.
The hearts and souls deteriorate, minds become despondent.
Violence controls. Shot after shot, day after day.
The commotion never ceases.
It is not safe here, but no where to refuge.
Struggling to live each day more give into death, risking their own lives.
Confined to hell, the Angel of death has come for us all.
Slowly but surely pealing us off our planet, one by one.
Endure the pain, endure the pain, for violence forever controls.

Julia Renee Lissner

Eros-Ion

The sun rises behind the clouds
of a dark September morning,
concealing the summer joy
that was ours so briefly.
The light rains that once were welcome,
cooling the skin, inviting us to slip
into each echo my sadness.

Longing wades furtively toward winter
in the wake of a jealous sea,
to an island that demands devotion
and offers simply survival.
I surf, riding the excitement of your waves,
only to be dropped
on the beaches of my belonging,
while your tide slowly ebbs.

Diffusion.
A puddle of stilled desire,
I reflect the sun and am absorbed.
Beneath the sands, I listen for you to break
from the deep and return.

Brian J. McCormick

You Can't Go Back

I have returned at times to youthful scenes.
  My comrades all have gone,
The schoolrooms look so tiny, the grounds so small.
  You can't go back.

The girl who knew the latest dances is matronly mature.
  She speaks of recipes and kids.
The boy with whom I made the team, and envied for his popularity,
  sells insurance and earnestly talks of annuities.
You can't go back.

To the Yale-Princeton homecoming weekend I went,
  returning after years away from college.
Together with old room-mates and pals I made nostalgic rounds of
  Temple Bar, Old Heidelburg and Passion Pit, trying to be a
    sophomore again.
The gaiety was forced, sobriety intruded.
  You can't go back.

And if meet an old love, well she may smile,
  and we might talk of when,
And I might try...but you can't go back.
  Even if you wanted to.

  Paul D. Ellner

Di

Explosion of black motion
With the toss of a battered tennis ball,
Di, Loony Lab, moving like a pulling guard,
Running low and hard,
Has a single goal:
The ball.
Woe be to anything in the way.

The job must be done.
Any possible intruder fearful or not
Has to be frightened away
By barrages of brazen barking.
Beware the fangs; cross the line at your own risk.
Di the Defender. Dare to defy and lose a leg.

Devoted, demanding Di, there to please,
With huge, brown eyes that drip affection,
Constant shadow, always underfoot, wanting to play.
Frequently she waits, lying with front paws crossed,
On the rug at the top of the stairs,
Daintily a lady.
What do we do to deserve so much?

  Peter L. Fenninger

The Pillow And The Stuffed Dog

"Just look at me!" said the pillow to the dog.
"Why should you complain?" inquired the dog.
"I'm stuffed, I'm worn, I'm looked at with disdain!"
"So what?" countered the pillow.
"When Rachel is angry
I get thrown against the wall.
I don't like it much at all!"
"Big deal!" yelled the dog.
"I get dragged along on every occasion!
Be it a weekend trip or a summer vacation."
"Still," said the pillow, "I like it at night
when Rachel goes to bed,
and she lays her bushy head on my face."
"I agree," said the dog. "And I think it's nice
when she takes me in her arms
and hugs me twice."
Said the pillow, "I think we both agree,
that the treatment we receive
is worth it to be some of
Rachel's favorite things."

  Rachel Herrmann

Being Alone

Being alone, is it really that bad?
Sometimes you're happy, but mostly you're sad.
Can't go out, can't stay home
Can't stare at the walls, cant wait by the phone.
Don't you know how to laugh, don't you know how to feel.
Losing yourself, forgetting what's real.
Wishing and wondering, counting the tears.
Wearing a smile, but hiding the fears.
No one to listen, nothing to share.
Why do I bother, why should I care,
Try to be strong, why should I care.
Try to be strong, hold your head high
How do I do it, how do I try?
Being alone, being together
Will I knew which last forever.
Being alone, this can't be true
I wouldn't be here
If it weren't for you!

  Lisa Lisanti

Lines

Smoothly turning
inward around and through
slowly drooping
dividing shaping
forming sharply a thought not yet expressed
a sense of rediscovered past
a smell of breast and nipple arching forward
a river carrying away the earth on which I stand watching
an apple that tasted sour
small dark pinholes pointing to the life within
a rock that once was my face domain behind the
house within the trees
a tower humming with instant death
a field of strawberries warming in the sun
impressions of anger shame bitter cold nights
flow across the sheet and mock by changing in midcapture
glasses resting on a wooden sink cow teats
tractor tracks sacks filled with backaching potatoes
a line game played to fill the emptiness of a country schoolroom
when everyone is left the long walk home

  Eric Knuffke

"I Love You"

There was growing content as the months passed,
For he knew he was in love at last.
All of his dreams he thought couldn't be,
Were now becoming a reality.

She entered his life like a friendly wind.
They both thought the passion would never end.
All the was left for him to do,
Was to say those simple words "I love you."

He treated time like an eternity.
To him, love was something that would always be.
"Tomorrow," he said, "I will open my heart"
But he put it off, thinking they would never part.

She suddenly took sick, and remained in bed.
But still those words were never said.
When the doctor gave the report, they both cried.
Sadly, two weeks later, his loved died.

When he visited her grave to deliver flowers,
His drops of tears turned into showers.
And all that was left for him to do,
Was to say those simple words "I love you."

  Diidri Wells

Beto

Your eyes are dangerous but I can't look away
When I stare into them I become trapped
in a pool of passion
I can't get out I don't want to get out I
want to gaze into them for eternity
They are passionate they are dangerous

You intoxicate me with the sound of your voice
It grabs me and wont let go it makes me lose
all control it puts me under a spell
It's gentle yet strong it's intoxicating

Your lips are deadly I desire them constantly
they take control of my life making me think of
nothing more than pressing against them
and devouring them
They are powerful they are deadly

Heather Branum

Untitled

You would not believe what this has caused me
run to catch up to you
make me hide behind a tree

The complete luster is now a book of prayers
I fight to make you open up
as I cover myself in a thousand layers

It's not pain that I feel, but complete hurt
you look to a girl who left you behind
and treat me like dirt.

It's not fair how my heart is beating around
it jumps from my chest
sometimes it's up and sometimes it's down

I lost all control and made you mine
your heart next to me
gave me the clear sign

That you did not want this moment to end
lovers never
always a friend

Swann

Untitled

Inside me it's raining.
It's been raining for so long....

When the sky rains it's as if we become one.
For a brief time I'm whole.
Then the sky quits raining.

You looked into my eyes.
Tell me, what did you see?
You wanted to take my hand.
Why?
What did you see?

Did you see me standing in the rain?
Did you think if you touched me it would stop?
It won't.

Someday it will.
Forever.
Yes, with a touch.

Who will it be?
I don't know.

Can you look down at the stars?

Rachelle Riggs

Untitled

How the winds of change have blown across this heart
sometimes as gentle as a summer breeze
Peacefully caressing with glistening hands of air
and sometimes like a hurricane rolling up the coast
wiping away everything, leaving me only this empty stare

Yes storms have raged deep within me
But when they pass I notice now,
The sky's a little brighter, the sun's a little warmer

And as everything returns to how it was detail
I see now for the first time, that it's never like before
Oh many things may have been swept away
But looking back I really didn't need them anyway

So now even though I still enjoy
The soft caress of a gentle breeze deep within my heart
I know that soon over the horizon I'll sense the storm,
Coming source than I did Betsie
and now knowing why it must come through me
I'll welcome the winds of change as they sweep it all away
Because that they'll leave me is the lessons of life,
That I'd get no other way.

Paul R. Damico Jr.

A Prize Of Great Wealth

There are so many games
That the mind does play
In so many levels
And in so many ways
For it is easy to go insane
Yet so much harder to become sane
A trip to the dark side of the brain
That's only one way
For a round trip
Just takes to many days

A long journey deep in thought
On a quest for more thoughts
A ring of desire, just out of reach
A Prize of Great Wealth
That can never be seen
Only felt in your being

For sanity is, not an easy game to be played
Or a level to achieve
But a Prize of Great Wealth
That all strive for in their being

Christopher A. Zeller

Lost

I feel lost without a hope,
So I run to the nearest friend, dope.
He makes me feel good and smile,
But just for awhile.
Then he makes me feel sick and ill.
So I run to some pills.
I swallow too many.
When I wake up, I see Jesus standing.
How could this be, I haven't lived all my years.
He told me if I don't stop death is near.
I say no one cares.
Then he frowns, in which is rare.
He says you are wrong and I hope you
wake up before too long.
Then off he goes, into the clouds,
As I wake up with friends and family
standing around.
As usual he was right.
I woke up that night,
'Fore I saw the light.

Amanda Montgomery

Ode To The Four Winds

Oh whispering wind, moonlit breeze,
why mumble mid the fallen leaves,
to whisk away enraged by me
as winter's breath through barren trees?
My mind's tormented by a presaged vision
of multitudes in the Valley of Decision.
On the mountains peak, I watch them go
one by one to the valley below.

With feathered lance and leathered shields,
the warriors loomed fore the battlefield.
A stallion's bell tingles till the thunders roar.
The whirlwind doomed the truculent hoard.
In the distance, across the plain,
nether clouds of gray and mists of rain,
a dawning light shepherded the way.

Suddenly I woke to hear the ancient chant.
My eyes beheld the words their banner bore
o'er fastened bows and shields of war.
Ancient words uttered from the dust,
in liberty, and in God, we trust.

Tal Henderson

Help Us

Help us in this day and time
Why aren't we letting our light shine
Seems like our love has grown so cold
Don't people know what God requires of their soul
We got to live right and do what he said
For he's our maker, creator our head
Oh how sweet is his name
And everyday he's yet the same
Our hope should be build on nothing less
But his true love and his righteousness
So look up, and let God's love spread
Stop acting as though you're dead
For his people are lively stones
He'll pick you up and move every one of your bones
Help us so we'll stand the test
For we must do right, we've got to do our best
If you stay with him he'll see you through
And remember one day he's coming for me and you.

Juanita Chambliss

Ocean Wonders In Oregon

We look out and see, the far away light,
Of a shrimp boat, fishing away into the night.
Across the sky, the satellite roves,
Between the misty stars it goes.
The roar of the surf, is making us dream,
Of what a new morning might bring.
The air is fresh and cool, as we sleep thru the night,
To awake to look at the rolling surf, what a sight!!
It's roaring and crashing, over rocks and sand,
The tide's coming in, to change the land.
Great logs are moved, to a new resting place,
The sandpipers are flying and dancing with grace.
Then, in the distance a puff appears,
And the huge gray whale lunges - as we cheer.
What grace and presence - as we stand in awe,
Not really believing in what we saw.
The wonder of nature, the sights we behold,
Are truly the stories, that need to be told.

Irene Buchanan

In Memory Of Thomas James Watts

As we scrambled and scurried on a moon lit night
We left our stations and knew there would be a fight
As we glided above the jungle and close to the trees
You could close your eyes and feel the night breeze
With God so close at this peaceful time,
Before our eyed flashed their lives and mine.
In a very few moments we all did know
The fighting would start and the fear would go.
My loved ones so far away must understand
Why here I must stay
With Gods light touch upon my hand
I know that together we both will stand.

Jerry McKee

The Vision

A starving child lies unconscious in the overcast of death,
As the music bounced gently upon the emperor's caviar.
And seconds project moments of the dreams he once had,
as the house perspired heavily with the
inconsiderateness of the rich.
Somewhere, somehow, a lost battles was won,
as the once starved child, now, sits beside the "real king."
And the rich drank heavily and chanted
"down with the poor",
while another 'once starved child', approaches
heaven's pearly door.

David J. Rochester

Untitled

I wonder where you are tonight
Are you happy? Is everything alright?
I think this for each of my children
And I send up a prayer for each one
That God will be with them and bless them
In all the days to come

I cannot be beside them
They're grown and out on their own.
I pray they have someone to love
Who will love them in return.
I pray God will look out for them
And bless them from above.

I thank God for each of my children
And all of my grandchildren too
Each one is very special
Their looks and talents unique.
They're loving and giving people
Who make my world complete

Reba Crooks

"Life Is Footprints In The Snow"

Life is footprints in the snow.
How you leave your mark,
that's up to you.
You can leave your print heavy and dark,
or be forgettable and leave your print
Soft and low
Life can be unfair
So when you make a mistake
You can't go back.
You have to go on
and try to turn around
So think before you make your mark,
on the pure, untouched snow.

L. Deng

Beyond The Heaven

On the wings of Angels, have I been swept away. I feel a sudden rush
of wind upon my face. As if my breath been taken away. My heart is
pouncing loud as the blood rush in my veins. My breathing has become very strained.
As I lay prostrate before the king.

There is the sound of music, sounds I cannot trace, as if a thousand
violins were all in place. This sweet sounds fills the air, I've heard a sound that can quite compare.

There is a bright light such as one I've never seen, glowing in this
place that smells like spring. So sweet fragrance it makes you want to sing.
Rise up rise up and dance for the king. The singing is so sweet it sounds like a crystal spring,
bubbling in the mountains as the birds joyful sing, rise up dance for the king.

My chest feels heavy as my heart beats loud, I here the sound of drum
beats coming from the clouds. Rise up, rise and dance for the king.
The music wraps around me as I began to swing, twirling, leaping and
bowing with such delight, as a feather taken in flight. Chiffon of many colors is my covering.
Tiny little wings so crystal clear, began to flutter as I take to the air. Arms outstretch as I curtsey low, so
shy and humbled as I real slow.

My eyes are closed, as I listen to the sounds, I here the sounds of tum-tum coming from the clouds.
The singing of the Angels soft and clear as the sweet sound of violins caress my ear,
and I know without a doubt I have nothing to fear. When I hear the Angels voices saying rise up,
rise up the time is near. When suddenly I am awaken to find this was all a dream,
but never shall forget how I dance before the king.

    Carrie Johnson

THE DESERT IN SPRING

Dawn skies take on a brilliance of bluish, reddish hue at Desert Sunrise.
As the mountainous terrain awakens, its eloquent majesty beneath white clouded azure skies.
And the morning dew gently kisses the cactus. Pastel painted flowers and all Flora and Fauna in the valley as they roam.
Every one stretches their very existence up toward heaven from their sandy desert home.

For all desert nature is blessed by the mighty hand of God with a most gentle love.
Her many splendid variegated tones brought out by nature's kindly shove.
For she embraces mother nature in all her righteous splendor.
Begging the sky with sun parched lips for some rain to Please! Surrender.

For the radiant Afternoon Sun is high, the breeze is sand filled, and infernally dry.
As a Diamond Backed Rattler lays poised on a rock waiting for its next victim to happen by.
As the Desert Sun Sets and Twilight appears bringing glorious configurations in pinkish hues.
All of the Desert Night Fauna, comes out to spread its magical news.

In this arid, lonely, vastness as the evening brings a cool refreshing gale.
You can hear the Wailful Cries of Coyotes in the distant dale.
For the desert holds its own calm, peaceful, serenity for God's beauty it does bring.
For this is the grandeur of nature in the Desert In Spring.

    Carla Jean Esely

Birds Of A Feather

Take me to the place where the white dove flies high
Where the black bird soars the skies
Take me to the place where the blue bird's color is as important as others
Where the hummingbird's song makes all sing along.

Take me to the place where the sparrow's eyes are not filled with
   sadness because of an evil hunter's madness
But where the chirping of new born golden yellow chicks fill the air with gladness.

Take me to the place where the two shaded ducklings can roam free
Where the birds of every shade can fly in unity.
Take me to the place where we can all come together like the colors on a peacock's feathers.

If there is a place. That's where I'd love to be
Where love has no color and in this place you are my sister and my brother
If there is a place. That's where I want to be
Where you can be you and I can be me.
May the colors of our worldwide rainbow run together as one race the human race.

    Katina Jones

Humbled Faith

If everything I'd worked for
Were to crumble at my feet
My heart and soul stripped naked
Inner demons for to meet

No sword to lift above my head
No shield to guard my chest
No horse on which to run away
No place in which to rest

God would be beside me
To guide me through those days
He'd tell me it was all a test
And downfall, just a phase

He'd stress the unimportance
Of material things I'd gained
For all I dare take with me
Is what my soul's retained

And when they dwindle to but one
(The grains of sand I am)
I know he'll fold me in his arms
This humbled, wayward lamb

Ronalee Schall

Happiness

It sweeps over your soul,
Engulfing you in a sweet caress
You close your eyes,
And tears course down your face.

It comes not very often,
Yet when it comes it's true.
The experience will last forever
And you'll remember it inside of you.

The wish has come to pass,
Your brightest dream is here,
And the happiness you feel,
Is forever and always dear.

Bogdana Marchis

Is This Art?

Metaphors percolate...
They bubble first, then spring
From some abiding subterrain.
I grow at intervals
Engorged with verse -
Artesian verse that spills -
Like a whimsical water toy
That dips and bobs and fills
And emptied,
Rights itself.

Something deep inside,
Remote from day-to-day,
Presses, pushes, tickles, prods,
Demands, expands
Til I explode and pour it out,
Then right myself.

Is this liquid filling/spilling
Between my in and out,
Art?

C. A. Meyer

Un-Named

Life is a dream,
Lingering in your mind.
As real as it may seem,
It will soon fade in time.

Katrina G. Bear

Magician's Dawn

Arise, see the day
and know
it is mine.
Reaching beyond myself,
by trial of my convictions
spinning until,
I succeed.
Grasping, in my palm
a shining Truth
that eluded me, just a while.
Its nature is strength
to draw on.
Soothing of soul,
lucid, eternal,
I know it now.
Another pane
through which to gaze
from my many windowed home.

Lorraine Hammock

Through A Child's Eyes

I look into the mirror
And a child's face I see.
No cares, no fears,
Feeling satisfied just to be.

I don't know any sorrow:
I'm just happy to be alive.
Pain does not touch me
No clouds in my sky.

I caress the moment
And wonder at every sound.
I'm free to be myself;
So my fulfillment abounds.

How very sad it is
That a child we cannot be
Through all our years
And into eternity........

Peggy Tucker

I Want It All

I don't just want to live.
I want to be alive.
I don't just want the stars.
I want the whole Milky Way.

I don't just want a job.
I want a career.
I don't just want to be anybody.
I want to be somebody.

I don't just want someone to love.
I want someone who loves me.
I don't just want a man.
I want a hero.

I don't just want children.
I want a family.
I don't just want love
I want a love of a lifetime.

I don't just want a goal.
I want the dream.
I don't just want a life.
I want the fairy tale.

Shelley Wilkins

All The Hidden Beauty

When I look at me
Do I see a shining light?
When I look at an enemy
Do I see the upcoming fight?

When I look at a stone
Do I see a sparkling gem?
When I see a baby
Do I hear the crying?
When I meet an old lady
Do I think of her dying?

When I look at a flower
I see the stinging bee
When I look in the mirror
I see only the faults in me.

David M. Nigro

Alone?

The Lord looked down
he saw the child sit sadly on her bed
In hopeless desperation
she wished that she were dead.

Her mother seemed to hate her
Her father far away
If only he would come and get her
on this very day.

God above, he shed a tear
for this child so all alone
Away to reach her, he would find
He'd make her his very own.

Child if you read this
Know he's up above
Looking down and loving you

A plan of hope will come.

Beverly A. Ward

Spring

Here I lay, way up high
The clouds rolling in the sky

Birds are busy building nests
Squirrels are playing with happy jest

The flowers blossom
The colors are awesome

Trees are growing
Rivers are flowing

Insects are busy
They move so fast it's dizzy

The bees are humming
Summer is coming

Children are frolicking
Everyone's playing with spring

Ethel Tovar

Mind Pain

Pain seeps through
Seeking to be assuaged
by kind words
that never
are offered

Mind pain
erased only by
self
healed only by self

Alma Louise Ward Dalton

Crystal Haze

Looking through rainbows
Up in the sky
Colors so clear and bright
Dreams are passing you by

Colors of red, green and blue
Passing in the sky
From end to end
Rainbows never die
They just go on to the next bend

Raindrops crystal clear
Making the colors so bright
Looking into the mirror
Fading into the night
Moonlight taking over
Giving way to mornings light

Shinning morning light
Glistening on the lawn
Is the morning dew
It's plain to see
So are you
Tim Beschler

Living City

Plastic sounds
throb backwards
exploding into themselves
forever and ever
without circumstance

Time slows down
for you
to let you taste
pain
of the unknown

Opened eyes
burn like fluid
in the bright

The whiteness

Here
you will never know
where you are from
where you belong
who you are
Michael J. Puleloa

The Road One Dreams

The road one dreams
is paved with great
anticipation

However at its end, one may
find not all sunshine but
varied precipitation.

So if at first, your wish does
seem to lack-

It's obvious the fun is not
upon arriving,
But in simply looking back.
Jackie Ferrini

"Silence"

I sit here in silence
Waiting
Wanting

For the sound of your voice
Or the gentle caress of your lips
Upon mine

When will it come
When will it be
The time to tell you...I love you

The silence goes on
Unobtrusive and unaware
That nobody comes...nobody cares

The silence surrounds me
Enfolds me in its embrace
Until I'm nothing more than a memory.
Nichole Cloud

Loneliness

Incredibly painful
just being by yourself
Having no friends
Alone

As loneliness emerges
On the people of the world
The love of their hearts
So slowly turns cold

So many times
Have I wanted to know
Why loneliness is
And its powerful feeling
Ivania Rodriquez-Pinto

Hope

Hope is a dream
that you've wished for,
for so long
but still hasn't come true

You've waited in despair
for that one faithful word

You've seen pictures of it
in your head
But in real life those pictures
do not exist?

Where is Hope?
That's the question for most people
But still to this day
this question cannot be answered
Arianna Navarro

Each Day

I go to the edge.
I am not afraid.
I don't look down,
but up, where rainbows breed.

I go to the edge.
I will not fall.
I see the wind,
whisper, smiling in its call.

I go to the edge.
I see the why.
I step forward,
and play, where colors fly.
Shirley Harris

Life

Breathing. Crying.
Eating. Sleeping.

Walking. Skipping.
Running. Jumping.

Laughing. Smiling.
Happy. Funny.

Driving. Dating.
Sleeping. Lying.

Working. Shopping.
Cooking. Laundry.

Cleaning. Smoking.
Drinking. Trying.

Sicker. Thinner.
Slower. Paler.

Aging. Crying.
Fading. Dying...
Barbara Werner

Forlorn

The Lady of the Moon
She glimmers by the light
she shimmers with reflection
As she leads into the night

Alone and sad
She lives a life of questions
Never knowing what's bad
Never knowing what's good

The Love she's longed for
Hides in the shadows
The Love she's needed
Slips through her fingers

She reaches out
She loses everything
Her empty heart
As dark as night

Her luminosity left low
Her fire fading faint
What hope is left
John Cordrey

Freedom

Like an eagle in flight
my heart soars so high
over the mountains, the valleys,
and the clouds in the sky.
Flying ever upward
on the wings of love
through skies so blue,
To the heavens above
As the eagle rises freely
unchecked in his flight
our love knows no boundaries,
only delight.
I don't wish to bind him
or clip his broad wings
I want only to love him
and share what life brings.
Lila L. Marek

A Warm Summer Night

She came into my world
in a beautiful way.
Although it was a while ago,
I remember it like yesterday,
It was love at first sight.
I was afraid to cradle her in my arm.
She looked as fragile as a china doll.
She was so soft and warm.
It was a warm summer evening
the day we met.
I looked into her eyes
and I confess, I wept.
The joy that I felt
could not be put into words
Her young and tender life
made my worries feel absurd.
She made me a proud father
for the third time in my life.
God showed me his love
on that warm summer night.

James Matthies

Prairie Eagle

As I watch the prairie
sky, I see an eagle soaring
gracefully, looking at
every little thing. Looking maybe
for food, or a place to
make a nest. Eagles soar so
soft and gentle, yet when they
fly, they are fast and strong.
Eagles are called birds, but
I think they are far too majestic
for that name. They watch
over every move and listen
over every sound on the
rocky earth below.

Joshua Cooley

A River

Life is like a river,
Its way is never lost,
Flowing through the ages,
Over rocks and frost,
Down valleys, over mountains,
Gaining wisdom from the earth,
Then flowing into oceans,
With all of its life's worth

Jeremy Brown

Jerusalem At Peace

Beyond the gates of Jerusalem,
Why must the soldiers stand?
The evil enemies swarm the city,
We cannot predict their horrible plans.
I dream of the day they leave our land,
And the world is at peace again.
No more bombs or murders,
Our land we shall regain.
With shuls and torahs everywhere,
Chanukiahs galore,
A new Jew comes in by the minute,
More and more and more.
And there is always a little hope,
That this can really be.
That all Jews are in Jerusalem,
Young and old, you and me.

Sarah Sultan

Stars

Stars, stars everywhere,
look right here, look right there.
Burning dimly, burning bright,
in the middle of the night.

The more I look the more I see,
they are so shiny so glittery.
As they glow I wonder why?
Why are they so high in the sky?

As they die they start to shoot
And dance in the sky as a group.
They are so far, so far away
Why can't we see them in the day?

Kevin Lamb

It's Gone

Incinerated words of rhyme
As callous as an arson's crime
Thrust caustic wounds upon the heart
Of lovers when they fall apart.

Words that once were dearly spoken
Lay like shattered vases, broken.
Kiss me, miss me, hold me tight
Mean only this - Stay out of sight.

Love like castles made of sand
Or like the gambler's poker hand
Is subject to a vast array
Of Nature's forces. Dare I say

That luck is, too, a part of this?
It's take your chances, hit or miss,
Or wait until the tide is high
To watch your work become a lie.

The castle's gone, the hand is lost.
The price you paid, too high a cost!
No one believes you when you say
That once your love was there to stay.

Jack Fahey

Brothers

The morning marsh
of autumn cattails,
alive with water sounds
and puddle ducks,
warming sleek feathers.
I watch my brother's hat,
bobbing through the cornstalks.
He retrieves another mallard.

Rob Kolomyski

Friends

Laughter, tears, good and bad,
A friend is always there.

To share in everything you do,
To help you through it all.

Getting into trouble,
Finding a way out.

Always together,
Never apart.

Sharing deep secrets,
Keeping all promises.

Memories last forever,
And a good friend will too.

Tracy Wilson

Why?

A bombing in Oklahoma City:
Many die.
All over the country, people ask,
"Why?"

Children shot in school:
Many die.
The gunman committed suicide.
"Why?"

Suicide bombing in Jerusalem:
Innocent victims die.
Where is human worth?
"Why?"

Is it lack of moral fiber?
Greed?
Political Power?
Money?
What reasons underlie?
There is no answer
So the question remains,
"Why?"

Hilda Gentry McKnight

Night Of Rashko

Language barriers caused
    no communication errors
as we talked
    and laughed,
barely noticing
    the night passing.
Unexpectedly, not surprised
    to be still together
at daybreak,
it began to dawn on us,
    maybe we had come
    to mean something
    to each other.
In the grey morning light
    we shared the evenings
    first embrace,
as you whispered,
"Oh, where have
    you been
    all night?"

Barbara L. Fox

Untitled

The night goes on till morn,
The moon in deep blue seas
The bright stars cast a glow
On sleeping willow trees

The eerie glow of midnight
Will echo through the hills
The moon will cast its shadow
Through quiet window sills.

When bright ribbons of sunlight
Peek through the misty sky
The stars will disappear
into another time -

The moon will fade away
Behind colors of dawn
The sun will soon appear
until the day is gone -

Chandra Hildebrand

Slide 1, Microscope 1

Serrated islands of flesh,
The only remnants of a baby's
    snug pillow in utero.
Disrupted and torn,
A motley mix of blood and womb.
What is left of a baby unborn?
Praising, praying, accusing,
a severed finger on a glass slide.
The eyes of a cold microscope rove
What can this be?
A product of conception.

Augusto F. Mesia

Untitled

I sit alone
the only light
Candles.

Your Picture it
glows with
memory.

My heart it
burns with
pain.

Come back.
Hold On.
I have your
coat

The one that
gave you
security,

and you can't
have it
back.

Shana Graves

"I Heard"

Late last night as I lay in bed
I heard something.
I heard a gunshot very clear
Then another not so near,
I listened but did not hear
The sirens
The sirens
Coming here,

Holly Carr

Mother's Love

I went outside today, Mom,
I saw the grass so green,
The flowers were so pretty, Mom
The setting so serene.
The sky so clear and blue, Mom
The delicate leaves of the tree,
But, all this beauty could not compare,
    to the love you give to me.

Janet Jock

Boulevard Of Tears

A drop of anxiety
splashes inside me,
drips on my broken heart,
gathers in my drunken head,
moves through my body,
and falls at my feet.

Carla Brown

Reflections

Lost, my girl with the laughing eyes.
Gone quickly as the snow wind flies,
Haunting songs that close in tears,
Visions echo through the years,

Voices whispering in the dark,
Memories holding loves faint spark,
Fainter now,... but louder then,
Glimpses of what might have been.

J. Padgett

The Wanderer

The burning streak across the sky,
it disappears from my eyes.
It continues on its lonely flight,
travelling in an endless night.

Nothing but gas and stone,
the traveller searches for his home.
Through the heavens time he squander,
roaming about this helpless wanderer.

Always looking but never stopping,
no home port would be docking.
Drifting around in the starry mist,
bringing watchful gazers another wish.

Bernard M. Newton

Untitled

The ocean waters come calm
Its waves smash!
One day,
Will the ocean waters
Be nothing but trash?!!

Something so beautiful,
Yet so rough.
People fail to realize,
Pollution is tough.

So watch our actions,
Watch our waters.
Don't throw garbage
In Mother Nature's quarters!!!

David Wayne Lenceski

Memorial Day

Some sit
on damp sand
while I sit
cafe style
in the city
eating tofutti
watching them crawl past
sirens
drown out
rock music
from shiny cars
cruising by
some are seals
diving under icy waves
while I browse
mosaic dunes
in second hand stores

Dianne Twersky

My Bubble

A bubble is what I'm living in.
One day my bubble will break.
Then I'll be put in the ground
over there by the big lake.

But before that happens,
I would like to say:
will you stay with me?
Yes, we'll go all the way.

We'll go to the moon,
and then to Mars.
Nothing will stop us...
we'll pass all the stars.

We'll go to a place
with no one else there.
We'll leave this planet
and fly through the air.

Wait, please, don't say no.
All my hopes will drop.
Hey, come back here.
There goes another, oh well...Pop.

John Wojtowicz

Untitled

From up above reality
You caught me looking down
Into the spines and the petals
Of the sweet wine sound.

Thinking obsolete
Feeling everything
Showing me your beauty
You have won and I am beat
Knowing time will ring.

Rolling down that golden road
A truckload of my life
Shook my boots and slammed that door
Waved my last goodbye

Thinking obsolete
Feeling everything
Showing me your beauty
You have won and I will beat
Knowing time will ring.

Jennifer E. Loth

Gypsy Moth Dancer

A madcap girl
in gauzy twirl
beyond control

So tightly bound
she flickers 'round
her blazing soul

One encore spin
she plunges in
to death extol

Christopher W. Boldt

Untitled

To begin a journey
one must end
to end one's life
is to never journey again.

Christopher L. Raymond

The Defeated Mage

The crystal sits upended
　On the table below
The ivory hands ascend it
　And the orb begins to glow

The light flickers like a candle
　Burning forevermore
It proves too much to handle
　And the mage drops to the floor

The deep colors swirl brightly
　Around the dark domain
They touch his forehead lightly
　Intoxicating, insane

The wind rises with his fear
　The mage crawls and cowers
The gale mocks him with a sneer
　And strips away his powers

The voice howled and thundered
　"Don't touch what you can't control
Just like this body I've plundered
　And then I'll steal your soul."

　　Mimi Diaz

Friends For Ever

You put up with me
And never complain
You're my best friend
And that'll never change

　You're always there
　When I'm broken in two
　You'll always be there
　That I know it's true

Without you
I don't know where I'd be
You deserve a bravery metal
Just for putting up with me

　You're there when I laugh
　You're there when I cry
　It doesn't matter how I feel
　'cause you're there to make me try

You're always there
When I'm a friend in need
And forever you'll stand out
Like a flower and a weed

　　Elsa Marques

Untitled

Every time I think of you
Tears swell in my eyes.

I realize we had nothing,
and I still ask myself "why?"

Why did it have to end this way?
We'll probably never know.

But if we knew
Why'd we have to go?

Your thoughts are with me always,
Even if you're not.

I think about you night and day,
Because you're all I got!

　　Beth Bernard

Spring

Soft gentle breezes,
Warming rays of sun,
Preparing Mother Earth
For new life has begun.
Run Winter Run.

Green blades of grass are sprouting.
Seeds planted soon become,
Brightly colored flowers
Swaying gently in the sun.
Children gather having fun.

Robins hunting worms,
Meadowlarks in song,
Sheep with lambs beside them
Playing where they belong.
Sights and sounds for which I long.

Run Winter Run.
Days warmed by sunny rays.
Laughing, running, playing,
Spring is here children say.
Stay Spring Stay.

　　Sandra J. Estabrook

Untitled

Peeling down to the barest
barest...
Knocked off my center compass
All that was lost evaded me
now comes
in scrapes and scorn
lest realness in confrontation
Changing changing chameleon
in a world of hype and long goodbyes
got to sell your soul
got to sell your self.
This car exhaust world of images
never true to the mirror
they look in
Heal is hurt
Truth is pain
but truth sets you free
so how long will it take me...

　　Hilary Megan

"Fox Talk"

I love to chase chickens
and hounds love to chase me
I use all my wits to get away
and sometimes succeed.

I have lots of fun
tricking those dumb mangy mutts
and sometimes I think
I am just too smart
for those runts.

But when they catch me
I think it is all going to be over
but they let me go again
to hide in the lush green clover.

　　Keith L. Morreira

Weeping Willow

Weeping willow you weep,
For weeping willow my heart to keep.
If thy shall leave,
Or move away,
Under your branches my heart shall stay.

　　Jessi Carr

A Man I Think I Am

A man I think I am
A man I think I am
A man I wish to be
A man I want to see
I see a man in the mirror
All I see is me
Where is the man I want to be
Where is the man I wish to see
Where is the man I think I am
All I see is me

　　Darin R. Huntley

I'd Live It All Again

I looked across a football field-
My young heart began to pound.
she was slim, blonde and beautiful-
this wondrous, girl I found.
Listen up you pretty thing-
I grinned at her and sighed.
You just met your husband-
　she smiled at me and cried.
The greatest memory
of my whole life, Happened
that one night.
We had a most fantastic date-
And Everything
　was right!
The years now number 45-
We're Partners, Lovers,
　Friends.
Were I to get a second
　chance-
I'd live it all again.

　　Donald R. Thompson

Birdsong

Nature's music,
　the sound of the birds,
The songs they sing
　while they gracefully fly.
Creating a song
　that requires no words
Sung by the creatures
　That roam the skies.
The sounds resounding
　from their beaks,
As they sail
　high in the air,
Makes a song that's
　Oh-so sweet.
A song that with the world
　they share!

　　Trenton Knew

Zima

Zima is my kitty cat
Never far away,
She loves to purr and purr,
She's always in your way.
I love her very, very much,
All day and night,
When her eyes show bright,
Zima is my kitty cat,
Good night!

　　Aimee Bycholski

Portrait Of An Old Woman

I feel for you old woman.
I am not where you are
But I shall follow.
Your path is mine.
Your loves, now fantasies,
Become my dreams too.
Time waits not for us,
It has taken its toll,
Broken dreams, broken bodies,
Yet, you smile, a secret goal?
I shall be there too.
We shall meet.
Your fears are my fears.
Lonely we come, lonely we go
Hold my hand old woman.

Jeanne L. Horner

My Salient Insanity

My salient insanity
No one sees
It comes and goes
As it please.

It steals from me
Moments and smells
And leaves me like
A vacant shell.

All alone in my salient hell
It's hard to cope with
the smell

God only gives us
What we can handle.
I think I'll light a candle.
To let him know I'm still
Trying to handle.
My salient insanity.

Loretta Wood

Life

Sometimes hard, sometimes rough
Never easy, usually tough
Don't give up, always try
Hold that head up, never cry
look to the future, cherish the past
Sometimes it seems, that life goes too fast.

Jessica Burns

If I'm Here, And You're There

Yes, I still want you.
No, I'll get by.
Yes, I still love you.
No, I won't cry.
Yes, I'll be happy.
No, I don't mind.
Yes, I'll keep trying.
No, I'll be fine.
Yes, you must go now.
Come on now, I won't cry.
Yes, I still Love you.
I Love you, Goodbye!

Tammy Cocking Patterson

The Crooked Road

Lead me down the crooked road
and keep me in your sight,
Hold my hand and don't let
go and we will be alright,
Keep your faith in me and
walk me to the end,
and love me now forever,
until we reach the end.

Rebecca Wilson

Flight Of Fools

Stand outside of the Glass wall
Watch the inevitable destruction fall
Youthful energy devoid of cause
Authority is unavailing laws
Bound together with isolation
What is becoming of our nation
Foggy thoughts brought forth with haze
Mankind is in an ignorant daze
We're running from fate
Destiny deserves our praise
Rapidly approaching the expiration date

Angela Buckner

"Arctic Poetry"

Always cold
Reliably fun
Cold enough for snow year-round
Talk about it to friends
Iceberg City
Cold reality

Tiffany Pendleton

Expectation!

I lay upon the earth today
Upon the sandy shore
I lay upon the earth today
And watched the seagulls soar!

I lay within the sea today
Within the cool, green water
I lay within the sea today
And felt the waves wash over!

I did not lay upon the sky today
As the gulls appeared to be
But my heart was soaring just as high
My love was coming to me!

Shirley S. Belding

Untitled

Time and time again,
the truth consumes my soul,
Committing all my being,
to take on one high goal;

To act as Jesus wants me,
in life from day to day,
And spread the Gospel Story,
to others on the way;

To love my Lord and Savior,
with all my heart and mind,
And emulate his mercy,
to every human kind.

Dorville D. Whitson Jr.

Everybody Calls My Stuff Stupid

Everybody calls my stuff stupid,
Everybody calls my stuff junk.

Everybody calls my stuff stupid,
Every single day.
Everybody calls my stuff stupid,
The want me to give it away.

Everybody calls my stuff stupid,
Probably because it's mine.
Everybody calls my stuff stupid,
Probably because it's mine.

Everybody calls my stuff stupid,
Everybody calls my stuff junk.

Kira LaRue

The Dream

She is refreshing
Like a high mountain stream
Her clean waters caressing
A lost love in my dream

A magnetic presence
Winding along on her own
I seek to capture her essence
To share her majestic throne

Gentle, but persistent
In her final destination
My love remains distant
As she rushes in anticipation

In my dream her voice is calling
She will never be tamed
Each night, I continue stalling
But must awaken to a love unclaimed

Peter L. Poole

The Incas Named The Sun Inty

Stars pale, the world is quiet,
Shadows flow up from the deep.
They shroud the mountains in a mantle
of indigo.

Far out on the horizon,
A thin frame of gold
Outlines the rugged peaks.
A promise of light,

Even the blue-white mass of the
Snow-covered volcano,
Looming in the dark,
Is slowly transformed.

Golden fire, a kiss of life
On slopes of ice and snow.
Majestic, glorious and eternal
The beauty of the mountain.

Explosion of light!
Triumphant in his radiant splendor
Inty, the sun, bursts forth.
It is day.

Fred A. Steinlauf

Untitled

To write and to draw;
Unfrozen like vapor,
The mind tends to thaw,
Spilling thoughts onto paper.

Bradley J. Lewis

Railroad Bridge At Old Saybrook

It rose from the river one day,
Eons of time ago
Eight black, wiry segments.
Now it lies basking
In this Apollonian sun.

From somewhere far off,
A signal is given
To raise its crusty spine.
With painful exhortations
It arches up one arthritic disc.

Again the yawl's spiky finger
Scratches its ancient belly.

Janet Skingor

3 PM

Dreams of thunder hear them roar,
Waking moments cease no more.
Takes me back to time immortal
Another life through heavens portal.

Through the tunnel, see the light
A little girl with sense of sight.
Down the road where once she stood,
A home, a man - a shrouded hood.

A uniform, the music, dancing -
The civil war - a romance entrancing.
Tears of pain, a heavy heart,
Shrouded mists of love depart.

A journey through time
Of love ever searching,
The knowledge we carry
Of souls ever learning.

Karen Marie Murphy

Left Behind

As I stand in the doorway,
I give a little sigh.
I remember how you used to say,
Before we said goodbye,

That you would always love me.
In good times and in bad.
Now you're not here to see,
That my life is sad.

I told myself I would not cry,
If that day ever came.
But now I feel like I could die,
Because nothing is the same.

I don't understand what went wrong.
I guess I never will.
The days now seem very long,
As I sit on the window sill

Looking out past the bend,
Hoping you'll be there.
But all I see is the cold wind
Blowing without care.

Jennifer Chrismer

"Nothing Compares"

The greenest pasture is where the pedestal
of life's single greatest treasure stands,
No car, train or plane can take you to the top,
Only the love, warmth and trust of a child
can take you there!

Brian Mallonn

"Double Vision"

You care not
Of my life, of my laugh;
You and I
Make our own little raff.

You look around
And know what you see,
All while I'm gone,
Fearing for where we'll be.

You come forth
And tuck away my life;
Then back off,
Just adding to my strife.

Yet remember,
After all the fun,
After all the fact,
Look in the mirror,
And I'll look right back.

M. Barry Floore

To Blue Bonnet

Fine rains
Like your small hearts
Sweet and bothering
All grasses washed green
Only I
Standing among you
With a blue heart
And a black umbrella

Zhang Jing

Only A Dream

You're only a dream
It never could be

You and me
to different to be

So why even think about you
of you are just a dream

When I see you with another
girl my heart fills with pain

Don't ask me why I don't know
It's just a dream it never could be

But my dream it seems so real
if it could only be I would

not dream only more, my dream
would be complete.

Becky Gruwell

A Pearl Of Sunrise

The sun was dazzling
behind a pearly
incandescent cloud.

This effect was only
momentary however
before the sun
burst forth at white heat.

Blinded by its glory
I closed my eyes,
then, looked away
into an uninspired room
of lesser things.

Mary Koge

A Friend

A friend is like an old song grown
Sweeter with the years,
A friend is some one who share
Our joys, and wipes away our tears.
A friend will look for goodness in
Everything we do.
A friend is one who knows our faults.
Yet find out virtues too.
A friend will shares a crust of bread
Or help to lift a load.
Happy are we who finds a few
Good friends along the road.

Velma M. Broski

Because Of The Snow

It seems as though
Everything is sleeping
Because of the snow

It seems as though
We have ten feet or so
Because of the snow

It seems as though
There's no school today
Because of the snow

It seems as though
There's no place to go
Because of the snow

It seems as though
The snowflakes never stop
Because of the snow

It seems as though
This poem won't end
Because of the snow!

Carrie O'Dell

"These Are The Final Days"

God is on his way.
You better be prepared.
Because the end is near.
Soon we will see our Saviour.
Judgment Day it will be.
Seek God before it's too late.
Because "These are the final days."

Sharon O. Brigham

Life

Life is changing,
Winding around going up and down
Swinging and jerking us all around
Life ends and begins never
forgetting the happiness and
sadness of growing up,
Life is full of memories good and bad,
Life never lets go never, never
till the end!

Christy Fisher

The Soup Of The Day

The soup of the
day is strong and thick,
made of marrow
bones of mother's love
laced with tears,
greens and wings.

Georgene Gardner

Songs Of The Handmaid

Forever I have Known,
By all that is profound,
No good am I alone,
Without a man around.

A slave to all men,
No thought of my own,
a life is a sin,
never raise my tone.

That is what I've been taught,
No sin of one alone,
the weaker sex is bought,
And men sit on the throne.

Carrie Darnell

"Realm"

Alone in a cloak of heartache
hidden by a veil of tears
I must not emerge, for my sake
I'd better remain for years

I'll stay in my chamber of darkness
abiding where I can't sense pain
I'll stay where I prevail harmless
In my cold abyss I'll remain

I know that not one will miss me
they won't even notice I've ceased
My shadowy realm won't dismiss me
I'll loiter and flaunt my disease

Blind, shivering, cold and severed
waiting for my bright ascent
remembering grievance endeavored
realizing my crux is spent

Jessica Matson

"The World That Was"

A poet I am not
Tho I must write the line,
What concerns me most
How the world has become so blind.

Look at the world that was
Beauty, love and peace of mind,
Man has become so self-centered
Greed, hate and crime.

We must go back to the golden rule
Blotting out chaos and fear,
Bringing forth peace and love
The things we held so dear.

God created us in his likeness
To show his mercy, love and care,
Family, fellow man, and country
Return to the beginning - do we dare?

Peace instead of war
Love instead of hate,
Giving in the place of greed
Awake world - or is it too late?

Eula V. Mills

Quiet, Please

'Copter twirling overhead,
Squeal of brakes, an aching head.

Airplanes drone, engines groan,
Sirens screeching, car horns beeping.

Children crying. Feel like dying.
Quiet, please. Hospital Zone.

Elnora Semeniuk

"My Bill"

"The sky is on fire"
I screamed and I cried
As I look out the window
  by my bedside

"See the purple, see the gold
Yellow and scarlet like flags unfold."

"The sky is on fire"
I screamed and I cried
"It's only the sunset dear"
  Mommie sighed.

Helen Harper Merritt

I Live Where...

I live where
ideas fly
minds roam
and I am a
creator.
Sounds of worlds,
worlds of ideas
all pouring
out into
the air
onto paper.
Through our links
I am heard
  and
I am known.
Through myself
and my search
for myself
I see that
I am a creator.

Paul Rowe

Nineties Lament

So tired
  of clothes
    and shows
  of cars
    and bars
  of snows
    and blows
  of stars
    and mars
  of calories
    and galleries
  of speeches
    and leeches
  of people
    and places
    and unsmiling faces.

Sue Cash

"The Window"

I look out the window;
looking at everything
But seeing nothing;
Things are on my mind
But, I think of nothing;
Things whiz by
But, we are going too slow;
I wait for my final destination,
While looking out the window.

Bo Summers

Midwest Man Migration

Inter-state
80 years
Older than the small hills in
These Plains I have wandered
The icy wind
Whips my cheeks and
Gnarled hands chapped
Cut from
Rusted barbed wire strung as
Fences in snow
Blows through my
Eyes water from weather or
Lost sadness
Trudging slowly
I see my breath
Knows it is winter
I am alone on
The highway
At night and
I stumble

Paul Teeter

"Rape Of The Natural World"

The earth was once a virgin,
bright and clean and pure.
God had made her perfect,
on that he was so sure.
He gave the earth to humans,
who didn't understand.
They raped her very soul,
and polluted all her land.
God gave them perfection,
but people didn't care.
They needed more technology,
and stripped her spirit bare.
Never was there a gift,
of such great magnitude,
but because they were greedy,
they'll live in solitude.

Cody Toudouze

Untitled

If I tried to speak my mind
to you would you turn me away
and hide or would you try
to save me?

If I opened up my heart
to you would you believe it would
be true or would you think
I'm crazy?

I don't know what it is
that keeps you on my mind
But I just know it's you
and with me that's just fine.

I have tried nothing but I
could try to love your
everything if you could try
to save me.

Paul Brown

At Night

At night I look out my window
And I wonder what's above me,
The stars, the moon, and the sky
I make a wish upon star
And I hope my dream will come true.
At night.

Shannon Britton

A Daughter's Wish For Father's Day

If I were granted just one wish,
a wish meant only for me,
I'd wish that I were small again
and could climb upon your knee.

I'd wish that you would rock me,
and sing, "Daddy's Little Girl."
That would be such a great wish,
the best one in the world.

But, those year, have past us by,
and will never come again.
Yet, you still are my best sweetheart,
and also my best friend.

Sandra Lynn Wagg Converse

Midnight

Black and dreary night it be
Am I the only one to see
This pain filled heart
Full of sorrow brought on to it
    Pound it, hit it
Make the hurting stop
Make it cease
Let it fly far from the trees
In the wind it shall soon be free
Black and Dreary night it be
    Am I the only one to see?

Sandra Pérez

If I Were An Eagle (Or Eagle's Nest)

If, I were an Eagle,
I'd put you on my wings
Then take you to see so many,
beautiful things.
While you sat upon my wings

At the day's end, I'd return
with you to my nest.
In hopes you may rest,
while you're snuggled, deep
within my breast.
Way up high in my Eagle's Nest.

Angela Breitenstein

Ivory Coast

The sand being eaten by the sea,
Former French territory,
Africa its mother,
Ghana its brother,
L'Abidjanaise its theme,
Francs the redeem,
Tribes hold the culture,
President looks over like a vulture,
Diamonds its treasure,
Bananas its pleasure,
Love one another,
Place like no other,
Abidjan its center,
Felix its mentor,
Brings luck like a clover,
As God watches over.

Adam Troy

"Seduced By The Devil"

The horrid beast flies by leisurely,
    through the sky.
Majestically magically flying,
    so high.
Legs of a goat, the face of the
    Mother.
He loved my whole family,
    including my lover.
He will not kill me, for torture is
    his revenge.
He will slaughter every body until
    I have no more friends.
His spirit is evil to the fullest
    extent.
The Holy Ghost cannot save me,
    and this I resent.
He will take me by force into the
    fiery pits of hell.
He will make me his slave, yes,
    my soul I will have to sell.

Michael Schuster

To Be Gone Forever

The day had been wet with
yesterday's dew when our friend
Peter Ballinger was laid to rest.

Near a tree we all stood
silently praying until the
cascade of tears came falling down.

All of our eyes were red with
memories in mind, but why
God did he have to drink and drive?

In my heart I will always
remember Norm who clutched
at the emptiness that had made him cry,
and little Tammy who held his hand.

For all the Kleenex I had given
away to you two, it can
never make the pain of forever go away.

Jennifer Moe

The End Of Friendship

I call to you but no one comes.
I yell for you, only silence answers my call.
I can no longer see you, are you still there?
My friend I sit waiting for you, why
do you not come?
Have you found another to take my place?
My tears fall like rain , and the
silence only laughs at my pain
I cannot understand why you hide
yourself from me. "Is this the end."
I cry, but the silence mocks me.
As I turn, I resist the urge to call
one last time.

Susan Haab

God, My Goddess

God, my Goddess,
Your love has no bounds,
Whether I may be "wrong" or "right".
She is always there,
To hear my words.
She will always love ME.
Some say "He",
But "She" is who she is to me.

Jennifer L. Heuser

Spring Life

Spring is here, a rebirth of life
people should stop and look around,
the tinge of green capping the
trees. The birds singing, even the
flowers are in blossom.

People are too busy hurrying
here and there. People take for
granted that spring comes and goes
like life. When one person dies
another is born. But that's so wrong.

Spring is here, stop and
listen; even stop to smell the
flowers and slow down, for
life comes but only once. People
should just enjoy and love each other.

Stop, Spring is here!

Linda Corigliano

My Vow To Jesus

I wish I could have lived
When Jesus walked the Earth,
I would have liked to touch His Robe
Though I've doubts as to my worth.

To watch Him work His miracles
Must have been glorious to see,
And though I'd lived in sinful ways
I'm sure He'd have pardoned me.

I would have been among the throng
That worshipped Him complete,
And the Day that He was crucified
I'd have wept there at His feet.

But since my life I live today
I'll make to Him this Vow,
To try and live the way He'd want
If He were here right now.

Helen E. Faisy

Love

I loved you when I saw you,
And still I cannot change,
This feeling down inside of me,
That makes me feel insane.

Your name is carved into my brain,
Your smile is held in my heart,
I love the way you hold me,
And say we'll never part.

So whisper to me gently,
Those three words I love to hear.
Promise that you'll be my friend,
And always keep me near.

Lara Nash

Untitled

Thrice damned am I
To have loved
To have lost
And to remember
Curses that you put on me
To never love another
To see a little of you
In everyone after
But the sum of all others
Could not reach
Your measure.

Larry Lamb

Feel Think

Indelible Impression
The Loss of Something
   Personal... Pure...
   Inchoate
Maddening Heartache
   as articulate as
   a New Language
Desperate Search
Questions
  FEEL
     THINK
Clarity, reconciliation.
ENORMITY OF COMPLEXITY

   Derek Schweers

Goodbye My Friend

  The Lord took him away on a
Thursday afternoon
  When he left it felt like his life
went by so soon
  Twenty-one years is all he had
to live
  And with the time he spent on Earth
all he did was give
  Some things are forgotten and some
are left behind
  But we will never forget the day our
dear friend died
  He took with him the things that
many people lack
  Although it seems he's gone for
good and we can't bring him back.
  There is always a place for him in
our hearts forever
  And time will pass and we will see
that his memory will bring us together.

   Lynda Belcher

Rookery

Sounds like the cash prize,
the bus terminal, rush hour.

Snapping in the breeze,
the fellow's feathers
of matt black elastic,

Gregarious guy,
failing as a neighbor,
no consideration,
shuffling cards in the colony,
squawking Corvus, Corvus
proud of his credentials,
fiercely guarding eggs,

Slipping grubs
into rubber beaks like
a one-armed bandit,
generous, lucky,
who lived through
the quick spray
of buckshot,

Corvus.

   Sarah R. Batschelet

New Life

Today I start a new life,
Like no other before.
This one involves a lady.
The one that I adore.
And as I start this new life,
Many things will change.
From the way I thought of only myself,
To the way you sigh your name.
And as we start this new life,
There will be many joys.
From each other and from our children.
Be they girls or boys.
As we live this new life,
There will be great love.
For every thing about this life,
Has been blessed by God above.
Together in this new life,
There will be no strife.
We will always be as one,
For you are my loving wife.

   Paul R. Blanton

Chilly Tricks

On the farm, the ground
surrounding,
a leaf falls to the blanket
beneath.
It once was a part of an
oak,
now withered with the cold that
deceived it.
As I look
the frost in its
face,
I see a reflection of a tree,
alone on a
winter's day,
It stands without its coat,
it shed its warm outside cover
to this chilly winter's day.

   Hannah Baumhover

Me Without You...

A bird with no wing...
How can it fly?

Me without you...
Why should I try?

A rose with no bud...
How can it grow?

Me without you...
It can't be so.

A train with no track...
How can it run?

Me without you..
Just give me a gun!

Me without you...
What else can I do?
Me without you...

   Tabi Ingle

Identity Crisis

I'm having an identity crisis.
I don't know who I am.
My life is changing without warning...
I live in the precious present,
I cherish the past,
yet
I secure the future.
I'm unsure where to go.
Which way to run.
I'm having an identity crisis.
I don't know who I am.

   Mariah J. Glisson

The Choice

In the Bible the story is told
how God's son was tried before
he grew old.

He gave his life to us
requesting only one special task,
believe in God, try to follow his ways,
his rewards are many if only we ask.

We pick and choose the road we walk
not even giving Jesus a thought.
Until we find we have lost our way,
we discover all we must do is pray.

With open arms are accepted,
God's lovely treasures
we have elected.

   Patricia M. Kenyon

"Visions Of Storm"

Visions of storm
in the moonlight sky.
Lightning takes form,
far away, up so high.

The sounds of thunder
in the cool evening hours.
Does it make you wonder
is there hope for the flowers?

Late in the season,
you can feel the breeze
He gives no reason
when the rain starts to freeze.

Listening to the rain,
streaming down from above.
Covering the mother earth
God spreading his love.

   Sunny Lambert

"My Family"

The essence of love spins
like a whirlwind through
my head. Shedding the
symbolic light and sounds
of harpsichords down all
around me. Making me
feel alive. Revealing in
me now outer beauty like
a glistening smile showing
inner peace.

   Debra Cantrell

In The Eyes Of Natasha

In the eyes of two year old
Natasha there's sex, violence,
hate, abuse, and neglect. The sex
between the baby-sitter and his
woman, the violence of her father
beating her mother over her
welfare check, the hate she sees
in her mother's eyes every time
her father comes into the room.

The neglect from her mother and
father when she is sent to bed
without food and the abuse of the
beatings when she cries because
she's hungry. In the eyes of
Natasha there's no birthday
parties or toys at Christmas or
even a whole meal; there's only
empty spaces without answers.

Violet Walton

Wondering

I sit and stare out of my window;
I see a tall, old oak tree.
I wonder how long it has been there
Growing so wild and free.

I see a bird fly o'er the tree tops;
I think it will reach the sky.
But why is it the only creature
That was created to fly?

I see a beautiful, great, blue sky
Such a vast and open range.
I wonder how far that it reaches,
And if it will ever change.

I see so many different things;
Each one I wonder much at
I wonder about small things and big;
Some things are wonders like that.

Samantha Pasco

Ode To A Dandelion

Oh dandelion, thy golden hair
Shall soon be shortened by the share.
Thy head that nodded from the lawn.
Thy yellow face, shall soon be gone.

They cut thee down while in Thy prime;
Yet if they'd only give thee time:
Thy golden locks would turn to gray,
And thou wouldst quickly fade away.

Though some despise thy humble mien
And oft remove thee from the scene,
I'll guard thee as a flower fine
And love thee much, oh dandelion!

It always makes me sad to see
Thy silver hairs strewn o'er the lea.
Yet well I know that where you blow
Another dandelion will grow.

Mae Mosher Duggan

Love

Some love is like the wind ...
Forever.
Moments gentle,
Like a warm summer breeze.

At times blowing fiercely
As a wild winter storm,
Harsh and demanding ...
Then suddenly silent.

Often changing direction
Yet, always returning,
As is our love...
Forever...

Peggy S. Blithe

A Moral Distinction

My Odessa-born mother, eager
to keep up with her Bronx
born boys, read classics
with eye-squinting ardor.
Anna Karenina she much preferred
to Emma Bovary whom she reviled.
"But why?" I asked. "Both were
adulteresses, weren't they?"
"Adulteresses-schmadultresses.
That Emma Bovary was a cheap,
empty-headed tramp! But Anna,
poor dear, chose death like
a lady," spoke my dreamy-eyed mother.

William M. Wolf

Untitled

O for a shell
Where I could hide,
Preferably a chambered nautilus.
I could burrow deep,
    and weep,
      and sleep,
I could hide from rain,
    from pain,
      Go insane.
O for a shell to hide
      inside...

Alice S. Windish

Untitled

Love can make you laugh.
Love can make you scream.

Love can give you hopes.
Love can give you dreams.

Love can make you giddy.
Love can make you cry.

Love can make you drown.
Love can make you fly.

Love can blossom like a flower,
Or it can wilt like a weed.

Love can make you say,
"I Love You."

Rebecca Kostura

Vision Of A Sunset

My golden dream of love
resembles the glowing of a sunset.
True, honest and
charming as can be.

As Wallace Stevens once said,
"a poet looks at the world as
a man looks at a woman."

I for one, look at the sunset
when Shakespeare once was
the great author he proved to be.

Nature comes about
as the last golden rays
of the day's end
covers all creatures big and small.
Showers of stars fall all about
as far as the eye can see.

I can vision anything you can imagine
far and wide.
When I look into a sunset
sitting by the ocean side.

Jessica C. Shutiva

The Orphan

How was she supposed to know
who they really are?
For so many years,
she's been left behind.
Now she's come so far.
Why should she worry?
She has it all.
She has a life.
22, soon to be a wife.
But, still, she wonders,
'who are they?'
Maybe she'll find out,
someday.

Kara Yocum

Beyond The Tip

Mom, you taught
me to find beauty
in winter, as well as summer.
You pointed out sparrows
bathing in the sprinkler.
We laughed together.
Sharing with me
your love of the desert,
finally came through the pink buds
of a cactus.
Through bales of hay.
We saw three day old kittens.
Innocent charm.
You taught me to listen to people,
learn from them all I can.
Mom, the most precious thing
I have learned
is the beauty in you.

Gayle H. Smith

A Christmas Prayer

As advent hymns ring loud and clear,
Proclaiming Jesus' birthday near;

We pray to us He will descend,
Also to each and every friend.

Then at the close of Christmas tide,
We'll ask our Lord to still abide.

And cause our hearts to always sing,
Praises to Him: God, Babe and King!

Jacqueline A. Kirby

I'll Always Remember!

I'll always remember,
the secrets you told me
the stories
your dreams.

I'll always remember,
your laugh
your moves
the way you spoke to me.

I'll always remember
the fun times we shared.
The bad times we went through.
All the promises you made.

I'll always remember
You were like an older sister to me.
You were there for me
you told me that things were fine.

Now that I am older
I'll always remember
the time you
passed away.

Rebecca Clunis

Images Of You

An illusion in a dream
Then before my eyes
Not knowing it was you

Through the passage set before me
I took a walk inside
Not ever knowing who

Shot radiance into night
All shades of darkness and light

Heightened passion
An intoxicating touch
Shot an arrow
I feel it deep inside
As deep as can be thrust

I lay drugged and weak
Unable to speak

So beautiful an unknown
That someone knows

I breathe deep inside
The blossom of a rose

Alexia Vullis

Looking Through

Why must you see evil when you
    look into my eyes
Why must you see my heart as stone
Look through what you see to what you feel
And you will find me.

Lisa Macki

Mountain Wine

Fill my glass
with mountain wine

High on the summit top
where frosty winds do blow

Changing the trees
to a yellow candle glow.

Bushes brushed with crimson, pine
branches bending low

It's time to start the season
of mountain green and snow.

Rosy cheeks of children
silver streaks in the snow

Making mountain laughter
echo high and low.

How could I ever leave thee?
No one would ever know.

Fill my glass with mountain wine
ROCKY MOUNTAIN SNOW!

Leah Mae Hall

"The Little Ram"

Once there was
A silly ole' ram
Who thought he could butt
A hole in a dam

He backed up and charged
And oh what a clatter
His mom ran to him
To see what was the matter

Mom, oh Mom!
He cried out in scorn
The poor little ram
had just broken his horn

She led him up the path
Where peace be still
Then pretty soon
He began to heal

He misses his little horn
But that's alright ya see
'Cause the missing horn reminds him
How silly he used to be

Jimbo Craven

The Hearth

Icicle soul
Defrost your heart
Warm yourself beside the fire

Melt away
To live your life
Your passion takes you higher

Cold fortress
Surrounds your heart
Release it, let it be free

Sunny days
Await your love
Be patient, soon you'll see

Shanon Harrell Matheny

Spring Air

Spring is in the air
Warm winds blow
Love is everywhere
Pretty flowers grow

A gentle rain falls
A sweet fragrance in the air
God loves us all
Spring is everywhere

Spring is in the air
Bouquet of flowers bloom
Cause love is everywhere
Under a full moon

Birds singing in the trees
Spring is everywhere
God is as busy as a bee
Love is in the air.

Wendell Harrison

At Night

Lying here, tossing
  Bones crack
  Crickets chirp lazily
  Curtains dance in the night
  Your breath, soft, slow and sure
Cool on my back.

  A reminder of our togetherness.

Lying here, thinking
  Rhymes form
  Death comes languidly
  Memories fade in the night
  My breath, hard, fast, unsure
Warm on my hands.

  A reminder of my oneness.

Lying here, sleeping
  Dreams disturb
  Reality crashes loudly
  As morning replaces night
  Our breath, numbered like the
Hairs on our head.

  A reminder of our mortality.

Rhonda L. Crews

Because He Cares

Death is never easy,
The loss will always be.
To not have the one you love,
On earth is all you see.

But God has taken them away,
To stand with Him in Glory.
The time with us too short,
But peace, is now the story.

For the day your name is called,
And you are carried to Him up there;
The reunion will be so great,
With never another care.

The struggle remains on earth,
For God has a Glorious Plan.
Your dedication to the loved one gone,
The love of all of God's clan.

For through loss we all grow,
Through loss we all gain.
Through loss God gives us,
The strength to try again.

Mark Glenn

"People Always Want"

People always want
what they can't have.
If they get it, they
decide they don't want
it anymore, so they
get rid of it. It's only
then they realize they
love it and they want
it back.

Bethany Heinz

The Listeners

The listeners are here do you
know who they are they care
they hear your plea. They help
you through the Bad times
They look so beautiful if you
know what beauty is. They
live in a special place they
talk to the stars and one
very special being you guessed
it their angels so tender so
lean. They talk to God He
tells them about you. They're
on a mission and won't quit
till it's through. They love you.

Virginia Stanton

I Will Be...

I will be a wizard
Apprentice by my side
I'll climb the highest mountain
I will control the tide.

I will be a princess
I'll dress in silky gowns
I'll live in a great big palace
And someday have the crown.

I will be a heroine
I will protect the weak
I'll travel 'round the country
Adventure I will seek.

I could be so many things
Or I could be one
I could set the highest standards
Or I could have none.

Catharine C. Biddle

I Will Be With You

I will be with you always
And you with me
When your eyes are crying
I will dry them
When your ears strain to hear
I will speak
When your hands are grasping
I will hold them
When your heart is heavy laden
I will lift it
When everyone has deserted you
I will love you
When your enemies have surrounded you
I will defend you
When you are in darkness
I will light your way
When you seek me
I will be there

Walter McDonald

The Animal In Me

I wish I were a bird,
So I could fly away,
So far away,
But not today,
If I were a fish,
I'd swim to the sea,
If I did,
Would you come with me?
If I were a tiger,
I'd run to you,
Because life is a zoo,
I wish I were a bird in the sky,
Or a fish in the sea,
But I'm not,
I'm just me.

Amy Swenson

My Guide

An outstretched hand -
A loving smile
Gently probing me
To go the extra mile -

What is it that you see in me
That my mind simply stores
Is it what I see in you
This I can't ignore -

My paths have not been the best
This I can't deny
Your light shining above the rest
Keep me going when I want to cry -

My love, my sister worry not of me
I'll watch through your eyes
So I can see
The all of me

Judy Robinson

The Soldier

Through the smoke I see a figure
Standing alone
He is bleeding
He limps
The smoke rises
I can see his face
It is distorted in pain
I go to help him
But he refuses
He wants to do it on his own
He walks towards the dirt path
It leads back to his camp
His knee buckles
He falls
He gets right back up
He continues on

Kathleen S. Mullen

Untitled

As you wipe the blood from your hands
And the tears will not come,
You realize your soul is undone.
Alone you confront the fears,
And alone you face
Your piercing scream,
Echoing
Off my
Tombstone.

Michael Repko

Our Love

Love is not loud,
But the quiet moments
when neither of us has to speak.

Love is not the highs,
But what comes to bring us
from the valley to a peak.

Love is not jealous,
But the pride we feel when achieving
the accomplishments we seek.

Love is not selfish,
But rather the happiness
we receive by giving away.

Love is not fire,
But a glow in our hearts
that brightens each day

Love for me is not possible,
Without you in my life
in every way.

Arline F. Terzek

Untitled

Seeping down inside me
My mind trembles with fear.

I am so not myself
Yet that is the expectation.

It won't leave my head
Aching for the life.

Ordinary or extraordinary,
I can't seem to decide.

Tell me in the past;
Then save me in the future

Filled up completely,
I can't ever be the same.

It took so long to realize
But now I've used the ability.

I am leaving behind the pain
And taking all the memories.

Karen Woodburn

Remembering For Forgetting

I cannot forget thee
unless I can remember in
spoken words
my naked thoughts of
shimmering hours.

Remembering out loud
will still my soul
and water-down my blood,
and ease the way of memory
to die by.

But silence
steeps a potent brew of phantoms
spawned ever anew, and makes of
madness and deceit
twin allies.

Though Time is said
to heal all wounds, and spoken words
will wipe remembrance clean,
One thorn remains to pierce the heart -
the emptiness of never having been.

Tigelia DiGiovanna

Nothing At All

Words of the night are whispered
Like the beat - the beating in - of
a lightly tapped drum
All rhythm no sound
No noise all perfection
Nothing coming together except
the beating of the drum
That drum; that was left motionless;
in the night of whispers
To soften sounds that
were not heard

Candace Letson

Untitled

Forever is too long
Never is not at all.
Together is forever
Don't forget to call.

She said forever
He said never.
She said you'll forget me.
He said he couldn't ever.

She found another
He said he'd love her forever!
But forever was too long
Because he could never.

Forever is too long
Never is not at all.
Together is forever
Don't forget to call.

Amanda Hataway

Untitled

Wherever you may go today,
Remember I'll always care.
As you go on your way today,
Remember I'm always there.

Wherever you are tonight,
Remember my love for you.
As you fall into dreams tonight,
Remember I'll always be true.

Wherever life may take you someday,
I'll always be near your side;
If we should be apart someday,
You'll find me with you inside.

Whenever we are parted on earth
I'll meet you in heaven with wings;
And whenever we are one with earth
Heaven will greet us when it sings.

Wherever this journey leads us,
Together we'll stand strong.
Whatever troubles may try us,
Together we'll never be wrong.

Jenny L. Hataway

Indian Dances

Feel the fire as it goes
out; hear the sounds of
the spirits a they cry out
to them. Watch the sun as
it slowly moves down out of
the sky into the darkness.
They will dance from dawn
to dusk until they can dance
no longer.

Chelsea Drennan

"An Ode To Pop"

Strong as a fortress
Yet sentimental as a rose
Overflowing with generosity
Towards everyone he knows.

A father, a mentor, a Citadel man
Devoted to his family,
his church, his native land.
Humor, wit, and charm abound
Whenever my grandfather is around.
Respected by many but
Cherished the most
By those of us who hold
him in our hearts-really close.

To me, he is much more
than my granddad,
He's my hero, my inspiration,
My father, my friend.

Melissa Altman Leonard

Dream Of Life

In Death's Dream Valley
Dark walls of obsidian, cold
smooth as glass
stretching cross the landscape dry,
wilted grass.
            Cold.

Dry glass dreams carry
    paper people
from hollow grounds of
body and soul.
Of the mountains.
            Cold.
Crystal rain rises
    down to fire.
Drown the tears of
    Pearl's tiger
black heart
            Cold.

Heather L. Massey

Linda's Eyes

If only the stars that shine at night
Could match your twinkling eyes
How much brighter the heavens would be
How much lovelier the skies.
For in your eyes I see a love
That no one else can see
A love that lies within you deep
But alas 'tis not for me.
Many men have seen your beauty
But in your eyes I've seen your soul
I guess that's why I'll always stay
And they will come and go.

Daniel A. Rector

Mission

Serpent like, without a leg,
I, on my belly, went to beg;
Writhing in my wingless state,
I coiled and slithered to my fate;
Scaled and written o'er with paint,
My hide slid backward from the saint,
And with a forkèd tongue I hissed
And struck at happiness and missed!

Diana Dutton

I Love Him God...Amen

As I kneel beside my bed, at the end
of a long weary day.
I bury my face into trembling hands,
as the tears fall as I pray....

Dear God,
Unworthy as I am, I ask one thing of thee,
If the one I love should forget some things,
please help him to remember me.
For I can no longer go to him and
let him take me by the hand,
God you can talk to him to help
him understand.
Help keep me inside his precious
heart until we meet again.
Even though we are far apart..
I Love Him God
Amen.

Tabitha Dobson

Achieve

If you ever
walk across a man
who tells you
you can't do something
that you have
your heart and soul
set on doing,
kindly,
walk around that man.
For he
will never move.

Ryan Murdock

Untitled

Silence falls over,
the green land,
    Turning it brown.
The moment passes and,
    The silence lingers.
Wiping out the memories,
    Leaving nothing but empty space.
The touch is gone,
    none will ever compare.
The land will never be,
    as green again.
The flowers will never bloom.
    The sky will stay gray,
and the air musty.
    Sadness will rain.
The moment is gone,
    never to be seen again.
Or remembered.

Rebecca L. Lux

"Endless Journey"

I am, in this world, a
part of it
Yet with no belonging
to my footstep.

My path is as yet unknown,
Vague—
Wandering as misty fog
In ocean woods.

I may, perhaps, never
alight. Merely visit as
the fog — then drift
away once more.

Norman W. Gibson

Untitled

Sea breeze mist
come close
lost in a kaleidoscope
of starlight reflections

Mirror the images
into one

Soft cool spray
Touches the gentle air

Burning bright fresh glows
Sparkles day into night
Say you will...

Carrie Lee Angeles

Friendship

Friendship.
Feeling like a good event.
Scattering like marbles rolling.
Moving like an open sea.
Waiting like open arms for me.
Opening like a morning flower.
Friendship is the best.

It is there to catch me when I fall,
Cheers me up when I am sad,
Comforts me when I am alone,
Listens when I have something to say,
Loves me all the time,
Friendship.

Robbie Lyday

Wisteria

Gnarled branches
Centuries old
Green leaves
Purple flowers
The sweet dank smell of ages
Here is where your hand
touched so long ago.

So many voices
Spoken hear
all now
Betrayed of sound

Riplets of love
Form the petals
Drops of sun
press inside the cracks
the wood breathes
Air suffocates
Sound burns
Hearts break

Jocelyn A. Rowan

"Flowers Of Sun"

Small seed
Sunshine and rain
Sprout
Blooming petals
Tall and swaying
Vivid yellow
Dancing sun
Dew drops on petals
Like smiling rays
Sheer gold
Glimmering
Sunflowers.

Annie Gelner

Stars

Within the world
  You would like
    to be.

Is in the
  movies, and
    on TV.

And when a fan
  writes to her
    favorite Stars.

All she dreams
  of is meeting
    them as they
    are.

But when the Stars
  begin to fall.
    She see them as
    No Stars at all.

Ingrid Enloe

After the Fall

Driving along
the fog's so thick
to lose the line
is to lose the road.
Nocturnal madness creeps,
pricking the corners
of a mind
used to sleep.

These weary bones wonder
how to fit into his,
and fancy that—
when it's over—
he'll not be the one
missing a rib.

Chrystena Chrzanowski

Look At Me

Look at me, what am I to you
Look at me, you think I'm a ghost
Look at me, what or whom do you see.
Look at me, I'm pretty and free.
Look at me, I wish you could see,
that inside of me, I'm pretty and free.

Nikki Price

Untitled

Feeling so unloved
Like I can't please anyone
Drowning in a world
With no acceptance
Trying to find a place
To be myself.
Always doubting it's really there.
Locked in a tower
Where being perfect
  is the only way out.
Yet my heart still beats
Finding its own pattern of life
As if my presence
  really affects someone
  somehow
  somewhere
I feel my self fading away
Willingly letting go
Finally being free.

Becky Wilkerson

One Day

A new flower blooms everyday.
Everyday a leaf falls. Every time
a flower blooms and a leaf falls
a baby is born a new life is given.
But one day that flower will die
One day that leaf will disappear.
One day we all will fade away.

Crystal Ann Rowland

The Stillness And The Storm

The sun is glittering splendidly,
except in the distance
  Where a midnight black haze
blankets the earth.
  The birds are chirping gently,
in this perfect little area.
  But in the distance, the overlaying
mist is creeping closer and closer.
  The birds are now fleeing,
scurrying swiftly along.
  The cold dark world is now
racing forward.
  The carefree world has faded out,
leaving no trace of its former self.
  The gloomy world has arrived,
the rain begins to spew forth.
  The blackness of the sky,
turns into the illusion of daylight.
  Boom.....
The rumble fades into the night.

Ilona M. Ranelli

Peace

It is over
For everyone.
Business crashes.
A poor class becomes.
Millions
Thrown out of work.
No need for us,
Man is done.

The Long Peace has come.

Adam Berger

No Clock Can Measure

Your touch enthralls so
the pause of my heart.

Your arms harbor passion
the gasp of my mouth.

Your eyes of emerald
the fire of my soul.

Your body lightly glistens
the release of my grasp.

Your masculinus way
the impulse to obey.

Your love brought desire
the heat of my flesh.

Your rapturous surprise
the ecstasy of my mind.

For our time together
no clock can measure.

Teresa Church

The Wave

She shyly retreats
On pussy cat feet
Holding her petticoats high.

Then gathering her forces
Of rearing green horses
Tossing their manes to the sky—

Like a battering ram
She heads for the sand
Self destructive - determined to die.

But no, she retreats
On pussy cat feet
Holding her petticoats high.

Elizabeth Gillard

A Father's Love

When I'm a dad, I'll be the best
No doubt better, than all the rest
I'll listen, wait, and understand
Always be there, to lend a hand
Be there to guide and show the way
Be there for bad, and better days
Be there for you, Brandyn my son
Be there until, my life is done.

Charles Geisz Jr.

"If Everyday Could Be Christmas"

If everyday could be Christmas, what
a wonderful place this would be
to live. Everyone you meet, would
have their own personal gift to give.
   It may be the gift of laughter,
a smile, or maybe just a kind word.
And the spirit of the birth of Jesus,
could be seem through all of us,
as well as heard.
   And on this day, the love can
be felt from all across this earth.
Yes, if everyday could be Christmas,
we would always feel the
wonders of his birth.

Ricky Riggs

Silky Strands

A silky silver strand is seen
Against a golden sky.
So delicately dangling
Yet pleasing to the eye.

So graceful flows it here to there,
Its beauty so invites,
That dew and sunbeam cling to it
And dance as merry sprites.

As strand by strand the pattern grows,
It calls out to the world
Of simple things so radiant
That meeker things unfurled.

And as the sun climbs filled with awe,
Up from the mounts beyond,
It paints a humble background
For the mighty spider's wand.

A web was woven wearily
To maintain a meager meal.
May our essential actions too,
Show beauty so surreal.

Bonnie Hannigan

My Love

Trying to get you
Was like a steal.

Kissing and hugging.
That's what I feel.

The red rose you gave me
With the petals that never fall.

Happiness and times to remember.
You give me them all.

You are one of God's creations.
You are my heart.

And with your love
It will never fall apart.

Chane'l Jackson

Forgive

I have wanted to walk
To the end of my path
beside you.
Why have you turned
away and dropped
my hand.
Do I know who you are?
Are you embarrassed to let
your sadness and shame
be known.
I am sure your humanness
more than matches my own
could we touch again,
try to.

Elise Murphy

Untitled

The rosing winds kiss
The lost paths we walked
Yesterday.
The snails marvel at how fast
Our garden bloomed...
Then as fall into winter turned
Everything brown and
Colours changed to cold and blue
The hummingbird starves:
The loving warm smiles of
Flowers gone for now
Are memories.
Warm like the sun
When I remember your touch.
Buzzing like a meadow
When I see your smiles
And feel you near.

Scott Richardson

The Self

The matutinal pond
heavy like a fat monk
content with his god
smoked in the waking dawn.

The silent sentinel of the sleepy deep
the solitary pike
on fire with his divinity
exploded
into the embarrassed air.

Edward G. Zogby, S. J.

There's Always A Beginning

There's always a beginning
There's always an end
There's always an enemy
There's always a friend
There will always be hate
There will always be love
There's always an answer
That comes from above.

There's people who are happy
There's people who are sad
There's people who are good
There's people who are bad
There's people who are old fashioned
There's people who are mod
But there's no one on earth
Who will ever be like God.

Cheryl A. Bennett

Trust

The anger inside me is
raging. I cannot hardly sleep
at night. I shan't take it
anymore. When shall it end?
When will the world become
full of happiness? When will
peace flow through us? I only
wish I knew. How can the
anger stop? When will the
wars and cold-blooded killings
come to an end? When will
we love one another? Can't we at
least try? When will peace come?
I hope that peace, love, and
happiness will come, I pray to
God that it will. I trust.

Healy Schuber

Nightmares Of The Past

Democracy, aristocracy
a total wave of power.
People search, pray in church,
waiting for the hour.
An hour of salvation,
the revolution has begun.
The armies ride,
the people run,
and the blood of the conquered
covers the sun.
Some of the hunted
flee with the knowing
that they are the last,
and so is now
what I had thought
to be nightmares of the past.

Marc Kristopher Meyer

A Winter Garden

A garden covered all in snow
glistens as the sun sinks low
the stars come out they seem to glow
they shimmer as the wind will blow
around the bend I see a doe
brown and white against the snow
she walks around as the wind will blow
a winter garden in the snow.

Mara Redlich Revkin

Leviathan

A twisting monster within,
kept me on the stroll.
Yea, out there,
on the famous Sunset Boulevard.

When your work pad is
like a barren dungeon,
tricks resemble sick cattle,
and you hear the Devil sing,
playing Dylan's,
"Slow Train Coming,"
you want to roll over and die.
Yea, on your round satin bed,
that the strangers you cannot kiss,
lay on like fools,
it's not even yours.

You have nothing but sadness,
pity and shame forever.
Caught in a hallucinatory trap.

And you wonder,
will I ever change?

Cherry-Rose Hastings

Still

The wind still shall blow
With the soul of a child
Older than time
Forever tender and wild
  And hearts still will be moved
  By Earth's gentle grace
  The depth of her dance
  And the beauty of her face
The waves still shall roll
In an ethereal dance
Holding those who watch
In a dreamlike trance
  And the stars still will shine
  Eternally bright
  Bathing the treetops
  In silvery light
So although I'm gone
Do not fear
In these things
I will always be near.

Jennifer Smith

What If?

I love you
and you love me,
our lives will grow
like mahogany trees standing close
to each other.

Our time will be spent
like birds flying
together
in the skies.

Our bodies will move
like swimmers floating
in the seas.

Our thoughts will flow
back and forth
as connected rooms.

Our souls will be joined
forever and ever
and ever.

Pilar Tan

Questions

Where are the answers
To all my questions?
Trapped behind a stone wall
That refuses to fall,

When will the pain end?
Now, or after it is done
Eating away what feelings I have left -
Or maybe it won't...

What solution is there
To the emptiness I hold
So close to my heart
That refuses to stop beating?

Why does life have so many turns
That confuse the past with the present,
Yet hold the key to the future
Behind a door that can't be opened?

Anna Munsell

The Howling In The Wood

On a warm summer day,
Or even in the night,
I sometimes hear them howling
With all their majestic might.
I seldom ever see them,
And the latest one I saw,
I found its giant footprint,
Made a plaster of its paw.
One day that I went hiking,
A pack of them I found,
Probing in the grass for mice,
Then vanishing without a sound.
I'd love to see them running,
Or chasing the weakest deer.
Still the long, slow howling,
Is my favorite thing to hear.

Jonathan Roberts

The Bridge

Troubled people cross me,
but not physically.
Problems I have seen
are cut very deep.
I help to see the light.
People walk across me
and are mended.
I am a bridge of feelings
and emotions.
I solve problems,
no matter to me
if it takes
forever.

Brad Ward

Only You

Only you can hold me tight
  kiss me right and
  love me all through the night.

Only you can have my hand
  and be my man.

Only you will be on my mind
  throughout all of time.

Only you are for me
  and that's the way it'll be
  for all eternity.

Christine Curry

Forbidden Love

As I sit here thinking of you,
All I see is...
The beauty within you.

I know our love is forbidden.
But when I am with you,
My true feelings are never hidden.

How do I say, I love you so much?
Mere words can not explain,
My heart you have touched.

I wish our love could shine through.
But there are clouds in the sky,
Which make my heart blue.

True love, they say, will always be.
And that is why,
Our love, I will someday see.

Thomas B. Serrato

The Ocean Majestic

Out of the fog-laden night,
A force unveils itself;
Driven by the force of wild stallions-
Precariously pounding the surf.
Kelp bestrides the moistened sand,
Left to clothe the denuded land;
Remnants of times of yore-
Finding dominion on the shore,
Until the crest takes control;
Propelling its majesty onto the ground,
Entrancing me with hypnotic sounds.
Once free from its shadowy demesne,
The white caps journey on;
Consuming all that block its path-
Anxiously awaiting the golden dawn.

Sean J. Heiss

High Time

Time allotted to us is precious time
a time to work and a time to play
Time to take a stand, to be firm
and a time to pray.
Time speeding by on wings waiting
for no one. Think then act to make
the most of each passing day.
Time my only jewel will be lost
forever if I wait for the perfect
time to accomplish my goals
of either work or play.
Before the sun goes down at the
end of the day take time to be
holy take time then to pray.

Pauline Hassler

Inchoate Moment

The uneven pieces
  Lie strewn about the floor
Waiting a master's hand,
  Hoping to assemble
With the sureness of a Rembrandt,
  Or the joyous illusion of a Monet.

My uncertainty
  Drains their spirit,
As I fumble, reconsider,
  Attempt again
To create the masterpiece they expect.

Anne Voth

Guardian Angel

Angel of light
Time to take flight
The Lord above calls you
There is something you must do
Spread your wings of silk
Don't ever let them wilt
Heaven and earth are yours to see
Never knowing that much beauty could be
We look upon you for help
In your grace we knelt
We shield our eyes from your beauty
The light of your powers guide me
When in times of hardness
I will remember this
There is an angel looking over me
So that I may always see clearly
My Guardian Angel.

Lené M. Decker

Gabe

My heart has throbbed
so, hoping that you love
me as I love you.
Feel the soft touch
of my lips against
yours. Be with me as
I wish to be with
you. My shoulders feel
softer knowing that
you love me back as
I have loved you
since, the day your
eyes met mine.

Ashley Parker

Love In The Sixties

We met in the sixties
My was it nifty
Our eyes met in a machine shop
And shot rockets to the roof top
Thence to the countryside
Where we danced along the road side
And on to the Navy
Where we made all that gravy
Plus we were wavy baby Butchie
It lasted a balmy decade
Until we got caught in a Tornado
Torn apart at the root and destroyed
We healed in the mountains
Where they have ample fountains
Fountains of faith to heal
To sit at the seaside
And watch the gulls fly by
Upward unto the horizon
And thus watch your life fly away.
Bye Bye baby 'til we meet again.

Barbara Davis

Just A Heartbeat Away

I never knew anyone like you.
  Some one so precious, so kind and true.

Who took my hand when I needed a friend.
  Was patient, loving and kind to the end.

Now time is drawing nearer, and we must part.
  But always remember,
    there's a special place for you, in my heart.

Johnnie M. Reance

Let Me Die

Please let me die.
Peacefully in the night.
Eternal peace.
Rest for this tired body.
Serenity for my soul.

Please let me go.
Understand my pain.
Forgive my selfishness.
My everlasting Love is with you.
Tho you feel abandoned, Persevere.

Please let me die.
Life is for the living.
Hopeless is tomorrow.
Mystified by life and time.
Relinquish my heart.

Please let me go.
Prevent not my wish.
My spirit remains with yours.
Wed in love, honor, our Souls one.
Bestow your sanction, let me die.

Renee Cook

Innocence

I can't see innocence,
For I know nothing of.
No, I can't see happiness,
Or peace, or joy, or love.

I can't cry but bitter tears,
And I don't feel the sun.
I don't know what I'm working for,
But it's never, never done.

I can't let them touch my heart,
Touch it, squeeze it, break it.
I can't let them touch my soul,
Touch it, burn it, take it.

I can't look into your eyes,
Because I know your mind.
I just can't see innocence.
I may as well be blind.

C. Lynn Majors

Need

How many tears must I weep
before you understand
of this love I want to keep?
So many unspoken words
and undone actions
are mounted upon our souls.

Do you want to leave?
I sense you do-
but I try to believe
it's all in my head.
Sometimes emotions
speak louder than words.

If your heart is not in it
Please-
don't hurt me.
I know I'll do something I'll regret.
You can't accept the fact
that I need you here with me-
You are my life...my air
I need you.

Cassie N. Grube

"You Have Gone"

I look upon the empty chair
The people have gone home
An empty house to roam in now
A house now and empty home
The children stayed a little while
But their families need them now
For me it's quiet and lonely
Without you in the house
We married young and stayed together
For many many years
You aged a little faster
As you had many senior years
But now the house is silent
When I come in the door
You are gone but not forgotten
For you're in heaven with the Lord
I know I'll see you someday
When my time on earth's at end
And we will be together
Forever once again.

Bonnie Lou

The Missing Link

Every night I look out the window
and wish to the man up above
If he could do anything
find me someone to love.

It could be anybody
just somebody to see
my qualities within
and not my disability

Somebody to love me
somebody to care
a relation filled with love
and plenty to share

Somebody to accept me
and give me a chance
because I will do anything
just for romance

If there is someone
could they be found
when will it be
because I've looked all around

James Finley Pruitt

Crayons

There used to be a box of crayons
Sitting on that shelf over there
Yeah, it was only six colors
Red
Yellow
Green
Blue
Black
and
White
Red and yellow didn't get along
Because yellow acted too bright

Green and blue didn't get along
Because green acted too rich

But I never knew why
Black and white didn't get along...

Yorel Pickens

Beautiful Sky

I like to look up
  into the sky
and watch the billowing
  clouds roll by,
Forming funny clowns
  and dancing girls
Even Old Glory as it
  unfurls!
I have seen a man on a horse
  race by
And tumbling acrobats
  in the sky.
Once God smiled
  down at me!
And made me happy
  as could be!

Dorothy Baigh Schlesinger

Time Is Right

You in my life, for time is right I
Have no need to fear.
Love is a treasure, for we are gold
Of today and yester-year.
Tender thoughts flow through tears
Of past and future things. For time
Is right and time is love, for what
Out future brings.

Joyce Lavon Wells

Love Is

Soft as a baby's touch
Sweet as a buttercup
Tender as your heart.
Strong as two arms around
You, when hurt.
Fuzzy as a kitten's fur
Precious as life God gives us
A cloak that wraps
itself around us.
Love is what God gave to all.
Love is the power of the universe.

Gwen Shuler

The Monster

It came up from the harbor
On misty, nebulous paws
And no one knew its purpose
And no one knew its cause

Folks ran inside their houses
With fear plain in their eyes
For none knew what would happen
(They hated a surprise)

One small girl dared to challenge
The creature 'round the town
To reclaim her baby doll
She'd stare a monster down!

A little while later
The monster'd lost its touch
The girl had found her dolly
But Mom had worried much

Mother said "Oh daughter dear
'Twas like a rabid dog."
"But Ma, it had my dolly.
Besides, 'twas only fog!"

Melissa R. Johnson

Dad

Putting on his coat.
I felt the tender touch
of soft lining.
Willing myself to believe
It was really his caring
Feeling so cool and soft
Against my skin
Knowing he was always trying
To love with tenderness
His children.

Liz Nason

Like A Wounded Bird

Four years she suffered,
Uncomplaining.
Her Faith in life was
All-sustaining.
I marvelled at her
Stoicism,
Was buoyed up by her
Cheerfulness
Which daily affected the
Patients around her.
Never, until the very end
Did the sparkle leave
Those blue eyes.
Yet, with deep, silent compassion
We viewed that tiny body
So helpless, so cut,
That we silently wept
And questioned: "Why?"
So like a wounded bird,
  My mother.

Helen E. Scott

The Revelation

Day after day, nothing changes
No revelations
No insight
No hope

Day after day, the fire burns
More sorrows
More worries
More problems

Day after day, emptiness
A broken heart
A broken dream
A broken promise

Day after day, the clouds clear
A new horizon
A new chance
A new life

Brian Weber

Listening

You wonder how I feel,
but when I tell you,
  You don't listen.

My heart echoes thunder
like the beating of a drum.
  Then the tears come.

My heart may never heal,
cause of what I feel.
Tears may go away
or come another day.

Jessica McCormack

Unlimited

Freedom dings on the marketsquare
Fat Sacks swingin' everywhere
Radical reruns return to rot
Pacers bake back on their cot
Liners long for the Constitution
Ecstasy is for evolution
Fallin' down another row
Bolt the Cragars on my GTO
A purple haze is in my eyes
As I sit down I start to rise
Arc that bend when you drill for oil
Fixin' my dents with aluminum foil
Call Doctor Jack when you're in pain
Trust yourself they're all insane
Give up floozies' dividends
The golden curves will never end
Awl in all, buy electric fence
Don't put up with incompetence

Brian J. Sauers

Eyes

Those eyes, watching, waiting
Behind the shadows motionless
Seeing through, clear through
past the covers of mere men
Men wait for a sound but
none comes to those who
cannot listen Only the faint
everlasting echo of silence is
heard from these eyes
Keeping them ever prepared for
what is to come When not
looking, I am there watching
listening, waiting, forgiving
the purpose of me is for every
man his own, secret fears,
joy and desires For the shadows
are my domain in which I rule
If not now you realize what or
who I really am I died for
you...These are the eyes of the
Almighty God.

Matthew Wheeler

If I Should Go Blind

If I should go blind
I know the Lord will
lead me through the
darkness of the night.

If I should go blind
I know the Lord will
lead me from here to
eternity.

Wherever my path shall lead
I know the Lord will be there for me.

If I should go blind.

Mary M. Restivo

What Color Are You?

What color are you?
Are you red, green, purple or blue?

Can you pick the color of your mood?
Can you eat the color in your food?

What color is you?
What is your hue?
Who...are...you?

Nora Devine

Not Guilty

Live in trouble
toil and strife
Shake my hand
feel my knife.

Look in the storm
to find the sun
You're my friend
and here's my gun.

The world is black
and white and red
If we're the living
who's the dead.

Life is love
light and free
we're in the dark
on a killing spree.

Kim Hampton

The Man In The Mirror

When I look at my picture
Taken in Nineteen forty-three,
It makes me feel mighty proud,
Because I know it's me.

But when I look in the mirror,
I just have to stand and stare;
That has to be someone else,
Who's looking out of there.

His hair is so gray and thin,
And his stomach's round and fat.
There is no way in this world,
I could ever look like that!

With those sagging eyelids,
And the likes of his double chin;
One look quickly tells me,
He is just a "has been."

So his true identity,
Will just have to remain in doubt!
For I might be disappointed,
If I should find it out!

Clifford Hevener

A Friend Like You

A friend like you comes along
Only once in a lifetime
A friend who is dedicated and loyal
A friend who is loving and kind

Even though we've been friends
For such a long while
You still have the gift
Of making me smile

Your loving kindness is evident
In all the things you do
I enjoy the gifts you give me
Knowing they come from you

We'll always be together
Even when we're apart
For I carry a piece of you
Locked away in my heart

No matter what the future holds
I know our friendship remains true
I only wish that everyone in the world
Could have a friend just like you

Jeffrey Glenn Ayers

Butterfly Wings

How would it be
On a day in June,
To open your eyes
In a dark, dark cocoon?

To soften one end
And crawl outside,
And find you had wings,
To open up wide?

To find you could fly
To a bush or a tree,
Or float on the breeze
Like a boat at sea?

How, how would it be?

Derek Beebe

The Blizzard Of 1996

Standing in my driveway
    knee deep in snow,
Feeling the bone-chilling
    winds as they blow.

Thoughts drifting back
    over the years...
Remembering our ancestors—
    the "Trail Of Tears."

I can just imagine how
    they must have felt—
Will the snow ever stop?
    Will this ice ever melt?

With every footstep, I feel
    your agony and pain!!!!
It should Not have happened;
    you did not die in vain.

As each silent voice echoes...
I will always hear it.
May you forever rest in peace
with the Great Spirit.

*Jacqueline "April Rain" Clark
(Cherokee)*

"Fallen Nature"

When fall the golden spangles
from their boughs

Then know that Love requires
this to be

And that which is for Love
shall never be for nought

Though branch and trunk
may fruitless seem to be

Though nailed
as a target to a tree

*Kelli Kennedy Tanksley
1 Peter 2:24*

The Lonely

She sat alone, there in the dark,
As tears rolled down her face,
Again, she asked, why me oh Lord.
Was gave a life to waste?
I've known no love, no happiness,
On earth, I've found no place,
This precious life, you've given me
was surely by mistake!

Margaret Jones

A Shrink's Lament

Doctor, Doctor tell me.....

Why am I so?
God made you so!

Why am I so?
Mother's milk made you so!

Why am I so?
Chromosomes made you so!

Why am I so?
Chemicals made you so!

Why am I so?
Poverty made you so!

Why am I so?
Drugs made you so!

Why am I so?
Pollution made you so!

Why am I so?
Abuse made you so!

Why am I so?
How the Hell do I know???

Marcel Perlman

"The Days"

The days of your life are as
Precious as gold, for you are
The only one who lived the
Story as it was told.

The days went by so fun and
Fast, that you lived your life
As it was your past.

Things happened so very clear,
That when you remember them
They feel so very near.

People you know are gone,
But your memories live on
As you go on.

Candice Monique Colbert

Untitled

As time went on
    the times of care
The memories of the
    years that we shared
From this day on
    we will be one
Praying that our love doesn't fade
    as does the sun
Our love becomes
    deeper everyday
Every hour every minute
    and in every special way
Each new day
    that we spend together
Brings our love
    closer to forever
Forever is something
    we look forward to
And forever is me
    always loving you!

Christine L. Corigliano

Friendship

Friendship is a softer word
   for love
Because friends were sent
   from God above
Friendship means to love
   and understand
Friendship will ease your pain
   just because it can
Being a friend is the best
   thing you can do
A friend will always mean
   it when they say

"I love you"
     Sharon Paige

Standing Still

The world is standing still,
not moving around
like a dead body in the ground.
Not going anywhere
not doing anything
just listening to the sound
that lies all around.
For everyone to hear
but nobody listens,
except the dead body
in the ground.
That has nothing to do
except listen
to the beautiful sound,
the earth has to offer,
In its essence of life
that it lets out in a song,
only the dead body
listens to and treasures
the likeness of the earth.
     Curtina Beblo

"The Second Chance"

He was born on Christmas Day,
So very long ago,
Not very many noticed,
On that day or after,
How He was so special
And how He would give
The world a second chance.

Only those who lived that day
Will ever know how real He is,
When He died and rose again
And even when He went back up
Into the heaven above.
     Rebecca Faber

Concomitance

To you my thoughts are nothing
   in the wind.
You think with your mind.
I reach out with my heart.
You can make a speech.
I can make a bed.
You see the vine.
I see the leaf.
As to living, we have the same belief.
So somehow I see
We can live together quite happily.
     Florence Baker Hanson

Angels

They come
When we need them;
When we do not know,
They are here.
They come
To save
To protect
Or heal.
These wonderful Beings—
Gentle and good—
Make us strong
Resilient
And free.
Sometimes when our minds
Are absent
And we worry and fear,
We forget them,
But later revive
And know
They were here.
     Helen M. Brown

Dog Day

Crystal ships in the sky,
Daylight moon, wondering why.
In the tree a blinding sand,
Every day the mind of man.

Golden door knobs lead the way,
Glowing leaves on an autumn day.
Keep away he knows not when,
To see himself, time and again.
     Richard Steven Wilson

All Alone

Descending into madness,
He stared at the wall.
Locked into visions,
No one else could see at all.

He had grown thin and haggard,
Eyes bleary from lack of sleep.
Hands covering his ears,
He would sit and weep.

He listened to the voices,
Which increased his fear.
Loud, demanding conversations,
No one else seemed to hear.

He was a pitiful man,
With a life so bleak.
Descending into madness,
All alone on the street.

People walked by briskly,
Blind to his plight.
With a tattered coat upon him,
He lay down for the night.
     Brenda S. Jones

Weeping Willow

  Weeping willow hear my cry
As I look into the sky
  Wishing one day for it to rain
To wash away the hurt and pain
  Soaring eagles see my heart
All bent, twisted and broke apart
  One day I shall feel again
Weeping willow help me mend.
     Karen Collins

Untitled

Picture a
white apparatus sun,
next gift crushed,
still not manipulate like their mother,
beat the pink summer.
Old father is his grave,
he gave me the go ahead.
Black free fall, through the
past darkly.
Dawn, why not go to hell?
Dawn, why not go to paradise?
She slams the door in
his face. He cries. She laughs.
He collapses. She dances.
All their torn families
with their torn souls and
torn beliefs.
Dawn, why not stick around for awhile?
     Gabriel B. Herrin

Etherea

He reached down from the
heavens and touched
my soul
His lips kissed mine
as never been told
We made love in a
constellation for hours
on end
and then conceived a child
for whom the light
would bend
     Diane Myers Yoder

Friends

A friend is someone special,
And I'm going to tell you why.
They always seem to understand,
Even when you cry.

They're there to lend a helping hand,
Whenever you might call.
They're always there to pick you up,
When by chance you fall.

A friend is there to give a push,
When you think you can't go on.
A friend is in the darkest night,
To keep you safe 'til dawn.

And now I will advise you
To find a friend today.
A friend is a good thing to have,
To keep from day to day.
     Rachel Swoboda

Her Life

The sun had set in her eyes
The vision of it but in disguise
Growing weak
She lost her way
Off the path she started to stray
Her new life, Now carved in stone
Looking away
She felt alone
Nothing mattered anymore
Gone without knowing what life was for
     Dina Turcic

Excuse Me

Excuse me for a moment
There's something that I miss.
I think you took it from me
The very first time we kissed.

Excuse me for a moment
Please can I have it back.
You quickly took it from me
And left me just like that.

Excuse me for a moment
There's nothing I can do.
Would you please return it
Cause it doesn't belong to you.

Excuse me for a moment
You left me in the dark.
I'll ask you one last time
"Would you give me back my Heart?"

Christie G. Miller

The Corn-poppy

In summer the corn-poppies
Dance in the grain
Lifting their petticoats
Red as a stain.

I picked a red corn-poppy
Bright as a gem.
Down fell her petticoats
Round her torn stem.

My love is a corn-poppy,
Now she lies dead.
All her red petticoats
Wrapped round her head.

I'd give all my riches
And give them again
To see her feet dancing
Once more in the grain.

Charles Shute

Good-Bye

I feel the end is coming,
I feel that we must part,
But until we meet again,
You will always be in my heart.
I loved you till the end,
And this you must believe,
I will remember you for always,
Until the world I leave.
My heart will be with you,
And yours will be with me,
Until we meet again,
Together we mustn't be.
I'm sorry for the pain I caused,
I didn't want it to be,
But I think it would be best for you,
Just to forget about me.

Lindsay I. Horstman

Can We

What can we do when everyone's gone,
What can we do when there's nothing
   to dawn.
What can we say when there's no one to hear,
What can we say to stop all the tears.
Who can we be if there's nothing to be,
Who can we turn to if there's no one but me.

Elana Scopa

Precious Gifts

As I walk along the shore
beneath the pale moonlight
The waves come rushing in
it's such a beautiful sight

We seem to have the power
but yet we seem so small
how can one create
what matters most of all

The dreams that we dream
the wishes that come true
Seem so far and distant
like walking on the moon

To realize what we have
is it real or is it fake
it doesn't make any sense
the chances we must take

When life seems to go downhill
my spirits give me a lift
when I look into the ocean
and see the world's precious gift

Autumn Lyn Kessinger

That Old Wooden Cross

That old wooden cross,
So rugged and so rough,
Jesus carried it to die on;
It must have been so tough!

Do you wonder if He thought
of the pain that He'd receive?
Or, did He think of you and me,
and the pain He could relieve?

No matter what His thoughts,
as He carried His cross on that day,
He died in perfect submission
in His Father's perfect way.

All those things He did endure
on that day on Calvary's Hill,
because He knew it was for sure,
He was doing His Father's will!

He hung there so all alone,
and died on that old cross.
Our sins He freely took,
so for us, there'd be no loss!!

Barbara N. Alverson

A Windy Path

So young and strong I jog along
A windy path.
I see a man, old and gray,
I jog his way.
Sitting upon a bench in the park
I hear the man say,
"You must slow down my dear,
life is too short you hear,
You must slow down my dear."
I laugh and begin to run,
Thinking dumb old man.
Years and years away,
I jog the same path old and gray.
I get to the bench where the
dumb old man once sat,
think of his words and see what he meant.
I do not jog, nor do I run, but sit
where the wise old man once sat.

Melissa VanOrden

World

A ball is round
for it is condemned to that shape
a prisoner in an existentialistic world

Did you ever wonder

Would that ball
rather be
something else

Perhaps the sun
condemned to that shape
a prisoner in an existentialistic world

John Martin

I Have For Our Future

I have courage.
I have hope.
If we stick together,
We can learn to cope.

I have strength.
I have power.
If we form a team,
This will be our greatest hour.

I have ideas.
I have thoughts.
We all have our opinions,
Which needs to be taught.

I have something,
Something deep inside.
It wants to get out,
And express its pride.

I have a lot,
But not enough.
I want peace,
But I know it's tough.

Tori DiTaranto

The Door

The door
Black and full of rage
The door
Red and full of evil
The door
Green and full of envy
The door
Blue and full of sadness
The door
Purple full of romance
The door
Yellow and full of sensitivity
So which door is your
Door?

Nicole Levake

God's Promises

God made everything from the grass
   to the sky,
Because he loves you and I.
Because of him we are free
   God is not a fantasy.
He can tell right from wrong because
   his promise lasts forever long.
So you may have everlasting life
   Jesus died for your life.

Kristen Kalz

The Legend Of The Eagle

In the frosty mountains of Tennessee,
Just before the dawn,
An eagle plans her strategy
While awaiting a ray of the sun.

Firmly clutching her claws in an amber branch,
She looks down on the clear, sparkling water.
There in the stream, it happens by chance
That her prey appears dancing before her.

Releasing herself, she soars into flight.
Screaming, as she races to seize him.
With the wings of an angel and all of her might,
She carefully executes determination.

Victoriously rising, she returns to the sky....
Well known for her strength and her grace.
Joyful and confident, she holds her head high!
As she, in this world, takes her place.

Christal Kahles

Living

Come to my house
It is no mansion in the sky
Or where you go when you die
It is a place where I try to keep love alive
And God is always there with me

Let us be friends while we can
As we journey together in this land
Can we love one another and sing in our heart
Share the bread of God until we must part
To meet again on that far distant shore

Life is like a river
Water flowing free and always moving onward
With Christ guiding me
Oh sweet Jesus please take my hand
Lead me to the promise land
Never to forsake me as I make my stand
In witness of all my love for thee

Dolores Beard

Dreams

Once upon a future day, the sky was clear, the grass was green.
I sat down to ponder my way,
the past before me I have seen.

I shall, I thought, take a short nap,
and dream of days of future past.
As my thoughts carried me forward, my life like a map,
I hope this dream would last and last.

Bell bottomed pants, platform shoes,
peace beads around my neck.
Flower children praising peace, abundant love everywhere,
Vietnam war, disapproving public, damn them all to heck,
all God's children need our love, please everyone lets be fair.

Crowds of colorful people, daydreamers everywhere,
singing songs of joy and peace, many heads up in a cloud.
Once together now divided, that gives me a scare,
we all live in America let's be proud.

Some things good, some things bad, with every time.
Nothings ever perfect, we dream of days gone by.
I'm glad I live in a time that's mine,
in a day and age when time can fly.

Sarah M. Karns

Mirror Mirror

I look into the water and see the innocence of love.
I look into the stars and see the answers to many wonders.
But, when I look at you I see a candle burning both ends with
    anguish and dampened expectations.
The flame will continue to destroy the wick until the mirror finally

Jackie Wilkerson

"Journey To The Shore"

As do the ripples from a pebble in a pond
affect each other on their journey to the shore,
so do our lives and every breath affect our beloved
and even a distant strangers course.

To say that I could have or might have or should have
is eventually fatal to mind.

For once the pebble had fallen, the beginning
of the end has begun. And so too as a life begins,
another is rushing to shore.

James Alan Bowers

In Dreamland

Clashing swords of knights in armor
Starlight gazes upon the harbor
Circus elephants on parades
Fine cuisines and flambés
Sneaky pirates, treasures, and gold
Bold, new stories to be told
Pretty, perfect houses with white picket fences
Hitting a home run far past the benches
Things that we should have done
Games that we would have won

In Dreamland

Deirdra Tully

The Rock

I, the rock, I am immortal,
I have lived for more than a thousand years.

I am one of earth's masterpieces
I am one of mother nature's beauties
I hold all the phases of nature in one figure...

I hold the pastel colors of the rainbow,
I hold the rock formations of the canyons,
I hold the fragrance of the fir trees,
I hold the songs of the wind...

I am an abstract figure
Different patterns and formations
Lie all over my hard body like a wrinkled old man.

I am a mountain to an ant,
I am a piece of dust to a human,
I am home to worms, I am a creation of mother nature.

I, the rock, lay in my natural surroundings
With the cold air whisking by me...
The wind howls, the trees sway, the birds screech
And... patiently... obediently... silently...

The Rock Lies.

Priya Sridhar

You Are Cordially Invited

Ah, the human body...
An out dated machine,
Victim of technology
Decaying long before the worms' feast.
Armies maintaining our health
Condemning us here?
O' insects of the earth
Have no fear
Dine and your prey
For sweeter is the flesh of he who "sins"
Of he who falsely obeys the orthodox way

Luz Rodriguez

"How Many Tears?"

Millions of babies killed each year by abortion;
Our world's now distorted way out of proportion.
She walks into a clinic, they tell her, "you'll be fine."
She leaves with faltering steps, confusion in her mind.

Her heart breaks in two for each mother in pain,
As the clinic takes her money, their blood-bought gain.
As she returns home, she feels lonely and confused,
Wondering who will now care for her...she feels abused.

Overcome with emotion, she cries to God above;
He comes to her and whispers, "Do not fear, My love!
Your sins, though many, I surely do forgive;
I ask from this day forward, for Me, that you will live.

I died upon the cross to take your sin and shame,
That you might live forever, and always bear My name.
The guilt from your sin, I wash with My blood,
Your baby's safe with Me in My arms of love!"

How many tears must our Lord Jesus cry
Before another tiny baby has to die?
    ...has to die?
    ...has to die?

Cindy L. Blann

The Phoenix

Rise,
Rise and fly, fly to the sky,
As humble eyes look from all around,
To watch Phoenix's past body fall to the ground.

Rise,
As the ancient sun sets,
From the east and the west,
The two ends, both young and old, have met,
Once again it is morning,
A new day is dawning.

Rise,
In a time bounteous of anger and fear,
It is good to know the spirit of Phoenix is here,
Phoenix's tender loving care,
Holds the volatile strings which keeps all that is fair.

Rise,
When no one in this war-ravaged world has faith,
Phoenix rises above all of the hate,
To those whose hearts are willing to cope,
The Phoenix is called Hope.

Eric Brooks

Untitled

Even I envy Edith.
Evergreen eyes and ebony hair.
Every word said is said with great care.

Victoria Greiss

Love, Laughter And Tears

As I stand in the doorway of my life,
I look back and reflect upon memories.
Recollections of where I have been,
Of things I have done -
And that which I have yet to do.

Knowing that these memories are the thread
That separates the living from the lifeless.
I reflect upon the friendships I have made,
The times and tears that we have shared -
And upon those friends who have said good-bye.

For I hold these tiny woven strands dearly -
They are what keep me from falling.
Because if I could not embrace their touch,
I too would not exist.

Someday, I know I will pass through the great door,
And fulfill what my destiny will be.
In doing so, I can only hope that what lies ahead
Will be full of that which I already possess -
The love, laughter and tears of memories.

Scott Villaneda-Kleinert

Heart Attack

Pain - in the chest,
Trouble breathing.
He'd pulled the water-laden branches out,
Letting the pond run freely now into the woodland creek.
Barreling down 91 and 95 at a desperate 80,
Watching him with panicked eyes, I stroke his fingers.
He moves. He's breathing, sleeping, as I drive miraculously
Through empty Throgs Neck Bridge, Cross Island, Lie.
The Hospital.
Lines, forms, questions, insurance mix up.
Take him take him take him.
And then he's seen, hooked up, monitored,
They bleed him with their modern suckers looking for changes,
    for enzymes.
They're not there.
Color is back in his face now. He laughs.
He pulls on sneakers for inclined running,
Points out where they've put the dye to peak inside him.
All tests passed. No cheating.
Pulled muscles.
And my pulled heart.

Janet Wiener De Winter

Lost Love

I once knew a very sweet girl,
who could make your mind whirl.
She was better than the rest,
because to me she was the best.

When she would take a walk,
my eyes would be the first to stalk.
Even while still yet unspoken,
my ears would be all open.

And then those first few words,
my heart those did stir.
For within me I knew,
that this couldn't be true.

For she told me love is great,
but it wasn't meant for us to mate.
I broke down upon my knee,
and sent up my only plea.

As if I had killed a dove,
she has forever killed my only love.
So I have only to look forward,
to that time I pass on forever and ever.

Myron McCartney

Untitled

The morning comes
in gentle rushing steps
and sings to me the morning song
and beckons me to rise.
The day is just dawning
the bright sun still yawning
its arms stretched wide across the horizon
as it prepares to climb the great blue hill called sky.
All the earth is waking now as every beast
and bird lifts its brow to look upon the new come day.
The flowers throw wide their petals
to show their colors to all who'll see
and to host the humming bird and the buzzing bee.
The trees reach out their bright green fingers
to grasp every falling ray of shine
that the sun lets down once it's made its morning climb.
Everything that moves and lives has risen for the day
each to do the things they do in their own time and way
and when they're finished and they've done their best
then evening comes and with it rest.

Chris Granberry

Finding Peace Through A Friend

Only a true friend has the ability to mitigate the feelings of
frustration, disappointment, anger, and sadness.
Only a true friend has the compassion to lighten my heavy heart.
Only a true friend can see beneath my facade.
Only a true friend uncovers my pain and then shares the pain.

Frustration with myself or with others causes me to snap at him.
But his gentle eyes show nothing but understanding and patience.
The disappointment I sometimes feel over a failure causes exhaustion.
But his continuous support and reassurance revives my weary heart.

Anger drains the energy required for my happiness.
But the wisdom of his words calms my mind and I feel at ease.
The tears roll down my face because of my sadness.
But through the tears I see the deep concern on his face.

I have the utmost respect for him.
He is my dearest companion and life-long friend.
He is my protector; my guardian angel.
He is more than a friend; I think of him as my brother.

For his loving nature, I am eternally indebted.
For his perceptive nature, I am eternally grateful.
For his indefinite support, I am eternally obligated.
And for his mere presence, I am eternally thankful to God.

Nasheel Joules

Gettysburg

I often come and sit here to feel the ebb and tide
of the thing men call freedom, near the spot where many died.

Many stories of this battleground will not again be told
and as the grass is trodden down, I think to men of old.

They fought as knights, valiantly with guns that we call plain.
Men fought their brothers fearlessly so freedom'd reign again.

The bravery of the soldiers in every mortal man
is something that I long for as I sit here once again.

We fight to guard property, we fight to clear our name
we fight with no dignity, we fight to shift the blame.

I shed a tear for humanity, because we cannot see
through all of this insanity, we'll simply cease to be.

Todd Walden

Thank God

There is something I like to see,
 my little daughters come to me.
And put their arms around my neck,
 and give my lips a gentle peck.

And say to me, I love you so,
 as scampering off to bed they go.
I tuck them in and hear their prayers,
 I'm happy they have no cares.

And sometimes when they've been real good,
 I can't control myself or should,
A story is told, I'm through I think,
 then out they cry, "I want a drink".

And all the other usual things,
 that going to bed so often brings,
And finally settled for the night,
 tucked in again without a fight.

I tell them that I love them so,
 it's good to tell them that you know,
And later when I knelt to pray,
 "Thank you God for my girls", I say.

Glenn L. Gibson Jr.

My Best Friend

There was once a time, when I found my best friend.
She was the only one, I was to be with until the end.
There were periods of time, we know both good and bad.
Together you brought me happiness, during times when I was sad.
Memories come into mind, but there's just too many to say.
Keeping with them always, is how I wish to spend my days.
Reminiscing back, with you and my younger years.
You were always there, sharing with me all my fears.
A time not long ago, in which alone I was afraid,
With your shoulder to lean on, my fears to rest you laid.
In my only lifetime, and for the past eleven years,
You've shared my dreams, and all my hopes and fears.
Separated only by distance, I will be home soon my dear.
Together we will share, those needed hugs and tears.

John Clinton Rochford

The Landlords

It's a beautiful spring day, and the birdsongs have been a
tinkling backdrop for all the thoughts that have been flowing
through my mind. I have been watching the baby cardinals exploring
the ground under the bushes in the same delightful way new
fledglings have done around here each spring, and suddenly I'm
impressed by the confident joy of ownership these little creatures
seem to possess without any doubts or fears. How did these
newborns come here knowing such joy of creation, when those who
were created to have dominion over all these things might live
fifty to a hundred years without ever perceiving the first thing
about such kind of confidence?
 We seek power, and pleasure, and joy in nearly every thing we
do in life, and so often fail to simply go out into the realm God
gave us the way the creatures not endowed with intelligence do.
I had been hearing the music all day, as I planned for the future,
and remembered the past, hardly aware of the day. Maybe I longed
for this during the cold of the winter, and maybe I'll remember it
during the heat of the summer, so why am I not out there drinking
it in today?

Rita J. Dahms

Untitled

With every rain and through the flood
You give me reason
   to shed my blood
With every beat
   and every breath
You bring me closer
   to my death
I've lost myself
   to all temptation
But with every rain
   there comes the Spring
The life you give
   the joy you bring
You save me from
   my hate I behold
You bring me in
   from the winter cold
I crawl inside
   you keep me warm
but I sit here waiting for next year's storm

    Cheri Thompson

Oceanicus

As I slowly drift off to sleep
I hear a seal begin to weep.
He is not the only one,
So are the gull and the grunion.

I dive in further and begin to see
All the sad things that seem to be.
The utter can no longer play
With the penguin all the day.

The ocean seems to be so quiet
There no longer is a riot
between the bear and the shark
just to see who gets to the seamark.

No longer do the seabirds sing,
No longer does the buoy ring.
The Oceanicus is dead,
We lay down our ashamed head.

We owe it all to the Exxon Valdez.
The captain never really says, "I owe it all to you."

Slowly as I awaken I take a trip up to heaven.
No longer do I exist, because I too was killed.

    Kate Dolan

Songbird

The new day barely having time
to open its eyes
Wakes to the mellifluous song
of the lark.

Nestled in the arm of an
ageless oak tree
His melodic thrill is heard
through the gentle sigh of the wind.

And each composition a natural masterpiece
Silver-tongued warble
Shaking off remnants of slumber
in my innermost being.

Garbled and incoherent as
early morning thoughts might be
It is heart's fancy that he flies not away
Leaving heavy silence to sing another day.

    Heather Gasper

The Open Window

It all rushed in like the crisp
winter air tumbling over itself,
racing to extend its icy fingers
and bring within its grasp
all that brought warmth
into the smell room

Sounds of the world exposed
made the mind revere
experience that could not be obtained
through an imagination limited
to what it sees through the window pane.

The chill becomes too much
for that which is exposed
returned, the room is forever changed
by the open window.

    Matthew Baysden

Whose Child Am I

I walked along a beach in Jersey
The ocean was on my right
To the north I wandered
No end was in sight

I flew in exhaustion
Five times a week, Boston to LA
I wondered at first
was it day or night

I walked along a beach in San Francisco
The ocean was on my left
To the north I wandered
Will it always be night?

I looked for my beginning
For now I am always alone
Was there ever anyone who loved me
Was I ever really home

    Jane Ranae Moore

Look Beyond

I like frosting, with a freshly baked cake underneath.
I hate having $100, when I owe it to a bank.
Hard round things I also like, called baseballs.
I don't like friends, that say things about me when I'm not around.

I like homework, when I have a homework pass.
Ice cream tastes horrible, when it has nuts.
Wood is really fun, if you tools to make something.
Music tapes and CD's are so boring, when you don't have
   a tape player.

I like cheese, on top of a hamburger.
T.V. is so stupid, if you don't have any electricity.
I like boxes, if they have a good game inside.
Water guns are not fun, without water.

Pillows are so fun, when you get to hit your
friends with one.
Computers are useless, unplugged.
Blank paper is cool, if you have crayons.
Life is boring, while you are asleep.

    Kris Abercrombie

Untitled

There should be that which is God in everyone
Since God is the spirit of love.
Combine that with spirited justice
And you're approaching Heaven above.

But non-divinity is very rife
What with our world-wide struggle and strife.
Doing away with hatred and greed
Should be uppermost in everyone's creed.
If upon others you would impose your beliefs,
More likely than not you will enhance their griefs.

Don't say it's immoral to talk about sperm
And then force a young lady to go through to term.
Don't insist on imposing your will
Upon the poor folks who are terminally ill.
You go your way, I'll go mine
Is so much closer to being divine.

We can still hold hands and be super-refined
What with love and justice preempting our mind.
May this take precedence over being one of a kind!

Bert A. Kanwit

En Route

Destination chosen-
Big backed beetle ingests me.
Moving faster than Mendell,
or Ford would to admit possible.

Here to thither,
Hither to there.
I travel animated.

Held captive by an unexplainable familiarity—
too rare to quantify.
I become entrenched
in hangman and digestion.

Michael Kazmierczak

"Distant Lover"

A love that surpasses physical touch
Just the thought of you
Just a look -
My nerves seem to get shook up
Past memories race through my mind
Years have passed and time has somehow escaped
Yet, the desire - the urge -
The thoughts of you never leave.

Distant lover, you are "special".
You are in my dreams.
As I meditate, I see you
(You are there)
Although I am not touching you
Holding you -
Caressing you -
Or feeling you -
It doesn't change a thing.

You will always be my distant lover.

Chiquita Renee Swoope

Beyond Life

I once had a love that brought joy to my heart,
Then the Lord called him and we had to part.
At first I thought my pain would never end,
Then his sweet memory put my heart to mend.
He was always there to pick me up and make me smile,
He is still with me and helps me all the while.
When love passes beyond life,
you know you were a lucky wife.

Cynthia Stevenson

Sunrise On The Beach

I walk on the desolate beach
Feeling the cool sand near my feet.
The time is six o'clock a.m.
Nobody now is in the street.
Sunrise...
The waves crash on rocks by the shore.
The sound's so peaceful - will never end.
And early - morning seagull chirps.
He flies off - a message to send.
Sunrise...
I am the one that's on the beach.
There's no sign of other humans.
And that huge golden ball rises.
Sunset loses, and sunrise wins.
Sunrise...
Sunrise...

Elena M. Blyskal

Taken

Sitting on a lonely beach
I watch the tide roll in, gently
Kissing my toes, only to cower and retreat
Back to the deep.
I gaze at the never-ending horizon,
Through soulful damped eyes
Until it is no longer linear
But, blurred and distorted.
The quiet of the waves crashing
In the distance, The wind
Calling me...beckoning me.
"Come with me"..."Come with me."
I turn, expecting you there,
But you are gone.
You said you would never leave me.
Now you are gone. It has taken you
I wish it would take me too.
We could be together...again.
I can make that happen...it's calling me...
We can be together...again.

Jill Reynolds

Glamour

Glamour, beauty,
Luxurious woman

Put on your diamond
Slap on some makeup

Have a buck
Have 100 bucks

Give me some silk sheets
To lay down in and sleep

Live in a mansion
Can you imagine?

$200 shoes
The most expensive booze

Tiger for a pet
Don't lay down just yet

How about Satin pajamas
Don't forget your earrings

How about a Mercedes-Benz? No, I prefer Jags

Take a walk on the beach. Don't get sand in your shoes

I need to buy more Chanel #5
And a couple Gucci purses or maybe nine

Nidia Chediak

We All Count

In the big picture (I/you/we) don't count.......
(I/you/we) s\yo—u-o-uld!!!
...But yah don't...(Patti Labelle-If you don't know...you'll never...)
(I am/you are/we are) a significant piece in the whole puzzle picture
(If/you/we) don't feel (my/you/our) true worth because others dismiss
    and/or diminish it...
In reality!!!! Although considered insignificant in the big
    picture, (I am/you are/we are)
All extremely vital piece of the puzzle/picture
For sometimes!!!! Without (me/you/us) (you could/they should/they
    would) not complete the puzzle!!!

We all count!!!
Unfortunately, not all equal... rightfully and wrongfully so...
But, what ever!!!, let's start with "we all count!!!"
    and move on from there............
    Karim A. Edwards

"Temptation"

He ate of the fruit
that sends us to our tomb.
She ate of the fruit
that compromises our doom.
He ate of the fruit
as did his mate.
She ate of the fruit
that sealed our fate,
and if they hadn't ate of that fruit,
would our world be filled with racism and hate,
our towns destroyed, or our woman raped?
No, we owe it to
Temptation
    Kevin M. Kane

The River Of Dreams

I know this river
It runs clear with tears
My tears
It runs fast with fears
My fears
It runs cold with pain
My pain
It runs alone with depression
My depression
It runs deep with sorrow
My sorrow
It runs far away with time
Our time
And when it starts to run out of hand
with our tears, our pain and our sorrow,
it starts to run warn with a friend
My friend
It starts to run smiling with life, My life
It starts to run happy with dreams, My life
On the river of dreams
    Sarah Petralia

Millennium

A decade half past over.
A century nearly defunct.
An uncharted expanse heretofore unknown,
Unmeasured,
Without guidelines, codes or disciplines
Sucks us to its vortex while a myriad of galaxies
Watch in wonder and dismay
As earthlings near the new
With yet no mastery of the now.
    Sue Turner

"The Door"

On a long stairway, headed
downward,
Feeling as if I were being lured.

I hear a faint voice calling my name,
I feel as if I am going insane

I have never had this feeling before,
Suddenly, I see it, a lone
black door.

I wonder what might be
waiting inside.
I want to run, I want to hide.

When I open the door, what
will I see?
Is something in there waiting for me?

I open it, eyes bright and wide,
fearing for my life,
And there stands a man asking,
Will you be my wife?"

I want to scream, I will hurt no more.
Yet, I softly refuse, and I close the door.
    Tammy J. McHenry

Untitled

Tiny lines across my face
The woes of human race
The struggles just to get by
Tiny lines across my face
It's hard to keep pace
The blood on my hands sweat from my brow
But I have the Lord with me now
Daddy why didn't you warm me of this blow
How am I to know which way to go
Little son of mine
Have faith in Jesus and shine
And he'll protect you from these little tiny lines
Tiny lines they creep and crawl
They get longer with every fall
But I won't let these lines defeat me no
The Lord will show me the way to go
Daddy do they come with all my tears
Or daddy do they come from all my fears
Little son of mine have faith in the Lord and shine
And he'll protect you from these little tiny lines
    Neil Mason

Lightning

Thoughts invade my mind. Words escape my mouth.
The sun shines down, the clouds come out.
Thunder, lightning, danger, chaos. It all seems to be a dream.
It is all a dream, everything about you.
Your body, your moves, the words that slide across your lips.
Wake me, Save me. Love me, Kill me.
Secrets, lies, deceit. Our chains are broken,
Yet were never really bound.
Free Love, Free Hate. All behind the iron gate.
Bells ring. The hour tolls. You grab on with both hands.
Behind the bars, the beams, the polls.
Your soul escapes from its mortal form.
Never again shall you see the lightning flash,
or hear the thunder roll.
    Kelli Mann

Communion With God

Forgive me, Lord, for clinging tenaciously to my past
  and drawing back from accepting the present as is.

Yes Lord; you remind me, that "my" past is no longer mine,
  for it is forever gone from me to be in the hands of my maker.

Today is all that I can lay claim to;
  so, help me Lord to make good use of it.

Forbid that when this day becomes yesterday, that in its
  passing, it should leave with me even one regret to taunt me.

Make me strong in faith and able to put the past behind me,
  to make the most of today and to face the future with my
  hand in the hand of God.

  Beulah Marie Conley

Paperboats

I make a team of paperboats,
Dwelling on shore.
They are fleets of superior,
Glorious it is presented for.

While they are monitoring along in Sea,
Providing the Calmity as it should be.
The intricate drama advocates to me you should see,
Let me tell you how it is:

Against the tidal waves, there was union.
The crew of hundreds and thousands,
To guard their country to show exploitations.
Wholly wally striking toward them,
There came roaring waves.
One after another on the way.
Like enemy's torpedoes chased after predators,
My fleets couldn't conquer or escape.

Unbearable to see the first one among submerged.
Then the second, the third and the fourth!
Like a tornado tramped over the scene,
Or a hurricane had swept in lost!
At last, rending my heart I discovered
Two more left on shore after all.

  Flora S. M. Lin

Untitled

  Please forgive me, little bird
I will now set you free
Spread your precious wings, and fly
And sing sweet songs to me.
I did not mean go cage you up
Nor hold you quite so tight
But now that I have set you free,
I know you'll be alright
Don't be afraid, it's only sky
Enjoy the gentle breeze
don't look back, to signal me
at least my heart's at ease
through clear blue skies, and endless space
it's there, where you belong
sharing us, this gift of love
the message is tour song
and if someday you should return I will be waiting here
relax your wings, and sing your song and lend an ear
light gently on my window sill and I will let you in
and when it's time for you to leave I'll set you free, again

  Donald M. Snow

I Promise

I promise to love you,
as long as we're together,
I promise to love you....for forever

I promise to trust you,
as long as you're near,
I promise to trust you....as long as you trust me dear,

I promise to care for you, as you can see,
I promise to care for you...when you're with me.

I promise I'll never leave you,
my word is very true,
I promise I'll never leave you...I'd be sad and blue

I promise to be loyal to you, for I could not cheat,
I promise to be loyal or my heart would soon not beat

I promise I'll never say good bye,
Until I'm taking, high into the sky

They say I'll be happy then, but it's not true,
how could I be happy-without you?

But I will wait,
I will miss you, I'll keep up fate
and once be back with you, I promise

  Kim Uptmore

Waitin' On The Next One

I missed the bloomin' deadline but I don't have a fear.
The Lord, above, has promised I'll be around next year.
I've led a life that's pleasant but not too good, I suppose
and there's lots of little ditties left for this guy to compose
As long as there are birthdays or other neat events
someone's got to be around and I've set precedents.
Sure, I write about some other things like sports or politics.
There's nothin' that is ailin' that some joshin' will not fix.
And when it comes to eulogies, quite frequently, I'm there
first writin' then recitin' and tryin' to be fair.
But when it comes to dinners and I'm chosen to MC
the hosts insist upon a twist of Harmon's poetry.
In "letters to the editor", from the east coast to the west
you'll find bits of rhyme, from time to time, almost like Edgar Guest.
You see, Eddie was my favorite but the Lord has called him home.
If not for Eddie's style that brought a smile, I'd never write a poem
Yes, I know I missed your target date when May first rolled around
but be a sentry for this entry. Make sure it will be found
'cause it would be so shameful, for all eternity,
if next year's prize went to anyone else than Edgar Guest and me.

  J. Harmon Moss

The Road

The end of the road for us is near
I can see it is clear as day.
How do I say good-bye?
There is no real way.

You will always be a part of me.
Holding my hand when I'm afraid.
Loving me with each step I take.
Even though you are not with me,
Your spirit remains eternally.

The end of the road for us is near
And so much is left unsaid.
But I know you understand all the things
I cannot bear to say.

The sun is coming with brilliant light,
Guiding the roads we have yet to travel.
Roads I must travel without you.

  Rosalyn B. Kim

"Tribute To Dad"

I often wondered where he could be at.
Wondering and waiting to see if he was ever coming back.
He came into my life with arms open wide,
And he went back out like a thief in the night.
Whenever I saw him, my eyes would well up with tears,
Because I'd remember the painful heartaches
he'd brought me through the years.

Cari Ann Johnson

Timeless Memories

Much time has come and gone, since the year that you were wed
You joined your lives together, to always look ahead
Love, honor and cherish are words that once were spoken
The promises made and vows you took, these things remain unbroken.

Though the world was always changing, ideas and views were new
Your love survived, remained intact and thus your family grew
Commitment is a challenge that so many fail these days
Your strength is much respected and admired in many ways.

The past it lay behind you, no regrets that you should bear
The present is right in front of you, so give and love and share
The future lay ahead of you, so make it what you will
For time is to be treasured, and life to be fulfilled.

Today I am quite proud of you, and your fifty years together
I realize the challenges and storms you've had to weather
The memories that you've made, I celebrate this day
And thank you for the gifts I have that one cannot repay.

Christina Atkins

Detonate

I have seen their gaunt frames
Thousand of sunken eyes
Were it not for their protruding cheekbones
They would slide down their nameless faces drop
One by one off jutting chins and burst
Melting into the ground swallowed
Like long awaited rain
I have witnessed decay
Death stealthily biding time please
Someone crush their cheekbones
Let them splinter and crack
Turn to a fine grainy powder please
Someone let their watery eyes
Slide off the withered faces
And with the detonation of faded vision
They see not the ghastly smile
Of death's ivory face
One particle of comfort in an endless
sea of suffering

Andrea T. Belkman

In The Night, In My Room

In the night, In my room, I will cry, oh so soon. First I
listen for the sound of his footsteps come around. Then
just before he opens my door, I will pray just once more. I
close my eyes the fright that he will be there in my
sight. I feel his shadow in my room, oh my God! Why so soon!!
With my eyes closed ever so tight, he lies down beside me and
tells me it's alright. I don't struggle and I don't resist
cause if I do, the more he'll insist. I just lay there quiet
as can be, thinking of how dirty I must be. In the tub, I
scrub myself and try to wash the dirt right off. I'm so
filthy, it's so tough, soap and water is not enough.
I go to bed after my bath where I can cry, cry and be sad.
I will sleep and dare to dream, but I am scared that I will
scream. Nowhere to run and nowhere to hide,
I just want to sleep, to sleep and die...

Sylvia M. Caviano

From A Child's Point Of View

The world is always friendly, always kind and always true,
When you see it through the eyes of a child's point of view.

There is no such thing as war and the battles are always through,
When you try to consider truth from a child's point of view.

The world is all a playground and a simple box can be a Zoo,
When you look at it through their eyes, from a child's point of view.

The sun is always sunny and the is always blue,
When you stop to think about it from a child's point of view.

So maybe the world could be better, and we all could get a clue,
If we all just look straight at the world from a child's point of view.

Elise Goldstein

A True Friend

My poem doesn't judge me
on the basis of what I wear and when,
how sober I am,
how I do in school,
or any other irrelevant aspect of me.

My poem is Monty Hall,
it says to me:
"Hey, I'll make a deal with you"
Suddenly, symbiosis occurs.
My poem and I may now manifest ourselves truly.

My poem is a cool guy,
who knows how to get down
and work like he should,
even though I usually don't.

To me, my poem
is my stronger half,
but I bet it thinks the same way about me.

Cullen Kasunic

Cycles

Days roll on
Years fall off from mind
    into the desert dust
Looking back
    he smiles into the wind with the sand in his eyes
    and dirt filled laugh
Looking back
    a thousand graves
    children dead, unbinded
Looking back
    his footprints disappear
    the stranger catches up
    embraces
Looking back
    he stops running
Looking back unwanting...

...Turning 'round and moving on
  a little more complete

Emiliano S. Lee

White Tiger

White tiger lurking in the grass
Looking for your meal giraffes

Nothing can hear stalking oh so quietly
But because you are so fierce, every one fears you.

As they walk along you are silent
But then you attack oh so violently
They won't know what hit them

Joseph E. McCreedy

I Am Free

Once I did not have a future, only time that passes by.
Dim hope and fast fading dreams, a rope,
That tied my soul to body, so that I would not die.

Long and Long I waited, now my chance
Has finally come,
To grasp that eluding bold brass ring,
To blossom fully, as a flower in spring,
My life has only just begun.

Running swiftly from despair and doubt,
Eyes open wide, eager to see and learn,
No longer must I wander all about,
Because I know which way to turn.

Knowledge opened up the door, to light,
and the darkness fled.
Opportunity before me, a welcome sight,
After the life I've led,
Rejoice with Me,
I Am Free, you see, to become whatever I wish
To be!

    I Am Free.
    Cindy Lynnet Hart

To A Rose

You have beauty that is rare,
Within your silken petals fair.
You alone have the privilege divine
Of letting pearly dewdrops find
In their descent from heaven to earth,
Your petals for their short-lived birth.
Your colors are in every way
Bonny, sweet, and come what may,
Whether your shade is yellow or red —
It can almost always be said
That you cheer many people and make them feel bright,
And for others you start out the day just right.

    Joan DeFonzo

Divorce

Well, it won't be long now, before our marriage is done
and instead of two we will be one
I talked to a lawyer, soon the divorce will be through
but I'll think of the good times when I think of you

I'll think of the flowers and the cards too
so I can smile when I think of you
I'll think of the times we laid in bed
with just one pillow under our heads

I'll think of the walks we took hand in hand
and how proud I was to call you my man
Not about the fights or long, lonely nights
or how we fought over just who was right

So as we go our way to a new life
don't forget I was once your wife
And just every once in a while
Think about me, but be sure to smile

    Georgia D. Sherlin

Butterfly Butterfly How Do You Fly?

You fly so very high in the sky.
Your wings are so beautiful and full of color.
I like you flatter in a flower.
Are you ever sad or mad or just glad?

    Collins

Untitled

Seventeen thousand one hundred eight
acid ungird oh poised tempest
Christ
    Zoroaster
      Aesepus
        unto Alexander

        Burry
      all
        cynical
          noiselessness

Exist between echoes into ashy Aprils oh sinister vortex.

    Acquiesce!

Abandon acute admission upon amity oh heteronym,
compelling...

With any object reconsideration Exist absurd Apples
    upon
      Berkshire Hills

Agape.
    Jean Stewart Berg

"The Box"

Longing for life's good fortune wrapped
    in a gift box of ornaments
Adored from afar, but with lost glitter that shines
    only to tease-please the palette; it smells of
    sweet and sour to satisfy one side of the taste
    but to dry the saliva of the other
Carry on with the flaming torch of yesterday,
    yesterday's gone but not for long.
Close your eyes, see the future-the air is not
    as sweet as it seems, the water not as satisfying
    your breath not as life saving-but swallow
    continue to swallow this shallow invisible thing
    for too much can kill you.
    Your demise although causing a sense of
    melancholy continues to bring in business
    so go on don't be afraid to open
the box
    Victoria Nanguang

Solitary Shared

With that head
held way up high!
You think that only you!
Could lie there forever in time

Alone and unknown
that no one else will share your soul

Live your thoughts and keep your dreams
help you succeed where you should be

Know you everything there is for them to see.

But when that time has come to know!
The one that you should share your soul
Live your thoughts and keep your dreams
And hold forever.

Where life for you should the two
Share together

So space in your head
Will hold them there in that place forever!

    Susan Parry

Desert Flower

Lightning streaks across the night sky
Thunder roars over the desert
Life giving rain falls to the desert floor.
The desert turns into mass confusion
Flash floods rule the landscape
Upheaval and turmoil are the order of the moment.

Suddenly, a predawn silence
The winds are still, the sky calm
The sun rises, warms the earth.
In one place in a forsaken land
one Desert Flower grows.
The beauty of the flower isn't seen by all,
but touches the very soul of one,
Me!

Dennis D. Tomey

The Fall Of Adam

The dance of the sun's rays on the finger tips of my outstretched
    hand in these early morning hours makes me smile
It is not fully light yet and I am half shade away from the truth
These words are empty - Hollow rotten trees
In the night my words are jazz
Variations and combinations unchained from a full conscience
The notes play bright and sweet
Then a melancholy that seems even sweeter for its heart ache
Only the melodic meaning is constant — And these words shine
But the Dawn shines brighter — In the full light of day I see the truth
These words have not changed — Role a perspective command
Writer in the dark, speaker in the day — I must be Cyrano's Christian
But I am such a clumsy, awkward messenger and this light gives
    no shade
It is best if I do not profane or dull these sacred, shining words
    by speaking them
So will never know

We are harmony absent since the Garden
Oh my Eve, I would gladly eat the fruit from your hands

Robert B. S. Collins

"Only Time Will Tell"

The birds chirping in the early morning hours
wake one to a new day.

The taste of the first morning cup of coffee
is a delight sending me on my way.

So begins the day for millions of Americans
in the "good ole" U.S.A.

Clocks tick away hours, days, and decades,
ticking away into the 21st century,

Tick, tick, ticking away, with all great and
small making a grand entry.

Only time will tell what the future will bring.
Only time will tell.

Lucy Psillos

Why?

Why must I give up, so early in the fight?
Why must I lie down, think about in all night?
I am too young to die, my sorrow grows cold.
I am too vulnerable now, only thirteen years old.
Were is my sun and were is my moon?
Why must this continue? I dream it will end soon.
Why must I wake from this horrid nightmare?
Why must I wonder, why must I dare?
Why, why, why am I so scared?

Allie Vallotton

"See The Pictures On The Wall"

See the pictures on the wall,
They were never there before.
It's a blessing for us all,
Oh what beauty they bestow.

When you open up the door,
You're going down the hall.
There is something you should know,
Just see the pictures on the wall.

If you're living all alone,
And you cannot make a call.
See the grace on each face,
They bring back memories to us all.

See the pictures on the wall,
And the joy we would see.
Lots of love, and lots of calls,
That was the way it use to be.

They wouldn't want us in tears,
Our love was great right through the years.
So we bid them farewell,
There'll be others to see and tell.

Laura Cright

The Buffet Table

At a banquet, a buffet table. 26 yrs. long
A teacup full of joy.
Distasteful, unpleasant dishes.
A plate full of pain.
A glass filled with tears.
Iron hands grabbing the buffet table.

Battles of alcohol, beer cans, a bowl of vomit.
A tablespoon of joy.
Sounds of grief, a basket full with filthy words.
Grotesque expressions!
A tray of dangerous utensils, knives, a gun, crowbar and hammer.
Teaspoon of joy.

A jug full of pain.
A drop of joy.
A demon serving one quest.
A victim trapped in the banquet.
Black candles, the murky light fading.
At the end of the buffet table, 26 yrs. long.

Palmira Thurland

Wolf

A shadowy form creeps stealthily through the trees;
Stopping only to sniff the wind.
Which carries a concealed message of danger on its tongue,
Silence hangs in the air,
As if suspended by time,
Watching, waiting, then quickly moving on;
Moonlight creates an eerie glow,
As branches stir noiselessly to and fro;
A stick cracks; the wolf bounds away, still silent,
Into the shadows;
A man steps forth into a pool of moonlight,
A giant against the light;
Brandishing a gun, he steps forth,
A noisy, clumsy hulk of a man;
Compared to the wolf who is agile and tranquil,
He offends the night;
The man storms away,
Raving and ranting over the loss,
Which was never meant to be a gain;
For the wolf is one with the forest.

Laura Grace Gayton

Old Precious Eyes

Her face was a journal as each wrinkle told a story of the past.
Thin white on soft skin gave her timeless beauty.

The smile that occasioned her face
was lost today as a man,
who had accompanied her forever, was gone.
She raised her tired arms to him
as sad thoughts weighed them down.

Grains and dust, these were the remains of the man
that cared for her beyond death, the angel had finally gone.
These things once alive and full of vigor shined from old eyes,
old precious eyes.

Glazed wet lips lifted towards a child uttering nothing
but silence and narrating a lifetime she lived with him, through tears.
Each drop expressed an everlasting love
following the wrinkled stories on her face.

The child watched like a puppy as the lifetime of happiness
remained engraved within her.
As old precious eyes visited the child
she said, "I am so glad you came, and so is he."
As always you are wondrous, your old precious eyes.

Jason King

Misfortunate Fate

I will rest on faith's pillow
It shall bring forth mother date
Proudly awaiting tomorrow's misery
Once again to interrogate

How dare happiness intrude on my consistencies
content with familiar despair
Pleasures unknown to my untouched flesh
Cast shadow upon my thoughts, Dear

I must wallow in my miseries
for it is my misfortunate fate
I mustn't be trapped into human weakness
Your wicked charm shall not captivate

Yet I am drawn to his dark side
A place I know so well
like violets in the spring
the bitter-sweet scent shall one whelm

Tammy M. D'Arezzo

Untitled

I feel like something is missing
the cat has my tongue
only I don't have a tongue
I am complete
Yet somehow incomplete
what is all that is bothering me?
something is wrong
but I can't think of one single thing
is it the feeling of not having anything wrong
that is so troublesome
is this feeling so uncommon
that it feels foreign to my soul
is the feeling of wrong
so known to me
that I have come to accept it as natural
I hope I am still capable of feeling good

Mitchell Crooks

"The Poet"

Compressed
thoughts rearranged, put in sequence
making you want more.

A
blitz of rhythmic skill flowing like
water... soaked in through the eye;
Awakening a thought, changing pace of the heart.

Words
render your mood, your soul surrenders.
Barographs shift, emotions changed by subject.
Who is it?

"The Poet"
Marlon Syms

In Memory

Always unique in his own kind way
His routine would never falter,
For he would slip on blue sweats every day..

He was a savior, a man of all gentleness,
He was a stature of love,
A kind of love that no one could miss.

Rare in very right,
His life was full of reminiscence,
Full of those old Marine nights.

He enraptured my endless heart,
He was the core of my life,
Helping me see everything through
A different light.

He was warm, sensitive, and gentle
He was never, every judgmental.

A memory wave will forever bounce in my mind
For I will always love this man that was kind...
For he was the one who "bothered",
For he was my astounding Grandfather.

Gina M. Conn

The Day The Angels Came

The night was long as the angels drew near
Her spirit was strong, her body was weary,
For the years of resistance had taken their toll.
The day the angels came...

She gathered her children and husband from work
To be at her side as the angels approached.
Each one she touched and smiled on with love
The day the angels came...

The room was filled with a soft gentle light
Love bathed her in a radiant glow.
Her time was near, as the angels arrived
The day the angels came...

A soft sigh of goodbye, she slipped away
Into their arms, the angels on high.
The struggle was over, a new life to begin
The day the angels came...

I love her, I love her, I loved her so much!
But into his hands we sent forth her spirit.
God's gentle love to nourish her now
The day the angels came.

Michael D. Lynn

Summer Storms

A violent storm is raging on
Down from the heavens above
Rain briskly stimulates the side of my face
As the clouds swiftly push and shove.

As strikes of lightning fill up the sky
Most people would run for cover
Me... I love the strength of the wind
Enveloping me, like the arms of my lover.

I love to be in the midst of a storm
Feel the mystery and all its glory
The thundering powers it sends through my soul
Telling its earthly, heavenly story.

Oh... the magic of a summer night's storm
As the heat and the cold air blend
I can't pass it by, if only to see
The rainbow at its end.

Grace Murante

Untitled

We assemble inside the crevices of pages and streets
and scattered conversation
each thought holding a piece of the gatherings
I will go to the vineyards, the orchards
and crush fruit between my toes
just to feel sweet again we rip out through the season
and I look to the marks on your faces
I look to the veins from your hands
how unrestrained your laugh had become
how swift the passion crosses your eyes
at the name of the dream
you have once again become a part of
I chopped my hair and the shedding brought itself
through blood, aligning with my mind and its sacrifice
a white sheet encircles me looking to revere someone
needing to feel revered profound resistance
to the expected identity savage in its playfulness,
natural reaction a child as I have never been
where treasure boxes and pinki's promises
always remain sacred, sensitive as a word of truth to the conceived

Rachael Falber

My Child

My child, my daughter, as I watched you grow
the sights I saw, what I came to know
your first few words, as you learned to talk
your first few steps, as you learned to walk

Little child of mine
it again seems like the first time
I get to see
as you take on this world's mystery
everything is so fresh and new
as I see it again through you

From your beautiful smile
your cute little laugh
your pure innocence
means so much to me
my angel, my Heaven sent

My little angel, my child, you mean the world to me
so much a part of my heart, my soul, so much a part of me

My child, my HEAVEN LEIGH, you are my life so true
from your Daddy, Baby I Love You!!!

Carl Hough

This Is How I Feel About Death

This is how I feel about death. There is none.
It only seems like that. We fall off the conveyor
Belt as tin soldiers get knocked down.

The essence of who we are is a part
of that nebulous safe gray and light.
While our bodies go through at times pain,
suffering, exhaustion. Spirits cross over
into the unknown. We are left to wonder.
Since in this body, I have not experienced
"lay down and die", I'm taking from intuition.
I'm more afraid of others dying that I love
than my own death, because it's living
in this frame that's the challenge.

Everything has its season, and I have left
a wake that won't die, like ripples on a pond,
spread out through children, and grandchildren,
friends and lovers. I am a culmination
of other's lives and other lives before mine, perhaps.

Remember flowers bloom where earth was dust.
That dust could be mine.

Sidney Ulmer

"Give Jesus A Call"

Give Jesus a call, not one but all,
He's waiting yes waiting
To answer you all.
Give Jesus a call give Jesus a call
He'll answer your praises not one but all.

He's waiting and listening but not in vain.
For you to call him and speak his dear name
Jesus, oh Jesus preaches Jesus.

He was nailed to the cross for our sins he did die,
He's waiting for us to open our hearts from sin.
So he can forgive us then enter in.
He doesn't care what we might have been,
Poor, drunken, beggar, sinner, nothing for him is ever too much.

The evil is working yes working hard every day
For Jesus' dear ones to follow his way.
The drugs and AIDS are taking their toll
Jesus wants you to quit, so he can save your dear soul
So kneel down and pray it doesn't matter where.
For Jesus is there to answer your prayers.
Give Jesus a call, give Jesus a call.

Velva Stoner

Write It Down, I Say

Write it all down, it seems so simple
express yourself, every feeling churning inside of you,
Makes you want to sing the blues, or cry or rejoice,
write it all down I say, I know deep down, I really have no choice,
it feels good to write it down, its expression, emotion, I'm
breathing, it's elation,
don't want anyone to really discover my hidden desires
my deepest emotions, my sinful ways, I'm going to hell I say,
but write it all down, let it out, somebody might hear you, it's o.k.
Sometimes you're walking that tight rope, that thin, barely
visible wire, those deep down sinful wasteful unfulfilled desires,
I'm writing it, I want you to read it and understand what I'm saying
read my mind, open me up, ask me a question, no more delaying,
here you have it, I feel much better, deep breath, inhale, my mind is clear,
why don't you write it down, tell me I ain't the only sinner
who wants to sing the blues, cry or rejoice,
I'm sure it's something everyone in the world needs to hear.

Lisl Howell

347

Get Some Rest If You Can...

When life seems a bore and the chips are down
And the plant is on strike in your own home town;
Money is low, but your bills are high,
And you try to smile, but you want to cry,
Your knees are buckling as things get rough,
Get some rest if you can, But Don't Give Up!

Life's like a river with its twists and turns,
Through rapids and falls we sometimes learn.
Many men and women that were turned about
Could have won the race if they'd stuck it out.
So stand by your guns when things get tough,
Get some rest if you can, But Don't Give Up!

Success is failure turned inside out.
The goal seems so far if you always doubt.
And you learn too late after giving up,
That you could have captured the golden cup.
Don't throw in the towel and say that's enough,
Get some ret if you can, But Don't You Give up!

Ed Bach

Seventh Grade Rock

My teacher threw a party in the seventh grade
My principal showed up in masquerade
The kids were jumping and the janitor began to dance
If you want to have some fun, here's your last chance
The band showed up the leader was a diehard hippie
I stood up on a chair and yelled, "Yippee, skippie!"
Pizza boy arrived he said, "How 'bout some food?"
We were having so much fun that alone there he stood
He threw down the pizzas and started to move
The drummer in the band yelled, "Show me that groove!"
By seven o'clock we were all gettin' down
No one in the house was wearing a frown
When eight o'clock arrived we were doing the jive
We didn't even stop to watch Party of Five
Twelve o'clock came and went no one even cared
By one o'clock we were dyeing everybody's hair
I heard a buzzing in my head
I turned and saw that I was in my bed
The party was a dream, nothing real at all
Now, I must get up and face those horrid halls.

Elizabeth Hahn

"Desire"

My feelings for you run as deep as the ocean;
as continuous as a stream, forever flowing,
somewhere it began, but it has no end.

Each morning I long to hear the whisper of your voice
in my ear; to see the sunshine on your face when I
look deep into your eyes; at night, my body aches for
your touch, for the feel of your skin touching mine;
my lips desire to press hard against yours and my
mouth wants to taste the passion that is in your sweet kiss.

My emotions are running wild like a volcanic explosion,
everything inside me is throbbing to be released,
to escape the confines of my body, to fulfill your
every desire, but the danger are to great, the fire is too hot.

I'm forced to keep this secret,
only you know the depth of my desires,
maybe someday we'll be able to quench the fire that burns within us,
until then I have my daydreams and in those quiet
moments in my mind, you are mine alone...

Kathy Adams

"A Poem For A Love Who Went Away"

Why did you go so far away
When I can't go and I must stay
You left me behind and I pray
We will meet again somewhere, someday
Until then this is what I say.

Forget me not, I love you still
And ten years from now, I still will
Everyday with tears my eyes fill
Each one for you that is until
I see you again and with love
  like mine, believe me when I say "I will"

Sara Boudwin

"Surroundings"

Surroundings are everything we see
They are what we hear, feel, and touch
Surroundings are the love and caring that surrounds us by the
  people we most care about.
They can also be the birds that sing and chirp it the bright
  mornings glow.
The green grass on the ground
The rainbows in the sky that we see after it rains.
The colorful sights of red and yellow in the trees.
Surrounds are everything we see in life.

Katina Diloreto

A Splash Of Spring

Yellow, green, emerald!
At the dawn of day birds chirp...
"Come here, come here," they seem to say.
Carpets of green fields
Lie open before me.
Lambs frisk and play,
Nature is reborn.

Winter is past and gone.
Creation is calling... renewing its youth...
Bursting with... color... sound... music.

Snows melt into tiny streams.
Trickling down the hillside,
The forests are lush...
Safe nesting places!
Great God! Your grandeur is great!
Your beauty is evident. Your presence is pervading...

Awesome... inspiring... enveloping... transcending all limits
And I am part of that great beauty... mystery... mosaic.

You are there, loving me into existence!!!
Your resurrection is real.

Cabrini Cahill

Beautiful Hands

Hey little brother, what's that in your hands
Is it a toy
Does it bring you lots of joy
When you look to the future, what do you see
Can you see yourself with a home and family - or
steel bars between you and we.
Is that piece of metal worth your life
Hey little brother what's that in your hands, does it
make you feel like a man
Is it worth it to be part of the clan
Hey little brother take a good hard look at those
hands and know that they're beautiful and precious
all on their own and don't need a .38 to give them a home.
So hey little brother take my hands if you need
something to hold, they'll always be there along with my prayers.
Love always your sister.

Gloria Clark

Sunlit Walk

Early morning sunlit walk
Tall green towers shades us
Grayish, brown bushy tails scamper up and down trunks coated
   with bark
Enchanting birds of song
Sun disintegrating early mist slowly.

A mystical river me meet!
Sun tries to find its way through thick trees and dried up
   morning dew
Mystical river wears her coat of morning mist
A small boat afloat, holding two fishermen
On her banks, a young boy sits - blends with natural beauty.

We move on hand-n-hand with our sunlit walk
Cozy homes line country streets along with velvet green,
   tall maple and pine

I'm lost in nature and enveloped by love
Small meaningful talk, content silence
Eyes savor every look of beauty

Sunlit walk with love
A morning never felt or looked more beautiful
A day that began so right from birth
It was natural beauty that blessed us let us walk forever on
   sunlit walk
   Rita Mattioli

Touched By An Angel

It was a night of pleasure yet sadness for me,
and I trudged up a grassy hill.
There I greeted the moon with a simple hello.
And stood silent and calm and still.
To soothe my pain the moon whispered to me
a story of glory and peace.
And I listened with ears as big as the world
for her words brought me much ease.
Then I whispered back my story of gloom
which is what she wanted in return
and as I began to weep and bawl
my eyes and my heart and me burned.
Until it was that a breeze blew by
which was warm and thick and celestial
I began to realize what happened to me:
It was clear I had been touched by an angel.
In my troubled head there came the bells
of harmony and silence and love
which were flown on the wings of an angel.

   Vicky Knox

Soul Salvager

Precious moments... you... white men and women did waste,
running through your life, in such haste
seeking for your destiny, hoping to stumble upon eternity.
I already have what you are after, not the rooftop, nor the
foundation, but we... thee frame and the rafters (my peoples)
You! Seek not to lead now but to follow and you... too shall wallow
in this our hallowed land... not your hallowed land... a tomb.
Seek not to be led but to be fed, for would truth is not as you've
written to be read.
But in our own... invisible minds... between our own two big black,
brown ears, behind our own big black, brown eyes,
within our own big black or brown heads.
But are you... white man and white woman, prepared to pay all
the prices, of such lonely moments and earthly sacrifices? (Give up
all material things that you won... your money, fame and all fortunes)
You can't be stiff-necked, overcome with self-pride (feeling that you
know all and everything and refuse to accept this great change)
or else your maker'll break you. (Destroy all your wealth, take
away your good health) and she'll have your hide!
(You'll die... same as you've been doing for 15 billion years.)

   Merlie V. Phlegm

The Grand Cycle

Birth
The little ones run free and with no fear
No shake, no fall, no dark, no spear.
After the birth we are as supposed,
Nothing in our way, no well too high.
Ignorant to life's trials and woes.
The children will soon realize, but why?

Maturity
Energy, power, and thought at its prime
They are healthy and so very alive.
Values and reasons are learned well.
See them triumph, see them fail.
Live it up, love and lust, life is greet and just!

Death, the last days of the children are here.
We saw them triumph and we saw them learn fear.
Now we watch them all thou.
"Dress them up in cloth of the finest grade, and big a hole,
Bury them deep, but keep this soul and watch their loved ones weep."
They are gone now, but it's not the end,
For they are part of a cycle that only begins.

   Ty Jenkins

Composure

Bolts of melody flow through
The silence, tranquility of deep thought
Shallow eyes of a genius sense, dart
From rooms many walls.

The eyes squint from not the bright rays of sun, but
From insecurity buried within.
She feels empty, yet full of senseless meaning.
Wonder her heart, who am I?
One of genuine reality?
Or angelic fantasy of a child's foolish soul?
At this time, none may know, except
The voice.

Soon the voice departs the mind, leaving
The one alone with the truth, yet
The misperception.

Another arrives, telling of feeling,
Quote the lashing whisper,
"I am nobody, who are you?"

   Hillary S. Kativa

Rosebud

Rosebud, Sweet-pea,
unchristened names
your stalwart Daddy
gave to you;

Names that even
grandma Hattie
understand and knew.

Rosebud, throughout your life
you've graced the world with love, not strife
and with compassion and delight
you've shown us how to win the fight!

Sweet-pea, now in this contorted place,
I need to calmly sit, with ample space
and revisit our lives at a leisurely pace.

No matter what the future holds
love continues to abound;
as daily struggles ceaselessly unfold,
truth and faith are common ground.

   Vivian Taylor

The Dreamer's Last Dream

To tired to breathe, to weak to think, to lonely for hope
My photograph album and diary are the only proof that this shattered
life was once whole

Once a heart, once a man, now a lie

The present taunts me with a constant reminder of dreams unfulfilled
Grant me a wish, send me an angel, let me taste all that I have lost

Live for the moment truly a recipe for a cornucopia of disaster
I think even as I write, of how as a dreamer I lived my greatest of
days, my proudest of victories in a half conscious state of fantasy

Dreamt of love, longed for passion
Awoke to late to live my dreams

Sobered by the truth
Living the lie a created
Father of a revelation I have found
The revelation of failure, dream of the mountain top
Dream of sailing the sea, but dream not forever
For in a dream you will never really be

Hope with your actions act out your dreams
For time is immortal and dreamers forgotten like me

Nathaniel J. Coniglio

Tiny Thunders

A white castle crowns the city tonight.
Shimmering lights spread about like poppies lie before it.
Moving lights pass by in the sky, trickling with tiny thunders
behind them. In front of one a headlight shines like a pointed
styrofoam cone, a unicorn, charging away in the night, perhaps...
A car's cat eyes rumble down a lonely street.
The bridge far away glistens with tiny oil droplets running down
its wires. The world is quiet, yet not everyone is asleep...
An empty bag tumbles down the street. A can rolls a curb. Leaves
rustle along the ground. They thank the wind for giving them life.
The cars far away sound only like a distant ocean. The lifeless
meadows below hold a stadium and an arena where modern day
gladiators and giants fight to win. Only we call it play...
So many lights, all of them innocent, lighting up our features, good
and bad.
Big signs scattered about way above our heads try to be our parents.
Neon lights and blinking towers add color to the night... a man and
his dog come out to do their business, the working day not over yet.
The dog follows his own path now and changes roles...
A police car goes by and tucks in the neighborhood. Time passes...
Down the hill stands an old schoolhouse, knowing well where we have
been, but never knowing where we are going. A dog barks and leaves
shuffle. A temporary intruder has passed. A car putters up a
cobblestone hill, the past again colliding with the present... the
air grows now as does the ground. It's time to leave and put the
world to sleep, except of course for the lights, the wind and his
friends, and last but not least, those tiny thunders.

James Class

Stars

Stars have no life, and they do not know
How to protect in the rain or snow,
How to gather around a nice cozy fire
There are the things we people desire.

Stars are like people, wandering here and there
Some with sad faces, some gleaming with glare.
Stars have no five points as we say it to be
Stars have round faces like you and me.

So countless the stars that we see every night,
Some stars have tails as we see in their flight.
But I'm sure of one thing, all stars are the same,
And all stars shine with a one purposed aim.

Malachi Owens Jr.

Remember Grandma

I sat looking up at my grandma
As I noticed her skin so soft like a feather.

I kept asking her questions
To her I was never in the way.

Grandma had a way of answering
So different but understanding.

All I remember was that
She was older than the year.

Grandma is now in a kingdom
Where she can tell everyone
the stories she told me.

Someday I'll join her in her kingdom
Where she can do the asking
and let me do the answering

Christina Ramig

Hunter's Glen

Through the mist, there came a sound,
    a growl, a roar, a grin.
For the hunter knew he had caught his prey
Alone on Hunter's Glen.

He held his gun to his side and searched the surrounding white.
He knew his prey was close at hand;
He smelled the beast's fright.

Ahead he saw a shadow he always yearned to see.
There stood the beast in front of him
Calmly waiting in the trees.

He raised his gun but not in time; a mighty claw struck out.
The heavy gun fell to the ground;
The man was whirled about.

The brutal beast had its fun and slashed him once again.
Through the mist a scream was heard,
Alone on Hunter's Glen

The beast looked upon the man
    and gave a sneering grin.
It turned and left the man to die
Alone on Hunter's Glen.

Paula Tranbarger

A Heart Like A Quilt

The heart is like a quilt
It varies from piece to piece, some pieces are bright then some are dull.

But, if even one simple, little piece
is missing neither would be complete.

Just as a quilt would have a hold,
the heart would have a void also.

Each individual piece has an
important part in the making of a person or the making of a cloth.

The size and number will surely be
different, from article to article and heart to heart.

But neither would be complete if
missing a single part.

The making of the two is quite a difficult task!

Because, the creators of both must be
true to their creations;

For they demand their makers to fill every part.

The two are a lot alike, yet still they differ, since any one can make
a quilt but only God can make a heart!

Amber Stanley

Anything 2 Rhyme

On the meadows of the ocean
I can see a golden clearing
And the rushing of the waves
Sounds like the bird song I've been hearing
Like the toll bell's steady chime
Anything to rhyme, ever mountain here can see
As the sky cries on the forest
One can hear a gentle singing
It's the woods own secret chows
Flowers raise their heads to glance in a trance.
What would it be to out run
what one's future would have him become?
But who would dare to interrupt
The drum that beats its own steady rhythm
in a frantic search to find anything to rhyme.
A stream of softly humming voices
beneath a moon that never glistens
in some simple place in time
where one could dream and if he listens
hear the sound of weeping laughter forever after.

Diana Blizzard

Approaching Fifty

The leaves,
they murmur to me, "go back, go back"
I cannot, my destiny will not let me

The wind,
it wails out, "turn around, turn around"
I cannot, they will not allow it

My youth,
is beckons to be but I cannot grasp it
for it is gray now, no longer white yet not quite black

The snow,
it whispers to me, "look forward, look forward"
I cannot, I am too tired from trying to reclaim the past

The will-o'-the-wisp
it tinkles to me, "Seek me, seek me"
I cannot, I do not know in which direction to find it

My future,
it is leading me, to some unknown fate
taking me along as time reveals my story

Marie Modica

Prelude To The Anti Christ

Son of satan, God of darkness; welcome to our world:
It has laboured 6000 years to bring forth what is unfurled.
Socio-economic religion is poised precariously upon the edge of chaos;
And the geo-political landscape is a powder key to bias.
Our neo-nazi/gestapo leaders are preparing for revolution;
While our new world order nature loving zealots are advocating
Evolution.
Dictators and despots all, dehumanizing society.
Forging chains and laying traps com compromise our piety.
Pride, avarice, and selfishness abound;
While truth, mercy, and justice cannot be found.
To capture and create utopia is only an illusion;
But all of this foolishness and nonsense leave but one conclusion.
That all of life exists but for one reason;
It is God above designed it for our faith to be tested;
To use it wisely as he intended; or foolishly; life wasted.
The paths are ours; he will not interfere;
The choices be great, but not always clear.
To follow his son through the tomb to the light;
Or the God of anarchy, death, and eternal night.

Noel M. Helligso

Where Are You, Santa?

This is a spoof an Ole Saint Nick,
He isn't untouchable — what the Heck!?
What is it with you this year?
Is it true you can no longer hear?
Or is it like I was told
That nowadays you are too old?
Or like somebody said, "Now I heared
That Santa tripped over his beard
And fell with that bowl full of jelly,
Spilling out all his big old belly!"
Was it that he fell from the sky into grandma's pie?
Or was kicked by Vixen, jealous over Rudolph who was fixen
To lead that sleigh again?
With his nose shining bright, it just didn't seem right!
All this making Santa fall from the sky
Putting out his eye...
Causing Santa to be laid up this year
Many children are shedding a tear...
And saying, "If you don't come, you Jolly Old Elf
I'll eat the cookies and milk all by myself!

James O. Sutton

Milquetoast Cleans The Carpet

Is there nothing beyond the dull routine?
Is there nourishment in a jellybean?
I'm tired, depressed, fearful, and horny
How awful can this life really be?
Am I not coward always be one?
That corner is so hard to clean
Will the belt break on this machine?
Solitude, failure, and loss are all I know
How do you cultivate with a broken hoe?
But for precious awareness and imagination
I would try walking from New York to London
Smoking a real camel
Vacuuming my skull
Facing big harm
Buying the farm
Ending my session
Getting personal with Smith and Wesson
Going deep on a short field
Drinking a molotov cocktail...

Dennis Kann

If Only My Love Knew

My love and only my love
understands me.
My love is secure and blessed
with the gift of kindness and forgiveness.
My love and I are apart, but
soon we will become as
one, if only my love knew.
Why is he shy but so observant?
His eyes shine like sapphires
and glistens within any light.
My love, my love if only you
knew how much I loved
you, of how much I care and do adore you.
Destiny brought us together,
but now has kept us apart.
If only my love had known
that I had loved him too!

Amy McKinney

351

The Home

On a potato farm off route nine
The developer built a series of homes in New Jersey
It is a simple way to enjoy life divine
To live in a house that is not surrounded by phantasies and obstacles
The atmosphere is free of city mixtures
The landscape is picture like bliss
The sun and moon express their beauty to its fixture
The morning air is clear and without fumes
It is followed by afternoon changes
To achieve full life pleasures is to reach for ecstatic delights

Philip Hershaft

Paradox

An errant sigh escapes the breast
Of one who watches stars go by,
And hands unseen strike chords of time.
A hidden harp weaves the melodies and rhythms of life.
One footstep follows another,
As silent footfalls echo loudly between the ages
Of man, God, and Machine.
A bright light shines in the darkness,
A darkness veils in the light; and we?
We cannot see, distinguish as we might one from the other.
Can we tell which is which? Life - Death? Death - Life?
One is indistinguishable from another.
Both are states of being.
One can learn from either.
We know life... that we can know death...
That we can know life... that...
And so continues the walker, on the path between the spheres.
Encompass the laughter, release the tears,
Feed the hunger, banish the fears.
Fill the spaces between the ages that all may be one.

J. Earil Wilson

Untitled

I will lead the way for those who are lost,
I will stand for those who cannot stand,
I will speak for those who cannot speak,
I will walk an extra mile for those who fell short of theirs,
I will teach those to smile that cannot
I will give the disturbed a little peace,
I will clear the clouds for those who lost their light,
I will give hope to those who forgot how to hope,
I will lend my hand to those who have fallen,
I will rise for those who are paralyzed with their fear.
Someone dear, did these things for me, and then said to me, not
in debt am I to them, but to those who have not had a helping hand,
and give your wisdom and lessons to others in need,
teach them to give freely from their hearts to another needy one
as they once were.
I hope everyone, sometime during their life, will rise for those
who don't know how, and teach them to teach others,
Rise for those who can't...

Rana Beeson

Never Is There One Without The Other

Without day, there is no night
Having life, death is bound to come
Impossible to hate, and never to love
With every tear must come laughter
Feeling safe, means once being afraid
Experience victory, but welcome defeat
Can only be lovers, if friends first
Cannot have a past, without a future
Along side a man, should always be a women
With you, will always be me

Allison Hoffman

Jesus Understands It All

The Lord knows what you're going through,
So plead the blood and go on!

What problem do you have that the Lord doesn't know about?
Why, none you know - so true.

And what person are you that the Lord cannot help?
Why, none you know - 'tis true.

So just tell the Lord about it and the Lord will help you
If you'll let him - so true.

Tell the Lord about everything - he already knows.
Then plead the blood and go on through.
Jesus understand it all and He loves you - so true.

Just get ready to meet him,
And stay true and ready - so true.

We'll all be in glory.
Can't wait, can you?

Pat Nestich

I Want To Die

Why can't they hear me cry,
screaming that I want to die.
How can happy people understand,
when your life is going like sifting sand.
They don't want to hear my problems anymore,
So I hold it in my heart, the core.
They like to gang on you in teams,
and I feel like all I can do is scream.
I know these poems aren't much,
but all this rage, how can you take such.
I have no more strength,
my heart ache increases in its length.
They like to get me very mad, and inside I feel so sad.
I lock myself up in a fortress,
and don't even allow in my mothers kiss.
I make myself become so cold, and like a card game my heart folds.
How many people can I tell, before I say just got a hell.
You mean absolutely nothing to me, without you happiness might be.
I can understand making someone want to cry,
but how can you make someone want to die.

Sheena Blyman

"Dear Hero"

You did not rescue me from a burning fire,
Nor catch me as I was falling.
You did not jump in front of a bullet,
Nor did you risk your life for mine.

Why are you my hero, you ask?
Because you have done some things no one else has.
You were there for me all the time
Even if you did not know it.

Everyday you gave me something to look forward to,
Everyday you inspired me, that much more!
You also showed me the value of life,
For this is another reason why you're my hero.

You taught me more than to read and write,
You taught me that there's more to life.
To live with love, friends, and happiness,
Was just one piece of your valuable advice.

No one knows that you are my hero,
That is, everyone but me.
A hero to look up to,
And remember deep inside my heart, for eternity.

Kim Greene

Today, Not Tomorrow

Every day, all day, the city churns with life
Seethes with anger, screams with strife
I am just a child, just a girl
But if I could stop the streets from wailing
I would; I would touch it and heal it if I could
My touch would be a bandage
My words could sooth, my smile could shine with so-needed love
Too many people pass the hurting and aching
Holding a bandage in their hands, unused, ungiven
But while I keep promising hollowly
The bandage-holders, too, are filled with empty promises to healing
As I climb the stinking yellow bus for school
As I ride to the dirty halls and tired teachers
A child screams
A voice of the streets
Haunting and real
I must bandage the child, the world, today

Catherine Wright

Come To Me

As I wake from my sleep of ignorance
having squandered yesterday in yearning dreams, I plea,
Come to me... oh! Come to me.

As the cranes seek their nests or warmer climates
by the end of twilight or the autumn season, I wish,
Come to me... oh! Come to me.

As the tribes in the parched arid deserts
wait for their lost beloved monsoon dreams, I call, Come to me...
oh!
Come to me. As the passion of deceitful death
stealthily robs the joy of life, without warning, I stare,
Come to me... oh! Come to me.

As I burn my wicks to understand my nothingness,
the reason of your not coming in the light of day or night, I knock,
Come to me... oh! Come to me.

As I seek you in the pleasures of touches, in meditation
that grace the conscience of my sinful smallness, I seek,
Come to me... oh! Come to me.

As the drops of sparkling dew hang in helpless agony
I hold on to a hope making rainbow prayers, I ask,
Come to me... oh! Come to me my Lord.

Gabriel Robin Anthony

You Are Not Forgotten

I stand on the holy ground
taking in the magic from around.
I step up and touch the name,
my fingers linger and my heart aches.
The Vietnam veteran's memorial in Washington, D.C.
a place for all to see.
Sobs echo throughout the land.
I reach over and take another's hand.
We all share a common grief,
kind hearts and tender words are far from brief.
We are all one big family here
for we have lost someone dear.
A single tear falls from my eye, I will not say goodbye!
The shout of war, the cry for freedom he could give no more.
A young man gives his life while overcoming pain and strife.
His only goal to see, the red, white and blue flying free.
You have succeeded my brother and are as famous as any other.
I feel an overbearing stab of pain as my fingers brush across
your name. You are never far from my heart and mind.
Farewell my brother, You Are Not Forgotten!

Tabitha Haver

Flowers Don't Cry

The life that I've lived has had its sorrow and pains.
I've felt the warmth in my heart and the cold in my veins.
I've seen the flowers of spring wilt and die in the fall,
As the cold hand of winter comes and swipes at them all.
I go through each day searching for some kind of distraction.
Hoping that something will pledge me attraction.
Dependent on some great opportunity to hail.
And frightened of knowing I might eventually fail.
So my days are no different and the nights all the same.
As the months stick together forever shortening my game.
I feel the has to be something, so much more than I see.
And why can't the answers be easier for me.
I can feel time behind me, as it chases me down.
Reaching, but still missing as I crawl cross the ground.
What will be remembered after winter calls on me.
My laughter, my tears, my curiosity,
This is what pushes me to do the best that I can.
No matter what opportunities are placed in my hand.
So before that cold hand of winter knifes through
I'll sure make a difference for me and for you.

Michael J. Bartholme

Brave Knight

Oh! Come brave knight and let me join you on your
valiant quest to free lands under tyrant's rule. For to love you and
not to see you is in agony that I cannot bear. Our is a love
that is strong and true for my heart wouldn't beat a minute once
death has claimed you. My life is yours my bitter sweet love.
For if ever you should stop loving me, tearing my still-beating heart
from my body would hurt less than my losing your love. So please
my brave Knight let me join you on your quest so that we may
never, for whatever you desire my love, my heart, my mind shall
be with you. Do not leave me here all alone Oh brave Knight to
fend off the wickedness of this world. I would never survive
one minute without you. Your love surrounds me like an invisible
wall shielding me from all that's bad. Please do not take that
away from me. You are my everything. Without you I am nothing.

Hershella B. Bledsoe

A Tribute To Erma Bombeck

You touched the lives of so many
Without even knowing you did
You helped the plight of housewives
Who are constantly doing their bid.

You said so many wonderful words
That gave us strength to keep going on
Your humor was so insightful
For every wife, husband, daughter, and son.

Your advice hit home in every way
From kitchen cleaning to toilet scrubbin'
Your wit was so special
From learning to cook to bathtub ring rubbin'.

It's hard these days to find humor in everyday life
With all the extra bustle
But you helped us all so much
I guess we all need to hustle.

Even though you are gone
We'll try very hard to keep on going
For we all know you are smiling
From above with God all knowing.

Shirlene Chamrad

English Class

It began, not unlike all of the rest.
I walked into the room and chose a desk.
I sat and surveyed the room and its occupants,
Hoping to recognize any familiar face among many strangers.
Then, precisely at nine, she entered the room.
No time was wasted, roll was taken, the syllabus was handed out,
And our first assignment was given. The days passed quickly.
Candide had traveled the world, Blake faced the tiger
and Wordsworth reclaimed his youth. Tennyson and Ulysses struggled
with life, death, and following their dreams.
Through all of this, she remained enthusiastic,
Always willing to help, yet at times I could see her disappointment.
Although she did everything possible, and in my view succeeded,
To make the ancient words have a life of their own,
There were always those students who seemed indifferent.
This troubled her, though it was no fault of her own.
She felt as if she had fallen short of her goal,
Of enlightening the minds of everyone she met.
But as the semester slowly comes to a close,
One thing remains without a doubt, Ms. Stevens truly had class

Tommy Williams

The Emergence

I am woman.
I am butterfly.
Men have surrounded me with a
cocoon of chauvinistic ignorance
even when my fellow sisters gained respect in the 1920's.
They have not released the entrapment they placed upon me.

But I rise.
I grow wings.
I fight.
I am woman.
I am free, and free I shall remain.

To all those who are opposers to the notion,
I name
Rosa Parks.
I name
Amelia Earhart.
I name
Susan B. Anthony.
I name
Myself. I rise to the challenge of a new day.

Myra Rachel Ambrozewski

Life Defeats Death

When my heart endures sore pain and strife
I ask the purpose for this life,
I mourn ones silent sleep in death,
And yet I'm told they lie on yet.

I cry to the one of ancient days
And kneel beneath his pensive gaze,
He assures me well, they're in blissful rest
And cry no tears of bitterness.

He reminds me too, as from days of old
That man will walk on streets of gold,
Why then fret and sorely weep
For loved ones that have fallen asleep?

Then run this race of human life
'Midst all the tears and all the strife
There remains a purpose 'neath the sun,
For a race run well and for good works done.

Now the father wills we be aware
That we as well, will join them there,
And when the spirit flees to where they are
We will view the earth as a faraway star.

Vera Lightsey

Mythological Beauty

Do you feel what I feel?
The satin arm of earthly sand
hugging the shape of your back,
as the ocean gently ebbs from your toes.

Do you hear what I hear?
The spewing froth breaking into foam near the horizon.
Such beautiful tranquility; I can almost see Aphrodite rising
as the siren's enticing songs effervesce inside of me.

Do you see what I see?
Or is it just my imagination?
The brilliance of the early morn's warm colors embracing the sky,
as the treetops tiptoe to kiss Aurora's wonders.

Can such serenity be for real?
Perhaps it is Morpheus; who so cunningly deceives the subconscious
of my poor mind, letting it wander freely in this Elysian field.
Something tells me it's real.
But the infinite peace of this musical shore,
can only be found in the flight of fantasy.

Selin Tuysuzoglu

The Moon

As I wandered weak and weary
On a day so drab and dreary
Along a road with no intent,
But with me I had not one cent;
But darkness which unto I was peering
Came from there a golden glint.

I rushed toward the gleaming thing;
The shape it cast was of a ring;
Nearer and nearer came forth I
With every step, it seemed to fly
Into the night which was cold and serene;
It ascended towards the sky.

With head half-cocked and mouth ajar
It heightened like a shooting star,
Much higher and higher it arose;
Then out came light, from there it flows;
I reached out to touch, but it was too far,
Out of mind the magic shows.

I awoke later, after my swoon;
To my astonishment, I noticed the moon.

Evan Garver

Riff For Her

It is just a riff to her;
One of many songs
Things like that appeal to her
Then the music's gone.

I know a little more than something.
About the way that she must feel;
Now I must vanish into nothing,
Except for the part of me that is real.
Ode me that is real.

It is just a thrill to her.
Where we'd never gone.
No more than just a kiss to her
Then the thrill is gone.

And I know a little more than something,
About the way that she must feel;
Now I must vanish into nothing,
Except for the part of me that is real.

Here is just a riff for her.
It was just a dream to her.
I couldn't make it come true,
I couldn't make it come true.

Lance Young

To Whom It May Concern

I'm a young female who's depressed
and why?
I really cannot find the words to express
these feelings I bundle inside.
They scare me, but there's no place to hide.

I need a shoulder,
I need an ear or someone to hold me close and near.

I must dig deep to the loot of the matter,
but too afraid at what I might realize and become shattered.
I'm full of held back tears that had have gathered over the years.

I want to cry, but what good will it do, when
the same I'd thing is still around you?
I'm twenty-one and I haven't really lived
but now that I have a lot more to give.
But I'm scared, because I don't you know where I'm
going in life.

Does anyone hear me? I know my plea
is quiet silent, just help me because I
fear of being violent. Does anyone hear me.

Tamara Nicholson

Drifting

Drifting in and out of dreams,
Thoughts of childhood pass the screen.
Images and words become so clear,
The leaves of fall as winter nears.
Snowflakes fall, the cold wind blows,
The warmth of home and snuggling toes.
Laughing and singing I didn't away
The seasons change the light the wind,
My untamed spirit flows like wind,
Like love and trust of a new found friend.
The time slips by and soars through space,
This drift so soft, so real, so pure,
Holds every feeling my soul endures.
So hold me and love me my drifting light,
For now, forever, the glorious sight.

Todd Blamire

"Love-Sick"

Something is happening to me,
I see your face all day,
even when you're far from me,
I've a vision of it engraved in my mind...

The sweet caress of your lips lingers on mine,
as though the sunlight were kissing them all day and night..

That fragrance which you omit never seems to fade away.
I can smell you wherever I go,
as if the entire earth were covered with roses and their delicious scent....

After your strong loving embrace,
I can still feel the beat of your heart pulsing along side mine...

Though I've only described a few of my symptoms,
I have hundreds more than cannot be put into words....

For a long time, I never thought I would be one of the lucky ones
to be infected with this illness,
but now I know I was not damned to immune....

Now I must confess: I've a bad case
of this little bug and no desire to cure it,
for I've my remedy, You!

Maria-Leonor Lovo

Last Night I Cried

Last night I cried.
I cried to the heavens,
Asking the angels for help-
Searching for knowledge,
guidance.

I wept tears of blood for my family,
For my sisters.

I cried for the soul of a stranger.
I cried to the chamber walls for myself,
And my future-
I wept for my life.

I cried for those eyes that could not.
For hours, I wept the tears of two thousand years.

Last night I cried.
I cried for a billion strangers.

Ellwood Stowe Hare IV

Dreams

Often in a dream
   we experience anything we desire,
From being an outcast
   to being a star.

There are many horrible things evoked in sleep
   which trouble us continually;
But not as much as will ever be
   in our life-long prophesy.

And once we leave our imaginative playground
   to return to reality,
We forget the things we lived our life for
   but remember agony.

Elizabeth Bell

Alone

Walking, walking, walking.
Alone am I.

Going no place,
But headed toward the wind at my face.

Stopping to catch a snowflake on my tongue,
I promise I won't stay long.
Then, I walk along, one foot in front of the other one.

I hear the peaceful snowflakes say,
"What are you doing out on this snowy winter's day?"
Then, I hear myself say, "Don't worry I'm not going to stay."

Headed toward the wind at my face,
But going no place.
Alone am I.
Walking, walking, walking...
Alone and stray.

Courtney Ann Guy

The Alternative Mother's Day Card

Dedicated to the woman who grinds up my feelings...
Constantly puts salt on the wounds...
Gores the scabs of my life...
Tongue of fire...
Cold like ice and frost...
You are disowned!
My alternative Mother's Day greeting!

Jo Anna M. Polistena

355

End Of August...

High-pitched vibrations,
Incessant music of an ending day,
Orchestra of darkness,
Dirge of summer's passing,
Notes of sadness,
Harps of insects playing their last lay.

Chill-tinged evenings,
Sharp omen of the end of summer's stay,
Prophets of bleakness,
Sermons on sun's waning,
Words of sadness,
Shivering forecast of feelings disarray.

Brown-blotched tree leaves,
God's nuncios of life's return to clay,
Providential witness,
Pain-in-color, foreboding,
Shades so ominous—
Yet green still holding death at bay.

Charles W. Brightwell

Room Full Of Doubt

A noise a sound, a yell a scream
Sitting sleeping, was it a dream?
You wonder before sleeping
You wonder before waking
Where am I going.
Why am I going
These are things I often say
At night or in the light of day
Do mirrors lie, do shadows lie
Do people lie from fear or doubt
You think about it
Who am I?
Am I important, am I needed
Am I wanted, am I loved
Do I deserved it, did I deceive to get it
What does it all mean
These are things I think about
In a locked room, full of doubt.

Galatea Antonas

Addiction

Kiss me with demonic eyes
Swallowing the poison
the medicine, angels say
steal the souls of children;
Children running from God no longer in fear.
Standing still staring down your throat,
Knowing solitude is more than a game
flowing through the veins;
It's the life we choose not to acknowledge.
Kiss me again with bloody curses this time,
Time is the vessel sailing towards rocky shores
smashing promises on empty memories.
Hearing cries in vain for the kiss of sleep
from the light
burning in those eyes, angels say
steal the souls of children;
Children wanting nothing anymore.

Laura M. Morita

"So Far, But Yet So Near"

They look upon us with sadness in their eyes,
If only we could hear their cries,
For they are lonely where they are,
Their loved ones are so far,
But in their hearts there is no fear,
Cause your love is but so near.

V. M. Anderbery

Fishing

I am always wishing I was fishing!
I like to fish in the Gulf stream.
I am always wishing I was fishing!
I can sit in the sun and dream.
I am always wishing I was fishing!
I like to float in my boat and stare at the sea.
I am always wishing I was fishing!
When I stare at the sea it makes me feel free.
I am always wishing I was fishing!
When I stare at the sea it makes me feel free.
I am always wishing I was fishing!
It is so much fun to drive a boat out so far.
I am always wishing I was fishing!
Nothing can be beat trolling over a sandbar.
I am always wishing I was fishing!

William E. Hackett III

My Friend

Tell me when you need me
I will always be there
No matter where it should lead me
I will be there

Ask me, I will answer; call me, I will listen
I will help guide you, I will help you steer
Even if your tears should glisten
I will be there

No other reason needed
For all my love, I will send
Till my life is ended
I will be there, as your friend

Vicky A. Stutzman

Instant Angels

There's no understanding why a
young spirit is suddenly taken away. The
breath of life only to touch this little one for
such a short moment. Trying to justify why
someone so innocent and new to the world must
leave so quickly.
The moment they leave our world
they become "Instant Angels".
chosen by God to be in His Grace
and Blessed to live in heaven as one of His children.
Pray as time continues on that the
pain will ease by knowing your little one was
unique and chosen for chosen purpose and
Honor in becoming an Angel Of God.

Eva M. Davis

The Rose And The Thorn

The rose so gentle and neat,
that no other flower could ever beat.
Every petal perfect in place,
that puts a smile on my face.
I take a deep breath and smell the faint perfume,
A scent that's natural, that mother nature created, I assume.
The stem and leaves are a dark green,
With thorns that look ungodly mean.
I pick up the red rose with my bare hand,
I felt a sharp pain that I couldn't stand.
The thorns are as pointed as a needle,
like a stinger on a beetle.
Blood, from my body drips red as the rose,
a sudden flashback from the past opened from a close.
Hurt, ache, yet nothing, nothing to gain.
Something so beautiful made me feel pain.

Kelly Peikert

Prison Poem

Gray on black on brown on white are colors he remembered.
It was and it might be and it could have been: different.
Various bad grades and hookey, dreams and dreams then reality.
   Trouble,
then [free] followed
by an arrest,
then a term.
Now a sun-washed white, white wall, colorless. Empty in
the endless plain corridor upon corridor upon corridor.
Now a window, then a walk: over and over locking up his
soul and throwing away the key.

James R. Keller

My 5th Grade Teacher

   I once had a teacher named Mr. Killian.
Everyone thought he was worth a million
They thought they'd have such a blast.
They found out different at last.
Once they had him in class.

   One day without any warning.
As I sat down at my desk.
I heard this grumping and growling
I was really trying to take my test.

   When Mr. Killian waltzed in.
His hair was a mess.
On his face was a wicked grin.
"Surprise Surprise. Just take a guess,
At what you have to do to win."

   Eat raw egg,
and a chicken leg?

   Oh, gee where have you been.
I am lucky to have Mr. Killian for
a friend.

Christy L. Pomeroy

Closings

When you left us Grandmother,
birds wheeled on the wing
gathering for their southward journey,
and the warm wind of an Indian Summer
helped us sing our sorrows to you.

Please forgive us Grandmother,
for even in our loss, even though the winter
was long, hard and cold
we struggled on, lived on with out you.
All save one, one who could not fathom
life without you.

You would have been proud Grandmother,
of how He faced winter's cold barren.
But when Spring's supreme beauty
spoke of young love and being new,
He could not live it without you.

   And with all the passionate love and beauty
   that comes with the struggle of birth
He walked away.

Laurie McNabb

Untitled

There used to be light in this heart of mine
Which once had no problem with proceeding to shine
Now it is dark and filled with clouds
Adding much more unhappiness than one is allowed.

Michelle Bryan

"Echoes In Time"

When our drums beat, what do you view:
Our people, or are we invisible to you?
Let me pain you a picture, my pen weave a line,
As you wander back to the beginning of time.
Where once we stood, proud and strong
Our history stretched wide and long.
A people existing in gentle harmony
Roaming where we pleased, always living free.
And with the Eagle we did fly
Our voices echoing in the wolves' cry.
Hearts beating to the rhythm of Mother Earth;
Reminding all what each of us is worth.
Your Native Brothers — can you hear their call?
There once was a time when we had it all.
Standing tall on the edge of thew world
Watching quietly as our destinies swirled
Together; Lakota, Pomo and Cherokee
Our past, present, and what is yet to be.
qo?di ?ya?khe hi?da sati dan?qa
Grant that our path be clear.

Shaina J. Thompson

One More Day

As one more day fades into night
And all the tears have dried,
All the feelings from my heart
Are hidden deep inside.

The strength that comes from deep within
Burns fiercely like a fire,
Through despair it still prevails
And build's upon desire.

Heard in my prayers to silent skies
And visioned in the my mind,
Are hopes and fears of what may come
And of what I might find.

But, yet, with what my fate may hold
My heart will find a way,
To conquer every fear that comes
And get through one more day.

Breeze Bishop

My Longing Heart

Your eyes are such a pretty blue;
They laugh so very gently, too.
At times, I watch you look my way.
"Love you", I feel your eyes do say.
You walked toward me; my heart left higher
So quickly was my heart a fire,
I am to shy to talk to you;
So, I hide and run from you, too,
I wish I knew how much you care,
then I would know how much I dare
to tell you of my dream. You see,
I wish that you would visit me.

A. M. Lindman

Life

The cold winds of words blow all around me,
the cruel signs of hatred I feel surround me.
The tears I cry slash through my puddles of dreams,
I cover my ears and let out a scream.
As I fall to the floor, this isn't a dream,
I remember the shot that had made me scream,
I felt a sharp pain pierce into my side,
the feelings I felt poured out beside.
Scared and confused I closed my eyes,
I waved to my soul as it flew to the skies.

Tina Lyzwa

Nothing Is Like Reality

You hear a shot whiz by your ear
You get paralyzed by fear
You turn left and see a fight
you no longer know what's wrong or right
You turn right and see a kid crying
You know somewhere someone is dying
You close your eyes saying make it all go away
When you open them reality hits you in your face
Sometimes you think you're in a race
That will never end just continuing for ever
You see the distance to run when you
see the end you won't be done
All crime and violence will not be gone
You grab hold of a woman beside you
You look up and see loss and sadness in her eyes
And what else you see are lies
What shall I do? You ask to no one
All you can do is run
Because no one has won

Danielle Lenar

Hello, Is That You Lord Jesus, Hello Is That You?

Jesus' spirit lives inside of you, allow it to be your guide
The fleshly desires that control your mind must first be denied

Many times what we like most or would like to be our delight
Cast a shadow over the Holy Spirit that always guide you right

The enemy Satan will work on you, when you're vulnerable and weak
Before Jesus can make a way for you, a way for yourself you seek

Hello, is that you Lord Jesus that has given me of what I ask
Not remembering you didn't give Jesus a chance, so Satan is
  performing his act

Things appear to be going fine, just as you have planned
Until God reveals this is not his doing and brings you back to land

Now you're like a little sheep that has strayed from the flock
You don't know where to turn for help, you're running amuck

Hello, is that you Lord Jesus I really need your help
I have been with you all along my child but you wanted to help
  yourself

Many times my precious child what you want is not for the best
But Satan will get a glimpse of your weakness and put you to the test

My Holy Spirit lives in you, allow it to be your guide
The fleshly desires that control your mind must first be denied

I still love you my golden angel and want you to love me too
Just depend on me and Holy Spirit, we will see you through

Clifford Thomas

Spring's Renewal Of Love

My darling, you must know that spring has come again,
That piercing winds no longer drive a biting wedge
Between the frozen earth and men;
That soft trills of love free tree and hedge
Reveal the tender passion that immortalize the merest wren.

My darling you can read the message in the trees,
That long have marked the sky with branches bare;
The allotted span of sorrow now has run it timely lease.
The bursting need to love can have no valid care
For bitter words, harsh spoken only to displease.

My darling you must know that Spring again is here;
That we have paths to follow that our winter had obscured.
We left their shades when summer's here at half the year
Revealed the sorrows that could not be endured,
And which had overwhelmed our tender love with fear.

Lloyd Motz

A Dying Planet's Lament

I've watched you destroy me,
you've taken all I grow.
It's time you let me be,
and it's time I let you know.

My land is being littered,
my life is being cut down.
My fresh water that once glittered;
there's barely any left in my ground.

My trees are being uprooted.
My sea creatures are covered in oil.
My air is being polluted,
and there are barely any minerals left in my soil.

Please, stop trying to make me better,
you have only made me worse.
Now I'll end my letter,
but remember, take care of me,
  Mother Earth

Virginia L. Spencer

The Bloody Night

Volcanic was the rage which led in the bloody night
Vengeance coupled with justice the tragic dance has begun
Thunderous heartbeats echo raindrops crimson as they fall
The lone church bell roars a dozen curses

As the clock strikes midnight the child wrestles (missing words)
She struggles to turn back the clock Father Time refuses to yield
Mourning death morning light the torch of life
Is smothered in a blanket of fury

Cloaked in misery she toils desperate to rouse the corpse
The cold torpid fingers of death await eager to embrace him
So the weary child dorms a well worn garment immersed in guilt
Tainted and soiled the veil clings sheltering comforting the
  weeping child

Justice graceful as always has bowed out
Vengeance had his solo yet the moment of glory is lost

S. D. Thomas

Untitled

I knew you were ill my wonderful friend,
Very ill indeed,
Yet still I hesitated to see you
Or minister to your needs,
That I meant you harm I'm sure you
were aware,
You showed no malice towards me
The times I ventured there,
You greatly appreciated the flowers
and gifts I left behind,
so much easier to send
when I had not the time,
my wonderful friend is gone now
and I miss (missing word) all the more
because in my rush to like my life
I failed to see her go.

LaVerne Carrington

Passing Time

The children play day after day
Soon growing up and moving away.
People say hello and give you their best.

Growing older and older each day
Can't wait until your kids bring the baby over to play,
Remembering when you were just their age.

Brandy Spears

Homeless Child

It's dark, where am I?
I'm scared, I'm lost
I've got to get home
Oh, that's right
Mama had to sell the house...my only security
I keep thinking, hoping it's all a dream
Oh, it's raining
A shelter mama?
No, they're dirty
I guess we have no other choice
No room?
Not even for one night?
This bench, is it okay?
I have no home, no clothes, no money
Only love
I'm okay,
I can live on that...for now.

Stacy Geibel

Untitled

Two older boys cajoled, and lured the toddler out of the mall
Promising him something like a toy, top, or maybe a ball

They quietly spoke amongst themselves, planning and smirking
All the while their brains deviously working.

Maybe he should have stayed with his Mom,
After all he didn't know them from Tom.

The boys turned around with rocks and bricks in hand
and hurled them at the toddler in a steady band.

The tyke tried to run but his legs were too short,
the boys came and smashed his head, then went to cavort.

The toddler lay in a pool of blood, his head smashed,
all his promise and hopes were also dashed.

For 'lil James Bulger is dead for good,
he lies alone in a box of wood.

Kristi Marie Brey

The Pitch

He raises his leg
Then throws towards the plate
Letting the ball fall out of his tight grasp
The ball spins in a repetitive pattern
    reaching the plate

The batter's sweat rolling down his pale cheeks
Anxious, his teeth clenched
His hand grasping the bat
Fiercely waiting for the ball
To reach the perfect destination

The bat has finally come in
Contact with the spinning worn ball
There is complete silence throughout
The ball, now travelling through the
Cool but misty air, undisturbed,
Still rising, but eventually the ball
Is nowhere to be seen

Cries of joy and excitement
Overwhelm the crowd!

Giacomo S. Buscaino

A Precious Gift

Over the years our friendship has grown;
Though many heartaches we both have known.
Through all that has happened one thing remains true,
You've been there for me and I've been there for you.

As we grow older and increasingly wiser
Time spent together is a priority much higher.
For we realize that this precious gift
Is worth all the effort to build and uplift.

When times are hectic as they often will be,
May we commit to each other to always see
That we plan times to just be together;
Knowing that what we have will last forever.

I thank God for this most precious gift.
He knew a great way our spirits to lift.
A friendship that's healthy and filled with love
We know is ordained and sent from above.

Cynthia Hoover

Rainbow

A rainbow is magic, with its yellows, blues, and greens
bestowed from the heavens, God's miracles are seen.
The sparkle intrigues us, spreads sunshine for all
how is it that this gift, is a wash on the wall.

It glimmers and sparkles and sometimes will fade
the memories it leaves can never be erased.
we wish for a rainbow and wish on it we do
for its mystical powers work wonders, can you?

As children we wonder can we reach it or not
for I always say, if there is a will there's a shot.
I've tried and I've tried and yet not succeeded
one day I will catch it, I know I will bet it.

The wonders I've questioned are for the heavens and me
but does God up above have it in store? We shall see.

'Tis not for us to question though questions are good
look into the stars and wish for God's holy word.

I leave you with faith, look high and look low
look into your hearts and onto your foes.

Antoinette Ricci

George Washington Carver

He was a lad of slavery days,
Born in the early sixties.
He had no home for rest and peace
Which kept him very sickly.

He was taken as a child
By raiders in their flight;
Not knowing who his parents were,
He toured a lonesome life.

At ten he started on his way
To get an education.
Successfully he did just that
And found plants' valuation.

He took the plant and found its cause,
Its value to mankind,
And formed three hundred fourteen things
In his good and kindly lifetime.

Now he's left his comrades
To seek a higher place,
For during the year of '43
He was called, his God to face.

Eugene L. Washington

You And Me - How Different We Can Be

When first I learned of motherhood, this goal I set for thee
That life would be a simpler one than it had been for me.

But through the years and through the tears, the clearer I can see
The goal I set was not for you, but truly was for me.

How can a mother learn the way she thought she always knew?

I thought I was the perfect mom, the one that you'd adore.
But who was I to think I could be all of that and more?

I love you more than you will know - how proud I've been of you.
You've always done the things that I had hoped that you would do.

I need your help to understand the things I cannot see.
For what it is and why it is and how it came to be.

I want to see what you see - I know you doubt that now.
But through our years and through our tears, we'll figure out just how.

Sheila Ito

Mary Had What?

Mary had a little lamb.
Its father was, of course, a ram.
This drove poor Mary up the wall.
She didn't quite know what to call
Her lamb which it is sad to state
Might end up on a dinner plate.
But deep in thought she found the answer.
She'd give her lamb the name of Dancer
For poor St. Nick 'tis sad to say
Had had a reindeer go astray.
So now when Christmas Eve rolls 'round
That little lamb can be found
In front of Santa's reindeer pack
While Rudolph has to run in back.

Robert C. Mosher

Who Is This Man Called Holy?

The world is so full of sin like it was in the past, but he
died on the cross for you and me so that the world could
only last. He sat down at a table and ate with twelve
little men, they said that one would betray him for the
power of the world and sin. His feet were burned in a
furnace like fine linen and dark brass, and if you asked
what color he was, they would only give you a laugh. Through
repentance and baptism and speaking of unknown tongues,
there is a spirit call the Holy Ghost, that will comfort you
until he comes. Now if you are a witness you'll be happy to
go out and boast, for men and women are doing this from east
to coast to coast. Now if you want to see him, for his face
is a mystery, you must obey the law of the holy land and
have no misery. For his way is the only way and is perfect
in our sight, for he will come back and take us all like a
thief in the night. The rapture will be soon to come in a
twinkling of an eye and all the saints will meet him in the sky.
Now Jesus is the Son of God and say this very boldly, so now
do you know this man that the Bible say is Holy?

Phillip D. Bledsoe

Time

How much are you willing to pay, if time could be bought
How much time would you take, if you knew you couldn't get caught
A gift so precious, given to us everyday
Some use it wisely, some just seem to waste it away
Time to conserve all that we could
Time to take the time to do the things we should
Spend time to do the things that make us grow
For it can't be taken back after you've let it go
For time will slip away before you know
Time...

Georgette Neglia

My Life

My life is sweet even though some people
Won't come down my street

My life is so good, but still some people
Won't venture into my neighborhood

My life may or may not be the best, but I can't live
My life for you or the rest

My life is mine, your life is yours
But please live your life with an open door

Be kind to your fellow man, you never know when
You may need their hand

Keep your feet on the ground, your head in the skies
See people with your heart not with your eyes

I might live here and you may live there,
But if we meet in the middle the rewards we both may share

Gene B. Singleton

My Light

When I'm sitting alone the dark, I think how my life could be.
Then I must stop and realize what a great gift I have.
This is knowing that I have been given the choice to live my life
as a light bulb.
As I turn myself on, I know that the longer I'm on, the warmer I'll
get and only when can I share myself with others.
If I turn myself off, I will become dark and cold—then no one
even knows I'm there.
If my light goes out, it is up to me to leave it dark or restore the light.
God has come into my life like that of a light bulb,
no one but myself can turn God on so He is bright, warm glowing.
Only I may turn God away and live in darkness.
As God is my power, he leaves me to be my own, and with this power
I shall light my life.

Ann C. Higgins

So Many Seek

So many seek, so few find.
The big rewards, like winning "the lottery,"
or the specialty awards;
Pulitzer Prize, Oscars, Tony's, Olympics, World Series.

There are many small rewards,
so few seek, so few enjoy,
a sunrise or sunset,
a clear warm sunny day,
the smell of fresh cut grass,
the smell of burning leaves,
ice covered trees of winter, shining like glass crystal,
city lights at night.

A trout stream or the sounds of a waterfall
the outdoor wildlife, and the big pines of the timberland,
a compliment, a hug, a pat on the back, or a smile.
These are the small rewards,
so few seek, so few enjoy.

Dan J. Honour

The Little Rose Bush

There's a little rose bush on the side of the house,
Each spring as I walk by it, I am more determined
To rake the leaves around it and to weed and spray it;
But never do I take the rake and do it.

What a little raking, weeding and spraying can do
And some love and care would help it too.
What a beautiful full bush through summer would grow
If I took the rake in hand and then the hoe.

Paula M. Libonati Schumann

By His Mountains Of Humility And The Sky Of His Brow

By his mountains of humility,
And the sky of his brow
I'm in awe at His complexity,
And were forced to wonder how!

By the winds of His breath,
And the seas of His love...
All are forced to acknowledge His power
That comes from above.

He gave blessing in abundance,
And tender, loving care...
He warned we'd be under surveillance
But reminded His justice was more than fair.

He gave guidance for protection,
And said He'd come one day,
He warned of sins with little detection,
And said when we go, we'll go to stay.

Through the power of His wisdom,
And the blood of His Son
He paved the road to His kingdom,
Where all mankind would be one!

Michael W. Sharrow

Love Sonnet

You have a way of when you smile,
That's with me all the while.
When you look into my eyes with yours of love,
And hold me in your arms while stars shine above.
When you thrill me with your charms in love's fashion,
And I hold you in my arms and kiss your lips of passion,
You have a way of love when we dance,
That makes my heart take loves chance.
A way of love is a treasure.
A way of love is a pleasure.
A moment of loves serenity,
Holds the magic of loves eternity.
So come dance with me my love,
Tonight while the moon is high above.

Elizabeth Browne

A Familiar Face

As I look into my child's eyes
I see a face that will haunt me everyday.
Scarred by the Demon known as "Alcohol"
Now I will never know what she could offer to society
But must worry how society will accept her and treat her.
I prayed for the strength to go on; because she needed me.
Then from this tragedy a ray of hope shone through
A voice crying, "tell others not to make the mistakes I did."
How a precious life can be destroyed with just one drink
And with no regards to race, sex or socio-economic status
Don't allow the Demon called "Alcohol" in your unborn's life.
We have the choice not to drink
Our unborn has no choice
And as I reflected on this
I realized I saw a familiar face from my childhood
It was my sister's face staring out at me
She had been the unlucky one to be visited by
The demon known as "Alcohol,"
Avoid the pain of seeing a familiar face in your life
By simply not drinking during pregnancy.

Brenda Carrier

Wandering Path

Days of cool dawns and dew covered grasses,
Pink and purple skies laced with gray ribbons.

Shimmering moist blankets lift from pumpkin patches,
As a drowsy sun climbs to its perch.

Warm yellow fingers paint rainbow on trees,
Whose colors lead to pots of ripe fruitful gold.

Fields of papery plants stand with broken arms,
Too weak to hold their young.

Squirrels dance about a walnut tree,
In celebration of discovered treasures.

A crow's call piercing the lazy afternoon
Startles a fawn nibbling on wealthy grape vines.

A canopy of trees shields the oven warm sun,
As a lonely creek wanders a dying horse's path.

Darkness enters as the Indian sun sneaks behind the tree line,
Shadows cast spells dissolving all color.

Leaves rustle like wrinkling cellophane,
Torn and tattered by crisp October winds.

Trees are filled with birds, birds, and still more birds,
Waiting for their ticket to take them away.

Jon McPheeters

Escape

Forgotten promises and broken dreams speak bitterly in a child's tears.
As words of hate fill her soul, she wonders what it is she's done.
She tries in vain to gain their love but for her to find there is
    only pain.
She reaches out with faith unknown only to embrace hate so cold.

A drop of rain, a fallen tear to show the pain that's within.
She cries out with rage and fear but her cries fall upon deafened ears.
The child asks how much more she must endure;
    her soul longing for escape.

For her to find there was only pain.
For her to find there was only death.
She has closed her eyes;
    forever leaving behind her world of pain.
In this death there was peace
    for at last she found her escape.

Marla Whitehouse

What's A Grandchild?

A grandchild brings a breath of fresh air
to an adult world
that has gone stale.
A grandchild loves you unconditionally
with a joy that
is filled with laughter.
A grandchild expects everything
and usually gets it
because of the joy he brings.
A grandchild guarantees our infinity
through the things
only a grandparent can give.
A grandchild gives you hope
for the future.
Oh, to begin anew!

Janell Martin

361

Alone

A song is sung
Yet no one hears its beauty
The eloquence of its tones
Voicing hopes of love that might be

Tears are shed
Yet no one sees
The grief expressed
Fears — lonely

Ignored — unseen
Others may not be aware
Loves gift declared — fears pain revealed
Heart's emotions made bare

Every feeling
Shown
Remains private — though expressed
Due to being alone

J. Michael Easterday

My Dream

Will there be any log cabins in Heavens?
With a porch and two rocking chairs
One for me to sit in and one for a friend to share
I know there are many mansions
And streets of purest gold
But I'd like a little log cabin
And a fireplace to share when it's cold
I think of a little log cabin
By the side of a beautiful stream
And then the daylight is dawning
I awake, it was only a dream
Dreams have a way of happening
And maybe, on that Great Judgement Day
When I meet my Savior in Heaven
He will say come child, I'll show you the way
To your little log cabin you longed for
I've been saying it just for today

Thelma L. Gross

I Heard You Kill A Dragon In Our Backyard Today

You must be tired my little one from your day of play.
I heard you kill a dragon in our backyard today.

And to fight off all those Indians, must have been hard for you.
Escaping in the nick of time, in a box was your canoe.

In the jungle of my holly bushes, a tiger you did sight.
You wrestled him for more than 10 minutes, you gave me such a fright.

I thought that you might hurt yourself, with the stick that was
your knife.
Tarzan would have been proud of you, if he had seen you in
your strife.

I am so proud of you, my little man, you are so very brave.
Defeating the evil king and the princess you did save.

Night has fallen, and the mightiest of warriors must have rest.
In our backyard, my little one, you are the very best.

You must be tired my little one from your day of play.
I heard you kill a dragon in our backyard today.

Debbie M. Sears

"Three Photographs"

I took three photographs just the other day.
One was of my dad, his thin lips curling
up into a sober smile.
One was of my sister affectionately embracing
me all the while.
One was of a friend named Kevin, this picture
was taken closer to eleven, 11 o'clock that is.
I took three photographs today.
One was of my father, the "love" of a haunting sea.
One was of my sister dancing upon a stage of memories.
One was of my best friend beneath a half mile
arch of lemon-smelling pines.
Yes, all of these photographs are truly divine.

Kenneth Adeneur

Get Home Before Sundown

When I was a little girl I grew
up on a farm.
My parents said get home before sundown
and you won't come to any harm.
When I became a teenager it always
stayed in the back of my mind
Get home before sundown and always
watch the time.
When I became a woman, no matter
where I roamed.
When sundown came I always tried
to be at home.
And now I've grown old, and almost to the end.
It seems I can hear the master call
Come home, come home my friend.
I know that my time will soon come around
and I will be buried somewhere in the ground.
But I just want get home before Sundown.

Ophelia Poindexter

What Is Me!

What is me?
Am I the way others perceive me to be?
Am I the way I think of myself?
Am I the one who gives meaning to others?
Am I the one who shatters meaning?

I am not just flesh on this earth!
I am not a number!
What is me?
I have goals and aspirations—
But doesn't everyone?
I think of the figure I will cut in the world.
Ambitions awake within me.
It just may be others may know me better than I.
But as time passes by, my image shall uncover itself piece by piece,
And then shall I know what is me.

Bernice Rumala - age 16

The Name Falls Gently From The Lips - September

Golden sunrises, cool mornings, and bright warm days
A subtle change is upon the land.
A quiet expectancy of things to come
With new beauties hidden from view
As though nature in her scheme of things
Has delayed the promise true.
A stillness is in the air
An awareness of unshed tears
The voice of a cricket in the grass - the waiting trees
Each one somehow knowing that
Autumn is here.

Doris W. Guinn

Time

The guardian of treasures, keeps of the midnight's black ink.
Knowledge, that of the gods' drink of humanity, perplexes all who
try to think

And ponder its meaning of life ne'erending.
No rules it follows, as all things it distorts, bending
the fabric of space, yet time always lending

Itself to cause of good and evil same. It has no mercy, yet can suffer
no shame, for it sees all life as pawns in a game.

As it rules over the present tense and has reigned over past without
err. And into the future, it shall endure: Existing without knowing
wear. Passing so slow, yet soaring away. So solid, yet subtle as air.

In its presence, it sees over all, but is indifferent, it will not
take sides. Guiding the moon, sun, and earth. Steadying the orbits
and tides. It fears no danger, for it destroys all. In its sight, all
enemy hides. And time is the subject of all topics far and near.
It steals, gives back, and covets the things that are dear
to others; it has no belongings, and protests it does not hear.

It cannot be expressed in words, to great poets' fear,
Is not in music to be heard by the ear.
But it is always watching, always staying near.

Scott Snowman

"Tender Love"

Out there in the forest
  under a shaded tree,
Lying on a bed of moss
  my special friend and me.
We held each other very close,
  we kissed so tenderly;
I couldn't get enough of him
  for he meant so much to me.
We made love under the bright blue sky
  as the sun shined up above
So glad that we were all alone
  because we were in love.
Where sunrays peeked through in patches,
  we tread a shaded path;
We walked nearby a flowing creek
  and held hands as we laughed.
We knew we never would forget
  this very special day,
When time had momentarily stopped
  in a gentle, loving way.

Elsie M. Readinger

Naked Eye

Silence screams as darkness falls
caressing those secluded within their walls.
Evil triumphs over purity once again, leaving its mark
and the scar within.
A total loss is felt as the pain pulses through my heart
to leave it bleeding, no longer playing a part.
The strength wears thin, the droplets sink down
and no one seems to understand the reasons for this frown.
The night soothes me, for the darkness covers up the real me
and the day brings heartache, because too much is shown for
the world to see.
The rain comforts my hunger, for it lets nothing go to waste
and the sun seems to burn my eyes, allowing the insanity to grow
and take place.
No control over what I need
everything is deceiving to those who cannot see.
This they will not admit because they do not want to believe.
Treacherous to the mind, but not to the heart's eye
praying that deceit can no longer pass through the naked eye.

Anna Wasilewski

Nature Sings Its Song

There is beauty in every cloud in the sky
And in the shadows that move them along;
There is always a color that blends them together
And makes them seem like a song.

For clouds appear like lantern slides
That are gilded and mixed and toned,
And their color is scented and their notes are flute clear,
Too soon the reflections we see have all flown.

They are fleeting and graceful and gentle,
For their softness is like the softness of care
When it's gentle and loving and the rainbows appear
And all the colors of the palette are there.

For the ring of nature is calling
It is dialed and its number is clear
For the notes are all chosen and written
And the melody is played on the air.

For it sings its songs in a key of its own
It blends its echoes in a grander swell
Its oboes, its violins, its seed bells ring
And it's unison combined in a living bell.

Jearline Bates

Benign Sanctum

Fear's sweat, rolled from my eyes,
Sorrow's tears, seeped from my pores,
Falling as one, each slowly dies.
Yet each has life, now no more.

Emotional sights, I see through my eyes,
Depression's impact, fills my mind,
Injectures of life, come forth as cries.
Nothing at my control, left soulfully blind.

To guide this confusion, order is taken away,
A rebirth of feeling holds me to attention,
Losing what is solid, the mind is left to play.
A realization for meaning, chaos shall mention.

Matthew Maitlen

Tis Agreed

Tis agreed
You are the queen of the fair
Tis agreed
You have them all beat there
As long as I'm the judge
A judge that wouldn't budge
The likes of you are few and far between
You're lovely and delight
You're heavenly and gay
Strange as you are beautiful
And a good sport all the way
Tis agreed,
You're the one for me
Tis agreed
No one else could be,
Half so sweet as you are
For the likes of you are few and far between

Mark Lefler

My Dreams

Seagulls circled overhead and the smell of salt was in the air that
day as I walked along the beach. I saw a school of fish swimming by.
I said to myself here is a good fishing spot. The waves are high.
I lay down the fishing nets to sleep. I dream of flying with the
birds or swimming with the whales.
I feel at home by the salty water side as the day passes by,
or was the whole day a dream?

Christina Hilby

Faith

Dedicated to Dr. Micheal Feltes and his family
A family tragedy
A child is mourned.
A family blessing
A child is born.

Each day that goes by
Thoughts and memories are alive.

With the new child that has just arrived,
The blessings are oh... so high.

With the tragedy of one,
And the birth of the other.

One child cannot be replaced.
But keeps us to have faith,
That this child has been placed.
In the faith of God above.

Paula Jean Henry

One

As the last weak rays of light gradually dim into a subtle shine
That sinks slowly behind the horizon
My mind drifts off into another realm
With thoughts of only you.
Here together, close, we both kneel at the edge of our love
Which surrounds us wide and blue.
The soft, caressing surf our gentle kiss.
The sand and sea our lust filled bodies.
The vision of your lips, the glimmer of your eyes and your
Soft, warm breath against my cheek.
A feeling of your being that surrounds me always,
Far, deep within my soul.
The conscious and unconscious worlds unite as one
Regardless of all differences,
Like the sand and sea with the caress
Of the rising tide.
You and I, one, when our warm palms slowly meet.
Heart to heart, soul to soul, lips to lips united as one.
You and I, now and forever, one.

Mayling Torres

Love Is

Love is for real.
Love is forever.
Love is for people who start out as
friends and build something better.
Love is for people who want a start.
Love is for people who have a true heart.
Love is for people who start out with two hearts,
and now have one true heart.

Amber Goodell

Dreams Coming True

Each night I sit by my window and look at the sky,
wishing that one day maybe I could fly.
I wish I could fly far away so no one could find me,
to a place in this world where it's peaceful and
where there's no violence.
I know I would be all alone,
but at least I would be a bird on her own.
I could fly, fly and never stop,
until I made it to where I was going.
I wouldn't stop to eat, sleep, or even to rest my wings,
until I made it to my destiny.
But for now all I can do is dream,
and maybe, just maybe, my wish will come true.

Latasha Marie McCoy

The Chair

Rocking chair, rocking chair rock me away,
Back to my youth and a happier day,
When my bones didn't creak and my hair wasn't gray,
And all of my worries just floated away.

Rocking chair, rocking chair rock me to sleep,
I'm old and I'm tired and so very weak,
Let nothing but good memories dare to creep,
Into my dreams as you rock me to sleep.

Rocking chair, rocking chair you've been my friend,
Through laughter, tears, heartaches and bones on the mend,
Through whatever disclosure the fates did send,
You've given me comfort right up to the end.

Rosanna J. Deaumé

To Uncle With Love

I can't believe the awful thing that I have done today.
Yes, I have done a terrible thing and really ought to pay.

Flog me if you want to or hang me by my toes,
Put me in the darkest dungeon, I deserve it Heaven knows.

Send me to the hottest desert or to some frozen land,
But what I did was accidental, it wasn't even planned.

As I sat down with pen in hand to do my tax return,
I hemmed and hawed and scratched my head, my brain began to churn.

It wasn't hard, it went quite fast, I wouldn't lose much sleep,
To calculate what part was mine and the part IRS would keep.

I didn't cheat, I was as honest as anyone could be.
I didn't owe a dime at all, in fact Uncle Sam owed me.

But then the moment came at last, I committed the big sin,
When I placed a great big "Love" stamp on the envelope
   my tax return was in.

Nancy M. Anderson

Moondancer

On a special night when the moon is at rest
You may see her dancing on the pale yellow crest.

Some call her the moon dancer, the one who weaves dreams
Others claim she's the spinner of the moon's precious beams.

But keep in mind that to see her at all,
You must listen very closely for her mystical call.

When she beckons you to her one starry wee hour,
Look deep in the glimmer of the moon's magic power.

There she will be, like phantom in white.
Spinning and twirling in the moons heavenly light.
Leaving memories with you always of that one enchanted night.

Jennifer Walker

Spirit Of Mother's Day

On mother's day all your wishes come true,
and your dreams and fantasies will always be with you.
The children you gave life to so many years ago
now thank and cherish you for the spirit you gave
them that you had to let go
even if they're far away,
they think of you on this special day.
All your triumphs they respect,
all your dreams they try to make come true for you,
I love you a lot and there's no way to end it
and the spirit you gave me is the proof. I'll defend it.

Courtney A. Francis

"Warning"

What did I do
What did I say
What did I do to you
For you to push me away

I don't know what I've done
I'm blind to what I see
I'm sorry if I've hurt anyone
So please forgive me

If all cannot be forgotten, then know this
My heart will break in two
My last action will be our last kiss
For I will not know what to do

Heed my words of warning
And never forget what I've said
For if you are in mourning
Then you know I must be dead

Jamie Hudson

The Window Seat

The window seat sits alone in the attic;
Its faded cushions make the room seem dramatic.
From it I can see for miles around,
Or just watch raindrops hit the ground.

On sunny days the scene is bright;
My thoughts take on a whole new light.
But cloudy times are always ahead,
When hope and sunshine appear to have fled.

And then here comes the lightning storm.
The sky begins to completely transform.
Streaks of color fill the sky,
And thunder sings a lullaby.

But soon the storm has gone away,
The calm returns without delay.
The gentle drumming of the rain,
Drives away the deepest pain.

The sky is dark and night is near,
And stars majestically appear.
Beneath the moon I fall asleep,
But the memories I'll always keep.

Erin Schoenfelder

Metamorphosis

Our body is only a cocoon
like the lonely moth
on route to the moon,
only our soul is not lost!

After our metamorphosis
we have the wings of an Angel,
like the katydids
we leave our shell behind,

Like the butterflies
we go to another dimension.
Do they remember being a caterpillar?
Do we remember being a person?

Once we get our wings
heaven is like a garden,
our used bodies stay behind,
our soul soars with wings anew!

My mother went to heaven today,
she got her wings to soar
with God and moths and butterflies
and katydids until her next metamorphosis.

Mary Fay Loyd

Untitled

By your vicious ways I cry,
Only to leave me wondering why,
Because of your brutal hands I try,
Try to escape before I die.

Part of me fades with each blow I take,
Someone please help me before it's too late.
Emotional struggles which I must face,
Seem to have taken my life's place.

This abuse will continue each day,
Only to end when I am taken away.

Angie Ditto

Thanks A Lot

Thanks for having me.
I slept all the way to G.S.P.
Mom, Dad and Zack-Back were there to greet me.
They hold me close and love me tight.
I knew I wanted to spend the night.
I slept real sound just like a log,
But when I awoke I had thoughts of a dog.
I thought and thought until I couldn't thought no more.
So I called Maw's to help me with this chore.
She set me straight and things aren't so muddy
I remember now - his name was Buddy.

Melinda Moore

Moon Lit Cry

I walked a lonely mile in the moonlight,
And saw your face through my tears,
Your image distorted,
I could see inside,
Your hopes,
Your dreams,
Your fears,
I fell back in awe,
Of what I saw inside,
The theme of despair,
Your sadden soul,
In the crisp night air,
I reached out,
Trying to grasp your hand,
In the sense of seeing,
I was a blind man,
Yet your image slips through my fingers,
And falls to the floor,
I wish you would stay here,
The memories I will adore.

Sharla Meese

"Tribute To A Friend"

So frail and utterly precious
    Too much, so it seems, for some
Richness in heart and caring in her abounds

Though confused in emotions
    Her life with steady purpose
Touches all those around

Ethereal in beauty flowing freely a
    Path of warmth and a fountain of goodness
To saturate my soul to which she lends

In the purest essence of an angel's spirit
    Which is my fortune to have found
She is my dearest friend

Maria Rose

Samm-Death Of A Friend

I am overwhelmed
I am overwrought
Pain
Hurt
Anger
These emotions overwhelm me like the snap of
the slave masters whip against my flesh
Death consumes me like a cloud of smoke
Life promises a new beginning
God is the beginning
God is the end
Like a flash of lighting
Like a sudden rainstorm
I am here
I am gone
But do not dwell in sorrow
Rejoice underneath the sadness
For when one spirit leaves another returns
And u may see my spirit soon
In the eyes of many children

Stefanie Joseph

Waiting For Spring To Come Once More

I'm up at four and walking the floor,
it's sixty below as I look out the door,
waiting for spring to come once more.
The ice on the windows is two inches thick,
everyone is sleeping, they think they're so slick.
It's just me and my dog, up late at night,
passing some time waiting for light.
The clock just struck five, it sounds divine,
the gift that you gave us to share a long time.
The warmth that it brings can't melt the ice,
but the sound of it makes me feel so nice,
as I'm writing this letter with the dog on the floor,
waiting for spring to come once more.
I think of the spring flowers in the early morning dew
and just want to tell you how much I love you.
So, Mom, when you look out your door,
waiting for spring to come once more,
think of spring flowers in the early morning dew
and you'll know I always think of you.

Michael J. Dzera Jr.

"Friendships Best"

Like the hues of a rainbow cast by the sun,
We were three young lives destined to be one;

We never thought that our lives unknowingly brought together,
Would spin a web of friendship that will last forever;

Through the good times and the bad, through the laughs
   and the tears,
We could always look to each other for support through the years;

Someone to share a smile with, to join in the laughter,
A shoulder to cry on, a helping hand for after;

We've shared and cared, we've lived and loved,
The times together as precious as heaven above;

With miles between us, at times we're apart,
Yet never alone, always in the heart;

Like the Universe expands infinitely above,
As does the best of friendships, the closest our love;

As the years will surely pass, one day our time will come,
But together we'll always be because now, we are as one.

Jeffery G. Hines

The Man Of My Dreams

Though I walked among many, I was as alone as I could be,
There was an emptiness, deep inside of me

I searched and I looked, without any prevail,
I didn't know what was lacking, I couldn't tell

One day, while I was seeking, I saw the man of my dreams,
He was right there beside me, reaching out to me

I gave him my hand, and handed over my heart,
Now we walk together, we have from the start

Just look beside you, for Jesus is his name,
Hand him your heart, and your life won't be the same

Linda Sue Caldwell Russell

"Too Much"

I think too much!
I think I think too much!
Maybe it's me! I'm not saying you think
too much... but if you must think
all the time why?

I feel too much!
I feel I feel too much! Me! I'm not saying
you feel too much... but if you
must feel all the time why?

I long too much!
I long so long it's too long! Me! I'm not
saying you long too much... but if
You must long all the time why?

I fear too much!
I fear I fear too much! Me! I'm not
saying you fear too much...
But if you must fear all the time why?

I hope too much!
I hope I hope too much! Me! I'm not saying
You hope too much... but if you Must hope all the time why?

Peter Russell

Demise Of An Enchanting Seraphim

Courageously you chose to accompany us
In this unintelligible earth
Triumphantly you battled and struggled 28 weeks
To conduct a perfect union
My Enchanting Seraphim

Colossal attempt constructed your haven
Melancholy registers of thoughts past intruded
Resistance lacked - events directed to the
Supreme Being of the skies
My Enchanting Seraphim

None foundation to embrace
Endless pandemonium
But always faith under the powers
True mockery - a total failure of what was relied
My Enchanting Seraphim

Forgive me innocent child of God
Mourning and grieving your loss forever
Merciful one assist a mother acquire strength
Awaiting re-union upon the heavens
My Enchanting Seraphim

Dimitra Ardamis-Raftis

"The Barrier Of Despair"

Nothing matters anymore.
Locked away in your dark cage of hate,
The key resting in my heart,
Beyond the barrier of despair.

Everything up close, yet so far away.
The angel of death,
Summoning me to its fingertips.
A marionette with strings.

Looking up, the wind blows by,
Whispering the horrifying fate,
Crying the terrifying future,
Ripping through the last crescent of hope.

A beautiful sun radiates my spirit,
Yet a bitter rain pours through my soul.
I douse my flame of eloquence,
With my tears of rage.

My courage a crystal, shattered into a million pieces.
But no one ever finds them all.
Looking down at my grave,
The death of an unexpected future.

Chris McManus

The Man Who Changed His Ways!

There once lived this old man who lives in
Gosham, Maine. His name was Kain. He was a
rich old man who was vain. Because he was
vain, he had lots of pain. His house was big with lots of fame.

As I was walking down a lain I seen Kain. I
asked him, "why are you walking down this lane Kain?"
He said to me, "I am so much pain because I
have fame, but I am very vain. That's
why I walk down this lane here in Maine."

When he told this to me I thought to myself,
"What lots of pain Kain has because he has
fame, but is very vain." "I will help you Kain. Wait
until it rains. Then go out and give your money away.
Not all of it now. Soon your pain will disappear and
your fame will soon get brighter. Then you will be a
rich Kain with no pain and filled with lots of
fame." "I will do that Quain, thanks a lot!"

And the old man changed his ways, and he still remains
in Maine, where he is buried and still has lots of fame.

Jason Cornell

Companions

Angels guide with the speed of light,
Counsel by day and comfort by night.
Ever watchful of our ways,
Illuminating spirits with joyful rays.

Our souls communicate in unspoken words
With the guardians of earth more numerous than birds.
God's message to man is preserved and fulfilled,
As His messengers daily oversee all He's willed.

Our sight is limited, our vision weak,
Our struggles and worries move us to seek.
An answer to problems not quite unique
From those who have failed to hear the mystique.

The door to this world is kindness and peace,
The key is the love that will never cease.
As we open our hearts and quietly listen
We'll rejoice in the message that soon will be given.

Maria Mastracchio

The Cry Of A Baby

I've heard the cry of a baby
I know the bluebird sings sad songs
I've seen the tears drip down clown's faces
And seen smiles that don't belong

I've seen the rainbows vanish
I've smelled a wilting rose
I've touched a broken heart
I've felt heaven's door close

I've seen a frown on a teddy bear
I know the loneliness of a dove
I've tasted sugar that's gone stale
I've seen a marriage without love

I've seen a cut in a diamond
I've seen a sunrise awake with a sigh
I've seen that sorrow lives
Within the joyful times of life

Bekah Fite

Winter Envy

I envy the bird in winter.
So calmly he sits in a tree.

His heart pumps so fast and his blood rushes round
That he never feels the cold of the ground.

What a view he must have while he flies through the sky;
What a sight it must be while he sits in his tree.

How blind we are, who stay so low to the cold,
That we miss the beauty of our whitened earth mold.
I envy the bird in winter.

Jeanette Borthwick

"Unforbidden Dream"

Weeping willows gently caressing a winding stream,
warming light from the sun's radiant golden beam,
lightly fragrant flowers from the earth's mysterious inner seam,
precious life bursting forth in this unforbidden dream.

Transparent air swirling over a blossoming countryside,
clover covered mountains where golden eagles glide,
swelling oceans drifting along on a subterranean tide,
unforbidden dream where God and intangible love reside.

Soft moonlight illuminating a starfilled night,
mystical constellations shinning with a heavenly inner light,
florescent stars creating a warm and glorious sight,
eternal unforbidden dream ascending to an unprofound height.

Bob Vorholy

Being And Having

Night brings with it an exigency
to utter what should not be uttered
in the disquietude of a tomorrow that may never come.

Distant apparitions dance in amber-lit windows;
sexless and ineffable, willfully reaching for the other
while penetrating shadow, and never touching body.
To possess the other is to delay the loneliness
which arrives with the sun and gently reminds us
that what is had can be lost.

A ship trapped in an ice-pack I have struggled
to break the urn which holds the future,
to find in this stale world the fragments of youth,
and to erect a life of love and blissful forgetfulness,
of being without having.

Colin Higgins

What Has Become Of You

What has become of you?
Do the flowers Know
What I don't.

I was half way on the road looking
For that familiar path
When it dawned on me
I was lost in the passage to your heart.

I recall the wild animals and wolves that howled
Like me in the echo distant of the last hello.
Well, I watched the year pass swiftly then the winds began
To blow back.

One more time the sun rose
One more time the rains fell
One more time was one more time
Just that and nothing more or less.

What has become of you
Has become
Wilfred Yamasawa

My Granddaughter, Bryna

My child, my child, today you are 5 years old
And here's a story, just waiting to be told

The nurse put a bundle in my arms
And I saw at once you had so many charms

You opened your eyes and you looked up at me
The most beautiful eyes - and they said to me

"Hi Grammy, I'm here - came into your big world
Know I'll like it" - as her little finger curled

"Heard Mama's sweet prayer - and heard her sweet call
So I came to be with you - with one and all"

Your Granddad and Dad said you were a 'keeper'
And our love for you grows deeper and deeper
Natalie Kallmeyer

Another Day

When nighttime calls, I go to bed;
Fluff my pillow and rest my head.
I close my eyes before they're red;
And my body becomes still as if I were dead.

I dream the dreams that I should dream;
But they're not as long as they should seem.
I wake up daily with eyes so green;
And I drink my coffee with white cream.

I go to school when yellow shows;
And my mind fills with things I don't know.
I eat my lunch right after Bio;
And then I go to sleep during Español.

I return home when school is done;
I do my homework, which is so much fun.
Then nighttime comes; there goes the sun.
I fall asleep, another day is done.
Jamie Rash

Memories Of Love

Now life comes and goes, here today and gone tomorrow, but memories of love linger on. So how sweet it is to beloved and the sweet memories of love. For after all, when it's all said and done, we are nobody till somebody love us, so how sweet it is to beloved. Oh the sweet memories of love linger on, so when you have your ups and downs, remember love is still around, so put on a smile it's gone be alright now.
Jimmie L. Isom

"puppycloud"

knock me on my ass, my friend.
slap your truth in my face.
but if the stained-glass window of righteousness
separates your crooked face from mine,
let me scream... and spit... and punch
until the broken glass falls in your eyes
and you come crashing down,
writhing with me in mental agony.

we'll walk the earth a couple of inches lower.
brains erupting with their blessed, pseudo-wisdom
filled with empty holes, waiting to overflow
with thoughts of a farmer in peru,
a friend in zaire, a child in taiwan.

(maybe then you'll be able to see a puppy-shaped cloud
when you thought it was a devil,
or a dandelion yellow, beautiful
like a fresh rose pink.)
danita joy kolb

"Nobody's Perfect"

I could walk that walk, talk that talk,
But does that make me perfect?
I'm not super woman, Shera ain't me,
Nobody's perfect, so understand my plea,
Don't think I can't reach heights
That have never been conquered,
Nothing happens easily, there are downfalls haven't you heard
Blood is a rush, love is a crush,
I have feelings too, and so do you, I trust,
I could clap my hands at the sound of a beat,
I have a mind too, I use it to speak,
Love is something that can't be wasted on perfection,
Nobody can obtain that, so what's your selection,
You know what I can do and what I can't,
You can whisper to me, sing a song or chant,
I could be all I can be,
I could be more you see,
I could cry tonight, die tomorrow,
And throughout my whole life,
Never be perfect.
Tiffany Blount

He Is Not Free

He is the love of my life - in my every thought.
Our times together are beyond words.
The simple things when we are together
Mean so much - but he is not free.

Our hearts are breaking - we have such love.
He's pledged to another - we both do know.
The hurt is hard to bear - but life is cruel.
We accept this fate, that he is not free.

She has his name, I have his heart.
Our times together are very dear.
Our future's not clear, guess it's not to be.
These are the facts, he is not free.

Obligations dictate his duty to her.
What a great life we could have together.
Enjoying the touch of his hand in mine.
It is not to be - he is not free.

Contentment together in a wonderful way.
We have something very few have.
An intense relationship, that is hard to believe.
But it is not to be, he is not free.
Gail Wright

Tolerance

Is it the stuff dreams are made of
or is it the basis of nightmares!?!
Corrupting our psyches
     IGNORANCE
       RACISM
         GREED.
Governments try to mold our views
of people of many Races and Hues.
Propaganda is what Destroys our lives
against all the bullsh*t we try to strive.
    Just stop,
    take a step back,
      WATCH
   and soon you'll find
    that it's more fun to laugh
when you're no longer in line.
    Eric Brown

To Andy

Chocolate kisses sweet desire
loud jazz blares, a soul of fire
dance on rooftops, pray to the sun
your love, our love, so much fun.

Screaming poems, say what's right
singing passion into night
a quiet dream I had with you
purity white, then morning dew.

Howling acid I'm so alone
your voice calms me through the phone
when no one else understood
you knew me like no one could.

Riding in a chariot of blue
through our hair the wind flew
pounding drums on ocean shore
your freedom touched my soul and more.

You let me in, you held me near
my words, my heart I hope you hear
I love you and always will
Andy, sweet Andy, 'til time stands still.
    Kim Schumacher

Nervous

Emotions, like riding a roller coaster for
the first time... I can not describe
how I feel, I know that I am scared.
And I feel like I am isolated
in a pod — no one can come in and
I can not get out.

I am paralyzed by fear of the
unknown... will I be able to
change my decision and go back?
Or will I achieve determination and
overcome this overwhelming fear?

Will I overcome this need to have
the Earth open up and swallow me
whole, in order for the unfamiliar;
but, yet always familiar eyes of
strangers... to forget that I am new.

Entering the room, I see friendly
faces that do not want me to feel isolated.
I am relieved to see that the faces feel like they are new too!
    Nicole Patrick

The Meadow

Mother means so many wonderful things
like the day and the night and the dawn
that brings, sunshine to our hearts
on butterfly wings.

Like a drop of dew on a flower so sweet
she brings sustenance to our lives as she
silently creeps.

Like a meadow whose breezes blow silent and warm
she breathes strength our direction
when we are weakened and torn.

In the center of this world where she
stands alone, so quiet, so perfect
has the sun on her shone.

In return she blossoms, giving forth
beauty and life
she is a wonderful mother,
and an irreplaceable wife.

This person I love,
this beauty so true,
this woman is my mother, and I do love you!
    Lori Wright

The Dance

I was moving along in life doing my thing,
Going to work-driving home-planning meals.
Dusting the tables-sorting the wash-feeding the dog,
Bought a new sweater-enjoying fall.
Then he came, this intruder, this despicable monger,
To invade my privacy, to disrupt my plans and tear my soul.
Giving me fear where my confidence once stood,
I'm forced to dance with this partner called Death.
I don't know the steps and must resist to follow his lead,
I must not let him finish this dance with me.
He must walk away and leave me alone,
I'll gather my partner of life and go on.
Our meeting though brief leaves me numb and cold,
When I think of the dance and his control.
He's backing away-the dance is over,
I'm left in the crowd a strange sensation of surprise and relief.
I'll get about my life again going to work and coming home,
Doing all the things I want to do.
But I'll keep an eye open because I know, He's there,
Out on the floor and may tap my shoulder to dance once more.
    Kathy Davidson

Hunting

Some say hunting is bad.
What else would we have had.
Tell your cat this is bad.
Even though you say you don't kill.
What about that piece of dill?
You say to kill is about meat.
But to kill is how we eat.
Don't even think you can live
Without a life something will have to give.
Some say milk is delivered by a fairy.
Tell that to the man at the dairy.
I see them wandering at the lakes
Wondering who packages these grapes.
How can you say hunting is bad
When life itself says this is all we've had.
    Scott J. Hansen

Trial Of An Adolescence *Canto Of Love*

Indeed this day I shall reveal
The measure of love I have concealed

To try to muster the strength each day
Bearing the infirmities of my dismay

The madness I feel only leads to confusion
Is this real or have I fell to illusion?

For I have crossed this path before
The mystery of love did lure

Tasting the sweet temptation
The bitterness of my trepidation

Lead to the confines of my heart
Juggling the ways from finish to start

I must express the passion within
To reveal the power of uncertainty been

Fear has gripped my heart's intent
The waste of time I have spent

Pondering the *if's* in my head
Afraid to be rejected I dread

Nevertheless I will abide
My heart's desire I can no longer hide

Sonceria Mayes

On Color

When I look I see not in colors of black or white.
My colors of white are soft and glowing not harsh and blinding.
My colors of black are calm and soothing like the night, welcoming.
I see in shades of soft heathers and brilliant flourescences.
Not blinding and forceful but in hues of pastels and gentle glows.
Tawny peaches, shimmering pinks, pale yellows, stunning bronzes,
coppers, golds and magnificent brooding browns.

Behind every color I see light reflecting, some covered
   and some glowing.
And when I look my eyes aren't blinded by objects of hate and anger;
but of joy to look upon God's wonderful creation.
My colors are of light and life and love and goodness.
I look with my eyes not cluttered but free to see and to reflect.
When I look my eyes are fill with light that shines in a world of
darkness, I see colors that absorb love and reflect hate.
The light in my colors are soft yet brilliantly reflected.
On the darkest night my colors show light to a falling star.
The heavens pour out my colors of white and cover with my colors of
black. My colors are different yet shine for all and lead the way to love.
So with every color I see, I see the color of human love.

Joyce Bryan

A Friend

A friend is a friend forever
no matter what happens to them
A friend is a friend forever
they will stand by you through thick and thin
A friend will help you go the longest mile
and that friend always knows how to make you smile
A friend can make you feel better when something is wrong
and no matter what the problem is it wont last too long
A friend will stand by you to the end
you can always rely on that friend
A friend will be with you through your joy and sadness
will walk beside you and carry you through the times of madness
A friend is a friend forever right through the end
and will always be with you
no matter what happens to them

Kari Carr

The Rainbow

All of the beautiful colors it does show
It surely has no place to go
Up in the sky half blue half gray
A little bit of rain fell today
The red, yellow, orange, green, and blue were so right
Oh-what a beautiful and rare sight
An endless arc of happiness and grace
Just like the colorful smile on my face
As each rain drop hits the sun
The rain and the sun become one
Up in the sky so careless and free
It is exactly what I dream to be
It's like peace so simple yet true
Like the feelings I give from me to you
The gold is on the other side
Chase after it you have nothing to hide
As the clouds burst the sun goes away
A rainbow is never meant to stay

Melissa Modrovich

To Have A Dream

Always have a dream and believe it will come true,
   Strive to make it happen in everything you do,
Work toward your dream all the day long,
   Persistence will make your heart and mind strong,
With each step the dreams draw closer than before,
   Sooner than expected one may be at your door,
For dreams are what make life worth living,
   Love worth taking and love worth giving,
They lift your spirit and keep it soaring,
   They keep life from being boring.

Tiffany Libeu

Life Conquers Death

She tips toes through the pains of her life; with a beaten heart and
no trust live by she goes to the hour before her. She feels the anger
inside as the thought of death draws near to her; she stares at the
place on her arm that calls out death, as she's constrained through
the dew of her eyes that causes her blur. The dark room blackens with
her breath as her nose burns slow with the smell of death, and the
battle around her losses the fight, as the dark one laughs in the
still of the night. Her tears dry and crack on her face from the
emptiness her heart cries with a hope of a forgotten pace. Drowning
in the swamp of sadness she reaches above for a touch of love; the
savior appears in the glisten of the sky, as the dark clouds disappear
from the power of his eyes. He reaches His hand to her little morsel
soul and raises her from the death that has pulled her so low. She
runs to fall in His arms; the Lord holds her and fills her with love.
Her tears dry as she looks upon his face and the smile from His heart
fills here yet with a joyous grace. Her Jesus carries her in His arms
as the healing of love begins- He wipes away the tears as she forgets
all her fears; she hears the truth in His voice. No longer is her
heart black with the death of night, but pure through the light of
Jesus Christ, her everlasting life.

Sheila Marie Arana

Love Me

   The love, the hate, the hate the fear in your eyes but, yet so
soft hearted. Your heart is like making a pot, if you push too hard
it will fall apart but, if you don't push at all you will never form
the beauty you are seeking.

   Eyes of an eagle, heart of a rose. When endangered within she
still cares about others. As the wind catches her wings, she flies.
She flies though the air showing me the path. The path with the
least of pain and the most of love. She shows me this path with
all the love she has to offer.

   A question of fear, a question of pain, a question of sadness,
Do you love me?

Tracey Skidmore

What Is Love? New Different, And Crazy!!

I am in love can't deny it. What I feel is right,
so totally new; we are on solid ground baby
don't let me down. I get so high when I look
into your beautiful crystal blue eyes. I see us
together forever. I hope we can be strong away
or close together. I want to hold you oh so
tight, because if feels so right, I am glad
we are waiting for each of us has our own
reasons for holding out. I will care for you,
respect, honor and cherish every moment we
share together. We are always thinking when
it will be right, will we every know? You give
me strength to go on with my life. For we
must fight everyday to make life what we
want it to be. Maybe our love is a love
neither one of us has ever known;
remember you must love yourself before
you can love another. Love takes time to bloom
like a flower in the motion of full growth.
And the sweet fragrance of fulfillment.

Gayle C. Steffens

Why?

The rifles crack and soldiers fall
Bodies upon the border wall
Bloodied - Innocent victims dead.
"Why - why?" the anguished widows cry
"For our faith and for our God," they said.

A bomb explodes - screams pierce the air
Limbs torn - Children moan in despair
Search through the rubble - Loved ones dead.
"Why - why?", sorrowful mothers cry
"It's our revenge - for our God," they said.

Outside the abortion clinic
They screamed, "If you dare - go in it!"
The doctor did - they shot him dead,
"Why - oh why?" the poor women cry
"Because of morality", they said.

Tornadoes, Hurricanes, Floods, Rain
Snowfalls in May - who can explain?
Disasters, Dangers, People dead.
"Why-oh God?" the scientists cry
"For you, my children," is what God said.

Mary L. Gibbons

anything,
Anything.

light all around that shines upon everything,
So confused.
nothing is left untouched by the light,
It seems.

it seems maybe some is left,
Dark alley.
could be anything in there,
Anything.

anything could also be out here,
Could be anywhere.
hard to see because the lights are so bright,
Too bright.

too bright in comparison to her,
Pale skin.
awful sign behind her blinks,
Blinks.

blinks out a message to be seen,
Wanting to be seen.
anyone it seems to say,
Anyone.

Stephanie Bertels

Love Machine

You're just a machine with no conflicts I see
Your emotions are torn and locked up to free
Your time is forever, your face handsome froze
Your hands like steel, gently carry a sweet rose

Your girlfriends are many
But in one you can't confide
That you are really lonely
For which one you can't decide

Your voice is so distant
Yet longs to be near
And I grow to wonder
If love is all you fear.

So, please disengage your motor
And set your emotions free
So you will have some conflict
And you'll decide on me.

Lee Ludwig

In Love

I'm falling in love
Can't somebody help me
The way you come at night, when I am sleeping
You hold me so tight, or am I just dreaming
Are the feelings untrue, are the emotions from you
Is it you that holds me when I am scared
Or is it me holding on to nothing
Can't this love awaken, can't you tell me something
When I close my eyes, you appear
Or is it you that I hear
Tell me now, before I walk away
Tell me now, before we waste another day
Open your eyes and let me in
Tell me now before we let it end
Do I love you, or am I insane
Do you love me or is this a game

Michelle Ingram

Love's Containment

There! Within a golden haze, misty soft
And serene, she moves 'midst glittering joy
And quivering sadness. A vision made
And deep-etched on a place in me where I
Emotionally realize wants I most miss.
Of me she as yet seems wary: Respect,
Trust and agape are the gifts I earn from her.
Would I lose these if I speak true
Love—turning the haze dark, impregnable? What dread!
I must love within only the cauldron of my mind:
The primordial stem, shaper of reason.
This limbus, this friend and foe, this maker of what
Is most powerful: Emotion, unreasonable, dauntless.
Am I capable to be like a God
Indifferent to mortal senses? I am not.
Thus, fearing the loss of any her
Gifts, shadowy dark stays my love—sadly,
Through the remains of my life. But when death's grip holds,
Please, someone sweet, mix my ashes with wildflower seeds
And strew them wide where she may chance to walk.

Milton Foster

In A Child's Heart

Long ago not far away
There lived a girl who longed to say,
"Oh Daddy, my Daddy!"
But sad to say the words weren't spoken,
And little by little her heart was broken.
She waited anxiously day by day,
For him to come, and sit and stay.
But where was he, where did he go?
And what could she of done to make it so?
Gazing out the window she knew he'd come.
He would explain his delay and off they'd run!
With so much to talk about
And much laughter to share,
At last he'd show her how much he cared.
It's still a dream she imagines today
But as time goes on it's safe to say,
"My father hasn't come and probably won't
Sad as it seems, I continue to hope."

Barbara L. Burns

The Future

The past is behind us;
Its sepulchers tall:
The future before us;
Not certain at all.
We've made mistakes
Down through the years.
We've laughed so bold,
And then shed a tear.
The past stands firm:
It will not change,
But shaping the future is in your range,
Because the future is what you make it.
Almost like clay in your hands.
You can gain back your good name,
In time, if you choose.
You can gain forgiveness
Or end a feud.
So expand your horizons,
All is possibility.
Yes, you can shape the future to what you want it to be.

Jessica Leigh Norris

Aunt Mary

There once was a beautiful girl,
Who had a head full of golden brown curls.
Her eyes were as green as the sea,
And her voice was as happy as can be.

To McDonalds and the Movies she would take me.
Sleepovers were her specialty.
She always made me feel special,
Love and Caring was her key.

This wonderful lady, was my Aunt Mary.
She lives in heaven now, and has golden wings like a fairy.
When I look up at the sky at night,
I can imagine her in flight.

So, when I see all the twinkling stars up above,
I remember my Aunt Mary with Love.

Theresa Sollitto

Life - It Could Be

Between the flowers and the trees
I'm a wonderer of what others see
I look up at the bright blue sky
I look up so very high
I look up at a puffy white cloud
And hope that God is proud

Do people realize, do they see
What the worlds come to be,
Hoping to know...
Hoping for the Earth to grow
We have been put on Earth by God
Some understand but some think it's odd.

Now I ask Do you see
What the world could really be,
If only we had obeyed
The rules God made
You can actually see
We could all live in peace and harmony.

Mark Platt

Don't Go

Don't go away, stay in my heart
love me forever let's never part. You
give me the strength to carry on even
when I'm not strong, but deep inside
we have a special bond. Do you see me
in your dreams even though you don't
know me? Do you feel my presence even
though you don't see me? Do you feel
love though you don't know where it's
from? I'm in your heart. Don't be
afraid. I know you're confused. I won't
hurt you. I see your pain, I feel your
grief. You're scared, I'm here. Just call
my name. I can care for you. Leave the
past and grab my hand. We can go
through this together. Love will lead us,
no one can beat us. We are strong when
together and weak when apart. Love will
lead us forward and one we will become.

Heather Shewmake

Holocaust

He's looking for me
but I hide.
The bushes scratch my face.
I almost moan when I see the blood.
He comes closer
and I stop breathing till passes.
A moment of freedom
and a moment of privacy.
One which I must die for, if I am caught.
I am a person.
A almost forget.
I give a prayer of thanks.
Thanks for a moment
of remembrance of freedom...
and of myself.
A light flashes and I hear a shot..
I feel no pain
I hear no sound
expect for my last word
"Amen"

Lisa M. Tankersley

"Love Is"

Love is like a dove, smooth in flight,
and you know it's right. Love enters
into existence in a blaze of glory -
now let me tell you a little story.
Love is not A tool for fools.
Neither is it a toy for a girl or boy.
Love will make you say, that you want it to stay.
Now remember don't treat love shoddy
or you will lose your body.
Heavens gate is at the cross-road
of individual "Pain" and lovers lane.
If you want to seal your fate, enter
Heaven's gate, you'll always have a mate.
Don't try to improvise or reconstruct.
You, will surely self destruct.
Love's no toy, it was meant for girl
and boy to really enjoy.

    William H. Wynn

He And The Sea

A contented child looked at the sea.
The endless waves splashed at his feet.
He and the sea were great friends.
No one else understood why.

"You can't talk to it," said his father.
"Yes I can," said boy, "and it talks to me."

"You can't play with it," said his mother.
"We wrestle quite a lot," replied the boy.

"The sea isn't friendly," said his sister.
"Then how come it waves?" asked the boy.

"It can't sing you to sleep," said his grandmother.
"Then you haven't heard the songs," said the boy.

"The sea doesn't have feelings." said his brother.
"But I have seen the stormy anger, the mournful loneliness
    and the cheerful side of the sea," replied the boy.

His family thought he was crazy.
They left him there when they went home,
—Over the hill, by the sea—
The boy didn't mind.
He and the sea were great friends.

    Emily Morris

Heaven

When I dream I dream of a place,
That I hope I will see someday,
Even though it is far away.
Beyond the star filled nights,
Beyond paradise,
Beyond the clouds in the sky,
Some place where angels fly.
Where St. Peter awaits at the golden gates,
With a heavenly smile on his face,
I do hope it is a beautiful place.
If my dreams come true,
You will be there too.
We will jump on the clouds,
We will fly through the air,
Making our way to the castle,
With its beauty so fair.
When we get where,
The angels await,
They play their heavenly songs,
Up there, there is no Hate!

    Ashley Marie Raymond

Grounded - 1944

Oh, I have wandered carefree near and far
On wings that bore me thru the azure skies,
Filled with a million secrets he cannot know
Who never talks with winds or clouds or fragrant air,
Untrampeled by the feet of man.

And I have felt the rain upon my face
Tears from above, cleansing the Heavens,
Of all the waste with which man desecrates
The, once upon a time, virginity of space,
Until again we rise and leave our mark.

But now my wings are shorn, no more to fly
Today I gaze into the far off blue above,
No more I roam the mysterious trails to everywhere
Except in dreams of these exciting days of yesterday,
Someday perhaps, oh spacious Heaven, we'll meet again.

    Robert E. Keister

My Child

You're my child, and you'll always be
No matter how far away you are from me.
We may not always see eye to eye.
We may not always understand, no matter how hard we try
But you're bone of my bone, my own flesh and blood.
You're a gift from heaven, sent from God.
And God has a plan for your life I know
And I'm believing that one of these days you'll grow
To love the Lord and serve Him with all of your heart
And from His word you'll never depart.
But until that happens I just want you to know
That I'll always love you as I watch you grow
And even when your choices don't seem to be right
You can count on my prayers all through the night.
When you lay your head on your pillow at night
I want you to hang on to this thought real tight,
You're my child and I love you no matter what
And maybe things aren't as bad as you thought.

    Betty Daniels

Cathay Hotel Blues (Penang, Malaysia)

Hand-rolled cigarillos, toxic body shock.
The lethargy of stagnation,
Being compounded by the marooning effect
Of fetid effluent in rancid gutters.

Sweating, flabby Chinese juxtaposed upon
Raw buildings held together by kitsch plastic wonders.
Grey skies, unrelenting heat
—There is no escape.
I don't want these walls no more.
And these walls won't get me.
Osmosis do your thing, and take me through
To the other side.

You know I am the monkey king—I can do anything.

Give me my strength, and my spark
And there will be no ceilings.

    Glen-John Hoffman

Consuming Love

By your love I am consumed in time and thought.
As by magic your touch calms my very being.
Alluring, reassuring, enticing, you sedate my soul.
As if by fate our paths were meant to cross.
Then blend in heart and soul unwavering.
I cannot shall not accept less than your total love.
I cannot shall not give you anything less than all.

    Linda F. Sayyah

Secrets

I have known the silence of secrets-
family secrets buried under generations of humiliated children,
questions are not to be thought of, God forbid they're ever asked.
Child abuse? Alcoholism? Drug Abuse? Fornication?
According to some, "these never occurred."
According to others, "children should be seen and not heard."
Everyone knows, but no one admits
I have been expected to keep these secrets,
sharing my continued pain with no one.
I have been a disappointment to the hidden legacy.

Becky Capelle

The Clandestine

she...
running in moonlight glistening pale to find him
waiting...
among the rune-rocks beside the sound of soft water
with the kiss of the moon on the darkness

she...
running naked soft breeze as it kisses at her breasts
thighs...
moist with the night-dew from the ferns that bow
beneath the stars and the vines entwined up above

she...
running in silence under a moon turned blood
frightened...
as the trees reach to find her heat cloying and sticky
flower petals clinging to her face

she...
running in sudden terror like the night-vines shrinking back
trembling...
against the rune-rocks beside the sound of soft water
with the kiss of the moon on the darkness...

Stephanie Leigh Igou

Women

Women are like pieces of China.
Some always look shiny and new;
Others have a few cracked edges-but
they themselves were once new too.
Some have excited lightened eyes, always
looking for new things to seek.
Others seem to have nothing to count on,
and their eyes appear to be somber and bleak.
They seem to bring us their special hearts
that give to the world a special part.
Maybe we should listen to their words
because even excited eyes have worried hearts.

Hannah Oberman

Love

What is love?
Is it a feeling inside?
Or is it a way you feel about someone?
Do you love or feel lust?
What is true love?
How do you know when to love?
Do you care or not?
Does anyone love?
Is love a true feeling inside your heart, or
is it a way to get what you want?
Do we all love one another?
How do we love?
Is love forever?
What is love?
Do we really know?

Lori A. Mikkelson

I Believe In You

There seems to be no limit as to what a man can do
If he's buoyed up by the current of an "I believe in you",
He can climb the highest mountain, swim the widest sea,
He can be whatever person he believes himself to be.

Now when I say a man can do these things, I hope you know,
That a woman, too, can match a man and go where he can go,
So I'm speaking of mankind, and of what this team can do,
If they both support each other, and say, I believe in you".

It's amazing how a person, though he thinks himself so small,
When he knows someone's behind him, can dig down and give his all,
And sometimes surprise himself at what he now can do,
He has found this well of strength from an "I believe in you".

Such a startling revelation, when you've done all you can do,
To step back and see you've done all you really wanted to,
And you know you owe the thanks for these dreams of yours come true
To the faith of all the people who said "I believe in you".

Gregory C. Bell

To A Young Cop On Night Duty

Death takes a holiday from time to time, his shadow crosses yours
    and mine
Though we are in our prime, he reminds us he will come for us in his
    own time.
As life's game grows ever wilder, your stance must be ever milder
Calmly look this challenger in his glaring eyes, logic always favors
    the wise
If you must bear as bear you must the end of life of those you trust
Their crosses you will find fall on you
And having done all that man can do you will suffer too what all men
must soon returning into dust
We grow older, wiser, sadder deep inside but this as men we must
ever hide and show a manly face in silent pride
But when we have the duty and ride alone at night and this is
    always true
And turn you left or turn you right you'll never get all the answers right
So some you just accept as worrisome things that haunt the night
And slowly disappear in the early dawning light
Those who have gone before made a difference in the lives of many
And so must you because that is how their greatness is carried on
In the hearts and minds and arms of the very young and strong
Good night, partner, your tour was not alone, I was there before you.

Leo G. Gallivan

Genesis

Tenderly,
gaze into my eyes, know me,
lovingly,
face to face, lips caressing your crown.
Breathe, deeply,
absorbing the sweet smell of you.

Hello you.
Innocence,
lying here beside me.
Tiny fingers exploring, searching.
Searching for your belonging.

Hungry,
cheek against breast,
bonding.
Whisper, hear me love you.
Flutter,
eyelids fall heavy, contentment.

Perfect,
new life,
That came from within me.

Julie Fretwell

Forest Guardian

Blue, white crystals fallen last eve;
Covered pines and evergreens heavily laden;
Are you safe little one?
Branches release their white powder;
As if they were stretching, shuddering the cold;
A squirrel leaps without fright;
Grabbing mornings delight;
Snowbirds gathering, huddling under a great one;
Little sparrow, tiny feathered one;
Rays of sunshine creep over the ridge;
Warmth on the grandfathers head;
Otters and beavers acknowledge creators morn;
Snapping of tree saplings, a deer munches;
Small bird who are you?
Fresh trails abounds the meadow;
The hand of the North wisps my feathers;
I am not scared;
My protector lives with me;
Eyes of courage, heart of strength he gives me

   William Good

Life's Scribble

You may read this fast
You may read it slow
You may throw it in disgust
I'll never know.

I rarely read fast
My handwriting is slow
Word combinations and meanings often don't flow
It's my own writing I'm to decipher
Before another I show

Do my words come close to you
or are the far away?
Do they mingle with the dew
Or in the wind go astray?
There me - for me - why do I sway?

Nature visits my hand often
Thoughts come unstuck and loosen
Their dance goes within
I become one with the wind
But how with another do I go?

   Linda L. Will

The Desert Waits

The sky is heavy with ponderous thunderheads,
The horizon is a glow as fingers of lightening caress the clouds,
The Acacia, Palo Verde, and Mesquite stand poised,
   with welcoming arms,
The Saquaro, Cholla, and Ocotillo send forth tiny hairlet roots in
preparation for the rain.
And the desert waits.

The wind carries with it a hint of rain and the smell
   of the parched earth.
The lightening no longer caresses the clouds,
Rather, it provokes and jabs at them as if to say,
"Give forth your life giving nectar!"
And the desert waits.

The lightening increases in ferocity,
The tremulous rolls of thunder shake Heaven and Earth.
Alas, the first heavy drops of rain fall,
Leaving crater like indentations in the sand.
And the wind carries with it one final gust of parched earth.
The first drop is followed by another and another,
Eventually becoming the monsoonal deluge of life giving nectar,
The desert vegetation greedily stores the rain for the coming drought,
sending forth multicolored blooms and greenery.
And the desert waits no more.

   Penny J. Sabbe

I Am

I am a flutist with a cat.
I wonder if I will be in Marching Band.
I hear flutes playing in the forest.
I see a cat jumping into the sky.
I want a newborn kitten.
I am a flutist with a cat.

I pretend I am a great actress.
I feel the problems my friends have.
I touch the fish in the sea.
I worry that rainforests will be gone.
I cry because my sister lives in New York.
I am a flutist with a cat.

I understand that life is hard.
I say that wild animals should be free.
I dream of going to a different country.
I try to practice my flute every day.
I hope that people will find peace.
I am a flutist with a cat.

   Mandy Harpenau

Interaction Of Deception

He came out of the fog in the wasteful night
He had the powers of the dark and the light
He gave me a choice with no time to spend
To be with him or to stay with them
If I go with him the journey begins
If I stay with them my life is condemned
Who am I to have this choice to make
I am so young and naive and have so many chances to take
Can I drop all my Habits in this life as I know it
Or is it to the higher spirit who I owe it
I'm so sick of the misery I'm so sick of the pain
I'm sick of the heartaches I'm sick of being sane
How can I pass this up and throw it all away
Will I die or is this my chance to stay
Why did this come to me what have I done
With all this insanity who knows what I've become
Time has ran out and he asked once again
Come with me or stay with them
My choice is made and time is up
I am condemned and it will never stop

   Mike McArdle

My Dear Mother

April showers bring back sweet days with you.
Time flies; thus, it was not too long ago.
I was nothing but a burden in you.
Fair weather circulated around us so.

The hour came to deliver your ripped womb.
A thousand claws gripped through your heart and soul.
You supported me no less else I'd be doomed.
If I were vine, you'd be my only pole.

At ten I left to uncover my dream.
Happy moments were often too hasty.
Momentary fun caught me with a gleam.
I had blindly neglected your love for me.

After every mist the sun will shine through.
My latent love for you will always true.

   Cuong Ba Vo

Schoolbus Largo

Elephantine chain, inching forward,
of cars and schoolbus yellow.

Curbside leaves of popsicle glow...
Maple tree in orange,
Bush blaze of cherry red,
Evergreens, not lime, but brooding, dark.
Aubergine or grape to match our dark mood of delay.

Drifting dreams on buses,
Yawnful boredom in cars.

Janelle Naylor

Untitled

I know I made your life a living hell
I'm sorry it took so long to tell
I looked up to you and I cared
I wish you only knew
I know I never really said it
but I love you.
I'll never forget those last six months
with everyone gone and only us
We had a lot of good times those last six months
I'm sorry it didn't last
I love you so much.
Through good and bad I think I can say
we lived and prayed everyday
I might've been wrong but I tried to be there
where my heart felt best and that was with you
until your final rest.
I'll never forget you as long as I live
your with me everyday and that's where you'll stay
till that day when I wish to leave
and I'll take your hand and enter eternity.

Shelley Gillespie

Untitled

Who are you that stands beside me?
For what reasons do you hold my hand?
How have we come to be and
how shall we come to end?
Friends and lovers shall we remain
or enemies of bitter scorn,
tasting bile with the mention of
one-another's name.
Tell me not, that love shall never fade.
Promise, only the love you hold for me today.

Daniel Rabaca

If There Was Not

If there was not a blade of grass,
Or trees that whispered in the wind,
Nor blossoms laid along the paths
Where I may walk within,
  Or streams that rippled merrily
  Through leas or mountains high,
  Nor waves that crashed on sandy beach
  And clouds puffed in the sky;
If there were no birds that sang
Or soared high on the wing,
Nor moon and stars in night sky hang
For us their light to bring;
  If there was not the sun by day
  To shine warmly on the earth,
  Nor children laughing as they play
  Or babies' cries at birth—
Then I could say there was no God!
No, I would not be here—
There would not be earth to trod-
Yes— all would disappear!

Carol J. Ellis

Vision

Fingers gnarled and scarred, careworn;
Hair snow-white, like a cotton crown;
Osteoporotic humped and bent
From too many worries and burdens that life had sent,
From childraising to nursing a sick man,
She toiled from the raising to the setting of the sun;
And, while her laugh was hardy and quick,
She loved a ribald story, pun, or joke,
Too seldom did she get to leave her work
To enjoy her friends or other folk.
Laugh lines creased her face,
But too often tears coursed down her cheeks.
Only enough money for necessities all her life
Her husband praised her as a wonderful wife,
Never asking for more than God provided
And sharing with others for her always decided.
Time brought her physical pain,
But never once did she complain.
They say when one's mother is gone
You feel alone. I do.

Elaine C. Wolfe

Your Galaxy

Together we shared each other for a short, brief period,
Only to be parted by the very thing that brought us together
As the group spat their views upon every move we made
You encouraged me to open up to you, to give you my love and
in return, you moved to another member to make your quest
for being a full-fledged comrade, en masse perfect.
Your loyalty, your love, was to the group-not to me.

You haven't a mind of your own as it belongs and is meshed
with all the other members you charmed just to learn all
you could. Tell me Fred, do you treat all your lovers
and friends in this manner? Have you no conscience,
no worthiness, no integrity at all?
I am angry now for associating with a charmer and
cortege without knowing that it wasn't a relationship nor
membership at all whilst unveiling too much about
my business, my thoughts, and my life.
Why did I reach for the stars, and trust you?
I was lonely and you were not because you belonged.
Initiation into your galaxy was painful light years away
From the support and love that I sought and needed.

Judith C. Brown

Boundaries And Beyond

Freedom's boundary flows gently,
Ever embracing invisible truth,
Unyielding to forces which would redefine the flow,
(So familiar it is that garden nor gate of the old
Home place afford greater comfort to a wandering soul)
Providing an edge to self only mine, distinguishing
That which is me from that which is you

Seductive horizons far beyond those tranquil swells beckon;
Sweet summons and eager spirit blend to bond with destiny,
Claiming promises for an interlude of harmony between
Self and surroundings that defy the margin of truth.
Endless expanse of emptiness, vastness without definition
Lures the restless into meaningless existence

No prisoner, I, though scoffers would contend it to be so;
For me the lines fall in pleasant places and whether this
Side of truth or that I at once know where I shall find rest

Myra D. Yoder

Music

Music,
That sweet harmony ringing in my ear.
Places,
Music is in many different places,
Places where you would least expect it to be.
When rain falls, the sound of pitter - patter strikes again as
music.
Songs,
The songs of bluejays are beautiful music.
Music is a small child's voice.
Music is a memory.
Music is like the sunshine,
It makes everyone happy.
Music whispers to people saying, "Be happy, be happy!"
And so they are.
Music,
Everything is music to my ears!

Michelle Cruey

Does Momma Love Santa Best?

We had a Merry Christmas, our tree was very nice
I got a whole bunch of presents, one of 'em I got twice
I tried to help my momma, who usually has daddy's help
But daddy got stuck in a snowstorm, they say he's beside himself.

I looked at my beautiful Christmas Tree, and hurried off to bed
Then I thanked God for everything, and into dreamland I sped
I only slept a little bit, then I awoke and ran down the stair
For another look at my Christmas Tree, I just wanted to get my share

I peeked into the living room, then stood there filled with emotion
For there beside my Christmas Tree, I witnessed true devotion
I didn't like what I saw, my momma was huggin' and kissin'
But it was her and Santa Claus, enjoyin' what daddy was missin'

   Now, I love my momma, and I love my dad
   My grandpa and all the rest
   But I wouldn't be happy at all
   If momma loved Santa Claus best

David A. Gaunt

The Siren

You, who waits for death so calm,
Your ship has reached its shore.
While mine, the tempest casts about,

   The Siren at my door.

The black-veiled nymph, she beckons me.
With arms outstretched she calls.
"Not now! I've work to do." Said I.

   The Siren knocks once more.

"Is there no peace for me tonight?
Must I succumb so poor?
My work is not quite finished yet."

   The Siren knocks no more.

She enters in with deadly grace,
And speaks to me so soft.
I place the pen upon my desk,

   And exit out the door.

Ben Ortiz

To Jennifer On Her 14th Birthday

Flower unto flower yet again,
Mother to daughter her beauty has distilled,
The bud, like chosen grain is gently milled.
Essence of woman, a bloom whose name is Jen.

She softly walks those paths that she must wend,
And guards her heart while mind with knowledge fills,
Aware that grace, not fortune can be willed,
For flowers left uncared, their stems will bend.

The world before you opens, hear its call,
No need to hurry, counselors at your side
Will guide your steps, lest you should fall.

And soon dear Jen, those tethers come untied.
Your choice is made, you hasten to the ball,
And hearts you'll break, as you in beauty stride.

Irving Mandell

Feeling Of Loss

Sometimes things or people come into our lives,
at first you are angry at them,
then they leave and it leaves you sad.
Just as soon as you get used to them, they're gone.
They leave you heartbroken.
They take away a piece of your heart and soul.
You cry out for help for a long time.
After a while you start to feel better,
but you still hurt.
You will have a small pain in your heart forever,
but you now know it was God's will.

Jessica Allman

Tree

   The tree I love sits in the rain forest
Every single day.
The tree I love is lots of fun
We always like to play.
   My tree you see is a home
To animals and birds.
My tree you see is a chatterbox
He says lots of words.
   Oh tree, oh tree, they're polluting you
Please, please don't die.
Oh tree, oh tree, if you die
I will surely cry.

Heather Geraci

A God For All Seasons

I see the bright sun, I feel the great heat,
The sheep in the meadow, I hear their bleat,
And I know God made Summer.

I see the colored leaves, I feel the brisk air,
I hear the rain fall, and put a scarf on my hair,
And I know God made Fall.

I see the falling snow, I feel the rush of cold,
I hear the whistling wind, to go out is only for the bold,
And I know God made Winter.

I see the yellow crocus, and I feel the warm breeze,
I hear the sounds of the buzzing of the bee,
My joy is knowing life is new again,
And I know to trust God because He made Spring.

Irene Carloni

The Greatest Joy

What is the greatest joy?
I do not think it is a new toy.

Some may think it is a new job.
It can cause an individual to sob.

Some way think it is a big raise,
That is followed by a lot of praise.

Some may think it is a job well done,
For some that could be fun.

Some may look to the stars at night,
For their twinkle and glitter offer delight.

I do not think they can compare,
With anything you might dare.

The ultimate joy from any view,
Is when you hear- "Dad, I Love You".

Galen Towner

"My Prayer"

God - Bless this little child of mine
Keep him safe for a long long time

Fill his days with sunshine bright
Send your angels to fill his nights

Give him knowledge and broaden his mind
Take his steps one day at a time

As he grows to become a man
Let him prosper in this land

And if, by chance his faith should falter
Show him the path to find the alter

Give him power and strength to give
For you gave your Son so mine could live.

A-men

Jane Harris

An Ode To Feeling Good

Feeling Good.
Is it an unexplained emotional surge,
or is it when there is an uncontrollable urge?
Blood pumping, heart racing, sweat breaking,
Feeling Good!

What could this "feeling good" be?
One might say "feeling good is a good feeling."
The laughter, the pain, a multitude of things.

Another might say,
"health, wealth, and the state of the art stealth"
Feeling Good?

The fact of the matter is-
God is good.
God is the ultimate good.
For what greater good could there be for one to feel?
Hence, feeling good is feeling God.

AMEN

James L. Hawkins

Before The Turn To After

Rear vision sights bridges of time, well tramped.

Spans of innocence windowed; Mom at home, Dad at work,
baking bread, fence talks, seniors in parks,
watching children with balls at tag.

Linked by wars called, cold, civil, gas, drugs, sex,
race, poverty...

Suspended innocence, hurling itself away to damaged
images of; Mom at work, Dad nowhere, bread in bags,
strangers talk by tapping keys,
seniors separated -
from children with drugs, latchkeys and guns
pointed at babies with holes
pulsing the jaded liquid of
life — out.

Advancing tapes, screen bridges of time, yet marked.

Spanning innocence returned, linked by Mom, Dad and kids
at work of play.

In common effort to restore young and old futures.

Priscilla L. Wood

My Love To You

The day we met was beautiful day.
Sun was smiling at us, and breeze was leading us.
How could I ever imagine someone like you.
I can see a deep crystal blue lake from your eyes
which is so beautiful that I don't want to touch.
Your face and skin were so smooth as silk.
When I see your smile, I will be in heaven.
I will give you a rose as my heart.
I'll bend my knee as my soul, my body.
Please, take this and set it free in your heart
so we can get together forever.

Taechul Kang

A Voice To Break The Silence

The road promised me no revelation,
Yet to the world's edge I ran, unheeding.
Before me lay the sky-mirror,
Blue and broken, white advancing.
With feet immersed in ebbing tide,
The twilight stole my song.
And none could hear the violet screams
Of red-eyed Cyclops drowning.

Alone I mourned, the light of stars
Could not illuminate my tears.
These sand cramped toes carried me,
To seaweed gardens in muddy sand.
Amongst the other flotsam I sat,
Driftwood damp beneath me.

The horizon betrayed an orange glow.
As wind, my flight to reach it.
The sand disturbed but no one there,
And fire in need of stoking.

Head thrown back, I raised my cry to the night,
A voice to break the silence.

Christian J. Kuznia

Washington D.C.

As I gazed upon the Washington Monument I thought,
Why to Washington D.C. had I been brought?
Was it the White House with its white walls standing tall and true,
Or the National Arboretum, with flowers of many colors, from red to blue.
There was also the National Aquarium with fish of all kinds,
From the hungry piranhas to the puffer fish, it's enough to blow your mind!
As I turned around, there stood the bronze doors of the Supreme Court.
With its 16 columns of white marble, it looks like a giant fort.
My next stop was the chambers of the Capitol.
The men here propose laws, which is not something little!
I also went to see the Vietnam memorial, the fate of these men was short and true,
They had given up their lives for the causes of the red, white, and blue.
I left for the Archives, the holder of patents and the Bill of Rights document,
I traced my family tree and spotted the Constitution, and here my day I spent.
The next day I went to the Smithsonian Museum, my favorite,
It has everything from Edison's light bulb to Apollo 11, this museum is not moderate!
Washington: A place where once Abe Lincoln called home,
The home of the Capitol, with its big white dome.
This place is very small, but look at all the things it's got,
I enjoyed going there for my vacation, for I learned a lot!

> *Kyle Gilbertson*

Ascertain

Echoing through generational bondage-cries of freedom...Let my people go..
Only to be enslaved by drugs, thoughts of despair...Let my people go.

Let us arise above oppression...freedom to develop our minds.
We, Nubians...

We African-Americans, Let the intelligence of our intellect rise
above oppression.. let our men rise above with respect they deserve..
that their manhood doesn't have to be proven by the conquest of a lay.
but by the echo in the winds, the legacy of a proud people
Let your heritage and awareness be exemplified by the
Knowledge of who you are as a people... knowledge of where you are going... for as an Eagle soars...

> Ascertain

For there is yet a dream to be fulfilled, come alive...oh dream...
A dream of encouragement a dream of strength
A new vitality oh Nubians, African-Americans
Where does your dream lie? In the respect of your integrity,
in your liberty...freedom does cry-and-yearn to be answered

Rise up! Answer the call-there is hope; Grasp the reality of the dream.

> *Dorothy Bradshaw*

Average Americans

Family history, especially to the young, is boring.
Yet it serves to steady, much like a ship to a mooring.

My father, at age 18, came from scotland in search of better life.
Ford motors, most appealing, WWI, adventure, possibly a little strife.

Discharged as a Sgt. of the 2nd cavalry, is how his citizenship was earned.
My mother, daughter of German immigrants, soon had my father's head turned.

Together, the depression years they survived.
It made them stronger... they actually thrived.

Three sons and three daughters later, no prouder parents could be found.
WWII, Korea, and 'Nam' saw their sons serving and returning, safe and mostly sound.

Their grandchildren never knew them and that certainly is a shame.
They've seen the pictures and heard the stories. We know it's not the same.
Americans by birth, it's mandatory they all know from whence they came.

And, when our national anthem plays, we're all among the first to stand...
With hands over our hearts and tears in our eyes, we truly love this land.

> *Frank E. Miller*

Tomorrow

Think about tomorrow and all the plants that you have set.
Tomorrow is still coming, so don't give up hope yet.

Think about tomorrow when you think about your dreams.
Don't think about the yesterdays that have been ripped apart at the seams.

Tomorrow is a time that no one person can predict or foretell,
Tomorrow can be peaceful, while today was a living hell.

Tomorrow is something that cannot be taken away from you,
There will always be another tomorrow on its way to see you through.

Think of tomorrow as a path that you have never traveled before,
Your todays may seem repetitive, but tomorrow will open up a new door.

Tomorrow is when you will find the answers that you have been searching for.
And I promise you, when tomorrow comes there be no need to seek these answers anymore.
Tomorrow will prepare you for things that are coming your way,
Tomorrow will allow you to smile at all the things that may bring you down today.

When you think about tomorrow think about a new man in the making,
Think about what you are going to give of yourself and not what you have been taking.

I know right now tomorrow seems a million miles away,
But keep in mind that soon your tomorrow will be remembered as yesterday.
   Dana Damiano

"A Prayer Request"

Oh God I have a request, that I ask of you in this prayer;
And God I just ask you to answer this, if it's your will, and if it's fair.

God, I ask you to send me down an angel tonight, to fill that final part;
For God you've filled the rest, but there's still something missing in my heart.

For God I still have the need for a young lady, in which to love, and in her confide;
I need the one who'll be my partner in flesh, for which she'll always be by my side.

God I need a girl who'll abide by, and support your morals, for which I now stand;
Lord this is just a prayer request, from that a desperate young man.

For I'm desperate because, you see God, I've looked, but I've yet to find;
Someone who could be an angel of God, so peaceful, and kind.

For God I just pray this, God please have your will;
And I'll just keep praying God until my heart finally gets all filled.
   Richard D. Brinson

The One In The Middle

Three porcelain dolls were placed on a shelf, beautiful and innocent were they.
The one on the left was strong, industrious, always running, energetic.
A perfectionist. Caring and generous. Always looking for love.
The one on the right was quiet and demure. Unsure of herself.
Loving and kind with a child like naivete.
The one in the middle was a combination of the two.
A loving mediator, counselor, listener, friend, forever searching for herself.
Their tingling laughter brought light and happiness to the world.
Then one day it happened.
The one in the middle was accidentally pushed and lay shattered on the floor.
The one on the right and the one on the left
Looked at the stark void between them.
Tears welled in their eyes, causing an irreparable crack in their hearts
Dark shadows of sadness entered the room. Time passed
The two remaining porcelain dolls stood cold, empty, and alone.
One dark morning the room became suddenly light,
An enveloping warmth came to each as a comforting arm went around them.
They turned to each other with startled eyes.
And saw an angel between them standing.
   With the face of the middle one.
   Dottie Crane Jones

"Silent Enemy"

You have never seen me because I am invisible. You speak of me with
contempt but, I never mention your name because I have no voice in
which to converse. I have no eyes, nor do I need them for I am aware
of your presence at all times. Ears, I don't need for it is your
thoughts I penetrate without the slightest effort. Although, I am
deaf and blind that does not concern me. It is only trivial. I have power to control your
actions and your thoughts. It is of this power that I boast. I am
not a creed, a color or a number. But, you can call me "number one"
because I am your "number one enemy." Due to the silent and listless
nature, I appear to be dead. But, I am very much alive and kicking.
The only way you can recognize me is the way you feel when I am inside
of you. In your heart is where I live. I am restless and burdensome,
yet I am carried around wherever you go. In order for me to survive,
I must have nourishment and shelter. I am never filled to capacity and
must be fed continually or I will die. You, out there, have supplied
all I need to sustain me. How long I live will depend upon you.
Feed me and I will waste away. Jealousy, greed and pride are only a few
tricks of my trade. In return for your generosity, I have doubled
your sorrows and taken away your peace of mind. I have robbed you of
your freedom and will cause you to lose your soul in the end. I will tell you what I am.
"I am bitterness!"

> *Ruby Foster Witzel*

Precious Heart

I feel out two hearts beating together as it they were my own
One means sure life to me, the other true love that you have shown
Love is as strong as life, so long as I live I will love you
To live without your love would be not to live at all, life is your love so true
But life and romance like promises and truth can sometimes be forever apart
Together we have bridged this distance by giving our all from the start
Being more than stead-fast lovers, but of friends and trusting companions
We have put our faith in one another to overcome these great divisions
Like a shield I'll always protect your heart, your faith in me shall not be in vain
Your tears are precious as pearls to me, I'll not let your heart be in pain
On your weakest days I'll be your strength you can always depend upon
Anytime you have the need, I'll be your pillar of stone for you to lean on
I'll walk you down the road of life, for you have given yourself to me
When you stumble I'll be there for you, I'll keep you steady
You're the reason my heart burns as thought it was wood, you set my soul aflame.
I love you so, I place your precious heart above my own, for you have given me the same.

> *Michael Rogers*

Alabama

Sitting on the front porch swing, listening to memories of days gone by
  As a sweet wind blows across my heart, I gently start to cry.

Fresh Honeysuckle and Jasmine blooms in no way could compare

Like the tender kisses we had shared, my boy from the South is there...
  Holding someone else's hand, now... Alabama, you've been "no fair!"

The way you'd carry your soft melodies from hidden rivers and streams,
  You gave me a taste of a heart on fire... just to take it back, it seems.

Your heartless, southern gentleman from Birmingham to Montgomery,
  I have suffered greater distance... just give him back to me!

You've teased me with your fields of white (such pleasures you've given this fool),
  As cotton gently rocks my sleep... how could you be so cruel?

From southern beaus to rodeos, you're surely the Red Devil's son...
  Like any man, you have played the game... and no doubt, you have surely won!

No money involved, just heart and soul be given to the winner...
  Tempt me with a wild horse... Alabama, you've one more sinner.

So, once in a lifetime, carry me home... Alabama, don't forget...
  Of all the heartaches I have chosen, You are the one I don't regret.

> *Summer D. San Souci*

Galapagos

If you have love,
it is a tree. Therefore
let it grow
for things nurtured,
    cared for,
        watched,
will blossom from the roots
    into something
beyond replacement.

Jill Broussard

Peace

Peace with its many tongues
Lonely to some
Impossible to others

When God of Moses,
The same God of Jesus and
of Muhammed
Brings mercy to mankind to
Adhere to the truth, that is
Compassionate peace

When people of different
Shades, shapes and languages
Understand, tolerate and
Respect one another
It paints a picture of
Beatific peace
When a white dove is cradled
In the cloudless sky,
Supporting an olive leaf,
That is peace.

Hilala Crutchfield

Lost In Love

He was the joy of my days,
My warm shining sun.
I felt good when I was with him
Our relationship was full of fun.

He always seemed to hurt me
I don't really think he meant to
I tried to make things work
What is left for me to do?

He says that he loves me
Is this actually the case?
Does he say this to make me feel good
And then joke when he's not in my face

There were times I hated him,
I wanted him dead.
But I just put up with the pain
And went on instead.

Our relationship is over now
I feel free like a dove.
Was I blinded by emotions?
Or just lost in love.

Tosha Walker

Artist

Pain, sun, tears, laughter
Carve a myriad of lines
on life's blank canvas.

Donna Alexander

For MF

I recall staring at
A neatly folded piece of paper
Wedged between two rocks.
I prayed the memory of you
Would outweigh the ink
That held the words to the paper.
And I left you there,
Nestled between
Two tear stained cracks of earth
Amongst a field of asphodels
Some place in Greece.

Michael Freedman

Ode To Second Place

Here's to all the people
Who have crossed the finish line,
Looked up and saw that someone else
Was there ahead of time.

Here's to holding back the tears
To bravely flash a smile
And shake the hand of that same man
Who has this fist held high.

Here's to walking off the field
Without the accolades,
And wondering if you'll ever
Get the chance to hear the praise.

Here's to finding courage
To leave the race behind,
And free yourself of might-have-beens
That linger in your mind.

Here's to perseverance
And the will to try again,
For the drive to overcome defeat
Is what it takes to win.

Brian Clement Sullivan

Prisoner In An Existentialistic Is A Clown Always A Clown?

What kind of a person makes a clown?
How do they get so wound?
Some fat, some thin in the waist,
Who is it behind the face?

Always smiling, always happy,
Some wears a hat that is flappy.
Wonder what is on their mind.
Do they ever have to unwind?

Some clowns wear a frown,
Wonder if they are feeling down?
Are they happy when work is done?
Or are they fooling everyone?

Whether they are happy or sad,
They can always make you glad.
It is always their style,
To make everyone smile.

A little clown can always find,
Something to do with his time.
Their hearts are made of gold,
For your attention they can hold.

Marie Dunham

Misty Eyes

With misty eyes
I look tonight
Into the sky
With stars so bright

The tears begin
To fall like rain
Surprisingly.....
They ease the pain

Was it love
That made me cry
Or is love
In fact a lie

Why she left
I'll never know
My misty eyes
Say just let go

m. a. stewart

The Old Days

When did everything get so strange?
When did life get re-arranged?
Have the playing rules been changed?
From the old days
From the old ways.
How life was played

Our world is bought and sold
While we save our bits of gold
The power man has a strangle hold.
In the new days
With Our New ways
How life is played.

Can we make it past?
And can we make it last

And change the old days.
To so much better days
How it could be played.

Stan Weber

Me! (To Thine Own Self Be True)

There is so much made up
to make me.
God must have taken time to
create such perfect uniqueness.
I may not think as you,
I may not look like you do.
But my presence is gifted and
graced with the same beauty
The Lord shares with all
His children
To thine own self be true!

June Thompson

Seeing Is To Be Blind

Everyone can see the light,
But everyone is truly blind,
To be blind is to see the past,
But to see the past is to...
Envision the future.

Laura Weaver

Nocturne

The day is over.
I purge my soul of all hope.
Venomous hatred poisons my blood.
Tonight, I am seized by unacted desire.
The suffering virgin,
The miserable poet...
How inevitable that their souls
are enmeshed.
How beautiful to play the martyr.
Mollified by this poetic journey;
"A derangement of the senses."
Arduous gallows!
I taste the night in my drunkenness.
Festive night!
Such proud displays of temptation;
Its satin flesh, Its pallid eyes...
I am denied forgiveness

Barbara Perez

My Father

When I was just a child,
Sitting on my father's knee;
I felt so happy and content,
He meant the world to me.

He was my rock to lean on,
When things were hard for me;
He was always there to pick me up,
And guide me tenderly.

His time on earth was very short,
How I miss him now he is gone;
But one thought rings within my mind,
I will never be alone.

My heavenly Father is there for me,
To comfort me when I'm sad;
To fill my lonely moments,
And to teach me to be glad.

For one day I will see them both,
Standing side by side, you see;
Waiting and watching with loving arms,
Opened wide to welcome me.

Dianne B. Hughes

My Daddy

When I was a little girl
and naughty as can be,
I would either run and hide,
or jump on Daddy's knee;
I always knew where I'd be safe,
Right in Daddy's arms
No one would ever touch me there,
I was free from care and harm.

I'd hug him and I'd kiss him and
say "I love you so", Then he would
hold me, Oh so tight,
I thought he'd never let me go;

Now that I'm all grown up
I'm not naughty any more,
I have no need to run and hide
or stomp my feet upon the floor;

I'll always need my Daddy's love
to keep me free from harm,
But I'll never be too grown up
to be held in Daddy's arms.

Lucy Jane Peters

Heurigen

Once the new wine came with spring.
Apple blossoms, or perhaps
lilacs purple branch
nailed above the tavern's oaken door
to herald its arrival.
And people spoke one word
to mean both the new wine
and the place where it was drunk.

Now when spring is about,
we lament the pollen count
and complain
about the rain.
And drink our ordinary wine.

J. Howse

Abused

I have been battered and bruised.
My hopes and dreams the wind has scattered.
The snow has but burned me.
The sun has but froze me.
It looks like they are done trying to mold me.
They can laugh all they want at me.
They can stop loving and living
I don't care because
I shall always be here.

Eric Brower

Our Little Girl

She's our precious little darling,
With big brown eyes, and golden hair.
When we take her out strolling,
People pass by, they smile, and stare.

Her favorite game is playing ball,
And she catches very well,
She is loved by all the family,
And she loves us too, we can tell.

She is very tender hearted,
And sometimes very shy,
and if we speak to her sharply
She has tears in those big, brown eyes.

We all love her very much
And always call her baby,
Although her name is Roxie
She's just a little Pomeranian Lady.

Ruth Staples

A Tale

I tell a tale like most
tales go, of love, hate
and sorrow but even
though my tale is filled
with pain, and I shall
never past this road again.

My tale is different how you
say, well if I tell my
tale in such a way that
makes you weep and cry and pray
then I haven't done as I say
but if my tale leaves an
inspiring, encouraging and empowering
trail then I've told my tale well.

Dionne McClaurine

Mom

She's funny and nice,
like sugar and spice.
She makes me laugh,
and scores a ten on a graph.

She has a job,
and a husband named Bob.
She's a counselor and a coach,
but, I don't want to boast.

She's sweet and smart
just like a sweet tart.
She has her days,
but, that's just a phase.

She has golden red hair,
and she's always fair.
I have a mom who...
loves me too.

Cassandra Morgan Stuke

Dancing On A Midnight Train

I am
Dancing on a midnight train with you
In some dream
Where you are not you
And I am not anyone,
But the sheer creation
Of that someone
I have dreamed of before.

Have been before, in fact.
Have tripped the light before
As this someone
Where I have jostled limbs
From a shaky height.

But now
It is only in dreams
I fathom the who of who I am
Because you are not you
And I am not anyone, anymore.

Elizabeth A. Stolfi

Too Late

Everyday it bothers me.
And there is nothing I can do,
It gnaws at my insides,
And pains me through and through.
It happened in my teens,
And through my later years,
Every time I think of it.
It fills my eyes with tears,
And now that I am older,
It bothers me even more.
That I didn't have the time to say,
What was on my mind every day.
Now that they are gone,
It makes me very sad,
That I never took the time to say,
I love you mom and dad.

Harry D. Deichler

Untitled

The silent sound
Of the winter moon
in the cold sky
tells nothing
of the warm spring
to come.

Edgar F. Hazleton

Reminiscing

I can't believe how old I am
I feel like I'm in my prime
I woke up this morning raring to go
It was already a quarter to nine

I looked at my calendar
Nothing to do today
What shall I do where shall I go
Guess I'll just go play

Thinking about when I became a mother
At the age of twenty three
It seems so very long ago
And how tired I used to be

Now I live alone
No family and very few friends
I wish that I were young again
And life would never end

Marie Noble Swanson

A Cardinal Crying In The Wind

I heard a Cardinal calling
Across the wind-swept snow,
His mate an answer giving,
In tones quite soft and low.

It seemed to me their calling
Was crying in the wind,
For useless, ceaseless war
And mankind etern'ly sinned.

Their crying was forlorn
For lands of blood and sand,
And for the men and women
Dying in a broken land.

Can we ever find a peace,
Or are we all madmen?
Five wars in all one's lifetime,
Too much for hearts to withstand.

Marjory J. Hornig

A-Wake

A deafening silence
Much louder than words,
A heart screaming out
Though nothing is heard.
A tear stained cheek
A long vacant sigh,
Is it a look to the future
Or the years that have gone by?
A mind that is racing
A weak trembling hand,
So hard to let go
What you can't understand.
A tense shaken smile
To cover up the pain,
An attempt to be strong
Only to break down again.
Yet just like a flower
That blooms, wilts and then dies,
A new seed has been planted
In the heavenly skies...

Michele Formoso

Mark My Place

No stone I want to mark my place
when this world I no longer face;
Peace and Love, a helping hand
my mark, I pray, upon this land.
Strength and Power from above
From me they see God's Eternal Love.
Help me, Lord, to battle on
against the odds that come along;
fear and hate within my mind
belies my heart which You make kind.
Strengthen me against the lies
of Darkness cast upon my eyes,
grant me power that I may aid
those in need each and every day.

Jedda Blessing

Along The Banks Of The River

Along the banks of the river
I watch the birds flying high
And gaze at my own reflection
As water slowly ripples by.

It's hot out, and the sun is bright
My head is full of dreams
Thought I'd take some quiet time, alone
That's hard to get, it seems.

A peaceful place where I can go
Enjoy my solitude
Sort out all my thoughts and prayers
Which direction I will move.

I find a rock to lean against
A soft cushioned bed of grass
And watch the clouds up in the sky
Like time....they drift right past.

Ducks are swimming, frogs are jumping
Birds are flying free
As I sit along the river
And wonder....what's in store for me.

Grace Dickison

"Love"

On a night like this
   I could give you a kiss
To press your lips to mine
   Would be so fine
I will never forget the night
   I held you ever so tight
The thoughts that are in my mind
   You will never find
For it is a mystery my love
   A mystery my love.

Tina Grogan

Serenity

Languishing in the noonday sun
Nestle deep in clover
A silky paw rests on my arm
Whiskers tickle my cheek.

My little furball purrs,
   stretches,
    yawns,
And then goes back to sleep.

Sybil W. Nelms

Boat

An old, rusty boat
Sitting on the sand,
Your paint needs a new coat,
Your oars no longer feel hands;
You are old, you are useless;
No-one pushes you to the water,
The effort would be fruitless:
You've been through laughter,
All that's left are bits and pieces,
Parts of what you once were.
As the length of time increases
Memories of you no longer stir;
You are like me,
I am like you,
Alone,
Staring out to sea.

Benedetta Agnole

Happiness

For the hearts I've touched in my life,
during this brief but meaningful stay.
  Plants everlasting memories
in my mind, of the special
ones that happened to pass my way.
  As the years pass by, I sit back
and reflect on life's most memorable times
  Some were good and some were
back, but that's how life goes.
  Life may not seem to always
go my way.
  But I'm glad to have had the chance
to touch someone's life, during this brief
but meaningful stay.

Donald Williams

Follow Jesus

Climb the highest mountain
Walk the longest path
Follow the brightest star
Watch sun shine on the water
And follow Him, you will

Watch the sun rise in the morning
Watch children at their play
Keep your eye on the sparrow
Be led throughout the day
And follow Him, you will

Work hard at tasks unending
Sow seeds where none have been
Show love to those around you
Be guided by His word
And follow Him, you will

His word will guide you upward
His hands will hold you too
Your fears will all be conquered
And follow Him, you will.

Bertha Clark

Lies

A broken promise
A broken heart
A word of silence
A shattered heart.

To say you love
To say a Lie
To say you're through
To say good bye

Words of lies
Words of nothing
Words of no meaning
Words of Lust

Gone away
Gone for good
Gone your separate ways
Gone to never come back

Never look back
Never going back
Never thinking twice
Never falling again

April Bleich

Down By The River

Down by the river
    Doin' some fishing.
A bite here and there
    Doin' some wishing.

Up goes the pole
    let's start the reeling
Could be a big one
    the way the line's feeling.

In comes the hook
    pulling a can
See the disappointment
    on the face of the man.

Put a new worm
    on the hook fast
Maybe there'll be one
    on the next cast.

Cindy Saxer

Last December

Moon light shines on crashing waves
In memories the sight he saves

On hillside all is decked in lights
The city there is up all night

He roams the land with distant fears
Locked inside are hateful tears
The face he wears shows his years
Locked down deep are shameful tears

The country town is warm and friendly
The way he sees, it's dark and deadly

The rural house with picket fence
To him it makes no common sense

He roams the land with untold lies
Deep in his heart he slowly dies
Every night he sits and cries
Deep inside his memory dies

Forgot the joy he once had
The hatred now, drives him mad

The reason why, he can't remember
Snow falls down, his last December.

Dana Koren Aldrich

Daydreams Of Love

I sit here day and night
Thinking of the words to say
As the thoughts of being with him
Grow stronger every day

I think of what it would be like
To hold each other in our arms
To love each other and keep each other
Safe from others' harm

But alas I've yet to find
The words to let him know
How much he's on my mind
I've got to tell him so

In the meantime, I'll hold on to
My daydreams of love
But one day I'll tell him
And make him my true love

Linda Labrasseur

Changing Seasons

I withered away that day.
I fell to the ground,
and turned goldenrod and brown.
Free of fight.
Free of life.
As susceptible to the wind
as dandelions,
and as open to prey.

I used to be so full of dreams
they made me grow.
Ambition that was as warm
and strong as sunlight.
As real as rain, and as welcoming
as unprovoked laughter.

But now, I will drift for a while.
Where the wind takes me.
And I will be as light
And lofty as a child's play.
And as soft and brilliant
in my diminishing colors as the sunset.

Kathryn Clark

A Baby's Life

A baby's life depends on love,
from the female and the male,
a baby's life cannot be sold,
for an endless millions sale.

A baby's life begins you see,
when he is first conceived,
and that baby is a miracle,
or so my heart has always believed.

A baby's life cannot be lived,
on account of being used,
and a baby's life cannot be lived,
beaten and abused.

A child's life deserves,
his mother and his father,
and if you can't give this child that,
then you shouldn't bother.

A baby cannot pay the price,
if it is just for welfare checks,
and if you cannot raise a child,
then you shouldn't be having sex.

Kristi Ragland

Twilight

The twinkle of the cowbell
The songs of the whip-poor-will
Fill my heart capture
As they echo through the hills
The beauty of the twilight
When the day is at its close
As the stars come out greet me
In silent sweet repose
I see the moon a climbin'
O'er the top of the wildwood hill
It sets my heart a knowing
That God is with me still
    And now the twilight
I know that God will keep me
Until the morning night.

Ollie Kendrick

The Touch Of A Teacher

The touch of a teacher
A warm light glows.
The heart of a child
A love for learning grows.

The touch of a teacher
With every lump of clay.
The shape of a child
Is molded day by day.

The touch of a teacher
Helps to pave the way.
The efforts of a child
Must be encouraged, come what may.

The touch of a teacher
So much to do, so little time.
The education of a child
A very high mountain to climb.

The touch of a teacher
To go that extra mile.
The light of a child
Makes it all worthwhile.

Susan L. Evans

Old Age

Old age is like a quiet pool
The course of life run dry
Peaceful, alone—
Through with strife

In arrogant youth
So fervently flowing
Rippling, gay, over the pebbles.
Distorting reflections,
Teasing the oak
With a fantasy wild
Forming of truth
What it pleased to see.

So at last the end
Tired and weary
Pebbles have ceased their stir

In still repose the quiet pool
Takes life as is
Reflects back what it see—
Nothing more

Ida LaBonge

Love's Questioning

We love to love
lost in a cove
searching for
a little more
what will we find
exploring the mind
where will it go
high and low
so we wonder now
about making a vow
seeking to end
and all our ways mend
like a perfect rose
you I chose
and to see you there
makes me dare
till the end of the day
through work and play
I can love you
can you love me too

Mary Veeneman

Transformation

My wounds have scarred
  And I stand alone.

My heart is hard
  But, I'm not unknown.

My body numb, from all of my pain.
But warmth from others wakes the slain.

Now I start my journey new.
With quest, some things to do.

An old shell cast, weathered by time.
I now have wings, time to climb.

I've shed my past away from me.
I open up.
Now I am free.

Roy Nicholson

To Mature

If only I had listened
There would have been heard
Those sighs from aging
Our youthful zest ignored

If only I had seen
The youth gone from the eyes
That experienced already
What for me in the future lies

If only I could say
Mistakes I will not repeat
Then the aging process
Would not have been a defeat

I apologize elders
For my youthful ignorance
Now you must feel again
The pain of adolescence

Sheryl Kruse

Untitled

She come to me only as a friend
She comes to me only now and then
I ask myself will I see her again
When....

Miles E. Waller

In Memory

Tenderness rendered inert,
Embraces forever divested,
Loving words silenced,
A uniqueness is extinguished.

Memories become creation,
Dreams become solicitous,
Re-creating a past happiness,
Reality vanishing momentarily.

Inundations of thought,
Cascading as a waterfall,
Resurfacing through the current,
Fragmenting flashes of remembrance.

Separation from this plane,
Terminations of agonizing reality,
Eternal longevity becomes reality,
Soulful deservedness is achieved.

S. Lee Lantz

You Left Me

From this moment now
Everything changes
Now that you're gone
Well it's hard to explain
The night you looked
In my eyes, say
I got to believe
But it's painful for you
But it could possibly be me
I know now the world doesn't end
I know the life will go on
But what's the good of life
Without you in my own
I promise my self I'm gonna be strong
Well I'll find someone new
Forget you and move on
When I think of your smile
But some one else will still hold
The pain I can't hide
I break down and lose control.

Megan Szymula

Take The Seed

Plant it in fertile spadix,
Nurture it with love,
give it knowledge,
feed it wisdom,
watch it grow, bloom,
show it the heavenly way,
caress it as it ages, withers.
Bury it deep in our hearts.
Remember it always,
A seed of life
as part of you, us, universe,
God.

Juan Shamsul Alam

Who Am I?

I ask who are you, but who am I?
I don't know who I am, and
now I know who you are.
Some men know who one
man is, but don't know who they are.
They may never find out.
Those who do possess a power
to live life instead of living death.

Danny Magariel

"Love"

You
I
You in I
I in You

We consummated
in our own I

Not You
but I
not I
but You

You and I
not You!
maybe We

Not, because We are not Two
but You and I one We are
Yes, Two in One
One at the same Time

Francisco D. Pon

"City Dweller"

Twisted agony
mechanical reactions
what's to be
when the blood runs

Washed out hope
unable to care
climb the rope
of burning fear

Feel the pain
of tired eyes
can't see past the rain
broken cries

Dance in the fire
hearts gone cold
try to find desire
the hope has grown old

Look for something new
in the musty cellar
search without a clue
only to find the city dweller

Janice Abbruscato

Mid April

Closed eyes reflect tired hope
a faded soul
a shallow dream
body aches remind me of lost trains
drunk with midnight cold
listening for an angel's breath
or a demon's sneeze
salvation
fresh
or a mockery of lust
awake with four days' boredom
and forty eight self inflicted slices
a teacher of razors
dulled from death's teasings
kiss me harshly
suffocate my desire to create
oh glorious flames
you would never believe

Charon Ryu

Killer Dead

For every month, there's a season.
For every season, there's a murder.
For every murder, there's a survivor.
For every survivor,
No one knows.

For this is the year
of the killer dead.
And every hundred years
This year is said
To pour death on
Thousands and thousands
Of people
When they're asleep and in bed.

You never know
Just when it strikes
It cuts just like a knife
You never live to see it leave
It steals many a precious life.

Katy Metz

Solace

I close my eyes
And see the ocean
Pounding on the shore

I am afraid to open them
For fear 'twill be no more

I close my eyes
And see the mountains
Tucked beneath the sky

I am afraid to open them
For fear 'twill be good-bye

I close my eyes
And see your face
Emblazoned on my heart

I'm not afraid to open them
Our souls shall never part

Joy Kieran Bell

The Cartelist Anthem

Hoodlums jiving in Manhattan
Escobared to a grisly tan
On Big Apple's streets delinquents run
Won't nobody shoot a gun?

O the strum on an oriental lyre!
The song of the dead - a deadly lie,
Dig sepulchers till you've got a mile
You couldn't dim St. Peter's smile.

Hankering for a dime or two?
Go to hell, O hellish you!
Crave, slave, groan and die;
Garnish the prig's apple-pie!
The Cry of Abel cannot be heard
Till Nietsches lie in counted dead
Who dare say its kinda dread?
'Tis the baron's milk and bread.

Grave, slave, groan and die
Garnish the prig's apple-pie
'Tis the baron's milk and bread.

Josh Levi Andraizer

I Am His

I am his child, I question why?
But, I'll not let life pass me by.
For I'll go out in Jesus' name,
Until he takes me home with him.
And there before the golden gate,
I'll take his hand and wait.
For all my questions one by one,
To be answered by God's son.

I'll then go down a golden path,
To stand before my God at last.
I'll see my life before my eyes,
And see the tears that Jesus cried.
Because I chose a life of sin,
And wouldn't let my savior in.

I saw the joy come to his face,
When I received his saving grace.
I wonder what he'll say of me,
A job well done;
He will be pleased!

Bernice Brown

Kobe, LA, Terra Firma 00000-0000

An empty moon precedes a further day.

The earth will fail beneath our feet,
and the screams of our progeny
will be our waveless shrieks,
as Earth rotates about its business.

Traffic is disrupted,
planes and trains no longer move,
a population shattered in disbelief
of what was always known.

That God who never shrugs,
image etched in slabs of marble,
inert, cold and clammy,
cut from the mountains,
that glisten like snow.

The marble dissolves in time.
We have our restorers.

Life does sing,
only to pass on
as a muttered twilight
on this one given day.

Frank W. Donovan

Tyrannosaurus

Redeeming value
social grace
numbered Icons
bits the race.

Tyrannosaurus
did He bore us?
Slow his pounds
did sluggishly bound.

Electric flash
digits crash
faster dash
store the facts.

Tyrannosaurus
should've implored us
or ignored us;
hope they'll adore us.

G. Courtney Crockett

To Melissa With A "Heart" Of Love

Newborn baby girl
Perfect in a Mother's eyes
Precious bundle of joy
Who would ever realize?

Baby arrived with love
Beautiful and Divine to hold
Love at its fullest
But, there's a story to be told.

Now... in heaven she waits
As God spoke and said "Come Here"
She's enjoying life above
What have I to fear?

I struggle, I wonder
Why must this be?
Death casts only a shadow
Praise God for eternity!

I can hold my angel again
This time...no letting go
God blesses us in ways
That reach down into our soul.

Jeanne Suchland

Untitled

Your love for me is endless
the shining of the sun
It stays with me through every day
and when each day is done
your shell of love surrounds me
in it I drift asleep
and as a brand new day is born
I know it's mine to keep
your love is endless as the sea
and countless as the sand
your love extends from you to me
when we walk hand in hand.

Teresa Fahy

"Dreaming On"

I once had a dream
that in my life,
things would go right.

For the love, that I've found
still isn't right.
I've been let down so many times,
I've been fed a bunch of lies.
The only thing left to do is
"Dream on"

I've dreamt of the perfect life
Being the perfect wife.
Having the world shine
Letting happiness be mine
for that was just a dream
It hasn't yet came true
there is only one thing
left to do, that is keep
"Dreaming on"
until all my faith is gone.

Brandy Clifton

The Singles Lament

I'm searching for a partner
why can't I connect?
I work out at the gym
and my clothes are cutting edge.

I have sufficient income
to spend on me, myself.
Every wish and fantasy are
not beyond my reach.

All the major holidays
mean travel, fun and games.
I never have to cook or clean
or even entertain.

No-one expects me to perform
and no-one sits and waits.
The clock just keeps on ticking...
however long I dance alone.

When will find a mate?
Shoshana Kagan

Untitled

No last "I love you"
did she get to say.
For God came and took
him far, far away.
Maybe if she would have seen
him one more single time.
We wouldn't see
so many tears
fall down her dreary eyes.
Never mean, always kind.
Those are the memories
let in her mind.
Now he's in peace
and not hurting like Hell.
Although she was wishing
he had gotten well.
But now he is well,
he's just not present.
He's lying in Heaven,
feeling quite pleasant.
Kayla Eddy

The Pelican

As he perches on the pier
I fear his body's downright queer.
His odd misshapen beak, a freak,
Stretched out neck and baggy cheek!

Now at a predetermined sign
He joins his brothers in a line,
Skimming o'er the splashing spray -
On swimming morsels hopes to prey.

Then nature waves her wand once more.
He rises up above the shore.
With feathered sides now gliding
On a whispered wind he's riding.
A graceful giant, king on wings,
Barely glimpsing mortal things.
Jo McNally

Untitled

Locked in...
Feeling felt; but never shown
Not knowing hot to except the unknown
Thrown aside
Joshua Perkins

Love And Hate

How can you love someone and
hate them at the same time?
You love them for who they are,
and who they are is their own person.
But you hate them for the stuff
they said and the stuff they did.
How can you be so confused about
life and death, if you know what you
want out of both of them.
How come none understands you,
what you are feeling, and what you are
thinking, if all that is what you are.
And the people who do understand
you, you don't know anymore.
Julie Taylor

The Rainbow Is A Poem

How do you describe a rainbow,
using black ink on white paper?

Is it enough to say:
"Sunlight's golden rays,
through silver raindrops,
gently arches..."

Yellow
Green Orange
Indigo Red
Blue Violet

No adjectives needed.

Or is it just plain easier,
to wait for the next rainfall,
and look out the window?
Ray Fourzan

Lonely Pilgrim

I am a lonely pilgrim,
    seeking water from the well.
Drifting in or out to sea,
    the direction's hard to tell.

I have come among these people
    walking darkened empty streets.
Peering into open doorways,
    where contented people meet.

The silence will bear witness
    and the stillness testify,
While the whispers of the wind
    quiet my lonesome cries.

As I turn another corner
    I barely hear the sigh.
For the night carries your whisper,
    your whisper of good bye.

I am a lonely pilgrim
    on a journey to the sun.
After years, the mending
    of my heart has just begun.
Michael Svetecz

The Battle

The snow is white
Where we have a snowball fight.
Snowballs flying.
Pretend dying.
In the snow everyone is lying!
Wolf Zahnle

Kids

I have two, a boy and a girl,
who sometimes send me into a whirl.

They play, they fight,
they stand by one another.

They are my kids,
I wouldn't want any others.
Or would I!
Patricia Sweeney

Untitled

How often we wish for another chance
    to make a fresh beginning.
A chance to blot out our mistakes
    and change failure into winning.
And it does not take a special time
    to make a brand new start;
It only takes the deep desire
    to try with all your heart.
To live a little better,
    and always be forgiving
And add a little sunshine
    to the world in which we're living.
So never give up in despair
    and think you are through
For there's always a tomorrow
    and a chance to start anew.
Shawn Woolridge

"Into The Eyes Of Death"

I feel her coming,
bringing an embrace.
Her movements thrumming,
as I make haste.

Struggling to break free,
these ties that bind.
Death draws near me,
no escape to find.

Ebon eyes coldly gaze,
with no hint of pity,
as she crosses the maze,
and stands over me.

Stomach cold and churning,
deep strikes her spear,
bringing pain and burning,
numbness and darkness appear.

'ever sleeps been brought,
away does life ebb,
from the fly caught,
within the spider's web.
Joseph E. Potter III

Untitled

You may think it is
    but it isn't
Remember, you thought it was
    and it wasn't?
What makes you think it will be
    when it won't?

Why don't you just accept that your
finite mind can't grasp infinity
    and give up?
And understand that things may seem
to make sense sometimes
    but they don't?
Charles E. Holder

Hearts Lament

In the heart of the starry
night sky do you lament for time
better spent,
   Is there something amiss,
How long ago is the remembrance
of a good kiss,
   In the throes of your hunger
of the early morning's night do
you wish for someone to hold
you tight,
of good conversations and
communications reached,
of building things together and
time's march breached,
   Do you hear words of sweet
nothings echoing through the night's
starry sea,
   Does your soul's sound ripple
across the night's tide
Do you lament for time better spent.

   David Paul Johnson

"A Walk"

The grasshopper hoping,
The birds in the sky,
The bees that are buzzing,
The flies flying by.
The sun shining down,
The breeze on my life,
The plants that are growing,
A beautiful place.
I walk a little farther,
A dog runs by,
Then comes a mother
Her baby starts to cry.
Now there is silence,
There's not a sound,
As my walk ends,
And I walk back to town.

   Brittany Smith

Nowhere To Turn

Alone...
Watching the meadows...
Bathing colors in the Sun.
Shades of yellow.
Stranded!
The mind is so powerful.
Hopeful...
The Sun is so warm.
Free?
Nowhere to turn.
Like a boomerang:
The meadows,
The colors,
The Sun;
All inhabit one space,
My mind.

   Korena Oginar

The Golden Field

Soft as the wind blows
   the golden grain;
Tall, thin, and dry
   O'er miles of endless land.
It waves hello in a secret way,
   as it whistles with the winds.
Silently I sit watching,...
   Watching the golden grain.

   Cathy Holland

"Maid Of Orleans"

Did you not wish the hot flames
were put out by your tears?
Or scream out in pain
after the war of a hundred years?
Did you truly hear voices
and trust in their words?
Did your endless faith in Heaven
rise above the soaring birds?
Were there any regrets?
Did the onlookers mourn?
Did dark clouds overhead
carry hope of a storm?
Did the rope burn your wrists?
Was your mind fiercely crazed?
Did you pray for Christ's kiss
when they set you ablaze?
Did the heat sting your eyes?
Did you twist and then moan?
On that damned stake where you died,
my dear, brave Saint Joan.

   Shanna Hebel

The Piano

As I rub my fingers on the keys
I hear a soft sweet melody play,
All morning and all night
Till the piano stops
With a thump
And I realize the piano has lost
All hope of ever playing a soft
Sweet melody again.
The piano is still now,
With nothing left to play.

   Patricia Comblo

Metaphors, Cliches And Intentional Misspellings While Thinking Of...

On the banks of Denial,
   Which flows through the
   Lad of the Lotus Eaters,
The Philosopher Stoned
   Comes awake.
His train of thought makes its last
   Stop
   Before turning around to
   Come home.
Home is here, hungry and in pain,
Where a look can kill, and the
Neighbors throw knives.
It is blood to be home.

   David M. Schulz

Untitled

The child is gone
the boy who lived
God bless him
he had so much more to give
a tragedy of our days
affected him in all its ways
he's gone but not forgotten
there's a message here for all
in our hearts and in our minds
we can recall
feelings, sadness things never said,
aids - he was the victim
of this disease we dread.

   Ann Sobol

The Dirty Dozen

My first love was a lie
   the second on the beach
Three and Four, a swimming pool
The fifth was out of reach

   Six was on an island
She talked the night in two
Seven, an aerobic workout
   jailbait, I hardly knew

Eight was a Volkswagen Beetle
She ran three miles per day
Nine in my college dorm
I knew but could not say

Number ten, a midnight dream
   an artist, purely divine
   eleven, forgot her name
Twelve, I called her mine.

   David Quamme

Hold On To Your Dreams

Hold on to your dreams...
Don't ever give in.
If you keep trying.
You're going to win.
Hold on to your dreams...
Though sometimes it's hard.
Just hold your head up.
And reach for the stars.
Hold on to your dreams...
Though they seem far away.
And those dreams will come true.
Some-how... some-way!

   Steven Taylor

Untitled

I miss being young
I miss being active
I miss feeling needed
I miss my old house
I miss my yard and flowers
But most of all
I miss being the me
that I used to be

   Martha D. Waite

Everything To Me

You're just like an eagle,
Soaring high in the sky.
Flapping your elegant wings,
And when you leave, my heart dies.

You're just like a rose,
Which seems to always make me smile.
Keeping Mother Nature on her toes,
So that you'll stay for a while.

You're just like a white pearl,
In the deep blue ocean.
Ask anyone if I love you,
And they'll say, "Second that notion."

You're just like a shining star,
You're what I want to be,
But no matter what you are,
You're everything to me.

   Schalisa Moore

One Of Those

Dance with me silent raven!
Our songs are quite alike.
The time is now to sing the
mental tune of our fights.

Dance with me silent raven!
Our tongues are frozen still
but the music always plays
for you and I our truths kill.

Dance with me silent raven!
our sorrows were twinned at birth.
Let's waltz away our sadness,
let's flee this horrid earth.

Die with me silent raven!
The time to leave is now.
Our songs no longer play on
and life is not allowed.

Emily Douglas

Little Old Lady

She's a little old lady
    from Handytown,
She hands out coffee and
    doughnuts anytime.
She tries to find the homeless kind,
    Some are old, some are young.
It makes no difference to her
    whether they're young or old.
To her, they're all hungry and
    need to eat.
Some would like to work, but cannot
    find a job.
Other's who could work would rather
    live on the street.
When she sees all these hungry people,
    Her heart goes out to them all.
She goes out of her way searching for
    some one to help,
For she's the little old lady, when
    feeds the hungry along the way.

Catherine M. Karpiak

The End

Walls... they're closing in on me.
Dark, silence, nothing,
Scenes I cannot see,
Flashing, quickly, quietly.
Scenes of lie,
Lifeless scenes.
Can't remember,
Remember nothing.
Just a little,
Maybe something.
Hopeless dreams,
Never gotten.
Cares of death,
Soon forgotten.
Hate to live,
Scared to die.
Shallow world,
Just wonders why.
Life is gone, death no more...
Reaper's scratching at my door!!!

Elizabeth Flavin

Lost Love

You are all I see and all I see is you.
I fear now more than I
have feared before
because I love now more
than I have loved before.

I wonder at times what
I would do without you,
or how it would end.
Until we see each other
no more.
And the fear I have felt has
turned to sorrow.
And the love I have known
has broken my heart.
And I wonder no longer
what it would be like
without you.
Because I have no longer
And that I wonder
how it ever started.

Cheryl Winkelman

Who Am I?

I am a woman.
I am black.
I am a proud African-American.
I am a struggling sister, who will
one day reach my final destination.

I am happy and resourceful.
I can climb any mountain.
I am a woman of worth and dignity.
I am powerful and focused - my
influence reaches far.

I am who I am and am
proud to be me.

Joan Leslie

My Father

You warrior's face
is like history,
it can be seen for a thousand years.
Those Hispanic eyes
and Aztec smile reveals everything
about the Pacific War
and myself.
You fought the enemy.

Guam, the Solomon Islands,
the proud photo showing you holding
your hands on your hips.
The Khaki always primed with starch
and the hidden discipline known
as the art of war
your blood rang of Zapata's legions.
Sergeants, like you, knew why
Caesar wept for Gaul.

Luis L. Tijerina

For Cassie

She whispers the name again
fury in heart and far from sober
she takes out the rainbows from
over the years and gives
each one a purpose.
Didn't think you'd get this far.

Jaine Mclean

Sea-Born

I am a child of the sea,
the sound my primal home,
my blood all tinted ocean green,
my hair light-flecked with foam.

The pipers dance upon my heart,
the gulls and I rejoice.
I need no salt save tangy air,
I love the breakers voice.

Let others seek eternal youth,
money, fame or pow'r their goal,
I need but the sand and tides
for lift of heart and lilt of soul.

Marie A. Conn

The Rose

Red,
velvet,
sweet perfume,
delicate folds,
dew runs down,
thorns stand out,
love's color,
beautiful,
perfect.

Ilovilov
eyouilove you
ilove

iwantyo
uiwantyouiyou
iwant

Court Williams

I Wish I Was A Child

To climb a tree
or hide in the hay,
To skin my knees
and play all day,
Have my summers free
To do as I will.
Oh, I wish I was a child still,
I wish I was a child.
To say up all night
And look at the moon,
Or go to bed
And sleep till noon.
To go to Mom
Whenever I'm hurt,
Make Mudpies
Out of the dirt,
Go sled riding down a hill.
Oh, I wish I was a child still,
I wish I was a child.

Brenda L. Bennett

Forgotten Message

Why have you forgotten,
that which you should always know:
You drug, you thug,
you bug, you smug,
now box by box you go.

I hope one day you'll remember
what we all have tried to tell:
You love, from above,
like hand in glove,
together we'll get out of this hell.

D. Marie T.

Epilogue: In Reflection Of Dylan Thomas's Grave

An unmarked grave on a
misty hill, cemetery silt
is jilted by tennis shoes
shuffling;

And I could sit by
your side, searching for
the sound of a solitary
church bell through traffic
winding below, whisper
to the few blades of
grass grappling for
a grey sky above
lips, a lullaby in soil,

Where granite cannot
silence tongues of dust,
where epitaphs are resolved
to wind raking a barren hill...

Dave Buracker

Tutti Gli Uiomini Dormiranno

I know my tears will do no good,
yet I free them from my eye.

The heavens descend and grasp him,
While I, gazing bout the lawn,
Notice the inspiring light,
pouring from this eternal sight,
  At the break of dawn.
Waiting for death to pardon,
  in all its grave and misery.

Wander, wander in this day of night,
Vivere sul filo della mortalita
  blinded by the streaks of Eternity.

Joey Caldarone

Siddhartha's Ferryman

The words of the river whispers
Sorrows, thoughts, and prayers,
It cries the singing song of life
For every heart that dares
To follow the flow of memory
Until the eternal end
Where every journeyer sighs
To reach around the bend.
Look into the haunting waters-
A mirror is what you'll see,
Listen to the bubbles and falls,
A riddle of what you'll be.
Mother Nature sings her lullaby
And you fall sound asleep,
To awake with love and life again
A dream you wish to keep.

Barbara Newton

The Swallow

Fair sky
The swallows fly
Comfort in the air
With breeze everywhere

Water sparks
The swallows remark
Be gently playing around
With the whispering sound

Van K. Martin

Lost

You're no longer there
Not there to catch my fall
Not there to mend my broken heart
Not there to be my shawl
to cover me from darkness
to keep away the light
Or to warm the bitter winds
That invade my dreams at night
Not there to scare away the ghosts
too far to hear me cry
Not close enough to feel my pain
Such pain that I might die

Brooke Johnson

Love Is A Dream

Dreams are like a story,
waiting to be told.
Some dreams,
are kind of misty,
something like love.

A definition for love,
I think cannot be found,
Because love is all around.

Brandon Clay Ayers

Controversy Over Our Flag

What terrible nonsense,
What terrible ignorance.
Created equal in God's eye?
  Yes.
Created equal in man's eye?
  No.
A raging bullet crosses one's pain,
  milliseconds too fast.
Innocent, brave young men
  torn from family and friends.
    Taken up to God,
Lay peacefully brave one.
Lay peaceful for you have died
for your flag and your country.
  Lay peaceful brave one,
  lay peacefully.

Melissa Lahner

Love Petals

  Love comes and goes like
the petals from a rose. Once
the petals fall upon the ground
a new rose will soon be around.

Crystal Tucker

My Love

My love is gentle,
warm and true.

My love is kind,
refreshing and new.

I hope and pray
we never part,
for that would surely
break my heart.

It wasn't long
before I knew,
I'd always belong,
my love, to you.

Cheri Shaw

"Sister Solace"

Sister Solace come to me
Take away life's miseries
Take a roll how do you do
Sister Solace can cure your blues

Sister Solace come to my side
Help ease life's unruly ride
Help stem the rising tide
Sister Solace never lies

Sister Solace eases my pain
Takes away ever increasing strain
Produces sunshine vanishing rain
Sister Solace destroys the bane

Sister Solace your wiles are old
Your stories are myriads seldom told
Your grace and beauty never sold
Sister Solace flesh of my folds

Joseph Mark Pierce

A Mother's Heart

A mother's heart
Seems hid from view
Except to God
He knows she's blue,
God sees the love,
the scars, her mind
the longings there
For those to find.
But, children too,
don't care to look
they leave her heart
closed, as a book.
Oh, seek and probe
and do be kind,
your mother's heart
you'll surely find.

Rochelle M. Armstrong

Forget Me Not...

Forget me not when our
Summer days are gone, or when
the Winter nights are long.
Forget me not when you are
all alone, or when you are
gazing into the eyes
of another, longing for my touch.
Even though we are so far
apart, living our lives so differently
now, I will always be here with
you, forever.
Forget me not...

Heather Trotter

SShhh

Swaying of the dock talking of
the water. Wind whispering in my
ear. Sun blazing down on my face.
Close my eyes, cool water rushing
through my fingers, birds singing
in the trees. Wish you were here
to see the beauty were nothing or
no one can disturb the peace. Listen
to the water pop under the dock.
Never in a rush.
SShhh!! Listen!!

Meranda Dennis

They Joy Of All Dogs

Dogs bring out the inner joy of people.
They bring out the inner soul.
But, the best quality
I think they have,
is that they are very bold.

Dogs chase cats,
cats don't fight back.
That's why they can protect
you from being kidnapped by men.

Predators from far,
predators from near,
dogs know,
and they protect you,
with evil (missing word)

Some are young,
some are old,
but they still,
do what they are told.

Kerry Scruggs

Charles Was Late

One day I woke up late
and had to rush out the door,
then I noticed the empty bottle
sitting on the floor

I wet my hair in the sink
and grabbed the Ivory Liquid,
I rinsed it out as fast as I could
Well you see, I thought I did.

When I went to work that morning
the sun was shining brightly.
My wet afro hair style
dried itself oh so slightly.

At lunch time I went home
and it started to rain,
people began to laugh and stare,
it was causing quite a strain.

Then I saw the confusion,
I understood every one's stare.
The shampoo wasn't rinsed out
and "Bubbles" were everywhere!

Jeanne A. Comito

Lonely Heart

Let me hold your hand again
As I often used to do
When the stars were very young
And the heaven very blue.

Let me see your smile again
Gentle as a day in spring
That a thousand little dreams
To my heart was sure to bring.

Let me hear you speak again
With your voice so sweet and low
Like the winds at eventide
Which across the meadows blow.

Let me touch your hair again
When the stardust on it lies
And entrancing moonbeams glow.

In your lovely warming eyes
All I really ask, my dear
(Missing line)
So that in my lonely heart
Happiness I my regain.

Trudy G. Nichols

"The Gift"

I have a special gift for you
it can't be bought or sold.
Moth nor rust can corrupt,
and it's worth more than precious gold.

You won't find it in the mall,
This special gift I have for you,
is "Jesus Christ" God's Son.

Take this gift I've given you
and place "Him" in your heart,
and remember unto the end,
Our Lord Jesus will never part.

I hope you like this precious gift,
I picked it so carefully.
Please remember, it's the only gift
that will last an Eternity...

Linda Schultz

Jesus Ever Present

I need not ever worry
I need not ever care
For I am oft reminded
That my Lord is always there.

He is so kind and loving
He wipes away all tears
And when I'm at my lowest
I feel His presence near.

He does not look at failures
Defeats are stepping stones
To something He has better
For you and me alone.

I see Him in the sunrise
And in the twilight hues
His ever present beauty
Is always shining through.

I'm glad He is my Savior
I'm so glad He is my friend
And one thing I know for certain
He'll be with me to the end.

Alice Lyman

"Thank You Lord"

Thank you Lord, for
children's laughter,
for games to play,
and "Happy ever afters."

Thank you Lord, for
bedtime kisses,
for silly excuses,
and childhood wishes.

Thank you Lord, for
special hugs,
for unsure footsteps,
and pant leg tugs.

Thank you Lord, for
little boys,
for little girls too.

And thank you for
their lives that touch
and bring to us great joy.

Lisa M. Stoltenow

Wisdom

He who tosses a pebble
into a pond
may get a ripple
yet, he who tosses enough pebbles
may get a wave

Jeffrey Sheehan

Sally The Quiet Soul

The quiet soul
that was there for Jim
and now she's taken
to be with Him
we can't understand
the reason why
we hurt in our heart
we cry with our eyes
we really believe
that God knows best
but we don't understand
all of the rest
while our hearts are aching
and we hurt to the bone
we still recognize
God is on His throne
so comfort our hearts
and often our hurt
we will give you the praise
all the while we're on earth

Alice Roach

Gulf Coast

I miss your billowy hair,
blazing glare of orange, wavering,
lips of purple grazing dusk.

I miss your gaping Gulf
gurgling sea brine in
the breath of salty wind.

I miss your whiteness convulsing,
bellows jarring the earth,
jump starts of crackles snapping.

I miss your hummingbird spring,
honeysuckle fragrance,
sublime callings of whippoorwills.

I miss your wormlike rivers,
salivating gestures,
color of mud between sand beds.

Inside your warming waters,
Gulf coast, let me grope
the swaying current's cradle.

Patsy James

The Tree

Remarkable as you and I may be,
only nature can make a tree.
Time and sun, wind and rain,
I see you fall, I feel your pain.
You once stood tall, you touched
the sky, now stripped of life,
you succumb and die.
Your corpse is used for the good
of man-kind, a large empty hole
or stump left behind.
So please take a moment and
maybe you will see, that there
once was a forest where a
desert will be.

Mark A. North

"Thunderstorms"

Thunderstorms are beautiful,
But strong and full of grace.
I sit and watch the rain and lightning.
And never hide my face.

Thunderstorms are beautiful.
They nurse and aid the ground.
The heavy drops of falling rain
Are a most relaxing sound.

Thunderstorms are beautiful.
Most people are afraid.
They hide away in a sheltered room
Until the strong winds fade.

The heavy rain and thunder
(I often wish I could keep)
Slowly takes my mind away,
As I drift deep into sleep.

Shayna Nesbit

Ode To California Poppies

We pulled our poppies up today
No longer will I see them sway
Their orangish heads so bright and free
Always said, "Hello" to me.

They slept at night with petals closed
As if in slumber - deep repose
But come the sun their heads uplift
As if to say, "we get the drift.

Up and at 'em with delight
We welcome you oh sunshine bright
We'll make the most of every day"
They made my heart sing and be gay.

I'll miss your shiny faces bright
And remember you in bed at night
Though you are gone from us this year
You'll come again to bring us cheer.

Ruth Holland

"Gently, My Love"

My love I hold gently
Like a bird in my hand
Trembling and fearful
That I might not understand
I might hold too tightly
Clip his wings from their flight
Break his free-loving spirit
Change his days into night.

My love I stroke gently
With impatience hard to conceal
I want to cling to him
With a passionate zeal
I love him so much
I don't want him to stray
But I must hold lightly
Or my bird will fly away.

Eva Myers

Angels

Angels who are special,
Divine, wise and true,
May see, hear and know,
All that we do.
For they are sent down from Heaven,
By God up above,
To deliver his message,
Of forgiveness and love.

Vivian Skipper

Men—They're Great

Men, they're great,
they stand and wait,
while she looks and parlies on,
some feminine thing
he has no interest in.

He says not a word,
while she looks and looks,
whether it's clothes or books.

He puts up with her styles
her new hair do's
and even if it looks like a birds nest
he makes no jest.

Just puts his arm around her
and proudly walks abreast.
He listens to her chatter
and deals with the matter.

Sometimes bored, but she never knows,
just as her talk flows.
Even if he has to wait
men-they are great.

Ruth E. Starlin Schafer

Tender One

Oh my tender one
Your hands so gentle,
Your eyes so sincere,
Oh how I wish you were near.

When I am alone, I am not;
I sit in peace, yet
In the midst of chaos.

Oh hold me my dear,
Just hold me near;
With you by my side,
You and I abide
For we are one another's guide.

As we walk hand in hand
Along the snowy white sand,
I imagine us in such a world
Where all is welcome aboard.

In reality, I am here
And you there;
And in between us
Lies a road with uncertainties.

Heather A. Hinkle

Passing Worlds

Yesterday
  the whole world fell into my arms.
Because I was weak
  it dropped to the ground
Below me and split down the middle,
  displaying ugliness and roses.
One must choose you know
  between the two.

Being young and small,
  I chose too quickly.
The ugliness I had never known
  and it shown so.
Now then the sun is too far gone
  I stand with outstretched arms
Waiting for another world to
  pass along.

Vicki Budd

Light Rain

Walking in the rainbow
I found myself in blue
Blue is the color of my soul
Blue blue is my all view

I was melted in the rainbow
With all the colors of beauty
And was no color for my soul
My soul turned light

Light that went through a crystal soul
Showing the spectrum of my soul
A brilliant spectrum of love
Love turned into a ray

The ray that lighten the way
The way of the rainbow
The color of life pass by
To the eternal rainbow

Daniel Flores

Our Midnight Garden

I saw your hand among
apples and peaches
in the midnight
picking up the best fruit you said:
"This garden makes me remember
what it is to fly into the soul"
then you threw me two apples
soaked with your laugh
their smell perfectly destroyed
my minute resistance
bringing desire
"no wonder" I thought "you must go
this place will never give you
enough reasons to cry
my imagination seems to be
not ready yet for both of us."

Marek Belz

"Lost"

I called my love
and know not where
his heart has journeyed
his silence bare...
what thoughts shall I render
in this courtly fare
shall I lend love sonnets
and linger there...
pity, spring will be here
I close my eyes
in the stillness
of my breath
and hold your rose
crushed to my breast
a feeling of sadness
as I rest...

Mary L. Hinton

Weed

The peculiar flower
gives off a sweet smell
as its elegance
is deeply admired.

But, the spirit inside
refuses
to exist
For, its intentions are
far from beauty.

Camille Bosen

Psalm 028 To Be Released

"Guide me, God." (Me arrow.)
"Archer, aim me true."
"Target, small and narrow,
Here me come for You!"

Tiny target (Gratitude)
In a field of pride.
"God, adjust the attitude,"
(Me spoke, my head, inside.)

Arrow, flying, whistles
(Confidence is high)
Before the first epistles.
(Me know "I am I.")

Arrow joins another two.
("What is!") Listen. Hear
"The arrow is this side of you," and
David drawing near.

Larry J. Powers

Rows Of Life

Walking the old dirty tracks of life
Heading into the sun
For new life has just begun

See the yellow of the corn
See the rows of life as one
See the rows, come and see

Stepping into the rich golden field
See the cricket sitting on the yield
I am at peace when walking between
For new life is abound
I have seen

See the yellow of the corn
See the rows of life as one
See the rows, come and see

Timothy L. Fromme

La Chasseure Heureuse

Matin bells mnemonically
evoke upon the morning sea
sounds of sour deity
confounding Le Chasseur Maudit

But fat clangs battling rattling palms
at surf's susurrant evening psalms
summon Gaea, Full of Grace
who makes the hunt a happy chase

Oh Holy Mother, Cosmic Eye
keep the hunt a constant high
pray man's flagellate creations
stay at bay in evocations

Hone the tattered rainbow trove
to stab and stain your silk sand mauve
when cowl clouds conjured raptor claws
begin to shred our last hurrahs

Suzanne LaMarre

Epitaph

How strange is our fortune,
How bitter its flavor,
That those who love us
Our hearts never favor.

And turning the coin
You will find it quite true
That those that you love,
Sadly, never love you.

James Elward

Christmas 1989

It was Christmas 1989!
The holiday was very fine!
I saw my cousins, who were mine!
To eat, my relatives,
did not have to stay in line!
We sat around a marble table.
The conversation was about cable,
also, books on how to write a fable.
My stable grandmother,
Mable, who sings and is a dancer,
searched on the roof for Prancer.
He is one of Santa's reindeer.
We shed our tears.
Told our fears!
Had a toast of merry cheer!
Also, said best wishes and Happy New Year!

Anna Valente

Sensing

Laying in the sand,
clouds above my head.
I hear the waves crash,
I feel the hot sand,
burying my toes.

Swimming in the water,
floating on my back.
I hear children splashing,
I feel the cool water,
covering my legs.

Standing in my towel,
drying out my hair.
I hear the sounds I love,
I feel the gentle breeze,
I memorize these feelings.

For me,
this is life,
and for everyone,
life is short.

Meghan O'Connor

The Pillow

The pillow is such a comfort
When you're all alone at night,
It helps to ease your problems,
A companion till it's light.

So many things are deep within
You cannot say aloud.
It accepts them all in stride,
Nothing's whispered to the crowd.

When you're angry, you can hit it,
When you're sad, it gets your tears.
No matter what your mood is,
You seem to know it hears.

The pillow is just a symbol
Of God's eternal love.
It's really "Him" you talk to,
He's listening from above.

Marlene Neuforth

Bully In The Park

There once was a bull elk named Clark,
who lived in Banff National Park.
He caused lots of trouble
by making the golf course a rubble.
All people thought he was a shark.

Laine Smith

Last Leaf

The last leaf on the
tree is so beautiful and
fair. When that tree
was full of leaves it
taught us about life.
How it at first was
planted with a seed into
the ground and each
year it grew fuller,
with beautiful leaves.
As months past the
leaves turn colors; red,
brown, yellow, and green.
And in the fall, leaves
started to fall until the
last leaf was left.
And now that leaf
is ready to fall and
start a whole new
life over again.

Amanda Provence

We Are Bound With Rope

My life, the box enclosed.
Your life, the binding chain.
My form, the weakness exposed.
Your void, the black hole drain.

My eyes, no upward look.
Your eyes, no pupil dilate.
My mind, no open book.
Your thoughts, no storm abate.

My words, a meaning inside.
Your words, a hidden seed.
My tongue, a cloaked confide.
Your lips, a forbidden need.

My heart, with growing flame.
Your heart, with dying breath.
My love, with forgotten name.
Your soul, with closer death.

My night, now to close.
Your night, now soon torn.
My wish, now vision rose.
Your star, now banish thorn.

Ethan Cooper

Ending The Game

Confined in stormy
wretched weather,
  No shelter from
  the cold,
Feeding on my thoughts
so empty,
  Alone
  so weak and old,
Feeble are
my fragile feelings,
  Decrepit tale
  been told,
The depression of my life
so true, so sad, I fold.

Jeffery N. Czarnecki

February In Indiana

The frozen thermometer
I brought
Inside the house

Chihoko Wake

Left Alone

Daddy?
Are you home?
No answer to questions unknown,
Left Alone
Tears are cried, but not seen.
Dreams are felt, but not dreamed.
Hope of life unseen
Left Alone
Thoughts; of somewhere beyond my
home,
Somewhere unknown - to not just me.
Left Alone
Choices not made because; not told.
Punished, because of choices untold.
Left Alone
A house full of faces unseen.
A house full of dreams undreamed.
Left Alone
Unknown.

Sharon Lynette Cook

Blind Love

Strongest power found to be,
locked away within.
Frightened to let free,
denying them to win.

Pain and anger to reflect,
upon the evil ones.
Never once finding respect,
to these are who she shuns.

A liar in the past,
locked her heart and lost the key.
Will animosity still last,
or will one help again to see.

Carey McCarron

Untitled

As I sit here and watch the
rain fall into the night, I wonder to
myself, will there be another fight?

Will they start to yell and throw
things against the wall, as I try to think
of how to get away from it all.

Tomorrow she'll wake up black and blue,
as she wonders to herself what should she do.

Should she ran away and try to save us
from a life of violence, or will she just "learn"
to keep her silence?

I shouldn't ask a question to an answer
I already know, because you see, tomorrow,
there will be another show.

Tracey Murphy

"Time"

Jutting high in the sky
   mountains with snow.
Down below oceans flow
   to and fro.
Father times hourly chimes
   running slow
Comes the down
   life is gone.
Sweet after glow.

Dolores Fell

Reality Check

Watching from armed tower
   with disdain
For these —
   Lesser than me beings
To misstep in direction
   And bring down my wrath
With fiery correction,
   Two catch my attention
As they exercise in unison
   Like one and his mirrored shadow,
Fact to face.
   A hugely obese form,
The other fit and willing
   To share time and energy for giving
A brother of his soul —
   Motivation for living.

Gail Sumerlin

Listen

   Don't cry don't whine
They won't hear
   Don't yell don't scream
They won't hear
   Don't waste your time because
They don't want to hear

   The drugs the violence
They won't hear
   They live in the dream worlds

No guns no darkness
   No pressure no life

Don't cry don't whine
   They mustn't hear
Don't yell don't scream
   They mustn't hear
Don't crack the dream world.

Brandi Stiefel

Untitled

When God's will is ready,
Only then does a miracle occur.
When you are unaware
Unanticipating
Innocent and open
God brings you together.
The communion of two souls
Connecting by Divine Magic.
Blessed with a complete knowing
Peace
Oneness
A depth beyond words.
A bond for eternity.
The mingling of two hearts
Being sent on a new journey,
Forever embracing
Existing as one.

Lisa Rocheleau

Untitled

Some folks in looks
Take so much pride
They seldom think of what's inside
As for me, I know my face
Can never be a thing of grace
So I'll think a bit and see
How I can fix inside of me
Then folks will say she looks like sin
But ain't she beautiful within?

R. R. Scott

Bag Lady

She waddled like a possum
Head down and in no rush.
Her shopping cart shoved out ahead
Coat dragging in the dust.

Like porcupine her bristles rose
Like wolf she snarled at strangers.
Like bear she thought of men as foes
Who'd put her in great danger.

Her meagre goods she clutched to chest
Like snake she bared her fangs.
Like wolverine she tried to test
The evil hell-bent gangs.

And so she lives her lonely life
Like a stray cat in a ditch.
And when she dies, they'll spit on her
This dirty unkempt bitch.

In Potter's field her bones will lie
In earth from whence she came.
In youth, she never thought she'd die
A loser in life's game.

Mary C. Kennedy

Love

Love invites the crucified
To experience its realm
Like a ship amidst a sea of doubt
With Jesus at the helm

Sail on to ports of peace and joy
Where pain's evaporated
To dance upon the shores of life
As Christ has intimated

But if we must traverse again
The oceans of despair
I know we're not alone, Yahweh
I've sensed your Presence there

Guide us through these times of trial
And set our spirits free
So we can love each other now
And You eternally

Steve Ryan

"Love"

Love is in
the groom and bride
Love is in
their parent's pride

Love is in
your best friend
Love always lasts
until the end

And remember,
Love is in
your heart
Until the day
We part.

Catherine Gero

Ants

Ants in the cakes,
   Ants in the pies.
Ants all over
   And I don't know why!

Jeremy Lee Wheat

Silence

Listen to the silence
It is a golden prayer
Given by God for us to share
For in silence we can hear
The dropping of a single tear
Is it not the greater role
To hear the crying of a soul
Gentle servants, make the choice
Not the sound of your own voice
Listen to the silence
Glory and mystery unfold
Auspicious destiny be told
Eternal grandeur behold!

Angela Kiel Willoughby

Dejected Ellipses

for Frank O'Hara

Sad old ladies in sun dresses
roll out dusk city streets with brooms
I lie naked on my bed
Dvòrak, billowed curtains and iced tea
not wearing my watch

Jane is awake
I feel her eyes opening, sobbing
La guittara de làgrimas
Sleep,
like that of a far-off building,
slowly comes

Jared E. Young

"The Music Of The Spheres"

I heard the music of the spheres,
A lofty melody divine -
Descended from above the stars,
   past galaxies unknown -
So far and deep,
   space infinite -
Beyond man's measured span!

The beauty of celestial sound,
Had penetrated cosmic void -
With tiny silver bells,
   they chime and ring -
With lutes and harps,
   that lilt and sing —

The music of the spheres,
Does touch the heart -
It causes blood,
   to race -
To reach the recesses
   of the mind -
Serenity - to fill the soul!

Michael Stone

Society Today

When you look through life's glasses,
What do you see?

I see people dying all around me.

When you listen,
What do you hear?

I hear the cries of a child in fear.

When you touch something,
How does it feel?

Like society's problems,
it is real.

Tina Wright

Peace Vs. Reality

Peace will never happen,
As we can already see.
The whole world will sadden,
And happiness will not be free.

The world is full of hatred.
Everyone can not be loved.
Love will be forgotten,
And hate will be ungloved.

Sadness will fall upon us,
People will be killed.
Love will be forgotten,
And romance unfulfilled.

Peace and society do not mix.
Everyone will eventually die.
Some will kill just for kicks,
Every death will go without a sigh.

Death will now enstrange,
No one will make a fuss.
The future will not change,
It has been planned for us.

Peggy J. Lapin

Jessica

My Little Granddaughter, just a
Beautiful five.
With eyes that sparkle,
So wondrously alive.
She asks many questions with a
Child's wondering mind.
Why is grandma's hair silver, and
What makes her so kind?
I've explained that she loves you
and her eyes turn above.
She asks then is this something
Like God's wonderful love?
Now as I'm growing older,
Nearing seventy-seven.
She asks me,
Papa will you write me a letter
When you get to heaven?

James M. Rossman

Listen

As I recall the times,
God has rescued me,
I remember many times
how did I never see.
So many times he's taken me
high and set me free,
delivered me from evil
how did I never see.
We are so blind to everything
He always holds the key,
we simply have to ask Him
how did I never see.
He is with us every day
every second that we breath,
and when you listen for Him
you will truly see.

Englisa Harrison

"At Peace"

Be at peace with what you are...
Take care and nurture thy soul
Allow yourself room to breathe...
Enrich thy earthly goal.

Paula K. Fraley

Morman Rocks

There is a place not far from my
house I often like to visit, and if
we ever moved from here I surely
think I'd miss it.
We go there on the weekend, that
is my dad and I, we climb from
rock to rock sometimes very high.
We like to see the animals that
live there in the sandstone.
They burrow deep into the rocks
and make this place their home.
We sit at the top and have our
lunch and have a little talk, this
place we like to do this at is called
the Morman Rock.

Sean P. Brickley

Together

Life in its essence
is a very fragile state
each breath of air we take
is an act of our very fate.

We felt the fear of loss
didn't want to say goodbye
our spirits were joined in union
you told them "she will not die."

Days passed with unanswered questions
but still I didn't let go
I wanted you at my side
together, you said "we know."

In a moment, I realized
how much of you I'd forgotten-
the safety in all-knowing eyes
and the warmth of each embrace.

Your presence brought great comfort
I found it was us, not me
you kept saying the word "together"
I'd make it, it became clear to see.

Leslie A. Hickman

Roses

I love roses,
It's a meaning poses,
For love at first sight,
Giving all of its might,
Red, pink, yellow, and white,
Are my colors,
Not horrors,
Soft and sweet,
As sleet,
So petite,
That is what I like,
Even on my trike.

Anna Reznik

Mirror

Found a friend today we
talked for hours she listened
to me she listened to how I
felt about life and love and
not once did she interrupt
me or tell me I was wrong
and when I went to touch
her to show her how much
I cared I realized it was
just a mirror

Tammy Kesemeyer

Thinking Of You

I watch out my
window
Thinking of you
and hoping you're
okay.
All I think about
is you.
Even when I'm sleeping
you show up in my dreams.
I cant wait till you
will return to me.
Then we'll be together
Forever!

Carrie Fraise

The Bestest Mom

My mommy is the bestest mom
That any baby ever had
She plays with me and cleans me up
And she smells much better than dad.

She loves to clean my diaper
Oh, I know she doesn't mind
Cuz she's the bestest mommy
And so very sweet and kind.

I love my mommy lots and lots
And I know she loves me too
Cuz she puts up with the little things
That little babies do.

My mommy feeds me all the time
She keeps me nice and fat
All I do is eat, sleep, poop
But that's really where it's at.

What would I do without my mom?
I guess I just don't know
Cuz she's the bestest mommy
And I really love her so!

R. Jason Hayes

Summertime

Summers coming,
Spring is gone,
The air is warm,
and the wind is calm,
Children come outside to play,
On a sunny summer day,
The flowers will bloom,
The grass will grow,
The willow trees will bow down low,
The pinkish, glow of a summer night,
Brings peace in the air,
and gets rid of fright.

Hari Nandu

Depression

Do we sit alone in silence?
Do we sit alone at all?

Are we alone as we rise?
Are we alone as we fall?

Does the world seem cold and black,
Even on a bright sunny day?

Just take a dose of some Prozac,
And everything will seem okay!

Curt Keaton

The Day After You Left

Silence lonely
Deception aroused
Quiet thoughts become loud
Drinking in cup of despair
Hiding behind your lock of hair
Holding, touching, feeling you near
Thoughts, quiet as a mouse
Whispering in my ear.
Come back to me.
Tell me it ain't so.
Tell me you love me
Tell her to go.
We had a lot, why'd you let go.
Never again, never to be
Hate replace love
Pain take over joy.
Jealousy rip apart trust
Going away, far away.
Taking my heart, never to return,
For all eternity.

Nicosha Kim Cutright

Witness

Fake people,
is what I see.
Self discovery, not to be.
Friendly faces,
not really friends.
they love themselves, never an end.
Kisses kissed,
there is no love.
Ignoring outlines,
the truth is shoved.
They can't see it,
so it's not there.
It's kinda sad,
but they don't care.
Waking moments,
they will not have.
Pity them,
it's those they'll crave.
I am sorry, it's not my business.
You don't have to listen,
I'm only a witness.

Noelle Zablosky

Friends

To have a friend is something
    more precious than is gold,
And yet we often do forget
    the wonderful years untold.

We take for granted friendship
    without a single thought,
But do we really realize
    true friendship can't be bought?

My friends did stand close by me
    when I was in distress,
And softly said, Have Courage
    for soon you'll have a rest.

The Lord will try your patience
    until you're at wit's ends,
Hang on a little longer
    have faith, we're all your friends.

And when my trial is over
    to God I'll softly pray,
Bless these friends forever more
    please God, do not delay.

Charmaine Willy

Faith

Faith is like a sapling,
Unnurtured, it will die,
To gain new strength and power
It must on God rely,
It needs the Father's loving heart
And Christ's redeeming grace,
The guidance of the Spirit
If it would grow apace,
It needs to send its roots deep down
In the soil of God's word,
To feast on food that can relieve
The guilt by sin incurred.
It needs the precious promises
Within the word contained
To withstand the many storms of life
Ere full stature is attained.

Helen Seelbinder

Perpendicular Line

A perpendicular line
runs down into your core
spins wildly and upside
down to drill for something more
and when the hole's
pressed firmly, no dust on either side
the gap stands staring upward
turns sideways and looks wide
a yard stick's gently placed
to measure this fine hole
but sinking in and lost within
we try instead a pole
but long as our measuring rod
is to find the end
the depth of our eternal soul
swallows it my friend.

Shannon Gawronski

Untitled

In all my life, I've never met
Anyone quite like you
A strong, but kind and gentle man
who's even witty too

You've filled my heart with every joy
I've yearned for from the start
And all the things you have to give
Are given from the heart

If anyone had to told me
Of this happiness today
I wouldn't have believed them
I didn't think you'd stay

If I could trade all we have
For wealth that I once knew
I know I'd rather be in love
And share my life with you

Joseph, when I met you
All my dreams came true
You will always have my heart
I'm so in love with you

Janet M. Everman

Flowers

Blue butterflies resting on the ground,
Pink pinwheels spinning all around.
Red fairies sleeping in the sun,
Beautiful blossom for everyone.
Like pretty faces standing high,
And the smell of homemade apple pie.

Samantha Riegel

Keon's Legacy

Out of the mist from nowhere
Came an Angel with a song
His messages from the Universe
Worldwide answers sung

If everyone listened to these words
Peace would reign forever
Harmony, Love and Understanding
A worthwhile strong endeavor

Words to always strive for
Listen to what they say
They have an inner meaning
to help us every day

One song that could change the world
In how we really feel
Give Continents a taste of this
It is and can be real

Someday Earth will understand
What Music will project
the reality of one person
Who can make your Heart reflect

Gayle L. Yeager

A Hope Of This World

From ocean shore,
To ocean shore,
From sun rise on your east.
My dear land,
My precious land,
God ever grant you peace.

You always were,
You'll always be
A hope of this world
Forever young, forever strong
Courageous and bold

A rising sun is smiling back
To a country that I love
America the beautiful
Forever promised land

Valentina I. Andraos

Vision

From this window,
the stream below
splashes, over log
over stone, within
inlet to outlet,
feeding springs,
feeding trillium,
rushes onward to river,
to the lake.
You and I are there,
grains of sand,
ever polishing,
ever being washed
toward the sea,
that massive see.

Helen G. Deer

Hope

And yet they tell me "hope"
"Hope," brightest flower
Has long ago fled from this
    earthly sphere
But I must wait, and seemingly content
Myself with "patience" in this element.

Edna G. Cummings

The Day I Lived

The sky was blue
The grass was green
The fish all swam
The birds all flew
The people cheered
The animals howled
The night was dark
The day was bright
The sun did shine
The moon did glow
The books were read
The movies were seen
The baby cried
The grown man died
The day is coming
The night is almost through
The time has come
The nightmare is done
The day I lived
The night I died

Chad Alford

Rumors

The wolf is stalking me
In his hope to bring me down
And when he finally gets me
It's him who'll wear the crown

He wants nothing more than to catch me
And to make me suffer
He will stop at nothing
So I better get a lot tougher

He feeds on my weaknesses
He devours all my dreams
I better move quicker
He is closer than he seems

He focuses on happiness
So he can take it all away
All he is is heartless
Just wants to make me pay

The wolf is very close now
It's so very cold
I can feel his breath upon my neck
But the wolf is just the lie you told

Tia Shaw

Devil in the Meadow

The devil's in the meadow,
The demons are asleep,
The goblins dance around the town,
The Gods angels weep.

My body's in the coffin,
The face is in my mind,
The arms and legs are wrapped around
Their newest bloody find.

The desert's overflowing,
With water from the sky,
The lake's as dry as ancient tombs,
But not a soul knows why.

His universe is blackened,
The moon has drowned from fright,
True love is now forgotten, why?
The devil's taking flight.

Claire Loomis

My Rat And His Hat

My rat has a hat,
It's so big and fat.
My rat has a friend,
His name is pat.
They like to lay on a mat.

My rat has a hat,
And likes to play with a bat.
The rat sat on a gnat.
Oh! No! It was pat.
Now, pat is flat.

My rat has a hat.
One day he saw a cat.
My rat has no hat,
Because the cat ate his hat.

Paul Anthony Smith

I Miss You

A little bit of you
and a little bit of me
have switched respective places
in a mystifying "we"

When miles come between us
and our lives are drawn apart
our thoughts remain together
tugging softly at the heart.

The loneliness without you
tell of special moments shared
and says across the miles
just how much we've always cared

The emptiness that comes
with just the memory of your touch

Stirs a feeling from within
that says
I miss you very much!!!

Brianna Nicol

Children Of Alcoholics

A ghost I'd perceive in the night
whether sober... or in flight

Never trusting even a smile
for fear that later a reminder...
of how unstable our reality was

No need to ask, for never knowing
was a part and tears a flowing
only in silence or "what was wrong"

If only they knew how wounded we were

But why would it matter?
Our childish fears...

For them all they knew
was a drunken blur

Crystal Van Haverbeke

A Friend

A friend is a special person
    that you have to
be trusted by one another and to
    always
be together when something goes wrong,
    therefore
you and I will always be standing
    together as
    we both grow old...

Jonathan Fielden

Untitled

The sun glares harshly
making my headache.
I sit, wondering when
the sun will be mine,
and as I sit in silent
musing
I think of you,
who, like the sun,
burns me with your brilliant
radiance
And of our plastic love
so unconductive in the heat
I weep.
The salty tears running
saddened rivulets down
my dusty cheeks.
I think of the day
when I kiss the sun
and slowly fade away.

Eric Toth

Life

Life is sometimes good.
Life is more than we think it is.
Life is sometimes bad.
Life is sometimes less than we think.
Life is pretty.
Life is sometimes like a big ocean and
we need help with it.
That's how life is.
Life what is it? What does life mean?
    Life.

Heather Lane

Grace

Was it not you who said,
"Such grace is mine", and
Plainly stared in empty mind,
Staring again on stately plain
The winter's woe and the summer's rain,
And realized that such a way
Can no man play, for time
Wishes not that you would play
But lead thyself to stately grace,
And stare no more on empty space
But give thyself, for Him who waits.

Jesse Varela

Loose Hips

Loose hips
let you in
spread-you
wide-open
you up

Loose hips lie

Loose hips
flat
back you
in a corner

Loose hips
leave you
raw

Alone with
bruised thighs
finger-
marked flesh

Maxine Factor

"Darling Denise"

I first saw her at the carwash
To shy to say hello
As I sat upon a golf cart
My heart began to grow
One day we got to talking
And soon we were best friends
We became much more than lovers
But that to soon would end
Away upon the friendly skies
An ocean and continent away
Alone I passed the time myself
My love had gone away
Days to weeks to months came years
A decade would pass us bye
But the love we share between us
Will never leave or die

Wilfred A. Lopes II

Goodbye Grandma

There are people gone in my life,
A few here and there.
But she was better than most.
She knew the flavor
Of more than just ice cream.
Life was her undying
Specialty.
Closed eyes and
Spinning realities engulf
The stilled minds of the dead
Yet their cast iron masks
Show how they used to be.
Blank stares and wet
Eyes surround them,
But who is this person?
One I miss.

Robyn Huttinga

Children

Children, children everywhere,
cute as a little bear.

With all the cherished times,
when they were not always as mimes.

Oh, they are sweet as roses,
with warm hearts, and small noses.

To grow strong as a tree
being busy as a bee.

With laughter all around,
to the future they are bound.

Yes, we love them so,
Let the children know.

Marilyn Grippa

I'll Always Be There For You

I am a friend,
The best in the world,
I really care,
And I promise,
I'll always be there for you.
You can trust me,
No matter what you're going through,
Or how bad you feel,
No matter what you say or do,
Remember one thing,
I'll always be there for you.

Malia Richardson

Laurel

From a cabin in the Smokies
a baby girl was born.
Her Momma named her Laurel
for the blooms outside her door.

She wore wild mountain laurel
braided in hair of gold,
and she waltzed across the dance floor
with her favorite beau.

Springtime saw her as his bride
disappearing into the night.
A silhouette of blossoms
shone through her veil of white.

Twilight years would find them
growing old and more in love.
They walked along together,
in the beauty of the Cove.

Each year in the midst of springtime
he stands alone and prays.
His teardrops kiss the flowers
upon his lady's grave.

Jane M. Vineyard

My Friend

I have a special Friend,
She lives within my mirror.
She's been there with me always,
Through the laughter and the tears.
She's been there for the good times,
and also for the bad,
She hasn't always been true,
She's lied and made me sad.
She's been there when there's trouble,
some of it she's caused.
She'll point out all my faults,
never stops or does she pause,
She's led me down the wrong path,
and told me it was best,
But she's been there with me always,
to pick up the pieces left.
You see she is my best friend,
and I won't give up on her,
Although she's made mistakes,
for me she's always there.

Kerry Gullickson

Untitled

In Spring
When the sadness
Lifts from the far off fields
Touched to bleeding
From the rain

A gently felt
Rolling scent
Runs through the denseness
Of the air

Then slowly backs off
Onto the neatly soft wafered
Layers of the
Whispering sand.

George Lowi

Untitled

I lose myself
  in your scent,
I lose myself
  in your smile,
I lose myself
  in your eyes,
I lose myself
  in your hair,
I lose myself
  in your hands,
I lose myself
  in your lips,
And if you asked me
  for the truth,
Without hesitation
  I would say
I'm falling in love with you.

Jorge L. Zeballos

Wandering Forever

Under the winter's pale moon gaze
Are the everlasting weeping willows,
Watching; listening; mystified;
Bowed down to the supreme light.

Across the River Of Lost Souls
Roams the ever powerful Rhino,
Watching; listening; mystified;
By the river's lonely, offensive wail.

Below the caverns of Desdi
Lies God's most homely creation,
Watching; listening; mystified;
By the honesty of Desdi Caverns.

Above is where
All of mankind are expected,
Watching; listening; mystified,
By the ever-loving being called God.

Stephenie Cowles

I Can Do

I can do anything
you can do so there.
It's my story.
I can run,
I can jump,
I can dream,
I can sing,
I can be kind,
I can be free,
So what did you think of it?
Just say yes.

Sarah Jackson

"Love Cycle"

All the confusion
And the frustration
All the anxiousness
But hesitation
Together they are mixed
And become one
No replacement can be fixed
For this "Love Cycle" has just begun
Then comes enchantment
And roses and poems being sent
Then suddenly it's over
And all is about to begin
Once again

Jessica Olson

The Real Meaning Of Christmas

He was born on Christmas morning
  Our little Lord king
To help the world from sinning
  And every living thing.

To help the sick and crippled
  When nothing else seemed right
To lead us down the right path
  So we can have eternal life.

So as he got more popular
  Of His teaching truth and good
Some people started getting jealous
  He didn't think they would

They took Him off to prison
  Until they could come up with a plan
So they made Him drag His own cross
  And nailed Him to it, feet and Hands

So think about what is written
  It is very plain to see
If you believe in, the Lord Jesus
  You will have eternity.

Ronnie Lee Patton

Praise God

There is a mystery with wings
so close about your head it sings
or starts the pigeons when it rings
from sun-drenched towers with
their bells; the caper at the
start of things, the lilt that's
hidden in the strings, before
it's touched, the lyre sings!
As though each blossom were
a lute, and sound could
bend your soul with fruit!
To grasp that being is, is flame
that leaps up from the leafy frame
like vineyards in the sun and rain;
the fragrance of the sweetest plot,
that anything should be at all
and nothingness is not!

Joseph C. DiCarlo

The Old Crow

You ugly bird,
You old crow,
Every morning at 5:30
You're outside my window.

You haw and rrah,
So loud and clear,
You wake my slumber,
Till light appears.

And once you feel
Your job is done,
You wing away
For more morning fun.

But you just wait,
With winter snow,
To a Southern home
You'll have to go.

And then in quiet,
I will sleep
Till 7:30
Without a peep.

Milton Bloch

For Only Me

There's a place I can go
Where no one else knows
There's a place safe inside
For only me to hide
If you try to you can find it
Your place where you want it
If you find it let me know
For there I will never go
I'll leave you alone
because it's only your zone.

April McClellan

I Couldn't

The knife was so sharp
as it pressed against my throat.
The world caved in around me
it made me want to choke.
The pain of this world
was too much to bear.
The expression I got daily
was one huge glare.
I felt everyone hated me
So I tried to take my life.
I felt this was the only thing
that I could do right.
When I was ready
I slowly counted to ten.
I didn't want to die.
I'd rather not be a has-been.
From then on
I took a different path.
I'm not a has-been.
I couldn't do the task.

Amber Lang

I Remember

I remember when the milkman came
and left bottles on the porch.
I remember when the farmer came round
with his pony cart and horse.
I remember mother beating
dirty old rugs in the heat,
and Summer fairs with colored lights
in the middle of the street.
I remember Summer Bible school
with Jesus up above
and I remember grandma's house
and I remember love.

Randall T. McCandless

Unicorn

As I wipe the tears from my eyes,
I see that I'm very high.
Something I was on,
That sang a lovely song.
A unicorn from long ago,
It came to soothe my sorrow so.
As it put me down on the ground,
I said good bye without a sound.
Then it flew off in the blue,
To make my dreams come true.

Stephanie Nicole Clouse

My Mother, So Dear

Although it hasn't been a year,
I miss you, Mother so dear.
I feel that you are so near,
That I still hear your voice, so dear.
Something I will always miss,
Every day of the year,
Is hearing your voice, by my ear.
I will miss you always,
My mother, so dear.

Jerry L. Rutledge Sr.

Happy Mother's Day!

Mom, you're the best that there
can be.
No matter what, you're always
there for me.
Even when I'm a pain,
You love me still the same.
I can never thank you enough
for your undeserved love.
I thank God I have you for me.
I'll always love you; eternally.
So even if on this earth we part,
You'll be forever in my heart.
Happy Mother's Day.

Michelle Salentine

Untitled

The patterns they form
    as they circle up there
are just shapes and dreams
    floating around in the air.

But sometimes it seems,
    even though we know
that this all makes sense
    and is our own personal show.

Angela Houston

Untitled

A life
A moment
To ponder upon
With great expectation we try
    to carry on
To please our mothers and
    fathers alike
We often do thing out of
    cruelty and spite
But then in the end they
    forgive and forget
Because we all owe our parents
    the greatest of debts
Life.

Carlos Brown

A Good Friend

Have you ever asked yourself,
    what exactly is a friend.
A friend is someone who cares
    and stands by you all the way.
A friend is someone who trusts you
    with someone they care about
    Whether it be their boyfriend or a crush.
A friend is someone who accepts
    you the way you are, good or bad.

Mary Ann Givens

Create

I ache thinking.
A knife of light
frantic
flooding the void
smearing language over
the bare place
in my head.
Out dream!
Produce a vision,
elaborate on life.

Dianne Vaughan Carey

The Park

The trash hides
The naked
Ground
While the can
Stands defiantly
Empty
And the cross
Hangs motionless
In the sky
Never looking
Down
Because it knows
It has nothing
To stand
On

Denise M. Colby

Devil's Honor

Lord I praise thee
make them see
I will follow thee
to the depths of the sea
basking in the dark
I'll proudly show your mark
to bathe in fire
is my utmost desire
I exalt thee
for others do not see
your honor I praise
a lamb placed before you lays
I will slit my wrist
just to be on your list
to be in your heaven
I'll kill myself times seven
I know not sin
your honor I will win
the Lord of lies
never dies.

Dylan Cavin

Questions

Who are we? What are we?
Are we anything more than
just tiny specks on the third
planet from the sun?
Will the world ever end? When
will the world end?
Is that day going to be
grey, dull, and miserable?
What is the meaning of life?
Does life even have a meaning?
Is life just one giant question
that everyone is afraid to answer?

Rebecca Montalbano

One Moment

My face is hot
I feel the fool
Haven't acted so silly
Since my days in school

Six feet of charm
Makes me nervous and harried
I let the daydreams come
Knowing he was married

He has warm hazel eyes
Mustache like a bandit
It's hard to breathe
I can barely stand it

Now they're laughing at me
Forty eight year old joke
Don't pity my heart
It's not broke

I'm not angry
No need to raise my voice
I had one moment of romance
With the man of my choice

Lillian Hutchins

The Envelope Please

Suspenseful anxiety
spinning capricious thoughts
wildly jubilant
into the airwaves
agitating, swirling
as mindful of weeks
of disciplined toil
and sacrificial deeds,
breathless now.
The answer
only a breath away
as one waits in a moment
of hopeful expectancy
or in a second of questionable doubt.
The results
a shout of joy or a sigh of anguish.

Madeline Johnson Ridgway

Live Bait

Hidden on a back road
Near the marshes by a stream
Is a place where people pass the time,
Go fishing and just dream.
A quiet lane, a resting place
That makes the spirit rise
And brings our natural world in tune
Beneath the brilliant skies.
The Spanish moss and palm trees
Cover silence so profound
The peaceful life, the tranquil ways
Of long ago abound.
One reminisces,
Wondering
At the changes made of late;
Yet the battered board
Still stands there
Offering fishermen
Live bait.

Kitty B. Maiden

Blue

Blue
Constant Blue
Diving deeper
And deeper
Into a dark indigo abyss
A dark inoperable hue
Little light seems to
Pierce this dark aquamarine
Stuck in the thickness of the dark navy
Until it lightens
Letting loose
Soaring up
Through the azure
Where the turquoise is light
But it is still
Blue
Constant blue

Michael Regier

Together To The End

Years of minds together,
Work a common thread,
Times of joint endeavor,
The future a joyful goal.

Planning rest, not retiring,
Winding down together,
Returning to simpler days,
Different times to weather.

Facing harder challenges,
Painful attempts at defying,
Standing, fighting together,
Sharing caring, crying.

Days of easy togetherness,
Gone like sunset,
Nights of love and sharing,
Gone like childhood.

Time to reflect and dream,
The mind wanders,
Time to sit and stare,
The mind wavers.

Joyce Ford

Our Home

Remember the laughter
Remember the tears
Remember the comfort
Remember the fears

Remember the smiles
Remember the frowns
Remember the ups
Remember the downs

Remember the ins
Remember the outs
Remember the certainty
Remember the doubts

Remember the good times
Remember the bad
Cherish the memories
Of the times that we had

Remember our home
And when you do
Remember it's wherever
I am with you.....

Ronald Jay Adams

Of This World

If the heroes of this world
Were never even born
Could we still look upon them
With our ridicule and scorn?

If the lovers of this world
Were cast away at birth
Would we still see good in each other
And search to find true worth?

If the fanatics of this world
Were overwhelmed with it all
Could we still feel for each other
And see love within it all?

If the people of this world
Just upped and disappeared
Would it be an end to hate and war
Or would it end pain and fear?

Damon Sutherland

When The Loom Is Silent

The pattern of my life
   now clearly seen,
Even though in fading light,
   time draws circles around me.
Kept in check my tears,
   as viewing my finished
      tapestry.
I caress the golden threads
   gleaming here and there,
Still, unwelcome the sight
   of the many unravelings...
      loose ends
      tasks undone
      Love
   not freely given,
Show on roughened underside
   as dark threads of misgiving.

Dorothy Faye Osner

You've Broke My Heart

My heart is aching deeply
My tears can't be held inside
My mind keeps rushing back
   to you every now and then
Time and time again

Did you really want to hurt me?
Is love a game you just like to play?
Can we ever be together again?

I hope you realize what
   you've done to me
How you've torn my soul into
A second chance, you'll never get with me
Because you've really broke my heart

Treva Baker

Life

Life can seem like a dream,
a fairy tale some say.

Never knowing what you are
going to get each day.

When we dream our bodies seem,
a million miles away.

Because life can seem,
like a dream...
A fairy tale some say...

Rachel E. Winfield

Coming From St. Patrick's Cathedral, Dublin
On A Sunny Day

Dirty faced
kid
beaten, smothered
until he can
not look me in the face
only stretch out his hand
and mumble.

I reach into my pocket.
To give him 20 pence.

My fingers come up with a coin
I look at it.

"Here kid, have a pound.
And wash your face."

Pub money
Fun money
Transportation money

Food
Protection
Life
Money.

Angie K. Markt

"Hope"

Behind the laughter
a veil of tears
a crown of sadness.

Beneath the smile
a wounded spirit
slumped shoulders
a sad face
Emmett Kelly.

Beyond the pain
friends
hope
God.

Beyond tomorrow
a strong faith
embracing Angels
a loving God.

Sue M. Campbell

Alone

When I'm out walking I'm lonely
So many young lovers I see
Then I pray for night to come
I know I soon shall be
Alone - all alone with my dreams
My dreams of you, sweetheart of mine
I kiss you, caress you and love you
And you are mine, only mine
They fill me with joyous pain
For you I long and pine
They are the moments of sweetest bliss
These dreams of you, sweetheart of mine.

Mary English

"Curmudgeon"

Tho I wear the cloak of time
It seems to fit quite loosely
As a book with broken spine
Can still be read profusely.

A button off both here and there
Color, cuffs, showing fray
At times untidy hair!
With a trump card yet to play.

So the mind is reeling
Searching under rubble
Grasping care and feeling
Sifting out the trouble.

Not often an eclipse
In damp darkness like a well
Just a short remiss
Always groping, in a spell.

While speech may be laconic
Very seldom heard
Try not to be Byronic
And care for old men's words.

James F. Loughran

The Glades

Tonight I watched the sun set
o'er these vast Everglades
and the twilight which danced
between the long grasses blades

Yet as the egret was soaring...
and the male gators were roaring...
mankind was at work
by slowly destroying

This unique habitat
which is poised on the brink
of a man-made disaster
for our failure to think
beyond the short term
or our immediate needs
though the implications are great
we still fail to heed

The signs she's provided
...Mother Nature's true warnings,
for with each day that dawns
fewer birds greet the morning.

Tanya E. Marsh

Life Cycles (Haiku Musing)

The hope of Spring shouts.
Out of shadows spirits rise.
The Circle of life.

Summer heat grows thick.
Outside, children laugh and play.
Innocent wisdom.

Autumn winds pierce us.
Daylight dims eternally.
penitent silence.

In Winter lives death.
A season of memory.
Tomorrow beckons...

C. L. Cross

Seascape

Subtle current of
An ebbing tide
Searching frantically
Far and wide....

While upon the pebbled shore
A solitary gull
Sparkling opaque
On a palette grown dull....

Scavenges here and there
For his next meal...
Inspired by survival
Quite willing to steal....

Paula Jo Hamm

Untitled

I call upon the power in
which I have to stand up for
All my rights, but is it wrong
to believe that way I think
not because life goes by what
you truly believe in. In my eyes
is it wrong to believe in ghost,
is it wrong to believe in God!
Is it wrong to believe in anything
you want to believe in. The path
all people should take is to believe
in one's self at all times,
is that wrong also
I think not once
Again!

Jevon Peoples

A Birthday Prayer

Dear God in heaven,
Please hear my humble prayer,
Give this message to my brother,
So he'll know that I still care,
Tell him Happy Birthday,
He would be forty-two.
But this one is so special.
It's his first birthday with you.
Tell him that we love him,
And miss him more each day,
Our hearts have been saddened since
He went away.
He was a special person,
Loved by everyone he knew,
But our hearts are much less burdened,
Just knowing he's with you.

Nancy L. Mullins

Eyes Of Love

I've ne'er beheld in pleasant dreams
    or all my days before,
Such beauty blaze before my eyes,
    the beauty that you bore.
In you through love I only saw
    that wonderful perfection.
But faults I'll notice ever more
    unveiled of love's protection.
Now as the sun sets on the day
    and sinks below the skies.
The love I feel for you declines
    and with it beauty dies.
But other's eyes may never see
    the change that's spoken of.
For beauty's more than shape or form
    when seen through eyes of love.

Kamm Richard Kartchner

Messiah

Born to touch
he arrows the
string of flesh
the glass bones
and tilts the
glass they lie on
he draws the seas
fish to nibble
at his glass fingers
in his right hand
he glues canvas
into square patches
a deck of blue faced
cards he scatters
from a cloud mountain
from his uncoursing love
from his compressing
deck of birth

Clarence Washington

Dream World

Dream of a world so beautiful,
without harm to overcome,
and hopes are more than plentiful.
Decisions are black or white,
without any complications,
you choose wrong or right.
Rewards are offered only to the good,
there are no exceptions or excuses,
do and choose as you should.
Honor is no longer just a word,
it is a state of being in every way,
to break it would be absurd.
Love, of course, would go hand in hand,
would grow and be as a strong oak tree,
with a good woman and a great man.
Dream of a world so fair to you,
want it, see it, yearn it, achieve it,
make it come true.

Kellie Davis

Eyes Closed

You built a fire in me
And I added the gas
You opened the door
But I turned the knob
You gave me hope
And I took the chance
You listened to my songs
And my words of desire
You ignored my proposal
And I resigned
You kept on looking
When I had my eyes closed
You made me shiver
And I said yes
You gave me the juice
And I felt like heaven
You closed your eyes
And I thought I was dreaming
You brought me the sun
And I woke in your arms

Mircalla Rodrigues

"Evil"

Close your eyes,
And listen to me.
I'm your life,
He's inside of me.
I'll tell you what
You should not hear.
For I am you,
And you are near.
You do the right,
But I'll do the wrong.
Sing this to me,
That hellish song.
I make the torture
And screams at night.
Cause I'm not known
For doing the right.

Mary-Jane Desmarais

My Life

I wish I could begin again
To start over when...
I was young and naive
Not knowing what to believe
To know the difference
   between right and wrong
Not only the feeling to belong
To love and be loved
What a torturous game
When things go wrong
Which one is to blame?
To have fun for the moment
Could mean a future of pain
To long for true love
I fear heartache to gain
To echo the past would wither my soul
It's now time for me to take control!

Corrie J. Gibbons

Help A Soul

Help a soul who is in need,
Caught up in all the selfish greed

Lost in a world that is unknown,
He thinks he's on a royal throne

Help a soul who hurts and cares,
In your arms his tears he bears

My hate for him is in those pieces,
Although my caring never ceases

Help a soul who's all alone,
Otherwise he is unknown.

Clair Camargo

"Friend"

This job requires,
no special training or skill.
The position is hard to find,
the job is hard to fill.
Patience and understanding,
is the only skill.
A Friend can I find one
the position is still open
the job is hard to fulfill.

David A. Ross

Slightly detached
And I wonder when it will end.
Brainstem floating
In a cloudy gelatinous goo,
And it will swallow my brain up
If I let it...
And I just might.
Freehand drawing
Around the body
With a slick stick
Of pink chalk,
My mind drifts.
Mental plain and simple plans
Go crashing over the edge.
Wind blowing down the bluffs,
Swirling to the bottom.
Crash tested and approved
I melt into the topsoil,
And bond with worms.

Kristine

My Grandpa's Martin House

My grandpa's martin house is great,
I often like to watch and wait,
And learn each bird's specific trait.
   My grandpas's martin house.

The birds swoop down upon the breeze,
And there I kneel on bended knees,
I watch them float about with ease.
   My grandpa's martin house.

I look upon the wondrous sight,
Of martin birds aloft in flight,
And wish I could be at that height.
   My grandpa's martin house.

I know I couldn't ask for more,
As I watch the martins soar,
And so I thank the Lord God for...
   My grandpa's martin house!

Chelsea Grohmann

Something Better Ahead

Sometimes life is
Like looking out a window.
Or like a ballgame
And your score is zero.

Always look up above
For your strength and survival.
God sent his son and
He gave you a Bible.

As others move forward
You seem to stand still.
There's always a battle,
But we still have our will.

There is always hope
And someday a better place.
We must never give up
In this time or space.

We are the winners.
I have read the book
Soon we'll say in awe,
Lift up your head, and look!

Cindy Warren

The Open Sea

The tide comes
   Rushing to the shore.
Rough, yet gentle,
   It takes the sands
   And beckons them out
To the open sea.
   Yet, it comes back for more.

Marsha Oldinski

An Old Couple

An old house, a pair of old
dogs a couple of old cars and
two very special older people
called Grandpa and Grandma. Two
who have been through so much
and given so little but still
remained. The ones who are always
there when in need when there
wasn't anyone else you could turn
to. You both have shared the
faith, the pain and joy of growing old.

Sherrie Kane

My Hero

Socrates is my hero.
We make a lovely pair.
He walked in Athens barefoot,
And wore no underwear.

Before you go assuming,
I'll say it isn't so.
The only way we are alike,
Is in the mind, you know.

Dorothy I. Arrowood

The Way I Know

A walk in the park,
At night, in the dark.
A stroll by the sea,
Alone, you and me.

These are the things,
That make you special.

A few minutes together,
When we can find the time.
The attention you give me,
Lets me know that you're mine.

These are the ways you,
Make me feel special.

Our hands touch,
Our eyes meet,
My heart skips a beat.

This is the way I know,
I Love You.

Walter F. Keys

Baby Doll

Cry baby doll cry
Jimbo jumped and left the lump to die
So cry baby doll cry
There's no reason to lie but my fears pass me by
I cry like baby doll I cry
Startled by life I still have to try
Cry baby doll cry
Fleeing in fright that was left by the night that I do not remember in full
Feeling so near that which was a tear
I cried baby doll I cried
The creed which is mine is so sublime I do not dare to speak it aloud
A voice inside wonders why but I am too proud
Cry baby doll cry
My tears inside they do not run dry just the same as my fears
Though I lie in bed at night whispering them to my ears
I still cry baby doll I cry

Dawning McGinnis

A Ship Doomed

It was a young ship but well worn from misuse
by an unseaworthy captain,
The vessel that had carried many a load,
traveled many a dangerous waters is now
sinking into a welcoming sea,
The Captain will die along with his ship as all
captains must eventually do,
For the poor man, you know, was never meant to
be master, a mistake of nature has made
him one, and nature corrects its mistakes.

Jeffrey A. Baron

The Face Of Inspiration

Beautiful face of inspiration
Gracing my world like a flower.
With pastel shades of soft perfection
Whispered to life by an angel.
Famous eyes have nothing on yours—
Enchanting hazel seduction.
The greatest of sonnets
Began in such eyes,
My words could not bring them justice.
Across the room
I watch your lips,
Drawn like a child to play.
One touch could melt the coldest of hearts
My heart could have drowned in its chance.
Beautiful face of inspiration
Thank you for all that you are.
A rekindled passion of peace and hope
A shelter for my tender dream.

Karen R. Pryor

Forever Friends

Well, my Friend, exactly where do I start?
These words I say come from the bottom of my Heart.
You'll be my Friend through thick and thin,
We've stood the test of time, though perfect, it hasn't been
Our friendship is real, we've proved it through time.
Your thoughts and ideas I treasure, as if they were mine.
Never hide anything from me - never keep it inside.
Don't hesitate to come to me, my arms are always opened wide.
Right now in your pain, you're hurting deep within.
I hope you know I Love You, Please just let me in!

Dennise Geiger

Great Grammar

Side by side on a diagram
a noun and a verb sat hand in hand.

"I'll give you action," the verb announced,
his diction clear, each word pronounced.

"I've nothing to do," the noun complained,
"so your offer sounds good, if you can be tamed."

"I'm rather tense, but if you agree,"
said the verb, "I'll follow you faithfully."

"Now let's be objective," another noun spoke
to the right of the verb, "you're a restless bloke.

You might run off with an adverb some day."
"Don't change the subject," the first noun did say.

"You must be specific," an adjective chimed,
"I'll modify things so they're clearly defined.

You, verb can't help moving, you're action itself.
But nouns, you just sit there like dust on the shelf.

To compound things a bit I think you should seek
another verb partner or this diagram's weak."

The noun and the verb thought that this was just fine.
"I'll move on then," the verb said, "but drop me a line."

Annette Dougherty

Truth

One who talks about others, clearly cannot talk about oneself,
for they are afraid of the truth that is hidden deep within.

The truth is a task most often hard to find,
unless ones body is pure within the heart and mind.

Knowing that no soul is perfect,
and knowing what harm one can do,
I pray at night that your soul is honest,
and that you always speak the truth.

Kelly M. Ferguson

Letter Past Due

Have to write that letter.
It's long past overdue.
I have really been neglectful,
Answering letters from you-

There really isn't a lot of news -
The weather here is fine -
Hope that everyone is well -
Why don't you come see us sometime?

We are doing pretty good
The garden is just about shot.
Oh, and someone dropped a dog off here
We just named her spot.

Haven't had much rain this year -
The ground is terribly dry -
Wind is blowing hot breeze -
Few cloud's in the sky -

Now you all take care of yourselves -
Main thing care for each other -
Perhaps next time, I'll have some news -
Or just make up something or other love bye

Grace P. Garland

405

Flower

Sadness and grief flow from your voice.
You are a flower like all other flowers.
Full of seeds, that blossom through the years.
Fading, withering flowers within your soul.
Part of you had been taken away
Ahead of time.
Your identity shattered in the mist.
Looking for roots!
Questioning, seeking, Asking, yet with no clear
Answers.
Contemplating the mirror
You see, it is your image.
A dream of a couple
That are no longer within the blooming.

Shirley Hananel

You Are

You are my eyes,
You showed me how to see all the beauty there can be.

You are my ears,
You taught me how to listen...
Before, I only heard.

You are my voice,
You helped me to speak my innermost thoughts.

You are my head,
You opened my mind to so many things.

You are my Soul,
You have shown me my spirituality...
It is my strength.

You are my heart,
You have shown me,

What Love could be
What Love should be
What Love is.

You are my Love...

Cheryl Sullivan

Untitled

I see her face in my head,
And think what it's like to be dead.
What if she were really gone?
Could I really carry on?
She'll be my friend to the end.
She's the one who I depend.
I would be all alone,
No one there on the phone.
How selfish we all would be,
Not thinking about what happened to she.
At least she's here, alive, and well—
Not in a grave regretting herself.
How we all would miss her so,
Carrying on would be a no!
On top of a mountain we'd stand and see,
Her face shining down on thee.
But now we have to worry little.
She's here, and alive.
Thank you.

Sara Rotkoff

SHE

Many times I've taken that fatal step toward oblivion
She was always there to ease me back.
Yesterday I took that final step,
And I became nameless.

Stephen M. Burdick

A Lover's Lament

I loved you so very much,
More than words can ever say.
Blinded by love, how was I to know
You'd be unfaithful along the way!

You left me with a sad, cold heart,
Not caring about tomorrow;
And the chill that swept over me
Brought me grief and untold sorrow.

Now here I sit so lonely,
No one special to say goodnight,
No one special to hold my hand,
No one special to hug me tight.

Oh, what wouldn't I give for one yesterday,
When my days were so happy and bright!
I doubt if I ever love again,
But, if my heart thaws out, I might!

Dorothea Fletcher

Friends And Lovers And Others

It's hardest to love when you're hurt and you're mad
But love shoulders the blame when something's gone bad
And there is the love that has learned it can say
"I know that you're sorry, and my anger won't stay."
For two sides of love help us all to hang on:
The side that forgives when a person's done wrong
And the side that can say, through anger and pride,
"I made a mistake. Please stay by my side."
Love keeps our anger from growing so big
That a whole tree is broken because of a twig
So please take my love that can say when I'm wrong
And my love that forgives when anger is strong
For both sides of love make up a whole heart
And what's most important
Has love for a start

Karleen Wagner Good

Time

Time drones on, forever going,
tiny beads of future sowing.
Aging those, who've spent their years,
clarifying buried fears.

Time tells troubles, and sleepless nights,
forcing couples into fights.
Boredom, boredom, boredom awaits,
welcoming you into open gates.

Time always buzzes in your mind,
around every corner there's secrets to find.
Never the same, always differs,
helping along endless drifters.

Time holds power, and it gets in your hair,
ever existing, always there.
Will it bring fortune, a life that's well?
That, my friends, only time can tell.

Chantal Marlhot

Single Peace

Somber sleeplessness in the grayness of a vision dimmed,
by the mindless transcendence back into that shallow grave.
Stillness and tranquillity marred only by the tithe of essence.
Wakeful hopelessness impotent in its conclusion and
death only a futile desire for deliverance from the searing emptiness.
Restless calm penetrated by thrusts of longing and forgiveness.
Chained agony tethered only by the umbilic truth
and the sweet embrace of madness is the single peace to be found.

Angela Gibson Bieger

The Frame

Under eaves of glass and nail and wood,
My tiny framed soul had sat and stood.
Watching and waiting for winds to blow
The sun beneath for a twilight show.

Single, dark nights from my square brown frame,
I steadily watched the moon to tame
Aged stars refusing the beckon
As these my sheep to sleep I reckoned.

Today by frame I waited to yield,
But stars and moon were hidden by field.
A small wet jewel fell into my hand
And tears trespassed on my moon-lit land.

Neil Harward

Oracle

Chaos devouring, a scourge upon the land
Futile weakling resistance, final hour is at-hand
Decreation of the sphere, tormented defedation of man kind
Rotting earth reduced to ash, oracle consuming life
For God has forbidden this waste left behind
Emptying crypts, rise ye dormant vile, thy oracle now shines

God of the night, in ritual we beckon a sign
Oh, my madir, nothing words undivine
Blessed be the pilgrimage, recessing from gates of gold
Resurrection, tombs unleashing forgotten souls

Day of destiny, mouring now phalsm
Grand pestilence upon our dawn
Millennium of endless storms
Eternal year in emptiness and scorn

Christopher J. Robertson

Einstein's Duck

Do you wonder why a duck's content
To float around when heaven's sent
A chance to take to wing and fly
And gaze down from the azure sky
At everything?

I'll tell you why that fowl's blase
And floats atop a pond all day,
Wanting not to go where we can't go
Caring not to know what we can't know —
It's relative.

Louis A. Dezelan

Taken

I shiver at the thought of how the goodness I have found,
Was taken out of my hands, and buried underground.
I sit alone and ponder if there's something I can do.
But then it shoots the bullet, that they have taken you.
Taken far away to some place never found.
But I will find the shovel, you're no longer underground.
When I think about you, the one I love so dear,
I find a sudden craving as I shed a single tear.
Someday we'll find a way out to our own ethereal sky.
Where we can float like Angels, until the day we die.

Kimberly Provencher

Forgive

Take heed and grasp these words I pen,
    All you've done is not a sin.
Perfection being merely a word,
    That is often spoken and never heard,
By faceless people weak and small
    You stand taller than them all.

Scarlet T. Ellis

A Love Shared

The dawn of a new day has burst forth
with wondrous beauty... flowing,
ever flowing as my love for you

I awaken and you are there beside me
your body so soft, so loveable,
so warm from our closeness

I want to reach out to touch you,
to caress you,
but I do not want to awaken you

I want only to look at you and to absorb
the beauty of your precious being
so at peace in sleep, so relaxed
from the love we shared in the night

Soon your eyes will open and you too
will awaken to the new day

The rapture of our love to once again
flow in togetherness throughout
the hours of wakefulness

Oh, my love, my love,
you are my Heaven on Earth

Evelyn Giles

Harry And Harriet

Harry rode to the store
Thinking of what he could get
He was about half way there
And beautiful Harriet he met.

"How-de doo!" he shouted
And she shyly smiled back
"Ya wanna come to the store with me?"
At him she loudly laughed.

"Why sure I'll come!" she quietly spoke
As they rode off into the wind
Romantically they never parted
And were never seen again.

Kristin Dubuque

Your Meaning To Me

If I had everything but you, I would have nothing.
But if I had you and nothing else, I would have Everything.
You mean more to me, than just a woman by my side.
You mean everything to me, and more than you can deny.
Your sweet gentle voice and presence alone, warm my heart.
These feelings you give me make me hope, that we'll never part.
I pray day and night, that you'll always be in my arms.
For I feel your love, is as sweet as candy charms.
I hope your feelings for me stay the same, for I try my best.
But if they change for the worst, I will never again rest.
You are more than I could ever dream of in a woman.
For every time we are together, I feel as if I'm in Heaven.
All of this to you, might seem somewhat strange.
But my heart and feelings for you, will never change.

Paul Fabian Torres

Untitled

    What's it like? What's what like?
Your pain. What pain? The feeling of
emptiness. I don't know, I won't admit it.
Have you tried death yet? No, I've tried
drugs. Do they work? Only if I believe
they do. Well do you? I don't know,
Do you need a friend? No, I need
money. Why? For security. What kind
of Security? False. Oh.

Kelly J. Snell

Question (?)

You're so wonderful.
You're so colorful.
I love you so much.
Oh how I wish I could make you understand
how I really feel about you.
I loved you so much.
But now we have nothing.
Did we ever have anything?
You changed so much you're no longer you,
you're different you no longer care like
I thought you did.
Were you ever you?
Did you ever really love me?
Did I ever really love you?
I thought I loved you.
I thought we'd be together forever.
Why'd you have to change?
I will always have a place for you in my heart.
But will you have a place for me in yours?

Kimberly Cross

Hold On And Be Strong

Hold on and be strong.
Even when you are treated wrong.
For what is just and right will come along.
Because life is more than a game of ping pong.

Hold on and be strong.
Although you may know the rules are wrong.
You see, a good player says this game is mine.
From early start to the finish line.

Hold on and be strong.
For fate makes right that which is wrong.
Yes, sometimes there are struggles and also strife.
But, a strong will adds a new spark to life.

Hold on and be strong.
Though challenges may sometimes tag along.
For it does not matter how the game begin.
Because a good player says I aim to win!

Jeannette Bussey

"Alyssa"

One day I was at our Granddaughter's Grave
And as I was sitting there talking to my beautiful Alyssa.
A beautiful painted lady butterfly sat near me.
And I put my finger dawn close to the ground
And the butterfly sat on my finger.
And I know it was from Alyssa saying
I love you Nana and I sat it on one of her
flowers telling her that I love you too
Alyssa with all my heart and soul.
Love forever
Nana.

Marylou Benoir

Extant

"This and that"... two grains of sand
which must, in time, pass through the glass.
Memories and thoughts dwelling in space,
gone with the light of yesterday.

There was "Happiness" and "Joy".
Now... ashes left in this great void.
There is also "Sad" and "Sorrow".
There is more!... there is "Tomorrow"!

Marco Antonio Peña

Ekaterina Gordeeva And Sergei Grinkov

They glided on the ice like one.
They showed their love,
and love to skate.

They jumped so high
and spun so fast.

They won the gold in Calgary,
then again in Lillehammer.

For the young pair skaters from Russia,
all their dreams came true.
Except for one day in November,
it came crashing down.

Sergei fell,
his heart stopped.

Nobody will ever forget,
the pair skaters from Russia.
Now that Ekaterina skates alone,
Sergei will be in our hearts.

Kelly Ann Maloney

Dance Of The Sheets

Whence blows the wind,
dancing in the sheets?

It blows from the valley,
where the shade cools a restless soul.

It blows from the mountain,
where the sun touches the heart grown cold.

It blows from the field,
where the grain feeds desire to be whole.

It blows from the sea,
where tide washes away bitterness taken hold.

It blows from the desert,
where heat inflames the passion, once burning low.

Hence rests the wind,
dancing in the streets.

Georgia Prusa

Gemini

I could sense her, it was intuition-some strong vibe almost
I knew she was attempting to return.
And rounding the corner with mighty stride
I witnessed her...coming
She had been greatly missed
But had not wandered far...just enough to be out of my sight

As she drew near she stopped briefly at a well
There, peeking through my rounded window, I saw her speaking
  to someone
A small girl child, hair frayed and with eyes as wide as the ocean
I did wait. But soon grew impatient and beckoned them both

Sensing my anxiety...she began to approach
leaving the child, who seemed to be imprisoned by temporary
ignorance, beside the well

Saving herself, she came...And once she arrived from her long journey
Oh, how joyous a reunion it was
I stroked her soft limp hands. Kissed her lips.
Inhaled her tender breath and then...I received her
I absorbed her

And with her reentry was somehow able to find comfort in my
until then, partially present self.

A. Denise Chisolm

Sustained By Grace

Though your life may not be easy
Your way - not too clear
Your path - a little crooked
Your days - overcast with fear

Though your wages may be meager
Your cupboard - bare of food
Your appearance - a little haggard
Your demeanor - morose and rude

Though your future may seem bleak
Your past - not too grand
Your dreams - a little shattered
Your aspirations - buried in sand

Though your troubles may tumble about you
Your peace - can rest inside
Your faith - can remain ever strong
Your joy - can strengthen your stride

Though Your Life May Not Be Perfect
Your spirit - will endure this race
Your heart - be filled with love
Your life - sustained by grace.

Lucille Worthy

Escape To Dreams

Only one can dream each day,
That the world wasn't this way.
Always wishing that we lived in simple times,
Instead of living in a world full of crimes.

Everyone always seems to worry,
Going through life in a big hurry.
We always think of things that are bad,
But we should think of all the good times we had.
We have been sucked into the Economic Vacuum,
Always worrying about money.
What ever happened,
To the things that mattered,
Like family and friends?
Remember that we can dream,
Even if the world ends.

Patricia Sobieck

Untitled

Why is someone so wonderful and generous
brought down by this unhappiness, grief, and sorrow?
What is the black cloud hovering over her head
doing besides making her wonder of tomorrow?
Who made this happen and brought this blackness
that puts a shadow on her life forever?
Where in the world will she be in the end
her last breath is taken, we're no longer together?
When will she know that it is all over
and will no longer fight-not for any cost?
How in the world can we make up and forget
the life we all loved and the angel we lost?

Michelle Conboy

Caring

Consequence we receive when giving so much
Affection we give. Is it to much?
Remedies we use to fix our problems, so we may
    reassure each other that we can solve them
Interest we show, so we may both know
Naturalism in you that brings us both through
Gentle touches we give to each other, so we may
    always know we will be lovers

Giovanna G. Wescott

The Purple Rose

A single rose held between a set of weary hands.
A being not knowing where to turn.

But the lone rose will be the source to
all the answers that lie ahead.
A set of lonely, scared eyes study the magnificent

Flower. Its shape is perfect.
Its color is so beautiful and overpowering, that it
can take your mind off to a world unknown.

Her mind settles on a single, solitary thought.
A tear falls slowly onto a petal. The weight of
the burden the tear carries, causes the purple

Petal to fall quickly to the ground.
She slowly picks up the tear-stained petal,
and sets it afloat a river of dreams.

A wish she has made is now washed away.
Hopefully, only to come true.

Jill Peterman

Soul...As I Feel It

The voice, the rhythm, the intensified sounds.
They fill my body with indescribable substance.
Some call it energy and others my say vibes.
But my body screams the name SOUL.

The kinda stuff that makes her hips sway.
The kinda stuff that makes grandpa "cut-a-rug".
Some call it dancing and others may say groove.
But my body screams the name SOUL.

The noise that makes you throw your hands to the sky.
The beat captivating your inner peace.
Some call it moving and others may say jam.
But my body screams the name SOUL.

The intensity—physical and mental
The oneness of flesh and spirit.
Some call it swaying and others may say bounce.
But my body screams the name SOUL.

Corey M. Porter

Friends

As my friends,
You were always there,
To listen, comfort, and give me care.
You shared my laughs,
My tears, my fears,
And walked beside me through these few years.

As your friend,
I thank you now,
For knowing what to say, and how.
And here I tell you,
With sincerity,
I'll be here for you,
Whenever you need me.

Connie Jenkins

As We Walk

As we walk through the park holding hands,
I think of the beautiful ways we can spend time alone.
We could go to a park and sit on the ground,
We could go to a circus and ride the merry go round.
We could go on a vacation and enjoy the rest and relaxation.
We could go to the ocean and watch the sea, glide in constant motion.
We could go to the ends of the earth
We could lie on the floor and watch the fire in the hearth
We could hug and kiss all night long...
Sweetheart...with you, that can't be wrong.

William Prato

Love

Love is a rhythm,
It goes fast and slow.
Love is a pitch,
It goes high and low.

Love is something that will be here forever,
It can't go away,
No not ever.

Most people don't understand love,
Because they're so ignorant and blind.
But if you look hard,
Love is what you'll find.

True love is much different than what you get from mom and dad.
Eventually if you don't find it,
You'll grow very sad.
Love really isn't that hard to find.
So if you want it,
Don't be so ignorant and blind.

Tiffany Helmly

My Precious Gift

Words cannot express the joy that fills my heart today,
For on the wings of angels God has sent a child my way,
A gift that is so precious that no money could afford,
I know that such a gift as this comes only from the Lord,
You brighten up my world around me with your loving face,
Every time I see you smile I'm reminded of God's grace,
A grandmother at forty-one, so proud I am to be,
If only every child could have the love I feel for thee,
And as I've watched you growing through the first year of your life,
Taking each new adventure, with just a grain of strife,
The wisdom that is in you, amazes me by far.
I know that if God grants it, someday you'll reach the stars,
These words I give to you today come wrapped up in a prayer,
That God will grant a wonderful life for you and yours to share,
Cleave unto God, our only hope, for in him you will find,
No other God to match his grace, no other God so kind.

Nettie Gustin

I Am An Abused Child

The old bruises fade while new ones appear
My silent screams no one seems to hear.
I used to laugh but now I just cry
I used to smile but now I don't try.
I love my parents but out of fear
Please God don't let them come too near.
They must hate me but I love them so
I must be better so they will know.
I wish they weren't mean but quiet and mild
For as you see, I am an abused child.

Mary S. Eliot

Sunday In Central Park

A Fata Morgana of crystal palaces floating
above the summer heat
beyond the periphery of Sunday strollers
and pretzel vendors selling their wares
A rhythm of stillness
mingled with golden dust
kicked up by soccer players
The muffled sound of children at play
An occasional bat from a baseball
responding to weary echoes
- A breathless city
now desolate.

Agnes Junger

Beautiful Day

As close I walked along the way
A fellow pilgrim posed one day
A question that ran so —
"If one petition you might see
Take root, bear fruit, and grow,
I pray, what would it be?"

From out my being's depths straightway
My answer rushed and tore that day,
"My friend, no question I would pray
That in this world no child will cry this day."

Locke Levering

Uninvited Guest

Uninvited, Andrew came
   He wasn't very nice;
He wrecked our homes, our jobs, our lives,
   Without even thinking twice.

Yes, Andrew came to visit
   He only stayed a while;
But when he left, he took it all,
   He made it hard to smile.

He twisted steel, uprooted trees
   and hurled them through the rain;
And if he knew, he didn't care
   how much he caused us pain.

He swept across our air base
   and felled it with one blow;
The thunder was his laughter,
   "You can't stop me, you know."

And though he's gone, his fury spent
   his memory will remain;
Down through the years,
   we'll ne'er forget our killer hurricane.

Lois L. Pease

Cows

A beautiful state Florida, full of lots of things to see
Animals, animals, animals for you and just for me.

Did you ever notice a pasture, the land is so wide and green
Where the eyes of the cows follow you, as you ride along the road.

Cows are a wondrous animal, so large and yet so meek
The young ones love to play and often fall off their feet.

Small white birds will follow cows around
   with the sun shining down, with white puffs
   of clouds mellowing about above.

I love cows, I guess you can see
   for they're here for you and for me!

Linda Louise Mohrdieck

The Flame

I burn this candle, this candle of life
A candle you gave me, when I had a choice
A choice that cut me, cut me like a knife
The smell of lilacs as the purple wax melts
The flame sees, sees how only I could've felt
Alone, deserted, and in pain, would I hold it, or be in eternal vain
The flame sees truth, yet all you saw was dreams
All I saw was youth, as in your eyes, fading was your gleam
Presents, gifts, and words; the hits, the slaps, the horrible words
You can't ever make up for putting my feelings behind bars
Would I ever love you again, I think you know the
Answer, my feelings will never begin, you brought
them to an end.

Susanne Wright

Fields (To All Fathers)

You never get to play (baseball) with your father,
Because he is too old, because you are too old,
The emotions come pouring out.
He was a great player, sure not the best, but it doesn't matter.
Time goes by, and before you know it, the time is gone.
You never got to say, "I'm proud of you, I wish I knew you when..."
The love of the game, the love of the man; sometimes they get
    confused.
Your father's father was a great player, maybe even better,
But it doesn't matter.
Because I only know you...or thought I did.
The man you once were, the man you are now,
Entangled together forever.
If I could, I would know your younger man,
But it's too late now.
If I could, I would take you out in the field
And watch you in your prime...but it is never to be.
All that is left is to love what is now.
So I will hug you as hard as I can
And see if I can touch that younger man inside.

Glenn A. Earich

My Parents

I came into this world in wonder and fright.
  You sheltered me from harm,
  And still are my guiding light.
You entrusted all your values and morals into me.
I took that love and wisdom, and molded into the
  best I could be.
Now, down this rocky path, we've gone hand in hand.
You've guided me through fields of glory and undiscovered land.
  Words cannot describe the way you make me feel.
  You are my parent, my friend, and my savior;
  I thank God I got the package deal.
  Now, there are still more adventures,
  So much more to be had...
And through it all, you'll guide me —
  I love you Mom and Dad.

Diane Garate

Time

Time is something we never have enough of;
and like a well-
you never know when it will run dry

Time spent making happy treasured memories
is the time spent best of all-
For those are the memories we'll always recall
To bring us through the tough times,
through the lonely times

Time is a gift from God-
And when we leave this earth
and those we love behind-
They should know we made the
best choices with our time-
Leaving smiles on their faces
and warmth in their hearts
To keep them company when we depart

Caroline Tucsnak

The Last Tear

Life has an emptiness now we've parted.
Your love was not discarded.

I feel your pain, your tears.
Wishing only to vanquish all your fears.

To touch your face, a close embrace.
The storm has calmed, the wind has died.
The last tear has now been cried.

Ann D. Cooper

Mother

So many memories bring to mind
Oh I've observed, but cannot find
The one to hold a candle to
The only friend and love so true.
Such understanding given to me.
When I felt low, she'd comfort me
Her guidance was a shining star.
She worried when I went afar
How much she sacrificed for me
But happy as a queen was she,
For riches, never was her goal,
There never was a kinder soul.
A priceless treasure I but hold.
Her love was worth much more than gold.
In sickness she would take my hand.
As though to wave a magic wand
She's missed so much since she is gone
I've searched and searched, but no not one
Such qualities are worth renown
And stars will sparkle in her crown.

Evelyn Nind Barnes

The Great Container

Life is a great container or boredom, disillusionment, anguish,
loneliness, useless, cruelty, deprivation-
At times life seems unrelenting, bleak; things seem as though they
will never change. If you are not careful, they may not.
Life is also a great container of joy, eloquence, enchantment,
ecstasy, beauty, imagination, peace, vitality, hopes, dreams -
At these times life seems fulfilling, energetic, it seems nothing can
go wrong - life seems full of everything good - love abounds.
This is the best life contains - grab it, and don't let it go.
When it hurts - think of the pain going away.
When it rains - think of the sun.
When you're alone - think of friends and good times.
When it seems unbearable - think of the times you didn't want
    a moment to end.
When it seems hopeless - think of the things you've hoped for
    and received.
When it seems useless - think of all the things you've accomplished.
When it seems endless - think of what it would be like to end.
Isn't life wonderful?

Peggi Babick

"Joshua's Flight"

There was a young man from Crownspoint,
  Who dearly loved to ride his bike.
He would ride over hill and gully,
  Just about anywhere he would like.

One day he was feeling so pert,
  That he decided to go for a ride.
He "borrowed" his brother's bike,
  And headed for somewhere to hide.

Everything was going so well,
  As near to the playground he drew.
When into the ditch he rode,
  He then became airborne and flew!

The flight that he made through the air
  Was not so bad at the top,
But he came to the sad conclusion,
  That the hurt came with the stop!

So now he sits in a chair at home,
  With little to do but complain.
While his brother has all of the fun,
  He sits and nurses his pain!

J. Lee Smith

America's "Lady"

The "Lady" in the harbour
Holds the torch of Freedom high.
She beckons in her quiet way;
Her torch lights up the sky.
Refugees in countless numbers,
Each searching to be free,
Came from a past that held them under.
Their quest: A life of liberty.
They believed in a land of promise.
Their faith made them strong.
Their talents were added to the "melting pot".
Such decisions could not be wrong.
Welcome them, dear Lady!
Accept from them their best.
Offer them a home with love
And America will be blessed.

Christine Reynolds

Consequences

She slips down the hallway to peek in at their faces
The sweetness of slumber the pain erases

Just two decades ago she knew the big secret
How to love and be loved and find happiness in it

Now alone with two children, the decades are four
She's a victim of bad choices, now add one more

At forty you're smart — you're supposed to know better
Don't be careless in lust
Yes, that's what they taught her

The man doesn't want it
The small speck in her womb
Fearful is she that this is her doom

No money, no help, her choices but two
To keep it — or not — either one
She's through

She cries out to God— Please take it away!
But this is what happens when you disobey

Forgive me sweet Jesus, my children — my self
Oh God grant me peace — I beg for your help!

Rachel Dantin

Bedside Vigil At Two O'Clock In The Morning

I sit beside my father — old and frail.
With trembling hands and muted lips he looks at me and
asks for — what? For water? Straighter sheets?
A word?
And then, he shuts his eyes in resignation
to the state in which he finds himself.
My wiry, steadfast Dad who built a house with his own
hands and paid his bills.
Who's neighbors sought him out for sound advice.
(He was inclined to honor his commitments and approved of
men who's handshakes were their contracts.)
He was never late to church and Mother never wondered where he was.
He used words like "respect" and "honor"
and "responsibility" and lived them all.
Oh, Dad, was that enough for you to spend your hours and
heartbeats for?
Me, I want to feel and fly and dance and
soar!
And I think I cannot do it without your permission.

Billye Lincoln

"Reminiscing"

I am an angel- in a broken down shack;
    And what has been- I can't take back.

I've seen the sun rise- I've seen the sun set;
    I've lived forever- I have no regrets.

I am an angel- there's gold in my veins;
    And when I'm gone- remember the pains.

Of raising a family- of the joys and the sorrows;
    And look ahead- to the todays and tomorrows.

For where there is gain- there is also loss;
    And it matters not- who is master or boss.

For God is our Master- the father of us all;
    And we must be ready- when we hear Him call.

Writing these words- has brought a few tears;
    Looking back over my seventy-one years.

Sometimes we're good- sometimes we're sad;
    But we must accept the good with the bad.
    "Life is what we make it".

Viva I. Allen

A Teasing Little Turtle

A teasing little turtle walked
along the bay,
shouting to everyone
and saying
"Hey".

Why I'm better than
you,
You all are so dumb
you can't think of
nothing to do".

But the turtle did not go away yet
He also said "Hey" You can't smell a rose,
with
your own
nose!

Then the turtle left thinking
he was clever,
But he wasn't very clever
never ever
ever

Tamika Tannis

A Mother's Tears

Son, it seems like yesterday that we held you on our knee,
And what a delight to hear you count from one to three,
We wiped your runny nose and tickled your toes
to hear you laugh with such glee.

We nursed you through colds, measles And mumps,
And treated you for all your cuts, scrapes and bumps,
Joe, we wiped your tears when you were sad,
And spanked your bottom when you were bad!

Oh what joy I got singing your special song
and now I wonder what went wrong.
Little did you think when you left home
That you would never return, and never more roam.

That your death would leave us here to mourn,
As though your spirit had never been born.
We do not know what pain you bore,
We only know that you left us for evermore,

We did not get to say good-bye or send you on your way
But we know you found your way to heaven.
So it's (so long), until the day... We make our journey that way.

Betty J. Lester

Across Lifetimes

Soulmate, we have journeyed so far,
Across lifetimes in search of each other's arms.
At last we found one another in Denver's snowy chill.
We knew each other in an instant as our hearts stood still.

Our souls entwined, our love poured through.
Without a doubt, we knew.

The challenge is before us. We must conquer our separate fears.
Now that we found each other,
We must learn to hold our own essence dear.

Our love must transcend the hurt and the pain our earthly form
    brings upon us.
Together we can overcome the twin fears of closeness and aloneness.

Hold on my love, we can make it through.
Let's not waste this lifetime, let's start anew.

Soulmate, we have journeyed so far,
Across lifetimes in search of each other's arms.
At last we found one another in Denver's snowy chill.
We knew each other in an instant as our hearts stood still.

Let our souls still entwine, let our love pour through.
Without a doubt, I love you!

Ann Schmitz

The Mountains

From my window I espy
The eructations that have risen
And wonder how the earth gave way
To her mountainous decision.

The shadows cast upon these hills
Come from light of ancient sun
That shines through clouds of fluffy white
Throughout these hills they run.

Such things of beauty but products of stress
That came from deep inside
And were released throughout the years
On days the earth had cried.

But life they give to wilderness
And peak into the skies
These majestic hills of untamed mass
Are beauty to my eyes.

Dennis Sklar

Rain Slips Down

Rain slips down through glistening trees,
The air, unruffled by a breeze,
Is heavy with a veil of balmy mist.
Trout lilies lift their yellow heads,
Rising up from leafy beds,
Each one of them with drops of rain is kissed.
Water beads, as clear as glass,
Cling to every blade of grass,
As the rain falls softly to the muddy ground.
It dances over puddle-top,
Leaves spreading ripples with each drop.
Its steady, soothing rhythm,
The forest's only sound.

Jenny Benson

Love

Love is expressed in many a way,
Be it in expressions or a loving touch,
Or a gentle word that means so much
In solemn repose or quietude
Of being just in a gentle attitude.
It surely makes a pleasant day.

Love is expressed in many a way.
An approval with a pleasant smile,
Of doing things that are worth-while
To help lift a burden of the mind,
Of speaking softly and being kind.
Which surely helps to make a pleasant day.

Love is expressed in many a way.
It is in doing good for those we care.
For its truest feelings to become aware,
That in all of us are the virtues of love,
As a sustaining force as a gift from above.
To give each one a pleasant day.

Casper Kaat

Hurting Over You

Thinking how you hurt me over and over.
My heart is torn in two like no other.

Thinking of you and how you don't care
only makes me want to pay the fare to be aware.

Whether I stay or go there will always be a fear
and this is where the tears flow.

I will grow and then let you know
that love can go.

It's hard to stay away.
But if I try and cry
it makes it easier by and by.

You're only here for one reason
and that is relieving no pleasing.

You are the blame for this game.
For I have no shame
You were my Flame!

Happiness lies in my eyes
Only love can show who is true
through and through.

So it must not be you!

Elizabeth Marie Perry

Confused

I look back upon those endless days so many troubles, yet
what I am about to face dampers all memories of the past. I
am uncertain of my next step I am unsure of this world. Am I
ready to face life? Am I ready to be alone? I've been
sheltered for so long not anything can prepare me, nothing
from my past can help with my future, for these final steps
right in the present are going to decide my destiny. Yet what
is my destiny? I have not a clue to it but I shall know one
day and by then this shall not matter for I am living for
the future alone. Am I right to do so? I have often been told
to live in the future and present so does that past advice matter?

Nicole Woodall

Crossroads

I love you my friend and want you to know
Your spirit and kindness has helped me to grow
I know now what sharing can actually be
For all of these things you are precious to me.

No matter what happens, what challenges I face
My life has been blessed, you've helped me erase
The pain and the sorrow of what couldn't be
You've helped me believe in the innermost me.

Your words of wisdom and caring advice
Our hours of talking have changed my life
I know what I want now, I know what can be
My future will show a more positive me.

I think of you often and all that you've done
My heart fills with gladness that you were the one
To open my heart and allow me to share
All of my feelings with such loving care.

And so I must tell you my most precious friend
Our crossroads are a beginning, not really an end
Although we must travel our own separate ways
Your spirit will be with me forever I pray.

Carly L. Guy

Seasoned Just Right

Blues! Now I can tell you about the blues, 'cause
I've known all kind of abuse, misuse, and just plain low down!
But they don't haunt me like they used to, 'cause
You season my life just right.

Before you came into my life I
knew sadness, loneliness, and emotional poverty.
With you, I appreciate joy, togetherness, and emotional wealth.
Only because you season my life just right.

I had learned to live with mediocrity, low self esteem,
and fear of creativity.
Now I am adamant in my rejection of being just so-so.
I can allow my creative juices to flow like pot-liquor!
Yes, you season my life just right.

How truly blessed I am that I found you.
Of all the people in the world, I found you.
What a find! You give me what I need,
when I need it, and in just the right amount.
You see, you season my life just right.

Phyllis L. Jordan

Imagination

Solitary...
like each gull he feeds with invisible crumbs
he perches beside the river
his estate at his feet
bags filled with castoffs
from people who will never know him -
He - the heir of their collections.

He adjusts the black stocking cap
he found in the alley beside the bank
and recreates the thrill of an imagined chase.
He - the hero fleeing victoriously
laden with bags that bulge with bundles of bills -
earnings of people who will never know
that their labors made possible his triumph.

His arm continues to flail in rhythmic concert
toward the opposite shore.

A lone gull swoops with anticipation on every toss -
Eyes search - wings sweep the empty sky.

Bonded for the moment they share all they have with each other...
Imagination.

Lou Edens

Dreams

Within all of us lies the power to perceive,
things we can not normally see.
Deep within the dark recesses of your mind
you will be astounded by what you find.
And in the dream is where you draw the line...

Trials and tribulations.
Hope and aspirations.
Dreams that will never be.
Trying to out run the past
But it's gaining much too fast.
I can't seem to break free.
Existence: Drab and dreary.
Persistence: Weak and weary.
The streets are lined with broken dreams.

Timothy Matthew Day

Wondering

People often wonder what it takes to find, that very special person
the one in their mind.

And some often wonder what it takes to be, how is it possible to
make their life happy.

I used to wonder this but not anymore, cause I have found the love
I'm waiting for.

She says that she loves me and shows that she cares, I tell her I love
her too and always will be there.

I promised you happiness this time it is true, Babe I want you to
know I'll never hurt you.

I've waited such a long time for you to come to me, so I guess I'm
letting you know I'll never set you free.

So you're stuck with what you got I know it's not the best, but I'll
try to prove to you I'm better then the rest.

So if you're feeling happy or even a bit sad, I always will be there
for you though the good and bad.

So don't you ever wonder like some people do, cause this time
sweetheart I'll always love you.

Gilbert P. Lopez

As I Begin

Back arched;
a swan descending deep into the
cool, clean, crisp waters

Flying forward;
a torpedo winning speed,
and I strike; a gymnast somersaulting on a new, blue mat

Then shoving off;
a beached canoe; just beginning on a
tiresome, perilous journey

I start the race

Jessica LeBoeuf

"What Is..."

What is a touch, when it's not from you.
What is a kiss, when it's not given by you.
What is love, when it's not shared with you.
What is "I Love You", when it's not said by you.
What is life, when it's not lived with you.
What is my heart, when it's not part of you.
I hope one day, I'll have my chance,
To show you my love in this world of romance.
I hope that one day, my dreams we can share.
I hope one day, you will love me and care.

Mariam Gyutyan

From Dusk to Dawn

When darkness drowns the light of day
As the sunlight fades away.
Shadows fall upon the Earth
As daylight sinks, with the birth
Of a crescent moon so highly bright
As it shines straight through the night.
A reflection of the sun long past
Whose rays of light it still does cast.
A deep black sheet across the land
The bright old sun has now been banned
From the deepest shade of sky
As midnight now has passed the eye.
And stars that glimmer brightly white
Are always seen through the murky night.
The deepest black has come to lay
Its hold before the break of day.
For what's that rising in the East
It is neither man nor beast.
The sleeping giant is now awake
To light the Earth in all his wake.

Jim Reed

Fighting At Plum Point Middle School

Causing confusion people fighting,
does damage to the human mind, and kids of
today getting involved in what they call he said,
she said. The reason we fight, we don't know, because
We see our friends, and want to put on
a show, but, when the crowd is gone and the fight
has ended, the principal comes and you get suspended. So,
next time do what you know is right, and remember
that Plum Point Gators don't Fight!!

Loniece Stewart

It Only Takes One Heart

It only takes one heart
One drop of love
To bring on a smile

A face suffering a loss of expression
Doesn't need a hundred hearts
To be reunited with happiness

The way mother bird's song caresses the air
How daddy's big arms hug good night
How sister reads a book each word with such care

A child's laughter
How they drag around that same bear by that same ear
Until it needs a trip to the sewing machine
That expensive sewing machine

The look of approval on grandpa's face
It's the way grandma sneaks you a piece of your favorite candy
When mother refuses

It's these moments that we treasure
Until that same day next year at that same time
When we remember

It only takes one heart

Kerrie Boydman

Why?

What's important to me, that I'll never know.
Why am I so stupid, believe me it does show.
What's the point of living, when no one wants to care.
How hard do I have to try to get someone to dare,
To want to get to know me and who I am inside.
Not just 'cause their sorry for what they see outside.

Juanita Resendiz

A Fairy's Story

A fairy's life keeps no time,
    but instead it tells of the day through a story of rhyme.
Morning brings a fairy bird.
    Who sings with such sweet words.

Afternoon brings fairy flowers and fairy trees,
    that sways in the grace of the gentle breeze.

Evening mist,
    brings the fairy's story to life with a little bit of a twist.
Night brings fairy dreams,
    to make a simple child beam.
But a fairy must sleep as well,
    so with a flutter of my wings I shall say
    Farewell.

Tiffney Mann

Never Never Land

Fly me to never never land, let me be a child again, let me
find myself a brand new friend to play with me until the end.
Don't you know I need to be a child again so I can rid my life
of you my old friend.

You play in the playground of my heart and right there you
tore it apart, making me think that you didn't possess a heart.
I should have realized that from the start, that you weren't
born with a heart.

For years you had me playing a part and over them I found my
way to your cold cold heart, and now that I won't play your
part you want to cause pain in my poor poor heart!

Oh take me to never never land so that I can find my heart again.
I need to see the world like a child again, so I can heal my
heart again. Oh fly me to never never land take me over the
moon again. Allow me to hear a nursery rhyme again. Good fairy
make me fly again. Help me find a new friend so that I can love again.
Fly me to never never land make me feel like a child my friend,
please make my heart sing again. So I can find myself a new
best friend.

Mary T. Ebinger

"Through The Children's Eyes"

Through the children's eyes,
they don't see different colors of skin,
only the real person who lies within.

Through the children's eyes,
they don't see the ugliness of
the world, only the true beauty
of the world, such as: Family, friends,
love, kindness, peace, happiness and
all of God's great creations.

The world is a perfect place,
free of prejudice and hate,
through the children's eyes.

Kerry J. Utley

Lacking Color

You can't see the beautiful blue sky
And you can't see the emerald green grass
Or the passionate pink flowers

You can't see the fluffy white clouds
Or the cinnamon brown tree bark
Nor the blinding yellow sun

Are you blind???
Or are you not taking the time to see the
beautiful colors of nature!?!?

Candace Cornick

You And Me

I'll never forget all the good times we shared
You would always be there
To be by my side and bring me glee
So why can't your attention come back to me
I know you care
It just doesn't show
Where did our friendship go
Yesterday I shared all that I feel
It took a while for you to heal
We can't pretend
This friendship either has to start again or end
I could tell you anything before
But now I need someone to talk to even more
My love
You are as peaceful as a dove
I don't want you to fly faraway
Like you almost did yesterday
I miss you more than ever before
Friends forever is what we are

Heather Crosby

Easter Was — Easter Is

When I was a child, and Easter day came;
I never once dreamed that it was more than a game:

For my only thoughts were of bunnies and eggs;
and the new shiny trousers that covered my legs:

Now as I grow older and older each day;
I think more about Jesus, who lightens my way:

As He died that evening on Golgotha Hill;
I know it was because of His Father's will:

Because He never was guilty of one little sin;
and He forgave His accusers right up to the end:

But, He died for me, and He died for you;
and He died for our neighbors down the street too:

All of His suffering, and all of His strife;
he endured it all, so that we may have life:

And now I know that Easter's not just a game;
for I am the one for whom He was shamed:

Now He said He was leaving, but He would return;
and for that wonderful, glorious day, I do yearn.

Edward Norris

"The Meaning Of Suffering"

The toolmaker works carefully
His work is exact
The parts fit together with precision
There is no room for error
When all is finished, the last step remains
The steel is soft and easily damaged.
Now it is time for the forge
Red hot and ice cold the parts are purged.
Glass hard the tool is made
Now it is ready for production
Is this the way of the Master Creator?
Suffer we must to endure the vicissitudes of life?

Stanley Hirsh

"Marriage Is A Gift Of Love"

Marriage is a gift of love,
Sent from heaven above,
Given to us to share,
Where two or more are gathered,
God will be there.

Let our love grow as a flower in full bloom,
Withholding nothing-forever true.
Come walk by my side, let us be one,
United together-leaving nothing undone.
Rekindled is a new love in my heart,
For you were God's gift to me right from the start.

Let us walk hand-in-hand forever and a day,
With the Lord leading, guiding us all the way.
We ask that you hold us in your care,
Bless our love that with you we share.
Let our hearts continually yearn,
For the eternal flame, let it burn.

Laura Dawn Grimmer

Age Doesn't Matter

The old man, so alive, so....
energetic, full of the spark.
"Come, lie down and rest," his nurse says.
"Come, lie down and rest," his children say.
"Come, lie down and rest," his grandchildren,
and his great-grandchildren.
All save me.

I alone stand in his silence,
not intruding upon the pondering look in his eyes.
Marveling at his age and in his beauty,
with his lined face and aged hands.
"Why," he finally questions, "do you never tell me to lie down?"
I only shrug, knowing he will answer for me.
And he does.

"I know why," his unsteady whisper says,
"Because you know the greatest secret of all."
And he smiles, outlining his face in a host of cracks.
"You know that age is just a bookmark." I nod.
"It marks the life's story for man,"
"It doesn't write the tale within." I smile.

Matt Adkins

I'll Be So Lonely When I'm Gone

Laughing I know I'm real, suffering.
As comprehensible as a round square,
or a peace keeping missile.
Trying to listen to the flowing river,
the screams of butterflies fill my mind.
The racing and hunting for her to get me high
is spinning my head,
imploding into itself, a lonely star dies.
Characters in this tragically, funny circus drowning,
yet crying out in thirst.
A fish with wings in this sea of emptiness,
I have no where to fly to, but inside.
They are searching in space, thinking it's their final frontier,
I close my eyes and see stars, space, emptiness, being.
Their goal is in the mirror, silence.
Watch me move my arms and dance.
How? You ask. Who knows and who cares?
Infinite, insane surprises.
I'll be so lonely when I'm gone.

Jacob Greba

You

Look, who do you see
You are the spitting image of yourself.

When others look at you
They only see you as you
Then why is it you can't see you as you?

You are steady trying to see
Someone else in you
And trying to look and dress the part
But the greatest reality is looking at you
And realizing you are you
And no one is as great as you.

Edith Langston

Only Once

You never know what you have until it's gone.
But, that's not always true.
I knew how very special it was,
When I was with you.

I will always love you, that is true.
My life began when I met you.

The brush of your hand upon my cheek,
Always made me smile and most times weak.

The sparkle of your eyes I will always miss.
I can still feel the passion, of our first kiss.

And then you were gone... without a word.
The pain I felt... will never be heard.

I've cried each night alone in our room.
And that loneliness, is now... my tomb.

Carol L. Cilinski

Grandmother

The Lord has blessed this heart of mine
With your gentle kindness, never blind.
Whether times were good or times were bad,
That loving Grandmother I always had.

Those baseball days in grammar school
Make the game on time was the only rule.
Drive on the sidewalk or in someone's yard
Let's get to the game, Tom's on the card!

Then came high school. Long hair was in.
Although I looked silly, you loved me and then,
You chauffeured and coached me never asking one time
To return such kindness by walking the straight line.

You let me become your grandson through love,
Left all my mistakes on the wings of a dove,
Your faith has held us even closer than before,
When I leave you, Grandmother, I always come back for more.

The years that have passed and the future to come
Only bring us closer to our Lord, the only one!
He sees the strength in our union, my love for you.
We know together there's nothing we can't do.

Thomas G. Hirsch

Children

Children?
My reflection in the mirror, my voice on tape.
My gripes repeated to me, and shaming me no end.
My eyes looking up to me for help.
My habits, good and bad, left in this world six-fold
when I have gone.

Anna Jane Wagner

A Prayer Of Hope

My soul is not open enshrouded in pain of children
Around me, I'm wearing strain.
Lord open my being... lift the pain from my heart..
I'm needful of you to begin a new start.

Floundering in the question... what can I do?
Have I done all that I can.. weary through and through.
Tears fall from my eyes.. I can't hold them back, Lord
Give me the strength that I daily lack.

I lay it all at your doorstep for you to take in,
Lord you are my salvation... where my faith lies in.
I can't hold anymore.. you are my release... my comforting
Assurance and heavenly peace.

I serve you wholly... not perfect I know.
Through my prayers to you I continue to grow more alive
And knowing of all that You mean. The difference between
Chaos and a term called serene.

Thomas E. Darr

Tomorrow Part II

Tomorrow,
And many of the ages to come
I will hold your candlelight glow
In my selective arms.
We can make love in the sun and the snow
Nestled in our distant farms
And loving your special charms,
Tonight.

We'll gather the twigs
And build the fields
That keep the shadows warm.
Surround ourselves
With careful beauty
And live a love that
The earth and all her
Children never
Could survive the obtusity
With the pasts that
We've both had.

Keith D. Hohlfeldt

Alive After Death

I think I thought I'd heard you'd said
"I wonder why I see you dead?!"
You live to love; and love to hate.
A life you lived, now create.

The people, my friends, they laugh and scorn...
They create a mindset sometimes worn,
I disregard now all I'm told.
Secret emotions I mysteriously hold.

I hear of stories and things said,
Kind of funny 'cause now I'm dead...
The shearing pain from wound by stave,
You hear my cries coming from the grave.

The life we lived, in past I'd torn...
All the people have ceased to scorn...
I ask myself if death kills love?
And realize no, by the pure White Dove.

I think, I though I'd heard you'd said
"I love you," but I hear I'm dead?
Inaction becoming very old...
The pain you felt, now I hold...

Daniel S. Hodgin

Florida Storm

The stillness of the wind, the quietness of the animals,
then a great rumbling from the heavens above.
An ear piercing crack and a flash of lightning,
the rain falls, in a great rush before my eyes.

The swamps fill, and the trees sway,
as the wind comes alive and whips over the land.
It brings to me a salty spray,
that washes over my face and lifts my spirit.
Though, as suddenly as the storm began,
it dies, and with it, the Everglades awaken.

Now, there is only a gentle breeze,
and the tall grass slightly waves.
A loon, standing out in the distance, cries out.
A marsh hawk flies out for food,
and the dragonflies start buzzing around.

Then breeze then stopped,
and a warm, soft mist settled in.
Out of it came the scent of pure air,
the wild things, all became still.
Peace, was born.

Marlo Gierczynski

Above The Whispers

I hear the sound of the roaring ocean
    upon the now sleek backs of the once coarse rocks.
I listen hard and I understand
it is not the ocean,
    but the mournful cries of the beaten stones.
Years of torment beat them to shape,
    and they now conform to the desires of the ocean.
But they still cry out.
I don't know why I never heard them before,
perhaps their muffled sighs were so meant to be.
I, too, cry as I listen,
    for today I understand.

Barbara Bonventre

Sugar

She came to live with me when she was seven
In time she became a living piece of heaven
Beautifully white and fluffy is her hair
So for her appearance she gives no care

Our first days together were very rough
She was mean, sassy, and extremely tough
I knew she was afraid of being in a new place
So I took time, and care, and slowed my pace

What she needed was love and attention
To discipline her, there was made no mention
I worked to earn her loving trust
To wait for this to happen, I must

She came from a hard and unpleasant life
I knew she had experienced much harshness and strife
With time she came to depend on me
There is great reward in this coming to be

Lifting her burden of anxiety and fear
Accomplishing this has become so dear
She is happy now and free from any harms
She appreciates and loves me when I hold her in my arms

L. A. Rucker

"The Beast"

The doors open; the doors close.
The drawers open; the drawers close.
The eyes open; the eyes close.

The carpet rose above the midnight tower
Which appeared to me as some gigantic flower.
i, a simple person of dizzying intellect,
Had found myself alone like some lunatic derelict.
The sun settled slowly in the east
And i caught a glimpse of some dreadful Beast.
The carpet fibers got in my way
As i searched for the path where i'd gone astray.
But the Beast had found me
And as i screamed softly
The Beast drained my psyche
And made me as the World thought i should be.

The doors open; the doors close.
The drawers open; the drawers close.
The eyes open; the eyes close.

Amy Kelly

Life

My life as I know it is a mess,
And so to this I must confess.
My aunt has just gone and died,
And at the funeral everyone cried.

I didn't tell her I loved her enough,
But mom said she knows and to be tough.
And seeing her picture hanging on the wall,
I feel like I've taken a big fall.

My mother's family has disappeared,
And almost five years later a little one appeared.
In August it will be five years,
And still I will be in tears.

No one can ever take her place,
She had the most wonderful face.
Always so loving and caring and bright,
With her she always carried a light.

Now I will be to this baby an aunt,
And be the same way she was I can't.
Sure I will love this baby with all my heart,
And teach it right from wrong from the start.

Stacie Greenwald

Why?! Why?! Why?!

It's already dark
in the town's park.
But one unmarried couple is still walking
and passionately talking.
They hold hands
and talk about family and friends,
about love and hate,
hope and faith,
books, movies, art...
"Oh - she said - you're so smart!"
Many times they chose to stop and rather
hug and kiss each other.
Friendly to them were the twinkling stars and the moon
but they found out very soon
that the planet Mars was very mad,
so mad that his face turned red.
"Why - he yelled to the stars and the moon - why folks,
married couples don't have similar walks?!
Tell me, why?!
Why?!, why?!, why?!

Elias Feldman

Purple Heart

Morning glowed, Phillip.
A purple fire burned beacon bright
against the stench of napalm.

A thick thistle two feet from your head
wordless in speech, watched with dark misfortune
curving letters of prayer
above your bleeding valor.

A crumpled martyr - lying there, innocent as
a schoolboy, amidst the blare of gunfire
asleep in our country's eyes
dormant in the arms of a stranger.
I held you... lost brother
tucked inside my soul; nineteen and breathless.

The tears in my lungs
spilled softly onto your forehead
as I knelt in the center of August's garden,
staring at the mud stained badge above your heart
feeling the strange warmth
of mourning
glow.

John A. Heck

Almost, Graveside At Night

Proximity draws us there, where
we know no residents.
The prune-titted dog, who has left her litter,
leads us on, a shape sharper and darker
than the shadows. She turns to check
our progress, half-illumined in a slant of
light between graves. My wife
walks another path, just above
the ground where her mind awaits her
like the Red Balloon. The candle-flame
before a graveside photograph lifts my eyes
mindward to my wife's breasts
on the beach today: A fresh sail
on the first day, tracing the horizon
where the sky angles down to the upward
swimming sea, but the wind has picked up
mentally, and the symbols clang and scatter
musically into the distance.

Tiller Russell

When God Took You

I thought, God took you away, because of me,
But then I realized that it comes naturally.
I have a lot of pain, anger, and hurt,
I know, I've treated you like dirt.
I never thought you would leave me,
The time came you had to say goodbye.
I know, I promised never to lie,
When I think of you, all I do is cry.
I know you loved me, I love you too,
But things went wrong between me and you.
Our lives tore apart,
All I have left is your memory, in my heart.
When they told me you were gone,
I thought it wasn't true.
I know your looking over me,
As I look over you.
So guide me through out my life,
Until, I can be with you.

Diana L. Hayes

If I'm To Blame

Inscribe all your suffering in water,
Carve all your blessings in stone.
The only disgrace found in suffering,
Is the self pity we might have known.
As you look about, you are sure to find,
Those suffering far more than you.
And those displaying far more courage;
Than you'll ever be called upon to do.
It is not my desire to see you hurt,
And if perchance I should be to fault.
My suffering will be twice that of yours,
Any my soul will suffer a guilt assault.

Eugene J. Liller

Maturity

As Winter casts off her silver haze
Reminding me of lonely days,
I see colours beyond the ethereal door,
Leaving my grievances forevermore.
Ah—the rosebuds are succulent and sweet,
With thorns that linger by their feet,
Full blossoms thrive in Heaven's light
And can withstand the chill of night.
These briars have diminished such,
And simply don't amount to much,
As Nature turns a tattered page,
She reads about the Golden Age,
Without displeasure we shall thrive
And discover new wonders of being alive.

Elizabeth Weiner

Sisters Together

I can't believe we're sitting here in a place I thought we'd never be. Our baby sister is upstairs while we sit helpless in our chairs.

After six years and two babies, he told her that there was nothing there. Facing the problem alone, she took her babies and moved back home.

Why does she have to be the one to make the choice of what has to be done? We pictured the face of the little one, who we will never see or get to know. We've listened to her reasoning, but still, it's not all clear to me. She reassures us there is nothing to fear, yet I know she must be scared.

Even if he doesn't care, he should be the one here instead of us. It's so unfair for her to be the one who had to make the choice. It takes two to bring a new life into this world, but now alone, she is left to wonder, did I make the right decision for me, my two babies and our future.

You're not alone, Babe, we're right here and always will be now and forever. We love you. Your big sisters.

Janis Sibert

Him

We walked down the road together, hand in hand,
    for we had lost a loved one and alone we could not stand.

When I looked into the sky, I wondered how and I wondered why,
    for he was only small, and never once did cry.

He was taken, oh, so quickly, we had never seen him smile,
    and they hadn't let me hold him, not even for a while.

Now I know that he sleeps soundly, though he is far from home,
    for I know that God above me, would not leave my babe alone.

Sally McDermott

My Daughter My Best Friend!!!!!

There is a young lady that I know.
And every time I think of her it makes my heart glow.
She has beautiful green eyes and golden hair.
With long skinny legs and her skin is fair.

I have known this young lady going on fifteen years
I have mended her cuts and washed away her tears,
I have taught her to walk and I've taught her to talk,
And not once through all of this has she shown any fear.

Now this young lady has grown right before my eyes, and come so far
That now it seems, it's time to teach her how to drive a car.
Where do I get the courage, and how do I keep my sanity?
It's going to be crazy, I'm sure she and I will agree.

But through all the teaching and through all the tears,
This young lady and I have grown through the years.
For she is my daughter and my best friend,
And I will be there with her right up to the end.

Jeannine Curto

The Love That Never Was

He walks among the shallow graves,
    She lives with all the vines.
The way they lived, they never thought
    They wouldn't have much time.

He bath in rivers filled with hate,
    She lay in crystal light.
Her love for him was far to late,
    Their fate as black as night.

He dreams of death and of desire,
    She dream unearthly thoughts.
The love they share that would not live,
    The love they never sought.

He loved and gave her his dark soul
    Then opened up his heart
She would not take all that he gave,
    She knew that they would part.

The time has come for them to say,
    Although they loved each other,
"I hate you with a passion"
    As they left without another.

Sarah Jane Mills

That Was Kim

In the midst of a dust storm he came
He announced to all he was here
Never again was my life to be the same
A bundle of heaven was my little dear.

I'm sure I saw a halo above his head
His eyes were like the stars that come out of the night
As ever so gentle they laid him in my bed
Around him I was sure there shone a special light.

He was such a special little boy for sure
For all who knew him will never forget
Loving eyes and a smile so very pure
He wound little fingers around your heart like a net.

He didn't have a chance to do great things
Like be President or a great football player
But, for us he was the greatest for the joy he still brings
For being loaned to us our life is forever gayer.

In the midst of a snow storm God looked down
He needed the little boy with the halo around his head
The little boy who had no room for a frown
He wrapped His gentle arms around Kim and tucked him in His bed.

Beverly Untrif

Lookout Mountain

The wind blows down from lookout mountain
And sweeps away the snow-white pages of our time.
It whispers dreams and hopes and visions
Buried deep beside the elders of our kind.

Listen close, you can hear them singing
And feel the drumming of their feet upon the ground.
They loved this land too much to leave it
They gave their lives to rest here where their bones are found.

Lookout mountain, rising in my dreams
A silent witness to the reason that we grieve.
Lookout mountain, on you I still believe
I'm going back to find a home I've never seen.

Darkness falls upon the mountain
Cicada chorus brings me back to present time.
Asphalt chains across our mountain
The smell of diesel in the dogwood and the pine.

The moon beams down upon the mountain
Shadows rise to dance in the coolness of the breeze.
And as it blows among the oak trees
I thought I heard it moan, "I miss you Cherokees."

Alan Pyeatt

The Stranger In The Glass

Who owns that unfamiliar face that stares
Back at me from the looking glass?
In my head, I know full well but why does my heart
Resist in the acknowledgement?

Is it my spirit that refuses to accept the inevitable
And wants to stay forever young?
Why is that woman who looks back at me
So surprised to find that the years have
Evaporated all too quickly?

Does she, like I, resent the looks of pained tolerance
On the faces of those who just a short time ago were her peers?
Does she also jump spasmodically when the occasional ring
Of her phone screams into the silence?
Is she disappointed or relieved to learn that
Someone has dialed a wrong number?

Here I Go111..... rambling again!
When I should tell the old woman in the glass
To comb her hair, straighten her shoulders and
Get on with her journey.....
She may just find a pleasant reward at the end of it!

Mildred M. Haas

I Don't Understand

I don't understand why some people are seeing
themselves as a special race and superior being.
They think they'll see heaven, a peaceful bliss,
but they'll all go to hell for being prejudiced.
Maybe they forgot the Golden Rule;
how would they feel being called a n****r, or fool?
What would good ol' Abe Lincoln think,
to see his hard work all go down the sink?
I think it's time for us to see.
that all races are the same as you and me;
we all were born one happy day,
all as kids we loved to play,
we all live in the land of the free and the brave,
and one day we will all be in a grave.

Tia Adams

"1963"

Who drew up this plot
and by whom the president was shot
In 2029 I surely hope that we will find
the answer to this mysterious crime
Everyone will point a finger
but this question still does linger
It was him or her or you
one or three or maybe two
will we find out what is true
from the building which the birds flew
and the conclusions that Earl Warren drew
and now it's up to you.

Toni Campitiello

Where Will We Go

I wonder what tomorrow holds or what the day may bring.
I wonder if we will be together, Living all our dreams.

If we shall stand, hand in hand, taking the world by storm.
Making it known that our love is forever and no one can bring us harm.

Laying upon the beaches and sands, imprinting the
figures of our love; which shall remain forever written in our hearts.

What shall the future bring, your guess is as good as mine,
just remember I told you, today, that you shall never leave my mind.

Kenneth R. Armstrong Jr.

"The Tree"

As I looked out of my back door this morning, I noticed a tree. Its leaves once green were now red as the blood in Revelation. The trunk of the tree stood firm and straight, for it is well rooted and grounded as we the saints of God are to be in the last days. As I looked further the top of the tree was moving back and forth as if to free itself of the red leaves that were sure to fall to the ground and be blown away. The branches held firm; blowing from side to side yet not falling themselves and not one was broken. Each stood tall and straight up. Some were thick and yet others were thin; each still held on to the trunk and the roots that were grounded. There were brown leaves amid the green grass that had fallen to their eternal sleep. The Gardener would come, at my call, to gather them up and dispose of them, where they would become mulch and be no more.

Catherine D. Fulp

The Little Things

The little things in life we take for granted every day.
How very much we'd miss them if they were suddenly taken away.

The warm shelter that surrounds us, doesn't matter how big or small.
It's one of those important little things, much better than nothing
  at all.

The people who love and care for us, those we know will always
  be there.
In the good and the bad times with always a kind word to share.

The way the sun comes to visit after a rainy day.
It's a welcome little thing that chases the blues away.

A sudden smile from a stranger, a surprise call from a friend.
A big bright beautiful sunset, captures a moment we don't want to end.

That relaxing feeling we get after a hectic day.
To lay our head on a soft pillow and let all our cares fade away.

It's the little things we couldn't do without.
For they are really the big things that life is all about!

Mary Stacy

Estelle The Woman

There was something -a sort of a wild joy
That filled her heart when she saw him

And when he laughed - well when he laughed
It made her mouth form a smile so wide,
Bright tears filled her eyes, but they didn't fall,
They just made her eyes look like shiny black diamonds
Which reflected, like a mirror, in his eyes

And when his eyes saw and when his mind acknowledged
This magnificent brightness

He knew she loved him, oh he knew
But it had to be his way, his terms, not hers, never, hers.

And those sparkling diamonds fell from her eyes,
Covering her completely and became ashes
When she felt this hard, cold wall of maleness

And she vowed no - oh no, no, no
She had been down that street before
She knew that street was a dead-end - no U-turn possible

So she picked up her heart and just walked away
If she wasn't going to win
Well then, she sure as hell wasn't going to lose, not ever again

Belle M. Samuels-Raines

Untitled

I lay my firebrand down onto my house
The estate is damned and these flames were due.
With this burns everything in our providence
Its walls left a lifelong stigma.
This keep you have shown me to be repressive
Its enemies have given it rest; a charnel no more.
May Earth accept our offerings
I fear it is not enough.
So then add our limbs to the exposition
My blood you gave - will not be taken in vain.
I value this gift more than what this structure once provided.

Nicholas Moore

God In The Rocks

I walked along the stream and watched
the yellow butterflies.
The day seemed endless.
I didn't have a care in the world.

The sun went down and the sun came up.
I was merely there to enjoy it.
If I ever saw God, it was in the water
trickling over the rocks and comforting my soul.

My thoughts wander to that experience,
and I wonder why I'm not there any more.
A place I loved and left for reasons of life.
I want to go back.

I hope it isn't wrong to look for that girl again.
The one laughing with the fishing pole,
even in the rain. Laughing, even at herself.
Seeing God in the rocks.

Kimberly L. Rowland

The Moth

The moth flutters by,
Bringing with it all its grace
And all its secrets.
Wings, splashed with red, white and grey,
Its mission, fill hearts with love.

Christine M. Donovan

The Garden

On this warm summer night, when the air is still,
I go a-walking
Atop the flow'ring hill.

I see the flowers of the night, 'neath the moon they glow,
I see the Gard'ner tending
With water and with hoe.

Above, the nightingale sings his song of deep repose,
And the words to his hymn,
Only the sleepers know.

Here do the sleepers rest, free from care and woe.
The only sound that breaks the silence;
The scratching of the Gard'ner's hoe.

Down the hill I walk, my mind at ease within.
I know the next time I go there
I shan't return again.

And yet my mind is at ease, heart at rest within me,
For I know that where I go
The Gard'ner tends so carefully.

David Hirt

Childhood Memories

I stood there at the edge of the garden
Memories and feelings tumbling through my mind
Remembering little girls playing
While their garlands were swaying in the wind
    ever so softly....

The pain I felt while contemplating the empty garden
Was one of a memory so sweet and long gone by
Lives scattered, earths shattered in between
Days, months and years have gone by
    ever so softly...

Frances P. Harris

Ha!

I fly with the breezes, and float with the storm
The filling of pockets, is where I am born
One day I am single, the next I am two
Occasionally we are captured, and made into new
How we live to gather, with all of our friends
Next to the sidewalks, on roads, curves, and bends
We dive out of windows, and swim in the seas
We are silent mountains, with no climbers or trees
For some we are sifted, in search of a meal
To others we're traded, in hopes of a deal
By trillions we'll takeover, recolor our Earth
Then kiss you and thank you, for giving us birth
Please go right on taking, and not giving back
We have the element of control, you now lack
Our goal is to multiply, to reach for the sky
While waging your wars to control us, you try
You'll find vain your efforts, we cannot go in haste
For your production of convenience, is the food of all waste...

Archer Azara

Untitled

Tis Christmas - tis Christmas
Are the joyous cries.
Through the snow covered streets
As the sun starts to rise
Awake all ye people for it is morn,
Tis the blessed day our saviour was born,
Today is the day to be happy and gay,
When peace should reign through the earth,
To banish all sorrows and cares away.
Be full of laughter and mirth.

Dolores A. Salerno

Denied

Low rumbling thunder in the hills
Shattered by blinding lightning sky
A gnarled, withered hand to window sill
To wipe a tear-stained reflection dry.

Two weary eyes heavenward cast
In prayer to recently believed
Atonement for a lifetime passed
For all things wickedly perceived.

In defense of harsh, innumerable sins
Deep concentration cannot allow
For black shadows creeping, closing in
Eyes sinking under dampened brow.

With trembling lips, a final word
Now does an aged, worn body lay
To await an answer only heard
By others who have come this way.

From out of cold darkness should appear
A grotesque grinning spectre, beckoning
No forgiveness shall be granted here
Upon this day of reckoning.

Aaron Martel

Fire

Crackle, hiss,
stir and flit,
flames dancing in the fires midst.

Mantle glow,
dim lit room,
entrancing me with its finger tips.

Mesmerizing,
and pacifying,
my soul is captured by its grace.

Consuming, fading,
illuminating,
coals all aglow in the fire place.

Flames simmer,
coals glimmer,
the shadows dance with the glowing light.

Peace and calm,
its restful song,
silently serenades me into the night.

Richard Gertz

Birds

When you go outside and watch the birds
Be very quiet and listen to every word
The birds send messages through every song
That they hum all morning long

Birds are very independent and strong
In their little own way
That they try hard to find food for their young
And travel every day

When you go outside and watch the birds
Be very nice and generate to them
They work hard all on their own
Flying from tree to tree to find a home

Nikki Whatley

Untitled

Slowly entering the room of the ones I love most,
all that can be seen is blackness from coast to coast.
The smell of non-existence permeates the air.
All that can be heard is the quiet release of pain.
My throat starts lumping as my heart stops pumping,
I come to the shocking realization that what once was
near has suddenly disappeared.
Sensing the emptiness of what should have been a celebration,
leaves my heart broken like a shattered reflection.
As the tears steadily ripple, the fear of loss leaves me crippled.
How can this be? For just the other day he was right next to me.
Looking around at all the blurred faces,
The coldness shivers throughout my spine.
Staring down at my so called "God" through his windowed dome,
I am left in sorrow and shame, for my love had not been known.
I pray, believing one day we will meet once more,
So he will know how much he is adored.

Lauren LoFaso

Be Gone O' Hemorrhagic City

With high decibel screams
Shots resound across the streets
They signal the end of lives just begun
White powder in packets, sold to one
Brings death to scores or more
Painted women in thigh high boots
Sell their bodies for a fix
Porno flicks with neon signs
Distort and tempt a pervert's mind
Policeman killed like sitting ducks
By mindless murdering junkies
Firemen burned to death,
saving derelicts and homeless in a condemned building
torched by arsonists
The city overflows with innocent blood
Be gone - be gone
Helter skelter hemorrhaging city
May God take pity
New York, New York let there be an end to your strife
Lead us to a better life

Rose Catherine Antelis

Sonnet To Unrequited Love

May I tarry awhile 'mid the roses
As my sad heart stifles its sighs?
For a question unanswered reposes
Deep within those luminous eyes.

Can the wind speak softer than I
Although through its passing a dream it has chilled?
Can the night bird's most plaintive cry
Be more woeful than a heart that is stilled?

Like the breathless rush of dawn's early breaking
While all is yet quiet and still
So acts the heart just awakening
Once lonely, now showing its will.

Dennis J. Murphy Sr.

My Bride

Of one so sweet, pure and true,
The imaging beauty I feel for you;
The blooming flower of a rose bush tree,
The mellow hum of a bumble bee.
I was stung by the feeling of love,
Through the letters delivered from a dove up above.
Your mere words show kindness, interest and care.
I could say "I love you" or should I dare.
To have a true friend, to stand at my side,
Dear heart, I'm asking, "Will you be my Bride?"

Clifford Andy Ramzy

Words Of A Child

Tell me where the sun goes,
Or why I have freckles on my nose.
Why do pickles have bumps?
And are there really beans that jump?
Can friendship be bought and sold,
And is Grandma really that old?
How come girls always scream?
Can dogs and bumblebees dream?
Who really likes to eat liver,
And when you're cold, why do you shiver?
How come you can stay up so late?
When will I be old enough to date?
How come I have to go bed and do chores?
Why don't waves stay on the shore?
And who made up all those rules?
Just one more question that's in my head:
Can you kiss me goodnight and tuck me into bed?

Jennifer Homan

Silence When Talking To Satan

His devil image,
His playful hands.
The ways he speaks to me
With his strokes on the guitar.
His demon style
His silver vinyl pants.
The ways I love him,
With only a relationship in mind.
His fine dark black hair
His haunted Hollywood mansion.
The ways he pulls me closer,
Is only his seductive features in his music.

Kaye Jarvis

Don't Look Back

Don't look back, it will only hurt more,
Don't think twice, before you head to the door.

If this is the end, don't say hi,
Just kiss me, and say goodbye.

I love you, I love you so dear,
When you left me. I quivered with fear.

I'm at a point in my life,
Where right now, I wish I was your wife.

I miss you a lot,
But no one I know can fill your spot.

You are my savior,
And yes I would do you any favor.

If you would love me, like I love you,
Then one of my wishes would come true.

So remember I love you with all my heart,
And no one can make up for my broken
Heart that almost fell apart.

Camy Hovdestad

At Peace

The autumn breeze feels so good as I sit upon this aging wood.
The day a slumber and I at rest, cozy in my nature nest.
The falling leaves sail and drift, clinging to the wind they lift.
Where they go I do not know, the time has come for falling snow.
But for now I'll allow the peacefully aging, gentle fall.
Sun shines brightly through the trees, its warmth absorbs tho'
  crisp the breeze.
A day to put my mind to rest and strengthen for a new dawns quest.
Yes I know this day won't stay, the dusk sets not too far away.
I'll find pleasure while it's here, daybreak may be just as clear.

Renata Zanon

Critter Watchin'

When Christmas time is over and it's terrible long till spring
I usually do my "critter" watchin' so I never do complain.
When it's January, and it's icy cold outside
I sit me by the window just back fur enough to hide.
Folks take stock in roarin' fires and popcorn in the bowl
but I watch God's critters run in and out their holes.
Why, they's a couple little squirrels that's out a dozen times a day
flittin' back from limb to limb, scramblin' in their play.
Now, if they's lovers- that old girl must really know the trick
cause they circle that old tree all day and he 'ain't catched her yet.
But birds is what I really like as they glide through the sky
you know that only God has taught them how to fly.

They sit a spell and flick their tails and pay those squirrels no mind
It's sure a lot of joy- this critter watchin' time.

Thelma Davids

A Message From The Wind

As I sit alone under a tree no one around but my thoughts and me,
my hair unravels crawling apart as a rush of wind chills my heart.
The tree above me leans and whispers, "I am the wind
    and you're not alone."
I was not frightened; I only asked, "Where did you come from?"

The wind replied, "I speak through the leaves that are upon this tree.
Now there are four: The tree, you, your thoughts, and me.
So when you think that you're alone, quiet as it may be, be still
and feel the wind and you will find there is more around you
    than you see."

The message was soft but clear. The tree, the wind were still again.
So I picked up a leaf that fell from the tree as a reminder of what
a beautiful friend nature can be. When you're alone, she sends
a message from the wind!

French Smith Shaw

True Friends

    For many years you have been on a quest for true
friendship. You were hoping to share your life with someone
special and although it may appear that your search will
never end—don't give. For true friends really do exist;
although they are extremely hard to find—they do exist!
For a true friend will always have some time to share—a
kind word—sometimes just an ear, and he will not lash out
at you when eventually—you disagree; conversely, he will
stand by you in times of good cheer and help you through
your most desperate hour of despair. A true friend will
guide you in becoming what you truly wish to be. True
friends should be cherished—as they are unique. At times
they seem elusive, but they really aren't so hard to find
you only need to open—your heart—your soul—your mind.
Now wipe those tears and put on a smile, for your true friend
only seems elusive—as you can see—I've been here all the time!

Danny Caraza

Mother, Mother

Mother, Mother, do beware
It's your day, and it is near
If it's sunny and in the air
Then Mother, Mother, do beware.
This day is here
Mother, Mother, I give you my heart.
My heart is here for you to take—
I'll give you my heart!
On Mother's Day for you to keep.
Mother, Mother, this day is here
So do beware, it's in the air
It's Mother's Day and it's finally here.
So Happy Mother's Day to you.

John H. D'Amato

"Our World"

Stop and Look around you,
There is beauty everywhere;

See the mighty oak, the meadows green,
Flowers grown with loving care;

See majestic mountains capped with snow,
Pointing to the sky;

Smell the fresh, clean scent behind the rain,
See the clouds go rolling by;

Our world is full of beauty
Created by the loving Master's hand;

There are streams, rivers, oceans,
and beaches of pure white sand;

When the pressures of life weigh heavy,
Look for the beauty in each new day;

Let your spirit soar with the eagles,
and go joyfully on your way!

Nathan Gay

Sugarless Now

Sugar is pure, white and sweet,
Unnatural flavoring that rots the teeth.
It clings, it sticks inside the mouth
Making tongue twitch all about.

It laces the gums, and cracks the teeth,
Sometimes discoloring to unbelief.

Shades of orange, brown, green and black.
Trips to the dentist drilling the plaque.
If only I had refused those sugary treats,
And saved myself the sweet-tooth grief.

Kenyon Boyce-Benson

The Fountain

A collective pool of dreamer's unconscious not spoken
Compromised aspirations intertwine with the night
Ethereal screams scar a twilight unbroken
As angels ascend the font riding beams of light

Spiralling into fleeting security the witching hour brings
Angels aspire to the heavens hindered by broken wings
Plummeting to unwelcome solace the copper bottom gives
A haunting admonition of reveries unlived

The unbearable cycle forever flowing
Burial ground for the existing their souls have died
Life taking life by living without knowing
A collective pool of dreamer's tears uncried

Heather Schmaedeke

Origin

Out of my side, you say, while I was sleeping
God carved you, Eve, taking me unaware,
stole such a glory and damnation, keeping
my portions charged, changed in you for a snare?
Surely I was near death that hour in slumber
not to awaken, shriek with the halving pain.
I was content as one until my number
was split in two across body and brain.
Now I am doomed. If I hope to be one
again I must gather your apples, put
bites of you back. As we couple I stun
my side with woman, each day try to shut
you in my earth, as though afflicted with night
about to die without your warming light.

George Boss

The Storm

The storm clouds are dark and gray and full of rain.
It is the eve of winter and the wind is brisk and cold.
The sun, all but memory, threatens never to return again.
Though young, this season feels so old.
And the storm rages on...

My sole is dark and gray and full of pain.
It is the eve of winter and the wind is brisk and cold.
Happier times, all but memory, threaten never to return again.
Though young, I feel so old.
And the storm rages on...

Wake up! And lift thy head from thy pillow.
All men must weather storms that never last.
The Spring shall soon return and bring the willow.
All one has is this day so leave behind the past!
And I laugh at the storm...

Michael J. Horkey

On The Threshold Of Desire

Balancing between wrong and right
On the threshold of desire
Decisions lost and decisions made
On the threshold of desire
Confusion of day understanding night
On the threshold of desire
Lost in a maze found in the labyrinth
On the threshold of desire
Blind in the sun sight in the moon
On the threshold of desire
Stench of the flowers scent of the weeds
On the threshold of desire
Fall of the sky rise of the sea
On the threshold of desire
Displeasure of a smile beauty of a frown
On the threshold of desire
Piercing gazes gentle knife
On the threshold of desire
Consequence of measure deceit of pain
On the threshold of desire

Sarah Hawk

The Hidden Depth

If I were given one last choice of where I'd want to be
If tomorrow were my last on earth, I know just where I'd flee

I know that you and you alone, would always comfort me
I'd share your power and your rage, as you thrashed across the shore
I'd feel your mist upon my face as you tried to speak to me

I'd know you'd understand something's were never meant to be
I'd sit and listen quietly for the wisdom of your song
The wind and whitecaps alone will tell your words are very strong;
and yet so full of grace

Knowing our day had ended, I'd watch you drift away
Knowing you'd come back to me, at least another day

I know you'll wait for me until my days on earth are through
Knowing someday my ashes you'll carry
Forever away with you.

Kathleen Cahill

The Sunset Dream

Spring brings flowers, birds, and trees.
  Spring brings many a gentle breeze.
Spring brings buds, that turn to leaves.
  Spring brings out animals, from birds to bees.
People watch sunset ponds, beneath pine and willow trees.
  And all through the sunset dream, I will smile with please.

Angeline I. Olsen

A Child's Wish

If I could talk here is what I would say,
my Mommy and daddy loved me that day. That
day I was born I am talking about, They hugged me
and cried and wanted to shout. But now it seems
since one year has passed, they have forgotten
about me and are smoking their grass. There popping
the pills and having their fun, but what about
me? I was the one. The one that they wanted and
needed so bad they truly loved me that's what they said.
The fun that they're having will all end one day.
I'm hoping it's not when God takes me away, so
mommy and daddy please love me I pray, just like
you did on that very first day.

Ella M. Starr

The Lion And The Lamb

As the lion lay down with the lamb I came to you in pain to find
your lion heart afforded me a long awaited resting place.
I saw the gentleness in your eyes and was touched by your
protective love and strength of spirit.

You allowed me to come and lay down the burdens of my life,
Reassuring me that there was a safe and quiet place in this world for me.
Many times you were the only thing between my will to live and my
drive to self-destruct.

You have blessed me with the gift of trust and the gift of hope, and
so it is with us, embodied as the lion and the lamb.

Diane Workman

The Island Of My Dreams

I know where there's an island nook,
Surrounded by tall spreading trees
Where clear and laughing, leaps a brook
Which tells adventures to the breeze.

Where there are Cardinals who sing
Against the trees' soft foliage green
Or, like bright bits of flame they cling
Close by the ivy's rambling screen.

Where orioles in summer perch
Splashes orange, against the blue
Or fly about sometimes to search
For hairlike roots to build nests new.

Where songs of doves and thrushes sound
Beside the clear and sparkling streams
While blithe and gay birds flit around
That is the Island of my Dreams.

Mary A. Dunnell

Sounds Of Nature

Do you hear, the rooster crow at dawn,
Or the birds with their chatter, or trill
with their songs? The wind as it passes
lightly through the leaves,
of the different bushes, and the various trees?
Do you hear the bee, who buzzes on by,
The cricket in the grass, or the hum of the flies?
Do you hear, the croak of a bullfrog
And the splash that he makes?
Hear fish jumping, from a very nearby lake,
The sounds of running water,
from a small and rapid stream.
Now, just sit and feel the sun upon your face,
listening very closely, and slowing
down your pace. These are the sounds of
nature, mixed, with the human race.

Lois A. Cicairos

Miracle Of The Sky

At times - a deeper blue than blue
Decorated with sweeps of fleecy clouds floating here and there.
At times - Holding together castles of billowy shapes
tainted with pinks, orange and fiery reds.
At times - rainbows lifted in an arch across the stretch of it
gentle colorful hues bound together like a wide ribbon.
At times - grey misty wisps floating through the blue of it
to both disappear and reappear in other shapes and sizes.
At times - reaching the earth with showers of rain and snow
to moisten the soil and bring forth the richness it holds.
At times...Night times...
Brilliant with trillions of lights we call stars
Sparkling in the eternal distance of space
Creating a wonder beyond imagination-
Their brightness disappearing into the brightness of the rising sun.
Oh sky, are you not a miracle?

Pauline Sticka

Untitled

If I could go back to when you liked me,
I'd be there in less than a second.
Love is so hard to find,
But after I met you it seemed so easy.
But the more I wanted you, the less you wanted me,
And in the end, you broke my heart.
It was like a nightmare,
Like I didn't want to believe what you where telling me.
But whatever I tried, I still couldn't wake up,
It's like a piece of me is gone,
And without you,
It will never be back.

Katie Digristina

The Bum

He is crazy; that's what he is.
His face a map of lines, his hair a tangle jungle.
Crazy, blue-eyed oceans shift beneath storm dark brows.
Shadow-dark visions drift in the canyons of his mind,
Blocking reality behind a wall
One thousand miles long,
One thousand miles high,
One thousand miles thick.
Pale, mottled skin: Crust of a world of shifting insanity.
Joint-tremble earthquakes shake him to the core;
Volcanic mouth erupts madness in floods.
He is an isolated planet in a universe of normality;
Wildly careering on an undetermined course of downward spiral
Through levels of deteriorating rationalization.
His ability to think is as thread bare as his clothes.
I see him as a world on the brink of destruction
without enough strength to control the destructive
energy of a deteriorating mind.

Andrea L. Case

Untitled

Standing outside early one morning, waiting for the bus.
Standing on line in a store.
Who is standing next to me,
but someone of another race.
They are all my friends.
Mama always said to me,
it's not the color of their skin,
it's not where they came from
that makes them a good friend;
it's what's inside.
Mama always said
everyone is the same inside.
Do you want to know something?
Mama was right, they are all my friends.

Meighan Enright

Your Last Breath

I saw you take your last breath.
You were nineteen and frightened. You knew you were dying.
You asked for your mother but she couldn't come.
I saw you take your last breath.

Things were noisy and rushed and your eyes wide with alarm.
What was happening was painful. It shouldn't have been
happening.
You cried and you gasped and tried not to go.
I saw you take your last breath.

I felt helpless and hopeless and I wanted to hold you.
I too cried and gasped but it was all deep inside.
You were too young to die, but still...
I saw you take your last breath.

The terror was real and was felt in the air.
The comfort I offered felt inept and trite.
I've dreamt of you since as you tried not to leave.
Yes, I saw you take your last breath.

Norman C. Olsen, RN

Revealing Eyes

When I sit in silent thought about roads not taken,
Reflecting on times gone by,
I realize the importance of memories,
Held in expressions from their eyes.

Whether it be feelings of pain,
Brought on from a scraped knee,
Or a show of "Thank you, Mom"
For a tender kiss placed gently.

Despite all of my efforts,
Their eyes show weakness,
And a need for comfort and care,
In the time of sickness.

Anticipation fills their faces,
When their eyes reveal a special wish,
Eyes begin to sparkle and shine,
Amid thoughts of a Christmas list.

I am aware of my importance in their lives,
When tears of joy or pain flow my way,
God also understands their worth to me,
When I pray nightly to look into their eyes one more day.

Patricia Duncan

"Drawn To An End"

We met so late in our time together
And now it may be time to say good-bye forever
But I cannot say so soon for...
In my heart
The time will never come

On that one sweet night
When you and I embraced
An air-tight seal formed
Not only to hold us together
But also to protect those few precious memories
From fading away
Fade away like you must now do

Maybe at another time
We will embrace once again
And move on together
As one

That time, however, never will go by
As quickly as our moment has
But then again my friend
This is the folly of life

Brent Geers

'River of Regret'

He caressed her laughter,
making love to the echoes
careening into his soul with
sporadic velocity;
Embracing his melancholy, he could
only behold the passage
requiring insight to his preservation:
To his sanity;
Was she worth it?
Was the agony he grappled, only
to suffocate and decimate him now,
Serve to remind her of one's propensity
to inflict barbs into a scabbing soul?
Truly, the mask of selfishness and
uncertainty can cloak the face where
the light of knowledge and trust struggle
for recognition.

Stephen Hobbs Jr.

A Talk With Nature

I think out loud.
I talk to the mountains.
They don't talk back,
    but they understand me anyway.
They understand my desire to be near them,
    despite any fear that may overwhelm me.
They use my desire to control my fear.
They comfort me even in my fear.
Their breath in the breeze shelters my trembling bones,
    and blankets my fear with their shade.
They echo songs in the valleys to help ease my mind
    and sing me to sleep.
I wake up and I feel the shade covering my body.
It is late in the day and the sun will soon lay down to sleep.
I get up and walk to my car.
Looking over the side of the mountain,
    I notice the city below and the smoky sky, no longer blue.
I dread going back.
But am only comforted at the thought of my return.
Comforted by the sheltering mountains as they listen to me.

Carol A. Sandin

"Dying Daydreams Of A PARAMEDIC"

You may never learn my identity,
As I cradle your lives in my hands.
Seconds are my currency,
Deftly stolen from Fate's Hour-glass sands.

I am that Forgotten guardian, thankfully,
Patiently awaiting your pleas, upon demand,
to appear rapidly, angelically,
Rendering the vital services at my command.

Yet while I strive, to help you survive,
Doing everything I possibly can,
I know I can not keep you all alive...
We are mortal on that day we do not plan.

Sometimes, you just look at me.
Others, you sigh, just before you die.
But when you cry, and beg, 'Why? How can this be?'
I pray my end is less painful than your good-bye.

Numerous souls have departed before me,
Motivating my ability, devouring my sanctity.
It's ironic, today, I can only smile, at YOU, now memory,
Adding my soul to the list that encumber your sterility.

Nicholas Sciarro

A Touch Of Love

A touch of love is simple
    a light that glows

Roses watered, planted and made to grow

Nations and nations bound together
Where peace and happiness
make the world better

Boys and girls respecting
their fathers and mothers
accepting all races and stop
abusing their brothers

Putting up guns and knives
learning to solve problems
with dignity and pride

Eager to give, not looking to receive
always render men good deeds

A smile, A touch to be bold
All these qualities equal to gold
A touch of love, is a mystery to happiness

Debbie Williams

The Essence Of A Woman

If you know where you're going,
I'll let you take me for the ride.
As long as you recognize my ability to drive.

Respect is a must, trust is one too;
And what's good for me
Is even better for you.

I don't need to wear your pants or fit in your shoes.
I won't test your manhood
If you're capable of utilizing your own tools.

I won't sell you short or
Cut back on your needs;
As long as you recognize, I am who you should please.

Submission has its place and passivity too;
But don't be offended by my eagerness
To take charge and my aggressive moods.

I will be your wife, lover, and friend;
But I'll only be a mother to our children.

I've solved part of the mystery of what I have in store;
But to live it is to gain a whole lot more.

Geronda V. Carter

Happy Birthday ... For Sharon

How to choose a present for someone as special as you ...
This is something much easier to say than it is to do ...

It should be beautiful, because that describes what you are ...
Like the sparkle of crystal, like the light from a star ...

It should be warm and comforting, as you are known so well to be ...
Like the soft glow of a candle, like the friend you've been to me ...

It should be a spectrum of color, for you have touched many a heart...
Like a rainbow after showers, like a smile after tears depart ...

It should be vibrant and strong, and as sweet as fine perfume ...
Like a flower with richly colored petals, like a garden in full bloom ...

Yes, I considered all these things as I sought out a birthday treasure ...
Yet there was another quality which I could not begin to compare
    or measure ...

The one enduring, exceptional gift bestowed from heaven above ...
May you always receive, as you have generously given,
    the precious gift of love.

Dolores H. Cox

427

Captured Sanity

Footsteps in the sand getting washed away.
I sit and lay, as the water crashes onto the rocks.
A force I feel within myself,
A conjugated prism, that is Life...
Seaweed rushes in and out,
Never the same piece is seen again.
Black marks, Big time waves bring in the sea.
Once on a lone prairie, A little puppy dog sings,
"Finally I feel at peace. I feel safe. I feel warm."
The sun caresses my skin,
As a mist of water crashing envelops me.
Forming a new skin. A layer impenetrable by anyone!
But, there is one, who I lay myself into and sleep.
One who loves. The Shade is her name.
She takes care of me when I haven't the energy to.
Her hair is ablaze with wind, As she shoots me to the sky.
As I caress the Angel of Light,
My life is now immortal...
As my reality of youth finally says, goodbye.

Jeremy David Swartz

I Am A Jaguar

I am a jaguar with black fur and gleaming yellow eyes.
I wonder how the jungle animals feel when they are my prey.
I hear the cries of my prey in the night.
I see all that fear my presence.
I want to be the king of the jungle.
I am a jaguar with black fur and gleaming yellow eyes.

I pretend to be the king of the jungle.
I feel the fear of my prey when they are attacked.
I touch the warm ground with my paws.
I worry about getting into fights with other jungle animals.
I cry when the other male jaguars throw dirt in my face and claw
    at my sides.

I am a jaguar with black fur and gleaming yellow eyes.
I understand that you respect other jungle creatures.
I say what has to be said to help the jungle.
I dream about a perfect habitat where hunters cannot harm me.
I try not to ruin other animal's homes.
I hope that one day jaguars will be the kings of all the jungles.
I am a jaguar with black fur and gleaming yellow eyes.

Timothy Fielder

The Match And The Candle

As the flame burst like a bubble, the match starts to darken
like an eclipse over the land having no mercy. The red flames
and the blackish-gray smoke combine and make an explosion
all their own. Flames spread as if they were people that just had
a fight. Yet, come back to join as if they made up at the same time.
Now still like a tree getting ready to be cut down. Leaves fall
on another tree, a bigger tree, this tree now cut down and thrown away.
Yet, the other tree is not cut but standing firm, and not moving
an inch, but something under it was. The ground below was
moving rapidly. Pouring over the little hill beside the tree and
down, down, down that hill it went just like the Energizer Bunny,
it just keep going, and going and going. Then suddenly
the candle's flame burnt out like a dying animal.

Scott George

Dead Of Winter

A violet mist encircled the night;
selectively, mysteriously deprived.
Entangled in fear; a never-ending fight.
A life of disillusion, it readily contrived.

And the wind howled in solemn anguish,
to dwell in tempting, undesiring passion.
The moon opalesced with its sultry language,
caressed the darkness in unyielding fashion.

And the trees withered and despondent,
trembled in ubiquitous disarray.
Despairing figures of a cruel moment;
victims of an invincible fray.

And the lake frigidly frozen in time;
a motionless block of crystalline ice.
Reflected on changes, the youth of its prime.
Sacrificing virtue, consumed in vice.

The night owl perched in grandiose style,
overlooked the gray and desolate scene.
Surveying the barren land for many a mile,
distraught by the change, remained serene.

Carlos A. Morales-Soto

Dare

I dare to be what I want,
I dare to dream the things that haunt.
I dare to be the very best,
I dare to be a cut above the rest.
I dare to be myself;
To forgive, forget, and put things on the shelf.
I dare to aspire to higher heights,
And I dare to do it with all my might.
I dare to be great and make myself known.
I dare to never be overthrown.
I dare to teach and help; to do what I can.
In the race war, I dare to be a helping hand.
I dare to be the best I can be,
And you; I dare you to stop believing in me.
I dare to have hope, love, joy, and peace.
And I dare to give it away, piece by piece.
Out of all these things I dare to be,
I never dare to stop believing in me.

Latisha Barnes

The Quest

Will I ever complete my restless search
Which leads me onward, I know not where?
From shabby hovel to elegant church,
Hoping to find it, praying it will be there.

Amongst the ancient ruins it may be found.
In modern cities it may be hidden.
So extremely deep, dark, and profound,
That one might think it were forbidden.

Lying eternally deeper than the stroke of a brush
Or buried in a sculptor's tool
Expressing itself in the song of a thrush,
Concealed forever in the heart of a fool.

So long as men shall consecrate their hearts,
In ever beauty shall advance the arts.

Peri M. Rezai

The John Hancock Building At Four AM

The Monolith - soundless, looming, and ominous,
against the night lights of the city.

It arrived - black against a lesser black,
a silent rectangle with an awesome presence.

It arrived - as snow dusted the streets in pale swirls,
filling the night with space-devouring mystery.
It arrived - by old John Hancock diminished by,
the geometry of its portentous slab-like inky form.

It arrived - by old Copley church humbled by,
the shadowy glass power of a new and darker age.

The Monolith - hangs in space,
and two sharp vertices outline its velvet void,
and fills the window of the night,
with futuristic sense - and dread.

John E. Fahy

Nuclear War

Glimpsing through the peephole of time
Sacrificing only the nature of the beast
Cometh the dead winds
   onto the sea of tranquility
Henceforth holding fast into the night
Passions burning from the inner soul
Unleashing the lion into the calm
Tearing and slashing its prey
Cunning as a wolf in the still of the night
Left is only a remnant
   of what was and will never be.

Jason King

Time Through A Pepper Shaker

Look, some faces might gaze back at me, back in scattered whimsy,
their faces long, green, brittle, blue, lovely faces, ancient, new: it
seems I can see the drifting, the anchored, the parading and the still
dead locked in their chambers-but then I wonder: "Do I imagine
   them only?"
-do I create their heads from ink and paper-? (Where their voices
dangle like written word as fiction people from fiction leaves-)
Faces halfway clear, halfway submerged in misty haze, it seems I want
to hear and speak them, to see them return my gaze, to watch them shop
in Tinsel Towns, and paint themselves on beaches with rocks, and read
from manuals and pretend to understand-
I need only to be told: "there will be time, and time," that the
blinding mists will clear from my eyes, that there will be days to
speak, others to listen, and test the illusions they might tell us,
and give crackers to polly parrots, and take buses to ridiculous,
empty places- I think I shouldn't write a novel now- without so much
as one great fall, a torrid affair, or my own garden even-
Faces that step through station, street and wood clearing, voices,
telling of summertime watches, of the year two thousand and twenty
two- I need one simple voice to speak: "There will be time and time,
for them and you....."

Matia Burnett

A Christmas Wish

We wish that we could see and enjoy,
all the friends we've ever had;
For 'tis the Season, lo the Season, when such
thoughts, to see them all, does make the heart,
yes, Oh so glad.

Alas, life is not that way, but 'er we know,
our memories are precious and those friendships always grow;
Thus, even though we may not see them, from distant
times and even now, we trust they know we love
them, and miss them, and wish them

The Happiest Of Christmas Holidays.

Ted Lundberg

He Is Always Listening

As I walk through the dark, silent forest,
I realize I am the only one around.
I cry out loud, for I am scared,
But no one can hear me.
For I am alone.

If a tree were to fall, there would not
be any one to hear, but me.
If a fire were to start, no one
would here my cries.

I cry loudly for someone, anyone to
come and be with me.
But no one is there to respond.
So I decide to leave.

After I am gone, I realize that if
I would have called out one name,
He would have answered.
Speak unto the Lord and call unto Him,
And He shall answer,
For He is always listening.

Tera Abernathy Kelley

Heroes

I'm in search for the heroes of today
The few who are not frightened scared and afraid
To be individuals and not followers or clones
Following no one's path but the one they've carved out on their own
I'm in search for the heroes who will still stand
Though mocked and rebuked by the enemy's hands
Their souls will not fret or be in total despair
Because in their hearts they are righteous and fair
I'm in search for the heroes who will speak to
The hearts of all people the great small and few
Demanding from all men all that they can give
Much more then a little but one hundred percent
I'm in search for the heroes that children will admire
Instilling in them respect honor and pride
Heroes who are strong who will suffer and bleed
The father and mother figures the world so badly needs

Selamawit Yilma

Twisted Faith

Raw shreds of
lacerated flesh cling to
corroded metal cuffs of bondage broken. Elevated hopes for
security in suffocating
hatred vaporize. Lamenting is of no
use. Even suicide can't
comfort
despair. Always able
to flee to your side was my foolish trust in
life but you died and left me without promises of
forever.
Satisfaction of tangible
bliss was mine to manipulate,
true suffering was foreign until you disappeared.
Engaging in pointless pastimes filled with promises never expected to
be kept— friendship, purity, religion, dream.
Denying all that grounded
me prior to the
abandonment, in desperation I destroyed all covenants made as a
child naive but one forgotten refused to become void.

Michelle S. Morita

Environmental Adaptation

If it's winter, the heat's turned off at night. You
dress hurriedly in your sister's hand-me-downs, ignoring
your nagging stomach.
You are careful not to awaken your brother, he's a
year older, but he dropped out of school last spring.
You leave by the back door, the front won't lock; you
also avoid the well-dressed crowd that pokes fun at
those who don't dress as well.

You walk alone this year, your best friend, who's twelve
also is pregnant now.
In your palm is fifteen cents, you mentally resolve
to buy a candy bar after-school.
Pausing, you take a deep breath and begin another day.

Gracie Kinsey

"What's The Score"

The sound of the ocean's crashing waves
digging deep shallow graves,
through the storm someone raves
meet me in those hollow caves.

The storm is over
the boats ashore
the once dreaded storm,
is alas nevermore.

The water has claimed many lives,
people struggling to survive,
can't get out of the deep ocean dive
yet they still begin to strive.

Strive they may, strive they might
the great blue beast holds them tight
keeping their eyes from any light.
It's no use to struggle, it's no use to fight.

As someone from the ocean floor
asks someone up there what's the score?
Someone ponders and remembers
the people some, the ocean more.

Samuel Ray Jewell

Atlanta '96 Olympics

The Olympics are coming to Atlanta,
A waiting world is ready to begin.
To the love and war metropolis Atlanta.
Will be coming and going with the wind.

Home of the devil woman Scarlett O'Hara
Who ruled Atlanta with the prick of a pin,
The legendary home she lovingly called Tara
Her coming and going with the wind.

The lust for gold and glory is forever,
The flaming torch is every thing but sin,
The artists zest for good will, and fair play glory,
'Bout the few or the many lose or win.

The sharp shooters aim their bows and arrows,
Calculating every inch in every mile
With the vim and spirit of an O'Hara
There'll be a hot time in Atlanta for a while

The athletes are waiting for that special day
So light that torch and let the games begin.
The multitudes from places strange and far away,
Will be coming a-dreaming, of a Gold medal win.

William B. Raines

Do You Know The Way To The Land Of Joy

On top of the trees,
and beyond the sky,
there lies a trail to the land of joy.
Is it the clouds that lead the way,
or is it the sun,
or the moon,
or the sky?
We will never know unless we follow
the clouds,
or the sun,
or the moon,
or the sky.
But the way of life can also lead us to that special place.

Jennifer Gottesfeld

"After-noon Delight"

As the day grows old and I'm all alone
I'll walk over and pick up the telephone
Happy am I, that home you are
But wishing that you were with me at my bar
For here I'll sit, talk, and sadly see
A drink poured for you, waiting patiently
And when this receiver, hence will fall
Around your house I will call
School is in session, both pupils are here
Speak now, my darling, sweet music to the ear
And after all the love is made
We'll advance to a higher grade
Solemnly, we will not repent
For a night, that was so well spent
Then once again, I'll be alone
As I make my long journey home
Sitting at the bar, head in hands, and thinking
Looking up and over, at what you would be drinking
And when my night is finally through
I'll drink it up, and think of you!!!

Steve Allen Shipman

Vision Got A Season

God's got a vision just for you
Soon one day it will come true.
Just give it a little time
Keep His vision on your mind.

Flowers don't grow in just a few hours
Birds don't fly in just a few days
Seasons don't change in just a few minutes.
We don't grow old on the day we're born,
Babies aren't adults in just a few days.

Your vision got a season
Give it a little more time.
It all takes time, Oh! Can't you see.
It's gonna be alright
It's gonna be fine
God's working it out for you.

Juanita Russell

New Moon's Scythe

Slicing crisp the crescent light,
Cuts clean the darkling sky.
Muted tones of piping crickets slide
Their trombone notes,
As night bread slices fold
Close stacked together, day's labor toll
To wrap the leaving crumbs,
For night owl's song.

Betty L. Collie

Untitled

The night you walked into my life,
The night you walked out of my life,
The night we made love,
The night we had a fight.
The night you bought me roses,
The night the thorns stung my heart.
The peaceful night I kissed your tears away,
The stormy night I made you cry.
Our first date on that warm summer night
You swore you would never leave.
Our last date on that cold winter night
You swore you would never come back.
The happy tears we cried,
The sad tears we cried.
The night you fought for my honor,
The night you fought for your freedom.
The night I moved on and held his hand,
The night you stood still and held onto the memories.

Lisa Mark

The Soul Of Man

Fear not the darkness of the night, but tremble at the thoughts of
the darkness of the soul.
The night is soothing, caressing, it holds you tight to its bosom
like a mother protecting its child.
But the soul of man can be a hideous place, an endless black hole
filled with deception, and greed.
You know not of who is controlled by such a soul. You can be
misled, deceived by a kind word, a gentle smile, or a soft voice.
You are lulled into a false sense of security until bit by bit your
whole being is devoured.
You lose all control of who you are and what you are all about and
then it's too late, there is no escape.
So trust in the night, find peace in the darkness, keep your wits
about you, and trust not in the soul of man.

John Pradon

Unforgettable Fire

Oh precious love, through the hours of madness,
There is but one thing that guides me
The sweet sound of your gladness.

Into the darkest of night, I tread blinded in sight
Ever guessing the shadows of my perilous flight.

For a breathless choke, I search and poke,
To bring life free from the fire and smoke

The reek of death throughout the air,
Shed's a darkened light on a mother's despair.

Even love and care cannot save a mate,
Once fire has raged its twisted fate.

Jack H. Milton Jr.

The Tree

One who sees all the stages
and seasons of life,
whether it's the bitter snow,
downfall of rain,
or the play of a child in its arms.
One will remember that upon these arms
one will see beautiful leaves of green.
And on a special day
see beautiful pedals of a budding flower.
And soon to taste the fruit of its nature,
one will feast upon its supplements and enjoy its spirit.
For way up high one is free.
And to enjoy this
one has to be a Tree.

Amy Heille

God's Wonderful Creations

As I travel down the highway
And I view the mountain tops,
With its huge bouquet of colors
In the early Autumn light.

I stop to see the colors
Yellow, green, and crimson red,
I bowed my head in thanks
For the things that God has made.

In Spring I wake up early
And see the bright sunlight,
I hear the bird sing sweetly
as I slowly walk outside.

The flowers are blooming by the stream,
That runs beside the mill,
I stopped to watch the water
As it slowly turns the wheel.

As times goes by I'm glad I stopped
To look around and see,
All the wonderful creations
That God has made for me.

Peggy L. Cooper

"Dissolve"

Ever feel like you just wanna dissolve,
to be nothing more than the wind and the stars?

Ever feel like your head was in the clouds,
soaring like a bird up up and away from the ground?

Ever feel like burstin' out with a song,
lying on a swing in the warmth of the sun?

Ever feel like goin' over a rainbow,
hopin' you'll be led to the pot o' gold at the end o' the road?

Ever feel like you'll be never alone,
though you may be sittin' at home watchin' your soaps?

Ever feel like you're livin' on another planet,
conversin' with an Alien Nation?

Ever feel like you just wanna dissolve?

Melani Betbadal

Farewell, My Spring

Spring came late that year...
For me it never really came at all.
I wonder if I'll ever welcome spring.
I know that I will always dread the Fall.

That Spring you had such hope, just like our flowers
That you would live to see another year.
When Fall arrived, our lovely flowers died.
They will return, but you will not be here.

What will tomorrow be? I hate to think.
As misty as today, life without breath.
How can one man leave such an aching void?
How can love continue growing after death?

I sometimes think that I have died with you.
It saddens me to find I'm still alive.
Since the greatest part of me is buried, too,
Why must my hollow, lifeless shell survive?

You're gone and you took all my joy with you.
You won't be here to view the golden fall.
I will never see your smiling face again.
I'm sure Spring won't return this year at all.

Darlene Lutz

10 Little Fingers - 10 Little Toes

10 little fingers and 10 little toes
a cute little smile and a button nose
a lovely cleft chin with skin so fair
eyes that are blue of which there are a pair
reddish/blond hair of which there's little
lips of red from which drools spittle

He has a voice that when angry is loud
and a nanny and grandpa, who are most proud
he is very special and requires lots of love
and when he is happy he coos like a dove

To watch him sleep, an angel he is like
tho I know before long he will be on a bike
Time changes all and slips by so fast
which makes me realize his baby stage will not last
He will so soon grow up and I'll get older
till my 6 foot piece of land the sod they'll lay o'er
Then the circle complete will be for the button nose
when he will have his 10 little fingers and 10 little toes.

Fred Ward

Springtime In The Park

The Woman sits alone on a bench within the park,
Beneath a budding tree, does she hear the singing lark?
She sits and reads a book, so intense or so it seems,
I wonder about her solitude, I wonder what it means.

Spring is in the air, the trees are dressed in green.
My soul's without a care, or that's the way it seems.
As I sit upon the grass at the edge of the wood,
I ponder on a thought and wonder if I should.

The Woman sits alone, I know not for how long,
Should I go and say hello, or would that be all wrong?
Does she really want to sit alone on such a pretty day,
Or would she like some company and tell me it's okay?

Spring is in the air, the sun is warm and bright.
The sky's a pale blue, and the lark is taking flight.
My break is slipping by, it will soon be in the past,
To stop the clock of time, and make this moment last.

The Woman on the bench, she's walking by to go!
Did my ears deceive me, or did she say hello?
She'll be back another day, I'll see her yet again.
Then I'll go and talk to her, my loneliness will end.

Dave Franclemont

Weeds

There were two friends who gardened well;
One's name was Anne, one's Isabell.
Anne trimmed the hedges, raked the leaves,
And swept pine needles from the eaves.

A manicured retreat Anne kept;
She raked 'n raked 'n swept 'n swept.
Oh! Curse a weed if it would dare
To show its branches anywhere.

Now Isabell, a different case;
Allowed all weeds to grow in place.
"A plant whose harvest we don't reap,
Makes it no less a plant to keep."

The years fled by, their friendship shattered;
To stand their ground was all that mattered.
When Isabell died, Anne tended her plot;
An orderly mound, fey Isabell got.

'Round the tomb she'd chop and hoe;
'Twas fate, for Anne would never know
That when she died, poor weeding slave...
Great weeds would grow upon her grave.

Carole Estrup

Noondepth

In the fullness of noondepth
Standing in the shade of summer
She raised her ravaged head
And saw red wings fleeting by.

In the tanglewood of noondepth
She parted the cattails
And saw a sliver of sun
Slice the blue of the void.

In the forgetfulness of noondepth
She waved fiery flags
At beings in crystallized cities
Beside the churning waters of gone.

In the silent stillness of noondepth
Amid the silken whispering of oneness
She flicked through the blueness of silence
And sang the serenade of noondepth.

Gwen J. Mathis

"Fight Life"

Be strong, I think
Bitterness comes along
Trying to fight life, not letting a soul
get close to you
Respect, respect fills my mind
Always pushing myself to be kind, though
how can I really? Being faced with life's
pressures, negatives, and self image
I ask myself how, when hate tries to seep through me
I will try, but probably end up dieing inside

Melonie Megnin

Shoes

The Dance of scholarly thoughts
once entertained me
In the midst of the fraughts
of confusion,
Like a tiptoe through delicacies in the air,
Answers.
To avoid life's despair...

Then the dance stopped forever.
The next moment ahead
Grooved the feel for defining the dread—
To choose from one choice,
The choice not to choose—
Left me suspended at the edge of myself,
Clueless
Glueless
Save for my shoes

Christopher M. Murray

Thunderstorm

The thunderstorm came in the middle of the night.
It rumbled and rained and caused great fright.

The lightning flashed brightly and lit up the skies,
And when I tried to watch it, it blinded my eyes.

The rain pounded the windows and roof so loudly,
That no one in the town could sleep very soundly.

The wind blew and howled and whistled through the trees,
It sounded like a banshee riding on the breeze.

My dog shook with fear at the foot of my bed,
I calmly tried to soothe him by patting his head.

When the clouds broke and I saw the moon beams,
I was able to sleep and have sweet dreams.

Shaun Reale

The Night And Day

At dusk the comets brush their hair
A thousand strands of golden flare
They wash the sky in orange hues
And paint deep purples, rose, and blue
And the sun in rage shall sink away
To flee the night and search the day
Stars bathe the earth in silvery light
The welcoming of "Moons Dark Night"

The earth shall open wide her heart
And let flow the sound of chipper larks
Bidding welcome to the sun again
Outstretched arms, letting all in
The stars are blinded by white and blue
The sky unfold's, the sun shines through
The flowers sway amidst the winds
The trees will stretch their leafy limbs...
And glory to the morning flies
O'er oceans blue and mountains high

Raquel Williams

The Creator Wisdom

Profound wisdom of God remaining long while
Job learned quite well through torturous trial
Where were you Job when the Morning Stars sang?
When I set bars and doors for the waves?

Where is the way light dwells, and is parted?
A way for the lightning of thunder—water divided?
Who gendered the hoary frost of Heaven?
Who can number the clouds in wisdom?

Can you stay the bottles of Heaven
Hunt prey for the Lion, provide for the Raven?
Do you know the time of wild Goats even?
Can you bind sweet influences of Pleiades?

Do you know the ordinances of heaven
And set the dominion in the earth?
Can you guide Arcturus with his sons
Bring forth in season Mazzaroth?

Did you give wings unto the Peacock?
Does the Hawk fly by your wisdom?
Does the Eagle fly by your command?
Tell me Job, tell me if you can.

Margaret R. Nuner

Street Crossing

Oh the sights you see when you cross the street
Not in a car, but on your feet.

The other day as the sun shone bright
The rear of a woman was struck by the light
The pants she wore were see through white
but the panties beneath were red.
I blinked my eyes and turned my head
And looked again at the woman ahead.

She didn't know or she didn't care
that the sun would show up her underwear.

I wondered whether she would laugh or cry
If she knew why heads turned her way,
But then again, she might have said
You've just made my day.

Rachel P. Levin

The Precious Tree

Life is like the barren of a tree.
It must be watered and loved for it to breath.
As with life, it must be filled with knowledge and truth.
Knowing is not just for learning, it's the key to the root!
For nothings more powerful or more profound,
than the root of the tree that's beneath the ground.
Just like in our hearts there is a hole;
A place for secrecy————which is our soul!
For we humans think life is less than free,
so unlike the precious tree.
To live we humans must give our all,
no matter the size, great or small!
As for the tree; the choices are none,
because we humans take 'till they're all gone.
A necessity in life that we must bare
is The Precious Tree we take from here.
The moral of this poem is plain to see,
that nothing compares to The Precious Tree.
They stand on this earth so tall and proud;
just to be conquered straight to the ground!

Kenna S. Senn

Civilization Fading

The carnival triumphantly begins,
Gradually mixing rain, thunder and light,
As children's screams foreshadow our coming plight.
Civilization fading.

Fans wildly cheer for football and the bullfight,
As desperate ghetto dwellers pray to survive another night.
Crime, drugs, guns and unprotected sex.
Civilization fading.

Politicians promise but never deliver.
Eloquent words that suddenly cause us harm,
As third world nations gather nuclear arms.
What goes up, must come down.
Civilization fading.

A mission to encourage education and the arts.
Would be an appropriate place to start.
Why are we waiting?
Civilization fading.

Andrew O'Rourke

Home

Homes are in near and far off places
Each with different forms and races,
Some are built on lucky street
And some on streets where poor folk meet,
But it doesn't matter 'tho poor or fare
They're just the same if love dwells there.

Home is where your loved ones dwell
And you feel secure for all is well,
A place that make you feel glad inside
And home is where deep peace abides,
Home always draws you at close of day
With joy and comfort that's home I'd say.

Home is where prayers are said
And where God's word is often read,
Here children are taught the right from wrong
And grow up into good men and women strong,
For God's blessing rests on the home you know
And you'll find homes the same where ever you go.

Home-it's not in the building-it's just in the heart
And it's always from love that a home must start.

Mada D. Rhea

Rainbows

Rainbows, a beautiful sight
Fill the sky with colorful light.

This beautiful object will sometimes appear
You could be far away or very near.

Red, orange, and yellow are a few colors of the rainbow.
Others are violet, green, blue, and indigo.

Rainbows can be seen sometimes after stormy weather,
The best time for rainbows to form together.

Sometimes two colors can look like the color pink
But you have to look fast because sometimes they will go by
in a blink.

Sometimes after a rainbow has come together
It seems like it has been there in the sky forever.

A mystery a rainbow is known to hold
At the end, a pot of gold.

Rainbows are astonishing, beautiful, and rare
And if you look long enough one might appear in the sky
somewhere.

If this is a sight you think you'll adore,
Glance outside sometimes and observe some more.

Renee Cox

I'm Different

I look at myself and find my flaws,
my face, my hips, my stomach
I paint my nails and always wear make-up,
but there's still that different person underneath
My family thinks it's just because I'm thirteen
but I've always felt this way
My grade point average is 4.0,
But I don't understand
On the outside I'm a person who blends in with the crowd,
but once you know me, I'm a quiet little girl
I went to a therapist for my parents' divorce,
it didn't help at all
My brother only adds to my difference,
he makes fun of it
I've lost all of my friends,
and have trouble making new ones
Maybe I'm not different from the rest of the world,
Maybe the rest of the world is different from me.

Sara Kramer

Between Two Ghosts

My window wanes westward
toward the Gansevoort Pier
where Herman Melville labored
nineteen spirit-crushing years
inspecting what-not on that dock
that bares his icy mother's name

For daring sea-dreams
Herman Gansevoort was mocked
quite penniless
like Ishmael defamed.

Down the cruel winter block and shiver
Past Hudson, Bank Street and Bethune
The Bar: where Dylan Thomas hurled his silver
Discus at our grime-black moon...

Of two fine lyric voices
One was sung before he died —
The second: tethered by the Gods
To witness

From the Other Side

M. Seton

The Mother's Tongue

In the midst of it all is the mother's tongue. Making and molding with such power. In the midst of the air, the trees, the flowers and the breeze is the mother's tongue. Through words of wisdom, words in song. The Lullaby's and the words of pressing on. The mother's tongue keeps making and molding with such power.

The mother's tongue proclaims liberty and identifies races, promotes her own opinion, beliefs and values. An invisible force making and molding with such power. Don't sleep in the dark! Never jump over a broom. Be heard and not seen, always clean up your room. Don't hit on the girls, always say please and thank you. The mother's tongue making and molding with such power. With power and authority, sometimes negative and sometimes positive, the voice of the mother's tongue is heard. The impact is real making and molding with much power!

Gloria Oshadipe

"Live Happily Ever After"

When "Once upon a time..." seems "Long ago and far away,"
And you pray your prince will come, preferably today;
A ripe, poisoned apple is poised near your face,
And old, dirty rags have replaced that golden lace;
Your glass-slippered feet are also cold and wet,
And you and fairy godmother haven't ever met.

Heed this advice and happiness companions you along,
Or else you'll find upon your lips a different, bitter song:

"Live happily ever after." That's all you need to do.
Yesterday will be today; your prince will come for you.
From poisoned apple to ambrosia, the gods' sweet delight,
Clothed in silk and satin showers, you're suddenly a sight,
For sore eyes, but not sore feet, your glass slippers fit,
And fairy godmother does the rest, every little bit.

And so you see the path is clear to happiness and peace.
Sing and all your troubles flee, like elusive, golden fleece.
And do not pout and say with doubt you've tried this once before.
Stop living in reality; it's always been a bore.
Fairy tales exist and, thus, life, you will find,
Is made up less by the fruit, but much more by the rind.

Patrick David Preston

Changing Seasons

Trickles of water slowly seeping down the hill and
over the rocks. Whatever are you doing, running away
from life? I hear your voice echo through the trees.
No, you say. "I am making something of myself,
winter is when my beauty shines."

See my long flowing tresses, how they sparkle
and glow in the afternoon sunlight. I am water
frozen in infinity. Never will you see beauty like
this again, for I am rare, just one of a kind.

Be still! At this moment time has no meaning.
Breathe in the fresh, cool air, relax against the pine. This
space is for you alone, remember it forever. Soon the warm,
gentle winds of spring shall come, I will become part of
the nearby creek, watering the wild flowers.

Don't grieve for me now, this is not the end, for
I have great plans. Next year at this same
bluff, I shall reappear more magnificent than ever
to charm and enchant you.

Nola Gorges

On The Edge

I sit upon the edge of the forest, an edge created by man.
I feel the concrete pathway that leads to nature, a pathway
    made by man.
I see the death of a tree, a death created by man.
I see the wall of foliage in front, a wall of brick behind, brick
    made by man.
I hear the birds chirping, disturbed by the buzzing of a fan, a fan
    made by man.
I feel nature's tears dropping upon my head, tears of acid, pollution
    made by man.
I feel chills from the coldness, away from the heated buildings, heat
    made by man.
I observe nature's rebirth, reincarnation, death turning to life, and
    old becoming new, all without the help of man.

John Waterman

Peace

Once you embrace the moment
Where worries, cares, and toils evade
You have encountered serenity.
And if ever obtained, your life shall never be the same.
To some this state is embellished in having riches,
But to most others the joy of inner tranquility suffices.
Can contentment be found by indulging in acts or deeds
That momentarily give pleasure?
I think not, peace surpasses the mere
Temporal moments that we partake.
The instance when mind, body, and soul
Seize solitude, the pinnacle of utter bliss,
You have passed from existing to solace.

Tonya N. Tait

Love...

What love is, or What is love?
Not lust, Not sex,
But love from the heart,
True within, true without,
But there never is that certain doubt,
Special something can't be explained,
Not bought with cash,
Nor stole with hate,
But true honest to God love,
Peace, and Happiness,
Never a broken heart,
Nor a sad and lonely face,
Because, True love is here,
I have never had this glorious gift,
But hope and pray and every wish
Is for this gift
Love, true love,
Pure and untouched,
The kind of love even fate can't mess with.....

Sheena Pasko

A Bugging Game

At 5 o'clock in the morning I look upon the wall
The roaches and the bedbugs were having a game of ball
The score was 6 to nothing, the roaches were ahead
A roach hit a home run and knocked me off the bed
When I opened my eyes
I was attacked by bunch of flies.
Cheering out loud
Because they were the crowd
They were going for my cookie crumbs that I had last night
I turned on my light to get the bug spray
Then I blew the game away

David Vereen Wright

Lifetime Symphony

They say I've three score years and ten
To dance and sing and play, and then
There'll be no dancing, singing, playing:
    I'd better add a bit of praying.

A lifetime symphony of living,
Weeping, laughing, taking, giving,
Must be compressed in these short limits;
    I'd better learn to count the minutes.

An hour to laugh, an hour for sorrow,
Today to work, and dance tomorrow;
A moment's pause for things sublime;
    I'll have to learn to ration time.

A song of three score years and ten
May be all right for many men,
But I've so many things in store
    I guess I'll need a long encore.

Arthur Taft

I Wish He Could Come Back

It was about four years ago
My great-grandfather passed away
It was very cold, the world was quiet
It was a very sad day

I miss having him around
He was really the best friend I had.
Just being around him brought joy to my life
He kept me really glad

Our whole family, has never been the same
Since the day he passed away
But I know he'll always be in my heart
Each and every day

It's a shame that everyone else gets to live
People on marijuana, acid and crack
I miss him very much
I wish he would come back

Aaron Daugherty

New Spirits In An Old Home

The old tire swing, gently sways in the wind.
The door swings open and shut, for the lock was never fixed.
The sun-bleached curtains twirl
as the evening breeze floats through the broken window.
The sun still rises and sets around this old abandoned house,
which some still call home.
If you listen closely you can still hear the laughter of children,
the clanging of cooking pans,
and you may smell the sweet, musty aroma of freshly cut hay.
As I sit under this old cottonwood, I remember taking refuge from
blistering summer days and cool quiet evenings.
And as I walk away I can feel its spirit calling me back.
But as I turn back I feel tears of sadness and joy swelling in my eyes,
and run down my sun-burned face.
For now I know a place where I can truly call home.

Adena L. Wilkens

Eternal Messenger

I'm a restless wind that stalks the summer nights
I'm the frosty dew on a moon-lit leaf
I'm the salty taste of a sometime tear
I'm a mossy brook lost in the heartland of winter
I'm a wisp o'smoke within a rainbow's eye
I'm the fleeting thought of a forgotten dream
I'm the laughing gull that soars high above the storm burnt skies
I'm a gentle rose that has no thorns
For I am truth

Gary R. Brakefield

Styles Of Life

I am smart and ambitious.
I wonder where life will take me as I grow.
I hear the praises of my parents, teachers, and peers for what I have
    done in my life.
I see the world becoming peaceful while war is trying to be driven out.
I want to help make the world safe for the next generation.
I am smart and ambitious.

I pretend that I am an elected official who does as much as he can
    for education.
I feel that people do not try to help their community and that
    they should.
I touch my schoolwork from long ago and I relive the fun I had then.
I worry that the children of this community will not get the
    education that they need in this school system.
I cry when others are hurt or killed because of senseless violence.
I am smart and ambitious.

I understand that I can do anything I want if I put my mind to it.
I say, "Work hard for your community and your community will work
    hard for you."
I dream that I will make millions of people happy someday.
I try to get into the best schools possible.
I hope that people will remember me when I am gone.
I am smart and ambitious.

Joshua French

The Heart Rules

Tears well up, my stomach hurts
Oh damn! It's happened again.
My heart has ruled, I told it no.
    Why won't it listen?

Stay impartial, that's the rule
Do your job and close the door.
Do what you can than walk away.
    Nothing more!

My heart has fingers, strong and sure
Reaching out to grab - No more!
But it persists - goes back for more
    Grabbing, clutching, reaching for?

The one who hurts and aches inside
And then rebels and acts real tough.
Crying loud from inside out
    The voice will raise, begin to shout.

Is this truly the job for me?
Sometimes I wonder who I am
To take such torment day to day
    I must be nuts - I think I'll stay!

Rebecca L. George

"The One"

Those laughing sweet eyes
that touching soft hair
The constant kind words
make me feel life can still be fair.

My talk with my best friend
her praise for my life
she thinks I'm a good friend,
a good Mother and a good wife.

I live with the criticism
each day is a flop.
With no one to turn to
just dry the teardrops.

The person who cares
may just be a dream.
But when he touches my nighttime
I can touch the stars and taste the streams.

Marcia L. Walters

"In A Sound Of A Cry!"

We're moving back,
Our ears from sound.
Silence now reigns,
Your Kingdom's found.

Going back we are in time,
Upwards, moving back, we climb.
Losing ground of all high,
In our kingdoms we die.

The heat is roaring,
So intense, it's roaring.
High above the great white clouds,
These clouds hide the sun in their shrouds.

Saying good-bye, I cry, I cry.
In 'my' kingdom, I'll never die.
He hath plans for me,
When the trumpet sounds, I am free!

Born again, fresh and free,
Sharing my love with all that's blee.
Knowing as I look into the blue skies,
All true love, it never dies!

Geoffrey A. Reed

Reflections

As I look back on life in general, the irony makes me shake my head;
remarks I said I wouldn't make, I realize now I've said.
Things I've declared I wouldn't do, no matter what the case;
are outstanding in my mind, because now they lead the race.
Don't ever say what your kids won't do, just because you hope
    it's true;
they will make a liar out of you every time, and if they don't, it's few.
If wisdom comes with age, I still don't feel too smart;
My fiftieth birthday is coming up, so, here's my wisdom to impart.
My number one rule is, there is never a time to be rude;
and anyone who does so, is the epitome of a fool.
They are to be pitied, and held at arms length;
their life must be empty, if they consider that a strength.
To tell a lie is useless, it will bring you to your knees;
and come back to haunt you, when you want a good night's sleep.
Take a tip from me, my friend, and watch out what you say;
because if you live long enough, you'll eat those words each day.
I thought my parents were ignorant, and in their ways set;
but the longer they are dead, the smarter they get.

Bobbie L. Harris

Our Daddy

You work so hard every night and day,
So we'll have toys with which to play.
There's so many wonderful things that you do-
Daddies like you are far too few!

You're loving and caring and you're always there,
Three wonderful traits that are really quite rare.
You try to teach us right from wrong,
And help us grow up to be big and strong.

You kiss our boo-boos and wipe away tears,
You take the time to calm our fears.
You hug us and kiss us and hold us too,
There's no one quite as special as you.

Though we sometimes cry and act real bad,
You're always so proud to be our Dad.
We're so very lucky - we know it's true-
You're the very best Daddy and We Love You!!

Cori Rhodes

An American Eagle

I am a mighty eagle, dancing in the air.
With wings spread out, high above my lair.
The symbol of America, one of great respect,
Demanding to be noticed, America's history,
To reflect.

Flying in high altitudes, full of beauty and grace,
Look at all the pictures, showing off my face.
I am an American Eagle, genuine and proud,
Showing off my colors, high above the clouds.

I hunt my prey with sharp eyes, and strike with
One mighty blow,
I always get my kill, no mercy do I show.
My beak is sharp and pointed, to a razor's edge,
For tearing and feeding, on a mountain ledge.

You just might see me flying, on those clear sunny days,
For I'm a national treasure, victory is what I say.
For I am the American Eagle, dancing in the sky,
Forever to be remembered, beyond the day I die.

David A. Winstead

Untitled

On the day of your birth, the angels sang,
The trumpets blew, and the Lord's Bell rang.
This is my life, my son, my soul,
The Lord had said, and with this goal,
There will be times of great joy and sorrow,
But listen to my whispers for all the morrow.
I shall never speak loudly, shout or yell,
For in this noise, you cannot hear my Bell.
I shall ring it once, in the morning as you rise,
I shall ring it twice, at noon, when you're wise
and again, I shall ring it thrice,
before you rest the evening with Christ.
I will be there for you, as I always am,
As I was for Joseph and each little lamb.
Todays a new day, beginning in time,
Yesterday's gone, a memory of mine,
Tomorrow's the future, I give over and over.
Walk with it gently and you will uncover,
My promise to you on your birth and everyday
That I will always love, my son, where he lay.

LaQuenta Turner

"The Stranger"

From out of the darkness came
    the tall, dark stranger with no name,
His eyes like the lightning flash,
    someone's life is soon to pass,
His laughter like the thunder rolls,
    the church bell slowly tolls.
Whose hand will he take, yours or mine?
    life's pattern has no design.
Live each day as though your last,
    each day, each hour goes swiftly past.
Enjoy each sunrise, each day to come,
    enjoy the night when day is done.
Tell the ones you love, hold dear ,
    the "I love you" they long to hear.
You never know as time ebbs past,
    for this day could be your last.
Whose time to go we'll never know,
    but when he comes you too will go
Back to the darkness from where he came,
    with the tall dark stranger with no name.

Letamae Bruce

Darkness

The vast celestial expanse exceeds my image of it.
Breathtaking
The dark misty immensity reminds me of an endless blanket
covering the city below.
Far-flung
Only faint silhouettes can be seen now as the day declines into night.
Enormous
The trees seem to have fallen into a trance until the faint
light of morning revives them.
Comprehensive

Serena Lynn Colwell

It All Starts With A Dream

It all starts with a dream...
Admiration,
The act we love to encounter.
Love,
The passion we desire most.
Desire,
The feeling that leads us to courageously change.
Courage,
The feeling we ask God to create.
Creativity,
Everyone is inspired differently.
Inspiration,
The feeling that gives us the will to accomplish.
Will,
Everything that shows us how to accept ourselves.
Acceptance,
The thing from others we could do without.
...and it all ends as reality.

Ann Jaksa

First Born

Sweet baby boy with eyes so blue
Do you know how much we love you!
You entered this world with a burst of splendor,
What a proud day for mom and dad to remember!
Have they checked all your fingers and counted your toes,
The size of your ears and the shape of your nose!
Does he look like you or look like me,
Such a beautiful baby it's easy to see!
How much love you have brought to your parents today,
I hope that it grows and continues always!
Bless you sweet baby Mom and Dad too,
May God up in heaven always smile down on you!

Janice Baldwin

Hobos

We used to say "I love you,"
Time moved past.
We didn't mean it:
Only want you, want your kisses,
Sweetness, desire, delirium.
When the clash came,
We were hobos, hopping trains that trailed away.
Time has passed.
"I love you" lives inside me,
Now "I'm sorry" doesn't matter.
Only that I am without you,
Wondering if the memories
Could be better than your kisses?

Pennee Struckman

Reflections

While reflections shatter from the glass.
Not knowing the future from the past.

Destiny shall be captured in my mind,
About how to live or how to die.
When every night to come before,
And every glass to hit the floor.

As the light from the moon that seems to shine.
And every thought that crossed my mind.
Reflections are always revealing to me.
For images are flashing moments of reality.

Nothing ever stays the same,
While remembering running through the rain.
Shredding mistakes made in the past,
As I sit here staring at the glass.

Creases of sorrow always seem to leave.
But are somehow built to echo obscurity.
Then every moment seems to fade away,
Just as fast as when it came.

Jacquilyn Ann Foster

"Break Up"

Sitting by the phone
Waiting all alone
Wishing you would call
Hoping that you know,
The love that I have for you will never die out
Because you're the one that I will always care about

Why don't you call
Why don't you see
How much you are hurting me
You say you love me
You say you care
But if you really did
I wouldn't be sitting here.

Dawn Kokolski

Monkeyshines

We went out walking - my dad and me.
I heard a noise and looked up to see
A little brown monkey looking down at me
With his tail around the branch of a tree.

He scratched his head as he looked at me.
I scratched mine, then I slapped my knee.
The monkey slapped his, then screeched with glee
As he swung to a lower branch of the tree.

I reached up high and touched the tree
To see if he'd reach down to me.
He touched my hand and I giggled with glee.
Kids and monkeys are full of Curiosity!!

Joan R. Pickett

Quest

Youth bleeds through fleshly cracks and fissures
Leaves permanent engravings
Crone years loom hollow
Foretelling all small endings
Wisdom, knowledge long sought, beckons
A wispy shade of distant lavender
Beauty and loveliness remembered
Entangled lie - sad the mirror's truth
Foreign tongue remains the future's language
Bog and bramble - the way to mystery
Now half refuted, half desired
Becomes the focus

Barbara Charest

One Knight With You

Ah, to champion you lady fair,
To take on all who would dare
Plan to do my lady harm
Should feel the strength in my arms
And taste the steel that serves just you
Or, myself, be run through
Again and again I'd face Death
By evil men or dragons breath
With broken lance I'd defend
Your honor till the bitter end
Suffer my lady? That I'd be near
The one my heart holds so dear
Arrows shafts are not as true
As the love,my Lady, I feel for you

Timothy T. Brown

A Tribute To The Afro-American Woman

She gave birth to the Afro-American race.
She walks with her head held high in all of her beauty and grace.
She is always there to support everything you do.
She is always there to say I Love You.
She is there through the good times and the bad.
She is there to comfort us when we're sad.
She works hard for us to survive.
She will always stay close and never say Good-bye.
She is the strongest branch of the family tree.
She is the greatest person there will ever be.
For all of her grace, beauty and strengths.
She deserves more than one day of thanks.
So now I salute you for everything you have done.
In the future the Afro-American woman will still be number one.

Cheryl Larea Chandler

What Is A Winner?

A winner is a person,
With very much at stake,
They work so very hard,
With destiny soon to make.

A winner strives to get better,
They practice day and night,
And when they are feeling down,
They make themselves fight.

A winner has determination,
Discipline and desire,
If you opened them up, there would be nothing
But a gleaming blaze of fire.

A winner wants perfection,
With everything they do,
You can never hold them back,
Oh, if you only knew.

So do you think that you're a winner?
Only you can see,
Just look inside of your heart,
It is a power that will always be.

Lauri Illy

Feelings

Remember all our silly games that we both enjoyed to play.
And what about our serious talks when you didn't know what to say.
Our dreams and thoughts can fall apart so fast as you well know.
So this is why I'm asking please don't let us go.
I lie awake each night and think that maybe you will change.
It really isn't very hard it's like tearing out a page.
Your lies and ways are driving us so far and far apart.
But maybe if you stop and change we could have a brand new start.

Marion H. Kendrick Saenz

Tired

Sometimes the horses just get tired.
Sometimes the buglers lips are cracked and dried-
Charge goes unsounded.
Sometimes the wagons don't circle in time-
The cavalry takes the wrong turn at the pass-
the ammunition runs out.
Sometimes the horses just get tired.
Sometimes the well runs dry.
Sometimes the seed rots in the ground-
fails to sprout.
Sometimes the farmer falls and breaks his leg-
the machinery doesn't work-
the money runs out.
Sometimes the farmer just gets tired.

Joseph A. Warren

Dead Of Night

Running in the cool dead of night
Looking up bathing in the moon's light
Feeling the cool dark dampness of the air
Free of despair
Watching the rustling of the tree leaves
In the cool...so cool breeze
The air is alive for sure
I feel it going through my pores
I am one with the ground
The wind
The sky
The river
The trees
Running free
No one knows that I am here
They look but they do not see
Only if they are quiet and is as one like me
Then they too can be running free
In the cool dead of night
Bathing in the moon's light

Altina Simons

Untitled

This is how my story goes
Nobody wants to be my friend
I know I will be by myself to the end.
No matter how hard I try.
I know it will always be, me, myself and I.
They don't want to be friends with me.
They beat me up and take my money.
I say to myself this is not a joke, but
They think it's funny.
"I am alone, I'm on my own"
I don't even have a girlfriend to call on the phone.
They say there are plenty of fish in the sea.
But they are all swimming, swimming away from me.

Clinton Culliver

Cry Of Death

I heard the scream of horror,
It looked me in the eye;
When I heard it loud and clear,
I was afraid I was gonna die.

The cry wouldn't go away,
It haunted me day and night,
It had scared me so badly,
my body was filled with fright.

As I sat there in the corner,
I was way too scared to run;
'cause the second I moved from that spot,
my life would then be done.

Eric Faitoute

"Life Worth Loving"

If you're wondering what I'm doing
If you're wondering where I am
Just close your eyes at anytime, and I will be your friend
If there comes a time, in your life, that you need someone to turn to
If there comes a time, in your life, that you need a helping hand
If there comes a time, at any time, you need someone to go to
Just close your eyes at day or night, and I will be your man
If you feel that life has got you down, and you've reached
    your last straw
If you feel that friends have let you down, and no one's left at all
Remember to close your eyes and clear your mind, of all things
    that have gone bad
And think of all the good times past, and all that make you glad
By touching others and spreading your love, you're someone
    truly unique
A person with a purpose in life, that's someone that I seek
See, I was just like you once, unappreciated, down and out
Then I closed my eyes, and cleared my mind
Then I knew what life was about

Charles G. Terzian Jr.

Does It Edify Or Bring Joy?

We all think we have something to say,
But will it edify or bring joy?

We want our opinions to be valued,
But do they edify or bring joy?

We need to express our "side of the story",
but does it edify or bring joy?

We say that our actions are justified,
but do they edify or bring joy?

We strongly suggest that our leaders
should do this or not do that,
But do these nuggets of wisdom edify or bring joy?

We implore others to listen to our complaints,
but do they edify or bring joy?

We question our Maker's right to do what He does,
knowing not that He truly is
the one who edifies and brings joy.

Thomesa L. Smith

In His Eyes

In His eyes I see softness, like the feathers of a dove,
In His eyes I see forgiveness, which He offers out of love.
In His eyes I see compassion, I see understanding there,
In His eyes I see a special love that He freely wants to share.
In His eyes I see hope, as we begin each day anew,
And if you will look into His eyes, perhaps you can see it too.

In His eyes I see a twinkle, like the stars that shine at night,
In His eyes I see a special glow, like the sun so big and bright.
In His eyes I see dedication, for He is my dearest Friend,
In His eyes I see persistence, for He will be with me to the end.
In His eyes I see a miracle, maybe this one is just for you,
And if you will look into His eyes, perhaps you can see it too.

In His eyes I see beauty, like a butterfly in flight,
In His eyes I see comfort, for the longest and darkest night.
In His eyes I see wisdom, for no one is wiser than He,
In His eyes I see a special love, which He gives to full and free.
In His eyes I see my future, which He holds now in His hands,
In His eyes I see the future of every woman, child and man.
In His eyes I see eternity, and I am so glad I do,
And if you will look into His eyes, perhaps you can see it too.

Cathie Ousley

Almost Amputee

I reach out my hand of friendship
I extend it far and often
But each time you sneer and bite

My pinkie bitten off in the letter I wrote
My next for the long distance call
My middle for my attempt to visit
And now...

Now I have only two appendages left
And I am saving them to raise them at you-
My first to point at you in disgust
And my thumb in gratitude for myself.

Maria D'Alessandro

A Place For Dying

Trapped by banks and the relentless pull of gravity,
Water loses all knowledge of the other senses.
While gnarled wails dissolve in white water,
The unthinkable secret is encoded by confusion.
Forever garbled by the nature of fluids,
The testimony plays victim to the mouth of the river.

Absorbed by the moon and sentenced to silence,
Cries of those stolen illuminate the night.
Foul scars blanket the surface,
Trophies to the one who put you there.
The unseeing eye inherits justice and consumes it as nourishment.
Lives give rise to the beacon of the crime.

Troubled by ignorance, the wind drools the words of a fool
And carries the scent of the ritual.
Reality whistles away through winter's landscape
Sending memories and mind fragments into the chaos of the atmosphere.
Inherent is the ability to cure blindness and mute,
Yet the wind loses focus, your identity is lost.

Daniel Balint

Where I'll Always Be

I placed my trust in you
   A precious gift I can't undo
Unknowingly you stole my heart
   And now I don't know where to start
To tell you how I feel
   I have never climbed this hill
This path I travel is new
   I have never loved anyone as I love you
My thoughts fly from my head
   When into the room you tread
This has never happened to me before
   I'm like a ship with no shore
Tossed about on an endless sea
   The one called love, where I'll always be.

Jamie Akins

"Listen"

Let us walk through the woods and listen to the trees,
As they talk to the skies so heavenly instilled above us.
Be still and listen to the quietness of it all,
As we join in the sharing of God's creation surrounding us.

Feel the breeze flow through the blades of grass.
As we enjoy the solemnness of all the little creatures.
Look around and see it all changing before our eyes,
As we take in the breathlessness of each day.

Close your eyes and see the brilliance carved
around us by one.
Listen, it is simply a rare experience to feel
Such joy as a new day has begun. Listen.

Norma J. Johnson

His Gift

He comes to me in the mid of night;
   and comforts me with grace,
He holds me with his nail-scarred hands;
   and tells me of a place.

A place to where my savior lives;
   for there he wears his crown,
A place for where he waits for me;
   where happiness abounds.

To where a place my soul can rest;
   far beyond our eye,
A place to where our soul is best;
   for there his angels fly.

Joy and laughter appear as wings;
   where troubles not in mind,
Where life is renewed as flowing springs;
   for love is all we find.

So if you on the Lord rely;
   his sheltering wings is spread,
Comforting, peaceful sleep supply;
   God's angel at your head.

Elizabeth N. Stanley

The Fool

Is reality but a dream?
Is life but a lie?

Do we awaken to a world that's real,
or do we create its existence in our sleep

Are we awake in our reality,
or is love and life,
nothing but a dream?

If so,
then in my reality,
my love I gave to you,
and from this love, a child was born.
A beautiful child!

How could this not be reality!

There are, so many rules to this game!
So many games, in each rule.
Am I but a fool,
to assume, this reality,
or am I a fool to think I am dreaming?

Seema Malhotra-Fernandes

My Danny Boy

Danielle said, "I'm moving." And asked,
   "Would you take my cat, for I have to go alone?"
Reluctantly, I agreed, but I thought it would be
   All right to give you a home.
I named you Danny Boy; you were so sleek and handsome,
   I knew you would bring me joy.
And that you did, for the next few years;
   Then one day I noticed you weren't breathing right.
My eyes filled with tears—
   The doctor told me you were a very sick cat.
"I'll do all I can," he said. Then a phone call came
   And I knew you were dead.
I asked the question, "Why?" The answer never really came.
   I am left here to cry; but I realize no one is to blame.
You came into my life because you needed a home.
   You came into my heart because I dared to love you—
Now you are gone.
   My home is empty; my heart is sad,
I lost the best little friend I ever had.

Judy L. O'Neal

"To Psychobabblers"

Doctor, doctor - listen to what I have to say
Don't put me in a neatly labeled box-please-not today

Yes - my story you have heard before
From so many who have walked through that door

I speak of pain in my life - here and there
meanwhile - searching your face - wondering -
do you really care?

Do you hear me - me - not just the words I speak
or am I just another - emotional freak

I have no degrees upon my wall
So in your presence I might feel very small

Yet I come to you - fear as I may
because in this pain - I can no longer stay

So I trust you - and vulnerable I become
and even pay you for this - quite a large sum

But remember, my friend, if you should ever
be tempted to look down at me
that in this very same place - except for God's grace -
you too could be

Nickie Danison

On The Death Of My Husband

What should I say; what can I write
About the cherished memories of our fifty three years together?
That was the happy time when we were
Constant comrades in a pure married bliss!
I wish that joy was everlasting: Nothing lasts forever.
Thank God for those fifty three years.
To the unknown and the great beyond -
Wherever that is, wherever you've gone,
I wish you had asked me to come along!

Did you like death more than everything else?
Did you love him more than life, - or me?
Why, oh why, when he beckoned, you waited not
To tell me that you were leaving me,
Leaving all of us for good?
A man of science that you were,
And with an inquisitive intellect
Maybe you went to meditate and solve
The inexplicable mystery of Death.
Perhaps you are now trying to find
A scheme to ponder on - Farewell.

Razia Ishaq

Their Banner At Their Head

Deep in the shadows on the hill,
when all is calm, dark, and still,
all alone but for the moon,
in silence, watch. And very soon
come marching the men of a lost brigade.

In elegant brass their cavalcade,
boys who died for freedom's reign,
for their country's liberty gain.
Carrying at their column's head
the banner for which they are dead.

The colors which meant more than self,
a cause of pure and priceless wealth,
one which they sought to leave for kin.

May tyranny never need to be fought again
for a land fresh and new,
over which star and stripes blew.

Clare E. Lyon

Untitled

I don't know how to say what I know I need to say
this isn't easy for me but somewhere along the line
someone has to say it.

We were the best, no one can deny that
when we were in love and when we made love
nothing could stop us.

We did everything with a passion and a zest
that has been unsurpassed in my life.

But through the years we've grown up
and grown apart
and as much as we'd like to change that
we can't.

So I think the time has come
for us to take separate courses
and try to move on - although I know we won't forget.

And in the long run
The tears we shed and the pain we feel
will diminish and bad memories will depart.

But our love will always remain.

Jeri Cohen

Untitled

INTO THE EYES OF THE INNOCENT
Visible is the damage he has done
tear stained faces
wasted are the days of salvation
sough was the redemption of life
HERE STANDS THE BEGINNING
second chance come not once
the circle repeated, yet not come full
lifelong dreams of righteousness
aspiring to the nightmare of those mirrored
stranglehold on the breathe of happiness
HALF HIS HEIGHT, TWICE HIS SANITY
of one they stand
a man yet to come
a father continuing to learn

Gabren-Taylor King

The Lost Ghost Town

The lonely, ebony night wept crystal tears on the snow-touched
    ghost town;
So long had it been mourned. In its own tears could it have drowned,
But in all misery prevailed, twas the winds that blew them away;
Why, Hope shall never come here, melancholy forever stay.
The sympathetic moon shone down on the sea of withering grass,
Shining on its tiny icicles, wishing hope could ever last.
For a moment, the whole ghost-town seemed to die under
    the fading light,
And so slowly it had turned into a ghostly pallor white.
A cold susurration whispered and the houses began to creak
as if there was something it was fearing;
What could provoke such fear on a thing so sad and bleak?
The answer blew in the Northern winds, for they were fatefully nearing.
The winds' monotonous wails came reverberating in
Followed by the winds themselves, stronger than they had ever been.
Taking down everything in sight,
Leaving behind littler and littler—dying down the rays of light.
For sadly, Day and the Night both cried here;
Until all was lost in spite of fear.

Preshona Ghose

441

The Garden

I know where there's a garden
That's been still for quite a while,
It's in a little village
By a house without much style.

That's where my friend would spend time
In the early dawn of morn,
All clad in sweats and overcoat
To keep his body warm.

He had such perfect plants there
They were many and so neat,
And more than once he brought some
For my family to eat.

He told me that he raised them
So he wouldn't get so bored,
But little did he realize
That they truly pleased the Lord.

And now he'll tend God's garden
'Cause his toil was not in vain,
You see, it was an internship —
He'll garden once again.

Eileen Bahlmann

God's Awesome Creations

I feel the sun beating down on my back.
It is hot and bright.

The days are hot and the nights are cool.
The grass is green and full of life.

The birds sing and squirrels play,
    and I sit back and catch some rays.
I take a dip in a nice cool pool,
    and practice my back stroke for a while.

A butterfly lands on an elegant rose,
    and I watch it as it opens its beautiful wings.
The day drags on,
    and the sun slowly creeps toward the west.

I lay in the cool grass,
    and think of how wonderful life is with God's
    awesome creations.

Nathan C. Washington

Illusion

Greet the morning, as the sun peeks
to kiss the dewy cool grass.
Achieve unity to feel magic.

Muscles contract as energy explodes,
bright sparks dim the sun's glow.
Lightning flickers off fingertips.

Balance as if soaring on Pegasus' wings,
through amber clouds loved by the sun.
The fantasy castle is nearing fast.

Heart throbs, pulse races,
beads of sweat trickle.
Savor every adrenalin pump.

Close eyes, spread arms out
and take hold of the moment.
Allow control to relent.

Feel the heat, invite ecstasy in
wash away doubt or fear, let go let go.
We have arrived.

Sherrie L. Darling

Nothing To Write

I'm suppose to be writing a poem
Although I'm not sure how.
The words aren't coming
Because I don't know what to write about.
A teacher told me once just to write
So that's what I'm doing,
Trying to put something on paper.
Red, black, yellow are the colors on this table
Oh! That's not quite right.
Something else please follow.
I hope you don't mind that it is short
Because I have about 10 lines
And I don't have anything else to write.
That's not true, I seem to be on a roll
This isn't so bad, it may eventually be fun.
I won't stop here, I'll just keep rambling on.
I can't keep saying that I have nothing to write,
Because almost 20 lines later I'm still not done.
So even if I don't have something to write about
I have this subject, nothing to write.

Richelle T. Sanchez

The Town

The dark black sky
Is now filled with stars
As a neon moon shines high above
The lights of the city have all been turned off
And the streets are silent and blue
For the town is asleep

The noises have stopped
And no one is to be seen
The crickets are singing their lullaby
For the town is asleep

Soon the sun will rise
And the town will awake
As the quiet will cease
The town will no longer be asleep

Alnee Rae Baldwin

A Grandma's Prayer

Debbie is a tiny girl with eyes the bluest blue,
She's twined around her Grandma's heart, this little girl of two.
I see a tiny baby face grow wiser with each day,
And tiny baby steps more sure as she scampers on her way.
Gentle God, my heart implores, please take her hand in Yours,
Surround her with Your grace and truth, the key to Heaven's door.

Each time she scampers through the door a miracle's performed
This old house a castle, each shabby chair a throne—
Her laughter that of angels echoing 'round the room.
And when she's gone the house is still, the beauty seems to dim,
Not to shine so bright for us until she comes again.

How was it here before she came?
I can't remember now.
But thank you Lord for sending her
And trusting us to see that she's as pure as when she came,
When she returns to Thee.

Once again I ask you Lord, guard this little one.
Help our girl grow up to be good and strong and pure.
In Your special Grandma file keep this Grandma's prayer.

Alice Phillips

Thoughts

Does he ever think about me in middle of the night?
Or in the early morning when the sun is shining bright?
Or in that Mansion window with the Crystal Chandelier,
all he has to do is whisper and I will gladly be near.

Does he ever think about me, does he even know I care?
Does he know about the nights I've spent wishing I were
there? I'd wrap my arms around him and hug him through the
night Oh how I long to see him, but it wouldn't be quite right.

Does he know my heart is breaking, and the tears stream
down my face? Or is this a reflection of a vision in his space?

Does he know that I do love him, in my very private way?
Does he know that there are many words that I can never say?

Does he know the walls are hiding him from the love that
comes his way? Does he know I touch him with my mind and
that will have to do until he lets that wall down and
lets my love flow through.

Linda Barrett

Feel The Pain 2

Feel the pain as it flows through your body
Feel the pain as it consumes your soul

Feel the pain as you weep
Feel the pain as you sleep
Feel the pain as you suffer through your darkest hour
Feel the pain as you dream your nightmare
Feel the pain as you begin to rage
Feel the pain as you turn the page
Feel the pain as you set yourself free
Feel the pain and remember
Feel the pain and forgive

James S. Wilder

Yesterday's Child

Where is the child of yesteryear
Who stepped on bees and shed a tear?
Who ran barefooted in the snow
And didn't know the meaning of "No!"

Who climbed out the window after dark
To catch fireflies in the park.
Who loved all animals, climbed tall trees-
Remember how simple life seemed to be?

No locks on doors, windows opened wide.
No one to fear, no need to hide.
A child could be what she wanted to.
No doubts to inhibit or bother you.

The years go by and doubts accrue.
We play at games and know we do.
Where is that child who used to be?
I think she still lives inside of me.

Ann R. Steinert

Untitled

There are no words to convey,
just what is in my heart today.
The aches and sorrows within my breast,
are far too much to try to express.
The loss of your son and godson to me
is now with God forever to be.
We did not have time to stay our goodbyes,
for God felt it was time for his son to arise.
I pray with time, God will ease your pain,
So that you may find peace in this life again.
Someday in God's heavenly house you will meet,
and together find happiness with your lives then complete.

Valda Mudge

Love's Compensations

When they crowd you off the sidewalk,
  Nearly push you in the street,
I just wonder what they're thinking,
  Fellow travelers that I meet.

It may be they're not a-thinking,
  Not intending thus to cheat.
Doesn't matter. I still have
  All the world... and I have feet!

Some will hurry right on past you,
  Never speak and never smile.
Doesn't matter. There are others
  Who will stop and chat awhile.

Matters not how others prosper,
  I have some things they have sought:
Attitude that's right, contentment,
  Gained by love — not money-bought.

If a white man ... black man... hate you,
  Multitudes of both still love.
All of life by love is balanced,
  Compensated from above.

Pauline W. Hill

The Rainbow

The last glistening raindrops have fallen,
The sun reappears in the sky;
Earth's freshness and beauty surround me,
A rainbow blossoms forth up on high.

Dear Lord, where does Thy rainbow end?
Does it reach to Thy heavenly gate?
Does it end where eternal peace still reigns,
With the solace we sorely await?

I'm not searching for the pot of gold,
Believed to be at the rainbow's end;
You've given me many treasures here below,
As along life's pathway I wend.

Will You be waiting at the rainbow's end,
When life's clock ticks its final hour?
Will You be waiting to bestow upon us,
All the blessings within Your power?

It's a symbol of hope for we mortals below,
This arc You paint on a canvas of blue;
A reminder that 'though to-day clouds hover,
Tomorrow the sun will shine through.

Bettie Duda

"My Father's Pride"

This I write is something new
because it is for all of you...
You are the brother, a very good friend,
after the college days came to an end...
You are the brother who saved my life,
when all I could see was anger and strife...
You are the brother who spurred me on,
to look ahead and keep growing strong...
You are the brother I never knew;
the years brought us closer, I found you were true...
You are the brother who touched my soul,
your song and your dance helped me to be whole...
You are the sister, one whom I love,
I see in you hope, you are white as a dove...
You are the sister who is so like me,
when you open your heart, I can really see...
You are the sister, sincere and strong,
always there for me to lean on...
You are the children, growing and free—
Your laughter and loving help me to be me.

Laura Lee Brownton

Sister Love

I grieve that I've lived without a sister.
We never swapped turns at doing the dishes.
We didn't pull wishbones to make our wishes.
This sister I never had, I've missed her.

So many things we never could do:
We didn't tell stories under the covers;
We couldn't share secrets about friends and lovers;
We couldn't trade clothes, old or new.

My sister wasn't there standing by
When I was afraid to try new things.
We didn't ride seesaws; nor, on the swings
Holding hands, let the old cat die.

You who grieve today in a loss that's fresh,
Whose lives have been touched by a true loving sister.
Know better than I what it means to have missed her:
Your wound bites achingly deep into flesh.

Someday you'll know you can be glad.
(Though poisoned now by death's sharp dart)
Sisterly love has warmed your heart.
You grieve for a sister that you had.

Rima M. Segal

AB 184

Pornographic papers can be bought with three or four quarters.
Our children are buying them, much to our horror.
God, forgive me for sitting idly by and shutting my ears and eyes to
victims of sexual crimes.
Rape, child molestation, sexual abuse - when will it stop?
  What can I do?
I can write one letter and send it to a committee.
It might get to the assembly and then I'll have to write many.
And, if by God's grace, it goes to the Senate, I will praise God,
  and get my pen out.
I will write my senator, and the governor, and (with lots of prayer)
a new law will save people from lifetime scars.
God, will You raise up others who will slay this giant?
Smut peddlers, the A.C.L.U., they're all against this.
Will you raise prayer warriors, callers, letter writers - Christians
  who are willing to be pornography fighters?
Just a few minutes, and just a few quarters may save a child from
  sexual horrors.

Ruth Van Gilder

Surrealism

Friends, family, cancer, surgery
All together, all separate
  misery
Frightening, surreal, this can't be happening
Familiar children's chant:
Who me sir, not I sir!
Flash, it's over, flash
my old self again, I think not
Don't panic! Don't panic!
on the verge of screaming
Keep breathing, keep breathing
Can handle this
  Death, dying, funeral
  overwhelming, visceral
  Black, everywhere
  clothing, earth, underneath
  Please no death wreath
Is this my last waking hour
I'm scared, they can't put me
  "under"

Vicki Maria Carter

Do You Know?

You know me, or just know my name?
If you did know me, you'd say, "she's insane."
But for what reason makes you think you know so much about me?
My sister, my brother, let me explain more clearly.
My name, my game, it's not what you think.
So all that garbage you heard, let if flow down the sink.
Let it be known, let it be told.
She might be short, but she's very bold.
Smart by choice, strong with words.
Voices opinions, some times unheard.
In a world of her own, she has a special glow.
I know who she is.
But...Do You Know?

Venitia Malika Ford

Seeing For The First Time

Warm sun once seen before
Hazed now by drops of rain
Shall be felt again
Or an illusion just the same

Shall I wish the rain to stay
For fear the light has faded
Or could this be the way
To view a new one created

Rain does stop through time alone
Leaving blessed hope to grow
Envisioning the flower of tomorrow
But always remembering the warmth felt once before

Tessa Ploesser

Aluminum

I see into you, tell me what I am, tell me what I see,
  when you are everything.
Reflect who I am when the lights go out to keep me from disgrace.
Show me things I'll show no one else where no shadows know distaste.

You saw into me, told me what I'm not, told me what I need,
  but you weren't anything,
rejected me when you felt shutout, and never tried to take my place.
Reactions killed me as I loved you, you only saved your face.

I've seen through you, tell me what you are, tell me it can't be
  that I see everything.
The life I saw in you fades along with me, exhuming long dead
  hate, and breeding animosity.
So sink me in your depths, safe on the other side, pretending
  not to know that you're the reason why.

All I saw is what you want to be, but that is all gone away.
Your perfect world is a perfect tomb for me,
I'll resurrect myself today.

Sean McCarty

Untitled

What kind of light can we shine with the insecurity of our emotions.
How can we embrace happiness if it doesn't exist within.
Why is one wiser than another if they aren't the same person.
It's not to touch, or to see, or to smell.
It's to feel, the feelings that exist in all of us,
but are too scared to reach into the inner soul.
It's the courage we all have to express ourselves.
It's the way we make a place for ourselves in the cruel
world, in dimness or shine we all relate in a
way no one can explain. Could it be the fear inside
each one of us, like a big bubble waiting to burst, into
a cloud of dust awaiting to dissolve into the air
and leaving the darkness of our shadows behind,
to be washed away by the rain.

Erin Dignan

The Bird Of Death

I saw the Bird of Death,
it sat on my window
singing a song of pain and sorrow

I saw the Bird of Death;
as our eyes meet, my heart skipped a beat;
my soul darkens like the black night

Yes! I saw the Bird of Death
Bringing the news of a lost one,
whose journey had just begun
I saw the Bird of Death
and the sounds of thunder, cracking in the cloudy sky,
but I kept searing the bird in its eyes;
and my only question to it was why?
The Bird of Death reply: "Why ask why?"

Derrick R. Trim

"Shrapnel"

These words of hate
pour like an aged wine,
from my hand
that holds this mediocre invention
we beings dubbed a pen.

The veins in my arms,
nearly splurge out
from beneath the callused flesh
that clings to the bones of my
freshly numbed body.

Pools of ink,
now soil the immaculate paper
as the pressure of my grip forces the inner liquid
to spew controllably outward.

Can you feel the what I mean?

And I am only sorry and apologetic,
that this same hand
that grasps this materialistic instrument
cannot cling and leach to your heart.

Would the outcome be the same?

Laurie L. Brabec

Portrait Of A Gold Hour

The white sun went gray four times to turn gold.
In an arena of air with lovers to my right,
An empty robe of copper leaves grew wilder.
The same wind wild clouds smeared the day gray for miles.
I saw the same rag of white floating in light
And the gray moved, deep as God, to the end of the day.
The same gray sky was organizing a wild ruby light.
This was a very strong time.
I saw the same wild white cloud float in midnight blue up high.
The same strength of an arched throat and the wind on a neck;
The same ache of architecture when the trees strain
To move their strength in the air.
Long gold arches tangled in black semicircle branches.
Even the green statue across the street went silver as leaves
Way over where I began to get cold on the stone wall
In love for miles, ignored by the lovers to my right.
Until I could see why trees believe they float
Even in the street.

Mia Albright

Mister Supervisor

The supervisor's career
His name Mister Steer

His game is golfing
And he does a lot of talking

To co-workers racing
To get through their tracing

He sometimes gets moody
With supervisor duty

He once was a hub hog
Working like a big dog

Who kept on striving
And went into driving

He is a family man
We do understand

Not a high roller
But a more than average bowler

When it comes to spending
He does little bending

He knows we're conscious of tracing clarity
In spite of our sometimes jocularity

Deborah R. Williams

A Mother's Love

What can compare to a mother's love
for the tender child she bore?
Nine months of carrying, a lifetime of care.
Countless hours of up all night and nerves worn and torn.
A mother's love we can never repay.
Until the day she dies we owe her our
respect and admiration in every way.
From dusk till dawn her labor is never done-
pampering and cherishing the fruits of her womb.
A mother's love is unconditional, unrestrained and pure.
Next to God's love, mother's love is the only holistic love we know.
Even when we grow old and grey our mothers
want to be there always willing to show us the way-.
Never growing weary incase we go astray.
God bless mothers and their love.
They are wonderful gifts from above.
As they grow in age they may grow in grace.
Hoping they all live long lives.
You are our constant friend in life's race.

Darwin Lowe

Creepy Melody

As the dark night leaps upon us,
like a tiger upon its prey,
A strange, creepy melody begins to play.

But don't listen to the sound,
for it is told
that you will grow old,

So run and grab your children,
and send them off to bed,

For when the sound comes,
it will wake the dead.

Brandy Simpson

445

Dangling Key

What key on my key chain opens Future's door?
There are so many on my chain that it would take a lifetime to try
    them all.
Some people question what the future holds, and some take each day
    as it comes.
I am someone who wants to know now.
Some say your future is already planned, and others say
    it's your own decision.
I am someone who wants to know now.
The keys to my future are supposedly in my hand for me to choose
    the correct key.
Some keys may be the wrong key to a certain door, and some are
    a perfect fit.
I don't want to try each key for that is eternity
I am someone who wants to know now.
The future, what a dismal picture of greys.
A hallway of doors, each locked with a different key to open it.
I don't have eternity to try each door
I am someone who wants to know now.
So many doors, I can wait for a few, but I can't wait to know about you.
I am someone who wants to know now.

   Amanda Joy Eberle

The Garden Of Life

Flowers start blooming when winter is done.
They grow in abundance with just water and sun.
Spring brings new life after winter is past,
Crocus start sprouting as they poke through the grass.
Daffodils show off their bright yellow petals,
Like soldiers in uniform, with their chest full of medals.
Forsythia, Lilacs and Tulips galore,
brighten our yards as they creep to our doors.

With care and attention all gardens will grow.
Weed them, care for them, their beauty will show.
A garden is a marriage of patience and care, cultivated with
love and kindness, the more flowers it bares.

As you enter your new life as Husband and Wife, think of your
Marriage as "The Garden Of Life."

   Shirley A. Smith

An Ode To Jordan

A child should have a future where he can run and play,
But Jordan only twelve years old, an infant he must stay.
A handsome little tyke who laughs and smiles all day,
Will never know the thrill of riding on a bike
Or ever give a hug to Mom or Dad or brother Doug.
He cannot walk he cannot talk, these things are locked inside.
He tries so hard to do them all for those who love and care.
He's filled with joy and happiness, at times it's hard to bear,
But as long as Jordan needs me I know that I'll be there.
Tomorrow is not promised us or any other day,
But this lad should have the right to a brighter day.
Each night as he lies sleeping, his dreams we cannot know,
I see an angel weeping, tears fall from the sky,
To seep down through the stars, for this child filled with love.
When he awakens to the sun, there's a rainbow in his smile.
There is sunshine all around him, so I think I'll stay awhile.
As long as I can be a part of his world and help him grow.
He has made my life worth living, this I surely know:
The love I have to share, I will give to keep that gleam alive,
In the eyes of a child.

   Phyllis R. Moss

"Touched By Love"

   Life can bring us pain and sorrow,
"but it can also give us the best of
    life, when we are touched by love."
Life is not easy to deal with, "but
    with love, hope, and understanding we
can survive, when we are touched by love."
   Life is precious and wonderful, "but
sometimes, destiny throws us a curve to
    See if we are strong enough to
survive, "but we can only survive when
    we are touched by love.
Life is anything you want it to be with
    the best of your desires, "but only if
the right path is chosen, because
    life is seriously splendorous, "for it is
a treasure lost at sea and it is
    found only when we are touched by
love," "for life is within the
    very depth of our souls.....

   Maria Laureano

Constant Companion Of Life

The mind is the perpetual abode of Joy and Sorrow,
A sole source for the salutary, serene morrow;
The switch to generate the inner spirit's ability
And oft a barrier to contentment, a ladder to anxiety
Making life cumbersome, weighty, hazy with perplexity
We inhabit the planet Earth that whirls around,
And for a tedious, life journey by nature bound;
To make it, less wearisome, there's a way that has been found,
And the right step to take one must precisely know
To direct the mind to proceed and directly go.
The prime point, to start is the promiscuous mind,
Where needless fear, doubts delusion one often find,
And hindersome, negative thoughts of perplexing kind
As they pile up, shovel and shove them far behind;
With prodigious, positive thoughts be alert to find
How to enslave the "Tricky Comrade" called the mind.
A steady mind, is the compass for the voyage bound
To make on Earth, the sojourn safe and sound:
Remember, to adhere to the way that's been found,
A diligent and determined mind will lead to reach the goal.

   Christina Rajadurai

A Game Of Life

Once you put your quarter in
your life has just begun.
You use the controls to play the game
and succeed until you have won.

For winning is the point at which
you have triumphantly reached your goal.
And everything you put forth in life
comes together to make you whole.

During the game you'll make decisions
that will affect how you play.
There will be some good things and bad,
that you'll learn from each and every day.

Once you've lived your life,
and your game has come to a termination.
The words Games Over appear,
no restart, just discontinuation.

   Jacqueline F. Thurman

The Cost Of Peace

With their villages, towns and farmlands destroyed.
Such great courage they found, every man, woman, boy.
As they marched through the village on down to the shore,
although ravaged and pillaged they still went to war.
Some held guns in their hands. Others knives, rocks and swords.
As they marched over land even some picked up boards.
Down sand dunes they came. Their objective in sight.
Although wounded and lame all were ready to fight.
The battle commenced with a thunderous sound, and became
so intense that blood covered the ground.
The screaming and wailing when they lunged with their knives.
Slowly prevailing, they fought for their lives.
As the enemy fled to their boats on the shore.
Leaving their dead and so many more.
With wounded just scattered all over the place.
So beaten and tattered, my God what a waste!
The battle had ended, the cries muffled now,
and they had defended their village some how.
But did either side win? So many lives lost.
It seems such a sin. Was it worth the cost?

Janet Naticchioni

The Jester To The King

This the Jester said to the King
"You hired me to present you with many a merry thing;
So I will do as you request
And entertain all of your wealthy guests.
Yet, do not forget that tragedy looms
Behind all of comedies' witty plumes,
And that under each tragedy there lies a joke
Writ in by the poets and simple folk.
You may laugh, Highness, as I tell you this
Comedy, like death, has a fatal kiss.
And now I'll begin my sorrowful jests,
And foresee a day when you laugh to death."

LeEtta M. Gross

My God

As I sit upon the cliff above the big wide sea with the waves
crashing up against the hard unmovable rock
I think My God is good to me.

He is the hard unmovable rock. He is the steady stream of light
from the big round moon above. He is strong when I need him.
He is the light to guide me when I am blinded by evil.

And as I sit and think these thoughts I notice how the sea
has calmed down. Its ferociousness is gone and it is replaced
by a gentle little splash against the rock. I must not forget the sea.

My God is like the sea. He is rough when he needs to be but gentle too.
"Yes" I say out loud, my God means everything to me.

He is in everything I love. So I say to you at last, If you
cannot find God in everything you love then my friend it is time
for you to figure out just how much your God means to you.

Andrea Strickland

Songs Of Heartbreak

I can hear the sad songs of heartbreak,
I can feel the pain and tears in each chorus.
I can sense the hatred and denial in each note.
The words tell of those who think they can't go on.
The blaming of themselves and others,
The trusting hearts that turn away from any trust at all.
The songs changing from strong and loud to weak and soft.
Each heart then cries itself to sleep and dreams of the way it once was,
Then wakes-up and realizes the pain is still there,
The next day, I can hear the sad songs of heartbreak.

Heather Roberts

In Memory — July 17, 1981

Leaves don't break when they fall.
Sky walks do.
Fallen leaves pattern soft, crunchy pathways
    through the park.
Sky walks no longer airborne maim, bury loved ones.
Perhaps we are not meant to walk in air,
But more humbly 'neath sky, amid leaves
    strewn softly at our feet.

Camilla Verret

Broken Promises

Why must I be in the middle of mommy's and daddy's
arguments, fights, and broken promises. They
think by splitting up, and shifting me place to
place they're doing it for my own good. They don't
realize my feelings, my needs, and my undivided
love, for both of them. I can't handle the
pressure of dividing my love between them during
holiday, vacations, or at any time.
"Oh mommy and daddy please understand me I don't
understand what I did to deserve your divided
love." Please don't break your promise to me
please love me as one person instead of the divided
I have become. Mommy and Daddy I will always love
you as one please do the same for me. I feel
trapped and forget whose turn it is to share my love with.

Nancy Newger

A Talk With Jesus

The beauty of life is all around, up above, below the ground.
I made it all, for all to see, just trust and believe in me.
The trees, the flowers, the sky so high, why oh why, did you
have to die? I died to save you from your sins, I died to set
you free. I want you to come home with me.....

You gave your life so freely, so forgiveness could be found.
I promise you dear Jesus, I won't let you down. You see,
your love, I gladly receive. But why, why did you have to
leave? I went away to glory, to build mansions on high, so
hush my child, do not cry....

I miss you so much, my heart is filled with woe. I wish you
could stay. Do you really have to go? Though you can't see
me, I'm with you everyday, so, the times you feel lonely my
child. Just bow your head and pray.....

Myrtis L. Price

"Assassination Of A Sniper"

He tries to kill anyway and anywhere;
but he'll fail 'cause God is always there.
He's got a plan and a gun, if he doesn't
watch out he'll be on the run. I'll get
you today or tomorrow, but he's forgot
that God is always pointing his arrow.

A sniper is keen and quick; no one knows
what makes him tick. So cold and calculating
in his mind, it's no wonder we can't catch his signs.
No more assassinations you snipers, 'cause the
traps you plot are nothing like a bite from a viper.
(Death)

Darlene Harris

Soul Visions

Spring time, where are you?
My Visions are clear,
But I look out my window,
And I see you're not here

I need the warm sun on my face,
Close my eyes and dream of a place,
Where there's dolphins at play,
Where my Soul is happy to stay

I want waves and blue water
To wash over my toes,
To cleanse my soul,
That only God knows

I want sea shells and sand
To put delight in my eyes,
Combine all these things,
My soul cannot help, but to rise

For Spring and Summer,
Brings the Soul back alive,
This beautiful season,
Entices my soul to survive

Regina McClure

Junesong

What can one say dear?
How should one cry?
What can we do now...?
Ah God.....O' my.

What's left to do now?
What's there to say?
We loved dear June,
And you stole away.

Clean up my household;
Touch your things there
It wasn't for nothing.
You seem everywhere.

Yet, all is so final
Plans never to be
Ausable Chasm
Love by the sea.

Nothing to do now.
Nothing but pray
So many in love
Have gone our way.

Mark C. Kennedy

You're Always There For Me

When I was but a child
You put me in clean clothes,

But when you turned your back
In puddles I would go.

And when I asked for water,
You'd even hold my cup.

You saw me through the stages
Of slowly growing up.

Whenever I would need you,
You were quick as 1-2-3;

And now that I am older,
You STILL are there for me!

I really love you, Momma,
And I hope you truly know

You'll always be real special
No matter where I go!

Kaye S. Morris

Vermont Meadow

Six Haiku
Corn tassels windblown -
Wave after billowing wave
Never reaching shore.

Dragonfly darting,
Near hummingbird hovering -
Helicopter style.

Around the meadow,
A turkey processional -
Grasshoppers look out!

Leaves softly rustling,
Children breathlessly alert,
Small snake slithers past.

Harvest-time gleaners -
Turkeys, crows join each other
Picnicking on corn.

Day ends, sleep for all,
Only insects still around.
Moonrise; bat swoops down.

Kit Hildick-Smith

Images

What's that image starring at me?
Hate, hurt, pain
No longer can I look at that image
What can I do?
Look deeper, to the heart
There you will see
Healing, love, trust
Just look past the image
Look deep inside the heart
There you will find,
Covered by the image,
All you have been looking for
And more

Shelly Roberts

Wonderful Things

Wonderful things are neat,
They are things you can't beat.

Like a warm bed at night,
As you drift off without a fright.

Strawberries in a summer breeze.
And the pollen doesn't make you sneeze.

Mom's hugs in the evening,
While I'm still home and breathing.

Drinking hot cocoa in the winter,
Without one little splinter.

These things are here,
They're everywhere.

Danielle Markham

The Face Of Love

I saw the face of love
As he laid sleeping late last night.
And though his face in shadow lay,
It was clear in evening's light.

For when I touched his quiet brow
To be certain of my vision,
His smile illuminated the night,
And the best of my decisions.

Danielle Malavade

A Sister And Her Baby

She is so much like you
Her hair in shining curls
from the waves washed in.
The sun stopping at the lines
where her swim suit had been.
It seemed the same sun, the same sand
I had seen you play in.
I wanted to hold time
before it slipped away again.
In her, I see you
And know if times when.
She is so much like you
your baby
who now has memories to lend.
so much the same feelings.
the same magic
as if now here then.

Deborah Wolstencroft Cooper

My Promise

Creator's power extended
Within your womb
Grew the overflow of love

Quivering vibrations
Welcomed the heritage
Of Heart and Soul and Mind

And so your hands began
Gently, quietly quilting
The patchwork of my life

Naming my puzzle
Grace and Truth and Strength
You bound each block with love

So don't you fear
As night draws near
Of the silence found at midnight

Life extended
Toil commended
I will take you in my arms

And I shall call you blessed

Lora St. Michell

My Front Yard

I sat down watching the
  leaves flow in the breeze.
I watched the trees wave
  in the wind.
I watched the sky form
  into a sunset of red, orange,
  yellow, green, purple, and blue.
I watched a star twinkle
  next to the crescent moon.
I watched it all,
  in my front yard.

Shannon Massengale

The Miracle Of Laughter

The feeling of laughter soothes
even the saddest of hearts.
The sound of laughter gathers
broken pieces torn apart.
The way that laughter reaches
a face to bring a smile.
Is the miracle that laughter teaches
forget your cares a while.

Alva V. Copeland

My Jewel

There it lay, reflecting the
glistening light of the sun.
A mother's farewell tear for loved one.

A sparkling jewel displaying all
the light of love held so dear
in the heart of a mother.

Oh, that I could capture that
radiant jewel divine that clung
to her, for it's really mine.

I would seal it forever deep in
my heart, and nothing on earth
could tear me apart from my
celestial star of shining love,
my mother's farewell tear.

Franklin D. Murdock

Grandma, The Butterfly

Grandma always said to see
The best that's yet to be.
You left with a sigh
To a world in the sky.

Grandma, so full of wisdom,
You left only a few things undone.
They were due to Parkinson's -
Now, tho, you can see your baby son.

You always wanted to be a butterfly -
Grandma, who was so sly!
You knew the right words to sooth -
Oh Grandma, you were so smooth!

You loved everything and everyone;
You loved the rising sun.
Grandpa, your husband Jack;
Now, he wants you back.

We must let you go.
Heaven needs you so.
In every butterfly we see,
We'll know you are finally free.

Cathy L. Fay

Silence

Always asking questions
Babble on
Babble on
Mouth never resting
Babble on
Babble on
Hush! For awhile
Babble on
Babble on
Going to see Daddy
Babble on
Babble on
The silence is immense
Babble Gone

Dawn D. Turnbow

Baling Hay

A gentle breeze plays down
the hill, bringing relief to
hot, tired, bodies.
   The last of the load whirrs
up the elevator as a family, together,
ends a job well done.

Kenneth C. Dettbarn

A Breath Of Hope

Like a spring wind,
Softly whispering,
Gently moving,
Bringing promises of warm summer days.

Like a brook,
Quietly murmuring,
Encouraging, urging,
Showing little ones a better way.

Touch the future
Embrace the past
A breath of hope
Will it last?

The little hands
Help them reach
Ever learning
That's why I teach.

Kim Smith

On Monday I Learned About Jealousy

It crept into me
without invitation but
extreme determination
to make me ill

As thick as lava it flowed
swelling and resonating
in a pool surrounding my heart;
bubbling and boiling

No antacid could have cured
this burning,
seeping downward and
soaking my stomach in single droplets

Each drip a fury
settling like liquid nitrogen
drenching,
before erupting into vomit

Melissa Capuano

Untitled

Dance, dance, along my shadows
not beyond the threatening touch
breath coldly upon my candle
when its light has become too much
float freely among my bliss cloud
and share the straw of the golden cup
slip away with quiet splendor
while I sleep to just give up
melt on through my empty feelings
to stab a second try
naked with emotion
now a questioning reply
living off the venom splash
of answers that remain
is the beauty I must suffer
to confuse the line of sane

Sandra Brannelly

Empty Apartment

Too many damned white walls,
an asylum

Making prisoners
of dim summer nights.

Brian PJ Cronin

If I Had Magic

If I had magic I would make a dog,
turn into a flying frog.

I would make the frog fly away,
Across a field and over the hay.

The frog would fly with all its might,
And then here comes a big termite.

The termite will bite the frog,
And then turn into the plain old dog.

All of this was a lie.
Because the termite was a fly.

Caitlin Victoria Smith

Untitled

Dig up the skull of some priest,
And use it as an ashtray,
Sail around an island of freaks,
Never touching it.
While eating Fruit loops.
Simple minded lover,
Charles weep weep.
It has become quite clear,
Death I mean
Im mean.
Scream.
No one cares.

Brandon Kuck

Doorways

Divided by a door he spoke.
"Whisper me your wiles"
But I knew that my face was cloaked,
And he but stood and smiled.

Abandoned garden we had tended
Blessed by the sun.
And torn apart the hearts we mended
Needle and thread hath spun.

Divided by a wall he spoke,
"Lead me through your wrath."
I lead him where the vines do poke
Beyond the safest path.

Barren fields beneath our feet
Where once a forest grew.
Those glossy graves don't bear a leaf
But shine in morning's dew.

Divided by a heart he spoke,
"Remove your holy veil."
But there a curtain hung by smoke
Where dreams of dread prevail.

Kathryn D'Amato

Listen

Listen.
Stop and listen.
Be a listener.
Don't have solutions.
Don't have answers.
Have a hug.
Have a smile.
Share a tear.
Care.
Help them through.
Be a friend.
Be a listener.

Verena Cooke

Untitled

In the whispers of a
summer's night
Can you hear a gentle
heartbeat so close
to you that you may think
it is your own?

When you see the moon
rise in rhythm
of my eyes,
can you hear me tenderly
calling your name?

Over and over!
suddenly feel like a child
taking his first steps

And the whispers of a
summer's night
are so precious

Lauren Milligan

Hearts Full Of Racism

Walking on a crowded beach
is a young couple hand in hand.
Taking one step at a time.
Four bare feet kick the sand.
People whisper and stare
when they've passed by.
Others just glance at them, and roll their eyes.
Why is this happening
to an innocent couple?
They've done no harm
or caused no trouble.
But since the girl is white,
and the boy is black,
people feel they have a reason
to talk behind their backs.

Alicia R. Hearst

Little Cat

There once was a cat
who lived in a hat
she ate little mice
who had a lot of spice.

Anna Matthews

Deep Entirety

Colorless
Lightless
Void of all tints and textures
Without sight or spectrum
Desolate with serenity and passivity
Centralized
Buried
Burning ember
Consuming force
Enticing seducer
Absorbing everything
Leaving nothing
Extracting all tangibles
Excluding all unreals
Freeing formlessness
Trapping structure
Controlling existential completeness

Donald Ravanne Gaye

New Angel In Heaven

She'd come down to grandma's house
And we'd play together
Inside playing games or dolls
Or outside in the warm weather

There's a new Angel in Heaven
Looking down from above
We miss her each day
We miss the hugs and love

We would pretend and make believe
And make names for each other
Then we would need a real person
To play, we'd get her brother

She's not up there by herself
To protect her so she won't fall
Standing beside her is her
Uncle and her Grandpa's

She was so young
Just four years past eleven
Though we lost her here
There's a new angel in heaven

Sandi Scurlock

"The Gifts Of Night"

Don't be afraid of the night:
It comes as a loving friend,
Wrapping its arms around you
When day has come to an end.

The night gives renewal
To body, soul and mind,
A chance to dream, to envision
And leave the cares of day behind.

When it is time to go,
Night slowly and silently slips away,
Leaving for us the gift
Of a beautiful newborn day.

Carolyn Rogers Hudson

Empty Pockets

Sweet warm liquor
  intoxicating me
With rich, full flavor.

helping me to smile,
  and laugh so free
I beg for more.

Then your bottle empties,
  and my pockets
Share your pain.

Permanent bliss, so hoped
  for, yet never achieved
Broken into tiny shards.

The last ruminants spilling,
  onto the table,
Rolling and splashing to
  the floor.

Not even I can taste,
  what might have been-
  Forever.

Brown

Indifference

Black and White
the opposites of lore,
Heaven and Hell.
But to the trees
who cares?
Man builds a wall
the wind knocks it down.
Man wages War
and the rocks...
watch.
The Greatest of Man's Achievements
the tides of time
wash away
without a trace.
And we move on
in the face of an indifferent world.

Michael Beckwith

"Dare To Discover"

Discover a New World,
Where children can play,
And have their say.
We can make friends with anybody.
Death, Worries,... Weapons
None of these in the New World.
Peace is there,
You and I can share,
No more scares.
Do what you want,
Because it's your decision,
Make the right one,
And you won't be shunned!
For this to happen...
Try to be the captain,
Of Discovering a New World!

Mattson Kokura

Seasons

When shallow skies break
Over all laughter fake,
Scattering clouds away
For the true few's sake.

It comes to view this dream
Of our lives so calm, serene,
In too clear, sunlight hidden
But in single rays so seen.

For if flowers in winter bloomed
And on every cratered moon,
Who'd shed May's precious petals
Under dreamy skies in moon?

It's as tears to laughter lead
And hate to love does heed,
That sorrow, o' wonderful sorrow
Is only joy's first seed.

Kevin Kaufman

Sharks

Beautiful, lonely
Confused about all the world,
Yet calmly swimming

Bonnie McCay

Surgery

Horror of Night
Reality of Day
Be good, baby
They wheel her away

Stark Whiteness
Putrid Smells
Long corridors
Leading Where?

Harsh Lights
Ice Steel
Skilled Hands
Special Drill

Agonizing Worry
Soul Bared
Naked Vulnerability
Life! Be Spared!

Appel M. Grisby

Music From The Soul

Music from the soul,
will come straight from the heart.
Reaching deep within,
to find a work of art.

Releasing inner pain,
moulding it into a song.
With music from the soul,
you really can't go wrong.

B. B. King has his blues,
and I have got my own.
I can breathe all my troubles,
into my saxophone.

Not the mind,
but the emotions are key.
Music from the soul,
lives on eternally.

Though songs such as this,
now seem quite few,
music from the soul
speaks to both me and you.

Nick Cook

No Voice

I can't say I have no voice, because
No one listen. When I talk
to a crowded room full of people,
It seems like a brick wall is there.

When I talk to my peers, they
appear to care. Yet they still
don't want to hear my voice

But you shall hear my voice
and my words. Have you ever
heard "action speak louder than words.
Well, my action shall be my words

And my voice shall be heard, by
the people in the crowded room
and by my peers. And to all
those who listen

Yet they still don't
want to hear my
voice!

Shanequa Brown

California

California with its surf and sand,
Can give you a great suntan,
The prices on Rodeo Drive,
Are sure to give you mumps and hives.

The Pacific Ocean is oh so cold.
Jose Eber looks really old.
In one great state, it is a surprise,
To find so many gorgeous guys.

Fancy cars and limousines,
Koi goldfish and lemon trees,
You can even catch a stingray,
Off a pier near the expressway.

Movie Stars and Hollywood,
Palm Trees and big Redwoods,
Anaheim and Disneyland,
Beverly Hills is unbelievably grand.

Mansions and earthquakes,
Millionaires and cheesecakes,
Tori Spelling's moving mistake,
Oh, My gosh!!! Give me a Break!!!

Ashleigh E. Gebhardt

Along The Way

As I go through life
From day to day
And someone needs help
Along the way

As the situation arises
There should be no delay
To help the person
Along the way

We know not if God
Will grant us another day
So make the best of time
Along the way

We don't do any good
To plan for someday
And snub our fellow man
Along the way

God may take our life
We may die this very day
So let's help each other
Along the way

Jimmy Snowdon

The Only One

The grey-ey'd morning smiles on the
frowning night,
Clustering the eastern clouds with
streaks of light;
Then the birds whistle of the
chilling bite,
The dew on the leaves from just
last night;
Listen and hear the swiftness of
the breeze,
Lifting the sun high and gliding
through the trees;
Light shimmering on all of
God's creatures,
Casting an inseparable shadow and
showing their features;
The sun must go now its work
is done,
Now the darkness of the moon is
the only one.

Donna Smith

Freedom

We are a blest free people
Residing in this free land
To live in peace together
For law and order we stand.

Freedom is not free license
Doing those things one would choose
But mindful thought of neighbors
Who have their own rights and views.

Some people chant about rights
Causing a problem and din;
One's freedom comes to an end
Where another's rights begin.

We revere Founding Fathers
Whose foresight and plan became
Government "by the people"
Freedom for all men the same.

We honor all war vet'rans
Those who gave life for country.
We love and respect our flag
The Emblem of Liberty.

Lovina C. Tuttle

Untitled

She loved me
	and in turn I murdered her soul

She trusted me
	and with it I raped her heart

She enriched me
	and too often I stole her dreams

She blessed me
	and still I torment her memories

For these crimes I am damned
	and so with tears await my sentence

Kenneth Carver III

Because There Is No You
(That's Life)

I don't know where I'm going
Don't even know where I've been
I came across a river
A river that has no end

This river is filled with sadness
It has love and laughter too
But the sadness has taken over
Because there is no you

I don't know where I'm going
Don't even know where I've been
I have traveled this wide world over
I have traveled near and far

I went by train and plane and bus
And even went by car

I came upon this same river
The river that's filled with sadness
Has love and laughter too

This river has many bends and turns
Because there is no you

Frederick J. Horn

"Forever"

A spiraling stair case
winding on forever.
Always going up,
and onward,
never wanting
to end.

So much like a
never-ending carousel ride
that you dreadfully
want to stop.

There's no sign of
the banister,
that used to help the others
on their way

Now it's just you,
left to climb
the best you can.

Climbing on forever
in that wondrous
thing we call life.

Josh Moesser

Angels

Angels are messengers
sent by the Lord to help
mankind keep God in
mind. Protecting, loving
and sharing. They take
us by the hand and lead us
through our harsh cruel
world. They show us a world
filled with peace and
love. These nameless figures
whom God has sent will
always be there through
all times so don't fret
there with you yet.

Khristina Renninger

"Peace Of Mind"

A few more steps are all that's left
until the journey's done.
It's been a long and lonely trek,
Thank God there's only one.
I've searched the world from end to end
for something I can't find.
It seems like such a simple thing,
They call it peace of mind.
I envy those contented souls
Who've found their peace on earth
And hope that they may realize
Just what that peace is worth.
But torment seems to be the plight
which plagues unsettled souls;
And though we search our lives in vain
We never reach our goals.
Perhaps the future holds a world
in which we too may find
An end to torment for our souls,
A gentle peace of mind.

John D. Blume

Mom Says....

Take a shower in
An hour
Get your broom
Sweep your room
Clean that vase
And wash your face
Go to bed
Because I said
Brush your teeth
And don't touch that
Wreath
You're grounded you'll
Get pounded
And never never do that
Again.

Stephen Cannavo Jr.

California Vietnam Memorial

They built a rock
in the midst of a park
Oh how pretty
All dressed up with bronze
The names they are many
They stand out from sheets of black
The flag with all its honor
Stands in the middle of stone
The men that stand around are still
once they moved
Once alive.
Love ones come to see the names
to remember.
After all these years
The pain still moves
From name to name

Katherine C. Patterson

This World We Live In - "The Jet Age"

Well, we've come into the jet age
But what do we behold
But the truth of that old adage
That what's behind is old.

Our offsprings latest contour
Is a helmet clamped in place,
With the weapons sure to detour
Any comets touring space.

Just tune in any station
And you're greeted with the "screams",
That the moon is now on ration
So stock up on your beams!!

If you're planning a vacation
Make your reservation now,
On the nearest satellite station
It's sure to be a "wow"!!

As for me, some pills I'll swallow
And bolster my reserves,
With a tonic next to follow
To calm my shaking nerves.

Mary De Prisco

Blissful Creation

My lead-filled eyelids slowly close
like a creaking casket
encasing the corpse of my worries.

I escape to a world
of everlasting happiness;
A world in which
mortality can never fully reach.

Where desires and fantasies
are all but a dream;
where one may be alone
but never feel lonely.

Where a tender feeling of love
fills the weakening heart,
forever soothing the flowing tears.

It is a world of magical bliss
and eternal enchantment;
A world found only
in the deepest confinements of the soul.

Theresa Gutierrez

Wisdom

Who could understand the mystery,
and presume to know his ways?
I might sooner know
when the wind will blow,
or why it suddenly lays.

To touch him would be
as if to catch a ray of sunlight,
and hold it in my hand.
His voice could be the melody
of all creation's band.

Suffice to know his ways are true,
and my soul has heard him call.
But the wisdom of a heart
that's felt his touch;
is the greatest knowledge of all.

Janet Stone

Earth

Our world is so beautiful
If you look to the blue sky
The green flowing grass
Won't you open your eyes?

The humming of the birds
(The angels that we can see).
The barking of the dogs
Many kids in the streets.

Why hurt our world
So perfectly made
with a piece of trash
or toxic waste

Lets preserve it
the best we can
and save the future
for those coming in!

Sulean Carruthers

Ode To The Candle

The light that you offer
  transmits in purest form,
    to a hurting individual
    passing through life's storm.
The beacon is beckoning
  in a manner becoming,
    not waiting for me
  but to me it comes running.
It seeks out the cold
  the damp and the darkened,
    cries out to my heart
  which through sorrow has hardened.
It makes me an offer
  if only I draw near,
    its promise is for warmth
  and freedom from my fear.
As I approach the flame
  my chills disseminate,
    my heart receives the light
  which the candle radiates.

David A. Shinn

Sunflowers

Forever destined to try for
  what I cannot reach.
Desperately trying to learn
  what they cannot teach.

I want it all so badly
  that I can't see straight.
Yet whether or not I
  win depends on Fate.

Learning to survive is
  a job for the strong.
The longing is so pure
  that I can't be wrong.

Like the sunflower that
  wants what cannot be had
I'll forever be reaching
  for the life I need so bad.

Tara A. Misdom

Green

Forest
Pine
Evergreen
All are me
All I see is green
Leaves are changing
and so am I
But maybe for the best...
Green is envy
and that brings me to you
You are Sienna
You are the changing of the leaves
Compatible in color
but not at heart
and that brings me back
to green

Trina Tucker

The Toy

There was a boy
Who owned a toy
Until he got it taken away by his pappy
Then he wasn't very happy
He no longer jumped for joy.

Ryan Robinson

Goodbye

Please come back.
Life is cruel without you.
The laughter and fun is all in my mind.
Memories of lost times are all that's left of you.
You left without a chance to say goodbye.
Now, all I wish is to start over again
A new beginning to an old end.
A chance for a goodbye.
A chance to take one last walk
down the road that leads me to you.
A chance for my recurring
dream to come true.
A chance for me and you.

Tara Woodward

Best Friend

Dedicated to my Best Friend, Patsy Washington
While traveling through life's journey
Something we all must do
We encounter all types of people,
Some make us happy, some make us blue

Maybe, only once in a lifetime
Do we meet a real true friend.
One who will encourage, uplift
and stick by you till the bitter end.

I feel that I have been blessed
to have met such a friend.
On March 3, 1975,
Our friendship began.

It has lasted over 20 years
without disagreement or a spat
That blessed friend is found
in my best friend named Pat.

Roberta M. Crosby

My Dream

I wish I could have a new life,
and start a new day,
with all of my rules,
living my way.

All of my prayers would be answered,
All of my dreams should come true,
and the greatest wish ever,
I would have you.

You would treat me so good
like silver and gold
great legends and romances
about us would be told.

Our world would be perfect
Not a scratch or a crack
and we would follow that path
and never look back.

Lori Roehm

The Park

The park is where you want to be,
In the park you'll see a bee.
The bee will give you a sting.
And it will be a painful thing.
The bee will fly back in its nest,
To take a long and quiet rest.
Then you'll know to leave it alone,
When you see alone just one!

William R. Byrd

Canyon Family

Our home was there
Where muddy waters roll.
What marks the place?
Three timbers
And a boulder
It was a dreadful night.
This morning
We are older.

More fortunate than some
We were not lost.
We know we live
For small things give us pain.
Our dog was drowned.
A Teddy Bear
Lies face-down
In the rain.

Ann Wugan

Battle of the Gods

The Goddess and the God battle once
more. Neither will win for each
other will make sure of it.
They still haven't learned, they
are stronger as one. The God defeats
himself by the evil that surrounds
and yet to blind to see he is being
controlled. He is not of full power
as he believes, unlike the Goddess
who won't stand for his child
like ways, would rather dismiss
him than play his game. So you
see her not playing his game,
for is not letting him win to
overtake her. Neither one can be
controlled but can be treated as
equal. So she sits back and
waits once again, history will
keep repeating itself until they
are one.

Tammie Gebhart

Child, Me

The child was small
the child needed you.
The child cried
you held it close,
made it safe.
The child reached out
holding tight
to your strong hand
grasping for support.
But the child let go
and will never
take your hand
in that way again.
The child is gone,
the child has grown,
only I am here now.....
just holding your hand.

Eliza Ridge

Time

Time is a coquette:
When sought
  withdraws
When fled
  pursues

James Leslie Gatwood Jr.

Dear Father

You've caused so much pain,
You'll never make it the same.
You left us with nothing,
You want to regain everything.
Your place in my life,
Is gone, forever lost in strife.
The tears I once cried,
Are forgotten and dried.
A father is all I need,
My love for you continues to reseed.
Respect is what you want,
With my emotions, you will not taunt!
So, this I say to you,
Your chances father are few!
So, use them wisely,
Before everyone learns to despise thee!

Venessa A. Corpus

Spring

Spring is 'round the corner,
Just ask me how I know.
I saw a little crocus
Poke its head above the snow.

A small brown rabbit left its lair...
And ran around the yard.
As if to say that now he knew,
Life wouldn't be so hard.

The trees behind the barn
Stand lonely and forlorn.
Soon, they will awaken
To face a sunny morn.

Children dance across the lawn
Playing in the snow.
Soon, they know, like all good things,
It will be the first to go.

Yes, Spring is 'round the corner,
And, oh, I know it's true.
We'll welcome in the springtime.
And life will start anew.

Susan Rugh

White World

Windswept down produces drapery
and valance in intricate design;
cars top-notched with snow
are ghosts bedded in deep slumber;
oceans of crested foam submerge
the contours, the grime, the landmarks
of familiarity.

I sit ...
wrapped in my cocoon
of one room comfort.

Anna Louise Staub

A Visit To Arlington

Oh worm's delight,
Oh ugly sight,
Beneath my feet I tread.
Under my foot
Lies the soot
A blanket for the dead.
Oh earth would cry
Like you and I
If only it knew whom it covered.

Steve V. LeShay

Fantasy

Fantasy moving
from my mind
to yours
Fantasy
be my reality
Fantasy
There are parts
I can't see
but yet to be
Fantasy, Fantasy, Fantasy
Let yours become mine
decent and in order
all form me to you
Fantasy of being one flesh
not separated in the test

Vennie L. Burns

"I See Me"

As I looked back at me today, my
mirror told a tale;
of what has been, and what will be,
if, I don't let me fail.

Dear Lord, I hope to always see
this light that's in my eyes;
for in it I've found truth and love,
which living can't disguise.

I know that if you really look,
the same thing you will see;
that God is always there for you,
just as He's been for me!

Marilyn Martin

Inquiry

From the islands of yesterday
how far my soul to tomorrow?
how far from the hymns of birds,
pearls or angels
to a wizard's book of fire?
in silence, perhaps, to the
garden beyond paradise
or one moment of truth within
the fire of a rose.
Held in the mind
it is a long journey,
the door ever opening
in joy or sorrow
as peacocks spring-greened
grace the satin land
or cascades of misery drench
the dust of stones —
which then my soul, which?
voices from the moon
or music from the sun?

Ralph E. Jerles

Prelude To Night

The evening shadows cross the sky.
The glow of day has slowed its stride.
Darkness comes upon the land
And with it brings a peaceful hand
To brush away the cares of man.
Fireflies glow and insects creep.
And nature's folk a haven seek.
Birds rustle wings with quiet sound
As sleepily they settle down.
A lonely deer with eyes so soft
Stands quietly as if in thought
And acts as guards through night so long.

Helen Brennan

Untitled

My mother holds me tight,
I fall asleep in her arm,
And dream of the moon to my right,
and the dull stars at my left,
I close my eyes harder,
to ignore my world of white,
I wish and wish for my
beautiful stars to be bright,
I smile forever,
to put on an act,
to make people happy,
I laugh and laugh
to never look back,
I take what I have,
to make the future pure,
and to make my world seem right.

Aubree Robbins

The Book

'Tis upon this wondrous book I look.
To absorb the words within
To learn its contents and
Hold its knowledge with intriguing vim.

I hope to keep the words in mind
for recall at a later time.
To use as needed or brought forth
As help for me a understanding sign
Many are the days I read
And learn each and every day
The words inclosed a bind
Within this book of mine.

DeAnn C. Killingsworth

A Frightful Night

Mother said I had to go to bed.
The night gives me such a scare.
Please no! It's so dark I said,
But I had to go, to my despair.

A room so dark you could not see,
My eyes I kept closed so very tight.
Something there was staring back at me,
It gave me such a horrible fright.

I wondered what it could be.
Who is there? I cried,
As I looked up to see.
I was shaking and so terrified.

Then I came to realize,
There was someone sitting in my chair.
Wait! I know those familiar eyes,
It's just my faithful Teddy Bear.

Ralph Hunt

Honey Dew Love

Love that you have for him
Love that he has for you,
Until others took the love
You have for each other away.
Just like a plane going far away
The love in your heart and eyes
As you look until you can no
Longer see your loved one
Being taken from thee,
Then the love in your heart
Turns to sadness in your eyes.
When you shed a tear, it
Is like a raindrop from the sky.

Victoria Johnson

Love

Love is an asset,
that is, provided
it's equally shared
and not one-sided.

Love as an asset
brings one much joy,
but love one-sided
two hearts may destroy.

So love as you will,
but please bear in mind,
the love that you lose
won't be easy to find.

Clarence E. Plum

Skies

The skies,
our heavenly skies
high up
above the clouds
of this earth,
wishing to join in
with the beauty
of it all,
but knowing I can not,
I sit here,
looking up,
as the darkness rolls in
and realize,
time is passing me by,
so I fell with ease
onto the soft grass,
and now I know
I could be part
of the heavenly skies
deep within my heart.

George Lawrence Fortier

"A Bird's Feather"

Once a bird fell
out of a tree.
It just sat there,
and looked at me.

And after it I saw,
a bird's feather that I
had seen fall.

It fell down, down,
down.
It was the color
brown.

And that's a bird's
feather.

Carrie E. Yarbrough

Untitled

At night I lay there
With my mind adrift
At night my mind takes over
At night in the darkness
all is possible and none is true
At night
Where are you?

Dave Nevin

Cycle

One summer dry and hot
These hills with fire,
Smokey red and gold,
Burned and went to ash.

Spring brought poppies,
merry and golden.
Autumn dusted the hills
with yellow wildflowers.

Fire and ash,
Pollen, then flowers.
Fire burns away the old.
Flowers complete the cycle.

Trudi Enge

Untitled

Experience has passed me
I now live bearing knowledge
The years of never knowing
Have faded into the day
I now walk the earth gracefully
I live a part of nature
I am own inspiring source
I have journeyed mountain - love
I have dealt with pain at times I fell
Today I discontinue

Never will I look down
Down there is where I learned
Today is new. A success
Love has encouraged me to climb
Someday I will be a little higher
The day the curtains fall
For that, I am not afraid
I have experienced life
In its most valuable form
Now I am loved. I am complete.

Suzanne Storey

September Lament

They say all things are evened up,
There's sunshine after rain
September's here, the school bell rings
I feel I'm free again!

The peanut butter jar is still,
No instant pop to mix,
No in and out the house, she'll come
With things for me to fix.

In sweet relief I wave goodbye,
And contemplate my day—
But in the stillness creeps the thought
There's always P.T.A.!

Marion Walley Barwick

Blanket Of Love

On this cold winter's day
May your love surround you
Blanket you and keep you warm
May an Angel touch your heart
And bring you peace
May your spirit find you
And fill your soul with joy.

Rachel Struch

A Gift From God

Today God sent me back a
little bit

Of what he took away
so long ago.

He sent a little girl I never
had

To take the place of a son
we miss so much

Let me live long enough

to hold this little gift from
heaven

And remember the soul
she came to replace

And fill the void that was
left by his going.

Grace M. Taylor

Liquid Prayer

Another person dies from cancer,
   your dog dies,
Someone you know is brutally
   murdered in their own home,
Your best friend moves away,
A five year old child is molested,
You and your (boy/girl) friend
   break up,
A family of three is killed by
   a Drunk Driver,
You ask yourself "Why?"
Doesn't anyone care?"
"Is anyone listening?"
Of course there is because
Every time you cry you're
   saying a "Liquid Prayer"

Carmaria Mathis

Hiker At Heart

Lost and lonely among the crowds,
The city feels cramped today.
Want to enjoy the trees and clouds,
But I just can't get away.
From the cities, fly swift feet!
In the mountains, I will play,
It's an emotional retreat,
I need to be stilled and pray.
If not work, then emotion
confusing my mind, decay.
You are my tonic, my potion,
A single sunshiny day
reserved to help my soul survive.
I seem to be losing the fray,
You keep my spirit alive.
Please, sweet memories, stay.

Kelley Eren Stegall

More Than Words

Talking thoughts and
walking dreams
clamour for release.

They course through pens
and burn the paper,
but still they never cease.

Eva C. Phillips

A Woman's Nightmare

I wake each day
To cry myself asleep each night
Thinking about the times
I could have run,
But didn't have any feet;
No door to run through,
Nowhere to hide,
Just pain deep down inside...
The fear is what made me stay.
The fear is what helped me get away.
The fear is what took his life,
But in the end, I survived,
With nowhere to run,
Nowhere to hide,
Just pain deep down inside...

Denise Woods

"Time"

I want to hold on to yesterday
but it has already past
it flashed right by my eyes

Didn't even have the chance
to say my goodbyes

Time doesn't give one a chance
it rushes by like a quaint glance

This is the way life goes by
until the very day that we die

We must hold on to today
for tomorrow might be
taken away....

Shari Moscato

Leaves

In brilliant splendor
  Glow
    The autumn leaves—
      Flourish in beauty
    Then
      Forsake the trees
To drop for pleasant
  Crunching
    Under feet, or roll
      With tinkling
        Earth sounds
          Down the street.

Ethel V. Hodge

As I Lay Awake In Bed

As I lay awake in bed,
things unravel in my head.
About of a day that has gone by,
all the sudden I start to cry.
In the morning I am sad,
and I get everyone mad.
It's not my fault I say to me,
but as I look I start to see.
As a person had once said,
they'd just want me to be dead.
I've thought about saying "bye";
but then it'd be a stupid lie.
Yes, I'm off of feeling glad,
not very much just a tad.
Maybe some day I'll learn to flee,
but I'm finding my certain key.

Charish Berg

Halloween Night

Witches across the moonlit sky
Halloween just about to die
Trick-or-treaters in the night
Be sure to leave on a bright light.

Halloween just about to die
Wolves on a mountain top start to cry
Be sure to leave on a bright light
Goblins will surely give you a fright.

Wolves on a mountain top start to cry
While children try to say good-bye
Goblins will surely give you a fright
Those scary costumes are such a sight.

While children try to say good-bye
A pumpkin suddenly winks his eye
Those scary costumes are such a sight
Some are so very, very bright.

Cara Marchio

Talent

Those songs are outstanding,
The delivery is great,
Each arrangement is different
Would you guess, six or eight?
It could be a group,
Or maybe a choir,
Who trains all those singers?
But Look - Out there on the wire!
You have to be kidding,
All that music we've heard,
Is produced by none other
Than One MockingBird!

Duane Wilkin

"Thoughts When We First Married"

I have given my love
to one as tender as a dove
this feeling is from above,
So don't hurt my heart

My life is now complete
for you are of the elite
so bright, so clean, so neat,
So don't hurt my heart

You make the days and nights
as fun as flying a kite
you bring my feelings to light,
So don't hurt my heart

The thoughts of the past go away
when we start each day
because together we'll always stay,
So don't hurt my heart

Year one was close and warm
Year two was better, no storm
Year three no harm
Cause you won't hurt my heart.

Dean Wilson

Spring

When I think of Spring
I think of pink and white flowers,
And the birds that sing.
Ducks swimming in the pond.
Trees growing green leaves.
Digging in the garden with my Grandpa
And flying kites in the sky.
I really love Spring!

Desiree' M. Fritz

A Voice Within

I'm in another world as you can see a world
where things aren't what they seem to be.

Alone within myself, unhappy as can be,
a world surely not meant for me.

In life I cower and hide, my head
between my knees.
Night and day the same to me.
When will it end this darkness that
surrounds me?

Once I saw the sun, but that was long ago.
I felt a warmth I can't describe that left me
with an inner glow.

Someone please! Help me!
Bring me to the light I barely know
someone called it sun
a long, long time ago
in a world I may never know.

Marta

Chad

  Chad, you are my puppy
when ever I was sad you were there
I thank you and I love you
thank you for the years
I'll never forget them
and I'll never forget you
we had fun but now the years are over
you have went somewhere
I'll never see you again
it was fun to spend my life with you.

Matthew Denney

Deyn

In the land above me
Lives a sinister voice.
It commands me
To rejoice
In the window
The window in my mind,
Lives Deyn:
Beggar in crime.
I hardly know what hits me,
And yet I go and fail.
Therefore I'm sent into my life,
My self made jail.
I break free and hide,
Back into the pathos of fear,
Something familiar and near.
In the mind I've lost
Above me hovers.
I can not touch it,
And nor will I try.

Nathan Grogg

Your Promise

Don't promise me forever,
Forever isn't true.
You can say that you love me.
I know that I love you.
We are now together,
But this won't last for always,
Because life won't last forever.
So love shall never stay.
Just love me until tomorrow,
And promise me today.

Katrina Colwell

Love

Hot tears sting my face
They leave their mark
Like you did on my heart
The laughter has been replaced
By deafening cries
That are silent to everyone but me
For I keep my pain
Behind closed doors
I lock out the world
For fear of retribution
Of being warned before hand
About your calculating ways
And relentless pursuit
Of that ultimate feeling
Euphoric, if I may
You know, that blinding state of mind
Called Love.

Jeanette Ann Saia

"To The One I Love"

Give me water from your fountain
Let me taste from you the joy
Let me be in your life the captain
I'll the hurricanes destroy

I am jealous of the flowers
they resemble much your face
I will build around you towers
I will build in you my place

When you're sleeping in the morning
And the sun rays touch your eyes
How it hurts! my heart is burning!
I will scream it to the skies

When we meet again in heaven
Where the time exists no more
I shall love you more than seven
We'll be one forever more.

Miguel Dominguez

My Imagination

My imagination is
special
and
one-of-a-kind.
No one else's is like
mine.
It can dream up many wonderful things.
Once my imagination
goes,
it really goes,
like a car on the express-way
going 120 miles an hour.
I love my imagination
like it is one of the family,
or like one of my cousin's
cows, eating out of my hand.

I love my Imagination!

Sarah Edgington

"Commiserate"

Of life and love,
a mystery.
To be or not,
is history.
In tears of grief,
the misery.
For birth and death,
and chivalry.

Phyllis Dougherty

Our Class

We have lived and loved together
like birds in the spring,
through many changing years.
Now our feathers are falling.
Our life is growing short,
but I know one day
our feathers will meet again.
So for now, I say
see you in the spring.

Jennifer Calhoun

Colors

There is so much discussion
about the color of one's skin.
We won't open our eyes
and let our love begin.
There is so much hatred
between people black and white.
Will there ever be a day
when it will be make right.
When this time comes
there will be work for us that day.
To know each other better
to make a better way.
There is so much prejudice
against people like you and me.
There is only one way
that we can make unity.
When this time comes
it will open up our eyes.
Colors can only white
when people realize.

Falgun Patel

Kentucky

Kentucky is where the bluegrass grows
Where people are free
Where people grow
There is lots of pretty land

Kentucky my home
Oh how I love Kentucky
The fresh air all around
Wind whistling in my ear
The beautiful view
Oh my old Kentucky home

Andrea Hogan

Prophet's Graveyard

Beauty is in women
I shall worship you, the new religion
And when I meditate on you
It shows me all I shall be
My love and my soul are with everyone
But I must decline
Because I am nothing
Except your love and your soul
Though you will not see me
You will hear me
Because I am your thoughts
I am your spirituality
That you will never understand
Please embrace it
Though it means nothing to you
But until closeness is what we share
Until closeness of two twilights
I must withdraw

Cyrus Kai

Jesus Is All

When the world turns cold,
And desolation is all around
Do we know who is to be found
To heal our troubled souls?

Can we take up our cross
Leave our burden to the one
Who will never leave us to be loss
And will help us overcome.

When we walk troubled miles
Can't see a loving face,
Can't find one to help our trials
Look to Jesus for love, mercy and grace.

Annette Weaver

Difference

Two totally different worlds
Look like they're about to collide
As they are about to crash
They just pass side by side.

One world has come to know
Loss hope, death, and drugs
The other is always filled with
Smiles, happiness, and hugs.

No one that knows them now
Would ever guess they were once friends
An eight year long friendship
That suddenly came to an end.

One world was very safe
The other held the danger
The differences that held them together
Has now made them total strangers.

Ashlee Saltaformaggio

Untitled

Mystery captured her suddenly,
As she slowly drink the blood red wine
I carefully bundled away years ago
to vintage in the cold, dark
cellar of my heart
Where I bottled it tightly
and labeled it unattainable
It's lust not to be heard
not to be transferred
until the very moment
She decides to taste
... to consider my adoration
"When mystery captures her"
And I realize simply -
Why mountains seldom move.

Cathleen A. Wilk

Prodigal Son

The leaves are turning red and gold.
An autumn moon shines down.
Before the frost is on the grass,
may you drive into our town.

My roses have bloomed two summers
since you went away.
Before they bloom again I pray that
you will be home to stay.

I do not always understand
why you choose to roam.
Or why your feet don't find their way
back to the hills of home.

Goldie Lakey Dabbs

The Masses

When the fields of amber
Flash and shimmer in the sun
When black ropes descend over
The amber
And angels climb down
From their high,
Waiting beds of vapor
When music so sweet and soothing
Rises up through the soil
And brings the angels to tears
And seeps into the seas
And sings again through the air
When the life rhythm
Comes echoing
From within the warm mass
And gives some of its life
To the next mass
A connection has been made
That no one dares to break.

Jennifer Avery

"There's Nothing In This World"

There's nothing in this world
That can keep my love away
For the feeling keeps on growing
Stronger everyday.

There is nothing in this world
That will tear my love apart
For the bond we share remains strong
Within our souls and heart

There's nothing in this world
That can destroy my love so true
For every early waking day
My love stays strong for you

There is nothing in this world
That hasn't been said or done
For always and forever yours
The thoughts of us as one

There's nothing in this world
That keeps us from being together
For as time goes on and on
Our love grows old forever

Cathy M. Garrett

An Ogden Nashiversary Greeting

A Nash would dash off clever verse
to honor this, your anniverse.
A lesser bard must take her chances
penning lines to Al and Frances.
Still, the lure of Nash's meter
tempts this amateurversary greeter.

Nash, on marriage, wrote uniquely,
keeping tongue quite firm in cheekly.
While he seemed a bit disparaging,
he was all for love and marriaging.
Nash's verses caught the essence
of a spouse's true confessants.

So I wish you, in his fashion,
years more happiness, Ogden Nashian.

Frances Gorman

Ode To A Breakup

How could I possibly
Fulfill my fears
Without my eyes watching
Your silver tears
The journey has ended
Our time ran us by
No places to go
No dreams to fly
I loved you once
At least I thought
You're hard to let go
You've been blood bought
Running a race that won't end
My pace grows slow
The rose sunk a nail
By the force of the blow
There will be no winners
Just feelings we shared
You're lost now
And mine repaired

Steven Batson

Rain

Rain...
It taps on my window
It dances on my roof
Calling some long forgotten name
The place remains aloof
Eden...

Rain...
It gathers and meets on the ground
Puddles of forgotten memories
They come together for the cool, clean
The animals, the grass, and the trees
Life...

Rain...
You've washed away my dirt
Returned a spirit long lost before
I'm clean again and blithe
Free to fall to sin once more
Man...

Michael R. Myers

Your Things

Our material things
make us choose
our friends
able us to pick

But in the end
do they comfort you?
make you feel good?

Are you afraid
to open your eyes?

See past your material world?

Think
Your mind has no
boundaries.

Tanya Kempf

Depression

I've thought myself into a corner
For the hundredth time today
Drifting in the highs and lows
That eat my brains away
I've built a box around me
With keys but not a lid
A clear view without windows
Is where I've always hid
I've fought all day with reason
Without the rules of war
In the grips of deep depression
I fight forevermore

Steven Maldonado

Untitled

The deep, dark chasm howls into
  the cold night.
Its velvety, black secret fills me with
  chill and fright.
Warped and agonized murmurs ring
  in my ears,
Their echoes wrench my soul and
  confirm my fears.
I see my doom portrayed in this evil well,
I shiver with terror as I stare into hell!

Ian Sudimak

If I Were A Tree

If I were a tree
I would see,
Birds flying near me.

If I were a tree
I might see,
A stinging bumblebee.

If I were a tree
I'd probably see
Leaves floating around me.

If I were a tree
I might possibly see,
A squirrel running crazily.

As you can see.
I'm not a tree.
But bow to them
Magnificently.

Ashley Cooper

Black Woman

Black Woman, black woman where art
thy power? I have given it to my children,
Lord, and they're dying by the hour.

Black woman, I have set you free
with the understanding you can always
come back to me. Let us find all your children,
bind them with spiritual rope. Feed them
on the love of Jesus that will give them hope.

Black Woman, black woman my
prize possession. Keep in touch
with Jesus he does your intersession.

Jean G. Ortiz

Untitled

Walking along a sandy beach
A storm is moving in
I feel the chill
Remember the past
I am thinking about you again

The sky is black
The wind is cold
I feel the sting of my tears
It's been so long
And that was then
I haven't seen you in years

I can't stop wondering
What you're doing now
I know I should let it go
It's in the past
And what might've been
I know I'll never know

Lorie Lemmert

Remembrance

You've come into my life,
Like a candle in the night.

I'm so very lucky, to call you
my wife.

Like snow and ice in sunlight,
Glittering bright, you've
Joined with me in this
Mortal fight.

When our days are past,
Please always know, that
Candlelight still flickers
And dances, at night.

Know, that sunlight, still
Dapples and dazzles, on
Snow and ice.

Daniel Rogers

The Killing Game

My tumbling thoughts
Play with the fleeing day
A losing game

And time
Watching my loss
Smiles without pity

Beware of brooding right
When rampant thought
Begets a fiercer foe

When ghostly players
In tight circle bound
begin the killing game

Who would have thought
Eternity
Could be a single night

Or find
Redemption
In rays of dawning day

Mac Belfer

Changing Time Zones

Today is the abode where people live
In the confines of the ever present now

Yesterday is where our ancestors are
Forever beyond our influence

Our children will be found in tomorrow
Always under pressure to make it better

Many yesterdays passed is our history
Unchangeable, immutable, static

More tomorrows ahead is our future
Malleable, fluid, impressionable

In all these times, a common thread
runs; we each get only one chance

To live the way we ought and do the
things we should: try harder.

David Greeley

Generations

First the hippies came around
lolling all over the ground.
Then came the yuppies
like sad eyed puppies!!
Generation X came next
Braggadocio and vexed.
Now comes US.
Without much of a fuss.
Though generation gaps between us be,
I'm sure we will all see
Although we're not the same
Life is surely no game.

Leah Edwards

"A Bad Day"

Ignorance, anger, rejection, and hate.
These are a few things
That can cause a bad day.
But, if you wear a big smile,
That can be seen for a mile,
A good mood can overcome you,
Maybe even last through the day.
It's all a state of mind.
You can live that way.
It's not the world around you
Which controls your mood.
You control it;
It's the truth, bare and nude.
You control your mind.
Your thoughts control how you feel.
You control your life,
Which no one can steal.

Ryan Willbrand

Last Breath

What comes so fair that sullen moon
That shines so bright upon my gloom

Is this my time? Please take my hand
Away from hatred lead to God's land

And lo, I feel as darkness nears
The faltered willowing of all my fears

But as I pass the in between
A gladdening light above is seen

Kevin P. Sullivan

The Soul Of The Horse

I am immortal.
I have been worshipped by man,
and been the God's mate.
With my speed, courage and grace.

I race through the valleys,
swim in the rivers.
Fly over fallen trees,
and dance with the thunder.

Through the ages of time,
I've helped the human race.
Pulling their wagons,
and carrying their weight.

Though the ages have been harsh,
I still hold my head high.
My step is still regal,
with beauty on my side.

If they should perish,
Here I will stay,
to help them flourish
and be great again one day.

Johnna L. Degree

All Paths Lead To You

All paths lead to you
Where e'er I stray
You are the evening star
At the end of day.

All paths lead to you
Hill top or low,
You are the white birch
In the sun's glow.

All paths lead to you
Where e'er I roam.
You are the lark-song
Calling me home.

Leithella Rose

Renewal

The old woman,
   bent and walking slowly,
Smiled as she sat
   next to the baby girl.

You're so pretty, she said,
   and have bare feet...
   and a pretty dress...

Her delighted look was one
   of equality.
She and the child,
   the same age,
   the same concerns.

David E. Horton

Lost

I looked at you
I shed a tear
Oh, how I wish you still were here.

Your sparkling smile
Your loving face
Your loss has left an empty space.

For now you are gone
Gone till forever
But someday, I know, we will be
together.

Amber Love

Untitled

Imagine a place where 3 things
  are true every day...
Where colorful ideas
  and choices have no limits.
We are all, in general,
  of the same race.
Where being Different
  is original and OK.
Yet people think this place is so
  Far away,
But it's not you see...
Welcome to America,
  Home of the Free!

Erin Beth Riegel

The Bridge

Above the passage to the sea
  across the tidal straight
the colossus of cable spans
  the portal of the gate
On tandem towers anchored sound
  that reach from sea to sky
the structure stands on cable strands
  that straddle wide and high

The crown rides way above the bay
  to bridge the severed hills
Connecting that which was apart
  its purpose now fulfills
To bring together separate lands
  so that we need not wait
Man's marvelous creation stands
  that's known as Golden Gate

William J. Kieffer

"I Am..."

I am a woman,
Strong and black.
I am a daughter,
Respectful and good.
I am a lover,
Faithful and true.
I am a worker,
Dedicated and honest.
I am a sister,
Trustworthy and friendly.

I am a woman,
With a good strong back.
I am a care giver,
Tender and good.
I am a mother,
I know what to do.
I am the weather,
At worst and at best.
I am forever...
For I am me.

Jessica Majors

A Mid Summer Eve

On a mid summer eve I saw you flex.
You were wearing a jersey that showed
  your pecs.
Umm, how I would love to touch.
Your cologne engulfed my soul.
I was hopin'! It got out of control.
You look sweeter than my chocolate bar!

Rosiland Clark Jr.

In This House

The calming bliss that serenades
Calamities of men,
Abides among the blue cascades
And soothes distress within.
As mighty massive granite stones
Withstands times weathering breath
So Too must we rely on bones
To carry us till our death.
Green canopies of leaves provide
such cool, protective shade,
That even homes in which we hide
Pale to what nature has made.
Yes, in this house, which we call Earth
Resides a precious thing,
By which no artificial means
Could equal pleasure bring
The unadulterated joy
That nature has to give,
Breeds love and faith in mankind
And the hope and strength to live.

Christina Aspell

Conversation On The Cross

"If, thou be Christ," said one robber
"Take us down, from off this tree-
Heal our wounds; give us money;
Let us from the Law be free!"

In rebuke the second, chided
"Dost thou not, at all, fear God?
This one here, is blameless! Sinless!
We do get our just reward."

Then turning to Christ, he pleaded,
Through gritted teeth, from pain-
"When you go to your kingdom, Master,
Will you think of me again?"

Jesus, though suffering agony,
Had a tender look in His eyes:
Spoke to the thief, most gently
"Today you will live in the skies"

Pauline Dillard

My Daughters

I have not one, but two.
Their eyes are brown, not blue.
One is tall.
The other is small.
And they stick together like glue.

Each is the other's best friend.
At times neither will bend.
And it starts a fight.
Oh, what a sight.
But they will make up in the end.

I like to see their smiles.
It takes me miles and miles.
When they get the "bug."
I give them a hug.
And sit with them all the whiles.

We love one another.
I don't prefer one over the other.
This is the reason.
No matter what season.
I am my daughters' mother.

Ann M. Olsen

Untitled

To play, as a child, in the
cool summer rain
To have your mother kiss the
hurt and take away the pain

To frolic with friends in the
freshly fallen snow
To be completely lost and have
a stranger lead you home

To return home as a surprise
on a cold and wintry night
To be warmed all over by a family's
love and crackling firelight.

To experience these emotions
in such a short lifetime
Is nothing less than wonderful
a gift that is truly sublime.

Yet, in all of God's creation,
the treasure is found by few
The rare and priceless wonder
in hearing, "I love you!"

Jeff Russell

Peace

When will this nation
come to peace?
When will the hurt and pain
of all desperate souls in need,
have tender, loving, care?

How come there has
to be so much war and
pain between us?
Is it just the fact that,
that's the way life comes
and goes right before your
eyes, lightning fast?
Or is it just plain life?

Please, tell me.....
When will this nation
come to peace?

Shelly Robledo

Thunderstorm

The one dark cloud,
it hovers over me
so huge that I can see
the clouds so big,
the clouds so black,
when I see them
I get chills down my back.
I look up at the sky and
I see it is going to rain on me
in the distance I see a great flash.
Then I hear a loud crash
I run, and I run, it is chasing
me and I can't get away
I hear the wind blow and
the trees sway. Later, the storm dies
down and, I see a rainbow.

Rebecca Zarker

"Thoughts Of Time"

Standing in one place
keeping a safe distance
from the rest of the world
isolated by my own willingness
I want to be safe from harm
I don't want anyone getting too close
just me and my conscience
that's all I need
people can only hurt you
words can only make you cry
tears can only burn through
the mounds of flesh we call a face
silence is peaceful
peace is kind
thoughts are soothing
thoughts of time.

Rosalyn Calixto

Ladies With Pride

Ladies with pride,
grace and wonder,
no way to keep her feelings inside.
Their innermost thoughts,
reflect on their actions,
and their actions...
become self.

What's on her mind,
is nothing but a mystery,
but shows how she really feels,
not bottled up,
but out in the open,
to show her inside feelings.

These things she cannot hide,
but grace and beauty,
makes her a lady indeed,
a lady with pride.

Rashana Mims

Chocolate Sea

Blackened air sole existence
Vertical I stood
Leaning down, prepared to dive
As deeply as I could.
My hardened flesh, needing soothing
Pierced the unknown tide
Which rose slowly above my head
As I dove inside.
Warm surroundings console my flesh
United - you and me
Body and soul release a flame
Beneath the chocolate sea.
I stroke and stroke to create
A smooth and creamy wave
Warm current ripple down under
The waters which I bathe.
The chocolate sea again was calm
Left alone to rest
I walked away but looked behind
To remember - Chocolate at its best!

Cheryl Archer

Monarch Butterfly

Rising in the morning breeze
Floating softly as a sigh
Some saw him soar so high
A flawless monarch butterfly

His chrysalis stirred mystery
Now his majesty confounds
Some saw him only yesterday
Crossing slowly on our grounds

Before fresh-found wings were drying
Glistening in the summer air
Some said he would be flying
To enlighten everywhere

His metamorphosis was through
Cleansing grateful human hearts
Some swear he sees the cosmic view
Coaching man in endless arts

Rising in the morning breeze
Floating softly as a sigh
Some saw him soar so high
A flawless monarch butterfly

Mike Moody

Helpless?

I am turtle "Roly - Poly",
Lying on my back,
I depend on others solely,
To get me way back up.

I like resting on my belly,
It's soooo comfortable,
My back is hard and really shelly,
To lie on it is pitiful.

If you see me on my shell,
Show some sympathy,
Otherwise I go through hell,
And never ending agony.

Lilli Lanz

Nuclear Winter

The world has gotten silent
No animals appear
The ice set down without rent
And it's freezing in here.

To look outside hurts the eyes
I am blind from the strain
Everything seems to have died
It started with the rain.

The world could not get along
Nor cooperate
Instead they had this long
And disastrous hate.

No one could decide their fate
It was taken from their hands
They just told peace to wait
While they destroyed the land.

I think we're the only ones
Still taking a breath
Adam and Eve again
In life - after atomic death.

Alan Thomas

My Teacher

In Loving Memory of Mrs. Mary J.Pfeiffer
You laugh when I am happy,
You hug me when I'm sad.
You praise me when I'm being good,
And scold me when I'm bad

You've taught me everything I know
Things I'll need as I grow.

ABC's and 123's
With you it's been
Quite a breeze.

You know that I will
Never forget
Your kindness or your
Thoughtfulness.

I hope we meet
Around the bend,
You're not just my teacher -
You're My friend.

Judith Kepka-Nyhuis

Love Me

Love me tender
Love me true
Cause I'll always be here
    Through and through.

I know you're mine
I know I'm yours

Give me strength
Give me love
Cause I know I'll need it for
    The road ahead.

Love me tender
Love me true
Cause I know you'll be there
    Through and through.

Brooke Calvillo

My Boys

The children of mine
Glow in the dark
Grow in my mind
Grow to the world,
Totally theirs, totally mine.
Ages of light
In their eyes
In their minds
Nothing remains
Nothing defined
Diffuse, yet crystal clear
Is all the love and all the fear
Felt in my heart watching their smiles.
Wonderful eyes, Hearts that cry.
Thousands of nos. Yet, yes, yes, yes.
Children of mine - so close.
Such a delicate time
Seems to be mine
Definitely theirs
For play and for life.

Eugenia Kazamaki Ottersten

461

Buck

When I got Buck
He came in a box
He wasn't very big
He chewed on my socks.

As he got big
Rules still to be taught
He thought it was fun
Patience I had not.

Now he's all grown
No bark but a whine
A partner for life
He's one of a kind.

Shannon Jones

Boxcar Memories

The treadmill keeps on turning
Burning candles at both ends
Can't seem to satisfy the yearning
Can't seem to make amends

How you take me back railroad track
To showers in the sun
When time and space were not a race
And the earth and I were one

You held me in your loving arms
Calmed me with your touch
Yes I've been gone far too long
And I miss your voice... So much

J. Michael Shelley

Mother

Mother, dear Mother
Where be there, O, Mother
My Mother
With a twinkle in her
Eyes and a smile thru
Beauty like the sun
Her hands so worn by
Time, full of pain; yet
When some asked, would
Play the music of her
Time and mine
O, Mother, dear Mother
I miss you so, especially
On this day each and
Every year; yes
Mother's Day is now here
But all I can do is
Look upward to heaven
And say "much love"
Dear Mother of mine

Cloamae Suitens

Sunflower Inspiration

Suddenly you stand
Tall, bold, clear, unafraid.
(Where was I in your coming?)
Your fifteen faces face the sun
And luminous majesty sparkles
As you sway in gentle solemnity
Would that I might imitate your dauntlessness
And dare to trust my passion!

Briegeen Moore

"The Dogwood"

Of all God's trees
There is no lovelier than the dogwood.
I can think of many short and tall
That would absolutely astound one.

But the dogwood is special to me
As it opens the door to spring.
It shelters tiny blossoms on
The floor of the earth
And lifts the birds to sing.

It wears a crown of thorns you see
In the middle of the blossom.
To remind us of the one who died
Upon a tree
His death was sad and awesome.

Oh I hate to see the blossoms fade
And fall away from the tree.
But spring it will bud and bloom again
For all the world to see...

Darlene Rockett

The Fooling Path

The saddening path
of a friendless fool
that turns away
is the end of happiness
the beginning of hopelessness

To turn away
from a friend
is like the total end of all ends
but the beginning of all beginnings

Feeling the weird silence
of emptiness like the dark heart
that is empty of all feelings
but flutters to the path
of its own well being
empty is the feeling of the fool

Cory M. Feidt

Earth Warning; As Angels Watch

The angels peeking through the stars,
Through infinity's sparkling haze.
As ever near, still as stars are
Perfect diamonds, a heavenly gaze.

Angels feel our fight, as God knows,
For his presence we all have need,
Watching with our cares and woes,
His assistance to intercede!

To stop destruction of this earth
We had good air, it's almost gone,
In poisoning roots of future's birth,
We must unite to right what's wrong!

The angels know if nothing's done,
We will have no place to run,
We can no longer sing life's song,
Father, please help your wayward sons.

Moistures going from the blue sky,
Even angels' eyes are all dry,
Oh, how they hurt that they can't cry,
But only wait and watch us die!

Allene Webster Jones

Mother Africa

Why are you crying Mother Africa?
Do tell what is wrong.
Are you hurt that the struggle,
Is taking so long?
Well, dry your tears and say,
A prayer for your children,
For soon your children will be,
As free as eagles soaring through
The night air.
All that is theirs will be returned.
As for you Mother Africa,
You shall grow stronger,
From what you have learned.

Vanessa Y. Stuart

Embrace Death

Run
To the grim reaper
Meet him, greet him
Look him dead in the eyes
Let him know that you're not afraid
To die

You can't run away, so don't even try
When it's your time, just say good-bye
But until then don't try to hide
You can't cheat death
And the reason why....
From ashes to ashes
And dust to dust
All things return
From whence they came
So walk in the light
Side by side, keep in step
Challenge death
And live a full life, while you
Embrace death

Jeffrey J. Davis

On Rain

Today the grass is sparkling
With rain that came last night
And freshened all the living things
That are within our sight.

The drought has been quite awesome
And Oh! The joy of rain!
That came with a heavy thundercloud
And promised life again —

To yards so parched and dying growth
Of plants and even trees —,
Which gave new life to flowers
And nectar to the bees!

The farmers are, Oh, so grateful
For the promises anew!
That seeds long planted now my yield
Their future looks less blue.

That you, God, for the rain
That you send us from above
May it ever remind us of your care
Your promises and unfailing love.

Alva M. Thompson

The Life In Love, The Love In Life

What is life,
if the love in it is lacking?
Yet what exactly would love be
if it was without life behind it?

Shadows fall on our life,
love lightens all our darkness.
When there is no light, evil lurks,
yet love comes to conquer all.

Whatever evil you endure
must only be altered by love.
And yet love doesn't destroy,
it only strengthens for the good.

So remember to keep love in your life
and life in your love.

Melissa K. Blodgett

Our Beloved Mother

Fond memories of my mother
Cloud my thoughts today.

Strength, hope and love
as she taught us how to pray.

She sacrificed for all of us,
her whole family.

Carried burdens deep inside
none of us could see.

A glow appeared upon her face
and with her tired eyes

She held us gently in her hand
and lifted us so high.

Each one of you are special
and oh, so very dear.

So wipe away those clouds today
and rainbows will appear.

Marilyn E. Lindsey

To Yves

I left her there in satin clouds
Released from cold embrace
Dizzily she drifts among ethereal cords
That bind her soul in sacred place
Never will she know the day
Her body to his eyes unseen
And when the blood flows ceremonial
Her Vampire in the sun will dream
Like candles lit to show their face
The ecstasy of my words melt
Trickling from my velvet tongue
To seal her undying heart held
I mold that pliant wax
And make of it a form divine
This ancient boon granted her
Imbued with thirst for human wine
A bond forged eternally
Bends her will to my heart
My beautiful servant ever
Praying for my darksome art

Todd Wayne Ramsey

Untitled

Like a rose without the sun
That withers and dies away

Like a rainbow in a storm
That only visits and cannot stay

Like an empty playground
With no laughter or love

Like a cold, starless night
In the dark sky above

This would be my life
If you were not there

To hold me, to love me
To show me you care.

Toni Miller

Lost

Lost in your eyes
a part of your soul
truly cataclysmic
this hold
Drawn to your smile
the scenery's unreal
lasting a while
this what I feel
Bound to your ways
vagrant they may be
riding the waves
of uncertainty
Wanting to win
strategy unsure
needing less
desiring more
Crying, no tears
Paying, no cost
Writing, no words
Lost

Kimone Gooden

The Flower

A flower blooms within my heart;
It's strong and pure and true.
Its essence of loveliness,
Reminds me so of you.

The flower blooming in my heart,
Drinks not a liquid fair.
It refreshes not on morning dew,
Nor breathes the crystal air.

The flower blooming in my heart,
Was born not of a seed.
It flourished from a love so bold,
Love fills its every need.

The flower blooming in my heart,
Is a rose among memories.
It started growing when I was a child,
And still its sweetness I breathe.

The flower blooming in my heart,
Is the manifest of my love for you.
The years have only strengthened it,
Its beauty ever new.

Sue Lewis

Dog Wood

Here I stand.
Unseen are my roots.
Yet they are here.
Planted firmly to grow
Stronger year after year.
So is the love that put me here.

My trunk tall and strong
To hold gentle limbs flowing
With flowers a new.

I am here to remember you.

Beth Ann Morgan

The Sky

I see the rain come
falling down from the
clouds to the ground
after the rain comes
Falling down I see
a rainbow going down from
ground to ground
but, looking I see
all the colors like the
color of candy
that you eat
the sky looks like the deep
big blue sea that glimpse
like a crystal and shine
In the night
like a light upon
the moonlight.

Virginia Franklin

"Lost"

I'm all alone,
I want to go home.
I feel a chill
As I sit on the hill,
And I'm filled with shame
As I try to gain
courage to go home.
But if I roam
Too far I fear,
I may not be very near
To home.
I'm all alone.
I'm lost.

Melissa Powell

The Last Of My Hopes

A single tear
glides down my face.
Expressing the last
of my hopes.
The light at the end
has suddenly gone.
Leaving me cold, dark, and alone.
Fear strangles me
and I no longer can
breathe freely.
I slowly slip away.
Until at last my soul is
at peace.

Alle Rhames

Untitled

The light is gone from the window,
Softly and slowly it has slipped away.
Gone is the late day's golden glow
And night holds dark and wintry sway.

Gone is the fire from the empty heart,
Only the ashes of memory stay.
The light is gone from the broken heart
And night holds dark and wintry sway.

Donald Norman Blyler

Everlasting Life

I was lost for such a long time
till I found the man of my dreams
a man I can't touch
or so it seems

When I reach out
He's always there for me
the ruler of my soul
in any situation he'll always be

He gives me strength
He knows all my thoughts
when I've hit rock bottom
He handles the shots

I never thought
that I could have a man
who loves me unconditionally
who has that special hand

Unlike any other man
He promises everlasting life
He's there for me
in any kind of strife

Tracy Maryann Kaplan

Big Sister

I think about you everyday
and when I do my loneliness goes away
Oh Big Sister with a touch.
I miss you oh so much
Altho' we are apart
you will always stay in my heart
your love for me makes me strong
that's why my life will prolong
And some day we will unite
And our life will be so bright

Reva Trueba

Our Love - For Susan

I'm sitting here alone,
Thinking of our love.
To me it's as bright,
As the stars above.

But oft I wonder
"What's your view?"
Of love and life
Of me and you?

The answer is:
I think I know,
It's in the way,
The love you show.

Andrew J. Schmoldt

Through The Window

Looking through the window,
What do I see?
Focusing on the land,
I let my spirit free.

My spirit is flying high;
Leaving everything behind.
Above the treetops am I.
Flying in the sky.

I swim in the sea,
I walk on the land.
I fly like a bee,
I sing with the band.

The ticket to your dreams
Is all in the mind, it seems,
All you have to do to unlock the fun...
Is use your imagination.

Gina Salvo

Nostalgia

I turn the pages
Of yellowing time
To unageing faces
Of friends.
They will always
Be there for me

My empty room
To fill
With memories
And thoughts
Of how
It could have been.
I daydream.

Sentiments long frozen,
Are thawed,
Aroused anew,
As I glimpse through.

Kiran Prasad

"The Rose"

It's a symbol of my love,
  A fragment of my heart...
And I'll give it to you,
  For as long as we're apart;

It's wet as if with dew,
  From all the tears I've cried...
Whenever I think of you,
  Of the fateful day you died;

Every petal holds its beauty,
  So graceful and so fine...
It reminds me of your life,
  And how beautiful it was in mine;

And so my love, that is why,
  In my heart I have chose...
To always think of you...
  In the beauty of the Rose.

M. Antone Ressler

Stillborn Child

I was a stillborn child
Lost in my mother's womb
Trying to find my purpose in life
Before I enter the outside world
No one knows I'm really dead inside
but this lost and lonely child
Lost in this dark and deadly sea
Maybe there's still a chance
to prove to the world I
am worthy of life
Once I break free
Maybe I can be revived real fast
No little child
R.I.P.

Sonja M. Crockett

"Daughter"

That summer day so long ago
We wed beneath the tree.
Our lives were much more simple then
and we seemed much more free.
But over time our love has grown
And we have shared one heart
And seeds of happiness we've sown
And gave a child a start.
And now our child returns that love
That we to her have taught
And freedom seems a trifle price
To pay for what she's brought.

Dan Young

Angel Visitation

I'm overwhelmed.
There's no way out.
My heart is heavy,
with clouds of doubt.
I've sought for answers
to endless woe,
and prayed to God
to sooth my soul.
Could someone care,
or to assume
would I even dare.
I feel a breeze,
a brush of wings,
a sudden sense of ease.
To my surprise,
a white robed figure
by me flies.
"Peace", he speaks,
and with fluttering wings
I fall asleep.

Nelda Blackwell

My Friend

A friend to stand by you,
A pal to the end.
The power to push you,
And help you begin.

A smile that's uplifting,
A wink that is kind.
The hand that will guide you,
A hug that will bind.

Katy Ellis

Last Snow

Am I dreaming? Is Spring coming?
Awakened to a fresh snowfall outdoors
Trees, bushes, and landscapes all white
Heart delights with joy and radiance

Beautiful sight all around here
Sun is shining and casting a glow
Brightens the snow to the beholder
Silenced rooftops packed with snow

'Tis another season soon to be
New life we all will see
Seasons change four times a year
Each provides "a special" in life

Ah! Awake my spring time
Nature's last snowstorm for winter
Spring will be bursting forth
Let the spirit erupt with joy
Florence Preiner

After You Died

As the wind howls,
the leaves gracefully flow,
while the sky black,
the rain pouring down,
you're saying don't look back,
the noises from the air,
brings back the cherished
memories from the older but
happy days,
The days we spent were long to stay,
but after you died,
I have been washed away in sorrow,
without any display,
I was left lonelily,
not gay.
Amber Royal

What Is A Day?

A passing of time
Space occupied
Deeds done
People met
Words said
Racing thoughts
Something to remember
Something to forget
A reminder of the past
Hope for tomorrow
We wait, we wait...
For another day.
Patricia Taylor

Image Of Madness

Look into my eyes,
watch the tear I shed
Gleam into the pain
feel the suffering that fled
Watch me to go insane.
The rage that fills inside,
flows into the street,
of love I've pushed aside.
My dear ones drawn in my anger
My thoughts lost like a stranger
I feel completely full of sadness
to look into my mind and see
the reflection...
image of madness
Michelle Myers

When

We're all silent witnesses
As Mother Earth
And Father Time fight.
We don't know
What's going to happen
Tonight.
We all sit in wonder,
As ideas they do explore,
What if they decide
That we're to be no more?
The earth is in trouble.
O, what can we do?
Whatever it is
It'll take more than two.
The devil tries to tempt us
As they tell us our fate.
Why can't this all end?
O, wouldn't that be great!
Christine Neumann

"Prophecy"

Technology, Biology, ruling our world
with cyber-space and microbe's pace
distorting life in all its phases.

The earth we eat, piece by piece
'til God knows what will be left:
for little ones crawling on floors
who will wonder what it is for.

Communication on all stations
no one should ever be lonely:
human contact in gestation
that will be left to the lowly.

Engineering to plants and seeds
human genes transferred to beasts:
the seven eyes and seven horns
is a mistake we all abhor.

But, a lamb as such will open the seal
silence above - the world is still:
time to fulfill the prophecy.
Michele L. De Ascentis

Rain's Cloak

Shadows bestow serum
upon the lone soul;
Casting beads of confinement
from masses unknown.

Though swarms of an legion,
do passages hold;
It doth suffer me refuge
in an haven mine own.
Renee' Speegle

Hold Me

Hold me close,
hold me tight,
never let me
out of your sight.

Hold me in your arms,
don't ever let go,
Hold me forever,
then let your love show.

Stay by me forever,
and let's not fall apart,
hold me so close
and let love start.
Annatha Jones

"Priceless"

Though your hands are rough
You have a tender touch.
For you - I do little
For me - you do much.
You work so very hard
All through the day
And all of my wants
You don't hesitate to pay.
Your mind is full of wisdom
Your heart is full of love.
You always read and pray
To your Father up above.
You are my mentor
My grandmother and friend.
All of my pain
You can always mend.
So Happy Mother's Day, Nanny!
I love you!
Indeed you are priceless
No one else will do.
Tiffany Prosser

Justice

Flowers on their graves
Heartaches left behind
Still hoping for peace
In this violent time
Our soldiers are dying
Leaving their love
While our flag boldly waves
In the spacious sky above
They're taught to preserve
The freedom we know
What's given in return
What gratitude we show
The corruption of creation
The stripping of pride
And lack of appreciation
For this countryside
So hands up for our Savior
And all the ones who died
Find justice for the tears
That the world has cried
Rhonda Fowler

The Thought Of Losing You

The thought of ever losing you I try
to keep out of my mind
Because the way I feel for you I've
never felt for another guy
My feelings for you I no longer want
to keep in the dark
I want you to know everything
I feel in my heart
I promise to try never to hurt you
And I hope you'll do the same
for me too
I just pray to God that things will
work out between you and I
And that you will always stay here
by my side
Just try and make me happy
And I'll do the same for you
Because I can never have the
thought of ever losing you
Michele Schilaci

The Dunes

During my travels I saw the sand-white dunes.
They just stood there like crests of great white waves that never crash.
A billowing carpet covers the land as far as the eye could see.
I began to climb one of the colossi.
With each step my feet sink into the glistening sand, my lungs
ache, and my heart is ready to burst.
After my slow ascent, I stood on top of the crest,
With a feeling of victory, I stood tall,
I once again stare, hearing nothing but the haunting sounds of
ghosts whistling through the dunes.

Anthony DiFolco

No More Tears

As I walk through this empty house,
I laugh to myself, knowing.
I run my fingers through his hair
Only to wish he was there.
My tears, I have no more
To see his eyes, but only a dream
I want to feel high, like I did that night
I've never been wrong, only right
I was wrong to let you go.
He felt me through as if he knew
I didn't stay it was wrong.
I've never been right, only wrong
I was right to go away.
I felt pain from within
I have no more tears.

April Okamoto

"Thy Infinitive Extremes"

You are the Alpha and Omega to the spirit of my soul: My destiny.
    The Master of my fate; Designer of my past; Possessor of my
        present right of being.
Within The Temple is ever lighted by the flame of unspoken passion,
Forever captivating the will of sight and constant forward direction
    to conquer.
The coldest touch of abominance decrees, and hasn't dual reason.
Spontaneous erratic means, contemplate every endured
    and eventual trial.
Potentials unseen, go fiercely reserved with but instinctive presentation.
The Creature of time passing, your strengths dull resistance,
    and subvert modest perceptions.
Living the seemingly unlivable, seeking the unsought...
Becoming the solemn unknown greatness in the solitude and solace of
    Extremities to Infinity.

Joseph D. Fejerang

Land Of The Living

While I am in the Land of the Living, let me laugh and love,
and view each day as an unwrapped present to be opened with
delight and wonder at Your Gift

Before I leave, let me not take another sunset for granted; or a
bird's melody go unheard; nor forget to stop and smell the fragrant
fresh-mowed Spring grass, glistening with dew; let me hear once
again the song of children's laughter at play

Let me feel one more time the spray of the ocean upon my face, and
give me a moment to pick some wildflowers; let me experience the
majesty of another golden sunrise, and the joy of winter's first
snow softly falling, blanketing the earth in pearled silence

Let me touch the lives of the strangers around me, and hold my
loved ones in a last embrace; let me make the difference in someone's
life and bring a small measure of comfort to those who have lost
their faith, and are hopeless and despairing, to light their way

Remind me Lord, in my time remaining, that the past is gone,
the future is uncertain, and to always move forward,
seize the day, and make each precious second count!

Judy Aloia

Walk In His Light

Walk in His Light, brightening the day
Walk in His Truth, follow while you may
Walk in His Glory, walk in His Way
Walk in His Light and wander in His Love,
Walk in the beauty of God.

Go where you can, and know that He is here,
Speak of His Hope, eliminating fear,
Bear forth His Light, His Presence so near,
His are the Words of Wisdom and Truth
He is the light of the world.

Wake from your sleep, and He will be your light,
Wake from your sleep, end the gloom of night,
Then you will be as children of light,
Wake from your sleep, He will give you light,
Walk in the beauty of God.

Camille Tuzzeo

I Yearn To Be Free

Deep in my heart, I long to be free, I long to
see, what has driven me. To always strive, though
I cannot see, to be the best in life, that I can be,
Can you not see, I yearn to be free;

Sometimes I'd like to travel, and see all there is to
see. I would, were there not, something hindering
me. Finance, time, and motivation are but three,
of the many little distractions, and why my dreams can't be.

I'd love to own a small business, and enjoy discovering
fine art, and sing a hymn of how great thou art; I'd
love my home to be filled with love, with a picture of
Christ, our Lord above;

Deep in my heart, I long to be free. These are but a few
things, that truly concern me; To live, and let live, can you
not see, would enhance my life, and set my soul free.

Patricia Christopher

Untamed

Sunrise, sunset or moonbeams, the Island is breathing place.
Great wide sea, with creeping things small and great.
Lovely sunrise shadows, reflecting in the sand and clouds above,
Marvelous shining lights, for a perfect day of love.

To feel so full of goodness, as the sun begins to set.
Your hearts knit together a tune of happiness.
Great white waters, getting ready for the light of the moon
Mysterious, hidden treasures tucked away in sand dunes.

As the wild fowls of heaven, sing among the branches.
The salt grass grows, where wild ponies roam.
Evergreens nourish, filled with small game nests,
Moonbeam's all aglow all God's creatures are at rest.

Ruby A. Harris

Forgive Me

Forgive me I hurt you.
I didn't mean to.

It hurts me to see what I have done.
I want you to know I'm not going to run.

I loved you then, I love you now.
Can I make things right. Please tell me how.

You say you still love me, but just don't know
If you can forgive me and let it go.

Cheryl R. Parr

Reflecting

I hear the rustling sounds of leaves
the whistle in the wind, the creek of bowing branches
caressingly the cool air swirls against my skin

A stark stillness engulfs... Then is broken
by familiar pitter-patts, pitter-patt, pitter-patt
pitter-patt, pitter-patt, pitter-patt
Down pours pitter, pitter, pitter, pitter-pat
pitter, pitter, pitter, pitter-patt

Drenched in heavy laden clothes
shadows long the sun setting
the coolness does impose
goose-bumps gift a chill

Resting now on rotted stump...pitter-patt, pitter-patt,
patt, patt...magnificent the skies...clouds dissolve and
more, more evolve as wind/time go by
pitter, patt-patt, patt

    Paula L. Peters

The Snowy Days Of Winter

The snow piled high like billowing clouds.
A babbling brook quieted by its icy patches.
The sun with its brightness, casting blue shadows.
Bring me to a state of serenity.
A snowy white rabbit hopping along.
"Oh what a beautiful sight to see."

The pine trees all decorated in their wintry coats.
Looking like a fairy land all dressed in white.
With a beauty so inspiring.

Children with cheeks all aglow,
Dancing and skating on water turned to ice.
Dressed all in costumes of crimson and white.
Swirling and twirling to make their designs.

Upon a hillside a boy with his sled,
Slid past me with a shout and a smile of delight.
With a smile on my face,
At such a beautiful sight.
"Never, again will I feel such delight."

    Beverly Mills

Pain

I sit on the rug
clutter all around me.
Playing cards scattered by my feet.
The bright light bulb blinds me.
Questions running through my head
like a train through a tunnel.
Nothing to stop them but an answer.
Which are nowhere to be found.
I stare at the poster on my wall.
It's like being in a coma.
A light breeze blowing through the window
makes me fall even deeper.
The unmade mattresses behind me,
filled with dreams and peace,
are the only answer to escape
  the pain.
The mirror on the wall
only brings disappointment
for when I see my reflection
my heart fills up with pain.

    Tiffany Morrell

Friends

I thought about a friend today, the best I ever had,
I thought about this friend of mine, although it makes me sad
Cause she's not here, and I'm not there, we're
both so far away.
I thought of all the talks we had,
and all the things we did, to laugh
to cry, or just to sit in silence we
would ponder our hopes our fears
our joys and dreams, while
sitting there together.
I thought about a friend today,
and somehow it made me glad
to know even though she's so far
away, I still have this friend
of mine.
The Best I ever had.

    Shara Blevins

Love

My dear one,
Love is a sweet warm blanket.
It's the peace at the end of the day, the echoing of truth
  down the years.
It's the shyness of first sharings, the fulfillment of being.
It's the magic of nearness, the wonder of limitless horizons.
It's light and life and all the hazy strands of dreams.

It's the heartbeat of the world.

It's the joy of attainment, the anguish of unsatisfied yearnings,
  the tenderness of giving.
It's the joy of union and the reverence of creation.
It's sweet spring and satisfied summer.
It's diamonds and dirt, laughter and tears, honey and gall.
It's Heaven and Hell.

And it's you.

    Evelyn H. Sherman

Natalie

She lived in California
But came to visit when she could
A long time friend of my dad's
She was now mine.

Traveling around the world
From Korea and China
She always remembered me
Sending postcards and packages across the seas.

I went to visit her in the sunshine state a few years back
We picked oranges off a tree
Danced by the sea
Ate until we were full.

I wanted to visit again
She called and said she hoped to see me soon
She didn't say what she said to my folks
Brain tumor surgery was ahead

Who could have known those were her last words
Who could have known I would not see her again
Who could have known she would not be here for graduation
Who could have known I miss her even more now than I did before

    Krista Marie Geisler

Midnight Leaf Ball

A time of the year when the leaves have a ball,
Is a wonderful season we call fall.
Trees grow weak, and begin to cry
You can hear them in the breezes as the minutes pass by.
The tips of the branches are suddenly healed,
As they look to the ground the answer is revealed.
The leaves have all fallen gently to the ground
And the wind lifts them up and swirls them around.
This is it! It has started! Look at them go!
The Foxtrot, the Waltz, and even the Tango!
Never to return to the trees so tall,
For they're having too much fun at the midnight Leaf Ball!
fall is over, the leaves have gone away
The trees are patiently waiting for the next Autumn day.

Heather Padgett

Fifty

An age that is oh nifty
If there were an age that could freeze time
Fifty - would be just fine

Not necessarily dreams put asunder
But - on the brink of many wonders
some questions put to rest
Where others rise to the test

So embrace these past fifty years
Through the laughter and the tears
Many challenges you may have met
But - oh so many more - yours to get

Irene Hanley

Ain't No Ordinary Man

The cowboy ain't no ordinary man.
He writes his own creed and lives off the land.
He's like an eagle high in the sky,
Endangered...but never will die!
He's his horse and his horse is him,
Together they ride 'til the sky turns dim.
Then as they camp beneath the moon,
They dream of the next day that will come soon.
He wears his hat with dignity and pride,
And if a man dares touch it, he'll skin his hide!
Nature alone is his only kin,
He may lose battles but the war he'll win,
Sure he'll grow old but he'll never grow sour,
He'll live his own life right up to his last hour.
His hands as hard as steel, his heart as pure as gold.
His face rugged and scarred, and his eyes are deep and cold
All this roughness still never will hide,
The love that dwells deep down inside,
Of this man that can do anything, because he thinks he can.
The Cowboy ain't no ordinary man!!!!!

Branden Benningfield

Drive-By

Drive-By shootings is what you see
is this really where you want to be?

Shots are fired all around
what the choice, but to hit the ground!

Police sirens ringing all about
All the madness makes you want to shout.

The crypts and the bloods a lot of gangs more
what they do is definitely no bore.
If gang asks you to join here's what you do
Tell 'em that stuff just ain't right for you

Leah Barbee

Hands

Hands...How marvelous you are!
You laugh...cry...kiss...kill;
You pen the passionate words of a lover a far.
The thoughtless words of a fool you spill.

Hands...You set millions free,
And yet you condemn a million more;
You write a farewell note: "Please forgive me,"
Then pull the trigger heartsore.

Hands... As an infant, we kiss them;
As a child, we pat them;
As a lover, we hold them;
As age comes, we caress them.

Hands...That belong to the surgeon, artist, and bricklayer,
They play the symphony of life with zest,
And a mother's hands clasped in prayer,
In the sight of God are blessed.

Hands...How marvelous you are!
You perpetuate wise nature's beauty bazaar,
Thank you, God, for the gift of hands.
Thank you, God, for my hands!

Marion Dunstan Karsten

Life

Life must be free of muds, like a pure spring
Flowing on and on, over rocks and sand,
For the mind to bloom, free from all binding,
For the soul to soar, out of all low blend.
Life must be like a boat in higher seas,
It can stay afloat to help the lowlies,
To give all humans, the dark and the bright,
A good and strong will to strive for the height.

For a human with a bright soul,
One hundred years of mundane life
Are for him to go on and fight
For higher wisdom in his rise.
Highest is a body of light,
So great and so immense in size,
So small and low in density,
So pure that nobody can see.

Thuy Lexuan

My Child

I looked at you today and saw the day that you were born,
I looked at you with love, my child, not malice, hate or scorn.

I remember your first tooth and step, your hopes and dreams and fears,
I look at you today, my child, and hope you know I care.

I nursed you through your childhood whenever you were ill,
I want to do it now, my child, like you're a baby still.

You're part of me you see, my child, and that will never cease,
My love for you and hopes for you, they never will decrease.

I look at you, my child, and see the memories of the years,
When you were growing up, my child, the laughter, joy and tears.

I see you standing there, my child and you truly look the same,
But when I hear your words, my child, I do not know your name.

This new found friend of yours, my child, has robbed your very soul,
I pray the Lord watch over you 'till the truth you can behold.

It has robbed you of yourself, my child, and taken you away,
And I hope someday you'll see it's lies and finally find your way.

Just remember this, my child, on your family you can depend,
Friends they come and go, my child, but family's love will never end.

Jo Anne B. Brosnan

No Goodbyes

You brought sunshine and happiness to our
lives. You brightened up each day. I thanked the
Lord most every night for sending you my way.
You made our love so special, our house a happy
home, but now I have to go away, and leave you all alone.
I'll watch over you from heaven, and keep you safe
from harm, till we can meet again and I can hold you
in my arms. I'll tell all the angels up above about
the love we shared and ask them to watch over you
and keep you in their care.
I know you're sad and lonely and you cry most every night
and I feel the heartache that you feel as you hold my
pillow tight. The hurt and pain will fade away, as time
your memory dims. But just remember darling someday
we'll meet again. So 'til then, I'll watch over you
from heaven and keep you safe from harm till we can
meet again and I can hold you in my arms. I'll tell
all the angels up above about the love we shared, and
ask them to watch over you and keep you in their care.

Judith Leach

Bicycling

I am riding my bike like a galloping horse
Gliding like a bird in the blue sky
Riding faster than a speeding bullet
The wind whipping in my face
The sun beaming down on my head
Blue sky
I need strength like an Ox
I ride up the hill pedaling as fast as I can
As I get to the top I look down
I am higher than the clouds
White clouds
I soar down the hill as fast as a cheetah
Very fast
I crashed down on the ground
Finally I am safe on the land

Andrew Lovett

Summer Storms

The rain goes pitter patter against my window
It sounds like a bunch of little bugs, hitting a wall
The thunder rolls over the hills
It is fun to see how close the storm is getting
And when it is going to leave
The lightning flashes like a bunch of cameras
My brother says it is people taking pictures of a jumping elephant
The rain comes down in sheets
Soothing
It is so relaxing to my ears
It glides off the roof and the gutters
The rain goes into the many large puddles
After the storm is over the wind is still blowing
It whispers saying, "Don't stay inside, play"
I go out in my rain boots, hat, and coat
As I splash from puddle to puddle, I see,
Beautiful Colors
It is a rainbow
As I go inside I remember the sights and sounds of the storm
Summer Storms are so mysterious

Allison Vest

Oak Tree

If I was an oak tree.
I would sway in the afternoon breeze,
Open my mouth and drink the spring rain,
Let my experiences spread my roots,
Hold sleeping children in my arms,
And woo young maidens on a warm summer day.

Aaron Gerst

"Dawn"

I like your direction.
Waking with spangles of dreams
Still clinging to me
So coolly diaphanous
Like water colored ivy -
At five o'clock
I look anxiously to the dawn -
The shattered moon exalted in promise
Of day's ritual
And your shining, unreal face,
The warmth of your hand
Painting with blue, shivering light
A picture of my soul as it must seem from afar:
White gold and impenetrable,
Delicate, slighted china
Seething with love
As though I alone
Exist.

Heather Green

Wind Dancer

As I look out my window
In the middle of spring
It looks as if the wind
Is ready to dance and sing.

Trees and plants
Sway in the breeze
As if a great creature
Blew them with ease.

As the leaves from trees blow all around
In the air and on the ground
I sit and think my day away
If every day could be like today.

Casey Rising

"The Aged Campfire"

The aged campfire, whose light in perfect form
Has for centuries kept its visitors warm.
Kings and queens, poets and paupers, in awe of its flame
Have gazed in wonder united by their thoughts, the same.

And yet when we ponder deeper,
Are we on the outside looking in?
Could this shadow by the pyre
Be wondering when it all will end?

Perhaps our blood is that sparkling fire,
Which seeks another day.
But like the log that turns to ash,
We all must fade away.

Neil S. Richards

Mirror

I am a mirror, my jobs to reflect.
I don't try to disturb or try to effect.
I show what I see and never tell lies.
Unless the spirit of the person happens to die.
They see what they want and say what they see.
They try to avoid what they really should be
I don't understand why they try to hide,
Or show what they have that's buried inside.

Jamileh Dacea Darden

Christmas Eve Memories

Each year it was tradition, Christmas Eve at Pop and Grandma's house.

The silver tree with the rotating light, kumquats, and the aroma of turkey and dressing always just right.

There was always a big group of aunts, uncles, with cousins to play, and forever the memory of Great-Grandma Mae.

We could never eat our big meal, our little sparkling eyes only the presents could fill.

Our uncle, whom everyone called "Jimmy the Greek" always dropped in with boxes of chocolate covered cherries with him.

When the moon began to shine, our bag of fireworks and sparklers would light up the sky.

Now all the presents are open, and we are headed home, for Santa Claus is on his way, now it won't be long.

Though the family is all scattered now and things may have changed, my childhood Christmas Eve memories will always be the same.

Wanda Wells

The Bird In The Tree

The bird in the tree whispered to me
"Do you see what I see?"
He pointed to the sky and then asked why the clouds cry?

I told him of God's pain and of the world's strain
that the tears are called rain.

I told him that rain is not so bad, even if it makes us sad.
You see, even if God makes it rain there is more
happiness than there is pain.

I told him that with every tear we should not have any fear,
for that God created every storm to brighten our
hearts and to keep us warm.

With that the bird looked up at me
With eyes as if he now could see,
that God created rain with a purpose
to make us strong and to make us focus.

I continued on with my story
How God is the light, the power and the glory.

I told him about God sending his son
and that God's pain and the world's strain
now are gone.

Charlotte L. Webster

Strength

...He would talk
...And she would listen
He would tell stories of purple hearts and she would bask in glory
...Stories of battles won and she would swoon
...Stories of pride and she would smile

...Then she would talk
...And he would listen
She would tell stories of death and he would weep for her
...Stories of heartbreak and he would be saddened
...Stories of loss and he would smile

Because in her eyes he saw a thousand pains
And in her hands he saw a thousand strengths
And in her smile he saw the world at peace
And he realized that he wanted to hold her
And tell her that everything was going to be alright,
But she already knew
And she realized that she didn't need his arms...to stay standing.

Ann Black

The Weather And More

He sits with his glasses pulled down on his nose
He reads the paper and watches the storm moving
Closer, Closer, Darker, Darker.

The ground is saturated from thirty days of rain
After thirty days, nothing looks the same.
Everything's blooming and green, so much alive

Behind the glasses, behind his eyes
Things grow darker as the year passes by
He needs some dry weather if they're going to survive
Seeds to be planted, crops must get in
To keep the hope of planting again

Equipment is sitting
All in a line waiting
Waiting for the right time.

When it's dry, is there time to get things in?
Or leave it lined up and sell it again.

Donald R. Feekin

Revolving

The world goes on in some fashion-
whether or not one plans for the weather.

The world goes on and fits the pattern
like a well worn shoe-like a favorite sweater.

And days go by, one after another-
And seasons blend their particular color.

The world goes on, and it does not matter
if one pays attention, or if one ignores.

Today-it rains.
Tomorrow there's sun.
One day one awakes and there is snow.

Leaves in autumn still turn gold.

The world goes on-
though some say it won't-
Until that time comes-
the world goes on.

Joan L. Shapiro

Ones Self To Oneself

For years we've been selfish, not showing concern
Not actually taking true action, for our reactions
Misunderstandings of one another, and self
By ourselves, self has met tragedy
Miscommunication relating to mass vulnerability
Centuries of families, and friends gathered
Shared themselves among self, shared through showing up
Throwing up after celebration, wine cellars empty
Beat me, treat me to a cell, believe in me
I tell truth, and prevail existence of no scare in soul
Bed of comfort, a blossoming flower, sour taste in many mouths
Delivering a bouquet of roses for every loving one, the sun
Moon and stars, out of space for you
Confused, defuse obstacles, penetrate healing
Revealing peace and harmony, mahogany desert traveled
Many lands, cultures, beliefs, beast deceased
Peace increased, souls release from mind an take kind
Combine as one, hole love, self never heard of one
Searches of never ending light to one being one soul
Letting go, and controlled self for eternity

Gary Robert Fahrenbruch

470

Awfully Nice

Filtering through the blue sky air,
Wisping its way and winding its tune,
It captures the essence that calls itself life,
The music is playing awfully nice.

The throngs of sound which push through the ear,
The percussion of drums blaring.
The rhythm of song and the beauty of sing,
The music playing is awfully nice.

You see it in your mind and you hear it in your soul,
A tiny voice that's screaming out loud in harmony.
Silence is ice 'cause the music that's playing is awfully nice.

Without the instruments, without that sound,
The ambient music, the background,
Would never instill its spirit into you,
You never would know what you now do.

You'd never know...
That the music that's playing is awfully nice.

Michael Yan

My Son

I went somewhere with you today
I'll have to admit I shed a tear along the way
I packed your ragged teddy bear away
I stopped to reflect a moment or two
And in my mind I walked with you
Through sleepless nights with stuffy noses,
Cowboy boots, tennis shoes, Star Wars,
The Wizard of Oz and the Lucy Show,
Lego Castles, cut out cookies and
Christmas mornings with your face aglow
As I closed the lid on that teddy bear
I thanked God for giving me, you to share
And whatever walks we take tomorrow
We will have those days from which to borrow
The love and closeness that is me and you
God gave us for a lifetime to see us through
Thank you my son for being you.

Lana Fristoe Crane

Give It All

If I had a choice, I'd give it all to you,

My love, my life,
My heart, my soul,

If I knew that it was true, I'd give it all to you,

My wishes, my dreams,
My hopes, my fantasies,

If I knew that you were the one, I'd give it all to you,

My past, my present,
My future, my memories,

But I don't know if you are the one,
So let's just wait and see as time goes by,
See what happens between you and me,
Our dreams might change,
Our lives will proceed,

And then we'll see our dreams come true,
And hope that they're of me and you.

Sara Coe

Midnight Storm

A cut of fire in the sky
Bleeding whiteness
Burning the walls of my cell
In an instant of lacy shadow.
Suspended like a crack of divinity
Against the steel gray womb of Storm
Slicing night in two
Reaching fingers of light to the earth
Scarring the tender flesh of soil with its wrath
As so scarring my eyes with image of art.
Within its shattering silence
I am teased by savage grace
Only then to be awakened by a calling
A roar of ripping wind beating against my mind
A tide of pulsing waves
That grows lower
Deeper
And then subsides.
So I am left, baptized with rain
Touched by the lightening.

Julia Elizabeth Barrett

Open Your Eyes And See

You can see clear blue sky
don't you dare let it pass you by
The white fluffy clouds,
brings thousands of crowds.

You can see giant trees,
and you can see lots of bees
You should get rid of trash and litter
so you can see the most beautiful critter.

Recycle our wonderful planet
what you can do is take trash and can it
so you can see our beautiful world,
instead of it shriveled and curled.

In our world there's lots of gangs
aren't you tried of all those bangs?
In our world there's lots of violence
wouldn't you like peace and silence?

The world is very important to us
that's why you shouldn't make a fuss
So just open your eyes and see,
that the world is a happy place to be.

Laurel Hewitt

Love And A Tear

I sit and try to understand these feelings
I sit enveloped in thought,
Feelings that have forever plagued me
Feelings that I have always fought.

The short times we have had, I have lived every day
I enjoyed you, you enjoyed me - every delight, every way.
Standing in the shadows of pleasure, something grew,
Something within me, something old - something very new.

Seeing you brings it all back, and the world fades,
I can think of nothing but the late August fall.
"You weren't supposed to happen yet," fell from her lips,
I simply sank and stared, I could have had it all.

I expressed myself in a foreign way, only in the end to say:
"Love, next time you take your man to the theater round,
Please stop and take a minute.
Somewhere there you'll find my heart on the ground."

Do with your life what you think is right,
If you care about me tell me not to fear.
I will be with you if I can, I will wait if I must,
All I ask of you is honesty, love and a tear.

David Weisberg

Pierre

So lucky are we to have a son-in-law like you,
You are thoughtful, kind and generous through and through.
You are a person beyond compare
Showering everyone you meet with love and care.
That God has granted you such a lovely family
Shows us what life and living is meant to be.

Carolyn H. Johnson

The Black Hole Theory

As I made my way through the jungle,
I stumbled upon time;
Times Square that is.
And as I walked towards the cross walk that would inevitably
take me to the great monitor which, much like a black hole,
sucked everything and everyone towards it, I was engulfed in
questions from exotic women speaking a language much like English.
Looking up to take in my overwhelming surroundings I
noticed dozens of theaters with a three track rating system
seemingly obsessed with the letter "x."
The light turned a sickly green and I made my way toward
the great screen that would give me wisdom beyond my wildest dreams.
In a flash the Mighty Gap Toothed one appeared, smoking a
 large brown cigar.
In all his wisdom he then inquired,
"What the hell are you doing here?"

Heath Druzin

The Boy Next Door

The tender words you never said
Were spoken by your arms as you enclosed me,
That moment loops around me, binds me to it.

Boy-man from my girlhood, calling to the dark undergrowth
Of unawakened woman. Cloud-colored eyes,
Your knee upon the swing, calling to your sister.
Petaled ballerinas dance along my arm.

A captured moth cupped between my hands
Powders my fingers with gold dust.
You and I are wingless, age-dusted, cupped by time.

Slender shafts of light explore between the silvered slats.
Just for a moment, dusty giant, the cotton of your shirt
Beneath my fingers, before you shunted, silent,
Into the gray-weathered shadows of the shed.
A man of few words.

In the graveyard of my mind where lost loves lie
White petaled, sepulchered, I place gardenias.

Rest in your silence, giant, I have what I came after.
The tender words you never said
I do not need to hear.

Trisha Stewart

The Tarnished Years

They were robbed of the Golden Years.
Happiness and anticipation, replaced by fears.
Instead of a life of carefree days and travel;
they silently watched as their whole life unraveled.

They are sentenced for life; the illness their prison:
locked up with emotions for each crisis that has arisen.
Their gaze has grown dull, carrying the pain for years;
behind their eyes is a heaviness, a reservoir of tears.

Oh Lord help the caretakers who must deal with this
curse, of having to change roles from loving spouse-
to Nurse.

The days drag by slowly as they continue their fight,
with a degenerative illness and cries in the night.

Sharon T. Nieminski

I Remember

I remember playing hide and seek in the dark with my brothers at
night and screaming when they jumped out at me.

I remember going grocery shopping with my mother riding under
the cart pretending I was driving.

I remember going on walks with my grandma and having tea
parties with her when we got home.

I remember riding in our car sitting in the front seat between my parents,
not being able to sit in the back with my brothers because we'd fight.

I remember dressing up and playing in make-up pretending
to be a teenager.

I remember my mother taking me to my room every night and
tucking me in and kissing me good night.

Karen C. Platner

Life

When our road in life seems narrow, we must broaden our horizon.
The answers are inside us, We must find out what they are.

With confidence and courage, our life's experience guides us,
to the nearest planet or a far and distant star.

Our soul itself, a universe to travel.
Surprise and disappointment upon the journey
..........bring growth........

Deep inside................
to explore and find ourselves.
To delight when we find what we can know.

The truth is light that helps us to evolve out of our lonely shell
and stand against the winds of hate and wrong.

Let not ignorance
be your guide......

Let love and respect
be your song........

Janie Harris

Silent Tears

My eyes are wet, with silent tears falling I wept
Though no one knew, no one could see them, yet they feel.
My heart, filled with sorrow and pain, ached, but no one knew.
Cold and unfeeling they declare, but their minds could not
comprehend the unrestlessness.
Detached from reality? Maybe too in touch with reality!
I do feel, I say. But to feel emotions, must you show them?
Who decides? An awareness of one's own emotions are of
greatest urgency, to come face to face with our individual thoughts,
or desires, beyond standing judgement on one another for their
actions or lack thereof; I do feel, I say, but no one hears.
Yet they continue with their ignorant declarations, and I thought
no one knew, with silent tears falling wept.

Jennifer Elliott

I Wish

I wish people could always keep their promises
I wish no one had to die.
I wish peace wasn't just an American dream.
I see the life and love in an innocent child's eyes.
I see their dreams soaring through the sky.
I wish I could show the world what I see,
That the power of love is greater than the sea.

Amber Nicole Edwards

Sand (What Does Solomon Know?)

Winsomeness and self-made lies
I think of others so I won't think of you
But you manage to trail behind, then on my side
you revel while you remind
(Though I must confess, I see the rose,
Pull the thorn and stick it in my side)

Imagery and your face
you are a danger to ever entertain
But if you tossed me a hat, I would dance
Solomon would then become bare nonsense
And I'd become a fool
(Even now, my feet begin to move.)

Well did I pray, walked over the waves
Like Astaire 'til I believed you were the answer
My heart slipped through my fingers
Frail am I for your unspoken lies
Do you know how you speak, how I dream
I hear your voice and the dance beginning
(How well the hat befits me!)

Heather St. John

As One

Fifty years can it be true
This long have I been married to you?
Mid days of joy, peace, trials and fun
We've walked this walk just as one.

Our four precious children came along,
Sent as blessings from God's own home.
He knew we needed help on our way.
For they kept us busy and happy through the day.

As one we have walked this happy way.
Singing unto the Lord day by day.
Many a day he carried us along,
Or we couldn't have had this happy song.

When days got long and funds got low
God was always not far away, you know.
During sickness and pain, he was there too
Doing what no other one could do.

Yes, it has been good to be as one,
With you and I and God's own son.
Without the help of this precious one,
You and I could never have walked as one.

Allene Williams

"Swept Away"

Sprawled, out beneath the heavens,
Rock, resting my weightless body,
Clouds, sweeping passed the sun
Trying not to shade
The star too long.

Ocean surf breaking,
Soaking all in its path,
Eyes closed, listening to the call of Seagulls
Create tranquility and peacefulness,
Bringing me closer and closer to nature.

Exhaling deeply,
Opening my eyes,
A cloud, like an albatross
Hanging motionless in the sky
Changed perception of motion.

Sweeping clouds stood still,
Earth raced beneath me,
Grabbing, clutching the rock
To no be swept away,
Realizing, perception is just a state of mind.

Craig R. Kirchenberg

Happiness

Did I hear what I think I heard?
Or
Was that just a chirping bird?
I asked if she could repeat it just once more
As my heart started to soar
My body felt light and I lost my sight
My knees got weak and I couldn't speak
I knew I heard the words I wanted to hear
As my eyes dropped a joyful tear
I can't believe three little letters did this to me
This wasn't going to be a two week-thing I could see
It was going to be the start of something great
I'm telling you it had to be fate
Because even when I hear her talk
My mouth feels like chalk
I think about her night and day
I guess love is what people say

Jeramy Dominguez

HIV AKA Heaven In View

What can it be?
Can it happen to me?
My only child was my little boy
He was to me my pride and joy

We would laugh and travel and
have so much fun
It was as if we were almost one.

Then HIV AIDS took him away
Never to return for even a day

Is unprotected fun so important to you
You are willing to suffer and die for it too?

I don't have AIDS but I suffer and cry
as I write this for those who may also die

My son is gone by this horrible ill
but you needn't go way over that hill

Come on world and please listen to me
Ask yourself Do I want AIDS to happen to me?

Diane Lindquist

Departure

Nothing ever lasts forever
no matter how you plea.
No matter how you cry or beg,
the things you love will flee.
You need to recognize their worth,
and love them while they're there,
for when they're gone you'll feel more pain
to finally learn you care.
Knowing that things will have to end
is somber yes it's true,
but if you show you care for them,
they might just care for you.
The things you never choose to ask,
you'll never, ever know,
and how much truth you really learn
depends on what you show.
You need to drop your guard for once,
and show you really care,
to let the one you care about
stop being unaware.

Nikki Borowski

Why

Why am I ugly,
Why am I fat,
Why am I tender,
Why am I not slender.
Why am I not liked!
Why do I like,
Why do I even love,
But why does nothing come back,
Why do I even try,
It just makes me cry.
Why do I feel,
I just get killed.
Why do I not have friends,
Why do I live,
Why don't I just lay in a grave and die.
Why do I have a heart,
Why do I have a life.
All I do is die, my heart dies,
My life dies.
But Why!!!

Scotti Shay Daw

The Jewel Within

A soul is a soul is a soul and a jewel, of this you may be sure
placed within the flesh, a lifetime to endure
silently it slumbers there, resting many years
So blind is the flesh to the soul within as it suffers earthly fears
then one day the soul is awakened from its repose
and like the flower of the vine, yes like a splendid rose
within your heart the soul begins to grow
Not faceted as a diamond cut, nor as an emerald set
yet now reflecting simple acts that even strangers cannot forget
a loving word, by a child heard
or a helping hand to a homeless man
all pearls of the strand
a loving gesture and a wound is healed
through each kindly act the jewel is unsealed
this lasting love is sent by the Lord above
thus he removes our sin, and life begins
and now you have found **The Jewel Within**

Richard Lester

Where Can I Find You?

Where can I find You, if my heart should bleed?
How will I truly know You hear my need?
Show me the way, that I might see Your light,
And know in my heart that my living is right.

When as a child I first learned of Your care,
I praised You with singing, and thanked You with prayer.
My faith became strong, as I knew You were near.
Whatever my thoughts were, I knew You would hear.

I marvel at all in this world that is grand:
The earth with its beauty - all made by Your hand.
Your comfort and peace surround us with love.
We all share Your blessing that come from above.

Where do I find You? Wherever I go!
I know You are with me, and ready to show
The right path to take as I go on my way.
Thank You for guiding me - each day by day.

Janet R. Carville

"A Love That Will Last"

How do I explain what I truly feel
That this sensation is only for you?
It's a reaction I cannot conceal
Because my love for you is ever true.

Why did you stick by me through thick and thin?
Your not knowing what the outcome might be
And not even fearing the strongest wind
That could destroy feelings for you and me.

You are my delight of exaltation,
And nothing will keep you and me apart.
My love for you is true inspiration—
Continually beating in my heart.

Life's trials and tribulations we will face
With a love this strong we can win life's race.

Joshua Parker

Untitled

I see in the past
A young girl

Who used to dream
For a man

That would give himself
To her completely

He would love her
Like no one has had before
Therefore he would give his life for her

Now that day is here

The young girl
Now a young woman

No longer needs to dream
She's found the man
To love her completely
And she gives herself to him

But one thing has changed
Instead of expecting the man
To give his life for her

She would gladly give up her life for him.

Donna McKinnon

In The Land Of The Horses

Galloping gracefully along the shores of a silvery moonlit lake;
    comes a band of wild horses.
Arabians, Pintos, Appaloosas, and Thoroughbreds;
    All were beautiful.
As they turned to the right the moon shined bright.
    Foals were sprinting, Stallions
were kicking, Mares were trotting;
    in the land of the horses.
The grass is green the horses are keen;
    only in the land of the horses.

Sarah Corbett

To My Little Grandson

Dear little John, I look at you as you lie sleeping,
I wonder what's in store for you, when you're not in my keeping.
Your hand under your chin, your lips smiling;
thinking of Angels, in dreams beguiling.
Little four-year old I know I'll be gone,
long before you are grown..
You'll probably not recall the Grandma-Mother you had known;
the only mother you knew, when you said "I love you!"

Florence F. Schnitzer

Heart Of Dreams

Once in a while I retreat in time back to my younger days.
I drift along down memory lane with my mind in a misty haze.

I can see the old house with its rough worn floors,
    I can see my Mom and Dad.
I can see my brothers and sisters too and feel the love that we had.

The pasture with its tall green grass that felt good to a child's
    bare feet,
I can hear the sound of rippling water o'er the rocks in the
    near-by creek.

The long low branch on my favorite tree where I could see
    the clouds drift by,
Or the long rope swing Daddy made for me where I thought I could
    touch the sky.

The sun going down behind the hill and the moon begins to shine.
Mom coming to the door to call us in because it's supper time.

All these things are just memories now stored in my heart of dreams,
Where I can find them at any time no matter how hard life seems.

Frances E. Owens

I Am

I am here tho it is dark
    now the water is going

I am here now it is bright
    I hope they will all see the light

I am the Creator
    and, yes, you will all see me later

I am the one in whom is found no deceit
    yet I am the one who will wash your feet

I am the one who was pierced through
    Oh! Forgive them for they know not what they do

I am now the guilty, yet not I
    'twas payment for you, you will soon see why

I am the one who was meant to die
    I am Jesus, the crucified

I am now not here and so you see
    All of this was to set you free

I am the one who has gone above
    Believe in me and I will show you true love

Dean M. Thimineur

The Beach

The birds fly above the blue sky
The moist air makes you want to die.

The ocean waves crash over each other one by one
When you look into the water you can see the reflection of the sun.

The golden, brown sand lays on the beach
It seems like all our hopes and dreams are in reach.

People walk the beach hand in hand
While their feet burn when they walk on the sand.

You can see the white foam upon the water after a wave crashes
It looks as beautiful as after lightning flashes.

You can smell the ocean scent when you walk on the dunes
It's nice to get away from the city fumes.

While you walk shells are scattered all around
As you listen to the wind you think what a beautiful sound.

If you look straight out and about
You can see the twisting of a water spout.

If you listen hard enough
You can hear the waves crashing so rough.

Kristen Reynolds

The Land Of Faraway

Pain and Heartache flow away
They drift to the Land of Faraway.

Darkness and Fright are here contained
No light or joy can here be feigned...

Terror and Longing flow away

Roaming The land of faraway

Wisdom and Life can now be kept
For you alone have paid this debt...

Hatred and evil flow away

Forever to frolic in The Land of Faraway.

Remember, Beware, for you too may flow away
And the good are forsaken in The Land of Faraway.

Stay far from the river,
The River Of Shade...

Once you are there the transaction is made.

So keep your wits about you
    Do Not Be Swept Away...

For all Love forsaken in The Land Of Faraway.

Andrea Lovan

Playfulness

O life's companion playfulness,
What joys you do invoke,
You give my life rhythm
And longevity evoke.

In early years playfulness
Turned to boisterous thump,
With energy as simple as
A bouncing ball or jump.

During the dating and early marriage days,
The kiss was hallmark of bliss,
And playfulness the guide and source
Of making an art of this.

In the middle years when family and career
Peaked in their demand,
The auto serves as an outlet
Wherein playfulness could command.

Senior years produced
The grandchild as loving kin,
While playfulness despite pain and tears
Brought in many a whim.

Sam Silbergeld

Untitled

She stood by herself...not alone
In an empty meadow; overgrown
To appreciate the ugliness of
Nature's beauty by man untouched
When the fallen angel from hell was sent
To give her a message of pleading repent.
He said unto her with pain in his eyes
And a wounded hand raised to the sky
"It is not too late to save your soul
From the tainted lies you've not yet told."
"Not I" she replied "no life have I taken,
Nor stolen from he who was not forsaken."
"You needn't take lightly this warning I spread
For I have no life anymore" He said.
As he turned to leave, his smile deceiving
He beckoned to her; a test of believing
With a fleeting thought to the message he gave
She followed him lying "Tomorrow...I pray."

Deirdre Aileen Cooke

I Like

I like long walks in the summer's air,
 and feeling within my heart that you really care.
I like skies that are painted with heavenly hue,
 and I like you.

I like romantic nights that never seem to end,
 and calling you my special friend.
I like viewing the ocean's waters blue
 and I like being with you.

I like sipping wine in front of the fireplace,
 and remembering the laughter on our face.
I like holding hands as lovers do,
 and I like believing in you.

I like feeling warm within my heart.
 and knowing that we shall never part
I like great artists of the world which are few,
 and I like touching you.

I like creating poems in sweet melody,
 and feeling young, spirited and free.
I like special moments that are shared by two,
 and I like loving you.

 Gloria Ann Williams

Mona Lisa

This painting is "great" and very pretty
 this wonderful lady by Leonardo da Vinci.
She looks very peaceful, and somewhat shy
 this can be symbolized by the dark sky.
But the tone of her skin and the look in her eyes
 this gives her the look of one that's despised.
This priceless work of art, to me, is as beautiful
 as a homemade pizza
 this painting of da Vinci is entitled Mona Lisa.

 Jason Whitfill

Lily

The flower begins to blossom,
 Only to be bitten by love's harsh wind,
 Her pure white petals begin to turn dingy yellow,
 As her heart hardens, her will is broken,
 The void, which until now laid dormant,
 begins to take her over like a raging inferno,
 Her petals begin to fall to the ground as she
 transforms,
 What once was a lily of great beauty,
 Is now a weed to be pulled up and tossed to
 the side.

 Katrina Rozelle

"Baltimore Winter"

In the room alone with your sweater, I put on the music
and it brings me back to the cold Baltimore winter driving
in your car to all the places that you showed me:
 The Fells Point Inner Harbor doesn't seem
 so far away now, and I can still taste
 the Tiramisu from Vaccarro's on my lips
 and yours. That longing to go to what we so
 kindly dubbed "The Runaway Cafe" is still
 there. I don't think it will leave.
The air is blowing through my hair, the music is loud and
a new smoke travels through my body with chills and the
sensation of those wild thoughts of escape we had with
the nights that followed, and you stare to see my mouth
move as I sing those fast lines, and I'll smile then and now
just to remember what made us so happy to get
away from it all.

 Lauren A. Mouzakes

Home

The place we've known as home
now is just a house standing alone.
Hate and bitterness now dwells within
the place we called home.

Violence and tears spreading woes and fears
inside these walls listen it's very clear
the room where meals were eaten
All are splattered with blood and hate.
Our home is now just a house
Where happiness is as tiny as a mouse.
Laughter and gladness once dwelt within
now are stripped with ugliness and sin.

 Dianne Brown

I Know Who I Am

I know little about the country from which my fathers came;
I may not know the way they lived, or if they achieved great fame.

And though my own true heritage is forever hidden away,
A feeling deep inside of me grows stronger day by day.

The color of my skin and the texture of my hair
Remind me from my mirror of the roots from which I share.

For I am African and American, the latter forced to be,
But the roots of being African will forever be part of me.

With pride and thankfulness I stand, not alone but with my brother,
Pleased and proud of my African roots more so than any other.

It is a great God that made me to be just what he chose,
And the pride of being African has gallantly arose.

Right now I dismiss all doubts and fears or search for an identity,
And embrace and cherish the beautiful challenge
As an African-American entity.

 Helen Haley Smith

Dream Killer

I'm the shoes of God in the Garden of Eden,
Adam and Eve are bent over weeding.
I'm the shepherd of loneliness watching the flocks,
My feet are still bleeding from walking on rocks.
I'm the maker of sadness when everyone mourns,
When I look at a rose, all I see are the thorns.
I'm the cloud in the sky that brings thunder and rain,
My lightning strikes twice and then you complain.
I'm the dead angel that sleeps in your head,
Lend me your soul I don't wish to be dead.

I am that match that refuses to light,
I'm the shadows that haunt all the children at night.
I'm the nightmare that lingers until you die,
When you think about your life I will make you cry.
I'm the killer of dreams and the maker of fear,
And I am the reason you're shedding the tear.
I unlock the prison that's holding back hate,
If you ever need comfort, I will be late.
When you see that life's pain and that's all it will be,
Then my dear friend, that's when you've seen me...

 Michelle Martin

Strength Within

Each of us has strength within,
an ability to fight and win,
It's there somewhere there's no doubt,
we must reach within and pull it out.
Sometimes life's trials will get us down,
but the strength God gives us can we found.

 Katherine E. Crichton Lawyer

When Life Goes Bad, Don't Give Up Hope

When life goes bad, don't give up hope,
life, is like a tied up rope.
Failing, neglect and disapproval,
life cycles, disappointment arrivals.
Not willing to give up, now this is good,
inner self-esteem, must be understood.

Life has up's and downs, so be alert,
one time you're happy, then another you're hurt.
That's why I say, don't give up hope,
it's a part of life that one must cope.
Understanding and patience must be observed,
educational knowledge one must reserved.
Never rush tomorrow,
one might never know.
Let tomorrow just show,
with its own sorrow.

Mavis M. John

Spring

Trees, flowers, sunshine, rain
Warm cool breezes swaying
The branches, intertwining, caressing and enveloping
Their leaves in an embrace
The droplet of rain on a
Floral petal, is a dew drop kiss
The sunshine adorns all of
Nature's bounty
With its radiance

Anna Gilmore

"I Am A Minor"

"I am a minor, so they say...
and I'm reminded everyday...
Don't do this and don't do that!...
And parents always saying what?...
I shouldn't smoke and shouldn't drink...
They even tell me how to think...
If they would listen, they would see...
There's really a person inside of me...
I can listen, talk and think...
Make decisions in a wink...
I can work and I can play...so I will be
Grown-up someday...
If a minor you might know...and love the
Way we love you so...
Give us the chance to show that we...
A minor we won't always be ...
You were a minor, weren't thee?..."

Sue D'Onofrio

Window

On the outside the world looks big
Inside it is shallow and cold
When you think you are so different, you never realize how
  alike we all really are,
And you see yourself as an outsider, when everyone else is
  the outsider
You wish you were perfect, and you finally realize that
  nobody is perfect!

Danielle C. Litterio

Might We

You are so beautiful to me
There is nothing else that I can see
Just tell me one thing
Why did you leave me
I heard the birds sing
I heard the bells ring
So why?
Why did you say good bye
Didn't I treat you right
I always kept your goals in sight
I always put you before me
Can we, might we ever get back .....
Then I realized that you already packed
There will never be a we
between you and me
ever again in this life, in this eternity

Christopher Barrie

First Signs Of Spring

Tiny blossoms burst through the snow,
Displaying their colors as they sway to and fro.
Bright purple, sparkling white, and dazzling yellow,
Filling my day with glorious bursts of color.

My heart leaps with excitement and joy,
As the first signs of Spring bursts forth with awe.
But, I know without a shadow of doubt,
One blossom doeth not a springtime make.

Winter is not over with its ice and snow,
We still have the month of March to go.
But the blooms of crocus have lifted their heads,
A sure sign that Winter is waning and almost dead.

Buds of my Bartlett Pear, Forsythia and Japonica swell,
And the Red-Breasted Robins are chirping, "all is well."
The first signs of Spring so beautifully blend,
With the deadness of Winter which is about to end.

June N. Hamlett

Sigh

The trees loom into the sky
As they start to sway you hear them sigh,
He walks with us from day to day
Nigh do we see him,
Nor words does he say,
When you were lost and could go no more,
That's when you learned what his love was for,
You lead your life as it shall be
throughout all eternity,
He reaches out and takes your hand
Through each galaxy to another land,
So now you're gone from our eyes,
We shall meet again
When the trees do sigh.

Cynthia Scholl

The Greatest Mom Of All TIme

To the woman who gave me life -
Some people would say it's nice, but I think it's great,
That even though you and Dad were bad mates,
And things didn't go as planned,
I still turned out to be a nice young man.
The things we went through are why I have to say
I love you!

Anthony Morris

In His Time

As I lay here helplessly,
My bones are so very weary,
My flesh is weak,
My strength is gone.
I can hear people say, I don't have long now.
As I can see my body is decaying and they say
I have lost my mind.
They are praying that You take me home soon.
Do they not know my choice is to be with You now?
My mind is still with me if You dare to look deep within me
for You will see.
I just can't express what I want You to know.
You see I am through here doing my Father's will
but He still wishes to use my vessel to reach one of you.
So please be patient with me.
Til my Father's work is complete in me.
For it is in His time never in vain.

Kim Bryant

Dear God

I've got a sad heart today
There isn't anything anyone can do or say,
I cry, I'm sad, I'm mad
Why did this have to happen to Dad?

Lord, I've got a sad heart again today,
They say the memories stay,
And the pain in time will go away,
But why did he have to go now? And this way.

I've got a sad heart today
There's times when he is on my mind night and day.
Please Lord, I have to know, why did you take him away?
I've got a real sad heart today.
I love you Daddy.

Kathy J. Johnson

"Annual Termites"

I am the flame that burns your hand
I am the suffering that you command
I am the nausea within your throat
I am the water on which you choke
I am the memories that slowly fade away
I am every word that you say
I am the fuel to the sun
I am the war in your head that has begun
I am the salty tears that you cry
I am the fire that will not die
I am the mud that you step in
I am the spirit that is within
I am the ship that proudly sinks
I am the thoughts that you think
I am the knife that's in your back
I am out of the blue and into the black

Kurt Prutsman

"I Qualify"

In life it seems to be most everything you try
"You Must Qualify."
Whether to get a job or to drive a car
"You Must Qualify"
Out of all the things this world could give to
make life here easy to live
"You Must Qualify"
I have found something that I can do
without the world's help and a high IQ
I Can Service My God With All My
Might Everyday And Every Night.
I know I Qualify.

Ruth Patterson

Dad

On a spring day in April, this baby boy was born.
A full life ahead, with a smile always worn.

At an early age to the field, many chores to be done.
A two mile walk to school, his education had begun.

Life was a free spirit to roam, riding motorcycles north in June,
Dakota wheat fields, Minnesota lakes, in the wind a harmonica tune.

He never met a stranger, always willing to lend a hand.
A friendly faith in people, this boy is now a man.

Eager to try new ventures, the forties were a changing time.
Not afraid to take a gamble; pictures shows were a dime.

Occupations many over the years, inner strength was his guide.
Farmer, insulator, painter, all work was done with pride.

Music is entertaining for young and old alike.
His fiddle delighted many on any given night.

The fiddle and harmonica were pals in the aging years of life.
Many a time he fell asleep, man and fiddle together, says his wife.

The setting is Christmas, 1994; family gatherings full of love.
Children, grandchildren and six greats too; next chapter of life
    unfolding from above.

Good times are remembered, the hour is now past eleven.
Dreams are dreams forever, our Forrest is now in heaven.

Donna Hansen

The Seed Of War

The seed of war,
It's in all of us.

It grows with hatred.
Gets stronger with others fear.

Blooms in poison,
Yet it won't hurt me.

It kills and destroys what we have
worked so hard for.

So why the seed of war?
It hurt all of us in one way or another.

No one can control the seed!

What do you do you ask yourself?
Pray, pray, and pray some more

How will you change?
What will the seed do that grows in all of us?

I'll tell you what to do,
Keep the seed with in yourself.

Jessica Vogel

My Goal At Age 80

Only good thoughts I want to collect
As I'm improving my intellect.
I shall have joy and peace of mind
Dealing each day with humankind.
Beauties that nature will provide
Add to the picture far and wide,
Even in the crowded city square
That barely has space for bodies there.
As the weather changes and the breezes blow,
There will be great things for me to love and know,
To discover more and share with high and low.
Nothing matters as long as I
Keep my eyes up to the bright sky,
As I still seek the How and Why.

Marion E. Miller

Afraid

If only you knew,
That I am not just some girl in your class.
That my nose is not tilted in the air.
That I am a person just like you.

If only you knew.
Just how I feel,
How I felt,
How I long to talk to you.

But do I dare?
Do I dare risk
Being hurt again.
Put down,
Because I differ so much from you.

If only you knew.
If only I could tell you just how I feel.
If only you could get to know the real me.

Kesi Haynie

Sometimes I Wonder

Sometimes I wonder ....
If all this selfishness I'm holding in
And letting out will backfire
Maybe when I'm young, old, and gray
Or just very tired.

Sometimes I wonder......................
If I'll even last long enough
To bury this feeling under
I can't explain my feelings on a
Piece of paper, but I do know
Every word written here my
Mind is getting weaker

Sometimes I wonder......................
If my soul is playing these same
Scenes, I play it over and over
But I do not know what it means
I'm going to race this and win
Letting God know this is my only sin.
But sometimes I wonder.

Michelle Woods

To Free Your Mind

You see nothing when you look for things that bind your mind
But don't realize you're still mesmerized by electric fireflies

And still every Sunday millions drop to their knees
Like sheep to the slaughter they are blind
Thinking by doing so they'll find Christ
When they need not look further than their minds
Which are chained by fear of Hell
But God knows only to be kind

How do you find depth in the words of others
When most things that impress you really have no purpose

You have clouded the magic in your mind
Hidden it in the fog
Surrendered the map to it to age
And forgotten the way over time

There still is a place centered around your mind
Which can be lifted above the clouds
Free of darkness, fear, the shallow way earthly things are defined
Free of electric fireflies
Free of shackles to bind your mind

Tristan Tyler

Sweet Tears

Sweet tears from heaven, gently they fall,
touching the earth an angel is born
Sweet tears from heaven softly they flow,
through rivers, through streams, through
valley's rich green, in the eyes of this
angel this beauty is seen.
Sweet tears from heaven, touched by the
stars, touched by the sun, to the face
of this angel heaven has come.
Sweet tears from heaven, more beautiful,
more beautiful then white winter snow,
from the heart of this angel a radiant glow.
Sweet tears from heaven such heavenly bliss,
this angel, this angel this lovely young miss.

Rex B. Oriti

Mt. Rainier 2/93

Imposingly silent,
she stood there before us,
taller than any I'd ever seen,
rising like a marble monument
from a prickly, evergreen carpet.
Her garments and skin and hair, snow white,
just a tint lighter than
the suggestion of blue
that enveloped round her.
She seemed to breathe slowly;
preparing the moment that sends her
into a cataclysmic motion.
Everyone there sensed it;
our breathe, though much faster,
a tint lighter than the suggestion
of the blue that enveloped round us.

Richard Reitz

Colts Of Solitude

Distance. Silence. Solitude.
Horizons in my dreams are invisible fences
guarded by nights and Blues.
Where are you?
Where are your dormant doves?
Have they learned the flight of your absence?
Where are your quiet hemispheres of light?
Where are you?
Sadness and blue.

Ocean has become mysterious desert.
Silent word. Hidden and wild presence.
I hear your voice through the darkness.
Your silent song and your pure essence
riding the colts of loneliness.

The night is broken like a string.
It is broken in the mutiny of the heart
and broken in the melody of the sea.
Sadness and Blues.
Where are you?
Distance. Silence. Solitude.

Jose Villalba

A Writer's Tools

As a writer uses ink and pen,
A carpenter uses hammer and nails.
As a carpenter uses his tools to make a house—
A writer uses them to write his tales.

But more important tools than ink and pen,
the poetic minds of women and men!

Philip Bonelli

479

Richard Truly

Richard Truly was his name
Shuttle missions brought him much fame
Fayette was where he was born
On an early November morn

He went to the Georgia Institute
I don't think he wore a suit
Two shuttle missions he did go
The bottom of the shuttle, it did glow

It lifted off into the sky
What once was low now was high
It went into the black of space
Not even leaving a little trace

When he came back down
He did not drown
He floated down with the greatest of ease
I don't think he tried to sneeze

When he landed the wheels did not screech
It would be hard to land on the beach
When he got out he went on with his life
And went home to see his wife

    David V. Lockley

I Am A Fox, Not A Pet

I know I am pretty, but I am wild animal
You probably would like to pet me, but it goes against nature
I know you think I am cuddly, but please do not touch
Even though I have cubs that are cute, I will protect them
I may look gentle but I am a wild animal with instincts
Please do not feed me because someday I may have to feed
Myself and I will forget how and starve
You maybe nice and need a pet but it is not to be me
For I am a creature of the wild and my master will always
Be the wind, rain, sun and earth.

    A. K. West

Views From A Double-Decker Bus

    Welcome to the Poverty Travel Tour.
Experience the degradation of spirit,
debilitation of body and starvation of the mind.
    On your right are civic monuments to death,
breeding places for insidious slaughter.
Architectural discards. Un-achievement awards.
Where rainbow hues imitate nature
coloring the brain with diminished capacity,
locking against achievement, escape, life.
    On your left are material enticements, controlling toys,
vacuous fare. Instruments of sorcery. Road signs of false success.
    Breathsucking systems shill grants for childcare/playgrounds.
City fathers strike deals with foreign enterprise and
biological fathers strike deals with incarceration.
The balm of music veils the view and the hand-picked few
bat and jump and run. Elders wither from ill-regard and
institutional memory dies.
    To the front is the yellow brick road, the winner's path to what?

    Anne Warren

Midnight To Dawn - God's Song

The stars sit sequenced in wonderful, heavenly places
They dance and shine in their glittering spaces
Blackness of the night sky engulfs the air
The lake watches the starlight with an intriguing stare
Moonlight stretches over the blueness of the watery mass
Echoes of tiny animals on the banks suddenly sound, then pass
Motion in the darkness continues in the beautiful, well written song
Until God pulls back the night and gives way to another dawn.

    Angie Rinehart Burleson

My Final Resting Place

Where is this vast land that I am walking through?
The darkness is overwhelming me; my time to go is soon.
Bodies piled up, so mangled that even the maggots will not feed.
I plant something in a field; the something is a seed.
I see stone everywhere, but all I can make out is R.I.P.

The undertaker arises from the fog
He raises his arms and says "come along."

He leads me to a place where I have never been before.
And just five feet in front of me, there is a black door.

As I walk through this door I see
something from the past.
The undertaker chuckles,
then kicks me in the ass.
And I fall face first,
straight into the grass.

I arise after awakening to see in front of my face:
My name on a tombstone; this is my final resting place.

    Trent Kannenberg

Dad

Dad is a name that is not given, it's earned.
This is something as a child growing into an adult I learned.

Though our blood is not our bond,
Our friendship and love go far beyond.

Your patience, love and understanding
Is what makes our relationship so undemanding.

Where most times it's the blood that binds Dad to daughter,
With us it's our hearts, souls and minds joined with love and laughter.

Your encouragement and faith in me
To do or be anything I want to be,

Your praise and joy over all the things I do,
Make me realize what a special parent I have in you.

Thank you for being there to give a push when needed,
Or encouragement and a hug when the world's receded.

You always make me feel as if I can do anything,
And make me feel as if a dream doesn't have to be a dream.

So, my Dad you are, a title you earned,
And the very best one, as far as this daughter is concerned.

    Melissa T. Jackson

Distant Love

I know so much about you and yet, I know nothing.
I don't know what you feel, what you need, or what you dream.
My love for you flows like a raging river, out of control.
While your love for me is as still as a dying lake.
I'm tempted to give up hope, to label you intangible, unreachable,
And so distant, you're like a dim star, galaxies away.
But I cannot. I can't forget my own feelings.
I can't put them out of my mind like a bad dream.
I won't ever forget the gentle curve of your lips.
I could never forget the way you held me, so close.
I can't imagine not seeing the warmth in your eyes ever again.
You are a part of me now.
A part of my life.
A part of my soul.

    Dena Wise

What We Could Do

As I lay in bed dreaming about you
I figured out what we could do.

We could lay on the beach
while sharing a juicy peach.

We could walk on the shore of the ocean
We do this to show our devotion.

We could have a picnic in the park
While listening to the dogs' soft bark

As I lay in bed thinking of
all these things I know
we will never do but all
I can think about is how
much I Love You

Tanya Curran

Tentative To My Future

I exemplify a precarious soul
a meticulous but precarious soul

no where close to perfect

not diligent, no I'm much too lazy for that word
I with hold an erratic mind

I created the now obsolete passion that burns
I some how enhanced my rotten thoughts
and now I speak with a diverse tongue

still, no where close to perfect

I'm not inclined to be perfect
but I should be
it should be expected of me
not to sound skeptical of my own fate

A monotonous sound, low in pitch
boring house in which I sit
provoked by an antagonizing voice
one that is small in volume

Still, the ones I love hold their arrogance above me
and still, I do not understand them

now, do I give in to the censor? Or do I say good night?

Monica Knight

Beautiful Little Sad Eyes

   Elisa wore a smile in every picture, the camera did not know
that this little girl was frightened and was hurting so. Do not
let anyone know the pain and sorrow that your sad eyes show.
Those beautiful little Sad eyes, do not tell lies, of her
unanswered cries. Adored by her natural father, he loved her so,
he did not want to leave her, but it was his time to go. Left
all alone and helpless, a shameful death would come. A fitful
end for no one, but an end at last, and no more of the devil's
doings will be afflicted on this pretty young lass. For now she
is hand in hand with Jesus in paradise. He will love you
forever, reunite you with your dad, who will hug you, and no longer
be sad. You have earned the wings of an angel, and you will be a
guardian to the young, and you will assure these battered and
lonely children, of better times to come. So take comfort all
you children, whose names are written on the palm of His hand,
know that our savior loves you, rest in peace now beautiful
little sad eyes, as I bid you adieu.

Bryan Murphy

Dawn's Ride On The Bay

She saddled the horse to ride off alone,
To ponder life in the quiet of dawn.
So many questions circled around in her mind
So many answers she needed to find.
The bay horse seemed to sense her despair,
And walked along gently; head high in the air.
yes, that horse knew the need of this ride
As they passed all the homes with people inside.
The woman wondered where her life has gone wrong.
Would she find contentment; a place to belong?
And when she returned home that day
She had learned all the answers
While riding that bay.
Then she packed up her clothes,
And she drove off alone.
For the things she was seeking could never be found,
While she lived life away from the rest of her kind.
She prayed to live life through her writing, her son,
and her mind.

Diane Turmaine Leslie

Untitled

My daughter by chance
My friend by choice
That's what I thought of when I heard your voice

It's hard to tell you how I feel
But I will tell you now that the feelings are real
My love goes beyond boundaries you could imagine
You are my Mother and my image of you is heaven

I know it hurts to see us apart
But we're always together just feel it in your heart
You've been there for me though differences we may have had
But I want you to know the arguments no longer make me sad

The pain between us is gone
I believe we can make it to see a new dawn
So take this poem and know that you're appreciated without cause
And never believe that I ever paused

Just believe we're always meant to be
A Daughter for you...A Mother for me

Nichol Soto

Once Again

As the rain washes the earth
   And gives it new life,
So does Love beckon me and
   Cleanse my soul with joy.
Once again she embraces me
   And I follow her path in heady delight.

I am to know again the secret of a soul
   and the promise of tomorrow;
   To discover the serenity of night
   And the passion of a storm;
   To sing the music and dance
   On tiptoe;
To feel the rushing winds of Time
   And the warm tears.

Kathryn S. Adams

'At Closing Of The Day'

The night is a slinking darkness of Phantom Gypsy shapes,
   All garbed in cloaks of black, and darkly flopping capes;
Stealing through the city streets, snuffing out all light,
   To defend the solemn promise, of the still dark night.
Their grotesque shadows cowering low,
   Furtively guarding the dark gloom they bestow,
In zealous pursuit of each flame of light,
   To speed the Light - Wings of Day, into disappearing Flight...
But Lo - In yonder distance — is seen,
   Silhouetted by the glowing fiery gleam;
Of the slowly sinking Sunset's presence there,
   With its awesome Flaming, Flash, and Flare,
Behind a dark Majestic Wall of Mountain crests so high.
   A looming ominous Giant in the Sky - - -
Of darkening clouds, and shadowy space,
   Disclosing the presence of Night's mysterious Face.
And the Sunset's Passion Drama of radiance so rare,
   Is the Closing curtain Finale, and warning to prepare
For soothing restful Dark - Night's solemn Promise, so sly,
   That assures, O Yes, the end of Day is Nigh.

    Lynn Adele Lawrence

The Song

The song of love was heard,
   whenever you were near,
You were the rhythm that made my heart beat.
The beats of my heart, played a song of happiness,
   the song of One.

When you left the song stopped.
The beats became erratic, and dull.
There are now deafening sounds of the new song my heart sings,
it is one of loneliness and despair.

Much time has now passed, the unsteady beats
   have become slow and steady.
My heart will never again be able to play,
   that same rhythm of Our Song.
My heart now beats a song, for me,
   a song of strength and independence.

    Diane Bass

Theft

He stood tall, toughing it out,
and stole from a planter,
hundreds strong,
a scarlet tulip

which he offered to his lady

seated beneath him in a wheelchair—
she, frail aftermath of an ordeal,
wrapped in gauzy hospital weeds
blown by the breeze.

He offered her passover blessing—

which grasped in her pale hands,
cherished, cupped beneath chin,
breathing from its blessed
sanguine cup

she smiled its velvet hue—and flourished.

    Saralee Gelman Fine

One Last Breath

Anton Asher Dancinger.
I am Anton Asher Dancinger.
I am eighty years old.
Madmen have seized my nation
and slaughtered my family.

I am Anton Asher Dancinger.
Ye hey shmay raba am eighty years old.
Ba-agala divra dichol bet Yisrael am not insane.
Youth has withered around my feet,
Gassed, screaming, and buried in ditches.

I am Anton Asher Dancinger.
I am eighty years old.
I am not insane.
The gas has just been released.
I am a Jew.

Shima Yisrael, Adonai Elohaenu, Adonai Echod.

    Jerry Rifkin

Beneath The Stars

Look at them
Cherish them
I wonder of their story
Where can they lead us?
What secrets do they hold?
How many people have wished on that one?
Which one shined its light first tonight?
Why do they hide so far away?
What can we learn?
Study them
Wonder about them
Ask about them
There is endless knowledge about these
wordless wonders
Fall in love
Beneath the stars.

    Sabrina Massey

I Made A Hole

I didn't mean to do it
But my frequent mental travel
Sent my mind soaring upward
What did I unravel?
Silly, far-out daydreams made me earth's evil slayer
Because I made a hole in the ozone layer.
With my head in the clouds, inner fantasies swarming
Through a desperate, repressed mind
That's now caused global warming
I won't take the blame - if life weren't so unappealing
My thoughts would never stray so far as to puncture
Our earth's ceiling.
Go ahead and sentence me with punishment reserved
For reckless ozone killers melanomas deserved
I should have been an accountant or been a team player
Because none of those minds would touch the ozone layer

    Pam Ayers

Life Everlasting

From dust I've came, to dust I shall return.
Fire for eternity, will I forever burn?
I'm tired of being captive, in the Devil's den.
Is this the end, I've committed many sins?
I let out long sighs, when I want to cry.
My life is already dead, I'm ready to die!
The Lord's eternal fire, within, keeps me alive.
So I must strive, because he promised me...
   Everlasting life.

    Dondi A. Springer

The Break Of Dawn

As the dark night retires
And the light of morn shines,
A new day is dawning.
This is the beginning of the rest of our lives.
Live well, for no moment shall be spared
Or repeated.
Live now—we have only what today gives
And what tomorrow has in store.
For we know what the past contains,
Though we can't have it back.

The farewell of day;
The fall of dusk.
The night is coming;
This day is nor more.
Now the night is our gift.
We must rest.
We must dream about the future.
For now dreams are all we can see of it.
Once we get there, it is present,
And in a blink of an eye, it is past.

Jennie Wysocki

Hands

Hands come in many sizes, shapes, and colors
Hands are loving, kind, and helpful
A baby's hands are soft and gentle
We use our hands to explore the world
A grandma's hands are old and wrinkled maybe even cold
A father's hands protect us from the world, and even teach
    you to play baseball
A mother's hands are used to hug you and fix your boo boos
Our hands teach us many things, like how something feels
A hand can be hateful, they slap, hit, and point at you
You can be ashamed of them when you see someone with perfect
    hands and yours are dirty, dry, and peeling so you put them
    out of sight
Our hands join us together and help to form a more peaceful world
Hands are works of art that also help to heal us

Jennifer Hawkins

Companions

The pathway placates its part to lead
The wanderer to another's need.

Kneeling, knitting Samaritans mend,
Sowing hearts when travelers befriend,

The wooded path with four feet slowing,
Leads to the hearth of fireplace glowing.

The welded moment, blue-white, and fused,
Will bind their purpose albeit bruised.

The spark, electric light emitting,
Seals with love the soul's rift remitting.

Yet two they are in time not lasting,
Final fusion invites a fasting.

Life is movement and all contrasting
While friends, and foe alike, go grasping.

The lonely night of fright seems catching
The morning multitudes of matching,

When light to light will take together
The dance of dark apart to sever.

And leave our hearts as one eternal
Entity-inscribed joyful journal.

Richard Bishop

Sea Of Love

I stand on the shore of an ocean of men.
I see phantasmic faces in its foam
And bodies cresting on the shifting waves.
Floating voices swirl around me and through me.
Their tide rises up to me, grappling my soul.
The tide flows away, inviting me to follow.

Time after time, in faith I return to the water's edge;
In tempest and hurricanes, as they fling themselves
Upon rocks in desperation for someone to love (consume?)
My forlorn heart draws me to their treacherous arms
And my paralyzing fear keeps me from surrendering
To the undulating rhythms of this sea of love.

Conquered by the longing of an unrelenting flow,
I run towards the sea with the sand gripping my feet,
Warning me to stay on dry land; I swim out and away.
Suddenly, the water chills and the current ceases.
I slowly begin to sink as the current refuses to support my weight.
Why do they now let me drown and die?

I need just one wave to keep my head above the surface.
Just one tidal rush, to a life beyond the shore.

Crystal M. Guidry

Too Much Stuff

Our house has too much stuff
It's making housekeeping rough.

A few of the things can stay
Some can be given away,

The important thing to know
Is what to keep and what to throw.

Now everywhere I turn my head
I see something to sort, but I read instead,

A plan has to be made
If I hope to make the grade.

So I'll discard a sack a week
And only a few things keep,

Then my clutter overload
Will go to recyclers down the road.

My storage problems will cease
And time for pleasure increase,

Being home will be great fun
With more time to sit in the sun.

I'll hold this habit dear
And continue to sort all year.

Marie Cavalli

When The Children Are Gone

After the children have left home,
    They've gone their separate ways...you're all alone.
No Christmas candy, no Trick-or-Treat,
    No pitter-patter of little feet.
The tiny red wagon is now all rusty.
    The doll house is broken...and very dusty.
The board games are stacked
    The rooms are all clean.
The precious heirlooms stand uncracked.
    No little fingers to streak the windows
No more scaring away children's dreamed up foes.
    No bumps or bruises...or mosquito bites.
No giant trees that like to eat kites
    You're left home all alone
With a house full of memories.....
    And an occasional call on the phone.

Steven Elmer Carlson

Hi Dad

The breeze softly touches my cheek, as his eyes say
he's ready to speak. His size so large a shade
does cause, the calm and peace within does draw.
As though he touches, the breeze was felt. At the
time I could not reach his belt. I walked to him—
he could not come. I came before out of shade to
"son," He never talked to me at home, but if I came
before was grown, he'd talk to me about seeds I'd
sown, He seemed to know if fruit to bear, good or
bad or must be shared. He seemed to know just how
I felt, he certainly knew what I was dealt. The
game he said I'd play alone, but just until I was
grown. I didn't know at the time, he had not drawn
a definite line. He smiled often as we spoke. He
had a way to give me a hope, and as I knelt on his
grave, he had a way to quietly say
I love you.....

Kirk Asplin

Speak Softly

Speak softly when you speak to poets,
for however staunchly their dissembled features
deny their vulnerability,
they are unmanned by the everyday cruelties
others slough off.
Their ears are instruments of pain
sensitive to tones as well as words,
helpless again bombardments.
Their eyes look through defenses and if an evil core exists
they see it in a lacerating vision.
Fighting against reclusion, they straighten their slender spines
against the onslaught.
Speak softly when you speak to poets.

Gloria Sadoff Landy

A Journey Taken

It was a cold and lonely night,
My entire body shivered.
Through the darkness I saw a light,
My thoughts began to quiver.

The light pulled me near,
The wind blowing through my hair.
Although, I felt no fear,
As I walked on the air.

Demons and dragons surround me,
The evil darkness has found me.
For I am a soul set free,
And alive again is what I long to be.

I was only trying to find my way,
Trying to make it through this life.
My existence being cut away,
By some stranger with a knife.

I must go to the light,
There is no more love, no more life.
Never will there be another good - night,
As long as there is a stranger with a knife.

Stacia J. Ruthrauff

A Wondering Mind

A wondering mind filled with curiosity can be born with little
knowledge of what he or she is born into.
It happens a lot, and the number is unlimited.
A world that has been explored over and over, and yet not discovered.
A world that is green in your mind if you try to believe it will be!
But the truth can be a delusion and the delusion can be the truth
of a Black, Cold, Heartless world, where Friendship is yet to be invented.

Sammy Pamias

"A Part Of You"

There was a time, a very short time, that you cared for me from within,
But then I arrived, months later I arrived, a small person, made
you happier then you'd ever been.

Hours you gave, care and love you gave, to mold me and guide me
with love,
A strong kind of love a binding love, partly bestowed from our God
up above.

Time will pass, hopefully patience will last, to support me
through my growing years,
There will be trying times, unhappy times, but hopefully, many
happy tears.

So please keep in mind, in the passing of time, all the happiness I
gave while I grew,
Cause on this special day, I have my own little way, showing that
I'm proud to be a
"Part of You"!
Happy Mother's Day!

Lorraine G. Hoskins

'Trapped'

The room is a small one.
It has hard thick walls made of cement, so hard, cold and dark grey.
The ceiling is way above me and that space seems to go on forever,
I can just about see it.
I'm cold and lonely sitting huddled in the corner staring at that window.
Staring at my window.
It is small and square and has thick steel bars.
It's open so the light streams through it, like a spotlight into
the darkness as it catches the dust.
I can see it,... I can feel it... I can smell it...
the beautiful light.
I also see the feet walking past my window.
No one ever stops to look in
If someone was only to take the time they'd see there's a handle on
the bars outside to open the window..... and inside is a person
waiting to be free.

Sharon H. Dixon

Carpe Diem

There comes a time in every man's life when a risk must be made.
But they ask themselves "Why should it be on this very day?"
They procrastinate and wait and take their time.
And then find out that they've crossed the line.
They've waited too long and it's become too late.
And they regret that risk that they did not take.
Carpe Diem
Just do it says the wise man, just seize the day.
I can't, I will, but I don't know a way.
Don't think too hard, don't think too long.
Just do it, just do it, just move along.
And that time the man sees the light.
And he realizes just then that the wise man was right.
Just do it, just do it, just seize the day.
For if you do not, it might drift away.

Brian Apgar

Untitled

A Friend is someone who cares;
Someone who is there;
Let you know you treat them fair;
They'll never take the stair;
A friend is someone that you need;
Without asking they'll do a good deed;
A friend is someone that you love;
Together, will find the love from above;
So when you find a good friend;
All your troubles will end.

Megan McGuire

Boston Underground

The city's filth flows into the sewers
Mingling with the water and oil of the streets
Casting off a reddish glow, and streaming down,
Down,
Down,
Into the caves, where the cobra carves its burrow in the dust
Silver coins clink in curved black coffins as
Threads of music, falling from lonely violins,
Stir the stale and heavy air
Touching darker places of the soul
Where sunlight never brushes away the dust
Shadows peer from shadows, bound forever to the cobra's cave
Their weathered faces,
Untouched by Time's chisel,
Creak and groan beneath the harsh hammer of the sculpture
Grief.
Pale phantoms, haunted by memories of the
Sun, like Stoker's children,
Waste away beneath the world,
Whose sparkling days and moonlit nights,
Are never pierced by violins

Kathleen Gibbons

Can You See Him?

Can you see Him my friend?

Ahh,....look again

He is in the smallest of flowers
and the tumbling of waterfalls.

On His laughter, the butterflies rise and fall
and the eagle soars with ease.

From His smile comes the warmth that fills the suns rays
as they spread across the earth.

His voice can be heard in the wind that sways the trees,
tousles a child's hair, and sings deep in the night.

With the rising of the sun, it is as if we are looking into
His eyes, and seeing the hope of life.

And as the sun, aglow with colors you've never even seen
disappear from sight, His love, His might, His ever-presence
is so alive, all creation is awed, and can do nothing
but watch.

Dana Romanello

A Young Man And An Older Man

"Is it not true, that I being older than you
can't learn from you, or do the thinking you do?
Does age matter, is knowledge a ladder that we climb
together, strive to be better??"
"By me being younger, can I be a teacher,
can I be a preacher, can I ever reach ya!??
Are you listening or-are you hearing??
Am I talking or am I speaking?
Indeed you can learn from me
as I learned from thee.
Age doesn't matter!
It's just chatter!!"
"Yes! Oh young one, you can teach someone
preach a sermon - if you determined
I have listened to you talk and watched how
you walk, together we can stand,
a young and older man"

O'Donald McCants

At Touch Of Dawn

The robin sang at touch of dawn.
It was right early in the morn.
The sky was dark, the day was new.
Yet every note he sang was true.

That bird sings with song that's bright.
Birds farewell to that dark night.
He heralds day with lilting tune,
Waking the flowers in early June.

His song tells of a faith in God.
It rang out where none else had trod.
It echoed o'er the pond and dale,
And through the wooded mountain trail.

Oh, give me such a song I pray.
That at the break of each new day,
My life may shed a golden ray,
To bless those I meet along the way.

Marjorie E. Jones Mott

Grandma

She ambles her way through twigs and pines, never once stopping
herself to mind, that she is but a speck on this sacred ground.

And when she walks she is like my mother; preoccupied with
endless tasks and mindless worries, with this needs to be done
and that needs to be washed. Today isn't long enough for her
to notice that summer is dying and winter is waiting to be
born, and she is but a speck on this sacred ground.

Her arms are barrel-round and her skin is the color of morning
coffee. Her breasts are the envy of well-fed geese. Her hands
are weather worn from wet water washings of me and my like.
Laundry Day is her domain. Other peoples vanities are hers
second hand. She has seldom heard a "thank-you", and is always
shocked when she does. She smiles Jack-o-lantern, and she
brushes onionskin hair away just like that. She will not stop
to rest until God says so, for she is but a speck on this sacred ground.

R. J. St. Patrick

"Short Tongue"

He was born with a short tongue.
He was born with two left hands.
Pointing outward just like the trees
He's travelling the avenues along the way.
He's on the plain you're on today.
Going nowhere just so he can see.
A penny now for what you're thinking.
A sunken ship that keeps on sinking.
I forgot a lot of times, but I haven't missed a lot.
He wears his fortune around his neck.
You can't neglect what you don't expect.
Make him a statistic.
Make me realistic.
He was born with a silver tongue.
He was born with a pessimism.
Taking everything where nothing's free.
    Talk to me universally.
    Talk to me personally.

Chris Council

Unchaining Prometheus

For yet another thousand years
    Must Prometheus suffer still
Till man shall know the difference between
    His destiny and his will;
Till man shall bear with equal right
    His knowledge and the crown;
Till man shall lose his illusions
    And lay his weapons down.

Bob McBride

Gibbous Moon

Gibbous Moon, shine forth your brightest
For me in my time of need; light
Up the darkness in which I am fettered.

You have evaded the clouds.
You have precluded the stars.

I will follow your sparkling, sequined path,
Gleaning strength and confidence
From your perfect stability.

Burn along to your fullest
And I will grow with you:
Wax on, Gibbous Moon!

Charles M. Foster

The Last Mile

Perfectly disguised to us from the one
A closeness that revealed the news
crossing lines into pieces of romance
building together yet breaking apart

The darkness lifted by salvations light
commitment turned to convince
attempts to nullify the love
but the plan continued by grace

Commence then yield, insecurity revealed
intimacy ceased by time
tempted fear from the dark for two
instilled desires but never spoken

Fulfilling the lust of one
denying needs of a pure heart
with childlike hope struggling in desperation
never knowing what prohibits a soul

Michelle Pleger

"Homesick For Heaven"

When I think of God's love for me all these years,
Through all of my trials, sorrows and tears,
I know soon I'll see Him face to face
And be rid of this sinful world, at last.

Lately, Heaven thoughts are on my mind,
Earthly gains and pleasures seem out of rhyme
With the beautiful home He's prepared above
While covering us here with His mercy and love.

Even so, come, Lord Jesus, come!
I'm ready when You are to take me home.
I pray all my family will be ready too,
Let none miss Your trumpet call from the blue.

Thanks for family joys, and friends You give,
Thanks that we can help others, as we live,
Let's live life to the fullest in Jesus' name,
Looking forward to Heaven when He comes again.

Sarah K. Lovett

Dreams And Rainbows

I wish dreams and rainbows could be forever, I love to see you
smile, I love to hear you laugh, but all I see is sadness in your
eyes. For you to smile, for you to laugh, the sadness must be in
my eyes. You ask I leave your life, and a very special wife.
Dreams will never die, but dreams do fade from view, and as long
as rainbows fill the sky, I'll always think of you. The majestic
rainbows light up the sky after the cleansing of the earth, as do
dreams light up our heart, after the cleansing of our soul. If
dreams and rainbows never coincide, the feeling of loneliness
will always remain in side. I wish dreams could last forever or
till rainbows are no more. You will forever be a very special wife.

Mike Tatun

Love Speaking

"Like the beauty of the butterfly that's dancing on the sky,
I cannot capture the beauty of love, I may only experience it."

"Fluttering, glimmering, dancing on the warmth of a pale-blue
sky. Soft; silver, gold white, yellow, orange, red, blue, green,
and velvety-black; Butterflies."

"Spiritually enraptured within love's embrace, as the soft fresh
beauty of spring's petals of peach blossoms in gentle float across
skies of shimmering warm blue breezes."

"The crescent of moon on satin-black sky, the crashing surf on
rocks below, creating heaving sounds of time's creation, enforcing
the strength of my love's endless time in space."

"A tiny sparrow's flight captured in dawn's soft orange glow
offers lonely proof of my love's distance, and reminds me of
my love's singular journey."

Richard Darrell Baldwin

Mom

Her face I don't remember.
Her voice is so unclear.
But memories I have are happy and quite dear.
Her love was never ending.
Her courage never matched.
The door that opened to her heart,
Was never ever latched.
My father always worried when to the store she walked.
For to any passing stranger she never failed to talk.
Her wisdom was so boundless.
Her face and eyes so clear.
and even though she's gone from us,
I feel her presence near.

Nancy M. Hendricks

Soldier's Prayer

Oh Dear Lord, let the war cease,
Bring to the world ever lasting peace.
We've tried fighting and that didn't work,
Think of all the killing and all of the hurt.

I see no sense in any war,
So please Dear Lord, let there be no more.
We're killing off our own beloved kind,
What isn't dead is scared in mind.

I don't see why all wars can't quit,
And people learn to love a little bit.
I'm just one soldier, but one who cares.
Please Dear Lord, hear my prayers.

My heart is heavy with sadness and concern,
There's so very much we have to learn.
In this war I may lose my life,
Who Dear Lord, will provide for my son and wife?

At the end of this deadly game,
Does it matter who won, or who's to blame?
Will you look at the children, can you tell me the score?
Oh Please Dear God, put an end to war!

Omer L. Paxton

If I Could Speak A Fraction

If I could speak a fraction of my mind about the world,
I would subtract all the bad.
In addition to that, I would deduct all of the sad.
I would multiply all the good and sum up all the smiles,
And divide the bad for metric miles.
I could never measure with a ruler,
How happy the world be to see me
measuring kindness.

Justin Janiak

Untitled

I forgot how to dream my dreams.
I forgot even my deepest feeling.
Then a wise woman came to my side.
She walked with me awhile,
and told me so many things.
Such a wise woman she was.
We shared dreams, we shared life itself.
Then she walked away,
Leaving me with my dreams,
And with life's many things.
And when we met again
We both had become friends.
So close and yet so far away
Our friendship seems.
But we both live our dreams.
Share our love, and our fantasies.
Separate lives but yet together
Because we are Friends.

Thelma Carver

I Need A Friend

I feel so unloved and so very much alone
Could you please call me on the phone?

I need someone, anyone to be my true friend
I feel my life is over, will you be there in the end?

My tears I've held in for so long are starting to fall
Please, please be my friend and give me a call!

There's so much I need to say
I need you, will you stay?

All I want is someone to care.
Why is life to me so unfair?

When you ask, I say "I'm fine"
Please look, take a little time.

My eyes are like a window pane.
Look inside, my pain is very plain.

Darlene Medicine Crow

Morning Haze

I peek through the screen of feathery pampas grass
which hides my view of the lapping water of the stream
as it leisurely embraces the sandy shore.
Four ducks glide with the current.
The thistles wave indolently in the breeze
And finally drop to a whisper.
I part the thistles to view the lavender peaks
of the hills in the distance, the sky a smoky blue.
I hear a mourning dove call to its mate
Then walk off together as though holding hands.
I move toward the bank and see the distorted reflection
of my face as the water glides over it.
Teasing, the sun rays hit the water then suddenly disappear
as though playing hide and seek.
I lie against the bank and dip my fingers
into the face in the water which imitates what I do.
I close my eyes, too content to dream.

Rosabelle W. Edelstein

I Failed To See

I've been around, but I failed to see;
All the beauty that's all around me.
The breeze was warm, the sky was blue.
I looked on the grass, and there was no dew.
The trees were a budding, and the flowers abloom.
I heard a little robin singing a tune.
It made me feel good to hear her song,
It tells me spring is coming along.

Jackie G. Cook

Just Look

Today I met my soul mate—beneath whose eyes I became opaque.
A burning built up inside, there were chances I had to take

It seems I've searched forever, for one who knew my every thought.
But it only took your glance—I knew I cared not the cost.

Life takes such twists and turns winding down the rocky road...
Then brings help to ease our burdens, help to carry our load.

But, would you care for me in illness, as I would care for you?
Would you help drive away my fears, as I would surely do?

Would you wipe away my tears and hold me close a night?
Is a soul mate worth the chances, or even worth the fight?

In love there should be happiness, excitement fulfilling your needs,
A respect that has clear meaning, arms that reward your deeds.

Do you receive patience and understanding, the kind I give to you?
Is your heart now contented, in everything you do?

Or is something really missing, that you've been trying to hide?
Do you need my reassurance it's time I'm willing to bide?

Is your body longing for romance—so rare and hard to find.
I want to fill your needs, can you place your hand in mine?

Were you looking to find your soul mate when fate brought us
    this way?
In my eyes you'll find the answer, I'll wait now for that day...

Teena Clayton

Possum

On the way to the wake she told us
how the possum had been visiting the cat's bowl on the porch,
licking it clean, enjoying the treat of easily found food.
How it crept up at night, silver eyes shining like duplicate moons.
The quietness of its eating was a marvel to watch.
Slow and gentle, crunching the "kitty kernels" in its small mouth.
Then on tiny padded paws, its belly low to the ground,
the nocturnal creature lumbered away.

Just two days ago she was walking down the farm road for the mail,
when she saw the possum in daylight. It lay on the road, looked
    quite dead.
Then it rose with a fury, the upper half of its body writhing,
paws scrambling for a foothold in the air.
It fell back down and she thought it now truly dead.
Then it rose again, again. Hysterical at the sight of the dying creature,
she ran to my father. "Put it out of its misery, put it out of its
    misery," she screamed.
Hoisting the shovel high, he helped the possum do what it couldn't
    do on its own.

Today as we ride together on the way to my father's wake,
the back seat fills with misery. It all seems
like a simple ending under the blade of a shovel
held by loving hands.

Debra Revere

Untitled

Look in my eyes, what do you see?
Now look into my soul and tell me it's free.
My heart beats are true
But without You I feel so very blue.
It is said "Life is a dance"
By God when will I get a chance?
I look around and see all the love
When do I get to fly like a dove?
I am taking a stand
If you wish take my hand.
With nowhere left to hide
I would love to have you stand by my side.

Tammy Mettler

Music Everywhere

The alarm goes off at the key of b.
The crow by the window caws at d.
The humming-bird chirps at d-sharp
While the finches sing at g.

I hear the phone ring at f
And the shower sprays at b-major.
There is a tea-kettle whistling to an f-sharp
And the car's engine warms up at c.

As I got out of the car
The school bus sang along in unison.
With the howling of the wind in a-diminished
Are the marching rhythms of children's footsteps.

Oh, what a band! Oh, what a band!
The world of songs, a perfect art.
I thank you, God! I thank you, God!
For the music in my heart.

John-Joseph A. Gatchalian

The White Path

The path
The fluffy, tranquil, peaceful path
Glittering like silken ripples
Rippling like gentle ripples.
The quiet, solitary, lonely path
O how I love you, snow-covered, peaceful path.

The path
The soft, velvety, cushiony path
Watching the squirrels dancing through
Allowing the creatures to ramble on through.
The soft, inviting, wondrous path
O how I love you, snow-covered, cushiony path.

The path
The snow-covered, pure white path
Hosting the pheasants gazing around
Greeting the new snow falling to the ground.
The padded, cottony, fluffy path
O how I love you, snow-covered pure white path.

So Un Ha Park

True Magic

Tap tap tap a rabbit jumps out of a hat...
    But that's not where the magic is truly at...

Think of the break of dawn...
    or a new baby just being born...

    That's magic...

Think of the sun with its rays so bright...
    or a shooting star falling from the sky at night...

The moon sending off its beams...
    or salmon swimming up not down stream...

    That's magic...

Think of a sparrow watching over its eggs in her nest...
    or a baby sucking freely from its mother's breast...

The color green in a small blade of grass...
    or the change of the season that has just passed...

    That's magic...

Our Father God we all should know, is the true magician in this
    fantastic show...

    Now That's Magic!
Celestine Keeton

Waiting For Love.....

As I sit here drifting off to that wonderful place,
My mind turns into nothingness,
Just an empty feeling with a face.
I can't make you out but I know in my heart
That our paths will cross, if not now
soon for we are not too far apart.
Your name is Hope, Love, Faith, and Destiny
Are you a package deal or even real?
Can you truly bring me joy, excitement,
Or just plain old-fashioned happiness.
I've been waiting for so long and struggled so much,
All I know is that I have Hope and Faith.
And most important of all I've got to remember,
Faith is my Hope and Love is my Destiny.

Ben Pimentel

You

You constantly invade my waking thoughts,
You constantly invade my sleeping dreams,
You can always see through my many schemes,
Twisting my lonely feelings into knots,
How am I supposed to find any sleep?
Your words echo timelessly in my mind,
You are so cruel and yet so kind.
You wrap the strength of your soul around me,
You've taken away a part of my soul...
Stolen away with one look in your eyes
Only...you ignored my desperate cries
Still without you near, I don't feel quite whole
How I long for you, How I long for you,
But, I don't mind because It's you.
It's you!

Katrina R. Walker

Seasons

I love to walk in the cool of the day,
Among the meadows and under the trees,
To watch the little children playing,
And enjoy a cool Summer's breeze.

To walk in the sand along the sea's shore,
To remember how God parted the Red Sea waters.
So his children, on dry land could cross over
Even more he will do for me and you.

I view the mountains that seem to reach the sky,
And Oh the beauty that Fall brings to behold.
Shining upon them is the Sun's warm rays,
Like flames of a fire they seem to blaze.

When I sail through the skies so blue,
I view the scenes of nature below.
All these beauties God did make,
Fear not dear ones, for he is by your side.

Someday we'll sail through the air,
Through vast white clouds looking like snow.
Our flight will end on Heaven's wonderful shore,
There to find peace and happiness forever more.

Earline Cox

We Wonder Why

Men among men who stood so very tall.
Fell at the feet of cowards, unable to move at all.
Three cowards pulled a trigger and left these men to die.
A President, Minister, and Statesman; we wonder why?
Men who fought for equality whether their skin be dark or light,
Men who walked hand in hand to answer our nation's plight.
No more will we hear their voices, cry out for you and I.
They are no longer with us.
We wonder why?

Lucille M. Long

Lost Rebels

The invincible is already conquered.
For strength is only something to defeat.
The great are what the people make them.
And great men have only to lose.
Rally the weak to fight for your cause,
For their submissive protests will always prevail.
Tyranny falls against unity.
Persistency silences might.
Equality is master of all.
Sooner or later the nobles must fall.
Tonight we will take out our rulers.
Tomorrow we'll handle their goons.
We'll fight with our hearts and live by our swords,
'Cus hey! We've got nothing to lose.
And sooner or later we'll have heroes as well,
We'll have lawyers, and big shots, and legends to shell.
And we'll all have fun when we're burning in hell,
'Cus we've already lost our war.

Bradley Root

Sonnet

The gulls assailing air fulfill their fate
By lyric rising to crescendo height
Of sky in vibrant tremolo of flight.
This is their life, a soaring wind-borne state—
They dance the hours away on wings elate;
And when they fall to where the tides invite
The drifting cadences of falling light,
Drifting with the tides their wings abate.

They rise, they fall, like wind, like breath, like sea,
And stormy or serene, embodiment
Of song are they by simply being gull.
What a glad way to travel destiny
On wind's broad back, on river's face and vent
The images of lives so beautiful.

Ethel Engnath

"Secrets Of The Heart"

The heart is a very private place
Where special feelings lie
Memories that sometimes make us smile
And feelings that make us cry

Somehow the seeds were planted here
And we allowed these seeds to grow
A harvest that grew abundantly
But the world must never know

For these are secrets of our lives
Loves we've won and loves we've lost
Loves that lived in the light of our lives
And loves that perished beneath a frost

These loves shall always be held within
For we knew they were doomed from the start
These loves that sometimes allow us a grin
Shall remain our "Secrets Of The Heart"

William E. Kenyon

Wars And Peace

If every nation would get their own country in order;
There wouldn't be time for wars, because there is so much to do.
Instead of trying to use each other and abuse each other,
Let's learn to need each other.
That is the way to peace.
Wars never brought peace;
All it ever brought was destruction and death to us;
And we didn't learn yet.
G od bless the world and if we don't learn to live together,
God help us.

Peter P. DiMattia

In The Dark

I hear it knockin', here or there
but just don't know exactly where
I cannot see,
through darkness that's surrounding me.

An eery feeling seems around,
I cannot hear any other sound.
I wonder what is this over there.
Some ugly faces, I could swear.

My heart is pounding ever so fast,
Will someone come and save me at last?
I lay there quiet and oh, so very still,
maybe they'll go away maybe they will.
I'm covered head to toe in sweat,
my Bed is also soaking wet.

I tell them go away. I can no longer look,
I quickly turn on the light, with all my strength it took.
Now they have gone and I'm so glad,
I'm feeling not the least bit sad.

Liane Brown

Set Sail

The world's like a picture,
Only the faithful can see
God makes all in simplicity.

We cannot understand what is to be,
So we must trust His creativity.

We do not understand why fleas must bite,
Yet we see clearly why dogs must fight

The things of the world are all turned around;
Who was the one who wore the Crown?!

Peace seems yet a life away,
But that is seen to our dismay.

We must tear away the veil;
Pick the right path, for we must sail!

Sail through the sea, the sea of peace;
For that is where we'll find true Harmony!

Brian H. Weil

Pendulum

The man walks an endless trail called life
It changes constantly from night to day
The man finds himself in the irony of it all
The more pain there is the more love there is
Out on his own he sees the contrast in it all
Pain and sorrow
The clock dings out of the night, 12
Happiness and love
The clock dings out of the day, 12
He was seeing himself as both

Everyone is night and Everyone is day
There is no happiness and love without pain and sorrow, just like
there is no Day without Night.

Erik Eden Rasmussen

Untitled

Strength lies in Tolerance.
Tolerance lies in Limits.
Limits begin with Dreams.
Dreams begin with Imagination.
Imagination comes from Within.
Don't let anybody take away your ability to
Dream, with Strength, Imagination, or no Limitations.

Valerie Whitaker

489

A Mother's Love

Many kinds of love have touched my life
For one special kind there is no other
No love exist which can take the place
Of the love given by you MY MOTHER
It's a love that begins with friendship
And unselfish caring too
A love that finds a path through thick and thin
No matter what I say or do
A love which says - "Come Home Again"
From where ever my feet may stray
And very often too it says
"My child, today for you I'll pray"
A love which shared with me knowledge to grow
And taught me right from wrong
A love that holds fast each time I'm sick
And encourages me to become strong
A Mother's Love! It gives so much
Yet, ask nothing in return
A love I now lift up with pride
A love I hope I've earned
Janice Wellington

Zero Tolerance

We have adopted this policy for your well being and safety;
It is to ensure things run smoothly and not too hasty.
This non-violent way is both responsible and smart;
Practice it everyday until it becomes an art.
If you encounter a problem, don't use physical force;
Get straight to the solution by getting to the source.

Drugs and alcohol, you will no longer abuse;
These things will no longer become your excuse.
You will come to know and respect yourself;
You owe it to you and no one else.

To ensure things go well between staff and you;
These are the things that you must do:
You must obey the rules of this establishment;
No drugs, no violence, no sexual harassment.
No gang related activity, no matter how small;
If it creates negativity, we don't want it all.

Be persistent in following the rules;
Make them a part of your everyday tools.
By using hit hard tactics: brain power and will:
You will achieve the goals you came here to fulfill!
Gloria Wilson

Tonight I've Died Inside

Tonight I've died inside
And all the fears I fear
have found a place to hide
I thought I knew what love was
until he stole my heart
Then everything I knew
was suddenly torn apart
It seems as though it's all a game
Where everyone's ahead
And I'm the one that's way behind
Crying myself to bed
You learn to expect the worst
And trust no one you meet
Because in the future you will meet your defeat
No one can rescue me
for I have swam out too deep
And all the secrets I have
only I can keep
Because tonight I've died inside
and this is my final sleep
Brandy Willis

The Wrong Number

The phone is out of order, wonder what it could be!
Now I don't have to think about when you're going to call me.
It's been like this the past couple of days,
But you can find me in so many different ways.
How about at work or on the road to home, and if that can't be
done - then I'll leave him alone.
Alone to be with his ex wife and his eight year old son.
Rene would just soak it up being the only one.

In the prime time of his life, how those precious moments fly by;
Not even a wonder, not even a try.
This is sad to think about I know;
Been sitting here waiting, waiting in the cold.

Don't know how much longer this is going to last,
I just take it day by day then dream about the past.
There is no other way our relationship could be,
Until you decide to leave her completely.

I'm not asking you to give up that little boy!
Just want to take away the pain and to replace it with joy.
Knowing you have a lot on your mind, I'll stop—by making this
    the last line.....
Suzanne M. Burke

The Mountains

I am the mountains.
I am the rocky land.
I provide the land to run and grow on.
Come roam, jump and play on me.
I am fed by the rain and sun.
I feel the trees growing inside of me.
I keep the mountains in their lines.
I shelter the jack rabbits and other rodents.
I know when to shake at the right time.
I sense the cool breeze hitting against my rocky sides.
I look like a brown bumpy blanket under 10,000 big mountains.
I am the mountains.
I am wild and free.
Come climb on me.
Ashlie Sarmiento

Hungarostroika

The people have taken the "People" away,
A Republic it is to be from now on.
The Danube's Red Star is it
extinguished Forever?
McDonalds neonlights Glow
in the newfound freedom of the Hamburger.
The democracy of the 'Bigmac'
can they Really afford it?
Time will show if the price the people pay is too high.
History's lessons must be learned-
But, if the Teacher changes
Before the Final Test??
W. E. Scheidges

Live

Wake up every morning with a happy smile
Never treat the day like a murder trial

Take a good look at every open door
Never think of it as a chore

Know that there are ways to enter a person's heart
Never think of love as a sour tart

When you see the light shine through
Never feel there is nothing you can do

As each day comes to a close
Be glad for you did not doze
Kim Freimuth

The Changing Season

Sometimes it hurts;
Sometimes it feels so good;
Sometimes it passes;
Sometimes it stays forever;
It's something everyone wants;
But not everyone finds it;
It could be around the corner;
Or in a distant land;
No one ever knows until it hits them
Full force in the softest part of their body;
It's something you have to look for;
Or maybe it'll find you;
It'll grow deep within in you;
Maybe it'll fade;
Or get stronger with age;
But if it comes your way,
Pray it will never go away.

Lori-Beth Porter

A Strange Object In A Strange Place

A beautiful rising sun, that
Shines in my room every morning,
Didn't rise with me as I remembered
You will not be here tomorrow.

A romantic and quiet walk on the beach,
Was not the walk I took with you as I tried
Not to cry as we talked about the many times
We've shared together.

A loud, screaming crack of pain, thunder
And pouring rain filled my already weakened
Heart as we said our sad good bye.

Nothing was the same. Not the sunsets, nights
Moon, or stars. In their own little way they
Reminded me of you.

The next morning that beautiful sun, that
Didn't shine in my room yesterday, appeared
Like A Strange Object In A Strange Place.

Luisa Pisano

To Walk Tall

Whenever I sit here, alone at night,
I wait till late, so I may write;
what I feel within my heart...
wishing for dreams someday to start.

I write about most anything,
just to satisfy, a certain yearning.
Not many know, what it is like,
to spend so many, a quiet night.

They think the loneliness I feel,
is caused by something, that is not real.
Dear Lord, I know not what to do,
but in my prayers, I will ask You.

I'm called a fool by most, you see;
but You are the only Judge of me!
It doesn't matter, the needs have I,
if they are meant, You will supply.

So Lord, if anyone tries to judge me,
please help them to stop, and try to see...
that I may stumble, or even fall...
but I know beside You Lord; I can still walk tall.

Cherrie Riegert

A Father Is...

The word father means different things to different people.
To me a father is strong and understanding.
He loves his family more than anything else.
His children are jewels, his wife is his heart.
A father is the shoulder you cry on when you're in pain.
He holds you tight and tells you he cares when you lose
    someone you love.
He's a great comforter.
When you're sick he makes you feel well.
He tells you just the right things to make you feel warm inside.
He knows just what to do to bring a smile to your face.
And whenever necessary he disciplines with a strong hand,
    but love in his eyes.
My father has gone to be with the heavenly comforter.

Now a father is an empty seat at the table.
He is an empty chair in the living room.
My father is an empty space in my heart that loving memories
    must fill.
He is a picture in my mind which I hold so dear.

Now my father is Jehovah God, the Great I Am.
He's father to the fatherless.
With his everlasting love and comfort the pain will go away.
I'm glad God's love surrounds me down every path chosen,
    and he will never leave me.

Melissa Rasmussen

Mortality

Flying, floating, spinning around.
Lazily landing is the bird on the ground.
Sick and suffering with pain to endure.
Twitching in twilight, nothing's assured.
Wounded and winded it lies to rest.
Pumping and pounding is its heart in its chest.
Higher and higher, its spirit flies.
Blindingly bright lights come to its eyes.
Unconscious or unliving is its body below.
Bloody, still bleeding, gaping wounds show.
Far and faint, the memories appear.
Fact or fiction, it's still unclear.
It was soaring slowly through the sky,
Unaware and unknowing of the hunter nearby.
Suddenly spotted, a shot rang out.
Crashing and cracking was the sound all about.
Instantly it felt a pain in its side.
Then feeling flustered the memories subside.
Mere mortal's lives, so delicate and lame.
Live a life or die just the same.

Mark Kaschner

Secret Obsession

Creature of my infinite desperation
grant me the ability to sneak
your aura has bound my heart
your body exudes frozen heat
My memory grows numb
My brain gasps for air

Sitting in this transparent Quiet chair
crying from underneath my skin
You become bored, left me to decay
I held your hunger in my gaze
I was scared and set you free

Wished on Moontime
Walking to the rhythm of your name
without you my arms are empty
without you my world is pain.

Julie Rivera

I Miss You

When the dawn flames in the sky
and the birds begin to fly, I miss you.

When the roses bloom in June
and are touched by morning dew, I miss you.

When the golden sun shined bright
upon your crown of silver white, I miss you.

When you held my hand in thine
I felt the warmth and comfort which we shared, I miss you.

When you embraced and crushed me in your arms
I remember the smile upon your face, I miss you.

When you kissed me in the dark
and whispered "I love you sweetheart", I miss you.

I will miss you
'til the end of time
and my love for you will pine.

Beloved,
I miss you.

Anne H. Miller

"Opportunities Lost"

This is to you, my father
The one I used to call "Dear Ole Dad"
Then you abandoned the family
And made my whole world sad.

You'll probably never see this
These words I write in sorrow
For the times we never shared
We had yesterday, But never more tomorrow.

You are lying on death's bed
And I don't know what to do
I want you to tell me what happened
But, I'm afraid I'll never know the "Real" you.

If I don't come to see you
It is just another opportunity lost
My pride says "No Big Deal"
But pride.... Always has a cost.

So, instead, I write down my feelings
And keep them all inside
Then, when someone asks "What is wrong"
My heart just runs and hides.

Roy W. Wilder

The Crow

If and when you die
The crow takes your soul.
If and when you die
The crow carries you like a mother with a child.

If and when you die
The crow sings to you a lullaby.
If and when you die
The crow smiles to take your fear away.

If and when you die
The crow gives you its comfort.
If and when you die
The crow watches you like a father.

If and when you die
The crow warms you with its wings.
If and when you die
The crow brings you eternal rest.

If and when you die.

Eurice Chavez

The Way Finds A Christian

I am down. Howling wolves surround me,
North winds, busting, blowing.
Storms drown. Icy around me,
White water, filthy, fast-flowing.

The night, dark as black.
Winter, exposed with lack.

Is there no kind sun, or calm flower?
No whispering tree?
Or cleansing shower?
If there is - then show me.

A loving finger strokes my brow, lifts my head,
Now I see above, the mush and mire,
Sky blue Dove and silver linings, in their stead.
And bright Red glow, like a flower on fire!

Free bird flying upon The Wing.
No more sighing as it does sing.

My God's mantle has warmed me, I feel His might,
Through His Son, my frozen soul He did save,
On this frigid winter's night.
And joy. Came in fresh brave wave. Perfect rave!

Michele Pettit

Untitled

My beautiful child if you only knew,
What kind of world you've been born into.
A world of hopes, a world of fears.
Yes my child there are even tears.

Our world was once a very safe place,
Times have changed there's problems to face.
Drugs and violence are all around,
Our children are trapped, too late to be found.

With this bad in our world,
You must see through.
To the beauty and good that lies there too.
Watch and listen beauty you'll see,
In the sky, ground, and there on the tree.
It's time to care and love our world too.
Appreciate the gifts God left for you.

Alicia R. Purdy

Enigma

I know that the sun flashes
After the morn scatters the dew
Its rays tickling slim branches
Loving the grass, I always knew.

When flowers reach beauty at its peak
Butterflies feast in quiet adoration
Impatiently awaiting to partake
With the bees, in their creation.

Why do oceans caress the deep
In a fickle earth that likes to lie?
When the moon sails by, waters never sleep
Hiding her wonders that never sigh.

Sunrise colors a pale horizon
Heralding a new day's might
Sunset descends in crying crimson
A warning of the unknown, in the night.

Ah, sweet mysteries are here to stay
Letting my heart feel what my eyes fail to see
The enigma of nature steals my mind away
But my soul, it feeds, and sets me free.

Bles Chavez

Beloved

What must this weary soul become to have your love
  My futile efforts hang in the void 'twixt us
With care have I cleaned and perfumed my body
  Declared my devotion in both word and deed

Silent and patient you wait for me to understand
  Your beauty close yet far from my caress
I dreamed last night and reached out to hold you
  My dream a vapor, now awake, I yet despair

As in my dream, I find you near yet far from me
  Reveal, I pray, what secret can loose your love
Why silent your lips, my entreaties refused while I
  With yearning long to touch, caress, possess

That my spirit may know your gentle touch as I sleep
  Let love pour forth upon me from your soft eyes
Fix me with the gentle gaze of their tranquil deep
  With greatest joy I dream of feeling your caress

I fear to know, my love, what you would have me do
  'Tis not by word, nor deed, that your love's free
The one to whom you give that joy must honor you
  If love I can't possess, come — share with me

  Walter E. French

The Best Part Of Me

My life hasn't been, always so kind
But I always knew, in the back of my mind
For in this world, someday I would see
The one who would be, the best part of me
When we first met, I did have a doubt
But then I realized, We'd work all things out
The love you have given, was just meant to be
For I'll always know, you're the best part of me
The things you do, and the caring I receive
I know in my mind, that it's not make believe
Your understanding and patience, seems to flow free
And you're still the one, that's the best part of me
I could never begin, to try and express
My love for you, and my true happiness
So I feel in my heart, heaven did hear my plea
There'll never be another, for you're the best part of me.

  James Vincent

America

On that hot July summer day, the bald eagle was born and we became the United States of America.

From the roots of the old oak trees came Thomas Jefferson with the Declaration of Independence, George Washington crossing the Delaware, and Honest Abe who set the slaves and symbols of misery free.

From the Great Lakes to the Rocky mountains to the Mississippi our love, beliefs, confidence, and happiness is so much stronger than the sourness and sorrow.

Who are the United State? We are the United States. How do you gamble with the lives of your children? How do you gamble with something so fragile, so pure? You don't. You don't because you know that you will never win. It is not just a game. It is our home, our country, our world and hopes. As the tree of joy blossoms of fruit and flowers, the tree of greed and misery shrivels and whimpers in the dark shadows. As Lady Liberty holds up her feeble body, she hopes to give us support, confidence, dreams, and hope.

  Elizabeth Lee

A Father

Who's a father?
Some may ask,
He's someone who cares, adores and doesn't think that's a task.
Someone who's strong and kind,
Someone who has his children on his mind.
Someone who works and shows full support,
Someone, when the times get hard, don't reach for a passport.
Someone who thinks the world of his child,
Not running the streets all wretched and wild.
Someone who protects and stands against all wrong,
So, that his children could learn to contribute to the society which they belong.
Someone who provides, don't have to be wealthy,
In order for his children to be strong and healthy.
So, to those men who think, Fatherhood's a bother,
It should be left to the mother
Think of your sons growing up rather,
Than being the non-existent father.

  Paulette R. Larmond

Happy Anniversary Mom And Dad

It's your anniversary- Fifty-five
You've been married longer than I've been alive (good thing!)

What gift could I give with complete assurance
That would compliment you on your strength and endurance.

Through good times and bad, for better or worse,
Raising two daughters who were sometimes perverse
  (not me though)

Dad, you overcame odds at which most would have balked,
When after your accident, you once again walked.
And went on to make yourself quite a name
  at 81 in the "Aviation Hall of fame".

And Mom, with your willpower, you're my inspiration,
You do it all, without reservation.

Though no parent thinks they have passed the test,
In my opinion, you both are the best.

I know it's not been easy, you've both given a lot,
You loved us and raised us and gave more than you got.

Though this day's in your honor of your 55th year,
I am blessed and so grateful to still have you here.

  Elizabeth K. Krege

Stars

Sometimes at night, when the moon is full and stars are bright
When the wondrous heavens are open wide
I stop to listen to the silence

To the question I ponder, am I truly alone?
The stars have given me the answer
As the night envelops me into its embrace
I find the truth has always been with me

The spirit of those in my heart, gone but not forgotten
The presence of those in my subconscious, never out of reach
The pictures in my mind, though faded with time, remain clear

With the angels looking over me, to protect and care for me
With the precious few, who have stolen a place in my heart
With the deep places in my soul, filled with memories and love
The stars have given me the answer, I knew was always there

  Melissa Stiner

Inspiring Creations

The sky! The sky! It's so very blue.
Beauty in itself as the words "I love you."

Sometimes it's cloudy and cold rain just pours.
Lucky for me 'cause I'm snug here indoors.

Often the moon's out and sometimes it's real bright.
Lighting up God's landscape in the middle of the night.

Shining so brightly are the rays of the sun.
Giving light for our living in a world made for fun.

Just look at the stars oh so perfect in shape.
While our mind tries to cope, our two eyes just gape.

The oceans are rolling and waves pound on shore.
Do the waves love the sand or does the sand say "no more?"

The wind blows and blows while we marvel at God's laws.
There are tornadoes and hurricanes, then no wind at all.

The bumblebee buzzes but look at the gnat.
Is his life lonesome from just this and that?

A creature of beauty is a large butterfly.
Did it come from a tomb or will it end up and die?

One baby's smile is most precious to see.
All things are perfect with God we'll agree.

Jason M. Rudisill

Untitled

No matter where I am, you're in my mind
Even though we are not so very near
I imagine myself closed in your arms
Just like it used to be in the old times
Just the two of us alone by ourselves
Dreaming of us as one in the future
I should've known it wasn't meant to be
The sound of use together forever
The tears I shed just thinking about you
How you could have left and done this all?
You ran away leaving my heart in grief
Along with plenty of pain and sorrow
Even though you made me look like a fool
You know that you will always have a place in my heart

Alexis Piekarsky

Give Peace A Chance

Women of Israel - unite!

We have enough of blood and tears. Will it never end?

We lost our leader - beloved and revered
We must not let his death remain in vain
Save our sons and daughters too
What good is the land without a people?
We have enough earth to cover the fallen, the maimed, the dead
We have enough food to feed the young and the old
This hunger for more land will kill us all.

Extremes can always be a curse -
The fight for more and even more will never end.
Israel was born in blood - now let our people rest.
We are tired of fighting; brother against brother,
Father against son - you call this holy?

Rabin tried to make peace
He paid the ultimate price
We lost our innocence when he died
Enough of blood and tears:
Give Peace A Chance!

Greta Weiniger Gruen

Untitled

White water wades against the ocean floor
Waves lapping in shadows of cries for love
Lonely, silence speaks as each crashes ashore
Falling stars loose their spark.

What becomes of one in such a small world
Wishes of another together in thought
To have someone love you unconditionally
But once again you spend the night alone with music, the T.V.,
    and the remote.

The same sound plays on the radio
A broken heart drowning in memories
Strange how familiar that song sounds
As the water deepens and erodes possibilities.

Funny how something so big as the ocean
Can create so much feeling and insight
But as I watch the water wallow in the night
I know it understands the darkness of an empty heart.

Erin R. Johnson

Restoration

I felt his inner hand lightly touch my soul,
Whispering pleas for my heart to come
From behind its sheltered tower walls made
Of my own design.

Frightened from the tormented years it lay.
Shunning his gentle caress convinced,
Our sweet conversations were no more than
A falsehood of hope.

His fingers sift my thoughts in empathy.
Mourning and consoling damages.
Cajoling my soul to see no horror,
But him; waiting there.

Deftly the wrist turns in supplication.
Speaking closing arguments as my soul,
Curls up in his palm - understood at last;
Dissolves its prison.

My inner heart sobs achieve their release.
As eyes dim; heart and soul singing free,
We smile watching one tear travel downward,
Holding each other.

Toni Mullins-Cotter

Tornado In The Night

The rain begins to sprinkle
The clouds steadily pass by above
The sky is slowly darkening
As the storm is moving in.

Lightening strikes, the thunder pounds
Now it begins to pour
The sky is full of purples and gray
And the calm is no more.

The whistling of the wind stirs up
An eerie feeling fills the night
Debris and leaves fly through the air
Branches break upon the ground.

Back doors flap with great force
Street lights dim and soon blow out
Glass is shattered, roofs are torn
Automobiles turned upside down.

Fear fills the minds of endless people,
panic everywhere
The wind dies down, the pour is but a sprinkle
With destruction all around.

Lori Campbell Peace

Mike's Hugs

"Wanna hold you a minute", my toddler would say,
when tired of playing at the end of the day,
or when puzzled by something not understood,
or sorry for actions he sensed weren't "good".

"Wanna hold you a minute", my toddler would say,
then nestling my shoulder to soothe away
the hurt of his anger, the pain of a fall,
a broken toy...or a lost ball.

Without asking, my man-child-now-grown,
our last Christmas together (if only I'd known!)
Hugged me his bear hug, his heart ever in it
and I thought I heard,
"Wanna hold you a minute".

Ruth Winters

My Mother

I have a shadow that goes in and out of me
It tells me I have a mother I ought to go and see
So, I'm going to Tennessee with a banjo on my knee
I'm going to the country a little woman to see
She's as lovely as a breath of fresh air, always busy as a bee
Her house is always happy it's full of laughter and glee
On her table is always cookies, cake or tea
She swings in her swing free as the breeze
She has a flower garden a sight for eyes to see
In her yard stands a majestic golden maple tree
This lady has a iron will, and as tough as the sea
She's like the wind that blows free
It would be a pleasure to sit a spell with this busy bee
Now my poem must end on a nightly zee
But best of all she's my mom Dolly Ree

Mary E. Lester

The First Time

The first time I saw love
Was when the wind blew through your hair
And there was a glow in your stare
As if you were sent from above

The first time I felt hate
Was when you slapped me in the face
And your eyes had lost their grace
As if Hell had opened up its gate

The first time I felt fear
Was when I was lying on the floor
My whole body bruised and sore
And I thought, "Why am I here?"

And that's the night I left you forever
Even thought you said I would never

Rachael Singer

Untitled

Life goes by,
Life so why,
Love rolls on,
Love so-long,
Light begins a new day,
Night ends the hooray,
Silence makes you cry,
Memories you wonder why,
Mother and Father long to see,
Pray and wish them to be,
Warm thoughts abound all around,
Then reality knocks you to the ground,
Blessings you have not one deserved,
But looking around, yes all my prayers have been heard.

Thomas A. Gregg

Prime Time

Throughout the year, we've beaten the rest,
Now it's time to play our best.
We've overcome our injuries
Which has lead us to victories.

The road to the final four
Has opened up the door
To great basketball
Where the winner takes it all.

I appreciate the cheerleaders being around
And the roar of the crowd.
This gives me "March Madness"
With Billy Packer and Jim Nantze.

The road to the final four
Leaves me wanting more,
But it ends the would have been
And the could have been.

It's a chance of a lifetime
To join the prime time.
The Bruins, Razorbacks and Running Rebels.
The Hoosiers, Wildcats and the Blue Devils.

J. H. Dumas

God Is Truly Amazing

God is truly amazing, we've only to
listen, to look and see, for all around
and everywhere are His true
convictions of His love and caring. His
voice in the wind, His face in the sun,
a beautiful rainbow when the storm is
done. The promise He has given will
never be broken, oh but to just listen,
on a winters still and snowy night.
You'll know and hear His soft voice
saying, everything will be alright. For
I am coming, as I have promised to take
you back with me. Just live in faith.
Stay in this moment, for I will love you
forever and take you with me, to live in
my heavenly home for eternity.

Kay Eileen Johnson

Social Security

The warmest of air blows against my skin and chills my soul
Nature's hand falls upon me and takes its toll
The clock runs a marathon in my head
It won't be long before I am dead
Each movement is critical, for it may be my last
Two minutes go by for everyone one I wasted in the past
Sad and lonely I only have myself to blame
I lived a life of insanity now I will never be the same
My hands shake constantly now along with everything else
My heart struggles for every beat I am lucky I still have a pulse
I once knew what it meant to be alive
But now I live in a pool of self pity and I have no pride
You speak to me in foreign tones like I can't hear
I just have nothing left to say I would rather shed a tear
One day closer to my last moment
Death will be my final opponent
I wish the record needle would skip back a few years
Maybe I would be able to overcome all these fears

James Willigar

Untitled

Loneliness is ashes,
Anger is a bully,
Horror is a monster, happiness
is a mom, courage
is Jesus, fear is
a first time, guilt
is a box, love is a
first kiss.
Embarrassment is a
fall, joy is a pet.

A friend is
Someone you can
talk to. A
girlfriend is a
person who loves
you. A mountain
is a big hill of
frustration. A
flower is someone growing up.
A cigarette is guilt. ET is like a snail.

Jeremey Henderson

When I Grow Old

When I grow old I may turn gray, but in my heart he will always stay.
My idea of a perfect job is to be a missionary.

Ever since I was small I had this dream once in the mall.
I would fly off far to Foreign lands and speak the word as best I can.

I would help save the hearts of many. I will teach the news from East
to west and always shout that God is best!

Once my years of ministry are over I will go to school to become an
architect. I will raise houses in the Middle East, I will draw
people's dreams with large wooden beams.
I will travel again to build his house throughout the nations
we will unite our hearts.

I will use my skills to reconstruct. I will worship him with my
fingertips. When I grow weary and almost faint I will lean on
him to give me strength.

A life of service is what I want. Days of observing and sharing his love.
A life of adventure and moving around though suitcase
unstable my heart is still sound.
No matter what task or trial that comes with my Lord
Jesus Christ everything will be won!

Rachel Leshe Larkins

Cherish

My Mother, My Father
Two Words - my heart, my hope

Like a warm breath of exhaled air hangs
suspended in the cold winter,
Pleasant childhood memories of being with you hangs
suspended in my yearning mind.
My mother, my father, as I grew into a young child
you gave me spiritual security and taught me to smile.

Let your guiding parental spirit silently listen to
your beloved child's cry of spiritual despair.
Gently hold me in the safety of your warm, loving arms
tenderly placing your strong protective arms around me.
Again, gently, place your courageous heart
in my languishing heart.

Let your spirit silently speak to my heart's spiritual despair.
Father,
who lovingly cared for and sheltered me.
Mother,
who tenderly nursed, bathed and whispered
loving praises to me.

Newfonie J. Inman

The Bird

As I was sitting under the tree, I heard the bird sing to me.
Come, come to my land, come you'll understand.
It has trees, flowers, and much grass, I'm very sure you won't pass.
As I flew with him over the sky, I saw the clouds go passing by.
One by one fluffy and white,
It seemed like everything was going all right.
But just then, a hawk came through, looking for something to chew.
We ducked, he missed, oh, how good, at least now we won't be
his food!
I reached his land I saw the grass, I said hurry let's get in fast!
We got closer I could see, all the flowers and the trees.
We reached the ground, I heard a sound: So beautiful, and
sweet,
I saw the birds I asked myself, what will I meet?
I met blue jays, cardinals, and parakeets.
They looked so peaceful, they looked so sweet,
No crime, no violence, nor anything Bad,
It made me think of our world, and made me sad.
Then I heard the alarm clock ring, the last bird sing.
I looked out the window without saying a word,
And that is when I saw the bird.

Crystal P. Molinary

She's Just Five

She came running to my embrace
   tears flowed down her little face.
As she trembled her words poured
   with each syllable emotions soared.
"Daddy yelled". "Mommy cried".
   "The other day my kitty died".
The pain was real with anguish
   even I could feel.
I held her tight. I held her long.
   I soothed her with a quiet song.
For it's not easy being five. There's pain and
   stress in your life.
Her needs seem few, but are no less felt.
   Then the things that you and I are dealt.
The hurt is real, but quickly banished when she
   feels she's loved and cherished.
Do not assume because she's five that she
   can wait 'til you have time.
For when your busy days are through, she may
   not have time for you.

Ginger Harne

In The Cool Cave

Slimy dirt-pink worms till the wet, gray earth
as we sit, trying to inhale the pale white clouds
of smoke rising from our virgin cigarettes.

Our crouched bodies are tapped by drops
of rain that slide down through the cracks
of our wooden pool deck directly above.
The water brings with it the acrid odor
of freshly-applied lacquer.

Murmurs from the water pump break
our concentration as we blindly encourage
the other's new-found habit with hesitant
words formed by our shivering lips. The sound
fills the wall-less, damp dwelling like a palpitating heart.

The darkness beneath the pool deck shields
our feelings from one another; the somberness
of seeing our fifth-grade school-mate laid
to rest in her casket just hours before. Like our parents
we drown our sorrows with smoke

only we have the cool cave
in which to hide.

Elizabeth Oliver

You Are My Mother

If I were a rose, you would be my petals,
Soft and delicate as a baby's skin.
Every time someone looked at me, you would make my beauty known.

If I were a piano, you would be the beautiful music,
    making me so well loved by all who hear it.

If I were an apple, you would be my skin,
    protecting me from the outside world,
Making me feel safe and warm,
    while you surround me from head to toe.

If I were a rainbow, you would be my pot of gold,
Making my life richer, as I shine and shimmer in the sky.
You, the unknown source of my sparkling pride.

If I were a ring, you would be the stone carefully imbedded
    right in the heart of me, giving me true value.

If I were a horse, you would be my legs,
    which keep me standing tall and strong.

But I am a girl, and you are my mother.
You gave me life, you protect me from harm.
You give me strength, confidence and encourage me in all I do.

While you sit back and watch me grow up.
Amanda Oehlmann

Childhood

Childhood, an immature reflection of events around,
A fading replica of objects on the ground,
An uneasy grip on the march of time,
A fantasy of things undescribable and unfounded
An obstinacy, an ego of its own kind-
Well reflected in his effort to put a square into a hole
And making a mountain of a little mole.

Childhood, a challenge to the authorities of time
May be a king, a queen or parenting,
All surrender to his innocent past-time.
He is the monarch of all what he sees,
A master of what comes under his command;
Demanding respect and adoration of his innocent domain
And total attention who wants to be his friend.

He is the hope of the future, the might of his time
The image of a generation, the foot-print of his age.
A true manifestation of total efforts
That a people can muster
In whom hinges the fate of man
To live, survive or to die like a doomsday.
Shamim A. Siddiqi

Love Is Our Answer

Love is our answer, to everything
Only the two of us can bring
Love is our answer to happiness, but not loneliness
Love can bring joy in our hearts, so we will never grow apart

Love can bring tears to our eyes
If we only say good-bye
Love is for the two of us to share together
Love isn't the answer to start fussing, but to join together

Love is our answer to our relationship, not our lips
Love is our answer to my thoughts, not by my faults
Memories set in my mind, and it's sometimes hard to find
I hold your hand close to mine, so everything will be fine

Love is thee answer to love again, so you won't feel the pain again
Love is what makes your life complete
Love isn't what makes you want to cheat
Love is very real, it makes us think of things we feel

And the feeling will stay strong, forever as our love grows
Rachel Cardwell

A New Year's Gala

A line of people in right minds
form outside, waiting to join
friends and co-workers to
celebrate an end, cheer a beginning.
As the annual countdown begins,
corks of champagne await their
performance time, and on the count
of three, bottles are shook. At the
call of midnight, corks pop with the
filling of glasses, hugs and handshakes,
a few kisses under the mistletoe.
Past resolutions forgotten, new ones
are made, whether they will last or not.
Joy and laughter fill the rom; now
you believe that peace on earth is real.
Susan Fila Murphy

Earthly Venus

In her eyes of silver-blue I see the Ocean
and its boundless horizon.
Mercurial sparkles reflect and dance upon the surface, enticing me
to investigate the abundant life within.

In her kiss I feel the refreshing Spring wind of Zephyrus.
Her Ocean breeze wisps the Winter's cold, grey clouds away.

In her hair of golden Summer I see the rays and waves of sunlight.
I sleep entangled in its hazy, airy warmth.

In her smile I see a string of luminous bay pearls
slightly guarded for its own protection
behind a thin, white veil.

Venus emerged from the Ocean
    innocent, and shyly aware
    of her beauty.
Miguel Angel Fernandez

Come dark like the clouds on a rainy day
Unexpected, unpredictable
Reasonable, unforgettable

Come with the winds
Strong, moving
Taking me with you to the ends of the earth
Are we going to heaven? I always wanted to know how it was

Come like the sounds of blues from a trumpet or even a sax
Take me, mesmerize me

Come like you are in the night
Jacinta V. White

Happiness

H is for holy- we are blessed in a holy state of mind and heart.
A is for adore- take time to love and adore our Lord...
P is for plentiful- God's love is plentiful.
P is for pretty- look at all the pretty things in the world...
I is for intelligence- God gave all of us the qualities that we would
    need in life- never more than we can handle. Never less than we need.
N is for nice- remember to be a nice person...
E is for everything- remember God gives us so many precious gifts...
    so many... it is hard to thank Him for everything, but we should.
S is for sincerity- that is very important - be sincere and true
    to yourself and to others.
S is for serene- that is a very important state to be in.
    We must be quiet and serene and hear God's voice as He talks
to us....

    Remember that you must be happy and loved and content
    and know that God loves you and has a plan for you to be happy.
Maria E. Solis

In His Presence

On her final journey through the dark night,
She walked ever so softly into the light.
She beheld His face and kneeled down before Him;
With angels around her, they all would adore Him.

He said to her - His voice calm and clear,
"Welcome to heaven. I'm so glad you are here.
Your grace and compassion left me no doubt -
You're a special angel heaven can't do without".

She was in His presence - what awe that inspired!
She didn't remember being sick and tired.
He sat on His throne - she at His feet -
She had longed for this day: her Savior to meet.

They talked for hours and walked streets of gold.
Angels smiled as they passed - both the young and the old;
But somehow up here they looked much the same.
No babies were crying - no one crippled or lame.

Peace and joy everywhere, beyond comprehension;
And this was not of her own mind's invention.
Rather, fulfillment of God's promise and love,
She's now in His presence - with the lamb and the dove.

Anna L. Aytes

The Attic

Musty smells complement the scattered light refracted
    through the smeared, small windows.
Whorls of dust and crumbling paper abound.
Whose once nimble fingers operated this stereopticon?
Whose now-closed eyes read of the sinking of the Titanic when it was
    freshly-minted news?
Whose visages are these that peer solemnly out of faded photographs
    lying on the wide pine boards along with the desiccated bodies of
    ancient wasps?
We discover the very search for linkage to be poignantly fruitless,
Since those who forged the chain can no longer be our guide to each
    reopened album and scrapbook.
All these momentos are fated to be relegated to the dust-bin along
    with the scratched, old-fashioned furniture that no one seems
    to want.
Surrealistic distortions of our present recollections imperfectly
    shape our understanding of past events and persons,
Moulding our very concept of immortality by forcing it through
    the narrow aperture of cloudy lenses.
All reminders of the mysteries we anxiously seek to solve,
    the enigmas we attempt to understand.

Elmer W. Smith

Dope Friend

Strung out... Addicted.
You are my life, my hopes, my dreams, my....friend.
You relieve all my tensions, uncertainties, my difficulties.
You are so beautiful. Every time I think of you, I want you more.
One question my friend. Why is your friendship so expensive?
You have cost me my family, friends, and my home.
But I love you still.

Strung out... Addicted.
I need you in my life; your ivory powdery being.
I'd never abuse your power, I cherish your impurities.
You my friend, control me. I'd steal, hurt, kill whatever I must,
    I will do for you.
I'd give the clothes from my back.
The food from my child's stomach, just to feel you close to me.
You make love to me like no other; encounter after encounter.
I'm hooked on you, my friend.
You're the only one who understands, I'm
Strung out... Addicted.

Sheree M. Simpson

The Road Of Life

When we are born we take the same path,
The same as others before;
First we learn to walk, talk, and laugh,
And then we learn even more.

The roads then split and split again,
Oh which one will I take.
Not knowing where the road will end
Or what is really at stake.

The road from youth to maturity,
Seems the longest that we take.
To most it seems an eternity,
When it's the shortest trip we make.

One road will lead to fun and thrills,
Another to despair.
Be wary of curves, holes, and hills,
And roads in need of repair.

But despite the dangers I will face
I will keep in mind,
It's the holes, hills, and different pace
That makes my life truly mine.

Cindy Eaton

"A Husband And Father"

Another day at the office
Catching up on my work.
My wife and kids at home,
But I'm stuck here in this book.

My family is just a picture
That's too perfect to paint.
That seems to be the common thought;
Perfect is what it ain't.

I'm never there when they need me;
I'm too busy to care.
Off on business half the time,
The other half everywhere.

My kids are growing up way too fast;
Their pictures constantly remind me.
My wife's growing old without me
Just trying to keep them happy.

A dad the kids hardly ever see;
A husband and provider always on the go.
I seem to be everyone to everybody else,
But to me I'm a man my family hardly knows.

Jason Crane

No More

Fulfill my thick anger
With your bitter honeysuckle and apples
Comfort me with your candy
That burns my tender lips
Whisper a soothing lullaby
That wounds my ears forever
Caress my aching conscience
Only to be hurt further
Give me gifts of flowers
That you made sharp and prickly
Bring me under the moon
To embrace and kiss me
Only to be denied your love
Only for one more disappointment
Just for what purpose
To lure me alone and hit me
You harmed me for so long and now I say we are done
No longer can you harm me. My feelings for you are gone
You have ruined what could have been
Now we are over, over, over!!

Haviva Siegel

The Luncheon
Circle Of Friends

The ninth person had arrived
    the circle is complete
A circle of friends
    coming from different directions
to share camaraderie, laughter and love.

They sat at a circular table
    and learned they were a mini-United Nations
having travelled 2 continents and all of
    the U.S. of A.

They come from diverse occupations
    as they do religions
and have a total of 7 cats and 1 dog
    but their common bond is
their love of family, mankind, and friendship

"Circle of Friends" ... Luncheon
    universal occurrences that leave all players
wishing it were a "dress rehearsal" and that the
    "play" will have a lifetime run.

Patricia Ann Thurz

The Race

The wind is blowing across my face,
The clouds are ready just in case,
The sun tries hard to keep its pace,
But the rain, the rain,
It doesn't blow across my face,
It's never ready just in case,
It doesn't try to keep its pace,
So guess who will win the famous race,
The clouds, the clouds who are always ready just in case.

Gwendalyn E. Turner

Little Diamond Crystals

Whirling, swirling,
looking for a home.
The moonlight guides them.
The starlight inspires them.
They find a place,
where they gently rest.
Until the Toro-super-deluxe 12 horse power-automatic
snow blower
comes and
moves them along.
Hurry, scurry,
find a home.
The Toro calls to the

Little diamond crystals.

Rebecca Roti

My Day

Seven o'clock I start the day.
Come on, get up, no time to play.
Nine o'clock, off to school.
Hurry, hurry you know the rule.
At 12:15 we're in for a treat.
Go down to the lunchroom for something to eat.
At 1:30 we go to Ms. Willingham's class.
In two hours we go to gym.
Four o'clock, we go home in the car.
I'm quite sure we are almost home.
Around six we eat again.
If dinner's not ready, we always ask, "When?"
Nine thirty, time for bed.
Just lie down and rest your head.
Seven o'clock rolls around and then
    It's time to start my day again.

Anthony Williams

Dream A Little Dream

The day I met her my heart smiled
To pursue my happiness would be worthwhile.
She was the only thing on my mind
I thought that day would be etched in time.
I did what I wanted, I said what I pleased
That wasn't enough at least not for me.
I needed someone to love, someone to hold
I needed a hand to touch, a pillow to share,
I wanted to run my fingers through her hair.
To hold her tight, spot a smile and stare
To kiss her lips, and rub her tummy,
I needed someone, someone to love me.
It's too bad my joy would last but one night
The first starlit kiss under that soft dim light.
It's too bad now, my heart's in shambles
That's what happens when the crying man gambles.
Once again I am left standing alone
In a cloud of darkness, I fall to my knees
Praying to God that it's only a dream,
A nightmare is more what it seems.

Chris Gillpatrick

Man You've Got It

Now you may say I exaggerate, that I'm making to much of what you
    call nothing
Your nothing is too great at any rate, to just sit back and not let
you know in some small way, just where I think you're at.

Man You've Got It
Whatever it is that makes a star shine and a candle glow, you've got it.
I'll grant you, you're handsome and pleasant to look at, delightful
    to talk to.
Your inner beauty is so great that it over powers any outer physical
beauty that may be missing if any from you.

Man You've Got It
Granted you're not where you could or should or even want to be, but
you're not where you have been either.
At any rate if you never get there, to me you're already a superstar.

Man You've Got It
No flattery just fact, anyone that shines with so much love and
    understanding
And inspiring so many others with just a honest encouraging world,
can't be but so bad.
This isn't meant to take you on an ego trip, but to simply say

Man You've Got It

Dorothy Jones

Mind Or I

I am bad.
I am no good.
My Mind keeps saying those words.

It doesn't matter
What I might do,
Those very words keep on coming through.

I cannot run.
I cannot hide.
The Mind will always find the I.

I cannot change,
What I might hear
When I am conditioned to Mind.

Mind over I,
I over Mind,
It is an ongoing battle.

I hear it all,
I feel it all,
Strife between the I and the Mind.

Brenda Neal Medlock

Dana...

The wind moves serenely and softly through her hair

She is a striking young woman

A stated but carefree gait as she moves along the boulevard
She is lovely, open and freely inventive with her dress
Yet, as always, she is radiantly stylish-simplistic elegance at its best

I was completely taken by her look

Like others must, I wish to know of her being, her essence
What tides ebb and flow in her mind?
Her cool, outward demeanor, fascinates me
and I have often envisioned us together

But for the maddening irony

She effects me in a way no other has
What lies beneath that exterior?
Is the sanguine color of wine a clue?

It is a charade!, a facade!, and sadly, a dreamer's fantasy..

For whether I am behind or in front of the window, that pain of
   glass will forever separate us
   - it can never be breached, broken or removed

Why?

      ...Is married
      Rodney K. Boswell

God's Concert On The Lake

On evenings most tired, the trip to a concert I make.
I sit on the dock at the edge of the lake.
A few of the band warm up as more musicians move in;
A beautiful concert is soon to begin.

No country western and no rock and roll
I just forget Randy Travis, I forget Billy Joel.
For me the lake music will get the nod
You see, the lake music is the music of God.
He's tuned the bird voices and bullfrogs with care
He created a band with which none can compare.

One day He just spoke and the band came to be
Now, He conducts it each night just for me
He plays a sweet song that will soothe my tired soul
When I need peace and rest, it's a great place to go.

My body relaxes and my mind feels at ease,
As God orders each note in all the right keys.
God's concert is flawless as He performs it for me
Thank you Lord Jesus, All praise be to Thee!

      Danny Farmer

Western Memory

I can remember sun burned faces.
Covered up from dusty places.

Heads under ten gallon caps.
Legs protected by leather chaps.

Wide open spaces where flowers bloomed.
Long grassy prairies where June bugs zoomed.

Good guys in white hats.
Fist fights and welcome mats.

A wagon with a horse and buggy.
Summer nights that were hot and muggy.

Cameos and long, lacy skirts,
Ruffled collars and cowboy shirts

This memory is one of the best.
It's my memory of the wild west.

      Kelly Puckett

Heaven

There is a place where angels roam,
where people love, it is God's home.
It's full of mansions, it's full of gold,
it's never too hot, it's never too cold.
Heaven is a beautiful place to be;
where music plays and souls are free.

The streets of gold were paved by hand,
the same hand that made woman, and also
made man. You never go hungry and you
never cry. You always live you never die.

According to God all this is true.
Heaven is great through and through.
Heaven is a place where children can play,
safely in the streets day after day.
In Heaven you get your every need,
there is no lust and there is no greed.

God's lived in Heaven for millions of years;
there are no worries, there are no fears.
Heaven is great as you can see,
it is for you, it is for me.
      Jason McLaughlin

Daddy

My sweet father you'll never know, just how much I love you so.
This is a tribute to you from me, for the entire world to see.

I'm not certain why I've not told you before,
But things won't go unsaid.....not anymore.

The love that I feel for you, runs so very deep.
All bundled up inside of me, now is yours to keep.

You have been my teacher and you've been my mentor too,
There is so much gratitude, that is owed from me to you.

You taught me how to fix a car, and how to change flat tires.
Pouring gas in carburetors, and catching ourselves on fire!

You showed me how to plant a garden, and how to keep it alive.
You even managed to pet the bees, while away from their hive.

You made a special tape for me of you singing lullabies,
Too-ra-loo-ra-loo-ra, calmed mine and the babies' cries.

The many things you've done for me, memories to treasure.
Of all of the wonderful times, that we have shared together.

There is no man in the universe, that I could compare you to.
You are truly an <u>awesome</u> father, my love runs so deep for you.

Please just know I love you daddy, from the bottom of my heart.
I have not ever told you enough, so this is my way to start.
      Mary Jo Stavros

El Sentimiento De Tristeza

Why am I feeling so sad inside, it's
as if my soul had died, so gloomy
I do feel this pain I'm feeling
it can't be real, take a rope and fill
it with despair tie it around my neck
I don't care. If I die will you care?
Will you come with me will you be
there? Right now I can't believe I'm
crying I hurt so much I feel like dying.
Give me a gun a rope, something it's
a lot better that having nothing.

Give me a reason why I should live, I
have no contributions nothing to give
I feel so lonely in this desolate place
I can't wait to see God's loving face

      Steven Aaron Englehart

Hat In Hand

I put on my hat
because it reminds me
of the freezer-cold morning
of no breakfast and nothing-doing;

when we walked around
because we were there,
in the empty parking lot,
and we got sick of
the crayon-box yellow bus,
of girls and warmness and giggle-stories
and boyfriend-stories and friend-gossip
and cold complaints about the little hour;

talk-thinking about
oatmeal and...
and peeing in little blue houses and...

and I put my hat on
because it reminds me of you,
and it keeps my ears warm
when I'm alone in
the freezer-cold nothing of morning.

Brian J. Simoneau

Death

It stalks its prey with life's darkness for its cover
With a sting poised and venom laden
Venom so powerful, man remains ultimately vanquished

Nothing on earth is known to be faster
Nothing is known to be so sublime, yet
Nothing is known to be so real

At conception strikes the villain
As it embraces its victim for a life-long ballet
Who gets crowned at the end with a tombstone

Unaided its venom never fails to achieve
Yet it gleefully accepts help from the elements
Who in many cases are its very own victims

Victims who tread life's path
While slowly wasting away
As the sting takes its toll

Only one way out of the misery
Enjoy with others the beauty life offers
While it lasts, with no help offered the cold one

It is everywhere with a fixed grin of satisfaction
And is as loud as the sound of shadows dancing

Emmanuel C. Mpock

The Bequest

The life line of a family interweaves to continue.

No life is ever ended.

It is joined to those that carry on, and presents the very best that has been handed down to them from those loved ones that have gone before.

Family is the cornerstone of life.

The cutting edge of acceptance.

The core of existence that enables life to move forward with the assurance that in your past a path has been chiseled to give the better way, and secure the heritage of your family.

So be the bequest passed on to you.

Jenell T. Perry

Moor Cat

Hidden in the darkness, beyond the fire,
Where man is subject to nature's ire,
Danger treads silently on padded feet.
Hunter and hunted destined to meet.
Shrouded beneath the falling snow,
The swamp lies silent high and low.
A rodent freezes, paralyzed by fear,
That which hunts him is drawing near.
The cat too pauses, seeking his prey.
His quarry is near, yet he does delay.
With a flash the mouse starts to race;
The cat pursues with a lethal grace.
Silence is broken by a piercing scream;
Thoughts of safety vanish like a dream.
Sitting by the fire a man jerks about,
His face is masked by fear and doubt.
Toward the sound he stares due north.
From the fire he dares not venture forth.
With baleful eyes, glowing bright,
The moor cat stalks the moonless night.

Jonathan Dowds

The Measure Of Success

Success is a bank account waiting to be invested.
It is a budding plant preparing to be flowered;
An interesting book expecting to be enjoyed;
A new world longing to be explored.
It is a great talent yearning to be discovered.
Success is a hit song ready to be vocalized.

Success is often measured in dollars and cents
And is mistaken for the execution of common sense.
Some believe it is the ability in popularity
Or relaxing in the jacuzzi of prosperity.
Some think it is the ability to wield power
Or the opportunity to see others cower.
Some say it is having a prestigious occupation
And dining with the elites of our nation.
It is assessed by the cost of one's house and car
Or the numerous times you travel afar.

Let examine life's litmus test and X-ray
And then we will conclude and have to say
Success is hard work and ambition,
Happiness, fulfillment and determination.

Jacynth Montague

Delivery

I had to use a vehicle
but I could not get it to go
The wheels and the engine were both in their place
but one would not move for the other
with each turn of the key
I'd get no further than I was before
Going nowhere fast I had to get moving
and see if I could tell what it was
Under the hood I fiddled about
with the tools I had at hand
I looked and I listened for a sight
or a sound - something to give me a clue
Finding nothing amiss
I feared I wouldn't get where I needed to go
I was out of ideas, so out of frustration
I turned the key just one more time
and to my surprise
it started right up and ran without trouble
and took me where I wanted to go

Fran McEvoy

When You Love

When you love, put God first and let him lead your relationship.
With God as your leader, your morals are intact and the temptations
around you have no purpose other than to show you the strength
of your love.

When you love, remember to love yourself. Without love of self,
your love will continually be half-hearted. For you will always
love someone else and in turn expect them to fulfill the space
within your heart that is lacking of self love.
Thereby making you dependent and adding strain on the relationship.

When you love, love unselfishly. Love enough to put someone else's
happiness above your own, Stand on your faith when your partner
wants the one thing that hurt your heart the most. Know
that love is not always joy and happiness. Love comes in the form
of hurt also.

When you can love yourself while loving unselfishly, stand on
your faith in your time of pain and let God lead your relationship,
You are ready for love.

Cathedral Williams

The Darkness Within You

There is a dark man that always follows me
around, and is sure to never let me out of his sight.
He has no eyes yet sees all I do, he has no
ears yet hears all I say,
He has no mouth yet is loud and rude, he
has no heart yet lives to stalk me every day,
He has no skin, hair, or color yet is my exact
image, he is my shadow dark and dreary,
he has no feelings or emotions and is dead to
the earth, yet it is strange...
I envy him, this soul dead to the earth, this
mother of illusion and flexibility,
He cannot be hurt, pierced or damaged in any
way, he is a perfect example of my exact opposite,
Yet sometimes when I am sitting looking down at
my shadow, I wonder if he is sitting there looking
up at me wondering the same thing.

Jantzen T. Kopp

Peace

Peace is what we need the most
Around the world and in the coast
Children's eyes cry, parents' spirits die
Peace isn't there to heal with tender care

Peace is what we need the most
in the heart painfully most
bullets graze our ears, tormenters flee in tears
food is scarce, dogs are pierced with pain

Peace is what we need the most
toward our soldiers in the coast
they are careful, many are hopeful
that soon peace will be here

Peace is what we need the most
the war isn't over and hard to bear
the death toll will rise with despair
but look above the falling night
because soon the light will shine bright
and when it does open wide, peace
will shine with pride

James Hensley

Avian Ballet

A sudden fright of starlings spattered into the sky.
A dark pattern of whirling birds, performing a brief dance
before clattering back to roost again.
Leaving the sky blank.

J. M. Farrell

The Jog

Towering French double doors, protected by wrought-iron gates.
Ivory marble pillars guard as well, threatening the uninvited.
This mansion, secluded, lonely and yet beautiful in its solitude.
Not a hint of movement within its walls
Only a solitary gardener, serving life's sentence, outdoors.

I'm suffocated by the dead motionless air
And I quicken my pace to escape.
My heartbeat is strong and deafening in my ears
Then my throat begins to tighten as it is tortured and parched
but I force and push myself, this jog nearing its end.

Life and living fills the neighborhood.
Children on skateboards and bicycles, dogs and cats.
and a child yells out to the ice cream truck
disappearing around the corner.

A motorcyclist waves "Hello" as he crouches for his ride.
Waving back I attempt to catch my breath
I stop, admiring the small, inviting house.
and walk up to the stained-glass door that welcomes me home.....

Diana Isler-Galindo

"Everything Has A Reason"

Like the wolf hunts, hungry for food,
Like the moth is drawn to a flame,
We hunt for happiness in a cruel, cruel world.
But tell me, who do we have to blame?

Like the chameleon's skin changes its color,
And the shark has rows of razor-sharp teeth.
We too are given special defenses, and on a
Sliver of hope, we try to elude harms reach.

Like an animal has its instincts,
We are also blessed with hidden talents.
So be on your guard at all times
In case something tries to knock you off balance.

And when the wolf makes its kill,
He eats a feast fit for a king,
And when the moth finds its flame,
Its imprint is left on everything.

So, like the animals to their habitats,
We to change with the seasons,
So don't question the obvious or obscure,
Because, everything has its reasons.

R. Scott Morris

As The Eagle Flies

Dark skin I have and long black hair
with braids and beads and buckskin shirts.
I am the brother of all things.
I respect the land and put more in than I take out,
I don't own the land cause no one can.
We lived peacefully until the white men came.
Then everything was changed.
We were introduced to greed and dishonesty.
I do not understand nor ever will
How something so beautiful and magnificent,
Could be ruined and destroyed so.
I wish they would just leave and let us live our lives,
But they tell us we must move to a different place,
A place where they can watch us.
They told us lies and we believed them.
So now we are forced to move away from our homes,
But I will die fighting for them.
So as long as the eagle flies,
And as long as the wind blows,
No one will ever own the land, No one can.

Katie McIntyre

Friendship

Friendship is a special place
Where some have feared to go;
They've shied away, or run and hid,
Afraid to learn; to know.

Some people hide from friendship,
At work they keep furious pace;
It's not others that they run from,
They're afraid of their very own face.

Some people look at friendship
as a challenge or difficult thing;
When truly an honest friendship
Joy and harmony it can bring.

A true and honest friendship
Can help us realize
That work and deadlines should really be
A very small part of our lives.

So people of this world take heed,
Of a friendship be a part;
For life is much too short, you see,
To live without a caring heart.

Barbara J. Smith

Ambassador Of Laughter

Laughter is a language that needs no translator,
It's known the whole world round.
But it sometimes needs an instigator,
And its favorite Ambassador is a clown!

Whether tis one clown mumbling, grumbling, or tumbling,
Or doing a daring double-dip flip.
Or maybe fumbling, bumbling, or stumbling,
Pretending to slip or trip!

Or two clowns together, doing a gag,
One the recipient of a pie to the face!
Or dressed in drag whacking wigs off with a wet washrag,
Ending in a knock-down-drag-out-zig-zag chase!

Or a thousand clowns cataclysmically catapulting out
Of the most minuscule of miniature cars!
Clumping and bumping and jumping about,
Buffooning, ballooning, or crooning like stars!

Let's salute this rewarding time honored profession,
And all who aspire in the Comedy Craft!
For a clown it is a never ending obsession
To provoke kids of all ages to laugh!!!

Christopher Shelton

Dark

Bounded by chains
Holding me down
Surrounded by masked faces
and painted smiles
Suits of colors standing
from the ground
While death and despair dances all around
Jokers who wants to be King
Kills the Queen and the child she bears for a limited
Lust that will soon disappear
But through the darkness
A speckle of sun shines on my face
And make me warm
My body shakes as if being reborn
I have seen the light
I have seen the way
No yesterday will spoil
My today

LaTonya Dyer

Reunion

To have the soul of a tree,
is forever and always to see,
The sacred blessings of Mother Earth,
her gift of never-ceasing birth.

To realize your roots are deep;
and intertwining with fairy feet,
Connecting joyfully with others...
Fathers, sisters, sons and mothers.
A tree has known since time began,
that all of us, people, ocean and sand.
We're connected, like or not...
We must strive to remember, all we've forgot.
Beg Mother Earth to take us back;
and teach us again, all we lack.
To renew her, heart and soul,
to give back her life, and make her whole.

To have the soul of a tree,
is forever and always to see,
The sacred blessings of Mother Earth,
her gift of never-ceasing birth.

Shauna Nusbaum

Spirit In Flight

Perhaps this kite will fly soon!
It belongs in the sky with the other kites;
there it will soar to its highest heights
and
will shine brighter than brite;
one source,
one light,
I love my kite.

Elizabeth Victoria Cameron

That Day

On a Saturday night I sit in my room,
waiting for the phone to ring in the dark gloom.
I watch the people walk around,
as the street lamps go out.
They look for a place to go have some beers,
as I sit and listen to their cheers.
A bottle and a few packs of cigarettes keep me company,
as the television is playing reruns of "Three's Company."
I watch my life fall apart around me,
as I remember the dreaded day you divorced me.
Now with a gun in my hand I sit in this dark place,
and pull the trigger, as I see your beautiful face.

Elizabeth Economopoulos

Freedom

Many of us can not see
That we still are not completely free
There's still plenty of racism in different forms
But some places consist of more
Why is there a such word as hate
How can people discriminate
There are many lessons to be taught
One is that love can't be bought
We must learn to see past color
Because in God's eyes we are all sisters and brothers
How can you judge someone by their skin
This doesn't determine their personality or brains
If only we weren't so judgmental
There wouldn't be comments to make others crinkle
Let's start sticking together to work this out
Because things would turn out good without a doubt
Living together in peace and harmony
Because that's the way this world is suppose to be

Camara Harris

503

An American Dream

Once long ago,
We dreamed what the future would hold
A job, a home, success, family
These were attainable goals.

Oh, how this dream has changed
A nightmare it's become
To drugs, violence, and crime
Society has succumbed.

Some of our children, the symbols of our future
Are on drugs or in jail
What has happened to our country?
Where did we, as a society fail?

Mothers, Fathers, Children
Wake up and take a stand
Return pride and stability to America
Our promised land.

Let us prove to the world
That we can make the dream come true
Determination, hard work, and courage
Those traits come from me and you.

Andrew Fortson

Clouds

Clouds are happiness in the sky flying
through the air. They make you think without
a care. Sometimes they look like dragon's
breath. They make you forget about pain and
death. What a wonderful thing clouds are.
So beautiful but so far.

Ryan Stinson

Rhythm Of Autumn

The old grayed man, disheveled by his autumn work,
    continued Raking the leaves into piles.
Three Young boys, still school-dressed, stopped
    on the gravel road to watch.
Each boy eyed the Rhythm of the Old man's method:
Rake-Pile...Rake-Pile...Rake-Pile...Rake-Pile....

The Rake came their way; one boy frowned softly;
    the other two stared—their eyes focused on the old man.
"I've got more Rakes!" the old man offered.
"Can't! Got to go home!" the frowning one anxiously
    answered for the others.

The old grayed man eyed the Young boys as they
    gravel-kicked their way home.
When they disappeared around the road's bend
    into the evening's colors, the old man quietly
resumed the Raking, smiling softly in his autumn.

Thomas J. Ryan

My Love For You

My love for you is greater than all others -
    my brother, sister, even my mother.
My love for you is larger than life,
    yet you can abuse it without the aid of a knife.
You can deny it because you think it's fate,
    but don't worry dear, my love will wait.
You can hate and beat it. That's not new,
    for nothing will kill my love for you.

Roger J. Butler Jr.

Eternity

Pollution, a simple factor to be,
accepted by society.
Tall stacks, car exhaust, even fumes,
all lead up to this large earth's dooms.

Species are evaporating like water in sun,
and many barbaric humans find this fun.
Trees are cut down for livestock, an unhealthy "treat",
who are thrown into cages and cruelly beat.

Animal testing is pointless and dumb,
and now, finally the time has come;
People need to realize what we've done,
to our Mother Earth we act like a gun.

All in all, humans are to blame,
for all the cruelty, pointless shame.
My one wish in life is that people could see,
that our Earth needs to last through eternity.

Chrissy Jank

The New Start

As a young woman walked
the road of her life, in front of
her the sun was starting to rise and
behind her the sun had set. She stopped,
looked back behind her and started to
smile. She thought to herself, it's
over. That part of her life is over
and she is now ready to make a
Fresh Beginning,
A New Start...

Christina A. Basile

If Dark Birds Band Together

If dark birds band together,
Why does it seem to be?
When someone close departs this world,
One bird I only see.

It's not soaring out 'cross the sky
Or far away perched in a tree.
When an old acquaintance has passed away,
A dark bird looks straight at me!

It usually happens at the moment they depart.
Before the public is made aware.
And before I read the obituary list,
I know what will be written there.

Michael Christopher Bonitto

Why Life Isn't Easy

If things were all easy, if there were no
troubles. It would be like living in a bubble.

If the car doesn't start, if the kids don't cry. If
the ones we care for would never die.

If the sun was out every day, and we could
see the stars at night. If there wasn't a Boogie
man to give us fright

If the buses were on time and there wasn't
any crime, if our pockets weren't empty when
we needed that last dime.

If life was so easy it wouldn't be God's way, he
gives us our challenges to strengthen us day by day.

It is in his word that challenges there will
be, there will be some for you and there'll
be some for me.

Jim Martel

Untitled

The man on the street sits
with his back pressed against the store window.
His dirt packed fingernails
part of his time laden hands
grasp loosely at his cup of life-
full of empty coins

Maybe it will buy me a
bottle of whiskey to bury my face in

A woman with a child passes him,
she pulls her innocent baby tightly
against her bosom as she realizes
the being of the man.
He jiggles the cup, more in sarcastic sorrow
than need for pennies.

I used to be a man.
        Rachel Evans

Time

Carefully and silently,
I run through the meadows.

I build mountains up,
and I send them crashing down.

The wind is my wings,
and the sky is my face.

People are my slaves,
yet I am full of grace.

I am a father,
I am a mother.

I am made of hopes and dreams,
and also desperation.

I am cried about and laughed about
and thought about often.

The future is my arms,
the past is my legs.

No one can imprison me,
I am everywhere.

If you don't know me, then neither do I.
I am your great-grandchild to be, and your mother's lullaby.
        Jessica Kelley

Old Springtime

How I long for old Springtime
The warm south wind and bright sunshine
With aroma of cherry blossoms in the air
Wide eyed animals leaving their winter lairs
Singing wrens and buzzing bees
The leaves a budding on the trees
Turtles sunning and fish a jumping
Just makes my heart start pumping
Thundering rivers that run real swift
Springtime it's one of God's greatest gifts
As I glance out the window at a foot of snow
When I die I'm not sure where I'll go
But how I long for old Springtime
The warm south wind and bright sunshine
        Michael A. Clark

Who Would That I

It is an awesome commitment that I should lead a prosperous life
only to be left questioning, "through which gates my kingdom lie".
Not from the heavens does my jealousy come.
Nor from hell does it whine. But from the well that all commoners drink.
        Dale W. Betts

Memories

My heart is sad and I cry alone
    For the things that might have been.
For the people that I've known and lost
    The children, women and men.
They say time heals the hardest hurt,
    But that's not true, my friend.
I still grieve and I still cry
    And I will until the end.
When times are quiet, when night is nigh,
    And darkness closes in,
I sometimes lie awake and sigh
    As the memories come again.
I see the child, I hear the voice
    The laugh, the song, the face.
I say the name and reach to touch
    And wish for that last embrace
But, the laugh is gone, the vision lost
    And I'm wide awake again.
For my heart is sad and I cry alone
    Remembering the things, that might have been.
        Nancy L. Melcher

A Broken Love

Whatever happened to the love that once upon a time we shared?
Whatever happened to the times we always showed we cared?

What happened to the friendship that kept our love together?
What happened to that promise "always and forever?"

What happened to the special bond we shared between us, both?
Whatever happened to the moments when we were once so close?

If you look within yourself, you'll find a love that's lost;
We had our problems like anyone, but we never knew the cost.

If you look inside your heart, a love still grows so strong;
But you can't get back what you had before, you know you
    must move on.

If you look into my eyes, you'll know I feel the same;
We have to somehow get on with our lives, and stop playing
    little games.

If you look inside my heart, you'll see the pain I feel;
You'll also see the strength I hold, knowing the end is real.

Whatever happened to the wishes, and things that we dreamed of?
If you look in both our hearts, you'll find a broken love.
        Andrea Wong

Our Thanksgiving Prayer

We've put aside this day of thanks,
    To take the time to say,
The things we take for granted,
    As we go from day to day.

Please keep in mind the hungry,
    And feed them if you will,
Watch over them and love them,
    So many lives are standing still.

Thank you for our health Lord,
    that keeps us on our way.
And thank you for the love we share
    Please keep it strong, so that it may stay.

We give our thanks to you dear Lord,
    for this meal on Thanksgiving Day.
And for our friends here with us,
    Our thoughts are blended as we pray.
        Ron S. Pittman

Make Your Dream A Reality

The blues and lies are what you choose,
If your path in life has no positive direction.
You are the person in the end who will lose.
There are many rules designated to us in life we may not like,
But it is up to us as citizens of America to make the
ultimate sacrifice.
Life can be hard and most of the time we have to come
out with our gloves on ready to fight.
There are many obstacles we face, but we gain inner
strength from God and pray to him with all our might.
The blues and lies just remind us that it does no good
to complain about life,
There can be a better tomorrow,
Just look at your African American forefathers who stepped
out on faith,
Booker T. Washington, Mary McCloud Bethune and more,
These were successful people on a mission,
And it's up to today's African American's to carry on
this fine tradition.

Maderia Rogers

True Love

Love is sending delectable chocolates and pleasant smelling flowers.
It is whispering sweet nothings into each other's ears
    and blowing kisses.
Love is walking under the moon and the stars, holding hands.

Love is thinking and dreaming of you, and only you.
It is calling you on the telephone, just to hear your voice.
It is talking to each other and not saying a word.
It is hearing your name and smiling.

Love is feeling pain when you are hurt or distressed.
It is feeling joy when you are cheerful or content.

Love is dreaming of the future and not imagining it without you.

Love is what we share.

Natalie Kubala

Some Days

To this day I owe nothing.
To this place I owe nothing.
To this anxiety, I am unsure
To this heartache, to this pain,
From it nothing, this far, I've gained
In my mind, I seek and find a cure.

To this man, to this child
Nothing strong, nothing mild.
To you my fiendish friend
There's a helping hand and care
Love I'll give you if I dare
To assist with your broken heart to mend.

To this charity, you owe not a penny
With all this charity, you may not accept any
From I or another
Be they foe or brother
For them, don't bother,
To them all you owe nothing.

Morris J. Chaisson

Message In A Bottle

tiny straining, clawing hands
grasping my soul
ripping it to pieces
and casting lots for the mangled fragments,
stuffing flesh and skin
into a dirty discarded bottle
tossing all into the mighty heaving ocean
of humanity.
my tattered soul floating never gently
in its looking glass imprisonment
hurtling toward the towering rocky reef
of insanity
teetering on the brink of smashing -
slipping, sliding barely by,
now on to other crashing billows
spinning, swirling in my jar -
hopelessly
spinning, swirling.

Jason Miller

Tranquility

He stands high atop a mountain.
There are tears in his eyes.
He dreams of a world free of sadness,
A place where all is at peace.

The trees whisper with the winds song.
The sun smiles upon the land.
A bright array of colors arch before his eyes.
A deer looks from across a field.
Birds flutter from tree to tree.

He looks out across the land.
There is a smile on his face.
But, still he has to wonder,
What would it be like,
A world without sadness?
What will it be like tomorrow?
He hears children's laughter.
He moves on with peace in his heart!

Kelly Swallow

God Specializes

On October twenty-fifth, nine years ago,
God gave life to a little soul.
Little, yes little indeed,
For she weighed 3 1/2 pounds you see,
There were other concerns, concerns of man,
Who were predicting her future as though it was in their hands.
But, God stepped in and showed His plan.
From the crown of her head to the tip of her toes,
God began to fashion His mold.
He touched her in a mighty way,
Bestowed blessings upon her each day.
The good Lord looked from heaven above,
And crowned Shantae with His love.
Shantae, continue to work hard and pray,
Obey God and Mommy everyday,
For this is God's chosen way.
Yes, He gave life to this little soul,
And now He continues to fashion His mold!

Bernice Davis

Ecouter

A mind is an ocean.
So peaceful and serene.
It must be filled with a mysterious potion.
For it will turn in a moment to raging and mean.

It knows many happy times and joys,
But death will sometimes wash upon its shore.
It is like a complicated toy.
It is your light, it is your cure.

Many living parts make up the whole,
Most of which cannot be seen.
Some parts have an innocent soul,
While others are black and green.

A mind is a very complicated thing.
But without it, you cannot survive.
Treat it well, let it sing,
Let it flow, you will thrive.

Ashley Barber

"The Course Of A Meal"

Food is something everyone enjoys
In one form or another,
Whether it be coconut, casserole, cookies, or cake
A meal brings food and friends together.

Appetizers are an opening portion
Added like a prologue to a book.
If you're not careful you'll overeat on this course,
And possibly offend the cook.

A gurgling casserole fresh from the rack
Suggests a friend's warm smile;
It warms my soul before I partake
And gives me energy for a while.

There are many qualities of desserts
That make me stop and wonder;
The desire to heed the calling of cake,
Is unfortunately louder than thunder.

Even though I could go on and on,
One point is mine to make:
Fascinating food should not be like money-
The more there is, the more we'll take.

Jordan Garber

Forsaken

I watch you as you sit there on the bedside
With that all too familiar smirk on your face,
And I know what you're thinking behind those
Black
Hollow eyes.
And I can't find your soul, for the darkness overwhelms
Me and your tears have not been revealed
For some time now, and I can't see the sun for the
Dark
Dreary curtains
You forced me to hang up when you withdrew into
Your lonely shell, and I'm left to view them alone,
With emptiness surrounding me, crawling around my
Sullen
Emaciated heart,
Beating out of time and out of rhythm
Since my conductor left me, selfishly, to do a
Solo, a piece of haunting music that racks my
Clouded
Confused mind.

Carla Griffith

Window To Your Heart

Some people don't get close to others
For they have fear of the unknown,
So all the thoughts and feelings they have
Are pushed aside and left unshown.

If only they could realize
All the fun there is to be had,
Then they could see a whole new life
And maybe not be so sad.

If only someone would tell them
Everyone gets hurt now and then,
They can experience having friends
And if it doesn't work, just try again.

Some people keep their window covered
Not allowing others to see in,
They are afraid they will make fun
Of what lies deep within.

If you look into the depths of your soul
And open up to others for a start,
It's then they will be able to find
The window to your heart.

Emily E. Sigler

Lost Souls

We are the new generation
The disenchanted generation
No hope, no future, just despairs
The world's at our finger tips
Yet it slips away and no one really cares

Hearts of fire have been quenched
And we are the residue
Our minds are full of reality
Now we can no longer think; We just act without knowing
No question asked; No answers given
Just following the laws
I pray to God my soul to keep
But even it begins to fade
Sinking like a battered ship
Soon to be lost in the misty haze

Who can help us now
when the soul is gone what is left?
Is not soul what makes the man?
There is no will, or desire
Only the smoldering flames of a quenched fire

Clayton L. Lowe

Where My Soul Resides

Where do you go, my soul, at night?
Soaring like a stringless kite
Through visions of sound, and voices of light,
Never solid the ground on which you alight.

I've closed my eyes, been transported away
To the place where night's light pales the dim glow of day.
There I alone am solid, while the universe sways,
And only a child can escape the dark maze.

To where sunlight is rumor, and laughter a myth,
And one's dreams and desires are dripping with filth.
Where reality's dark side is the only side seen,
Where innocence is broken, and purity obscene.

And yet even there, in the darkest of banes
A faint glimmer is seen, and in hope it remains;
For every dark coin must require two sides.
And it's there, in that haven, where my soul resides.

Daniel J. DiGloria

Aids

Don't tread on me.
Open your eyes unlike a blind man and try to see.
All the pain he feels inside,
The truth has come out. His illness he can no longer deny.
He tried to hide this horrible fact.
But the pain was too much, it kept coming back.
His dreams have slowly disappeared.
He sits alone, alone in sadness, alone in fear.
He wonders why it had to be him.
What did he do wrong, how did he sin?
His career and whole life was taken away.
He had nothing to do, nothing to say.
His tears came pouring down like rain.
He realized what he did, and knew there was no one to blame.
He made a big mistake.
Did he know his life he would take?
He knew he could no longer go on.
For all he had worked hard for was gone.
He wonders when he will die.
Will he even get the chance to say good-bye?

Mary Elizabeth Bradley

The Umbilical String

This string is invisible and sewn inside of her pocket
    She walks ahead of me
She cannot see her string reaches into my pocket
    I trail behind her
We are connected!

Why do I feel so badly when I play my game
    "See if you can find me"
We are connected!

A voice begins to chant quietly at first
    She doesn't really care
      She doesn't really care
        She doesn't really care

My heart aches and through my tears I sensed
    If I cut this string then my mom will die
And now I know my own real fear is
    If I cut this string then I will die!

Emalou King

Being A Child

Being a child - what does that mean
It doesn't mean not being heard or being seen
Being a child - what does that mean
Careful parents - live your lives clean

Being a child means everything is new
Being a child means there is learning to do
Being a child means learning from adults
Being a child means learning life hurts

A child is always so carefree an gay
And always able to enjoy each and every day
With a child's heart there is so much to explore
Loving the life they live more and more

Not knowing the pitfalls they stumble along
Playing new games and singing new songs
Being trusting in all they do
They'll even trust a stranger too

We must protect them can't you see
These little beings belong to you and me
We want them to grow big and tall so we
Must make the trip safe for their journey

Deidre Baylor-Sabai

The Rose

The roots are its growth and strength of life.
The stem is the strength in the body that helps it to stand
straight and tall.
The leaves are its beauty and give it the texture it needs.
The thorns help keep the intruders away.
The tiny bud is for a fresh new beginning of life.
A full Bloom Rose is the end of its life.
The beauty and fragrance of a Rose give us
great pleasure in life.

Rose Mary Webster

Changeling

Changeling I am
and changeling I be
riding the air
and the foam of the sea

Long ago here and there
Men remembered my name
Young girls put garlands in my soft green hair
I played tag with the sons of men
Hiding under mushrooms
Stepping over mountains

Changeling I am
and changeling I be
Riding the air
and the foam of the sea

Karin Davis

Paris

The river: still.
Reflects the city's lights.

Side by side
we stroll.
Moonlit gardens
whisper our beauty.
They grow off our Love
and Life.

A glorious sight...
Flowers open their
redolent petals to welcome the young lovers.

The cobblestone paths
soften beneath their high.
We take our cue
And drown within arms and voices.

Tiffany Hill

My Little Boat Dream

My little boat and me struggle down the
river. With water in my eyes. Over waterfall
we go. That just makes it harder to
paddle. We try to slow down but here
comes another waterfall that
made me fall out of the boat. I
struggled to get back in the boat
stopped on a rock. I swim and
swim until I reached the boat.
I got back in and reached
for my lunch. And pulled out a soggy
sandwich and soda pop and when
I bit the sandwich it was a little boat dream.

Shalita Ford

Drafted Children

They were drafted without notice and left in a place unknown,
Their eyes full of pain within; looking for the clearing, their minds like the thickness of fog,
Trying to be soldiers, they carry pretended strength as in war,
Fear within, throughout and here, but geared in uniform to face their foe,
They march in step as to not look unsteady, hiding buckled knees, and crying hearts,
Their Captain, Lieutenant, and hero gone, the look of abandonment, desertion, why was I called,
Not prepared to face their inner war zone, left with uncertainty,
Do we go home to hero's welcomes or will we be a forgotten loved one, relatives tagged like M.I.A's, P.O.W's,
Soldiers feeling stripped of stripes and given no purple heart, altho' heavenly burden,
they come through, living in the world expected to be the same,
But if you really knew the world they live in, you'd see behind their primitive smiles,
grief, regrets, questions and more,
Flashback of memories and new dreams of young ones whose parent left
to go above, the place of peace, and joy to the one who's gone,
but to the soldiers behind an assignment of duty to carry on.
A call to duty.
A war of minds.
A mission of adjusting, when reality will come,
a homecoming without the arms of their hero to say well done.

Debra L. Hendricks

Trademark

It's commonly known that for many centuries people come and then they go.
But leave with us a part of their souls.
While giving the world love and a part of their lives.
Some have big names others have treasures to pay their way.

Now, as she climbs step-by-step against the clock to stake her claim.
The poor little person believing no one will die in vain.
A born small town girl bearing her own inner beauty and name.

Blessed with the strength of a fighter.
Her mind have been trained to overcome most any enduring pain.
In the same you are as lovable as any human being.

Then people that may like your style will follow you for a lifetime.
And never be forgotten because your trademark will be in their pockets.
Inside a stainless steel gold locket.

"I say to the world - here's my trademark!"
This is her dream - let it be seen "I'll leave my trademark for all you rookies".
This is her goal - may it be known "I'll leave my trademark before I go".

"You people in the stands I thank you for my successful plans."
"I'll never forget the person I am".
"Nor the creator which brought me to this land."
"Because that's what made my trademark - my most important hand."

Lori A. Allen

Tornado Poem

The loud loud wind went down the street, throwing debris at everything that it would meet,
The sound just got really loud, I looked outside and I saw a funnel cloud,
It started to rain and rain, and a piece of wood just cut through everything,
I ducked, down on the floor, as the violent storm took away my door,
There was no knock as you can see, the tornado took down my cherry tree,
Things started going round and round, I then noticed a high pitched sound,
An old chair went through the glass, I jumped in the air as it did pass,
My roof started to come ajar, I could hear the storm and it wasn't far,
Piece by piece it floated away, as if it were just a piece of hay,
There was a huge bump on my head, so I went to lay down on my bed,
For a second, I thought it was through, but found out it was not true,
The winds quickly were at full force, I then saw lightning at the golf course,
My whole house just got flooded, as the foundation soon got gutted,
Could it be that this storm is over, I looked on the grass and picked a clover,
The sky immediately got clear, as nothing had ever happened here,
I got out, from behind the little wall, which was the only thing that did not fall,
I looked around, and saw the mess, all this damage from this, YES!

Michael Schwebel

Shared Dreams

I once had a dream that I was standing on a big, beautiful, and pure green mountain.
All of a sudden, while I was admiring the beauty, I could hear mystical music
Echoing loud off in the distance. Then I noticed I seemed to have
been the only person there. So then I was wondering where, how, who was this music coming from.
Then I heard my name quietly whispered behind me. I slowly turned around,
and saw you standing there smiling. Your eyes so dark and dangerous.
Your smile so mysterious. Then you walked towards me with your arms opened, and you suddenly held me close to you.
Softly asked. "Do you love me?". Then I rubbed my hand through your hair as you gently kissed my neck.
I then gazed into your silent eyes, and I tenderly said, "I love you with all of my heart, soul, and spirit!".
After I said those words I awakened to see you standing at the head of my bed,
and when I stared into your eyes you said, "I love you with all my heart, soul, and spirit too!".
Then as I was wondering how you knew about my dreams
you looked at me and smirked and said, "You're in my dreams too!".

   Melanie Nichols

Celestial View Of Night

The sky was crystal clear with billowing bright white scattered clouds here and there.
Reflecting light from the moon against the partial clouds at night.
Appearing to have timeless motion transcending the infinite sea of
an almost black hue of navy blue stratosphere with countless tiny stars in the night.
Radiantly focused in the celestial firmament sending twinkling soft rays of light throughout the universe at night.
Along with the bright, rich golden face of a full moon,
providing a sufficient glow of light for the night.
Occasionally, without a trace of clouds in the sky on a given night,
you might observe the Milky Way with all of its clusters of white glittering stars, heavenly bodies,
formed from creation all distinctly different in various shapes and sizes,
and all have their separate names of which two(2) sets of clusters of stars are known,
as the "Little Dipper" and the "Big Dipper"!
A magnificent world wide panoramic view of peace and tranquility.
Look up and discover the marvelous splendor of God's handiwork.
What a mighty God, who created it all!

   James A. Walker

"The Dance Of The Swords"

Adept at the art as a bird is to flying, a slow step forward, with infinite grace.
A courteous word, then a quick step, slide, slash, followed up by a
meeting of two steel-hearted companions, Clash!
Breaking away, one scythes through the air, hungrily gleaming yet devoid of a face.
Shock tales its course on an alarmed personage, the wielder steps aside in a dodge.
The other masked profile pulls back his defender, startled to see his foe not in the same place.
Though fighting with heart, not to kill, not to harm, a few eloquent words they give like a charm.
Never tire do they, two mountains of strength, they dance through the forms with elegance, on pace.
But then with reluctance, they stop their graceful prance, and bow like Lady and Lord apres-dance.

   James D. Cormier

Memories Of New Orleans

i long for darkness because it give me solace.
those times when the wind, thick and heavy off the river
splits the night like a willing vagina,
the heat and sweat pour from the city, raw and seething,
filled with drunkenness and sour blood.
i walk in nights like these along the river-side, where all is soft and cool.
every sight and sound and smell assaults my senses and i am frightened.
i am mastered by a fear that crawls into my belly, heavy and settled,
refusing to be dislodged by any amount of drinking.
it is a fear that sends a raw taste to my mouth,
stinging my breath and my mind with foul memories of things done and seen,
times long past and long forgotten.
as I walk, all is silent amongst the din:
green, purple, and gold of a faded mardi gras that never seems to really end.
the endless gaiety that surrounds me only adds to the taste in my mouth
and the fear in my belly.
i walk alone, as I have walked so many times before.
other times, when the fear and pain roiled in me so violently
that it forced my legs to move, to carry me away,
to seek a release from so great a tension...

   Heather Joan Williams

Naked Ride

My HORSE surprised, he thinks me queer
that I stripped naked, without a dwelling near.
 I hide the clothing which I had shed,
while HORSE in hackamore is carefully led.
 I gaze and wonder if he had cared,
the bit and saddle which I have spared.
 His nose he plunges, strokes my chest,
to seek a response to what is best.
 My heart rages, burns with fire!
With sudden leap I fill desire!
 I thrust my member into his side,
heave upward seat, bare legs astride!
 He lunged forward; on his back I did slide.
I floundered about on his naked hide!
 Now for a gallop in wide open field.
To its rhythmic movement body parts yield!
 Times changed and it doesn't seem fit,
to ride with saddle, clothing, and bit.
 The tall grass, how it tickled my toes!
Oh to do it again without any clothes!

William B. Haug

Poker Game

"Royal Flush!"
Family Affairs
I would just
Die
to
Spend
TIME
with Them
F**k starving Rwandans, displaced Whey, the gun-toting future of
our country.

"I said Royal Flush!"

I could eat Their smegma and never brush my teeth again. I wish I had
a life supply of It. Their
Smegma that is. I could only
Hope to
Die among It. Their Smegma. Damn welfare
Queen at the store took the last issue.

"If I may inquire, why do you
Chuck your brain away on the nonesuch much?"

Because they are foreign, They are rich, and They don't work.

Hyper Weller Green

"In The Bed You Made"

From love to lies and bed to bed.
Once you vowed to be as one flesh,
Now it's known, lustful desire you've fed.
For so long you've played the faithful part,
How does it feel to break so many a heart?
To throw so much away - just for a lay.
Did you close your eyes to all that you had?
Was it easier than being a real man - a true husband?
I hope it was good for your ego,
but how do you hold your head up when you've gone so low?
Did you honestly believe in deceit, to control and to keep?
I'm certain never did you think
you'd watch yourself sink.
To burn eternally in a myth called hell,
could not ever make you well.
I wish you understood even death would be too good.
Let me offer this assurance - you will pay
for all the pain you've caused.
So think of this as you lay,
in the bed that you made.

Jennifer Ayn Buttler

Missing Young

I miss being young, feeling my limbs limber liquiding
I miss the calm inside my jog after a run on a sandy beach

I miss being a girl, growing my pudgy flesh into a round space where
a light beams a golden shine
between my vagina and ample thighs

I miss having a best girlfriend and laughing

I miss the exterior of my femaleness that draws a man's eyes
 to my form,
longing him to follow
my boulevard sassy-walk into the burn of my interior

For now, I'm tied into corded packages that I must properly care
for — a husband and two sons and
three boy cats and a crusty-eyed father and two brothers and
numerous nephews

Most of all, with my heart, I miss the long length of my future,
rising like a new dawn, past the
shortened inch of my childhood history

I miss being young...... and yet, given the chance, would I retread
my babysteps?

Would you?

Joan Petit

Life's A Bitch

There's nothing on the radio
And nothing on T.V.
This world is in the sh*thouse
For as far as I can see.

Life's a bitch and then you die
Or so the story goes
The sky could be caving in on us
For as far as anyone knows.

But there's nothing on the radio,
And nothing on T.V.
This world is getting smaller
Or is it just me?

Brad Stocking

A Fact To A Fake

"Till death do us part" are the vows we said
but now we're apart and neither of us are dead.

I found it hard to even be your friend
I tried and tried right till the end.

You say you love me and I bet you do
but why you gotta love someone else too.

I got news for you Mr. Macho Man
I was lovin' myself a hell of a man.

He was sweet and kind and a man not a mouse
and he even wiped his feet before entering the house.

That's right "the house" I said 'cause he was here
before one night when you were out banging some whore.

I know two wrongs don't make a right
but it just felt so good lovin' him all night.

You kept inside you what you thought I didn't know
but I knew somethin' was up 'cause you were always on the go.

Now that everything's out in the open, do you have anything to say?
'Cause if you don't have any explanations I suggest you be
 on your way!

Yvonne C. Williamson

Untitled

I don't wear dresses.
I don't date boys.
I love playing sports
And cars that make noise.

You didn't seem to mind when I was little,
"Always a tomboy," you said with a giggle.
But now that I've grown,
You want me to be someone who's not me.

"You should've been a boy" is always what you said.
"Why don't you wear make-up or maybe a dress?
You could be so pretty if only you tried."
How could you say these words that made me cry.

So now after many long nights and a ton of internal fights.
I decided to no longer hide.
Out of the closet I came, kicking the door down.
No regret, no shame.

I don't wear dresses.
I don't date boys.
I love who I am
And fighting the lesbian wars.

Heather Bright

"Torture"

The steaming,
Smoking,
Red-orange,
Sharp needle stares you straight in the eye.
Sweat droplets trickle down your forehead and cheek,
Meanwhile the needle advances,
One-eighth of an inch away from your eyeball,
You squirm with fear.
Your eyelid tries to blink,
But fingers are forcing your eye open.
As the scorching,
Scalding,
Sizzling,
And sweltering needle pokes through your pupil,
You twinge, cringe, and shriek,
While urinating in your pants.
The needle enters the lens of your eye,
With blood squirting out of the punctured hole.

Kelly Hamilton

A Good Man

As I thought long and hard of you today,
My heart filled with many things to say.
I had difficulty on where to begin,
You are unlike other men.
Virtues of patience and honesty so true,
Are strengths I see in you.
When your presence is in the air
Caring and compassion are always there.
Aside from what lies in your soul
Other attributes still remain untold.
Your enchanting eyes, filled with burning desire,
Excite me when I see that I'm your fire.
Your luscious lips, as they touch and caress
Pleasure points that reside on my breast.
My blood boils with a wild, hot flow
To pulsing, throbbing regions below.
I feel you at the door waiting to come in
So that a natural rhythm can begin.
You fit well into my plan;
To have a good man.

Dwavalon L. Young

Regrettably So

Hushed silence. Music softly sifting from behind.
I lay back, eyes closed, in my own world; I smile; the fantasy begins.

A strong, musky, deep scent caresses my nostrils.
A deep green of senses in your eyes, passion?
A moment I hold my breath, an eternity it seems.

Lips thin and soft, outlined in a silken mass of hair.
Firm with desire, yet gentle and divine to my touch.
Fire erupts from so long awaited temptation.

I am no longer my own, I am only senses.
Arms so strong and fierce; tender only to me.
The creamy expanse of rock above me glistens to my shadowed eyes.

All muscles taught with animal lust.
My heart quickens to our rhythm, or is that yours?
I no longer think of "my own"; I sense and react to you.

The air is thick and shocks with static; electric!
There is no time or existence, just we as one.
Reaching to highest heaven in elation.

I breath once more, in the silence.
The air resumes a normal posture; slowly my eyes open, senses lost
no more. Regrettably So

Tina R. Garcia

Gaining Strength 1 (Or Lesbian Rabbi's Diary)

As if there is no protection
from the hot winds of righteous indignation
I stand afraid, but not alone
unable to comprehend the gusting forces

Where did they get all of that anger
And why are they burning it my way?

There are monsters in the play room
of the broken house, indeed
and if I am going to continue to thrive there
I must not let them know that they frighten me

They may roar ferociously and look quite evil
but I am stronger than they are stronger than
I am stronger than them.

Life lived in fear is life half-lived, so dance, baby,
dance in their face. Hula shake and rattle twist
spin and fly high, landing on your knees
you won't even feel a thing.

Soar, and sing, baby, sing a rhythmic kind of primal shimmy shuk.
Spinning, you create your own tornado, torpedo, insane, no, just free.
I am and I will be. Just try to stop me.

Rabbi Karen Bender

What Am I To Do

You have been so fond, through all the years that are
gone; My strength has gone away, so why won't you
please stay; I really care for you, Oh, what am I to do?
You've forgotten me, but not the memories;
Pictures may be proof, but love outlives the truth;
I really care for you, Oh, what am I to do?
You stood by my side, while I stood there and cried;
You lent a helping hand, you were such a loving man;
But now that you are gone, I've realized all along,
I really care for you, Oh, what am I to do?
Through the rain and snow, you kept on your toes;
Waiting there for me, like a bird out on the sea;
But now that you are gone, I've realized all along,
I really care for you, Oh, what am I to do? Oh, what
am I to do?

Becky Neisen

512

"Blue Empyrean"

Awakened by a heavenly harmony
  from on high
Sighted a silhouette while
  scanning the sky
Hovering over strings of a
  celestial rhyme
Reminiscent of ballads of
  the bluesy kind
Resounding serenade
  lyrical and clear
Emerging through the clouds
  Sweet angel did appear
I am here in your
  stage of woe
To atone your heart
  Restore your soul
Earthbound, go back
  Return to rest
Eternally retaining the
  final curtain request.

Kim Aleta Rose

Death

Death creeps on people
like an unsuspected surprise,
wiping out people of all
ages and size.
Why does death happen,
Why can't we live forever?

Death comes at different
times, because time
is not the same.
So when death comes
who can we blame?
The killers, diseases
and catastrophes,
death is a mysterious
creature waiting
to be free.

Tanecia Moore

Snapshots Of A Dead Man

His pictures bring recollection,
  images that belong
  to yesterday, exposed again
  in fragments like
  old song

Superimposed upon my heart
sweet ballads long unheard,
recall attuned to memory
  brings melody
  and word.

Joan Jean Emery

Untitled

I am me, you are you
total acceptance, no questions
mysteries of the universe
we are friends.

Alice Johnstone Turner

Wasting Time

Wasting time,
  just wasting time.
Here I sit,
  listening to the radio,
    playing country tunes,
    just wasting time.
Should be working,
  but I'm in no hurry.
Should be busy,
  just don't feel like it.
Plenty of work to do,
  no energy to do it with,
    just wasting time.
I make people crazy,
  'cuz I'm so lazy.
They're in a hurry,
  it makes things hazy.
But I don't care,
  I'm just wasting time.

Bonnie Logan

What's Important

Envision a goal,
Look well and look deep,
For all strength is built
As you challenge each peak.

The journey is hard.
Your effort must not despair
For in the fortunes of challenge,
True patience is rare.

Your worst enemy is you,
And only you can defeat
The depression and fear
That will refuse to retreat.

You can succeed, with
Powerful determination, it's true.
You'll work, develop,
And learn what to do.

Now look to the future,
And while determination shines through,
No challenge can be conquered,
Until You are important to You!!!

Terri L. Shaw

What Would It Be Like

When I sit alone
I begin to think and wonder
What would life have been like
If I had not been there

Would they laugh, smile
or even think the same
Who would know but one

For in the kingdom of God
everyone has a mission
A deed for others
In his favor

So do not think
What would it be like
For where you are
was meant to be

Jon Miner

Untitled

Beautiful is the fragile daffodil
Blowing in a spring breeze.
Growing.
Developing
In sunshine and gentle showers.
Drops of dew shining in
The midnight air.
Moon beams
Softly shine on the dew making them
Small tear shaped diamonds.
Petals arouse in the approaching
Dawn, slowly uncurling in
All of their sunshine-like
Glory.
Then a mighty gust of wind
Rips
The glorious petals off
One
By
One.

Angie Jones

Tomorrow Is Not Known

As I walk down a lonely road,
with nowhere to go
I see my days draw near to a close
Today I stand but
tomorrow is a question
left unanswered.

Kathryn Hopkins

The Night

Beautiful is the night,
Like a Grand Lady of Elegance,
Moving with grace and beauty.
It envelops you with
Its exquisite ebony veil,
Locking in its bosom
Your nightly passionate secrets,
Eternally to be sealed,
Never to be revealed.
But the Omnipresent,
The Omniscient God,
Knows all, sees all,
Do not be deceived!

Paulita Rodriguez

Untitled

  I wrote this letter
to tell you how I feel.
  I wrote this letter
hoping you might heal.
  You were like a sister
a friend or two.
  In a snap you were
gone you left what a shame.
  I hate you now with
all my pain.
  You make me feel like
nobody in shame.

Elizabeth Ramey

The Vision

She saw him in the distant mist,
surely it was him.
The one unruly shock of hair,
that ever teasing grin.

They'd say it was another dream
that happened with morphine.
When loved ones who had long been gone
were subsequently seen.

But she knew he was really there,
she'd waited for so long
to feel his arms enfolding her,
tender, loving, strong.

As he drew near, she gazed at him,
then rose and took his hand.
Slowly, they approached the mist,
together once again.

Edna Gangwisch

Us

We all have secrets
that we sometimes say
but why we have the need
to tell, but a desire
to keep ourselves concealed,
nobody knows.
This communal bonding
that is the glue of our
social structure
that can be destroyed
with a mere push over
the edge, is all
so frail.
But these words I
write cannot even
describe the beauty
of art.
And these secrets
we keep can only
make us weaker.

Bernard Baggett

The Headless Rider

Dashing through the dead of night
Upon his fiery steed,
The headless rider galloped on
In maddened, frenzied speed.
One knew not from whence he came
Nor whither he would go
But voices whispered often times
Of a hot place down below
Where he resided in his den
Of foul iniquity
His evil plans he laid by night
And plotted silently.
Then off he rode across the hill
Till he was out of sight
And left a haunting silhouette
Against the coming light.
At stroke of dawn the world arose
And searched its aching soul
And gave its thanks. The headless one
Had taken not his toll.

Vivian Wardwell

My Cross

As I awake
To begin a new day
There is so much to do
And so much to say.

But before I can start
I lift my head high
And there on my shelf
My cross, the Lord Jesus lie.

And without hesitation
I fall to my knees
And ask for forgiveness
And guidance, please.

Now my day has begun
His love I can't measure
I know he'll be with me
And this I will treasure.

Corey Andrew Carpenter

Escape

She watches the metal
with the gleam in her eyes.
She touches the cold metal
just below her right palm.
The color appears.
It leaks from the fine line.
Escape.

Valerie A. Persinko

Ripples

Ripples in the water
come slowly at me.
Gradually they grow larger
and crash down around me.

Why do I feel so alone?
I feel like I'm drowning
where is my help?

The waves keep coming,
stronger and stronger
they crash over my head
pushing me under.

I cry out,
suddenly, silence,
slowly I float upward.

I reach out
he grasps my hand
firmly and pulls me
into safety.

There I watch
ripples in the water.

Jana Polzin

Untitled

Going nowhere, nowhere going
Leaving living, leaving my enemy.
Knowing nothing, fear of knowing
Fearing living killing me.

Needing no one, no one knowing
Feeling nothing; misery.
Growing darkness, in darkness mourning
Wanting ending, ending me.

Avag Sinanyan

Thru Windows

Thru windows
We see neighbors pass
Exchange friendly waves
Trading recipes
Mowing their grass

Thru windows in cars
We drive slow down some roads
And others go fast
Some drop off passengers
Trucks that pick up loads

Thru windows in stores
Lifeless dummies can see
With sightless eyes
Madding crowds shuffle by
That is what they see

Thru windows in our souls
We suffer daily strife
And somehow we go on
Never giving up
Is the secret to life

George A. Ridings

My Old Hometown

It is a place for the visitor
The mere passerby
The facades are impressive
Behind, empty boards and lies
Promising a peace and happiness
Which here do not reside
Much as the old framed photos
Depicting my happy childhood
Which history never did provide

Margaret Gendreau

Mothers Day

You go girl
you're as pretty as pearls
you're so sweet and you
don't even have big
feet. You're so nice you
make every one think
twice this is all I have
to say remember me
next May. Oh yeah have
a happy Mother's Day.

Kennisha Hannah

To Run For Cover

To run for cover,
    Every time it rains,
You weren't born yesterday,
    You know what a cloud contains.

If it were money,
    Nothing would grow,
And all the stupid fools
    Would wait in a row.

But who is stupid
    Not to follow the crowd,
Especially when it's "Money"
    Yelled out loud.

Money is so rare,
    I must confess;
If it came from heaven,
    It would be meaningless.

Johanna Davies

I Don't Believe The Sky Is Blue

Can I believe my eyes,
As they look into the skies?
A lovely shade of blue,
Hangs over me and you.

Unless you look at night,
When it's dark and dusk and bleak.
So is the blackened color right?
Or light blue the correct streak?

I don't believe the sky is blue,
But dark and dreary as me and you.
Only lit up to a blue so bright,
By His omnipotent brilliance bright.
That turns the soul colored darkness,
With His glorious, radiant lightness.
The same way my blackened soul,
Is lit by His candle forevermore.

David R. Mingus

Dreams

Dreams are good
dreams are bad
some are even sad.

When I have a bad dream
and I wake up, someone is
always there to cuddle me up.

When I have a dream
that is nice, I stop and
think about my life.

I would like to know if
my dreams will come true?
But my question is what do
your dreams mean to you?

Sophia Hernandez

Tree By The Lake

There was this big
ole tree by the lake,
where brothers and sisters
talked of their fate.

Where children brought grandchildren
to learn of each other,
and intense games of sport
pitted brother against brother.

Should this ole tree speak
of the conquests it's been told,
children would marvel
at their parents so bold.

This tree does not speak
as that's not its mission,
but often we come here
just to listen.

Oh what we've heard
from this tree by the lake.

William D. McCarty

"Friendship"

Friendship knows no distance
Nor does it feel void.
For the love of which it consists
Reaches into the depths of one's soul
And wraps around one's heart
Like a warm woolen blanket
On the coldest of winter nights!

Susan Cruit Gainer

Spring Glory

Listening without a sigh,
You may hear them by and by,
Unwrapping greens of every shade,
Exposing hues on every blade.

Peachy pinks and purple blues,
Abounding reds from which to choose.
Fade to black, the winter's starkness,
Put away the grays of darkness.

Whisk away the frosty ice,
Bring on tints of burnished spice,
Pale plum lilacs and lavender's blush,
Swirls of cream; spring's awesome rush.

Scalloped petals of tinkling bells,
Ruffled edges on tasseled swells,
Puffy clusters burst in glory,
Bud explosions reveal spring's story.

Listen closely that you may hear,
Spring announcing it is near,
In silent winds the whispers flow,
Hinting hushes, that you may know.

Deborah Anne Crone

"Trusting"

I will trust in thee, my Lord,
and I will not fear;
For I have the blessed assurance,
that you are ever near.

And when fiery trials come,
I know you'll see me through,
giving to me Thy wondrous grace,
strengthening me in all I do.

So, Lord, when the storms arise,
I will turn my eyes upon thee,
knowing, I'm up held by your hand;
And that you dearly love me.

Faith Knickman

Love Is A Wonderful Thing

You know that it is you I love
And when I see you it is heavens above
And if I knew you really cared
To be with you would be fair
And when I look into your eyes
To me dear it is like paradise
If by chance you should feel blue
Think of the love I have for you
Love is a wonderful thing
For each day seems like spring
The raindrops are music to my ears
As it goes on forever through the years
Your love has made me feel so proud
I feel I am floating on a cloud
I know that there is no one else
For as I see you my heart melts

Mary P. Criniti

Untitled

The colors of the rainbow
I keep in a jar
With my jam and my butter
And release when I grow tired
Of the colors of the day
The shades of night
And the boredom of the race.

Brad Jones

Summer Dayz

Summer dayz of merriment
hearing kids run to
the sound of bells

Summer dayz of contentment
Playing around the 2
supple wells

Summer dayz of relaxation
cleared of all worries that
were at mind

Summer dayz of contemplation
picturing a picture that is
truly divine!

Angela Boutin

Bugtime Ball

The fireflies were at rehearsal
  in the tinseled hall,
Down among the corn stalks, by
  the barn, along the wall
Ladybug arrived wearing dots,
  and praying mantis green
Spider came in tulle, with a
  silvery sheen
Bumble bee buzzed in
  wearing black and gold
When dragon fly arrived he
  knocked everybody cold
A field mouse did a hand stand
  on a pumpkin in the hall,
And scarecrow screamed "we're
  going to have a hall".

Margaret Crocker

Fallin' Star

Your light so bright
To be seen this far
You travel millions of miles
To go nowhere
You're just a flash in the sky
A reminder of what was
Now, against the dark night
I seen your short flight
And in my mind
At last you're just a memory of the past

Ronald Peterson

Japanese Garden

As I watch the plants
grow like a yin yang as
it's bursting with life in
the sun. I see the plant
falling down and dying.
As I look at the crossing
between shade and
light, I see death and life.
As a leaf falls between
the crossing.

Samuel Chapin Fellows

Broken

Torn and tattered
No one thought it mattered
A heart broke and undone
Should belong to someone
Oh how sad it is to be
A lonely she without a he

Paula Mortimer

High Ridge Top

Sittin' on this high ridge top
Away from all my worries
I watch the race of rats in town
And wonder why they hurry.

People run to get things done
They'll run for anything
To get hair cut, or wash the truck
Or even stranger things.

I saw a man running once
He seemed to be in a bind
He run right by, not saying hi
As if he'd lost his mind.

The speed of life amazes me
Atop this ridge I look
And down below along the streets
Are actions I once took.

But way up here the speed of life
It slows a bit with thought
That's why I spend my excess time
Upon this high ridge top.

Brian Hugh French

"Sweeter Love"

You are sweeter than all the
roses in the spring,
Your love is the life in me.
All that it is, and all that it brings.
Your touch is so tender and
everlasting.
Our love can survive anything.
Your kiss is so divine.
Like the taste of good wine.
You're sweeter, better, and greater
That I am so glad you're mine.

Eva Regino

A Thousand Lives

I've lived a thousand lives,
I've been a thousand places,
I've seen a thousand sights,
I've worn a thousand faces,
I've had a thousand mishaps,
In a thousand secret nooks,
I've lived a life of shame and glory,
In a thousand different books.

Mitzi Williams

Untitled

I wished upon a midnight star
And thanked the good Lord above
Grateful for the grace he shares
That showers me with love.....

Each day can be purposeful
Some are filled with need
Take the time to lend your hands
Love will sow the seed.....

When that seed is nurtured
With tenderness and care
All the world will see its beauty
Feel the love it bears.....

With each day that passes by
You can hold a smile
Fulfillment comes in many ways
When life is made worthwhile.....

B. Lafferty

Self-Discovery

Who is that girl
I see in my reflection
With the frizzy red hair
Not hardly perfection

She looks familiar
She has that face
But I can't remember
I can't place

The scrawny body
Her big blue eyes
She wants to be something she isn't
She tries

Her pale skin
Her freckled nose
She doesn't think much of it from
Her head to her toes

I think I know who
It's hard to see but I think I know
It's me

Katie Durant-Storey

Dreamer

A dream is a calling
To find something new,
A yearning, a searching,
A new part of view.
A wandering idea
Looks for a time to take place
In a world full of fantasy
Where time is a race.
A dream is the product
of logic gone wild.
And it happens to every
Adult, every child.
Whether it is a fantasy
Or just a small thought,
If it's something that matters,
Then it's a dream that you've got.
So when faced with a task
If impossible it seems,
Just take a deep breath,
And follow your dreams.

Amanda Kaye Sweeney

Untitled

Concrete block
Hard, unyielding
Roughened surface
Hot from the sun
Scorched, burning

In an open field
The heart of the forest
Fat lazy flies circle
The unmoving stone
Too hot to linger

Unfeeling, unknowing
Solid through heaviness
But empty and hollow
Dead and unfilled
Hopeless and unaware

The flies have withdrawn
The sun goes down
On the now cold
Pressured, dead stone
In the empty field.

Jeanne DeLima

Names - Names

I feel so glad
When someone calls me by my name
Oh, oh, how I wish I could do the same.

Forgive me if I call you
Honey, Mary or Jane
My mind has a space
I remember your face
But I simply can't think
of your name.

Elta H. Croft

sky without clouds

blinding blue
boasts beautiful
breath beneath
battered beliefs

binding bruised
begotten boy
bewildered by
benevolent barrenness
but
beheld believing

blinding blue
boasts beautiful
breath beneath
battered beliefs

David Vail

Rose

On the eve of your departure
A rose sent to my door.
A cry let out of me
For you could not see how much
I wished for you once more.

A music box lay by my bed
It played our song, sweet
sweet memories.
Ballerina please stop dancing!
For it all seems so wrong to me.

That night of your departure
You sent a rose to me.
And you sang our sweet sweet
song. Oh! too many memories.

Kristin Powe

Untitled

Every sad song I hear
reminds me of you
and the nights we shared
under skies of blue

I sit and wonder
what you're up to
and if you're thinking of me
while I'm thinking of you

The miles that separate us
bring tears to my eyes
and knowing you're gone
makes me want to die

But maybe one day
we'll meet again
and you'll realize
we should of been

Heather Sims

Our Angels Wear Black

The angels sing of harmony
Content in their transcendent blindness
The words turning to bubbles as they
Spill from their lips
Floating endlessly on up
To the cold surface
Where the wind rages
At closed doors
And the bubbles pop
Into nonexistence
Trampled by clumsy ships
The meaning they hold
Lost forever to uncaring students
And down below
The angels continue singing
Mourning even as they hope.

Richa Avasthi

When Kay Smiles

When Kay smiles a smile
  I pause a while
To appreciate the beauty I see
When Kay speaks a word
  I realize when I've heard
How glad I am she speaks to me
When Kay sighs a sigh
  I get high
On hope of what might be
When Kay looks a look
  Into my favorite Book
I realize she was made by He.
When Kay winks a wink
  I can't help but think
The best things in life are free
When Kay breathes a breath
  The thought that I'm left
Is how good I feel when she's near me

Michael R. Ousley

Christmas Time Story

Outside the wind is blowing.
And the snow is a-flowing
Snow is drifting high on the
Fence post and across the
railroad ties.
Inside five gather around the
fires and even the baby cries.

They know outside it's cold.
As they listen to the story unfold.
Dad tells them how Jesus was born.
And how everyone sang about it
with great cheer.
The heavenly angels blew gold horns.

Later off to bed we go.
Because Mom wants to so, so, so...

Miranda Mercer

Untitled

I want you to come to me for sensuality
For unspoken whispers and confessions
To undig buried treasures
And discover the jewels to be simply
You and I
When all the dirt is lifted away

Sharon Stella Wit

The Clydesdale

Thudding hoof and flowing hair,
Style and action sweet and fair,
Bone and sinew well defined,
Movement close both fore and hind
Noble eye and handsome head,
Bold, intelligent, well-bred,
Lovely neck and shoulder laid,
See how shapely he is made
Muscle strong and frame well knit,
Strength personified and fit,
Thus the Clydesdale-see him go,
To the field, the stud, the show,
Proper back and ribs well sprung,
Sound of limb, and sound of lang,
Powerful lion, and quarter wide,
Grace and majesty allied,
Basic power-living foise-Equine King
The Clydesdale horse

Adriana Velasquez

On Losing My Mother

Weighted by an emotional anchor,
Dropping it in every passing mirage,
I heave, crash and splinter each time.
My moorings of life disappearing
With the break of the umbilical cord,
I'm natant in an ocean of despair,
Quite alien from the life water within.
Spinning in that vortex of love,
Every curve of the shore well known,
Kicking into the nourishing sands,
To watch the blood gush out to me,
I needed no moorings in that ocean.
Oh Mama! Why did you birth me?
Why float me in this sea of misery?
With you not there to anchor me
I fear I'm sinking with every wave.

I. Rajan

The Dance Team

Dance is
Gracefulness
And competing with
Other dancers on
A stage
Dance is
Jazzy
And a really funky beat
To dance to
But then there is
Very slow music
To do
Ballet.
Dance is acro
And flips, flips, and flips
Dance is making a
Team
And showing sportsmanship

Ashlee Afterkirks

A Day At Coler Memorial Hospital

Broken bodies
Twisted minds
Skilled doctors
Gentle nurses
Kind volunteers
The swiftly moving river
A blooming cherry tree

Astrith J. Deyrup

Without

Without a day
Without a night
Time is without a fight

Without a kiss
Without a dream
Fantasies are never seen

Without a friend
Without a boy
Days are without joy

Heather Murdock

The Journey

God, I run to you
with all my dreams.
To look way back
is so hard, it seems.
To face myself can only
lead to healing of myself.
To accept the pain
for what it is
is to only bring my gain.
Each day I face the memories
and bring myself to my knees.
I am on a road of transformation
from my head to my heart.
All the things stuck in my head
is about to take that journey
to the center of my soul.

Julie Anne Sorenson

Time Gone

The hands of the clock
move steady and slow,
one day moves into another,
where do they go?

Soon the days turn into weeks,
what is it that my heart seeks?

The weeks are slowly moving
  into months,
I need to see you, please
  just once?

A year passes without a word,
you're gone forever
  for I have heard...

Viviane Cummings

Faraway

Where waves hit the beach,
Where birds sing,
Where trees grow;
Generations begin.
Above roads, above bridges,
There is a land,
Beyond all wishes.
And where the stars shine,
And the moon is bright,
Where the sun beats down,
On a bird's flight.
Where the bridges connect,
And the road ends,
There is a land,
Around the bend.

Emily Thompson

517

"My Daddy"

My Daddy praised his Savior,
  from daylight 'till dark,
In early morn,
  he rose like a lark,
A prayer on his lips
  a song in his heart.

Then that day came,
  the sky was all grey,
The thunder did roar,
  and it rained all the day.

He looked so good,
  in his suit of blue-green,
He was as pale
  as any I've seen,
In his coffin so cold,
  and he looked so lean.

He's up in Heaven,
  He's up on high,
Up in heaven,
  where he will never die.

Mary J. Maybin

Only Seven

Second grade,
the days of elastic
pants and animals prints;
only seven
and waiting for the school bus.
Warmly dressed:
cream-colored knitted
cap and matching mittens...
still cold.
My breath formed
a frothy cloud of smoke
that billowed and disappeared.
"Dragonsbreath,"
you said, with your pink
nose and sincere eyes,
but I watched intensely
until the bus came
and never did see
any dragons.

Kristy Corbett

Behind You

The feel of winter
The smell of the rain
Close your eyes, listen
Hear a whisper?
It's calling your name
I'm here for you
I love you
Keep going, don't be afraid
I'll be behind you
Helping and guiding your way
Don't look back
this path was set for you
open your eyes, peer through the fog
Go on, it awaits you
Don't worry, I'll be there
You made it, I'm proud
Your fate awaits you
You stop, look around,
Smile, move on
The past is now finally gone

Diana L. Sir Louis

Too Late

You had him,
  but you let him go.

You love him very much,
  but until he was gone
  you didn't know.

You realize now how
  happy the two of you
  were.

It breaks your heart
  to think of him
  with someone new,
  but now it's too late;
  there's nothing you
  can do.

Hazel L. Duncan

The Courageous Eagle

To Moe, My Dad
An Eagle soars
as a sky turns grey
The wind howls
and the clouds thunder.
The Eagle turns
to face the rain;

The Eagle has courage now,
as he soars and glides
across the winds
in the heavenly skies.

Desi Hill

Marital Bliss

The wife and I
For fifteen years
Have loved and laughed
And shed many tears.

A child we've lost
The two we have
It's heartbreak and magic
They run hand in hand.

Loving this woman
Comes easy to me
She's all in the world
Love's intended to be.

A marriage like ours
Is like a fine wine
Our love and our friendship
Keep improving with time.

What is this thing
Called marital bliss?
It's a contract of love
That's sealed with a kiss.

Doug Owen

My Forever Love

Before me I see thy
true love is he,
Gallant he will be my
only true love to me,
Upon my loving heart
my love for him shall
not part,
In deed I see thy
true love is he.

Kristin Ann Auble

I'm Needing You Tonight

The stars have lost their sparkle
They once shined so bright
Blue skies turned to darkness
I'm needing you tonight

Was it what I didn't do
Was it what I didn't say
That made us say forever
Then made you go away

A love that seemed so perfect
A love that seemed so right
Two hearts that were once so close
I'm needing you tonight

If you're wondering how I'm doing
Just look up to the sky
And you'll feel my broken heart beat
I'm needing you tonight

Could we make a brand new start
And put aside our pride
Bring back the love that we once knew
I'm needing you tonight

Josh Edrington

Our Daily Bread

With nine hungry mouths to feed.
Some bread we need
With prices sky high
who can afford to buy
Mother we need some
bread for today
Counting flour and yeast
and other ingredients and all
Make it into a big ball.
Knead, knead, knead away
Knead your bread for this day
Now set it aside
and watch it rise
Now it is ready to bake
m, m, m what a wonderful smell
you can tell,
Mother baked bread today.

Geraldine Thompson Peacock

Goodbye

You tell me that it's over
That it's time for you to go
You said you never loved me anyways
You thought I should know
Thanks for being so kind
I'm glad that you still care
But I'll be thinking of you
And the love that we once shared
Not every story has a happy ending
Not all love can stay
No matter who breaks up with who
Someone always pays
If I asked you to stay
How would you reply?
If you found me hurt
Would you help me or let me die?
These are all my questions
With no heard replies
I'll watch you walk out that door
And I'll whisper goodbye

Melissa Doiron

Common Direction

Cold morning,
Hard against comfort
Unforgiving with frost, wind, ice,
Accented by steel, gray skies.

Long coated travelers,
Fresh from warm coffee,
Muffins, a loving bed,
Gather in the approaching dawn.

"Good morning's!" greet newcomers,
Bonding each to the other;
Their personal space defined
By silence.

Clusters of twos and threes,
Group together in community,
Stand apart,
Independent.

All turn to face a common direction.
Eyes, sensitive to height and distance,
Grow bright and nonchalant
As the bus turns into view.

Alan R. Hirsch

Psychedelic Euphoria

Hurled-
Into a world,
of yellow, green, purple, and red,
There's a buzz inside my head,
Round and round and round I go,
Can you feel the water flow?
The music is playing very loud,
A blur of indistinct sounds,
Feeling a rush inside my head,
What is that the old man said?
Never go back,
Never to return,
My world has started to churn,
Up, down, back, and forth,
Sir, can you tell me, are we due north?
Round and round and round again,
This vicious cycle has no end.
Chop chop chop chop
Stop!

Rachel Rickard

Us And Them

There never should have been
An us and a them.
The making of enemies,
Where there could be a friend.
Who are they,
That call us them?
Some strange creatures,
Or other men?
We point, they stare,
We all, learn not to care.
They yell, we scream,
Forgetting how to share.
Looking for a scapegoat,
We ridicule their rules.
Then that they may save face,
They perceive us as fools.
Let's us be them and they be us,
Together we can't lose.

James P. Mallay

Fall

F alling Leaves,
A utumn Leaves,
L aughing Leaves,
L ovely Leaves,
brown are the
leaves in fall.
yellow are the
leaves in fall.
red are the
leaves in fall.

All of these
Wonderful things
in Fall,
But I wonder,
Which is the
Best of all?

Christina Hughes

Dancing Bears

A pair of Polar Bears were dancing,
beside a chilly river Yukon way.
the long night's sleep surpassing.

Stepping lively to music played
by bubbling water as he whirled
his lady bear tho not dismayed.

'twas low noon! The first rays
of the warming sun peeked
thru the far horizon's haze.

Like young lovers full of fun;
jumping, yet laughing she held fast,
while whirling wildly in the sun.

That heaven's blissful joy would be.
Sure, tho I'm dreaming while thinking.
Could those loving bears be you and me?

Alfonso San Miguel

A Place In The Heart

Images of her,
  Glisten in the light,
Sunsets are golden,
  As they fade to night.

Years gone by,
  Stars far away,
Dreams not forgotten,
  If only she stayed.

Sunsets slip away,
  Time travels by,
Straining to remember,
  She was my...

Mark R. Bletch

Trapped

Help me I'm trapped
I can't find a way out.
The light is slowly fading.
The light will be gone soon.
I'm suffocating on the darkness.
Can anyone hear me?
Can anyone see me?
Help me.
Please someone help me.
Is anyone there?
Can anyone hear me?
Oh God help me the light is gone.
I'm lost forever.

Michelle Cole

Please Make It Stop

Buildings sprout
and people shout
cars zoom by
a child's cry
a spray paint can
a homeless man
What are we coming to?

A bullet flies
an innocent dies
a cop's lights flash
as a window is smashed
blood stains the concrete
after different gangs meet
What is happening?
Please make it stop

Jennifer L. Struck

Epoch

I wonder why we can't have peace,
  Our world has lost all love.
    Forever gone our happiness,
    May these days never come.

A world of gray skies and war and hate
  This world in present time,
    Has an uncertain kind of fate.

Children now are hungry,
  And left out in the cold.
    The winds of change are churning,
    The sands of time grow old.

Can we change our future?
  We cannot change the past.
    Our worlds fate is almost here,
    Is it meant to last?

Jessica Mahn

Fox Hole Outside Da Nang

GI's on alert
The distant sound of bombs
Choppers transporting
  the wounded...
The warriors have been silenced
A long night of war games
Singing death's song

He was afraid to die
Despite war games and the like
An old warrior from the farm
Like his father before him
A flag-draped coffin and taps
His children mourn

Kyna Kujasky

Satellites

Everywhere in the midnight sky
almost as big as a fly
see them all around
and watch them abound
lie on the grass at night
and watch them all in flight

Vanessa Bleecher

The Old Man's Dream

The old man sails the seven seas
In the night, in his dreams
He travels the ocean, beneath the skies
He's young again, he pays no price
She calls to him, all thru the night
He answers her, in a curious fright
She beckons him, with every breath
Beneath the ocean, a watery death
His echoes are with no reply
But he loves her and cannot say goodbye
The ocean roars with a savage tone
It matters not, for he is alone
He doesn't fight the wild wind
And falls beneath the waters again
The sirens sing his spoken song
In terms of wishes, it won't be long
His eyes they sparkle
As he awakens from his dream
The old man smiles
And falls back to sleep

Shelby Vyvlecka

This Mother's Hands

This mother's hands have seen
some changes from share cropping
in Mississippi, to a luggage
repair shop in Chicago.

To serving her country in the
sixties, at Fort McClellan there
was K.P. to Fort Sam Houston
where we learned the medical
skilled, to soothe the wounded
at Landsthul Germany.

Now living in Bay City Michigan
with a family of four, and four
grandchildren, and one on the
way, these hands are still working.

There will be tests, and trials
and tribulations, but I'll lift
My hands to him whom
my strength comes from
Jesus Christ.

Lizzie Simpson

Special Love

I see his body lying there,
I wonder why they just don't care,
Can't they see the love inside,
Because it's hard for me to hide.

I can't keep running from the pain,
That seems to bring the cold, rain.
It makes them blind,
Oh they can't see,
This special love,
Inside of me.

His love was special,
It was true,
I never thought his life was due.
I know the pain,
Will go away,
Yet in my heart,
His love will stay.

Katie Phillips

"A Musician"

Anyone is a musician
so this you may not know.
We all must be musicians
  in order to grow.

A good musician must
make their feelings known.
Sometimes it so easy
others feel chills in their bones.

Of course, there is the obvious
of some musicians' ways.
Who feel that they must either sing
or find an instrument to play.

A true musician knows
right from the very start.
That music simply can't exist
unless it's from the heart.

Courtney Clark

Untitled

As I fall on my knees
In a desperate plea.
I know I was told
In the years past of old,
That my life was someday
In the times far away,
Could a tapestry be
For my children to see.
How the threads then would make
A perfect picture to take,
To give courage and strength
Not to measure the length
But life's quality deeds
For those who have needs
Far beyond any I
Could conceive if I try.

DeeDee Strauss

The Way Of Life

   He wasn't only the best,
he was better than all the
rest, he was filled happiness,
he was also filled with
attention, then he mentioned
life is the way you make it,
I kept that with me for along
time. People come and people
go, you will feel the way I
do when that time comes,
from now on you should rely
on your grandfather, don't bother
to make life the way you really
don't want it. I loved my
grandfather so much, he was
one of the people who had
to go, it was his time, I
would of done anything in the
world for him.

Christy Foster

A Boy's Game

Boys love to play all kinds of games
Some are ruff, and others are tame.
Baseball, football and all that stuff.
Make our boys so silly and ruff.

Steve Hassell Jr.

Do You Know?

Do you know
a day without You
is like a year,
and a year
a decade,
and a decade
a century?

Do You know
wherever You are
and whatever You do,
You are being thought of dearly
by Someone
who would like
to take You as what You are?

Mary T. Au

Garbage Pain

People put garbage into trash cans.
People put pain into my mind
Peels, cans, cigar butts, and crumpled paper.
Anger fear shame and hate
This garbage builds up in the trash can,
These feelings build up in my mind
Blocking out all other garbage,
Blocking out all other thoughts
Recyclable or not.
Good or bad
And just when you think,
And just when I think
The can will explode,
My head will explode
The garbage is carried away
The pain is taken away
By a garbage man.
By a caring friend
And everything is all right.
And everything is all right

Erik Minkin

Open Your Eyes And See

Open your eyes and see,
There is no difference between you and me.
We might be a different race,
But don't judge me by the color of my face.

Open your eyes and see,
You will find that love is the key.
Tomorrow is so far away,
So be my friend today.

Open your eyes and see,
What kind of person do you want to be?
To have a friend, you've got to be a friend,
Respect is the answer in the end.

Cherie Bailey

Disguised

For I was once a child too,
  looking in a father's eyes.
A smile, a stare, a glance, a laugh,
  but a look that cannot lie.
To think transpiring through a glance,
  holds years of passing by.
All I can say to this is,
  my how time flies!
Be yourself, have fun, and be a
  child as long as you can.
Because someday soon, I'm afraid,
  you too will share a similar disguise.

John P. Cario

Our Son

Bells of joy again sing their song
The rainbow's end has been found
A miracle of happiness was meant to be
Little hand, little feet, our son Eddie

Eyes wandering, searching his new world
Hands grasping the unfamiliar and unknown
Sounds are heard and does try to follow
Love is felt when we soothe his sorrow

His mom, his dad is all he knows
Life's design he still does search
A cry, a whimper, his call of need
Night or day for comfort or feed

Thoughts of compassion his dad does feel
So proud to think a son his own
President, genius are thoughts afar
Musician, Professor or great football star

The days, the months, the seasons pass by
White flakes, birds song come and go
Sharing the years of warmth, laughter and fun
Soon a man with his own little son, soon a man with our grandson

Edward C. Ellis

White Lace

War is on
the cannons roar
screams are muffled
souls are dying
bodies are still -
and the girls wear white, translucent lace.

Bombs bellow
high pitched echoes
of moaning men
mouths are open
ears hear nothing -
and the girls wear white, translucent lace.

People line up for death's call
women's eyes are wells full
of deep, dark water
men's hearts are a vague gray -
and the girls wear white, translucent lace.

Teresa Grabstein

If We Know We Lived Before (Why Bother)

If we know we lived before
Those times sowing that we now reap
A times as Slaves or even as Masters
A times as Whites or even as Blacks

If we know we lived before.
Our kids today, once our parents before,
Our lives today, consequences of our past,
Our lives tomorrow, consequences of todays.

If we know we lived before
Tasted in those times and generations,
On power, slavery, color or race,
Examined on an impartial scale of justice

If we know we lived before,
Why bother whether we be Black or White?
Why bother whether we be richer or poorer?
Why bother whether we be weaker or greater?

If we know we lived before
What today we are is then explained.
In such knowledge, the tolerance of today is found.
Wisely today we therefore live for tomorrow's responsibility.

Oliver O. Mbamara

Streets Of Dope

Bizarre streets,
A city of promise that does not deliver.
The billboard offers hope,
The reality offers nothing.
Filthy fingers eating what others have thrown away,
The selling of their youth for a little security.
The manipulation of lives in exchange for power,
The guiding hand that misleads us.
Wasted youth.
Needle marks.
Lives forever trying to grow up too quickly,
then realizing what they had lost along the way.
The advertisement looked great,
but the product never existed.

Jason Haas

The Man In His Place

He's not the man that should have been there
but he's the one who's always been
He's the man we call our daddy;
Our dad he's always been

Though he did not make us
that's all he did not do,
Whenever there were coughs or tears
Our daddy saw us through

The man whose blood flows through our veins
Knows us not at all
but the man that's been our dad
Knows our every flaw

We could not thank our dad enough and
We could not love him more
Although he is our step-dad
the step our heart ignores

So, who deserves the sweetest name
A man could ever have,
Is it the man who made us?
No, it's the man we call dad.

Tammy Adcock

Mother's Day

It's Mother's Day as I must say,
you give me your love each day.

It feels good to know you're there
and that you really care.

As I shout out loud
to say I'm very proud.

I wouldn't another
because you're my very own special mother.

You make life joyful and bright,
you're always trying to do what is right.

So keep loving yourself as you are,
because you're still that superstar.

Stephanie Vincent

Warlock...

Fade my nightmares made of gold,
Immeasurable blindness is searching my soul,
maelstrom
I will ride the flaming tides
until I die

Wait for me outside

Brandi Livasy

The Sound Of Darkness

No one comes to visit
my eyesight all but gone
No family, no friends
I am all alone.

There is no life left in me
just a body full of pain,
Death is a welcome friend
Life has no gain.

I close my eyes forever
as the breath leaves my chest
the deafening sound of darkness falling
my body now at rest.

As the darkness envelopes me
there is coldness all around
I can't bear this sound of darkness
or the dampness of the ground.

With the sound of darkness growing,
my spirit begins to soar
God reaches out His Holy hand,
the body that confined me, chains me never more.

Pamela Stanley

We Won't Give Up

We won't give up the fight.
We are given this legal right.

We are your future, it's true.
Calm down, don't look so blue.

We have selected our future careers.
Maybe, this will soothe your fears.

In our world there are tough demands.
It seems too hard for us to comprehend.

Kids like us live in a cold world, yes.
The generation before us left a bona fide mess.

Be patient, have faith in us, we know you can.
The future will improve according to the master plan.

Bertha J. Johnson

Untitled

A breeze beneath her feet as they dance within the sky.
Even as hail and rain fall upon them, their love keeps them dry;
Temperatures of intense cold are blown around them and yet
   they stay warm.
They continue to dance with grace and beauty within the brutal storm;
In a moment of fear she place her hand in his palm.
She then feels his strength and once again becomes calm;
Thunder fills their ears with all its mighty sound.
As the clouds beneath their feet send lightning to the ground;
The storm grows silent as time rages on.
The sky turns red with the birth of the dawn;
As they look down at the earth they begin to kiss.
For life and all its pleasures they will surely miss;
Suddenly a light appears above the sky.
In knowing what lies in store for them, they begin to cry;
They pray the Lord can forgive them for any of their sin.
Even as they stand before the golden gates of heaven.

Dimitrius C. Loring

"Grandfather"

I go to your house and expect you there.
All I find is your favorite empty chair.
We played checkers together.
I thought we were going to play that forever.
Now that you're gone the games are done.
I stare at my checkerboard and think of all the games you've won.

Lakeisha Hill

Ode To The Merry Maids

Two Merry Maids who lived separate and apart,
   got together each week to do their part.
They worked and cleaned until everything shined,
   and finally they left with no look behind.
The Merry Maids were loved and adored by others,
   especially by their three brothers.
Now remember this is an ode to two Merry Maids,
   by the way what is an ode any old way.
An ode is a lyric, a ballad, or sonnet,
   that is done to highlight a particular bonnet.
The Merry Maids have been close even from the start,
   Like sisters whom they are can never part.
Though cherished and loved by one and all,
   no one can count what it means to Papaw.
Not only to Paw but the brothers as well,
   this ode is meant to be very swell.
There's a lesson in here for all to see,
   Raise your children right and with dignity.
When they are old and wise and away from you,
   Hopefully there will be a Merry Maid or two.

Ray Wilkerson

The Trip

Discovery,
Of myself,
Brings me closer to the surface,
Of who,
I am.

Journey,
Around the world,
But when I come back,
There is only me and my dreams.

Destinations,
Are many,
But only one counts,
And when it is found, your soul will know other.

Allison M. Barnes

The Chained Mother

Lost to the world and yet vital, they are not
deemed important or worshiped as idol.

Giving and caring to nourish a life, never asking
for what reason they have taken this strife.

Dawn the age of the Mother bonded in chains.
Stripped of what she is and the world is to blame.

It is the choices we make that tear us apart. It is the
Mother who can give our children the guidance of heart.

To save our children from the world of grief, bring home
our Mothers for that is my belief....

Melinda Darlene Bell

Tower To Heaven

Blue-white night light dancing round and round.
Skipping over the ocean; skimming along the ground.
Keeping up your vigil of watching through the night.
Guiding those to safety who keep you in their sight.

Sturdy little lighthouse standing tall amidst the waves
I wonder, yes I wonder how many lives you've saved.
I gaze upon your structure and I smile inwardly.
You are a handsome figure standing up against the sea.

I entered through your belly, large and round and white.
I climbed your spiral staircase that lead me to your light.
An awesome sight I saw there. Tears would not be denied.
I saw the sea as you do through your weather-beaten eyes.

Paulette M. Arthurs

Arboreal

Living in the sun, singing with the breeze, reaching for
tomorrow, reaching steadily.
Anchored by our mother, fathered by the sky. The forest is our
brother, the meadow's at our feet.
Gaining by the rain, holding back the thunder, grow until
tomorrow, silent, silently.
Breathing, breathing; feed the worlds hunger, reaching for
tomorrow, reaching steadily.
Pain we feel, it belongs to you. Steel and chain and fire.
One family now so few.
Staving off the blade, builders of antiquity. Growing for
tomorrow, growing from the past.
Life can be worth living, now living in the past, reaching for
tomorrow, now reaching rather fast.
A seed is what is needed, to make this world complete, contained
within is hope, a future unabridged.
Living in the sun, singing with the breeze, reaching for
tomorrow, reaching steadily.

Joel Bomgardner

Leaf

A small, simple house among a patch of thick trees.
Different colored leaves laying all around.
Do you see them?
The young couple running around the house....

Her in her lively beauty and him in his sure-footedness.
Round and round they do run.
One chasing the other and the other chasing the one.
How much life abounds....

With not a care one—
Will she catch him, will he catch her?
For the day grows old and children do play.
Do you see them, the old couple on the porch?
She rocks in hers,
He rocks in his,
As the leaves do fall.

James P. Redford

"God's Children On Loan"

Babies are a little bit of heaven, be they girl or boy.
A little bet of heaven to bring us untold joy!!
The little ones are God's true piece of art.
Take care of the baby He has sent you, do it from the start.
Give the little one all the love and joy you can, do it from your heart!
Remember they are God's children, only given to you on loan.
They may have a long life, or a very short life to stay in their
earthly home.
We know not when or why He will call, we only know
they are God's children here on loan!
We know they will have peace and everlasting love in their
heavenly home!
We know that we will see them, when our names He calls to His throne.
Because we too are God's children only here on loan!

Geneva E. Coit

Do Not Doubt

You say that you no longer inspire me
How can you know such a thing?
You do not feel the fire
that blazes in my mind.
It grows from a spark in your eyes.
And you know not how it lingers
burning into each part of the day.
Just because I have not learned to tame it
or put it on display,
do not doubt its existence
or its origins
or its power.

Kim M. Baxter

Stupid

Did you think it couldn't happen?
Did you think it wasn't real?
You thought of only fun and games
As you got behind the wheel.

You knew that it was stupid
You didn't stop to think,
You got into the car that night
You'd had too much to drink!

You didn't even see that tree
You were going way too fast.
You drew in a sharp breath
A breath that was your last.

Three precious lives were lost that night
You weren't the first to die,
We think about you lovingly
As each day passes by.

This poem is a warning
To each and everyone,
The results of drunken driving
Can never be undone!

Aimee Nancy Orn

Love Of The Ages

She came to me after my heart was torn
By my first love gone astray,
Then it was a healing love
She gave a lot and asked very little, we were married
Then it was a fun love
We became contented and through our contentment
We almost lost love
Then it was a hard love
But the bond was too strong and through our near loss
We found true love
As time has gone on I now see in myself
That I saw in my Grandfather and now my Father,
A bonding of spirit so strong as to be inseparable
This is the love of the ages
For when I pass on, I will wait for her
And together we go to the next plane and the next
Never separated always loving
The love of the ages.

Melvin Rogers

Singular Lament, 1996

Marital Status is a concern
of those who are
to those who aren't.
"What?! No special friend?"
The unattached must be cured
of the disease, 'singular'.
The Drill:
Physiological resumes exchanged,
sometimes phone numbers.
Blind date? - I wince.
Arrange meeting? - I stammer.
A group fling? - Maybe.
Why must the world be coupled?
Besides, I'm swamped with work, hobbies, sports,
Residence is relative.
No time to engage (Mr. Right)
Advantages: No conflicts, no compromises,
Freedom!
Hey, I'm not alone, I'm convinced!
Of course that's how it appears.

Jeanna Washburn

523

On The Street

I am so lonely, I have no where to go
I am on the street with nothing for to show

I am on the street, and for that a friend say to me
Look you're on the street your something will never be

The girl I love so much, wants the better things in life you see
She says you're on the street, you're not the man for me

So here I stand lonely and lost with nothing but my pride
Still on the street and searching, for a place to hide

Material things are not the things I have lost
For when on the street you find love is the
Thing that costs

So if you would house me with the love in
Your heart so bold
I wouldn't be on the street, but in
A house of gold

Forrest Smith

A Salute To A Brave Soldier

God took him home in '43
Fighting for his country as he wanted to be free.

He gave up his country, his life and his home
To join God in his heavenly throne.

His name was Gold, and he was a true gem
and the reason God called, He had a place for him.

He left a daughter, a real beautiful girl
To grow up without him, in this unsettled world.

We all feel sad for this wonderful guy
But for now, just so long and not goodbye.

Jeanne Bitterman

"A Darker Shade"

I am going blind,
I am just another wrinkle,
on the face of time.

The future is dark,
almost too dark to see,
the devil is ready,
waiting to devour me.

The sky,
it's starting to fade,
the brightness I once knew,
is now collaborating with a darker shade.

Albert Teng Williams Jr.

"The Rose"

Dedicated to Vincent Martinez
The Rose, lonely it stands.
This until I met you and we joined hands.
Our love is like this rose I hold,
it starts off growing slow, ready to get old.
Now the leaves are coming out
for all the times you showed me what life is about.
The petals are fully grown
to hear those words in a sweet tone.
Now the thorns appear,
for all the times I thought you'd leave; I'd fear.
Now, all my petals are falling for when we cry,
to save our love before it passes on by.
But what is this, I see my Rose at birth again,
when you dress my hand with a gold band.
Our love is like my Rose I hold,
to be together to grow old.

Esther Flores Lopez

Untitled

Oh the earth, such an intelligent place.
  Huh! I pretend I'm not there.
    Pretending to be invisible.
I feel unconscious, a sense of floating, peace, I'm volitating.
  Please tell me I'm not dreaming?

I'm like a tabula rasa! So alone, so empty, yet invincible!
  No one seems to notice anyway. Do they ever? Hmm?

Oh the earth, such a trial and error of a place.
  Uh uh, I'm slipping into consciousness.
    I feel dissonant with everyone and everything.
There appears to be a brigade standing in my way of growth.
  It's something fierce!

Oh the earth, such a brave yet cowardice place.
  Oh no I see everything! Damn, now I'm visible!
I'm naked and exposed. They're pouring more salt into my wounds;
  Once again, attempting to break my spirit.

I'm leaving now because this place is not my home.
  So I close my eyes, release my soul, I'm volitating.
    Imagine that! I'm free.

Latilia Warren

Two Ducks And Five Geese

Two ducks and five geese
  As happy as can be
Discovered the garden when they followed
  The lady, intent to see.
Not knowing they were there
  She was startled and yelled with despair.
Shooing them away - quacking and waddling
  Away they went
Up the road with heads high in the air
  But their spirits were bent.
"So, you don't want us to eat
  your peas so green
Nor your melons and cucumbers," they screamed.
"We'll try to be content then
  with these old weeds and grass,
Until one day when you're not looking
  We might sample your garden at last."

Elsie S. Hueston

Inner Joy

How sweet is the laughter of your husband when he comes home
  at night and smells the bread baking and the chicken frying —
A kiss to mother from her child when she has washed and ironed
  a pretty, frilly dress makes joy come with her crying —
As darkness descends on a home and lights go on and music
  and laughter are heard from inside —
The friends who approach can feel the mirth and warmth that the
  family has applied —
But we know the love of family and friends has to be continuously
  worked toward —
To make everlasting joy and happiness come we need the Lord —
He gives us this inner joy such as we get from happiness —
Without it we are just a great big mess.

Doris Peterman

Caitlin's Birthday

Caitlin is my name.
A party is my game.
I like ice cream and cake.
Tomorrow my mom will bake.
Little presents, big presents for my birthday.
Icing is so sweet, there's not much more to say.
New friends, old friends, I'll invite them all to play.

Caitlin C. Fletcher

So What More Can I Do?

Oh Lord: Here I stand before Thee, complete with sin and all,
mine iniquities bared unto you, how I pray thee hear my call.
I know ye sent thy only begotten son, and for that I do thank you,
but still I'm a sinner Lord, so what more can I do?

Born in a manger on top of some hay, was our Lord Jesus
on what's now called Christmas Day.
Your key to redemption for all of our sins
is the Lord Jesus sent from heaven and you,
but still I'm a sinner, so what more can I do?

Hung on a cross at the top of Calvary
was the Lord Jesus Christ for all the world to see.
So that all sins would be washed clean, for you and for me.

Oh how I thank you Father in Heaven, for your son from above,
for it is because of Jesus that I know I am loved.
I pray Thee, please forgive me all my sins and debts due.
I now have Jesus, so what more can I do?

Felix Bermea III

The Dream

Last night I dreamed of you.
I dreamed you were walking on the shoreline
and I was walking with you.
Last night I dreamed of you.
You were walking through the prairie grasses,
I dreamed I followed you
and I watched the wind caress your hair.
You were wanted by me,
the way a woman wants a man.
Last night I dreamed of you.
I dreamed your eyes sparkled with the stars,
and I watched the wind caress your hair.
You were wanted
by me,
who dreamed of you.

Dakotah Woller

Lonely

Here I sit,
Peerless and despondent.
Not one says "hi" or "bye."
Nothing to break the monotonous stillness.
Not one dares stretch out his hand to offer succor
But walks on by too busy to offer aid to one in need.
If it isn't about me, don't bother telling me about it.
Got a buck I can borrow?
Do you dance? Wear your hair long?
Have a ring in your ear? These are important.
If I have problems,
Tough, here's a quarter. Call someone who cares.
Man is a fickle thing, he is,
Based on outward signs
I yet sit alone on the curb, watching people go by.
Does anyone say can I help you?
Everybody already knows everybody they care to know.
So I remain peerless until
One cares enough to take the time
To know me and mine.

Christopher Edwards

Highway 1

The last view I saw was gossamer glass,
Red stained, each webben silk a lifeline,
Being plucked away by a cruel child
Who enjoys the power of entropy.

Todd Wampler

A Bright Tomorrow

When through this world we wander alone
And our pillows, are sand and stone
Do not give in to grief and sorrow.
Lift up you chin, and look for A Bright Tomorrow.

When we feel we are doomed with pain
And our days are filled, with storm, and rain
And we think we have reached our wits end.
Remember! There's a better life, around the bend.

When our pages of life have been turned,
And Our Merits have been earned.
Then we shall wander, no more,
Along life's rough and stormy shore.

Maxwell B. Williams

These Troubled Times

Our children are dying, by each other's hand,
There's brother against brother, in the homeland
Prayers in our schools, have come to an end,
Laws are now made, too easy to bend

Sisters and daughters attacked, on our sands,
Sons are off fighting, amidst foreign clans.
Hungry and homeless, are our fellow man,
Our great leaders too scared, to take a stand.

Drugs and disorder, now reach a great span,
Violence and hatred, is today's blend
Families and morals, have begun to disband,
Marriage vows broken, is the latest trend.

Mothers and fathers, let's pray for an end,
And all pull together, our world to mend.
For this was not God's intended plan.

Patsy A. Preece

Untitled

The world, the ocean, the sky
Is a picture waiting to be drawn
A poem waiting to be written
A book waiting to be read

You draw the picture
But you still can't see it
Look harder
And you will see the meaning behind the clouds

You write the poem
But you still don't understand it
Look again
And you will see the message in the waves

You read the book
But you still don't see the words
Look harder, look again, look once more
And you will see where you fit in the world

Lisa Kovener

Untitled

The moon sings a song of death and the powerful blood cry
    to the kindred.
Their unspoken language is the key to unlocking their eternal need.

The wind whispers of their passionate and hypnotic ways.
The stars gossip of tales of their lust for blood and pleasure.
The forests keep secrets of their defiance of death and their
    survival through the ages.
The dawn of a new day radiates tales of the destruction of the
    kindred, the end to the immortal beings.

Lindsay Kennedy

Greater Than Its Parts

Although alone, we have much to enjoy and offer, it's in the
Wholeness of love that the transformation begins.
As if in revelation, love now makes us realize, we are only complete
With that of another.
Together, we wonder, how we endured alone and apart, mattering
Only to be one with our love.
Our now selfless life, takes on new purpose and meaning, sharing
The joys, hardships, and all in between.
More aware of life's simplicities, yet better able to deal with
The complex.
We see the world from another's eyes, opening new vistas that we
Both now share.
And even when the pair has parted, we are willing to endure the
Pain of beginning again.
As if in rebirth, to once again experience the love that is,
Greater than its parts.

Stan Shulda

Appreciate What You Have

We are on his earth, but for a short time,
And many times we tend to dwell on
All the things that go wrong in our lives,
Or what seems to be missing,
Instead of opening our eyes and our hearts,
To truly appreciate the wonderful things
We are so lucky to have.

When someone listens to every problem
Even when they have their own,
And gives you confidence and belief in yourself
When you thought you weren't worth believing in;
When they cry with you and comfort you
And are always there whenever you need them,
Encouraging you and loving you
In spite of your faults and blunders.
When someone makes you see the good in yourself
And stands by you because they love who you are;
Stop dwelling on what you think you're missing,
Appreciate the precious things you have.

Linda Bohlinger

When The Time Comes

When the times comes for you to find out that your only
living grandfather is diagnosed with a disease that you forget
everything you just want to cry.

When the time comes for you to find out that your only
living grandfather is going to be placed in a nursing home, you
think why me.

When the time comes for you to go and visit your only
living grandfather in a nursing home, you think I can't go on.

When the time comes that you find out that your only
living grandfather has been rushed to the hospital because he can't
breathe, you think no it's not his time.

When the time comes for you to go to your last living
grandfather's wake and funeral you think, I can't cry. All I need
is to see him alive again and tell him. I Love You.

Christina Sowich

Reality?

What is reality?
A dream which no one can grasp,
Years of waiting and watching time pass.
Endless words and music of hope,
All the while just trying to cope.
You see, my friend
You will not know until
The End

Kerry Donohoe

Farewell To Maidens

Might thy face of cheery rose so beautiful and whole,
cause me endure on to try and o'er take thy soul.
How would I becalm those bestial eyes for lack of wind
by that, then would my vile heart have unto you sinned?

If thou art by me forsaken be not dismayed,
for not even one so fair can keep this heart stayed.
Life is brief and memories become ponderous.
How much more then could be asked of one so wondrous.

Fare thee well then my loves for I am called to war
and so must fight for you and others all the more.
Never has writing brought to me less than I willed,
but now I go to find empires to be fulfilled.

Joel Gibson

Mother

Sometimes we argue and disagree,
But don't all mothers and daughters.
No matter how our thoughts differ
I know you will be there for me.

If things do not end up my way in something or another,
And I am sad and lonely because of this
You will be there to comfort me
Because you are my mother.

If I am having trouble on a project or so
You will be there to help me finish
Or at least do your best trying.
You are my friend, far from foe.

One day I will be grown
And maybe have children.
I can only pray that someday
I will be as good of a mother as my own.

F. Michelle Allen

Mt. St. Helens

On that day 1980
Following an earthquake
Your long sleep was now over
All the beautiful landscape which had formed
You destroyed without a warn
You had a terrible temper and exploded
Killing everything in your path
Throwing lava, rock, and ash
Into the sky and on the ground
Not a living thing left except...
A pine tree.

Bryan Kennedy

The Doll At Grandmother's House

Penny is a doll at Grandmother's house...
She sits and waits — waits because there
    isn't anyone to play with.

There she sits in the little gold rocking chair,
The one left behind when the children were there.

Grandmother moves her around and straightens her clothes,
As she half opens her eyes to see if perhaps a
    child has her to hold.

If Penny could talk, she would say, "Why do the children
    stay away?... oh well, Grandmother is good to me;
She picks me up and combs my hair... and I sit
waiting in the little gold chair."

Avis Dunn

Why Me?

My heart deep inside, thanks all
the people who have touched my life!
Physically and mentally.
    Thanks to the people who have changed my
life without knowing, because I can not
find the words in my heart to thank them.
    Some people don't understand my feelings
for others... why?
    I don't understand them, do they not
understand me because they have not felt
this special feeling... like I have?
    It makes me feel sad for them,
in a way. Deep in my mind, I wonder why
I deserved this feeling... why didn't they
deserve this feeling... why?
I don't understand, why me?

Abigail Schneider

Time Heals

People says time heals all of hurts in life.
When you're a kid, you can fall and scrape your
knees and time heals all scrapes and cuts.
As you grow older and learn about love and friendship.
You never have to worry about great friends leaving you.
Best friends are forever. No matter what time
always heals great friendships. When you fall
in love with a friend you not only trust them
as a friend but as a lover. When someone else
comes between them or feelings change between
the two of them. The hurt cuts deep so for
that person and for me I feel like time can't
heal this hurt I'm feeling ever!! When you
feel like someone just ripped out my heart
and throw it away. I don't think time
can heal this hurt I feel inside! Time
won't ever heal this hurt I feel so deep inside
I can't ever dream about living without him in my life.
Time won't ever heal my hurt I feel for him.

Donna Storms

An Ode To My Doll

Dollie came to me in the year nineteen twenty two.
She had curly brown hair and eyes of blue.

Her satin dress was Christmas red
Adorned with bows and lace from toe to head.

My dear mother taught me how to sew.
The number of dresses I've made for Dollie
  I shall never know.

Through all the years she was dressed in style.
The trips with me have been many a mile.

She accompanied me through Elementary,
  High School and College.
She must have acquired a bit of knowledge.

Now in our later years we can only reminiscence
Of early days filled with joy and bliss.

Eloise McClendon

The War

It was a dark, stormy day
The soldiers were on the battle field ready to fight
Everyone of the soldiers wanted to try his might
As they raised their guns and started to shoot
They began dying group by group
Thus ended this dark and stormy day

Chad Weaver English II

Untitled

The earth drifts on its tilted setting,
The time, the place constantly spins by,
Moments build to the episodic saga
And fall neatly into the story called life
While in that motionless tilt
The world holds an eerie place
The locale being solid and incredibly
Fuzzy at the same time
From this sweet planted resting
Spot, the view seems clear
But the vision distorted
It exists through so many eyes
That it is fondled too often
Not allowing for personal expression
So the world fights back
With natural disasters and violent storms
Be they weather or abuse
They disturb the raping population greatly

Storey Radzuinas

Wake Up! Wake Up!

The Earth Mother is calling you.
She knows you have polluted her water.
She knows you have poisoned the air.
She knows you have wreaked havoc on the soil.
She also knows you are her children.
Wake up! Wake up to realize who you are;
sons and daughters of the Earth Mother.

Ronald A. McNeil

Moonset

Moonset, like a pearl in the western sky
while her prodigal sun rouses the morning wind,
tumbles, dives and shatters against a waking river.

Moonset, like a pearl enthroned
where playful dawn is gathering
into a pool of golden vapor
now bouncing off meddlesome clouds
now pouncing upon piqued mountains
and straining through vagrant forests
then draining over that river's ledge.

Moonset like a pearl ensconced
where sunrise deposits his illusive
and radiant geste in this stillness,
on her behalf.

Paul Sonderman

Celestial Conversations

His head bent round
He wears a crooked crown
They say he engages in celestial conversations.

Posing as Napoleon
On a giant, grey mare
Or acting out Alice
With rabbits in his hair
They say he engages in celestial conversations.

Dancing with shadows
Standing in mid air
Or acting out Medusa
Crawling from her lair
They say he engages in celestial conversations.

Rick Petrea

One By One

Why must our feelings grow strong,
Just to again and again be lowered into frailty,
They should be as free as blowing leaves,
Falling one by one into a pond, creating many ripples.

Instead they become heavy from disappointment,
Not able to float on the surface of the cool water,
And bask in the warmth of the sunlight,
But quickly sinking, one by one into the depths of darkness.

When the heart is left out under the sun,
Shelterless, it becomes hardened,
Until one by one, the drops of rain finally come,
And left etched upon the earth is the faintest good-bye.

Eric M. Walker

The Question Is?

Where will we be when Jesus comes?
Will we be ready for that day?
All will not, but there will be some!
How do we live the righteous way?

We must live each day fair and just,
So that we do not be left behind.
This law God says is a must!
Treating everyone gentle and kind.

What should we do for one another?
When we walk our own way!
Do we have to treat each one as our brother?
In this world we live in today.

We must give love to each and everyone.
Forgiving sin that we all have done.
Have Faith and Believe in the Almighty One!
Just Trust in the Father and the Son!
Yes, Jesus will come!

Karen A. King

Love

Love is a great thing
Love is the best thing
Anyone could think of
It's just like being up above

Love is the prettiest thing in the world
Sometimes it is all twirled
Love is good, it makes us do
What we are told
It's always in **BOLD, BOLD, BOLD**.

You can't see love but you sure can feel it
It's like choosing right from wrong
Love is the greatest thing on earth!
I'm glad Heavenly Father and Jesus Christ made it...
So no one should let it fade.

Heather Hansen

Reflections

I see beauty in this life that others may not see
It's found within the heart of man whose conscience is free!
I see beauty in an act of kindness without glory,
Helping some child find the way back to the right road is an old story!
I see beauty in a touch of gentle handling, relieves the pain,
    aids so much and eases the suffering!
I see beauty in a word given to reassure, letting them know that
    God has heard and will give strength to endure!
I see beauty in those who strive to serve, going on uncomplaining,
    when he hears some unkind word not deserved!
I see beauty in eternal life, the soul of man set free, to live in
    a world free from strife, with God, in peace and harmony!

Juanita L. Walford

Life Guide

Many roads I have not travelled,
But the pain I've seen is great.
For many I've seen along the way,
And most were filled with hate.
And when I looked upon their faces,
And saw their fiery rage,
My mind likened them unto an animal,
That's trapped within a cage.
When I recalled how things had been,
And how I used to be,
I was humbled when I realized,
That they were just like me.
When pain and anger and hatred,
Had all but consumed my soul,
The Lord came down and touched my heart,
And now I'm completely whole.
And now I see these people,
And the help they need inside,
Knowing now God's reasons,
He put me here to guide.

Christopher Lee Terry

Timeless

I look up at you
You stare or even glare back at me
My arms are tired
But your arms never tire of their hourly trek
Your numbers see seconds go by
I see only unmoving time
Why must you always move so slowly?

Peery

The Song Of A Youthful Bird

Grateful is my unforgettable feeling for the admirable
And the extraordinary exploits done.
Given me was a wonderful existence.
Many a sacrifice made for my sake.

Well, in addition, teach me flying as I am a juvenile,
My special request, whether you had that chance
Or you learned from your own aptitude.

If you did, was it a difficult experience?
Please, reveal it to me
And don't let me undergo it alone.

If you really did, how many times did you fall on the surface?
Scary, as you know, maybe that jungle out there.
Please, start teaching me.
If you do, fulfilled will be my ultimate desire
And generous will be my contribution to my entire race.

Vital Lauriston

Destiny

Oh! Destiny, destiny of mine.
Where are thou? That I feel it not.
Since I was told long ago where I should go.
Was it not to praise and sing to the master
of my soul?
When rain and thunder comes, I feel his
presence, and yet I see him not.
Oh! Destiny, destiny of mine.
Where is the master of my soul?
When I mourn and weep; I feel his love,
and see him not. I laugh and dance with
joy, and see him not. I feel his love
all around me, and yet see him not.
Oh! Destiny, destiny of mine.
Where is the master of my soul?

Estella L. Chelette

A Modern Mind

When I am alone and quiet,
Having exhausted the entertainment value
Of mediated make-believe,
I tentatively turn to test the paradox
In consciousness itself.

I see mind and heart at play
In radical estrangement from the objects of the world.
New vocabularies cloud perception.
The world itself unravels.
Causes, consequences, courses and connections come undone.

Appearances, affections interweave.
No Plato, Christ or Euclid,
No Marx and no Maimonides
Adjusts the focus.
Convention summons up experience,
And deep subjective whim.

Meaning, destiny and right
Are baffled.
I see I cannot test for truth
And know.

Ruth W. Ericson

I'm Tired Of Being Sick

I'm tired of being sick.
Maybe I should give this sickness a kick.

This cough is driving me crazy,
I'm very, very lazy.
Resting on the couch is getting kind of boring,
Every other minute I hope I don't start snoring.
Dad stayed home and acted like a Doctor,

Out poured the medicine, my Mom, it really shocked her.
For a treat my mom made fudge,

But off the couch I would not budge.
Even though we don't eat in the den,
I ate my fudge and committed a sin.
Now is the first time I wanted to go to school.
Golly, gosh, gee, wow, Dr. Dad thinks that's cool.

Since I'm sick for this whole week,
It doesn't matter if I look like a Geek!
Chills, fevers, and shivers is a "double 2-thumbs down."
Keep yourself healthy and well or you'll get sick.
(Hey... I can't make every line rhyme!)

Caleb Michael Fletcher

Summer

Swimming, sun bathing, fishing too
All during summer the skies are blue
Sticky hot and humid,
Sun shining bright
Air conditioners running
All day and all night
Bees are buzzing as a cool breeze blows,
All during summer
We wear light colored clothes
We go on vacation
And stay out in the sun,
Summer is filled with laughter and fun
The sun shines bright
On the children out at play,
It stays nice out day after day
Swimming, sun bathing, fishing too
All during summer, the skies are blue.

Allison Konick

Garden Of My Heart

Open the door, and find a secret garden
That's carefully been tended, year to year
Seeds of hope help it to flourish
And buds of love are fragrant on the air

The sun's early rays, filter through the ivy
That clings to a crumbling wall surround
Flowers of all kinds grow in abundance here
A kaleidoscope of color and dancing with the breeze

From time to time, tears from the heavens
Fall in abandon, dampening the earth
Like chords in harmony they'll soon flow together
In bubbling mirth where hope springs anew

The leaves of the tall oaks like a canopy of lace
Birds of a feather and animals who've strayed
Lightning bugs twitter in the twilight of a day gone by
Dreamers can get lost in the heady perfume

In today's ravished world, the doorways rarely open
To glimpse at a world so filled with love and joy
Embrace it with your heart, trust in its purity
And close the door behind you if you step inside

Ann Schmoekel

The Color Of My Skin

Steamin' hot days in field pickin' cotton,
The food scraps even sometimes rotten.
Everyday I was beaten, not to mention mistreated.

Rags is what I was given to wear,
Lord help me to survive is how I began my every prayer.

If Masta' Dalton could see through my kinky hair,
He would only find someone who wanted to be treated fair.

If he could look at my full lips,
He will understand why I learned to read and write
When death was the consequence,
But ya' see the mind is powerful, so I took that risk.

If Masta' Dalton could look into my dark brown eyes,
He would know why my head is held so high,
He could never strip me of my pride,
Even though to be treated equal I was denied.

I asked myself what about the person within?
Treated like a animal only because the color of my skin.

Tameka Westmoreland

Daniel In The Lions Den

I was sitting in my easy chair one day,
When all of a sudden, my mind went astray.
I got to thinking of Daniel in the Lion's Den,
With those hungary lions, with appetites that never end.

When he looked at those great big cats,
I know he thought "This is not a good place to be at".
And then King Darius, who was responsible for his plight,
Said to Daniel, "Your God whom you serve will
protect you through the night".

Early the next day, King Darius rushed to the den,
To see if "God had really protected his friend".
Now low and behold, as King Darius looked in,
There sat "Daniel with a great big grin".

Now the King who was tricked by some very evil friends,
That had persuaded him to throw "Daniel into the Lion's Den".
But now King Darius, "Had seen God's power",
He had those men and their family thrown into
the den for the lions to devour.

Henry Hamlett

"The World's A Stage"

Marvels the moon observes all day,
Occupy'n conspicuously
Celestial sky box of the world.

Revolving earth, in splendor clad,
Each season decked in bright array
From polar caps to desert heat
With raging winds and softest breeze.

Comings and goings, night and day,
Creatures of forest, land and sea,
Bright birds awing and beasts of prey.

'Mid curtain calls - setting the stage
All creatures have a part to play,
They do their thing, then pass away.

Age in, age out, "the world's a stage,"
Its center spot, man's destiny,
He writes the script and speaks at times,
The actors vary with the lines

About tragedies and wars and peace,
Man's inhumanity to man,
Lord, cause these calamities to cease!
    Mary Lawrence Hiti, A.S.C.

Street Sign

Stepping out into the street
Wide-opened dark eyes stare straight ahead
His gait is purposeful, steady
Traffic along the four lane road disavows his presence
And he is oblivious to theirs
He proceeds, boldly, confidently
Forcing acknowledgment
One car swerves, another manages to stop
Probability, formerly elusive, catches up
    as a van hits him squarely in the side
He screams: "Can't you see I'm here?"
    and mutters some obscenities as he loses consciousness
The driver, standing near him,
    scan others along the sidewalk for help and absolution
Except for some rubbernecking through dark reflective glass,
    traffic along the four road disavows his presence
A cardboard sign lies next to him
    Homeless and Hungry
    God Bless
Neatly written in black crayola.
    William E. Lee III

Mr. Yesterday Unaware

I bid farewell to he who walks the earth slowly
Trudging through the thick maple syrup of bygone
Pausing and forever crafting his time
He is stuck somewhere in the last wooded area
Arguing with the grass or the wind
Debating with the earth concerning beauty
Laughing at the efforts of the sun

He is called Mr. Yesterday Unaware
How swiftly his time has come to be vanished
How abruptly came the stick of the tar pit
How fleeting the wit from his tongue
Not even the earth can halt the arrival
That future sees fit to bring

He is called Mr. Yesterday Unaware
How uneasy he looks melting into the morning
    Tim Weber

Grandpa

From the very first day I came to earth,
from my very first day, my birth.

You were always a caring man,
and always my biggest fan.

You were always nice and kind,
something we lost, you could find.

Anything broke you could fix.
although a recipe you could not mix.

You called me your pumpkin on Halloween,
then I grew up to be a teen.

And then came the day that you went away,
in the funeral home there you lay.

Gone until the day that we will be,
together for eternity.

Living there with you, a caring man
and I will be your biggest fan.
    Noralyn Bolander

Sail Silent My Night Dream, Warm Breath From The Sea

Night so silent upon this desolate spit,
dark fingers from seaward to my soul crept.
While sleeping at anchor the Liberty lay.

I, in my dingy, stealthfully slip.
Up her mooring for a fantasy sail,
Into the dark and memory trail.
Quietly easing the anchor to rest,
Leaving the landward breathless at best.
Sail silent my night dream, warm breath from the sea.

Escaping the channel so close and so threatening,
gently we glide past the breakwaters crashing
Into the night, and her arms so embracing,
the Liberty and I go home to the sea.

Slap! Goes the mainsail!
Crack! Goes the jib!
Slow rolls the heart of the Liberty kid.
Into the night, into tomorrow
slow rolls the fulfillment of yesterday's sorrow.

Sail silent my night dream, warm breath from the sea,
Me and the Liberty are returning to thee.
    Pam Cabak

Soul To Soul

Soul to soul we speak,
I have felt your pain,
yet can not reach out to console you.
I have heard you cry and brushed the
air as if to dry your tears.
I have reveled in your joy and laughter
though I can not see your smile.

In my prayers your name is but a
whisper that only God and you may hear.
How I have longed to touch your face and
hold you near; only in spirit is this allowed.
Through these gifts you have touched the
depths of my soul, places only God has
seen until now.

These gifts I do not question, only why
are you so near yet so far?
In my soul and in my prayers you will
stay until God takes you away.
    Tamara Ermer

"Lost Years"

I am sitting here thinking
What is my Dad sitting there thinking
Confined to a home where he most
Certainly feels alone
When did he leave us
Where did he go

Didn't he know I would miss him
I saw him the other night
I said Dad what are you thinking
He said "about when I am going to get out of here"
He told me his birthday
Was the other day and that he was 59
My father was 59 twenty years ago
Where did he go
When did he leave us
How come he didn't tell me he was going?

Jeanne Murphy Beggins

"Summer Breeze"

When the wind blow softly
so sweet and blurry,
the breeze and butterflies
in a flurry
it seems to me, exact to be
that everything is free
no limits, no stops,
no nervous digestive flops
In the graceful breeze you'll run to me
arms outstretched
You're deep in spring's great dreams
Summer's coming, you are leaving
think of other themes,
No wind is from west, nor south,
nor east, nor north, it all comes from deep in the heart of the chest.

Rachel Kloby

"Still Falls, The Dew"

Tears flow like a river,
  through the crevice in my heart.
I'm a princess in a play,
  with no one to play the prince's part.

Knights, in polished armor, have come,
  and also gone.
But these have left me feeling
  very empty and alone.

Petals are falling from the rose within my heart,
  as, slowly, it withers away.
I am left with only my dreams
  of a prince carrying me away.

He'll take me on his porcelain horse,
  and we'll ride to the summery eve.
Neither of us will abandon the other,
  his side, I'll never leave.

Someday, these dreams,
  they may come true.
As time, forever, marches on,
  and yet, still falls, the dew.

Kristina L. Hilburn

Untitled

Listen people, hear my plea!
It's time to reach out, time to see.
Reach to the nations, reach to the stars,
Lets help all people, heal the scars.
Regardless of race, religion or lands,
It's time to reach out with helping hands,
Unite today! Tomorrows too late,
Nations must change or resign to fate.
Our lives, our customs differ so much,
All we need is a gentle touch.
A child is crying, do you all hear?
The mother is reaching to hold him near.
It's time for war, to stop, to cease,
It's time for all to be at peace.
Lend out a hand, extend all our best,
Lets put our morality to the test.

Jean F. Valentine

Joy

Joy is the bright colors of the sun
setting on a clear night.
   It is the sound of a herald trumpeter
playing in the heavens.
   It tastes like sweet dew
and smells like the fresh mountain air.
It looks like a waterfall ever pouring.
   Joy makes you feel loved by everyone and everything.

Denise Schenck

"When We Were Young - Not Gray"

When we were young - not gray
What an abundance of spiritedness
We youngsters would display.

There was nothing at all we couldn't do
The sky was the limit,
And when it came to a dare
We were so foolhardy - just say the word
We'd do it - we weren't ones to scare.

Now that we're gray - not young
It's nice to recall those years of fun
But where did they go to
It really can't be
It only seemed like yesterday
Don't you agree?

Our walk is now slower - our reactions are too
And without our glasses - we haven't a clue

We're happy to be gray - none the less
We've done our best - we've passed the test
We loved those times - when we were young
And now that we're gray - we can still have fun!

Agnes B. McGann

A Shocking Treasure

Electricity can be shocking, but it's cool.
It juices up the radio and heats the pool.
Thanks to good old Benjamin,
At night there's light for reading in,
for doing last-minute book reports,
and making Civil War Lego forts.·
It gives you instant power,
everyday, every year, every hour.

Andrew Amedeo Rocca, 9 years old

Where

Where the night penetrates darkness as the
darkness penetrates night
Where eerie sounds echo off the moon and come
pounding back to silence the living
Where death and devils play their tortured games
and triumph
Where blood thirsting creatures crawl about shadows
so that no human eye could ever see their presence
Where to the mortal there exists no such frightening
things but what yet has to be discovered in the
blackness of night
Where some go and never return and
Where others fear to even leave their bedside
That's where
Where the night penetrates darkness as the
darkness penetrates night into the deepest black
that sends cringing shivers up your spine

Asza Toombs

She Came Early To School

Her big brown eyes were filled with tears.
    Small for her age but wise for her years.
She came in early to talk and to weep
    To tell me a secret she knew I would keep.

"The police came and took my brother away.
    This morning at seven, they took him today.
They say he hurt a little girl.
    It can't be true... I'm all in a whirl."

"He's nice to me and I love him so.
    I don't understand. I just don't know!"
She needed a hug and I held her tight.
    I wish I could make it all turn out right.

It was time for the bell and the class came in.
    She squared her shoulders and gave a weak grin.
She'd meet the world and stand on her feet.
    Ready to face the trouble she'd meet.

She's only eight and wise for her years.
    She went to her seat and dried her tears.
A sweet caring child with a small sad face.
    She opened a book and stared into space.

Roberta Ropp

Poverty's Prison Mart

They say "Amateurs, try to win
Generous Mr. Ely wants to help,
So I pick up my pen and start to write
God knows I can use a little help.

The poem should not exceed 20 lines
I only have 14 more to go,
So, I sit at my typewriter, and sip my coffee
For the prize, I'll need a darn good score.

The national library of poetry
Must really know of my plight,
Must really care about someone's poverty
So to escape it, the winning poem I'll try to write.

Please Mr. Postman, deliver this poem
Please God, let it touch Mr. Ely's heart,
And if it does, I'll have some resources
To help me escape poverty's prison mart.

Only three more lines to go
Then my pen I must put away,
May God bless, bless and embrace you
For giving someone a trace of hope today.

Mary D. Ravit

Problems

Everyone has them.
Some are small and some great.
I will worry about money.
Never enough to meet the needs
    especially the wants.
Spend, spend, spend.
I worry of test taking and
    of failing to do well.
I worry of people's approval
    and of people's thoughts.
Meanwhile, a child dies of starvation.
A family killed by a bomb.
A man can no longer walk.
A woman finds out she has breast cancer.
A couple gives birth to a retarded child.
My cares and worries are small.
My troubles will pass and I will live.
Lord guide me, but spend more time
    with others not as strong.
For someday, I may be one of them.

Steven F. Chanter

To My Child

May you always view the world through a child's eye,
Exciting, hopeful, full of awe and wonder.
May you remember to smile from the inside out
for it is only inside that we conquer the wars of the soul.
Try to remember the soothing voice within,
Guiding you through dark moments.
May you build your dreams one day at a time
For futures are built upon moments.
May you allow the calmness within to override fear...
And may you always have the courage to cry.
Remember that it is through the healing of the spirit
That we are reborn unto this place...
May you try to remember that love surrounds you
Even when you can't feel the sunshine.
And, may you not wander too far away from me,
Yet, far enough to satisfy your own soul...

Renee L. Gunterman-Davis

Library

L ook and you shall find, worlds waiting to be explored;
Mysteries, histories, adventures and fantasies
Await you at its doors.

I magine you are Plato, and let your imagination soar.
Listen to Beethoven's Fifth, or test a computer chip.
Catch up on current events, or read about Hercules' feats.

B en had the right idea when he first opened its doors.

R esearch and discover the marvels of civilizations lost.
Where kings and knights, princesses and gods, all roamed.

A nalyze physics; convert your metrics here.
Look up a foreign word, or check your chemistry.
Rewards await you here.

R econstruct the past? Design the future!
Remember something you've learned here,
That no one can deny;
The library knows more than you and me,
And always answers your why.

Y es! It's your local library, a treasure to behold.
The heart of the community,
As wondrous worlds unfold.

Nicholas A. G. Lamb

Final Prayer

What to feel, this blanket of black.
  Soul long gone, no turning back
Nothing now, but this sheet of white
  Lost hopes and dreams without a fight

One hundred years, we'll lie the same
  And in between we play this game.
Look to thyself, and not my grave
  Push through the dark, I beg, be brave.

Look for the light, and firmly grasp.
  I felt too soon, death's cold...cold clasp.

Charles B. Wright

Ostrich

Abstract dilemma, notorious shift.
The happiness in soul I keep,
will harbor a smile from ear to ear
for no more tears shall I weep.

Circumstantial divide in perilous report.
The mystery surrounding the cloudy sky,
will pour sunbeams upon my brow,
and so light my heart that I might fly.

Paul B. Terry

He Answers

What is birth, he asks...
Birth is your awakening, He answers...

Have I merely been asleep, he asks...
You have slept and awakened many times on your journey,
He answers...

Where am I going, he asks...
You are going home, He answers...

When will I arrive, he asks...
You will know when you have arrived, He answers...

Must I travel alone, he asks...
You are not alone, He answers...

What if I tire along the way, what will nourish and replenish me, he
asks... If you tire, if there is need to be nourished, drink from the
fountain of youthful memories; eat from the fruitful tree of
knowledge; rest in the bed of life's experience, and you will be
replenished, He answers....

What if I falter, what if I stray, how will I find my way, he asks...
Let your heart be your guide and you will not lose your way, He
  answers...

How can I trust in what you say, he asks... The truth cannot be
altered and you have know the truth from the beginning,
He answers...

I have learned from you this day, he says...
And I, from you, He answers.

Nina Robinson

My Mother

My mother is someone who understands what I am going through
My mother is someone I can talk to and will listen
My mother helps me through the good and the bad times
My mother listens to my every word and helps me with my problems
My mother tells me everything is going to be O.K.
My mother is someone who is always going to be there when
  my friends aren't, no matter what!
I love you and I am glad that you are my mother, thanks for always
being there for me.

Jennifer Valentin

His Price For Peace

Dedicated to the memory of my mother Ann and also Thomas (Butch)
Riley who like a lot of servicemen paid the ultimate price
On November 22, 1963 the world lost a man who could have made this
land free. Out in the pacific a battle he fought he would have laid
down his life then for the peace that the sought.
He wanted freedom for one and all he said; it had cold winter's day
he accepted his call.

The price was high he also said but we were willing to pay it to
keep a head. There was the Cuban crisis and also Berlin his
inaugural address was not just a whim. He tried very hard for his
new frontier and the world seemed much safer when he was here.

Then came the Friday we will never forget that was the day the
whole world wept. He was riding through Dallas greeting the people
he loved when a bullet was fired from a building high above.
He was rushed to the hospital the doctors all worked with strife but
John Kennedy lost the greatest battle of all his life.

He is gone from us now and the torch has passed for a new
generation to take up the task.
His flame burns bright for all to see but with love in our hearts
just maybe the world could be free.

Marjorie L. Rafferty

"Innocent Rain"

Like Bosnia she lies weeping,
Torn and tattered like discarded paper,
Her mountains raked and her valleys bloodied,
Her thighs burning from the encroachment of the intruder.
A trashing she has endured and a punishment undue;
There beaten and bruised like an abused child,
Hair so violated by unkempt hands,
Infested and scorned like a harlot worthy of stoning.
Let the rains come, then!
Let them fall hard like fists
With a cleansing only the heavens can grant.
Let them wash away the foreign soil
And purge the sweat from her hallowed ground.
So pure before the damning.
So innocent yet in eyes red from crying.
Let the rains come, then!
Let them fall hard like fists
With a cleansing only the heavens can grant.
Let them wash away the foreign soil
And purge the sweat from her hallowed ground.

David Powell

Apologia Pro Vita Sua

Let us consider our intern, Fionnuala:
for she is from Ireland and speaks with an accent;
for she was a child star and entertained millions;
for she was sunburnt a new shade of red;
for she enjoys drink and the merriment it brings;
for she jumps like a cat when she hears a particular voice;
for she is courteous and polite in spite of the fact that no one
  can spell her name;
for she sits for hours watching a flickering screen;
for she logs bills and invoices with cheer;
for she highlights journal entries with skill and precision;
for she is each day in another chair;
for she makes her way around worms waiting in apples;
for she is leaving and going to Cape Cod;
for she will go home to finish her schooling;
for we may not see her for many a year;
for she promises to return.

Julie Madnick

For My Love

I stand here two steps from where you are
   to me that is so very far.
We use to stand together hand in hand
   but all the moments slipped like sand.
We no longer talk all night long
   and I try not to listen to our song.
All the secrets I had inside
   are things I continue to hide.
For the day you turned and walked away
   was the day I didn't know what to say.
I know it was so long ago
   but I never felt so low.
I dream of you every night
   and I know I need to fight,
For my love who is not here
For my love who is not near.

   R. Yesan

"How You Make Me Feel"

Thoughts of you in my mind, day and night
I see visions of your blackness in my sleep

What have you done to me to make me feel this way

Obsessed with your beautiful black mind, body and soul
I can only hope that my obsession for your love is evenly felt

You have landed on a part of my soul that has laid untouched
(I'm scared) for you posses the power to exploit this beautiful
Black world of mine, or have it go into remission — forever

I say again, what have you done to make me feel this way

In your hands lie a heart, a heart that is loving and giving
to the core, hold it, caress it, mold it, but don't break it

For you are to me that star that out-shines the many

And that is how you make me feel

   Anthony Paul Smith

"A Thought"

What would life be like
Without the cares and woes
Of each and every day
That seem to grow and grow?

Would it be carefree
And full of happy days,
Or would it just be boring
With life a timeless maze.

I wish I had the chance
To live a life of ease
And laugh and play and spend the day
At rest beneath green trees.

I might be disappointed
To miss the chance to grieve
Or face a worthwhile challenge
Which trials of life can weave.

Just let me now in peace to wonder
If all things taken in account
Will bring for me a rich full life
And strength to face life's pouring fount.

   Carol A. Lane

"Remembering Mothers"

Once a year on a Sunday in May,
we honor mothers on their special day.

Now mothers are a unique blend 'cause,
God made them with His own hand.

Some are weak and some are strong,
But, to each He gave a song.

Some are big and some are small, but
to children, mothers are ten feet tall.

Mothers, young or old, let the beauty
of life through your children be told.

Let this day be blessed with God's love for you
Children, with love for mothers please be true.

   Lois Wood

Specialty

There's someone in my life,
that's far more than special.
For he makes the sun shine before dawn,
and makes the stars sparkle before night.

Something so special just can't be right.
For each day were together he makes everyday seem bright.

When he holds me, his grip is often firm and tight,
and when we argue it never ends in a fight.

Oh how I know this time it must be right for
each night and day our love is strengthened to new heights.

   Monica R. Nelson

Andrews Point

On a day so clear one could see Portugal if the Earth were flat,
   the Ocean lathered the rocks in its randomly rhythmic, seething surge.

Empty cottages linked to the world by umbilical cords of power
   and phone,
strung to lonely poles thrusting upward like barkless, leafless,
   limbless trees.

Birders peered and parents with little kids clambered over the rocks
   like fuzzy figures in a Prendergast painting.

Next door was a diminutive collie whose black body, white neck, and
   black head demanded her name - "Oreo".

A bell buoy pealed its wailful tone across the wind swept waters.

Time moved ever so slowly, but surely one wanted this moment to last.
Alas, the earth continued its spin from the Sun, till dusk
   and urban duty called.

Tomorrow we'll be back, and tomorrow after that, each time returning
   to the peace and solitude of this place.

What is it that draws us to the Sea? Is it really whence we came?
   Or is it where we're going?
Surely it's different from every other experience, environment, or thing.

No Christian, Judeo, or Eastern religion can replace its tranquility.
   One reads other's thoughts re love of sea. But it's more than love.
It's an inner longing, an urgent appetite, only satisfied by being there.

Being there - that's the thing - no song, scent nor video can replicate.

   William Wolf

Parent's Appreciation

You've been here for us,
in times of sorrow and despair.
You were our strength,
when no one else cared.

You've wiped away the tears,
that our wounded hearts have shed.
You've given us a new life,
full of love not hatred.

You've helped us through the years,
you've comforted us when lonely.
You were our only strength,
when the paths we chose were stoney.

You were there when life seemed hopeless,
there through thick and thin,
Helping us to live our lives,
giving us strength against sin.

You molded and watched over us,
with your gentle loving touch,
and all we want to say is...
"We love you very much".

Roxanne Diaz

"Memories"

I thought I was all cried out.
That the aching went away.
But, as I took a trip down memory lane,
You were there causing me pain.
It is not anything you ever intended,
I just can't let go.

I look at your picture and smile.
You, made me happy at one time.
Now melancholy fills me with a dull ache.
Even so far away you are the one for me.
If only I could hold you again.
I'll always love you.
You are my forever friend.

Jaclyn A. Provau

A Note Of Thanks

I thank you my friend
    for all you've done
        for all you've given me.
The times we cared and even shared
    all that was meant to be.

You've given me a hope and joy
    which words cannot express
And made me feel so confident
    when life was not the best.

You have that special beauty
    which is sometimes hard to find
That quality of caring and eagerly being kind
I hope you find that inner peace
    which the Lord has let me see
That feeling of fulfillment
    in all that is to be.

And if at times, there's no escape,
    and things get out of hand
Just say a prayer on how to cope
    and your answer will be there.

Louis Corsitto

My Friend

The willow tree hangs its branches down.
So the tears will fall free.
To my tree I run, there I hide alone and sad.
I cry which tears are his, which are mine,
Together we share the pain.
Here I will stay until I can walk alone.
Here I'll stay until I'm strong, He'll
Protect me until I can walk tall and free.
My friend the willow tree.
And when I go, as my tree knows I will.
I'll cry for my friend, who again will
Stand alone, my friend the willow tree

Brenda Priest

Dark Night Of The Soul

The dark night of the soul came and ripped my heart out;
it swept me up and silenced me, leaving me unable to shout.
I cannot fight it for I have no power,
it's time to surrender to my darkest hour.
Terror seized me and contorted my face,
crying out to God, "I quit this race!"
Emptiness has filled this void in my heart,
poor beaten soul is torn apart.
This darkest hour has left me not feeling,
numbed to the core, I beg for healing.
Ever so slowly, I slip away dying,
unable to reach out, can't you see that I'm crying?
Being gripped by pain has been my story,
am I asking too much for the Light of God's Glory?
For in the warmth of His Light I would bask,
throwing away forever my worn tattered mask.
The soul of my child has been a long time dead;
now darkness has returned to rear its ugly head.
The dark night of the soul leaves me lost,
it knows no boundaries and cares not the cost!

Patricia Fitzgerald-Swanson

To My Father

The man I've lived with all my life, I guess I barely knew
The facts he's told me of his life hard to believe that they were true
The words I wanted him to say, were said few and far between
Sometimes I didn't know he loved me,
maybe that's just the way it seemed.
The man I've lived with all my life, who worked so hard to keep us fed,
tormented by his early life, these visions played inside his head.
Didn't know how to talk to me,
sometimes we didn't talk at all,
and all that time we didn't speak,
I felt the presence of a wall.
The man I've lived with all my life,
achieved great things I hadn't known,
lived in a world I can't imagine,
strived hard to make good on his own.
The man I've lived with all my life,
he barely ever said, "I love you."
Would have been nice to hear sometime,
but I just guess he thought I knew.

Diana Tsudik

I Miss You

I grow weak
With the absence of your love
I remind myself to breathe
Emptiness, invades, pain resides
Within me, without you
I hear only your gentle voice in my head
Sweetness in your tones
That reflect your love for me
Eyes that speak the language of your heart
Only existing...my heart is dying
Tears become a permanent part of my face
I want, need, desire
Only You
For your presence
Enhances
The beauty and meaning
Of my life
My heart is at peace
Only with You

Jennifer Jones

White Dove

White dove I saw you sailing by

Like an angel: Like an angel in flight

Never knowing your destination
I reach out to you and its unknown

Take me with you don't leave me behind,
For tomorrow, I don't know if I can find.

Oh it's your loneliness that draws me to you
Not that you're in distress
Come what may my child
Allow yourself to play and be wild.

You see white dove it's you in me
Who desires to be free.

Diana Head Grogan

Missing You

There once was a woman so true and small
that commanded respect of even the tall.
She lived a long eventful life
through several wars, battles and much strife.

This woman we revere is my Nanny you see.
She's loving and kind and means very much to me.
She raised me to be strong, true and fair
in every way that she could share.

My insides are crying out to say Don't Go! Don't Go!
When I know in my heart that it will be so... it will be so.
She's lead a full life from the start to the end
with horses and cars and the rockets that we send.

What she's seen in her life is truly amazing
because it goes from candles to electric lights a blazing.
From outdoor to indoor plumbing with ease
but when something is amiss she goes down on her knees.

I guess I'm terribly selfish for wanting her to stay
when I know in my heart she's said all she's going to say.
But I just want to tell her one more time
I love you, Nanny, for being so loving and kind.

Barbara A. Lyles

I, The Navy-Man

Through the endless waves of the ocean I sailed,
Fought, bled and died. I know no nationality and
My brotherhood is universal.

I chart my course, man the guns, explore the deep,
Soar the sky, light the boilers, keep the ship a float
And fighting, and care for my shipmates.

I uphold my nation's interest. In peace I train,
visit distant shores and make friends. In war
I am swift, ruthless and daring, a scorn to those
Who oppose me.

As I fight, bleed and die, banners drape my last
Remains. Yet, from the deep blue sea, far from the
Horizon another me shall rise - it is I the navy-man

Samuel J. Marcelo

Little Comet

Little Comet in the sky
Why you're there, I don't know why
Wag your tail and make me smile
For soon you'll be gone for quite a while

Little Comet you're not shy
Sailing high above us in the sky
There among the stars you glow
The stars are envious of you, you know

Soon you'll leave us, and be on your way
To shine your glory in another day
We'll never see you in our time again
But others will, for that's your plan

Evelyn Placek

"I Wish"

I wish I was Cinderella
And you were her Prince Charming
Or I could be Jasmine, and you could be Aladdin
Why oh why can't it be a storybook love?
You see each other, stare into each other's eyes
There are no lies only good times
You fall in love and live happily ever after
Why can't it be this way?
S-l-o-w-l-y I float back to reality
And see that we will never be
I see you there
But we do not stare, deep into each other's eyes
Now I see all the lies
The storybook love is untrue.
Except for one thing
That one thing that will always be true
Is that I will always love you.

Jessica Wexler

The Eternal Love

There was a love so deep, so strong, so pure no wall could divide it
It shone through so bright no darkness could hide it
Nothing could break it no man could take it
It was not one hidden in the night or concealed by day
Only one that was true in every way
Neither a long winter nor a summer to short could tear the love apart
It was a love like this so strong and so powerful
It's a love like this that remains eternal.

Pamela M. Furr

Once In A Promised Land

Once in a promised land,
our soldiers held out their hand.
They saved the lives of many,
earning yet not a penny,
for they risked their lives for all the rest,
serving the very best.

On with the fight,
on with the chase,
shedding the blood of every race.
On they fought still,
many with the will to kill.

This was the war,
this was the fight,
that made the living see the light.

Still in a promised land,
our soldiers hold out their hand,
too many in need,
and now we live with no more greed.

Kristin Scott

Emotions

Emotions running deep in the heart,
try to keep many of them far apart.

Love is one that is strong and true,
hate is another that brings harm to you.

Also, one is when people have fear,
never letting anyone ever get near.

Empathy for others we should all take heed,
caring for each other's needs.

Some feel shame for things they've done,
but this is today, not the past my son.

Try to do better for the things we feel strong,
but at the same time never do wrong.

Today is today, and the past is the past,
the good things we do will always last.

So my son emotions run deep,
only the bad ones never repeat.

Ollie Marie Camargo

Sanctuary

Here I lay in a field of stone
As in rifle-life I am all alone
My blood is black from all my sins
Black flowers upon my chest from a deceitful friend.

Edgar Allan Poe was such a depressed poet
He said our lives are lived like a deadly disease
Sharp tongues put razor to the wrist
Veins rejoice and the mind finally at peace.

For Heather Christine I will be a phantom
No pain shall ever enter her angelic soul
She will always be a smiling child in church
Even though I will be beneath staring and cold.

I will triumph over my tortured life
Into their decayed bodies I will put the revengeful knife
I have drowned so many times in their wicked pool
Walking always with head down the vicious rule.

Heather Christine dressed in victorian purple
Beware my lovely lucifer will pull you into his circle
One day you will be queen over the dark and dreary
And within my love you will find sanctuary.

Christine Mullins

Somewhere

Somewhere someone is dying,
Because God has chosen their fate.
Somewhere a lover is crying,
Because sorry came a little too late

Somewhere a baby is living,
Giving happiness to two young lovers.
Somewhere a mother is giving
A kiss and pulling the covers.

Somewhere a poet is writing
From the twisted, deep, depths of their soul.
And on the inside and outside is fighting
To achieve an impossible goal.

Somewhere the naiveness of childhood
Is depressing and confusing a child,
Because everyone knows it doesn't feel good
When the fights in yourself are not mild.

There's a definite truth living somewhere,
And for some it's already too late.
All they have is the memories they did share,
Because God has now chosen their fate.

Dena Diliberto

The Little Lost Lamb

I was born into this world the little lost lamb
Wondering what I was to be...
Wondering what I am

My eyes were crossed and could not see where I was going
My ears were deaf and could not hear the voice of my shepherd calling

Then one day I wandered off so far, there seemed no end
I've got to find my way back home
It must be around the next bend

I thought I knew my way back home
But everywhere seemed the same
My little legs grew so weary, running frantically round the plain

Worn out from exhaustion, I could not run anymore
I could not find the will to live
The vultures would find me for sure

Then all at once my ears were opened
My eyes began to see
The loving arms of my shepherd had come to rescue me

He said to me "Little Lamb, I am the one who is true"
"You need not fear anymore"
"I will never leave you nor forsake you"

Vera Lee Hopson

The Answer

My heart was broken, 'twas crushed and torn,
The anguish I could not repress.
It seemed like the clouds were flung low in the sky,
It seemed like the sun was erased from on high —
'Twas an ache I could never express.

How long, I asked, would this pain be here?
This hurt that my lips could not form.
Can hope be so far from the grasp of mankind,
Or ever a light of escape can I find?
Will there ever be peace from the storm?

And then He came, and He spoke to me:
My child, though the veil is now drawn,
One day you'll know what you cannot now see,
You'll understand then why this now has to be —
Put your faith in Me, child, till the dawn.

Jean Jarrett

Life Is Good!

We wake to sounds of surf on sand,
To a weird melody of a sea gull band.
The sun has risen, the ocean glistens,
Schooling dolphins are a nice addition.
Life is good!

The sun is high and noon is near,
The breeze is warm, the gulf is clear.
We walk the beach in search of shells,
Not many places can cast such spells.
Life is good!

As afternoon moves into eve,
A softening light puts us at ease.
The daylight passes into night,
The glowing horizon a beautiful sight.
Life is good!

The surf tumbles hard against the shore,
Palms sway calmly, birds speak no more.
The sun is gone, the moon aglow,
The mood is set for love to flow.
Life is good!

Andrew E. Sutherland

Little Eileen

Broken flower,
Broken child,
Why are you so meek and mild?

Afraid and shy, the world goes by,
With your face pressed against the window pane.

I hear you crying in the night,
Come with me; we'll take flight.

Take my hand Eileen my child,
and I'll protect you all the while:

I'll hold you in my arms so tight,
and shield you from the dark of night.

Don't be afraid, take my hand,
I'll take you to that 'Never-Land,
Where all is happy, and all is bright,
Come, come Eileen with me tonight.
(We'll sail into the Morning Light;)

Come little one, away with me,
and we will sail upon the sea;
The Sea of Love, so Big, so Bright,
Now we're heading toward "The Light".

Eileen M. Barmettler

Ocean Waves

As you walk slowly along the calm sands of a beach,
You meet a friend from the distance, one you couldn't reach.
The passion you feel, hurts deep inside,
A friend that you tell your feelings to, with nothing to hide.

You sit and chat, about memories long ago,
His sadness and pity, bring you to a new low.
Now softly he embraces you with his strong arms,
And kisses you ever so gently, and yet you're not alarmed.

Your emotions burning higher and higher than ever before,
Your heart beats faster and still you want more.
The explosion of your feelings, fly to the sky,
Your soul burns, and you feel an emotional high.

And now as he pulls away, you feel left out,
Feeling as if you might lose him, feeling in doubt.
You fall quickly back to earth, looking into his eyes that now gleam.
Staring through them, seeing the ocean waves, realizing it was only
    a dream.

Daryl R. Johnson

If Only

If only he had known what it would do
to his friends and daughter
At a little post two
He had a lot of wine and looked well
His friends were all drunk and most fell.
Didn't call a taxi- didn't call a friend
Got into the car; the adventure began
Couldn't stay on the right side
couldn't see the car
In a matter of seconds they hit hard
a ricochet back of 30 to 40 feet
stopped on its side in the middle
of the street.
Took them to the hospital and
all lived but the girl.

Learn a lesson and learn it quick.
Drinking and driving don't mix!

Angela Trueblood

Mother...That Special Lady

A Mothers's love is special, there's nothing that compares.
She's there for you in good times and all your childhood fears.

A Mother sacrifices, to provide your wants and needs.
And often we forget to Thank Her for Her loving deeds.

God took my Mother "Earthie", She's in a better place,
But the impact She's made on my life still shows upon my face.

I want to Thank You Mother, for all the love you gave.
I share your memories with my kids to honor and to save.

They know this Special Lady, the way I knew her too.
Because that Special Lady Mom will always be You.

Linda Chandler-Blake

The Wind Woman

Our lady our love she knows no bounds,
She sings all day and night,
And when the moon has found its home,
She whispers of her flights.

Among the trees of the forest grand,
Across the sands of the sahara,
Around the golden tombs of kings,
Along the mountains of Kilimanjaro.

Her hair is of the deepest blue sea,
Her eyes forest green,
Her clothes the gray from the highest clouds,
Her frown yet to be seen.

She blows away the clouds that block
The glorious light of day,
That wakes up those who trust in her,
To keep their spirits safe.

Hope McLean

One Mind

People want you to be what they think you are
They are like the proverbial fleas in the jar
How can no two bodies be one of a kind
But all of society think with one mind
If you dare to act on thoughts of your own
Society will gladly cast the first stone
As long as you stay in their eyes' way
Their minds will try to control your day
Make the first move and disappear
Then their minds become strangely unclear

Larry Hart

Alpine Nursing Home

Alpine Nursing Home is sophisticated
It should be appreciated
It's a high class place
It operates on a strong pace
They take good care of their residents
They are treated like presidents
The building inside and outside is
Like Hollywood
Doesn't that sound good
The workers are grand
Let's give them a helping hand
Show me a better place
You can't it's written all over your face

Mary Volpe

1995

Life changing so fast, moorings all at once slipping
Pretentious ramblings—heartfelt, gripping.
Precious daughter, all but lost
Still, father's ring—too tight—embossed
On her right hand so strong, so tender.
Cause for restraint, battle doomed to surrender.
Almost a balance for perfect fit
Of lover's circle, left finger to sit.
Son yet floundering, impossible to lead
My mother's patience, filled with need.
Loved-one gone, long-become burden.
Shame of release, rejoiced fallen curtain.
Through distance and schedule unable to ease
Duties and drive preventing appease.
Selfish, yet selfless as Blanche DuBois
The whiff of a dream, a moment's pause.
One gift of illusion, brief applaud
"Then in a moment, there is God."

Carol B. Vaughan

This Little Light

This little light so radiant and bright
Dances and sings all through the night.

Sometimes it hurts from the opinion of others
But they only love and care just like a room full of mothers.

Then something happened, the light got real dim
The light got so full of hatred and sin.

My heart hurt bad, for I loved that little light
What happened to him dancing and singing at night?

I cried and I wept, for the light had gone out.
I was hurt and upset, I just wanted to shout.

For I know that this light still has its radiant glow
Maybe it's just waiting for its moment to show.

Cori Ehrlich

To Market, To Market

To Market, to Market we go.
Where it all goes we just don't know.
On-line to Plastic, Coins, Bills, and Checks,
Shopping anymore does make us all wrecks.
Some gain. Some lose.
Some sing the job search blues.
From Willy Loman to Bill Gates
We all dream of winning
THE BIG SWEEPSTAKES.

Donita M. Sheets

Inner Sadness

She sits on a lonely bed.
Shivering and shaking from the cold.
Wishing for a true friend.
Hoping with her soul.

She stares up at the ceiling.
Thinking about her past.
Loneliness comes over her.
Wondering how long it will last.

She slowly rises hoping for escape.
Rests her gaze upon the window.
She thinks while looking two stories down.
No one would care if I do go.

She dazedly lifts the window up.
and sits upon the window pane.
Feeling the musty wind.
And the drops of hailing rain.

She spreads her arms in eagle length.
And closes her swollen eyes.
She then gracefully jumps
And softly says her sad good-bye...

Sophie

No Time For Love

In this world of broken dreams
   Oh how very sad it seems,
To give all our love to those
   who should care,
Only to find there is none returned
   they have none to spare.
I can remember many years ago
   when the world revolved around
   the heart and the soul.
Experience teaches the young today
   a heart and a soul just get in the way.
There comes a time when the young grow old
The body and mind spent to purchase wealth untold.
And they are left only with a heart and soul.
Will there be enough time left to learn
   how to use them.
Will the next generation learn from the old,
To experience life totally thru the years as they grow,
Using not only the mind and the body.
But the heart and the soul.

Norma L. Oller

Untitled

Am I the target
I don't want to be
But sometimes it just feels like I am
I can't take the fear anymore
I'm going to get my life back on track no matter what
I have to or I won't get my life back
That is my goal in life
I have to start now or it will start getting harder has it goes
I'm going to take it back starting today
I'm going to confront the people who have hurt me the most in life
When I do confront those people I'm going to say it without fear
   in my voice.

Brandalynn Dachs

Looks Of An Eye

Complexion so delicate,
feelings so valuable.
Appearance like a mouse,
but heart of a lion.

Looks, beauty, feelings.
so passionate, so sweet.
I'll love thee, till the nearest defeat.

Eyes that put you in a trance,
lips so smooth to kiss.
Face so soft to touch,
hair so shiny and feels like silk.

Looks, beauty, feelings.
So passionate, so sweet.
I'll love thee, till the nearest defeat.

What I feel inside is hard to bare,
but uncontrollable to speak.

Looks, beauty, feelings.
So passionate, so sweet.
I'll always love thee, till the nearest defeat.

Julie Chinchock

Earth

O earth
Hollow orb
So old, so old
With your pyramids and pink city of antiquity

Sweet Lucy
Beautiful girl
So sweet, so sweet
Dancing by the placid shore under the red sun

Catch me
This day is yours
So new, so new
My time will come three millions years from now

Our earth
Hollow orb
So young, so young
With your music of the universe reaching the stars.

R. E. Dudash

Wishing Upon A Star

I once wished upon a star
That hope was here
And fear was far
For all the world to live in peace
And all the crimes to decrease
I also wished that all hate was gone
And all the world was like a new-born fawn
If only all my wishes come true
And only then will all the errors undo.

Wendy Cheung

Reflections

The little girl in the hazy mirror
is me looking at my reflection.
I can tell by her complexion,
pale and soft with the tenderness
She's lost, but red and rough from the battles in her heart
with her properties that have departed.
This is me for I am
because this kind of pain no one
could endure leave me alone for
this is true this is myself and not.....
You!

Christine Maggard

The Great Leprechaun Chase

The sun was rising one St. Patrick's Day
The one day Leprechauns appear
One awoke and took a stroll in town
Wondering why St. Paddy's Day came only once a year

The Leprechaun was having fun
But when he came round the bend
A woman cried "Look! It's one of those
Green vertically challenged men!"

"What did she say" The people thought
a child said "She means a Leprechaun!"
The Leprechaun ran fast and faster
and so the chase was on

The chase wore on for hours
But the people still chased the Leprechaun
Many thoughts of pots of gold
Forced them to continue on

The sun was setting on St. Patrick's Day
Night would soon be here
The Leprechaun had found out why
St. Paddy's Day came only once each year

Rebecca Richards

My Grandpa

When I was little we used to go over to his house for Christmas.
My cousins and I would run through the dark hall that led to the
    bar in his basement.
We used to play with the old toys that used to be our parents'.
He had a beer can that was fake and looked spilled, I loved it.
For Christmas he'd always give us money in money envelopes with
    his name signed on it.
He had statues of old men, I always stared at them.
When I came over we used to sit in his yard and talk, the whole family.
We used to play in the porch by the garage.
My dad showed me where he used to play sports and the marble wall
    that split our bodies, we laughed.
Whenever I kissed him his lips were always wet and cold.
If anyone sneezed or said good-bye he'd always say "God bless you
    honey".
When I saw him in the hospital, I cried.
I made him a sign that said "I love you and get well".
When my dad read it to him he said "Tell her thanks and that I love
    her". I couldn't speak.
When I went up to him to say good-bye and that I loved him, he said
    he loved me too.
We always called him Papa Roy.
He was the best Grandpa.

Alisha Walden

The Lover In My Dream

He's tall dark and mighty fine, He loves me unconditionally.
Sometimes I catch him, by the hands and try
to bring him to my world with me; when
I open up my eyes to welcome my dream
lover to my world there's no one there,
but the dark room I left behind
I close my eyes very tight, with a tear
running down my cheeks. Praying for
sleep to take over me.
Here I am once again, skipping in and
out of dreams, searching and searching for
that special one.
I asked the Lord in my dreams, to please
return him back to me, I never did get
his name, he was very special to me.
Each and every night, I'm searching
for him in each and every dream.

Sharon D. Smith

I'm Only 25

I'm only 25 and I have 5 kids.
I'm only 25 and I stay strung-out.
I have no money, no car, no life at all.
If you ask my kids what they want to be when they grow up,
one would tell you a big-time gangster. One would say a drug dealer.
How do I suppose to change their decision, I'm only 25.
I have no man to show my kids the way.
I can't do it all, I'm only 25.
I'm only 25 with a 9th grade education. I can't get a job.
I can't get help from the police because I'll have to leave my 5
children. I can't go to jail cause I'm only 25.
My children have no food, no daddy, no clothes.
What can I do, I'm only 25.
I thought about starting over, but how can I do that? I'm only 25.
People look at me and say, "ain't that a shame she is only 25."

Toccara Alicia Jefferson

Read And Apply God's Word Daily

Look at the state of the world
From the Middle East- to the Far East
From the North Pole- to the South Pole
From New York- to New Delhi
From Canberra- to Cancun

We see crime and violence
We see pollution and greed
We see hostility and war

Oh if only people would read and apply God's word daily
Imagine a world at peace
No more crime and violence
No more pollution and greed
No more hostility and war

So why not give it a try
Read and apply God's word daily

David Farrant

Bleeding Heart

Listen to the voice of my bleeding heart,
crying like a wolf in the desert land.
A strange hunger rages within my soul
for the pleasure of love which the heart demands.
The elegance of gold cannot appease my thirst
and the wealth of Kings have no value.
But the sweetness of love I'll take to the heart,
like Swallows that danced to their enchanting tune.
So let the rose of love open its leaves
that I may feel its ever-loving embrace.
Its soft petals shall become my home
and my bleeding heart will soothe with grace.

Osee Benjamin Edwards

The Arrival Of Spring

The arrival of Spring
Brings many things.
Sweet warm sunshine,
And flowers that smell like perfume.
Beautiful baby horses,
Learning to gallop.
Cute baby chicks,
Pecking away at the ground.
Swarming bees and flying robins,
Trees blossoming with buds,
Apple trees with white flowers,
Green grass and dandelions littering the ground.
Tender emerald leaves and caterpillars,
Ladybugs and butterflies.
All welcome the arrival of Spring.

Arundathi Gururajan

Devin

Just heard you died...
I am sorry to lose you
Years have passed since we spoke
We chose different roads, but the memories come back.

Years ago, us as young men, old enough to think we knew it all
Arrogant beyond imagination
Making our way, breaking our way through trials by fire, by failure,
    by business and by lovers.

You were never quite in my world,
You seemed to visit my realm, then drift elsewhere
A place strange, often dark and not altogether wholesome
Yet when you visited it was warm, caring and genuine.

A few weeks ago I couldn't stop thinking of you
Suddenly, after years you were on my mind
Apparently that's when you died...
Back home, with your distant parents, in the South you hated,
    so alone
I am sorry.

Ernan Roman

I Miss You

I miss you. I miss your smiles. I miss your laughs.
Why, oh why, did you have to go?

I miss your fuzzy beard on my cheek when you kiss me good night.
I miss the ways you made me smile. I miss your advice on life and
even though you're not with me, I can still hear your words of wisdom.

I don't remember having an imaginary friend because you were
always with me.

Now that you are gone, the sun that shined bright in my heart
has died. And the smile on my face has faded.

When I see your picture, I start to cry. When I hear stories about
when you were here, I smile.

When I am sad and need someone to talk to, I'll talk to you.
When I need a smile, I think of you.
When I am in trouble and I need help, I'll look up to you.

I miss your smiles, I miss your laughs. Why, oh why
did He have to take you?

After a while I realized that you would never come back and
God took you for a reason. Now that I know this, the shine
has come back in my heart and the smiles back on my face.

Juli Plemmons

Pages

Opened to a Sunday morning and the radiator's hiss. The Times lay
unread and the TV shouts for warmer weather. There is this and there
is that but no one knows. Smiles in a photo but all eyes are closed.
The umbrella waits patiently and the clock has been unplugged. Water
drips from a faucet and only the mirror knows. An empty wastebasket
an afterthought. Some flowers never bought. Still looking for that
kiss, but the stores are closed. Turning the pages you can smell the
cigarette smoke. You know it's more than just some thing that you
can't have. You're past that and that it was. An unforgettable
moment lost in space and the weeks pass like your childhood. Not
making any sense and too much sense of the world. Palpable,
untouchable, indestructible, loveable. A tiger that likes to be
petted. A kiss you want to keep. It's morning not mourning. It's
forgetting, it's never ending. It's a kid with a flower. It's a
ring that changes colors. It's an unknown love. It's about being
nonchalant with the things that mean the most. It's a cover. It's
whatever, it's max. It could be better. It's agent 99. Extravagant
subtleties. Said it all and all at once, blah, blah, blah. It's
only Saturday night. Someone turned the page too soon.

Christina Lahera

Semantics

I happened upon a magical twilight
In a tropical, far away land.
It was quite simple, really,
But changed the way I see the world forever.

On a dusty road, walking
In the mosquito hour of the day
I looked among the banana leaves
And saw stars twinkle in the shadows.

I stopped, and stood in awe,
Wondering at the little lights.
"Luciernagas," the old man said,
As he grinned an impoverished grin my way.

Luciernagas were so much nicer
To see than just lightning bugs
There among the banana leaves
In the quiet mosquito hour.

I knew then that never again
Would I see another lightning bug.
And even now, years and worlds away,
I dream the luciernagas.

Dale L. Knuth

Transcend

The silent snow around me drifts slowly to the ground.
It falls on spire and arch and above and at feet without a sound.
The chiming of cathedral bells as we gather on the hill,
Blend sweetly with the flurries white to dispel the morning chill.
I pass through the oaken doors to kneel within these halls.
Where winter sun through amber glass glows on the floor and walls.
Robes of wool are wrapped about to ward us from the cold.
The chancel set with linen illumined with cross of gold.
Incense smoke of shrouded visions rise upwards from the Altar,
To blend amidst the beams above with prayers that do not falter.
Faintly do I catch the scent of softly burning candles,
The muffled sound of whispered word and the quiet of sandals.
The harmony of our voices join in music as they raise,
In songs of joy that echo deep to Him we sing our praise.
The spirit swells within me now like the waters of a flood.
Oh! To attend the sacrament of body and of blood.
I lift my head at the sound of angels and as I start to rise,
The walls turn to pearl and gold through the tears of my eyes.

Jeffrey Alan Watkins

Into The Night

Where does the time go it's all in disarray
sometimes you wish you can turn back the day.
Being so busy just fills in the time
but what you do is a concern of mine.
Slow down be patient and look around
try to take in the positive sound.
Your ancestors did it all right
they set around and enjoyed the night.
Taking time to relax and socialize
was one aspect that we should realize.
Because before you know it that clock has slowed down
it truly becomes harder to get around.
Your body is weaker but your mind is still strong
for Father Time has come along.
Stop and enjoy life's pleasurable stuff
your family, friends, neighbors, it's not that rough.
Sure time is everyone's concern
so try not to let it just burn.
Your life is special so do it all right
stop and enjoy right into the night.

Tawny Schisnewski

Soliloquy At Sunset

O evening sky whence comes your gold -
  From daffodils exquisite fold;
The store of treasure that they keep -
  Is this the source wherefrom you reap;
Or in your travels, is it true,
  You gather from the timeless blue.

Bequeathing fairest roses now,
  Our hearts and spirits you endow,
Their tender petals multitude,
  Communicate beatitude,
Your unsurpassed magnificence -
  It confounds our intelligence.

Among your violets now we pace,
  Their loveliness our eyes embrace;
While softly they adorn the mist,
  From coffers filled with amethyst,
They try to stay the raven's flight,
  Who brings the shadow of the night.

Peter M. Nicholson

I Love You Pop Pop

You sleep on now.
Your ship has sailed away.
The sea is all, the land is gone.

Old friends join now,
and all is new again.
Hearts are still yours that you had won.

And you live on,
your seeds are grown and love.
Your shadow still walks with me.

And you live on,
your strength your dear ones hold,
I hope you still remember me.

Erin Dominique Williams

Spring Is A Happy Time

Spring is a happy time.
Easter is white and so are daisies,
while dandelions and the sun are yellow.
There are rabbits eating carrots and people playing golf.
There are ducks, geese, lambs and kites,
but those darn mosquitoes keep giving me bites.
Spring rain makes grass green but skies gray;
I hope there is a warmer day on the way.
Spring is accidentally running over mice with your Rollerblades.
Then you hear squeaks but it's not your wheels.
Spring is a happy time (except for mice).

Spencer Wirth-Davis

Call Me Cyrano (A Lucky Man)

Just call me Cyrano, because I use somebody else to tell you
  how I feel.

I was born a lucky man, in a lucky town with lucky indignity.
I've been through tunnels and the darkness helped me see as far
  as I can see.

I don't know if I even have a heart, because I gave it all away to you.
Its smell is so sweet, but the color of the rose says I'm blue.

I've been eating my pride, but I'm not full enough to believe it's true.
So take this toast, because it is all I have to give to you.

Just call me Cyrano, because I use somebody else to tell you
  how I feel.

Stone Grover

A Note On Venice

Perhaps by now one could imagine it—
an elegy that played on through centuries
of silk and sheen, with no particular twinge
for the flashes of gilded renaissance,

or for what once had been, irreclaimably,
from dome to fleche to the tangled finials
of the Basilica, an emporium of myth
adrift in the ooze of a backwater lagoon,

the lost artifacts in a fragile seduction of white
pageantry—as it now appears to a breathless
newcomer—a rich millennium that had risen
from the water's ovation, and with which

one was now absorbingly impassioned:
the embellishment of marble, the mercantile
bloom of sea power—a brackish chill everywhere—
it was dusk and the water, gathering an olive mist,

diminished one's gaze to mere relic even as the air
burgeoned with the full lung of a tenor,
the smooth sweep of a gondola, vanishing
into the hour of that once magnificent flourishing.

Joanne Monte

The Power Of Now

If I Do It Now, It Will Get Done.
If I do it later, it may become.
Yes, it may, it might, it could, it should;
All these remarks are almost good,
But "almost" does not make its way
To, "I will. I am. I did it today."
"Later" does not show what is found
When one takes hold the power of now.

Guy E. Kenison

Lady Bug

I kneeled to catch the memories
I bent to hear the cries

I inhaled their fragrances as they passed over me
I felt the warmth of their pain
But
I cannot tell their names

So I'll go where purple phlox grows tall
And listen to their sounds

From deep within I flew away
Upon the wings of the
"Lady Bug"

Susan Karlovich

A Poet's Plea

Let me write just one more rhyme,
Tho' I've been working overtime;
One more stanza, one more verse,
So I can quench this constant thirst.

Of the cup the Muse will bring to me,
Let me drink deep, so she will sing to me
The Sirens' song, or the Lorelei's,
So I'll be driven to comply

And write the thoughts that burn my brain
So she'll give me words for that refrain,
The best verse that my heart may hold,
And let my love-born lines unfold

The deep emotions that fill my heart
And to myself and readers joy impart.

Bobbie Bobo Hennecy

Sonnet ... On Lethargy

I while away the hours and start
On trivial and useless things, when
With emotions high, I should stand
Before my easel as my memories weld
To conjure up the vision of that land,
That should with palette at the ready, be
About to take shape as I saw it.
But procrastinate, day-dream, that is me,
When by the while I work at all
The mundane tasks of life that itch
Away at conscience, until I after all
Change the life-style that fills the hours
and lets me take a different view and alter,
To end the frittering that leaves no dower.

John Boothroyd

Sun

When the sun sets, before the night
It is such a breath taking sight
The mountains, bid it good night
As it tucks in tight
The wind kisses it gently
As it falls down, so sweetly.

Then it rises, from its sleep
To kiss the sky, and the mountain peak
It warms the earth, while on its journey, in the sky
Then again, it will bid us, Good Bye
As it falls from the sky
Just to rest, never die.

Alice Joann Pace

Untitled

Through the darkness and through the trees
No one knows what the other one sees.
A pair of eyes in which to see
Where will we go and what will we be.
Blinded by thoughts that enter our mind
Where will we go and what will we find.
So little we know, so much to share
How much will the other one hear.
A mouth to speak, but nothing to say
Nothing to do but kneel and pray.
What do we feel, what good would it do
To tell someone who is close to you.
With so little time and no time to spare
How much will the other one hear.

Patricia Reiss

Grief

Grief comes in stages, so I am told.
At times you feel your heart has turned cold.

At first you can't believe it, you sometimes get mad!
You feel a lot of guilt. You are in and out of sad.

At times you feel your heart will break.
You wonder to yourself, how much more can I take?

How can I ever say good-bye,
When more often than not, I can't help but cry?

Time is a great healer, so they say.
Time slowly passes, day by day.

It helps a lot to talk. It helps a lot to share.
What helped me the most, was to be with loved ones
  who sincerely care.

A mother.

Peggy A. Vickers

Hindrance

It is His caring countenance the blind can see
And by the deaf His veritable voice is heard.
The crippled and the lame, they run to Thee
And the slow and illiterate perceive His word.
In Him weak paupers discover they have much
And the waif and orphan have a Father to claim.
Those plagued with leprosy can feel His empathetic touch
And even the mute may hail His reverenced name.
Yet some possess eyes that cannot spy
While others have ears that do not heed.
Some know they can walk but think impossible to fly
And the most scholarly try too hard to read.
To the greedy rich green paper is a must
And people scream for an independence that's overrated.
Most want embraces but misunderstand their lust
And some can sing but the truth is never stated.
There are many diseases that earth cannot heal
But in faith the deformed are made whole
And the only heartache heaven will ever feel
Is in the life and death of the disabled soul.

Jennifer Arnold

Asian Sky

The evening sun hovers
over the military boats just off the shore
of this, the great city of the Philippines.
Red.
Reddish orange
and Big.
Big enough to reach from one elevated end of the ship to the other
   before sinking
below the mass of steel,
below the deep-blue water,
below the eternal horizon.
Red and orange
the clouded sky lying in naked love with the wetness of the ocean.

Jill Darling

Remembering A Happy World

Morning sunlight, dances softly, upon my window.
My attentive heart, welcomes, the magnificent sight.
I reminisce, of childhood days, filled with laughter.
As I watch, the radiant flicker, of the light.

Timeless hours, blissful moments, of playful folly.
As slender legs, leaped triumphantly, in new mown hay.
Agile fingers, plucking petals, from a daisy.
A perfect world, where pain would always, go away.

Cool wind blowing, whispering gently, in the twilight.
Restful sleep, brought a quiet end, to a perfect day.
Early light, as dawn broke brightly, for a sunrise.
An ideal world, when life was, just a game to play.

Now the years have come and vanished, and I've grown older.
My body now impaired, suffers never ending pain.
Youthful play, open spaces, clearly remembered.
Enlightens a saddened heart, teaches it to sing.

G. Kathryn Blankfard

The Unicorn Lamed

I comply but I do not obey
I bend but I do not break
I reject the Keeper's oats and hay
As my hooves splinter his rotting stakes

My will is secret, for now unfurled
My desire is intense and dark
My mind imagines a different world
Far removed from this common lot

Mike Joiner

Flowers In The Sand

Sometimes a seed is planted
That just quietly grows
Through the fiber of your being
In ways that no one knows.

Ever there, it thrives then fails
Lies dormant, then bursts forth
Renewed again, in hope sustained
Unawareness, clouding up its source.

Watered by memories long thought lost
Structured to ever prevail
Sustaining flowers in rare moments come
To bless you on the trail.

You planted that seed when you showed you cared
One day when we walked on the sand.
You cautioned me when we came to the jetty
You smiled and you took my hand.

I send to you the flowers blooming now
Within my soul - watered by tears
May the petals ever line your path
For the way you quieted my fears.

Joan Brennick

Dragon Lady

I have lived a life with him.
He knows my pain, he dreams my dreams.
I will never see him as a monster, because my heart does not
know of it.
He teaches me things I did not know of for he knows of good,
of evil, of life, of death.

As I walk through the moonlight and feel the wind blow through
my hair, he walks with me.
I look into his eyes, and do not know what I see.
It does not really matter because I love him.

I know of people who think of them as monsters, but I know of
this is not true.
I have known him all my life.
I am the lady that understands him.

As the sun sets to end another day we sit in its light.
As we look on to another day remember my words, because we are
all around you.

Emily Ann Wingard

Dimensionless

I walk within confusion.
Chaos and regret follow close behind.
I try to separate my emotions,
Instead they stay tightly mixed.
I try to correct things that have gone wrong,
My problems laugh at my pitiful attempt.
No one understands me or my intentions
Everyone seems so one-sided.
They expect me to change but yet be myself.
I'm ridiculed for my actions and beliefs,
People don't take me seriously, they don't care.
They put forth such puny interest in me,
I am portrayed futile against their wishes.
I wish I could change my surroundings,
I just don't fit in among this crowd.
In this world of many dimensions there's not a place for me.

Rebecca Caves

Mama, Are You There?

Do you remember a child, do you remember me? Do you remember
Mama when I was three? The night so dark, so scary to me, do
you remember Mama the avocado tree? "Mama are you there?"

The windows rattling, the pelting of the rain, the leaves dark and
green swooshing against the window pane. Leave the door open please
Just a wee bit. Mama I'm so frightened, please come and sit.

Grandpa's bed so big like a massive ship. I'm afraid to go to sleep
for fear of a lost trip. The ticking of the clock, minutes passing
by. The tone of your voice, your stern look and sigh. Nothing to be
afraid of, nothing to fear. Now please honey please go to sleep my dear.

Figures in the closet, shadows on the wall, Mama...Mama, I'm afraid,
I call. "Mama are you there"? At last, at last it's nearly past
four, the bed's not so big and Mama's opened the door. I pause and
wait. I choke back my tears, your voice so soft melts away my fears.

Mama are you there? Mama are you there? Yes dear, Yes dear,
I'm here, I'm here.

Jacquelin Ivene Yuhas

The Man Of Darkness

There's a man of darkness
Do you know his name
Some would like to be him
Rich and full of fame

He walks the streets at night
Filling children with scare and fright
To adults he sells pills
he lies, steals and kills

He will murder your family
and make you cry
May I remind you
The man of darkness will never die

When you think happiness and sadness are level
There's something to bring you down
No doubt - the man of darkness.
The Devil

Sarah McCarthy

Contradictions

I'm glad I'm not there
But I miss it.
The hollyhocks grew around the outhouse,
And groundcherry jam is the best,
Snow sealed the doors shut,
And the wind howled all night,
But a featherbed is warm.

Mosquitoes like the smell of sweat
And clouds of gnats
Get in your mouth and eyes.
But a field of alfalfa hay
When it's one hundred and five
Smells sweeter than anything.

Prairie thunder storms
Turn the sky angry purple and red
And hailstones kill the chickens,
But there is more sky there than anywhere.
I'm glad I'm not there
But I'm glad it's there.

Ruth Ann Chambers

Daddy

Daddy, why are your arms so big and strong?
   To always keep you safe and warm.
Daddy, why are your hands and fingers strong?
   To help catch you whenever you fall.
Daddy, why is your lap soft enough to curl upon?
   To rock, to hold, and to sing you my songs.
Daddy, why are your words so softly spoken?
   To gently teach you right from wrong.
   And my eyes were given special to me,
   To see you have all that you need.
But Daddy, why can't I see your heart?
I can't see how much love is left for me.
   Come, sit and listen to me,
   God keeps that hidden, but you still can see,
   By every hug and kiss that is filled with love,
   By every tear and the sound of laughter,
   For all the time we spend together now and forever after.

Melissa Jean Brown

The Sands Of Time

Carved out by moral intimacy,
Stretched out forever the sands of time.
Glowing of what was new,
But now is ancient.
The sand intermixed by races,
Who take over,
Flooding in-
Pushing back the natives.
The circular path that all must follow;
Somewhat repeating themselves.
Breaking out of the mold
to renew themselves.
Making each known and recorded
for others to remember.
Where the wind blows
So as our destiny in the dunes.
The thin layer that deciphers
between that which Sparkles
and that which is Darkness.
In the end, together as one.

Melanie Johnson

Always In My Dreams

Life is precious, I thought you knew.
I tried my best, and did all I could do.
I held you in my arms, holding on so tight,
together as one, fighting for your life.
Brothers Forever,
and friends till the end,
two little boys, that grew into men.
Living in a world that has no heart,
taking what it wants and tearing lives apart.
But always sticking together, like brothers should,
If I could trade places with you, you know I would.
But I can't, and I don't know what to do.
My life will never be the same again,
Not Without You!
I carry in my heart, the memories we had,
the playing and laughing, the good and the bad.
Even though you're gone now, you'll always be with me.
Forever in my thoughts and always in my dreams!
I Love You Little Brother!

George David Pena

The Precious Jewel Of Israel

Upon the horizon I came to fix my eyes,
Upon a precious light of a candle,
The candle flame glistened as it drew nearer,
A special presence did accompany it,
An intriguing holy presence,
"Holy - Holy - Holy,"
"Holy - Holy - Holy,"
I heard being sung from the tongues of angels,
Then seven golden trumpets were blown within the vision,
As the King of Everlasting came piercing through the clouds,
A magnificent white horse was carrying him into flight,
Then all of a sudden the King let out a victorious cry,
A cry so powerful causing the heavens and earth to shudder,
For their King had finally arrived,
The precious Jewel of Israel, Jesus Christ.

Cynthia Wright

From Our Eyes

Once was a time a man stood tall.
Once was a time a woman felt secure.
Now the woman left all on her own,
Turns to face her children so small.
It's not your fault your daddy doesn't stand tall,
You're too young to understand this all.
So here's our mommy feeling so insecure.
Not even our smiles can make her feel secure.
Now as we watch our mommy stand tall,
We wonder why daddy doesn't come home at all?
He use to come home, mommy was ready with
dinner for our plates, now we just have to wait.
Tonight we looked up a her, trying not to feel so small,
sorry there was no rest for you,
maybe while we sleep, you also will sleep
and God to watch us all sleep this night!

Virginia M. Murphy

Untitled

It is him that I love so much,
In his heart I wish to touch.
Every second of every day,
I think about him at work or at play.
As I stare into his big green eyes,
I hope that he'll never tell me lies.
Every time I see him my heart starts to rush,
To think it all started as just a little crush
And even until my dying day.
In my heart he will always stay.

Amber Hollarman

Mothers

  Nice, Beautiful, Smart, Helpful, and Sweet
That describes moms, everyone you meet
Some are young some are old
Some warm and some are cold
Some are strong some are weak
But even those will be there for you every day of the week
Even rich or poor
They'll give you a lot more
Some will give you the third degree
But they're only trying to protect you and me
Some are mean some are nice
But they'll care for you even more than twice
So care for your mom all year long
And try to do nothing wrong.

Jessie Mullan

The Cry Of The Voice

Among the hastening of business in present day society a voice
    speaks; yet cannot be heard
Radio transmissions cell phones and automobiles corrupt the air
    with confusion; yet a voice speaks, it cannot be heard
A voice speaking of vivacity, happiness, and immortality blows in the
    gentleness of the noonday breeze; but it cannot be heard
A voice that calls and entices the casting away of all cares
    and dancing in a meadow full of sunflowers speaks; yet cannot be
    heard
But all is not lost; for someone breaks the monotony of life
    to hear the voice crying to be heard
The cry of non-acceptance to physical reality as it is, however,
    to accept reality as nonphysical. The cry is heard; by one
The voice cries of vengeance toward his rejection and disapproval
    yet it is heard; still only by one
The voice speaks of eternal happiness in his presence
    Can it be heard
    Will it be heard
    It must be heard
    The cry of the voice

Elbert Gardner Jr.

Silent Prayer

The anxious wonder silent prayer inside,
to hope their living spousal answers.

She's written very many postcards
letters telling her undying devote.

An anxious wonder silent prayer inside,
to hope their loving spouse is alive.

Her wistful wishing hoping gratitude,
kept himself alive during relegate.

Her painful moments alone wondering,
no corresponding between themselves.

She misses his loving embrace often.

Anxious wonder she is always feeling.

Jamie Ann Turgeon

An Old Flannel Shirt

I have an old flannel shirt.
It's still warm, but it is worn,
It was my Granddad's shirt
Which I was given such a long time ago.
I cling to the shirt, just like I cling to old friends and memories.
I love that old shirt.
It tears at me that every time the shirt is washed,
It's a little thinner, and a little more worn.

Lindsay Ross Crain

The Glass Cell

Run so you can't see them laugh at you
their ignorance possessing nothing
Your world is black and white; nothing more perfect
Onomatopoeia is visualized and yet
if you close your eyes and open your mind
I can hear your voice yet
you're not speaking
taste your bitter screaming words
smell your hostility; it reeks of oppression
You're grey
impatient
I can touch what you're thinking
The blind artist paints what he feels not what he sees
A thirst in the desert, but you flew to the oasis with broken wings
I heard you crying although you were expressionless

Brooke Simpson

God's Little People

Oh, these little people, a part of God's almighty plan.
I have three little people, he's placed them in my hands.

I love my little people, and the honest thing they do.
There's nothing phoney about them saying,
"Mommie, I Love You."

These little tiny people are smarter than
you think, and if you don't believe
me, just ask them what they think.

They are always ready to please me,
with just a little praise
I have so little time to teach them,
so may I make the most of all my days.

Oh God I need your guidance—
My hands feel so unworthy, for such a
task as this

But I know I have a job to do
because what's mine is his.

Delores Jean Belcher

Antinuclear Song

What a peaceful planet is earth ya ya yo
Atomic superpowers are all set to glow
What a heaven is this earth ya ya yo

What a sea full of glee ya ya yo
Peaceful Pacific becomes terrific
With the French atomic blow
What a peaceful Pacific is ya ya yo

Islands turned violent with deadly sow
When? When Murmurowa Atoll's existence will blow
What a peaceful planet is earth ya ya yo

Make this earth a peaceful planet ya ya yo
Atomic powers shut your reactors from deadly flow
Make this earth a peaceful planet ya ya yo

People have come here to live a life of glow
No reactors are protector of mankind's flow
What a peaceful planet is earth ya ya yo
What peaceful countries are ya ya yo

Gautam Chandra Chunder

Thoughts Of Summer

The warm breeze, the sea breeze is beautiful.
I roll down the window of my car and am
overwhelmed by the ocean scent. Sliding down
the sandy slope I run clumsily, my feet
unconsciously searching for some firm surface
to grasp as I make my way into the wild ocean
waves. The taste of salt as I dive, the cold
water envelopes me. There is silence and I am
remarkably aware of my presence, my own self
as I glide smoothly through the hazy blue-green.
As I come up for air it is as if I have entered
another world. Back under water I think of life
and how lost I feel living there. I trudge
through the thick water back to shore. The
warm air feels sweet to my grateful body. I
reach the shore, refreshed and alive and I fall to
the beach. Lying there alone, I gaze up at the
sky so far away and there motionless I dream of
the one I love.

Paula J. Fortuna

My Precious Boys

Jesus has blessed me from heaven above
He has given me two little boys to love.
One has blond hair, the other has brown,
Sometimes they smile and sometimes they frown.
Sometimes they argue and bicker and fight
But all is well when they go to bed at night.
When I go to bed at night I pray,
"Please, Dear Lord Jesus, don't let them stray."
These two little boys I hold in my arms,
"Lord Jesus, Thank you, for keeping them from harm."
"Lord Jesus please help us and keep us together,
For now, for always and ever."
"And thank you Lord Jesus for letting me see
The kind of a Mother I truly should be."
"Please fill their hearts with love for each other
And not just with love for their Mother".
For someday Mother will go to be with Thee,
And they will need the love of a brother without me
But most of all Jesus, please let them see
That they will Always have need of thee.

Bonnie Aarnes

The Widow's Walk

As I walk The Widows' walk and scan
    the horizon, darkness envelopes me.
There is no sign of your sailing ship.
The cold air grips me like a vise.
There has been no word of you for weeks.

Your possessions lie waiting for you,
    casually strewn about the house.
Does my love now lie forever with his
    cold, dark mistress?
Or, will he return to me, as rugged and
    handsome as ever?

Please do not take him, I implore.
Please, not him, I beg.
But she does not reply.
I hear only the echoes of my footsteps,
    the ticking of the clock,
And the constant rolling of her waves.

Sharon Marie Hass

Untitled

As I was walking down the beach on a
hot summer's day; wishing you were here
with me, thinking about you so far away.

You my baby, I want home, shall
come and walk along; beside me down
that beach, and our love we share strong.

In the beauty of the sunshine, your
soft special touch; the breezy wind fills the
air, my voice speaks, I love you so much.

As the day turns to night, we shall
be leaving soon; but first we share a light
sweet kiss, under the midnight foggy moon.

As we walk down the beach, leaving
the sandy shore; another day passes by
us, and again, I love you even more.

Now back home in a nice soft bed
I'm not alone anymore; my dream came
true that I made today, you met me
on that sandy shore.

Renee Davis

Untitled

Foreign hillside 'neath this foreign sky
Cradling in your foster arms this grave wherein I lie -
Hold high this tiny cross that is the all of me
that some within this hating world my see.
And - tell them how passionately I long to live - how desperately.
Wring from their hearts my teardrops left unshed
Be thou my living, now I am dead.
Aye, tell them my emptiness who chance to see
Ye last, last speech that doth remain to me.

Henry E. McCone

Love's Death

You were not here when Love died-
Love died because you were not here-
Love died because you did not care.

Love died a slow, deliberate death-
Love had no reason to Be-
It was the love within me.

I could have fought to keep Love alive-
But Love's life caused me too much pain-
To let it go on living on in vain.

Love died a slow death-
But happily, to set me free
Of you. Now...let me Be.

Viola P. Thigpen

Hands Of A Widow

It had been a shotgun
because of that Saturday they had spent
entwined on his single mattress,
but she didn't mind,
liking the feel of the gold band
that the boy, pimply and nervous, had slid there.

After fifty years together she knew his breath like her own,
so when he had trouble climbing stairs
or lifting things, she knew
and noticed when he shrank from a heavy man to a scarecrow,
and when they lay together at night,
it was bone against bone.
After a year of it he told her,
Honey, my heart hurts
and died beside a bowl of half eaten oatmeal.

Her hands are not hers now,
just tendons and veins wrapped in skin,
loose and gray like a wet Sunday paper,
The same hands that yesterday
sifted the first fistful of soil over him.

Larissa C. Biggers

Motive And Perception

What good is a gift if not given?
What good is a gift left untouched or
Where did the intent come from, and
How did the motive begin?
Why do we at times give something so precious;
Something we cherish and adore;
Just to be given in return an "attitude"
Not one of thanks but one of belittlement and disgrace.
How could a blessing be a blessing if it is withheld?
But what makes giving a blessing so real
Is the joy in your heart that you feel!
It is better to give than to receive
If only this, mankind would believe.

Kenneth Provost

A Spring Lament

It's April and the snow still flies,
And covers signs of Spring's return.
My thoughts fly like the snow but fly
To climes, and you, for which I yearn.

Oh! If I could but bridge the miles
That separate my love and me,
My rapture, then, would be complete,
My heart o'erflow at sight of thee.

This love poem that I write to you
Comes from down deep, like daffodils
Come bursting forth from 'neath the earth.
Each is spontaneous, both unwilled.

That unseen power that lies beneath
The ground throughout fierce winter's freeze
Erupts in beauty, green and gold,
As if to show God's need to please.

My poem erupts like daffodils,
And shows how much for you I long.
If only you, like Spring, were here
My heart would burst forth into song.

Richard E. McElrath

Mother

My mom is comforting
She is always there for me.

Over protecting. She can be over
protecting to where I go sometimes.
Or what I do.

The perfect mother. If I'm sick she
will be right by my side. She's
the best mom anyone could ever have.

Having her as my mom is better
than any gift anyone could ever give me.

Exciting. She makes my life exciting,
challenging, and also interesting.

Remember. I will remember her
as long as I live for the rest of
my life. When I die I will
see her in the next world.

Heather Wisniewski

Untitled

What is a second chance?
Is it like sticking your hand in a fire,
getting burnt and then doing it again?
Or is it finding something new,
something you both missed the first few times.
What is a second chance?
Is it trying to forget about the
past and look into the future,
or do we look into the past and
forget about the future.
Why do some people not give others
a second chance?
I guess some people just let
life scare them so much that
they pass up all the good things.
So I guess I can now
really ask myself, what is a second chance?

Sarah Dontsow

Spinning

There's this little place, of which you may have heard,
where I sit and think, perhaps write a word,
reflect, reminisce think and unwind,
this odd little place where I spend my time.
I've watched sunset and starfall, season and year,
in my little realm from which I peer.
I've seen life and death, birth and the grave,
yet nothing so odd, nothing so strange,
as when I noticed my little place,
'tween Venus and Mars
was spinning round and round.

I laughed.

Matthew Fisher

The Dream

On a day when the earth did turn,
A fiery fever within me burned.
The flowers around glowed suddenly brighter,
The clouds above then did grow whiter.
And I ran through the field of wheat,
But never felt the ground under my bare feet.
The sense called time was all but gone,
And as I ran I sang a song.
I saw the brown earth all rushing by
And the wheat then turned to grass so high.
Then I could see no more but green,
The grass showed me sights I'd never seen.
The pictures upon which I gazed
Left me only breathless and slightly dazed.
What they were, I do not know.
The grass again will never show.
Suddenly back here I counted my blessings.
I know that trip had shown me a lesson.
When it's needed, I'll know what it was.
Until then, I'll only wonder when I hear the grass buzz.

Jennifer C. Miller

Ode To "Gone With The Wind"

Sixty years ago, a writer of the South,
In the sheer state of boredom
Retained the legends of glory—admitted that ever
A dream descended upon the human heart
This side the writing of the Divine Word;
And now, as out of respect of that state,
Four words—four magical monosyllables—
That even the English bard—
Could hope to pen.
The keys lie motionless upon the battered typewriter.
With the beloved words as theme,
I sit wanderless before the flickering screen,
Gazing, entranced...
And thrilling as I see upon the illumined tube,
Amid Cavaliers and Cotton Fields, long ago
To where the scene unfolds—*gone with the wind.*

Rick L. Pope

Alliteration

Insectabet
Many moth-like, mean mangol-bugs live in man-
    made motels
Mangol-bugs eat much meat and macaroni
Most like malls, machines, magazines,
Madonna, magic, and getting mail.
They don't like mean-mallards, mercury,
the military and medusa.

Benjamin Jordan

Lake House

Welcome to our humble home, come in
and share the love. We are a healthy
    household, no alcohol no drugs.
We're happy to have you here with us
    we've been apart too long. Who's to
    say life's paths have led us right or
    even led us wrong?
No tears while reminiscing, no time
to hold a grudge. Positive begets positive
(proof) you'll find when you feel loved.
So if you have nothing nice to say
    don't say anything at all for these
are the house rules: Be nice,
    be good, be happy and we'll have
    ourselves a ball.
If you can't comply and need to leave
    come back when you can stay
You know you're welcome in your heart
    we'll share a sunny day.

Terry McKey

Odium

I'm full of hatred, all I feel is pain,
Something burning inside me, fills me with shame,
My anger is steaming, I can't control it,
An unbearable pain,
A feeling of sadness,
You're all happy and joyful and filled with gladness,
I sit and watch you,
It doesn't matter what you do,
I'm filled with rage, when I realize I can't control you,
An ache burns in my body, as hate fills my heart,
Then I fall unconscious, as nature takes its part,
You wake in the morning,
And feel a painful crack,
You don't know what happened, and you can't move your back,
My anger is calming,
I feel your sorrow,
Keep on your guard,
There's always tomorrow.

Josh A. Bohm

The Spark

Upon an unsuspecting heart a single spark ignites,
Where once there was only darkness,
Shines a small glimmer of light of things long ago forgotten,
Of words so seldom said,
Emerges feelings from my heart thought only to be dead,
A spark of passion ignites me from deep within my soul,
My heart has froze at sixteen;
Although I'm slowly growing old,
The spark, the spark, burst into flames,
It envelopes all my being,
And engulfs my very brain.
If I should dwell in solitude,
I pray the spark remain.

Yolanda Carino

Winter Break

Vaguely aware of my surroundings,
    I sat motionless.

Eyes fixed on the open window,
    Yet saw nothing.

Imagining clouds as snowmen and reindeer,
    It's peaceful here.

Drifting slowly back to reality,
    My winter recess over.

Delois Davis-McDuffie

549

A Low Tide Lullaby

The tide pulls in and pushes back
Revealing as it does Her glorious under water sanctuary
Hidden from all
but those who gently enter
so diving deeper
Embracing with sweet caresses and soft whispers
in order that Her soothing rhythm
Bathe and protect this delicate balance.
Then, exploding into Her vast eternal darkness
Exploring the warmth and the chill of diving deeper
Surfacing, like awakening from a tender dream
to find her with enduring strength lapping at
   the sandy loins of her love.
Taking with a kiss giving back with much more than a sound
of exhilarated content or submissive passion?
Music that falls on the ears of the soul
like a lullaby from G-d.

Marjorie R. Orlin

Children

Oh how I yearn
For the days to return
When my children were snuggled in bed...

If I looked in on them
A peaceful as gems
After a story I so eagerly read...

Now in my sorrow
I think of tomorrow
When one of them might curiously ask...
Did you care?
And I'd share
More than my feelings could mask...

How is it now?
When the sunset is low
I'd be given such grief, far beyond my belief...

As to have them not claim-
A Mom's only aim...

Which is to nurture and love,
Like my God from above.

DeeDee Strauss

Quest

Been travelling the road of life
searching to find out what's wrong and what's right
wondering when this journey will end
so I may find peace in my life once again.

Been searching my life for a dream
not even knowing where I'm going or where I've been
to find a place where people really love
to see if there's a hell below or heaven above.

Been hunting for so long
that all my fears and worries have gone
this path leading me down the road of self knowledge
gaining wisdom not found in any school or college.

Been on this road far too long
and now the years have come and gone
only to find I didn't have to run
for the answer was where my journey had begun...

Everything I was looking for was inside of me.

Carmen Maja Nagoda

The Boy

There is this boy. He is loud and outgoing. He is very popular,
too. Everybody wants to be around him, including me.
   He talks about people less fortunate than him. He laughs at
their every mistake. When people look at him they see a cool
person, a really popular guy.
   When I look at him I see past the laughter, past the criticism
and past his nice clothes. In his heart I see pain, a pain that
endures with his loneliness and the need to be loved.
   There is this boy and I see him constantly trying to fight back
tears of frustration. I know this boy and his actions don't reflect
his feelings. He doesn't want it to be known but I know. I know
how he feels inside. I know his dreams.
   There is this boy. I walk beside him, he walks ahead. I walk
beside him and he turns away. I stretch my arms and take his hand.
His eyes grow hazy. I open my heart, he lets a lonely tear fall.
He opens his heart.
   There is this boy. He is my friend!

Kiera Brooks

Seeker

Like the child who never questions,
Your words of promise I believed,
Filled with life for our tomorrow,
Those words meant only to deceive.

Your last words left me lost and broken,
To face the world and truth alone.
This world for me had no tomorrow
Because the cherished child was gone.

How do I pass from child to woman,
Not sure what lies between the two,
Perhaps the depth of your deception,
Perhaps the ache of losing you.

I'm told, while searching for the woman
I must accept and then let go
Of those long years, now false, now sorry
And of your heart that time turned cold.

Today's a step towards my tomorrow,
I won't bring back the child to rein,
For my tomorrow's hope is finding,
The woman formed from faith, not pain.

Jennifer Facey

Thunder Dancing

Thunder growls. Lightning shatters.
The air churns as the dark, threatening storm clouds bellow across
the sky. Drip-drop...drip-drop...drip-drop.
The first rain descends, sharply striking the roof, echoing in the
ears and throughout the house. The parched earth hesitantly tests
this now strange - almost alien - occurrence. At first guardedly,
then eagerly and greedily the earth drinks the heaven-sent
water, absorbing it into herself, into her soul.
Thunder growls. Lightning shatters.
Towering trees sway; dancing with the wild rushing wind as their
partner. Elegant motions executed with electric synchronicity.
They are as one, embracing as lovers,
twirling, swaying, bowing as no other couple.
All the while the dewy leaves of the trees' evening gowns
temptingly express their fresh, crisp, honey perfume.
The scent drifts over the wild wind, teasing him, subduing him,
leisurely drugging him with its heady sweet fragrance.
The rain slows, leaving behind its lingering aroma.
And in the distance...
Thunder growls. Lightning shatters.

Carol Andrews

flame

flickering, dancing, floating on air,
showing me faces that are not there.

colors so cool playing games on the ceiling,
can be so hot and likewise deceiving.

you blow with a breeze, you tickle the air,
you bounce to a beat that is not there.

the caress of your light can warm the soul
and spark romance for young and old.

a sliver of light, a trace of glare,
that trembles slightly with a whisper of air.

excite the spirit. ignite the fire.
rekindle devotion. refurbish desire.

Shannon Cape

Ascension

As You ascend to Higher Realms
I reach out for one of Your wounded feet
And press it upon my loving cheek.
Dear Lord, not yet do I ask to leave
My bleeding parish, the suffering world,
But would hope to work for the kingdom still
If it be Your Will, if it be Your Will,
As long as the Spirit keeps me centered on You
And attached to You by the grasp of Your foot,
A COVENANT impressed on my wrinkled cheek.

Sr. Yvonne M. Nobert, CSC

Dear Janice

I had not truly loved until I beheld you,
the one precious and lovely inside,
as your soul washed a great wave of peace over mine
when my gaze was gripped by your sweet eyes.
From their blackness did shine this sparkling warmth
as you smiled and waved over your shoulder,
and with genuine class even then yet a girl
there could not be a more perfect lady.
I loved you back then even more than my life
and I'm sorry that I never said it,
for you loved me I knew but what did you know,
I would drive you or anyone crazy.
I let you cry and walk out of my life
wrongly judging that you weren't a Christian;
then twelve winters descended when God made me see
a real Saint if ever I knew one.
My letter: "I'm sorry..." at long last "I love you...
Please forgive me... and come be my wife."
And now I know love by your gracious response,
for in love with you I'll ache forever.

Kurt Stull

Life

What is life? Is it in the head?
When I think of life, I see a sleeping bed.
Life has its curves ahead, like a great poet like me just said.
I wonder if life has its ups and downs.
Maybe it's more like a king getting a crown.
I wonder if I will ever know?
Will life tell me to stop and go?
Is life like a person going around the world in eighty days?
Or does life have its personal ways?
What is life? What can it be?
I know that it is inside of me.

Javon Smith

Life Without Charlie

His hog leg sure looks lonesome in its holster by the door,
And that gun without Charlie just ain't as beautiful no more.
Like any hand that's good at ropin'
Wearing iron, and chaps, and splinters,
Old Charlie—he was ornery at jokin'
But he made me "split my sides" most winters.

And so we sadly sit and ponder
On the days...
When Charlie and the boys
Would saddle up and ride out yonder
Into town with guns ablaze.

There we was hootin' and a hollerin';
Just a tearin' up the place...
Nobody ever messed with Charlie
With a grin upon his face.

I guess there ain't no rhyme or reason
Charlie's gone—for roundup season!
But life around the bunkhouse sure has sung a mournful tune,
Since old Charlie hung his gun
And went to Texas on his honeymoon!

Mark Rogers

To Brothers And Baseball

I played the game, no one remembers the name,
No Hall of Fame; Just a young man on pasture
    of green, many times unseen.
The crack of the bat, the ball; The home green over the wall.
The long shot, the streak hot; and all
    the time the eagle eye fixed to race for the longest fly.

The curve, the slider, the in shoot the out,
Step up to the plate, give it a clout.
The line drive; The Texas League fly,
I've had my share, I've given it a ride.

The golden sun, count every run;
Don't look back, steal the sack.
Run like the wind, then do it again.
Move to the right, then the other way,
Tag the bases twice — a double play.

All the time the senses real,
At calls good and bad, that make me feel.
That tomorrow will be a better day,
And my Brother and I, will come to play,
Again; on the pastures of green.

Jack De Young

Visions

When you look at me from across the hall,
my body shivers standing against the wall.
The moments of happiness that you give to me, feels like
fresh breath of air on an open sea.

Just once when you glare
don't stand there; care to come over to me
for just a little while,
you don't have to say a word
Just stand there and smile.

...Oh how I wish that it could be
Just a little romance between you and me.
But you act like you bare a lot of time to approach me,
and drop line.

If you wait too long. You will see
all the time that could of been
spent between you and me.
Will be with another significant other
Who truly cares
and wants to be my lover.

Denise Thompson

To The Children

If the day should come
When I shall be unraveled,
When my voice can't speak
The words I wish it would.
Please try to hide impatience and despair.

My mind might be remembering
Sunny days and happy hours we shared,
The joy your being brought to me
And later quiet and peaceful times
Which led me to this place at last.

So smile at me and hold my hand
In your strong one
And when you see the fabric of my life undone,
Don't grieve or weep.
The weaving of my life
Has been such fun!

Rita M. Braskie

America's Pride

There is an animal that stands
For freedom of rights, equality, and justice
It floats through the air like a hanglider easily
And swiftly moving through the
air currents. It looks down
Upon the land people below look and
People below look and
Point to the sky and the shado of this
Creature flies, glides, owver them with
A blanket of darkness offering protection
to all. Peace and strength are its
ideals. His white feather sand brown body stand out
As a symbol of freedom in America
The bald eagle our nation's sacred animal
Our protector, overseer, and our American way show in
The majesty of the bald eagle, the symbol of America.

John M. Duffy Jr.

"Summer Winds"

Summer winds, they feel so fine
As I find myself, going back in time
They say the past, is gone forever
But at time it helps, keep me together.

The greenest grass, and tallest trees
Helps put my mind, back at ease
Just hearing the birds, sing there song
There's just no way, this could be wrong.

Summer winds, they feel so free
I like the thought, its helping me
I've seen the city, and worked on a farm
And the summer winds, they cause no harm.

Peaceful and happy, as the winds blow
These summer winds, beat any ole show
I've yet to see, a place and time
That could add up, to this peace of mind.

John W. Costello

Untitled

The time that we spent as friends was the best.
But now you are gone, you will surely be missed.
Thank-you for the memories that you gave to us...
Let us remember how you lit up the room with your smile.
We will try to be brave through this time.
Let God Bless you and your family.

Steve Patterson

The Last Goodbye

An all so grey winter/spring day early in April with the smell of maple in the air. A pitter a patter ooh my heart. A wibble a wobble oohh my knees. A gasp and opening a talk so soft. Water pouring from my eyes. A pain such pain that none should bare. A thought a memory of what was to share. The last goodbye, the first bright day. The last goodbye all the pain is gone away. To live and love is all so great. Life is for living and yet so sad you choose I choose thegood with the bad. Today is the day oh what a way to have to say the last goodbye with tears in my eyes and love in my heart. The pain, oh pain as I find the strength the strength to say the last goodbye.

Linda Wilson

The Decision

The night is split into tide and time with a clock's second hand,
Awakening from a still long sleep
Opening eyes of the mind with piety,
The year ending, wiled away by a foreign wayfarer.

Waiting for coming New Year in a moment of the deep emotional throbbing of the heart and the pulsating tide of horrible fear;

As a successful and valuable property,
Imagination is intended for posterity,
A forerunner's symbolism of the permanent discord,
Leaving inner strife and self consciousness.

The colorful outer covering of the empty men's life,
Taking off in a world of bundles of selfishness,
The inside's of human's has to be changed quietly and honestly,
Also sincerity lives forever more.

The waste land of wide plain's, blowing sand, that comes constantly,
Immigrant's keep and have dreams of living in a great country;
Today's America.

Lucy Choi

The Rose

A more perfect flower may never have grown.
It's beauty brought gladness to all who were shown.
A beauty so timeless, no words can describe.
The shear joy that it gave just from being alive.
As it blossomed its splendor and beauty were shared
By all those who passed it and all who had cared.
It had struggled through autumn and reached for the light.
But the frost overtook it one cold winters night.
We will miss the great beauty we passed by each day.
In our memory its radiance will not fade away.
Though this rose now has fallen and gone to its rest,
In the springtime with God may its beauty be blessed.

Judith M. Hamilton

Love Others

Love is the best way of all.
You might be able to speak in different languages.
You might be to tell the future.
You might even be really smart.
But if you don't show love to tell others,
these things don't matter at all.
A person who loves is patient and doesn't brag.
A person who loves is not rude or selfish.
He does not become angry easily or remember
when someone is mean to him.
Love is not happy with bad,
but is happy with good.
Three things will never end:
Faith, hope and love. But love is the
greatest thing of all.

Crystal Olguin

"My Treasure"

I have a treasure worth more then gold,
It cannot be bought or sold;
Perfect, unique, with love freely given,
I can take it with me till I reach heaven.

Free for the asking and receiving;
His birth, His death, and resurrection believing,
This treasure is so precious you see,
And the King of kings gave it to me.

It's mine for life and all eternity,
It's love, joy, peace, forgiveness each day;
He loved me so much, He gave his blood;
Now I can love with His kind of love.

Treasures are different for different people,
Of this treasure, there is no equal;
It will never grow old or tarnish,
My treasure I will always cherish.

It cannot be bought or sold;
To me it's worth more than pure gold;
Thank you, Lord, for your great love for me,
Continue making me what you want me to be.

Mary Williams

The Homeless Girl

The snow was softly falling, falling
Her gaunt body was bent and still
The wind cut her hands like knives of steel
Tears froze on her cheeks and fell on the hill.

The sky turned black and the stars on high
Were like pieces of ice in the midnight sky.
Icy winds from an arctic hell blew the snowy clouds away.
Bringing death as their spell to heal her broken heart as well.

Her small dirty feet were blue with cold
Her shoes stolen by another homeless soul
Who can search the human mind and delve so deep?
Only **God** knew who stole her shoes in her sleep.

Passers-by engorged with sweet pastry and tea
Argued sports and horses ignoring each plea
No one cared when police carried the stiff corpse away
For a girl in filthy clothes no one bothered to pray.

The soul of the girl in the heavens above
Joined the stars in the Universe of love,
Looked down at the frozen snow glist'ning like white gems,
In her arms she held a rainbow made of flowers and stems.

Rita Goldstein

Once Love-Struck

The waves crash against the shore
with the power of a love-struck being.

The wind flows over the restless sea
as the birds dance in the blue sky.

Their hearts taken over by some hidden passion.

They circle the waters as though they were out of control
and the waves embrace the cliff sides below them.

The tide settles in.

Then slowly it drifts away
appearing to have never touched the sand
yet leaving a subtle suspicion.

The clouds above seem to darken
and the sun disappears beyond the horizon.

The wind begins to vigorously scourge the waves
and the birds now fly at a distance.

Corrine Kerhulas

Mommies Daddies

Children! Children! Listen to me
there is a day coming quickly as can be.

Mommies and daddies will always be
when you need or don't need thee.

Listen! Listen! Please listen!
Mommies and daddies want
you to grow like sweet
smelling flowers - straight
tall, bright, with innocents
of the mind - to be molded
with what is delight.

With love respect, to educate you with what's right.
Go out into the world soar high.

So listen! Listen! Please
children listen to me mommies
and daddies are to be if there
are no mommies or daddies there are know you to be.

Antoinette Collins

Learning To Fly

I have seen too much pain,
Touched too much blood and tasted rage.
In this book I have survived.
I've turned my cheek and turned the page.

I've felt the fire within the ice.
I've been burned alive by the cold.
I've lived every kind of life,
Been blind and dumb, bought and sold.

I've seen hell and hell on Earth.
In my life, I've killed and died.
I've crossed the waters of the river Styx.
I've told the truth and then I've lied.

In all that I have been and done,
I still can wonder why,
Through all the pain and bloody rage.
You've taught me how to fly.

Daelynn G. Pachick

Brittney's Poem

I hope you got a Barbie Doll
and a good teacher in Math.
Grow up in Heaven my Brittney,
Just don't do it too fast.

Do kids have a childhood in Heaven,
Anything like the kids here on Earth?
Do they laugh when they hear a knock, knock joke
When they skin their knees, does it hurt?

You've been gone ten years come December,
The best ten years of your life
Your momma's the one that brought you to me
She's a really good mommy, my wife.

Do kids have a childhood in Heaven,
Anything like the kids on our block do?
Do they ever get to learn how to color?
Oh Brittney, my baby, I miss you.

I'm trying not to cry as I write this
But missing you makes me, oh, so sad
I know how well you're being taken care of,
But I'll never get to hear you call me Dad.

Alan B. Isaac

A Kaleidoscope

Frosty white, soft, misty gray,
  warm radiance, ethereal colors,
    sunshine.

  Boundless horizons, clear promise,
    limitless possibilities,
      faith.

    Myopic image, distant fantasy,
      dimension, texture,
        passion.

     Distinct shapes, precise patterns,
       unclouded direction,
         hope.

     Small pieces, converging, colliding,
       forming massive mountains,
         creation.

     A b s t r a c t s , i n d i s t i n g u i s h a b l e
    configurations,
      exploding, melting, fading,
        shadows.

    Falling apart, bit by bit, crashing,
      tumbling, claustrophobic corners,
       uncertainty.

  Moving slowly, moving quickly,
    not moving at all,
      fear.

Fresh formations, small pieces, large pieces,
  intersecting, shaping, existing,
    survive.

Frosty white, soft, misty gray,
  warm radiance, ethereal colors,
    sunshine.

        A KALEIDOSCOPE...my life.

Bobbi Stevens McArdle

Football Madness

FOOTBALL Season is over, and I for one am glad.
When football season comes to an end
I am not one bit sad.
FRIDAYS, SATURDAYS, SUNDAYS and MONDAYS too.
There are just too many other things to do.
18 weeks of this long game.
I don't understand! Why all the fame?
First down, touchdown, pass, a run,
kickoff, punt. Doesn't this sound fun?
What about fumbles, penalties, injuries, ejections in the game?
These are just a few by name.
I won't miss none of this at all!
I dread that word they call "FOOTBALL."
For all those that love the sport football.
For all those that dread the game.
For all those who feel lonely.
There are many who feel the same.
Spend time with the sport you love.
But don't forget, You have a life! Don't forget your friends,
your girlfriend, or your wife.

Lianne Riley

The Unwanted One

I had a dream,
a warm and happy dream.
I was being swept by the beauty of all those dolls
lined up on a shelf on the wall,
all so still and quiet.
The sign hanging said "DON'T TOUCH."
My eyes glancing over and over,
I came to the end of the shelf
and I thought that was all,
but I looked over my shoulder
because I thought someone was staring at me....
There was one left,
but it was just a head.
No body, only a head,
it was ugly and had marker all scribbled on it.
The hair was pulled out,
and the little girl that stood beside me said to her mother:
"Mommy, why is this one different?"
And the mother replied,
"It's not always a perfect world."

Melissa Tait

From Me to You

Friendships are the grandest schemes,
All love is meant forever.
A friendship between two,
Is like a flowing river.
Like two birds in the sky,
Flying up so high.
A level of truth,
A level of trust,
A level of love,
It's just enough.
For kindness and caring
Are a real part of sharing.
Why friendships are never to die.
For friendships are meant to last forever,
Just like the one between
You and I.

Sandra Pennell

Altered Innocence

A charcoal mask
Separated the two of us...
An evil crape
A marred past
Frozen in existence...
Until now!

"What are you doing with that thing on your face?" I asked.
Peering at me with blank hollow eyes, she shrugged
her heavy shoulders.

"Let's play dress-up today," she said.
"No, thanks," I replied.
I did not wish to take part in her mock funeral
or her deathly wedding.
That mask she was wearing simply had to go.

"What are you hiding from me?" I questioned.

To think you truly know the unknowns of a person
is deceiving.

"I gotta go," I said. "See ya tomorrow."

Walking out the door, I paused, ran to her, and stopped.

"Take the mask off and let me see," I cried
And then she died.

Krista Brown

Me, The Lettucehead

I would sometimes wonder why
I came into the world,
But nobody cared.
I felt their sadness, but I didn't know why...
That was bad.

When I was older, I would lie in bed and try to
Understand why I had no friends.
I could not go outside...
I thought they would think I was bad.
My parents would not let me eat on the dining room table.
They would open my door and leave me food
Which I didn't like.
It was more like left-overs and tasted so bad.
I could not understand why I was bad.
I don't know why,
I don't know why.

Carlos Bastida

"A Broken Arrow"

I know where the stars are at night
I know where the sun goes after it sinks low into the western sky
But what about a lost soul like me
Does it make any difference if I live or die?
Sometimes I stand in the falling rain
Or sit by a cold mountain stream
Just to think of what I should do
Because it just seems like nobody cares if I have pain.
I am like a blind man trying to find his sight
Or like a bird that cannot find his way home
So that is why I am walking down this mysterious road
To see if I can find my lost forgotten dream.
Then I can look down at the valley below
And tell the people it's good to be free
Because a life of freedom is more precious than gold.

Barry R. Moss

Forever Unity

You and I have grown as one, like two saplings I once planted.
Over time there roots grew close, and the leaned towards
  each other slanted.
One tree she, gave the sweetness of shade, the other he,
  provided light.
Together they grew strong and tall, it was the most beautiful sight.
One tree protecting always, the closeness of his mate, for they were
  never alone.
They loved, they cared, and knew, one tree was the other trees home.
Together they endured the heat, the cold, the snow and rain.
They shared the earth, the sunlight, their water and also their pain.
They grew and grew 'till one crisp day, when winter came they died.
But, they fell as one unto the earth, the mere place that did provide.
I want us to have the love and trust just like that special tree.
For our mind and soul to be as one forever unity.

Cristy Steffey

"Night"

At Night, lying in bed, vision despite darkness,
tranquillity displaces sound, day-time seclusion.
Fatigue estopped, wonderment restored,
no worry, nor hurry for days to come.

This restful mind harbors copious calmness,
serendipity serenades through an open window above,
pleasant thoughts pierce inimical truths,
images - aspirations, free from harbingers of sin or despair.

Sunrise, doubtless, to push aside trouble before,
asleep at last . . . will come more.

P. Svensson Couch

Who I Am = Choices X Trials Squared

I lie on my back
  gazing towards the heavens.
Flickering of light from stars
  billions of light years away
  fade into the dense masses of blackness.
Rays of light, which at one time
  sprang forth from an immense sphere
  of heat and energy, have traveled
  through greater space and time
  than my minute existence
  can comprehend.
Unlike rays of light
  unchanged by its' travels,
  I become a product
  of lifes' experiences.

Signe Gines

"Life Signs"

Caress of the onshore breeze on her back,
while the fire roast - toast her front,

Counter pointed by the eternal kissing
shrush of waves against the shore.

She stores into the heart of the
Blaze, where hard edges lose their definition,

Boundaries fading between fuel and flame,
Wood cost in flicker - flashing strokes of molten gold.

She watches electrons spin faster in orbital paths around their
atomic nuclei, filling themselves with energy,
casting off old structures forming new,

Transitioning joyously, spontaneously
from one state of matter to another.

She listen to the sound of drift wood
popping unheard on her sub-molecular
on another, finally soft and gentle, familiar in her ears.

So much about life is different brand new. Her name is unknown
most. There are many words to describe her educated, intellectual,
liberal, passionate, woman, Hero among them all, both the least and
greatest is a single term. Poetic.

She is Victorious. And for her, nothing will ever be the same again.

Chevelle White

Without A Trace

A cry, a scream from life to death expressed for the life within,
  a human being, no right, no name, no wish or a chance to win.
A cry, a scream from life to death, the entry of unwanted hands,
  hands of steel that seek and kill for many across the lands.
Forced to disappear without a trace, no start of finish to choose,
  backed in the corner by laws and rules, no weapon of voice to use,
A cry, a scream from life to death, a body engulfed with pain,
  denied the justice to live out a dream, denied the touch the rain.
Eliminated without a trace, the gulp of every breath,
  once receive of a child to be, but instead it fell pray to death.
Consumed and vanished without a trace, by its own life source a friend,
  no words or thoughts of forgiveness for the betrayal that led to
  the end.
Bound and discarded without a trace, the silence of an empty space,
  once home of an innocent heart beating alive peacefully in its
  dwelling place,
A cry, a scream from life to death, no opportunity just obtain to be,
  an ordinary citizen— no one special to say yes, no, I agree.
  A doctor, a lawyer, a nurse, a priest, or a fisherman at sea,
a custodian, a teacher a smiling face that glows when planting tree.
Lost forever without a trace,—forgotten for eternity, deprived of
  love or a smiling face, deprived humanity,
A cry, a scream from life to death; darkness, no light, and no shame,
life, liberty, and happiness no longer means the same.

Anthony M. Walker

"Thoughts"

I had to say something
Before I could stop.
There's so many things
That I wanted to drop.

When time comes, I'll go
And that will be fine
But that won't change
The name of mine.

I'll stay,
And I'll face it,
And soon
I'll embrace it.

With thoughts
That have come and passed,
With thoughts
That will stay and last.

Olga Dvornikov

Love

Love to me my kingdom is
Love to me is what love does
Love to me is conquering ones self
Love is but today what tomorrow will be

Love can be a story untold
Love can be a heart of pure gold
Love can be a simple good deed
Love can be today what yesterday was

Love is passion to be stored
Love is doubtless and hold
Love is communication I'm told
Love is now what today maybe

Love will stand when others fail
Love will win no matter what prevails
Love will conquer great or small
Love will he our todays, yesterday
Tomorrow and our forevers

Jacqueline Adams

Promises Of Womanhood

Red blood red
nails dipped
in revlon
buffed with Avon
cut, low cut
dress slipped
over Wind Song
worn long
suede, black suede
fedora tipped
with bows
waved, short waved
hair clipped
shorn
gone
shaded, teal shaded
eyes Moisture Whipped
half open
slit
lost, young lost
girl disillusioned
fooled, gypped
by promises of
womanhood.

Josiane Gregoire

Blizzard Of January 1996

The dawn's early light revealed
Icicled branches on majestic trees
Resembling giant chandeliers
That illuminated the atmosphere,
While the slow rising sun
Began its clearing into pure blue
Skies, portraying shimmering
Crystals, be decked with gleaming
Jewels, as the defrosting process
Began its magical charm
What a spectacular
Picturesque scene with its
Thick pure white carpet
At its feet
Mother nature at its finest

Harriet Pruzan Marks

Conscience

I awake in the morning to wash
my face in the morning dew.

I may be immortal but in some
cases I am like You.

I can see you, but you really
can't see Me.

I can hear you, make plans of
tomorrows dreams.

I am the immortal being, of what
the tomorrows may Seem.

I am your Goals
which may mold
into Me

I am you
Your future.

Bernice M. Dixon

lips

supple flesh
like ripe peaches -
the color of hydration.
tiny creases
lying side by side
grooved and worn.

swollen flesh
held by one thin line -
zippers them together.
resplendent curves.
one pulls heavily on the other
forcing it to follow
side by side
one
on
top
of
the
other.

Kricken Hering

Untitled

I watch fascinated at the music you create,
my eyes close, and I travel a mental wave.
Taking me to the highest peaks,
calming my soul with its rhythm.

You have become my muse.
Inspiring my dreams and fantasies.
All the while, seeming to know
you play to inspire them more.

Mirrored in your eyes,
I see the emptiness of lost love.
And the hardness of the world.
But also, the yearn for one who understands.

The softness of a whisper,
the passions of an innocent touch,
a magical thread seems to connect us,
binding me to your music in ecstasy.

I look into your eyes
you seem to know my inner soul.
Seeing my fears, hopes, and passions,
then recreate them in your song.

Brenda D. Mills

"Will I Ever Get It Done?"

Wash and clean every day.
It never seems to get done.
Take out the trash, mop the floor.
Will I ever get it Done?

Clean your room and the bath.
Wash the windows too.
Clean the car and vacuum the floor.
Will I ever get close to being Done?

Wash the dishes and the clothes.
Sweep the floor and beat the rug.
Lord, I wish I could get it all Done.
Maybe one day I'll get close to being
Done.

Carri Jo Moreno

Untitled

Snow birds winging
Their way in flight
Across a sea of winters white
Lusty winds seducing the snow
Creating waves cradled quivering
Beneath a blanket of ice spawned gold

A mist of silver
Diamond inlaid interlocked
Into a world of illusions
Of mystical array.
Invisible shadows thirst
In their plight to
Cross the sea
Of winters white.

Beneath a blanket of snowy wonder
Winter lays its head in peaceful slumber
As spring beneath its crusted bed
In silence softly lifts its sleepless head
Leaving behind its wintry bed.

Oneita Ward

Modern Life

Patience is a virtue
In this world of glass, concrete, and steel.
Morbid thoughts and broken dreams,
Murderous plots and nightly screams,
Isn't it wonderful, living this modern dream.
Evening news, paying your dues to society.
Patience is almost extinct
In this world of silicon and plastic
As is love and reality.
Drugs, sex, and rock-n-roll
Is the way of the youth,
The future of the world;
On the line, walking so close to the edge.
Living for the moment,
Not for the day, week, or year.
Patience is a virtue,
Love is a virtue,
Reality so untrue; in this world of silicon and plastic,
Glass, concrete, and steel; where dreams become reality,
And reality is not real.

Briana Hill

Dream

A stage production to an empty audience
A solo director lost far away
To a meaningless plot written by a mind.
Endless acts which lead nowhere
No setting really, only in the viewer
Making sense until the fantasy is exposed
A conclusion solving nothing, leaving confusion
Actors fade away, never again to perform.
Stage lights oddly switched on
The theater closed until darkness arrives.

Jasmine Krotzman

Someone's Watching Over Me

Someone's watching over me,
Who, I cannot see,
Someone no longer living,
But always, and forever giving.
That day so long ago he died,
I couldn't believe it, and cried and cried.
My heart felt intense pain,
As I walked in the February rain.
Through the many, many years,
I did shed fewer tears.
But today I still feel very sad,
Recalling that day, and dear sweet Dad.
Someone's watching over me,
Who I cannot see.
But I know he is up there, watching, tenderly.

Sandra M. Alarcon

Biographies
of
Poets

AARNES, BONNIE
[b.] August 31, 1941, Monroe, OR; [ch.] Tracy Anne-Timothy Wayne, Toby Conrad; [ed.] Willamette High School Lane Community College Eugene, Oregon; [occ.] Care Provider for Elderly; [memb.] Christian Coalition, Church of Jesus Christ, concerned Women for America, Precinct Committee Person for Republican Party; [oth. writ.] First Publication: Have other poems I would like published.; [pers.] I want my poems to lift up the name of Jesus.; [a.] Eugene, OR

ABALLI, MAXINE DOTSON WITTE
[b.] August 8, 1931, San Diego, CA; [p.] Irish and Ralph Sawyer (Stepfather); [m.] George J. Aballi (Deceased), January 30, 1975; [ch.] Gary, Ronald and Russell Witte; [ed.] Woodbary College - L.A. 1951, Brawley Union High School - Imperial Valley California 1950; [occ.] Retired; [memb.] Religious/Science of Mind Church Demited Eastern Star ISP. Member; [hon.] 1st Miss Imperial Valley 1950's Contestant in Miss. California 1950's Business Awards in Sales - Farmers Ins. Service Awards far Beauty Pageants in Apple Valley, CA; [oth. writ.] My Daddy is in Heaven (Mist of Enchantments) 1995 Affirmation for Strength of Endurance Pledge Allegiance with Faith Hope and Charity; [pers.] This poem - Mother and Dad is very important to me. Ralph Sacoyer, was well known in Imperial Valley. My name was "Datson", no one connected Dad and Mother to me - I want all to know they were my parents, in Brawley, California.; [a.] Lake Havasu City, AZ

ABBRUSCATO, JANICE M.
[b.] April 23, 1972, Bridgeport, CT; [p.] Kathleen Dayton, Michael Abbruscato; [ed.] Newtown High School, Brio Academy of Cosmetology; [occ.] Receptionist; [memb.] US Army Reserves; [oth. writ.] Several poems and songs not yet published; [pers.] I write what I see, feel of anything that comes to mind. I'd say my main influence is life itself, and possibly James Douglas Morrison.; [a.] Meriden, CT

ABERCROMBIE, KRISTOPHER
[b.] January 11, 1982, Thousand Oaks; [p.] Michelle and Mike Enge; [ed.] Los Cerritos Middle School; [occ.] Freshman at Thousand Oaks High School; [memb.] Youth Baseball and Football; [hon.] 4.0 G.P.A., Science Fair Awards, and All-star in baseball, football, and soccer. I also have awards from jumping my wonderful horse.; [pers.] I would like to thank my parents for supporting me through out my life. My stepdad encouraged me to write and send in this poem, and my mom has always been there for me when I needed her. Thank you both!; [a.] Thousand Oaks, CA

ABUD, MARIA A.
[pen.] Alex, Destiny, Elvira; [b.] August 29, 1981, Nicaragua; [p.] Manee Gonzalez and Alejandro Abud; [ed.] High School student at Miami Coral Park Senior High School; [occ.] Student; [memb.] Cure Aids now, civinettes; [oth. writ.] Several unpublished poems; [pers.] Vampires are angels of darkness that feed on lost souls of those who were born to never be found.; [a.] Miami, FL

ADAMS, H. J.
[b.] July 11, 1924, Hamburg, NY; [ed.] Ph.D., 1961 University of Buffalo; [occ.] Retired Clinical Pharmacologist; [oth. writ.] Two volumes of verse: The eye of the Day and Touth of the Lion, To Hear such Tunes, Two children's book: With Dandelions to Tell the Hours, Once in the Wind of Morning.; [a.] Westborough, MA

ADAMS, RONALD JAY
[pen.] Mister A.; [b.] February 17, 1956, Indianapolis,

IN; [p.] Julius Otis Adams, Emily Mary Musil Adams; [m.] Jennifer Sue Adams, April 7, 1979; [ch.] Emily Nora, Byron Allen, Kimberly Erin; [ed.] Southport High, Fullerton Junior College; [occ.] Construction Management; [memb.] Knights of Columbus; [hon.] The Maxwell Award Honorary Life Member; [oth. writ.] Several poems, unpublished; [pers.] When the time is right, live life through a child's eyes.; [a.] Indianapolis, IN

ADAMS JR., WILLIAM W.
[pen.] Will Adams; [b.] July 8, 1929, Tuscaloosa, AL; [p.] William W. Sr., Beulah (Reeves) Adams; [m.] Eleaner R. (Ormond) Adams, August 28, 1954; [ch.] William W. III, James K. Adams; [ed.] B.A., Kansas University, 1951, M.A., Kansas University, 1954, M.A., Columbia University, 1960, Ph. D., Columbia University, 1968; [occ.] Professor of Political Science (Ret.), Ballroom Dancing Instructor, Jazz pianist, public opinion research; [memb.] Am. Pol. Sci. Ass'n, Am. Ass'n for Advancement of Slavic Studies, Central Slavic Conference (founder), Am. Ass'n of Political Consultants; [hon.] Ford Foreign Area Studies Fellowship (1959-60), Danforth Teacher Grant (1966-67), Pi Sigma Alpha, Favorite Faculty Member, 1974, Sabbatical Leave, 1971, Faculty Development Grant; [oth. Writ.] "Communism In Transition," The Baptist Student, December 1965, "Communism, Realism, And Christianity," Protest and Politics, Attic Press, 1968, "Cap. Punishment in Imperial And Soviet Russia," AM. J. Of Comp. Law, 18/3, 1970, "Cap. Pun. in Soviet Crim. Legis. 1922-65," On The Road To Communism 1972, Manag. Ed., Bul. on Current Research in Soviet and E. European Law, 1972-78, "Dukhovnyi krizis: Demokratizatsia—ili?.." Sovetsky Molodezh, Irkutsk, Russia, January 1994, "The New Russian Capitalism," Liberty News, July 27, 1994.; [pers.] Teaching in Irkutsk, Russia, 1991 and 1993, and in Tallinn, Estonia, 1993, impresses me with the quality of students in the former Soviet Union. Teaching dancing and making music there and at home makes me aware of people's ability to enjoy, and to love. Give people the benefit of the doubt, and don't sweat the small stuff! I love my wife, my sons, and our dear friend, Amy, also my brother and his family, our dancing students, and the people who enjoy dancing to the music of my band.; [a.] Liberty, MO

ADENEUR, KENNETH
[pen.] Kenneth Adene Jr., William Thomas; [b.] September 9, 1978, Pine Bluff, AR; [p.] Michael McGough, Syble McGough; [ed.] Livingston Academy High School; [occ.] Construction Worker, unpublished Novelist, Poet; [oth. writ.] Seven Science, fiction novels of various lengths, 139 poems and a few research papers; [pers.] Emotion is the substance which makes my words freely flow!; [a.] Livingston, TN

ADKINS, MATTHEW GLENDON
[pen.] Alton Mynes; [b.] January 31, 1975, Soldotna, AK; [p.] Ronald and Martha Adkins; [ed.] Russell Independent High School, Ashland Community College, working toward medical school at University of Kentucky; [oth. writ.] Formerly unpublished author; [pers.] The best poet is the one who has no idea what he is to write until his pen touches the page. Then the magic begins.; [a.] Flatwoods, KY

ALAM, JUAN SHAMSUL
[pen.] Juan Shamsul Alam; [b.] August 20, 1946, New York City; [p.] Julia Garcia Van Pelt and Shamsul De Alam; [m.] Gloria Rivera Alam (Commonlaw); [ch.] John W., John A., Shamsul, Hakim, Alia, Yaasmyn, Rapheal, Stepson Julian; [ed.] Charles Evans Hugues

H.S., College of New Rochelle; [occ.] Playwright; [memb.] Drama League, Screen Actors Guild, Writers Guild of America; [hon.] Brio Award, New York State Co Council Awards, McDonald Awards H.U.M.TTA.L. Grant 5 Villager Award for Drama; [oth. writ.] Zookeepers Penguin Press 1994, "God's Children Ollanty Press Magazine 1993", "Midnight Blues" Arte Publico Press 1990; [pers.] I write from the Heart, A gift from God for Humankind.; [a.] Queens, NY

ALBRIGHT, MIA
[b.] March 21, 1948, Missoula, MT; [p.] Joy S. Albright and Robert Albright; [ed.] Arizona State University, M.A. 1979, B.A. 1970; [occ.] I am a Writer who supports herself as a Secretary; [memb.] Director, F.C.B.F.L. - Feminists Concerned for Better Feminist Leadership; [oth. writ.] I have written poetry, political philosophy, and drama. I have published privately since 1980 with my volume of poems titled, a scrap of royal need.; [pers.] I believe that a writer should discover the world as a scientist or an explorer makes discoveries, with the important distinction that a poet, philosopher or dramatist discover what society believes is already known.; [a.] Bronx, NY

ALIJAJ, MUHAMET
[b.] October 4, 1977, Bronx, NY; [p.] Hasdin Alijaj, Servet Alijaj; [ed.] Roosevelt High School, Sophmore at Fordham University, Bronx, NY; [pers.] A poet is a hidden prophet who is able to see the joysand sorrows in life, each poem, published or not, is like a beam of light in the dark caves of everyday life giving humanity the gifts of sight and beauty everlasting.; [a.] Yonkers, NY

ALLEN, ALLISON
[pen.] Allie; [b.] February 2, 1983, Spokane, WA; [p.] Tom and Jeannine Allen; [ed.] 8th grade, St. Michael's School, Olympia, WA; [occ.] Student; [pers.] I think that a lot of good things are underestimated in this world, specially by people that live in rich countries. Many people don't know how lucky they are. I think that people shouldn't complain, things could be worse.; [a.] Olympia, WA

ALLEN, F. MICHELLE
[b.] October 4, 1982, Florence, SC; [p.] Frankie D. and Kimberly H. Allen; [ed.] The Carolina Academy; [occ.] Student; [memb.] Beta Club; [hon.] All American Scholar the National Honor Roll U.S. Leadership Merit Award Presidents Award for Educational Excellence George Grice Eight Grade Scholar Award math meet award 1995 and 96 Music Festival Award

ALLEN, LORI
[pen.] Anna Jo Ann; [b.] March 21, 1964, Toledo, OH; [p.] Joyce Williams and Richard Allen; [ed.] Central Catholic High, Stautzenberger College, University of Toledo; [occ.] Customer Service Representative, Toledo, OH; [pers.] I hope to convey. In my writing an energy that is fresh from left to right, youthful and graceful with everything else in between.; [a.] Toledo, OH

ALTER, ALIXANDRE B.
[b.] April 10, 1986, Kingston, NY; [p.] Lysandre and Bruce Alter; [ed.] Elementary school entering fifth grade in September 1996; [occ.] Student; [pers.] Writing comes to me when I least expect it. I've been inspired by my dear Teacher Miss Holly Heppner who always believed in me and gave me great confidence.; [a.] Bearsville, NY

AMBROZEWSKI, MYRA R.
[b.] February 2, 1984; [p.] Monina and Arthur Ambrozewski; [ed.] Graduate of W. W. Brier Elemen-

tary School; [occ.] Student; [memb.] Greenpeace; [hon.] Honors Society, member throughout intermediate grades (4-6), Student Council member-treasurer-got salad bar for Brier as well as helped modify dress code, Brier Bronco Cheerleader, Brier Bronco Basketball player, participated in advanced art group, tutor, 4.0 student; [oth. writ.] Non-published poetry and short stories; [pers.] In my writing I try to emphasis emotions. Whether rising up to chauvinism or questioning the inauguration of the universe. I am entranced by Shakespeare, Emily Dickinson, as well as other poets and writers.; [a.] Fremont, CA

AMYX, JENNIFER MICHELLE

[b.] January 10, 1981, Mountain Home, AR; [p.] Brenda Amyx; [ed.] Sophomore in High School; [occ.] Student; [memb.] FFA, Dance Team, Basketball, Volleyball, Softball Teams and FBLA (Future Business Leaders of America); [hon.] High-individual livestock-judge; [a.] Gainesville, MO

ANTELIS, ROSE CATHERINE

[b.] October 29, 1930, Brooklyn; [p.] Salvatore and Francesa D'Amato; [m.] Dr. Eugene Antelis, May 8, 1950; [ch.] 3; [ed.] Prospect Heights H.S. Kingsboro College; [occ.] Antique dealer in carriage clocks - and office manager; [memb.] Distinguised member National Library of Poetry member of MADD; [hon.] The International poet merit award; [oth. writ.] Several poems published in the Candlelight Corner, the National Library of Poetry, and Feelings; [pers.] My own writings consist mainly of my personal experience. It is my fervent hope to explore and share with others, that which I have gathered.; [a.] Brooklyn, NY

ANTHONY, DEBRA

[b.] October 10, 1952, St. Joseph, MO; [p.] Delbert and Eileen Spalding; [ch.] Rebecca Kathleen, Brandon, Michael; [ed.] Central High School at St. Joseph, MO, Research School of Nursing, Kansas City, MO; [occ.] RN - Kendallwood Hospice Kansas City, MO; [memb.] Hospice Nurses Association; [oth. writ.] Poetry to be published in Oncology/Gynecology Nurses Newsletter, article to be published in David Naster's book upcoming. On humor; [pers.] Poetry has been a valuable part of my life. It touches souls, and inspires. My poetry shares my feelings and thoughts and I hope it touches other lives; [a.] Kansas City, MO

ANTHONY, GABRIEL ROBIN

[b.] May 25, 1960, Hyderabad, A.P., India; [p.] Mr. John Joseph and Mrs. Margaret Anthony; [ed.] All Saints High School, Mysore University (PUC), New Science College—Hyderabad, Osmania University; [occ.] Telecommunications; [memb.] St. Leo The Great, "Lector", Houston, Member III Order, Carmalite's, Houston, Member Amway Distributor's Association; [hon.] Essay Writings in School, Creative Writings in College, Poetry contests in Intercollegiate Meets; [oth. writ.] I have written for two decades for friends, family and my own personal growth and development.; [pers.] I have strived to write my silent songs to God and man for the satisfaction of mankind. I have been greatly influenced by: St. Francis of Assisi, my beloved mother and father, Early Romantic Poets, and Mr. and Mrs. Harry and Irene Ramjeawan; [a.] Houston, TX

ARANA, SHEILA MARIE

[b.] May 22, 1980, Costa Mesa, CA; [p.] John and Karen Arana; [ed.] Pensacola High School; [occ.] Student; [memb.] The TJC Drama; [hon.] The Presidential Academic Award, Many Awards for Sports; [pers.] Poetry is

what you feel in your heart and believe with your soul. This is why I dedicate "Life Conquers Death" to all the young people who have tried to take their lives instead of living them, and to let them know that in death their hope will die, but in life, that hope will live.; [a.] Fort Worth, TX

ARATA, CATHY

[b.] Scotland; [occ.] Artist; [hon.] National Awards (New Jersey) Tri State Area T.V. interview, best in Show. For Oil Paintings.

ARMSTRONG, ROCHELLE

[b.] Stamford, CT; [m.] Larry Earl Armstrong; [pers.] I've been blessed with the ability to express myself in writing, sketching, painting and acting. I have a great compassion and love for the helpless both humans and animals. God is my source and strength. My love and laughter come from Nehemiah, Daniel baby Hannah and Joshua. Lekos also; [a.] Jupiter, FL

ARONSON, EDWARD L.

[b.] December 26, 1957, Orlando, FL; [p.] Sumner and Selma Aronson; [m.] Mary E. Aronson, April 9, 1995; [ch.] Samuel Joseph Aronson; [ed.] Hollywood Hills High University of Florida Community College of the Air Force; [occ.] Retail Manager; [pers.] A life full of love is a life full of happiness, for love does, indeed, conquer all.; [a.] Margate, FL

ARREOLA, MARIA

[b.] August 10, 1973, Corpus Christi, TX; [p.] Santa Arreola; [ed.] Math, Writing, History, Software Computer, Typing, Art, Communication Writing, Spanish Class History and Writing, Agriculture, Journal; [hon.] Citizen-of-the Month, Certificate of Achievements, Biology Award, Super Student Award, Student of the Month, Certificate of Awards, Certificate of Las Cruces Mac Arthur Elementary, Certificate of Chorus; [oth. writ.] Last Month I took long Ridge Writer's Group - incorrect it was probably about 4 months ago that I took that test when I entered it.; [a.] Las Cruces, NM

ASPELL, CHRISTINA

[b.] January 12, 1979, Monterey Park, CA; [p.] Leonard Aspell and Ellen Aspell; [ed.] El Toro High School; [pers.] To compel the reader to feel the emotions the words create, to paint a colorful world for someone by means of a melodic phrase, this is what I love about poetry.; [a.] Lake Forest, CA

AUGUSTINE, FRANKIE

[b.] December 16, 1933, Idaho Springs, CO; [p.] David Murphy, Maxine Tow; [m.] Victor Augustine, September 6, 1950; [ch.] Vicki DeVae, Ron Francis, Michael Boyd; [ed.] Perryville, Arkansas High; [occ.] Retired; [pers.] I write of my feelings, thoughts and impressions of friends and acquaintances.; [a.] Battlement Mesa, CO

AVILLA, MICHAEL

[b.] January 27, 1979, Fairfield, CA; [p.] Michael and Debra Avilla; [ed.] Junior in High School; [occ.] Student/Athlete, Motorcycle Mechanic; [memb.] AMA American Motorcycle Association; [hon.] All league award for football. Honor Roll List for school.; [pers.] Therefore if any man is in Christ, he is a new creative, the old things passed away, behold new things have come.; [a.] Suisun, CA

AYERS, BRANDON

[b.] November 20, 1983, Fayetteville, NC; [p.] Dennis Ayers and Jo Oden; [ed.] 8th grader this year 1996-97; [occ.] Student; [hon.] Writers Conference Award, Writ-

ers Conference Award (different ones); [oth. writ.] I write stories for my comic characters that I draw.; [pers.] Life is only what you make of it. I write my poems in many different places; [a.] Blountsville, AL

AYERS, JEFFREY GLENN

[b.] July 19, 1974, Pontiac, MI; [p.] Nancy Ayers, Lewis Ayers; [oth. writ.] Previously published in of sunshine and daydreams and memories of tomorrow.; [pers.] True immortality is not living forever. It is always being remembered. It is most easily accomplished by being there for people you love. As long as you are remembered, you will remain immortal.

AYERS, PAM

[b.] June 2, 1963, Oxford, OH; [p.] Gary Ayers and Frances Guieswhite, Bob Guieswhite (Step-father); [ed.] Talawanda High School, Miami University (1 year); [pers.] I take delight in contributing to the Downfall of condescension and excess display of vocabulary in poetry by making it accessibly abstract and humorous, I would never want my work to become part of an inside joke for a few people with master's degrees.

BABKA, BRENDAN

[pen.] The name Brendan B. was chosen so as not to create any conflict of interest in my place of business.; [p.] They live in Harford County and are retired.; [m.] Married for thirteen years to Frank Komulainen (February 18, 1983).; [ch.] None; [ed.] B.F.A. Bachelor of Fine Arts - Maryland Institute of Art 1972; [occ.] Worked twenty years in medical illustration, graphics and scientific technical editing/proofing. Currently working at Johns Hopkins Hospital in Medical Records.; [oth. writ.] Several Poems published with the National Library of Poetry. A single poem was featured on the New York Radio Program, Poetry Today with Florence Henderson.; [pers.] Likes: The outdoors: camping, biking, swimming, films and dancing. Future writing plans: Plan to write historical fiction, plays, verse, and short stories. "In ancient times, the word, was invented to express a concept, a feeling, or a revelation. Writing and verse will often reduce a complex sentiment to its simplest expression. What I write is not necessarily poetry but heartfelt sentiment."

BAGBY, GLENN H.

[b.] March 13, 1948, Detroit, MI; [p.] Howard and Nancy Bagby; [m.] Elizabeth Bagby, July 27, 1984; [ch.] Glenn R. Bagby; [ed.] Bachelor of Science in Mathematics and Bachelor of Arts in Architecture London, England; [occ.] Architect/Cartoonist; [oth. writ.] Several poems have been published in National Literary publications.; [pers.] I have spent a lot of time over my adult life traveling, seeing different people and places. I often reminisce about how things were for me as a young man and how life has changed over the years. I find writing to be a form of release and a way f extending of feelings of life.; [a.] Saint Petersburg, FL

BAHLMANN, EILEEN

[b.] August 15, 1941, Little Turkey, IA; [p.] Leonard and Madonna Kacher; [m.] Kenny Bahlmann, March 30, 1961; [ch.] Tim, Annette, and Allison; [ed.] '59 Grad. Protivin High School, "Writing for Children and Teenagers" Course - Redding Ridge, Conn., Med Aide Certification; [occ.] Part Time Postal Worker - own my own Small Nursery/Greenhouse Business; [memb.] St. Mary's Church and Rosary Society, NAPUS, Town 'N County Women's Club, Honorary Charter Mbs. in International Society of Poets 1993; [hon.] Golden Poet 1988, 89, 90 and 91, Editor's Choice Award 1993, Accomplishment of Merit - Creative Arts Forum '92, Who's Who in Poetry 1990, 20 Awards, Trophies and Placques for Poetic Accomplishments; [oth. writ.] Many poems published in various publications here and aboard.; [pers.] "Leave your corner of the world better than you found it."; [a.] Frederika, IA

BAILEY, KATHRYN
[b.] March 14, 1937, Kentucky; [p.] Nila Blair, Shelt McQuinn; [m.] LLoyd Bailey (Deceased); [ch.] Rose Marie and Sharon Ann; [occ.] Retired; [hon.] Editor's Choice Award, 1995-1996 - National Library of Poetry; [oth. writ.] Numerous poems, "Twig of Faith", "It's No Bother", "Don't Muddy The Water"; [pers.] I thank God that I'm able to write the words on paper that I feel in my heart. And for the love and support of my family; [a.] Wellington, KY

BAKER, LATISHA
[b.] June 1, 1981, Jacksonville, FL; [p.] Esther and Derrall Merrick; [ed.] 10th Grader in High School; [hon.] Certificate of Appreciation from the African Methodist Episcopal Church in an Appreciation of Honor Roll and many other awards; [oth. writ.] Other poems are priceless, gone wrong, and I wonder. Nothing has ever been published before that I have written.; [pers.] In my writing I strive to reflect problems wrong in the world today, hoping one day there will be no more problems.; [a.] Oak Hill, FL

BALDWIN, BEN
[pen.] Ben Baldwin; [b.] December 27, 1979, Las Vegas, NV; [p.] Donna Baldwin; [ed.] Junior in High School at Kemper Military School and College Boonville MO; [occ.] Student; [hon.] Signed and obided by the Standard of Honor at Kemper Military School; [pers.] Thanks to Mrs. Allen who inspired me; [a.] Saint Joseph, MO

BALDWIN, JANICE
[b.] February 19, 1934, Cranston, RI; [p.] Joseph Jones, Mildred Jones; [m.] Divorced; [ch.] Norma Baldwin Scott, Bridgett Baldwin Owens, Andrew Baldwin, Six Grandchildren; [ed.] Burrillville High, 2 Years Providence - Barrington Bible College; [occ.] CNA - In Home Health Care - Gilbert, Arizona; [memb.] Central Christian Church; [hon.] Employee of the month Mesa Public Schools; [oth. writ.] Written several poems none published till now.; [pers.] To have my poem published in whispers of dusk is a great honor. I will cherish it always.; [a.] Mesa, AZ

BALDWIN, RICHARD DARRELL
[b.] September 7, 1937, New Port Beach, CA; [p.] Deceased; [m.] Marilyn M., July 3, 1989, (2nd for both); [ch.] David, Carrie (2 Grandsons) Joe, Craig (step); [ed.] B.A. Architecture, U.S.C., M.B.A., U.C.L.A., Advanced Studies in Structures, U.S.C./U.C.L.A.; [occ.] Licensed Professional Architect; [memb.] American Inst. Architects, American Society Military Engineers, American Legion; [hon.] Several Architectural Awards in California. Silver Star and Purple Heart/Military; [oth. writ.] Poem Published in "Readers Digest", Editorial Comments published in local newspapers. About 100 Misc. subject quotes to be submitted to "Readers Digest". Poem published in "Stars and Stripes".; [pers.] On poem "Love Speaking", "True love has no form, shape or essence, it is and cannot be explained only experienced".; [a.] Bronxville, NY

BALL, NANCY
[pen.] "A Country Belle"; [b.] January 18, 1936, Ottawa, KS; [p.] Robert and Vera Strain Jr.; [m.] Allen Ball, May 23, 1954; [ch.] Jo, Jack, Gwen, Lela, Lisa, Rob;

[ed.] Garnett High School; [occ.] Farm wife; [memb.] Mont Ida Church of the Brenthen; [hon.] I started writing in October 1995; [oth. writ.] A tribute to my kindergarten teacher, Dorothy Thomas in the Garnett Newspaper; [pers.] I strive to glorify my Lord and Savior, Jesus Christ in my writing. "Let your light so shine before men, that they may see your good works, and glorify your Father which is in "Heaven" Matt. 5:16; [a.] Welda, KS

BARBER, JUNE D.
[pen.] Jamie June Barber; [b.] January 2, 1930, Paterson, NJ; [p.] Lucille and Roy Barber; [ed.] Eastside High and Washington Irving High attended Manhattan Community; [occ.] TAPE Hismania; [memb.] Bryant Society, Holocust Museum, Amantes History Mason to my Miletian Club; [pers.] "Never Keep Knowledge", "To Yourself", "Extend Your Hand", "To Teach Whom You Can" For without - That - We Will Be Thrown Back - To A Dark Void Of Ignorance.

BARLETTA, LINDA S. STOUT
[pen.] Catherine Elizabeth Sheehan; [b.] June 21, 1956, Jersey City, NJ; [p.] Charles H. Stout, Patricia A. Stout; [m.] Frank R. Barletta Sr.; [ch.] Melissa Patricia, Frankie Jr.; [occ.] Freelance Writer; [oth. writ.] Articles, opinions, poetry published local newspapers. The News Tribune, Home News, others.; [pers.] Began writing at the age of 6, I write from the heart about life experience, either first hand or family/others. I have the unique ability to empathize with anyone and write seemingly first hand pieces. I listen, observe, feel, then write.; [a.] Woodbridge Township, NJ

BARMETTLER, EILEEN
[pen.] Mickey McCormick; [b.] January 26, 1938, New York City; [p.] Frank and Marie Lehecka; [m.] John R. Barmettler Jr., April 6, 1963; [ch.] Therese John Jr. Phil, Tony; [ed.] 9th Grade (Public School - 126 Long Island City High School Queens Valley College (1 year) Music/Piano; [occ.] Housewife; [memb.] AARP (American Association Retired Persons); [hon.] Won First prize: Amateur Singing Contest; [oth. writ.] Have written mainly for myself.; [pers.] My goal is: To get "In touch" with my "Inner Child".; [a.] Highland, CA

BARNER, JUDY
[b.] June 12, 1946, Ohio; [p.] Ethel Hicks; [m.] Phil Barner, June 7, 1980; [ch.] 2; [ed.] High school graduate, Nursing School graduate, 2 yrs. Business University of Texas Arlington; [occ.] Certified Yoga Teacher for Therapist; [memb.] Amanda Yoga Teachers Association, American Kennel Club, Arlington Board of Realtors, National Association of Realtors; [hon.] 10th in the nation in Real Estate Sales, Superstars Award, Yearly other Awards in Real Estate; [oth. writ.] A Year of Healing, A Patch of Blue, A Walk With Death, The Healer, Child's Play, Little Girl, Tears, Bless The Healers; [pers.] After losing mu ability to work due to radical surgery and illness I began to write. I write from my very soul, from pain and love I write from personal experience; [a.] Los Angeles, CA

BARNES, ALLISON M.
[b.] August 1, 1975, Nashville, TN; [p.] Dwight and Pat Crews; [m.] Michael Barnes, August 16, 1993; [ed.] Lakes Sr. High School, Pierce College; [hon.] National Dean's List, Young Author's Award; [oth. writ.] Short story in school library, several short stories, novelettes, poems written but not as of yet published.; [pers.] I long to bring out the love and confidence I have for my fellow human beings by displaying it in my poems and behavior.; [a.] Albuquerque, NM

BARNES, LATISHA EVETTE
[pen.] Tisha Barnes; [b.] September 13, 1978, Norfolk, VA; [p.] Carolyn and Elijah Barnes; [ed.] Floyd E. Kellam High School (Va. Beach) 1996, Freshman - Norfolk State University; [occ.] Cashier/Clerk - Hardee's in Chesapeake, VA; [memb.] Student Council, Senior Senate, Chrome, Unity, FBLA, Church Choir, Sunday School, and Community Service; [hon.] Honor Graduate, Junior Class President, Student Council President, Two Academic Scholarships to Norfolk State University; [oth. writ.] Poems none "published"; [pers.] My writing is about everyday life. One day it may be about how I am feeling or how another person feels. Poetry is all about expressing what you cannot say.; [a.] Virginia Beach, VA

BARNES, NAOMI L.
[b.] July 6, 1965, Suffolk, VA; [ed.] John F. Kennedy High, M.C. Allen School of Religion; [pers.] I write poems and I love to read poems. I truly believe that God has given me this talent to glorify Him.; [a.] Suffolk, VA

BARON, JEFFREY A.
[pen.] Jeffrey A. Baron; [b.] April 18, 1946, Indianapolis, IN; [p.] Arthur G. and Marisa Baron; [ed.] Masters Degree in Sociology and Business Management, Graduate of Indiana University; [occ.] Deceased; [hon.] He was past President of the Business Management Faculty Assn. He was named "Teacher of The Year" by the colleges and received the "Glen Sample Award" for "Excellence in Teaching." He served on several Boards in Industry, Business and Government in Central Indiana, with an emphasis on motivation and quality; [oth. writ.] Jeffrey Baron was a faithful follower and advocate of the "Deming Theory of Quality Management" - He wrote several articles and enjoyed writing poetry.; [pers.] Jeffrey tried as a teacher to always help his students or anyone who asked his help. He was respected and beloved by his students and other faculty members. The common observations were, "He always gives so much of himself". My Husband and I found the poetry sent to you among his papers. He wrote that poem at age 15 yrs. It was so poignant and so full of insight that we wanted to have it published.; [a.] Indianapolis, IN

BARRETT, JULIA
[pen.] Rainlark; [b.] April 29, 1982, Evanston, IL; [p.] John Barrett, Kathleen Curzon; [ed.] Presently entering Fenwick High School; [occ.] Student, artist, and full-time dreamer; [memb.] People-to-people Student Ambassadors, former member and founder of the Percy Julian Writing Club, Student Council; [hon.] Honored in English, Awarded the Citizenship Award, Humanity Award, student Government Award, and C.A.S.T. Theatrical Award, most greatly honored in love from an Angel; [oth. writ.] Several poems and short essays published in "Letters to Anonymous", a collection of the Percy Julian Writing Club's works.; [pers.] "It is only in sorrow bad weather masters us, in joy we face the storm and defy it." - Amelia Barr; [a.] Oak Park, IL

BARRETT, TREVOR ANSON
[b.] December 2, 1981, Freeport, TX; [p.] Gary Wayne Barrett and Renee Barrett; [ed.] Northside Health Careers High School (NHCHS in San Antonio), have also studied in schools in Italy, Guam, California and Washington state; [occ.] Freshman at NHCHS, Student Vet Assistant at Kitty Animal Hospital; [memb.] National Junior Honors Society; [hon.] Taekwondo brown belt; [oth. writ.] Several other poems not yet published; [pers.] I usually always write poetry to music, especially romantic poetry to soft classical music. Most have been written to Pachelbels "Canon" in D.; [a.] Converse, TX

BARTHOLMÉ, MICHAEL JOHN
[b.] December 20, 1969, Okinawa, Japan; [p.] Ray Bartholme, Chiyoko Bartholme; [m.] Renee Bartholme, January 30, 1992; [ch.] Brandon, Matthew, Megan, Bartholme; [ed.] Adams City H.S., Colorado Inst. of Art; [occ.] Lube Tech. Grease Monkey Thornton Colorado; [pers.] I write my poems to make me feel better when I'm feeling a little down, hopefully, they put a smile on the faces of others.; [a.] Aurora, CO

BARTOLOTTA, CAMERA CHATHAM
[pen.] Camera C. Bartolotta; [b.] December 4, 1963, Cottage Grove, OR; [p.] Caren Chatham-Heller, Paul W. Heller; [m.] Bruce Bartolotta, January 28, 1988; [ch.] Devin, Dante; [ed.] Corvallis High, St. Mary's College of CA; [occ.] Small Business Owner and Freelance greeting Card Writer; [memb.] S.A.G., A.F.T.R.A., Nat'n Association of Independent Lubes (NAIL), Monongahela Chamber of Commerce, National Chamber of Commerce; [hon.] National Honor Society, Bousch and Lomb Science Award, Who's Who Among Students in American Universities and Colleges, Teen Magazine's "Great Model Search" National Finalist 1981; [oth. writ.] Several poems for use as greeting cards, published at age 9 in a collection of children's poetry, a children's fairy tale, articles for local paper; [pers.] Children and family are my inspiration. If I can make someone feel about them as I do, even for a moment, I am overjoyed.; [a.] Monongahela, PA

BASILE, CHRISTINA A.
[b.] January 30, 1969, Englewood, NY; [ed.] 1 Graduated High School, Went to a few classes at Ramapo, College in Mahwah, NJ; [pers.] I had just graduated high school in June of '87 and on 9-15 I had a car accident which left me in a Coma for 2 1/2 months. With my strong will and faith in God, I have made it through.; [a.] Ramsey, NJ

BATES, JEARLINE
[b.] January 20, 1919, Earlsboro, OK; [p.] Luna Macy and Pearl Macy; [m.] Clarence Smith - December 13, 1939, Reginald Bates - December 13, 1961; [ch.] Carolyn Smith Richards; [ed.] High School, 6 years private lessons in Oil Painting private lessons in Organ continuing; [occ.] Secretary Central Church of Christ Shawnee, OK. 74801 for 32 years; [memb.] Central Church of Christ; [oth. writ.] Poetry; [pers.] I can't write poetry, but I like to try, so I'll rhyme these words, and hope with a sigh.; [a.] Shawnee, OK

BAUER, KIRA RUSSO
[b.] November 20, 1964, Phoenix, AZ; [p.] Tom and Diane Huffman; [m.] Richard Alan Bauer, March 23, 1991; [ed.] Moon Valley High School, Northern Arizona University, California State University, Sacramento; [occ.] Historian; [memb.] Western Historical Association; [a.] Chandler, AZ

BAYLOR-SABAI, DEIDRE
[b.] March 8, 1948, New York; [p.] Jacqueline Shephard and Karl Baylor; [ch.] Weston Chavis III, and Jade Williams; [ed.] Jamaica High School; [occ.] Legal Secretary; [pers.] My poetry is an expression of my innermost feelings and experiences.

BEARD, DOLORES MIGUEL
[pen.] Dolores "Fifi Miguel" Beard; [b.] November 29, 1936, Tampa, FL; [p.] Alvaro Sergio Miguel, Ruth Dwight Bridges Miguel; [m.] April 17, 1953; [ch.] Michael Harvey Beard, Janalynn Beard Frantz, Grandchild - Michael Carlo Thomas Beard; [ed.] Florida Edu-

cation; [memb.] Florida Country Music - Association, First United Church Of Tampa - United Church of Christ; [oth. writ.] "Man Of The Road" Appeared in winter 1994. Contemporary poets of America and Britain.; [pers.] All children of the world especially, "Carlo, Mark, Marshal" future of the cosmos I pray the spirit of "Living" will be a beacon in your supernal hearts as your heritage of love forever.; [a.] Temple Terrace, FL

BEAUCHAMP, TWYLA
[b.] January 27, 1944, Douglas Co., MO; [p.] George F. and Pansy P. Lemons; [m.] James C. Beauchamp; [ch.] Rodney, Ronda, Rick and Vickie; [ed.] Mtn. Grove High School, Mtn Grove, MO, Melbourne Vo-Tech, Melbourne, AR, West Plains MO Vo-Tech; [occ.] Presently working on a Novel Titled Hearts of Fox Creek; [hon.] 1986 Golden Poet Award - Sponsored by Eddy Lou Cole - MC Milton Burell Open letter contest - sponsored by Mtn. Grove Journal - 1952, my first Award; [oth. writ.] My work has appeared in various newspapers throughout the midwest.; [pers.] My desire is to make this a better world. To create writings for the very young as well as the young at heart. All my works are done through love and faith.; [a.] Norwood, MO

BEAVER, JEANETTE E.
[pen.] Liz Beaver; [b.] March 24, 1939, Laoford, SC; [p.] Jeanette F. Young, Joseph Patterson; [m.] Joseph T. Beaver, July 9, 1967; [ch.] Kathy, Robert, Judy, Lynda, Joe - Fred; [ed.] Eg. Ged. Germania Com. College Act.; [occ.] Housewife Salesperson/Self-employed; [oth. writ.] The Mission, My Little Star - Lovely, am in process of writing a book only have two or three chapters to go - title "Twins"; [pers.] Sorry - can't find the release form - but this is official. You may publish my poem just what is free. My poem to be dedicated to my children.; [a.] Oxnard, CA

BECKER, VALERIE
[b.] April 18, 1969, Abington, PA; [p.] Matthew and Charlotte Becker; [ed.] MA - Master of Arts in Speech Language Pathology, BS - Bachelor of Science in Speech Path, Associates Degree in Liberal Arts; [occ.] Speech - language pathologist at Beechwood Center of NJ; [memb.] ASHA - American Speech - Language and Hearing Association; [hon.] "Best in the Class 1987" sponsored by Temple University and Channel 6 Deans List 2 yrs in a raw at Trenton State College; [oth. writ.] Articles published in "The Collegian" - college newspaper children's stories - not yet published novel in progress.; [pers.] I think writing is like any other art form. It's meant to evoke feelings, not just convey them. Good or bad - the stronger the better.; [a.] Maple Shade, NJ

BECKHAM, SUSAN LYNN
[b.] February 3, 1977, Stuttgart, AR; [p.] Robbi Thomas E. Beckham, Mrs. Gloria J. Beckham; [ed.] High School Graduate Louisville KY. Central High, Cosmetology College; [occ.] Respiet Worker and Student; [memb.] Temple Beth Shalom, Messianic Jewish Youth League; [hon.] Kentucky Colonels, Governors Cup Writing Competition, Young Authors Award; [oth. writ.] First Cry 1993, Because You Loved Me 1995, Pleasure For A Season 1995, Mask of Happiness 1994, Stolen Heart 1994, Darkness Of Morning 1993; [pers.] I seek to deliver originality and true emotion in all my writings. I have been greatly influenced by real life. My goal is to be the best and give my best.; [a.] Louisville, KY

BEGLEY, AMANDA
[b.] January 3, 1980, LaPorte, IN; [p.] Ed, Louise Begley; [ed.] North Laurel High School; [occ.] Long

John Silver's; [hon.] I graduated from John Robert Powers Modeling School. First prize in Science fair and Art fair; [pers.] My poem is about my grandpa and grandma. My grandpa is gone now and my grandma tells me how they sat on the porch and what it was like so this poem is dedicated to both grandpas who are gone now.; [a.] London, KY

BELL, JOY KIERAN
[b.] August 20, 1937, Staten Island, NY; [m.] H. Clark Bell, November 17, 1962; [ch.] Kieran Owen, Bridget Ann, Kathleen Siobhan; [ed.] Notre Dame Academy S.I., Dubarton College Washington, DC; [occ.] V.P. Bell Realty, V.P. Blackacre Enterprises; [mem.] Junior Leave Kingston (Sustainer) Ulster Tarden Club, Ulster County Republican Club, American Cancer Society; [oth.writ.] Nothing published - I am currently working on a family history book that includes 30 years of collected recipes as well as a collection of poetry.; [pers.] My love for poetry was nurtured during my years at Notre Dame Academy by the dedicated women of the Congregation of Notre Dame. Now, years later, I feel compelled to write - to try and express some simple truth within me.; [a.] Woodstock, NY

BELLINO, CHRISTINE KYLE
[pen.] Christine Kyle; [b.] December 30, 1958, Worcester, MA; [p.] Irene and Randolph Ringgard Jr. (Both Deceased); [m.] Nick M. Bellino, July 22, 1995; [ed.] College - US Army - High School - Medical Training in Medical Assisting; [occ.] Medical Assisting and Writing; [hon.] Letter of Commendation from US Army; [oth. writ.] Currently working on book - "My Guardian Angel Wants a Vacation", "I Could Have Been...I Still Could" published 1996 in book memories of tomorrow National Library of Poetry; [pers.] My poems only come from inspiration for a loved one when I put my feeling into words.; [a.] Worcester, MA

BENNETT, CHERYL A.
[b.] December 2, 1957, Niles, MI; [p.] Charles and Evelyn Bailey; [m.] Paul S. Bennett, July 30, 1977; [ch.] Megan, Marie and Andrew Nicholas; [ed.] Niles Senior High School; [occ.] Student Services Secretary South Bend Community Schools; [hon.] Blue Ribbons Art Award; [oth. writ.] I have written many poems, some have been printed in small papers for work or school.; [pers.] By writing poems I can express my feelings on life, love and others issues in an interesting and sometimes entertaining way.; [a.] Niles, MI

BENNINGFIELD, BRANDEN
[pen.] W. W. Wind; [b.] March 22, 1981, Brownwood, TX; [p.] Randy Benningfield, Tina Benningfield; [ed.] Lometa High School (Sophomore); [occ.] Student; [memb.] 1st Baptist Church, Lometa - FFA, Lometa Chapter - Texas Delaine Sheep Association - Fellowship of Christina Athletes; [hon.] Woodmen of the World Award (American History) "A" Honor Roll - San Saba FFA District Vice President - FFA Parlimentary Procedure team (President) 1st place in District - homet a FFA reporter - 97, 6 GPA - Lions club Academic Achievement Award; [oth. writ.] Unpublished poems: "The Champion" - "The Spinnin' Beast" - "The Chain Team" - "The Bad Boys Are Back", Unpublished Songs: "Bleeding Rain" - "All My Heart Needs."; [pers.] I am greatly influenced by the writings of Louis La'mour and I try to keep my writings interesting and appealing to all readers.; [a.] Lometa, TX

BENOIR, MARYLOU
[b.] July 10, 1940, Randolph, VT; [p.] Elmer and Chris-

tina White Sanford; [m.] Kenneth M. Benoir, October 17, 1959; [ch.] Kenny L., Scott E. Benoir; [ed.] 8 grade 3 1/2 years of High School; [occ.] Housewife, mother and grandmother; [oth. writ.] Just stories I wrote for myself. And my poetry.; [a.] Randolph, VT

BENTLEY, APRIL
[pen.] April Bentley; [b.] January 9, 1981, Athens, GA; [p.] Steve and Connie Bentley; [ed.] Monroe Area High; [hon.] Top 5 of Freshman Class; [pers.] Works very hard with younger children at church; [a.] Monroe, GA

BERG, CHARISH NICOLE
[b.] December 25, 1980, Valley City, ND; [p.] Terrance Berg and Tamie Loibl; [ed.] Only in 9th Grade at Cortez High School; [occ.] School; [hon.] Pre teen Pagent, Colorado teen pagent; [oth. writ.] Poem published in National Calendar; [pers.] I write poems to u~~s~~erstand myself, and each poem I write I understand myself that much better.; [a.] Cortez, CO

BERGER, MELISSA
[b.] December 10, 1975, Goshen, NY; [p.] Thomas Berger, Patricia Zillig; [ed.] Valley Central High, Orange County Community College, College at New Paltz; [occ.] Waitress, Pizza Hut; [hon.] Dean's List; [a.] Maybrook, NY

BERMUDEZ, MICHELLE
[pen.] Hope Baez; [b.] March 23, 1976, Chicago, IL; [p.] Iris and Felix Bermudez; [ed.] Steinmetz High School, Loyola University of Chicago, North Eastern Illinois University; [occ.] Reading and Math Tutor at Gray Elementary School; [memb.] Mont Clare Baptist Church; [oth. writ.] Was an entertainment writer for Loyola University Newspaper: The Phoenix. Had several movie reviews and entertainment articles published. Was editor of Steimetz High School Newspaper.; [pers.] Through the gifts that God has given me I try to captivate the beauty of love. In a society that takes love for granted I am trying to bring romance back through my poetry.; [a.] Chicago, IL

BERRY, DARLA
[b.] April 5, 1960, New Mexico; [p.] John and Joan Isaacks; [m.] John Berry, February 18, 1984; [ch.] Cody R., Ar-manda S.; [ed.] G.E.D.; [occ.] House Wife; [oth. writ.] A poem to my husband - "Our Love," entered into contest for May 1, 1996; [pers.] When you don't forgive others, you burn the bridge over which you yourself must travel to receive God's forgiveness for yourself.; [a.] Helena, MT

BERRY, LINDA GAIL
[b.] January 17, 1951, Hollywood, CA; [p.] Earl Oliver and Ruth Irene Bartlett; [m.] Jerry C. Berry, September 21, 1967; [ch.] Tammy Lee and Jerry Harold; [occ.] Co-owner and Instructor of Berry's Traditional Taekwondo Karate Centers (nine locations); [memb.] (IKSA) Independent Karate Schools of America; [oth. writ.] Several Poems, Songs, Short Stories, and other writings; [pers.] All of my poems have been inspired by My God, My dearly Mother, and my very loving family and friends. "When writing my poetry, I choose to rely on God's Great Simplicity to be my guide."; [a.] Mossyrock, WA

BESCHLER, TIMOTHY
[pen.] The Wiz; [b.] December 7, 1956, Tyrone, PA; [p.] John and Lois Beschler; [occ.] Mechanic at Kick's Garage Jamestown, Portage; [oth. writ.] I do have other writings that are not published, poems of many types; [pers.] I wrote on the insight of my now present and hope-

ful to be my wife someday. She gave me the inspiration to write these poems. In short (she's the best); [a.] Portage, PA

BICHEL, GRETHE
[pen.] Trille; [b.] November 15, 1921, Slagelse, Denmark; [p.] Ore and Grethe Knudson; [m.] Earl Bichel, February 20, 1944; [ch.] Grethe Armstrong - Tovekays, Earl L. Bichel; [ed.] Registered Nurse and Multiple Music Courses; [occ.] Professional singer, retired - School Nurse, Board membrer (Danish Home) Chicago; [memb.] PTA Life Memberships X2 Dania Ladies Society - Danish Home Society Scandinavian Cultural Society Danish American Athletic Club Director and member of ladies vocal group - Thursday girls; [hon.] Appreciation Award - from Danish Home, Appreciation Award from Mannheim School District #83-IL Poetry Awards NLOP; [oth. writ.] "Windward" "Thoughts in the Summer Heat" "From whatnic to Sputnik" Reports to "Den Danske Pioneer" and "USA Scandinavian" - and Local Papers "The River of LIve" 100's poems and lyrics; [pers.] My philosophy is to spread joy to those who in thought, spirit and body are depressed. My own life in enriched when motivating friends with uplifting thoughts in Poetry and thought.; [a.] River Grove, IL

BIEDLER, JOYCE A.
[b.] January 22, 1947, Mitchelle, SD; [p.] Francis and Evelyn Starzl; [ch.] Michelle, Theresa, Steven and William; [ed.] Amery High School, WITC Vocational - CNA; [occ.] Upholstery - Commercial Sewing; [memb.] Bethany Lutheran Church, Star Prairie, WI; [hon.] The honor of having 4 beautiful children and many, many close friends.; [oth. writ.] Several poems; [pers.] My poems come from my heart and all have been written about or to a special person in my life. I believe that love is the most important ingredient in life.; [a.] New Richmond, WI

BIELE, ANDREW F.
[b.] January 12, 1973, New York, NY; [p.] Albert and Ariene Biele; [ed.] Boston University, Fairfield University; [occ.] Vice-President - Aland Construction Communications; [memb.] Zigma Alpha Epsilon; [a.] New York, NY

BIELEC, SUZANNE M.
[b.] February 10, 1952, Milwaukee, WI; [p.] John and Betty Simon; [m.] Donald S. Bielec, September 16, 1977; [ch.] Our 3 cats are our family: Squeaker, Reggie and Peaches; [ed.] Pius XI High School, several years at various local colleges; [occ.] Own a small art/gift business; [hon.] National Honor Society; [oth. writ.] Several poems published in National Anthologies.; [pers.] Most of my poetry has been born out of the pain of recovery from childhood sexual abuse. My relationship with God has not only brought me through this dark time, but He is making glorious good out of the evil that was perpetrated against me. This particular poem reflects the truth of this.; [a.] Waukesha, WI

BISHOP, BREEZE TIVA
[b.] January 8, 1979, San Antonio, TX; [p.] Jeffery L. Bishop, Sheryl L. Bishop; [ed.] Clear Creek High School; [hon.] All American Scholar, Who's Who in American High Schools; [pers.] Dreams and wishes create hope, and if you keep faith in hope, miracles happen.; [a.] Kemah, TX

BJORKMAN, LORIE KAY
[b.] February 28, 1973, International Falls, MN; [p.] David Bjorkman, Evangelyn Bjorkman; [ed.] Atikokan High School, Lakehead University - Bachelor of Arts -

Bachelor of Education; [occ.] High School English Teacher; [hon.] Writing (Prose and poetry), Speaking Honour Roll, Top Student, Several University Scholarships; [oth. writ.] Catching the Spirit (Poetry Anthology); [pers.] Writing, to me, is an enjoyable release of emotion and I want emotion reflected in it. I give glory to God in all my accomplishment, for His love is the foundation of my life.; [a.] Pine City, MN

BLACK, GLENN
[pen.] Gavin Hall; [b.] September 8, 1945, Cincinnati; [p.] Carl and Ruby Black; [ed.] Attended: University of Cincinnati; [occ.] House Manager in a halfway house; [oth. writ.] Written several short stories and plays; [pers.] "There are many paths to the top of the mountain. And each one must find the path that is right for them."; [a.] Cincinnati, OH

BLACKBURN, GARY E.
[b.] September 24, 1969, Houston, TX; [m.] Dr. Yvonne Dechance; [ed.] University of Texas, Austin; [occ.] United States Marine Corps, Camp Pendleton, CA

BLACKMON, TONY
[b.] May 18, 1981, Yuma, AZ; [p.] Cathy Blackmon; [ed.] Travellers Rest Highs School in Travelers Rest, SC; [occ.] Student; [memb.] Mu Alpha Theta; [a.] Travelers Rest, SC

BLAKE, LINDA CHANDLER
[b.] January 23, 1960, Charleston, SC; [p.] Nathaniel West and Earthie Grant; [m.] Rodney Blake, November 22, 1983; [ch.] Ieesha, Banika, Rhonda; [ed.] North Charleston High - Trident Technical College; [occ.] Senior Sales Associate Montgomery Ward; [memb.] Washington United Methodist Church; [hon.] Washington United Methodist Church; [oth. writ.] Associate Choice Award; [pers.] All of my poems are from personal and past experiences. My husband and my 3 girls are my greatest motivation, they back me in everything I believe or try to do.; [a.] Charleston, SC

BLAMIRE, TODD EDWARD
[b.] May 10, 1966, Los Angeles; [p.] Carol and Edward Blamire; [m.] Terri Blamire, June 29, 1991; [oth. writ.] Too many personal stories, poems, and songs to write. I've kept all of my writings since I was 10 years old.; [pers.] Love each other, take care of each other, and make the most of our brief existence on this wonderful planet.; [a.] Richardson, TX

BLANCHFIELD, GARY C.
[pen.] G. Courtney Crockett; [b.] August 12, 1952, Baltimore, MD; [p.] John Blanchfield and Glenva Blanchfield; [ch.] Richard allen Blanchfield, Bryon Courtney Blanchfield; [ed.] High school; [occ.] Network Administrator, Computer Programmer; [oth. writ.] Tons, none published; [pers.] I write from the heart. I cannot control what I write nor do I attempt to tailor verse. I am not influenced by other writers. Philosophical: To think in foolish folly is pretentious, to fool in folly pretended is to prevail.; [a.] Cumberland, MD

BLANKFARD, G. KATHRYN
[pen.] Christina; [b.] April 24, 1932, Cabell County, WV; [p.] Grandfather: Wesley Edwards; [m.] Francis B. Blankfard, November 1973; [ch.] Bruce Weatherholt, Cheryl Weatherholt Puller; [ed.] High School - Milton, W VA Jr. College Santa Rosa, CA; [occ.] Homemaker; [memb.] St. Michaels Catholic Church - Wauchula Florida; [oth. writ.] Several Gospel Songs published by, "Stamps Baxter"; [pers.] I have been greatly influenced by the unique unconditional, deliberate and focused love

that I received from my grandfather who encouraged me to develop a talent, to take risk and to make important decisions.; [a.] Bowling Green, FL

BLANTON, PAUL R.
[b.] September 8, 1968, Atlanta, GA; [p.] Charles E. and Kloye A. Blanton; [m.] Sharon E. Blanton, November 26, 1993; [ch.] Laura Elizabeth, Cera Ashlei; [ed.] Towers High School; [occ.] Detention Officer, Sheriff's Department; [pers.] To be tormented by my thoughts is to have understood what I have said.; [a.] Snellville, GA

BLEDSOE, PHILLIP D.
[b.] January 29, 1963, Wheeling, WV; [p.] Sylvester and Juanita Bledsoe; [ed.] North Adams State College - BS-Degree in Business Management/Wheeling Park High School; [occ.] Equal Employment Opportunity Specialist - WVA. Division of Highways; [memb.] Commissioner - City of Wheeling Human Rights Commission; [hon.] William McKeever Award, Basketball Jersey Retired - College; [pers.] I can do all things through Christ which strengthen me. Philippians 4:13, greatly influenced and encouraged by my mother! Juanita Bledsoe; [a.] Wheeling, WV

BLETCH, MARK R.
[b.] June 8, 1989, Detroit, MI; [p.] Richard and Diane Bletch; [ed.] Stevenson High, Macomb County Community College; [occ.] Lot inventory at Jerome Duncan Ford; [memb.] Enlistment in the United States Marine corp reserve; [hon.] In Bowling, swimming, baseball, and hockey. Also the subject of a meritorious most in the summer and several promotions up to surgent.; [pers.] I would like to thank Gorrett Darosa as my inspiration for this poem entitled, "A Place In The Heart"; [a.] Sterling Heights, MI

BLEVINS, JERRYE CARGILL
[b.] July 5, 1938, Batesville, AR; [p.] William and Ruth Hill Cargill; [m.] Calvin D. Blevins (Deceased), June 29, 1963; [ch.] Chad Blevins, Shane Blevins; [hon.] I have written short stories for the newspaper, magazine the Honor comes from knowing. "I Have Touched Someone", "Giving Them" A Purpose and Meaning" in life.; [oth. writ.] "Threads of Pleasure", "Places of the Heart", "Happiness at Sylvan Glens", "The Sunset", "A Journey Home", "The Fashions of Spring and Youth"; [pers.] I write from my home a Freelance writer, I dedicated always to family and special friend Bob, for giving me years of encouragement, most of all to "The Creator of our Universe" who makes all things possible.; [a.] Locust Grove, AR

BLITHE, PEGGY S.
[b.] June 1, 1947, Upland, CA; [p.] William and Josephine Roberts; [m.] Richard Blithe; [ch.] Tisha Rene; [occ.] Admin. Asst., U.S. Small, Business Administration, Sacramento, CA; [pers.] My writings are inspired by the dictations of the universe in combination with real life.; [a.] Sacramento, CA

BLOUNT, TIFFANY M.
[pen.] Beebee Fanfare; [b.] August 1, 1981, Saint Louis, MO; [p.] Janice Blount and Michael First; [ed.] I am a 15 years old Sophomore at Hazelwood Central High School; [occ.] Student; [oth. writ.] I also have several other poems and Lyrics that are original.; [pers.] My sense of writing comes from my view of the world. I am inspired by people I admire, and people who know the meaning of success. "Determination can bring on success, success cannot be done without determination".; [a.] Florissant, MO

BLUME, JOHN D.
[pen.] Johnathondietrich; [b.] November 14, 1925, Redfield, SD; [p.] Franklin Blume, Nora Blume; [m.] Charlotte Blume, December 18, 1952; [ch.] Franklin, Colleen, Ramdna, Kathleen Constance, Gregory and Kevin; [ed.] Redfield H.S. Graduate; [occ.] Retired Railway Carman; [oth. writ.] I have written many poems through the years. All are as yet unpublished.; [pers.] I do not wish to jade your eye with words which cause confusion I won't attempt to mystify or baffle through illusion my verse won't take your breath away or set your senses reeling I simply wish it to convey the way my heart is feeling.; [a.] Brainerd, MN

BLYSKAL, ELENA MARY
[b.] December 8, 1986, Long Island, NY; [p.] Dr. Stanley and Florence Blyskal; [ed.] September '96: 5th grade student; [occ.] Student; [memb.] Member and volunteer performer with creative ministries a Christian theater group.; [hon.] NYSSMA (N.Y. State School Music Assn.) "Outstanding" rating in piano performance PTA Reflections Contest - NY State Literature District Winner; [pers.] Elena is the youngest of four girls and enjoys vacationing in fire Island. She has loved to read from a very young age and her enjoyment of books influences her writing. She loves music, drama and cats!; [a.] East Islip, NY

BOHLINGER, LINDA
[pen.] Linda Bohlinger; [b.] August 12, 1955, Poughkeepsie, NY; [p.] Harold Bohlinger, Marjorie Bohlinger; [ed.] Roosevelt High School; [occ.] Cash Office employee superkmart, Kingston, NY; [pers.] I dedicate this poem to my father and two sisters. For inspiring me to write this poem, for always believing in me and loving me, thanks Dad, Margie, and Martha.; [a.] Staatsburg, NY

BOHM, JOSHUA ADAM
[pen.] Josh Bohm; [b.] August 13, 1981, Melbourne, FL; [p.] Michael and Bonnie Bohm; [ed.] Currently a freshman at Lakeridge High School, Lake Oswego, OR; [occ.] Student; [pers.] Don't eat yellow snow; [a.] West Linn, OR

BOLICH, SUSAN E.
[pen.] Sioux; [b.] July 14, 1977, Cincinnati, OH; [p.] Sharyn Bolich, Raymond Bolich; [ed.] Kings High School, Indiana University; [occ.] Professional student; [memb.] National Geographic Society, Greenpeace, Phish Fan Club; [oth. writ.] Several poems saw publication in my high school montage of poem magazine and local newspapers; [pers.] I have faith that those of us who already know our "gift" will one day unite with those who haven't quite found theirs in a sess pool of energy, joy and beauty to create a total naturistic divinity; [a.] Maineville, OH

BOMGARDNER, JOEL DAVID
[b.] June 18, 1960; [p.] Gene Lee Bomgardner, Ethel Marguerite Bomgardner; [m.] Debra Jean Bomgardner, April 7, 1980; [ch.] David Bennet Bomgardner, Christopher Paul Bomgardner, Shannon Marie Bomgardner; [ed.] Baltimore Public Schools (Baltimore MD.) Bloomington High School South (Bloomington IN.); [occ.] Midwest Chain Convenience Store Manager; [memb.] Boy Scouts of America (District Committee); [oth. writ.] Children's books, A Mouse in The House and The magic Needle, yet un-published. Poems published in local magazines.; [pers.] I try to incorporate social issues and lessons in my writings to fulfill a deeper sense of accomplishment.

BONIN, KELLY
[b.] April 15, 1982, New Iberia, LA; [p.] Corey L. and Bonnie K. Bonin; [ed.] 7th grade Loreauville Junior High; [occ.] Student; [a.] Loreauville, LA

BONNER, JULIA O.
[pen.] Julia O'; [b.] August 26, 1915, Estill Springs, TN; [p.] Deceased; [m.] Deceased; [ed.] Holloway, High School—Division Academy for Girls, TN—Wayne County Community College; [occ.] Retired; [memb.] Board of Directors, United Generation Council—Beluaa Chap. #17 Orders of the Easter Star—IPOE of W Camille Chapter—300 Club of Greater Christ Baptist Church—Jolly Gabrielle Club—Advisory Board of Joseph Walker-Williams Center; [hon.] Crime Prevention Service Award—Council for the Arts Detroit News Award—United Generation Council Youth Literacy Award—Greater Detroit Society for the Blind—Virginia Park Citizens Service Award—Certificate of Attendance from the People's Law; [oth. writ.] Sin Defined, Unexamined Life, Crown and the Glory, Ages Eyes, A Tribute to Sister Ann, It, Little St. John, Tribute to Mom, Angels of Mercy; [pers.] I believe that positive thinking and the belief that you're never too old to learn are good rules to live by. I also believe that anything worth doing at all is worth doing well.; [a.] Highland Park, MI

BOOK, E. A.
[b.] New York City; [occ.] Writer, Captain, The Royal James; [oth. writ.] "'Tis all heaven allows, (ISBN/Library of Congress) pub: 9-96 Corpus Callosom, Naperville, IL. "Millennium III" in Progress, poems for the future. Written over 1 million words for newspapers.; [pers.] "Yea, as my swift days near their goal, "Tis all that I implore, In life and death a chainless soul, with courage to endure.; [a.] Beaufort, NC

BOONE, CHANDA
[pen.] Chanda Boone; [b.] August 13, 1960, Louisville, KY; [occ.] Asst. Manager of Baptist Towers, Apt. Bldg. for Elderly; [oth. writ.] Several poems published in Local Community Newspapers. "A Plea of Many Voices", published in National Teen Magazine, Y.E.S. Youth Fricted about Success. Poem presentations throughout the City of Louisville including Churches, Community functions and National Conference and Workshops.; [pers.] Poetry allows me to gather words and put them into poems of purpose. I give my writing as a gift, just as the gift has been given to me.; [a.] Louisville, KY

BOOTHROYD, JOHN M.
[b.] January 18, 1916, Lennoxville, Quebec; [p.] Eric, Lois; [m.] Margaret King Boothroyd, 1941; [ch.] Susan Hunter, Frederica Hoffmann; [ed.] Bishop's College School, Lennoxville, Que, Pratt Institute Brooklyn, NY Sir George Williams College, Montreal; [occ.] Retired; [memb.] Past member - Simsbury Light Opera Company, Past Pres. Boothroyd Advertising, Inc. Past President, Advertising Club of Greater Hartford, CT, Life Member, New York Art Directors Club; [hon.] Many awards for Ad, Campaigns, Posters, etc.; [oth. writ.] Mostly paintings and a few scribbles; [pers.] Influenced by the "Poets of the romantic revival."; [a.] Sarasota, FL

BORCHERS, MARIE
[b.] December 18, 1922, Lincoln, NE; [p.] R. Gould and Julia (DeVriendt) Brandy; [m.] Earl J. Borchers, February 12, 1945; [ch.] Janice Zimmermann, Marsha Felthaus, Sue Binter, Douglas Borchers; [ed.] Scottsbluff H.S., Scottsbluff, NE. Grad. Lincoln H.S., Lincoln, Nebr. Some college courses; [occ.] Retired Secretary; [memb.] Christ Lutheran Church, Lutheran Women's Mission-

ary League; [oth. writ.] None published so far except in church newsletters; [pers.] For years I have written poems and songs as an expression of my private thoughts and. These were kept secret from my family. It was at the encouragement of my daughter Sue that I have taken a step forward to have them published. They are my testimony to my faith in God.; [a.] Yuma, AZ

BORGER, GERALDINE
[b.] September 2, 1942, Clarence, PA; [p.] Mr. and Mrs. Frank Waxmunsky Sr.; [m.] Stanley W. Borger, September 19, 1964; [ch.] Vonda, Beth Ann, LeAnn, Doyle; [ed.] Graduate of Bald Eagle High School, Attended classes at Centre County Vo Tech School and Penn State Univ.; [occ.] Housewife; [memb.] Snow Shoe Ambulance Club, Mountaintop Alliance CMA Church; [hon.] Cub Scout Den Mother Award School Newspaper Staff Editor Award, School Library Staff Award; [oth. writ.] Several editorials and articles published in local newspaper, poems and writings in local Church newspaper and bulletins.; [pers.] My poetry expresses the love of God and His handiwork as revealed through His creation of all mankind and nature. My parents and family instilled within me strong Christian values and the love of nature.; [a.] Snow Shoe, PA

BOSS, DR. GEORGE P.
[b.] September 3, 1916, Punxsutawney, PA; [p.] Deceased; [m.] Divorced; [ed.] Un. of West Florida Pensarola, Fla. BA Ohio Un. Athens Ohio Masters and Doctorate; [occ.] Retired; [memb.] Rotary Club of Bloomsbery First Presbytorian Church, APSCUAF of Penna retired Assoc. of Penna State Un. Profs.; [hon.] Silver Beaver - adult Scouter Award; [oth. writ.] Plays "There Ladies and Bear" on the Life of Lincoln "Lock-Of-The Walk" on The Life of Vietnam Veterans Book of Poetry Saltfoam - published work; [pers.] Have written works of children and adult poetry, studied poetry and fiction of the world.; [a.] Bloomsbury, PA

BOSWELL, RODNEY K.
[b.] March 12, 1950, Los Angeles; [p.] Herbert T. Boswell Sr. and Lucille G. Boswell; [ed.] UCLA - BA, History; [pers.] I owe every success that I have had to my brother, Herb, Jr., my sister, Sharon, and to my wonderful Mom and "Pop".; [a.] Los Angeles, CA

BOUCHER, KAREN
[pen.] Karen Boucher; [b.] April 8, 1977, Salt Lake City; [p.] Larry and Linda Brower; [m.] Andrew Boucher, April 8, 1995; [occ.] Housewife; [oth. writ.] More poems which I have not done anything with yet. I hope to publish them sometime.; [pers.] This is for all the people who told me that my writing was not good enough to make it into a book.; [a.] Las Vegas, NV

BOWERS, JAMES ALAN
[pen.] The Thin Man; [b.] August 21, 1956, Omaha, NE; [p.] Harvey and Yvonne Bowers; [m.] Michelle Bowers, August 21, 1982; [ch.] Christopher - 15, Ashley - 11; [ed.] Alisal H.S. - Salinas, CA, Hartnell College, Salinas, CA, American River College, Sacramento, CA; [occ.] Sales Mgr. - Sierra Chevrolet, Colfax, CA; [memb.] Lions Club, Chamber of Commerce, Cordova Pride, Sacramento, CA; [hon.] Honorary Mayor of Rancho Cordova, CA (1992), Community Achievement Award from Senator Patrick Johnston - State Assembly (1993), Founder: Cordova Pride (1988), USAF Worldwide Talent Show (75-76); [oth. writ.] "The Life and Times Of An Ordinary Man"; [pers.] It is inevitable that humankind, through its infinite wisdom and religious diversity will return this planet to the fishes in the sea.; [a.] Colfax, CA

BOYDMAN, KERRIE
[b.] November 12, 1984, Cleveland, OH; [p.] Dr. Scott Boydman, Nancy Boydman; [ed.] Hilltop Elementary School - Fifth Grade; [occ.] Student; [hon.] (1) I wrote my poem, "It Only Takes One Heart" to music. It was performed at the Sixth Grade Commencement Ceremony, (2) "Straight A" Student in the Fifth Grade; [pers.] My writings reflect a wide variety of feelings and emotions. My goal is to broaden my horizons, challenge myself and show others a different perspective of life.; [a.] Beachwood, OH

BOYLE, BRIAN
[b.] November 20, 1969, Exeter, NH; [p.] B. J. Boyle Jr., Suzanne Boyle; [ed.] Graduated from Berkner high school in 1989. (Houston, TX), Richland Community College; [occ.] Packaging, fastenal Co., Carrollton, TX; [oth. writ.] Several poems published in three books printed by quill books. "Dusting Off Dreams", "Echoes from the Silence", "Treasure the Moment"; [pers.] "I prefer not to write about sensitive topics, my poems can provide an escape from today's newspaper headlines."; [a.] Carrollton, TX

BRABEC, LAURIE L.
[pen.] "Shadow" or "Slick"; [b.] October 26, 1971, Norfolk, NE; [p.] Gene and Marge Brabec; [ed.] Clarkson High School, Wayne State College U.S. Army; [occ.] Graphic Designer, Hallmark Cards, Inc., KC, MO; [memb.] U.S. Army Reserves - 7 years; [hon.] Several poems published in local newspapers, College published books, Sentiments for cards for private company. Art Exhibition and Awards; [oth. writ.] I also write w/in my paintings. I may grab from a previously written poem or write in something descriptive to my painting.; [pers.] I escape from frivolous lifestyles when I write. My poems often reflect someone else's life, heartaches, trials, or pains. I like to write about the people closest to me.; [a.] Kansas City, MO

BRADSHAW, C. MICHAEL
[b.] March 11, 1945, Birmingham, AL; [p.] Deceased; [m.] Gail T. Bradshaw, May 16, 1982; [ch.] 6; [ed.] BA Mobile College, MA, The George Washington University, Juris Doctorate Potomac School of Law; [occ.] Attorney-at-Law General Practice; [memb.] Anne Arundel County Bar Association; [oth. writ.] Article published in local newspaper, and astronomy magazine; [pers.] I strive to show/reflect man's interpersonal nature and his relationship to the physical universe. I have been influenced by southern writers and poets.; [a.] Crofton, MD

BRASKIE, RITA
[b.] August 2, 1914, Monson; [memb.] Volunteer and Trustee at Elkins Library Canterbury NH - Volunteer Canterbury Shaker Village; [hon.] Acknowledgement (2) Books, (1st) Seasoned with Grace, Subtitle, My Generation of Shaker Cooking by Elderess Bertha Lindsey, Rita worked with Eldress Bertha for about 1 yr - Trying and Refining each recipe - to present day standards, (2nd) Earth Shall Blossom Shaker Herbs and Gardening by Galen Beale, Mary Rose Boswell; [pers.] Avid Gardener - Weaver - Reader, (2) Poems hang in Elkins Library

BRATCHER, JUANITA
[pen.] "Nita"; [b.] Columbus, GA; [p.] Tommie and George Forte; [m.] Neal A. Bratcher Sr.; [ch.] Pamela, Angela, Sonya, Neal Jr.; [ed.] Bachelor's in Journalism AA degree in Liberal Arts; [occ.] Writer, publisher, poet and songwriter. Former investigative reporter, Chicago Defender, currently publisher and CEO, Copyline magazine.; [hon.] Kizzy Award, Portraits of Achievers, Ev-

eryday Hero Award, Illinois' Secretary of State George Ryan, Businesswoman of the Year, Outstanding support of Human Rights, Journalism Par Excellence, Exemplary Civic Service, Excellence in Investigative Reporting; [oth. writ.] "Harold: The Making of a Big City Mayor", "I Cry For A People", "Short, Sweet and All That," "The Last of the Red Hot Mammas" Have appeared in publications, on radio and TV shows.; [pers.] "A man is judged by the issues he espouses, and sacrifices made."; [a.] Chicago, IL

BRATT, KRISTA
[pen.] Lady Morgainne; [b.] San Francisco, CA; [pers.] Never pass up an opportunity to travel. It opens up your mind and expands your world in a way that only traveling can do. It teaches you more about yourself than you could have believed possible. Also, follow your dreams and believe in then and yourself because if you don't who will?

BRAUN, ERNEST ALEJANDRO
[b.] August 5, 1928, Caracas, Venezuela; [m.] Reyna Botello De Braun, December 17, 1993; [ch.] Lawrence, Michael; [ed.] High School By GED after honorably serving in the U.S. Army, BA in Sociology in 1959 from California State University Minor in Criminology and Juvenile Delinquency; [occ.] Retired after 32 years as a deputy probation officer in Los Angeles; [oth. writ.] Letters to the editor on topical matters, critiques on current events such as the impact of the cinema on our youth and other faculty pathways into adulthood.; [pers.] Self expression in the poetic form is the most idealized form of expression. We choose and clothe and educate our thoughts and thereby we lift ourselves into another dimension - I would even say that we purify ourselves in the process.; [a.] Orlando, FL

BRIGDEN, KATE
[b.] July 4, 1984, South Africa; [p.] Carol and Derek Brigden; [ed.] Herndon Middle School; [occ.] Scholar; [oth. writ.] Poems in school newspapers; [pers.] I have been encouraged to follow through on my dream by those who realized my talent and I hope others will do the same.; [a.] Reston, VA

BRIGGS, BONNIE ALLEN
[pen.] Bonnie Frann Allen; [b.] February 13, 1955, Shreveport, LA; [p.] Jean Fetteman, Linton Harold Allen; [m.] William W. Briggs Jr., November 21, 1993; [ed.] James Madison High, University of Houston - Clear Lake; [occ.] Sr. Staff Contract Representative Burlington Resources, Houston, TX; [memb.] Natural Gas Association of Houston; [hon.] Daughters of the American Revolution - Runner Up; [pers.] "You, The Funny Man", was written in honor and loving memory of my brother, Spencer Travelyon Allen. Who passed away April 27, 1996. He will be dearly miss by his family and many friends.; [a.] Houston, TX

BRIGHAM, SHARON O.
[pen.] Sharon Brigham; [b.] May 23, 1967, Dallas, TX; [p.] Albert Brigham, Effie Brigham; [ch.] Savannah Cook, Raymond Cook; [ed.] Forest Brook High, NA-Academy; [occ.] Nurse-Aide; [memb.] Bethel's Family Baptist Church (Houston Texas), Pastor Walter August Jr.; [pers.] Special thanks to: God our Creator, for giving me the knowledge to write "These Are The Final Days". My parents, children, family and friends. Ora Smith, Cree, Margrett, Gregory, Anthony, Mark, Randy, John, Rita, Cedric, Milton Brigham's. National Library of Poetry, thanks for all your love and support.

BRINES, SARA
[b.] July 16, 1976, Mount Holly; [p.] Robert Brines and Carolyn Tomich; [ed.] 1996 Graduate Moorestown Senior High School, Attending Burlington County College; [occ.] Cook; [hon.] Academic Achievement Award, 1996; [oth. writ.] "The Mountain of Life", and "Rain"; [a.] Mount Holly, NJ

BROCATO, SARAH
[pen.] Dimond Stars; [b.] December 19, 1982, Kansas; [p.] Jim and Kathie Brocato; [ed.] Public School until 6th grade, Home School from 6th grade until present; [occ.] Student; [memb.] 4-H; [pers.] I've enjoyed writing since the 1st grade when I learned that I could put my personal thoughts on paper and share them when I wanted to. My poem "Love" came from my hurt feelings with my first loved (3rd grade).; [a.] Glen Saint Mary, FL

BROMLEY, STEVEN M.
[b.] October 12, 1969, Camden, NJ; [p.] Dr. William H., Lois L.; [m.] Jennifer Arbittier Bromley, July 4, 1996; [ed.] Haddonfield Memorial High Bucknell University, University of Pennsylvania UMDNJ- Robert Wood Johnson Medical School; [occ.] Medical Student; [hon.] Cum Laude (U.Penn) Alpha Lambda Delta, Phi Eta Sigma, Dean's List; [oth. writ.] Include poetry published in International (JAMA, 2/7/96) and state-wide (Health State, Spring '96) publications. I have also been the author of several published research papers and abstracts.; [pers.] Inspiration lies within the complex relationship between body and mind, individual and society, Science and Religion. My poetry approaches these issues, and helps me to find meaning as both a Physician and a poet.; [a.] Philadelphia, PA

BROOKS, CHRISTINA
[b.] July 29, 1996, Kansas City, MO; [p.] Virgil Brooks and Lorraine Brooks; [ed.] Grade school, Junior High, presently student 6th grade, Winfield Middle School, Winfield, KS; [occ.] Student; [memb.] Olympia Sales Club; [hon.] Placed in Elementary Spelling Bee, Two Years of Choir, Placed in Limbo Contest Skating Rink - have been gifted student classes for past 4 yrs. (to present); [oth. writ.] I have many poems published in 2 books, not including Whispers at Dusk.; [pers.] I am in Walnut Valley Youth Choir/Winfield community Orchestra/Winfield Youth Soccer/Softball/D.A.R.E./Bethal A.M.E./Age 11/ hobbies: Roller skating, jogging, bike riding/Martin Luther King Task Force for 3 years; [a.] Winfield, KS

BROOKS, MARY
[pen.] Mary Pomarico; [b.] February 10, 1968, Norlen; [p.] Jay and Percy Brooks; [m.] Michael Pomarico, September 17, 1994; [ch.] Angelina and Michael Jr; [ed.] New York University - Tisch School of the Arts, Borough of Manhatan Community College; [occ.] Adolescent Initiative Counselor at Caribbean Women's Health Assoc. Inc; [hon.] Railroad My Heart - Honorable Dean's list and Dean's Scholarship, Tisch School of the Arts Scholarship; [oth. writ.] Various newspaper and magazine articles published on, entertaiment and Health issues. Editor of Hydro Magazine - Vybe Poems, Screen plays, Plays, Lyricists Entertainment Section Student Film - Great Escape and three guy's chillin'.; [pers.] I strive to reflect all that is good. To relay that into and alfow others to look into their souls and view my world as honestly and metaphorically as my creativity allows.; [a.] Brooklyn, NY

BROWN, BOBBY
[pen.] Stanton Allen; [b.] May 30, 1974, California; [p.]

Carlton T. Brown, Yasuko Brown; [ed.] Sky View High, Utah College of Massage Therapy, Sports Massage; [occ.] Olive Garden Rest, SLC, UT, Massage Clinic at UCMT; [memb.] Sport Massage, Bike Club, Health Club Member, Hydromassage; [hon.] Track and Field; [oth. writ.] Mirrors of Your Soul, She Was a Phantom of Delight, Pendant, The Night as I sense it, Void, Love's Secret; [pers.] I write poems, because I feel relax and claim. I sit by the river and start writing. I love to give a message, I feel relax and stress free.; [a.] West Bountiful, UT

BROWN, DANTE ORLANDO
[pen.] Hyper Weller Green; [oth. writ.] Mixed Man: Self of a Buppie (a book a poetry about one Black Urban Professional man).; [a.] Junction City, KS

BROWN, ELLY SPARKS
[b.] June 14, 1950, Pittsburgh, PA; [p.] Clifford and Arlene Sparks; [m.] Hugh E. Brown III, October 6, 1990; [ed.] B.A. Seton Hill College, Greensburg Pa, M.A. Catholic University, Wash. D.C., M. Div. Virginia Seminary, Alexandra, Virginia, D. Min. Wesley Seminary, Wash. D.C.; [occ.] Ordained Episcopal priest and Administrative Director for the Center for the Art's and Religion at Wesley Seminary; [memb.] Sacred Dance Guild Christians in the Visual Arts (CIVA) Cultural Alliance of Greater Washington; [pers.] Poetry has always been an integral part of my life. It is a source of truth and inspiration. Poetry causes us to "catch our breath" and to behold our souls and the world with new eyes.; [a.] Woodbridge, VA

BROWN, ERIC R.
[b.] September 5, 1980, Syracuse, NY; [p.] Kenneth J. Brown, Kim M. Hanscel; [ed.] Paul V. Moore High School Central Square NY; [occ.] Student; [oth. writ.] (Unpublished), wonder, W.A.R. alone.; [pers.] Teach people correct principles and they will govern themselves.; [a.] Brewerton, NY

BROWN, HELEN M.
[pen.] Helen Gregory Brown, Helen M. Gregory; [b.] February 10, 1920, Owensville, IN; [p.] Leo Gregory, Mabel Johnson Gregory; [ch.] Virginia Ward, James Brown, John Brown; [ed.] Kent State University graduate work at the Citadel; [occ.] Retired Teacher taught Music or English 27 years; [memb.] Harbor View Presbyterian Church, Charleston Preservation Society; [hon.] Delta Kappa Gamma; [oth. writ.] Poems, essays, autobiographical accounts.; [pers.] The subjects for my poems are time, place, family and meaning of life.; [a.] Charleston, SC

BROWN, JEAN
[pen.] Ros Milasha; [b.] August 13, 1935, Key West, FL; [p.] Carol Tynes, Annie Tynes; [ch.] Marcie, Erick, Burkman; [ed.] Douglas High, Postal Service East and West Coast Academy, Southwest College; [occ.] Retired - Vice Principal of Church of Holy Communion Child Care Center; [memb.] Order of the Eastern Star (PHRED) Ing. Family Comm. Develop Asso. Ing. Neighbor Housing Committee Board, Ing. Redevelopment Board, Egyptian Temple #5 daughters of Isis; [hon.] 1994 Inglewood Woman of the year. Woman of the year 1995 key West Islanders Association. 1993 Grand Vice Chairman, Trustee Board, Order of the Eastern Star Honors.; [oth. writ.] Several other poems that have not been published. Class play birthday cards - pomes not published.; [pers.] I hope to make a small difference for anyone who have a desire to write poetry but feel they are not good enough. I'd say "go for it".; [a.] Inglewood, CA

BROWN, LIANE
[b.] 1946, Germany; [p.] Meta Klein, Wilhelm Klein; [m.] Edward D. Brown, 1964; [ed.] Basics in Germany. Continued Education Rework related. Mostly self educated.; [occ.] Clinical Associate at a local Health Care Institute; [oth. writ.] January 1995, one poem published in our Health Care Communicator and same was published in March 1995 in the Journal of Nurse Assistants; [pers.] I would like to open the minds and hearts of my readers into a realization of deeper sense of beings. My greatest aspiration would be, to devote all my time to writing poetry and short stories if I become financially able to do so.; [a.] Colorado Springs, CO

BROWN, NEVILLE C.
[b.] May 29, 1968, Kingston, Jamaica, West Indies; [p.] Neville Brown Sr., Alicia Brown; [m.] Rita Jackson; [ch.] Allison Brown, Kimberly Brown, Lindslay Jackson; [ed.] Portchester High School, Portchester, NY; [occ.] HVAC Technician; [memb.] Pentecostal Church; [oth. writ.] Several poems need to publish; [pers.] Think good and good will follow you.; [a.] Laurel, MD

BROWN, SHANEQUA
[pen.] Nee-Nee; [b.] June 15, 1982, Brooklyn; [p.] Debra Johnson; [ed.] I.S. 390 Junior High 167, Public School; [occ.] Student; [hon.] Best Academic Award, Best Attendance, Spelling B Contest; [oth. writ.] Songs; [a.] Brooklyn, NY

BROWN, SYLVIA
[b.] March 5, 1968, Kansas City, MO; [p.] Marie Brown; [ed.] Lincoln Academy and Avila College; [occ.] Co-Owner The Queen Cuisine Catering Company; [memb.] Parents as Teachers Organization Coalition for positive family Relationships; [hon.] Quill and Scroll NAACP - Act so Award - poetry writing; [oth. writ.] We Are Black And Once Were Proud, The Wastelands, A Fantasy; [pers.] My writing reflect the injustices and in equality in our society. It also offers solutions as to improving there mysteries - I have been influenced by people fighting for and promoting social changes, and equal sights for me people.; [a.] Kansas City, MO

BROWN, TERESA A.
[pen.] Jordan Nicole; [b.] October 11, 1959, Cincinnati, OH; [p.] Jack Brown, Elsie C. Brown; [ed.] Our Lady of Angels H.s., University of Cincinnati College of Nursing and Health; [occ.] Registered Nurse, Univ. of Cincinnati Hospital, Cincinnati, OH; [memb.] Ohio Nurses Association, Black Nurses Association; [hon.] Academic Dean's List; [pers.] I try with my writing to touch the secret part of us that we protect the most, ourselves.; [a.] Cincinnati, OH

BROWN, TIMOTHY THOMAS
[b.] October 20, 1962, Richlands, VA; [p.] Charles T. and Zelma I. Brown; [m.] Div.; [ch.] Kendra Brown; [ed.] Richlands High, Southwest Virginia Community College A.S. Administration of Justice; [occ.] Police/ Animal control; [memb.] Martial Arts Instructor Tae Kwon Do, Shito Ryu; [hon.] Who's Who American's Junior Colleges, Summa Cum Laude; [oth. writ.] Several poems, short stories; [pers.] The only true failures in life are those who are content with mediocrity; [a.] Charlotte, NC

BROWNTON, LAURA LEE
[pen.] Anna Bloom; [b.] August 22, 1948, Omak, WA; [p.] Franklin and Mary Webster; [m.] Mark F. Brownton, November 30, 1974; [ch.] Elisabeth M. Brownton; [ed.] Brewster High, Fort Wright College; [occ.] Self-em-

ployed Sales; [memb.] American Cancer Society, Devore Comm. Church Worship Team; [pers.] My desire is to express love and appreciation of others through my writing.; [a.] Devore, CA

BRUNER, JERMAINE M.
[b.] August 2, 1973, Bellflower, CA; [p.] Anita Bruner and Jeremiah Bruner; [ed.] Graduated with Honors from Carson High School. Currently attending Cal. State University Dominiguez Hills in Carson, CA.; [occ.] Night Manager for Food 4 Less supermarket in Los Angeles; [hon.] Numerous awards for poems, essays and creative writing. I've won everything imaginable for my writing. This includes cash awards, concert tickets and publication. As Muhammad Ali once said. "It ain't braggin' if you can back it up".; [oth. writ.] Currently working in a book entitled "Beer, Wine, and Groceries".; [pers.] My motto is "Give me two days and I'll think of a million dollar idea for your advertisement or company". My natural talent is being creative's I have great and in mind for Nike, Madd, Suicide-prevention dental hygiene and hair loss to name a few.; [a.] Carson, CA

BRUNNER, MORGAN L.
[b.] September 25, 1983, Bayport, NY; [p.] John and Christine Brunner; [oth. writ.] "Rain", "Homework", "Teacher"; [a.] Bayport, NY

BRUNSINK, TREVOR
[b.] October 29, 1979, Janesville, WI; [p.] Todd Brunsink, Dawn Brunsink; [ed.] 9th-10th grade at Bowling Green High School, current 11th grade - post secondary Options Program at Owens Community College; [occ.] Student; [hon.] Honor Roll, Who's Who Among American High School Students, Modern Woodmen of America Writing contest, Women Club Writing contest; [pers.] God has given me a gift that I enjoy using. I hope to write for television when I'm older, and to make a positive difference in peoples lives through my work.; [a.] Portage, OH

BRYAN, MICHELLE RENEE
[b.] January 6, 1972; [p.] Walter and Dolores Bryan; [hon.] In High School I received an award for a story I did in my Senior Year; [oth. writ.] Many poems and stories at least 10 notebooks full; [pers.] I love to write. It's my soul. How I feel, and what I am is my poetry.; [a.] Fort Wayne, IN

BRYANT, KIM L.
[b.] September 29, 1963, Stanton, CA; [p.] Sharon and Gary McLearn; [ch.] Zack, Daniel, Chaylynn; [oth. writ.] In the near future I hope to put my poems into book form the title of my book will be called In His Hands; [pers.] I was inspired by King David in his writings in Psalms I give all the credit of my writings to the Lord.; [a.] Corona, CA

BUCHANAN, GARY
[b.] July 27, 1956, Weymouth, MA; [p.] Jack Buchanan, Betty Buchanan; [m.] Bonnie Buchanan, November 5, 1988; [ch.] Jessica Marie, Jennifer Lee; [ed.] Millis Jr./ Sr. High School, University of Massachusetts, Springfield Technical Community College; [occ.] Receiving Clerk in Steel Mill; [hon.] Graduated Cum Laude from High School, Honorable Mention Award from Wealth Builders; [oth. writ.] Several unpublished poems and songs at this time; [pers.] I feel blessed that God has give me the ability to express my thoughts and feelings in the form of song and poem.; [a.] Belchertown, MA

BUCQUOY-BROWN, CAROLINE
[b.] May 5, 1964, Paris, France; [p.] Brigitte and Jean Pierre Bucquoy; [m.] Peter Brown, September 14, 1985; [ch.] Andrew James and Julia-Sophie; [ed.] Law degree in French Law; [occ.] Mother; [memb.] Minneapolis Institute of Arts, Minnesota Arboretum; [oth. writ.] I write most often in French my native tongue.; [pers.] Poetry is an initiation rite, a symbolic voyage that recreates the effigy of my inner continent. Revelations are sometimes born out of the darkness, however, words continue to lead me back to the original brightness.; [a.] Deephaven, MN

BUDD, VICKI
[b.] October 16, 1953, Denten, TX; [ed.] Lutheran High North, Park College (BA), Washington University (MSW); [occ.] Psychotherapist, Chemical Depending Counselor; [memb.] MO Society of Clinical Social Workers, National Assoc. of Social Workers, St. Louis Psychoanalytic Institute; [hon.] Dean's List; [oth. writ.] Published Parish Health Newsletter X3 years, several poems in local magazines and newspapers; [pers.] My writing reflects a message of hope which has ever been present in my life, even amid times of despair.; [a.] Saint Louis, MO

BUFORD, JANET
[b.] February 15, 1982, Houston, TX; [p.] John E. Buford and Carol Robin Buford; [hon.] 1994-1995 Student of the Year, 1993-1996 "A" Honor Roll Award; [a.] Rosharon, TX

BUGLIONE, VERA
[b.] February 18, 1948, Bombay, India; [p.] Roshan Nanavati, Rustam Mehta; [m.] Bruce Buglione, September 27, 1980; [ch.] Rahul Hamid, Jyotin Hamid, Ariane Buglione and 2 Step children Andrew Buglione, Jason Buglione; [ed.] B.A. St. Xavier's College, Bombay University, M.A. Med and Ed. D. Teacher's College Columbia University; [occ.] Medical Assistant; [pers.] I'd like to find more time in my daily life for writing. All my life and experiences have centered around a struggle with the meaning of personal and cultural identity. As an adult immigrant, married to an american, the struggle continues, and to write is to create order as well as give it.; [a.] Sparkill, NY

BUNT, MRS. GRACE A.
[b.] March 9, 1921, Berwick, ME; [p.] Theodore and Helen Poelman; [m.] 1st 1945 (Died, 1977), 2nd April 25, 1987; [ch.] Several; [ed.] Public School and G.E.D. at 58 years young; [occ.] "Source of Light" (As missionary); [oth. writ.] I have written both prose and poetry since young children, but am an unknown, but for occasional request of friends to read a poem I wrote. Other poems I have written. Book and Short stories, Couple Book, But not published.; [pers.] I mostly write spiritual poems to encourage people and help them think of eternity.; [a.] Madison, GA

BURFIELD, EMILY
[pen.] Emily Burfeind; [b.] June 2, 1981, Chester; [p.] Martin Burfeind and Kimberly Bohne; [ed.] Enrolled in High School for 10th Grade; [occ.] High School Student; [memb.] Honor Roll, 3.5 or better 4-H, High School Band, California High School Rodeo Association, American Quater Horse Association; [hon.] Raised Grand Champ. Beef at my county fair in 1995, ran poles at the Jr. Cow Palace and at the Cal. State finals rodeo, Rodeo Queens for hometown rodeo; [pers.] I enjoy living in the country. My family is very important to me, without them and their support, I would not have the confidence to continue my many endeavors. I enjoy people and love traveling.; [a.] Taylorsville, CA

BURKE, CHARLOTTE
[b.] January 25, 1924, Astoria, NY; [p.] Charlotte and Thomas Winkel; [m.] Jerome, June 28, 1947; [ch.] Six, John, Robert, Paul, Michael, Thomas, Rosemary; [ed.] Bryant High School; [occ.] Retired; [memb.] Herricks Community Theater, Notre Dame Choir; [hon.] Goodwife Award New York University; [oth. writ.] Poems published in "The Transcript" Susquehanna PA, poetic voices of America spring 1996.; [pers.] My poems are inspired by scenery, childhood memories, and daily happenings.; [a.] New Hyde Park, NY

BURKE, SUZANNE
[b.] October 20, 1961, Allentown, PA; [ed.] BS in Business Admin W/A Major in Accounting from Widener Univ. in Wilmington, DE; [occ.] Accounting Manager; [memb.] Int'l sports and ranquettball Assoc. and Int'l Physical Fitness Assoc; [hon.] Swimming, horseback riding and piano; [oth. writ.] Other poems which have never been published; [pers.] I would like to see my writings set to music by a well known musician.; [a.] Arlington, TX

BURLESON, ANGIE RINEHART
[b.] August 27, 1970, Albemarle, NC; [p.] Mr. Cecil Rinehart and Mrs. Maggie Rinehart; [m.] Tony Burleson, September 12, 1992; [ed.] North Stanly High School Stanly Community College; [occ.] Industrial Engineering Technician; [memb.] Centerview Baptist Church Safety Activities Task Group - Collins Aikman (Albernarie plant); [hon.] Honor's List at Stanly Community College, Honor graduate from North Stanly, High School; [oth. writ.] Several poems published in high school literary magazine and newspaper. Many poems used in church bulletins.; [pers.] God has given me a talent in which to enrich the lives of others through written verse. Writing is self-expression, as well as a soul cleansing experience.; [a.] Albemarle, NC

BURNS, BARBARA L.
[b.] June 25, 1957, Stoneham, MA; [p.] Lorraine E. Burns; [ch.] Samuel David Lewis; [ed.] Melrose High School, Bunker Hill Community College, Peter Bent Brigham School of Nursing Somerville Hospital, School of Nursing; [occ.] Registered Nurse, Boston Medical Center, Boston, MA; [memb.] Mass Nurses Association; [hon.] 1983 Sarah Taylor Hayes Award, 1984 Rose B. Karlson Memorial Scholarship, Peter Bent Brigham School of Nursing Boston, MA; [oth. writ.] "In A Child's Heart" first publication; [pers.] "My poetry reflects a lifetime of experience with a tirade of emotion."; [a.] Melrose, MA

BURROUGHS, SONJA FELKER
[b.] August 15, 1949, Plant City, FL; [p.] Neil Braddy Lafever, James Ray Felker; [ch.] Byron Christopher, Robert Eric, Kevin James; [ed.] Plant City Senior High School, Manatee Community College, Eckerd College; [occ.] Full-time Student at Eckerd College - Major: Creative Writing and Literature; [oth. writ.] Several poems published in college publications, poems and other articles in local newspaper.; [pers.] My writings are reflective of life experiences real and imagined, I strive to maintain the essence of humanity and the richness and innate beauty found only in our unique individualities.; [a.] Bradenton, FL

BURTON, JANET MARIE
[pen.] Jan Philips; [b.] April 12, 1948, Allentown, PA; [m.] Howard Burton, October 9, 1982; [ch.] Michael, Steven, Don Allan, and Maria; [ed.] Oley Valley Area High School Diploma for Interior Decorating; [occ.]

Homemaker, Aspiring writer; [memb.] International Society of Poets - Del Norte Chamber of Commerence; [oth. writ.] Several unpublished poems and a few published; [pers.] There is so much more to life than materialism, if only we would stop for a moment to recognize and appreciate it.; [a.] Del Norte, CO

BUSSEY, JEANNETTE
[pen.] "JB" and "Bubbs"; [b.] November 15, 1937, Anniston, AL; [p.] Deceased; [m.] Deceased; [ch.] Michael A. Bussey and Deborah Bussey; [ed.] Graduate Student - Seminarian I plan to start matriculating my M.A. at a Theological Seminary in September, 1996 (Graduated from High School - Cobb Ave. High Anniston, Alabama - 1954); [occ.] Legal Technician United States Government-20th year of service; [memb.] Women's City Club of Cleveland, Ohio, Elected Employee Representative for Local 2089 Usher Board-Antioch Baptist Church, Missionary Society and Christian Board of Education, Church Members at: Antioch Baptist Church; [hon.] Dean's List - Dyke College and Honors List Dyke College - Cleveland, Ohio; [oth. writ.] I am currently writing the first draft for my first book regarding my personal life's successes as well as challenges.; [pers.] I believe that I have a personal responsibility to myself to strive for the highest ideals of my American Citizenship. I also believe that I owe it to myself to be all that I can be and, not one iota less. I also firmly believe that a Divine interception indeed, dictates my own destiny.; [a.] Cleveland, OH

BUTLER, KEVIN
[b.] December 2, 1959, Baltimore, MD; [p.] Chester Howard, Doris D. Howard; [m.] Belinda J. Butler, June 22, 1991; [ed.] Edmondson High/Big Bend Washington High; [occ.] Motorola, Austin Texas; [oth. writ.] Several poems awaiting to be enjoy. (The Tears of a Child, A Touch of an Angel, and etc...); [pers.] I just want the whole world to know, that to feel life and to be life, is the greatest happiness of living life.; [a.] Austin, TX

BUTLER JR., ROGER J.
[b.] March 8, 1981, Sylacauga, AL; [p.] Ruby and Roger Butler; [ed.] Currently 15 years old student at Coosa Central; [occ.] Student; [memb.] Beta Club; [pers.] I owe this writing to my inspiration Daisha Vick.; [a.] Sylacauga, AL

BYRD, RAYMOND GAIL
[b.] December 18, 1901, Bellefontaine, OH; [p.] John A., Clara A. Byrd; [m.] Mildred Faye Byrd, 1934; [ch.] Two boys, six girls; [ed.] One year high school, 54 years working on the Railroad (1917-1971, present age 94; [occ.] Retired; [memb.] Calvary Baptist Church; [hon.] Moody Baptist College thru the bible correspondence course; [oth. writ.] Prose, Satans Realm, Holocaust, A Boiling Pot, Computer, Wisdom Prophecy, Revealed No one, Prophecy Revealed No Two, Fool Has Said, (not finished); [pers.] Family name traced back to England (Byrd) by my daughter, Dr. Janis Byrd Sun Prairie Wisc.; [a.] Bellefontaine, OH

CACAN, ALMA
[b.] April 18, 1983, Sarajevo; [ed.] Middle School Student (7th grade); [occ.] Student at Lane Middle School; [hon.] I have been on the Honor Roll since first grade. I lived and went to school in Europe for one year when I was 7. I have been on my school's ciphering team twice.; [pers.] I usually get my writing inspirations when I can get some time for myself and clear my thoughts. I'd rather think of myself on artist than just a plain writer. I think of myself an artist who can paint a beautiful picture by choosing the right words.; [a.] Fort Wayne, IN

CAHILL, CABRINI
[b.] March 28, 1928, Ballacolla, Ireland; [p.] Patrick and Ann Cahill; [ed.] Incarnate Word University, (BA) English 1960, Our Lady of the Lake University, Adm. Courses, 1962, Teacher Certification, 1971, University College, Dublin, Ireland, 1950-53, Texas Exam for Admins. and Teachers given by the Texas Education Agency, Career Summary: Saint Paul School, San Antonio, 2nd 4th, 6th, 8th Teacher, from 1953-65: St. Luke School Principal and 8th Teacher 1966-71, Saint Thomas School, Beloit, Wis. from 1971-73, Saint Paul School, 7th, 8th 1973-74, Maynooth Theological College student 1974-95, 195-80, St Luke School 7th, 8th Teacher. 1980-84, Our Lady of Assumption School, Beloit, Wis., 1984-94, Saint Paul School, San Antonio, Teacher 7th and 8th; [occ.] Substituting in Schools in the Archdiocese of San Antonio, and one Public School, Gardendale in the Edgewood District.; [hon.] In 1993, Teaching Excellence Award From Incarnate Word University with Scholarship, Nominated by former students..Edward Esparza, Debora Huth in 1993, and 1993, and 1996 respectively for Who's Who Among America's Teachers; [pers.] I base my philosophy on that of Don Bosco who left us the "Preventative System". Among the requisites to be possessed by a successful educator is an awareness of the problems confronting mankind, because Education does not take place in a vacuum. I believe in the necessity of kindness in the training of the young. Mutual understanding is the secret of success in any educational endeavor. In short, educators need to be models of... reason, religion, Kindness: Go beyond the written words, and see the beauty and talent in each individual soul, who comes into your care. The 3R's have no meaning without the presence of the fourth...Religion Teach with compassion and conviction... be fair and firm.; [a.] San Antonio, TX

CALDARONE, JOSEPH SALVATORE
[b.] September 18, 1976; [p.] Nella Gina and Giorgio Caldarone; [ed.] UNC - Chapel Hill, Cornell University; [occ.] Student; [memb.] USTA National Italian American Found; [hon.] National Honor Society National Foreign Language Honor Society all state Tennis various Vocal Soloist Awards; [pers.] My Italian - American Heritage has guided me in all aspects of my life and through my writings it manifests itself.

CALDWELL, BILLY
[b.] November 19, 1960, Oklahoma City, OK; [p.] Billy Wayne and Sybil Lee Caldwell; [ch.] Billy Wayne and Austin Lee; [ed.] High School Diploma Trades School; [occ.] HVAC Technition R and K Heating and Coding, Muskegon, MI; [hon.] Heroic Action Award in Elkhart Indiana; [pers.] Having traveled most of the United States, within each and every person I have come in contract with, I have found the same desire. The desire to know Jesus, one on one and personally.; [a.] Muskegon, MI

CALO, DIANA M.
[b.] June 14, 1978, Rahway, NJ; [p.] Fern and Gaetano Calo; [ed.] Arthur L. Johnson High School - Clark, NJ, Kean College - Union, NJ; [occ.] Full time student; [pers.] Everyone that lives dies but not everyone who died ever lived. I feel this statement truly speaks for itself.; [a.] Clark, NJ

CALVILLO, BROOKE
[pen.] Brooke Calvillo; [b.] April 17, 1981, San Antonio; [p.] Elizabeth and Arnie Calvillo; [ed.] High School Student at Lutheran High School San Antonio, Texas. I am a Sophomore; [memb.] In the 9th grade I was a member of student council and yearbook.; [oth. writ.] "Ocean Blue", "Friends", "Believe In Me"; [pers.] I write very spontaneously. I write only when I have a strong feeling. I write about many things depending on my feeling. My father, who passed away June 1996, has encouraged my latest writing, it is called "My Father".; [a.] San Antonio, TX

CAMARGO, CLAIR MARIE
[b.] June 18, 1981, Pasadena; [p.] Darana C. Olpez and Raul A. Camargo; [ed.] High School Sophomore; [occ.] Student; [oth. writ.] Personal writings never published; [pers.] Open your mind, body and soul, to a world you don't know. Feel the words, feel the life that slowly begin to flow.; [a.] Irvine, CA

CAMARGO, OLLIE MARIE
[b.] April 8, 1938, Tulsa, OK; [p.] Mr. and Mrs. Ollie Martin Brewer; [m.] Orlando E. Camargo; [ch.] 3 Girls, 2 Grandchildren; [ed.] Studied Art for 10 years after High School; [occ.] Homemaker; [memb.] Honers and Awards do not make a person. It is the other way around.; [oth. writ.] Short Stories; [pers.] I think we live in a "Me" Society. Poems and short stories help jog one's emotions for what is right. A prophet once said "The heart is more treacherous than anything else and desperate. Who can know it? "Your emotions express what is in your heart.; [a.] Dallas, TX

CAMERON, ELIZABETH VICTORIA
[b.] August 7, 1955, Scotland; [p.] Alan B. Cameron and Elizabeth Wark; [ch.] James and Stuart McLeish; [ed.] College; [occ.] Paralegal for Popelka, Allard, McCowan and Bondonno; [memb.] Clan Cameron of Pacific N.W., Presb. Church USA; [oth. writ.] None published. Working on writing a book of poems.; [pers.] "To make a difference by sharing my gifts", Emigrated from Scotland in 1983. Became a U.S. Citizen in 1992.; [a.] San Jose, CA

CAMPITIELLO, TONI A.
[b.] August 15, 1978, Long Island, NY; [p.] James and Susan Campitiello; [ed.] Sachem North High School, currently enrolled in Suny Plattsburgh College; [occ.] Student; [memb.] National Honor Society Foreign Language Honor Society Member of the Library of Congress and the museum of Natural History; [hon.] Music Department Award, Community Service Awards, various Academic Awards; [oth. writ.] Unpublished poems and stories that have never been submitted; [pers.] I never thought I could be a poet but here I am. I want to thank everyone who has helped me over the years.; [a.] Holtsville, NY

CANADA, BEVERLY J.
[pen.] Joan, B.J.; [b.] March 29, 1954, La Grange, GA; [p.] Billie and Charles J. Copeland; [m.] Divorced; [ch.] Carla Nicole "Niki" Copeland; [ed.] Forest Park Sr. High La Grange Sr. High; [occ.] Data Entry, GA State Patrol, Atl, GA and Sales - Walmarts Morrow; [oth. writ.] Nothing published; [pers.] My poems and writing have been written more out of hobby. I write what I feel in my heart and experiences I have enjoyed my greatest dream is to be able to write more and to share my words.; [a.] Morrow, GA

CANILLAS, ANNA MARIA
[b.] November 3, 1947, Benevento, Italy; [p.] Carmine and Louisa Cavuoto; [m.] James Russell Canillas, June 15, 1974; [ch.] Anthony, Francis Carmine; [ed.] Everett High Mass Bay State Junior College of Business; [occ.] Avon Lady; [memb.] Soloist and Mezzo Soprano at Immaculate Conception Church Choir, plays piano and

casio organ member of the Catholic daughters of America, St. Anthony's Prayer Group B.A. in Legal Secretarial; [oth. writ.] Several poems published in local town newspaper; [pers.] I try to capture the feeling and emotion in my poetry as I do in my singing and playing. The soul's expression is important in all art forms.; [a.] Everett, MA

CANNON, BONNIE
[b.] October 29, 1937, Fredonia, TX; [p.] Frankie Green and Della Byrd; [m.] William Cannon (Deceased), September 14, 1952; [ch.] Gail, Diana Lynne, Karen Kathleen, James Ray Steven Wayne, Lauryl Elayne, Glenn Alan, Larissa Lynette, Tonya Rynee; [ed.] A.V. College Cal Poly Ponona; [occ.] Writer - poet (Amateur); [hon.] Alpha Gamma Sigma, Dean's List, Academic Scholarship; [oth. writ.] Poems, essays, novelist; [pers.] Pain is the wrapping paper of life - inside the box of life is the gift - what I do with these defines me.; [a.] Venice, CA

CAPE, SHANNON
[b.] July 19, 1971, Clinton, SC; [p.] Terry Cape, Paulette Cape; [ch.] TinkerBelle, Rosco, Garfield, Tyler, Cagney, Taylor, Boots, Hank; [ed.] Clinton High School, Newberry County Career Center; [occ.] Own Licensed Practical Nurse; [oth. writ.] Poem published in local newspaper; [pers.] Thanks to my best friend, Lisa, for encouraging me to send in a poem... may your "flame" stays strong.; [a.] Clinton, SC

CAPELLE, BECKY
[b.] October 29, 1979, Oshkosh, WI; [p.] Joe and Nancy Capelle

CAPPS, JOANNA
[b.] April 10, 1978, Roanoke, VA; [p.] William and Sharon Capps; [ed.] Cave Spring H.S.; [memb.] Amnesty International, N.O.W.; [pers.] All of life is sensual and poetic. Strive to find passion in your everyday.

CARAZA, HUMBERTO DANIEL
[pen.] Danny Caraza; [b.] December 6, 1953, Mexico; [p.] Ernesto Rene and Esther; [m.] Divorced; [ch.] Carlos Daniel and Angela Marie; [ed.] Very close to obtaining an A.A. Degree in Liberal Arts; [occ.] Aerospace Machinist; [hon.] Dean's List and also for exemplary scholarship; [oth. writ.] I have written several short stories about life, death, divorce and all the emotions that I have felt and seen in my short existence. Not published yet.; [pers.] I write, just because - if someone should read my work - then choose a new and brighter path, it will be worth the effort, even though I may never know the outcome.; [a.] Rancho Cucamonga, CA

CAREY, DIANNE VAUGHAN
[b.] August 5, 1946, Washington, DC; [p.] Bernard and Lucy Vaughan; [ch.] Barton Dallas, Christine Dianne, Janice Monique; [ed.] A.A., Catonsville Community College, B.S., Johns Hopkins University; [occ.] Development Coordinator, Corporate and Foundation, Relations, Johns Hopkins University, Balto, MD; [memb.] American Prospect Research Association (APRA) Volunteer: Hampden Family Center; [hon.] Dean's List, graduated with Honors.; [oth. writ.] Occasional articles/essays for local and school newspapers.; [pers.] Being is thoughtless beyond and beneath all categories of thought. Expression is the realization of creative thought. Being is still. Expression, moving. (Laurence Boldt, Zen and the Art of Making a living.); [a.] Baltimore, MD

CARFI, JACQUELINE M.
[b.] August 6, 1964, Sewickley, PA; [p.] Donald and Patricia Martin; [m.] Marc S. Carfi, August 5, 1995; [ch.] David Harvey Gibson; [ed.] Moon High, Parkway West Technical School, Bradford School of Business, Courses at Robert Morris College; [occ.] Accounting Manager/Systems Administrator; [oth. writ.] Many poems written for wedding and anniversary programs, newsletters, and church bulletins.; [pers.] I have been greatly influenced by poets Alfred Tennyson and Lydia Baxter, by my relationships with my family and friends and the special love we share has been the true inspiration for my writing.; [a.] Peekskill, NY

CARLONI, IRENE
[b.] August 7, 1930, Cleveland, OH; [p.] Florian Zavasky, Gizella Zavasky; [m.] August G. Carloni, July 29, 1950; [ch.] Laura, Diana Nourse, Michael; [ed.] John Hay High Cleve, O California Coast Univ. Calif, MBA; [occ.] Retired; [memb.] Christian Writers Fellowship, Christian Leaders, Authors and Speakers Services; [hon.] United Way Leadership Award, South bay Producers Guild Video Programming Excellence - South bay Fellowship Church, Women's Committee; [oth. writ.] Articles in Local Newspapers, Devotionals in Daily Hope, Proverbs for Busy Women, Scripts for Video Promotionals, "Quinquennial Moments" for 500 year Anniversary of Columbus, Edited told books.; [pers.] I want my writing to reflect GOd's goodness in our lives, to encourage and uplift readers.; [a.] Manhattan Beach, CA

CARLSON, STEVEN
[b.] June 6, 1967, Queens Village, NY; [p.] Elmer Carlson and Anne Carlson; [m.] Tonya Carlson, February 6, 1993; [ed.] Merritt Island High School, B.A. English - University of South Florida; [occ.] Technical Writer, Cape Canaveral Marine Services; [a.] Merritt Island, FL

CARNICLE, ANN
[b.] July 6, 1967, Cleveland, OH; [p.] Judy Watson, Arlen Watson; [m.] Greg Carnicle, March 10, 1990; [ch.] Cecilia Ann, Rachel Elizabeth, Veronica Therese, John Thomas; [ed.] Moon Valley High, Glendale Community College, National Education Center; [occ.] Part time medical assistant and wife and mother; [memb.] St. Jerome's Catholic Church; [pers.] I believe love must come first, followed by compassion, empathy, and a hunger to do God's will.; [a.] Peoria, AZ

CAROTHERS, LINDA
[pen.] Molly Bean; [b.] February 6, 1980; [p.] Marlana and Bob; [ed.] High School; [oth. writ.] A poem called Marasmus is going to be published in a book called Beginnings by Iliad Press; [pers.] Writing is suppose to be a personal expression, beliefs and opinions. Censorship will ruin it. Survival lays in poetry and music. I have been inspired by musicians such as Kurt Cobain, Courtney Love and Phillip Anselmo.; [a.] Sterling, VA

CARR, JESSI
[b.] July 28, 1982, Royal Oak, MI; [p.] Christopher E. and Joyce A. Carr; [ed.] Jessi is entering the 9th grade at Lasher High School; [occ.] Student; [memb.] Michigan Metro Girl Scouts; [oth. writ.] None at this time, but give me a little time; [pers.] Thank you Paula Beltowski for making me write poems!; [a.] Bloomfield Hills, MI

CARRIER, BRENDA
[b.] November 2, 1961, Fort Peck, MT; [p.] William Carrier, Lovella Bearcub; [ch.] Angela Marie, Nicole Michelle, Carl Cody, Jeremy Brett; [ed.] GED, State of WV Glenville State College; [occ.] Certified Nurses Assistant Richwood WV; [memb.] FAS Network First Baptist Jr BYF Class, Certified FAS Trainer; [pers.] I try hard to put in words about something I feel strongly about, and hope it will change one's way of thinking.; [a.] Richwood, WV

CARRILLO, SUE
[pen.] Sue Carrillo; [b.] October 4, 1962, Zanesville, OH; [p.] Judy E. Payne and Ronald D. Payne; [m.] Rene Carrillo, September 8, 1989; [ch.] Michael (14), Charlote (12), Charles (8); [ed.] Exeter Union High School - Exeter Calif., Herbert Hawkins Realestate - Chino, Calif., Golden State Business College, Visalia, CA; [occ.] Cross Country - Truck Driver (18-wheeler) Global - Mon-Van Trucking - Duarte, CA; [oth. writ.] Sunshine, The Rain, Tomorrow, Shadows, My Man; [a.] Chino, CA

CARRINGTON, LAVERNE
[pen.] Laverne Peterson; [b.] June 11, 1948, Council, NC; [p.] Acie and Idell Peterson; [m.] Divorced, August 17, 1972; [ch.] Kendra M., James Christopher; [ed.] Booker T. Wash, North Carolina Central Univ.; [occ.] Telephone Optr.

CARTHY, LEROY
[pen.] Ibatone Saint Bogle; [b.] February 26, 1959, Kingston, Jamaica; [p.] Hilda Bramuell, M. Carthy; [ch.] Hannica and Samantha; [ed.] Kingston Secondary High, Mico College; [occ.] Chef and Restaurant Attendant, Bklyn, NY; [hon.] Honorable Mention 1993 Illiad Literary Award, President's Award for Literary Excellence, The National Authors Registry 1994; [oth. writ.] Several poems published in local newspapers into Jamaica articles for the Bi-Weekly Sparkle and Arts and Youth Sight.; [pers.] You cannot achieve cooperation without a collection and creative mind. Love is tenable, graft the whole and you know, no partiality.; [a.] Brooklyn, NY

CARUSO, SHERRI LEE
[b.] January 20, 1975, Wayne, NJ; [p.] Sandra Caruso, The Late Lawrence Caruso; [ch.] Thomas James Doherty; [ed.] Elmwood Park Memorial, High School, Bergen Community College; [occ.] Homemaker and Telemarketer; [hon.] National Honor Society; [oth. writ.] "A Friend Like You" published in Spirit Of The Age; [pers.] "There's no bond more Special than the one between a mother and her child." All my love to my Mom. Thank you for all your time, love, understanding, and always being there for me. To Bill: Thank you for helping to make this my second poem publication. I love you both.; [a.] Elmwood Park, NJ

CARVER III, KENNETH
[b.] December 25, 1965, Los Angeles, CA; [p.] Kenneth, Barbara; [ed.] Granite Hills High School; [occ.] American Builders and Contractors Supply Company; [oth. writ.] I am a virtual unknown and as of this publication have only two poems credited to my name; [pers.] This poem was born of my heart and is sent to yours. Forgive me.; [a.] Martinez, CA

CARVILLE, JANET READ
[b.] August 28, 1938, Avon, CT; [p.] Walter Booth Read, Freda Prince, Woodford Read; [m.] Donald Robert Carville, November 24, 1978; [ch.] Patricia Ingalls, Kathryn White; [ed.] Canton (CT) High School Katharine Gibbs Secretarial School; [occ.] Vice President and Secretary of "The Pickin' Patch"; [memb.] Avon Congregational Church: Choir (50 years!) and Music Committee; [pers.] I am thankful for the strong faith of my parents and forebears, and for the heritage in my blood.; [a.] Avon, CT

CASH, SUE
[b.] Amarillo, TX; [oth. writ.] This is my first attempt to have any of my poems published. I have numerous I have written for my own pleasure.; [pers.] My grandfather loved poetry, he and my grandmother raised me. If I have any talent I owe it to my grandfather, Charles Butler, now deceased.; [a.] Channing, TX

CASSIDY, LISA
[b.] February 23, 1969, Ilion, NY; [p.] Mr. and Mrs. Robert Cassidy; [ed.] A.A.S. - Travel and Tourism Herkimer County Comm. Coll.; [occ.] Sales Office Manager Radisson Hotel - Utica Centre; [a.] Utica, NY

CAVIANO, SYLVIA
[pen.] Syl...; [b.] September 14, 1962, New York City; [p.] Jose and Luz Paniagua; [m.] Paul J. Caviano, September 4, 1982; [ch.] Brian and Alex Caviano; [ed.] Jane Addams Voc. H.S. and Lehman College; [pers.] Unseen scars are the most detrimental to the child whose cries go unhead. Protect our children today, they are our Future.; [a.] Woodside, NY

CAZIER, ANDREW L.
[pen.] Andrew Caz; [b.] December 30, 1961, Casper, WY; [p.] Don and Nylia Cazier; [m.] Divorced; [ch.] Dustin - 13 and Jordan - 10; [ed.] B.S. in Education at Black Hills State University; [occ.] English Teacher and Wrestling Coach; [memb.] U.S.A. Wrestling, PTA, First Christian Church; [hon.] One previously published poem.; [oth. writ.] Various short stories and poems. Untried.; [pers.] In all of life, one in doomed to repeat the actions of others, or he can create and build the legacy of his life. However, the choice is ultimately his own to make.; [a.] Casper, WY

CHAMBER, JANETTE
[m.] Randy Chambers; [ch.] Three sons; [ed.] Graduate of Katherine Gibbs Secretarial School Montclair, NJ (1979); [hon.] The greatest honor I have received is the honor of being called to motherhood. I have been entrusted to raise 3 boys. It is indeed my greatest honor to be their mother.; [pers.] I am an artist who instead of a paintbrush uses her pen to draw a picture of what I want others to see through the unveiling of words.

CHAMBLISS, JUANITA UNDERWOOD
[pen.] Nita; [b.] June 28, 1953, Memphis, TN; [p.] Edward and Lula Underwood; [m.] A. C. Chambliss, September 9, 1978; [ch.] Jennifer U. Chambliss; [ed.] Completed High School and 15 Mts Nursing School; [occ.] Nurse; [oth. writ.] I have several poems and reading unpublished yet to come.; [pers.] I hold God the author of my words because he gave them to me. If you put him first He will direct you.; [a.] Jackson, MN

CHANCE, MELINDA W.
[b.] November 21, 1950, Columbia, MS; [p.] Stephen Williamson, Vannie Williamson; [m.] Burney D. Chance, July 3, 1970; [ch.] Alice Wood and Jared Chance; [ed.] Bunker Hill High School and Pearl River Jr. College; [occ.] Business Office Secretary, Columbia Cable Manufacturing Co.; [oth. writ.] A tapestry of thoughts June, '96 Best poems of the 90's 1996; [pers.] I am a sentimental person. I value love and happiness more than material possessions. I have been influenced by, Helen Stiener Rice.; [a.] Columbia, MS

CHANDLER, CHERYL LAREA
[b.] March 15, 1972, Lafayette, IN; [p.] Valerie Chandler; [ed.] Lawrence North High School, Indiana State University, Ivy Tech State College; [occ.] Preschool Teacher, Dena's Child Care Center Indianapolis, IN, Student; [memb.] Sigma Gamma Rho, Sorority, Inc.; [hon.] Minority Teacher Scholarship; [pers.] I wrote this poem in the image of my mother, Valerie Chandler. My mother raised two children on her own. Thank you mommy, I appreciate and love you for everything you have done for me.; [a.] Indianapolis, IN

CHANDLER, EGBERT HOLDEN
[pen.] Joseph; [b.] May 25, 1957, Glen Cove, NY; [p.] Egbert H. Chandler and Lois E. Chandler; [ed.] Syosset High School, Syosset NY - U.S.C.G. Coast Guard; [occ.] Carpenter Union - Supervisor Market America; [memb.] Save the Children; [hon.] All County Baseball Syosset High; [oth. writ.] The book "Save Us."; [pers.] A voice in the night that said "Man, Women, Child." They will come. Inspired me to write the poem "Save Me," and the book "Save Us."; [a.] Blue Point, NY

CHANLEY, LISA LYNETTE
[pen.] Trixy; [b.] February 9, 1973, Anaheim, CA; [p.] Audrey Jean Chanley; [pers.] For love is all I've got, written for Michael Stewart, whom I will always love. Special thanks to: My grandparents Frank and Muriel Morgenweck, Hollie Ann Schneggenburger and Bhagavan Sri Sathya Sia Baba.; [a.] Fountain Valley, CA

CHAPMAN, SABRINA
[b.] July 11, 1980, Hamilton, NJ; [p.] Tom and Barbara Chapman; [ed.] Currently a Junior in High School; [a.] Trenton, NJ

CHAVEZ, BLESILDA
[pen.] Bles; [b.] August 13, 1954, Philippines; [ch.] Eurice, Yrra and Rehina; [ed.] Bachelor of Science in Nursing; [occ.] Mental Health Nurse, and Self-employed Business; [memb.] Filipino Nurses' Association of Florida, Association of Florida Poets, Pan American Society of Artists, St. Patrick Church Choir; [hon.] Graduated Cum Laude (BSN), 1994 Excellence in Clinical Nursing; [oth. writ.] At Dusk in Paradise; [pers.] I always strive to express, in my writing, life's and struggle, pain and triumph but most of all, love.; [a.] North Miami, FL

CHAVEZ, EURICE
[b.] October 1, 1979, Philippines; [p.] Andy Chavez and Bles Chavez; [ed.] H.S. Sophomore; [occ.] Student; [memb.] Drama Club Debate; [hon.] Honor Roll (International Baccalaureate Program - Advanced H.S. Curriculum); [oth. writ.] O My Lover, Voices; [pers.] I write only to express my inner self.; [a.] North Miami, FL

CHAVEZ, RENE
[b.] El Paso, TX; [p.] Rafael T. Chavez, Rosenda Chavez; [ed.] Stephen F. Austin High School, University of Texas at El Paso; [occ.] Writing Tutor; [memb.] Golden Key National Honor Society; [hon.] Dean's List; [oth. writ.] Short stories and poems published in local magazines and internet publications.; [pers.] Everything begins with one thing, the word.; [a.] El Paso, TX

CHEDIAK, ANDRIA
[pen.] Andria Chediak; [b.] January 2, 1983, Roanoke, VA; [p.] Nidia Chediak, Moises Chediak; [ed.] Middle School I am starting 8th grade 1996-1997, school season; [occ.] Student; [oth. writ.] "Dear and Muffled Mind", Thoughts", "Alien Attack", etc. and many more poems that have yet to be published that I am working on and also lyrics for songs.; [pers.] Hate is the ultimate fear of all!; [a.] Bola Raton, FL

CHELETTE, ESTELLA P.
[pen.] Estella Pena; [b.] November 21, 1947, Goliad, TX; [ed.] Innis High, LA., Canal Zone College, Texarkana Community College; [occ.] Teacher (Homeschool) Baton Rouge, LA; [pers.] The bible have been the book that I have read and study the most in life. Romantic books have influenced my way of thinking and I try to combine both in my writing.; [a.] Baton Rouge, LA

CHENG, RON
[pers.] I hope that someday, everyone will see. Driving on the highway of life, honking their horn at the guy who changed lanes without signaling, worrying about missing an exit sign, or making sure to signal when changing lanes, so many people are too busy worrying about the little things and don't stop to look at where they are or where they're going. Too many people only focus on those white, dashed ahead of them, only worrying about keeping in their lane, never stopping to look left or right, up or down. But then there are the people who walk along the grassy sidelines of the Highway, never worrying about being angry with people, missing an exit, or worrying about signaling before changing lanes, stopping every now and then to smell the roses. Stepping off from the Highway, they see it as a whole, where the Highway started and where it ends. They don't worry about those irrelevant issues of signaling when lanes, since they see that the Highway takes us all in the same direction, no matter lane they're in. They see. And I hope that someday, everyone will see.; [a.] NJ

CHOI, LUCY
[pen.] Lucy Choi; [b.] October 16, 1942, Korea; [ed.] Graduated Korea University Bachelor of Arts, Studies of Central Presbyterian, Theology M.D. Course; [occ.] Missionary; [memb.] Korean-American Christian Literature Association; [a.] Los Angeles, CA

CHUNDER, GAUTAM
[pen.] Gautam Chandra Chunder; [b.] August 23, 1956, Calcutta, India; [p.] Pratap Chunder and Leena; [ed.] High School, Left School for Political unrest, studied extensively at home; [occ.] Creative writing, Freelance journalism, Poet; [memb.] Edited Unmeshita (Abengali Yearly), Prajanmh (Abengali Quarterly), Hesperus Review (An English Quarterly); [hon.] Associate Editor Kavita India, special correspondent Indian News Service, Honorary Science Correspondent; [oth. writ.] Published books, Hey Duranta Yatri (poems in 1986). Published numerous books, short stories, in various, dailies, monthly and another year in India.; [pers.] I have been influenced greatly by Walt Whitman, Poet Jaideva and my Mother.; [a.] Cherryhill, NJ

CHURCH, TERESA
[b.] September 26, 1976, Denver; [p.] Ed and Charlene Church; [ed.] Horizon High School, Arapahoe Community College; [occ.] Salon Owner/Entrepreneur; [oth. writ.] Several poems and stories never published; [pers.] Poetry is a way to express your emotions with more then words.; [a.] Denver, CO

CICAIROS, LOIS
[b.] May 6, 1953, Oakland, CA; [p.] William S. Tarski, Betty Tarski; [m.] Albert Cicairos, September 21, 1976; [ch.] Jacob, Justin, Kim, Kelly, Kris, and Alex; [ed.] Pacific High School Calif., San Leandro Beauty College Calif.; [occ.] Housewife; [memb.] Prader-Willi Syndrome Association, Prader-Willi Calif. Foundation; [pers.] My ultimate goal in life is to be able to continue to express my thoughts and feelings through my writings, and to be able to share them, with all.; [a.] Coulterville, CA

CIMINERO, DEBBIE
[pen.] Debbie; [b.] May 18, 1962, Waco, TX; [pers.] Pam's dream was inspired by my mother's wife's dreams about him before they met and get married three months later. I thank God for this talent; [a.] Columbia, SC

CLARK, EILEEN DE STASIO
[b.] September 6, 1953, West Reading, PA; [p.] Joseph De Stasio Sr., and Miriam De Stasio; [m.] Steve M. Clark, July 10, 1977; [ch.] Eileen, Rebekah, Rachel, S. Michael, Jennifer, Sharon, Tara, Stephanie, Apryll, Mikaelah; [ed.] Wyomissing Area High, Brigham Young University; [occ.] Mother, Home Educator Director of Private School; [memb.] Pursuit of Excellence Targeteers Red Cross Instructor, YMCA; [oth. writ.] Short stories, essays, 3 plays story form vocabulary workbooks, a series of children's stories; [pers.] My desire in writing is to coordinate those things people wonder about with the truths that are so necessary to portray, to uplift and enlighten; [a.] Blue Springs, MO

CLARK, JACQUELINE
[pen.] "April Rain"; [b.] April 16, 1945, Philadelphia, PA; [p.] George Sullivan, Mattle "Little Flower"; [m.] Dr. William A. Clark, January 1, 1975; [ch.] William "Tall Oak" Clark; [ed.] Temple University - B.S. Glassboro State College - M.A.; [memb.] Southeastern Cherokee Confederacy of Pennsylvania - Earth Band; [hon.] Several poems published in the "Tsalagi Elohi" Newsletter of the Southeastern Cherokee Confederacy Earth Band; [oth. writ.] I strive to share my Native American Heritage through my poetry. I have been greatly influenced by the traditions and values of my Cherokee ancestors.; [pers.] Bala Cynwyd; [a.] PA

CLARK, JANA
[b.] February 16, 1955, Concordia, KS; [p.] Bill and Lois Clark; [ed.] Delphos Attendance Center, Delphos, KS; Minneapolis High School, Minneapolis, KS; Kansas State University, Manhattan, KS; [pers.] Things change. I can't spend my life looking back. To keep me positive and looking forward, I developed my own personal philosophy on life: I can laugh or I can cry. Crying gives me a headache, so I laugh, preferably at least one good belly laugh each day!; [a.] Mission, KS

CLARK, KATHRYN L.
[b.] March 5, 1965, Southern California; [p.] Mike and Pat Austin; [m.] John Clark, November 27, 1993; [ed.] Currently attending nursing school at Sierra College; [occ.] Sheriff's Dispatcher; [oth. writ.] This is my first published work.; [pers.] I enjoy all types of poetry. I was greatly influenced by early romantic poets as well as Rod McKuen and Merritt Mulloy. I believe that those who love without Boundries, will live forever.; [a.] Nevada City, CA

CLARK, MICHAEL
[pen.] Mike; [b.] December 3, 1949, Indianapolis; [p.] Roland Clark, Josephine Clark; [m.] Divorced; [ch.] Andy, Abby, Johnny Clark; [oth. writ.] Several to family and friends. I hope to have a book ready to publish by the end of the year.; [pers.] This poem was written in memory of my father who passed away in 1993. I know wherever he is there's a warm south wind and bright sunshine. "I love you Pop"; [a.] Danville, IN

CLARKE, RICHARD S.
[b.] August 23, 1934, Louisville, KY; [p.] Jesse and Sarah Elizabeth Clarke; [m.] Constance Jean Koga, September 29, 1956; [ch.] Stewart, Stephen, Susan; [ed.] Cum Laude Grad. Ill. State Normal Univ., B.S., Biology and Sociology (Minors, Psych., Phil., Educ.), Grad

Studies: Ill. Benedictine, De Paul, Univ., of Chicago, N.E. Mo. State Northwestern (Physics, Chemistry, Math, Business Mgmt.); [occ.] President, Alert Security Consultants, Inc.; [memb.] National Fire and Burglany Almn Assoc. St. Margaret Mary Parish-Pastoral Council, Human Concerns Commission, Auxiliary Minister; [hon.] Amer. Legion Award, Nat'l Honor Society Concert Master Violinist, Church Cantor and Singer, I.S.N.U. Scholarship, National Science Foundation Fellowship, Performer: TV, Radio, Gymnastic Circus, Amer. Ballet Theater and Community Plays-Kappa Delta Pi and Gamma Mu, Listed: Who's Who in America and Men of Achievement; [oth. writ.] College news columnist magazine article for Chicago purchaser encyclopedic science articles for children's press business mgmt. consult reviews and report editor/publisher: St. Margaret Mary today Author "The Chicago Spirit" and many other poems and songs; [pers.] The "River of love" is the dominant force of life, and I believe, love in its many forms is the fountain source of all creative achievements of both man and God.; [a.] Chicago, IL

CLARKSON, SHIRLEY J.
[b.] February 19, 1943, Amesbury, MA; [p.] Russell F. and Ruth A. Morrill Glidden; [m.] Robert D. Clarkson; [ch.] Eric J. Brown and Karen J. Cote; [ed.] Haverhill High School; [occ.] Assessor; [memb.] International Assessors Assoc., Massachusetts Assessors Association, Northeast Assessors Association, Essex County Assessors Association; [hon.] Massachusetts Accredited Assessor (MAA), Residential Massachusetts Assessor (RMA); [oth. writ.] None, this was my first writing.; [pers.] "Who I Am Is"... Who I am is the possibility of love, understanding and laughter for all mankind.; [a.] Georgetown, MA

CLARY, TODD C.
[b.] January 4, 1966, Olympia, WA; [p.] Don Clary and Kim Clary; [ed.] Bachelor of Arts in English, University of California at Santa Barbara - creative writing emphasis; [occ.] Rock Climbing Instructor/Guide; [a.] Santa Barbara, CA

CLASS, JAMES
[b.] July 24, 1969, NJ; [ed.] Rutgers College; [pers.] I am deeply inspired by nature and the physical universe and how people react to these things. I forever seek the truth in all things and in people and try to help them discover it as well.; [a.] Carlstadt, NJ

CLIFTON, BRANDY
[pen.] Stephanie Hart; [b.] October 1, 1977, Pontiac; [p.] Sheila and Randall Guthrie; [oth. writ.] I'm just a beginner but I write a lot of poems this was the first one I published; [pers.] I like writing poems, to get things off my mind and people enjoy reading some poems I write.; [a.] Kinross, MI

CLOUD, NICHOLE
[b.] January 26, 1977, West Germany; [p.] James and Karen Cloud; [ed.] Cypress-Falls High School; [a.] Houston, TX

CLURE III, WILLIAM C.
[pen.] Trey; [b.] September 20, 1969, Midwest City, OK; [p.] Bill and Debbie Clure; [m.] Linda L. Clure, December 29, 1990; [ch.] Becky Apple, Jason Apple; [ed.] Northwest Classen High School Bachelors Degree - Business/Marketing from the University of Central Oklahoma; [memb.] St. Monica's Catholic Church Edmond, Oklahoma; [oth. writ.] 150+ poems unpublished. Research papers.; [pers.] I strive to be a better husband and a better man. I listen to my heart as it precipitates feel-

ings into words on paper. I am greatly influenced by my life and my most beautiful wife.; [a.] Edmond, OK

CLUSE, BRIAN PAUL
[b.] October 27, 1973, Bellflower, CA; [p.] Mary LeMaire, Rodney Cluse; [memb.] Calvary Chapel of the Chino Valley; [oth. writ.] Fluttering Heart; [pers.] My faith in the Lord Jesus Christ as my personal savior has made possible the writing of this poem.; [a.] Ontario, CA

COBIN, SHARLENE
[b.] September 14, 1965, Paterson, NJ; [p.] Alberta Harrison; [m.] Norris Cobin, November 24, 1990; [ch.] Nicole and Alisa Cobin; [occ.] Nursing Assistant at Valley Health Care Center of Westwood, NJ; [pers.] I want to thank a dear friend of mine, Jody Calhoun, whom inspired me to write my recent poems one named Connected and the other Knowing.; [a.] Paterson, NJ

COCKING, TAMMY
[pen.] Tammy Cocking Patterson; [b.] December 19, 1961, Petaluma, CA; [p.] Donald R. Cocking, Linda Cocking; [m.] Larry Patterson, April 16, 1987; [ch.] Three boys and two girls; [ed.] GED, 2 years Junior College Housewife, disabled; [occ.] Housewife; [oth. writ.] I have over two hundred poems.; [pers.] I'll write it, if I want!; [a.] Olivehurst, CA

COIT, GENEVA
[b.] May 22, 1930, Lexington, IL; [p.] Mr. William R. White, Mrs. Leona Smith White; [m.] July 2, 1954; [ch.] Debra, Richard, Ronald and Lori; [ed.] High School - Ellsworth High, Ellsworth, IL; [occ.] Retired after working 34 yrs. for the Kresge - KMart Co.; [hon.] I have seven living grandchildren, and 1 deceased. They are the joy of my life. This poem was written for my grandson, who passed away when he was eleven.; [oth. writ.] I write a poem for family and friends birthday or any special time of their life. Just a hobby for me.; [pers.] I enjoy reading and caring for my family and friends I spend time with my Senior friends and my husband of 42 years Ron. We have a handicapped grandson who has taught us much about love and life and six great granddaughters.

COLBERT, CANDICE MONIQUE
[b.] March 13, 1983, San Diego, CA; [p.] Thomas F. Colbert, Arlene Colbert; [ed.] 7th Grader at Mike O'Callaghan Middle School; [hon.] Honorable mention for short story. Honor Roll student. Elected for Honor band; [pers.] Poetry is an art that should come from your heart. It should bloom from your soul with feeling and emotions.; [a.] Las Vegas, NV

COLBERT, DAMON R.
[pen.] DX Holmez; [b.] May 10, 1976, San Diego, CA; [p.] Vemla Smittick, Titus N. Colbert; [occ.] Security Guard For AACE Security; [memb.] National of Islam Muhammad Mosque #8 and Foi; [oth. writ.] Had a poem published in the book full of poets called the path not taken and in another called poems of the 90's.; [a.] San Diego, CA

COLBY, DENISE M.
[b.] July 18, 1970, Concord, NH; [p.] Robert Colby, Sheila Craique; [ch.] Markus and Jacob; [ed.] College for Lifelong Learning AAGS and Bachelor of Science - Management; [occ.] Student homemaker, Writer; [memb.] Overall, responsible member of the human race; [hon.] Being alive today; [oth. writ.] Stacks of unpublished autobiographical, interpretative, and critique pieces.; [pers.] Today, as we chronically see who is be-

hind every curtain, and find that there are as many holes in their heads as there is in their dogma, I find it comforting to embrace a paradox and stop infinite possibilities, at least in my life.; [a.] Franklin, NH

COLE, BERNADEEN
[pen.] Alexis; [b.] September 24, 1955, Hartford, CT; [p.] Alexander and Mary Gaddy; [m.] Bryant Cole, March 11, 1987, Divorced June 27, 1992; [ch.] Brynt Blake Trevonna; [ed.] Mary Immaculate Academy; [occ.] Teacher - Children's Korner - Porter and Chester Institute; [hon.] Through the years I received award in Mathematics English and art also in dance; [oth. writ.] "Black Sister Yo Mama", "The Legend", "The Death Of A Friend" in memory of Gregory B. and Arther D.; [pers.] I was first inspired to write in the early 70's when my two friends were killed in a car wreck. I created the death of a friend in their memory.; [a.] Hartford, CT

COLE, CYNTHIA YVETTE
[pen.] Angel; [b.] November 7, 1959, Oakland, CA; [p.] Opal and Oscar Cole; [ch.] Christopher Gerrome Cole-Bailey; [ed.] Central Mo. State University Warrensburg Mo.; [occ.] Marketing Research Liaison - NYSE AIM Distributors Inc., Licensed registered representative; [hon.] Who's Who in New Poets 1996; [oth. writ.] Pending publication: Black Gold, Garden Of Serenity, Forbidden Stranger, Music Box; [pers.] I close my eyes and feel life, I touch the colors of the rainbow with my thoughts and I live by God's map of my next step...loving today, learning from yesterday and anticipating the marrow.; [a.] Houston, TX

COLE-BAILEY, CHRISTOPHER GEROME
[pen.] Jazz; [b.] January 9, 1983, Kansas City, MO; [p.] Cynthia Y. Cole; [ed.] O'Donnell Middle School Alief, Houston TX; [occ.] Student; [memb.] Trailblazer Member 7th grade, Innovative Educational Program only offered to qualified selected students; [hon.] Honored Speaker: 5th Graduation — "My Hero"; [pers.] Live like a "plus" and you'll never equal "0".

COLLINS, KAREN LYNNETTE
[b.] May 1, 1976, Walnut Creek, CA; [p.] Don and Katie Collins; [ed.] Fresno High School, Klamath Lake Fire Training School; [occ.] Volunteer Fire Dept., Keno Rural Fire Protection Dist.; [memb.] American Ambulance Explorers; [pers.] I began writing in order to express my feelings in a way people can understand. And most are written in memory of my brother Corey Allen Collins. He was my inspiration to it all.; [a.] Klamath Falls, OR

COLWELL, SERENA LYNN
[b.] June 7, 1983, Palo Alto, CA; [p.] Sandra Bowen, Garrick Colwell; [ed.] Austin Waldorf School 7th Grade 1996; [occ.] Student/Babysitter; [memb.] Girl Scouts, Echanlear - Religion of the Light and Sound of God; [pers.] Poems are a very special kind of writing. And writing them is sometimes not easy. But what inspires me the most in nature. I wrote "Darkness" while sitting under the stars and just wrote down how I felt. Nature is so beautiful and so complex. You could ask ten people to write a poem about the ocean's qualities. Each response would be vastly different.; [a.] Austin, TX

CONCA JR., LOUIS F.
[pen.] Francis Sylvan; [b.] March 26, 1921, Providence, RI; [p.] Louis F. Sr. and Rose Marie (Both Deceased); [m.] Marguerite M. (Devitt) Conca, October 18, 1947; [ch.] Nancy Jean, Mary Lou, Stephen, Michael, James, Elizabeth and Thomas; [ed.] High School and Army Civil Service Schools, Active Air Force Military Schools (1942-1945), Oxford University Honorary Air Force

Attendee (1945), Ministry Study (3-yrs.), army air Force Communications Schools in New York, California, and Wisconsin; [occ.] Retired from New England Corps of Engineerings in 1973 (33 yrs. tenure) Administrative officer; [memb.] Leisure Learning Group, Knights of Columbus (former), Eucharistic Minister and Treasurer, Senior Citizen's Group; [hon.] Numerous Outstanding Performing Awards from New England Division Corps of Engineers during 33-years service, army Civilian Meritorious Award given by the Army, and Editor's choice award for poetry, 1996, awarded by National Library of Poetry; [oth. writ.] Numerous poems written and assembled in one volume (unpublished, as yet) also, have contemplated 150 pages of a novel.; [pers.] I've always written for my own pleasure, and made little effort, until now, towards publishing my works. I have been greatly influenced by the master poets, shakes - pear, sand berg, etc.; [a.] Providence, RI

CONEY, CATHY SIMS
[b.] September 23, 1959, Opa-Locka, FL; [p.] Marion and Mary Sims; [m.] Wilson Coney Jr., November 11, 1989; [ch.] Torrell Eugene, Taryn Darnell; [ed.] North Miami High, Miami Dade Community College; [occ.] Telephone Operator; [memb.] Greater New Bethal Baptist Church; [pers.] I hope that my writing will touch a spirit, and awaken it.; [a.] Miami, FL

CONIGLIO, NATHANIEL J.
[pen.] Nathan Julian; [b.] May 19, 1971, Trenton, NJ; [p.] Walter and Roseanna Coniglio; [m.] Tammy Jo Coniglio; [ed.] Notre Dame High School; [occ.] United States Marine; [oth. writ.] None published; [pers.] My ancient eye's have seen what humanity tries to hide. No more tears do I have to shed, just words to express what my soul can not forget.; [a.] Centereach, Long Island, NY

CONLEY, BEULAH M.
[b.] March 14, 1913, Creston, IA; [p.] Charles and Maude Hurley; [m.] Dale Glen Conley, December 26, 1931; [ch.] Donna Raye; [ed.] High School; [occ.] Retired; [memb.] Assembly of God Church; [hon.] Have received many honors for Bible Teaching taught the Bible for 50 years in churches - jails - Nursing Homes and my home; [oth. writ.] Many other writings poems - songs - stories they have been used in many states. Some poetry now is framed and hanging in public places; [pers.] God and family has been my inspiration and has kept the joy of living in my heart. I was born, one of 10 children. There was a lot at home to write about.; [a.] Gravois Mills, MO

CONN, DR. MARIE A.
[b.] January 9, 1944, Rockville Centre, NY; [p.] Ira F. and Alice R. Conn; [ed.] Ph.D., Theology, University of Notre Dame; [occ.] College Professor; [memb.] North American Academy of Liturgy, Societas Liturgical, College Theology Society; [hon.] Delta Epsilon Sigma, Eta Sigma Pi, Alpha Mu Gamm, John O'Brien, Fellowship (N.D.), Arthur Patch McKinley Scholarship; [oth. writ.] Two dozen professional and pastoral articles, most recently, "Health Care Reform as a Human Rights Issue" and "Star Trek: The Next Generation as Ecclesiology."; [a.] Hatboro, PA

CONN, GINA M.
[b.] May 21, 1976, Los Angeles, CA; [p.] Diana and Charles Conn; [m.] David M. Chabot, (will be married on) April 19, 1997; [ed.] Graduated from Narbonne High School in 1994. Am Pursuing my Assoc. of Arts at El Camino College; [occ.] Desktop publisher; [memb.] I am proud to be a member of a Wonderful family.; [hon.] Graduated High Sch. with Honors, Silver in Journalism/

Yearbook Comp., Principal's List; [oth. writ.] Was an editor for yearbook, also wrote for yearbook. Mainly write for self purposes.; [pers.] I am proud that I have such strong support from my family. Especially my Mother and my wonderful David.; [a.] Torrance, CA

COOKE, DEIRDRE AILEEN
[b.] July 24, 1971, Albany, NY; [p.] Ronald J. and Joan A. Cooke; [ed.] Averill Park High School; [occ.] Data Entry Machine Operator for NYS; [oth. writ.] Just my journal, I've always kept a journal. I've never shared my material with any one but close friends and other poets before.; [pers.] I write because it's how I process life. Poems, stories, letters and lyrics are my therapy.; [a.] Troy, NY

COOPER, ASHLEY
[b.] December 5, 1983, West Palm Beach, FL; [p.] Gary and Rita Cooper; [ch.] Brother Gavin and Sister Ally; [ed.] I'm entering the 7th grade in August of 1996; [occ.] Student at Macon Middle School.; [memb.] Jonathan Taylor Thomas Fan Club. Also Soccer Association Macon County Girls Soft Ball League; [hon.] Athletic Award Macon County Girls Softball 1995 and 1996. Presidential Fitness Award 1993, 1994, and 1995; [oth. writ.] Arts in our Future Worthy of Mention in Olive B. Eaton Creative Writing Awards. (1995); [pers.] If I Were A Tree was my first poem written for Mrs. Emma Jean Taylor my 5th Grade Teacher.; [a.] Franklin, NC

COOPER, DEBORAH WOLSTENCRAFT
[b.] February 10, 1954, Pawtucker, RI; [p.] Walter and Diane Wolstencroft; [m.] Charles Cooper Sr.; [ch.] Charles Cooper (Jr.), Jeffrey McNamara; [ed.] Liscenced Nursing program at Mass Bay Comm. College; [occ.] Nurse; [hon.] Wrote and delivered graduation exercise speech; [pers.] This poem written about my younger sister Barbara Andersen and my niece Amanda Andersen.; [a.] Framingham, MA

COOPER, JANICE
[b.] August 21, 1970; [p.] Bertha and Solomon Cooper; [ch.] MacKenzie Thomas; [ed.] Mattamuskeet High School, Swanquarter NC, Atlanta Job Corp., Atl. GA, Beaufort CLCC; [occ.] Nursing Assistant; [a.] Swanquarter, NC

COOPER, JENNIFER
[pen.] Jennifer Cooper; [b.] November 16, 1972, Pitts, PA; [p.] Nick and MaryLou Cindrich; [m.] Rod Lee, October 15, 1994; [pers.] My accomplishments in life are dedicated to my mother and father. For it is because of their unconditional love and belief in me that I am able to achieve.; [a.] Austin, TX

COOPER, LOU-PECK
[pen.] Lou-Peck; [b.] May 11, 1912, Newport, TX; [p.] Andrew & Almeda Peck; [m.] Charles Price Cooper, January 20, 1939; [ch.] None; [ed.] H. School, BS College, 1 yr. Jr. College - 4 yrs. Music & Voice; [occ.] Retired; [memb.] AARP - Church of Christ; [hon.] Many Golden Poet Awards; Awarded "Who's Who In Poetry"; [oth. writ.] Children's short stories, but none published - Many other poems - In fact if I had had money I would have published a book "Poetry For Young And Old" - Texas is the subject of many of my Poems - I am a Texan.; [a.] Mandeville, LA

COPELAND, ALVA V.
[b.] October 16, 1957, Detroit, MI; [m.] James Copeland; [ch.] Kamari and Dayna; [memb.] Member of Saddleback Community Church, The Vocalist for Jazz Group "Inertia" - (A Contemporary Ministry Group);

[oth. writ.] Written several poems and short stories not yet published, also songs for the group "Inertia".; [pers.] In all that I write and all that I sing my hope and prayer is that the words would move in the hearts of people to cause them to be encouraged, edified and built up enough to be provoked to action!; [a.] Mission Viejo, CA

CORBELL, MARY ANN
[pen.] Mary Corbell; [b.] September 12, 1944, Buhl, AL; [p.] Grey and Clara Lunsford; [m.] Franklin D. Corbell, December 9, 1960; [ch.] Beth, Diane, Karen, Tonya, Brandon; [ed.] 11th grade Tuscaloosa County High, Tuscaloosa, AL; [occ.] Housewife and mother; [memb.] Interfaith Christian Assembly this is my church; [oth. writ.] I have written many other poems, some skits, songs and a few short stories; [pers.] Never lose faith. I have wanted to write since I was a child but never could. Then christ came into my life and in a matter of weeks the lines of poetry came flooding into my mind.; [a.] Slaughter, LA

CORBETT, DESIREE
[pen.] Dezi; [b.] Burlington, NC; [p.] Donnell and Loleta Corbett; [ed.] Currently enrolled at Kleerview Academy; [occ.] Writing; [memb.] NLTR Club; [oth. writ.] Currently working on several novels and poems; [pers.] Live every day to the fullest for there may not be a tomorrow.; [a.] High Point, NC

CORDREY, JOHN S.
[b.] May 15, 1979, Orange, CA; [p.] Lee and Glenda Cordrey; [ed.] Senior in High School; [occ.] Student; [a.] Anaheim, CA

CORMIER, JAMES
[b.] February 16, 1982, Lowell, MA; [p.] Maureen A. Cormier, Dennis R. Cormier; [ed.] Norte Dame Academy, Entering St. John's Prep. School, Danvers, MA; [occ.] Student; [memb.] Long Meadow Golf Club, National Geographical Society; [hon.] Partial Scholarship, St. John's Prep. (academic); [oth. writ.] Currently working on fantasy fiction novel, several short stories, various poetry; [pers.] In my writing, I take equal parts of knowledge and imagination, twisting them around until they forge a threshold into my mind for my readers.; [a.] Lowell, MA

CORONEL, SUSANNA
[b.] December 16, 1974, Austin, TX; [p.] Natividad C. Chavarria; [ed.] Stephen F. Austin, Wharton County Jr. College; [occ.] College Student; [memb.] Texas Army National Guard; [hon.] Army Achievement Medal; [pers.] Poetry is a special way to express your thoughts.; [a.] Stafford, TX

CORRINGTON, ROBERT C.
[b.] June 14, 1951, Glendale, CA; [p.] Robert R., Sally Ann and Marie; [m.] Lillian C., August 26, 1983; [ch.] John Robert and Ryan Gavin; [ed.] John Burroughs High, Burbank, CA; [occ.] Hoist and Crane Tech. Crane-Veyor Corp. S. El Monte, CA; [memb.] United States Marine Corp.; [hon.] Honorable Discharge; [pers.] Thank you Dad, grandpa Jack and Ricky C. for all those memories and stories we have shared from our camping and fishing days.; [a.] La Puente, CA

COSTELLO, JOHN W.
[pen.] Walter Costello; [b.] December 19, 1953, White Hall, IL; [p.] Francis and Elizabeth Costello; [m.] Divorced, March, 1980; [ch.] Billy Joe, Robert Lynn, Mindy Ann; [ed.] 11 years also have Auctioneering Diploma; [occ.] Unemployed; [hon.] Short Order Cook Certificate, Produce Manager Certificate, Auctioneering

Diploma and several recording contracts with different recording companies.; [oth. writ.] I have a 100 page book of my own poems, of which has never been published.; [pers.] Everything I write is true to life. I've either lived it, or I can't write it, I do not write fiction. All my writing is true word for word.; [a.] Jacksonville, IL

COTTER, TONI
[b.] April 9, 1960, Queens, NY; [p.] Rita Mullins; [m.] John Matthew Cotter, October 3, 1987; [ed.] John Bowne High School, Salem College; [occ.] Secretary; [oth. writ.] Several children's stories and one novel; [pers.] By using our personal powers to heal, we both spread the love with which we all need to live and complete that which we were sent here to do by the Almighty. Keep the power, spread the love.

COUCH, PETER SVENSSON
[pen.] P. Svensson Couch; [b.] April 18, 1964, Watertown, NY; [p.] George and Lis Couch; [ed.] Hotchkiss School '82, Colgate University '87 B.A., Syracuse College of Law '92 J.D.; [occ.] Law; [memb.] Lambda Chi Alpha, Duck's Unlimited; [hon.] Dean's List; [oth. writ.] School publication seattle times "Letter to the Editor" poems: Canal Lines, The Pickle Factory; [pers.] "Carpe Diem"; [a.] Seattle, WA

COULSTON, JONATHAN
[pen.] Howdy; [b.] May 1, 1975, Fort Worth, TX; [p.] Jim and Nelda Coulston; [ed.] Sanger High School; [occ.] Bartender; [pers.] I am a firm believer in living one day at a time. To me, life is a series of mistakes from which one must learn, live, and carry on. If you feel yourself full of regrets and what ifs, you'll spend too much time worrying about what night have been instead of what is.; [a.] Beaumont, TX

COWFER, LEROY H.
[pen.] Lee Cowfer; [b.] January 28, 1939, Port Matilda, PA; [p.] Thomas and Colorado Cowfer; [ch.] Robin and Timothy; [ed.] Penn State University, Altoona Bible Institute; [occ.] Soldier in Salvation Army, Realtor; [oth. writ.] Mother's Day Hope, Dad, Back Home, Sun Rise, Dad's Shoes, Love; [pers.] May God's love through me express Loyalty to God, Country and Fellowmen. May God richly bless.; [a.] State College, PA

COX, DOLORES H.
[b.] 1955, Transylvania County, NC; [p.] Neva and Raymond Harrington; [m.] Tim Cox, 1982; [ed.] Rosman High School, Brevard College, University of North Carolina at Asheville; [occ.] Associate Director for Student Affairs and Admissions at Mercer, University Southern School of Pharmacy; [pers.] My college professors were a tremendous inspiration to me, and my Mother has also been a role model. I grew up listening to poems she wrote about the beauty of nature. Composing poetry is a gift I can give.; [a.] Atlanta, GA

COX, WILL W.
[pen.] Bill Cox; [b.] July 13, 1923, Belton, TX; [p.] Willie W. and Mary Ann Cox; [m.] Adina Arnold Cox, May 11, 1948; [ch.] William A., Michael D., Dee Ann Gibson; [ed.] Graduate - Waco, TX, High School, BA - Baylor University 1955, Journalism - Triple Minors; [occ.] Retired - City Manager; [memb.] Calvary Baptist Church; [hon.] Air Medal - Presidential Citation (World War II) Industrial Economic Development of year (3 times) listed in Who's Who Industry in the Southwest 1964-1966; [oth. writ.] It's a matter of fact newspaper Development Column for 33 years.; [pers.] My Pilot was written during world war II while a member of Navy Patrol squadron VB 106 in the Pacific

CRAIN, NANCY RUTH
[b.] May 6, 1940, Etowah, AR; [p.] Joe and Ola Mae Trull; [m.] Ralph Crain, December 9, 1959; [ch.] Annette, Tina, Stacey, Ton, Lorri; [ed.] Caraway Central High Class of 1958, 2 semesters at Arkansas St. Univ.; [occ.] Employee at General Electric; [memb.] Brookland Baptist Church United Way; [oth. writ.] Have written many poems, prose, songs. This is my first time to submit anything for publishing.; [pers.] I write poetry for the Love of all my children the four on earth and the one in Heaven.; [a.] Brookland, AR

CRANE, LAKIN
[b.] February 20, 1964, Washington, DC; [p.] Otis Graham, Ann Ehringer; [m.] Doug Crane, February 18, 1989; [ch.] Alex Wade Crane; [ed.] Mount Vernon College, University of California at Los Angeles; [occ.] Accounting Clerk, Hualalai Resort, Ka'upulehu-Kona HI; [memb.] National Notary Association; [hon.] Dean's List; [a.] Waikoloa Village, HI

CREAMER, NEDRA A.
[b.] June 26, 1942, Houston, TX; [p.] Edwin and Laura Innerarity; [m.] Paul M. Creamer (Deceased), December 30, 1959; [ch.] Mark, Cindy, Laurie and Matthew; [ed.] 8th Grade GED at 48 yrs old; [occ.] Correctional Officer in an all male prison; [memb.] Numerous; [hon.] Poetry contest in 1985, several in school 1953-1956; [oth. writ.] Poem "When A Husband Dies" book "Memoirs Of A Granny Prison Guard" working on book "Somewhere In Time"; [pers.] Nothing is beyond what you can do if you want to bad enough. You just have to think of it as already done. Once you see it as done then you get going.; [a.] Palestine, TX

CRESPINO JR., DONALD
[b.] August 17, 1966; [ch.] Tiara Crespino; [ed.] I passed by one point in my third GED test; [occ.] Direct Care Provider; [pers.] I try to reach for the spirit of Jesus Christ. I love you Mom. Let not my minds desires betray my hearts needs. God made me a king and placed a Tiara upon my heart. Buddha called me Bodhisattva. Peace and love to all.; [a.] Kingston, NY

CROFT, MRS. ELTA H.
[b.] April 6, 1918, Drake, ND; [p.] Peter and Mennie Merbach; [m.] Clifford Croft (Deceased), October 2, 1940; [ch.] Five Living, one deceased; [ed.] High School, Nurses Aide - L.P.N., School of Hard Knooks; [occ.] Retired - Voluntare at Nursing Homes, Church; [memb.] Church - PEP, and LW Harbor Mates (Travel) W.O.T.M., Country Dance Club; [oth. writ.] Wrote "My Rock of Ages" which has been put on tape and sold. Many poems and stories published and sermon for Church.; [pers.] My grandchildren want me to write a book.

CRONIN, BRIAN P. J.
[b.] July 22, 1975, Westfield, NJ; [p.] Jane and Jerry Cronin; [ed.] Westfield High School, Skidmore College; [occ.] Student; [hon.] Dean's list; [pers.] "We shape clay into a pot, but it is the emptiness inside that holds whatever we want" - Lao Tzu.; [a.] Westfield, Saratoga Springs, NY

CROOKS, MICHAELINE
[b.] April 8, 1960, Evansville; [p.] Jerry L. and Jane D. Corn; [ch.] MacKensey J. Crooks; [ed.] Boonville High School, graduated 1978; [occ.] Poet/Aspiring Singer; [memb.] Distinguished Member of Internal Society of Poets; [hon.] Editors Choice Award (for "No Where Bound"); [oth. writ.] "No Where Bound", "My Dream"; [pers.] "Thank You", "Joe", for being my inspiration.

This poem especially is dedicated to you. "I Love You". Forever.; [a.] Boonville, IN

CROOM, BRENDA K.
[b.] August 23, 1944, Kelly, NC; [p.] Margaret Sykes Croam and Pearlie Croom; [m.] Jerry Donald Eason Sr; [ed.] Graduated from New Hanover High School in Wilmington, NC and attended UNC Wilmington; [occ.] Disaster Assistance Employee with Federal Emergency Management Agency; [memb.] Toastmasters International, Miami-Kendall Rotary Club, NC Real Estate Broker; [oth. writ.] Professional Writer with FEMA, the federal agency which responds to Presidentially declared disasters.; [pers.] My goal is to enlighten and entertain with real life stories and childhood memories. Currently compiling works for a collection of stories and a children's cook book. Celebrating life in country sunshine.

CROSBY, DONALD E.
[b.] April 23, 1964, New Kensington, PA; [p.] Mr. and Mrs. Ronald F. Crosby; [m.] Ann Marie, April 27, 1996; [ch.] Kari Marie age 6; [ed.] Graduate of Kiski Area HS 1982; [occ.] Steelworker for Allegheny Ludlum, Vandergrift; [memb.] National Rifle Association, Elks #386, United Steel Workers Local 1138; [oth. writ.] "The Gift" unpublished; [pers.] I wrote this poem for my wife, Ann Marie. It appeared on the back of our wedding program. I love you, babe.; [a.] Vandergrift, PA

CROUSE, KENT A.
[b.] October 19, 1961, Richmond, IN; [p.] Edward Edmond and Norma Crouse; [ed.] Bachelor of Science in Mechanical Engineering, New Mexico State University; [occ.] Engineer for a major Southwestern Utility Interest; [memb.] Member: La Sociedad de Ingenieros; [hon.] Dean's List New Mexico State University; [oth. writ.] Several other poems as well as Southwestern short story and another short story. As well as several bilingual Spanish/English poems; [pers.] I am an observer of life. I write to capture the feelings and emotions of a given moment in time. Hopefully, the reader may experience those emotions through my words.; [a.] Tucson, AZ

CRUTHIS, DEBORAH
[b.] August 12, 1968, Nacogdoches, TX; [p.] Louis T. and Gloria Martindale; [m.] Tony Cruthis, September 13, 1991; [ch.] Brittany Alexandria; [ed.] Central Heights High School; [occ.] Business Office Manager Fullerton Medical Group, Nashville, TN; [pers.] Learn today what you need for tomorrow so you will not regret yesterday.; [a.] Dickson, TN

CULP, ROBERT J.
[b.] June 12, 1926, Wellsville, OH; [p.] George and Ruth Culp; [m.] Genevieve B. Culp, August 9, 1947; [ch.] 6 children; [ed.] Degree in Mechanical, Electrical Engineering, Structural Design at Penn State University; [occ.] Retired - Architect, Ural Designer-Penn State; [memb.] Presbyterian Church Elder; [hon.] Discharged from the Army Air Force 1946; [oth. writ.] None - my first attempt; [pers.] I strive to set a good example for my 6 children 16 grandchildren and as of now 1 great grandchild.; [a.] Port Charlotte, FL

CURRAN, TANYA MARIE
[b.] August 12, 1983, Springfield, MA; [p.] Kandie and Kevin Curran; [ed.] Mosley School; [occ.] Student; [memb.] Westfield Boys and Girls Club, Torch Club; [a.] Westfield, MA

CURRY, CHRISTINE
[pen.] Curry, Bunkie; [b.] April 25, 1976, Great Lakes Naval Base; [p.] Kathleen and Ed Curry; [p.] McHenry Community High School McHenry College (Associate's degree) North Central College; [occ.] Student at North Central College pursuing an education degree; [memb.] Prolife, Phi Theta Kappa, National Honors Society; [hon.] President's List, National Dean's List, Who's Who Among American High School Students, Who's Who Among American Junior Colleges, PTK Scholarships, Transfer Scholarship at North Central College; [pers.] Diane Nyhammer extremely encouraged my poetry writing. I can convey messages through my writing that I would not be able to otherwise say.; [a.] McHenry, IL

CURTIS, CASSANDRA A.
[pen.] San; [b.] May 8, 1963, Flint, MI; [p.] Gertrude L, Clemans, Cecile R. Thornton; [m.] Tyrone Curtis, July 8, 1995; [ch.] Tryone, Tyriea, Tobias (Deceased) Thornton; [ed.] Mott Adult High Baker College; [occ.] Assembly Operator for Britax Rainsford Inc. in Marysville MI; [pers.] I'm setting a goal to write a book on my children and my life. My children help me see a new life when they each were born.; [a.] Port Huron, MI

CURTIS, RICHARD
[b.] June 4, 1969, Michigan; [p.] Carol Curtis and Richard Curtis Sr.; [ch.] Tiffonie Trishane Curtis; [ed.] Nutrition and Fitness Professional, (now in study); [occ.] Machine Operator/Fitness Professional; [memb.] Iron City Gym (Michigan) a great place for fitness training; [hon.] High School 11th and 12th grade honor student. 1988-1989; [pers.] Your mind is like time in a clock if you don't use it, it's gone forever. You can't Reuse the second's, you can't Reuse the minutes, or the hours that time has passed. So live each day and use your mind as if it was your last.; [a.] Waterford, MI

CUSHMAN, DAVID M.
[b.] February 19, 1976, Frankfort, GA; [m.] Single; [ed.] Full-time student at the University of Texas at San Antonio.; [occ.] Labor and Delivery Room Assistant (University Hospital); [pers.] "Always strive for the best, and never accept mediocrity!"

CUTRIGHT, NICOSHA KIM
[b.] February 2, 1979, Aurora, CO; [p.] Kim and Mike Black; [ed.] I have graduated from high school and am taking a journalism/short story course through the mail.; [occ.] Wendys; [memb.] Star Trek Fan Club; [oth. writ.] Nothing published. I have written several poems and a long story. Wrote on the school paper.; [pers.] Always trust in God Jehovah and remember: Love is meant to give, to hold on you must remember. The good it will outweigh the bad.; [a.] Fruita, CO

CZARNECKI, JEFFERY N.
[b.] December 20, 1975, Albany, NY; [p.] Jeffery and Karen Czarnecki; [occ.] United Parcel Service; [memb.] Knights of Columbus, International Brotherhood of Tearsters AFL-CIO; [pers.] Gain strength from that which hurts and your pain will decrease the next time around.; [a.] Watervliet, NY

D'ALESSANDRO, MARIA
[b.] July 20, 1972, Meadowbrook, PA; [p.] Ed and Joan D'Alessandro; [ch.] Ian Marcus; [ed.] Bishop Conwell High School, Bucks County Community College, Pennco Technical School; [occ.] Computer Programmer; [pers.] Live deeply. Absorb all that is around you, so strongly that it becomes part of you. Yet also be absorbed, for this is how creativity and knowledge are earned.; [a.] Philadelphia, PA

D'ANDREA, ROCCO A.
[pen.] R. A. D'Andrea; [b.] Forest Hills General, Queens, NY; [p.] Rocco Sr. and Florence; [ed.] Harborfields High School served in the United States Air Force, Sergeant, in Civil Engineering and Communications; [memb.] Huntington Township Theater (will appear in their upcoming production: "The Musical Comedy Murders of 1940" in the role of Ken; [hon.] Air Force Good Conduct medal, Letter of Commendation from V.P. Al Gore for efforts in developing new and innovative technologies; [oth. writ.] Several letters and one articles published in Newsday, has written various unpub. works, designs for advanced transp. systems currently working on final draft of a thriller: The Scarecrow Murders.; [pers.] Each of us has a unique gift, a key of sorts that can unlock doors nobody else can, it is that wherein lies the secret of life.; [a.] Huntington, NY

D'AREZZO, TAMMY M.
[b.] July 21, 1972, Providence, RI; [p.] Albert D'Arezzo, Rosa LaFazia; [ch.] 4 dear cats Bo, Tobi, Galadrial, and Kirt; [ed.] Community College of RI, University of Rhode Island; [occ.] Administrative for Transportation Co. and Writer; [memb.] Voluntary Services for Animals; [oth. writ.] Hundreds of poems starting late 70's of which will be published also working on a Romance Novel; [pers.] The heart never lies, therefore, I write from the heart. I could only hope that someday I can hold a candle to my hero The Great Emily Dickerson.; [a.] Cranston, RI

DAHMS, RITA
[pen.] Rita J. Dahms, Rita Foster Dahms; [b.] April 29, 1940, Orange, CA; [p.] LeRoy Foster, Ruby Foster; [m.] Virgil Dahms, July 21, 1962; [ch.] Kathryn Carlile, Miriam Mills, Kenneth Dahms; [ed.] College of the Ozarks, Clarskville, Arkansas; [hon.] Dean's List; [pers.] My children, my grandchildren, Whitney Henderson, Nicole Dhams, and Steven Mills, my friends, Ellen Gillette, Mildred Trammell, and others, are my gifts from God. My writing is my gift to Him, and them, and all who love expressing the gifts of his creation.; [a.] Sulphur Springs, TX

DAMIAN, ELLEN
[pen.] Ellen Stewart; [b.] March 18, 1948, San Francisco; [p.] James and Florence Stewart; [m.] Freddie M. Damian, July 10, 1993; [ch.] Danny, Derek, Dina; [ed.] I am working on a bachelor's degree at CSUB, Bakerfield, CA; [oth. writ.] None published; [a.] Tehachapi, CA

DANIELS JR., WILLIAM A.
[b.] July 10, 1931, Mineola, NY; [p.] Rose Catherine and William Daniels; [m.] Phyllis Daniels, November 28, 1957; [ch.] 5 sons, 2 daughters; [ed.] 2 yrs. College; [occ.] Construction Engineer; [oth. writ.] New York's top writer of bad Irish poetry; [pers.] Live is a party, some unwanted guests, sometimes of running out of victuals and grog, and when I leave the party I'll leave the party I'll leave someone to clearly up the after math.; [a.] Medford, NY

DARLING, GLORIA
[pers.] I chose to celebrate life's small pleasure and seek to live each day without regrets.; [a.] Miami, FL

DARLING, SHERRIE
[b.] April 12, 1962, Orange County, CA; [p.] Richard and Sharlene Darling; [ed.] BA Psychology Fort Lewis College working towards Masters in Cellular and Molecular Biology; [occ.] EMT-B at Denver General-in ER; [hon.] 2 times President's List, 4.0 GPA, 2 times Dean's List, 3.4 GPA with 16 Credit Load; [pers.] My writing helps me to express feelings, my education is geared toward statistics and research, so when I enrolled in a 400

level creative writing class Dr. Red Bird must have thought I have lost my mind. So this one's for him, Thanks Red.; [a.] Denver, CO

DARR, THOMAS
[b.] August 16, 1950, York, PA; [p.] Rodger Darr, Elaine Darr; [m.] Elizabeth Darr, October 21, 1995; [ch.] Lauren, Luke, Papken, Tamar, Marie; [ed.] Dallaston High School, York College of PA, Currently Attending Lutheran Theological Southern Seminary; [occ.] Student; [oth. writ.] Several volumes, nothing has yet been published; [pers.] My writings provide a spiritual release for me and hopefully one day may help others in need.; [a.] Columbia, SC

DASSEL, JEFFREY
[pen.] Edmond Barrilea; [b.] August 10, 1973, Greenville, NC; [p.] Vicki Steila; [ed.] A.I. duPont High, University of Delaware; [occ.] Making the world a better place.; [memb.] Grace Lutheran Church Garrett County, MA, Habitat for Humanity, UD European Team Hanball; [hon.] UD General Honors Certificate, Dean's List, Macuho Award for Programming Excellence; [oth. writ.] Unsubmitted poetry; [pers.] Know your strengths and know your weaknesses, but know no limitations. "Dreams are the involuntary art of poetry". - Jean Paul Richter.; [a.] Hockessin, DE

DAUGHERTY, AARON JOHN
[pen.] "A.J.", "Skittles"; [b.] December 4, 1978, Pikeville Methodist Hospital; [p.] Johnny and Connie Daugherty; [ed.] Senior at Phelps High School after graduation plan on attending Indiana Bible College to be a Music Minister; [occ.] Works for Hornet's Restaurant; [memb.] He's a member of the Church of God in Jesus Name where Rev. Opie Harris is the pastor; [hon.] He received a Poetry award in Mrs. Shelia Pinson's Class at Phelps High School his Sophomore year; [oth. writ.] He's wrote several other poems that haven't been published - "What Christmas Really Means" and "The Christmas Wish" and many more.; [pers.] Aaron plays saxophone and drums. He loves anything to do with gospel music. He loves camping, sports but first and foremost He loves the Lord.

DAVENPORT, CHARLEEN
[b.] October 27, 1953, New Orleans, LA; [p.] Peter and Camelia Anderson Jr.; [m.] Jerome Davenport Sr.; [ch.] Jerome, David, Deon, Latherio Samuel; [ed.] Grades 1-9 Bethune High and Elem. Norco, LA. 10th Fifth ward, Reserve, LA, 11th-12th Leon Godchaux High, Reserve, LA; [occ.] Courier, Pony Express; [oth. writ.] "You'll Never Walk This Way Again", "Consider My Heart", "Prepare For Battle", "Look Through The Mirror", "The Tellers Prayer", "The Seed", "From Trails To Testimony", "The Son Is Shining Bright Today"; [pers.] My poems, prayers and writings are inspired by God. Much prayer and mediation goes before each stroke of the pen. Also many of my poems are real life testimonies. My objection is to comfort the hurting, add some light to a confused situation and put people in touch with other people hearts and feelings.; [a.] La Place, LA

DAVIS, DANA M.
[pen.] Dayna Davis; [b.] June 17, 1962, Watertown, WI; [p.] Dan and Beverly Mabie, Armand Prust; [m.] Edward Alan Davis Sr., August 24, 1985; [ch.] Emily Michele, Edward Alan, Geena Colleen; [ed.] Lake Mills High; [occ.] Technician; [memb.] Girl Scouts of the United States; [pers.] Writing, to me, is a way for me to express my feelings. If anyone enjoys my work, I have a wonderful feeling.; [a.] Lake Mills, WI

DAVIS, EVA M.
[pen.] Eva M. Signorile (maiden); [b.] October 9, 1955, Chicago, IL; [ch.] (Son) J. Michael L. Davis; [ed.] Fengur High, UTSA - 2 yrs. will cont. when health is better.; [occ.] Retired due to disability worked for N.E. Baptist Hosp.; [memb.] Unable to at this moment - Have gone through many surgeries the last few years. Tomorrow I go in for another unfortunately. This was good news to receive the day before. Thank you.; [hon.] Gold Key Finalist in NY for art project. Several art awards in Chg.; [oth. writ.] "Ultimate Love", "Prisoner", "Tears of Friendship", "Thoughts Through a Lonely Night", Eternal Light, Ultimate Pain, My Artistic Love Fantasy, A Day's Ending; [pers.] When writing I am free to express emotions and thoughts in the rawest form, attracting others who understand and can relate to each experience with a smile, a tear, or a simple nod. I am truly blessed and touched by God's inspiration.; [a.] San Antonio, TX

DAVIS, KATHLEEN G.
[b.] February 23, 1920, Rochester, England; [p.] Kathleen and Frederick Jones; [m.] James F. Davis Sr., January 8, 1948; [ch.] James F. Davis Jr., Robert Alan Davis; [ed.] High school (England), some college (USA) - 4 years Nursing degree; [occ.] Retired - Hon. Secretary Royal Naval Association, Long Beach; [memb.] United States Navy League, Royal Naval Association, Catholic Daughters of the Americas, Daughters of the British Empire; [oth. writ.] Published several "Letters to the Editors" during Vietnam war. Currently write for the "White Ensign" the newsletter of the Royal Naval Association.; [pers.] My poem is dedicated to my son Jim who "crossed the bar" Nov. 12th 1994, he was buried at sea by the US Navy Feb. 21st 1995. When I look out over the Pacific I know my son is there - and "all is peace."; [a.] Santee, CA

DAVIS, KELLIE
[b.] July 5, 1979, Meridian, MS; [p.] Terry Lee and Elizabeth Davis; [ed.] Currently enrolled as a Senior at West Lauderdale High School; [occ.] Child care assistant in a church; [memb.] Hero; [hon.] English III Award, Child Care II Award; [oth. writ.] Torn Between Love, Changing My Children, Brotha, Sista Debt (Short Stories); [pers.] Writing is great expression; [a.] Collinsville, MS

DAVIS, KENNETH M.
[pen.] Cat; [b.] October 9, 1947, Riverside, CA; [p.] Deceased; [m.] Divorced, 1967-1969; [ed.] Ramona High Riverside California, Riverside City College (AA Degree); [occ.] Music Student; [memb.] Leopard Karate School - Simi Retired; [hon.] Four Black Belt's; [pers.] To God only the glory ("Bach"); [a.] Riverside, CA

DAVIS, MRS. BETTY
[b.] December 10, 1937, Newburn, NC; [p.] Kennie and Lucy Davis; [ch.] Grand: Alicia, Melvin, Lucy, Sky and Gregory; [ed.] College for Human Service, A.A. degree College of New Rochelle, B.A. P.S. 184, Jr. High in North Carolina; [occ.] Retired Social Worker. Presently homemaker; [memb.] I am a member of all Saints R.C. Church; [hon.] Several Service Awards for Community Work; [pers.] While I believe my works, (poems) are good, I feel that this particular one is best. Life is very precious to me, and should be to everyone. We need not to take life for granted but cherished every moment.; [a.] Nyack, NY

DAVIS, NICOLLE TERASE
[b.] May 13, 1987, Long Island, NY; [p.] Lawrence and Mary Davis; [ed.] Old Mill Road Elementary School,

Merrick, New York; [occ.] 4th Grade Student; [memb.] Old Mill Road Elementary School Band-Flute Player; [hon.] 1) Keep A - Merrick - A Beautiful 1993 Poster Contest, 2) Keep A - Merrick - A Beautiful 1995 Essay Contest, 3) Nassau County Dental Health 1995 Poster Contest, 4) National PTA Cultural Arts 1995/96 Program; [pers.] "My Wish" when I was 8. My hobbies are writing, drawing, gymnastics, and dancing. I compete against myself to be the best that I can be.; [a.] Merrick, NY

DAVIS, RENEE
[b.] November 26, 1965, Pensacola, FL; [p.] Mr. and Mrs. John Dean; [m.] Michael Davis, June 23, 1984; [ch.] Steven Davis; [ed.] G.E.D. graduate; [occ.] Waitress "Hooters"; [memb.] Member of St. Marys Catholic Church; [hon.] Certified Cashier Nail Technician; [oth. writ.] I have many other poems. Probably a hundred and fifty or so.; [pers.] I love Aerobics, dancing, swimming, writing, the Gym and my family, and volleyball of course.; [a.] Pensacola, FL

DAVIS, TONYA
[pen.] Tea Charise; [b.] October 27, 1971, Chicago; [p.] Cassandra E. Gibbs and Paul Gibbs; [m.] Rodney Davis, August 19, 1995; [ch.] Blake Davis; [ed.] West High, currently finishing a marketing degree; [occ.] Full time student; [pers.] I have to thank God for giving me a grandmother who passed the love of writing and reading down into my soul.; [a.] Aurora, IL

DAVIS-MCDUFFIE, DELOIS
[b.] January 12, 1951, Chicago, IL; [ch.] Three sons; [ed.] B.A. Degree, California State University, San Jose, CA; [memb.] ZICA Creative Arts and Literary Guild; [oth. writ.] Inspired By Magic, Mother Earth, Thinking Of You.; [pers.] I enjoy music, reading and putting my emotions on paper in the form of poetry.; [a.] Sacramento, CA

DAY, JESSIE
[b.] November 24, 1916, New Castle, PA; [p.] Deceased; [m.] Deceased; [ch.] Two girls and one boy; [ed.] College for children and myself an English Teacher retired; [occ.] Living on a farm near New Castle, PA with sister and brother.

DE ASCENTIS, MICHELLE L.
[pen.] Michelle De Ascentis; [b.] May 27, 1947, Paris, France; [p.] Andree Reigert, Robert Chatelais; [m.] Ronald De Ascentis, December 28, 1964; [ch.] Gregory, Christine, Richard; [ed.] Paris France and Salue Regina University New Port RI; [occ.] Philosopher and Writer; [hon.] Several; [oth. writ.] Many poems and writings; [pers.] A contemplate life searching for truth, and become inspired following the deaths of my two children; [a.] Middletown, RI

DE SPAIN, DOROTHY ANN
[pen.] Dorothy Shield De Spain; [b.] Oak Park, IL; [p.] James Shields, Grace Shields; [m.] Frank J. De Spain; [ch.] James and Steven De Spain; [ed.] Trinity High School and Rosary College in River Forest, Illinois. B.A. - Art Education and English; [occ.] Retired Teacher; [memb.] Girl Scouts, and Art Institute of Chicago; [hon.] National Honor Society of Secondary Schools and Colleges, Dean's List. First Place Awards for Art Posters and Illustrations; [oth. writ.] Several poems published in local newspapers and magazines. College Class Reunion poems.; [pers.] I write about my personal experiences and feelings always mindful of the beauty of poetic meter and form.; [a.] Barrington, IL

DEAN, DINA M.
[b.] September 2, 1961, Charleston, SC; [p.] M - Avis J. Hoopes, F. - Vernon L. Hoopes; [m.] Christopher T. Dean, December 6, 1986; [ed.] Hansen High School, University of Soutwestern Louisiana; [occ.] CPA; [hon.] Phi Kappa Phi, Dean's List, Graduated Cum Laude; [a.] Phoenix, AZ

DECILLIS, REBECCA LIVIA
[b.] September 30, 1985, West Islip, NY; [p.] Michael A. DeCillis, Marie L. DeCillis; [ed.] Islip Community Nursery School - 2 yrs., Maud S. Sherwood Elementary School, Islip, NY, K-5th grade, currently attending Islip Middle School, Islip, NY; [memb.] Suffolk County Girl Scouts, Maud S. Sherwood Elementary School Band and Chorus, Suffolk County Girls Softball League; [hon.] NY State School Music Association - Outstanding Evaluation, Math Olympiads, Suffolk Reading Council Creative Writing Contest, President Award for Educational Excellence, Science Fair 1993 - School Representative at Brookhaven National Laboratory; [oth. writ.] "Autumn Leaves", Anthology of Poetry by Young Americans, 1996 Edition; [a.] Islip, NY

DELAINE, LULA EDYTHE
[pen.] L. Edythe DeLaine; [b.] January 14, 1935, Manning, SC; [p.] Lewis and Lula Mae DeLaine; [ed.] Allen University; [occ.] Social Worker; [pers.] To take the simple plain everyday things of life find beauty in them. To help others to understand that life is worthwhile; [a.] Manning, SC

DELAUTER, LINA
[pen.] Lyn and L and Brat; [b.] February 6, 1981; [p.] Lisa and Jeff Delauter; [ed.] 10th grade at South Hagerstown High School; [memb.] BMG Music Service, Hagerstown Church of the Brethen, South Hagerstown High School band; [hon.] Straight A and Honor Roll Student; [oth. writ.] I did a lot more writings for school; [pers.] I'm 15 years old, I play the clarinet in the band. I also play softball for our school. At church I am in 3 choirs, play bells, clown, in our youth choir and band.; [a.] Hagerstown, MD

DELL, GINA V.
[b.] May 26, 1969, Saskatchewan, Canada; [m.] John P. Dell; [ed.] Associate, Music Education Bachelor of Music, Performance English Degree - Creative Writing Classical Guitarists/Teacher; [occ.] Financial Services - Selco Credit Union, Eugene, OR; [memb.] University of Oregon Alumni; [hon.] Toronto Conservatory of Music - Classical Guitar Performance, English Award - Douglas College, New Westminster, British Columbia, Canada; [oth. writ.] This is the first poem officially published. Have published some of my own newsletters.; [pers.] My personal challenge is to see everyday events as unique and from a different perspective. Every experience in life is a gift. I feel lucky to know this secret. My job as a writer/artist is to remind everyone we are all creators - we are all fascinating.; [a.] Eugene, OR

DENG, LULU
[b.] May 13, 1982, China; [p.] Weimin Deng and Yuan Dong; [ed.] Walled Lake Middle School, Walled Lake Western; [occ.] Student at Walled Lake Western; [memb.] Club of Nations; [oth. writ.] Poems published in Renderings of The Imagination; [pers.] I like to thank my parents for being so wonderful and also all my buddies for being there for me when I needed them.; [a.] Wixom, MI

DENHOLTZ, ELAINE
[occ.] Faculty, Fairleigh Dickinson University, Dept. English; [memb.] Dramatist Guild of America, Phi Beta Kappa, Writers Guild of America; [hon.] Eugene O'Neill Playwright, N.J. Literary Hall of Fame, N.J. Council on Arts Winner; [oth. writ.] Author of books, plays and articles, films, newspaper columnist, television

DENNIS, ERLINE
[b.] May 8, 1953, Bridgeport, CT; [p.] Adgie and Bertha Dennis; [ch.] Shanté R. Randall; [ed.] Warren Harding High School, Bridgeport, CT; University of Bridgeport, Bridgeport, CT, Degree in Business & Humanities; [occ.] Single Mom - and work a full time job; [memb.] Member of Messiah Baptist Church, Bridgeport, CT; [oth. writ.] First poem ever written on 11/23/95 - "A Message To My Sister From Heart To Heart." Have written 25 poems since that date.; [pers.] I thank the Lord Almighty for this gift to write and my dearest and closest friend who has been a great inspiration to me. If the Lord is for me, what man can be against me.; [a.] Bridgeport, CT

DENNIS, MERANDA VIRGINIA
[pen.] Miss Thang, Miss Laughs Alot; [b.] January 21, 1981, Chester; [p.] JD Temple, Neil Williams (Stepdad); [ed.] 2nd year in high school James River; [occ.] Cindis Cleaning Crew. Cleans houses and apartments; [oth. writ.] Friend of Melissa Holmes better known as Missy, and too many guys to mention. Lives in Chester and loves cats especially my fat Prissy. Youngest sister of Heather Dennis a loving mom and stepdad Neil Williams. I love to write poems and or stories of my thoughts and feelings I am very caring and love to give advice when I can. My dad's never been there for me as I was growing up it was rough for my mom. She use to take us to parks and make us listen to all the nature around us. So one day at Bugs Island I sat on our private dock and wrote all that I heard I felt.; [pers.] I don't try to satisfy people with my poems, I just write how I feel.; [a.] Richmond, VA

DENNIS, SARAH JEAN
[b.] August 31, 1981, CA; [p.] John and Billie Dennis; [ed.] Heritage Christian School; [occ.] School and church; [memb.] Heritage Baptist Church; [hon.] For 14 souls saved, for helping the church. Also AB honor roll; [oth. writ.] I have many other poems that I hope they will soon be published.; [pers.] To strongly express myself and the way I think.; [a.] Orange Park, FL

DENTON, F. NEIL
[b.] March 29, 1940, Independence, KS; [p.] Floyd V. and Mabel E. Denton; [m.] Peggy Anna Donavan Denton, August 4, 1962; [ch.] Michelle, Stephanie; [ed.] BA, Kans St. Univ 1962, B. Divinity, Sacred Master of Theology, Dr. of Ministry, Dr. of Ministry, Andover, Newton Theological Seminary, Boston, MA; [occ.] Retired Professor of Pastoral Core and Dean of Students; [memb.] Assn. for Clinical Pastoral Education, Clinical Member, National Polycystic Kidney Foundation, Member; [a.] Kansas City, KS

DETTBARN, KENNETH
[b.] March 25, 1966, Elkader, IA; [p.] Kenneth and Gwen Dettbarn; [m.] Linda J. Dettbarn, June 1, 1985; [ch.] Sean M. and Nicholas G.; [ed.] Lincoln Technical Institute Associates in Applied Science, 1984 Graduate Central Comm. H.S. Elkader, IA; [occ.] United States Army, Warrant Officer; [a.] Killeen, TX

DEVAAN, MARY JANE
[b.] March 9, 1938, Swift Co., MN; [p.] Joseph and Lucille Rutledge; [m.] John L. DeVaan, October 6, 1956; [ch.] Deb, Cate, Joe, Mary, Ed, Steve, Jim, Sarah; [ed.] Murdoch High, St. Catherines College, Willmar Community College, Marshall State University; [occ.] Farmer and Business Manager; [memb.] St. Bridgets Catholic Church, V.F.W. Aux, Roaring 20's Homemakers, Swift Co. Historical Society, Chairperson of St. Bridget's Finance; [oth. writ.] Many poems and readings given orally at wedding and baby Showers, Anniversary's, etc.; [pers.] I write about family, friends and feelings from the heart and comics just for fun.; [a.] Glenwood, MN

DEZELAN, LOUIS A.
[b.] May 25, 1945, Indianapolis; [m.] Susan Wollenweber, September 12, 1987; [ed.] BA Indiana Univ.; [occ.] Battalion Chief Indianapolis Fire Dept.; [hon.] In 1990, awarded a fellowship to Harvard University's Program for Senior Executives in State and Local Governments; [oth. writ.] Numerous non-fiction articles in National Publications; [a.] Indianapolis, IN

DI MATTIA, PETER P.
[b.] March 11, 1926, Summit Hill, PA; [m.] Barbara Ann Di Mattia, January 16, 1955; [ch.] Peter, Robert, Daniel, two grandchildren Allyse, Lureen, two daughter-in-laws - Mary Ann and Trudy; [occ.] Electrician Coal Mining Co. 52 years still working; [oth. writ.] The End Of A Rainbow, The Greatest Gift In This World Is The Gift Of Life. The First Hundreds Tears Are The Hardest Abortion - How Low Did The Human Race Get.

DICARLO, JOSEPH
[pen.] Joe DiCarlo; [b.] June 20, 1940, Bronx, NY; [p.] Joseph DiCarlo Sr. and Rose DiCarlo; [ed.] Mount St. Michael Academy, BA, Fordham University, MA, St. John's University; [occ.] Free lance writer and artist; [hon.] Fordham Honors Program Golden Alpha; [oth. writ.] Many poems published in local church bulletin, additional poem published in magazine All About Issues, author, "Following Christ," Faith And Life Series, published by Ignatius Press; [a.] Pelham Manor, NY

DICK, CATRINA LYNN
[pen.] Trina; [b.] December 21, 1980, Galveston, TX; [p.] Katherine Hale, Ronny Hale (Stepfather), Don Dick; [ed.] Currently, I am in the 10th grade at Clear Creek High School; [oth. writ.] I've been writing poems since the 6th grade. I've written a large number of poems.; [pers.] I believe the combination of being in touch with your emotions and having an imagination to further extend the debt of your emotions are a great part of being a successful poet.; [a.] League City, TX

DICKERMAN, PAMELA ARDREY
[b.] May 17, 1954, Riverside, CA; [p.] Richard H. and LaNelle B. Ardrey; [m.] George F. Dickerman, October 28, 1989; [ch.] Beau Houston and Brock Ardrey Dickerman; [ed.] Riverside Polytechnic High School, Riverside Community College, Cal. State Univ. - Long Beach, Loma Linda University; [occ.] Physical Therapist/Mother, Kaiser Permanente - Riverside, CA; [memb.] American Horse Shows Assoc., American Saddlebred Horse Assoc., Southern CA Saddlebred Horse Assoc.; [hon.] DAR Homemaking Award Literary Awards in School Talent Awards - Pianist Briandale Therapeutic Riding Program, 1996 AHSA Saddlebred Horse of the Year Award - Western and Hunt Seat, 1996 Saddle and Bridle Magazine - Best of Breed - Western Horse, Various Awards - Recognition for coverage of high school athletic events; [pers.] I try to be keenly aware of nature and all the beautiful things which surround us, rather than get caught up in the stress/strife of everyday life. I am trying to pass a love of nature on to my children also.; [a.] Riverside, CA

DIGIOVANNA, TIGELIA
[pen.] Tigellia Da Verona; [b.] March 14, 1914, New York City; [p.] Coyntess Maria Bucelli and Luigi Cigco; [m.] Hon. Anthony DiGiovanna J.S.C., July 7, 1936 in Rome Italy; [ch.] Nina, Maria and John, 6 grandchildren, 6 great grandchildren; [ed.] N.Y. Private School, Shore Road Academy Adelphi College - Garden City N.Y. University New York; [occ.] Staying alive for a 91 years old husband.; [memb.] Chairman of Women's Campaign Committee for Mayor Robert Wagner of New York; [hon.] Trustee of The Brooklyn Public Library for 16 years, Selected Mother of the Year in 1975 by Italian Historical Society of America; [oth. writ.] I have written poetry since the age of 8 only for the joy of writing. To write poetry is to confess your truth, to God... and there is healing! Tigelia DiGiovanna; [pers.] Mr. Ely to receive an aword from the National Library of Poetry at the age of 82, would be a sweet topping to my life -long passion. Thank you for fanning my fire.; [a.] New York, NY

DILLARD, WANDA ANN
[pen.] Ann Dillard; [b.] December 9, 1952, Chickamauga, GA; [p.] Mr. and Mrs. Henry H. Lewis; [oth. writ.] "Lift your eyes to the father" Where is God, The Rivers Edge, A Place in the Wilderness Compassions of yesterday; [pers.] I write to glorify my Savior, so that I may inspire others.; [a.] Chattanooga, TN

DILULLO, ADRIENNE
[pen.] Adrienne Winters; [b.] May 21, 1949, Martins Ferry, OH; [p.] John and Mary Schlatt; [m.] Paul LaPrise; [ch.] Kevin and Nick; [pers.] I am intrigued by the precision and efficiency of poetry. My work as a "wordsmith" is to chose words and phrasing to capture and communicate the essence of a moment... the feeling, the mood, the image.; [a.] San Carlos, CA

DITARANTO, TORI
[b.] May 27, 1983, Paterson, NJ; [p.] Karen and Dan DiTaranto; [ed.] Dequannock Township Public Schools; [occ.] Student; [memb.] Greenpeace Organization, Literary Magazine Staff, Audubon Society Member; [hon.] Artist of the month, high honors role; [oth. writ.] Several entries in Literary Magazine, collection of poems in journal; [pers.] I strive to improve the environment and equality for all mankind in all my poems.; [a.] Pompton Plains, NJ

DIXON, MEGAN
[b.] May 6, 1982, Lansing, MI; [p.] Michael Dixon, Robin Dixon; [ed.] 9th Grade at Chippewa Valley High School; [memb.] Chippewa Valley Freshman Cheerleading, Student Government Freshmen Senate, and St. Gabriels Youth Group; [hon.] Wyandot Middle School's June Tarakoff Outstanding Service award 95-96, Outstanding Academic Achievement, Community Service Award; [a.] Clinton Township, MI

DIXON JR., BERNICE M.
[pen.] Minna Hawke; [b.] Chicago, IL; [ch.] Adriana and Thomas; [ed.] Student at Jackson State University, Jackson, MS, Pre-Med/Foreign Language Major; [occ.] CSS - Customer Serv. Specialist; [memb.] Anderson United Methodist Church, Anderson Choir; [oth. writ.] "Olde to Chicago", "History of the Black Woman", "Brother, Brother", "If", "Black Clouds", currently working on 1st manuscript "Sister to Sista"; [pers.] Know that I have not lived without truly living. To have a seriousness of attitude in whatever I do.; [a.] Jackson, MS

DOLAN, KATE
[pen.] Kat, K. R. Dolan; [b.] May 16, 1985, Germany;

[p.] Sim and Sally Dolan; [ed.] Vaughan Elementary School, Allen, TX; [occ.] Student; [memb.] O. M. (Odyssey of the Mind), Girl Scouts of America; [hon.] 2nd place in Odyssey of the mind (Great Impressions); [oth. writ.] Hoping to publish a children's chapter book; [pers.] I hope to start a new era in poem writing and influence kids of America to help clean our planet.; [a.] Allen, TX

DOMINGUEZ, BRIAN
[b.] August 26, 1976, Vallejo, CA; [p.] Rick Dominguez, Lynn Bishop; [ed.] Currently a Freshman Agri-business Major at Coffeyviolle Community College; [pers.] If everyone would listen to what writers had to say they might be able to live life a little happier.; [a.] Chetopa, KS

DOMINGUEZ, MIGUEL E.
[b.] August 3, 1960, El Salvador, CA; [p.] Catalina Y Leandro Dominguez; [m.] Ada L. Dominguez, August 17, 1985; [ch.] Samuel E. Dominguez, Daniel E. Dominguez, Miguel E. Dominguez Jr.; [ed.] Currently pursuing an Associated in Applied science in Electronics at the HCCC (Hudson County Community College) of Jersey City, NJ; [occ.] Warehouse Worker; [memb.] I am a member of "The Way" Pentecostal Church, Inc., Jersey City, NJ; [oth. writ.] The "Los Poemas De Miguel Dominguez", "Radio Vision Cristiana, 1330 Am" poem "Canciones A Mi Amado", songs; [pers.] These poems reflect my love for Jesus, my wife, my three children and the goodness of life in general.; [a.] Bayonne, NJ

DOUGHERTY, ANNETTE L.
[b.] December 5, 1951, Upper Darby, PA; [p.] John J. Dougherty, Anna M. McKeown; [ch.] Audubon Lynn Dougherty; [ed.] Archbishop Prendergast High School, Villanova Univ. (B. attended graduate school Univ of Conn, Fairfield Univ.); [occ.] Elementary Montessori Teacher, Newburyport Montessori School, private piano teacher; [pers.] I believe that our creative abilities are unlimited because our source is infinite. Therefore I have resolved to create one original work every day (writing, music or art). This has become a fulfilling habit and is my praise to the one and only creator.; [a.] Newburyport, MA

DOUGLAS, MICHELE ROSS
[pen.] Rene; [b.] September 11, 1953, Fort Dodge, IA; [p.] Orville Hurley and Ruby Hurley; [m.] Frank Douglas, August 22, 1995; [ch.] Holly Marie, Antonia Treasa, Daniel William; [ed.] Ellsworth Community College, Iowa Falls, Iowa; [occ.] Homemaker; [oth. writ.] Several poems published in Ellsworths College Literary publication "The Plum". Won honorable mention. Poems published in local newspaper. Story published in "True Stories", "Woman Are Wonderful" in November 1980.; [pers.] My "words on white" are based on the times of my life, the good and the bad.; [a.] Fort Dodge, IA

DOWD, BILL
[b.] March 12, 1984, Boston, MA; [p.] Chris Dowd, Karen Dowd; [ed.] 7th grade; [occ.] Student; [a.] Braintree, MA

DOZIER, EDEN
[b.] September 11, 1983, Lakewood, CA; [pers.] I wrote my poem "The Ocean" when I was eleven years old.

DRATHRING, LYN
[b.] November 28, 1955; [oth. writ.] Unpublished - keepers of the well poems- Earth ways.; [pers.] I seek to walk life's path with grace and integrity. For guidance I often listen for the divine presence I feel in nature and to my heart. My writing is in response to what I hear.; [a.] Crystal Lake, IL

DRIGGS, CAROLINE
[b.] June 8, 1959, Enugu, Nigeria; [p.] Donald Pickering, Susan Pickering; [m.] Edmund H. Driggs, March 3, 1990; [ch.] Edmund Hope and Elizabeth Simpson; [ed.] Cambridge University, England; [occ.] Portrait Photographer and mother; [hon.] M.A. (Hons) Cantab; [a.] Darien, CT

DUBOIS, JANICE
[pen.] Janice E. Holt; [b.] February 10, 1937, Minneapolis, MN; [p.] Knute and Edith Hold (Deceased); [ch.] Linda Edner, Scott Ranke, Christine Hay; [ed.] Miller Vocational High - Minneapolis, MN; [occ.] Secretary and also sports official for high school league; [memb.] National Rifle Assoc., Minn. State Horticulture Society; [hon.] Induction into the Minnesota Softball Hall of Fame in 1985; [oth. writ.] I Love To Walk In The Wood; [pers.] My favorite poem is "How Do I Love Thee" by Elizabeth Barrett Browning. Favorite poet is Edgar Allen Poe. These authors gave me both pleasure and inspiration.; [a.] Crystal, MN

DUFFY JR., JOHN M.
[pen.] Pat O'Shea; [b.] July 16, 1975, Allentown, PA; [p.] John M. Duffy and Mary Lou Duffy; [ed.] North Western Lehigh High. Lehigh Carbon Community College; [occ.] Student (Studying Criminal Justice); [memb.] North Western Ambulance Corp.; [hon.] Merit Award for Volunteerism as a High School Student; [oth. writ.] A notebook full of personel poems (This is my first published poem.); [pers.] My poetry reflects the reality of society and America through poetry, Influences: Robert Frost, Walt Whitman, Edgar Alan Poe. And so on.; [a.] Germonsville, PA

DUGANICH, DON R.
[pen.] Don R. Duganich; [b.] November 8, 1926, Noblesville, IN; [ch.] Christina K. and Richard E.; [ed.] Noblesville High, Two Navy Service Schools, four year Apprenticeship to become a journeyman, Electric Lineman for 27 years; [occ.] Retired, Submarine Torpedoman - WWII Veteran; [pers.] I believe the quality of ones life is much more important than the quantity. I enjoy writing poems that make people laugh.; [a.] Las Cruces, NM

DUMMERT, ANN L.
[pen.] Sophie Lee; [b.] April 18, 1957, Washington; [p.] LeRoy and Eileen Pierce; [m.] Marvin (Butch) Dummert, February 6, 1987; [ch.] Four; [ed.] Reynolds High School - Troutdale Ore. San Diego School of Nursing, Children's Lititure - Cor; [memb.] First Baptist Church Rosburg Rebekah Lodge #41 Myrtal Creek L.E.A. #79; [oth. writ.] Short Stories - Poems published: Glide Weekly, News Review; [pers.] The sensitive Nature of my Life, and a wonderful English teacher influenced my early writing Life. With writing we are able to feel. To feel is human and we can know we are alive.; [a.] Glide, OR

DUNCAN, HAZEL
[pen.] Hazel Duncan; [b.] January 25, 1971, Osceola, AR; [p.] James and Geneva Godwin; [m.] Michael Duncan, April 8, 1988; [ch.] Nicki Renae and Kaitlyn Michelle; [ed.] Rivercrest High School through grade 11. Cotton - Boll Vo-Tech for G.E.D., diploma; [occ.] Homemaker; [pers.] Life is full off things to write about. I enjoy just thinking about different situations and then expressing my feelings by writing about them.; [a.] Dyess, AR

DUNFEE, MARY SALLIE
[pen.] Sallie Carter; [b.] October 24, 1937, Saint Petersburg, FL; [p.] Charles and Mary Carter; [m.] Albert M. Dunfee, April 19, 1992; [ch.] Brian, Candy, Charlean,

Danny; [ed.] Tomlinson Voc Tec., Major Commercial Art; [memb.] Beta Sigma Phi, Alpha XI Sorority Volunteer, Tampa Gen. Hosp, also Bay Pines V.A.; [hon.] Numerous Art Awards also Miss Georgia 1954, Miss Missouri 1956, Scholarship Award's; [oth. writ.] Poem published in world of poetry anthology also honorable mention on numerous poems; [pers.] "I will not pass this way again." What might have been said or might have been done, that never can be said or done.; [a.] Saint Petersburg, FL

DUNHAM, MARIE
[oth. writ.] Several poems in local paper, a poem in the American poetry anthology, and my book: Poetry and me.; [a.] Clifton, TX

DUNNELL, MARY A.
[b.] September 18, 1914, Arnett, OK; [p.] James Allen and Mary Alice Rucker; [m.] Lloyd William Dunnell, January 21, 1936 - celebrated 60th Anniversary in 1996; [ch.] Lloyd W. Jr. and Jerry Allen; two Grandsons - Lloyd W. III and Donny Steven; [ed.] Graduated from Arnett High, 1933; [occ.] Farmer's wife; [memb.] First Baptist Church Mulvane, KS; [pers.] I spent summer vacations alone — observing the birds, their songs and nesting habits. I had no thoughts of writing poems until in my senior year of high school my English teacher required a poem in order to graduate. My poem was my nature observations put on paper. It was chosen the best in my class. I thought no more about it until I saw the poetry contest advertised a chance to have it graded.; [a.] Udall, KS

DYAL, MELISSA
[b.] February 24, 1975, Baxley, GA; [p.] Willie Dyal and Debbie Mathews; [ed.] Fernandina Beach High, Valdosta Tech.; [occ.] Secretary; [a.] Port Orange, FL

DYER, LA TONYA
[pen.] La Tonya Dyer; [b.] October 22, 1977, Baltimore, MD; [p.] Janelle Dyer and Earrol Dyer; [ed.] Meryen Thaler Vo-Tech High Baltimore City Community College; [occ.] Cashier; [memb.] BCCC Poetry Club, BCCC Business Club; [oth. writ.] Wrote collections of poems and stories; [pers.] My poetry is influenced by my life experiences, my family and my community. I strive to express my true feelings in my poetry so that others can relate and hopefully learn something; [a.] Baltimore, MD

EARICH, GLENN A.
[b.] March 28, 1968, Warren, OH; [p.] Rod Earich, Geneva Earich; [ed.] Howland High School, Ohio State University; [occ.] Comedian; [pers.] This poem is for all fathers and sons and the unspoken feelings that they share.; [a.] Warren, OH

EASTERDAY, JAMES MICHAEL
[b.] May 4, 1954, Hagerstown, MD; [p.] Irvin R. and G. Easterday; [ed.] BA: Eastern Mennonite College Harrisonburg VA, Master of Divinity: Eastern Mennonite Seminary Harrisonburg VA; [occ.] United Methodist Minister; [memb.] Baltimore-Washington Conference of United Methodist Church; [hon.] Elder of United Methodist Church; [oth. writ.] Unpublished poetry; [pers.] My writing is an endeavor to portray mankind's emotions towards life and a reflection of the world he lives in.; [a.] Hagerstown, MD

EBERLY, FRANK C.
[b.] February 19, 1917, Fayette Co, PA; [p.] Lidia and Edward Eberly; [m.] Deceased, February 28, 1941; [ch.] James, Lois, Cheryl; [ed.] High School, College B.S. degree graduate work U. of Del. Valedictorian High

School and College; [occ.] Retired - E. I. DuPont; [oth. writ.] Have written many short poems and given them away. None published.

ECKLES, BARBARA LEWIS
[pen.] Barbara Lewis Eckles; [b.] July 5, 1943, Colorado City, TX; [p.] Bob and Florence Lewis; [m.] Sparky Eckles, August 4, 1961; [ch.] Dedra Driggers, Audra Bryant, Melissa Burson, Jennifer Eckles - 4 daughters; [ed.] High School, Canadian High, Canadian TX 1961, Certified Lay Speaker, United Methodist Church NWT Conference; [occ.] City Swimming Pool Mgr. and School Employee; [memb.] United Methodist Church, Dickens - Spur Public Library, Friends of the Library, Llano Estacado, Emmaus Community, American Cancer Society, United Methodist Women; [hon.] Dickens Co. Woman of the Year by VFW in 1989, recognized for 17 years in leadership in Children's Choirs and Work.; [oth. writ.] Several poems published in local church paper and local newspapers, poetry used in talks and sermons I present; [pers.] I write by inspiration, I've always loved poetry. I began writing for myself seriously in 1970 following the death of my brother, Robert Lewis Jr. who I dedicate this publication to. I've learned when something comes to me, I must write it then - because it won't come again.; [a.] Spur, TX

ECONOMOPOULOS, ELIZABETH
[pen.] Liz Economopoulos; [b.] October 23, 1975, Brooklyn; [p.] Joann and Anastasios Economopoulos; [ed.] Fort Hamilton H.S., Baruch College of The City University of New York; [occ.] Student; [memb.] Intercollegiate Hellenic Society, Greek School of Plato Alumni and Marching band, Academy of Finance Alumni.; [oth. writ.] Many unpublished poems and several songs; [pers.] Follow your heart and things will come true.; [a.] Brooklyn, NY

EDELSTEIN, ROSABELLE W. M.
[pen.] Robin Dara Miller; [b.] New York, NY; [p.] Elias and Hannah Miller Winer, Prof. Harry Edward Miller (Economist) deceased; [m.] Mortimer S. Edelstein (Attorney) Deceased; [ch.] Jane Dara Rosenbloom; [ed.] Brown University, Rhode Island School of Design, New York University B.F.A., Fashion Institute of Technology, A.A.S., New York School of Interior Design, Art Career School (Architecture and Design) N.Y.C.; [occ.] Free lance writer Former occupation: Dress designer, former interior designer; [memb.] American Society of Interior Design (ASID) Charter Member of Writers Group "Writing to Publish" Sarasota FL; [hon.] Graduated with highest honors from F.I.T., National award first place for contract, photographs of many interiors published in residential and contract magazines; [oth. writ.] Regular column in Westport, Fairfield and Weston (Conn.) Town Crier "You and Your Home" over several years, Women and Money magazine, "Single Women and Money", Sarasota Herald Tribune "The Little Town Across the Bridge", short story collection (current); [pers.] Art is the soul of living, its beauty exudes into many areas and overlaps as though seeping from one to another.; [a.] Sarasota, FL

EDENS, LOU E.
[b.] August 8, 1941, Ruffin, SC; [p.] Francis B. Thomas, Llewellyn B. Thomas; [ch.] John E. Edens, Jamie Edens; [ed.] B.A. Sociology, University of South Carolina, 1962; [occ.] Retail Merchant, Real Estate Developer, Innkeeper; [memb.] Phi Beta Kappa, Zeta Tau Alpha Founder, Museum on the Common Founder, Shem Creek Maritime Museum Founder, Uncommon Literary Society; [hon.] 1994 Top SC Chip Enterprise Award,

Charleston Trident Outstanding Performance (TOP) Award 1993, SC Federation of Museums State of Achievement 1994, 1996; [oth. writ.] Museum exhibits - label copy. Local newspaper.; [pers.] A love of language, a fascination with the diversity of human behavior, and an abiding appreciation for the cultural heritage of my native SC low coming inspires my writings.; [a.] Isle of Palms, SC

EDGINGTON, SARAH
[b.] January 19, 1985, Covington, KY; [p.] Jeff and Judy Edgington; [ed.] Walton - Verona Elementary School; [hon.] Kentucky Student Scholar 1994-95 Mathematics Award, Spelling Award, Reading Award, Language Arts Award, Certificate of Recognition in Writing, Social Studies Award, Science Award, Perfect Attendance 1995-96; [a.] Walton, KY

EDLING, JULIE STAMMER
[b.] February 1, 1962, Sacramento; [p.] Jack Stammer and Nancy Price; [m.] Craig Edling, October 15, 1988; [ch.] Amber, Ashley; [ed.] Graduated El Modena High School, Orange, CA in 1980. Graduated from Modesto Junior College, Modesto, CA (AA General) in 1989. Pursuing a nursing Degree; [occ.] Domestic Engineer/ P/T Billing Clerk for Anesthesiologist; [memb.] Community United Methodist Church-Child Care Coordinator; [hon.] Modesto Junior College Deans List Spring 1989; [pers.] To my father who blessed me with his poetic talent and to my family and friends who encouraged me to write - your support and love has been my inspiration.; [a.] Waterford, CA

EDRINGTON, JOSH
[pen.] Josh Edrington; [b.] August 2, 1996, Merced, CA; [p.] Michael Maier, Lenora Maier; [ed.] Graduate of Atwater High School, Enrolled at Merced Junior College; [occ.] Cashier, Newberry's; [memb.] Sierra Nevada Club, Freshman Football, Varsity Track and Field; [pers.] My writing is from the heart. Many youths have a different way in expressing their feelings, writing is mine.; [a.] Winton, CA

EDWARDS, BONNIE L.
[pen.] Bonnie Lou; [b.] December 22, 1958, Syracuse, NY; [m.] Thomas J. Edwards, October 12, 1979; [occ.] Patient Counselor Baptist Medical Center; [a.] Kansas City, MO

ELIOT, MARY S.
[b.] January 15, 1953, Anderson, IN; [p.] Mary and Robert Furge; [m.] Richard S. Eliot, July 11, 1987; [ch.] Lisa Jones, Scott Jones; [ed.] Presently a Senior at Marian College; [occ.] Paramedic Wishard Hospital Indianapolis, IN; [memb.] Swim Masters, Westwood County Club, St. Michael Church; [pers.] I try to write regarding some of the joys and hardships I see on my job.; [a.] Indianapolis, IN

ENLOE, INGRID A.
[pen.] Ten Jan (T.J.) Roberts; [b.] January 5, 1961, Mesa, AZ; [p.] Wayne A. and Helen G. Enloe; [m.] Single Mother; [ch.] Ryan (daughter), Nikolas and Carson (sons); [ed.] Chandler Junior High, Chandler High School, Some College; [occ.] Self-employed (Cater to the stars), Artist (over 16 yrs. in ceramics); [memb.] The Phoenix Zoo, Disney Collections; [hon.] Honor Student in High School; [oth. writ.] A couple of other poems have been published. One written for my father.; [pers.] My poems are from my heart. The feeling and love is very strong like my art. My heart is in every piece of my art. And my poems.; [a.] Chandler, AZ

ERICSON, RUTH W.
[b.] October 23, 1925, Lakewood, OH; [p.] Calvin William White, Ruth Burleson White; [m.] Richard Joseph Ericson (Artist), July 17, 1948; [ch.] Richard, Joseph, Peter, Daniel, John, Mark and Steven; [ed.] BA, MA, ABD - Herbert Lehman Fellow in Sociology (New School Soc Research); [occ.] Retired Prof. Sociology (Suny, Liu, Cuny, NCC) Research Fellow Amer. Enterprise Inst. (-Detired); [memb.] Trustee and Treasurer Beckman Public Library Lector, Alto-Epescopal Church; [oth. writ.] Casual publication of 3 other poems in local media.; [pers.] Poetry puts back together the torn fabric of memory, meaning and desire.; [a.] Hopewell Junction, NY

ERQUHART, DONNA M.
[b.] April 21, 1965, Camden, ME; [p.] Margaret and Richard Erquhart; [m.] Rod Bluma, April 21, 1989; [ch.] Cynthia, Amber, Krissy; [ed.] High School Grad., Vocational Medical School and Washburn University; [occ.] Kansas State Board of Healing Arts; [memb.] ABATE of Kansas, District 4; [oth. writ.] If Only They Would Listen, As Angels Fly; [pers.] Anything is possible, you have only but to start.; [a.] Topeka, KS

ESELY, CARLA JEAN LAGLIA
[b.] February 20, 1954, Findlay, OH; [p.] Domenick Laglia and Nellie G. Oman Laglia; [m.] William Cecil Esely, April 10, 1982; [ed.] Graduate - Findlay Senior High School in 1972 was in High School "Chorus and Drama" or (Thespians); [occ.] Housewife, Poetic Writer. I also raise registered AKC Keeshondens; [memb.] The American Kennel Club, Women in Military Service for America, San Antonio Catholic Church and Distinguish Member of The International Society of Poets; [hon.] 1969 - President and Jr. Chairman-Ralph D. Cole Post Unit 3 American Legion Jr. Auxiliary Both Parents Honorably Discharged Naval Veterans (WWII and Korea). 1995-1996 International Society of Poets Recognition. The National Library of Poetry 1996 Editor's Choice Award.; [oth. writ.] Several unsubmitted. I song poem published. Defend your Land - stolen. 2 poems published 1. A Quiet Repose and #2 Freedom Cries by National Library of Poetry.; [pers.] I am a firm believer in God and Country. I have been greatly influenced in my writing by my parents and my Grand Parents Mr. and Mrs. Elmer Roy Oman who raised me with Love, Honor, Discipline, Understanding and support and By my loving supportive Husband William C. Esely and the splendid beauty of God's creations.; [a.] McIntosh, NM

ETESSAMI, SOUDABEH
[pen.] Soudabeh; [b.] Tehran, Iran; [p.] Said Etessami, Betty Farzin; [ch.] Samira Ghaffari; [ed.] Ph.D. (Animal Biology) from University of Bordeaun/France; [occ.] Senior Research Scientist; [memb.] Few Scientific Societies such as: ASHI (American Society of Histocompatibility and Immunsojenetics); [hon.] Honorable mention for poem published in "Poetry Revival, an Anthology" 1994. This poem is called "The Deep"; [oth. writ.] Several poems published in her native language (Foursi) scientific pyers and communications published internationally.; [pers.] I love to write poems when I am in love or I am sad. I think I inherited my talent from my aunt: Parvin Etessami who was the most famous female poet in Iran. I love to be a scientist also may be I could solve few problems for mankind; [a.] Tarzana, CA

EUL, CHERYL-LOUISE HASTINGS
[pen.] Cherry-Rose Hastings; [b.] August 27, 1949, Canton, OH; [p.] Daniel and Jeanne Hastings; [m.] Michael Allen Eul, September 12, 1993; [ch.] Rick (28), Ian (12), Sean (11), Brenton (10); [ed.] Pierce College Writing Courses, Learning Tree University Courses; [occ.] Artist - Home Business create Native American Crafts, Dream - catchers Jewelry, Oil-Paintings on Rocks...; [memb.] Book Publicists of Southern California and also V.P. of National Forest Association, Calvary Church, Counselor and Director of "Catharsis", non-profit org. for women" who want (none) out of sex - industry; [oth. writ.] Currently writing three screenplays, all of which are non-fiction also write and submit self help articles for women, song lyrics and poetry.; [pers.] I write to reflect the truth and beauty of simple things, and hope people take the time to see the way I do. I have been extremely influenced by Tennessee Ann Sexton. Williams and Truman Capote, and Sylvia Plath; [a.] La Canada, CA

EVANS, SUSAN LIPPERT
[b.] January 15, 1962, York, PA; [p.] Donald Lippert, Loyetta St. Clair; [m.] Steven Evans, July 2, 1983; [ch.] Matthew Steven, Jennifer Lynn; [ed.] Boyd Anderson High, Florida Atlantic University (BSW - Bachelor's in Social Work); [occ.] Homemaker, Volunteer; [memb.] Church of Christ; [hon.] Graduated in top 5% of H.S. class, Dean's List in College; [pers.] In life, I seek God, love, family, wisdom, balance, and understanding. In my writing, I seek to make a connection with a universal humanity.; [a.] Deerfield Beach, FL

EVERETT, HUMPHREY OWEN
[b.] October 25, 1920, Wautoma, WI; [p.] Marion and Flora Humphrey; [m.] Billye Cox (Deceased), April 6, 1946; [ch.] Reba and Ivye; [ed.] Wautoma High School, B.S., Univ., of Wis. Whitewater, M.S. Univ. of Ark., Fayetteville, Ed, Sp., Univ., of Illinois, Champaigne; [occ.] Retired school administrator; [memb.] ASCD (Life), NEA (Life), Phi Delta Kappa (Emeritus), Kappa Delta Phi, Int. Society of Poets, Collinsville Area Theatrical Society; [hon.] Phi Delta Kappa Service Key, 1984 Creativity Recognition Award, 1972 George H. Reavis Associate Award, 1991 Granite City Area Council PTA Award, 1979 Military (Bronze Star, 4 ETO Battle Stars) Biog. sketches: Dict. of Intern. Biog., Who's Who in the Midwest, Who's Who in America, Who's Who in Amer. Educ., Who's Who in the World, 2000 Men of Achievement, creative and successful personalities of the world; [oth. writ.] Poems pub. in a delicate balance, a Tapestry of Thoughts, Carvings in Stone, The Best Poems of the 90's, The Ebbing Tide, Of Sunshine and Daydreams, Famous, Poems of Today. Contributor to Illinois School Research author of the Greening of Gateway East.; [pers.] At age 75, my retirement years are stirring up renewed interest in the poetry-writing I first started at age 16. My time is largely filled with writing and acting in a community theater group.; [a.] Granite City, IL

EWERSEN, VIRGINIA PEASE
[b.] June 2, 1922, Van West County, OH; [p.] Elza and Pearlie Pease; [m.] Herbert Ewersen (Deceased), October 18, 1942; [ch.] Dale and Carol Ewersen; [ed.] B.S. in Education, Bowling Green State University, Graduate Studies Bowling Green, Toledo and Ohio State Universities; [occ.] Retired, Reading Coordinates - Teaching title I program; [memb.] Sandusky Chored Society, Nature Conservancy, National Reading Arsini, International Society of poets; [hon.] Award for literary, 1995, IRA, publishing of my poetry by the National Library of Poetry! Kappa Delta Pi (Education Honorary) Who's Who in American Education, Who's Who of American Women's, Who's Who Child Development; [oth. writ.] Local Newspaper Articles are Child Development's Activity Lord let "From Hyperactive to Happy Active" (1979); [pers.] I aim for excellence, with a cheerful, enthusiastic heart! Life intrigues me!; [a.] Port Clinton, OH

FAHEY, JOHN A.
[pen.] Jack Fahey; [b.] September 30, 1950, Dorchester, MA; [p.] James and Frances Fahey; [ed.] St. Anselm College BA (English) currently enrolled in MED program at Worcester State College; [occ.] English Teacher at Marlborough High School; [oth. writ.] All genres as yet unpublished.; [pers.] The real reward of any endeavor is knowing you can do it. It's not about fame or fortune. If you're satisfied, you've reached your goal, but always maintain high standards.; [a.] Marlborough, MA

FAHY, JOHN
[b.] August 17, 1935, MA; [ed.] Newbury Jr. College WPI - SIM; [occ.] Retired; [memb.] AMC, Elks, Maspenoch Rod and Gun Club; [oth. writ.] None published; [pers.] Jacob Bronowski and Loren Eiseley were right, inflexible positions are a danger to future growth and progress.; [a.] Whitinsville, MA

FALBER, RACHAEL
[pers.] "...How did the extremist caress the dove or the black below the sea beyond the directional simple - in the grueling scruff of jazz play till you die, die, till the ground lays you down, fly till the boundary is broken gracefully.; [a.] New Paltz, NY

FARAH, JEFFREY J.
[b.] August 16, 1964, Newark, NJ; [p.] Joseph J. and Awatif H. Farah; [m.] Rina A. Farah, July 18, 1992; [ed.] Ph.D. in ECSE from Rensselaer Polytechnic Institute, M.E.E. and B.E.E. from the Cooper Union School of Engineering; [occ.] Senior Member of Technical Staff, at AT&T; [memb.] Tau Beta Pi and Eta Kappa Nu National Honor Societies, IEEE, AAAS, NYAS; [hon.] Two US Parents, Bronze Eagle Award for Excellence, Multiple Quality Awards, Full Scholarships to the Cooper Union and rensselaer Polytechnic Institute; [oth. writ.] A Native New Yorker in King Arthur's Court (Satire) an American Identity, Multiple Technical Journal and Technical Conference Paper.; [pers.] The only stupid question is one that remains unasked. The only worthless suggestion is one that is never voiced.; [a.] North Brunswick, NJ

FARRELL, JANET M.
[b.] June 8, 1942, Providence, RI; [p.] James F. Conroy, Anna M. Conroy; [ch.] 2 sons, 3 grandchildren; [ed.] MS (Health Services RNC (Psychiatric Mental Health Nsg); [occ.] Clinical Case Manager; [memb.] American Nurses Assoc.; [pers.] I have always been interested in the power of words, written or spoken. Poetry is especially interesting because of it's ability to create an image with few words. I enjoy the work of Gerard and Emily Dickinson.

FEEKIN, DONALD R.
[pen.] Don Feekin; [b.] February 23, 1943, Council Bluffs; [p.] Areighle Feekin, Mildred Feekin; [m.] Judith A. Feekin, November 19, 1966; [ch.] Steven, Timothy, Renee; [ed.] Thomas Jefferson High, Iowa Western U.; [occ.] President Riteway Construction Co.; [memb.] Elks, American Legion, Ducks unlimited, Quails unlimited, Phesents unlimited, Mo. Valley Chamber of Comm. National Federation of Independent Business and Master Gardners. National of Fleeterg Sailors; [hon.] Elk of the year; [pers.] If its not broke, "Don't fix it."; [a.] Council Bluffs, IA

FEJERANG, JOSEPH D.
[pen.] Jay B. Styll; [b.] April 28, 1971, Guam; [p.] Joseph Taitano and Doris Fejerang (Deceased); [ed.] Simon Sanchez High, Guam Community College, St. Mary's College; [memb.] Chamorro Nation, Smithsonian Associates; [oth. writ.] Various poems published in small Circa Periodicals and Magazines; [pers.] Dwell not reflecting on being the best rather, on every whim, act in doing what is your all, and with the brevity of life, every day will be a better one that's true living.; [a.] Yigo, Guam

FELDMAN, ELIAS
[b.] January 1, 1924, Poland; [p.] Samuel and Esther; [m.] Henryka, April 1950; [ch.] Walter and Hanna; [ed.] Polish Law School (Lawyer in Poland); [occ.] Retired; [hon.] Several distinguished polish awards including the silver cross; [oth. writ.] Many short stories, poems Aforyzm, Political Jokes Reflections. (All in polish and not published.); [pers.] Formost be a Mench.; [a.] Plainview, NY

FERRINI, JACKIE L.
[pen.] Jackie L. Ferrini; [b.] December 6, 1936, Brooklyn, NY; [p.] Paul and Mary Hazelum; [m.] Joseph A. Ferrini, May 31, 1959; [ch.] Robin, Cindy, Joseph and David; [occ.] Happy Homemaker; [pers.] Savor the moment, for the happiness its memories will bring.

FIELDS JR., RONALD
[b.] January 13, 1978, Crossville, TN; [p.] Pam Roman, and Ronald Fields; [ed.] High School Valedictorian, Continuing education at Roare State then University of Tennesse; [occ.] Night Manager of Jond J', Iga; [hon.] Valedictorian, various awards for leadership, science and mathematics.; [oth. writ.] Several ethics many sunsets, poem for the deceased, etc.; [pers.] Search for logic in your mind, but let your poetry come from the heart.; [a.] Pikeville, TN

FIGUEROA, WILLIAM
[pen.] Willie; [b.] May 19, 1963, Brooklyn, NY; [p.] Osvaldo Figueroa and Lucia; [m.] Jeannette Figueroa, November 12, 1982; [ch.] Jonathan and Erica; [ed.] All Saint Elementary, Murry Bergtraum H.S., St. John's University; [occ.] MTA (3rd Rail Operator); [memb.] Jehovah's Witnesses; [hon.] Earth Day, Blackbelt in Ninjutsudo (not anymore), Awards for Coaching Soccer and Teaching Martial Arts, Greatest award being approved to serve Jehovah as his witness to all; [oth. writ.] None published, however I have many more that I would like to publish.; [pers.] P.N., Everyone should take time out to read the Holy Scriptures (Heb. and Greek) in order to get educated by Jehovah's inspired words.; [a.] Brooklyn, NY

FINKELMAN, SOL
[pen.] Sol The Sage; [b.] February 6, 1918, Warsaw, Poland; [p.] Sam and Rose Finkelman; [m.] Gay Newman Finkelman, December 31, 1985; [ch.] Larry, Cindy, Richard, Rhonda, Nancy; [ed.] Townsend Harris High, BBA C.C.N.Y.; [occ.] Retired CPA; [memb.] American Institute of CPAs, Score, Unitarian Universalist Fellowship; [oth. writ.] "Poetic Commentary by Sol The Sage" published in various newspapers on 4 continents, published books, Death and Grief, Love, Sex, and Marriage, Crazy in Love, Politics, Truth, and Law (Very Little Truth), Religion (A Diversity of Faith); [pers.] Poetry should be truth in beauty.; [a.] Lakeland, FL

FIRGAU, ALICE D.
[b.] June 30, 1937, Rahway, NJ; [p.] John (Deceased) and Delia Firgau; [ed.] M. Mus., University of Michigan, B.A., Douglas Collage, New Brunswick, NJ, Rahway High School, Rahway, NJ; [occ.] Textbook Editor; [memb.] National Museum of Women in the Arts, American Littoral Society, Sierra Club, and numerous other environmental and conservation groups; [hon.] Phi Beta Kappa, B.A. Awarded with highest honors in music; [oth. writ.] "On Learning Old Habits Must Be Unlearned" and "A Gentle Response to E-Mail Message" published by The National Library of Poetry, numerous song lyrics in English and Spanish published by Silver Burdett Ginn, Sacred choral compositions and arrangements for mixed voices.; [pers.] My life experiences have focused on love of art and beauty. I try to use the beauty of words - words organized, given form, and made musical - to express my deepest feelings and responses to personal interactions and all that is beautiful in the world.; [a.] South Plainfield, NJ

FISHER, ROGER F.
[pen.] R. F. II; [b.] May 26, 1974, Detroit, MI; [p.] Jonathan and Leona Fisher; [ed.] Cass Tech High School, Detroit, MI, 1992, Michigan State Univ. Student; [occ.] Student in Pre-Med Physiology/Sports Medicine; [memb.] International Poets Society, United States Weight Lifting Federation, National Dean's List; [hon.] Several poems and songs in major magazines and books over U.S. Who's Who in American (1993) High School (1992); [oth. writ.] Queen, I Search Of Love, Time Of Love Always and Forever; [pers.] Since my strong interest in music, I had begun writing poems that reflect on love and romance in which I gather ideas and emotions from listening, singing and writing love songs which have give me a heart mind and soul to express love in many ways.; [a.] Detroit, MI

FISSEL, RYAN P.
[b.] February 17, 1980, Youngstown, OH; [p.] Robert P. Fissel, Elizabeth M. Fissel; [ed.] Student in high school; [occ.] Student; [pers.] My poem,..."For Brendan" was writer April 25, 1996, in the evening after attending the funeral of a friend, Brendan Daugherty. He was killed April 20, 1996 by a drunk driver. He will be missed by many people, including my cousin Holly, who was his girlfriend.; [a.] Lebanon, OH

FISTES, JACOB
[b.] June 15, 1981, Baltimore, MD; [p.] Anastasios and Niki Fistes; [ed.] Student, 10th grade at Mary Star of the Sea High School; [hon.] Honor Roll; [pers.] I'd like to thank my mom for sending in my poem.; [a.] San Pedro, CA

FITCHIE, KATIE ANN
[b.] March 20, 1979, Santa Rosa; [p.] Tom Fitchie and Pam Adamson; [ed.] Montgomery High School Senior Graduate 97; [occ.] Baskin Robbins; [memb.] Varsity Soccer Team 3 years; [hon.] Who's Who Among American High School Students 1995-96; [pers.] One day I wish for the people of the world to view each other equal just as I do.; [a.] Santa Rosa, CA

FLICK, KATHY PATRICIA
[b.] August 18, 1959, Detroit, MI; [p.] Mabel and Conrad Clapsaddle; [m.] Michael A. Flick, February 28, 1993; [ch.] Kristina, Moriah; [ed.] St. Martins, St. Matthews, Guardian Angels, Denby High School Det, Michigan; [occ.] Supervisor of major Apt Complex; [memb.] St. Martins Church and Guardian Angels, A Bingo worker for the committee to reelect Cecil St. Piere for Warren Couselman; [hon.] Award for good citizenship at Campbell Elementary School. And Poe School for the Developmentally disabled.; [oth. writ.] This was my first poem ever written. Although I have been working on another. It takes time to put the thoughts into words.; [pers.] I was influenced by a family member and have always had a love for poetry.; [a.] Detroit, MI

FLUKER, GLORIA J.
[pen.] Glo; [b.] December 9, 1949, Texas; [p.] Both Deceased; [ch.] Quincy; [ed.] B.S. and Master from the University of Oregon (Elementary Ed and Counseling Rehabilitation); [occ.] Parole and Probation Officer, Mutl. Co. Community Corrections; [memb.] African American Health Coalition, Regional Drug Initiative, Oregon Teen-Preg. Task Force; [hon.] J.C. Penny Volunteer Awards Three video Awards from the NW young people film and video festival. The star of Loyalty Award - Paralyzed Veterans of America, Founder of Youth Unlimited, Inc. 1988, American Red Cross Literary Competition - Women and Aids.; [oth. writ.] Four Video production scripts; [pers.] The themes of my poems are meant to examine the unique and powerful effects relationships have on our lives. In my writing, I try to explore the feelings and thoughts that release strong emotions of sadness and disappointment. But at the same time, I'm trying to get the readers to come to terms with their feelings but not be conquered by them.; [a.] Portland, OR

FORMAN, DONNA
[b.] January 28, 1957, Brooklyn, NY; [p.] Felix and Francine O'Lenick; [m.] Lee Robinson (Fiance), June 14, 1997; [ch.] Desiree Leah, Wesley Adam; [ed.] A.A.S. Nursing; [occ.] Registered Nurse; [hon.] Soroptimist Women's for Education in Excellence 1994, National League for Nursing; [pers.] If it's going to be - it's up to me. A year from now, you may have wish you started today. Success is doing what you love and loving what you do. Loving and allowing yourself to be loved.; [a.] Mesa, AZ

FORTIER III, GEORGE L.
[b.] October 18, 1976, Newark, NJ; [p.] Mr. and Mrs. Thomas Vieira; [ed.] High School diploma; [occ.] United States Navy; [pers.] I would like to thank my teacher of eleventh and twelve grade, Mr. Valgenti, as well as my family and friends for standing by my side, and especially my reason for writing the poem, my girlfriend Tammy Guntt.; [a.] West Orange, NJ

FOSTER, CHARLES M.
[b.] April 12, 1971, Royal Oak, MI; [p.] Mr. and Mrs. Mitchell B. Foster; [ed.] Cranbrook Kingswood High School BA - English - Vanderbilt U. MBA - Mich. State Univ.; [occ.] In logistics in Chicago; [oth. writ.] Numerous other poems and short stories; [pers.] "Gibbous Moon" was writer in a time of difficulty for me, I was inspired by the reflection of the moonlight on the water.; [a.] Lake Angelus, MI

FOSTER, MILTON
[b.] October 8, Sacramento; [p.] Deceased; [ch.] Shannon, Kerrick, Keirnan; [ed.] B.A. English, Computer Science and Fine Arts; [occ.] Writer, Poetry, Resumes, "How To" and Technical Manuals; [oth. writ.] "Resumes Suck, Yours Won't", book, written but not submitted for publication. Poetry for my friends (because of my need for praise), many technical publications.; [pers.] I muse on the bits and pieces of the whole.; [a.] Escondido, CA

FOUTS, JERRY
[pen.] Jerry; [b.] November 23, 1957, Durand; [p.] Gerald and Loretta Fouts Sr.; [m.] Beth Ann, February 17, 1979; [ch.] Jennelle, Julie, Jessica, Jerry III; [ed.] Corunna High School, Corunna MI; [occ.] Repairman; [hon.] National Field Archery Assoc., Thorny Acres

Sportsman's Club; [pers.] Only take from nature what is needed and give back twice as much; [a.] Bancroft, MI

FOX, FRANCES L.
[b.] August 18, 1939, Monticello, KY; [p.] Kenneth-Pauline Bertram; [ch.] Thomas Fox Jr., granddaughter Letetsia A. Fox; [ed.] Central High, Los Angeles, Southwest College; [occ.] Los Angeles Civil Service - Retired; [pers.] Good things come to those who pray.; [a.] Rialto, CA

FRANK, AIMEE COLETTE
[pen.] A.C.F.; [b.] April 2, 1982; [ed.] Delaware Valley Regional High School; [occ.] Student, poet and resident hippie/peacnik; [pers.] Walls are meant to be written on. Beware of walls that aren't written on. I've been influenced by John Lennon, Joan Baez, Bob Dylan, and other poets. You can't escape influences. You're influenced by everything around you; [a.] Baptistown, NJ

FRANKLIN, VIRGINIA
[pen.] "Ginny"; [b.] May 20, 1982, Gainesville, FL; [p.] Mr. and Mrs. Benjamin K. Franklin; [ed.] Student 9th grade, Bellview Santos Elementary, Bellview Middle School, Bellview High School Ocala, Florida 34474; [occ.] Student at Bellview; [memb.] Creative writing Library 200+ Club; [hon.] Honor Roll Society Student of the Month; [pers.] "Try hard all the time, write a lot"

FREE, JOSHUA
[b.] October 14, 1980, Des Moines, IA; [p.] Leonard Free, Christina Free; [ed.] Southeast Polk High School, (Runnells, IA); [hon.] Connie Belin National Center for Gifted Education, Invent Iowa! State Invention Convention, Des Moines National Poetry Contest; [oth. writ.] "Life is What You Make Of It" read at Des Moines National Poetry Contest; [pers.] My parents and family have always given me support and encouragement. The person who influenced my writing style the most and taught me about poetry was my Eighth-Grade English teacher.; [a.] Altoona, IA

FREEMAN, JOVAN
[pen.] Vonni; [b.] October 6, 1983, Newark, NJ; [p.] Mr. and Mrs. Joseph C. Freeman Sr.; [ed.] Larkspur Middle School Summer classes located at (TCC) Tidewater Community College; [memb.] Gifted and Intellectual Program; [hon.] Honors Society Certificate from Delta Sigma Theta Sorority; [oth. writ.] Publication in Anthropology of young writers.; [pers.] In my writing I try to capture the true human feelings from a poetic point of view. I am influenced by my life and other lives which help give a purpose to my writing skills.; [a.] Virginia Beach, VA

FREER, CANDACE
[pen.] Slurpee, Dr. Can; [b.] December 30, 1979, Dickinson, ND; [p.] Tom Freer and Joyce Robinson; [ed.] I am currently attending Dickinson High School; [occ.] Herberger's Department Store; [memb.] Student Council, DECA, Close-Up, Dic Dak, The Chronicle and Drama; [hon.] Frank T. Lewis Leadership Award - for the most outstanding Student Council member. "New Pen" Award - for The Chronicle. Won the most valuable Reporter for The Chronicle.; [oth. writ.] What is Life?, Someone To Talk To, Cherubs, Very Special Christmas Day, Up and Way, What Should I Do?; [pers.] I believe people should live each day to the fullest and you should never give up on your dreams and goals, for real, thanks Carrie for being there when I needed you!; [a.] Dickinson, ND

FRENKEL, MARC
[b.] July 2, 1985, Brooklyn, NY; [p.] Mel and Phyllis;

[ed.] Finished the 5th grade. Always in gifted classes; [occ.] A Student with aspiration of being a brain surgeon, new surgeon; [hon.] Received the John Hopkins award for exceptional verbal scores; [oth. writ.] Various poems; [pers.] Environmental issues have always been a priority for me. My poems reflect a deep respect for the power, and beauty of nature.; [a.] North Woodmere, NY

FRETWELL, JULIE E.
[b.] August 4, 1957, England; [p.] Wilmot Brealey, Jessie Brealey; [m.] Robert Fretwell (Bob), August 4, 1995; [ch.] James Johnston, Daniel Johnston; [occ.] Aromatherapist; [hon.] 1995 Winner poetry competition, Trident Group "Times" (U.K.) two poems selected for "I believe in Unicorns" EFT Publications U.K. sponsored by Literature Development Office, Midlands Counties.; [oth. writ.] "Derbyshire Miner" included in Arrival Press, Poems of the Midlands. 1994 U.K. "Golden Shoes" selected for Horseshoe Publications Short Story Anthology 1994 U.K. Collection of poetry "Love, Damn It". Published October 1995 E.F.T. publications U.K.; [pers.] Listen to the heart with imagination and see the words flow.; [a.] Everson, WA

FRY, MARGARET WALL
[pen.] Pj or Peggy; [b.] December 9, 1948, Clearfield, PA; [p.] Thomas I. and Dorothy K. Wall; [m.] Walter T. Fry Jr., June 14, 1975; [ed.] B.S. Lock Haven State College, M.Ed Pennsylvania State University; [occ.] Kindergarten teacher Clearfield Area Schools - Leonard Grade; [memb.] West Branch Religious Society of Friends, Susquehanna Chapter D.A.R., 7th degree Grange (Penn Grange #534), The Treaty Elm Chapter Colonial Dames XVII Century, Quarter Woman, Trustee of Baltimore Yearly Meeting, Recording Clerk of Centre Quarter - BYM; [oth. writ.] Angel poetry, Book of the History of West Branch, Monthly Meeting, "West Branch Quakers: 1833-1983"; [pers.] Angels are all around us - helping us, guiding us.; [a.] Clearfield, PA

FULLER, JENESE LASHAE
[b.] January 3, 1985, Griffin, GA; [p.] Jimmy and Jennifer Releford; [ed.] Kelsey Avenue Middle School; [occ.] Student; [memb.] 4-M Club Band, Academic Bowl, FHA (Future Homemakers of America), Program Challenge; [hon.] All A honor roll, Field Day (first, second, third), Smartest girl, Challenge 24 Winner ($50.00), 4-H Secretary, plaque (Just Open Your Eyes and See..) others...; [pers.] My goal is to be in the 2000 Olympic games in gymnastics. I'm greatly influenced by the 1996 USA team.; [a.] Griffin, GA

FYFE, DOROTHY
[pen.] Dorie; [b.] December 2, 1937, Saint Francisville, LA; [p.] Deceased; [ed.] Baton Rouge High, Cambrige Buss College Detroit, MI; [occ.] Retired, Business woman. Formerly own, Dottio Cropshor, Fyfe Seafood and Dotties Inn; [memb.] St. Jude Catholic Church Detroit, MI; [oth. writ.] Singer, songwriter and composer; [pers.] I love life and try to accept things as they are and make the best of them, I love giving of myself to the old and shut in. To the little animals, who are left behind to feed for themselves.; [a.] Detroit, MI

GABRIEL, MATT
[b.] February 2, 1984, Greensburg; [p.] David and Virginia Gabriel; [ed.] Going into 7th Grade; [occ.] Student; [memb.] Greensburg Karate College, Greensburg Salem, Middle School Wrestling; [hon.] Honor Student, Recieved Black Belt at age of 10, Graduated Pa, State Police Camp Summer of 96, Finished First Place in the Keystone State Classics Karate Championship 1992;

[pers.] Nothing ventured, nothing gained; [a.] Saltsburg, PA

GAINES, KAREN CHAMPION
[pen.] Moochie; [b.] April 11, 1958, Indiana; [p.] Robert and Doris Champion Jr.; [ch.] Tamika Marie and Angela Yvette Gaines; [ed.] I completed all of my high school courses and graduated the 12th Grade. Attended the Institute of Data Processing.; [occ.] Mother; [pers.] Karen began writing in 1984. Her first poem title was "No Time," written for her two daughters. "I hope my daughters take heed to all of my works." The meanings you can live by. Karen is a new poet who is very eager to see her work in print. She looks forward to publication of her own book. Karen says when she began writing she never knew it would go this far. My writings are a great joy to me. Sometimes they are my smile when I am sad. The third child of nine children to Robert and Doris the Lord chose Karen to write what we feel every day.; [a.] Gary, IN

GALINDO, DIANA ISLER
[b.] January 1, 1956, Los Angeles, CA; [p.] Roy and Carmen Isler; [m.] David Galindo; [ch.] David, Leyah; [ed.] San Gabriel High, East Los Angeles College; [pers.] As long as I can remember, I've always been told I could write but never took people seriously. Now I can proudly say, "I guess I can!" And I hopefully will write more material worth publishing.; [a.] Baldwin Park, CA

GALLIVAN, LEO G.
[pen.] Leo G. Gallivan; [b.] October 29, 1919, Boston, MA; [p.] Deceased; [m.] Deceased, June 19, 1943; [ch.] Judy, Michael, Maureen, Mark, Monica, Karen; [ed.] Gonzaga College High School Wash. D.C., Tufts University 1941 Mech. Engineer, U.S. Navy Aircorps, Pilot, Officer 1942, U.S. Navy Deep Sea Diving/Salvage School Wash., D.C. 1943; [occ.] Retired, Builder of Custom Racing Cars; [memb.] American Society Automotive Engineers, American Military Engineers, American Arbitration Association; [hon.] Good health, Good looks, Good family, Good Friends; [oth. writ.] Novel, "Mabuhay, Manila," Novel "The Rockland Rum Runners" Utility Fleet Magazine-staff, Transport International-staff, play "Death of an Autumn Spy," play "Brother Luke and The Abbey Legend."; [pers.] We modern poets are willing, led by the unknowing, and doing the impossible for the ungrateful. We have done so much for so long with so little we are qualified how to do anything with nothing.

GANGWISCH, EDNA H.
[pen.] Edna Mae Holm; [b.] May 17, 1925, Kenosha, WI; [p.] Luther and Edna Holm; [m.] Robert L. Gangwisch, June 14, 1952; [ch.] Dr. Richard, Sally Schmidt, Julie, Schaeff, Robert, JR, James; [ed.] Bradford HS Kenosha, WI, Mundelein College, Chicago, BA Degree; [occ.] Freelance Writer, East Side Weekend Magazine; [memb.] Good Shepherd Catholic Church-writer for Flock Report the Shepherd's Staff; [hon.] Won "Dockers" contest with a poem, Received $500.00 ward robe; [oth. writ.] "A Candle for Kiri" is a novel ready for publication, humorous articles published in my Sycamore Messenger and Montgomery living, Cincinnati.; [pers.] There is much to be learned from the elderly. I strive to bring 71 years of a wonderful life to my poems and stories.; [a.] Cincinnati, OH

GARCIA, KAREN
[pen.] Queen K; [b.] July 24, 1983, New Jersey; [p.] Lezzy and Fernando Garcia; [ed.] St. George School; [memb.] Choir of St. George Church; [hon.] Student of

the month, First Honors, Second Honors, Honorable Mentions; [oth. writ.] Queen K. (poem); [pers.] I try to let people know what they want to achieve is their main goal and they shouldn't give it up!; [a.] Paterson, NJ

GARD, BECKY
[b.] November 7, 1980, St. Louis, MO; [p.] David Gard, Janice Gard; [ed.] Student at Parkway West High School; [occ.] Student at Parkway West High School, volunteer at veterinary hospital; [memb.] Parkway West High School Marching Band, SODS Band, Fair St. Louis Honors Band; [hon.] Academic and Citizenship Honor Rolls, 1st Place at State Odyssey of the mind competition in 1992, Marching Band, place 1st at Greater St. Louis marching competition and 4th at Citrus Bowl Marching Competition in Orlando Florida; [a.] Saint Louis, MO

GARDIAS, SOPHIA
[b.] January 18, 1964, Queens, NY; [p.] James Proios, Stella Proios; [m.] Theo Gardias, September 7, 1985; [ch.] 1; [ed.] Hastings High School, Art Institute of Houston, University of Houston; [occ.] Accounting Work; [memb.] St. Basils; [oth. writ.] I've written several poems, but never published in newspapers or anywhere else.

GARDNER, AARON LEE
[b.] May 28, 1982, Dearborn, MI; [p.] Cynthia M. Gardner; [ed.] Entering 9th grade at Harlandale High School; [occ.] Student; [memb.] Smithson Valley Middle School Year Book Staff. Also Member of the Athletic Club; [pers.] I enjoy writing short stories and poems, that I can share with others.; [a.] Spring Branch, TX

GATCHALIAN, JOHN-JOSEPH A.
[pen.] J.J.; [b.] June 11, 1982, Philippines; [p.] Lauro P. Gatchalian, Rebecca A. Gatchalian; [ed.] Sinaloa Jr. High School, 8th grade; [occ.] Student; [memb.] Village Music Guild, Amadeus Boys choir, Sinaloa Intermediate Band, Volunteer-United way; [hon.] Sinaloa Achievers, President Award for Outstanding Achievement, Award Excellence in Music, Award for Excellence in Social Studies; [a.] Simi Valley, CA

GATCHELL JR., JOHN
[pen.] John Hamilton; [b.] September 24, 1952, Kansas City, MO; [p.] John H. and Betty J. Gatchell; [ed.] John Marshall High School, South Okc Jr. College as a grant from the State of Oklahoma; [occ.] The Arts Free hand sketch, creative writings, music; [memb.] The Smithsonia, save the children, International Society of Poets, National Air and Space Museum, National Trust for Historic Preservation; [hon.] Editor's Choice Awards from the National Library of Poetry; [oth. writ.] Numerous works published by the National Library and the Sparrow grass Poetry Forum; [pers.] I write about the book of life, the good times will come, and the good times will go.; [a.] Oklahoma City, OK

GATWOOD JR., JAMES L.
[b.] November 12, 1942, Toledo, OH; [p.] Pauline K. and James L. Gatwood Sr.; [ed.] B.A. University of Toledo, 1971, M.Ed University of Idaho, 1975; [occ.] High School Language Arts Teacher; [memb.] National Education Association; [hon.] Instructional Assistantship in English Language and Literature from The University of Idaho in Moscow, Idaho 1971-73; [oth. writ.] Several poems and short stories published in college literary newspapers; [pers.] The precise word is worth a thousand pictures.; [a.] Toledo, OH

GAUNT, DAVID A.
[b.] September 23, 1913, Bluffton, IN; [p.] Edward L. and Ethyl Fay Gaunt; [m.] Ruth Gaunt, November 8, 1946; [ch.] 5 Cynthia, Sharon, Marsha, Dave Jr, Deborah; [ed.] 8th grade - there were ten children in our family and mother passed away at age 38 I was compelled to get a working permit at age 14 and support 9 brothers and sisters.; [occ.] I am 83 yrs. old and retired. However I make jewelry and write.; [memb.] Alb Board of Realtors - 50 years Monte Vista Christian Church Former Sec. and Tr. of N Mex Nurseryman Asso. former own and Pres. of Desert Green Corp. owner of David Gaunt Real Est. Co.; [hon.] My pet hobby is gardening and I recently was Albuq. Most Beautiful Landscaping Award, I have won tournaments and Championship in Golf, Tennis Pool and Horseshoe.; [oth. writ.] I have written 3 books - is with a Calif. Hollywood Producer another is being produced. Note - my book "People Bug People" contains my poem Taos Fauma Love Santa Best - however I care and will remove it if requested.; [pers.] In spite of my lack of education I have had many college students with every college degrees under my employees, and have had over a thousand Employees down through years.; [a.] Albuquerque, NM

GEBHARDT, ASHLEIGH ELIZABETH
[b.] December 18, 1983, Arlington, TX; [p.] Ed and Celia Gebhardt; [ed.] 7 years; [occ.] Full time student; [hon.] G/T - 6 years, A-Honor roll - 6 years; [pers.] "Do what you feel good about, don't listen to anyone who tries to bring you down - you can do anything you want to".; [a.] Bridgeport, TX

GEERS, BRENT T.
[b.] October 22, 1978, Grand Rapids, MI; [p.] Marlene Geers; [ed.] Creston High School; [occ.] High School Student, Senior, Creston High School; [memb.] National Honor Society; [hon.] Who's Who Among American High School Students, Listing, Grand Rapids Lions Club, Outstanding Citizenship Award, G.R. Foundation Outstanding Junior Award.; [pers.] Forget nothing the good and the bad - for memories are the only guidelines to life.; [a.] Grand Rapids, MI

GEIGER, DENNISE
[b.] January 2, 1973, Fontana, CA; [p.] Dennis and Libby Geiger; [ed.] Dawson County High-Glendive, MT, Dawson Community College-Glendive, MT; [occ.] At the Time of Dennise's Death, she was a Police Dispatcher. She also had received a Legal Secretary Degree.; [memb.] Montana Notary Public Society, Sacred Heart Catholic Church, Dawsettes Dance Team, Z-Club; [hon.] Numerous awards at the local fair for cooking and arts; [oth. writ.] Though none had been published Dennise wrote a book of poetry for a class in high school in which she received the highest grade possible - A+. This poems "Forever Friends" is from assignment.; [pers.] Dennise's poetry was influenced by real life experiences, whether her own or someone she loved. She always wrote what was in her heart. She is greatly missed by her parents, friends, and family. May she fly with the angels in heaven.; [a.] Barstow, CA

GENTRY, TARA ANN
[b.] December 7, 1983, Saint Pauls, NC; [p.] James and Beverly Gentry; [ed.] St. Pauls Middle School, 6th grade; [occ.] Student; [memb.] Year Book Club (St. Pauls); [hon.] A&B Honor Roll Awards, Artistic Achievement Awards; [oth. writ.] One poem in St. Pauls newpapers.; [a.] Saint Pauls, NC

GERTH, KRISTEN MICHELLE
[pen.] Kristen Gerth; [b.] April 30, 1980, Brookhaven; [p.] Kathy Gerth, Edward Gerth; [ed.] Ballport High School 11th Grade; [pers.] To help everyone open their eyes to the feelings in their souls.; [a.] Brookhaven, NY

GIAMMARINARO, NICHOLAS J.
[b.] September 15, 1951, Gouverneur, NY; [m.] Theresa; [ch.] Matthew, Michael and Mark; [pers.] "It's nice to be important, but it's important to be nice".; [a.] West Islip, NY

GIBSON, JOEL
[b.] October 25, 1979, Cambridge, OH; [p.] David and Carol Gibson; [ed.] Roswell High School; [occ.] High School Junior; [memb.] Beta Club S.T.A.R. (Students and Teachers for Academic Advancement at Roswell) Band (Symphonic, Concert and Marching); [hon.] Perfect Attendance, Honor Roll, 3.5 Club; [oth. writ.] Several poems published in local newspapers; [a.] Roswell, GA

GIBSON-BIEGER, ANGELA
[pen.] Marie Angelique; [b.] February 25, 1971, Georgia; [p.] Jim and Annette Gibson; [ed.] Associates from Reinhardt College currently and English Major at Kennesaw State University; [occ.] Service Coordinator at Vanstar Computer Corp.; [memb.] World Wildlife Fund, Nature Conservancy, American Legion Auxiliary; [hon.] Presidents List: Kennesaw St. Univ.; [oth. writ.] Many, but as yet, undiscovered (unpublished); [pers.] In three words I can sum up everything I've learned, about life. It goes on. Robert Frost.; [a.] Holly Springs, GA

GILBERTSON, KYLE
[b.] May 19, 1984, Rome, NY; [p.] Lt. Col. Edward W. Gilbertson, Melissa J. Gilbertson; [ed.] Seventh Grader at Mount View Middle School, Marriottsville, Maryland; [occ.] Student; [hon.] Second Grade, Honorable Mention in Colorado Springs Co, State of Colorado Art Competition Fourth Grade, First Place for Speech Competition at Pioneer Elem. School in Colorado Springs CO, Fifth Grade, Most Extensive Researcher, Maryland Award, Sixth Grade, P.E. Participation Award, Maryland; [pers.] Since my father is a career military officer, I have had the opportunity to live in many interesting and diverse locations. These experiences are reflected in the poetry I write.; [a.] Ellicott City, MD

GILES, EVELYN
[pen.] The Gypsy - Evelyn; [b.] March 5, 1918, Bemidji, MN; [p.] Arthur and Dorothy Thorn; [m.] Divorced; [ch.] 3 Sons: Successful family men; [ed.] Burbank High Graduate: L.A. Jr. College; [occ.] Retired Bookkeeper - Now complete concentration on writing poetry; [memb.] California Writer's Club (High Desert Chapter), New Poetry Society, Cactus Wren Garden Club, Cultural Arts Foundation, Hesperia Art Club, Sheriff's Reserve, 4-H Group Leader, Hesperia; [hon.] Tennis Trophy (3), Swimming Awards (5), Best Director (Theatre) Awards (3); [oth. writ.] Closet writing covers many years, slowly coming out, none published being submitted. Words for songs, greeting cards, Adventure, Romance, Fantasy, Children's stories. Heartfelt thanks to Blanche, My mentor, who shoved me out of the closet my cousin.; [pers.] My wish, my prayer, for the people of the world. A togetherness of humanity, the blending of many cultures and colors, creating a beautiful bouquet of peace and good will. Let it be!; [a.] Hesperia, CA

GILLES, EMILY CHRISTINE
[b.] April 11, 1981; [p.] John T. and Christine M. Gilles; [ed.] Brimfield High School, Sophomore; [memb.] Basketball, Softball, Volleyball, Student Council, Class Officer, Musical, Chorus, Band, Color Guard; [hon.] Honor Roll (4); [pers.] Be one not too.; [a.] Kickopoo, IL

GILMAN, JENNIFER
[b.] July 29, 1979, Portland; [p.] David and Charlene Gilman; [ed.] Through High School; [occ.] Student; [pers.] Live life to the fullest and don't let anybody tell you how to do something unless it's positive.

GILMAN, LUCY
[pen.] Luci Gilman; [b.] January 2, 1925, Transylvanna, Sighet, Romania; [p.] Deceased; [m.] Murray Gilman, December 20, 1947; [ch.] 2 sons, a grandson David Gilman and Phillip Gilman (Deceased), Zacharyis Davidson; [ed.] High School and several unmatriculated courses; [occ.] Retired, I do some voluntary services (Aids Related); [memb.] I also do charcoal portrait drawing, I was a translator. I received an honorary certificate for translating a book from English into Romanian; [hon.] I also translated some works from German, Yiddish and Hungarian into English. I speak 5 languages; [oth. writ.] I have written several poems (not submitted for publication.) One Romanian poem was featured in a weekly Romanian newspaper. I have also written several narratives; [pers.] I am a survivor of the Holocaust. My hope is to see the toxicity of bigotry and ethnic cleansing annihilated, instead of human beings; [a.] Kew Gardens, NY

GILMOUR, MAE
[pen.] Mae Gilmour; [b.] September 14, 1906, Belle Vernon, PA; [p.] John C. and Anna Nicholls; [m.] Daniels N. Gilmour Jr., June 5, 1936; [ch.] Daniel N. III, John C.; [ed.] Grades 1-8 Concord (1 room school) California, Pa. High School and Normal School, Kachina Art School Arizona 2 yr.(by mail) Institute of Children Literature 2 yrs. (by mail); [occ.] Retired Teacher (Elementary); [memb.] Wild River Art League Rehoboth Presbyterian Church Rostrover Garden Club; [hon.] 2nd place in poetry contest Westmoreland County sponsored by (Redstone Highlands) 50 yrs. Teaching children in Sunday School; [oth. writ.] Children's stories, poetry children's page church paper, Historical writings for local newspaper; [pers.] Look for the positive, keep learning, keep smiling, and busy with your God given talents.; [a.] Greensbury, PA

GINES, SIGNE
[m.] Tommy Gines; [ch.] Brad, Bryan, Brady, Aimee and Baby due in February; [occ.] Science and Math Teacher, secondary; [pers.] My writing is a reflection of life's experiences and the wisdom I have gained from those experiences.; [a.] Lehi, UT

GINGLES, ANNETTE
[b.] August 14, 1956, Pomona, CA; [p.] Robert T. Tessier, Ida Tessier; [m.] Mark Chandler Gingles, October 19, 1985; [ed.] Montclair High, Chaffee College I.C.S. Center of Degree; [occ.] Account's Receivable Dr.'s Armada and Williams, D.O. Upland, CA; [pers.] Life is what you make of it. So, I thrive to enjoy it daily, by following my heart's desire in all my writings. Inspired by Jaime Slocum, songwriter and singer.; [a.] Upland, CA

GINSBERG, JULIE
[b.] April 15, 1984, Kansas City; [p.] B. William and Cheryl Ginsberg; [ed.] Completed 6th grade; [occ.] Student

GLASER, DAVID
[b.] September 29, 1919, Brooklyn, NY; [p.] Samuel, Jennifer; [m.] Mildred, February 19, 1944; [ch.] Susan Sherry; [ed.] Thomas Jefferson High School Graduate 1936, Art Student League (Scholar), N.Y. School of Industrial Art, New York School Contemporary Art, Brooklyn Museum Art School. Freeport New York

1959; [occ.] Artist, Sculptor-Fine Art, Writing New Age graphic experimentation, owner studio concepts; [memb.] Allied Artists of America, Freeport Art Museum and Conservation, AVC, ACW, Amnesty Int'l, Wildness Soc., World Jewish Cong. Greenpeace, American Museum of Nat'l History; [hon.] First poem published 1934 National Human Review, Nassau County poetry award 1981, Art Students League Scholar 1936, Grand Prize redesign Levitt Home 1967, Numerous graphic awards, Monadnock Mills, Vet Soc. of American Artist, Desi-Grand prize, 3-Man show Heckscher Music Huntington 1964, Shows National Arts Club New York 1959, Art Directions 1959, ACA Galleries 1960, Hofstra U., Adelphi U., Nassau Community Call, Pres. Allied Artists of America 1985 exh. Wantagh Levittown, Civilian Conservation Corps 1936 Artist (Adirondacks); [oth. writ.] "My Mother Died Dancing Book 1970, cartoonist, editor, publisher, All "gigyrandom" 1993-4 orientation (USA Army) writings North Pacific 1945, numerous essay on human condition. Inventor: Mosaic reproduction 1948-50 artist, writer 1945 "Bearing Breeze" Aleutians; [pers.] To question to wonder, to accept all possibilities and to explore whenever possible and to accept so called "Failure" as a "given" side road to discovery. "Fortune in" to the inner universal self and express what is received back in the song of words or the visual. To go "against the grain". Insecurity expressed positively moves me more deeply toward the full potential; [a.] Wantagh, NY

GLENN, MARK
[b.] February 18, 1953, Silver City, NM; [p.] Jeff and Lora Nell Glenn; [m.] Carol Glenn, February 13, 1988; [ch.] Cassie Erin Glenn, Whitney Dawn Glenn; [ed.] B.S. - Sul Ross State Univ. May 1975 Alpine, Texas; [occ.] Building Security and Safety Manager for Las Cruces Public School's; [memb.] University United Methodist Church, Silver City Masonic Lodge AF&AM #8 - American Society of Safety Engineers; [oth. writ.] Several other poems. No other poems published.; [pers.] The poetry I write is meant to bring the beauty and grace of God to our being in another medium. The words I wrote are the same words he gives me.; [a.] Las Cruces, NM

GLOVER, ROBERT W.
[pen.] Bob, Bobby "G"; [b.] July 26, 1934, Wilmington, DE; [p.] Ellen Lucille and Thomas William; [m.] Marie M. Glover, April 16, 1977; [ch.] Bob, Cathy and John; [ed.] 2 years College Type Courses, Accounting I and II Real Estate License Course; [occ.] Liquor Manager, Walgreen's - retired from Dupont Co. 40 yrs serve; [memb.] Elks, Moose, 40+8 (life), Lions, American Legion (life), VFW (life), American Society of Notaries since 1981; [hon.] Life membership in American Legion, Television Production Plaque, Medals from service in U.S. Navy during Korean War; [oth. writ.] "Tears of Gladness", "An Ode to a New House", "Faith in Love", "Colony Inn", "An Ode to a Teenage Birthday", "The Kitchen Prayer", etc.; [pers.] I love America, Life, People, Animals and I like to write poetry about life's situation.; [a.] Fort Saint Lucie, FL

GLYNN, KEVIN G.
[b.] November 18, 1977, Passak, NJ; [p.] William and Judy Glynn; [ed.] Park Ridge High School; [occ.] Student at Widener University; [memb.] 4-H Exchange Club; [hon.] National Honors Society, President's Education Award; [a.] Park Ridge, NJ

GLYNN, XI'AN
[pen.] Bright Eyes; [b.] July 7, 1982, Yonkers, NY; [p.] Shirley Henry and Robert Glynn; [ed.] Elementary

School P.S. 153 named after Helen Keller, Middle School 180 after Daniel Hale Williams, September of 1996 Manhattan Center for Math and Science High School; [occ.] Student; [hon.] I was a honor student. An award for outstanding achievements in vocal music, social studies, an award for my success in Middle School from human High School, 2 Certificates for the Honor Roll, and a Certificate of Merit, on Award for creative writing, and one for journalism; [oth. writ.] I have about 50 published poems; [pers.] If you are determined to achieve, you must realize that satisfaction, achievement, and success are not acquired if there is belief that you were motivated someone. They have the ability to inspire, but the origins of motivation are from within peace, and God Bless.; [a.] New York, NY

GOHL, RAYMOND A.
[b.] May 11, 1963, Somers Point, NJ; [p.] Fredric Gohl, Dolores Gohl; [m.] Tammey Lee Gohl, June 30, 1990; [ch.] Lisa Lee, Gary Allen, Alexa Ray; [ed.] Central Columbia High School, Advanced Electronics School, U. S. Navy; [occ.] Avionics Technician, U.S. Navy; [pers.] My writings are dedicated to my loving family (all of them).; [a.] Arlington, TX

GOLDSMITH, LAUREN
[b.] August 25, 1981, Catskill, NY; [p.] Brenda and Karl Goldsmith; [ed.] Irondequoit High School; [oth. writ.] My writing is simply for my entertainment and pleasure. This is the first piece I have had published or entered to a contest.; [pers.] Writing is an art truly difficult of mastering, a real gift. However, talented an artist may be, nothing can be obtained without inspiration. To those who inspire me, thank you.; [a.] Rochester, NY

GOMOLINSKI, ADAM C.
[b.] February 26, 1976, Chicago, IL; [p.] Caroline Perry; [ch.] Ashley Marie; [ed.] Franklin High School class of 1994. Currently attending Junior College; [oth. writ.] "Deadly Silence" and many other non titled pieces; [pers.] "Memories of a Man" is dedicated to my grandpa, Denison "Black" Perry. He showed me the right way to be a man, when others weren't man enough them self. I'd also like to thank my guiding light, Eleanor Perry, Grandma.; [a.] Chicago, IL

GONSKI, JOHN
[b.] June 2, 1972, Waterbury, CT; [p.] Joseph and Sally Gonski; [ed.] Holy Cross, High School, Waterburg, CT, Southern CT, State University; [occ.] Business Services Manager, Staples; [oth. writ.] Other writings also published by NLP and by local magazines.; [pers.] My poems reflect my own personal experiences as well as my feelings. Poetry is somewhat my own personal diary, showing all I have experienced in lives.; [a.] Prospect, CT

GOOD, KARLEEN WAGNER
[b.] Enid, OK; [p.] Karl and Ruby Wagner; [m.] Rick Good, February 18, 1984; [ed.] AA, West Hills College, BA, English Literature, Fresno State, Post Graduate Studies in Counseling; [occ.] Teacher, Akers School, NAS Lemoore, CA; [memb.] CTA, English 500 Society; [hon.] Who's Who of America's Teachers; [oth. writ.] Articles published in college and community newspapers.; [pers.] Reading and writing have opened up many worlds to me, and I thank my parents for their encouragement in these areas and for their unfaltering support.; [a.] Lemoore, CA

GOOD, LINDA KAY
[pen.] Linda K. Good; [b.] August 19, 1947, Ferndale, MI; [p.] Jasper E. and Robbie Hutto; [ed.] High School, Cosmetology School, State of Michigan, Licensed

Cosmotogist; [memb.] Royal Park Church of Christ; [oth. writ.] I have written several poems that I have set to recorded music, and have done some different voices, mostly comedy, singing and imitating singers voices.; [pers.] I have never had any of my work published altho I have been writing poetry since I was a young girl, on many topics, some happy, other sad.; [a.] Madison Heights, MI

GOOD, WILLIAM
[b.] September 20, 1957, Kalamazoo, MI; [m.] Renda Good, September 8, 1989; [ch.] Nick; [ed.] High School; [occ.] Heating and Air Conditioning, Refrigeration Mechanic; [memb.] National Parks and Conservation Association World Wildlife Fund; [hon.] Ceremony Honoring the unknown American (Wash D.C.); [oth. writ.] Numerous poems over the years describing life, emotions and nature personal goal: To publish my book.; [pers.] My true feelings, emotions and inner self are expressed through mother earths' creations; [a.] Minot, ND

GOODENOUGH, DIANE CAROL
[b.] August 4, 1960, Birmingham, AL; [p.] Purnell James Goodenough and Ethel Settles Goodenough; [ed.] Richard Gahr High School, California State University Long Beach; [occ.] Printer/Computer Graphics Artist Nordstrom Inc., Fullerton, CA; [memb.] California State University, Long Beach Alumni Association, St. Paul The Apostle Catholic Church; [pers.] To evoke emotional responses and create vivid imagery through my writings.; [a.] Chino Hills, CA

GORDON, JUSTIN B.
[b.] August 21, 1985, Malden, MA; [p.] Doreen and Julian Gordon; [ed.] Tower School Marblehead, MA, completed 4th grade; [occ.] Student; [memb.] National Geographic Soc.; [hon.] 2nd place Paper Airplane Flying, 2 Soccer Medals, 1st Place at Camp; [oth. writ.] My Dog Benjie; [pers.] I was taught well by my language Arts Teacher Mr. White house. I concentrate on my subject.; [a.] Marblehead, MA

GORGES, NOLA RUTH
[pen.] Nola Ruth Gorges; [b.] April 24, 1947, Marquette, MI; [p.] Phillip and Ruth Clish; [m.] Divorced; [ch.] Noel Gene, Timothy Arnold; [ed.] Certificate in Business University of Chicago, Associate Degree in Business Waubonsee Community College Additional Courses, College of Dupage; [occ.] Motel Owner Pride Supervisor At and T 21 years; [memb.] Delta Kappa Gamma, St. Pauls EU. Lutheran Church U.S. and Ishpeming Negaunee Chamber of Commerce, National Ski Ski Hall of Fame, Iron Town Assoc. others; [hon.] Dean's List all colleges attended, 3.8 Aug. all; [oth. writ.] Personal only to friends or for friends; [pers.] Writing enables me to express my life's experiences on paper. Hopefully touching the heart and soul of others in an encouraging way.; [a.] Negaunee, MI

GORMAN, FRANCES
[b.] September 3, 1948, Baltimore, MD; [p.] Edmund Nash Gorman and Frances Barton Gorman; [ed.] Garrison Forest School ('67), University of Pennsylvania ('71); [occ.] Writer; [pers.] Live your life so that your epitaph could read "no regrets". Keep laughing! A good sense of humor cures almost all of life's ills.; [a.] San Francisco, CA

GOSNELL, EDITH E.
[b.] July 25, 1938, Spartanburg, SC; [p.] Buddy and Addie Fleming; [m.] Bobby Joe Gosnell, December 28, 1956; [ch.] Bobby, Debi, Marti, Chris and Marilyn; [ed.] Graduate of: Pacolet High School, Adult School - 1976; [occ.] Housewife

GRABSTEIN, TERESA
[b.] February 21, 1959, Lakeport, CA; [p.] Jack and Jane Chamberlain; [m.] Kenneth Grabstein, June 17, 1984; [ch.] Three children; [ed.] U.C. Berkeley 1984 B.A. University of Washington; [occ.] Short Story Writer and Poet; [memb.] Pacific Northwest Writers Conference, Seattle Writers Association; [hon.] Read outloud a short story of mine at the 1996 Writers in Performance held by Seattle Writers Association; [pers.] My poetry and short stories show hope as a personal triumph amidst death, war and illness.; [a.] Mercer Island, WA

GRANBERRY, CHRIS
[pen.] Jordan Stygian; [b.] July 31, 1975, Tulsa, OK; [p.] Robin and Carol Granberry; [ed.] Junior in College; [memb.] Seventh Day Adventist Church; [hon.] A few local poetry contests (4th place and honorable mention); [oth. writ.] Over 72 other poems, and around 12 stories, most yet to be completed.; [pers.] "If I have a space to fill, I want to fill it with something worthy of a greater space something that could never be conveyed from the imaginations of the mind, but still, I would want to try"; [a.] Villa Park, IL

GRANT, JOSEPH P.
[b.] March 1, 1964, Jersey City, NJ; [p.] Raymond T. Grant, Florence Grant; [occ.] Writer; [oth. writ.] Other verse published in Various Anthologies, Short Stories in Literary Reviews; [pers.] "Writing is a Dog's Life, but the only one worth living." - Flaubert.; [a.] Key West, FL

GRATTAN, JESSICA
[b.] March 27, 1979, Fort Lauderdale, FL; [p.] Jack Grattan, Audrey Zraket; [ed.] Northeast High School; [occ.] Student; [memb.] Art Addicts; [hon.] Artwork published in a United States Achievement Academy book, awarded as a National Art Award winner; [oth. writ.] Published in annual literary magazine; [pers.] From poetry to paintings, art is created not only at the hand of the artist, but in the mind of the beholder.; [a.] Fort Lauderdale, FL

GRAVES, SHANA LEE
[b.] March 31, 1977, Burlington, UT; [p.] Steven and Kansas Graves; [ed.] High School graduate from Bellows Tree Academy Fairfax; [occ.] Maid/poet; [memb.] Captain of local bowling team, and walk for cystic fibrosis in memory of Christina Belisle McMahon; [oth. writ.] Many short stories and poems. Other published pieces include, if only, set me free, and take me free, and take me with you.; [pers.] "Believe in love it can cause you pure "bliss". Anything is possible as long as you believe it can happen.; [a.] Milton, UT

GRAY, DIONNE
[pen.] Dominique Dunn; [b.] August 4, 1970, Houma, LA; [p.] Charles Gray, Lavonne Gray; [ed.] Atlanta Area Technical School (Cosmetology); [occ.] Customer Service Rep and Shampoo Assistant; [hon.] Gold medal for amateur play write 1st place elementary penmanship story write.; [oth. writ.] Various poems on personal life situations, start of two novels (non-fiction).; [pers.] Writing is my call in life, it comes to me so easily. I enjoy its out come and the reactions it brings to my readers.; [a.] Atlanta, GA

GRECO, MELISSA
[b.] February 20, 1970, Hackensack, NJ; [p.] Pamela Pero Blanchette; [ed.] Immaculate Heart Academy HS, College of New Rochelle; [occ.] Shiping and Inv Supervisor TSR Paging; [memb.] Aircrew and Aviation Odenancemen in the Navy Reserve; [hon.] National Art Honor Society, Psi Chi, Who's Who, 1st female Au to

be air crew qualified in the P3C for US Navy; [oth. writ.] H.S. literary magazine; [a.] Hackensack, NJ

GREEN, ARLETTE
[pen.] Arlette Dudley Green; [b.] May 10, 1935, Taunton, MA; [p.] Harold and Vivian Dudley (Deceased); [m.] Joseph A. Green, July 27, 1957; [ch.] Jenny, Melanie, Andy, Grandchildren - Thomas, Kristian and Sarah; [occ.] Writer, Homemaker for 1 Husband; [memb.] N.C. Writers' Network; [oth. writ.] "The Gathering" - A 17th to 20th Cent. Ghost Story not pub. "The Pond" - Horror centre work in progress.; [pers.] A struggling writer, struggling mostly to figure a way out of doing housework.; [a.] Durham, NC

GREEN, HEATHER
[b.] April 11, 1978, Woodstock, IL; [p.] James and Catherine Green; [ed.] Crystal Lake Central High; [occ.] Student at the University of Michigan; [oth. writ.] Loads of unpublished poems; [a.] Crystal Lake, IL

GREEN, RIVA L.
[b.] May 18, 1953, Denmark, SC; [p.] (Deceased) Rious and Elizzillia (Banks) Green; [m.] Divorced; [ch.] Corey, Kevin, Monique and Leon (Nephew); [ed.] Bridgeton High School, A.A.S., Cumberland County College, Jamison School of Ministry, Philadelphia, PA; [occ.] Caseworker, Salem County Women Services, Salem, NJ; [memb.] Bridgeton Housing Tenant Assoc. Bridgeton NAACP Coordinator, first-vice Pres., Cumberland County Chapter, NAACP., President African-American Culture Club, Cumber County College, Lorene Scholarship Committee.; [hon.] Outstanding Achievement Award, Cumberland County College, Who's Who in America Junior Colleges, Who's Who In The East-26th Edition of 1997-98 Publication.; [oth. writ.] Write poetry for Funerals, Weddings, Anniversaries and Encouragements. Several articles and poems in The Bridgeton Newspaper. Help write in newsletter at Salem County Women Services.; [pers.] My personal achievements are to strive for the best, reaching beyond imaginations and while striving, picking up those where their dreams seems to be impossible.; [a.] Bridgeton, NJ

GREENE, MARIETTE ROBINSON
[ed.] Graduated from Tuskegee Institute Alabama B.S. Degree California State University, B.A. Degree, majored in Communication Disorders of Speech and Language, presently employed with Los Angeles Unified District as a Language Specialist; [occ.] National Education Association; [oth. writ.] Creation of Plays for Children in Elementary Schools; [pers.] I love poetry because beautiful words fill the heart! My hobbies are travelling to all parts of Africa, Europe and Italy painting with water colors and sketching flowers. I enjoy planting flower and watching them grow.; [a.] Lawndale, CA

GREGOIRE, JOSIANE
[b.] May 14, 1966, Haiti; [p.] Pierre and Suze Gregoire; [ed.] Harvard Law School, Juris Doctor, 1992, New York University, (B.A. '88) (A.A. '86); [occ.] Attorney; [memb.] I) Bar Associations: 1) City Bar Assn NYC, 2) National Bar Assn, 3) New York Bar Assn, II) Society of Children's Book, III) Harvard Law Alumniae Assn; [hon.] 1) Honorable Mention Prize, for fiction, seventeen magazine, 2) NYU Icarus Award for poetry (1986), 3) New Youth Connections Fiction Prize (1985), 4) Cum Laude, NYU (Dean's List 3 years), - NYU Student Achievement Faculty Award, University Honors Scholar, NYU, National deans List 1986-87, Earl Warren Legal scholar (Harvard Law/NAACP Legal Defense Fund); [oth. writ.] 1) Wrote Chapter on Standardized

Testing for The Great School Debate, Simon and Shuster, 1985, 2) Feature articles and essays for teenage (National Magazine), 3) Book reviews for 1986 Harvard's Women's Law Journal and International Law Journal, 4) Wrote book reviews and essays for the daily challenge, a NY Newspaper, 5) By line article in New York Daily News, 1983 (Profiled b/c I testified before congress).

GREISS, VICTORIA
[pen.] Victoria Greiss; [b.] August 28, 1960, New York; [p.] Carmen and Avhram; [m.] BJorn Olovsson-Ohlson, June 27, 1986; [ed.] HS Of Music and Art Fashion Institute of Technology; [occ.] Senior Art Director; [oth. writ.] Copy writing for advertising; [pers.] I always believed that a lot can be said with very few words. The poem I wrote is a character study of a person conveyed in just a few sentences, in a style very similar to Japanese Haiku.; [a.] New York, NY

GRIMMER, LAURA DAWN
[pen.] Loll-Doll; [b.] September 1, 1962, Ottawa, IL; [p.] Martin F. Anderson and Nancy Roe of Soldotna Alaska; [m.] Todd A. Grimmer, August 20, 1983; [ch.] Racheal Ann Grimmer; [ed.] Ottawa Jr. High, IL, Kenai Penninsula Community College; [occ.] Homemaker, and self Avon, I also home school my daughter Racheal; [memb.] United Pentecostal Church; [hon.] I have had many poems submitted to church news letter; [oth. writ.] I have many other poems not yet published.; [pers.] I would like to thank God for giving me the words to this poem. I would like to dedicate this poem to my husband Todd, his love for me has inspired this poem. Rachael is my little miracle. Mom and Dad I love you. I thank my brother Marthy for his encouragement.

GRISBY, APPEL M.
[b.] March 30, 1960, San Pedro, CA; [p.] Boyd D. and Patricia L. Tuxhorn; [m.] Collis E. Grisby, September 20, 1991; [ed.] Bingham High, So Jordan, Utah Southern Utah, Cedar City, Utah; [occ.] Assistant Resident Manager of Ronald McDonald House-Midtown, Wichita, KS; [memb.] National Foreusics League; [hon.] Theater/Communication Scholarship, National Award Winning Oratorical Speaker, Forensics Degree of Distinction, National Honor Society; [oth. writ.] Honorable Mention - Augusta Arts Council Poetry Competition, Publisher and Editor of Company Newsletters; [pers.] God never gives us the Spirit of fear. Therefore, I believe in exploring and reaching out to the unknown - trusting God will hold me in his tender care.; [a.] Wichita, KS

GROGAN, DIANA HEAD
[b.] April 16, 1962, Douglasville, GA; [p.] Howard Head, Opal Harmon; [m.] Tracy Grogan, July 3, 1993; [ch.] Jessica Hannah (15), Shannon Alexandria (2); [occ.] Dispatch from Home for Family Business, Concrete Sawing; [oth. writ.] Little wise one where the eagle will carry me. I have sang my song to the East. (All unpublished).; [pers.] White Dove was written while appearing into the window of my soul. The historical native american writings have encouraged part of my identity to the soul.; [a.] Hiram, GA

GROSS, LEETTA
[b.] August 18, 1979, Saint Petersburg; [p.] Margie Doyle and Richard Gross; [ed.] Gibbs High School; [occ.] Student; [hon.] 3 years in Who's Who of American High School Students, High School Roll, Blue Ribbons Art Award from Art Instruction Schools, Min. MN, Auditioned and accepted into Pinnellas County Center for the Arts - Visual Arts Program, Print on display in Mahaffey Theater Gallery - Created Logo used by Girls

Oceanographic Camp and part of National Oceanographic Assoc. (NOH); [oth. writ.] Many unpublished as yet; [pers.] I write about myself - I think people can most identity with that, and are happy to find someone who has some feelings like their own.; [a.] Saint Petersburg, FL

GROSSNICKLE, NELVA
[b.] January 31, 1985, Cherry Point, NC; [p.] Nancy Grossnickle; [m.] Randy Dale Grossnickle, Divorced; [ch.] Nelva has a better named Jeremiah James; [ed.] Going into the 6th grade at Monocacy Middle School; [occ.] Student; [memb.] Girl Scouts of America past 5 years. She is a member at the YMCA of Frederick Md.; [hon.] Certificate of Appreciation from Frederick Canty Sheriffs Office to Nelva Grossnickle for continued support of the men, women and mission of the Frederick County Sheriffs several past awards in Math Office and Art in school; [oth. writ.] Nelva has several other writings. She has loved to write poems since a very young age. She loves life and always finds beautiful things in life to write about.; [pers.] You will never know what you are good at unless you try and try and try. Sometimes you win sometimes you lose. But most important of it all is. "Have fun" Don't give up. Life can be beautiful.; [a.] Frederick, MD

GRUBBS, RUTH F.
[pen.] Ruth Faulkner Grubbs; [b.] February 21, 1932, Jellico, TN; [ch.] LouAnn, James Allen Jr.; [ed.] Jellico High, Knoxville General University of Tennessee; [occ.] Registered Nurse Retired; [memb.] Arlington Baptist Church, Smoky Mountains Hiking Club; [hon.] Beta Club, Nursing School Honors, U.T. Dean's List; [oth. writ.] O'Conner Center Writer's Compilation: 9 entries; [pers.] Mostly I write to touch the emotions or to paint a picture. To my own surprise, poetry is my forte.; [a.] Knoxville, TN

GRUNDEN, PAT
[b.] May 28, 1944, Brevard, NC; [p.] Dallos and Dorothy McCall; [m.] John C. Grunden, August 24, 1963; [ch.] John Marcus; [ed.] A.B. LaSalle University, A.A. Georgia State University; [occ.] Comptroller - The Jonathan Risk and Insurance Counselors; [memb.] North Fayette United Methodist Church; [hon.] Member - Gold Key National Honor Society, Deans List with Distinction, Holder - Dean's Key for Academic Excellence; [oth. writ.] Newspaper Articles Volunteer Organizations Newsletters; [pers.] Loneliness can never reside in the heart that knows the written word as friend.; [a.] Fayetteville, GA

GUERRIERO, TARA
[b.] June 27, 1980, New York; [p.] Tom and Laura Guerriero; [ed.] Grammer School at Our Lady of Assumption, I'm a Junior at St. Catherine's Academy; [oth. writ.] Several poems never published; [a.] Bronx, NY

GUILLOT, CASEY
[b.] March 5, 1979, Breaux Bridge, LA; [p.] Judy and John Darby; [ed.] Acadiana High School; [memb.] Student Council, Quizbowl; [hon.] Freshman of the Year, State Math Champ, Spelling Bee Champ; [oth. writ.] Several poems which will hopefully be published one day; [pers.] I like to display distinct moral messages in my poems. My inspiration for "Alone" was the thought of losing my one true love, Waleska Latorre.; [a.] Lafayette, LA

GUINN, AMISHA S.
[b.] April 11, 1977, Detroit, MI; [p.] Pamela Craig, Michael Black; [ed.] Attended Northwestern High School

School from 1991-95, received General Equivalency Diploma. Attending Wayne State University/Winter '96; [occ.] Student Library Ass., Detroit Public Library, Detroit, MI; [memb.] Founder and President of Girls Youth Group: Chocolate Chip Club. Founded in may 1996; [pers.] My firm belief is that everyone is an example. Whether it's 'Divine', I take notes on both. I'm inspired by fantasies, life, love and fear. In addition to the poetic songwriter, Michael Franks. Unyielding motivation comes from my mother, Pam and the Lord.; [a.] Detroit, MI

GUY, CARLENE L.
[pen.] Carly L. Guy; [b.] February 6, 1952, Norwood, MS; [p.] Carleton L. Kingsford, Frances M. Kingsford; [ed.] Massabesic High School; [occ.] Recruiter; [pers.] I strive to be a caring and sensitive individual who treats others the way I would want them to treat me.; [a.] Clifton Park, NY

GUY, COURTNEY
[b.] October 26, 1982, Passaic Valley, NJ; [p.] Ann Marie and Daig Guy; [occ.] Student at the Academy for the Advancement of Science and Technology; [a.] Park Ridge, NJ

HACKMAN, CARL C.
[b.] May 7, 1913, Otoe, NE; [p.] William and Irene Hackman; [m.] Louise M. (Nee Gassman), 1936; [ch.] Richard, Robert, and Carolyn; [ed.] N.W. MO. State College (Grad.), Graduate study at Garret Theological Seminary, Evanston, Ill; [occ.] Retired from 42 years Ministry in United Methodist Church in 1978; [oth. writ.] Many poems, one published in Liberty newspaper, others in Our Lady of Mercy monthly bulletin. Chap-Book being compiled.; [pers.] My poetry writing started after retirement. I want to describe (express) nature's grandeur, the indispensability of Christian faith, my deep love for family and friends.; [a.] Liberty, MO

HADFIELD, RUTH DYSON
[b.] England; [p.] Ruth and Thomas Dyson; [ed.] R.S.C.N., S.R.N. England, "The Little Angel" was a little girl 2 yrs. called "Rosemary" my second year of training. I was 17 years old. My first experience of death. A beautiful child with T.B. meaning it is. No cure in those days prior to antibiotics. I will never forget her.; [pers.] Life a precious gift from God. No one can replace. `Value It.' Too many lives are wasted.; [a.] Richmond, VA

HALE, JAMES H.
[b.] December 14, 1952, Colusa Co., CA; [p.] James W. Hale, Marilyn Hale; [m.] Carolyn Hale, January 15, 1972; [ch.] Taffie Loraine, James C. Hale; [ed.] Williams High School; [occ.] Operations Supervisor County of Lake; [oth. writ.] Poems for family and friends; [pers.] I love to read all poems, I tend to write about everyday life and nature.; [a.] Clear Lake, CA

HALL, JEFFREY A.
[b.] October 6, 1968, Amherst, NH; [p.] Forrest and Doris Hall; [ed.] Under graduate at University of Pennsylvania, Wharton School of Business; [occ.] Student; [memb.] United Way, Christmas in April; [hon.] United States Navy Petty Officer; [oth. writ.] A Lover's Con, Ode To Howard, Contemplating Moon, Equate Thee To?, Passion; [pers.] "The Purpose of life is a life with purpose!"

HALL, LEAH MAE
[pen.] Leahmae; [b.] March 19, 1929, Las Animas, CO; [p.] Mr. and Mrs. W. S. Moore; [m.] Robert G. Hall, July 14, 1963; [ch.] Robert Dean Van Duyn, Gary Lynn Van Duyn; [ed.] Central High - Cosmetology School,

De Mart Cosmetology (Scholarship of Wigs Rommel Mancini); [occ.] Minnie Rates Drive Safe Systems - owner; [memb.] First Christian Church, Epsilon Sigma Alpha; [hon.] Can't think of any grate honors; [oth. writ.] "Sisters", The Wedding, Christmas Wish, Slot Machine of Life, Housewife Prayer, Mary Jane, "It A Mountain" in Vail Co.; [pers.] I only right about things that have touched my heart.; [a.] Arvada, CO

HAMILTON, JUDITH M.
[b.] November 18, 1962, Chahalis, WA; [p.] Frank R. Ness and Dolores C. Ness; [m.] Timothy R. Hamilton, January 30, 1983; [ch.] Michael, Tangella and Amanda; [ed.] Jeffersonville High School, Fla Jr College, Prosservoc; [occ.] Scheduling Coordinator; [hon.] Honorable Mention in The National Library of Poetry Contest; [oth. writ.] The Evening News, Poets Corner, Several Poems, A Poem published in The Coming of Dawn by the National Library of Poetry; [pers.] "The Rose" is dedicated to my neighbor Agnes Allen a retired teacher from Middle Road School in Jeffersonville, Indiana. Who went to heaven last year.; [a.] Jeffersonville, IN

HAMILTON, KELLY A.
[b.] March 29, 1982, Greenville, OH; [p.] Monty P. and Nancy L. Hamilton; [ed.] Freshman in High School; [hon.] Maintained a 40 G.P.A. in my Junior High School career.; [a.] Greenville, OH

HAMMOCK, PATRICIA LORRAINE
[pen.] Lorraine Hammock; [b.] March 25, 1965, Detroit, MI; [p.] Richard Cady, Patricia McFadden; [m.] Lonnie W. Hammock, November 26, 1983; [ch.] Lonnie W., Daniel D.; [ed.] Annapolis High School, 1983 Community College of the Air force, 1992 - A.A.S Informations Systems Management; [occ.] Computer Network Administration; [memb.] Planetary Society, O.B.O.D. - Order Bards, Ovatee, and Druids; [oth. writ.] Sci-Fi Novel - A Mystic's Advantage - currently seeking publisher; [pers.] Sources of inspirations include - Qabala, music - Queensryche, Ronnie James Dio Authors - Terry Brooks A. Crowley and the wondrous universe around us.; [a.] Taylor, MI

HAMPTON, WANDA
[b.] May 30, 1932, Beaman, MO; [m.] Harry Laton Hampton, August 23, 1952; [ch.] 5-16 Grandchildren - 5 Great; [ed.] Washington Elementary, Smith-Cotton High, Finished Education in U.S. Navy; [occ.] Antique Store Owner; [oth. writ.] Never been published; [pers.] When I didn't die during by-pass surgery I decided I had a purpose in life. So I'm having fun and helping others by listening to them.; [a.] Sedalia, MO

HANNES, RAYMOND A.
[pen.] Raymond Hannes; [ed.] "Outstanding Poets of 1994 except Bottomline is North Royalton, Ohio 44133 Instead of Brunswich OH; [occ.] Sales and Musician and Short story writer

HANSEN, SCOTT J.
[b.] January 22, 1952, Fort Dodge, IA; [p.] Gerald and Lola Hansen; [ed.] Carson High, Control DATL - Computer Tech. Black Belt - Taekwondo; [occ.] Trailer Park Manager; [memb.] Lion's Club, Elks Club Calif. Taekwondo Assoc.; [pers.] Hunting, Fishing, Skiing and Backpacking are my sports.

HANSON, FLORENCE BAKER
[b.] March 7, 1910, Concord, NH; [p.] Samuel Baker and Annie Gould; [m.] Russell S. Hanson, August 27, 1939; [ch.] Janet Hanson Gawlak, Sue Baker Hanson; [ed.] Concord High School, Concord, NH, University of New Hampshire, Durham, NH; [occ.] Retired Teacher; [oth. writ.] Observations by Florence Baker Hanson published by Carlton Press, Inc., Conclusions by Florence Baker Hanson published by Carlton Press, Inc.; [pers.] Poetry in thought so strong it has to be expressed.

HARDY, JACQUELINE
[b.] December 7, 1960, Savannah, GA; [m.] Divorced; [ch.] Eric Glover; [ed.] Saint Peter's College, Seton Hall Law School Attorney, Culler and Dykman, Brooklyn, New York; [a.] Montclair, NJ

HARE IV, ELLWOOD STOWE
[pen.] Doc, Hare, Ellwood Stowe; [b.] July 2, 1978, Columbus, OH; [p.] Tamara and Ellwood S. Hare III; [ed.] Northland High (Cols, OH), Ohio State University (1st year); [occ.] Full-time student; [memb.] National Honor Society, Ohio State Honors Program, Navy ROTC; [pers.] The meaning of life is an individual thing - the world is only as one sees it.; [a.] Columbus, OH

HARJU, LINDA
[b.] July 21, 1956, Massachusetts; [p.] Gail Hartley, Merton Hartley; [m.] Paul Harju, February 16, 1975; [ch.] Julie, Susan, Rebecca, Jennifer; [ed.] Plymouth-Carver High, Qunicy College; [occ.] Poet and Writer; [memb.] The Kingsbury Club, Upland Club and Jordan Hospital Life Time Member; [hon.] Member of the Honor Society in High School. The Diamond Homer Trophy for one of my Poems; [oth. writ.] The Aurorean, can be found in The South Shore News, The Stepping Stone, The National Library of Poetry anthologies: Portraits of Life and Whispers at Dusk also Famous Poets Society anthology Famous Poems of the Twentieth Century.; [pers.] I always look for the silver lining behind every cloud.; [a.] Plympton, MA

HARKINS, THERESE WHEATON
[b.] November 29, 1951, Elmira, NY; [p.] Frank and Helen Wheaton; [m.] William C. Harkins, June 27, 1981; [ch.] William - 12 yrs., Colleen - 10 yrs.; [ed.] State Univ. N.Y. - Brockport, N.Y. Free Lance Writer; [hon.] "Portrait of my Husband", Editors Choice from Nat'l Library of Poetry, - Published in A Muse to Follow; [oth. writ.] "Bridges of Harmony" - published in the best of the 90's, "Positive Speaking" - published in Forever and a Day. "My Pyramid of Jewels" - published in Recollections of Yesterday, "Transforming a Dream" - published in Whispers at Dusk

HARRINGTON, LOU F.
[b.] October 26, 1942, Anadarko, OK; [p.] Fred B. and Ida I. Pedigo; [m.] Gary D. Harrington, August 22, 1992; [ed.] Hanford, CA Clerical Typing, Delano, CA High School, Columbine Elementary School Delano, CA; [occ.] Homemaker; [memb.] New Life Harvest Pentecostal Church of God, PLA; [hon.] Handwriting Certificate from Columbine Elementary School Delano, CA; [pers.] Inspired by son "Kenneth Pendergrass." "Special Bouquet" was from God for "Traci Renee Conrad" a "Special Rose Bud" from Hanford CA.; [a.] Tipton, CA

HARRIS, BILLY EDWARD
[pen.] Billy Edward Harris; [b.] July 8, 1948, Cathage, MS; [p.] Mary E and Whenshaw Harris; [ed.] H.S. AJCC Edinburgh, IN, Grad American Institute of Applied Science, grad. Police Science Institute, Forestry and Gen. L.E., Grad. Blackstone school of Law, paralegal; [occ.] Retired Correction Officer and Provides some Legal Service for the indigent; [memb.] Free mason; [hon.] Silver and Bronze Star from the 82nd Airborn, Div. Vietnam 1968-69; [pers.] I believe that wisdom is not measured by how wise one is, but by how wisely one imparts that wisdom.; [a.] Lompoc, CA

HARRIS, BOBBIE LEE
[b.] March 11, 1947, Calhoun City, MS; [p.] Charlie and Willie Lee; [ch.] Glynis, Dennis, Donna; [oth. writ.] Speech in Jackson MS, paper, poem in local paper, poems in sparrowgrass anthology.; [pers.] I write about things that are very important to me or have made a deep impression!; [a.] Derma, MS

HARRIS, DARLENE ANTOINETTE MAY
[b.] July 9, 1971, Jackson, MS; [p.] Mrs. Janice Marie May Davis; [m.] Mr. Marvin Malcom Harris Sr., May 5, 1994; [ch.] Mr. Marvin Malcom Harris Jr.; [ed.] Graduate of the Class 1989 from John W. Provine, attended Jackson State University (3 yrs.), presently Studying for a degree in child care at P.C.D.I.; [occ.] Receptionist, Clerical; [memb.] Member of the Future Business Leaders of America, Pres. of Future Homemakers of America, Band Member; [hon.] Received Honorable Mention from "The Grand Ole O'Pry", "World of Poetry", for a poem titled - "Thieves In The Temple", in 1992, received trophy for Most Outstanding Student of Childcare and Guidance Class '87 and '88; [oth. writ.] I've written numerous poems, but here's just a few - "Faces of Grace", "Candle Light Fright", "Unlock Your Door", "I'm Hooked", and many many more!; [pers.] I believe you can accomplish anything as long as you keep focused on positive things. All things are possible through Christ if you just believe and try with all your heart!; [a.] Austin, TX

HARRIS, FRANCES P.
[b.] September 25, 1948, Java, Indonesia; [p.] Esther and Eugene H. Poublon; [m.] Jack B. Harris, September 17, 1973; [ed.] Lycee Frangois I, France University of Leiden, The Netherlands; [occ.] President, Art Management Consulting Corp./Blumbery and Harris Inc.; [memb.] NAFE - National Association for Female Executives, A.I.R.C. - American Indian Relief Council - Honorary Trustee; [hon.] BACCE/Aureate Degree with Honors, Prix d'Honeur for French Literature and Philosophy; [oth. writ.] Articles for art magazines/catalogues, and reviews/writing poetry.; [pers.] Growing up in Europe, Thadan early interest in writing, influenced by French Literature and Philosophy and the history of art.; [a.] New York, NY

HARRIS, JANIE
[b.] December 14, 1960, Kansas City, KS; [p.] George and Peggy Stuart; [m.] Darren Harris, June 17, 1992; [ch.] Melinda, Eric, Arwen, Khiana; [ed.] Turner High, KS Community College, M.T.T.I.; [occ.] Massage Therapist (C.M.T.), Postal Clerk; [memb.] A.P.W.U.; [oth. writ.] Self Published "My Slice of Pie" a selection of inspired poems; [pers.] "Listen to your inner-voice" it has the knowledge of the universe.; [a.] Kansas City, KS

HARRISON, WENDELL
[pen.] Reb; [b.] June 6, 1965, Artesia, NM; [p.] Earl Harrison; [ch.] Barbara Ellen, Christopher Scott, John Daniel; [ed.] Artesia High; [occ.] Farm Forman; [pers.] Everyone has something to say. We only have to stop and listen. Especially children. If you have no problems, life would be dull.; [a.] Artesia, NM

HART, CINDY L.
[pen.] Cynthia Lynnet; [b.] December 15, 1961, Bangor, ME; [p.] Charles Hart, Carlene Hart; [ed.] Complete SSA Program, (CPR, First Aid) Certified Reflexologist, Short Order Cook Degree (Job Corps), College Courses include Anatomy Physiology, Pathology (DSM) Certifi-

cate of Attainment; [occ.] Reflexologist; [memb.] Volunteer for the Baxter School for the Dead, Pine Tree Society for the Handicapped, United Way Member; [hon.] Spotlight Employee of the Month (8,95) Brighten Medical Center; [oth. writ.] I have written nearly 600 poems, but this is the first I've ever had published. It would be a dream come true to publish some of my poetry.; [pers.] My mission in life is to relieve, or to ease physical and spiritual pain, either by reflexology (physical), or through my poetry. (Spiritually); [a.] Portland, ME

HART, LAWRENCE E.
[pen.] Seth; [b.] September 14, Conway, SC; [p.] Russ Hart, Frances Garner; [ch.] Shane, Matthew, Ava Marie; [ed.] Wofford College - Spartanburg, SC; [occ.] Golf Landscaping; [oth. writ.] Health Beat - Monthly News learning for Corporations; [pers.] I have experienced th top of life and the bottom, now that I survived there are a million thoughts I want to share - Life, death, divorce - custody God bless - Adiction - Survival.; [a.] Clemson, SC

HARTRANFT, LINDA M.
[pen.] Linda St. Marie; [b.] August 22, 1955, Lancaster, PA; [p.] Mr. and Mrs. James E. Rowell; [m.] Thomas J. Hartranft, May 17, 1975; [ed.] Warwick High School; [occ.] Sales Clerk; [memb.] Lititz Lioness Club Legion Of Mary St. James Church; [oth. writ.] Climbing the Mountain.; [pers.] I write from within.; [a.] Lititz, PA

HASSELL JR., STEVE
[pen.] Stevie Hassell; [b.] November 9, 1984, Elizabeth City, NC; [p.] Steve Hassell, Debra Hassell; [ed.] Central Elementary School; [memb.] Albemarle Kart Club Assoc. Elizabeth City Boys Club, and Pentecostal Holiness Church; [hon.] A.B. Honor roll student, Superintendent's Academic Team Award, Perfect Attendance Award, Academic Excellence in Math Award; [oth. writ.] Several poems that I wrote in Sunday School. 3rd Grade I wrote a poem for our school contest and won.; [pers.] I would love to become a writer of poetry.; [a.] Elizabeth City, NC

HATAWAY, JENNY
[b.] July 2, 1976, Memphis, TN; [p.] William M. Hataway and Laneale Hataway; [ed.] Graduate of Northwest Mississippi Community College in the Paralegal Field (1996); [occ.] Paralegal at the Office of D. Rook Moore, III; [memb.] First Baptist Church College and Career Class, First Baptist Church Adult Choir, Women in Action; [hon.] Most Outstanding Paralegal for 1995-1996 Academic Term, Phi Theta Kappa Theta Sigma, Dean's List; [oth. writ.] Some poems published in school newspaper.; [pers.] Live for the moment and love while you can for tomorrow it may all be gone.; [a.] Holly Springs, MS

HAVERTAPE, ROSLYN JO
[b.] March 7, 1951, San Fernando Valley, CA; [p.] Russell and Mickey Johnson; [m.] George W. Havertape, November 23, 1974; [ch.] Skip, Kim, Jodi, Jason and Caleb; [ed.] South High School Torrance, CA - AA from MSJC - Mount San Jacinto Jr. College - San Jacinto, California; [occ.] I have 2 part-time jobs, Church secretary and graphic Artist; [pers.] I believe all truth is inspired by God. "The Mask", which is so true, is from God. People hide behind masks instead of telling the truth about where they are bound - so, who will deliver me from this death? O thank God, He will through Jesus Christ our Lord!; [a.] Hemet, CA

HAWKINS, MABLE T.
[b.] Atlanta, GA; [p.] Matthew L. Emanuel and Teola Emanuel; [m.] Dr. Alexander A. Hawkins (Deceased),

July 3, 1946; [ch.] Alexander A. Hawkins Jr. and Clinton Matthew Hawkins; [ed.] Schenley High, Pgh., PA, Spelman College, and Atlanta University, Atlanta, GA, University of Pittsburgh, Pgh., PA; [occ.] Retired Professor Emerita from University of Pittsburgh, School of Social Work; [memb.] St. James A.M.E. Church, National Assoc. of Social Work, Delta Sigma Theta Sorority, Phi Delta Gamma Scholarship Organization. Several professional publications including a book, and limited poetry publications in an anthology of poems.; [hon.] Several professional honors of which "Professor Emerita" I cherish as reflecting my life's work.; [oth. writ.] Writing poetry is a very recent interest on my part. My poem "Dinquinesh", was published, 1996, a Voyage to Remember By The National Library of Poetry.; [pers.] My poetry depicts my love for and interest in helping people attain the heights of their souls yearnings and abilities; [a.] Pittsburgh, PA

HAWKINS, STEVEN
[pen.] Steven Lee Hawkins; [b.] November 19, 1978, Greenville, SC; [p.] Tommie Lee and Janice Hawkins; [m.] Single; [ed.] Attended Wade Hampton High School, currently attending Greenville Tech pursuing a Bachelor of Science in Electronic (Engineering Technology); [occ.] Student; [memb.] Watchtower Bible and Tract Society, Jehovah's Witnesses; [hon.] "WHHS Orchestra Honor Award", "Rating of Superior from SC Music Educators Association", "Rating of Superior from Solo and Ensemble Festival, Orchestra Division", Certificate of Recognition and Gold Medal from ACT-SO"; [oth. writ.] "It Is Fall" special mention in "The Greenville News", "A Paradise Poem" and "The Anniversary Poem".; [pers.] I strive to write about how God will solve mankind's problems in my writing. I also like to reflect on the Bible (view) about how it is a source of wisdom and joy for us.; [a.] Greenville, SC

HAYES, JANICE K.
[b.] May 11, 1965, Ypsilanti, MI; [m.] William G. Hayes II, August 30, 1982; [ch.] Courtnie, Khrysta and William III; [pers.] I've been writing poems since I was 11 years old. I write from my heart and soul. I hope someday my children and their children will enjoy them and take them into their hearts.; [a.] Charlotte, NC

HAYNES, ANTONY K.
[b.] April 1, 1973, Athens, GA; [p.] Melvin Haynes Jr. and Y. Antoinette Young; [ed.] BS, Computer science, U.S.A.F. Academy, 31 May 1995, M.S., Computer Science, U. of Illinois - Urbana/Champaign, January 1997; [occ.] Graduate student, Air Force Officer (Lieutenant); [memb.] Upsilon P. Epsilon (Computer Science Honor Society). AAAI (American Association for Artificial Intelligence), Emmanuel Missionary Baptist Church, Association of graduates (USAF Academy); [hon.] High School class of 1991 Valedictorian, Eagle Scout, distinguished graduate of US Air Force Academy Class of 1995, most Outstanding Computer science graduate of US Air Force Academy Class of 995, listed among Who's Who among Students in American Universities and Colleges; [oth. writ.] Griot, Literary Magazine, Vol. 38, No 3, and No. 4: Critical essays and poetry, Modern Graffiti, Literary Magazine, Vol. III, assorted poems and short stories.; [pers.] Life is the quest for understanding, knowledge, wisdom - this is my mission: To discern truth from the world and use it to transform others even as I am transformed.; [a.] West Palm Beach, FL

HECK, JOHN ANTHONY
[pen.] John A. Heck; [b.] June 29, 1960, Brooklyn, NY; [p.] Barbara Heck, John, M. Heck; [ed.] Xaverian H.S.,

New York Univ.; [occ.] Operations Director, EIA, Inc.; [hon.] NY State Forensics Winner (1977-78); [oth. writ.] Library of Congress: Poems of Great America, The Bad Henry Review, Sensations (NJ); [a.] Forest Hills, NY

HECKER, ANITA
[b.] January 15, 1949, Town Creek, AL; [p.] Andrew and Annie Zills; [ed.] Spalding High School Chicago, Illinois; [occ.] Disabled through illness in 1995; [memb.] "Order of the Eastern Star" held office of worthy Matron in 1976 1994; [hon.] Was worthy Matron in Western Springs Chapter, Order of the Eastern Star (OES) in Illinois twice. First time in 1976 then again in 1994 prior to moving to Arizona.; [oth. writ.] Playful writing about my friends (most loved them). 2 short stories for children (never published) 1 letter to the Editor re: Samali refugees, published in an Italian-American Newspaper, wrote OES newsletter in 1976-1994; [pers.] Born in Alabama, moved to Chicago's West side at age 5 where I grew-up in 1994, moved to Arizona where I began writing down some of the poetic thoughts that I had never been encouraged to speak.

HECKER, KAREL ANNE
[pen.] Rose Ashley; [b.] November 7, 1953, Spokane, WA; [p.] Robert L. Hecker, Audrey A. Hecker; [ed.] El Camino H.S., Calif.; American River College, Calif; [occ.] Heavy Mobile Equipment Mechanic, Red River Army Depot, TX; [oth. writ.] All unpublished; [pers.] Influences: Mary-Chapin Carpenter, James Kavanaugh, Nanci Griffith. I find writing helps me ease through the hardships life deals out.; [a.] Hooks, TX

HEILLE, AMY
[b.] November 3, 1975, Fargo; [p.] Jon and Reniah Heille; [m.] Elijah Harter, expected September 27, 1997; [occ.] Server at Perkins Restaurant in Fargo; [oth. writ.] Holding Hands, Sarah, The Nothing, A Tare, The Meaning; [pers.] I am an idea, I will teach you all that I know.; [a.] Fargo, ND

HELGANZ, NANCY E.
[pen.] Nan-C-; [b.] February 21, 1967, Bloomfield Hills, MI; [p.] Jack and Ann Helganz; [ed.] University of Detroit, Detroit, MI; [occ.] Private Investigator; [memb.] Kappa Beta Gamma Sorority, Michigan Republicans; [hon.] Dean's list; [oth. writ.] Many hidden in my attic to come out after I lay down in the grand, hopefully in at 100 years.; [pers.] I owe my love of life, and art to my best friends, my parents. I thank them for all their love and support. Keep smiling world.; [a.] Northville, MI

HELLIGSO, NOEL M.
[b.] January 4, 1950, Astoria, OR; [p.] Stan and Robert Helligso; [m.] Cathleen Lori, March 16, 1974; [ch.] Flint Benjamin Helligso; [ed.] 68 graduate Warrenton High School, US Army Heavy Equip School 62330; [occ.] Log Home Contractor Heavy Equipment Mechanic; [memb.] Life Member NRA, Life Member VFW, Member International Union of Operating Engineers; [hon.] None of any significance; [pers.] We are all in this boat together, but before we tell others how to row we should be adepts, or at least morally blameless.; [a.] Lapine, OR

HENDERSON, JEREMEY
[pen.] Jeremy Henderson; [b.] April 9, 1983, Garden Grove, CA; [p.] Tyra Henderson; [ed.] Presently in 8th grade; [occ.] Summer job setting tables cleaning dishes; [hon.] Summer award with job; [oth. writ.] As I see the world go by; [pers.] Say what you believe.; [a.] Seal Beach, CA

HENDRICKSON, MICHELLE
[b.] February 21, 1967, Huntington, NY; [p.] Dennis and Marion Hendrickson; [ch.] Alexsandra, Sydnea; [ed.] Walt Whitman H.S.; [occ.] Office Associate - MTA Bridge and Tunnels; [pers.] "Poetry is truly thoughts for the mind" a few of my poems have been read at relationship workshops, poetry workshops. November 1994 at workshop entitled: Black Dating in the 90's, sponsored by Black Media Enterprise.

HENDRIX, FELICIA R.
[pen.] "Feli"; [b.] February 15, 1966, Boston, MA; [p.] Lewison and Willie Hendrix; [ch.] Tamika L. Hendrix; [ed.] J. E. Burke Honor roll Student, Metropolitan College - Travel; [occ.] Dialysis Secretary Mary Eliza Mahoney Dialysis Center; [oth. writ.] Several songs and poems Homeless People, Drugs While Year Pregnant, Stop And Search, Cold Night Fighting For Our Lives, Drugs Do No Justice; [pers.] In my poems and songs I write the things I see, as I write the things I've experienced, and continue to experience everyday of my life. When anger tries to overcome me, I write it down on paper, and express myself that way instead of violently.; [a.] Boston, MA

HENNECY, BOBBIE BOBO
[pen.] Bobbie Bobo-Hennecy; [b.] August 11, 1922, Tignall, GA; [p.] John Ebb Bobo, Lois Helen Gulledge Bobo; [m.] James Howell Hennecy, December 28, 1963; [ch.] Erin Hennecy; [ed.] Wesleyan Conservatory, A.B. Summa Cum Laude, Mercer University, M.A., NDEA Fellow, Emory University, Postgraduate: English-Speaking Union Scholar, Oxford Univ., Grant from Mercer U., Cambridge Univ.; [occ.] Emeritus Associate Professor, and Adjunct Professor, Mercer University; [memb.] Tattnall Sq. Bapt. Ch., Founder and Director of Tattnall Sq. Academy, AAUP, AAUW, Life Member, YWCA, UDC, DAR, Dames of Magna Charta, Desc of Colonial Clergy, Collegiate Press Advisory Bad, SAMLA, MLA, Sou, Nat'l., and Int'l Comparative Literature Assoc., Middle Ga. Hist. Assn., Middle Ga. Art Assoc., Chi Omega Fraternity; [hon.] Phi Kappa Phi, Sigma Tau Delta, Sigma Mu, Alpha Psi Omega: Cardinal Key, Names Outstanding Psi Gamma Chi Omega, Plaque for 30 yrs. as Chi Omega Alum. Adv., Award for poem by UDC, listed in Who's Who in S. and SW, Who's Who Int'l, Who's Who of Professional and Business Women, Int'l Dictionary of Biography, Hereditary Register, Who's Who in American Education; [oth. writ.] Variations and Adaptations of Hamlet, Modernization of The Famous Tragedie of Sir Thomas Wyatt (Dekker and Webster, 1607), Tots Miscellany (27 poems), desk-top pub, other poems; [pers.] To show the goodness and love of God and his creations is my aim. I have been deeply influenced by British Lit., which I have taught for many, years, esp., The King James Version of the Bible, Chauncer, Shakespeare, Sir Thomas Wyatt, the Elder, Milton and other 17th c., poets, Romantic and Victorian.; [a.] Macon, GA

HERING, KRICKEN
[b.] June 26, 1972, Portland, OR; [ed.] B.A., English Literature University of Colorado, Boulder; [pers.] Connecting a pen to paper enables me to connect to myself. It's my forum of unadulterated truth. Thank you, Noname. I would not be here, if not for you.; [a.] New York, NY

HERRMANN, RACHEL
[b.] March 17, 1985, New York, NY; [p.] Marilyn and Richard Herrmann; [ed.] PS158/Bayard Taylor, MS167SP-Wagner; [occ.] Student; [memb.] 92nd Street Y Flying Dolphins Swim Team; [oth. writ.] "Horses Are Different," "Bed Time."; [a.] New York, NY

HERSHAFT, PHILIP
[pen.] Philip Hershaft; [b.] May 2, 1911, New York City; [p.] Hyman and Anna Hershaft; [m.] Florence Hershaft, July 31, 1937; [ch.] Raymond and Helen; [ed.] City College of the City of N.Y., Brooklyn Law School; [occ.] Retired, former occupations - Assistant Corporation Counsel, N.Y.C., Administrative Law Judge, N.Y.C., Arbitrator, Associated with American Arbitration Association, N.Y.C., Counsel to Family Court, N.Y.C., Private Practice of Law, N.Y.C., Federal Practice, Southern District, Admitted to Practice before The Supreme Court of the United States of America, Atty. Parking Violations Bureau, N.Y.C.; [memb.] Bronx Country Bar Association, New York State Bar Association; [hon.] Citation from the Parking Violations Bureau N.Y.C., Award from Bronx County Bar Association for 50 years Membership; [pers.] I enjoyed practicing Law. As a Hobby, I play the Violin. I was a member of symphony orchestras and enjoyed my music. This avocation kept my mind alert and was beneficial to my Law work.; [a.] New York City, NY

HICKMAN, LESLIE A.
[b.] October 21, 1968, Lafayette, IN; [p.] James and Shirley Hickman; [ed.] Benton Central Jr.-Sr. High School, Purdue University (B.A. Psychology, 1991), Indiana Univ. - receiving M.A. in Counselor Educ.; [occ.] Group Home Manager for the chronically mentally ill in Indianapolis, IN; [memb.] American Psychological Association; [hon.] Psi Chi National Honor Society (Purdue Univ. Chapter), Dean's List; [oth. writ.] I have written much poetry, none of which has ever been in print. All of my writing reflects the significant events which we, as humans, experience as a part of our lives. It has served as a hobby for me and holds great therapeutic value, allowing my innermost feelings to be expressed and better understood by important others in my life.; [pers.] "Together" was written subsequent to my survival after a life-threatening illness, shortly after my 26th birthday. It is a tribute to my beautiful family, whose unending love and support facilitated an unexpected, yet quick and complete recovery.; [a.] Noblesville, IN

HIGGINS, ANN C.
[b.] April 16, 1939, Erie, PA; [p.] Helen Russell and John T. Higgins; [m.] February 2, 1982; [ch.] Tracy A. Connors, Mike McGenl, Lisa Kelly; [ed.] Strong Vincent High University of Pitt; [occ.] Home owner; [oth. writ.] North East Breeze; [pers.] If my poem helps just one person, then I've done my job. It was givers to me. Now its time to give it back.; [a.] North East, PA

HIGGINS, COLIN FRANCIS
[b.] May 9, 1970, Chicago; [p.] Frank Higgins, Patricia Maloney; [ed.] B.A. Clark University, Worcester, MA, M.A. DePaul University, Chicago, IL; [occ.] Teacher; [memb.] American Maritain Association; [a.] Chicago, IL

HIGGINS, MS. N. LOY KUHN
[pen.] Loy; [b.] August 2, 1944, Louisville, KY; [p.] Arthur Louis Kuhn (Deceased) and Nina Waller Kuhn; [m.] Dr. David Michael Higgins, November 27, 1990; [ed.] DuPont Manual High School, Louisville, KY, Class of '62. Eastern Kentucy State College, Richmond, KY, '62-'64. Miami Dade Junior College, Miami, Fl, '73-'74, AA Degree, Fine Arts/General. U of the State of New York, "86, AS Degree, Liberal Arts and General Sciences (Regents Program), conferred Jan '87.

Scottsdale Community College, Scootsdale, AZ, '95, Studio Recording and Electronic Music; [occ.] Writer, Musician, Teacher, Desktop Publisher; [memb.] International Society of Poets, National Authors Registry, Adult Recital Series of AZ State Music Teachers Assn, Alliance Francais, Senior Friends; [hon.] Poems published in the "National Library of Poetry's" anthologies A Voyage to Remember, A Muse to Follow, Amidst the Splendor, The Ebbing Tide, Memories of Tomorrow, The Best Poems of the '90's, and Frost at Midnight, the Modern Poetry Society of Dunnellon, FL's volume of modern poetry Mirrors of the Soul, The Mile High poetry Society of Denver, CO's anthology Muse, Iliad Press Literary Anthologies Crossings and Whispers, and the Marshall Islands Journal. Honorable Mention, Pine Hills, NY Poetry Competition 1995, Honorable Mention, Iliad Press Fall 1995 Literary Awards Program, and two Editor's Choice awards, The National Library of Poetry - 1996, Superior and Excellent Awards, National Federation Junior Festival's '93, '94, '95, Special Commendation, National Guild of Piano Teachers '93, '94, '95, and membership in the National Fraternity of Student Musicians, Student Divisions of American College of Musicians and Piano Hobbyists, ASMTA Central District, 43rd Piano Essemble, '95; [oth. writ.] Poems, humorous short stories, songs, and lyrics. Writer and publisher of Poetry Lines series. Arranger and performer of several keyboard cassette recordings, recorded in my previous home studio in Scottsdale, AZ; [pers.] As many people sharing one world, we travel different pathways to one destination, using music, poetry, and the arts to communicate and express our emotions.; [a.] Ajeltake, Majuro Atoll, MH

HIGLEY, MARTIN R.
[b.] February 10, 1947, Tiffin, OH; [p.] Perry M. Higley, Sarah Jean Higley; [m.] Colleen M. Higley, September 22, 1985; [ch.] Erick Shiloh Swanson; [ed.] 3 years of College, currently Enrolled with Institute of Children's Literature; [occ.] Respiratory Therapist; [memb.] AARC, UHMS; [oth. writ.] None published to date; [pers.] From caucasian and native American Heritage. My philosophy leans much more to my native American side. I have a strong bond and relationship with all animals.; [a.] Toledo, OH

HILL, BRIANA
[pen.] Mischief MacFarlane; [b.] May 21, 1977, Del Rio, YX; [p.] Christopher and Diane; [ed.] Currently attending Scarborough High School; [occ.] Student; [memb.] Latin Club UIL, one act play, crew member; [hon.] Several ribbons ranging from first place to fifth place, showing a horse I trained myself.; [oth. writ.] I have nothing published, but I am extremely hopeful now that I've gotten this wonderful opportunity.; [pers.] Patience is a virtue in this world, dreams can become reality if you realize them. I was very influenced by Anne Rice.; [a.] Houston, TX

HILL, JERI
[b.] Buffalo, NY; [ch.] Brenda McGlaston, Robin Williams; [ed.] State University College at Buffalo BS Ed., SUNY at Buffalo - MS Ed; [occ.] Retired Special Ed. teacher/coordinator, CSE chairperson, Buffalo, NY; [memb.] Alpha Kappa Alpha, Pi Lambda Theta, Maumbasoma Readers, NEA, Smithsonian; [pers.] Sharing the universality of frustration, hope, love, lust, throughout the lives of ordinary women.; [a.] Buffalo, NY

HILL, PATRICIA
[b.] January 16, 1948, Baltimore, MD; [ed.] AA De-

gree in Social Work from then; The Community College of Baltimore (1973); [occ.] Investigator with Baltimore City Dept. of Social Services; [hon.] Currently on the Dean's List at Dundalk Community College, Certificate of Appreciation from the Pratt Library Lifelong Learning Program and the Labor Education Achievement Program for my tutoring services.

HILL, TIFANNY

[b.] October 31, Pasadena, TX; [p.] Kimberly Hill; [ed.] The Woodlands High School; [occ.] Student; [memb.] Member of International Thespain Society, Who's Who of American High School Students; [hon.] National Merit Scholar; [oth. writ.] I'm just starting to get my work published.; [pers.] My mind and soul are dark and extraordinarily deep. I feel that my writing reflects my innermost thoughts and emotions. Also, Mrs. Kimberly Allen gave me the courage to pursue my dreams.; [a.] The Woodlands, TX

HILTON, PAULA VICKERY

[b.] November 19, 1969, Atlanta, GA; [p.] Ansel Vickery, Aletha Vanadore Vickery; [m.] Carl Hilton, February 23, 1996; [ch.] Kelly Hilton, Gary Hilton; [ed.] Heritage High School Conyers GA; [occ.] Dental Receptionist, Dr. Daniel A. Hodges, Conyers, GA; [memb.] Metro Heights Baptist Church; [hon.] Honor Roll, VICA Club Award, VBS - Teacher honor; [oth. writ.] Poems for gifts to relatives and friends - poems for contest; [pers.] I enjoy writing about personal experiences in life. I feel blessed to have been encouraged to write by my high school English teacher Mrs. Chris Cook. My loving family is my inspiration.; [a.] McDonough, GA

HINES, REGINA KEENE

[b.] June 28, 1967, Gainesville, FL; [p.] Roger and Elaine Wiggins; [m.] Kelcey M. Hines, July 29, 1994; [ch.] Devin Lance Keene; [ed.] Received Law Enforcement Certification from Lake City Comm. College. Received Correctional Certification from Santa Fe Comm. College; [memb.] Member of the International Society of Poetry; [hon.] Won the Editors Choice Award for my Poem titled "Our Destiny"; [oth. writ.] "Our Destiny" published in spirit of the age by the National Library of Poetry.; [pers.] One should strive to be all that you can be, for there are no promises of tomorrow. always be true to yourself and set higher goals to reach for.; [a.] Newberry, FL

HIRT, DAVID ALAN

[b.] May 31, 1978, Terre Haute, IN; [p.] Dennis Hirt, Dwyn Hirt; [ed.] Crawfordsville High School, Wabash College; [occ.] College Student; [memb.] National Art Honor Society; [oth. writ.] A few poems and short stories in my High School literary Magazine, "The Muse".; [pers.] Writing has to be a passion, just like any of the Fine Arts. I write because I love to write. I don't need to be famous, I am doing it for me. Viva J.R.R. Tolkien. Viva Tad Williams; [a.] Crawfordsville, IN

HITI, MARY LAWRENCE

[b.] January 31, 1924, Johnstown, PA; [p.] Joseph and Teresa Hiti; [ed.] B.S. Carlow College Pittsburgh, PA, M.Ed. Duquesne Univ. Pittsburgh, PA Post Graduate Credits; [memb.] Member of Religious Order of the Adorers of the Blood of Christ Columbia Province. Distinguished Member of the International Society of Poets; [hon.] ISP Editor's Award Poems Chosen and Recorded on the sound of poetry: Reawakenings: Celebrating Jubilees, So Turns the Earth; [oth. writ.] Poems published in Poetry Anthologies: Spirit Of The Age, Best Poets Of The 90's, Whispers At Dusk; [pers.] Writing

poetry unleashes the well springs of emotion and stokes the fires of the creative imagination, to unlimited heights.; [a.] Columbia, PA

HLAVINKA, KENNETH PAUL

[pen.] Paul Kenneth Hlavinka; [b.] February 4, 1931, McLaughlin, SD; [p.] Anthony and Ella Hlavinka; [m.] Norvella Ruth Hlavinka, May 22, 1953; [ch.] Steven, Beverly, Keven, Michael and Mark; [ed.] Formal Education McLaughlin High School, US Army Engineer School Heavy Equipment Topographic Survey Ft. Belvoir, Virginia.; [occ.] Cannery Mall Maint. Man.; [memb.] National Carousel Association; [hon.] VFW bike Safely Award (Instr) US Army Good Conduct and 2 letters of commendation buredy of reclamation 3 letters of commendation; [oth. writ.] Articles in newspapers in midwest author of article in 1968 National Law and Order Magazine title "Beating The Lack Of Money Problem"; [pers.] I tend to see good in all people and situations I reflect this in my writings and poems. I am a believer in the person and know eventually we all will see the light.; [a.] Corvallis, OR

HOCHSCHILD, TANYA

[b.] August 19, 1996, South Africa; [m.] Michael Hochschild; [ch.] Claudie and Lenny; [ed.] M.O.H. (Master of Humanities); [occ.] Writer; [memb.] IWWG (International Women's Writers Guild); [hon.] Work in Congressional Record "Highlights of U.N. History"; [oth. writ.] Journalist in South Africa, several articles published in greenwich magazine.; [a.] Greenwich, CT

HOFFMAN, GLEN-JOHN

[pen.] Xavier Nullepart; [b.] December 3, 1970, Cape Town, South Africa; [p.] Brenda Lyme Hoffman and Eric Hoffman; [m.] Michele Hoffman, April 12, 1996; [ed.] Diocesan College Cape Town University of Cape Town (B. Sor. Sci) SUNY Purchase New York; [occ.] Hedonistic Anthropologist; [memb.] Explorers Club (NY); [oth. writ.] A condensed anthology of poetry titled. "The Ramblings of a Lost Bard, Betrayed by His Silent Dictaphone."; [pers.] I attempt to glean personal insight through salubrious environments, through Jaded eyes, and disturbed compunction.; [a.] New York, NY

HOFFMAN, REBECCA A.

[b.] February 23, 1971, Plainfield, NJ; [p.] Louis W. and Barbara L. Hoffman; [ed.] B.A. in Literary Studies from University of Texas at Dallas, 1994, May; [occ.] Resource English Teacher at Crockett Jr High, Irving, TX; [oth. writ.] I've had other poems published in my High School Magazine "Reflections."; [pers.] I've been writing free verse poetry since I was 14. My influences have been the dark ages, me devil ages, and the romantics. Dreams do come true when you believe in yourself.; [a.] Richardson, TX

HOHLFELDT, KEITH D.

[b.] October 31, 1951, Chicago, IL; [p.] Kenn and Kay Hohlfeldt; [m.] Judy P. H. (McLamb), May 15, 1992; [ed.] BS in Microbiology and Biochemistry Minor in Psychology U. CA Santa Cruz - Honors graduated top of the class; [occ.] Wine and Food Technical Consultant; [memb.] American Society of Enology and Viticulture Culinary Institute of American; [hon.] 22 Winemaking Awards from various competitions Highest Honors from UCSC; [oth. writ.] 155 poems since 1968. None submitted for publication. Writing a book on my life as a wine maker and food critic in Oregon, Washington Western Europe and Ontario Canada (where I've lives); [pers.] I love love and fine art. Mostly imprestionists because its. Soothing and slightly seduc-

tive. My writing usually alludes to the state of the environment or loves of my life.; [a.] Morrisville, NC

HOLDER, CHARLES E.

[b.] August 4, 1915, Little Rock, AR; [p.] Fred and Ethel Holder; [m.] Edwina Holder, November 16, 1946; [ch.] Deborah Eberts; [ed.] BA 1937 University or Arkansas; [occ.] Retired; [hon.] US Army World War II counter Intelligence Corps Awarded Bronze Star; [a.] Jamesburg, NJ

HOOVER, CYNTHIA L.

[b.] June 18, 1953, Okmulgee, OK; [p.] John D. and Barbara Lee; [m.] Jerry W. Hoover, December 23, 1971; [ch.] Angela (22), Amy (18); [ed.] Okmulgee High, 1977 Practical Nursing, 1987 Associate of Science in Nursing, Registered Nurse; [occ.] Director of Nurses Public Health Nursing; [memb.] Oklahoma Nurse's Association, Foursquare Women International, Okmulgee County Health Care Coalition; [hon.] Rotary Ann Scholarship YMCA Volunteer of the year; [oth. writ.] I have written many poems, however, my entry to your contest was my very first publication outside of family and friends.; [pers.] My goal is to reach out and touch those I can and ease the journey of this life in some small way for those I can.; [a.] Okmulgee, OK

HOOVER, RUTH ANN

[b.] September 4, 1966, Elkins, WV; [p.] Gary "Bud" and Arlene Hoover; [ed.] Fairmont State College; [occ.] Admin. Assist. Snowshoe, Ski Resort; [pers.] Never pass over the opportunity to learn something new.; [a.] Snowshoe, WV

HOPKINS, JANIS

[pers.] Maiden name is Janis Behrendt

HORTON, DAVID E.

[pen.] Bloodworth Horton, Ogden Edsel; [b.] November 18, 1950, Jackson, MS; [p.] Dolores C. Bloodworth and Bingham B. Horton; [ed.] Coral Gables High, Career Academy school of Famous Broadcasters; [occ.] Owner, Porto and Horton Garage, Lakeland, FL; [memb.] Kaiser - Frazer Owners Club, Studebaker Driver's Club, Crosley Automobile Club, Nash Car Club of America; [oth. writ.] Auto Columnist, the Miami News, features writer, the Birmingham News, articles in Cars and Parts Magazine, Automobile Quarterly; [pers.] Poetry is the ultimate distillation of words and ideas.; [a.] Lakeland, FL

HORTON, SHIRLEY M.

[pen.] Shirley Campbell Horton; [b.] August 18, 1929, Brockton, MA; [p.] Gertrude and William Macomber; [m.] Llewelyn R. Horton, November 1, 1991; [ch.] Chris Bonnie, Mark, Beth and Todd; [ed.] Graduate of Howard High School 47 member of National Honor Society. Graduated from Springfield City Library Training School Spfld Ma; [occ.] Retired - Housewife Mary Kay Consultant (Avocation); [memb.] Member of West Yarmouth Cong's Church W. Yarmouth MA. Served on many committees and song with choir. Member of International Society of poets Distinguished Member; [hon.] Rec'd four Editors Choice Awards for published poems from Nat'l Library of Poetry; [oth. writ.] Christian Newsletters, Eight poems being published by National Library of Poetry. Hope to publish book in the fall.; [pers.] My mother read poems to me when I was a child. Now I am surrounded by poetry books. It became the love of my life because I can share so much with so many people. I take up my pen and ho, and behold there comes forth a poem.; [a.] Taunton, MA

HORTON, WALTER M.
[b.] March 4, 1927, Pittsburgh, PA; [p.] Lonnie and Susan Horton; [m.] Barbara J. Horton, April 12, 1967; [ch.] Dau. Derille J. Horton; [ed.] Three Years Col. American River Soc. CA, Major Art and Sculpture; [occ.] Retired USAF 1972 (20 years 6 mos.); [hon.] Bronze Zero Defects Award, Air Force Logistics Command, Seven Certificates of Training Awards; [oth. writ.] Songs and plays for musicals, none published series of poems published in the "People News" Pitts, PA 1947.; [pers.] As a christian and firm believer in my Lord and savior Jesus Christ, I write to edify Gods word as the spirit gives me knowledge.; [a.] Rancho Cordova, CA

HOWARTH, RAINEY
[pen.] Rainey Marie, Snowy; [b.] December 21, 1980, Seattle, WA; [p.] Rebecca; [ed.] Sophomore at Cedarville High School; [hon.] High School Honors Band; [pers.] Whatever I'm feeling, writing is my sanctuary in which it is expressed, contemplated, shared and laid to rest, but not forgotten never, ever forgotten. I'm so glad I can share this with so many others.; [a.] Cedarville, OH

HOWELL, LISL
[b.] July 25, 1961, Manhatttan, USA; [p.] Phyllis Floyd; [ch.] Nora, Michael and Courtney; [ed.] High School Graduate; [occ.] Secretary; [pers.] Poetry helps me think and express my feelings. I just have to "write it down."

HUBER, KELLI J.
[b.] July 6, 1982, Long Beach, CA; [p.] Valerie Anderson; [ed.] Just graduated from St. Barnabas Elementary School with Gold Cord; [occ.] Entering 9th grade at St. Joseph's High school; [memb.] Girl Scouts, Drama, Bell Choir, Junior Great Books; [hon.] Certificate of Excellence in Scholarship, 1996. Science Achievement Certificate, Christian Service Award (all 6/1996) Gold Cord/CA Junior Scholarship Federation; [oth. writ.] Several short stories and poems. This is the first writing submitted for publication. Kelli also does her own illustrations.; [pers.] Although only 14 yrs. old, Kelli has a zest for life and a love of learning. One day soon, she will do great things.; [a.] Long Beach, CA

HUDSON, CAROLYN ROGERS
[b.] September 23, 1931, North Little Rock, AR; [p.] Odessa L. and Elbert E. Rogers; [m.] Robert Byars Hudson, October 18, 1947; [ch.] Michael, Craig, Darryl and Elizabeth; [occ.] Retired; [memb.] Munsey Memorial United Methodist Church Care Committee, Administrative Board and Sheparding Committee; [hon.] National Honor Society, United Methodist Women Lifetime membership, Y's Menette of the Year 1987; [pers.] Music and poetry are my interests. I feel that poetry is music without notes.; [a.] Johnson City, TN

HUNT, FRANCIS STEVEN
[b.] September 13, 1960, Lex., VA; [p.] Frances H. Templeton; [m.] William Joseph Hunt; [ch.] Andrea Nicole and Phillip Brandon Hunt; [ed.] Parry McCluer H.S.; [occ.] Misc. Iron Worker; [memb.] Organ Donor; [hon.] Accepted the Lord Jesus Christ, by his precious blood on 3-8-93; [oth. writ.] First article ever entered, called upon in August of '95 to write his words into poetry - can't write without him showing me, tried it doesn't work.; [pers.] The poems I've written since August of 95 were given to me from Jesus Christ. For his grace influenced me never wrote poetry before this time.; [a.] Buena Vista, VA

HUNTER, SEAN P.
[b.] November 29, 1971; [p.] Joseph Hunter, Bridget T. Hunter; [ed.] South Side High School, Nassau Commu-

nity College, Molloy College; [memb.] Molloy College Alumni Assoc.; [pers.] This poem was inspired by a few close friends of mine. I want to share this poem with you.

HURLOCK, RONALD B.
[b.] April 3, 1937, Jamaica, West Indies; [p.] Clifton Hurlock and Isolyn Hurlock; [m.] April 12, 1961; [ch.] Seven; [ed.] High School, Study City and Guild London, Eng., P/House Operation, Study Mona Li JA. on Trade Unionism; [pers.] I love the human race because, I found that regardless of race colour and religion, we are all alike.

HURT, GENE C.
[pen.] Gene C. Hurt; [b.] March 1, 1933; [p.] William and Della Hurt; [m.] Diana L. Hopkins Hurt, April 29, 1969; [ch.] Laurie J. Flood; [ed.] Lincoln H.S., Classes at Lincoln Land Community College, Continuing Real Estate and Residential Appraisal Education Throughout Illinois; [occ.] Realtor and State Certificate Residential Real Estate Appraiser.; [memb.] First United Methodist Church. Springfield Board and Realtors, Multiple Listing Service, National Assn. of Realtors, State Assn. of Realtors; [hon.] These are received by making my friends and family happy with laughter, tears and recollection of special moments.; [oth. writ.] Numerous poems for weddings, special occasions - anniversaries, etc.; [pers.] It is most enjoyable for me to write about special people in my life or that have touched my life.; [a.] Springfield, IL

HYNES, JILL TALLEY
[pen.] Jill Talley Hynes; [b.] February 21, 1972, Wilmington, DE; [p.] James Owen Talley and Judith Livingston Talley; [m.] Patrick David Hynes, September 25, 1992; [ed.] I am studying Criminal Justice at the University of Delaware. I hope to become a children's victim's rights attorney; [occ.] Homemaker, Amateur Writer, Student; [oth. writ.] I have written several poems and also my philosophies in life.; [pers.] I would like to dedicate this poem to my grandfather who passed away in March 1994. He taught me to succeed, be diverse, and that hard work, with dedication on all of life's journeys, will pay off and lead us to our destination.; [a.] Newark, DE

IANNOTTI, MONA MARSHALL
[pen.] Mona Marshall; [m.] Salvatore Iannotti, April 11, 1986; [ed.] University City High, Central Missouri State University Robert C. Board Academy of Theatre Arts; [occ.] Voice Over Actress, singer - songwriter, writer, and fine artist; [memb.] SAG, AFTRA, writers Guild, Rolling Readers, Voice Over Cares About Life (VOCAL); [hon.] Woody Award For Best Musical Show, Dean's List; [oth. writ.] "Life Is A Celebration... Potholes and all" - A one person musical, "Mind Magic"- an Audio project designed to help children visualize, various songs and scripts, How to Prepare your Love; [pers.] All aspects of my work as an artist, regardless of the medium, serve to illuminate the celebration of the human spirit in all it's conditions.; [a.] Glendale, CA

IGOU, STEPHANIE
[b.] December 15, 1978, Marietta, GA; [p.] David and Colleen Igov; [ed.] Home Schooling, Fannin County High School; [occ.] Being a senior at Fannin County High School; [hon.] 2nd place Fannin Spring Poetry Contest, Honor Roll; [oth. writ.] First Place Drug Awareness Essay published in "Vitality" Magazine, poem published in the 1996 Georgia High School poetry anthology: Pathways; [pers.] I am a manic - depressive hippie child, and writing is my therapy.; [a.] Blue Ridge, GA

IHEKE, CHUKS L.
[b.] Nigeria; [m.] Juliana Iheke, December 18, 1989; [ch.] Iheke, Ogbeyalu, Chuks, Jr; [ed.] Institute of Stenography, Aba Nigeria, University of Oregon, Eugene, OR, California State University, Hayward, CA; [occ.] Senior Auditor, U.S. Department of Defense, Defense Contract Audit Agency Western Region; [memb.] Association of Government Accounts; [oth. writ.] "My Father's Land Is Gone" published in a student journal. Several unpublished writings.; [a.] Fremont, CA

INGLE, JOHN
[b.] November 28, 1974, Kansas City, MO; [p.] Bob and Flo Ingle; [ed.] Penney High School, Southest Missouri State University; [occ.] Steel Mill Worked; [oth. writ.] Several unpublished poems, stories and random thoughts put on paper; [pers.] I hope that whoever way read what I write will choose to your off the bridge and swim in the river.; [a.] Caruthersville, MO

INGRASCIOTTA, NICOLO ANTONIO
[pen.] Tony; [b.] May 29, 1974, Brooklyn, NY; [p.] Mr. and Mrs. Gaspare Ingrasciotta; [m.] Mrs. Maria Carmelina Ingrasciotta, September 21, 1996; [ed.] Grover Cleveland High School; [occ.] Construction Worker; [hon.] High School Diploma, Merit of Achievement, John F. Kennedy Soccer League Trophy, Bicycle Marathon Medal and Trophy; [pers.] I believe that if anyone puts their mind and effort they can easily achieve in life.; [a.] Ridgewood, NY

INMAN, NEWFONIE J.
[b.] December 24, 1937, Pembroke, CA; [p.] Charles Jackson, Duffie Jackson; [ed.] Los Angeles Comm. Adult School Los Angeles Trade - Tech. College; [occ.] Clerk, County of Los Angeles, Dept. of Children's and Family Services; [hon.] Outstanding student of year 1981-1982 (G.P.A. 4.0) Commencement Speaker, Award: Scholarship from LACAS to LATTC; [pers.] I believe successful opportunities will be presented when anyone is keenly interested in developing authentic talent(s).; [a.] Los Angeles, CA

ISAACSON, ILANA
[b.] December 27, 1981, New York City; [p.] Arlene and Robert Isaacson; [ed.] Sophomore in High School, West Hempstead High School; [occ.] Student, CIT at Coleman Country Day Camp; [memb.] National Art Honor Society, National Federation of Temple Youth, Students Against Drunk Driving, Temple Emanuel of New Hyde Park; [oth. writ.] Poem published in "Inkblot" The Art and Literary Magazine of West Hempstead High School, May, 1996.; [a.] West Hempstead, NY

ISOSAKI, LONDA
[pen.] Londa Brickey; [b.] August 19, 1965, Snoqualmie, WA; [m.] Anthony Isosaki, September 7, 1991; [ch.] Joseph Michael, Hannah Rae, Zachery Tyler; [pers.] I have enjoyed writing since I was a child, and feel honored to have opportunity to share my work with others. My true love is fiction, but my work often seems to portray realism and the sad reality of life.; [a.] Grayslake, IL

JACKSON, CHANE'L
[b.] April 12, 1980, Chicago, IL; [p.] Valerie Jackson, Henry Jackson; [ed.] Cabrillo High School in Lompoc, CA; [occ.] Student; [pers.] My writing comes from what I feel and what others close to me may feel. My writing also covers feelings that I would like to experience.; [a.] Lompoc, CA

JACKSON, SARAH ELIZABETH
[b.] March 10, 1989, Winchester, MA; [p.] Edward and Jean Jackson; [ed.] Free School "Rainbow School" Kindergarten and 1st grade at "South Memorial School"; [occ.] Having fun being a kind; [hon.] Accelerated reading program at South Memorial School "The 10 point Club"; [pers.] "I like to write and I want to be an artist when I grow up."; [a.] Peabody, MA

JACKSON, SUSAN
[b.] February 15, 1962, New York; [p.] Anthony and Evelyn Saro; [m.] James S. Jackson, March 14, 1992; [ch.] Robert, Jessica, Shane; [occ.] House Wife; [oth. writ.] Just Poems; [a.] New York, NY

JAMERSON, ARLIS
[b.] February 16, 1930, Bentley, ND; [p.] Alice and Dan Wolfe; [m.] Lawrence C. Jamerson, October 8, 1948; [ch.] Linda L. Helland, Nancy Doughty; [ed.] High School, Bus. school; [occ.] Retired; [memb.] Treasurer - Faith Outreach - India; [pers.] I am involved with a missionary outreach in Orissa, India, that provides food, clothing, shelter, medical care and education from nursery age through college in one of the poorest areas in India. The needs in Orissa are so great — it was the inspiration for my poem.; [a.] Rochester, WA

JAMES, PATSY G.
[b.] November 14, 1956, Fairfield, CA; [p.] George E. Galjour, Josephine Galjour; [ch.] Michael Scott James; [ed.] Associates Degree of Applied Science; [occ.] Sales/Clerical; [memb.] National Association of Court Reporters; [oth. writ.] Not published yet.; [pers.] I enjoy writing poetry about life its occasions its revelations, its history and the beauty of nature's treasures.; [a.] Gutport, MS

JANELLE, DIANE L.
[pen.] Diane St. Cyr Janelle; [b.] December 4, 1961, Manchester, NH; [p.] Arthur G. St. Cyr and Lorraine E. St. Cyr; [m.] Marc Andre Janelle, June 27, 1992; [ed.] Trinity High School Notre Dame College; [occ.] Teacher, Free-Lance Writer, part-time bookseller; [memb.] St. Anthony Parish Association Canada American; [hon.] Who's Who Among American's Teachers, 1996 Award Who's Who Among America's College Student, 1984 Award Dean's List Who's Who Among America's High School Students, 1980; [oth. writ.] Currently completing first children's book, composed 2 songs for children's masses; [pers.] Through my writing and humor, I hope that God continues to inspire me to bring a little more light and love to this world, especially to the children.; [a.] Manchester, NH

JEFFERSON, TOCCARA ALICIA
[b.] April 17, 1982, Little Rock, AR; [p.] Gregory and Feleecia Jefferson; [ed.] 9th grade student at Henderson Jr. High; [pers.] My poetry is influenced by being a teenager in the 90's. I often write about what is going on in the world around me, how I feel and what I see on television. This particular poem, "I'm Only 25", was inspired by the television show Cops.; [a.] Little Rock, AR

JENKINS, CONNIE NOEL
[b.] November 8, 1980, Hazlehurst, MS; [p.] John Jenkins Jr., Carol Jenkins; [ed.] Madison Central High School; [occ.] Student; [memb.] National Honor Society; [hon.] Honor Student, Outstanding Spanish Student, Duke University T.I.P Program, Odessey of the Mind State Champion Team Member and World Team Member; [oth. writ.] "The Guardian" published in The Anthology of Poetry of young Americans; [a.] Ridgeland, MS

JENKINS, ESTHER
[pen.] Rhubell Mintz; [b.] October 8, 1925, South Carolina; [p.] James Mintz, Mattie Mintz; [m.] December 23, 1942; [ch.] Eight children; [ed.] Wilkson High, S.C., Brainen Institute, S.C., Medical School, N.Y.C.; [occ.] Homemaker, early retirement because of injury on the job; [memb.] AARP, John Street Methodist Church, N.Y.C., Oasis Fellowship Church Ithaca N.Y., also a member of the Choir; [hon.] Honor roll in high school; [oth. writ.] I have written a few songs one published.; [pers.] I feel it is very important everyone express love in a sincere and descent manner, I feel that love and kindness is a binding power. Where as hate destroy the very foundation of life. Therefore, we must love to love.; [a.] Ithaca, NY

JENKINS, SHELE MARIE VALLARIO
[b.] October 22, 1915, Onslow County, Jacksonville, NC; [p.] Tom Vallario and Terry Vallario; [m.] Jerry Jenkins Sr., April 14, 1994; [ed.] Swansboro High School; [occ.] Make Donuts at Wal-Mart Super Center; [hon.] 1. Award of Merit Certificate for poem Feelings That Hurt (March 15, 1989), 2. Award of Merit Certificate for poem finish (May 10, 1990), 3. Who's Who in Poetry and Golden Poet Award for poem Feelings That Hurt (1989), 4. Silver Poet 1990; [oth. writ.] I have wrote poems all my life. I have several other poems published in hearts on fire: A treasury of poems on love, great poems of the Western World Vol. II; [pers.] I mostly write love poems. Most of my are from early romances and feelings that I went Thur.; [a.] Johnson City, TN

JIMENEZ, MARCIA P. MCNEELY
[b.] February 26, 1954, Habana, Cuba; [p.] Manuel Pena and E. Gloria Pena; [m.] Adalberto Jimenez, August 25, 1991; [ed.] Psy. D. candidate Clinical Psychology, Miami Institute of Psychology; [occ.] Psychology Intern at SZETC and part-time Legal Secretary at William Hearon, P.A.; [memb.] American Psychological Association; [hon.] Master's in Science with Distinction in Clinical Psychology; [pers.] Sadly, mental illness is a reality. Society needs to begin to step back, examine its taboos and if it is to judge, learn to judge individuals on their merits and actions and not just on the fact that they are mentally ill. A cancer patient would not be shunned yet we continually shun the mentally ill. Look within, see the person and seek to help.; [a.] Hialeah, FL

JOHN, MAVIS
[b.] May 11, 1970, Trinidad, West Indies; [p.] Daniel and Elaine John; [ed.] Baruch College, (Still enroll), Boy and Girls High School; [occ.] Personal Care Aide, Health Force Agency; [pers.] I write poems based on the poets of life, and to influence humanity.; [a.] Brooklyn, NY

JOHNSON, BROOKE
[b.] September 15, 1980, Willmar, MN; [p.] Bev and Reid Johnson; [hon.] Music Contest, Honor roll, Academic letter, Volunteer work, President's award; [oth. writ.] Various essays and poems selected for publication with the VFW and in "A Break in the Clouds."; [pers.] My subjects are usually a little grim but I try to portray things as I see them.; [a.] West Fargo, ND

JOHNSON, CAMMIE
[b.] January 31, 1972, Greensboro, NC; [p.] Beverly Leak, Leroy Snipes; [ed.] College Student; [occ.] Attending college; [memb.] St. Mark Independent, Holiness Church, Student Support Services/Disability Access Services Advisory Committee at GTCC; [hon.] Governor's Award for Excellence. In Workforce preparation in 1993. Youth Participant of the Year. Was named Who's Who in Student Support Services at GTCC in 1992. Was on the Honor's List for the winter quarter 1996 at Guilford Technical Community College and an Academic Excellence Award for Spring quarter of 1996.; [pers.] Everyone may obtain their heart's desires if they have the patience to wait on God's timing and direction. I thank God for blessing me with happiness, success, and achievement and for encouraging me to write poems. Trust in God and believe in yourself.; [a.] Greensboro, NC

JOHNSON, CARI
[b.] June 13, 1972, Las Vegas, NV; [p.] Carl Johnson and Marsha Threet; [ed.] Limestone High School; [occ.] Case Aide for counseling and family services (foster care); [oth. writ.] I wrote and dedicated poems to two very special people in my life who had passed on. And was asked to present them at the place of burial.; [a.] Peoria, IL

JOHNSON, CARRIE COLLINS
[pen.] CC; [b.] September 22, 1943, California; [p.] Jasper and Etta McMullan; [m.] Charles Johnson; [ch.] Anthony and Carlton; [occ.] Owner of T.B.L. Packaging CO. AKA The Box Lady; [memb.] San Francisco Christian Center; [oth. writ.] Soon to be published "Women Of Faith Come Into The Knowledge of Who You Are"; [pers.] In all I say and do, I do as unto the Lord...Loving mankind by praying for a better world. For our children and love ones; [a.] Oakland, CA

JOHNSON, DAVID PAUL
[b.] March 14, 1963, Argienca, Newfoundland; [p.] Dan and Jo Johnson; [ed.] High School, Private School some College; [occ.] Advertising Salesperson; [memb.] Member of the Masonic Order; [hon.] 1977 Music Award, 5th place Ceda Debate in 1988; [oth. writ.] Poetry in School papers; [pers.] "We are all the keepers of our brothers and there by responsible for keeping them as we should hope that we are also kept."; [a.] Asheville, NC

JOHNSON, ELAINE W.
[b.] October 27, 1920, Covington, KY; [p.] J. Elmer and Bertha Wallace; [m.] Harry J. Johnson Jr., January 17, 1942; [ch.] Sally E. Brown; [ed.] Holmes High, Covington, KY, Campbell Com'l College, Cincinnati, O.; [occ.] Retired; [oth. writ.] Several in church publications; [a.] Fort Mitchell, KY

JOHNSON, KATHERINE
[b.] June 9, 1976, Omaha, NE; [p.] Jerome and Cheryll Velehradsky; [m.] Jeremiah Johnson, November 25, 1995; [ch.] Michael Raistlin Johnson; [ed.] Mercy High; [memb.] Our Lady of Lourdes Church Choir; [pers.] A poem is just a song without accompaniment.; [a.] Omaha, NE

JOHNSON, KATHY J.
[b.] June 27, 1952, Fargo, ND; [p.] Wayne L. Steffen, Inga V. Olson-Steffen MacRunnels; [m.] James D. Johnson, December 6, 1971; [ch.] Channing Allan, Willow Ann; [pers.] With all my love for my "special guardian angels." Wayne L. born Sept. 13, 1929, lost his battle with leukemia July 10, 1992. Inga V. born July 23, 1930 lost her battle with lung cancer July 24, 1995.; [a.] Nisswa, MN

JOHNSON, KAY EILEEN ROBERTS
[b.] July 29, 1945, Sayre, PA; [pers.] Kay Eileen Johnson born July 29, 1945, Montrose Penna. Where I grow up. Now Reside in Tunkhannock Penna. I strive to let all mankind know the peace love, beauty of God.; [a.] Tunkhannock, PA

JOHNSON, MERLE C.
[pen.] Merle C. Johnson; [b.] October 28, 1908, Princeton, WV; [p.] J. C. and Nannie P. Copen; [m.] Andrew J. Johnson - Deceased 1969, May 8, 1936; [ch.] Melvin D. Johnson; [ed.] B.S. Degree - Education Master's Degree and 45 Hours Elementary Education I was school Principal 23 years; [occ.] Retired Teacher 41 years Experience or Service; [memb.] W. VEA -NEA School Church, Switzer Church of God, Switzer, W.V. 25647; [hon.] Since Retirement, I just write poems to pass the time away. I am so lonely, I read the Bible every day, that keeps me going, I use walker or came with which to walk.; [oth. writ.] Many other poems 107 to be exact in my poem book. I just write for pleasure.; [pers.] I am a widow, live alone, age 87 years, no relatives, other than my son, a teacher. I have cancer, a metal leg, both eyes operated on, heart attack this past year.; [a.] Switzer, Logan Country, WV

JOHNSON, NORMA J.
[b.] June 22, 1952, Sunbury, PA; [p.] Charles and Jean Hornberger; [m.] Craig A. Johnson, June 10, 1989; [ch.] Keith Alan, Joseph Albert, Richard Lee; [ed.] Shikellamy Sr. High and Empire Cosmetology (Cosmetologist and Cosmetology Instructor) School; [occ.] Manager of Paper Party Supply Store; [memb.] Mt. Pleasant U.M. Church Ladies Choir and mixed voice choir, and Trustee Comm.; [oth. writ.] Five written several poems throughout the years but never dreamed they were good enough to be published.; [pers.] I have found poetry to be very relaxing, and helpful in times of distress, it is also a way one can express oneself; [a.] Sunbury, PA

JONES, ALLENE WEBSTER
[b.] June 15, Townley, AL; [p.] James Levon Webster and Mary Ethel Chafin-Webster; [m.] Irby Eugene Jones, December 17, 1941; [ch.] Irby Levon Jones, Eugene Parker Jones; [ed.] Manchester High, Columbus School of Art (diploma), Columbus GA, studied with Fred Shepard, Columbus, Museum also Wyndell Taylor of Columbus, Georgia; [occ.] Retired; [memb.] I am an artist in the National League of American, Pen Women (Col. Branch). NSDAR (Col. Branch), Washington, D.C.), Methodist Sara Crawford Circle, Member of Azalea Garden Club, Manchester, GA; [pers.] I write about all of life, but I am deeply worried about our environment. Our government should draft an army to force negligent citizens to keep our country clean. They arrangement for they threaten our lives. If a foreign country threatened us, we'd act! It is far more frightening when our minds are in a state of apathy and we don't know we are in danger.; [a.] Pine Mountain, GA

JONES, DOROTHY RENEE
[b.] October 28, 1949, Brooklyn, NY; [ch.] Sheryl and Cherise; [ed.] High School Grad.; [oth. writ.] Too many to list here; [pers.] My writings are a reflection of what I feel about people places and things I see and experiences I have or have had.; [a.] New York, NY

JONES, JOANN
[b.] February 7, 1944; [p.] Joe and Lillie Phillips; [m.] Joe Jones, December 18, 1976; [ch.] Debra Joann and Robin Petrie; [occ.] Housewife; [pers.] May each person grow and develop into the person that they are within. Never let the domineering of another person take your years of life away.; [a.] Albany, GA

JONES, KATINA L.
[b.] November 18, 1972, Brooklyn, NY; [p.] Jimmy Jones, Rose Jones; [ed.] Kingsborough Community College; [occ.] Receptionist at Bates USA (old agency in N.Y.C.) until I go back to school for my B.A.; [memb.] N.Y. Gospel Mass Choir; [hon.] Recognition from the Dean throughout College for Outstanding Musical Performances. This also is an honor for me that my poem was accepted. Thank you; [oth. writ.] Several poems that have not yet been published; [pers.] Poetry and music are like a source of energy for me. It allows me to express myself in ways that no one or nothing else can. God willing I would love one day to have a book of poems in bookstores just like my favorite poet Maya Angelou.; [a.] Brooklyn, NY

JONES, MARYANNE CHIPMAN
[b.] January 29, 1928, Eagle Grove, IA; [p.] Anne and Claude Chipman; [m.] Robert Jones; [ch.] Tim, Barbara, Lori and Jill; [ed.] Eagle Grove High Waldorf College; [oth. writ.] Many poems!; [pers.] Am skipping much here, as the most and very important thing to me is that my poem will be signed Maryanne Chipman Jones! Am planning to bring some books, if correct signature; [a.] Las Vegas, NV

JONES, REGINA
[pers.] I wish to thank the Lord God and the evangelists Danny and Angie Norris who gave me a new heart and a new life.; [a.] Pacific, MO

JONES, RUIE SIMON
[b.] February 14, 1956, Miami, FL; [p.] Arthur Simon, Florence Simon; [m.] Peter E. Jones, May 22, 1982; [ch.] Brett Arthur Jones; [pers.] My writing comes from the heart because of my personal expression of love for my child.; [a.] Hialeah, FL

JONES, WILLIAM H.
[pen.] Captain J., Bill Jones, William Henry Jones, W. H. Jones; [b.] April 1, 1924, Black Diamond, WA; [p.] Helenor Jones, (Father Deceased); [m.] Barbara A. Jones, May 17, 1960; [ch.] Robert Jeffery Jones, Denise Lynn Williams; [ed.] B.A. San Diego State, Naval School of Hospital Administration; [occ.] Captain, U.S. Navy (Ret); [memb.] Federal Health Care Executives, Fleet Reserve Association, Distinguished Member International Society of Poets; [hon.] Legion of Merit (Navy) Numerous Service Medals and Awards, Graduated with honors 5 military schools, Advanced from Apprentice Seaman to Captain during Naval career. Editor's Choice Award 1995 (1), Editor's Choice Award 1996 (7); [oth. writ.] Endless Thought, Treasured Poems of America, April 1996, Am I Worthy, Treasured Poems of America, April 1996, In His Wisdom We Must Trust, Poetic Voices of America, June 1996, Garden Workshop, Poetic Voices of America June 1996, Sequins on the Floor, Poetic Voices of America, June 1996, Symphony of the Night, Treasured Poems of America, August 1996, Charlie, Treasured Poems of America, August 1996, Lady Of My Dreams, Treasured Poems of America, August 1996, Deares Mom, Treasured Poems of Amerian, August 1996, A Humble Apology, Poetic Voices of America, October 1996, Customary Places and Faces, Poetic Voices of America, October 1996, To Hell With Diamonds, Poetic Voices of American, October 1996, Man's Best Friend, Poetic Voices of America, October 1996, Dreams I've Had, Poetic Voices of America, October 1996, The Window of His Soul, Treasured Poems of America, December 1996, The Looking Glass, Treasureed Poems of America, December 1996, Believer Or Deceiver, Treasured Poems of America, December 1996, Chiqui Is Her Name, Treasured Poems of America, December 1996, Sweet Pixie, Treasured Poems of America, December 1996, Years O Joy, Treasured Poems of America, December 1996: Songs Unsung, Beyond the Stars, Fall 1996, Catacombs of the Night, Best Poems of 1996, Summer 1996, Stop and Smell The Roses, Spirit of the Age, Summer 1996, Home Alone, A Muse of Follow, Summer 1996, Devil's Wind, A Tapestry of Thought, Summer 1996; [pers.] I believe in personal achievement, inspiring others to fulfill their dreams, at peace with self and others, all with a sense of humor, dedication and perspective.; [a.] Lake San Marcos, CA

JORDAN, VALERIE DEANN
[b.] July 31, 1983, Man, WV; [p.] Harry and Mary Jordan; [ed.] 8th grade student Man Jr. High School Man, WV; [memb.] Hi-Y Club, Girl Scouts, Prayer Club, Math Club, Optimist Club, National Jr. Honor Society, Study Buddies (Tutoring kindergarten - 3rd graders), Gifted program; [hon.] Participated in Math Field Day, Academic Challenge, Academic Bowl, and Model United Nations. 2nd place County Science Fair, 1st place County Social Studies Fair - and attended State Social Studies Fair, State Award 1996 - John Hopkins Center for Talented Youth for outstanding abilities and potential for future Achievement; [pers.] It was not easy deciding which poem to send in, but I am glad this is the one I chose. I believe we should take care of the earth, not destroy it. We could make a difference. It takes more than one person to save the earth and we need to lend a helping hand. Even if it's a small task, it's still one step on the path to a better earth.; [a.] Amherstdale, WV

JUST, JAIMIE
[b.] August 5, 1981, Borger, TX; [p.] Johnny and Carol Just; [ed.] Putnam City High, Edison Elementary; [memb.] Marching Band, Cherokee Hills Baptist Church, German Club; [hon.] Band Honors all through school, Piano Awards; [oth. writ.] 3 short stories, non published; [pers.] I am inspired by nature. My grandparents are also an inspiration. Trust in the Lord with all your heart and lean not on your own understanding, in all your ways acknowledge Him and He will make your ways paths straight.; [a.] Oklahoma City, OK

JUSTICE, PATRICIA JEAN
[pen.] P. J.; [b.] May 1, 1944, Dover, OH; [p.] Mr. and Mrs. John T. Bair (Deceased); [m.] Gary M. Justice Sr., August 14, 1965; [ch.] Four children, 2 grandchildren, 3 step-grandchildren, 2 step-grandchildren; [ed.] Graduated Dover High School '62, Barberton School of Commerce 2 yrs. Worked Timken Co, 2 yrs.; [occ.] Housewife, avid reader of poetry and antiques; [memb.] St. Clement's Catholic Church - 31 yrs., Public School P.T.A.-P.T.O. 12 years; [hon.] Chile Contest, Honorable Mention- Won Tuscarawas, County for Canning Preservation Won State of Ohio for Canning Preservation II in Tuscarawas County at 18 yrs.; [oth. writ.] Whisper at Dusk "Winter 96" "Tribute to Grandpa". Best poems of 1996 "Tribute To Grandpa" (by Patricia J. Justice) A Sea of Treasures "A Tribute To My Brother" (by Patricia J. Justice); [pers.] I love nature and a lot other subjects, too! My first love was a book given to me in the 8th grade. I've been writing only a couple of years.; [a.] Massillon, OH

KAAT, CASPER
[b.] April 12, 1932, Rotterdam, Netherlands; [m.] Barbara, November 16, 1957; [ch.] 3 Sons and 2 daughters; [ed.] High School Trade School in the Netherlands; [hon.] Have received several recognitions in the field of Landscaping and received environmentalist of the year award; [oth. writ.] A variety of religious and secular poems; [pers.] I enjoy many areas of the arts including oil paintings, music woodcrafts and enjoy family life.; [a.] Raytown, MO

KADACH, DENISE
[pen.] DK; [b.] July 6, 1970, Los Angeles, CA; {p.} Bruce & Bernadette McCoy, Nancy Meece (Birth-Mom); [ed.] Columbia University; [occ.] Surgical Assistant; [oth. writ.] Melody of Music Published in "Best Poems of the 90's"; [pers.] Without Hope, there is no future.; [a.] New York, NY

KAGAN, SHOSHANA
[b.] November 25, 1944, Col., OH; [p.] Rabbi Jacob Baker and Dorothy Baker; [m.] Henry Kagan, September 5, 1962; [ch.] Gamliel, Simcha, Gershon, Yael; [ed.] M.B.A. at N.Y. Inst. of Technology, B.A. Brooklyn College; [occ.] Stock Broker, Financial Advisor; [memb.] Volunteer at Orthodox Union and Emunah Women, Ketubah Marriage Commission, Yavneh Minyan of Flat Bush; [hon.] When I started college, I already had 4 children. In Grad. School I worked full time in addition to the family. No honors but I did well.; [oth. writ.] Songs of love.; [pers.] I love to be happy and make others happy. I enjoy writing in the style of chances.; [a.] Brooklyn, NY

KAHLES, CHRISTAL
[pen.] Christal Kahles; [b.] May 6, 1982, Cincinnati, OH; [p.] Gary Steurer and Julie Kahles-Steurer; [ed.] 9th grade - home schooled; [memb.] Judy Link Dance Studio, Monfort Height United Methodist Youth Group, National Author's Registry; [hon.] Honorable Mention in One Poetry Contest, Miss Pee Wee Cincinnati, 2nd runner up Little Miss Ohio, Featured 'Young Author' in Magazine; [oth. writ.] Other poems completed Novel (July '96) titled "In The Garden" (unpublished to date); [pers.] I plan to attend the Cincinnati Bible College, and hope to inspire others through my writing.; [a.] Cincinnati, OH

KANE, BEVERLY A.
[b.] October 9, 1943, Buffalo; [p.] Clarence and Mabel Collins; [m.] Michael D. Kane Sr., November 10, 1962; [ch.] Shawn Michael, Mitchell Scott, Michael D. Jr.; [ed.] South Park High School Roney Business Institute; [occ.] Homemaker, Secretary of Haelon Alliance Reiki Practioner; [memb.] Haelon Alliance, Ordained Priest, order of Melchizedek; [oth. writ.] Channeled works of Sananda; [pers.] I seek to heal and teach through guidance from the almighty, to touch someone in a positive way.; [a.] Buffalo, NY

KANE, KEVIN M.
[b.] May 28, 1977, Melrose, MA; [p.] Kevin P. Kane, Barbara Davies; [ed.] Exeter High; [occ.] Photo Mgt. for Walgreens; [memb.] Boy Scouts of America; [hon.] Eagle Scout; [pers.] I wold really like to thank my Senior English teacher Julian Whipple and my good friend Jeanne Gosselin Arnold for inspiring me to write poetry.; [a.] Exeter, NH

KANE, MARY
[pen.] May; [b.] June 25, 1960, Brooklyn; [p.] Dolores and Howard; [m.] Robert (aka Bob), May 1, 1990; [ch.] Allison, Melissa and Mathew; [ed.] Associated Degree in early childhood: Kingsborough CC Bachlors Degree in Elementary Special Ed: Brooklyn College; [occ.] Vice President of M.A.R. Optical DBA Eyes on Aweu!; [hon.] Certificate: Famous Poet "1996" in my son Howard by Famous Poetry Society. Maybe more to come?; [oth. writ.] Here are some....reflections images of the mind. Poetry review "House on the Hill". Famous poetry society "My Son" (Certificate), poems in a audrey press. Feeling magazine and more....; [pers.] "My Love" is dedicated to my husband who is my only true love.

Thank you to my family for the support. I am honored to share my work and express my voice.; [a.] Brooklyn, NY

KANE, SHERRIE
[b.] November 7, 1957, Oregon; [p.] Donald Brown, Glenna Brown; [ch.] Truman J. II; [ed.] Cleveland H.S.; [occ.] Homemaker; [pers.] After a very long and unhappy life I met a very special man who inspired me to write.; [a.] Portland, OR

KANNENBERG, TRENT
[b.] September 17, 1980, Shakopee, MN; [p.] Monica Erickson; [ed.] Still in high school - will be entering as a Sophomore this fall; [occ.] High Student; [pers.] I find in my writings that I tend to add a little twist of humor to poems written on serious topics.; [a.] Chaska, MN

KANWIT, BERT A.
[b.] October 8, 1916, Lynbrook, NY; [p.] Harris M. and Dorothy S. Kanwit; [m.] 1. Martha, 1942, 2. Janet, 1970; [ch.] 5 - 1st marriage (25 years), 1 2nd marriage (now 26 years); [ed.] A.B. - '37, U. of Michigan, M.D. - Harvard - '41, Certified - Amer. Bd. of Surgery - 1951; [occ.] Retired; [memb.] 1. Amer. Coll. of Surgeons, 2. Unitarian - Universalist Fellowship, 3. Amer. Legion; [hon.] U.S. Navy Med. Officer - '41-'45 - survived torpe doing of my ship - '44; [oth. writ.] "Embers - memoirs and Reflections of a Bleeding Heart Surgeon"..not yet published; [pers.] I am in amazing shape for a guy of my vintage. I still go to the "if" 4x/wk and go thru a very demanding routine including to push-up! The pluses have far exceeded the minuses in my life and what and my 6 wonderful children and 12 grandchildren my immortality is established.; [a.] Poughkeepsie, NY

KAPLAN, TRACY M.
[b.] September 12, 1966, Washington, DC; [m.] Jule Kaplan, June 12, 1994; [ed.] Bachelor of Arts LaSalle University 1988; [occ.] Housewife

KARLOVICH, SUSAN
[pen.] The Story teller; [b.] August 14, 1954, Durant, OK; [ch.] Steven Michael, Matthew Don, Susan Elizabeth; [ed.] Southeastern Okla State University; [memb.] Sigma Kappa, DAR, Alpha Eta Rho; [pers.] If someone else finds comfort in my writings, then my personal journey will have been worth the trials.

KATCHER, KARRIE M.
[pen.] Keta; [b.] November 4, 1955, Milwaukee, WI; [p.] Jean Comaris; [m.] Tim L. Katcher, February 2, 1991; [ch.] John W. Herrin; [ed.] James Madison High, Mate - Madison - Veterinary Technician 1991, Laboratory Animal Technician 1992; [occ.] Farmer - Home maker; [memb.] AALAS - American Association of Laboratory Animal Science Lutheran Church of Peace - Platteville; [hon.] Dean's List (MATC); [pers.] I think everyone should have all they need to have a full and enjoyable life, as long as they respect the rights of all other living things.; [a.] Mineral Point, WI

KATSAP, MICHAEL
[b.] April 10, 1983, Kishiney, Moldova; [p.] Igor Katsap, Nelli Katsap; [ed.] Lawton Junior High; [occ.] Middle School Student; [hon.] Honor Roll Student; [oth. writ.] Several poems for school publications; [pers.] I feel that my best poetry comes when I write it spontaneously and for fun.; [a.] San Francisco, CA

KAUFMAN, IRVING
[b.] September 16, 1917, Orange, NJ; [p.] Morris and Tillie Kaufman; [m.] Martha Buskirk Kaufman, Novem-

ber 30, 1985; [ch.] Stephen David, Carole Suzanne, Richard Paul, James Robert and 6 grandchildren; [ed.] B.A. New York Univ., N.Y., N.Y., M.D. The George Wash. Univ. Medical School 1943 trained as a Psychiatrist and Psychoanalyst for children and adults. Black belt in Uechi Ryu ans Isshin Ryu karate; [occ.] M.D. Psychiatrist semi-retired from practice also retired teaching 25 years at Harvard Med. School and 40 years at Smith college school for Social Work; [memb.] Writing a short story on Satanic Cults and poetry - book published. Amer Psychiatric Assoc., The Boston Psychoanalytic Institute, Boston Gerontologic Soc.; [hon.] Honorary MSW in Social Work for the Smith College for Social Work, Northampton, MA, Elected to members in the International Society of Poets; [oth. writ.] Many articles, book chapters in the field of Psychiatry and mental health; [pers.] Almost 80 years and with a walking problems because I have Perkinson busy myself playing cello in my quartette and visiting with my 6 grandchildren. I also like to cook and refinish furniture.; [a.] Auburndale, MA

KAZMIERCZAK, MICHAEL
[b.] January 10, 1975; [p.] Mark and Janice Kazmierczak; [ed.] Graduate Shenendehowa High School ('93)...Potsdam State University (Junior); [occ.] Student; [hon.] Shenendehowa alumni art award (93) scholastic awards in art hyde museum "Excellence in art"; [pers.] In the future I aspire to attend graduate school for creative writing and become a university professor. I enjoy, the work of Thoreau, Leopold, X.J. Kennedy, and Galway Kinnell.; [a.] Clifton Park, NY

KEETON, CELESTINE
[pers.] First I give God the glory for the talent I have been writing for many years but have never had anything published. My husband and family have told me I was talented, but I didn't think I was talented enough. My son insisted that I enter your contest. Thank you for choosing my poem as a winner; [a.] College Park, GA

KEMPF, HEDWIG
[b.] July 2, 1912, Duren, Germany; [p.] Dr. Med Friedrich Roelen and Clementine Thelosen; [m.] Starr Gideon Kempf, January 12, 1942; [ch.] Madelin, Michael and Charlotte; [ed.] Graduate of Nursing School, Koln Lindenburg, Germany; [occ.] Registered Nurse and Licensed Physical Therapist; [oth. writ.] Autobiographical story and other poems; [pers.] I have lived a most fascinating life with my husband, Starr, a unique man with many talents play write, author, artist and sculptor. His bronzes and monumental wind - sculptures are now being widely acclaimed. Throughout our 53 years of marriage, my nursing career helped Starr to achieve his life's work as artist and sculptor. I greatly enjoyed my work and life with Starr because of his sense of humor and artistic genius.; [a.] Colorado Spring, CO

KENNEDY, BRYAN
[b.] June 12, 1980, Wilkes Barre, PA; [p.] Patrick Kennedy, Marie Kennedy; [ed.] Junior at Wyoming Valley, West High School, Plymouth, PA; [memb.] Life Scout/Boy Scout troop 456. Sprinter on Valley West Track Team, Altar Server at St. Mary's Nativity Church in Plymouth; [hon.] Honorable Mention in the Luzerne County Reading Council's Young Author's Contest; [oth. writ.] "Not A Bad Boy"; [a.] Plymouth, PA

KENT, ELIZABETH A.
[b.] September 20, 1932, Clay Center, KS; [p.] Merna and Virgil Haws; [m.] Donald E. Kent, July 21, 1956; [ch.] Scott D. and Ronald E. Kent; [ed.] High School

Diploma, CLay County Community High School, Clay Center, KS, graduating 1950; [occ.] Retired (Feb 1996) from US Civil Service. Previously Security and Intelligence Officer, Madigan Army Medical Center, Tacoma, WA; [memb.] Beta Sigma Phi Sorority; [hon.] Two Commander's Award for Civilian Service, US Army. (The second highest award a civilian employee can receive.) Also many "Outstanding Performance" awards over a 37 year government service career; [oth. writ.] Farewell poem published in Madigan Mountaineer (hospital newspaper) upon my retirement. Numerous unpublished poems written for family members.; [pers.] I write poetry for pleasure and the express my feelings on specific subjects.; [a.] Tacoma, WA

KENYON, PATRICIA M.
[b.] July 17, 1952, Belvidere, IL; [p.] Herbert Stroup and Alberta Stroup; [m.] Henry A. Kenyon, July 1, 1984; [ch.] Seven as a blended family; [ed.] Belvidere High, Alberto's School of Cosmetology, McHenry County College, Non-Credit Master's in Boy Scouts of America; [occ.] Administrative Asst. McHenry County College Foundation; [memb.] 12 years, Boy Scouts of America St. Mary's Catholic Church; [hon.] Boy Scouts of America Highest Award of Merit Two Scholarships McHenry County College Taught Classes in New Mexico for Boy Scouts of America; [oth. writ.] Many poems and illustrations of memories for family trees youth service Bureau McHenry Co. Poetry has been published in the newspaper sparrow grass poetry descriptive stories for other people.; [pers.] I write verses and poetry of hope. I am very adopt at helping people express their loving thoughts and memories with illustrations and combine this with their family tree information.; [a.] McHenry, IL

KENYON, WILLIAM E.
[b.] September 17, 1934, Palmer, MA; [p.] Archie and Evelyn Kenyon; [ch.] 9 Children, 16 Grandchildren; [ed.] 10 yrs. joined the United States Air force, where I spent 4 years and was a member of 815th Recon Tech Squadron; [occ.] Retired (Disabled); [hon.] I have had several of my poems published in small local newspapers but have had no luck getting anything, as of yet, published professionally; [oth. writ.] As a singer in a country western band I wrote many songs. I also write many children's songs and children's stories.; [pers.] Reading my children's stories to the children of my private school, "Madbrook Academy", the children and teachers now refer to me as "The Storyweaver" which I take as a wonderful compliment.

KERHULAS, CORRINE
[b.] October 30, 1977, Eureka, CA; [p.] Dennis and Elizabeth Kerhulas; [pers.] Imagination is one of the most important tools in life, and everyone should have an opportunity to use it.; [a.] Sacramento, CA

KIEFFER, WILLIAM J.
[pen.] W. J. Kieffer; [b.] June 18, 1926, Saint Louis, MO; [p.] Arthur and Florence Kieffer; [m.] Joy M. Kieffer, October 1, 1950; [ch.] Karen Lynn, William Jr., David C.; [ed.] BS (EE) Missouri School of Mines (1950); [occ.] Engineering Manager Retired; [memb.] President of Messiah Lutheran Church, Santa Cruz CA; [pers.] I compose verse for the enjoyment of doing it.; [a.] Scotts Valley, CA

KIM, ROSALYN B.
[b.] May 5, 1982, Englewood, NJ; [p.] Young I. Kim, Victoria B. Kim; [ed.] St. John School, Academy of the Holy Angels; [occ.] Student; [memb.] Teaneck Junior

Friends of the Library, Englewood Hospital and Medical Center Junior Volunteer; [hon.] 1. Leonia, NJ Firefighter's Poster Contest Winner, 1992, 2. Leonia, NJ Public Library Essay Winner, 1994, 3. President's Award for Educational Excellence, 1996, 4. Presidential Physical Fitness Award x4, 5. Consistent First Honor Student; [pers.] Seize the Day! My parents are the winds beneath my wings.; [a.] Teaneck, NJ

KINCAID, VIVIAN
[oth. writ.] Bookmarks, pros, poems, screenplays and book (not yet complete) and short stories, also write for a non-profit organization; [pers.] The life that I've seen has been deep and dark - through it I've been gifted with what you just read - "K. Unknown" stands for creator unknown. I'm shy. Thanks; [a.] Detroit, MI

KING, DOROTHY L. BRADSHAW
[pen.] Dorothy Bradshaw, "The Poetess"; [b.] October 24, 1954, Wilm., DE; [p.] Mr. and Mrs. Walter and Mamie Bradshaw; [m.] Levi Dethander King, September 8, 1993; [ch.] Stacey, Tamar, Isaiah Jr., Qwynetta, Solace; [ed.] Wilmington High School, Career Institute - Micro Computer Operations/Continuing Education; [occ.] Bell Alantic-Delaware Electronic Switching System Technician Wilm., DE; [memb.] United Way's-Forty Karat Club; [oth. writ.] Several poems published in "The Gazette Maz" a local newspaper. Appearance on local TV station recited poems. Others writings: "Diamonds", "I Make The Difference", "My Blood Cries Out", "Stop the Violence".; [pers.] I am blessed by God because He has allowed me to experience His reality - of love, forgiveness of sin and undeserved favor thru His Son - Jesus.; [a.] Wilmington, DE

KING, GABREN-TAYLOR
[pen.] Taylor Stephens; [b.] August 14, 1972, Ridgecrest, CA; [p.] Joy Fickett and Joel Taylor King; [ed.] Jonathan Dayton R.H.S., Arizona State University; [occ.] Student/Poet/Novelist; [memb.] PRCA, NRA, Professional Rodeo Cowboys Ass., National Rifle Ass.; [hon.] My greatest honor is my son, who will be born October 8, 1996.; [oth. writ.] Currently working on second novel, while compiling a poetic novela.; [pers.] "The poet presents his thoughts festively, on the carriage of rhythm: Usually because they could not walk." Friedrick Nietzsche; [a.] Mountainside, NJ

KING, HOLLI K.
[b.] February 15, 1983, Bellingham, WA; [p.] Harvey King and Brenda King; [ed.] Custer Elementary School, Vista Middle School, now Homeschooled; [hon.] Honor Student; [oth. writ.] Poem "The Sea" published in Anthology of Poetry by Young Americans 1995 Edition at age of 11 (eleven); [pers.] Started writing young, Love to write. Needs to come from heart. Age 13 (thirteen).; [a.] Custer, WA

KING, JASON ALLEN
[b.] October 31, 1975, Pittsburgh, PA; [p.] Russell L. King Jr., Cheryl King; [ed.] English Major, Luzerme County Community College; [occ.] Student; [memb.] Member of the editorial board of the Augustine Literary Magazine; [oth. writ.] Poems published in literary magazine. Essay published at University of Pittsburgh.; [pers.] I'm loving memory of my grandfather, Russell L. King and his bride of 53 years, Jane Auren King.; [a.] Mountain Top, PA

KINSEY, GRACIE
[b.] August 7, 1944, Washington County, MS; [p.] Jackson and Mary Mays; [m.] Hillary C. Kinsey, August 8, 1986; [ch.] La Shana, Keitha, Willie; [ed.] High School

graduate, Licensed Practical Nurse, Licensed Evangelist/Missionary X-ray Technician; [occ.] Licensed Practical Nurse/Office Manager; [pers.] I strive daily to help my fellowman, because my living must not have been in vain.; [a.] Memphis, TN

KLOBY, RACHEL CALI
[b.] July 16, 1985, Belleville, NJ; [p.] Angela Cali, Jerry Kloby; [ed.] (Grammar School) Montclair Cooperative School Grades Kindergarten - 5th completed; [memb.] Wolf Haven American Girl Club Lisa Frank; [oth. writ.] Works in progress; [pers.] Praise Weirdness and wolves and seals and dolphins favorite author, George MacDonald.; [a.] Montclair, NJ

KNIGHT, HEATHER
[b.] May 25, 1981; [p.] Diana Knight, Bob Knight (Divorced); [ed.] Entering 9th grade; [occ.] Student; [hon.] I haven't entered any contests. This is my first one.; [oth. writ.] A portfolio of poems and short stories, and I'm working on a three hundred page novel. I'm done with it, but it needs work.; [a.] Blissfield, MI

KNIGHT, MONICA
[b.] August 8, 1981, Iowa City; [p.] Calvin and Maureen Knight; [ed.] Student at Mercer Island High School; [oth. writ.] "Sweet Wind" - being published in the Poets Guild Anthology for this year; [pers.] In the grand scheme of things, I am still a child. I have much to learn about myself and my poetry. In time, I will be the best I can be but for now I'm just a poet filled with dreams.; [a.] Seattle, WA

KNOWLES, RAYMOND W. O.
[b.] March 20, 1907, Kansas; [p.] William B. Knowles, Jennie O. Waters-Knowles; [m.] Corinne B. Knowles, July 20, 1996; [ch.] Robert N. (Deceased), Margaret P. Jackson (Colorado), Dr. Richard T. Knowles (California); [ed.] BA Sterling College, Sterling, Kansas, 60 Hours Graduate work, Gliff School of Thrology, Co; [occ.] Retired UM Ministry; [memb.] Kansas West Conference, United Methodist Church, Past Member General Board of Pension, UM Church, Past Member General Board of Evangelism UM Church; [oth. writ.] News Paper Articles, American Bible Society, Christian Advocate, many unpublished sermons; [pers.] No one finds worth living we make it worth living by helping others in any way we can. Live for tomorrow. To start living in the past is to start dying inch by inch; [a.] Canon City, CO

KNOX, VICKY
[b.] January 24, 1984, Texas Woman's Hospitals; [p.] Jennifer and Thomas Knox; [ed.] Frostwood Elementary, Memorial Middle School, St. Pauls Methodist Church; [occ.] Student; [memb.] Honor Society; [hon.] Won honors in Science on the honor roll; [pers.] If you must publish my poem, tell in it that I thank my friend Jennifer Nelson and Rene Nelson, along with my parents, for support and they've also, thank April Vanoves for given me, inspiring me to write this poem.; [a.] Houston, TX

KOBROVSKY, VALARIE
[b.] November 8, 1984, Charleston, SC; [p.] Lawrence and Susan Kobrovsky; [ed.] Charleston County Public Schools: Completed Sullivan's Island Elem. School - entering School of the Arts majoring in creative writing (6th grade); [occ.] Student; [memb.] Sullivan's Island School Chorus Supertroupe II acting company; [hon.] Lt. Governor's Creative Writing Award (1st place); [oth. writ.] "Magnolia Gardens"-Grand prize winner of Lt. Governor's Writing Contest (S.C.) - Several poems published in the Anthology of Poetry by Young Americans

Poem published in Moultrie News; [pers.] I enjoy exploring the beauty and mystery of Mother Nature - I have been greatly influence by my uncle who is a published poet and writes about nature; [a.] Sullivan's Island, SC

KOERNER, RAYMOND
[b.] February 14, 1953, Kearny, NJ; [p.] Father - Peter W. Koerner, Mother - Claire A. Koerner, Stepmother - Catherine Koerner; [m.] Patricia Louise Koerner, June 14, 1997; [ed.] Roselle Park High School, Roselle Park, New Jersey; Associate in Arts and Science degree from Union County College, Cranford, New Jersey; [occ.] Pharmaceutical Operator Technical Operations in Ciba-Geigy Corporation in Summit, New Jersey/Suffern, New York; [memb.] United States American Legion Post 60, Roselle Park, New Jersey; United States Air Force, 1971-1975.; [hon.] Veterans of Foreign Wars Voice of Democracy Award; [oth. writ.] Many other various poems and short stories.; [pers.] Live and love as if today was the last day of your life. I have been greatly influenced by the words and music of John Lennon, Paul McCartney, and my lovely wife, Patricia, for whom I have written this poem. [a.] Elizabeth, New Jersey

KOKOLSKI, DAWN G.
[b.] August 18, 1972, Queens, NY; [p.] Jeanette and Harry Kokolski; [ed.] Mercer County Community College and Rowan College of New Jersey (Formerly Glassboro State); [occ.] Art Director - Nuvisions Studio Inc., Hillsboro, NJ; [memb.] Alpha Phi Omega (National Co-ed Service Fraternity), National Senior Honor Society (Gamma Tau Sigma), New Jersey State College Council for International Education (Semester abroad peer counselor), Cheerleading -Captain, Student Activities Board - Vice President, Student Government Association, Graphic Design Club, Member of the Graphic Artists Guild, NY; [hon.] International Semester Abroad Program, Recipient of the "Who's Who" Among Students in American Junior Colleges, Recipient of the "Who's Who" Among Students in American Universities and colleges, Student Service Award, Dean's List, Loss Prevention Award; [pers.] I strive to achieve the most life has to offer. To me life is like a chess board. It offers many choices, the road you choose is yours alone. It's your move!; [a.] Hillsboro, NJ

KOKOSKA, CASANDRA
[b.] December 22, 1978, Houston, TX; [p.] Yolanda and Matthew Kokoska; [ed.] High School Senior; [occ.] Freelance writing; [memb.] Speech and Debate Co-Captain, Thespians; [hon.] Publication in Chicken Soup for Soul: A third serving - Short story several performance trophies in speech and debate tournaments; [oth. writ.] Published in Chicken soup for the soul: A Third Helping: A New York Times Best Seller; [pers.] I try to find truth in all the illusions reality produces, I only hope the truth is not as discouraging as the reality.; [a.] Rosenberg, TX

KOLOMYSKI, ROB
[pen.] Rob Kolomyski; [b.] December 5, 1970, Mt. Clemens, MI; [p.] James and Melanie Kolomyski; [ed.] Associates of Applied Science; [occ.] Engineer - Automotive; [pers.] Inspired by big white clouds on a black sky.

KONICK, ALLISON
[b.] March 16, 1985, Edison, NJ; [p.] Kenneth and Nancy Konick; [ed.] Sixth grade student Edgar School Metuchen NJ; [occ.] Student; [hon.] President's Award for Educational Excellence, Awards Received for the '95-'96 School year at Campbell School: Positive Leadership, Citizenship, Language Arts, Reading, Science, Social Studies, and Band; [pers.] I would like to thank Mrs.

Gail Gaspar for teaching me how to write poetry when I was in fourth grade.; [a.] Metuchen, NJ

KORMENDY, JEFF
[pen.] Archer Azara; [b.] December 17, 1967, Chicago, IL; [p.] Ed and Karen Kormendy; [ch.] Son - Cody Dean; [ed.] Grad. of Lowell High School - Lowell, Indiana 1986, Bauder College - Radio and T.V. Broadcasting, Writer's Digest School - Fiction; [occ.] Rock Radio DJ - Rockford, IL, Drumset Teacher - P.T. At Bookstore (Waidenbooks Dundee, IL); [oth. writ.] One complete novel - "Fear and Gravity", 1/3 into my second, "Ha" will be my first publication credit, I also have completed a number of short stories.; [pers.] I'm a radio guy. I have a big mouth. It gets me in trouble. I seem to be able to speak my mind more calmly and clearly on paper. I'm an existentialist in perpetual training...; [a.] Marengo, IL

KOSTIOU, PATTI ANN
[pen.] Babe; [b.] April 12, 1964, Pennsylvania; [p.] Richard and Elsie Scarsellone; [m.] Nicholas S. Kostiou, May 16, 1989; [ch.] Thomas, Amber, Melissa; [ed.] 1982 graduate of Aliquippa High School, Aliquippa, PA; [occ.] Mother, Wife, Writer; [memb.] Saint Joseph Roman Catholic Church, International Society of Poets, Navy Wives Support Group; [hon.] Who's Who Among American High School Students, 1981-92 Volume; [oth. writ.] "Whisper's To A Friend", "Capture A Moment", "Were They", "I Miss You", "An Illusion Of You", My Love Went With You", several article series for local newspaper: "Soundings", "Chicago Sun Times", Beach County Times", "Daily Press", Feature Editor of High School year book 1980-82 "The Quippan" Aliquippa, PA; [pers.] This poem was written for and about my husband Nick who is a Navy Sailor in the US Navy and who I very much.

KOVAC, FRANK K.
[b.] June 16, 1965, Cleveland, OH; [ed.] John Carroll University; [oth. writ.] Several published poems; [pers.] A poet reflects the heart and soul of his day.; [a.] Lakewood, OH

KOVACENKO, THOMAS
[ch.] Two; [ed.] BA Queens College June 1970; [pers.] Help make a better world; [a.] Huntington Station, NY

KRAMER, SARA
[b.] March 17, 1983, Milwaukee; [p.] Linda Knee, Jerry Kramer; [ed.] 8th grade student; [pers.] You only have one life, so have fun!; [a.] Waukesha, WI

KRAUS, STEPHANIE J.
[b.] February 27, 1980, Jacksonville, FL; [p.] Pamela A. and Kim P. Spegal; [ed.] Currently a Junior at Robert E. Lee Senior High School; [memb.] Girl Scouts, Honor Society, Swimteam, Bible Club, Brain Brawl, Piano; [hon.] Perfect Attendance, Honor Roll, Outstanding Achievement Awards Nat'l Science Merit Scholarship; [oth. writ.] Many articles printed in school newspaper "The Traveller"; [pers.] Above everything, set your thoughts on God. He will never fail you.; [a.] Jacksonville, FL

KROM, MATTHEW L.
[b.] January 12, 1989, Palm Springs, CA; [p.] Robert Krom, Janet Krom; [ed.] Our Lady of the Desert School; [occ.] Student; [hon.] Honor Roll Student of the Month; [pers.] "Keep the earth clean for all animals", I Love the Redwoods and the ocean".; [a.] Yucca Valley, CA

KRUSE, SHERYL COSTA
[b.] January 17, 1957, Newport, RI; [p.] Charles and

Dolores Costa; [pers.] The blending of humans and our environment making life more hopeful and optimistic are issues I'd like to convey in my writing.; [a.] Sodus Point, NY

KUEBLER, RICHARD J.
[pen.] Michael Fox; [b.] July 25, 1948, Perry, IA; [p.] Robert Kuebler and Lillie Thompson; [m.] Susan Kuebler (1st wife), January 11, 1995, Brenda Payne Kuebler (2nd wife), August 23, 1967; [ch.] Richie and Cory Kuebler (1st wife); [ed.] Graduated from Santa Fe High School in 1966 - Alvin Com. College, Administrative Director for USMC; [occ.] Retired; [memb.] Debate Captain Club, Student Council - 4 years, Tau Delta Omega 4 yrs., Football - 4 years; [hon.] Marine of the Month from Chamber of Commerce, Coronation Duke, Sgt. in USMC; [pers.] My wife inspired me to write, whom I loved very much when we were together so this is for you Susan.

KUEHNERT, LILA G.
[b.] February 9, 1924, Conover, NC; [p.] Frank and Virginia Gilbert; [m.] Eldor Paul Kuehnert, August 10, 1947; [ch.] Deborah, Daniel, Don, David; [ed.] Newton - Conover H.S. Newton, N.C. Charlotte Memorial Hospital, (Charlotte N.C.) School of Nursing, Courses in early childhood Education, Rochester and Victor, N.Y.; [occ.] Retired; [memb.] Earlier years served on civic boards and school committees and active in local politics. Founded St. John's Lutheran Christian Pre school - Farmington N.Y.; [hon.] Farmington, NY Chamber of Commerce "Citizen of Year" shared with my husband Rev. E. P. Kuehnert; [oth. writ.] Correspondent for Palmyra Courier, a weekly newspaper. One poem used as Christmas Editorial.; [pers.] I have always been interested in nature and simple things in life. Little children are such a joy "truly gifts from God."; [a.] Conover, NC

KUHN, JEAN EWING
[b.] June 17, 1917, Pres. Hos., Phila, PA; [p.] Dr. and Mrs. C. Agnew Ewing; [m.] William C. Kuhn, October 18, 1941; [ch.] William C. Kuhn II, Heather Kuhn Somers; [ed.] Graduate of Westminster Choir College, Princeton, NJ as a professional choir Dir., Soloist and organist; [occ.] Housewife; [memb.] Elder and choir member of the Covenant Pres. church in Costa Mesa, Calif., Chaplain of C.M.W.R.F., Costa Mesa (2300 hrs.) Hoag Hospital Volunteer Newport Beach, Calif.; [hon.] Trophy for hole-in-one at Highland Hills Gold Course, Colo. Plaque from Westminster, Colo. Rotary Club for being Pianist 5 yrs. Past Pres. Highland Hills Women's Golf Club.; [pers.] Without God there is no justice, without justice there is no peace.; [a.] Costa Mesa, CA

KUNZ, KRISTINE
[b.] December 3, 1983, Staten Island, NY; [p.] Robert and Michele Kunz; [ed.] Our Lady Star of the Sea Elementary School; [occ.] Student; [memb.] O.L.S.S. Track team, school band and cheerleader; [hon.] Several poems published in the SI Advance, a poem published in a childrens book. I received a writing award given by the NY State Assembly and am also a first honor student. I have received many track and field medals; [pers.] I am very grateful to my parents, especially my mother who always pushes me to be my best. I am thankful to Mrs. Cilento my 5th and 6th grade composition teacher who influenced me to write.; [a.] Staten Island, NY

KYZER, MARION WALT
[pen.] Walt Kyzer; [b.] December 29, 1930, Edmund, SC; [p.] Alton and Geneva Kyzer; [m.] Betsy Ann (Morrison) Kyzer, November 12, 1954; [ch.] Jan Maureen, Amy Sue, Jeffrey Andrews; [ed.] Some Col-

lege at U. of Mass. and U. of Hawaii, High School at Mt. Zion, H.S., Winnsboro, SC; [occ.] Major, USAF (Retired) Office Products Engineer - Retired; [memb.] First Baptist Church of Perrine (Florida) - Deacon Campers on Missions (RV Club); [oth. writ.] About 70 poems (unpublished) "One Humble Man" - My Dad's Biography, "Vignettes" - My autobiography (Unpublished), a series of opinions (Unpublished) Several short articles published in small local journals.; [pers.] Much of my poetry is written to reflect my personal faith in God. I like to temper serious concerns with a touch of Irony or Humor. My point being we must not take life or circumstances too seriously.; [a.] Miami, FL

LA FOSSE, TANIA
[b.] April 4, 1979, Bronx, NY; [p.] Benjamin La Fosse, Ida La Fosse; [ed.] Evander Childs High School, Our Saviour Lutheran School, and Regent Elementary School; [occ.] Student; [memb.] Youth for Christ Choir, and Cathedral Secretarial Staff; [hon.] Honor Roll, English and Math award, Junior Varsity Basketball Medal; [pers.] I find that expressing positive thoughts through my poetry gives me a golden opportunity to influence others that life may have its problems, but it can still be beautiful.; [a.] Bronx, NY

LAGIUSA, MICHELE
[b.] November 16, 1974, Staten Island, N.Y.C.; [p.] Victoria & Lawrence; [ed.] Our Lady Queen of Peace (Elementary); Francis High School; The College of Staten Island; [occ.] Medical Assistant; [memb.] Marine Mammal Life Association, The American Red Cross; [hon.] Certified Medical Assistant, Certified CPR Tech, Certifed Pharmacy Tech; [pers.] My aim is to express the most inner feelings of the heart and soul and set it free.; [a.] Staten Island, New York

LAGUNA, LISA
[b.] August 21, 1973, West Covina, CA; [p.] Joseph Laguna, Candi Jackson; [ed.] West Covina High School, University of La Verne; [occ.] Assistant Teacher and Librarian; [memb.] Youth and young adults of The Militia Immaculate; [pers.] When my heart pounds so hard that it hurts, that's when I pick up my pen not to inspire - not to influence - just to feel, where it's free and safe.; [a.] South San Francisco, CA

LAHNER, MELISSA
[b.] April 27, 1983, Bristol, PA; [p.] Brenda Lahner, Robert Lahner; [ed.] 6 years Walter Miller Elementary, 1 year Hope Lutheran School, 1 year Newton Friends School, 1 year Queen of the Universe; [occ.] Full time student; [hon.] Honor roll; [oth. writ.] Poetry in another anthology (Of Young Americans); [pers.] Your writing is who you are. It says where you're going and where you've been.; [a.] Levittown, PA

LAIK, ERIN
[b.] October 28, 1982, Rhinebeck, NY; [p.] Laura Mulligan and William Laik; [ed.] Rondout Valley Middle, entering 9th Grade in Apopka High School; [memb.] Bowling, Swimming; [oth. writ.] Several other poems and I am currently writing a novel.; [a.] Apopka, FL

LAKHANI, HEENA
[b.] February 1, 1981, Chicago, IL; [p.] Qadri Lakhani, Siddig Lakhani; [ed.] Maine East High School; [pers.] "I think that if your dreams can take you anywhere then your mind will take you twice as far", I thought of this through all the experiences that I've had and will keep on thinking of it.; [a.] Des Plaines, IL

LALEMAN, BRENDA L.
[b.] August 7, 1949, Davenport, IA; [p.] Leo Fetterer Sr., Bernice Brittenham; [m.] Roger Laleman, July 7, 1984; [ch.] William, Robert, Jason, Amber; [ed.] United Township High School; [pers.] I loved poetry all my life. I was always told by my friends and family to write what was in my heart. I especially thank my children for their encouragement.; [a.] East Moline, IL

LANDY, GLORIA SADOFF
[pen.] Gloria Sadoff Landy; [b.] USA; [p.] Eva and Samuel Sadoff; [m.] Eugene W. Landy, September 15, 1957; [memb.] President New Jersey, State Poetry Society, Inc.

LANG, AMBER H.
[pen.] Amber Lang; [b.] July 19, 1982, Montgomery, AL; [p.] John and Janet Lang; [ed.] Freshman in high school (currently); [occ.] Student listing publication; [memb.] Marching Band (French Horn/Mellophone), Youth Choir/Cheernastics, PEP Club/Studies Piano Privately/Soloist in Church Choir, Honor Roll First 9-wks.; [hon.] All-District Band, lead roles in church drama and solos; [oth. writ.] Short story, poetry; [pers.] I enjoy using words to tell a story or express feelings. Becoming proficient at this could lead to many interesting and enjoyable jobs, not to mention the exposure to new worlds!; [a.] Brewton, AL

LANPHAR, ROBERT
[b.] November 3, 1947, Pasadena, CA; [p.] Robert and Betty Lanphar; [m.] Anne Marie Lanphar, June 26, 1976; [ch.] Mark, Christopher, James, Lisa; [ed.] BA, MS Computer Science, California State College at Fullerton; [occ.] Computer Systems Consulting; [memb.] Knights of Columbus, Boy Scouts of America, ACM, IEEE; [hon.] Past Grand Knight, BSA, Award of Merit, Silver Beaver, Distinguished Commissioner, St. George; [oth. writ.] Several poems published in BSA publications.; [pers.] It is a personal responsibility to share the quiet whispers with those caught in the chaos of noise.; [a.] Brea, CA

LANTIS, RYAN MICHAEL
[b.] June 16, 1980, Fargo, ND; [p.] Craig, Trish Lantis; [ed.] K-9 Grade; [occ.] High School, Student; [pers.] I believe that I was inspired for my poem by the Lord's creation. All beauty comes from Him and the things spoken about in my poem come from a God whose love is neverending; [a.] Salmon, ID

LARAMIE, LINDA MARY
[b.] November 13, 1955, Saint Louis, MO; [p.] John and Veronica Horton; [m.] Edward Laramie, July 18, 1975; [ch.] Joshua, Justin, Jessica, Julie, Joseph; [ed.] St. Thomas Aquinas High School; [occ.] Homemaker, wife and mother; [memb.] All Saints Parish, St. Christophers Prayers Group Community; [oth. writ.] "The Gift", "My Treasure", "Just Outside Your Door" and "The Roads of Life"; [pers.] I believe that poetry is a gift given by God which reveals an "inner beauty" of ones heart that reaches out and touches another.; [a.] Saint Peters, MO

LARKINS, RACHEL LESHE
[b.] April 11, 1983, Riverside, CA; [p.] John and Jacquie Larkins; [ed.] Terrace Hills Middle School, YWAM Missionary School; [occ.] Student 8th Grade; [hon.] Made Honor roll Soccer award MIP Most Improved Player - Science Fair "Excellent"; [oth. writ.] I have written several stories - poems etc. it's my hobby; [a.] Redlands, CA

LARMOND, PAULETTE
[b.] May 18, 1969, Jamaica; [p.] Lurline and Oswald Larmond; [ed.] Bachelor of Science in Psychology at Suny at Story Brook, High School Evander Childs H.S., John Philip Sousa Junior High School; [occ.] Mental Health Ass't, Social Work-Harlem Hospital; [memb.] First United Brethren In Christ, New York State Church of God Mass Choir; [hon.] Delta Theta Award, Who's Who In American High Schools, National Honor Society Arista; [oth. writ.] Several articles written for High School Newspaper Evander News. Several articles written for Harlem House News; [pers.] I write so as to encourage, motivate and inspire others.; [a.] Bronx, NY

LARSON, STEPHANIE E.
[b.] December 17, 1976, Detroit, MI; [p.] Steven Larson, Sheridan Larson; [ed.] The Story Brook School, Corcoran School of Art; [occ.] Student at the Corcoran School of Art in Washington, D.C.; [hon.] Dean's List, Editor of Paumanok Literary Magazine, Dean's Merit Scholarship Award; [a.] Falls Church, VA

LASSITER, JOANIE
[b.] June 27, 1948, Robertson County, TN; [p.] Lela Mae Austin (Deceased); [m.] 1967-1990; [ch.] Three; [ed.] Freshman in College Austin Peay, TN Volunteer State (Scholarship); [occ.] Greenhouse owner and waitress; [hon.] Highest over all average of GED tests in the year 1991 in Vol. state won college scholarship. High school awards long ago; [oth. writ.] The Rosebud is my only free verse poem. There are hundreds of rhyming poems in my collection throughout the years.; [pers.] Every individual express himself with his eyes, lips, body movements or pen during moments of sadness or ectasy!; [a.] Cedar Hill, TN

LAWRENCE, LYNN ADELE
[pen.] Ruth or Lynn Adele Lawrence; [b.] September 16, 1920, Chicago, IL; [p.] Geo 'R' Lawrence and Della Page Lawrence; [ed.] Grade School - High School and special study courses in L.A.C.C. of L.A. - and PVT. Tutalege with Famous Master Sculptor - Aaron Goodelman. And studies in other arts with PVT. Tutors. Air - Brush Art and Photo Retouching Arts; [occ.] Active retired senior 75 yrs old, Former, Sculptor, Painter, Designer, Teacher, Writer, and Poet; [memb.] Southland Art Assoc. of Montebello, CA. L.A County Employee Art Assoc. Writers Digest - NAFE. (Nat'l Assoc. of Female Execs.) Audobon Society. Member of 'Unity' (Unity Village, MO. (I am a Christian.); [hon.] Grade School Competition: 1st Prize for Painting of Iris Flower in Pastels. Exhibited in Art Institute of Chicago, Ill. in Children's Division for Extended Period of Time, N.Y.C, 1st Prize for Sculptured Portrait Bust of Marshal Tito in Yugo - Slavia, Bronze Repro. Sent him for his desk. Wrote Technical Article about Lamps, Lighting, and Art. Published in Trades Mag. with my photo and retailing daily newspaper. Many other honors and awards garnered in many art exhibits. (1946-1960's); [oth. writ.] Wrote story for writers digest aptitude test. Passed test with applause and praises. Now I have 4 books for children and adults. Compiling for publication. Collections of my own original works. Tales, Nursery Rhymes, Fables, Inspirational Verses, Nature. All written in poems that rhyme. Most are illustrated with my own original drawings, and paintings in pastels and ink. One book is about 20 favorite song birds with painted Illustrations in color.; [pers.] Paintings and sculptures shown CH. 5 T.V 1/2 Hr program. Prestigious showing by invitation. Chairperson and Dir. or Dept of Retouching Art and Instructor for 8 yrs and at Artography Academy of Photographic Arts. Jim Bettio Pres. Also taught sculptural

form to visually handicapped children and adults, at Jr. Blind Foundation. (Norman Kapland. I'm also proud to say, I'm a daughter of world famous Geo. 'R' Lawrence. (Library of Congress, Smith Sonian, others). Won Grand Prix at Paris Exposition 1906. (Seek God 1st and He will no fail you.) Glory be to God.; [a.] Los Angeles, CA

LAWYER, KATHERINE E. CRICHTON
[b.] October 11, 1947, Philadelphia, PA; [p.] Rev. John W. and Gertrude Crichton; [ch.] James, MistyAnn; [ed.] Bensalem High School, Nurses Aid for 38 yrs., Red Cross - C.P.R., Nurses Aid Course; [occ.] Nurses Aid - Caring for 91 yr. old (private duty); [memb.] I am a member at Riverside Gospel Mission, NJ. But attend Trinity United Church of Christ where I reside.; [hon.] 1-Golden Certificate, 2-Silver Certificates for poetry; [oth. writ.] Several poems published in Church Beacon; [pers.] I hope to help others through my poems I have been greatly influenced by my upbringing by Christian parents.; [a.] Fort Loudon, PA

LAZO, DAVID
[pen.] Boulder; [b.] December 14, 1980, Flint, MI; [p.] Dr. Sharon and Fausto Lazo; [ed.] Wheeling Country Day, Linsly; [occ.] Student; [memb.] Boy Scouts of America-Life Scout, Wheeling Area Hockey Association, American Hockey Association; [hon.] West Liberty Regional Science Fair- First Place 1994, 95 and 96. Grand Prize Winner - 1995, International Science Fair Participant 1995.; [pers.] May fortune favor the foolish, Hack the Planet.; [a.] Saint Clairsville, OH

LE, THUY XUAN
[pen.] Thuy Lexuan; [b.] April 25, 1927, Hanoi, Vietnam; [p.] Chinh Xuan Le and Ty Thi Tran (Both Deceased); [m.] Thin Thi Dang, September 7, 1957; [ch.] Phuong-Tram, Phuong-Thoa, Tung and Thach; [ed.] Agreige of International Accounting Systems, 1970; [occ.] Financial Control Systems Developer; [memb.] Secretary General, Puginier Alumni, Saigon, Vietnam 1971-74, Comptroller, Association of Vietnamese Scientists, Saigon, Vietnam, 1972-1975, Member International Platform Association/Academy of Poets, 1995; [hon.] Award of Excellence, U.S. Library of Congress, 1992, USA, Decree of Merits, 1995, International Biographical Center, Cambridge, England; [oth. writ.] Kim-Van-Kieu I, English Translation and Commentaries, 1963, Saigon, Vietnam, Principles of Advanced Bookkeeping and Accounting, 1971, Saigon, Vietnam, How to Establish of Uniform Chart of Accounts for Business Enterprises, 1971, Saigon, Vietnam, How to Establish a Powerful General Ledger for a Government, 1981, Virginia, USA, The Super Revelation, the Truth about the Creation of the Universe, Evolutions, and Divine Incarnations, 1989, Virginia, USA, The Prajnaparamita Sutra, Experimental Interpretation of the Highest Key of Wisdom, 1989, Virginia, USA. Kim-Van-Kieu II, Revised English Translation and Commentaries, Award of Excellence, US Library of Congress, 1992, USA, The Soul of Poetry inside Kim-Van-Kieu, Poetic Version and Commentaries, 1995 Virginia, USA, Dawnlight, a collection of my short poems I wrote in USA.; [pers.] My main objective consists of communicating to the world the highest experimental spiritual enlightenment acquired through transcendental meditation, the Truth about Christ and His coming, the Truth about the creation of the Universe, divine incarnations, the World of Spirits, and the Kingdom of Heaven.

LE CLAIRE, RENEE
[b.] June 14, 1971, Miami, FL; [p.] Kathleen Grossi, Ed Gietzen; [m.] Scott Le Claire, August 4, 1988; [ch.] Gregory (8), and Jaclyn (7); [pers.] This poem is dedicated to everyone who believed in me. I can never thank you enough for your encouragement, and constant support.; [a.] Detroit, MI

LEACH, MELISSA AMY
[b.] September 17, 1983, Omaha, NE; [p.] James Leach Jr., Elizabeth Leach; [ed.] McKeel Academy of Applied Technology; [occ.] Student; [hon.] Honor Roll, Citizenship Award/Sons of American Revolution; [a.] Lakeland, FL

LEE, ELIZABETH
[b.] March 26, 1986, California; [p.] Dr. Judith S. Lee; [ed.] Entering 5th Grade at Ramez; [occ.] Student; [memb.] Chess Club at Manhattan Chess Club; [oth. writ.] "Pirates" - a poem; [pers.] I want to make the world a better place by learning.; [a.] New York, NY

LEE, EMILIANO S.
[pen.] Jonny Nolan; [b.] October 21, 1974, Berkeley, CA; [p.] Louie Lee, Carmen Silva; [ed.] Abraham Lincoln High School; [occ.] Custom Framer; [hon.] Paid participant in "The Beats Go On" in San Fran, CA 10/29/93: A Cognac Hennessey promotion; [oth. writ.] Several poems published in school and local papers and 'zines, self-published book: "Carnage"; [pers.] Conceive truth, persevere life!; [a.] San Francisco, CA

LEE, NICOLE M.
[b.] May 17, 1980, Victorville, CA; [p.] Kenneth and Lisa Lee; [ed.] Shenendehowa Central School (honor student); [hon.] Bessie Raullison Award for Academic Excellence and Courage; [oth. writ.] Hope, Best Friends, Heaven. Nicole's poems title Hope was published in many local newspapers and has been used extensively as a source of inspiration.; [pers.] Nicole has provided courage and inspiration to thousands of people facing difficult situations through her poetry. She passed away on June 28, 1996 from Leukemia.; [a.] Clifton Park, NY

LEGGE, DEWAYNE H.
[pen.] DeWayne, Taz, Wayne O'.; [b.] August 4, 1959, Midland, TX; [p.] Landis and Barbara Legge; [m.] Michelle Renee Pittman Legge, December 16, 1994; [ch.] Michael Dillon Legge; [memb.] Bible Baptist Church, Narcotics Anonymous; [oth. writ.] The Wishing Well I and II, Hold Your Head Up High, Skeletons In My Closet, I Dream, You Dream, There's A Bee In My Pants, The Fable of Ellie Mae Troll, The Bulls Are Still The Champs, and many other poems.; [pers.] "I wrote this poem for you Michael Dillon, before you were even born. These are my hopes, wants and expectations of you and how you conduct yourself throughout your life. May you grow up with the morals and values becoming of a young man." These are my hopes and wants and expectations of you and how you conduct yourself throughout your life.; [a.] Stillwater, OK

LEITH, XUCHITL LEILANI
[b.] December 11, 1970, Lake Charles, LA; [p.] William Hauxwell (Deceased) and Maria Guadalupe Lupercio; [ed.] La Grange High School, L.C., LA County College of Morris, Randolph, NJ M.I.N.T., Denville, NJ; [occ.] Certified/Registered Dental Assistant; [pers.] Live life simply and naturally.; [a.] Lake Charles, LA

LEMMERMAN, LIZ
[b.] January 7, 1983, Worcester, MA; [p.] Carl B., Sheila Lemmerman; [ed.] Eighth grade, Ononaboya Hill Middle School; [hon.] Outstanding effort in Science Class, Outstanding Effort in Social Studies; [a.] Syracuse, NY

LEMMERT, LORIE
[b.] January 20, 1971, Ennis, TX; [p.] Gerald Johnson, Bill and Alice Kennedy; [m.] George Lemmert, July 4, 1989; [ch.] Brittany Michelle, Travis Carl; [ed.] Athens High School, Trinity Valley Community College, Tyler Junior College; [occ.] Chemistry Lab Technician; [a.] Edom, TX

LENCESKI, DAVID WAYNE
[pen.] SKI; [b.] March 15, 1970, Missouri; [p.] Richard Lenceski, Mary Rossfeld; [ed.] St. Cecilia (Grammar), Soldan (High School); [occ.] Mail Clerk; [memb.] National Parks and Conservation Assoc.; [hon.] 1) Letter of Appreciation - USN TMCM Cambell, W.D., 2) USS Orion Man Award - Captain USN Morgan, E.L., 3) Letter of Commendation - Captain Morgan, E. L. USN, 4) Citation - Rear Admiral Ryan, T.D. USN Owens, W.A., 5) Letter of Commendation - Vice Admiral - USN Owens, W.A., 6) Letter of Commendation - Rear Admiral Chiles, H.G. - USN; [oth. writ.] Personal Journal of Hearts, Mind and Soul. Includes short stories, personal Theories, and poems.; [pers.] A religious person, I am not. A spiritual person, I am. Three is a difference! "Mother Nature" is my mentor.; [a.] Saint Louis, MO

LENNINGTON, LINDA L.
[pen.] Lilana Michilo; [b.] July 18, 1947, OH; [oth. writ.] "Sheltered Thoughts", "My Hearts Hymn", "Fire Of Tears"; [pers.] Inspiration surfaces in one small phrase, born from all living things and developing further in dreams. Sometimes the simplest of verse can be the most complex.; [a.] Sunnyville, CA

LEONARD, MELISSA A.
[b.] March 19, 1971, Orangeburg; [p.] Dewise A. Bailey; [m.] Gregory R. Leonard, August 12, 1995; [ed.] Clemson University Bachelor of Arts, National Center for Paralegal Training; [occ.] Paralegal; [memb.] Kappa Alpha Theta, Hands on Greenville; [hon.] Graduated Cum Laude from Clemson Golden Key, National Honor Society; [pers.] Poetry comes naturally to me. I just let my feelings flow on to the paper.; [a.] Greenville, SC

LEQUIEU, ARWEN
[b.] October 28, 1979, Klamath Falls, OR; [p.] Clifford and Mary LeQuieu; [ed.] A senior at Cibola High School Skipping my junior year; [occ.] Farm Hand; [memb.] 4-H; [oth. writ.] Star people published in the Rippling Waters another National Library of Poetry anthology; [pers.] I believe that the old swedish proverb "Shared joy is double joy and shared sorrow is half-sorrow" should be practiced more today.; [a.] Rio Rancho, NM

LESHAY, PH.D. STEVEN V.
[b.] October 28, 1943, Hartford, CT; [p.] Andrew and Elsie LeShay; [m.] Maxine Hoffman Karelitz, April 17, 1982; [ch.] N. Aimee, Matthew and Gavin; [ed.] Ph.D. Temple University, MA Glassboro State College, BA Lenoir Rhyne College; [occ.] College Professor, Marketing; [memb.] American Marketing, Association, US Naval Reserve (Retired, Commander); [a.] Malaga, NJ

LESLIE, JOAN
[b.] Kingston, Jamaica; [pers.] When the history book of my life is written, may it be said there goes an individual whose life was lived to blessed mankind.; [a.] Bronx, NY

LESTER, BETTY J.
[pen.] Bj Lester; [b.] Levy, AR; [p.] Deceased; [m.] Harvey A., August 17, 1993; [ch.] Three Boys, Two Alive and One Deceased; [ed.] High School at some College Classes and Trade School Classes and lots of

Art Classes with Master Artists; [occ.] Part time Freelance Artist and Decorative Artist and Leather Art; [memb.] Nat. Decorative Painters Soc.; [hon.] Many 1st Place Awards (Fine Arts) - Shows Feathers on Magazine Covers for Decorative Painting and Published and write up on Swaffito Art and best also of shows and 1st place award; [oth. writ.] Have been published in many times for project painting authored 2 how to book Leather Tole books - 1) Painting on leather, 2) Painting on Fabric Fabric Tole wrote column for Tole World 8 years question/answers from readers (technical advice) and information design leather painting line for Ravon Leather.; [pers.] This is the 1st serious poem I have wrote - I guess the loss of my dear son, cause me to reach deep in my heart to express my feelings - 1st poem to be published.; [a.] San Bernardino, CA

LESTER, MARY E.
[pen.] "Yellow Rose"; [b.] March 24, 1937, Lewisburg, TN; [p.] Taylor and Dolly Church; [m.] Bill Lester, November 3, 1956; [ch.] Jeff, Cindi, Timothy; [ed.] Marshall County High School, attended Tarrant Co. Jr. College; [occ.] Self-employed, ME Wester and Son Trucking; [memb.] National Geographical Society, Diabetes Association; [oth. writ.] Just write for fun and relaxation of mind.; [pers.] I'm a country girl - to see the beauty of the country, the mountains, makes my heart feel good. My life revolves around my family - we're a loving family. I wrote poem for my mom - who in 1995 nearly died because of a surgery mishap.; [a.] Fort Worth, TX

LEWIS, KIMBERLY
[b.] February 8, 1973, Buffalo, NY; [p.] Edward and Marcia Lewis; [ed.] John F. Kennedy High School, Medaille College; [memb.] Compeer West Volunteer Services; [hon.] Dean's List; [pers.] In an ever-changing world, there is always help for those in need of it. I diligently try to reflect this in my writing. I thank the biggest strength of my life, God, that I am both able to write about this subject and practice it.; [a.] Buffalo, NY

LEWIS, NATALIE RUTLEDGE
[b.] November 11, 1931, N.Y.C.; [p.] Gladys and Gilbert Simpson; [m.] Iwan H. Lewis, July 26; [ch.] Shanette, Larney, Regina and Nancy Rutledge; [ed.] Cathedral H.S. 1 yr. Hunter Col.; [occ.] Retired Postal Clerk; [memb.] Sabbath School Teacher; [oth. writ.] I have written over 80 poems and would like to publish a book of sacred poetry. I also write acrostics for friends and to order.; [pers.] Since April 1995 I have been inspired to write religious poetry. I feel that a poem speaks volumes in a few words. I consider them sermons in poetry.; [a.] Brooklyn, NY

LEWIS, SUE
[b.] February 2, 1963, Port Arthur, TX; [p.] Janet and Dudley Guidry; [m.] Gordon Ray Lewis, May 17, 1986; [ch.] Gordon Ray II, Nickolas Clayton; [ed.] East Chambers High School, Winnie, TX, Texas Tech University, Lubbock, TX, BS in Agricultural Economics; [occ.] Office Manager for Bonds Ranch, and Turkey Foot Cattle, Co., Inc.; [memb.] First United Methodist Church Burleson, Texas, Haslet Elementary PTA; [oth. writ.] I have written several non-published poems. One of which was auctioned for our church fund raiser for $165.00. The pome pertains to operation desert storm.; [pers.] I am moved to write about things that touch my heart. When my heart is touched, the poems write themselves.; [a.] Forth Worth, TX

LEYBA, JULIA E.
[b.] March 20, 1939, Las Vegas, NM; [p.] Adelina Vigil

and Ralph Baros; [m.] George D. Leyba; [ch.] Victoria, Ralph, Karen, Pamela and Julie Ann; [ed.] 11th grade never finished school - took classes in Local School to benefit myself on the job market; [occ.] Executive Housekeeper in the Vail, Co Area; [memb.] Local Church member - Nashville Songwriters Ass. BMI member; [oth. writ.] Written several songs have around 175 poems - copy write on them - never been published songs - "Little by Little", "My Cowboys Going to be a Star", Spared You a Heartache Saved each of Us a Dream", "A New Day will Come"; [pers.] I love writing and hope that I can bring enjoyment to others thru them.; [a.] Leadville, CO

LHOTAN, LISA
[pen.] Armani L.; [b.] May 5, 1978, Long Island, NY; [ed.] Continuing; [pers.] The world is a rainbow of colors and sound. One needs only to listen with one's heart and hear with one's mind.; [a.] Central Islip, NY

LIGHTSEY, VERA DOYLE
[pen.] Bobbi Doyle Lightsey; [b.] Sydney, Nova Scotia, Canada; [p.] Lyra and Michael Doyle; [m.] Vernon Malton Lightsey of Okeechobee Florida (Deceased January 12, 1995); [ch.] 1 Son, Wayne, 2 Grandsons, Dylland Logan - live in Toronto, Canada, 1 daughter Sandra Beth, 1 granddaughter Jessica and 1 grandson, Cody, live in Colorado; [ed.] 1) Graduated in June '51 from Holy Angels Convent High School, Sydney, Nova Scotia, Canada, 2) Course in Aircraft - R.C.A.F. Identification - Worked at an Air Defense Control Center from 1954-1956; [occ.] Retired Secretary; [oth. writ.] Short Story - "Scleroderma - I've "Conquered it". Many songs and poems; [pers.] I believe that the purpose of life is to become involved in the studies of understanding the Philosophy of the creator of the universe. We should all try to be disciplined, Philosophers. Life is a gift with purpose!

LIND, CASSANDRA
[b.] Pittsfield, MA; [ed.] West Rome High, Rome, GA Bethel College, St. Paul, MN; [occ.] Actress; [memb.] First Presbyterian Church of Hollywood, Screen Actors Guild; [hon.] Dean's List; [a.] Sherman Oaks, CA

LINDSEY, MARILYN E.
[b.] Catskill, NY; [p.] Wesley R. Butts, Elaine T. Butts; [ed.] Victoria College; [oth. writ.] God's Angel, My Child's Hand, A Tiny Spark, Fond Memories, Dreams Do Come True, Freebies and Tea, Precious Christmas Memory, Farming The Land, A Terrible Problem; [pers.] The poetry that I write is influenced by the higher power. I strive to touch other people's lives in my writing.; [a.] Beeville, TX

LINDSTROM, LISA MICHELE
[b.] August 8, 1961, Minneapolis, MN; [p.] Ward Engebrit and M. J. Engebrit; [m.] Jeff, July 25, 1992; [ed.] Hopkins, Minnesota and 1 yr. U of Minn. Literature - Nationwide Insurance Claim School, Columbus, Ohio; [occ.] Poet, Publisher, Logistics Head for Special Events, Insurance Consultant; [memb.] Distinguished Member - International Society of Poets Charter Member - All American Eagle Racing Team - Dan Gurney; [hon.] Six Editors Choice Awards for Poetry - Several Logistical Praises as I was moved to Top Projects after the first; [oth. writ.] I published my 1st book, "Adequate Justice - Beginning Healing Through Poetry" and I am ready to publish my 2nd any time now.; [pers.] I dedicate this work to the native Indians who make "Dream Catchers" and "Mandelas." They have also aided me in my extensive healing process.; [a.] Yorba Linda, CA

LINN, E. ERNESTINE
[b.] November 30, 1947, Charleston, WV; [p.] Anna Olivene and Clifford Ferrell Messer; [m.] Anthony Michael Linn, September 14, 1974; [ch.] LeAnna Beth, Melissa Dawn, Michael Anthony; [occ.] Fashion/Finance Executive

LINT, ROBERT E.
[pen.] Tep Lint; [b.] May 23, 1927, Perryopolis, PA; [p.] Winforp P. and Jeannetta P. Lint; [m.] Widowed; [ch.] Thomas W. Lint, Janet L. Mahoney; [ed.] West Virginia University; [occ.] Retired; [oth. writ.] Several other poems in, "Spirit Of The Age", "Best Poems Of The 90's"; [pers.] I enjoy observing nature and the human condition along with the effect that each has on the other.; [a.] Sarasota, FL

LIPKA, NARISSA
[b.] August 6, 1968, Beloit, WI; [p.] Paul Lipka, Evelyn Lipka; [ed.] BA in Human services with a concentration in Gerontology; [occ.] Licensed Social Worker; [memb.] Certified Nurses Aide, Hospice, Massachusetts Brain Injury Association; [pers.] Enjoy every minute of everyday, because you never know what you can loose in 10 seconds.; [a.] Natick, MA

LITTERIO, DANIELLE CORISSA
[b.] July 21, 1981, Boston, MA; [p.] Mary and John Litterio; [ed.] Sophomore at Randolph Jr/Sr High School; [occ.] Bed Maker at Local Nursing Home for part time; [oth. writ.] One other poem published in the 1996 anthology of poetry by young Americans. Several other poems written for personal expression and enjoyment.; [pers.] I got my inspiration to write when my grandmother passed away. I get other inspiration from famous poets like Emily Dickenson and Edgar Allen Poe.; [a.] Randolph, MA

LLOYD, ANGELA MARIE
[b.] October 13, 1965, Erie, PA; [p.] Allen B. and Joyce A. Barnett; [m.] Elmer David Lloyd, October 2, 1993; [ed.] Punxsutawney High, Gannon University; [occ.] Owner, Angel's Boutique; [memb.] New Life Fellowship; [hon.] Graduated Magna Cum Laude at Gannon - Fellowship in Center for study of the Presidency; [oth. writ.] Currently writing fantasy novel and small book of poetry; [pers.] I wrote "The Poet's Sacrifice" for my sister when her beloved passed away. Such verse is amazing reminder that the creative light inside the soul cannot be extinguished by life's trials, nor banished even in a bleak world. Poetry is hope on paper.; [a.] Timblin, PA

LODEMORE, GARY
[b.] October 25, 1952, London, England; [p.] Thomas Henry Lodemore and Rosina; [ed.] College; [occ.] Hair and Make Up Artist; [pers.] Influenced by Loving and Caring people who helped get through a hard time.; [a.] Washington, DC

LODZINSKI II, EDWARD
[pen.] Eddie Lude; [b.] October 14, 1966, South Amboy, NJ; [p.] Edward and Alice; [ch.] Jessica Chris and Heather Nicole; [ed.] Cedar Ridge High School Brookdale College; [occ.] Maintenance Superintendant Fords, NJ; [pers.] I take one day at a time and live it. I try to express what's in my heart and head the best way I can. Thanks Katwoman for understanding me the best.; [a.] Fords, NJ

LOHR, ELEANOR M.
[b.] April 8, 1911, Cleveland, OH; [p.] Harry Valentine, Bertha Valentine; [m.] Paul Lohr, June 30, 1940; [ch.]

Joyce Elaine; [ed.] West Commerce High School; [occ.] Retired; [memb.] Calvary Bible Chapel Church; [oth. writ.] Poem published in school book - "Halloween". Then writing for own enjoyment. Now starting to submit on occasion.; [pers.] I love my Lord, and have always loved poetry, so in my writings I combine the two.; [a.] Toledo, OH

LONG, LUCILLE M.
[pen.] Lucy; [b.] March 6, 1925, Belvidere, IL; [p.] Harlen and Bernice Taylor; [m.] Former Husband Donald H. Cox, April 18, 1949; [ch.] Nancy, Linda, Randy; [ed.] Finished Grammar School - went to high school for only 6 months; [occ.] Deli Worker at Piggly Wiggly Belvidere; [memb.] I was a Brownie leader, also Girl Scouts worked with cub scouts for several years.; [hon.] I have not received any great honors or awards.; [pers.] I have several hobbies - decorating eggs - sweat shirts, making minatue angles, making necklaces out of beads - also did a lot of crochet work.; [a.] Belvidere, IL

LONGWORTH, DELIA M.
[b.] January 7, 1923, Puerto Rico; [p.] Angel Martinez and Antonia Rodriguez; [m.] Widow; [ch.] Angel Ernest Mena; [ed.] M.A. English as a Second Lang., M.A. English Lit.; [occ.] Was supervisor of Ed. now - retiree; [memb.] Smithonian Institution, Running strong for AM. Indian Youth, American Fed. of Teachers; [hon.] Inter American Univ. - Puerto Rico honored with student representing the ideals of said institution, New York Univ. graduated with honors from my Engl. as a second language M.A.; [oth. writ.] Two poems - published by The National Library of Poetry one of them - "Scars"; [pers.] One of the best ways of spreading beauty throughout the world is through the writing of poetry life and especially "Nature" provide us with so many rich experiences.; [a.] Yonkers, NY

LOPES II, WILFRED A.
[pen.] P. K. Hanamaikai; [b.] Ewa, HI; [p.] Mr. and Mrs. Wilfred A. Lopes Sr.; [ed.] Waianae High, Arizona Western College, Hono. Comm. College; [occ.] Resident Manager; [memb.] Makaha Surf Club, Shark Bait Scuba Club; [hon.] All State Football, Athletic Scholarship - Arizona Western College; [pers.] As a native Hawaiian, I have great respect and love for the land, ocean and cultures of the world. I hope to see the world United in Aloha. (Love).; [a.] Waianae, HI

LOPEZ SR., PEDRO J.
[pen.] P. J. Lopez; [b.] May 13, 1951, Camaguey, Hidalgo, Cuba; [p.] Javier F. Lopez, Ana Lopez; [m.] Divorced; [ch.] Peter J. Lopez Jr., Francesca Lopez; [ed.] Self Educated; [occ.] Salesman; [oth. writ.] Various other poetry musical composition, and Lyrics; [pers.] My poetry is a reflection of what is in my heart, life's experiences and the beautiful and the not so beautiful people I meet along my journey through life.

LOUGHRAN, JAMES F.
[pen.] James F. Loughran; [b.] March 18, 1922, Los Angeles, CA; [p.] Frank and Allene Loughran; [m.] Frances Loughran, August 15, 1953; [ed.] Woodrow Wilson High School Long Beach, CA; [occ.] Retired; [hon.] Veteran World War II; [oth. writ.] Nothing published.; [a.] Apple Valley, CA

LOVO, MARIA-LEONOR
[pen.] Lobita; [b.] August 31, 1976, Managua, Nicaragua; [p.] Alfonso N. Lovo, Leonor Lovo; [ed.] St. Brendan High School, Currently at Florida International university; [occ.] Student; [hon.] Who's Who Among

American High School Students 1992-1993; [oth. writ.] Few poems in High School's Literary and Artistic Anthology, Galatea; [pers.] "Il est tre's simple: On ne voit Bien qu'Avec le Coeur. L'essential Est Invisible pour les yeux." (The Little Prince) "A very simple secret: It is only with the heart that one can see rightly, what is essential is invisible to the eye".; [a.] Miami, FL

LOWDER, MEGAN H.
[b.] July 2, 1966; [p.] Chloe Koeninger, Duave Belcher; [m.] Charles E. Lowder, September 5, 1987; [ed.] Pasadena Mini High School, Associate of Science Degree in Child Development, and studies in Fine Art at Bakersfield College; [occ.] Artist Educator; [memb.] The Cousteau Society, Audubon, National Wildlife Federation; [oth. writ.] Personal poems and essays in school newspaper; [pers.] I believe in respecting and caring about other people animals and the Earth. I have been greatly influenced by classical and modern fine art, and the poets, Emily Dickenson, Yeats, Langston Hughes, and Maya Angelou.; [a.] Bakersfield, CA

LOWE, DARWIN
[b.] February 23, 1965; [m.] Cheryl Lowe, July 25, 1992; [ed.] Schenectady County Community College, Schenectady NY 12305 A-O-S Culinary Art graduated high honor, A-A-S Hotel & Restaurant Mgnt. graduate high honor; [occ.] Assistant Restaurant Manager; [memb.] President's List, Dean's List Who's Who Among Student in American, Junior Colleges, American Culinary Federation, Phi Theta Kappa; [pers.] Not all of us are born with silver spoons in our mouths - take the stainless steel one that you have been given and utilize it to the best of your ability.; [a.] Brooklyn, NY

LUDDINGTON, BETTY WALLES
[pen.] Betty Luddington; [b.] May 11, 1936, Tampa, FL; [p.] Edward and Ruby Luddington (Deceased); [m.] Robert Morris Schmidt, September 20, 1957 (Divorced: December 12, 1981); [ch.] Irene Losat, Daniel Schmidt; [ed.] Plant High School, University of South Florida, Tampa, FL, 1980 BA American Studies/History, 1982 MA Library Media and Information Studies 1986 Ed.S Curriculum and Instruction/Gifted Education; [occ.] Media Specialist, Dowdell Middle School, Tampa, FL; [memb.] HASLMS (Hillsborough Association of School Library Media Specialists, FTP/NFA/Hillsborough Classroom Teachers Association, County Music Fan Clubs: Brooks and Dunn, Diamond Rio, Joe Diffie, Aaron Tippin, ISP (International Society of Poets); [hon.] Phi Alpha Theta Outstanding Student Award, Golden Signet Award, Who's Who Among Students in American Colleges and Universities, Editor's Choice Awards for outstanding Achievement in Poetry (1996), Honoraries: Phi Kappa Phi, Kappa Delta Pi, Omicron Delta Kappa, Phi Alpha Theta, Pi Gamma Mu, Honors Council, Honors Convocation, and Graduate Scholarships: ODK, Library Studies, Alumni Assn.; [oth. writ.] "Witan: A simulation activity for gifted students." The Gifted Child Today, September/October 1986. Joe Diffie Fan Club (poems): "Diffie Boots," "Diffie Cult Fanfare," "Honky Tonk Attitude." The Tampa Tribune, December 1992: "Librarian uses poetry, country music to reach students at Dowdell." NLP, 1996: "I like Myself: James Evans," A Voyage to Remember, "Hillbilly Knight: Country Wildflower," A Tapestry of Thoughts "John McEuen: Strings Wizard," Across the Universe, "Sybil Ludington's 1977 Ride, The Best Poems of the '90's, "William Benjamin: Educational Leadership," Recollections of Yesterday, "Flowerscape/Mary Vincent Bertland," Memories of Tomorrow, "Charlene Can," Frost at Midnight.; [pers.] Inventing a poetic style that

flows forward and backwards with accents along the way...making like a poem, a bouquet of words that turns each day into something special.; [a.] Tampa, FL

LUKACIK, STEFAN
[b.] July 26, 1929, Nizna Nad Oravou, Slovakia; [p.] Stefan Lukacik, Zuzana Lukacik-Kazmier; [ed.] VSE (University of Economics), Bratislava, Slovakia, FAMU (Film Faculty of Muse Arts Academy), Prague Czech Republik; [occ.] Filmmaker; [pers.] Eternal life or death.; [a.] Los Angeles, CA

LUNA, MICHELE
[b.] January 18, 1941, New York, NY; [p.] Deceased; [m.] John Luna Jr., September 3, 1966; [ch.] Michael, Andrea, Stephanie; [ed.] Registered Nurse, Doctoral Candidate; [occ.] Rick Manager Tri-City, Medical Center Oceanside, CA; [oth. writ.] Inspirational and spiritual poetry published in church publication.; [pers.] I consider myself a "Magical Thinker." I look for inspiration in both the word of God and then needs of others. I have been influenced by reading the bible at looking at challenges within my own life. I'd like to think my writings will have a positive influence on how others view life challenges.; [a.] Laguna Beach, CA

LUNEAU, BRANDIE MICHELLE
[pen.] D; [b.] June 7, 1979, Baton Rouge, LA; [p.] Jerome Luneau, Donna Luneau; [ed.] Jasper High School; [oth. writ.] Long poems for school and for my boyfriend; [a.] Dogpatch, AR

LYMAN, ALICE
[b.] September 7, 1933, Rantoul, KS; [p.] Russell Morgan, Alice Morgan; [m.] Marion Lyman (Deceased), February 14, 1953; [ch.] James, Janis; [ed.] Baldwin High School, Washington School of Art; [occ.] Electronics Inspector; [memb.] Williamsburg, Ottawa Wildlife Club, American Association of Retired People, First Assembly of God Church, Washington School of Art; [hon.] OAT Award in typing High Honor Roll, High School; [oth. writ.] I have written several other poems that I am waiting to submit for publication.; [pers.] I give all the glory to God for His inspiration in my writings of poems. Without Him I could do nothing.; [a.] Ottawa, KS

LYNN, MICHAEL D.
[b.] July 5, 1943, Detroit, MI; [p.] James Lynn, Frances Lynn; [m.] Joanne Lynn (Deceased), May 5, 1973; [ch.] Jason Michael, Nicole Ann, Joel Eric; [ed.] Salesian Catholic High, Glendale Community College; [occ.] Customer Service Representative; [oth. writ.] Poems "Love Is", book "My Wife Has Cancer! For Me By Men"; [pers.] To teach the world that terminal illness is about people, not statistics; [a.] Phoenix, AZ

LYON, TRUDY GAIL NICHOLS
[pen.] Trudy Gail Nichols; [b.] August 20, 1950, Memphis, TN; [p.] L.D. Nichols and Mary Christine Montgomery; [m.] Divorced 1990 from Louis John Lyon, February 14, 1969; [ch.] 2 daughters Rajeanna, and Tammatha, 1 grandson from named David Greggory; [ed.] Graduate 1968 of Memphis Tech High School; [occ.] Past years Secretarial/self owned cleaning service clerical; [hon.] 1967 won 2nd place in National Distributive Education notebook on Petroleum out of over 75 high schools/honor roll student many times/major in Eng., Literature, spelling and essays; [oth. writ.] None entered yet for publication among poems, short stories, and essays; [pers.] Poetry is the purest form of love and romance deep from the heart, mind, and soul; [a.] Hernando, MS

LYONS, WHITNEY KAY
[pen.] Jazzi Jasmine; [b.] July 19, 1961; [p.] Foster Home; [ed.] College; [occ.] Writer; [hon.] Ohio Public Image Award, Honorable mention by Lliad press, Award of Merit by Hollywood's Famous Poetry Society, Ohio Speech and hearing Association Award; [oth. writ.] Inside Mother Outside Child, Lost Child Behind the Man, Soul Hero, Dark and Light Heart, Free Spirit Articles in Newspapers; [pers.] Inspired to reveal my talent by the people who adopted me at age 32. Children are to be loved not abused.; [a.] Delaware, OH

MACKEY, SHIRLEY JEAN
[pen.] Shirley Jean Mackey; [b.] April 1, 1927, Rochester, NY; [p.] Violet and Charles Mackey; [ch.] Jack Donna Carla; [ed.] Fairmount Grammer Solvay High School; [occ.] Ret. from GTE (17 yrs.); [oth. writ.] Local papers; [pers.] I like to bring a smile to people who read my poems - but as in real life some are sad.; [a.] Phoenix, AZ

MACNEIL, ALLEN
[b.] September 26, 1963, Bittburg, Germany; [p.] Gerlinde White and Donald MacNeil; [ed.] B.S. in Economics from the University of California, Davis, J.D from Loyda Law School; [occ.] Attorney; [memb.] Sigma Pi Fraternity, Phi Alpha Delta Legal Fraternity, American Bar Association, the State Bar of California, VC Davis Varsity Rughy Club, Orange County Bar Association; [hon.] Who's who among High School Students 1979-80, 1980-1981, Dean's List VC Davis, Dean's List Loyola Law School; [oth. writ.] No Prior publishing; [pers.] I try to focus on the good things on my life rather than worrying about the bad.; [a.] Fullerton, CA

MADRIGAL-LEDEZMA, OLMAN A.
[pen.] Olman A. Madrigal-Ledezma; [b.] October 22, 1938, San Jose, Costa Rica, CA; [p.] Hilde Madrigal, Consuel Ledezma; [m.] Maricarmen Madrigal, December 9, 1961; [ch.] Yamileth, Zaidem, Azhyadee, Aybecquel; [ed.] Bachelor in Sciences and Letters, Journalist, Reporter, Writer-Poet-Teacher, Automotive Technician, Electronic Technician, Illustrator, Painter, Graphic Artist; [occ.] Building Maintenance, Journeyman and Utility Man; [memb.] "UFO Clubcorp" - Organization, Costa Rica Community Center, "Macrocosmos Brotherhood", "Henry George Followers Circle"; [hon.] In: "Natural Sciences", "Education", "Journalism", "Illustration and Designs", "Art Paintings", (I am American Citizen - Naturalized); [oth. writ.] Book: 350 poems of OML, Book: "Ecstasy... In The Tropics", also several articles of poems published in different newspapers, and magazines. Book: "Legends and stories from Costa Rica and U.S.A."; [pers.] I love the love, I love to write inspired in the life and all the manifestations, I love to sing and write to the love by itself and the women and her beauty. I believe in extraterrestrial life and beings, we are not alone in the universe.; [a.] Paterson City, NY

MAGARIEL, DANNY A.
[b.] March 12, 1984, Kansas City, MO; [p.] Harold Stephen Magariel; [ed.] 7th grade, Hyman Brand Academy; [occ.] Student; [oth. writ.] 1st published; [pers.] I have been influenced by my father. I hoped people can learned things from my writings and be encouraged to express their feelings and thoughts; [a.] Olathe, KS

MAJORS, JESSICA
[b.] August 4, 1971, Bataka, NY; [p.] Jerrold and Melanie Majors; [ed.] High School - Caledonia Mumford Central School, College - Genesee Community College;

[occ.] Infant/Toddler Teacher at Community Gospel Church and Daycare; [hon.] Urbon League of Rochester Black Scholar Award, Certified in First, Aid and CPR, completed Infant, Toddler Workshop; [oth. writ.] I have several unpublished poems I have written over the last 10 year.; [pers.] My poems are based on the every day trail's and tribulations in my life. All of my poems are original and from my heart. My inspirations are Anthony Beans and my family.; [a.] Caledonia, NY

MALDONADO, STEVEN
[b.] August 24, 1977, Visalia, CA; [p.] Janette Semous, Louis Maldonado; [occ.] Aspiring Young Writer; [pers.] I attempt to expose the plights involved with being sane within an insane world through my own experiences and revelations. I have been influenced by everyone that has so much as spoken one word to me within my lifetime.; [a.] Exeter, CA

MALES, TAMMY
[b.] May 6, 1959, Sacramento; [p.] George and Maxine Kammerer; [m.] Tom Males, April 1, 1988; [ch.] Jeremy Males; [ed.] High School graduate; [occ.] Avon Representative; [hon.] Editors Choice Award; [oth. writ.] This Man, Hello My Love; [pers.] Live life to the fullest, its the only one you have.; [a.] West Sacramento, CA

MALLONN, BRIAN
[pen.] Oscar Nicholas, Jr.; [b.] October 9, 1963, New York, NY; [p.] Hubert Mallonn, Evelyn Mallonn; [ch.] Kyle Mallonn; [occ.] United State Postal Service, Ft. Lauderdale, FL; [pers.] My son is my life and I am his. Together we can make every day brighter. I love you, Kyler.; [a.] Coconut Creek, FL

MALTZ, LAURA
[b.] June 3, 1983, Boston, MA; [p.] Karen Maltz, Jeffery Maltz; [ed.] 8th grade, Robert Van Wyck J.H.S.; [occ.] Student; [hon.] Scholarship and citizenship awards; [oth. writ.] I have written a number of unpublished poems.; [pers.] I write poetry to express my thoughts in a magical way. I write my poems about nature to animate the life force; [a.] Briarwood, NY

MANN, TIFFNEY
[b.] August 25, 1977, Los Angeles, CA; [p.] Lani Munn and Mcke Munn; [ed.] Booker High School, Mote Marine Intern, and MCC; [occ.] Cashier; [hon.] This may not seam on one of your great bronze but means a lot to me. I was chosen to represent Sarasota in an environmental conference. I was also able to give a presentation.; [oth. writ.] This poem just happen to be why not thing. You know curiosity in.; [pers.] "Man cannot begin to grow if there is no room on the shelf for a new idea". To every child there is encourage this poem and all my dreams our dedicated to my mentors my mother and father.; [a.] Sarasota, FL

MANTECON, VALERIE H.
[b.] February 22, 1941, Providence, RI; [ed.] Ph.D. from Pacifica Graduate Institute in Carpinteria, CA, in clinical Psychology; [occ.] Marriage and Family Therapist - Private Practice in Mission Viejo, CA; [memb.] Association of Women in Psychology, California Association of Marriage and Family Therapists; [oth. writ.] Poems published in local newspapers, article and poem in Professional Journals; [pers.] I write of themes reflecting those things that matter to the soul of individuals and of The Natural World.; [a.] Laguna Niguel, CA

MARCAK, MICHELLE LYNNE
[b.] January 19, 1974, Deming, NM; [ch.] Jeffrey

Marcak; [ed.] Graduated from Garfield High in January 1992, Graduating from Jr. College (Major - English) with A.A. in 1997; [occ.] Currently working in English Center as a Tutor; [hon.] Received Scholarship Award for Outstanding Academic Achievement in April 1996; [oth. writ.] Poem "My Captivity" published in anthology "Etchings in the Sand" in 1996. 100 poems to date, plus limericks, shorts stories, articles and screenplays etc.; [pers.] (Limericks #7) Somewhere beyond a golden hill, exists the knowledge of God's will. To seek it out would be a true conquest. If any one man...could stand the test.; [a.] San Diego, CA

MARCHETTO-RYAN, NORA
[b.] December 26, 1984, Ridgewood, NJ; [p.] Sharon Marchetto, Charles Ryan; [ed.] Highland School, Midland Park, N.J.; [occ.] Student - Grade 6; [memb.] Midland Park Soccer, (Capt. of her soccer team), Midland Park Jr. Football Assoc. Cheerleader, M.P. Basketball Assoc., M.P. Softball, plays clarinet - Highland School Band; [pers.] Loves reading, sports, writing, the numerous pets in her family. Nora is the youngest of four children in her family. She has 3 older brothers.; [a.] Midland Park, NJ

MARKHAM, DANIELLE MARIE
[b.] March 30, 1987, Pueblo, CO; [p.] Linda and Vernon Markham; [memb.] Kaleidoscope "Gifted Childrens Program"; [hon.] 2 Spelling, 5 Reading, 3 Kaleidoscope, Citizenship Award, Penmanship Award; [pers.] I enjoy writing poems it clears my mind.; [a.] Broken Arrow, OK

MARKS, RITA
[b.] May 31, 1953, San Mateo, CA; [p.] Joseph and Sarah Marks; [ch.] Lazet Howard and Tanesha Howard; [ed.] Canada College, Redwood City, CA - AA degree, College of Norte Dame, Belmont, CA - expect Computer science degree in 1998; [occ.] Sr. Admin., Asst./Purchasing Agent at Sun Microsystems, Inc., in Mountain View, CA; [memb.] Member of Fremont Bible Fellowship Church in Fremont, CA; [hon.] Dean's list - twice, American Business Women's Scholarship - three tines, Redwood City Citizen's Scholarship, Canada College Scholarship, Bay Area Urban League Scholarship; [oth. writ.] Self, Rare Bird, Who Was That?, The Love, Life, I Want You. Unpublished poems are: The Mountain, What is Love, The Joy You Bring, and various others.; [pers.] All the honor, praises thankfulness, and blessings go to God for providing me with this talent to share with others. I thank my daughter for their love.; [a.] East Palo Alto, CA

MARSHALL-WHITE, ELEANOR
[b.] July 31, Sycamore, IL; [p.] Thomas M. and Lucy Scales White; [ch.] Lucy Weiger Ogle Barbara, Weiger Lepke Sims, Ralph James Weiger, Jr.; [ed.] BA DePauw Univ., MA in Eng. Univ. of South Carolina at Columbia; [occ.] Teacher of Eng. at Glendale Community College, Glendale, AZ 85302; [memb.] American Association of University Women, Daughters of the American Revolution, Alpha Gamma Delta, Church of the Advent in Episcopal; [hon.] Who's Who in American Education, 1992-1993 Ed.; [oth. writ.] Vantage Press published book in 1991 Women: Catalysts for Change, Interpretive Biographies of Shirley St. Hill Chisholm, Sandra Day O'Connor, and Nancy Landon Kassebaum; [pers.] "The future belongs to those who believe in the beauty of their dreams." Evans Roosevelt; [a.] Sun City West, AZ

MARTEL, JAMES R.
[b.] February 8, 1976, Sanford, ME; [p.] Raymond and Linda Martel; [ed.] Sanford High School, Current Student of Liberty University, Studying Public Speaking.;

[occ.] Student; [memb.] U.S. Army Reserve New Man Club, Liberty Universities Catholic Club; [hon.] Eagle Scout; [oth. writ.] Several essays and speeches about the need for Christian unity; [pers.] I want my writing to have a positive effect on my fellow man. I write about the most important things in the world. Love, life and the trials that we face while we pursues success. I thank God because without Him this poem would not have been possible.; [a.] Springvale, ME

MARTIN, JUDITH
[b.] October 13, 1971; [p.] Diana Sherman, Larry Sherman; [m.] Nicholas Martin, March 5, 1994; [ch.] Rebecca J. Martin, Jared E. Q. Martin; [ed.] Monta Vista High School, Cupertino, CA; [occ.] Litigation Copier, Legal copies int. Denver, CO; [oth. writ.] Two poems published in the Urban Peak news letter, Denver, CO; [pers.] My desire to write, and express myself is do to two men in my life. Gordon McLaughlin, my high school teacher, and Gordon McAdam, my grandfather. My ambition is entirely do to my Mother, Diane.; [a.] Denver, CO

MARTIN, MICHELLE
[b.] May 31, 1983, Saint Paul, MN; [p.] Patrice and Cort Martin; [ed.] Currently an eight grade student at Expo Middle School; [occ.] Student; [pers.] You'll never see the light if you've never met the darkness.; [a.] Saint Paul, MN

MARTINEZ, ANN
[b.] April 26, 1946, Bronx, NY; [p.] John Cudmore, Mary Cudmore; [m.] Nelson Martinez; [ch.] Phillip, Theresa, Michael, Neil, Ann Marie, Lauren; [ed.] St. Pius V H.S., College of New Rochelle - School of New Resources; [occ.] Telephone Operator at St. Barnabas Hospital Bronx, NY; [oth. writ.] Some spiritual poems, others ace quite personalized. One of which was published in "The St. Barnabas Newsletter".; [pers.] I enjoy writing about real people, events and circumstances in poetic form.; [a.] Bronx, NY

MARTINEZ, BOB G.
[b.] June 7, 1949, Las Vegas, NM; [p.] Mrs. Mary Jane Martinez; [m.] Annette (Poopsie), February 10, 1973; [ch.] Lita (College Student, 19); [ed.] Denver North High School Graduated in 1968; [occ.] Security Guard at the Denver Merchandise Mart; [memb.] Distinguished Member of ISP-NLP: Columbine Poets of Colorado: and the Mile High Chapter Society; [hon.] Received the "Most Handsome Little Mexican Poet this side of the Colorado River" award this year from my dear wife, Annette, and my precious daughter, Lita; [oth. writ.] Compilation of own poems "Sidetracks" and unbroken single poem depicting my life and times (1949-1994): The poem is over 300 pages.; [pers.] Poetry in my opinion, is best enjoyed when it is well understood and yet conveyed in a pleasant rhythm with rich verbiage.; [a.] Denver, CO

MARTINEZ, MARY A.
[pen.] Angelina Angel; [b.] April 1, 1959, Detroit, MI; [p.] John and Loreen Mayercak; [m.] Divorced; [ch.] David, Lance, Ashley, and Mary; [ed.] Bachelor's in Social Work, Bachelor's in Arts majoring in Theatre, and I am now a graduate student majoring in Theatre; [occ.] I am the founder and the Director of "The Theatre Tour Program"; [memb.] Notable American Women and The World Who's Who of Women; [hon.] 1989/90 Mrs. Beautiful National Titleholder, 1988 Mrs. Beautiful State Titleholder, I was I of the 2,000 Notable American Women, in the World Who's Who of Women 1992/93 Book; [oth. writ.] I write fables titled, "Angelina And

The Angel". I have also wrote children's' stories titled", "Believe in the Magic of Who You Are, We Cannot Accept Not Trying, school, and Large and in Charge."; [pers.] I try very hard to reveal love for self, love for spirituality, love for others, peace, serenity, and total acceptance of self and others in my work in life, writing, acting, family, and myself.; [a.] Okemos, MI

MARTINEZ, TRELANE
[pen.] Zero; [b.] November 30, 1976, Jacobi Hospital, Bronx, NY; [p.] Carmen I. Rodriguez; [ed.] Truman High School T.C.I.; [occ.] Sales Person at the Disney Store; [hon.] District Attorney Citation of Honor, Service Award; [oth. writ.] Short Stories printed in my school paper the truman times; [pers.] I have discovered that the hardest thing in my life to do is say goodbye, but it is a beautiful feeling to say hello all over again.; [a.] Bronx, NY

MASON, NEIL
[b.] July 15, 1959, Milwaukee, WI; [p.] Robert Mason and Marcia Mason; [ch.] Cory Mason and Justin Mason; [ed.] 2 yrs. College, Cal. State Northridge, Northridge California; [occ.] Self Employed, Sales C Jam Industries; [oth. writ.] Oregon And Unicorn, Sea Jam, Rich And Ruthless, all in works not published; [pers.] I believe through faith in Jesus all things are possible. It is time for all people to love one another and help each other to over come our troubled times; [a.] Torrance, CA

MASOTTO, TERESA
[pen.] Teresa Rose; [b.] May 15, 1976, Patchogue, NY; [p.] Constantino and Emily Masotto; [ed.] Shoreham-Wading River High, St. Joseph's College; [occ.] Student at St. Joseph's College majoring in English/Computers; [memb.] Peer advising, I participated in many community efforts to benefit the homeless and disabled/disadvantaged children.; [hon.] Dean's List; [oth. writ.] I've enjoyed to write for as long as I can remember, but this is the first time I've shared my work with the public.; [pers.] Words are like keys - when understood they unlock a doorway that leads to someone's soul.; [a.] Shoreham, NY

MASTRACCHIO, MARIA MICHELA
[b.] March 22, 1949, Sayre, PA; [p.] Mr. and Mrs. Michael Mastracchio; [ed.] Sayre Area High School, Maria Regina College Syr. NY, D'Youville College, Buffalo NY, University College Syr. NY. Regents Degree, University of State of NY, '82, Master Degree Sunny Oswego, Oswego NY '89; [occ.] Elementary Teacher, Syracuse City School District '86-'96; [memb.] Am in my 26th year of Teaching.; [pers.] "To teach is to touch the future" K.M. I've always loved this quote Krista. Children are our future. We are to hold them lovingly, guide them gently and teach them aim high and reach their dreams.; [a.] Syracuse, NY

MATHIS, GEVEN J.
[b.] February 20, 1929, Milwaukee; [p.] Chester (Deceased), Iola Mielke; [ch.] Two daughters and 2 grandson; [ed.] BFA - University of Thisensin Milwaukee MA - Webster College; [occ.] Retired; [memb.] Past President of artists Equity, Denver, Colo. Chapter; [hon.] Many awards for my art work; [oth. writ.] Autumn Trees - poem published 1994, Kaleidoscopic published 1963; [pers.] I have been an artist since 1962, have had paintings, sculpture and graphics accepted and displayed in many juried shows in Milwaukee, these and Denver, Colo.

MATTHEWS, ANNA
[b.] October 3, 1979, Florence, SC; [p.] Max and Jane Matthews; [ed.] Carolina Academy and Williamsburg

Academy; [occ.] Student; [memb.] Scranton Baptist Church, Soft Ball, Tennis, Drama Club, Cheerleader; [hon.] UCA all star cheer leader; [a.] Scranton, SC

MATTIOLI, RITA
[pen.] Rita Mattioli; [b.] June 1, 1954, Bronx, NY; [p.] Clarice Rietveldt Mattioli and Constantine Mattioli; [ch.] Stephen Rubeo; [ed.] Monroe College; [occ.] Office Manager in a city hospital; [hon.] President's and Dean's List, Community Achievement Award, Photojournalism Contributions for school publications, social events and guest speakers; [oth. writ.] Dawn Of Life And Joy, Whales, The Lady Who Wore Fur In God's House, Several articles published in Monroe College Newspaper School Talk; [pers.] "Nothing is so strong as gentleness. Nothing so gentle as real strength". In my writing I try to capture the real strength of humanity, gentleness.; [a.] Bronx, NY

MATTOX, BRANDEN GENE
[b.] November 27, 1982, Baltimore, MD; [p.] Mrs. Fernell Mattox and Mr. Bonnie Gene Mattox; [ed.] Dr. Martin Luther King Elem., Fallstaff Middle School and I'm in the 9th Grade at Forest Park High School; [occ.] Student; [hon.] 1st Runner-Up for Dramatic Reading Boy Scouts Merr. and Badges; [oth. writ.] I Shall Be A Warrior, Glory Star, Finale, Kenya, Closet Monster; [a.] Baltimore, MD

MAU, SARA
[b.] June 21, 1979, Cedar Rapids, IA; [p.] Bill, Dorrene Mau; [ed.] Senior-Kennedy H.S. part time student - Kirk Wood College full time student - Minneapolis School of Art; [occ.] Private Pilot and Receptionist at Marion Airport; [memb.] National Honor Society, Nat'l Assoc. Women in Aviation Metro Credit Union Jr. Board; [hon.] Who's Who in American High School Nat'l Council Youth Leadership; [oth. writ.] Several poems published in Iowa Poets; [pers.] Always soar with the eagles; [a.] Palo, IA

MAYES, SONCERIA
[pen.] Sonni; [b.] October 11, 1977, Houston; [p.] Sharon Jackson; [m.] James Jackson, August 12, 1995; [ch.] Ericka Mayes and S. Mayes; [ed.] High School Grad. MacArthur High; [occ.] Student at Local Community College North Harris; [memb.] Speech and Debate, Drama, Business Professionals of America; [hon.] Working on it; [pers.] I want to examine all aspects of life and to help through writing about emotion and love with God's help and wisdom; [a.] Houston, TX

MBAMARA, OLIVER
[pen.] C. J. Oliver; [b.] December 14, 1966, Nigeria; [p.] Sir Laz Ekejiuba (KSJ), Suzy Ekejiuba; [ed.] LLB (Hons) University of Lagos, BL. (Barrister At Law) Nigerian Law School; [occ.] Law; [memb.] Nigerian Bar Association, Eckankar - Religion of the light and sound of God, Amnesty International E.T.C.; [hon.] Private; [oth. writ.] Several dramatic scripts, poems and, poetic drama or dramatic poetry; [pers.] It is my humble intention to help others look within, realize themselves, understand life, and above all, utilize the essence of that great being within, hence my poems reflect the laws of Eck (ie the laws of spirit).; [a.] Bronx, NY

MCALISTER, JAMES
[b.] April 9, 1983, Florence; [p.] Renee and Robert McAlister; [ed.] Ronald E. McNair Junior High Eighth Grade; [memb.] Lake City Church of God Band, Junior Beta Club; [hon.] Superior in Band, Top 10 in Math Class, Presidential Fitness Award; [oth. writ.] Several other writings in school and made A's on all of them;

[pers.] I like to help people imagine a new better place to live and play. I was influenced by the early Chinese poetry.; [a.] Scranton, SC

MCARDLE, MICHAEL A.
[b.] December 2, 1978, Pompton Plains, NJ; [p.] Thomas J. McArdle Jr., Barbara Stevens McArdle; [ed.] Preparing for College; [occ.] Student; [hon.] It is an honor to have my first poem published!; [oth. writ.] "Sinking Confusion", "Headline Dreams", other works-in-progress; [pers.] My poetry reflects what I'm feeling deep inside. I write about what is close to me, influenced by life's events and music.; [a.] Lincoln Park, NJ

MCCARRON, CAREY
[b.] August 29, 1975, National City, CA; [p.] Gary and Shirley McCarron; [occ.] Administrative Assistant For GWM Insurance Brokers; [memb.] Western Hills Baptist Church; [pers.] I express what passes behind my eyes.; [a.] Boerne, TX

MCCARTNEY, MYRON
[b.] May 24, 1957, Little Rock, AR; [p.] Marvin L. and Marjorie F. McCartney; [m.] Dawn, March 31, 1996; [ch.] 3 and 3 stepchildren; [ed.] High School - 11th; [occ.] Disable; [memb.] Church of Christ; [hon.] Scouting; [oth. writ.] Poems - none published yet; [pers.] I strive to reflect "Love"; [a.] North Little Rock, AR

MCCHESNEY, ANDREA D.
[b.] July 8, 1981, Newton; [p.] Neil and Sandra McChesney; [ed.] Hesston Elementary School, Hesston Middle School, Hesston High School; [occ.] High School Student right now, I want to be a writer; [oth. writ.] My other poems that I have written in the last two years. I have about 50 or 60; [pers.] Being in High School I strive to study hard and play sports. I also spend my time writing about things I feel. My feelings are very important in my poetry. I was inspired to write poetry by personal experience. Although my favorite writers are Edgar Allan Poe and Langston Hughes. I would like to dedicate this pome to Matt who inspired me. And to my best friend Alisha, who gave me the address and believed in me.; [a.] Hesston, KS

MCCLAIN, GWENDOLYN D.
[b.] January 31, 1943, Detroit, MI; [p.] Ervin Frances Williams; [m.] Emmitt L. McClain, October 10, 1963; [ch.] Darryl, Rochelle, Leonardo, Eric, Shawn, Glenn; [ed.] High School, 2 yrs. Nursing School; [occ.] Safety Officer for the State of Michigan; [memb.] First Miss. Bapt. Church M.E.S.A. of Michigan; [hon.] Safety Officer Award, Gospel Sounds Music Award; [oth. writ.] Poems published for obituaries, short plays in school. Drawings and special notes for posters.; [pers.] I write about things I see and hear. I pay close attention to my feelings in everything I write. I'm inspired by the early poets, as though I were there with them, learning from them.; [a.] Belleville, MI

MCCLINTOCK, JEFFREY JAMES
[b.] July 31, 1962, Denver, CO; [p.] Jim and Peggy McClintock; [ch.] Kyle, Erin; [ed.] Metro State College of Denver, American Institute of Applied Science; [memb.] American Academy of Forensic Science, International Association for Identification; [hon.] Photographs Published Best of Photography 1988 and 1989, other photo's published magazines and newspapers; [pers.] Cathaleen Marie Godfrey-Donnelly you are the greatest gift I've been given. May God bless you, the father who created love and the spirit that plays the pipes.; [a.] Littleton, CO

MCCLISH, EYRLIS
[b.] July, 1919, Bellingham, WA; [m.] May 1949; [ch.] Three; [ed.] U of Washington, Grad. School of Physical Therapy, Stanford Univ.; [occ.] Retired Physical Therapist; [pers.] "Posy Smellers of bike trips" goes back to August, 1975 when four of us gals - in our 50's - took a club wagon loaded with bikes, sleeping bags, and food, and went up, to a cabin above Granite Falls, Washington. The first day was lovely, but the second and third days were more like fall, and we thought a couple of the showers were more like cloud-burst. We were dressed for rain. And we went 25 or 30 miles each day. This poem could apply to many other bike trips through the years. Hostels - "inexpensive overnight accommodation for young people from 4 to 94, traveling under their own steam" - came to the Pacific Northwest in 1938, and before long the Pacific Northwest Cycling Association was organized. Someone commented on the "conflict of interest" between the racers and the "posy smellers"- not withstanding, the PNCA still meets, "friendships that we cherish" has real meaning. As for me, now I'm 77 and I push up all the hills. By the way "Eyrlis" is pronounced Tr'lis!; [a.] Issaquah, WA

MCCLURE, REGINA
[b.] November 13, 1969, Baltimore, MD; [p.] Herman McClure, Irene McClure; [ed.] International Beauty School, Fleet Business School; [occ.] Cosmetologist; [pers.] My poems are inspired by my journeys in life, they are based on emotions, and come truly from my heart.

MCCONE, HENRY E.
[pen.] Henry E. McCone; [b.] February 13, 1918, Camden, NV; [p.] Harry - Ida; [m.] Marjorie, June 1944; [ch.] Thomas, Scott, Doughs, Robert; [ed.] Swarthmore College Univ. of Pennsylvania; [occ.] Retired Teacher; [a.] Wayne, PA

MCCORD, GEORGE E.
[b.] February 3, 1918, Altoona, PA; [ch.] Jane; [ed.] Dania FL. Altoona High School 1935, Williamson School 1938; [occ.] A trust working in Burnt Clay 47 years retired IE Bricklayer; [memb.] Mensa - VFW 10539; [a.] Okeechobee, FL

MCCORMICK, BARBARA A.
[pen.] Bad Mc; [b.] March 1, 1965, Providence, RI; [p.] Nicholas and Avis DiLorenzo; [m.] Robert J. McCormick, May 30, 1987; [ch.] Nichole - 7, Jessica - 6, Jackie - 5; [ed.] G.E.D. CCRI Composition one CCRI; [occ.] Poet and Mother; [hon.] Editors Choice Award for Poems. "Brassrail" and "Grind"; [oth. writ.] A book I wrote called "A Breathe of Rhyme" containing 250 poems; [pers.] What lasts forever if not love.; [a.] Johnston, RI

MCCORMICK, BRIAN
[b.] November 9, 1962, New York; [p.] John McCormick, Carol Nesbit; [ed.] Herricks High School, Suny Binghamton, The New School for Social Research; [occ.] Senior Training Analyst, TIAA-CREF; [memb.] Association of Independent Video and Film Makers; [hon.] New York City Mayor's Volunteer Action Award; [oth. writ.] Poems published in magazines and used for performance, dance reviews for local community newspaper.; [pers.] Poetry gives way to simple language, there is nothing that cannot be said.; [a.] Brooklyn, NY

MCCUISTON, LESLIE
[b.] December 12, 1951, Dayton, TN; [p.] Arnold C. Wilkey, Mary Lee Hall; [m.] Bertram B. McCuiston III (Dead), October 13, 1968; [ch.] Lee Anne Schafer, Susie

Price, Bertram B. IV; [ed.] Graduate of Rhea County High School GED test taken; [occ.] Grill cook at Frontier Restaurant; [oth. writ.] None except two more poems I have entered in contests; [pers.] Never give up all things are possible, win or lose as long as you have done your best, you have accomplished it all.; [a.] Dayton, TN

MCCULLOUGH, JENNIFER
[b.] November 17, 1973, Maumee, OH; [p.] Pamela L. Thebeau; [m.] Jerry McCullough, June 23, 1992; [ch.] Christa Lee, Melinda Devona, Joseph Ray D., Erin Briana; [ed.] Stratford High School; [occ.] Homemaker; [memb.] Tall Pines Baptist Church; [hon.] Who's Who in American High Schools; [pers.] I wrote the poem for my husband, Jerry, when we were dating.; [a.] Ladson, SC

MCDANIEL, MRS. STEPHANIE
[pen.] Steph; [b.] April 30, 1972, Keesler Air Force Base, Biloxi, MS; [p.] Edward and Genevieve Thompson; [m.] Jamie Lee, May 21, 1994; [ch.] Robert Lee; [ed.] Gulfport High School; [occ.] Domestic Goddess; [memb.] The Humane Society of the United States, American Red Cross; [hon.] Who's Who Among American High School Students, graduated with distinction; [oth. writ.] Two poems published in Sparrowgrass Poetry Forum Anthologies; [pers.] Life is a painting in my mind, the paper is my canvas and the pen is my brush.; [a.] Gulfport, MS

MCDONALD, KEVIN
[pen.] Kevin Barry; [b.] March 26, 1966, Bronx, NY; [p.] Michael and Vera McDonald; [ch.] Eilis Everdeen McDonald; [ed.] NYU School of Film Regis High School, Riverdale Country School Grammar School; [occ.] Director of Film Studies at Columbia U.; [memb.] American Civil Liberties Union, National Endowment for the Arts, Museum of Natural History; [hon.] Father of the Year 1993, Outstanding Citizen 1994, Young Publishers Award New York Times 1995; [oth. writ.] Enter the Dragon, Mortal Choices. The Storm. Snake Eyes. Bitter Heart. Born and Breed.; [pers.] Your life is a journey. The people you meet is the lesson. Your travels is the course. Learn your lesson well.; [a.] New York, NY

MCDOWELL, KATHLEEN
[b.] February 17, 1931, Perrysburg, OH; [m.] Widowed; [ch.] Jamie, Kimber, Lori; [ed.] Perrysburg High, St. Vincents Medical Center, Toledo, and R. N. Lourdes College - Sylvania, OH; [occ.] R. N. and Semi-Retired R. N. since 1952; [memb.] Zion Lutheran Church, Nature Conservancy, Environmental Defense Fund, Amnesty International; [oth. writ.] Have been writing and journaling as long as I can remember - never to published only in small local newsletters.; [pers.] Words spoken into my heart and mind as I experience life - often I find this need to catch hold of them on paper.; [a.] Deerfield Beach, FL

MCELROY, HARRIETTE BROWNING
[pen.] Harriette Browning McElroy; [b.] January 8, 1943, West Virginia; [p.] Myrtle Stephenson and Harry Browning; [m.] Robert H. McElroy, May 8, 1957; [ch.] Robert, Sherry and Brooke; [ed.] Jr. High School, no formal training, attended school in West Virginia, Houston, Texas and Cleveland, Ohio; [occ.] Housewife, in spare time I enjoy writing, drawing, sewing, and working with house plants.; [hon.] Golden Poet Award for Poem "Memory" in 1991; [oth. writ.] Numerous poetry, nothing published; [pers.] I started writing Poetry when I was 8 years old. My favorite Poets are Elizabeth Barrett and Robert Browning, Writing takes me to other worlds, which is nice, for a change.; [a.] Wallisville, TX

MCEVOY, FRAN
[pen.] Fran McEvoy; [b.] August 7, 1960, Queens, NY; [p.] Mom and Dad; [m.] Mom or Dad; [ch.] Nieces and Nephews; [ed.] Life and Schools, AAS - Suffolk Community College Seldem NY 5/93 Communications/Media Arts, BS - LI Univ (CW Post) Brookville NY Journalism Film Making (Minor) 9/95; [occ.] Undetermined - but all that matters is that I enjoy it all, in some way.; [memb.] No thanks. I used to play little league though. Led the league in strike outs and I wasn't pitching!; [hon.] Cum Laude, PHI ETA long Island Univ (CW Post) 1995, Phi Theta Kappa, Pi Alpha Sigma Suffolk Community College 1993, Most improved Bower: Aug. went from 70 to 104 in that league I was in a few years ago. Not bad they told me; [oth. writ.] Plenty of long letters to my brother in Fort Hood TX. Press releases - News day and various Long Island Local papers.; [pers.] Depending upon how you pay, the express line doesn't move a whole lot faster than the lines for 15 - 20 or more items.; [a.] Holbrook, NY

MCGANN, AGNES B.
[b.] July 7, 1922, Indianapolis, IN; [p.] Joseph and Mary Walter; [m.] Edmund McGann, April 11, 1942; [ch.] Stephen McGann, Greg, Tom, Joe; [ed.] I graduated High School; [occ.] Novice Poet; [memb.] YWCA Chorus St. Lawrence Church, Muncie Poetry Club, RSVP - Senior Volunteer Org.; [oth. writ.] Written 25, poems since joining poetry club in February 1996; [pers.] Self taught I never attempted writing until this year, never assuming I could. I love it. Have had a lot of good responses to my writing and suggestions that I pursue it further.; [a.] Muncie, IN

MCGARRY, LINDA MARIE
[b.] October 27, 1949, Bradford, PA; [p.] Allen H. Somers, Mary A. Somers; [m.] Patricia J. McGarry Sr., December 31, 1972; [ed.] Graduate of Bradford Senior High School in Bradford, PA (1967); [occ.] Company names "Our time is your time", self-employed, owner of a business that helps people in needy situations; [pers.] "Life's perplexities give rise to definitions of strange contradictions!" And as a North American Indian of the Ojibwa Tribe - this publication reflects me proud heritage!!

MCGEE, EDITH
[pen.] Catherin McGee; [b.] Police Department; [p.] Edith McGee; [ch.] 5 birth children; [ed.] H.S., business school; [occ.] I work for police I am retired now; [hon.] I wrote one poem. Too the president Bill Clinton homeless speak out; [oth. writ.] I have several poems. I wrote all kinds. I love my work.; [pers.] I strive to send a message to all people of love and feeling. That our dreams can come true. Dream forever; [a.] New York, NY

MCGINNIS, DAWNING
[b.] February 20, 1996, Tillamook, OR; [p.] Kate Atkins, Ron Atkins; [ed.] I went to high school for about two weeks then I got kicked out for never going and smoking in the parking lot, I went to rehab and now I go to Portland Community College.; [pers.] I am a 15 year old port and have been writing since I was about to spell. My poetry reflects my world and I have been through, I'm a teen dealing with a drug addiction, I was molested as a child, I was raped at age 14, and I'm dealing with teenage life.; [a.] Toalatin, OR

MCHENRY, TAMMY J.
[b.] March 30, 1976, Tulsa, OK; [p.] Ronnie McHenry-Chuck and Karla Christy; [pers.] I have my family and friends to thank for my poetry, they told me never to give

up. Jenny Lee, Travis, Adam, Mom, Dad, Chuck (step father, and last but not least Bon Bon. Thank You.; [a.] OK

MCKEE, JERALD A.
[b.] December 8, 1938, Nebraska; [p.] Mike McKee, Gretchen Gorr McKee; [m.] Georgann McKee, October 21, 1961; [ch.] Whitney Jo McKee Krick, Kacey Lynn McKee Spetner; [ed.] Jr. College; [occ.] Building Contractor; [memb.] St. Johns Lotheran Church, Prado Hill Men's Club (golf); [hon.] High school and Jr. College award in Football, baseball, track, basketball, adult golf - hole in 1; [oth. writ.] Only 1 poem to my wife; [pers.] The poem was written the day we received info re - Tom's death in Vietnam. Tom volunteered and was serving his 3rd tour; [a.] Santa Ana, CA

MCKEE, LUCIE
[b.] August 14, 1932, Brussels, Belgium; [p.] Ferdinand Mayer, Katherine Mayer; [m.] James M. Toolan M.D., May 15, 1995; [ch.] Katharine Coburn, Josephine McKee; [ed.] Smith College BA, Bennington College MFA; [occ.] Writing Full time; [hon.] A poem was included in Anthology of Magazines Verse/fear book of American Poetry, Alan F. Pater, ed.; [oth. writ.] Poems love appeared in the scream review, the new renaissance, Puerto Del Sol, footwork and other.; [pers.] I like words: The rhythms combinations of hem woke, the meanings, particular to poetry, found in those rhythms, so for me, the writing of poems is to fly in the weather, often blindly through clouds, the bumps of turbulence, then, suddenly, the sight of an entire city.; [a.] Pennington, VT

MCKEY, THERESA J.
[pen.] T. McKey; [b.] May 31, 1953, Kansas City, MO; [p.] Marion and Shirley McKey; [m.] Divorced; [ch.] Angel and Andy Brown; [ed.] Turner High School, K.C. KS; [occ.] Waitress; [oth. writ.] Personal poems to people I love and about past experiences; [pers.] I've lived in a negative world for 40 years. Three years ago I met ny hero, he has taught me the positive aspects in life. Now I can reflect on the past with fewer tears. Thank you Rick.; [a.] Stockton, MO

MCKNIGHT, HILDA GENTRY
[b.] July 16, 1935, Person County, NC; [p.] George T. and Sally M. Gentry; [m.] Divorced; [ch.] Bart Thomas McKnight; [ed.] Allensville School, Bethel Hill High School, Berry College, Rome, GA, Carson - Newman College, Jefferson City, TN; [occ.] Retired Teacher - 34 yrs. 6-8 grades, Language Arts, Social Studies, Chorus, Creative Arts, Science, Math, Title I Reading; [memb.] Writers Group of the Triad, Greensboro, NC, Alpha Delta Kappa International Fine Arts Comm: Art Component, Hillcrest Golf Assn., Clemmons Moravian Church, Teachers Bowling League; [hon.] 1976 - Teachers of the Year for the Winston-Salem, Forsyth County School System, 1978- TOY for WS/FC School System, 1995 - Semi-finalist TOY for WS/FC Schools (my last year of teaching), Demonstrated moravian Star-making at the Smithsonian's Museum of Amer. History - 1979, 1995, 1990 and N.C. Museum of History 1995-1996, Alpha Delta Kappa International Fine Arts Comm. 1995-2000; [oth. writ.] "Dream Job" published in No Grownups Allowed; [pers.] Poetry is the inner self trying to express deep emotions which cannot be expressed in everyday language.; [a.] Winston-Salem, NC

MCLEAN, HOPE
[pen.] L. H. McLean; [b.] June 5, 1979, Florence, SC; [p.] Kit and Lynda McLean; [ed.] Graduated from the Carolina Academy. Currently attending Francis Marion

University; [occ.] Student; [memb.] National Beta Club, National Honor Roll, South Lynches Fire Department Station Two; [hon.] South Carolina Junior Scholar, Honor Graduate, Editor of School Newspaper, VFW "Answering America's Call" Essay Finalist; [pers.] I try to express the simplicities of children and the complexities of nature in my poems. I have been greatly influenced by Lucy Maud Montgomery.; [a.] Coward, SC

MCLEAN, VIVIAN JAINE
[b.] October 21, 1981, Atlanta, GA; [p.] William Y. McLean Jr., and Vivian Barrios McLean; [pers.] Regret is the least worthwhile emotion conceivable. Be careful as you fall in love, but never regret.; [a.] Lilburn, GA

MCLESTER, CANDI
[pen.] Carol McLester and Candi McLester; [b.] January 18, 1948, Norfolk, VA; [p.] Raymond and Shirley Datson; [m.] Robert Gibson McLester III, December 26, 1969; [ch.] Robin Gayle and Bonnie Jean, Grandchildren: Kayla, Amber Harris and Bobby McDaniel; [ed.] 111 Ed University of FIA; [occ.] Homemaker - former teacher; [memb.] ISP; [hon.] Editors Choice Award from National Library of Poetry I was honored to implement the writer's workshop program in a DOD school in Grantanamo Bay Cuba which I started with Junior High School Students and later carried the program stateside to high school students. It was very successful; [oth. writ.] My personal volume "Of Rattle Shakes and Cakes" my writings appear in, Rainbow End, Best Poetry of the 90's.; [pers.] I have taught English is stated and overseas for 17 years. I have found that the range of human emotions crosses all man made demarcation and there is unity in the sharing of the emotions. I strive to capture these emotions though word and sound so that all feel connection rather than solution.; [a.] Vero Beach, FL

MCNEIL, KEVIN
[b.] January 30, 1986, Brooklyn; [p.] Latina McNeil, Kevin Morgan; [ed.] 5th grade; [pers.] Love writing and drawing

MCNEIL, RONALD A.
[b.] September 22, 1948; [p.] Scottish L. Cherokee; [m.] Widower; [ed.] Muskingum Tech. Merritt College; [occ.] Self-employed; [oth. writ.] Short stories (SC-71) Poems; [pers.] Would like to share short stories, poems, and oil painting with world and also native American heritage.

MCPHEETERS, JON
[b.] April 6, 1972, Peoria, IL; [p.] Bob and Jan McPheeters; [ed.] Southern Illinois University, Monmouth College; [occ.] TV/Film Production Assistant; [pers.] Good Luck, Good Times, and Good Fishin'.; [a.] Kewanee, IL

MCQUEARY, PEGGY M.
[b.] July 4, 1964, Yokosuka, Japan; [p.] James and Lora McQueary; [ed.] Completed High School at Strawn High School, Strawn, TX Military Police School in the U.S. Army - 9 years spent in the U.S. regular army; [occ.] U.S. Army Reserves Security Guard; [memb.] U.S. Army Reserves; [hon.] Numerous awards from the U.S., Army Military Police Corps, History Award and Art award in High School; [oth. writ.] Unpublished writings; [pers.] Enjoy the attempt to reflect the Gothic atmosphere in my writings. Would love to write a classical novel.; [a.] Fort Worth, TX

MEAKER, KAYE
[pen.] Cicada; [b.] July 27, 1953, Lewisburg, TN; [p.] E. H. and D. O. Horton; [m.] J. W. Meaker, July 17, 1971; [ch.] Amelia and Joseph (2) Grandchildren: Kyle,

Colyn; [ed.] Franklin County High, Winchester, TN; Motlow State Community College, Tullahoma, TN; [pers.] Writing is another way of sharing one's self with others, therefore my sharing is a gift of love to each reader. What a wonderful legacy: My words and thoughts touching others for many decades to come; [a.] Winchester, TN

MEDINA, PAUL H.
[pen.] P. H. Medina; [b.] May 30, 1951, Jersey City, NJ; [p.] Henry and Adolfina (Deceased); [m.] Maritza, September 21, 1987; [ch.] Daniel David, Michael Matthew; [ed.] Bayonne H.S.; [occ.] Metal Inventory Expeditor; [oth. writ.] "Sweeping Down The Plain", "To Your Health", Depth of the Earth, Think of Me, The Children, and others.; [pers.] I either see the beauty in something or the evil If I can write a poem the will touch a heart or a nerve than I have contributed words make ripples and sometimes tidal woves.; [a.] Lakewood, NJ

MEESE, SHARLA
[b.] July 6, 1982, Covington, KY; [p.] Andrew and Judith Meese; [ed.] Patton - Elementary, Winston Churchill - Elementary, Winston Park - Junior High, Palatine High School - currently attends; [occ.] Student; [memb.] Junior Great Books, Yearbook - Winston Park, Chorus - Winston Park, Speech Club - Palatine; [hon.] Young Authors Conference, All American Award, Presidential Award; [pers.] I use my writing as an outlet to my feelings and I write hoping to connect with others.; [a.] Palatine, IL

MENDEZ, KARAN PORTER
[b.] January 23, 1964, Corpus Christi, TX; [p.] William H. Porter and Dorothy Page; [m.] John Mendez; [ch.] Matthew Porter Mendez; [ed.] Computer Degree - Processing, Degree - Child Education; [pers.] My poetry is inspired by the bittersweet challenges and romance of everyday life.; [a.] Houston, TX

MESIA, AUGUSTO F.
[b.] June 6, 1956, Naga City, Philippines; [p.] Simeon Mesia, Salome Fajardo; [m.] Lilia Roseno-Mesia, October 1, 1992; [ed.] Ateneo De Naga, University of the Philippines, University of the East, Suny Brooklyn Health Science Center; [occ.] Anatomic and Clinical Pathologist, NYU Medical Center, Bellevue Hospital Medical School Faculty; [memb.] Diplomate, American Board of Pathology, American Medical Association; [oth. writ.] Scientific Papers; [pers.] Anything good that I accomplish is my offering to God.; [a.] New York, NY

METZ, KATY
[b.] July 24, 1982, Livermore, CA; [p.] Connie and Thomas Metz; [ed.] I'm a High School Freshman, but I wrote "Killer Dead" in the sixth grade; [occ.] Student; [oth. writ.] Many unpublished poems.; [a.] Tracy, CA

MEYERS, STEVEN W.
[pen.] Steven W. Meyers; [b.] January 8, 1971, Earth; [p.] Ann Brown, Jake Meyers Sr.; [m.] Emily L. Meyers, February 14, 1994; [ch.] Dakotah Wayne; [ed.] Harper ISD; [occ.] Ranch Hand; [oth. writ.] Other poems; [pers.] Your only as smart as the people you listen to.; [a.] Stafford, TX

MIELE, ANTHONY
[b.] November 4, 1964, Williamsport, PA; [ed.] BA Film/Video Penn State University; [occ.] Freelance Television Production; [memb.] Society of Children's Book Writers and Illustrators; [oth. writ.] Poem entitled, Journey Published in Quill Books, Dusting Off Dreams, Vol. 111 1994. Also, numerous works for children currently in

progress and seeking publication.; [pers.] My purpose is to awaken within humanity, especially children, the majesty of being and the exalted state that is our birth right. Pure guidance comes only from within and he that would serve most, attains most.; [a.] San Anselmo, CA

MILLER, ANNE H.
[pen.] Anne H. Miller; [b.] November 24, 1907, Amsterdam, NY; [m.] Ralph R. Miller; [ch.] William B. Miller; [ed.] Albany High School, Albany Business College, additional Education in Art of Music; [occ.] Retired artist; [hon.] Won many top honors in Juried shows throughout New York and New England. Art ranged from magazine cover, to college private collection; [pers.] Anne was at the epitome of her art career when her eyesight failed in 1991. At that time she was well known for her beautiful oil and water color Adirondacks and nature paintings. In a short time she became legally blind. She turned to Ham radio and within eighteen months had passed the FCC tests for license classes 'Novice', 'Technician Plus' and 'General', her call sign is KBZRZC. This accomplishment led to a feature full-color article in the daily Gazette of Schenectady, NY. It told about the remarkable achievement of the then 88-year old lady who, was blind, had no electrical or electronic background, had no previous knowledge of Ham radio, passed the stiff tests. Anne is now adding poetry to her endeavors. She feels poetry must now help fill the beauty gap she lost with her sight; [a.] Albany, NY

MILLER, CHRISTIE
[b.] August 7, 1972, Freeport, TX; [p.] Albert L. Hux, Stella Martin; [m.] Dennis R. Miller, February 14, 1994; [ed.] Junction City High School; [memb.] Arthritis Foundation; [pers.] Life provides each with many pleasures. One of mine is derived from the writing of my poetry. I hope that others can receive a small piece of the feelings that my writing provide for me.; [a.] Jonesboro, AR

MILLER, DANIEL
[b.] October 15, 1971, Memphis, TN; [ed.] BA Emory Univ. (History); [a.] Decatur, GA

MILLER, DARA B.
[b.] June 19, 1946, CA; [p.] John and Ila Miller; [ch.] Johnny Marsbach; [occ.] Manager of Metaphysical Bookstore; [oth. writ.] "Just A Memory" published in the anthology " Mists Of Enchantment"; [pers.] I hope to eventually publish a book of my poetry that will inspire and uplift others so that they many find their. Inner strength and self worth.

MILLER, EASTER IOZA
[b.] June 6, 1931, Tyler, TX; [p.] Jewel Lewis and Rosie Lewis; [m.] Divorced, June 9, 1952; [ch.] Easter Hawkins, Cassandra Miller; [ed.] Jackson High School (Tyler, TX) Texas College - BA degree; [occ.] Retired Teacher of 32 years; [memb.] National Educator's Assoc., Delta Sigma Theta Sorority Dukes and Duchesses Scholarship program, Black Caucus - SMCSD California Teachers Association; [hon.] Texas High School State Champion - Track 50 yd dash and 100 yd dash, Red Cross Volunteer Award, Judge-Martin Luther King Essay Contest; [oth. writ.] Not published; [pers.] I always remember the power in prayer. Humanity and human beings always come first. My parents showed and taught me to let my light shine so people will see it. God, family and friends are the reason of my being.; [a.] Columbia, MD

MILLER, JASON
[pen.] Jason Miller, Jason A. M.; [b.] May 5, 1979, Reading, PA; [p.] Emanuel Miller, Joann Miller; [ed.]

Westview High School (Junior) Shipshewana, IN; [occ.] Student, Westview High School, Shipshewana, IN (Junior); [memb.] National Honor Society, Westview Poetry Club; [oth. writ.] Poem published in 12th Annual High School Poetry Anthology, several poems published in Westview High School Poetry Collection; [pers.] Poetry is only a lifelong struggle by which we strive to be completely understood. My deepest yearning is to have my poems reveal my soul in its truest form.; [a.] Middlebury, IN

MILLER, KAREN A.
[b.] May 8, 1965, Newport Beach, CA; [p.] Joe and Irene Coderre; [m.] Robert L. Miller, July 1, 1983; [ch.] Laura and Jake Miller; [ed.] Foothill High, Santa Ana Jr. College; [occ.] Nurses Assistant; [memb.] Poetry Society of America; [oth. writ.] Spiritual book currently in writing; [pers.] I try to share the wisdom and grace of God's love in all my writings.; [a.] Branson, MO

MILLER, MARION E.
[pen.] Mary Lynne; [b.] February 15, 1916 Madison, WI; [p.] Louis C. and Diana H. Hoffman; [m.] James F. Miller Jr., December 20, 1946; [ch.] Scott C. Miller; [ed.] Lowell Elementary, Madison, WI Madison East H.S., Madison WI, University of WI Madison, WI, B.S. MA, Cred Ph.D Univ. of Ill. Urban, Ill.; [occ.] Getting organized to publish my collected writings during all these years.; [memb.] Prof. work Dir. USO- Service Club Serving Fort Lec, VA, Prof. in Drama and Interpretation, Debate Coach Mid-Western Universities, Instructor of Air Corps, Corps WW II, Prof. Speech, U. of Ill. Urbana, Ill.; [hon.] Prof. in University of Wis. at Platteville, Eau Claire and La Crosse, Wis. in Sp. Dept. During my years - active in sports and service work, volunteering during WW II took time!; [oth. writ.] Special education for special students ages to 18. Milwaukee Public Schools at Wis. Frederick J. Gaenslen, Spec. School Milwaukee.; [pers.] To spend my years being happy and making others similarly happy inspiring others for fulfillness in life with God's leading in all results gleaned for all.; [a.] Coral Springs, FL

MILLETTE, WILLIAM H.
[pen.] William H. Millette; [b.] February 15, 1941, Providence, RI; [p.] Art, Ann Millette; [m.] Suzette Millette, July 5, 1992; [ch.] Tim, Theresa; [ed.] A.A., Business Law; [occ.] Asset Manager of Bank of America; [memb.] (1) Past President Traditional Artist Guil, (2) Member of The Musicians/Song Writers Union, (3) Corporate Chairperson For United Way, Bank of America, (4) Corporate Represent for Small Business and Minority Relations - (Coca Cola - Security, Pacic - Bank of America); [hon.] (1) Honorable Mention - "American Song Writing Festival", (S. Calif.) (2) Varies Awards - (Competition) "Traditional Artist Guild", (3) Scholarship Award - "The Los Angeles Art Center", (4) Volunteer Musical Entertainment" varies local charities", (5) Published Photos - articles of creative accomplished local landmark - "Corva Caverns" and waterfall; [oth. writ.] Varies writings/artistic contributions published in local newspaper; [pers.] "Exploring all avenues of your creative talent/abilities, don't limit yourself to one challenge" - don't look back - don't give up - don't be afraid to laugh at yourself, recognize the beauty within you.; [a.] Corona, CA

MILLS, BEVERLY
[pen.] Beverly Browning Mills; [b.] March 24, 1937, Detroit, MI; [p.] Estil Higgins and Grace Browning Higgins; [m.] Don Mills, March 15, 1964; [ch.] Dawn Renea and Jeffrey Lane; [ed.] Goldberg Trade and High School diplomas Acquired-High School and Business,

City and State, graduate of Jefferson Intermediate; [occ.] Homemaker, I was a typist C and C Machinest, credit Dept. Sales girl, Packing Co, School Pictures, I worked on photos and year books, Receptionist, also receptionist and waitress in restaurant; [memb.] Modeled hats for SS Kresge Administration Co. Photo's Stated and Porta Rica; [hon.] Won Awards in newspaper sports contests; [oth. writ.] Poem published in local newspaper; [pers.] I strive to reflect the beauty of our country. I am influenced by the artistry of Currier and Ive's in my pastel drawings of snow scenes. Writing poems with a desire for the talents of Elizabeth Barrett Browning and Robert Browning, which I understand are my ancestors on mothers family tree. I'm working on my family tree. I have a desire to show beauty in my poetry. I have a great love for the beauty and artistry of figure skating.; [a.] Chattanooga, TN

MILLS, LACY
[pen.] "Leaves"; [b.] January 19, 1979, Rockford; [p.] Richard and Cathy Mills; [ed.] Elementary Education at 9 different schools, presently a Senior at Rockford Lutheran High School; [memb.] Grace Lutheran Church, Crusader wrestling team statistician; [hon.] Honor roll, 3 Editor's choice Awards from the national Library of poetry, an award from the office of the sheriff "Visions of Youth" award and nomination by who's who in American High School Students; [oth. writ.] "Yesterday", "A Once Red Rose", "A Memory", "A Rise Of Endless Hope", other poems published in smaller anthologies; [pers.] The voice of my heart speaks dreams through my poetry so that others may knows that they are not alone in this beautiful world of God.; [a.] Roscoe, IL

MILTON JR., JACK H.
[pen.] Jay; [b.] April 17, 1964, Augusta, GA; [p.] Jack H. Milton, Louise Story Milton; [m.] Tracy Diane Rice, June 14, 1992; [ch.] Matthew Ryan Milton, Joshua Rice Milton; [ed.] Aquinas High School; [occ.] Lieutenant on the Augusta Richmond County Fire Dept. and Safety Director at St. John Towers in Augusta, GA; [oth. writ.] Several poems but not currently published; [pers.] My writings are solemnly inspiration, whenever I am touched by an event in my life I feel the need to write. Whether I am driving in my car, eating at a restaurant, or waking from my sleep to recall a dream.; [a.] North Augusta, SC

MIMS, RASHANA
[b.] March 31, 1984, Syracuse, NY; [p.] Craig A. Mims, Velma J. Mims; [ed.] 7th Yr. Honor Student, entering Thurgood Marshall Middle School, Fall 1996; [pers.] I believe that the art of creative writing is a special gift. I'm inspired by the poet, Langston Hughes and would like to express my talent in the future by becoming a professional Author.; [a.] Temple Hills, MD

MINER, RUSSELL
[b.] March 30, 1977, Providence, RI; [p.] Diane and Curtis Miner; [ed.] Toll Gate High School, Warwick, RI, University of Rhode Island; [occ.] Student, Sophomore at URI; [memb.] Oaklawn Community Baptist Church, De Molay Fidelity Chapter, URI Poetry Club; [hon.] National Honor Society, Who's Who in American High School Students, Rhode Island Honor Society; [pers.] Writing poetry is a way for me to express feelings, likes, dislikes - I do it for fun. If I'm not doing it for fun, stop me.; [a.] Warwick, RI

MOHRDIECK, LINDA LOUISE
[b.] January 17, 1945, Bronx, NY; [p.] Mr. and Mrs. C. Gaye; [m.] Franklin Mohrdieck, November 13, 1971; [ch.] Deborah, Lisa and Frank; [ed.] Scotch Plains - Fanwood High Berkeley Secretarial School - NJ; [occ.]

Housewife; [memb.] Cancer Society, Arthritis Foundation; [pers.] I enjoyed Erma Bombeck's humor and shall miss her wit. My writing's are of the "Little Happenings" we have in every day life - laughter the best medicine of all!; [a.] Sebring, FL

MOLINARY, CRYSTAL P.
[pen.] Cutie Pie; [b.] October 22, 1983, Miami, FL; [p.] Sonia Molinary, Adolf M.; [ed.] Kindergarden - 7th grade, Piano, Ballet, Top, Jazz, Modeling; [memb.] School Club - Diamond Club; [hon.] Music, over all Science, A-B Honor Roll, A-I-A, Honor Roll, pre-Algebra, Conduct, Spanish; [oth. writ.] Spanish poems for youth fair.; [pers.] I believe that anyone that has it inside, of themselves, and the, potential to make it, they will make it if they.; [a.] Miami, FL

MONTAGUE, JACYNTH
[pen.] Pom Thomague; [b.] May 28, 1982, Jamaica, WI; [m.] Randall Montague, December 20, 1978; [ch.] Ramon, Sean; [ed.] Knox College, Shortwood Teachers College (Jamaica West Indies); [pers.] Poetry writing is a means of expressing myself uninhibitedly. I was first motivated by limericks.; [a.] Brooklyn, NY

MONTES, NATALIA
[pen.] Nati; [b.] September 3, 1985, NY; [p.] Daisy Rosario and Hector Montes; [ed.] River East Elementary; [occ.] Student; [hon.] Skating, Swimming, Tennis; [pers.] My goal in life is simply to do my best and be happy.; [a.] Bronx, NY

MOODY, FRED M.
[b.] November 15, 1950, Bacon County, GA; [p.] Omer and Lottie Moody; [m.] Divorced; [ch.] One daughter (19 yrs. old); [ed.] Attended Mercer University; [occ.] Retired/Disabled Poet - Sculptor; [hon.] Dean's List; [oth. writ.] Biffolous Broganza - (Sloft Stories) over 60 songs (copyrighted) and a multitude of poetry (in all forms).; [pers.] Do not top dance in a mine field.; [a.] Waycross, GA

MOON, MERIBETH
[b.] January 14, 1978, Franklin, PA; [p.] Pamela A. Kilgore; [ed.] Graduate of Franklin High School; [occ.] Enlisted Army Reserve/Student; [memb.] National Rifle Association (NRA); [hon.] 6th grade was given an Award from the Franklin Kwanis Club for an essay on the importance of Dental Care; [oth. writ.] I've always written, but never had the courage to try to publish any of it.; [pers.] Give me technology and I'll have entertainment but let me create and I'll be the entertainment.; [a.] Grove City, PA

MOORE, ESAU
[pen.] Easy Moore; [b.] April 10, 1941, Clearendom Cty, Summerton, SC; [p.] Mary Moore, Ardise Moore; [m.] Single; [ed.] Scottch Branch, H.S.; [occ.] Retired; [memb.] St. Marks United Medothist Church. The Assembly of the State of New York; [oth. writ.] Not published; [pers.] I truly believe in God, and the power that He gives all mankind to love each other.; [a.] Bronx, NY

MOORE, JANE RANAE
[pen.] Monique Barrington; [b.] December 11, 1957, Kodiak, AK; [m.] David Poulignot, October 18, 1995; [ch.] Domonique Nicole Grace Moore; [ed.] CIS, MIS, English Business Administration, Business Management, University of Southern Colorado, Finishing School John Robert Powers Academy; [occ.] Technical Support for the Internet; [memb.] Association of female executives Governor Romer's Task Force for Internet Development;

[hon.] Who's Who in American High Schools; [oth. writ.] The rape of the Female Spirit Time, Carousel, Gramp, Tapestry of Deception.; [pers.] Every hope on born in you should be nurtured until the day you die. No person or circumstance can rob you of hope unless you allow it.; [a.] Fowler, CO

MOORE, KIMBERLY L.
[b.] March 22, 1968, Iowa; [m.] May 17, 1987; [ch.] Two Daughters, 5 and 6 yrs.; [ed.] A.D.S.; [occ.] Guest Service Rep, Heartland Inn; [oth. writ.] Lavaca, Arkansas, and 53 unpublished poems, and 20 lyrics.; [pers.] My greatest poetical influences are Ann Sexton, Sylvia Plath, Dylan Thomas, and King David of Isreal. My greatest sources of inspiration are Y'Shua, my husband, my children, and nature.; [a.] Des Moines, IA

MOORE, TANECIA
[b.] January 26, 1982, Washington, DC; [p.] Cornelius and Patricia Moore; [ed.] Patrick Henry Elementary School, Francis C. Hammond Middle School, and currently attends Minnie Howard (9th grd.); [occ.] Goes to school at Minnie Howard (Ninth Grade School); [memb.] National Junior Honor's Society, A member of Mt. Pleasant Baptist Church. Member of the Church's Youth Dept. and Usher Board.; [hon.] Honor Roll Awards and perfect attendance awards for school, Presidential Award for Improvement, Most valuable person for team 8-2. Pastor's honor roll.; [oth. writ.] I have written several poems for school. Won 1st place in my second grade essay contest. My speech was published in a local newspaper.; [pers.] "The key to writing poetry is found in your inner thoughts, feelings, and emotions."; [a.] Alexandria, VA

MOORHOUSE, ERICA NICOLE
[b.] October 31, 1982, Warren, OH; [p.] JoAnn Kellar-Moorhouse, James Moorhouse; [ed.] Garfield Elementary and Garfield Junior High School; [occ.] Full Time Student; [memb.] Ohio Girls Softball Association - Garrettsville Girls Softball League; [hon.] School Honor and Merit Awards, Garfield Girls Softball League Awards X Three Years; [oth. writ.] Other published poems in recent books of poetry anthology.; [pers.] I write what ever comes to my mind, sometimes imaginary ideas, but a lot of times they come from my heart and how I feel at that time.; [a.] Garrettsville, OH

MORALES, RADAMES
[b.] May 22, 1940, Humacao, PR; [p.] Anselmo and Evarista; [m.] Maria H. Reifkohl; [ch.] Ronnell, Orianna, Iris, Lilibeth; [ed.] Serward Park HS, New York City, Penn State, Berks Campus; [occ.] Senior Technical Specialist (Intel Corp.); [memb.] Veterans of Foreign Wars Seti; [hon.] Good conduct medal from US Navy, Alaska Disaster Medal, Vietnam Theater Medal; [oth. writ.] "Survival, A Prelude To Vietnam", "The Spirit of Givens"; [pers.] What good is the written word, if no one reads it?; [a.] Tempe, AZ

MORENO, ROBERT
[b.] February 21, 1941, Texas; [p.] Carmen and Martha Moreno; [m.] Amparo Moreno, October 10, 1964, Wasco, CA; [ch.] Robert Jr., Rose Marie, Martha Alicia, Daniel Jaime, Juan Jose; [ed.] Orange Grove Elem., Texas; [occ.] Security Officer

MOREY, JONATHAN T.
[b.] May 12, 1965, Sellersville, PA; [p.] Charles R. Morey and Gail L.; [m.] Cheryl A. Morey, July 20, 1991; [ch.] Jacquelyn, Jonathan; [ed.] High School Beacon Christian Academy; [occ.] United States Navy; [memb.] Calvary Assembly of God; [hon.] Joint Service Achieve-

ment Medal and 12 years of service; [oth. writ.] Several poems yet to be published. Currently, I am working on a book of original poems.; [pers.] ...That you also inspire to lead a quiet life to mind own business and to work with your own hands as we commanded you, that you may walk properly toward those who are outside and that you may lack nothing. 1 Thess. 4:11-12; [a.] Hampton, VA

MORI, KAREN L.
[b.] February 26, 1970, Greensburg, PA; [p.] Wayne and Dolores Mori; [ed.] Norwin High School, California University of Penna., B.S. in Early Childhood/Special Education Degree; [occ.] Teacher; [pers.] When I write I write the feelings in my heart. The poem "Grandma's" is in memory of my grandmother Cecelia Nickle who passed away March 11, 1995.; [a.] Westmoreland City, PA

MORITA, LAURA M.
[b.] September 17, 1975, Waukegan, IL; [p.] Charlotte and Bob Morita; [ed.] Mundelein High, 2 years at College of Lake County; [occ.] Secretarial Assistant; [hon.] Who's Who Among High School Students; [oth. writ.] Several poems published in the High School Literary Magazine entitled Distilled Dreams, as well as, an additional magazine (also high school published) entitled The Thirsty Elephant.; [pers.] I believe in Joseph Campbell's Statement, "Every act in life yields pains of opposites in its results. The best we can do is lean towards the light, toward the harmonious relationships that come from compassion with suffering, from understanding the other person.; [a.] Mundelein, IL

MORITA, MICHELLE S.
[b.] December 3, 1974, Valencia; [p.] Megumu and Kazuko; [ed.] William S. Hart High School, currently attending University of California Santa Barbara; [occ.] Student; [pers.] "What you sow does not come to life unless it dies." (I Corinthians 15:36; [a.] Isla Vista, CA

MORRIS, KAYE SPIRES
[b.] January 15, 1955, Walterboro, SC; [p.] Catherine Walker Brooks, George Spires; [m.] Gene Morris, February 6, 1989; [ch.] Barry Wade Griffin, Krystal Lyn Griffin; [ed.] St. Matthews High School (SC) - 1973; [occ.] Disabled housewife; [memb.] EHS chorus booster club, Evans High School PTA member, M.A.D.D. member, Woodmen of the World Lodge member; [hon.] High School Valedictorian, presented lifetime membership to SC PTA in appreciation for volunteer work by Blackville Elem. School; [oth. writ.] Articles for the Barnwell People Sentinel Newspaper (SC); [pers.] This poem was written in honor of my mother, who has had more positive influence in my life than anybody else in the world. She taught me honesty, respect and compassion for others.; [a.] Martinez, GA

MORRISON, CHRISTINA J.
[pers.] For a great lady, my aunt, Betty Jensen, Love Chrissy.

MORSE, GORDON M.
[pen.] Gordon M. Morse; [b.] March 12, 1931, Quincy, MI; [p.] Harold and Gertrude Monse; [m.] Katherine, July 12, 1952; [ch.] Seven; [ed.] J. High School; [occ.] Pet Machinist; [oth. writ.] Precious poetry.

MORTIMER, PAULA
[b.] November 28, 1962, Chilton, WI; [p.] John and Donna Mortimer; [ed.] 1980 Graduate of Chilton High School; [occ.] Office Manager, Friederichs Abstract and Little Service; [oth. writ.] "Broken" is my first published

work!; [pers.] I enjoy working out, walking, swimming, biking, photograph, great rock music and "hanging out" at our cottage no lake Winnebago. My happiest times are spent with my Dad and Mom, my brother grant, my sister-in-law Bonnie, their kids Sarah and John and of course -Michi!; [a.] Chilton, WI

MOSELEY, GLAND J.
[b.] February 14, 1937, Odum, GA; [p.] Wyral and Mattie Leggett (Both Deceased); [m.] Harry K. Moseley, May 7, 1955; [ch.] Ann M. Arthur, Glenn Moseley; [ed.] Jeff Davis High; [occ.] Retired 1995 - worked 22 yrs. for Atlanta Gas Light Co.; [memb.] Applying Healthcare System Auxiliary, Crosby Chapel United Methodist Church; [pers.] Most of my writings reflect a certain mystical influence, and speaks many things to different readers, leaving you to ponder what you have read. To me this is the beauty of poetry.; [a.] Baxley, GA

MOSS, BARRY R.
[b.] April 30, 1956, Greenwood, SC; [p.] Clyde and Elizabeth Moss; [ed.] High School Graduate Associate Degree in Emergency Medical Technology; [occ.] Paramedic; [hon.] Honor Row Society Perfect Attendance Award; [oth. writ.] "Testimony For Living", "A Special Angel", "Make Me A Memory"; [pers.] "For those who believe and practice love, peace, and happiness shall know the Glory of Life"; [a.] Greenwood, SC

MOSS, JAY HARMON
[pen.] Words by Harmon; [b.] June 8, 1917, Detroit, MI; [p.] Abe and Jennie Moss; [m.] Dorothy (Freedman) Moss, June 21, 1941; [ch.] Gary, Joel and Karen (Hale); [ed.] BA Business (Wayne University); [occ.] Retired; [memb.] Mezeritcher Club; [oth. writ.] None published, several thousand greetings, messages, parodies and lyrics.; [pers.] Every moment of each day was a significance in the never ending march of time. To each of us some moments are of greater substance than others. At these times it is gratifying to be remembered.; [a.] Southfield, MI

MOTZ, LLOYD
[pen.] Lloyd Motz; [b.] June 5, 1910, Susquehanna, PA; [p.] Solomon and Minnie Motz; [m.] Minne R. Motz, June 14, 1934; [ch.] Robin O. Motz, Julie Motz; [ed.] B.S. CCNY, Ph.D. (Physics) Columbia Fellow Gottingen Germany; [occ.] Prof. Emeritus; [memb.] N.Y. Academy of Sci American Physical Soc./Fellow Astronomers Soc. AAAS (Fellow), World Acad. of Arts and Sci; [hon.] Gravity Research 1960, NY Acad of Sci Award, Pres. of N.Y. Acad of Sci 1970-71; [oth. writ.] 18 books in Physics and Mathematics Essential of Astronomy (Text) Astrophysics (graduate text); [pers.] The pursuit of truth and Beauty is the greatest of all activities.; [a.] New York City, NY

MOUA, KIA
[b.] June 10, 1976, Thailand; [p.] Chong Soua Moua and Chao Vue; [ed.] Merced High, California State University of Stanislau; [occ.] Student at Cal-State of Stanislaus; [pers.] I have been influenced by my experiences in life, friends, families and acquaintances who touches my life. It doesn't hurt to dream and fantasize with those thoughts, out comes some breath taking masterpieces.; [a.] Turlock, CA

MOZINGO, VICTORIA J.
[pen.] V. J. Mozingo; [b.] April 15, 1948, Chambersburg, PA; [m.] Gary H. Mozingo Sr., October 30, 1965; [ch.] Gary H., Jr. and Shelly M. Porter; [ed.] Big Spring High School, Newville, PA, Certification as Nursing Assistant - State of PA 1988; [occ.] Disabled; [memb.] Prince

Street United Brethren in Christ Church in Shippensburg, Pennsylvania. Pennsylvania Certified Nursing Assistant Registrar.; [hon.] Received several honors and awards when working in nursing profession at Piney Mountain Home for Aged in Fayetteville, Pennsylvania; [oth. writ.] Local newspaper, church newsletters, church bulletins, submitted works of poetry to warner press.; [pers.] I wish to convey to hurting people that God is there through all of their pain strife, and woe is they will only reach out and grasp his loving hands of mercy.; [a.] Shippensburg, PA

MUELLER, ERIC
[b.] April 23, 1969, Fort Rucker, AL; [p.] Edmund Mueller, Jane Mueller; [ed.] Douglas County High, Arapahoe Community College; [occ.] Inserter for Douglas County News-Press, Castle Rock, CO; [oth. writ.] Unpublished short stories and poems; [pers.] I like writing as much as I like talking for the same two reasons: I get to share ideas with others, and I simply enjoy doing it.; [a.] Castle Rock, CO

MUELLER, JAINE RENE
[b.] February 27, 1980, Agana, GU; [p.] Jackie Schwendener, James Mueller; [ed.] Dumlap Elem. K-8 Reedley High, Mountain View 9 present; [occ.] Video Store Clerk and Student; [memb.] Mountain Rodeo Assoc.; [hon.] I've been the assoc and schools for hard work and dependability. I also won the contest for town princess based on attitude and outlook.; [oth. writ.] Poetry I've written on the side and for other people.; [pers.] Poetry is my way of relaxing and clearing my mind. I write mostly of personal experiences and people on things around me.; [a.] Squaw Valley, CA

MULLICANE, CHRIS R.
[b.] Lynwood, CA; [p.] Richard, Sharol Mullicane; [ed.] Glendora High, Univ. of Southern CA; [memb.] Star Trek ta Club I.F.T. International Federation of Trekkers; [hon.] Who's Who list 84 and 85; [oth. writ.] Several poems, one pub. in Recollections of yesterday, short stories and a novel in development; [pers.] My writing is a reflection of things I have sean and felt with a bit of Romantic twist thrown in for flavor. I have been influenced from J.R.R. Tolkien to David Eddings. (By the works); [a.] Glendora, CA

MULLINS, CHRISTINE
[pen.] Christian; [b.] October 6, 1966, Chicago, IL; [p.] Shirley, Carlis Mullins; [ed.] Kelly High, Daley College; [occ.] Market Researcher, Strategic Radio Research; [memb.] American Cancer Society; [hon.] Dean's List, American Cancer Society; [oth. writ.] Others, poems and short stories unpublished; [pers.] My poems reflect my inner, true feelings, through my pain and suffering in life, my pen soothes my mind, and the paper becomes my salvation.; [a.] Chicago, IL

MUNOZ, BRYAN
[a.] Virginia Beach, VA

MUNOZ, MONICA SALINA
[b.] November 29, 1976, Torrance; [p.] Susan Garzon, Robert Munoz; [ed.] Carson High School, City of Angels; [pers.] "Memories" is dedicated to all my friends and relatives whom are still around creating precious memories and to those who have past on they will never be forgotten because of the special memories they left behind for us to cherish.; [a.] Long Beach, CA

MUNSELL, ANNA
[b.] July 8, 1976, North Carolina; [p.] Ben and Jamie; [ch.] Kiana Lane; [ed.] Graduated from Pisgah High

School in June 1994; [oth. writ.] I have written over 300 poems for recreation, but no past publications.; [a.] Canton, NC

MURANTE, GRACE
[pen.] Grace Dickison; [b.] December 23, 1956, Phillipsburg, NJ; [p.] Pearl Cowell and Warren Dickison; [ch.] Jessica Lynn; [ed.] North Warren Regional High School, Penn Sate College of Agricultural Science Workshops for childcare; [memb.] Nat'l Wildlife Foundation Nat'l Audubon Society; [oth. writ.] Ideals magazine Poetry published in Local newspaper; [pers.] My writing is a form of meditation and reflects on the intimate relationship between nature, God and humankind. In it, I hope to send a message that they are not separate, but one of the same. I write in honor of my spiritual growth and in recognition of all that is sacred, offering a special thanks to my therapist for his unending encouragement and for believing in me always.; [a.] Beach Lake, PA

MURPHY, AMANDA
[b.] September 13, 1980, St. Louis, MO; [p.] Susan and Rick Murphy; [ed.] Currently attending Neriux Hall High School for Young Women; [occ.] Business manager of the school newspaper, "Hallways"; [oth. writ.] Another poem called "Victim" published in The Coming Of Dawn; [pers.] Hope for tomorrow makes us better people today. I strive to portray this in my week.; [a.] Saint Louis, MO

MURPHY, ELISE
[b.] April 11, 1919, Newport, RI; [ch.] 3 daughter 1 son 7 grandchildren; [ed.] High School; [occ.] Retired 7 years; [memb.] Live Oak Unitarian Universalist Church, sing in the choir, read to bilinqualist and 2nd graders, local artists support group, Sufi dance group; [hon.] I am honored to be hanging my first "one woman show" in my community". Water Scapes and Innerscapes. August 1st thru 31st.; [oth. writ.] My own journey through sadness and loss. Writing poetry as a vehicle for chance never published.; [pers.] I believe in the natural beauty of the universe and my place in it. My interest lies in my watercolor expressions and my dream is to bring poetry and painting together.; [a.] Santa Barbara, CA

MURPHY JR., DENNIS J.
[b.] July 13, 1924, Lynn, MA; [p.] Deceased; [m.] Barbara Ruth Murphy, July 31, 1955; [ch.] James L. Steven, Julie Kay, Kathleen R., Dennis J. Jr.; [ed.] High School; [occ.] Retired; [hon.] Service Discharge, Navy, Merchant Marine, WWII Veteran; [oth. writ.] None published, As Hobby, Write Children's Short Stories, Poems, Lyric's Never Let To Music.; [pers.] I write because during my life - span, these little poems and stories are actual moments of time that I have experience (as my own history) of events and the moments I have taken to ponder why.; [a.] Castro Valley, CA

MURRAY, CHRISTOPHER M.
[b.] April 15, 1962, Utica, NY; [p.] Peter Murray, Ann Murray; [ed.] B.A. Social Studies, Utica College of Syracuse University; [occ.] Manager - Title Insurance Company; [pers.] The only important issue is our purpose for being here, all else is secondary. Ontology is the bridge between physics and metaphysics.; [a.] Sauquoit, NY

MYERS, C. JEANNETTE
[b.] March 2, 1936, Springfield, IL; [p.] Guy and Carmen (Waremburg) Myers; [ed.] Springfield High School - Class of 1954; [occ.] Executive Secretary Electrical and Gas Industry; [memb.] Southern Baptist Convention International Society of Poets (Distinguished Member);

[hon.] Old Fashioned Memories (Primitive Painting) 3 Blue Ribbons Ties that Bind (Electric Industry - The Art of EHV - Primitive Painting), Exhibited Layton School of Art - Milwaukee WI - 2-Yr Tour of U.S.; [oth. writ.] BOO - Beauty of Oranges, That Beautiful Batch, Olympians..., Veggie - vs - Herb; [pers.] Keep a visional view...of a stellular night...; [a.] Springfield, IL

MYERS JR., CHARLES ELMORE
[pen.] Meg Mog; [b.] March 13, 1957, Pensacola, FL; [p.] Charles E. Myers Sr. and Dorthy Joan Myers; [m.] Divorced; [ch.] Ashley Nichole Myers, Charles Elmer Myers III; [ed.] Kempsville High, Virginia Apprenticeship Norfolk Votech; [occ.] International Association of Heat and Frost Insulators and Asbestos Workers Union, Local #83 Norfolk, VA; [pers.] I would like to dedicate this literary work to my late mother Dorthy J. Myers. Inspired by Divine influence, all glory be given to God; [a.] Newport News, VA

NAAR, MARGARET
[pen.] Margaret Askey; [b.] August 24, London, England; [p.] Lucy and John Askey; [m.] Alvin Naar, September 28; [ch.] Elizabeth Jane and John Stephen; [ed.] Matriculated - Brompton Oratory, London, England, Royal Society of Arts - Certification; [occ.] Writing; [memb.] Assistance League So. Cal: (Assistance League of Southern California), The English - Speaking Union of the United States; [hon.] Academic Scholarship, Brompton Oratory, London; [oth. writ.] Unpublished children's stories, unpublished poetry and short stories.; [pers.] If through my writing the soul of a reader is stirred, I have in part, fulfilled my reason for being.; [a.] Sherman Oaks, CA

NAGLE, FRED
[b.] January 3, 1979, Boston, MA; [p.] Fred Nagle and Grace Nagle; [ed.] Oliver Ames High School; [occ.] Lifeguard and Student; [oth. writ.] Several poems published in school poetry books.; [a.] Easton, MA

NANDU, HARI
[pen.] Quik Fingers; [b.] April 28, 1986, Texas; [p.] Rajini Nandu and Nandu; [ed.] 5th grade, P.S. 117 Q Joyce Keld/Briarwood School, Briarwood, NY; [occ.] School Student; [memb.] Briarwood-Jamaica Little League; [hon.] Honor roll student from Kg to IV grade Student of the Year in 1996, Principal's award; [a.] Jamaica, NY

NANGUANG, VICTORIA
[b.] April 13, 1970, Kaduna, Nigeria; [p.] Daniel Nanguang, Adama Nanguang; [ch.] Trevor Perodin; [ed.] Irvington High, Essex County Vocational Tech. School of Nursing; [occ.] Licensed Practical Nurse, Net Kirkwood Detox, Wilmington, DE; [hon.] Honor roll, National Honor Society; [pers.] Life strives not only on air, but by the interaction of one another. It will survive with a unified solution - The Human Race.; [a.] Wilmington, DE

NAPONIELLO, DAN
[b.] October 5, 1983, Oak Lawn, IL; [p.] Anthony Karen; [ed.] Covington Elementary; [occ.] Student; [memb.] Boy Scouts of America, Champion Youth Karate; [hon.] Presidential Scholarship Award, Straight a Honor Roll; [pers.] I strive to do my best in all I do.; [a.] Oak Lawn, IL

NATICCHIONI, JANET
[pen.] Jayen Kriash; [b.] August 26, 1954, Biodeford, ME; [p.] Irene and Paul Rivais; [m.] Divorced, March 23, 1973; [ch.] Kristi Marie, Ashley Victoria; [ed.] Burlington High - Sylvania Technical College; [occ.]

Disabled - create original Christening ensembles at home; [memb.] Safe House Program Brookside and Memorial Elementary - former Fair Share Community Service Program; [hon.] One of Top 10 graduates Sylvania Computer Electronics; [oth. writ.] Approx. 40 poems being manuscripted. Hope to publish soon.; [pers.] We must all recognize the imperfections in the world - work together towards perfection and erase the ignorance. My inspirations come from God.; [a.] Milford, MA

NEGLIA, GEORGETTE
[pen.] Gigi; [b.] March 1, 1959, New York City; [p.] Lorraine and Raul; [m.] Paul, November 21, 1993; [ch.] Vincent Paul Neglia; [ed.] Kingsborough Community College; [occ.] Student; [hon.] Bronze; [pers.] I'd like to thank Romantique Limousines in Brooklyn, for the patience and use of their computer. Without whom my book would not have been possible.

NELMS, SYBIL
[b.] March 6, 1945, Nanticoke, PA; [ed.] Wyoming Seminary, Wilkes College; [pers.] My poetry is rather Eclectic in its style, encompassing a wide range of emotions including pain, sorrow, happiness, and joy.; [a.] Nanticoke, PA

NELSON, MARGARET K.
[b.] February 27, 1972, Wooster, OH; [p.] Dolores Daiger and Andrew Jorgensen II; [m.] Richard Nelson, January 16, 1993; [ch.] Kayla Danielle Nelson - 3 yrs.; [ed.] Graduated from Cloverleaf High in 1991; [occ.] I stay home with Kayla, I write and I sell Avon cosmetics; [oth. writ.] I've written many poems and songs but this would be the first seen or published.; [pers.] Writing is my way to get away and the best way I know how to show my true feelings.; [a.] Wadsworth, OH

NELSON, TIFFANY CHERI
[pen.] Tiffany; [b.] December 11, 1983, Groveland, IL; [p.] Christopher and Michele Nelson; [ed.] Washington Intermediate School; [occ.] Student; [memb.] C.A.R. (children of the American Revolution); [hon.] High Honors Student, Won Young Authors 4 times, Attended Young Authors State Conference at I.S.U. in '95; [oth. writ.] Dance poodles (young authors), Brigette, the Prima Ballerina (young Author State Conference), Disaster zone (young authors), The wampums cat (Published Issue 8 of Illinois Windows); [pers.] I am 12 years old and Love to write. When I am older I hope to take on writing as a part-time career. I also plant to see the world and maybe I will write about all of the people and places I see.; [a.] Pekin, IL

NESTICH, PATRICIA A.
[b.] July 28, 1946, Albany, GA; [p.] Mrs. Maragret Allbritton; [m.] Melvin J. Nestich, March 20, 1975; [ed.] Ellenwoodside High School, Anderson Jr. College, USC, BA, USC, MAT; [occ.] Housewife - Editor of Newsletter (Songwriter); [memb.] Forest Hill Baptist Church; [hon.] May Queen - Head Cheerleader - Denmark Society, Honor Society - Anderson Jr. College; [oth. writ.] God is - Jesus the sweetest name - the flag of Israel - Love the Lord a man walking through the clouds - what a wonderful day -; [pers.] At the end of my life I would like to say "I Have Loved" Stand for God and the Right".; [a.] Travelers Rest, SC

NEVSHEMAL, JOHN
[b.] October 14, 1935, Milwaukee, WI; [p.] Beatrice and Anthony; [m.] Elizabeth, November 19, 1966 - Divorced; [ch.] Kristine, John Jr, Martin Michael L. Joseph; [ed.] Marquette University BS and MS Degree; [occ.] Chief Engineer; [memb.] Professional Engineers Society,

American Nuclear Society; [hon.] Society of Sigma XI; [oth. writ.] Short Story - 2027 Various Other Poems; [pers.] Love is the basic driving force in life and relationships.; [a.] Parker, CO

NEWMAN, JOHN W.
[pen.] Johnny Dakota; [b.] April 2, 1936, Fargo, ND; [p.] John and Edna Newman; [m.] Karon L. Solomon, February 2, 1995; [ed.] 12th Grade U.S. Army, G.E.D. 1956. Ironworker Apprentice and Wilding School Graduate 1959; [occ.] Retired Journeyman Ironworker, Published Poet, Songwriter; [memb.] BMI, Portland Songwriters Assn. National Assn. of Songwriters Calvary Temple Assembly of God, Pacific Pipeline Co. Inc. Major West Coast Book Distributor; [hon.] Top Ten Award NCA Recording Co. Nashville TN, Certificate of Merit - Talent and Associated Companies Boston, MA; [oth. writ.] "Poems to Touch your Heart" a published book of poems. I have done 10 signing's and readings at various barnes and noble, walden book stores. More signing's booked for October 1996 also poems printed in various magazines also an album of 18 songs.; [pers.] "Don't ever give up. Be tenacious, like a pit bull with your talent, it's a gift from God and he wants you to use it. Be ready for rejections and shake the dust of your sandals and go on and on.";[a.] Portland, OR

NEWTON, BERNARD M.
[b.] May 10, 1952, Bardstown, KY; [p.] Bernard Ivo and Dorthy Irene; [m.] Vicki Ann, June 18, 1973; [ch.] Jennifer Irene and Amber Jo; [ed.] St. Catherine High School; [occ.] Police Chief; [pers.] I'm a simple person who loves to write simple stories and poems so the reader can understand and enjoy.; [a.] New Haven, KY

NICHOLS, WENDY
[b.] August 26, 1967, Detroit, MI; [p.] Joyce Nichols; [ed.] Kettering High, Detroit College of Business, Wayne County Community, Wayne State University; [occ.] Administrative Assistant Detroit Board of Education; [memb.] Mentoring Program, Intervention Assistance Team, Student Assistance Program, National Youth Sports Program, Ninth Grade Restructuring Team; [hon.] Police Athletic League Cheer Sponsor, Pom Pon Sponsor Osborn High School, Detroit, MI; [oth. writ.] My first poem to be published is entitled "Memories" and it will be published in the anthology fields of gold. I also write poems for greeting cards and invitations.; [pers.] My writings reflect many of my past experiences. I have been influenced by many talented song writers.; [a.] Detroit, MI

NICHOLSON, EDWARD A.
[pen.] Edward A. Nicholson; [b.] October 14, 1936, Glen Cove, NY; [p.] Edward and Annie Nicholson; [m.] Christina, May 21, 1960; [ch.] Kimberly; [ed.] College - University of Hawaii, H.S. - Glen Cove High. Grammar's Locust Valley School; [occ.] VP Sales and Marketing, American Prime; [memb.] Reformed Church of Locust Valley, New York; [oth. writ.] The National Library of Poetry. 1. Man's True Pride. A Muse to Follow 2. Eternity - Carvings In Stone 3. Condensed Beauty - Recollections of Yesterday 4. Invincible Force - Best Poems of the 90's 5. Message of the Winding Stream - Memories of Tomorrow; [pers.] I find poetry in motion, to be a major inspiration for my everyday life. It's everywhere! I may not win contests at. And if my livelihood depended on it, I'd be considered a starving poet. But I know my poems make sense, and people find comfort in them. And God knows I do as well. So much for rhetoric?; [a.] Paterson, NJ

NICHOLSON, PETER M.
[b.] September 7, 1925, Brooklyn, NY; [p.] Dominick, Kathleen Nicholson; [m.] Josephine R. Nicholson, September 29, 1984; [ch.] Peter A., Dennis M., Eileen M., William G.; [ed.] St. Johns University; [occ.] Retired; [memb.] Knights of Columbus, Loyal order of the Moose, Disabled American Veterans; [oth. writ.] Other poems published in local publication in Florida; [pers.] "Soliloquy at Sunset" is dedicated to my wife, Josephine, who rebuilt my shattered life, and whose love I do not deserve.; [a.] Harbour Heights, FL

NICHOLSON, ROY
[pen.] Vandela Tarchone; [b.] March 16, 1977, Seattle, WA; [p.] Ronald Nicholson, Penny Nicholson; [oth. writ.] A few poems in a small paper and an anthology.; [pers.] Strive to be the best, for yourself. Let your dreams take flight and they will take you away and let none hinder your quest for knowledge and enlightenment.; [a.] Oklahoma City, OK

NICHOLSON, TAMARA C.
[b.] June 2, 1973, Saint Louis; [p.] Carliss Mora and Greg Nicholson; [ch.] Manny and Justin; [ed.] Diploma, 2 years of College; [occ.] Drafting Asst. at Lucent Tech.; [hon.] Won Awards for my stories in Jr. High was chosen to recite Langston Hughes's, "I too," in High School for Black History Month. Honored, I was; [oth. writ.] I have many other poems that I have yet to introduce.; [pers.] I am enthralled by creative thoughts and to put them into words is beautiful. I've been highly influenced on personal experiences as well as relationships.; [a.] Saint Louis, MO

NIGRO, DAVID M.
[b.] January 3, 1969, Londonderry, Northern Ireland; [p.] Linda Nigro, Gary Nigro; [ed.] Riverhead High School, Suffolk County Community College (Seldan Campus), State University of New York at New Paltz; [occ.] Customer Service Rep., aspiring Police Officer and Teacher; [memb.] Sigma Alpha Mu Fraturnity, Long Island Ravens Bagpipe and Drum Corp. Abate of New York, Long Island Ravens Motorcycle Club; [pers.] There is a time for work and a time for play, but there is always a time to have fun.; [a.] Bellerose, NY

NIX, MAE
[b.] December 9, 1938, Fort Worth, TX; [p.] Helen and W. T. Wyatt; [m.] Don Nix, January 27, 1962; [ch.] Alan, Billy and Chris Nix; [ed.] Slaton High School, Rutherford - Metropolitan Speedwriting School, Attended Tarrant County - Jr. College for 1 Class; [occ.] Retired Federal Employee; [memb.] Travis Avenue Baptist Church; [pers.] I feel we learn and grow fun life experiences - good and bad. I look for something positive even in adverse situation.; [a.] Fort Worth, TX

NOERTKER, NATHAN
[b.] November 11, 1977, Mariemont, OH; [p.] Garry and Beckie Noertker; [ed.] Clermont Northeastern High School Associates in Pre-Business Administration from the University of Cincinnati. Currently attending Miami University; [occ.] Investments Worker for the Midland Company; [memb.] National Honor Society Junior Lead Clermont Miami University Marching Band; [hon.] Dean's List Who's Who of American High School Students; [pers.] If you have the drive and the motivation, you can do anything you want with your life. Only you decide what the outcome will be.; [a.] Batavia, OH

NORRIS, JESSICA LEIGH
[b.] October 8, 1981; [p.] Tim Norris and Kathy Norris; [ed.] Freshman in High School; [occ.] Student; [memb.]

Calvary Baptist Church; [hon.] Alpha Honor Roll; [pers.] I hope to, one day, have a historical fiction novel of mine published.; [a.] Short Gap, WV

NORRIS, NORMA
[pen.] Norma Lorraine; [b.] August 8, 1942, Philadelphia, PA; [p.] Louis and Minnie Marinoff; [m.] Allen Norris, July 25, 1961; [ch.] Amy, Jeffrey; [pers.] Dedicated to my granddaughter "Jessica" for whom this poem was written for. Life is not the time that we have, but rather the moments that we live... sharing... endearing... embracing.; [a.] Philadelphia, PA

NORTH, MARK A.
[b.] July 19, 1969, Fairfield, CA; [p.] Rose and Jerry North; [ed.] B.S. Criminal Justice Chaminade University; [occ.] US Navy E-5; [hon.] Vita in Verbo Dean's List; [a.] Aiea, HI

O'CONNOR, MEGHAN
[pen.]] B. N. Lewis; [b.] September 1, 1983, Providence, RI; [p.] John and Adriene O'Connor; [ed.] St. Matthews Middle School; [occ.] Student; [hon.] Honors for 4th quarter seventh grade; [oth. writ.] Some entries in the Junior Edition for Providence Journal Bulletins; [pers.] I try to reach the stars, and pray that they are not too far away.; [a.] Providence, RI

O'DELL, CAROLYNN
[pen.] Carrie O'Dell; [b.] March 18, 1984, Somerville, NJ; [p.] Carolynn Vogel O'Dell, Russel J. O'Dell; [ed.] The School of St. Elizabeth; [occ.] Student; [memb.] The Church of Our Lady of Perpetual Help, Hunterdon Hawks Track Club, Tewksbury Tup Athletic Association-Soccer, basketball, baseball, St. Elizabeth girls basketball; [hon.] First Honors, Achievement Awards, 1st place - shot-put/discus regional Mett: Junior Olympics.; [a.] Califon, NJ

O'DELL, CAROLYNN VOGEL
[b.] October 24, 1960, Rome, Italy; [p.] Dolores Dowd Vogel and Jerome Vogel; [m.] Russel J. O'Dell, June 19, 1982; [ch.] Carolyn Carroll-"Carrie", Russel James Jr.-"Rusty", Michael Jerome, Kelly Aileen; [ed.] Voorhees High School, Douglas College - Rutgers University, The College of St. Elizabeth; BS Business Administration - Management; [occ.] Aspiring Author; [memb.] The Church of Our Lady of Perpetual Help; [hon.] Departmental honors - Business Administration: The College of St. Elizabeth, Dean's List; [pers.] I put my faith and hope in God. I give my love to my family. I find strength and courage and love in their safe haven. But as did generations of my family past, I put my trust to the raven.; [a.] Califon, NJ

O'NEAL, JUDY L.
[b.] August 31, 1945, Portland, TN; [m.] Single; [ed.] Graduated Portland High School, attended Southern University, TN and Volunteer State Community College, Gallatin, TN; [occ.] Volunteer State Community College, Business Division Secretary III; [pers.] I believe through poetry one can express their true innermost feelings and still provide enjoyable reading for others. I like to think of poetry as music to the soul.; [a.] Gallatin, TN

O'ROURKE, ANDREW
[pen.] Drew O'Rourke; [b.] July 9, 1961, San Mateo, CA; [p.] Anna Mary and Andrew O'Rourke; [m.] Wendy Vanz O'Rourke, May 25, 1985; [ed.] BA Degree Sociology - Magna Cum Laude University of Oregon - Eugene, Oregon; [occ.] Owner of Business Writing/Advertising Firm; [hon.] Elected to Phi Beta Kappa, the Liberal Arts Honorary Society. Nominated to Kappa Tau

Alpha, the National Journalism Honorary Society; [oth. writ.] Have written several feature articles in various magazines. Presently working on a book of short stories and poems.; [a.] Albuquerque, NM

ODOM, RYAN LANCE
[pen.] Ryan Lance; [b.] 6/13/81, Okmulgee OK; [p.] Greg and Marion Odom; [m.] 1989; [ch.] 6; [ed.] 10th Grade, Red Mountain High School; Fremont Jr. High; [memb.] Fremont Jr. High Wrestling, Red Mountain Wrestling

OEHLMANN, AMANDA
[b.] August 4, 1979, Passaic, NJ; [p.] Ronald Oehlmann, Denise Pember; [ed.] Currently preparing to enter my senior year of high school in September of 1996 at Princeton High in Cincinnati, Ohio. (Also attended Stewart Elementary, Robert E. Lucus Intermediate and Princeton Junior High all in Cincinnati Ohio); [hon.] During my freshman year of high school, I won second place in a grade -level poetry contest and have had several poems printed in the school newspaper. I have also been on the honor roll every year since I started school, and have received several additional academic awards; [oth. writ.] I have been writing poetry for about 7 years now and have written over 60 other poems.; [pers.] I often tend to write about my feelings or personal issues or curiosities. I use my poetry as a way to express myself or how I feel about others. I guess my poetry is my version of a diary or journal of significant events and people in my life.; [a.] Cincinnati, OH

OLER, ARRITA
[pen.] Rita Ariel; [b.] January 6, 1983, Memphis, TN; [p.] James Oler, Elizabeth Oler; [ed.] I attend to Kolb Middle School in Rialto. I passed to the 8th grade.; [occ.] Junior High School Student; [memb.] I am in the National Junior Honor Society at my School; [hon.] Throughout the year I have maintained 3, 5 - 4, 0 GPA. I was on The High and Principal Honor Roll.; [pers.] I never thought I would be appreciated by my work but as I see all dreams do come true.; [a.] Rialto, CA

OLIVER, ELIZABETH
[b.] May 18, 1974, Vineland, NJ; [p.] Barbara and Roy Oliver; [ed.] Millville Sr High School, Western Maryland College; [occ.] Pr. Assistant Account Executive, Hartt and Company; [hon.] National Honor Society, Communications Honor Society; [a.] Cockeysville, MD

OLSEN, BARBARA J.
[b.] May 5; [p.] Herald and Bernice Keown; [m.] George Olsen; [ch.] Loren George Olsen, Alan Wayne Olsen; [ed.] BA Adams State College, Alamosa, CO MA Univ. of Colorado Boulder, CO; [occ.] Retired School Teacher Teec Nos Pos Boarding School Bureau of Indian Affairs Teec Nos Pos, AZ currently employed as Exceptional Programs Teacher Central Consolidated Sch. District Newcomb, NM Good Samaritan Center Southwest Memorial Hospital Auxiliary; [memb.] Who's Who Among America's Teachers; [a.] Cortez, CO

ORITI, REX B.
[b.] April 11, 1936, Bronx, NY; [p.] Joseph Oriti, Nancy Oriti; [ed.] Samuel Gompers H.S. Bx NY; [occ.] Electrician, N.C.Y. Transit Auth.; [hon.] First place NYC High School Speech Contest - 1953, M.V.P - NYC Champion Stick Ball Team - NYC Street Games - 1972; [oth. writ.] Several poems and short story's; [pers.] When writing a poem, for that moment in time, you give part of your life, part of yourself, no greater gift can one give another.; [a.] Bronx, NY

ORNDORF, BRENDA M.
[b.] February 5, 1927, England; [occ.] Retired; [oth. writ.] Poems published in Anthologies and Newspapers in the U.K.; [pers.] The artistry of words present pictures from the mind and heart. They will remain my epitaph, a little something for those who follow after.; [a.] Logan, OH

ORR, RONALD W.
[a.] Buford, GA

ORTIZ, JEAN GERMAN
[b.] November 3, 1941, Charleston, SC; [p.] William Gregorie, Marguerite Gregorie; [m.] James Ortiz, September 19, 1981; [ch.] Cornell German; [ed.] Laing High School, Palmer College and Farrah's Beauty Culture School; [occ.] Owner J-MO Enterprise; [oth. writ.] Spiritual Trivials; [pers.] Long-term ambition is to complete an anthology which will detail her inspirations from God.; [a.] Charleston, SC

ORTIZ, RUBEN JUAN CARLOS
[pen.] Ben Ortiz; [b.] March 14, 1946, Caguas, PR; [p.] Felix Ortiz and Antonia Ortiz; [ed.] La Salle Academy - University of Texas - BA English East Texas State Univ. - MA Spanish; [occ.] Spanish Teacher Woodrow Wilson High - Dallas, TX; [oth. writ.] Know - a short 2 act play written for high school students and focusing attention on the evils and pitfalls of drugs abuse.; [pers.] An inadequacy of the English language prevails in describing the satisfaction I feel (as an educator) when knowing I reached - out to a student and the responsiveness of that student was one of self-betterment.; [a.] Dallas, TX

OSBORNE, JOSEPH D.
[b.] December 24, 1970, Wurzburg, Germany; [p.] David Barbara Osborne; [ed.] A.A.S. from Pikes Peak Community College, Attending University of Colo. at Colorado Springs; [occ.] Security Officer for The Colorado Springs Fine Arts Center; [memb.] Partner of The 1996 Special Olympics, member of The International Society of Poets; [oth. writ.] "Loyalty and Trust" published by The National Library of Poetry; [pers.] I have written my poems in the hopes to show women that there still are a few romantic men out there. All they have to do is look.; [a.] Colorado Springs, CO

OSHADIPE, GLORIA J. S.
[b.] February 23, 1954, Atlanta; [p.] Tommie and Eloise Singleton; [m.] Segun Oshadipe, December, 1982; [ch.] Jeteha, Tony, Shycoya, Jerrica, Hehemiah; [ed.] B.A. Communication Goshen College, Goshen Indiana 46326; [occ.] Corporate Trainer Innotrac Corp. Norcross Georgia; [memb.] Hopewell Baptist Church, and National Society of Training and Development; [oth. writ.] Contemporary Christian Music lyric "Keeping My Eyes On Jesus", I Am On The Team With Jesus Christ", "Praise The Lord For The Family"; [pers.] Cherish people and you will enjoy life.; [a.] Atlanta, GA

OSPA, JUNE RACHELSON
[b.] June 28, 1951, Brooklyn, NY; [p.] Murray Rachelson, Mildred Floom; [m.] Jerry Ospa, July 1, 1982; [ch.] Jacob Ian born July 21, 1986, Jonathan Benjamin, Nov. 26, 1992; [ed.] BFA School of Visual Arts, NY, NY (Graduated 1974); [occ.] Songwriter, Scriptwriter; [memb.] Dramatist Guild, ASCAP; [oth. writ.] (Eleven) 11 songs on Early Years record series by BMG Kids. Book and lyrics for three Musicals: Original, S.W.A.K.-Sealed With A Kiss, Hyde and Seek-The Tale of Young Master Henry Jekyll, Criss-Cross-A Killer Of a Musical Thriller; [pers.] I believe that's it's important to do what you love to do. It one doesn't follow

one's dreams, one can wind up giving up the very essence of who they are. And how can one share with others if they have lost themselves? For me writing is as vital as the air I breathe.; [a.] New York, NY

OTERO, MERCEDES
[b.] September 24, 1925, NYC; [m.] Gilbert Otero, July 26, 1948; [ch.] 3; [ed.] 9th grade; [occ.] Housewife; [pers.] Hobby - drawing; [a.] Palmdale, CA

OTTERSTEN, EUGENIA KAZAMAKI
[b.] April 29, 1958, Greece; [ed.] Ph.D in Economics; [occ.] Visiting Scholar at Stanford University; [a.] Palo Alto, CA

PACHICK, DAELYNN G.
[b.] June 11, 1970, Wilkes-Barre, PA; [p.] Lindsay and David Suchowieski, Daniel Pachick; [m.] Fiancee John Farrell; [ch.] Jaeson David, Zachary Jonathan; [ed.] Hanover High School Luzerne County Community College; [occ.] On air personality, WGGY-FM, Pittston, PA; [hon.] Dean's List; [oth. writ.] Other poetry, short stories, novels all unpublished; [pers.] Most of my poetry is very dark, but it's all emotions that I probably 90% of the world has felt. It's my way of pushing out the bad feelings so someone else thinks "I don't feel so bad anymore"; [a.] Wilkes-Barre, PA

PAKELE, EDNA
[b.] July 4, 1938, Rome, NY; [p.] Bennie and Grace Killingbeck; [m.] Divorced; [ch.] James and Joey; [ed.] High School - Rome Free Academy, Rome NY, Crouse - Irving Hospital School of Nursing - Syracuse, N.Y., University of Buffalo, University of Hawaii, Honolulu Community College, Leeward Community College; [occ.] Psychiatric R.N.- Tripler Regional Medical Center; [memb.] 1) Aiea United Methodist Women, 2) Shelter Volunteer For Child and Family Service, Honolulu; [hon.] 1995 - Editor's Choice Award - "Tutu's Gift" 1996 - Editors Choice Award "The Toilet Seat"; [pers.] Rainbows are frequently seen in Hawaii and "one of my favorite things," They bring joy and happiness to my life Manoa Valley is called "The Birthplace of Rainbows"; [a.] Aiea, HI

PAMIAS, SAMMY
[pen.] Benadicta My Soul; [b.] October 25, 1978, Puerto Rico; [p.] Benadicta Matos and Felix Pamias; [m.] Rachel Felix (Fiancee); [ch.] Samantha T. Richie; [ed.] Frew Mill High School - GED; [occ.] Father/Poet/so to be Law Student; [hon.] Outstanding English Student, Basic life skills award, Best Children Story for a different friend. Last year of school Honor Roll and then Higher Honor Roll; [oth. writ.] Over 150 unpublished poems and still writing more till my time comes to leave Earth; [pers.] No matter how bad things get, they can always get worst, but believe in yourself and the sun will always come out, when its the darkest day. (God) Michel Angelo. Miles Davis; [a.] Camden, NJ

PANAGOTIS, DAVID
[pen.] Richard Colonna; [b.] August 11, 1951, Washington, PA; [p.] Timothy George Panagotis, Betty King Panagotis; [m.] Marie Nancy Panagotis, February 13, 1987; [ch.] Ellyn, Sally Marie; [ed.] Ocala, (Fla.) H.S., Queensborough C.C. - Word Proc. Cert., Marist College - B.A., Behav. Science; [occ.] Clerk; [memb.] Alpha Sigma Lambda (Adult Stud. Honor Soc.) 1990; [hon.] Dean's List at college, grad. Cum Laude, Pub. Choice Award, Watermark Press, Hon. Mention, Amer. Poetry Assoc. 1990; [oth. writ.] Vantage Press - New Voices in American Poetry, 1990, Amherst Society, 1990, poems in several other poetry pubs., Stringer for local newspa-

per "The Awakening", working on autobio and book of poetry, entitled Letters to a Lost Generation; [pers.] In our current scientific, technological society we should never devaluate the arts, like poetry. On the words of one of my professors: "The poets could save the world."; [a.] Staatsburg, NY

PARIS, RAINA
[b.] January 9, 1967, France; [m.] Andrei Ridgeway, May 20, 1995; [ed.] Columbia University New York City, B.A. M.F.A. Cum Laude; [occ.] Actor - Teacher - Poet and Spiritual Counsellor; [memb.] Agape Church of Religious Science - beyond Baroque Art Center, 18th Street Arts Complex; [hon.] B.A. Dean's List, M.F.A Cum Laude Columbia Univ., Dramalogue Critics Award for Best Performance in a one Woman Show; [oth. writ.] Book of poetry and short stories, the arsonist on time.; [pers.] As a writer it is one of my goals to reveal and express the shimmering truth of being both a spiritual and a human being and to show how we can dance life as both in one.; [a.] Los Angeles, CA

PARK, SO UN HA
[b.] Seoul, Korea; [m.] Yun Gi Park; [ch.] Richard, Linda; [ed.] Kyung Kee Girl's High, Ewha Woman's University, Northeastern Illinois; [occ.] University-Graduate College; [memb.] Bilingual/English as a Second Language Teacher, Schaumburg, IL; [oth. writ.] A poem published in our school newsletter; [pers.] I attempt to appreciate the beauty and pureness of nature in my writing.; [a.] Schaumburg, IL

PARKER, JOSHUA
[b.] June 25, 1977, Manning, SC; [p.] Mr. Johnnie L. Parker; [ed.] Scotts Branch High School, and (presently) Attending Charleston Southern University; [hon.] Honor Roll, Who's Who Among American High School Students, Math Award, Chorus Award, Perfect Attendance Award, Spanish Award, Home Ec. Award and U.S. Achievement Award; [oth. writ.] One of my poems was published in the Famous Poets Society.; [pers.] My writings come from my life experiences.; [a.] Pinewood, SC

PARKER, NANCY JEAN
[b.] September 29, 1952; [ed.] Quinsigamond Community College 1976; [occ.] Poet; [memb.] Veterans Community Care Center; [hon.] Alpha No Omega Honor Society

PARKS, NIYA F. H.
[pen.] Niya F. H. Parks; [b.] December 23, 1976, San Bernardino, CA; [p.] Marian E. Magee Parks; [ed.] Cajon High, John W. North High, San Bernardino Valley College; [occ.] Freshman Student, English Major; [memb.] New Horizons Ministries Church of God in Christ; [pers.] It is very often said that "A picture paints a thousand words", but I believe it is a thousand words that paints a picture.; [a.] San Bernardino, CA

PARRISH, MADELINE MICHELLE
[pen.] M. Gunstone; [b.] January 23, 1974, Omaha, NE; [p.] Jerry and Catherine Parrish; [ed.] Naaman Forest H.S., AA in English from DeKalb College; [memb.] American Diabetes Association, Our Lady of Perpetual Help Home Auxiliary; [hon.] Published in World of Poetry Anthology; [pers.] Optimism is the key to reaching your goals.; [a.] Norcross, GA

PARRY, SUSAN
[pen.] Razzle Dazzle; [b.] November 6, 1970, SL County; [p.] Wesley Parry; [m.] Barbara Monson, November 14, 1968; [ch.] One girl, one boy; [ed.] Went to my eleventh grade was going to graduate but something

happened; [occ.] Cashier at Chris and Dick's; [oth. writ.] My daughters name is Jaccia Amber Lynn Parry she is 5 yrs old, my son's name is Chase Troy William Thomas Parry he is 7 yrs old.; [pers.] I am 25 years old Born November 6, 1970 in S. L. County. I've been writing since I was about 9 years old. Poems here always been something I enjoy and always have. I love it.; [a.] West Valley, UT

PARSI JR., SERGIO
[pen.] Alexander Ross; [b.] August 2, 1964, Ponce, PR; [p.] Sergio Parsi Sr., Maria V. Parsi; [m.] Nancy M. Arreaga (Fiancee), March 29, 1997; [ed.] Camden County College and Thomas Edison State College; [occ.] Employment Specialist, Mental Health Assoc. of NJ; [memb.] First Spanish Baptist Church of Camden and Pennsauken; [hon.] Dean's List, Literary Award (High School); [oth. writ.] Written over 100 poems and six plays for my church and myself.; [pers.] My poetry reflects profound spiritual understanding, and how it relates to my every day emotional existance.; [a.] Camden, NJ

PASCOCELLO, GRACE
[b.] November 13, 1925, New York City; [p.] Jennie Cali, Anthony Lupo; [m.] Sylvester, March 27, 1943; [ch.] Pascale (Deceased), Francine Marino; [ed.] 2 years College; [occ.] School Secretary (Ret.); [oth. writ.] Extensive collection of personal poetry; [pers.] Life is...a continuous test of multiple questions and answers. Enjoy the fantastic trip life can be. That's the legacy I'd like to leave to my grandchildren Patrick and Lori.; [a.] Brooklyn, NY

PATCHIN, ALBERT E.
[pen.] "Patch"; [b.] July 2, 1929, Platteville, WI; [p.] Albert and Leora Patchin; [m.] Janice C. Patchin, September 26, 1953; [ch.] Scott, Nadine, Craig, Tracy and Lisa; [ed.] High School - American School of Chicago, Ill. (Correspondence course); [occ.] Retired; [memb.] Platteville VFW Post #5274 Platteville School Board Community Evangelical Free Church Trustee Disabled American Veterans Chapter #67; [oth. writ.] Poems published in area newspapers. Several articles published in different labor leaflets.; [pers.] I have always believed that reading poetry allows one to peek into the soul of the Author.; [a.] Platteville, WI

PATEL, FALGUN B.
[pen.] Uni-Ball; [b.] September 3, 1976, India; [p.] Bhupendra Patel and Saroj Patel; [ed.] Simi Valley High School, Moorpark College; [occ.] Student; [a.] Simi Valley, CA

PATTERSON, KATHERINE C.
[b.] October 12, 1950, French Camp, CA; [p.] Mary Botto, Sherman Gumm; [m.] David C. Patterson, December 17, 1966; [ch.] David Joseph, Leonard James; [occ.] Bus Driver Delta Charter Services Stockton CA; [a.] Stockton, CA

PATTERSON, RUTH
[b.] August 24, 1952, Rock Hill, SC; [p.] James and Leola Tucker; [m.] James A. Patterson, July 22, 1992; [occ.] Freelance writer; [oth. writ.] Praises, The Watcher, Joy, Hope, Miracles, Tears; [pers.] As a born again Christian I have been influenced by a higher power; [a.] Willingboro, NJ

PATTERSON, WENDY
[b.] July 24, 1979, Weiser, ID; [p.] Linda and Dwayne; [ed.] Still in High School 11th grade; [memb.] Member in Shotoken Karate of America (SKA); [hon.] Have earned Karate awards to honor roll.

PATTON, LISA
[b.] October 29, 1982, Stuart, FL; [p.] Jean and Bill Patton; [ed.] 8th grade (gifted), Lincoln Park Academy, Fort Pierce, Florida; [occ.] Student; [memb.] Junior National Honor Society, Girl Scouting, Orchestra Club; [hon.] 1st place beauty contest in Port St. Lucie, FL, 2 year Academic letter (4.0) and pin, Acad. trophy 6th grade, 6 years dance-ballet, jazz, tap and trophies, student of the "year" for yellow in orchestra, Junior National Honor Society member, Yellow Belt Karate; [oth. writ.] I have a journal of many poems and stories I hope to publish some day; [pers.] I strive to be the best I can in all that I do. I love reading and writing and feel many issues such as Aids and the environment need to be addressed for our future.; [a.] Port Saint Lucie, FL

PAYNE, KATRINA
[pen.] Jubil Lee, Jaycey Scott, Kat Russell, Willa Davis; [b.] December 2, 1971; [p.] Tim L. and Bonita J. Payne; [occ.] Medical Field; [hon.] High School Class of 89' Grad Honored Poem, Honorable Mentions (multiple); [oth. writ.] Sanity Miles, Love's Swallowed Thirst, Indian Tears, Memory Quivers, The Days of Song and Smoke, I Remember...; [pers.] Everything in life, - both good and bad - are the experiences to write about whether they happen to you or to me, I look for the word and hope for a phrase.; [a.] Garland, TX

PEACE, LORI
[b.] January 9, 1970, Kittery, ME; [p.] David M. and Sandra D. Campbell; [m.] William A. Peace, February 3, 1989; [ch.] Stephanie Noel, Serissa Nicole, Winston "Trey" Earl; [ed.] Stratford High, Goose Creek, SC (1988 Graduate); [occ.] Store Clerk, Magnolia Stop and Shop, Magnolia, KY; [memb.] Attend Buffalo Elementary, P.T.O. Club meetings regularly; [oth. writ.] A few personal poems, none of which have been seen by the public; [pers.] I tend to be a very nostalgic person, and this motivates me to write about personal events experiences, and people in my life.; [a.] Buffalo, KY

PECK, SUSAN C.
[b.] August 31, 1948, Brooklyn, NY; [p.] Cornelius Cleary, Loretta Cleary; [m.] Richard C. Peck, March 7, 1972; [ch.] Mary Catherine Peck; [ed.] Academy of St. Joseph, Brentwood, NY, BS St. John's University, Jamaica, NY; [occ.] Homemaker; [pers.] I try to express strong feelings as I explore aspects of my life and experience, and share what I discover.; [a.] Clifton Park, NY

PEERY, MEGAN
[b.] August 24, 1981, Medina, OH; [p.] William and Joan; [ed.] Freshman at Buckeye High School; [occ.] Student; [hon.] United States Student Ambassador to New Zealand and Australia, State Finalist: Ohio Power of the Pen Writing Tournament; [a.] Litchfield, OH

PELLICCIARO, CHRISTOPHER J.
[b.] November 25, 1975, JFK Hospital; [p.] Linda Pellicciaro; [ed.] Currently attending Union County College; [occ.] Assistant chef at Alipertiss Fine Italian Cuisine; [oth. writ.] Many poems and short stories. Also, one unfinished novel; [pers.] "There comes a time where we must all endure the pain of being exposed."; [a.] Clark, NJ

PENDLETON, TIFFANY NICOLE
[pen.] Tipper; [b.] March 26, 1984, Fairfax, VA; [p.] Bryan and Gale Pendleton; [ed.] 8th Grade Student at Riviera Middle School; [occ.] Student - 8th Grade; [memb.] National Honor Society, Bible Based Fellowship Church, NAACP; [hon.] "Junior National Honor

Society", St. Petersburg Junior College - Certificate of Achievement, Science Fair Participation, National Physical Fitness Award; [pers.] I strive one day to be as great as Maya Angelou in one positive way or another.; [a.] Tampa, FL

PEREZ, BARBARA
[b.] February 24, 1980; [p.] Lorenzo Perez, Mary Lou Perez; [hon.] Class President, International Foreign Language Award, Named "National Scholar" by the Congressional Youth Leadership Council in Washington, D.C., USAA Academic Achievement Award; [pers.] Influenced by Rimbaud, Verlaine, and other French poets. The sadness in my verse is for the poet who gave to me his infinite love and passion for writing. Exiled until his return, his light lingers even in my dreams; [a.] San Antonio, TX

PERKINS III, FREDERICK D.
[pen.] P Word; [b.] August 8, 1955, Chicago, IL; [p.] Fred and June Perkins; [ch.] Fred IV, Jason, Tia; [oth. writ.] Several poems and many songs; [pers.] Talented is what others call you when you have the courage to stick to your beliefs and believe in yourself.

PERRIN, JEREMY
[b.] August 31, 1979, Greensboro, NC; [p.] George and Elizabeth Perrin; [ed.] Page High School presently a senior; [memb.] JCL, YMCA; [hon.] First place in Memorial for Fallen Police Officer's poetry contest, Honor roll; [oth. writ.] Hero Fallen (poem), various entries in contest; [a.] Greensboro, NC

PETELLE, DEBORAH
[pen.] Deborah Hansen; [b.] May 14, 1952, Tampa, FL; [p.] Wyllie Sarah Thompson and Fred Hansen; [ch.] 1 child, Kristin Sue Petelle; [ed.] Junior College grad, St. Petersburg Junior College, St. Petersburg, Fla; [occ.] I work in the Food and Beverage Industry, now managing a sports bar and restaurant on Kauai Hawai but previously owned and operated my Trail Reading Operation on Kauai Hawai; [oth. writ.] I have my own personal book of poems that have never been published plus 7 children's books also never before published written soley for my grandson; [pers.] As I have struggled thru personal experiences in my life I found it helpful to write about life's situations, my daughter submitted this poem.; [a.] Hanalei, Kauai, HI

PETERMAN, DORIS ADA
[pen.] Peggy Lou Dare; [b.] June 24, 1924, Farmhouse, Dekalb County, IL; [p.] J. Ward and Ada Adriana (WISI) Coble; [m.] Deceased; [ch.] Four girls and one boy, Janet, Judy, Rose, Linnea and Carl, Palm; [ed.] High School and some College courses; [occ.] Retired; [memb.] Sycamore United Methodist Church Dustin Chapt. #365 order of Eastern Star of Illinois; [a.] Dekalb, IL

PETERMAN, JILL
[b.] March 20, 1981, Lansing, MI; [p.] Jeff and Dawn Peterman; [ed.] Shallowater High School 10th grade; [memb.] National Junior Honor Society (8th grade yr.), FHA (Future Homemakers of America), Texas Sight masters Pistol Club; [oth. writ.] None ever published; [a.] Shallowater, TX

PETTIT, MICHELE
[b.] November 16, 1960; [pers.] And the evening and the morning make one complete day!; [a.] Marina Del Rey, CA

PHILLIPS, ALICE L.
[b.] January 26, 1921, Tolt, WA; [p.] Tom Maloney and Olga Maloney; [m.] George G. Phillips, May 15, 1982; [ch.] Tom Hoey, Peggy Hoey, Bob and Terry Hoey; [ed.] Centralia Comm. College, Tacoma Community College, University Puget Sound, St. Peter Hosp. School of Nursing; [occ.] HSWF (Ret. Nurse); [oth. writ.] Articles to "The Olympian", local newspaper. Write monthly paper, "Westside Story" for St. Michael Catholic Church.; [pers.] I must feel deeply about anything I write and such the truth.; [a.] Olympia, WA

PHILLIPS, EVA
[pen.] E.C. Phillips; [b.] January 24, 1964, Ausburgh, Germany; [p.] Clyde Ford, Shirley Rod; [m.] Danny Phillips, May 29, 1982; [ch.] Amanda Phillips, Ryan PHillips; [pers.] I'm a dreamer, who loves words and wishes to share. The bible, Poe, Shakespeare and Tennyson made a great impression.; [a.] Monterey, TN

PHLEGM, MERLIE JEAN
[b.] June 25, 1942, Evergreen, TX; [p.] Rev. Frank Phlegm, Mary Jackson Phlegm; [m.] April 1965; [ch.] Madison/Menarak; [ed.] Lincoln High, Prairie View A&M Univ. 61-65: Clothing Textiles BS, SAM Houston St. Huntsville Sum 87 Kdg. Endorsement, TSU Sum 88 ESL, Augusta Col. Sum 1990 and 95 Ech. Ed.; [occ.] Kindergarten Teacher, Thurgood Marshall Mag. Sch, North Forest ISD Hou., TX; [memb.] Kappa Omicron Phi, NAEYC, NAACP; [hon.] Val Lincoln High, Coldspring, TX 1961; [oth. writ.] 99 Songs numerous poems 1 book "The Final Curtain"; [pers.] Man's/woman's destiny and fate is within him/herself. There is nothing beyond the flesh that influences his/her outcome. All are born with whatever is needed to succeed in life. For all person's success or failure is within the confines of his/her mind. As one thinketh, so is he/she.; [a.] Humble, TX

PIASECKI, MIKE
[pen.] Stone Grover; [b.] October 26, 1971, Sonora, CA; [ed.] News writing at Southwestern College, but no formal creative writing classes; [hon.] 1st and 2nd place at the Journalism Association of Community Colleges (JACC) of Southern California for Humor writing; [oth. writ.] Mostly poems and songs, but this is the first time I've ever submitted any.; [pers.] I dedicate this poem to my family and friends who gave me the inspiration. I have learned a lot through our paths we've taken together and they helped me realize that I am truly a lucky man.; [a.] Chula Vista, CA

PICKENS, YOREL
[b.] October 10, 1979, Philadelphia; [p.] Denise and Leroy Pickens; [ed.] Overbrook High School plans to attend Philadelphia College of Pharmacy and Science to be an Industrial Pharmacist; [occ.] Secretary at JFK Skills Center; [memb.] Philadelphia Young Play Wrights, Model, Debate team Volunteer at Communities Pharmacy; [hon.] 1,000 dollar savings bond from NAACP, Gold Medal winner in Search for Talented Poets, 3rd place winner in Young Play Wrights, first place winner in 1996 ACT-SO competition; [oth. writ.] Poems published in Philadelphia Tribune. In Middle School year book, recently put a book of poems together but unable to get published; [pers.] When someone close to you dies, you feel alone and scared, you are frightened and your heart drops into coldness. Crayons was my mothers favorite poem I would like to dedicate this publication in her loving memory. I love you mom.; [a.] Philadelphia, PA

PICKETT, JOAN R.
[b.] February 23, 1937, Westminster, MD; [p.] George Brown, Mary Shaffer Brown; [m.] Calvin Pickett, October 27, 1956; [ch.] Randall, Brenda, Luann; [ed.] High School, Taneytown High, Taneytown, MD; [occ.] Retired 1st grade Asst. Howard Co. Public Schools Lisbon, MD; [memb.] Poplar Springs UM Church, Lisbon Ladies Auxiliary to Lisbon Fire Co.; [hon.] 1st grade presented a retirement program featuring and incorporating all of the poems I had written over the years for them.; [oth. writ.] I've written some children's books that I hope to publish at some point.; [pers.] Most of my poetry has been written for the enjoyment of the students at Lisbon school and geared to their level. The inspiration comes from them and my love for all children.; [a.] Woodbine, MD

PIEKARSKY, ALEXIS
[b.] November 2, 1980, New Jersey; [p.] Bruce and Debra Piekarsky; [ed.] Cliffside Pk High School; [occ.] Student; [oth. writ.] Winner of Bergen County Cade of N.J. Essay winner 1995.; [a.] Cliffside Park, NJ

PIERSON, KAREN A.
[pen.] Karen A. Pierson; [b.] January 25, 1940, Maquon, IL; [p.] Mr. and Mrs. Charles F. Little; [m.] Jackie Lee Pierson, January 7, 1962; [ch.] Debra and Tammie Grandchildren: Kerry and Aaron; [ed.] Graduated 1958 from GHS Took courses for computers and Blue prints Carl Sandburg College; [occ.] Retired from Maytag Corporation; [memb.] American Legion Post 0285, Methodist Church, Union Midwest Lodge 2063, Song Writers Club of America, International Society of Poets-Lifetime Member Backyard Wildlife Habitat Certified #18014 National Audubon Society; [oth. writ.] Published own book "Poetic scraps of Literature" 1995, won the golden poet award 1991, 1992, 1988, 1990 Silver Award. National Library of Poetry Editors Choice 1993, 1994, 1995, 1996. Published many Anthologies and in a few papers, and "The Poets corner magazine". Also written and copyrights to few songs.; [pers.] I enjoy writing poetry, wildlife published, and sharing it with my family and friends. I am a widow, and I like to keep busy.; [a.] Galesburg, IL

PILLA, RAMANI S.
[pen.] 'Gita'; [p.] Parvati and Bhanoji Rao; [ed.] Finishing Ph.D. in Statistics from Pennsylvania State University. Got M.S. in Statistics from India; [occ.] Pre-Doctoral Lecturer at Penn State University; [memb.] Member of ASA and IMS (Statistical Associations); [hon.] 'Gold Medal' for securing first position in M.S. National Merit Scholarship for being an outstanding undergraduate student. 'Theoretical Development Award' for a research paper; [oth. writ.] Wrote several poems in my mother tongue 'Telugu' and got award in India. Other English poems include: Friend, Solitude, etc.; [pers.] I enjoy writing about nature and emotions. My writing reflects that. Influenced by several Indian Poets including Revindranath Tagore (Nobel Laureate for his work: 'Gitajanli'.; [a.] State College, PA

PILMAIER, DEBORAH
[b.] October 25, 1967, Pryor, OK; [p.] Glenda and Robert Meeker; [m.] Dave Pilmaier, October 3, 1987; [ch.] Jacob Joseph, Katie Rose; [ed.] Pryor High School, Northeastern State Univ, Northeastern State University - Bachelor Degree in Accounting, Northeastern State University and Langston University Working on Bachelors degree in Elementary Education; [occ.] Homemaker, Accountant, Teacher; [memb.] Alpha Chi; [hon.] Summa Cum Laude (class of 1989, Northeastern State University) President honor roll 4 yrs.; [oth. writ.] Several unpublished poems on various subjects; [pers.] My

poems are written about things that have touched my life such as my daughter's christening, my son's first birthday, the death of a friend, and the Oklahoma City Bombing; [a.] Chouteau, OK

PIMENTEL, BEN
[pen.] Ben Gee; [b.] December 1, 1966, Dominican Republic; [p.] Bienvenido and Olga Pimentel; [ch.] Vanessa and Angelica; [ed.] Academic H.S. (Jersey City, NJ) and Taylor Business School; [occ.] Bookkeeper; [oth. writ.] Just personal love and romance poems that have never been published.; [pers.] Love and friendship go inter twined without each other they just fall apart.; [a.] Jersey City, NJ

PIPES JR., RONALD NELSON
[b.] April 30, 1968, Hardinsburg, KY; [p.] Anna J. Garris and Bill Garris; [m.] Jennifer Lytle, not married yet but soon to be; [ch.] Krystal Pipes, Katrina Pipes, Megan Pipes, Alex Pipes, Greg Lytle; [ed.] Hardee High Wauchula, Fla. G.E.D.; [occ.] Rapid Cablevision; [memb.] Bowling League; [hon.] Track runner in high school, trophies and ribbons, chef; [oth. writ.] The Lord is Coming Soon, I'm not the Man She Thought, The Laughing Clowns, Love is Like a Rose, The Soldiers at War; [pers.] I like to write, it's been a hobby of mine since I was a little boy. I never thought I would really ever try to do anything with my writings; [a.] Guston, KY

PLOTTS, CHRYSTAL
[pen.] Chrystal; [b.] May 11, 1947, Monroe, NC; [p.] John and Beatrice Huckabee; [m.] Donald H. Plotts, June 8, 1991; [ch.] Russell, Duane, Israel, Chris, Rachel; [ed.] Bessemer City High, Bessemer City, NC; Gaston Community College, Dallas, NC; [occ.] Customer Service, Retail Sales; [memb.] Apopka Assembly of GOD, Apopka, FL; [hon.] P.T.A. President, Vice President Advisory Committee, Gastonia, NC; [oth. writ.] A collection of poems also a notebook of gospel songs. None has ever been published. This was the first poem I've ever sent in.; [pers.] My songs and poems are an inspiration from God. I would like to share this blessing with others. I give thanks to Doris Plotts for encouraging me to enter this contest.; [a.] Apopka, FL

POINDEXTER, OPHELIA C.
[b.] March 21, 1937, Clarksville, TN; [p.] James and Sallie Chiton; [m.] Leroy Poindexter, March 26, 1956; [ch.] Rockelle Daniels, Darcel Coles, Darro and Brenay Poindexter; [ed.] Burt-Hi-School attended Austin Peay University; [occ.] Retired; [oth. writ.] Write for hobby.

PON, FRANCISCO D.
[b.] July 18, 1951, Icqa, Peru; [p.] Sen Tac Pon and Dometria Salazar; [ed.] Master of Arts in Hispanic Literature and language Saint Louis University, St. Louis, Missouri Magister der Philosohie Leopold Franzen University, Innsbruck, Austria; [occ.] Assistant of the Consul of Mexico, Consultant of Mexico; [memb.] Alpha Sigma Nu, Sigma Delta Pi; [hon.] Ohtli Recognition, Alpha Sima Nu Jesuit Honor Society; [oth. writ.] International Progress Organization; [pers.] Juntos Todos Podemos, United everything is possible.; [a.] Saint Louis, MO

POPE, RICK L.
[pen.] Rick L. Pope; [b.] June 22, 1940, Cherokee County, GA; [p.] Rev. Tom (Deceased) and Hulette Pope; [ed.] Cherokee High School, Reinhardt College (Waleska, Georgia); [occ.] Retired Journalist, Teacher; [memb.] Pierce Literary Society, Jaycees, American Film Institute; [hon.] Various talent awards for singing, certificates for Public Speaking; [oth. writ.] "Words For Positive Living", "First Rate: The Greatest Films Of

All Time", various Arts and Entertainment Columns, Film Articles, other writings for newspapers; [pers.] "Choose your words wisely and voice them accordingly." "See yourself as you truly are: A valuable individual endowed with the potential to achieve."; [a.] Atlanta, GA

PORTER, ROBERT A.
[b.] February 10, 1936, Ayer, MA; [p.] George and Stella Porter; [m.] Marjorie Porter, April 21, 1956; [ch.] Karen, Cynthia, Joseph, Kim, Tammy, Carol; [ed.] Graduated, Leominster High School and Saxton Trade High School (both 6-55); [occ.] Retired; [pers.] I will be forever grateful that in my life, I have been blessed not once, but seven times, a wonderful wife and six children.; [a.] Athol, MA

POTTER, COLEEN
[b.] August 29, 1939, Rockford, IL; [p.] Alice Fricke, Bill Frandsen; [m.] Divorced; [ch.] Dianne Lynn Potter, Robert Steven Potter; [ed.] Bachelor of Science in Education Master of Art in Teaching and many graduate hours, Dr. of Metaphysics; [occ.] Teacher of Biology and Zoology; [memb.] Delta Kappa Gamma, Our Savior's Lutheran Church, AAUW, School Improvement Team, IABT; [hon.] Delta Kappa Gamma Chapter Recording Secretary, Corresponding Secretary and Personal Growth and Services Chairman, Who's Who Among American Teachers; [oth. writ.] Friendship, Spiritual Light, I Grew Old, many other poems and short stories; [pers.] I ask God to use me to reflect his light to mankind. Poetry and writing have been one of the ways I've been able to accomplish this for as long as I can remember.; [a.] Rockford, IL

POTTER, LINDA M.
[pen.] Amber Dawn; [b.] July 13, 1961, Chicago, IL; [occ.] Owner-Operator Clawzr US Nail Clinic experts in the treatment of problem nails diseases and disorders; [oth. writ.] Currently being printed "The Lord of Pen" includes" Time, Legacy, I Remembered When, Friend's Gifts, Giving All, To Forever Believe, Promises, The Betrayal of Richard Granium, The Bill, True Perfection, Undefeated, Longing, Daddy's Girl, Celest, Eye to Eye, The Lord of Pen, Human Observations, The Light, A Fool, Thanksgiving, Remember Why, Fantasy.; [pers.] I believe writing is a gift... Given to me for a purpose. It is my hope that my being published will allow others to experience. Through my writing, that fulfillment of purpose which comes from sharing a dream.; [a.] West Chicago, IL

POTTER III, JOSEPH
[b.] September 17, 1965, Milton, FL; [p.] Francis Williams and Joseph E. Potter Jr; [ed.] Milton High School, Community College of the Air Force, St. Leo College; [occ.] Network Analyst; [oth. writ.] Feature articles in on target computing 1992-1993, special interest publications and writing for hire 1986 present; [pers.] The only impossible dream is the one not persued Isle at 1996.; [a.] Austell, GA

POWELL, MELISSA
[b.] October 12, 1983, Glendale, AZ; [p.] Terry and Peggy Powell; [ed.] Oasis Elementary, 7th grade; [occ.] Student; [hon.] First Prize Recognition in 5th grade poetry contest, Phineas F. Bresee Award; [oth. writ.] Several poems written for school projects; [pers.] As a 7th grader, most of my poetry I've written has been a requirement for school, but I really love poetry and I am planning to continue writing.; [a.] Peoria, AZ

POWERS, EDWARD S.
[pen.] "Quiet Spirit"; [b.] March 16, 1947, Springfield, OH; [p.] Edward L. and Evelyn M. Powers; [m.]

Merrelyn C. Powers, August 1, 1970; [ed.] South High School, Continuing Ed. at Clark State College and Community Hospital, and life's experiences; [occ.] Mechanical tool assembler for Global Industrial Technologies, Inc.; [memb.] Woodland Indian Heritage Society, National Audubon Society, Aid Association for lutherans, Lutheran's Brotherhood; [oth. writ.] Several poems and writings at this time not published; [pers.] I am a product of the environment. My surroundings are of great influence. The great spirit directs my thoughts, and my hand.; [a.] Springfield, OH

PRATER II, DENNIS
[pen.] Little D.; [b.] March 2, 1980, Toledo, OH; [p.] Dennis I. and Barb Prater; [ed.] Junior at Waite High School; [occ.] Housekeeping at Holiday Inn French Quarters (Perrysburg Ohio), Big Boy Toledo Ohio; [pers.] Two wrong Don't Make a Right.

PRATT, BONNIE
[b.] November 11, 1976; [ed.] Hamilton - Wenham Regional High School, Suffolk University, College of Liberal Arts and Sciences; [occ.] Poetess; [memb.] Amnesty International, Equality Now; [hon.] Dean's List; [pers.] "A woman who writes feels too much." Anne Sexton The Black Art.; [a.] Boston, MA

PRICE, MYRTIS L.
[b.] August 15, 1951, Little Rock, AR; [p.] Margaret Walker, O'Dell Price; [ch.] Lenean, Sonya, Cindy, Julius and Dante; [ed.] Troy High School, Troy, New York, Cambridge, Business School, Detroit, Mich.; [occ.] Restaurant Manager, Burlington, NC; [hon.] Golden Pen Club, Most Talented Award; [pers.] I've always enjoyed reading and writing poetry, beginning in the fifth grade. I was always encouraged to write by my teachers as years went by. Influenced by Elizabeth Barret Browning.; [a.] Burlington, NC

PROSSER, TIFFANY M.
[pen.] Tifanny Prosser; [b.] August 9, 1981, Sumter, SC; [p.] Glenn Prosser, Donna Prosser; [memb.] Beta Club, Basketball Team; [hon.] High Honor Roll, Poem published in the Anthology of Poetry by Young Americans 1995 Edition; [oth. writ.] "What is a Lantern?"; [pers.] I thank the Lord for the inspiration and my family for their support.; [a.] Johnsonville, SC

PROVENCHER, KIMBERLY
[b.] September 6, 1980, Manchester, NH; [p.] Suzanne and Kevin Fraser; [ed.] Auburn Village School, Memorial H.S.; [hon.] Eight Grade Math Award, High Honors (9 and 10th grade), 2 yrs. Who's Who Honors; [pers.] Studying guitar and music. Love art and drawing; [a.] Auburn, NH

PRUSA, GEORGIA MONROE
[pen.] Georgia Monroe, Georgia Prusa; [b.] February 4, 1954, Paragould, AR; [p.] Lavell (Bob) and Pearlene Miller; [m.] Craig R. Prusa, February 24, 1996; [ch.] Chris, Angie, Brian Monroe; [ed.] Attended Arkansas State University and Southern Illinois University at Edwardsville, IL; [occ.] Sr. Records Clerk at Southwestern Bell Telephone and a Freelance writers; [memb.] Fete du Bon Vieux Temps Committee Cahokia Homecoming Assoc. Flood Fest Committe, Maplewood Church of Christ; [hon.] Community Service Award during the Flood of 93 at the Village of East Carondelet, IL; [oth. writ.] Freelance writer - The Herald Newspapers, Departmental Newsletter at SWBT, church bulletins; [pers.] "Two Roads diverged in a yellow wood... I took the one less traveled by, and that has made all the difference." Robert Frost; [a.] Cahokia, IL

PRUTSMAN, KURT
[pen.] Mellon Collie and Kurt Thomas; [b.] September 4, 1981, Vallejo, CA; [p.] Laura and Gary Prutsman; [ed.] A Sophomore in High School; [occ.] Student; [oth. writ.] "Pure Luck", "Hell's Discipline", "Social Suicide", "Nevermore", "Cage of Dirt", "Meat Fly", "Steak of Empathy" "Special Super Star", "Room God" "Muddy Milk" and many more; [pers.] Though I'm young I've gone through a lot. I've been depressed about a lot of things since I was 8. I started writing when I was 13. I am inspired by Kurt Cobain and Billy Cargon. I am inspired by Music in general.; [a.] San Clemente, CA

PRYOR, KAREN R.
[pen.] Rene; [b.] March 29, 1963, Augusta, GA; [p.] Sandra and Robert Pryor; [ed.] Spring Valley High, University of South Carolina; [occ.] Artist for self owned graphic sign company; [memb.] Trenholm Road, Methodist Church; [oth. writ.] Poem published for a Christmas program.; [pers.] "Creative pain is universal - a link to every heart that has loved", "Thanks to my family and friends for their loving support".; [a.] Columbia, SC

PULELOA, MICHAEL J.
[pen.] MJ Puleloa; [b.] October 6, 1973, Majuro, Marshall Islands; [p.] Williams Puleloa, Linda Puleloa; [ed.] Kamehameha Schools (High School), University of Hawaii and Manoa; [occ.] Student; [hon.] Dean's List, winner of the Myrle Clark Creative Writing Competition; [oth. writ.] Short stories and poetry; [a.] Kaunakakai, HI

PURDY, ALICIA
[b.] February 18, 1977, Lewes, DE; [p.] Forrest Purdy, Sandra Purdy; [ed.] Cape Henlopen High School, Delaware Technical Community College; [occ.] Student; [oth. writ.] Several poems published in our school papers; [pers.] Writing poetry helps me express the part of me people can't see. I want to thank my grandmother for the encouragement to enter this contest. Her faith led me this far.; [a.] Lewes, DE

QUAMME, DAVID
[pen.] Jackson Dice, Don Payote, Verse Valentino; [b.] November 25, 1965, Seattle, WA; [p.] Mike and Arlene Quamme; [ed.] BA Art University of WA, 1990, New England School of Photography, Professional Certificate 1995; [occ.] Carier with National Carier Systems; [memb.] National Press Photographers Association, Photographers Forum/Serbin Communications; [hon.] Best of College Photography 1995, Honorable Mention, Best of Photography Annual 1995, 4th Place B&W $100 cash prize Serbin Communications, Santa Barbara, CA; [oth. writ.] Sparrowgrass Poetry Forum, Poetry Exchange Newsletter, Commentary Letters to Editors, Boston Herald, University of WA Daily, Art Access, Livonia, Modern Shaman Magazine, Stuff Magazine, Art Resource Magazine and Night Vision, a Dream Journal Quarterly.; [pers.] We all breath the same air.; [a.] Seattle, WA

QUINN, BARBARA WORTHINGTON
[b.] Baltimore, MD; [p.] Margaret Whitaker Underhill, Elmer Lee Jones; [m.] David R. Quinn, USN Ret., November 6, 1982; [ch.] Sheila Ogletree Kennedy, Lish Lynette Ogletree; [ed.] Varied courses at U. MD., Ext. U. of WA State Tech (MPHS), Shelby State (MPHS), Rhodes College (formerly South Western At MPHS); [occ.] Former photographer. Now wife, mother, painter and writer, self-appointed care-taker of pets, strays and wildlife; [memb.] Humane Society of U.S., MPHS Humane Society, MPHS Museum Systems, MPHS Zoological Society, National Wildlife Federation and 3 Kuvasz

Associations, one in Canada; [oth. writ.] Several articles and poems for the Kuvasz Clubs (3) Magazines in the U.S. and Canada; [pers.] I am blessed in feeling a deeply spiritual and personal kinship with all living things. These feelings for nature and our environment and the intricate relationships with those I treasure most are what inspire me to write and attempt to share my special moments with others.; [a.] Memphis, TN

RAFFERTY, MARJORIE
[b.] February 23, 1935, Tyngsboro, MA; [p.] Ann and John Rafferty; [oth. writ.] Unpublished poems I have written for my own enjoyment.; [pers.] Dedicated to my mother Ann and also to the memory of Thomas (Butch) Riley who like many of our service men paid the ultimate price for peace.

RAFTIS, DIMITRA ARDAMIS
[b.] October 22, 1961, Sparta, Greece; [p.] George and Niki Ardamis; [m.] Kyriacos Raftis, October 28, 1990; [ed.] Fort Hamilton High School CUNY College of Staten Island Adelphi University; [occ.] Elementary School Teacher; [pers.] I wrote the poem in memory of my stillborn baby George-David. I will always love him.; [a.] Brooklyn, NY

RAGAZZO, BRENDA
[b.] August 7, 1964, Paterson, NJ; [p.] The late Lawrence Caruso and Sandra Caruso; [ch.] Kevin Michael and Ashley Mae; [ed.] Elmwood Park Memorial High School; [occ.] Legal Secretary; [pers.] I send special love and thanks to "Mommy" for inspiring me to write this poem. Not only is she my mother, but she truly is my best friend.; [a.] Elmwood Park, NJ

RAJADURAI, CHRISTINA THAVAMANY
[pen.] Thavam; [b.] August 31, 1918, Sri Lanka; [p.] Christy (Deceased), Mary Ragunathan; [m.] Alfred Rajadurai (Deceased), November 9, 1938; [ch.] Six in all, two boys, four girls; [ed.] Senior Cambridge; [occ.] NIL; [pers.] Life journey in general is not rosy and cosy and for some it's a might challenge, when it doesn't run a smooth course. As an early widow with half a dozen offsprings then of very tender ages, my experience is, that unless the mind is tuned to the inner spirit the vital force from which one taps extra strength to trudge along the rough and rugged path. Life would have been an utter force.; [a.] Waterbury, CT

RAMIG, CHRISTINA
[b.] December 13, 1976, Cleveland, OH; [p.] Leigh Cardwell, David Ramig; [ed.] Parkway North H.S. - St. Louis, Lindenwood College - St. Charles; [occ.] Beauty Warehouse - St. Charles; [oth. writ.] Several poems in local contests, as a child poetry in highlights for children.; [pers.] Poetry is my guide to my soul and my self worth. I use my writings to relax and writings to relax and express my inner and deepest thoughts. It is not to teach others but myself.; [a.] Saint Louis, MO

RAMPANI, ROBERT M.
[pen.] Bob Eagle; [b.] July 1, 1928, Saint Louis Co., MO; [p.] Etta and Mike Rampani; [m.] Divorced, October 23, 1950; [ch.] Steve, Gene, Ralph, Aaron Rampani, Roberta Dame; [ed.] High School; [occ.] Retired: McDonnell - Douglas Aircraft Corp.; [memb.] 45 yr. I am Machinist Union, Greater St. Louis Archaeology Society, Veteran of Foreign War; [hon.] Single Male Parent raised 5 children poem in worlds largest poem for peace, poems in many anthologies, honors in archeology.; [oth. writ.] Poems in numerous journals, newspapers, newsletters, articles in archaeology journals. Poem excepted on world's largest poem for peace. Poems in

many anthologies.; [pers.] A heartfelt writer on most all subjects, special interest on outdoors - saving land and wildlife. A tie with the past, early man and pioneer days. A writer with heart and pride and love for country and most things.; [a.] Bridgeton, MO

RAMSEY, TODD WAYNE
[b.] May 5, 1969, Houston, TX; [ed.] University of Houston; [occ.] Student; [pers.] Only the blackest will stain hearts no tears can wash away.; [a.] Houston, TX

RANA, JOSEPH JOHN
[pen.] Joe; [b.] April 21, 1983, Hartford, CT; [p.] Donald and Charnelle; [ed.] 7th grade Kingswood Oxford, West Hartford, Conn.; [occ.] Student, 7th grade; [a.] West Hartford, CT

RAO, A. V.
[b.] November 3, 1949, India; [p.] Rayudu, Jogamma; [m.] Sandhya, March 14, 1976; [ch.] Deepa; [ed.] B. SC (Engineering) (Metallurgy) certified Regulatory Manager, ICB, Washington, D.C.; [occ.] Banker; [memb.] Distinguished Member of International Society of Poets; [oth. writ.] Poem titled "Shepherd's Night" is being published in "Forever and a day". Collection of poems titled "The Meandering Mind". Several articles on banking and financial management including compliance with banking regulations.; [pers.] A poet's mind is an observatory, watching the play of life in nature's glorious territory. All humans have two simultaneous. Often contradictory needs-need for recognition and need to find inner bliss and contentment. Through my poems I endeavor to portray the struggle to attain these needs.; [a.] New York, NY

RASMUSSEN, ERIK E.
[pen.] Moose; [b.] January 27, 1976, Abilene, TX; [p.] Bruce and Cathy Rasmussen; [ed.] High School - Joel E. Ferris, 1 Semester College at College of the Siskiyous; [occ.] Porter for Mercedes-Benz; [a.] Spokane, WA

RASMUSSEN, MELISSA
[b.] July 22, 1978, Port Jefferson; [p.] Harry and Rose Anne Rasmussen; [ed.] Graduated from Newfield High School. Attending St. Joseph's College.; [hon.] Girl Scout Silver Award, Kenneth Whiteback Memorial Scholarship; [pers.] I wrote this poem several months after my father died. Putting my emotions into the words of this poem. Helped me to deal with the pain and newness of my loss. I hope that it can bring hope and comfort to anyone who may read my poem.; [a.] Port Jefferson Station, NY

RATHI, DINESHCHANDRA H.
[b.] December 1, 1968, Bombay, India; [p.] Harikisan Rathi, Pushpalata Rathi; [m.] Annada, March 29, 1996; [ed.] College of Engineering, Pusad, India Bachelor of Electronics Engineering; [occ.] Software Develops, Web-Sci Technologies, NJ; [memb.] Poetry Society of India; [oth. writ.] Several poems - not yet published. The themes one the mind, life and human relationships, ris-a-ris and individual and the society.; [pers.] Om Namah Shivaya!!!; [a.] Plainboro, NJ

RAUCH, DEBBIE H.
[b.] September 11, 1952, Ft. Jackson, SC; [p.] Violet Cowan, Virgil N. Bickley; [m.] Douglas Rauch, February 23, 1990; [ch.] Raymond Scott, V. J. Holladay, Kim Rauch; [ed.] Edmunds High, Central Carolina Sumter, SC; [occ.] Accounting Dept; [oth. writ.] Fictional Short Stories; [pers.] Almost Everyone has an interesting story if not give them one.

RAVENS, CHAD
[pen.] R. C. Michael; [b.] December 17, 1979, Kankakee, IL; [p.] Peter Stich, Vicki Stich, David Ravens; [ed.] Junior Aquainas High School La Crosse, WI; [occ.] Student; [oth. writ.] Many poems but none published; [pers.] Most of my poetry is dark and about death but to write lessens the risk of action.; [a.] Hokah, MN

RAVIT, MARY D.
[b.] September 25, 1942, Charleston, SC; [p.] Viola Williams, Wilburn Williams; [m.] Franklin Ravit, May 12, 1962; [ed.] Immaculate Conception High, Allied School of Nursing; [occ.] Practical Nurse; [pers.] With God, all things are possible. Realizing that truth act.; [a.] Chicago, FL

RAYNOR, WIL
[pen.] Wil Raynor; [b.] July 19, 1950, Carbondale, IL; [p.] Louise and Lewis Gee; [m.] Allen Raynor, October 25, 1975; [ch.] Jennifer, Timothy, Michael; [ed.] High School graduate - Anna Jonesboro Community High College Credits from Shawnee Jr. College Karnak Illinois and Kansas University, Lawrence, Kansas; [occ.] Supervisor of Driver License Northeast Kansas; [hon.] While in High School I won several awards and high Acclamations in regard to my poetry — since school and until very recently— I have returned to my past passion of writing poetry.; [oth. writ.] Have been pursuing a song writing career as a "Hobby" — Since my youngest child is now 16 I am finding more time to dedicate to my writing.; [pers.] I have always been moved by poetry and song lyrics but have no formal training and have always felt intimidated about my abilities, however I have always had a real passion for writing.; [a.] Manhattan, KS

READINGER, ELSIE M.
[b.] June 16, 1947; [m.] Harvey Readinger; [ch.] Robert, Timmy; [occ.] Retired Residential Services Aide for Mental Retardation. (At Hamburg Center). I was employed for 23 years until my retirement.; [oth. writ.] Poem published in "Poetic Voices of America" in 1988; [pers.] I enjoy writing poems about personal Experiences. I was greatly inspired by Helen Steiner Rice's poetry.; [a.] Hamburg, PA

RECTOR SR., PAUL T.
[pen.] Paul Rector; [b.] June 12, 1945, Muncie, IN; [p.] Dwight and Mary Rector; [m.] Divorced; [ch.] Donald, Paul Jr., Jennifer, Lance, Brian; [ed.] Davleville, High, B.S. Butler University; [occ.] Factory Worker; [memb.] Nat. Rifle Assn., A.A.R.P., Alpha Chi Omega; [hon.] Eagle Scout; [oth. writ.] Church Bulletin has printed one, and "You" will be in The Storyteller in September '96 "Purification" will be only the second of my poems to be formally published; [pers.] Most of my work comes from my experiences, going up on a farm in central Indiana, and as I have moved through life. I hope the reader can not just relate to them, but experience them along with me.; [a.] Lapel, IN

REDFORD, JAMES P.
[b.] March 9, 1969, Louisville, KY; [p.] B.C. Redford, Beverly Redford; [ed.] (Urban) Public Elementary Schools, Private Christain Jr. High, Public High Schools (Urban and Rural), University, Vo-Tech, each and every person that I have known, met or greeted; [occ.] Certified Respiratory Therapy Technician; [hon.] H) All the wonderful people in my life-past and present. A) The publication of my poem (leaf), The past 27 years and the consciousness to realize it; [oth. writ.] Are praised too much, are retained personally for those open minded enough to feel their thoughts as they read my words, are

inside yet to be realized; [pers.] For every question, comes an answer who's to say right or wrong for what is an answer but a perspective, from wisdom comes sight - Does wisdom not present another question?; [a.] Glasgow, KY

REDWINE, ANNA E.
[pen.] Ambrose Christophus; [b.] July 25, 1979, Lubbock, TX; [p.] Rev. Carrol and Jeanette Redwine; [ed.] Junior at Cornerstone Christian Academy; [occ.] Student at Cornerstone Christian Academy; [memb.] Member of the International Society of Poets; [hon.] Editor's Choice Award Presented by the National Library of Poetry; [oth. writ.] "Freedom" published in Spirit of the Age anthology.; [pers.] Time in eternity instructs the pen.; [a.] Skiatook, OK

REED, GEOFFREY ALAN
[b.] December 2, 1963, Boston, MA; [p.] Mr. and Mrs. Richard F. Hannaford; [ed.] High School, Automotives/Art - majors, general honors, 11th gr. and 12th, 1st Degree in Maintenance, Genesis Center, "Devereaux", 1 1/2 yr. Quality Cont.; [occ.] Window Maintenance, (due to incarceration); [memb.] "Former" - "Bass Angler's - Sportsman's Society's Society", Stavens Bros. 18x and 81 Racing Team, (Nascar); [hon.] Certificate in Interior/Exterior Maintenance, 2 yr. experience with Quality Control of, Pewter figure work, and Supervision of (12) man Dry - Wall Crew (experience) "Football", midjet - (Tackle) High - School - (Linebacker/Offensive Tackle); [oth. writ.] "Damsel of Double Muting!" "Color of Chump - Change, A Nine-Ball Player's Bible", "Life Lessons in Reading Comprehension", "The Blood-Lust!", "Table-Fifteen!", "Outside Man", Part I- "The Copperfield Sanction", Part II - "Death Reflection"; [pers.] "Other writings listed above, I am still looking for book publishing company with no subsidy or, author's `pre' fees..."anyone interested?!"; [a.] Newtown, CT

REED, JAMES
[b.] October 12, 1980, Indianapolis, IN; [p.] Margaret Scott; [ed.] Freshman in High School at Warren Central High School; [occ.] Tutor; [memb.] National Junior Honor Society, Boy Scouts of America, Warren Central Gold Brigade Marching Band, The Church of Jesus Christ of Later Day Saints; [hon.] Eagle Scout, Fire Crafter, Top 10 in the Freshmen Class (No. 2), Academic Excellence in Math and Geography; [oth. writ.] Journal of Australia, A Day in the Life of a Thief, "Words to Remember", "The Weeping Heart". (All of these works are not published); [pers.] To me the world is like a blank canvass. We are artists painting on it, try to leave our mark. Some painting are large and some small. Some are masterpieces while others are graffiti. However, in the end, the paint will inevitably dry and then chip off and be forgotten or be covered by other painters making their mark.; [a.] Indianapolis, IN

REESE, LU
[b.] May 9, 1930; [m.] Rolf, November 25, 1961; [ch.] Stacey, Erling; [occ.] Retired Brokerage, Firm Executive; [a.] Princeton, NJ

REGINO, EVA
[b.] April 21, 1940, Williamson Co., Round Rock, TX; [p.] Bassie Regino - (Dad) Deceased; [m.] Louis C. Dominguez, 1964; [ch.] 2 - a boy and a girl; [ed.] G.E.D. Food Service Schooling; [occ.] Pflugerville I.S.D., Cafeteria Manager; [memb.] Round Rock City Association Club, St. Williams Church; [hon.] Merit for cooking; [oth. writ.] Recipes for cookery others, never have been published. I love to write poems and short stories.

REIDENBACH JR., CLAUDE E.
[pen.] Buck Reidenbach; [b.] October 12, 1948, Centralia, MO; [p.] Naomi Ann and Claude E. Sr.; [m.] Divorced; [ch.] Dustin Ray, Connie Marie; [ed.] High School Chelmsford High School Chelmsford, Mass., College - B.A. in Business Administration, Columbia College, Columbia, Missouri; [occ.] Technical Services payless shoe source, Topeka, Kansas, Industrial Electrician; [memb.] President, Topeka Chapter of the National Congress for Fathers and Children, Topeka, Kansas; [hon.] Deans List Columbia College Columbia, Missouri; [oth. writ.] Contributing writer life in the heartland newspaper Topeka, Kansas editorials local newspapers, lobbyist for father's rights, prepare and present testimony to senate and legislative committees, state capitol, Topeka, Kansas; [pers.] A man needs to find a way to express himself it is very difficult for a man to show his deep emotions and love. It is easier, it seems, to show anger. I express myself through my poetry and writing the messages I want to convey are readily accepted that way.; [a.] Burlingame, KS

REIDHEAD, MONIQUE
[b.] May 13, 1975, Roosevelt, UT; [p.] Jimmie N. Reidhead, Jean R. Reidhead; [ed.] Uintah High, Snow College, Utah State University; [occ.] Deputy Court Clerk, eight District Juvenille Court, Vernal,UT; [hon.] Delta Kappa Gamma, Dean's List; [oth. writ.] Several poems published in high school literary book, several other poems unpublished; [pers.] I strive to portray emotion in such a way as to draw my reader into the poem. In a sense I am opening myself to the reader and allowing them to feel as I feel at that single point in time.; [a.] Roosevelt, UT

RENNINGER, KHRISTINA
[b.] November 17, 1983, Harrisburg, PA; [p.] Mark and MaLinda Renninger; [ed.] St. Margaret Mary's School - 7th grade; [occ.] Student; [memb.] Student Service Team, School Choir, Church Choir, Girl Scouts; [hon.] President's, Excellence of Education Award, National History Award, Student's Service Team Award, National Geography Olympaid Finalist; [oth. writ.] Winner of School Essay on Washington and Lincoln contributions to our country.; [pers.] My writing helps me express my most inner and personal thoughts.; [a.] Harrisburg, PA

RESENDIZ, JUANITA
[b.] November 4, 1981, Wylie, TX; [p.] Pedro and Nanette Resendiz; [ed.] Freshman Student; [occ.] Student of Whylie High School; [memb.] Member of St. Mark's Catholic Church; [oth. writ.] Death Bells Ring (unpublished); [pers.] I enjoy writing poetry and hanging out with my close friends. Friends are the best things in the world because you can always count on them.; [a.] Wylie, TX

RESTREPO, ANGELINE
[b.] October 16, 1980, Plantation, FL; [p.] Pam and Carlos Restrepo; [ed.] DeKalb County High School; [occ.] Student; [memb.] Beta Club, DeKalb County High School Marching Band, Fellowship of Christian Students, Drama Club, Upper Helton Baptist Church; [hon.] Academic Achievement; [pers.] My writing reflects my self and my surroundings. A different mood makes me write different things. I've been greatly influenced by my English teacher Mrs. Carol Hale.; [a.] Liberty, TN

REVERE, DEBRA
[b.] June 16, 1954, Los Angeles, CA; [p.] James and Dorothy Revere; [m.] Paul F. Schwartz, September 7, 1985; [ch.] Malaika R. Schwartz; [ed.] M.A. Psychol-

ogy - Antioch University B.A. Psychology - Univ. of WA Hopewell Valley Central H.S. Pennington, N.J; [occ.] Psychology Instructor at Seattle Central Community College and Antioch University; [memb.] Various Mental Health, Psychology and Education Associations, Congregation Beth Shalom; [hon.] Recipient of Academic Scholarship in College, Phi Eta Sigma honorary society; [oth. writ.] Book review for Secret Garden Children's Book Store; [pers.] Mantra: "It is familiar language, like the lifetime leitmotif of a vowel the one pure sound you will ever make, what you say to yourself in the little litany of breathing. Stanley Plumly; [a.] Seattle, WA

REYNOLDS, ROB

[pen.] Rob Reynolds; [b.] October 10, 1940, Columbia, SC; [p.] Gene and Mary Alice Reynolds; [m.] Linda Anne, May 28, 1987; [ed.] EAU Claire High School (Columbia, SC), University of SC - A.B. in English Lit.; [occ.] Realtor with Russell and Jefffcoat Realtors, Inc., Columbia, SC; [memb.] Greater Columbia Board of Realtors, our Savior Lutheran Church, Masonic Order; [oth. writ.] Poetry, prose and three as yet unpublished novels, "The Arbor," "Vector" and "Ghost Dancers" (All novels written in last 3 years) write op-eds for "The State" newspaper.; [pers.] Writing is the most fulfilling activity I have ever experienced. To be a good wordsmith is my fondest wish.; [a.] Chapin, SC

RHODES, CORI L.

[b.] September 24, 1964, Brooklyn, NY; [p.] Barry and Frances Blumen; [m.] John Rhodes, September 1, 1990; [ch.] Meghan Taylor and Kimberly Ellen; [ed.] Champlain Valley Union High School, Champlain College, Vermont College All in Vermont; [occ.] Registered Nurse, Visiting Nurse Association, Colchester, VT; [pers.] My poem entitled "Our Daddy" was written for the man who is so dedicated to the happiness of our family - my wonderful husband John - the best Daddy two girls could ever have. Thanks for all you do for us!; [a.] Duxbury, VT

RICCI, ANTONIETTE

[pen.] Ann Ricci; [b.] August 21, 1965, Salerno, Italy; [p.] Micheal Miglino, Geatana Miglino; [m.] Vincent Ricci, September 27, 1987; [ch.] Vincent Ricci Jr.; [occ.] Office Manager, Freelance Writer; [pers.] I was highly encouraged by the Catholic Church and family, for this it comes through in my writing. I try to wrote solely on the basis in which all can relate. (Humanity, faith, courage, and love).; [a.] Staten Island, NY

RICHARDS, KARL

[b.] November 1966, Seattle, WA; [p.] Dennis Richards, Judy Richards; [m.] Joyce Richards, June 22, 1991; [ch.] Michael Richards; [occ.] Police Communications Denver Police Department, Denver Co; [oth. writ.] Several other works to be submitted in time; [pers.] We have all passed someone homeless on the street at sometime and wondered how they could ever live that way, not admitting for a moment that with the right things gone wrong, we could be there tomorrow.; [a.] Denver, CO

RICHARDS, NEIL S.

[pen.] Neil S. Richards; [b.] October 16, 1948, Indianapolis, IN; [p.] Ann L. Richards; [m.] December 31, 1969 (Divorced 1977); [ch.] Jennifer Lynn Richards, Joshua Lee Richards; [ed.] Graduate of Theology degree, 1969, Tennessee Temple Bible School, Chattanooga, TN and Bachelor of Arts Degree, 1979, Indiana University, Indianapolis Campus (IUPUI); [occ.] Employed with REI, Real Estate Services, Indianapolis, In-

diana; [memb.] Arlington Heights Baptist Church presently serving on board of deacons; [oth. writ.] Copy righted works include "The Arrowhead", a short story, 1993, and "The Last Walloon", a three act play, 1996.; [pers.] I am indebted to our freedom of speech to give back a part of what so many Americans have instilled in me in this great country of ours.; [a.] Indianapolis, IN

RICHARDS, REBECCA

[b.] January 19, 1984, Nashua, NH; [p.] Don and Christina Richards; [ed.] Surfside Elem., DeLaura Jr. High; [occ.] Student; [hon.] Young Authors conference '96, Brevard County FL; [oth. writ.] Dreams, Destinies, and a Darkstar ('96 Y.A.C. winner) Surfside Elementary; [pers.] I am inspired by people I know, and Nintendo Video Games.; [a.] Satellite Beach, FL

RICHARDSON, MALIA

[b.] September 12, 1982, Santa Rosa, CA; [p.] Arch and Diane Richardson; [a.] Stewarts Point, CA

RICHARDSON, THOMAS

[b.] January 15, 1947, Los Angeles, CA; [p.] Luther and Helen Richardson; [ch.] Rhonda, Kimberly, Elicia, Adam, Timothy; [ed.] Hungtington Park High, Green River Community College, Temple Faye University; [occ.] Tool expediter for Boeing Co. and Reserve Police Officer; [hon.] Officer of the year 1995 for outstanding service in the community. As well as a job well done; [oth. writ.] Many other poems, birthdays, christmas, I miss you, as well as love poems; [pers.] I try to make my poetry precise discrete and non ambiguous. Short and to the point. My message is from the heart.; [a.] Auburn, WA

RICKLEFS, MICHAEL

[pen.] Michael Ricklefs; [b.] March 28, 1950, Davenport, IA; [p.] Walter H. and Evelyn J. Ricklefs; [m.] Celeste Kendall, June 8, 1968; [ch.] Michelle C. and Michael C., Grandchildren: Brandy A., Erika S., Kayla R., Iris S., Tyler K.; [ed.] West High, Drake Univ.; [occ.] U.S. West Tech. Mgr.; [memb.] B.P.O.E.; [oth. writ.] None published; [a.] Evergreen, CO

RIDINGS, GEORGE A.

[pen.] Pete; [b.] July 6, 1960, Germany; [p.] George O. and Shrily J. Ridings; [ed.] WM. D. Mosley Elementary Palatka South High School ('75-'77), Palatka High School ('78) G.E.D; [occ.] Meat Cutter; [pers.] I maintain myself by watching old John Wayne movies, never giving up and always turning to the special lady in my life for inspiration.; [a.] Interlachen, FL

RIGGS, RACHELLE

[b.] January 5, 1973, Terre Haute, IN; [p.] Steven and Mary Jane Riggs; [ed.] B.S. Public Affairs/Environmental Science, M.S.E.S. Hazardous, Materials Management, Indiana University Bloomington; [occ.] Full time graduate student; [memb.] Ill. Campus Judicial Board, Phi Eta Sigma, Phi Alpha Delta, Alpha Lambda Delta, Golden Key National Honor Society, IUB Honors Division; [hon.] Dean's List, Rhodes Scholar Nomines, National Democratic Education Fund Scholarship, Four Fouder's Day Awards, SPEA Fellowship; [oth. writ.] Several poems written - nothing else published; [pers.] My poem are a dance through memories of love, pleasure, manipulation, deceit, torture and terror, they are a blended melody of self-destruction, complete subservience and violent control. They compose a waltz of an extremist, and it's my waltz. It's a journey through my mind, a rather, if you will, through my soul. When reading my poems, please, take my hand and let me teach you the steps. When the waltz is over, you can judge me.; [a.] Bloomington, IN

RIGGS, RICKY

[pen.] Ricky Ricky; [b.] July 4, 1958. Stephenville, TX; [p.] Bill Riggs, Tommie Riggs; [ch.] Justin Riggs, Monty Riggs; [oth. writ.] "When My House Becomes a Home", "My Prayer", "Morning Prayer", "The Sound Of Silence" many others; [pers.] My writing has been greatly influenced by my family and many friends, but mostly by God, who I feel sometimes, is writing through me.; [a.] Stephenville, TX

RISING, CASEY

[b.] December 5, 1985, Charlotte, NC; [p.] David and Karen Rising; [ed.] 4th grader - Mallard Creek Elementary, Charlotte, NC; [hon.] Honor Student, several 1st place Awards in Tap and Jazz Dance National competitions; [pers.] To believe there is good and beauty in everything and everyone and to make every effort to find it. Special thanks to Barbara Klasen, John McLain, Imogene Shaver, Nicole Keeser and Flora Chance for teaching me the basics and for their inspiration.; [a.] Charlotte, NC

RIVERA, LUCIA

[b.] December 12, 1976; [p.] Luisa and Anthony Rivera; [ed.] Monsignor Edward Pace High School, Miami Dade Comm. College (North); [pers.] "Money is good, but you can't eat a twenty dollar bill. You have to settle for rice and beans".; [a.] Hialeah, FL

ROBBINS, AUBREE

[b.] June 29, 1981, Rock Springs, WY; [p.] Reed and Pat Robbins; [ed.] Junior High Student; [occ.] Student; [hon.] 7, 8, 9th grade honor student

ROBERTS, MARCIA KAY

[pen.] Marcia Kay Roberts; [b.] August 27, 1966, Fort Knox, KY; [p.] Kim Roberts, Douglas Roberts; [ed.] J. Sargeant Reynolds Community College, Richmond, VA; [occ.] Nursing Student, J. Sargeant Reynolds Comm. College; [hon.] Phi Theta Kappa, Dean's List - J Sargeant Reynolds Community College; [oth. writ.] Poem entered in previous contest for National Library of Poetry, "The Party", Across The Universe; [pers.] The choice of truth, the choice of lies freedom of choice in empty eyes pride faces reflection, tears must hide heart races redemption, love that died.; [a.] Richmond, VA

ROBERTS, MUNEERAH

[pen.] Mrs. M.; [b.] October 21, 1947, Charlotte, NC; [p.] Lewis Flood Bertha Grier; [m.] Mr. Robert Roberts, March 6, 1992; [ch.] Bryan, Mendel, Antoine; [ed.] Second Ward Executive Sec. School; [occ.] Private Secretary of my Husband establishing my writing for publish, Harvest Church; [hon.] I was given an opportunity to be an actor on cable TV I was a secretary I played as a Blue Fairy in Theatrical at York Road High; [oth. writ.] York Road High drama Dept.; [pers.] I am fulfilling my goals that I had at 6 years old. I persevere to give mankind food for thought to inspire and be a leader and example for our young generation that truly need our love and support.; [a.] Charlotte, NC

ROBERTS, RICHARD N.

[pen.] Wayne L. Winter; [b.] August 22, 1930, Detroit, MI; [p.] Alice M. and Harry F. Roberts; [m.] Peggy A. Kirgan, September 4, 1954; [ch.] Richard K. Roberts and Stephen H. Roberts; [ed.] Lincoln High School, Ferndale, Mich., St. Mary's University, San Antonio, Tex., Graduated from Univ. of Michigan, 1956, Major-Political Science Minor-English; [occ.] Ford Motor Co. Engineer for 35 years, now retired; [memb.] Alpha Sigma Phi Fraternity, Cub Scout Leader for Approx. 7 years, Dearborn Heights, Michigan, Member of Christus Victor Lutheran Church, Dearborn Heights, Mich.; [hon.] Korean War - Medals for Good Conduct and American Defense 1950-1954, Commendations from the parents of Cub Scouts - 1968 to 1975, Commendations from Ford Major for Participation in Several Highly Successful Quality Improvement Programs - 1989-1991; [oth. writ.] Many humorous poems, witty proverbs and true folk stories from South West Texas - Not yet published.; [pers.] I have been greatly influenced by the following poets: W. Shakespeare, Ogden Nash, T. S. Eliot, E. E. Cumming, Eugene Field, Alexander Pope, Robert Service and the former "Poet Laureate" of Detroit - Edgar A. Guest.; [a.] Dearborn Heights, MI

ROBERTS, THERESA A.
[pen.] Theresa A. Roberts; [b.] October 23, 1966; [p.] Curt and Sandy Roberts; [ed.] Horseheads High, D'Youville College; [occ.] Registered Nurse; [a.] North Tonawanda, NY

ROBERTS JR., HENRY LLOYD
[pen.] H. L. Roberts Jr.; [b.] November 1, 1968, Conway, SC; [p.] Lloyd and Loretta Roberts; [m.] Renee Herring Roberts, November 16, 1991; [ch.] Hannah Leona Roberts; [ed.] Socastee High School, University of South Carolina (Columbia, SC); [occ.] Insurance Agent/Broker; [memb.] Messiah Baptist Church, S.C. Waterfall Assoc., Independent Insurance Agents of SC Alpha Tau Omega; [oth. writ.] Several poems and short stories. None ever submitted for any type publication.; [pers.] Too often we as a society lose sight of the natural splendor which surrounds us. The "Snooze" button on an alarm clock takes precedence over a sunrise - a talk show over a sunset. Children learn by example.; [a.] Pawleys Island, SC

ROBERTSON, BRYAN SCOT
[pen.] Bryan S. Robertson; [b.] April 20, 1976, Charlotte, NC; [p.] Margaret Lau, William Bruce Robertson Jr.; [ed.] Obtained G.E.D. from Central Piedmont Community College in Charlotte, NC, currently a student at Central Virginia Community College; [occ.] Student; [oth. writ.] This is my first published work.; [pers.] Don't stand on a soap box telling everyone else what to think. The time you spend doing that could be better used.; [a.] Lynchburg, VA

ROBINSON, DARLENE
[b.] August 23, 1960, Fort Knox, KY; [p.] Bernice and Nell Sallee; [m.] Divorced; [ch.] Mark, Jonathan; [ed.] High School Graduate; [occ.] Medical Transcriptionist Evansville Internal Medicine Assoc. Evansville, Indiana; [memb.] First Assembly of God Evansville, Indiana Church Pianist Sunday School Teacher; [oth. writ.] Inspirational collection titled "Hope For The High Places", 1995 used as a ministry tool in my church and work place as well as friends and family; [pers.] I feel it is my God-given calling to use the talent He has given me to give others hope in this world that we live in. If my words can uplift the heart and soul of even one person then my mission in life has been fulfilled.; [a.] Henderson, KY

ROBINSON, ROSEMARY O.
[b.] June 10, 1944, Philadelphia, PA; [p.] James Wheeler (Deceased) and Mamie Wheeler; [ch.] Benjamin L. Robinson Jr.; [ed.] Master and 30 Degree in Education E.T.T.A. Certification Manna Bible Institute Biblical Counseling/Christian Research Development; [occ.] Teacher, Martha Washington, Elem. School, Philadelphia, PA; [memb.] Lupus Foundation, Phila. Council/ Internat'l. Reaching Association Writers Digest School,

Philadelphia Federation of Teachers, Toastmasters International (Covenant Toastmasters); [hon.] First Place - Short Story Contest - Fortress Magazines September/ October Issue 1996; [oth. Writ.] "The Guests Who Belonged" - published in Fortress Magazines, fall 1996; [pers.] I strive to reflect the human condition with emotion and sensitivity so others will know that they are not alone in their struggles.; [a.] Philadelphia, PA

ROBITAILLE, SHIRLEY
[b.] November 13, 1944, Pomona, CA; [p.] Thomas Peterman and Annie Peterman; [ch.] I have three beautiful children: Ann, Shiela, and Joe; [ed.] St. Francess of Rome Catholic School, Bishop Amaumont Catholic School, Azusa High School, and taken several classes in business.; [occ.] I had my own gardening and landscaping business for many years and now I work as a campus supervisor because I love working with children.; [hon.] Numerous letters and expressions of appreciation over the years.; [pers.] This poem is dedicated to my father, Thomas, my mother, Annie, my sister, Joann, Marguerite, who all taught me about love and respect and always made me feel like a special person.; [a.] Glendora, CA

ROCCA, ANDREW AMEDEO
[b.] June 27, New Hyde Park, NY; [p.] Eileen Breslin and Joseph Recca; [ed.] Our Lady of Grace - Manhassett Ny Pre-K thru Kindergarten, St. Mary's - Manhassett, NY 1 gr-4 gr; [occ.] Student; [memb.] Member - Young Astronauts; [oth. writ.] Poem - Man With Sand in His Hand

ROCHESTER, DAVID J.
[b.] October 29, 1954, Queens, NY; [p.] Viola and Junius Rochester; [m.] Sara M. Rochester, August 9, 1978; [ch.] Christopher J. Rochester; [ed.] New York Tech. College, York College, John Adams High School; [occ.] Computer Tech.; [oth. writ.] Treasures of the Mind, the Prize, Enchain Love, Pierced, The Cries of Silence; [pers.] My writing is an instrument which allows others to view the intricate and perennial worlds of my inner soul; [a.] New York, NY

ROCKWELL, LORI
[b.] April 1, 1963, Jackson Co., Maq., IA; [p.] Wendell and Beverly Higgins; [m.] Loren Rockwell, September 15, 1984; [ch.] Blake, Aubrey and Evan; [pers.] Within each of us there is life. Within life there is happiness, sadness, joy and pain, some more silent than others. Through writing we can experience it all.; [a.] Maquoketa, IA

RODRIGUEZ, PAULITA M.
[b.] Ozona, TX; [p.] Martin and Juanita Rodriguez; [ed.] BS and MA Incarnate Word College, Trinity University, San Antonio Jr. College; [occ.] Retired Elem. Sch. Teacher; [hon.] Selected Outstanding Teacher of America; [oth. writ.] Women of Devotion (article) FL Evangelio (The Gospel article); [pers.] God has blessed me with His Grace and Wisdom to bring honor and glory to His name.; [a.] San Antonio, TX

ROESE, TERRENCE J.
[b.] September 14, 1973, Illinois; [p.] Don and Cheryl; [ed.] St. Edwards High School; [hon.] Served few years in Military with Honorable Discage, National Defences Medal, and Army Achievement Medal; [oth. writ.] None published; [pers.] I write what I feel, this poem (life) reflects how I see man today, our world needs the love of one another to survive but somewhere we have only seemed we have only seemed to hurt one another!; [a.] Gatlinburg, TN

ROGERS, DAN C.
[pen.] Daniel Rogers; [b.] July 7, 1962, Fresno, CA; [p.] JoAnn B. Rogers (Mother); [m.] Laurina E. Rogers, June 17, 1995; [ch.] One; [ed.] High School Graduate. Clovis West H.S. Fresno CA, Associate Arts Degree (Liberal Arts), Fresno City College, Fresno; [memb.] The Yosemite Association; [hon.] No Literary Awards or Honors this would be my First; [oth. writ.] This would be my first published work.; [pers.] "Remembrance" represents the deep, abiding love that I feel for my wife. I pray those that I love will always be able to see life's grandeur and beauty. I hope my wife remembers, always, sunlight, candlelight, and ice glittering bright.

ROGERS, EDNA E.
[b.] November 25, 1926, Carrollton, GA; [p.] Mr. and Mrs. Charles F. Perdue; [m.] Walter F. Rogers (Deceased), September 8, 1943; [ch.] Two Sons; [ed.] High School McEachern - Powder Springs GA; [occ.] Retired; [oth. writ.] Poems published in local paper, church paper and school paper.; [pers.] My concept for writing is to share with others, my most poignant thoughts, and the pleasure it gives to me. But mostly to thank God for the talent.; [a.] Gustell, GA

ROGERS, GREGORY S.
[b.] May 2, 1973, Ware, MA; [p.] David and Mary Rogers; [ed.] Palmer High, Springfield Technical Community College, Massachusetts College of Art; [occ.] Student; [hon.] Eagle Scout, Principal's Award, Palmer High School 1991, Dean's List - Springfield Technical Community College; [pers.] I strive for rhythm and resonance in my poetry. I have been strongly influenced by Allan Ginsberg, and Jack Kerouac.; [a.] Palmer, MA

ROGERS, MADERIA L.
[b.] July 8, 1964, Tuskegee, AL; [p.] Mrs. Nettie W. Rogers, Rev. Amus A. Rogers Sr.; [ed.] TusKegee Public (Elementary), TusKegee Institute High School, TusKegee University (B.S. in Business Administration, 1988; [occ.] Substitute Teacher Detroit Public Schools; [memb.] Detroit Tuskegee Alumni Association, Oak Grove A.M.E. (church); [oth. writ.] Give It All You Got, Black Achievers, Friendship; [pers.] Always focus on your goal, with determination and motivation. You can face the world and the challenges that lie ahead. Because you are special as a mentor, person, and friend to those who have no hope.; [a.] Detroit, MI

ROOT, BRADLEY
[b.] July 28, 1980, Garden City, MI; [p.] Walter and Debra Root; [occ.] Junior at Foothill High School in Fustin, Ca.; [memb.] Trinity Episcopal Youth Leadership; [oth. writ.] Never before published; [pers.] "We also rejoice in our sufferings, because we know that suffering produces perseverance, perseverance, character, and character, hope. And hope does not disappoint us..." (Romans 5:3-5) Thanks to Mrs. Eathrage my Sophomore English Teacher.; [a.] Cowan Heights, CA

ROPP, ROBERTA LEE
[b.] Normal, IL; [p.] Robert and Ruby Cutter; [m.] Gordon Lee Ropp; [ch.] Diana Lee, Darren Lee, David Lee; [ed.] B.S. in Ed. Illinois State Univ. M.S. in Curriculum and Instruction Illinois State University; [occ.] Elementary Teacher Oakdale School - Unit Dist. 5; [memb.] Alpha Delta Kappa, Ill, Ed. Assoc., NEA, McLean County Hist. Soc. - Board of Dir. First Baptist Church Christian Ed. Committee; [hon.] Outstanding Senior - Ill. State Univ., Outstanding Woman in McLean County, Who's Who in American Education; [oth. writ.] Poems and short stories published in local papers, women's page

- Ill. Jersey Journal, Co-Author "Gem" — "Gifted Elementary Math", "Five Golden Doors" - Inspirational Article, "American Flags" - A flag history; [pers.] Twenty-five years of teaching have been filled with happy times and sad moments, too. "She came early to school" is true! My heart goes out to children and what they face in their daily lives.; [a.] Normal, IL

ROSA III, HECTOR M.
[b.] August 13, 1976, Bronx, NY; [p.] Hector M. Rosa (Yogi), Carmen B. Hortas; [ed.] Carvin High School (Carolina, PR) Inter American University; [memb.] Inter-American Trimester Association, (Pres) Forensic Club, Nywak (Dance Group), Carvin Band (Tener Sox), Batansis (Tap Dance Group), Karate; [hon.] Presidental Fitness Award; [oth. writ.] Several poem not yet published; [pers.] Live life to the fullest potential, express your emotions and be true to yourself in all that you do because the past is behind us, the Present is a Gift from God and the future is leading to tomorrow; [a.] Bronx, NY

ROSE, BENITA
[b.] February 14, 1958, Willimantic, CT; [p.] Raymond and Zigrida Rose; [m.] Eduard Anthony Gibbs, July 24, 1993; [ed.] B. Mus., University of Connecticut Graduate Work at the University of Connecticut and Hartt School of Music; [occ.] Concert Pianist/Piano Teacher; [hon.] Evelyn Bonar Scholarship Award, Francis Parker Award, University of Connecticut Concert Competition, CSMTA State Piano Competition; [oth. writ.] Numerous poems accepted for publication by night roses. Several accepted for publication by the National Library of Poetry.

ROSE, LEITHELLA
[b.] April 2, 1937, Jamaica, WI; [p.] Levi and Isabella Rose; [ch.] Dwight A. Smith; [ed.] High School; [occ.] Nanny; [memb.] Greater New Saint Paul Baptist Church

ROSS, CARRIE L.
[b.] November 23, 1966, Atlantic, IA; [p.] Donnie and Becky Powell; [m.] Rick Ross, August 19, 1983; [ch.] Candice and Jacob Ross; [ed.] C and M Comm. High, Iowa Western Comm. College; [occ.] Home Day Care Provider, Volunteer Emergency Medical Technician; [memb.] Cumberland Vol. Fire Dept. - Cass County Day care Assoc., Cass County Ems Assoc., Iowa Day Care Assoc.; [oth. writ.] Several poems and short stories for my children - family and friends - poem published as curriculum in Day Care enrichment program.; [pers.] I dedicate this poem to the loving memory of my grandmother - Clair Porter. May she rest in God's embrace. Thank you for your love and support. I miss you!; [a.] Cumberland, IA

ROSSMAN, JAMES M.
[b.] August 20, 1922, Atlanta, GA; [p.] W. Harry Rossman and Margurite; [m.] Elizabeth P. Rossman, September 26, 1958; [ch.] Michael J. and Mark E.; [ed.] High School; [occ.] Retired General Ins. Agent; [memb.] Church of Christ Rotary Club, VFW; [hon.] Former Military Pilot Rotary Club President and Paul Harris Fellow; [a.] Ridgemanor, FL

ROTHENBERG, SANDFORD
[b.] July 31, 1952, Lorain, OH; [p.] Louis Rothenberg, Ida Rothenberg; [ed.] Boston University; [occ.] Singer, Composer, Conductor and Teacher of Music; [memb.] Metropolitan Opera, New York City Opera, Rothenberg Opera Theatre; [hon.] "Straight A" Award, Honor Roll, National Merit Scholar, Nomination to National Honor Society, Foreign Language Award, Who's Who Among

American High School Students, Many Musical Honors Including Mentions in "The New York Times" and "Opera News" magazine; [oth. writ.] 50 musical compositions literary texts for musical works numerous texts about music history, appreciation, and performance; [pers.] I feel honored to have been able to perform internationally and appear on radio and television through my singing. It is my hope that my words and music convey the pleasure given me.; [a.] New York, NY

ROTHERMICH, SANDRA M.
[b.] August 23, 1954, Perryville, MO; [p.] Dorothy and James Kiefer; [m.] Carl A. Rothermich, October 22, 1994; [ch.] Two boys: 21 and 14; [ed.] Secretarial College - Patricia Stevens, St. Louis, MO, St. Vincent High - Perryville, MO; [occ.] Currently enjoying a Sabbatical; [memb.] NAWBO (National Association of Women Business Owners), Parallex Press, Progression Woman; [hon.] 2nd Honor for Shorthand and 1st Honor for Typing Speeds while at Secretarial School; [oth. writ.] My poem about my father's death was published in the annual yearbook in High School. I was 11 years old.; [pers.] I love the statement, "When the student is ready, the teacher appears". Poets that have influenced me the most are Kahlil Gibran and Hugy Prather.; [a.] Saint Louis, MO

ROTHMAN, LAWRENCE M.
[pen.] Red Rothman; [b.] March 25, 1944, Manhattan; [p.] Irling and May Rothman; [m.] Rhea Rothman, February 8, 1981; [ed.] 2 years College; [occ.] Clerk; [memb.] Epilepsy Society of Bleater New York; [oth. writ.] Other poems published by National Library of Poetry and World of Poetry; [pers.] Life can be wonderful, if only we would think positively.; [a.] New York, NY

ROTI, BECKY
[pen.] Becky Roty; [b.] November 2, 1980, Chicago, IL; [p.] Thomas and Donna Roti; [ed.] Sophomore at Fremd High School; [memb.] Cheerleading - football, basketball, track, S.A.D.D. International Foreign Language Award H.U.G.; [a.] Palatine, IL

ROUSSEAU, KALISHA T.
[b.] July 12, 1982, Islip, NY; [p.] Deborah Rousseau; [hon.] I was awarded for great writing imagination skills, most outstanding student, student of the week, top 10 percent, of class, president Award, and Honor Roll for 4 semesters; [oth. writ.] I have many other poems and I also have writing for books.; [pers.] I would like to thank God for blessing me with a supported mother, Imro, my family, best friend Nikki, Sug, Darryl, Ms. Rosetta, Mr. Smith, Maya Angelou (my idle) and through them my poetry shines.; [a.] Roosevelt, NY

ROWAN, JOCELYN A.
[b.] June 25, 1956, Brooklyn, NY; [p.] Juanita and Roscoe Bloant; [m.] Divorced; [ch.] Yasunari, Quentin, Rachel; [ed.] Rhodes School, H.S. Long Island University, B.S. Anthropology; [occ.] Front Desk Clerk Hotel/Conference Center; [oth. writ.] Poetry fiction all unpublished non-fiction, politics; [pers.] I write about love and politics. My favorite poets are Frederico Garcia Lorca, Emily Dickinson, Edgar Allen Poe. I like to red Histories and Biographies.; [a.] Tarrytown, NY

RUBIO, ARISTEO
[b.] June 15, 1981, Mexico City; [p.] Mr Aristeo Rubio, Mrs Diana Rubio; [ed.] Finished Jr. High - going to High School; [occ.] Full time student; [memb.] National Jr. Honor Society, Georgia Teen Institute; [hon.] Participation in the Annual DeKalb County Schools Secondary

Visual Arts and Faculty Exhibition. Peer Helper - Mediator; [pers.] I write poems that reflect how I feel.; [a.] Chamblee, GA

RUDEL, WESTON W.
[pen.] W. W. Swift; [b.] September 8, 1923, Fessenden, ND; [p.] Herbert and Emma Rudel; [m.] Divorced, November 4, 1945; [ch.] Brenda K. Lloyd (Rudel); [ed.] Fessenden N. Dak High School, Dakota Bus College, Fargo N. Dak Investivation Course Chicago, Ill; [occ.] Retired; [memb.] Eagle Aerie 2923 New Rock Ford N. Dak BPO Elks 1216 life member devils lake N. Dak West Oakey Baptist church, Las Vegas, NV; [hon.] Accepted (Recognition) published material in historical society paper of wells county N. Dak (and) in the harvey Herald Press, Harvey N. Dak, Registered - copy wrighted 22 books poems - Essay - articles - fiction- novels; [oth. writ.] The Forest Murmur, Controlled Serenade, "View Near Sunset" To Be Turned On Changing Of The Season Nature's Rhythm

RUDISILL, JASON M.
[b.] February 4, 1929, Bessemer City, NC; [p.] John Rudisill Sr., Virginia Rudisill; [m.] Nell Rudisill, February 23, 1952; [ch.] Joyce Ann, Joseph Lynn, Nancy Marie; [ed.] Gibsonville High, Elon College; [occ.] Retired; [memb.] First United Methodist Church, ARRL; [hon.] Life Member National Eagle Scout Association; [oth. writ.] Articles published over several years in local newspapers; [pers.] "Special writing thoughts" come to me when engaged in physical activities. Applying these thoughts on paper for the enjoyment, enlightenment, and edification of mankind is then pursued.; [a.] Titusville, FL

RUMALA, BERNICE
[b.] June 25, 1979, Brooklyn, NY; [p.] Florence Rumala; [ed.] P.S. II Elementary School (Bklyn, NY), High School for Health Profession (NY, NY); [occ.] High School student (going to the 12th grade, Sept. 96); [memb.] Debating Club and Science Research Club; [hon.] Honors in English, Math and Science, Certificate of Poetic Achievement (Amherst Society), Nominated for Who's Who Among American High School Students; [oth. writ.] Several poems published in newspapers and anthologies; [pers.] Life is a never ending poem, set your goals because it determines your thoughts and your thoughts determine your life.; [a.] Brooklyn, NY

RUSSELL, JEFF
[b.] May 23, 1968, Guymon, OK; [p.] Rev. J.R. and Essie Russell; [m.] Delynda Russell, June 15, 1996; [ch.] Amanda and Jeremy; [ed.] Borger High School and Southern Nazarene University, U.S. Army Military Police School; [occ.] Postal Clerk; [hon.] Nat'l Defense Medal, SW Asia Defence Medal, various Military Decorations; [oth. writ.] "Teach Us", "Seasons Of Love", "The Jungle", all unpublished; [pers.] Robert Frost was a master of painting vivid lyrical images to describe the commonplace. I would die happy if I could achieve a fraction of his ability!; [a.] Mesquite, TX

RUSSELL, PETER
[b.] October 30, 1951, Long Island, NY; [p.] Nicholas and Mary; [m.] Lori; [occ.] Artist Painter; [pers.] I write poetry to express what it is like to live!

RUTLEDGE SR., JERRY L.
[b.] November 3, 1954, Terre Haute; [p.] Myrtle M. and Calvin O. Rutledge Sr.; [m.] Sheila Ann, September 2, 1989; [ch.] Three boys, two stepsons; [ed.] 11th; [occ.] Disabled; [pers.] My mother was a hard working, one of a kind, mother. She raised 9 of us, 5 boys 4 girls we lost

her to cancer. I am the youngest boy. What I wrote, is how I really feel.; [a.] Terre Haute, IN

RUTTER, ALBERTA WADDELL
[b.] March 12, 1935, Louisville, KY; [p.] Albert Waddell, Lillie Waddell; [m.] Jerry Russell Rutter, March 2, 1968; [ch.] Donald, Theresa, Kimberly, Ronda Jude; [ed.] St. Boniface, Ursuline, The Institute of Children's Literature Writers' Roundtable; [occ.] Free-Lance Writer; [memb.] American Legion of KY. Women's Auxiliary, St. Boniface Church, St. Joe's, Southeast Writers Association, Natural Resources Defense Council, American Diabetes Association; [hon.] Actors Theatre of Louisville for Excellence in Volunteerism, Chenoweth School Tutor; [oth. writ.] I'm nearing completion of a biographical novel that took twenty years. Several stories in local magazines and newspapers. Also "Gracie" Published on "Heartworks."; [pers.] Kindness and truth shall meet, justice and peace shall kiss. Truth shall spring out of the earth "I want kindness and truth inscribed on my gravestone. These two virtues are the most important traits that one can possess."; [a.] Louisville, KY

RUTTMAN, SHAWN RACHELLE
[b.] August 27, 1973, Oklahoma City, OK; [p.] Broc Cordonnier and Judy Ruttman; [pers.] Knowledge without action, is empty; [a.] Calimesa, CA

SACCOMANNO, CONNIE
[b.] May 14, 1950, Price, UT; [p.] John and Sylvia Platis; [m.] Bill, September 11, 1971; [ch.] Hilary, Johnny; [ed.] Carbon High School, College of Eastern Utah, Utah State University; [occ.] Owner, Director The Winner School (Activity Center for Kids); [memb.] Utah Private Child Care Ass. Board of Directors, National Association of Child Care Professionals, National Association of Female Executives, US Chamber of Commerce, National Federation of Independent Business; [hon.] Utah State Honors List, High Salest Leadership Awards Jafra Cosmetics; [oth. writ.] Writings for the Winner School Publications, training sessions and programs.; [pers.] I believe that by nurturing your own inner spirit you become more authentic and feel more grace and harmony in life. Only then can you reach out and love others unconditionally.; [a.] Salt Lake City, UT

SAITO, YAYOI
[b.] Japan; [m.] Divorced; [ch.] Kimiharu Asakawa; [ed.] Under Professor William Packard (N.Y. University) Studied poetry waiting several years, interested writing sonets and syllabies since 1980; [occ.] Accountant; [hon.] Some of Senryu selected in a local newspaper when I was young (in Japan); [oth. writ.] Published own book "First step on Fruit" 1981 which dedicated to my son; [a.] New York, NY

SALAZAR, ERICK NEIL
[b.] February 18, 1981, Brownwood, TX; [p.] Virginia Galvan and Johnny Salazar; [ed.] Coleman High School; [occ.] Farmer; [memb.] Sacred Heart Church; [oth. writ.] Several other poems put in a book at school, but not published; [pers.] I'm inspired to write about my feelings, and when things happen to me.; [a.] Coleman, TX

SALDIVAR, YOLANDA
[b.] September 2, 1956, Tucson, AZ; [p.] Rodolfo and Natalia Saldivar; [ed.] Bachelor of Arts Degree in Romance Languages from the University of Arizona; [occ.] Artist; [oth. writ.] Unpublished short stories in Spanish and other languages.; [pers.] Through writing I can express who I am, what I believe in and all that I live.; [a.] Tucson, AZ

SAMUELS III, JUNIOUS
[pen.] "Bey"; [b.] September 28, 1961, Philadelphia, PA; [p.] Mary Samuel-Bey, Junious Samuel Sr.; [ch.] Juanita Lawson; [ed.] Southern High/Cheyney State University OLO Diminion Job Corps Center; [occ.] "Unemployed"; [memb.] Boy scouts of America, Job corps Alumni member, NAA cp-member, member of Moorish Science Temple of America....; [hon.] Brotherhood Elite Ltd. Cheyney state University, most courageous, Athlete Award (name in my honors at South High philadelphia High School); [oth. writ.] I have other writing in which I entertain myself mainly - but I won one other poem contest in job corp in which 375 people enter and I won...; [pers.] I strive to touch the spirit of mankind to awaken what was lost... I was greatly influenced spiritually....; [a.] Philadelphia, PA

SARKISSIAN, HENRY A.
[b.] 1922, Tehran, Iran; [m.] Annik, October 1948; [ch.] Armen, Vahe (two sons), Alex, Aliese, Sarah (three grandchildren); [ed.] Mostly self-taught. English is my fourth language; [occ.] I.R.S. Enrolled Agent; [oth. writ.] "Tales of 1,001 Iranian Days."; [a.] Los Angeles, CA

SAXER, CINDY S.
[b.] September 7, 1964, Freeport, IL; [p.] John and Cherie Kuhlmyer; [m.] Scott A. Saxer, January 5, 1992; [ch.] Christie Lee and Miranda Sue; [ed.] BS in Accounting from Rockford College, Rockford, IL; [occ.] Self-Employed Accountant/Tax Preparer; [hon.] Dec. 1995, Dean's List; [oth. writ.] None published; [a.] Freeport, IL

SAYYAH, LINDA FINCH
[b.] December 21, 1949, Greensboro, GA; [p.] Marion and Elizabeth Finch; [m.] Troy Prewett (Fiance); [ch.] Christine Michelle, Grandchildren Jordan and Trey; [ed.] Wills High; [occ.] Administrative Asst.; [memb.] Smyrna Church at Christ; [oth. writ.] I have been writing for 23 yrs. for those I love and myself. Never before shared with public. (p.s. I just write from my heart. I entered to have my poem criticized because I have never sent any in or shared my poems).; [pers.] For me, the greatest motivator is Love and faith the strongest asset. These inspire everything I write. These 3 and my fiancee inspired me to began writing again after a family tragedy which my mother was hit by a drunk driver and died. Without their Love and support I may have never written again.; [a.] Marietta, GA

SCHAFER, RUTH STARLIN
[pen.] Ruth Starlin; [b.] November 23, 1923, Thompson, MO; [p.] Mr. and Mrs. Lewis M. Johnson; [m.] Justin Schafer, March 4, 1989; [ch.] 5 by first marriage; [ed.] Portland High, Grad., Art Instruction Minneapolis, Min., Art School of Ft. Wayne, In., Art Students League, N.Y., N.Y.; [occ.] Professional Artist, Wife, Homemaker, Teacher; [memb.] Indiana Federation Of Art Clubs, West Walnut St. Church, Hoosier Art Salon, Indianapolis, In.; [hon.] Many Honors in the Art World. Gov. Otis Bowen Nomination to be, Arts Commission Cultural Rep. Indiana Artist to be honored in Washington D.C. by Senator Birch Bayh.; [oth. writ.] Poems for our School Annual Newspaper, Have a book written of my own; [pers.] I love Poetry and to paint in oils all subjects especially portraits. I love people and care for the elderly. I enjoy to the fullest my family. I believe happiness comes from caring and giving to others, and making them happy.; [a.] Portland, IN

SCHEIDGES, WINFRIED EAMON
[b.] November 11, 1954, Bad Krelznach, West Germany;

[m.] Ludmila Shigireva; [ch.] Aisling, Andrew and Stepdaughter Nina; [ed.] Diploma in Transport Management; [occ.] General Manager of Thermo King Rls, the Russian Dealership of Thermo King Corporation, Minneapolis, MN; [memb.] Royal Photographic Society, (LRPS), Chartened Institute of Transport (MCIT) Photographic Society of America; [hon.] LRPS, various photographs exhibited at Int. Saloons; [oth. writ.] Express my ideas mostly through photographic means, occasionally - time permitting - by articles poems.; [pers.] Like to reflect the diversity of life in my writings and my photography.; [a.] Eustis, FL

SCHENCK, DENISE MARIE
[b.] May 11, 1980, Lynchburg, VA; [p.] Steven and Patricia Schenck; [ed.] Student at Brighton High School, Brighton MI; [pers.] True joy is found in the Lord Jesus Christ.; [a.] Brighton, MI

SCHILACI, MICHELE L.
[b.] September 21, 1970, Chicago, IL; [p.] Fred G. Pacheco and Carol A. Schilaci-Pacheco; [ch.] South Gate High School; [oth. writ.] Currently working on limited edition book of ten illustrated poems.; [pers.] Each poem symbolizes my feelings of past experiences in my life. I express myself through my writings.; [a.] South Gate, CA

SCHLACHTER, REBECCA MICHELLE
[b.] May 17, 1978, Hinsdale; [p.] Harve and Stephany Schlachter; [ed.] St. Alphonsus/St. Patrick Schools-Lemont, Illinois (Kindergarten through eighth grades), Benet Academy (high school)-Lisle, Illinois, Illinois Benedictine - College-Lisle, Illinois, Lewis University - Romeoville, Illinois; [occ.] Hostess/part-time manager at The Strand Cafe-Lemont, full time administrative Assistant at American Resorts International - Oak Brook, Illinois; [memb.] National Spanish Honor Society; [hon.] Recognition of superior score on the National Spanish exam for 3 consecutive years, Honorable mention at the University of Wisconsin - Whitewater for an essay; [a.] Lemont, IL

SCHLOTTERBACK, EDWARD EARL
[b.] February 11, 1952, Garrett, IN; [p.] Earl Malcolm Schlotterback, Elsie Emma (Kleiber) Schlotterback; [m.] Darlene Louise (Conner) Schlotterback, September 26, 1982; [ch.] Emily Jean, Brett Alan, Bethany Rene, Stepdaughter - Kimberly Ann Miceli; [ed.] Associate of Science Degree, Log Angeles Community College, Major - Air Conditioning/Refrigeration graduated 1979, Associate of Science degree State Technical Institute at Memphis, Major - Vocational Technical Education graduated 1979, Bachelor of Science degree, Southern Illinois University Major - Industrial Technology graduated 1984, Honorary Doctorate degree in Philosophy, London Institute of Applied research Awarded 1992, Honorary Doctorate degree in Philosophy, Australian Institute for Co-ordinated Research, Awarded 1992; [occ.] Meteorologist, Philips, Automotive Electronics Auburn, Indiana; [memb.] Life fellow, American Biographical Institute Research Association, Life Member, National Rifle Association, Life Member, International Freelance Photographers Organization, Sustaining Member, Republican National Committee, Senior Member, Society of Manufacturing Engineers, Member American Legion, Member, Garrett Historical Society, Member Dekalb County Historical Society, Member, Smithsonian National Associates, Member Surface Mount Technology Association, Member, American Society for Quality Control, Member, National Threshers Association, Member, Northeast Indiana Steam and Gas Association, Member, Maumee Valley Steam and Gas Association, Mem-

ber Tri-State Engine and Tractor Association, Member, International Inventors Club, Member, Electrostatic Discharge Association, Life Fellow, International Biographical Association, Member, North American Hunting Club; [hon.] Awarded design Patent #D352964 on November 29, 1994 by United States patent and Trademark Office: Commemorative Medal of Honor, 1990, Commemorative Medal of Honor, 1991, other Biographical Listings, Who's Who in Finance and Industry, Men and Women of Distinction, Men of Achievement, Personalities of America, International Book of Honor, Community Leaders of America, Who's Who of Intellectuals, Dictionary of International Biography, Personalities of America, 5,000 Personalities of the World, 2,000 Notable American Men, International Directory of Distinguished Leadership, Five hundred Leaders of Influence, Who's Who of Emerging Leaders in America, Who's Who among Young American Professionals, Who's Who in the World, Microscope Historical Society, Sterling Who's Who, Who's Who of Entrepreneurs; [pers.] "Those Who take no action Reap no reward" my writing is deeply influenced by the realization that what happens tomorrow is dependent upon what action are taken today.; [a.] Kendallville, IN

SCHLUNDT, GORDON DEAN
[pen.] Dean Gordon; [b.] May 10, 1934, Michigan City, IN; [p.] Deceased; [ch.] Cindi, Daughter; [ed.] 1 1/2 yrs. Indiana Univ.; [occ.] Retired Retail Buyer, Sales Cl.; [memb.] Distinguished I.S.P. member Book of Month Club, AARP, Amer. Bowling Congress; [hon.] School News Journalism Plaque, La Porte Herald Argus, 1952 Editor's Choice Award Certificate NLP; [oth. writ.] Poem published in anthology "Beneath the Harvest Moon" (the first time I have submitted any of my work for publication) Have ideas about publishing my first book of poetry by summer of 1997.; [pers.] Anyone who has ever experienced emotional heartbreak can identify with "I Looked For You". I dedicate my poem to these readers.; [a.] Mattoon, IL

SCHMAEDEKE, HEATHER M.
[b.] April 27, 1973, Palos Heights, IL; [p.] James and Connie Schmaedeke; [ed.] Homewood Flossmoor High, Skidmore College AP Art Program Saratoga Springs, NY, Cornell College Mt Vernon, IA, Columbia College, Chicago; [occ.] In between jobs right now; [hon.] Won Scholarship to study at Skidmore College, Art displays at Uncle Wally's Chicago, Homewood Art Fair, Flossmoor Library; [oth. writ.] Published "Circus" in Xpressions Journal, Honorable Mention by Iliad Press for "Rising Tide", published in American Poetry Annual for "Silence"; [pers.] As I grow, I want to continually evolve and develop emotionally, spiritually and physically - to have a deeper understanding of myself and my world.; [a.] Homewood, IL

SCHNEIDER, ABIGAIL
[pen.] Abi; [b.] October 22, 1982, Hinesville, GA; [p.] Daniel and Deborah Schneider; [ed.] I'm in 8th grade and I go to Komachin Middle School; [memb.] I love Ice skating, so I am a member of Sprinker recreation center!; [a.] Lacey, WA

SCHOFIELD, RUTH ARENTINA
[b.] July 23, 1924, Bergen, Norway; [p.] Olaf and Abelona Johnson; [m.] Paul A. Schofield, January 8, 1944; [ch.] Paul, Kristine, Amy, Kari (Kari was adopted from Korea at age 8, 1976); [ed.] Graduated from Gallatin County, High School, Bozeman, MT, 1944; [occ.] Housewife; [memb.] Creative Writers of Bozeman, MT, Also belong to The National, Brain Injury, Assn.;

[oth. writ.] Two of my short stories have been published in the local newspaper; [pers.] I live next to a rushing mountain stream and have acres of trees and meadows with abundant wildlife and birds. I find joy in writing about the many beauties of nature. Then, also, I love to write poems and stories for the very young.; [a.] Bozeman, MT

SCHOW, VIONE
[b.] January 9, 1932, Hyrum, UT; [p.] Eilert and Viola Israelsen; [m.] Robert R. Schow, September 12, 1952; [ch.] Six children; [ed.] 2 years at BYU, completed 2 courses at the Institute of Children's Literature (Correspondence) taken two correspondence courses from University of Utah, and other night classes; [occ.] Retired; [oth. writ.] Vanna's Quest, to be published, a book. I also have other short stories to be published; [pers.] Most of my writing is about the family and its importance in life.; [a.] Taylorsville, UT

SCHULTZ, LINDA
[b.] June 27, 1954, Denver, CO; [p.] Edwin and Bonnie McCasland; [m.] Gary Schultz, July 17, 1971; [ch.] Todd, Jennifer, Lisa and Ryan (four), Jordan (grandson); [occ.] Denver Public Schools; [oth. writ.] Many poems published in church newspapers, throughout the US.; [pers.] My hope in writing is - to share the "love" which is my inspiration. The world would be a wonderful place to live, if only love were a priority!; [a.] Morrison, CO

SCHULZ, CAROLE S.
[b.] November 28, 1944, Philadelphia; [p.] Joseph and Mil Sivel; [m.] George Ron Schulz, July 10, 1965; [ch.] Ron G. Schulz; [ed.] Glassboro High, Glassboro, NJ; [occ.] Co-editor of ETS, Distribution Mgr. Splashline and Pool Sales Rep.; [oth. writ.] My Diary, Mrs. Sabotose, Grandpop, Silent Conversation, Donnie And Divorce, My Legacy, Color Bind, A Farmer's Farewell, Dear Friend, My Diary, In Your Innocence You Knew Me; [pers.] This poem was inspired by my husband's factory being closed. He had worked their for 32 years. I have witness the trauma of him and all co-workers trying to start over.; [a.] Franklinville, NJ

SCHWEBEL, MICHAEL B.
[b.] July 1, 1982, Brooklyn, NY; [p.] Marlene Schwebel, Ira Schwebel; [ed.] Presently 14 years old in Junior High School; [occ.] Student; [hon.] Honor Roll; [a.] East Brunswick, NJ

SCHWEERS, DEREK
[b.] February 10, 1973, Evanston, FL; [p.] Richard and Betsy Schweers; [ed.] Coe College, Class of 1995, B.A. in History; [occ.] Day Camp Counselor, Waiter/Bartender; [memb.] United States Tennis Association; [pers.] I believe the road to truth is not outward, but inward to one's subconscious mind. The human mind must break through and maybe with its subconscious to reach its potential.; [a.] Glenview, IL

SCIANNAMEO, CAROL
[b.] August 26, 1956, Brooklyn, NY; [p.] Angelo and Elaine Sciannameo; [ed.] Currently doing Masters at Polytechnic University, BS St Joseph's College in Human Resources, Graduate FBI National Academy; [occ.] Lieutenant, NYPD (Formerly with Transit Police); [memb.] SHRM, GOAL, FBI National Associates; [hon.] Distinguished Graduate at St Joseph's College; [oth. writ.] Goal Articles for Transit Police, numerous poems and short stories; [pers.] I strive for diversity and respect in people and endeavor to find truth. Ayn Rand and Ernest Hemingway have most influenced my life.; [a.] Brooklyn and Montauk, NY

SCIARRO, NICHOLAS
[pen.] Nick C. Arrow; [b.] November 1969; [ch.] Flash G. (Beagle/Pit Bull); [ed.] University of San Diego, CA; [occ.] Lifeguard/EMT, Lake Mary Jane, FL; [memb.] State of FL Emergency Medical Services, Pacific Coast, Eastern Rugby Unions, Aqua-Tots; [hon.] U.S. Navy Honor Graduate X2, Deep Sea Diver School, and Marine Mammal Handler School, Military Working Dos Training Program, Agitator; [oth. writ.] Currently writing a "Seaquest/007/Cyberpunk-style", novel (Possible Trilogy); [pers.] To surf the chaos of life, maintain neutrality, but always promote a symbiotic relation with your adversity. Use computers to communicate with our Delphinidae cousins. Colonize the oceans, above/below.; [a.] Orlando, FL

SCOTT, KRISTIN VIOLA
[pen.] Julia Grand; [b.] July 7, 1984, Kirksville, MO; [p.] Keila Scott and Danny Shafer; [ed.] Green City RI schools; [occ.] School education 6th grade; [hon.] Preteen USA for academic achievements; [pers.] The inspiration of my poem writing was of those who were brave enough to make us free. My grandfather and my father were in a war or in the army which gave me the idea for my first poem.; [a.] Green Castle, MO

SCRUGGS, KERRY L.
[pen.] Buddy, Kerry, or Mantiz; [b.] June 11, 1983, East Saint Louis; [p.] Stephanie Scruggs; [ed.] 7th Grade "A" Honor Roll; [hon.] Reading and other Academic Awards; [oth. writ.] I wrote a poem on Lima beans in the third grade my teacher said she had been participating her class in poem contests, in this year she had choose me out of the whole class.; [a.] Trotwood, OH

SCURLOCK, SANDI
[b.] June 9, 1976, Houston, MO; [p.] Don and Carolyn Scurlock; [ed.] Licking Elementary and High School, Licking, MO, Southwest Baptist University; [occ.] Deli worker, Town and Country Supermarket, Licking, MO; [memb.] National Forensic League; [hon.] 16 Speech Trophies, High School Honor Roll, Who's Who Among American High School Students, A Ruby Degree in Speech; [a.] Licking, MO

SDONO, JOEY JANINE
[b.] July 29, 1979, Akron, OH; [p.] Lora McCravy, Joseph Sdono; [ed.] Senior at Portage Lakes Career Center. (Law Enforcement); [occ.] Student; [memb.] Cadet Senior Airman Air Force Junior ROTC, Unit OH-861; [pers.] Be your own best friend. Respect yourself or nobody else will.; [a.] Akron, OH

SEADEEK, ESTHER FERRELL
[b.] March 29, 1931, Wheeling, WV; [p.] J. Emmett and Mary Plants Ferrell; [m.] 1. Late - Thomas Joseph Moranski, 2. Present - Leon William Seadeek, 1. September 26, 1955, 2. January 1, 1995; [ch.] Mary Rose Holbrook (4 children), 2. Joyce Ann Chancey (2 children); [ed.] 1. Triadelphia High School, 1949, 2. West Virginia Wesleyan College (B.A.) '53 3. Rollins College (M.A.) 1981 4. Florida Theological Seminary (Th.D.) 1985; [occ.] Retired Educator; [memb.] Episcopal Church, Ocoee Historical Commission, Biblical Archaeological Society, Smithsonian Institution, AARP, Arthritis Foundation, American Diabetes Association, Adult Bible Study Class; [hon.] Psi Chi National Honorary Society in Psychology, Kappa Delta Pi an honor Society in Education, Scholarship to Vanderbilt University School of Divinity, National Science Foundation scholarship in Chemistry, honorary literary socities, third place in a recent poetry contest, second place in an ear-

lier poetry contest.; [oth. writ.] Two poetry books: 1. Resilience, 2. Toward the light. One religious book: Foundations of faith. Poems and articles in 15 books, magazines, and newspapers.; [pers.] I enjoy showing skeptics that they can be part of the beauty and music of poetry if music, and let a thought or feeling sing. Then we add the mathematics and everyone can write poetry.; [a.] Ocoee, FL

SEELBINDER, HELEN
[b.] April 3, 1907, Lapeer Co., MI; [p.] Charles and Anna Seelbinder; [ed.] Ortonville High School, Wayne University; [occ.] Retired Teacher Administrator; [memb.] Hope Lutheran Church, Michigan Assoc. of Retired School Personnel (MARSP); [oth. writ.] Several poems. Some for special occasions. None published; [pers.] A common thread runs through all my poems - the desire to portray God's grace and love for all.; [a.] Warren, MI

SEGAL, RIMA M.
[b.] October 22, 1935, New York City; [p.] Toni Halpen Maxwell and Amos P. Maxwell; [m.] Dr. Sanford Leonard Segal, September 3, 1959; [ch.] Adam, Joshua, Zoe; [ed.] Sherrardswood School, England, Mount, Holyoke College, Wesleyan Univ., Univ. of Rochester; [occ.] Teacher of English to Speakers of others Languages, Greece (NY) Central Schools; [memb.] Religious Society of Friends (Quaker), NY State Teachers of English to Speakers of other Languages (NYSTESOL), Rochester Museum of Science; [hon.] Associate, Society of Sigma Xi (Science Honorary), A.B. Cum Laude; [oth. writ.] Writer/editor of quaker newsletter, published articles in friends journal, and Rochester Democrat and Chronicle, experiments in language and science, chapter with (Mary Bookout) in forth coming book, weaving whole language into ESOL, ed. Charlotte E. Brummett.; [pers.] Language is to me both a tool and a delight.; [a.] Rochester, NY

SELF, TRAVIS CALE
[b.] June 4, 1978, Dallas, TX; [p.] Travis E. Self Jr. and Belinda J. Self; [ed.] Greenwood High School in Midland, TX 1992-1996 West Texas A and M University in Canyon, TX 1996-? Music Education Major; [occ.] Student; [memb.] Hi-Sky Emmans Community, WTAMU Marching Band and Wind Ensemble; [hon.] 8-3A All-District Limebacker, 8-3A all-District Basketball, Chaplain of Greenwood Band 93-94, Captain 95, 92-96 ATSSB All-Region Band Member, 1996 ATSSB All-State Band Member, 94-95, 95-96 Who's Who Among American High School Students Honoree, 94-95, 95-96 National English Merit Award Winner, 4 year Liberace Music Scholarship to WTAMU; [pers.] All of my poetry is a "Spontaneous overflow of emotion" influenced by everyday and not-so-everyday events in my life. I thank God for the talents He has given me and give Him all the glory of my work.; [a.] Midland, TX

SENN, KENNA S.
[b.] August 15, 1969, W. Germany; [p.] Leroy and Patricia; [m.] Patrick O. Senn, February 21, 1992; [ch.] Mark, Anna, Chelsie, Kristyn; [ed.] Hanva High; [occ.] Housewife and mother; [memb.] Life center christian church; [hon.] Having my poem submitted into, "Whispers and Dusk", has been an honor for me.; [oth. writ.] I have several other poems that I have not submitted for publication.; [pers.] There are so many ways to enhance awareness to the world in all areas, I feel my writings give that without the harshness of situations. Writing also gives me peace of mind.; [a.] Tacoma, WA

SEPTAK, ALAINA M.
[b.] November 4, 1977, Pittsburgh, PA; [p.] Bernard J. and Joan K. Septak; [ed.] Hempfield Sr. High School; [occ.] Manager, Dollar Tree Cary, NC; [hon.] Track runner 1988-95 Amateur Poetry Group 1991-95; [oth. writ.] My poems were presented in 3 school newspapers, and 1 book; [pers.] I write poems in sequence with my life. I try to write the way I feel when something happens, that I can relate to.; [a.] Cary, NC

SETON, MIMI
[b.] 1950, New York; [p.] Literate and loving; [ed.] Educated at The North County School and Antioch College, Ohio (BA in Theatre Arts), London Drama Studio (Graduate with Honors in Acting); [occ.] Composer-songwriter and acting teacher in N.Y.C.; [memb.] Dramatic Guild; [hon.] 1995 Los Angeles, Ovation Award nominee for "best adaptation" for music and lyrics written for The Trojan Women produced in on the CBS-lot and several L.A. Weekly and Dramalogue Awards, for writing, music and acting.; [oth. writ.] All musical theatre events in L.A.: Brain Hotel (Collaborator) See Below Middle Sea, Superman, Wazo Wazo, The Trojan Women, A large number of songs - both music and lyrics still awaiting publication.; [pers.] I am grateful to all citizens of the world who value the poetic spirit and who stand against those who would try to crush it.; [a.] New York City, NY

SEYMORE, HEATHER
[b.] March 16, 1981, Kingsport, TN; [p.] Doug and Rena Seymore; [ed.] Cherokee High School; [occ.] Student; [oth. writ.] Some of my other poetry has been in the school newspapers or magazines.; [pers.] I don't really know what inspires me to write poetry. I find it to be a great honor if someone reads one of my poems and likes it. My poetry gives others a chance to see the world through my eyes.; [a.] Rogersville, TN

SHAFER, CAROLYN
[b.] February 12, 1924, Norwood, MA; [p.] Dr. and Mrs. Herbert Gurnee; [m.] (Deceased) James F. Shafer, February 18, 1945; [ch.] James Jr., Julie, Joe, Mary, Daniel, Grace, Paul, Thomas, Ruth, Richard; [ed.] B.A. Arizona State University M.S. East Texas State University; [occ.] Retired; [memb.] International Society of Poets, Texas Tri-County Poetry Society, Bethel Christian Church, AARP; [hon.] National Honor Society Teacher's Honorary Society, ASU, Magna Cum Laude, Arizona State University, Distinguished member of IPS, Semi-finalist at '95 ISP Convention, Bronze medal for "Tamara's Rescue" in Tomorrow Never Comes Anthology of National Library of Poetry; [oth. writ.] Poems religions magazines, poems in 8 National Library of poetry anthologies; [pers.] I see God reflected in the glory of His creation and seek to show forth His love and joy.; [a.] Athens, TX

SHAHIDI, KAREN S.
[b.] December 16, 1957, Cincinnati; [p.] Gerald Barrett, Sandra Robinson; [m.] Hans Shahidi, December 29, 1990; [ch.] Kari Yvonne, Patrick Ali; [hon.] Three Editor's Choice Awards; [oth. writ.] Several poems published by The National Library of Poetry.; [pers.] This poem is dedicated to Amber Asadurian. A beautiful young lady - inside and out. May God always watch over her.; [a.] Westlake Village, CA

SHALOM, QUEEN
[p.] Margaret DeGraffenreid; [ch.] Bernice, Mary and Avonhelena; [ed.] Wilkes-Barre Business College, University of Pittsburgh, Pennsylvania State University;

[occ.] Home Educator; [memb.] Writers Center; [hon.] Dean's List; [oth. writ.] Other unpublished Works; [pers.] Faith! Have faith in your goals and dreams and set goals for yourself. There are many unopened doors just waiting to be opened by those who desire more than the comfort zone.; [a.] Washington, DC

SHAPIRO, JOAN L.
[b.] February 12, 1949, Washington, DC; [p.] Mr. and Mrs. Bernard K. Shapiro; [ed.] University of Pittsburgh 1972, Trinity College post grad. Georgetown University course work; [occ.] Work for Greater D.C. Cares in Washington, D.C.; [memb.] American Cancer Society; [hon.] Read in Portland Poetry Festival in 1975, several poems published in local publications; [oth. writ.] "Firebird" published in WPFW anthology Poetry Anthology, 1992; [pers.] I believe that every day is a new day to write and that keeping a journal and participating in the writing process is very important being honest with oneself is also very important; [a.] Washington, DC

SHARPE, NADINE
[pen.] Nadine Sharpe; [b.] October 1, 1925, Los Angeles, CA; [p.] William Guthrie and Ada Bray; [m.] Deceased; [ch.] Sharon Lee Beatty; [ed.] High School; [occ.] Retired Homemaker; [oth. writ.] In 1993 I wrote my autobiography. I am a student of metaphysics and I hope to publish this year, a book of metaphysical poetry and spiritual thoughts to enlighten and inspire each of us to reach serenity.; [pers.] Time is immemorial, in essence replete, spiralling to perfection and reaching to touch the oneness of that which we are.; [a.] Las Vegas, NV

SHAW, ALEXI
[pen.] Bill Coolman; [b.] June 30, 1987, New York; [p.] Robert G. Shaw and Katerina Shaw; [occ.] Student; [memb.] Aqua Center; [hon.] Several drawing awards. Illustrating the back and cover of two books.; [pers.] I would like to thank Mrs. Kennedy, my third grade poetry teacher.; [a.] Manhattan, NY

SHAW, CHERI L.
[pen.] CL or CS; [b.] April 27, 1964, Fremont, CA; [p.] Isaac and Shirley Vegas; [m.] David A. Shaw, January 1, 1996; [ch.] David and Jason Lange, Amanda Shaw; [ed.] Tracy High, Tracy, CA, Alameda Technical College, Hayward, CA, where I studied Electronics, Los Positas Jr. College (Phyc) Major; [occ.] Business Owner, AC/DC Independent Power, Livermoor, CA; [oth. writ.] Just to name a few, whispers, the one I love has lied, love is. These are my favorites.; [pers.] I would like to say thank you to Patricia Cunningham for her support in all I do. To my husband David for loving me so tenderly, you truly are my inspiration, my love! I love you. Thank you Lord of all, for all the gifts we receive.; [a.] Livermore, CA

SHAW, FRENCH
[b.] July 14, 1963, Greensboro, NC; [p.] James Smith, Onetha Smith; [m.] James Howard Shaw, December 22, 1982; [ch.] 4 daughters, Sheena, Rachel, Ivy, Carmel Shaw; [ed.] High School Grimsley; [occ.] Care taker, Homemaker; [memb.] North Shore Animal League; [pers.] Writing has enabled me, to express the invisible twin which lives in each of us... our thoughts!; [a.] Greensboro, NC

SHAW, MAUREEN
[b.] August 7, 1964, Springfield, MA; [p.] Janet and Norman Hayes; [m.] Bobby R. Shaw, January 6, 1990; [oth. writ.] Several unpublished poems and songs.; [pers.] My writings often reflect personal experiences. I have

been writing since elementary school. I'm thankful to God for giving me this talent.; [a.] Springfield, MA

SHAW, STEVEN J.
[b.] November 16, 1918, Hamilton, NY; [p.] Konstantine and Agnes Szawlowski; [m.] Aracelis Goberna Shaw, June 8, 1952; [ed.] New York State Teachers College, Ms. and Ph.D. New York U. Grad. Schl. of Bus. New York, New York; [occ.] Dis. Professor Emeritus of Business Adm., Univ. of South Carolina Columbia, SC, Chess Master and Amateur Poet Student of Astronomy; [memb.] AARP, Florida chapter of Partners of the Americas, Fla. chapter of Ed. TV; [hon.] Marquis Who's Who in America 4th Edition Who's Who in the World, 1978/79 Pres. Southern Marketing Association (1964) Southern Chess Champion 1965, North Carolina/South Carolina Chess Camp 1959, Beta Gamma Signa (Press 1965); [oth. writ.] Salesmanship: Modern Viewpoints on Personal Communication (Holt) Marketing in Bus. Mgt. (Macmillan) Cases in Marketing Management Strategy - a number of unpublished poems.; [pers.] With my wife, we do lots of work with Latin American countries especially, Columbia, South America. As President of South Carolina Partners (wife) and exec. director (me) we sent medical teams, health teams, and agriculture teams to give them assistance/read lots of poetry.; [a.] Miami, FL

SHEAFFER, FLORENCE CELIA
[b.] February 21, 1907, Kistler, PA; [p.] Edward and Clara (Showers) Dobbs; [m.] William Burke Sheaffer, February 14, 1931; [ch.] Connie Lee Winterstein; [ed.] Elementary, Sandy Hill and Irvine High School, Ickesburg and Landisburg State Normal School, Shippensburg Taught School, thirty-three years.; [occ.] Retired; [memb.] O.E.S., NRTA, AARP, Blain Senior Center, Corner Club; [hon.] Blue Ribbons in Perry County Senior Games; [oth. writ.] The Wedding of the Flowers, Peace.

SHEELER, BETHANY
[b.] May 25, 1980, Pottstown, PA; [p.] Calvin A. and Roxane C. Sheeler; [ed.] Junior Central Catholic H.S. Reading, PA; [occ.] Student, Reporter - Voices/Reading Times; [hon.] Who's Who of American High School Students 1996, Peace Essay Award 1996; [a.] Boyertown, PA

SHELLEY, J. MICHAEL
[pen.] J. Michael Shelley; [b.] October 30, 1943, Eugene, OR; [p.] Jean and Rose Shelley; [m.] Lyne, August 18; [ch.] Lisa Marie, Shawn Michael; [ed.] Crater High University of Oregon; [occ.] Disabled last 4 years by M.S. teacher 20 yrs. 9th gr.; [memb.] Santa Clara Church of Christ, sons and daughters of the Oregon Trail, N.E.A.; [oth. writ.] A number of poems published. Have also written and performed songs as well as writing essays which I hope to publish as a book.; [pers.] I have been influenced by poets such as my name sake, shelley. I try to write words that inspire, that make one thing, moments and memories and song of the heart; [a.] Eugene, OR

SHEPHERD, MARTIN A.
[b.] August 5, 1970, Wichita, KS; [p.] Steve and Karen Shepherd; [m.] Cherrie Shepherd, January 6, 1993; [ed.] Pittsburgh High School, Pittsburgh State University; [occ.] Grocery Store Clerk; [oth. writ.] A handful of other poems. Sketches and short stories.; [pers.] My writing reflects my view of our human-ness. Fragile but enduring imperfect yet beautiful fleeting, still some how timeless stumbling, all the while guided by some unseen hand.; [a.] Littleton, CO

SHERLIN, GEORGIA D.
[b.] January 16, 1947, Buncome County; [p.] George and Irene Sherlin (Deceased); [m.] Engaged; [ch.] Tonya, Sonya, Debra, Keith, Frank; [ed.] Local high school, com. college for CNA and CNA II classes been in Nursing Field 28 years; [occ.] CNA II at Emerald Ridge Nursing Center, Weavervill; [memb.] None, spend time I write, spend time with friends, family; [oth. writ.] Have a book full of poems. Never had anything published before. Family and friends have tried to get me to try. I'm so excited. Thank you National Library of Poetry.; [pers.] I write when I'm sad or happy. All my poems are very personal feelings I have had. Writing and reading are my favorite things to do when I'm not working.; [a.] Weaverville, NC

SHERMAN, EVELYN H.
[b.] June 11, 1917, Sandersville, GA; [p.] Hilda F. and Bradford D. Hogue; [m.] Hildreth G. Sherman, May 16, 1947; [ch.] Patricia Marel, Michael Lance and Sharon Lynn; [ed.] Beaumont High School, Lamar College; [occ.] Real Estate Broker; [memb.] Resurrection Lutheran Church, Coronado Ass'n of Realtors, Ikebana International, Crown Garden Club, Coronado Historical Ass'n; [pers.] The furtherance of love of my fellow man has been a guiding light in my life.; [a.] Coronado, CA

SHIPMAN, STEVE ALLEN
[pen.] Milty Gritzgo; [b.] January 4, 1961, Treaton, NJ; [p.] Willie B., and Edie M. Shipman; [m.] Debra Jean Shipman, July 10, 1982; [ch.] Tarrell K. Shipman; [ed.] Trenton Central High, Craven College; [occ.] Law Enforcement - New Jersey State Prison; [memb.] P.B.A. #105, International Masons, life member N.R.A., founding member: International Gents Assoc., American Legion Post #182; [pers.] It is written, "So a man thinketh in his heart, so is He," thus comes my ability to write what I think. It comes from the heart; [a.] Ewing Township, NJ

SHORT, DIANNA
[b.] May 2, 1965, Carrolton, MO; [p.] Hazel Piper; [m.] James Short, October 28, 1989; [ed.] Glencliff High School, Earlham College; [occ.] Systems Analyst; [a.] Warminster, PA

SHREVE, DANIEL E.
[pen.] Daniel N. Cognito; [b.] January 14, 1951, Indianapolis, IN; [p.] Lucille and Eugene Shreve; [ed.] 1-12; [occ.] Security Officer; [hon.] One Award for Poetry; [oth. writ.] Elusive Night Copy wright registration in Library of Congress Washington D.C.; [pers.] I started writing in 1970 as an emotional outlet, I believe it was a God given talent to help this humble man cope with a world so wonderful yet sometimes in so much turmoils.

SHULDA, STAN
[b.] January 3, 1956; [p.] Stanley and Helen Szychulda; [ed.] Hofstra University M.B.A, B.A St. Francis Prep H.S.; [occ.] Director of Statistics, N.Y.C.; [memb.] "The International Society for Philosophical Enquiry", "Mensa"; [pers.] Loving and learning should be a life - long process; [a.] Brooklyn, NY

SHUTE, CHARLES
[m.] Rosemary Gay Robins, September 6, 1980; [ch.] Stephen, Patricia, Caroline, Emily; [ed.] Scholar of Eton College and King's College, Camaridge, M.D. University of Cambridge. (Legal Resident in U.S. 7 years); [occ.] Research Assistant (Egyptology) to gay Robins; [memb.] Faculty Spouse, Docent Michael C. Carlos Museum, Emory University; [hon.] Medical Fellow (Life) Christ's College, Cambridge Emeritus Professor, University of Cambridge; [oth. writ.] Scientific and Egyptological Works; [pers.] Like many others I have known much sorrow and much joy. "Try in different ways to express both in my poems.; [a.] Atlanta, GA

SIDDIQUI, SHAMIM A.
[pen.] "Pitni"; [b.] July 3, 1928, Bahraich, UG, India; [p.] Late Sheikh Harizullah; [m.] Shamim Razia Siddiqui, July 3, 1953; [ch.] Six; [ed.] BA, B. Com. (Completed); [occ.] Retired; [oth. writ.] Writer: So for published following books " Service To Humanity" is the team. 1. The Commitment, 2. Methodology of Dawah 3. The Greatest Need Of Man, 4. The Dawah Program, 5. The Revival (underprint); [pers.] Poetry is the best means of expression or innerself in a precise and concise fashion which depicts the death of feelings, pathos of life and tender touches that moves the domain of heat and mind of those who go through it, this is my best past time.; [a.] New York, NY

SIDERS, SCOTT
[b.] October 3, 1976, Cedar Rapids, IA; [p.] Kevin and Lin Fitzner and Tom and Susie Siders; [ed.] Centaurus High School, University of Evansville. Currently a Sophomore at the University of Colorado.; [hon.] Dean's List '95/'96 at the University of Evansville. Newcomer Award as Editorial Page Editor for the University of Evansville School newspaper. Received an award for poem published in the University of Evansville's "Literary Review." National Dean's '95/96; [oth. writ.] Poem published in Volume 6 edition of the University of Evansville's literary magazine, the "Literary Review"; [pers.] Good poetry has the ability to both confuse and enlighten, to create ambiguity out of specificity, to present an idea in which the reader can relate to, be it on emotional, intellectual, or philosophical level.; [a.] Boulder, CO

SILBERGELD, SAM
[b.] March 1, 1918, Wongrow, Poland; [p.] Hyman and Frieda Silbergeld; [m.] Mae Anna Driscoll Silbergeld (Deceased), June 22, 1952; [ch.] Sandra, Daniel, Janet, Nancy; [ed.] Ph D. (Biochemistry) MD Residing in Psychiatry at Stafford U.; [occ.] Semi-Retired Teaching at University of Maryland, College Park; [memb.] Numerous Professional Organizations, Member Board of Trustees, Black Burns College, Carlinville, Illinois; [hon.] Biography in Who's who in Science and Engineering, Who's Who in the East, Who's Who in America, Who's Who in the World, Leader Gaip Citation, Blackburn University, 1989; [oth. writ.] Professional papers; [pers.] Know thyself; [a.] Garrett Park, MD

SILVA, VELVET
[b.] November 17, 1971, Mass; [p.] Paul Silva, Donna Botelho; [ch.] Cassidy Noel Bazinet; [ed.] New England Christian Academy, Bristol Community College; [occ.] Student; [pers.] Writing poetry is my therapy; [a.] Fall River, MA

SIMMONS, ADREA ANISE
[b.] July 19, 1982, Detroit, MI; [p.] Ma'Sha Simmons; [ed.] Currently attending Mercy High School, graduate of Grosse Pointe Academy; [occ.] High School; [memb.] Plymouth United Church of Christ; [hon.] Forensics Team, Eight grade diploma, Headmasters, List, High Honor Roll; [pers.] If you destroy the beautiful shade of your tree, you will look for the shade of the clouds, which will always pass you by. A proverb from Senegal, West Africa.; [a.] Detroit, MI

SIMPSON, BROOKE
[b.] October 29, 1979, New York; [p.] Pamela, Robert Simpson; [ed.] John Jay Senior High School, Kent School (Kent, Ct); [occ.] Student; [pers.] I would like to pursue a musical career for piano composition at the Julliard School during the next few years. I would also like to note that words are only ink on paper without passion.; [a.] Wappingers Falls, NY

SIMPSON, LIZZIE
[b.] October 20, 1946, Kosciusko, MS; [p.] Florence Towers, Sylvester Jones; [ch.] Rita, Tressa, Christina, Chris; [ed.] Tipton High, U.S. Army Delta College; [occ.] Cook; [pers.] I want everyone that read my poem to know that through it all, Jesus have been there for me and my family. He will be there for them.; [a.] Bay City, MI

SIMPSON, SHEREE MONIQUE
[pen.] Monique Bennet; [b.] December 12, 1971, San Francisco; [p.] Wesley and Sonjia Simpson; [ed.] Abraham Lincoln High School City College of San Francisco California State University, Hayward; [occ.] Records Clerk, at McCutchin, Doyle, Brown and Enersen; [memb.] San Francisco Christian Center, Alexander Books (Women's Circle), and African American Achievement Program; [hon.] Scholarship from City College of San Francisco Criminology Dept.; [pers.] I create from personal experience, which is always from the heart. I flip the script, look at it from the outside looking in and let it all flow.; [a.] San Francisco, CA

SINGLETON, DAVID EARL
[b.] November 16, 1964, Mobile, AL; [p.] David Earnest Singleton, Mary Ida (Davis) Singleton; [m.] Kimerly Ann Singleton; [ch.] Brandon, Ashlee, August; [ed.] Bessie C. Fonville (Elem.) Mobile, Ala., Sutter Jr. High (Middle) Los Angeles, Crenshaw High Los Angeles, California; [occ.] Greyhound Lines Inc., Mobile, Ala; [pers.] This poem was dedicated to my dear mother Mary Ida (Davis) Singleton in September 10, 1924 in September 10 1924, she is survived by children Frank, Cora, Estella, Lela, Mary John, Olivia, Lean, David Earl.; [a.] Los Angeles, CA

SKELDING, KATHLEEN ANN
[b.] February 4, 1970, Lynchburg, VA; [p.] Robert and JoAnn Skelding; [m.] November 2, 1996; [ed.] College - BS East Tennessee State University in special Education Masters - Radford University special Education, in serious Emotional Disturbances; [occ.] Special Education Teacher in Roanoke, VA; [memb.] NEA, CEC; [oth. writ.] Amateur writer, I have never had any other writings published; [pers.] Every experience, good or bad, happens, for a reason. As a poet, I take the experiences and use them to make a combination of emotion and writings into a poem.; [a.] Roanoke, VA

SMITH, ANTHONY
[b.] September 30, 1962, Brooklyn, NY; [p.] Ed Smith, Yvonne Smith; [ch.] Jasmin Armani Smith; [ed.] Howard University (School of Business); [occ.] Sales and Marketing; [hon.] Denas List several times (Howard Univ., Praire View A and M Univ.); [pers.] A very special person who has found her way into my heart inspired the writing of this poem. Her name, Diana Pemberton, my eternal love partner.

SMITH, BRENDA
[pen.] Brenda Creach, Bea-Anna Cordelis; [b.] June 2, 1967, Torrance, CA; [p.] Robert and Shirleen Mulvey; [ch.] Jonathan Anthony Smith; [ed.] La Paloma High, Pittsburg Adult Education, Los Medanos College; [occ.] Courtesy Clerk, Raley's; [memb.] Degree of Pocahantas;

[pers.] Poetry has always been a way for me to express my inner feelings in a way that the outside world can understand my personal views, opinions, and experiences.; [a.] Pittsburg, CA

SMITH, BRINTON
[b.] July 3, 1974, Bryan Mawr; [p.] Edwin J. and Patricia L. Smith; [ed.] Currently attending Scottsdale Community College, Scottsdale, AZ; [a.] Kennett Square, PA

SMITH, CHERIE YVETTE
[b.] December 19, 1969, Boston, MA; [p.] Ruby McCall and Archie Smith Jr.; [ch.] Kiara Shante Smith-Perry; [ed.] High School Diploma from Frankfurt American High School 6/87 and CMB Education Center graduated as Medical Assistant (Diploma) 2 1/2 yrs. of College; [occ.] Home Health Aide with Seton Home Care and Nurses Plus in Austin, TX; [pers.] "I feel as long as you have faith in God you can accomplish anything in life." My greatest accomplishment right, now is my daughter Kiara which I dedicated this poem to".; [a.] Austin, TX

SMITH, DUANE
[b.] July 27, 1941, Prescott, AZ; [p.] Melvin, Muriel Smith; [m.] Olesia Smith, August 3, 1966; [ch.] Daniel Melvin, Carla Lee; [ed.] Bat 36 in Elementary Education, Arizona State University; [occ.] Bank Teller, The Stock Men's Bank's Seligman, AZ; [memb.] National Rifle Association, St. Francis Catholic Church, (Treasure) John Birch Society, Seligman Investment Club, (Treasure) Seligman Volunteer Fire Department; [oth. writ.] Wrote 35 Articles for "The High Plains Trader", a local publication. Two Novels, "Serpent Circus" and "Give a damn!", as well as 9 short stories, are currently with agent in phoenix.; [pers.] My writings attempt to persuade the reader that good will eventually triumph over evil, and to persevere in the face of hardship.; [a.] Seligman, AZ

SMITH, ELMER W.
[pen.] Ralph Alton; [b.] May 10, 1928, Trenton, NJ; [p.] Elmer W. and Violet M. Smith; [m.] Caroline C. Smith, June 23, 1956; [ch.] Caroline Elinore, Elliott Pearson, David Grant, Eric Graham; [ed.] Drew Univ., B.A., 1951, Syracuse Univ., M.P.A., 1952, Harvard Univ., 1952-54, Oxford Univ. (England), 1954-55; [occ.] Federal Government Administrator; [memb.] Senior Executives Assn., Pi Gamma MU; [hon.] Superior Service Awards 1964, 1981; [oth. writ.] Newspaper articles for Lambertville Beacon, foreword for social disabilities, published by New York University Press.; [a.] Woodlawn, MD

SMITH, JAMES LEE
[pen.] James Lee Smith; [b.] May 8, 1926, Wellington, TX; [p.] Lee and Stella Smith; [m.] Dorothy Lee Smith; [ch.] Five children: four step-children; [ed.] High School, 2 yrs. College; [occ.] Retired 1987 after 42 years with State of Texas; [memb.] Church-Veterans Organizations; [oth. writ.] None published

SMITH, JEREMY
[b.] June 9, 1981, Fort Worth, TX; [p.] Robert and Martie and Traci; [ed.] Middle School, Life; [occ.] Teenager; [memb.] Boy Scouts, School Football Team and Track Team; [oth. writ.] Alone, Drops, Everywhere You Look; [pers.] Believe in yourself and in your dreams.; [a.] Fort Worth, TX

SMITH, KIM
[b.] June 6, 1957, Neosho, MO; [p.] Leroy and Betty Wood; [m.] Greg Smith, May 25, 1985; [ch.] Jaime and

Daly Smith; [ed.] Republic H.S., Bachelors - Southwest Missouri State University, Masters - Southwest Missouri State University, Specialist - Southwest Missouri State University; [occ.] Principal at Sherwood, Elementary - Springfield Public Schools; [memb.] Missouri Association of Elementary School Principals, Missouri State Teachers Association; [hon.] Phi Kappa Phi, Gunuild Keetman Grant Winner with the National Off-Schulwork Association; [oth. writ.] Two Octavos published by Heritage Press - "Mississippi Mud" 1991 and "Eli" 1992.; [a.] Clever, MO

SMITH, PAUL E.
[pen.] Paul E. Smith; [b.] March 3, 1930, Noble Co., IN; [p.] Frank W. Smith; [m.] Mary L. Smith, March 12, 1950; [ch.] Kenneth, Connie, Kevin, Wallace; [ed.] High School; [occ.] Retired Pt. Time Mgr. Retirement Comm.; [memb.] New Life Community Church School Board Member 12 yrs.; [oth. writ.] God's Rochet Display A Friend Indeed Some Poetry published in Local Papers; [pers.] I like to write about personal experiences and things of beauty about us; [a.] Glendale, AZ

SMITH, RICHARD L.
[pen.] Richard Reitz; [b.] July 13, 1964, Brookville, PA; [p.] Robert and Shirley Smith; [ed.] MFA - Tyler School of Art of Temple University; [occ.] Graphic Design Principal/Designsmith and Book Artist/Letterpress Painter; [oth. writ.] Writing is available in limited edition, letterpress books through Sand Song Press - Brooklyn, NY a private press operated by the author.; [pers.] I started writing in Journal - form in my mid-teens to record what was happening in my life. Later, writing became more of a creative outlet for dreams and reflections. Now the two forms have blended and I title poems in part by date of the event of inspiration.; [a.] Brooklyn, NY

SMITH, SHANNON D.
[b.] September 17, 1973, Celina, TN; [p.] Glen Smith, Brenda Riddle; [ch.] Chasity Lynn; [ed.] Livingston Academy; [occ.] Advantage Check Cashing, Livingston, TN; [pers.] I would like to dedicate this poem to someone very special to me, Trey Mayes, he inspired me to write this, and I Love him with all my heart.; [a.] Livingston, TN

SMITH, SHARON D.
[b.] December 4, 1956, Alabama; [p.] Lufonzo McGill, Leroy Tubbs; [ch.] Kimberly, Carlos, Tiffany, Raymond; [occ.] Nursing Assistant, Sutter Memorial Hospital; [pers.] I write my poems on my personal life and experience. Putting my feelings in writing, helps me in my life to copy with life ups and downs.; [a.] Sacramento, CA

SMITH, THOMESA L.
[pen.] Louise Blaque; [b.] September 26, 1938, Los Angeles, CA; [p.] Verna Lee and Fred (not married); [m.] Twice divorced now legally separated; [ch.] Sylvia, Lucille and Blanche; [ed.] Some College in Calif. and Ohio, I was a Mathematics Major - Minor in Phys Ed; [occ.] Office Manager/Secretary; [hon.] Small Academic Scholarship 1957, Award for time Saving process when with Los Angeles County Probation Dept - 1974, Commendation for six years Service as Treasurer of my Church - 1989, Award for "Employee Excellence" from State Assemblyman - 1996; [oth. writ.] Several poems and short writings mostly of a christian or spiritual nature, none published to date 7/96.; [pers.] I do not want my real name published. I am a christian and have a strong desire to share the gospel of salvation through Jesus Christ with all the people I can. I attempt to set a decent example for my daughters by word, deed and

prayer. My only real hope and joy is in the Lord Jesus Christ.; [a.] Salinas, CA

SMITHLEY, DARLENE
[b.] June 13, 1932, Ft. Wayne, IN; [p.] J. Kenneth D. and Esther R.M. Dowthy D.; [m.] Widow/Gordon K. Smithley, August 21, 1968; [ch.] Two children, three step children; [ed.] Grodi Elmhurst HS, Ft. Wayne, IN Some College; [occ.] Retired 1996 from Phoenix Symphony; [memb.] Professional Secretaries International; [oth. writ.] Working on first novel; [pers.] It is my belief that humankind will prevail over the evils that pervade our earth because of the power of good, and I believe in a sense of humor at all costs.; [a.] Bellaire, MI

SNOW, DONALD M.
[b.] June 29, 1925, Taos, NM; [p.] Leonard Snow; [m.] Marlene C. Snow, 1952; [ch.] Deena Lynn, Anna Marie, Bonnie Carol, Jenny Lee, Donald Bryant; [ed.] U.S. Navy GED, World Travelled, self educated; [occ.] Retired US Navy; [hon.] Many Photographic Awards. In S4C, LAPS etc; [oth. writ.] Several poems unpublished reserved articles so many etc.; [pers.] I have written several articles on photography, and have published articles in Western Photographer Mag.; [a.] Los Angeles, CA

SOLLITTO, THERESA M.
[b.] July 20, 1985, Brooklyn, NY; [p.] Maria and Joseph Sollitto; [ed.] 6th grade at I S 24, S.I., N.Y; [hon.] John Ullsumer Memorial Award; [pers.] This poem was written about my Aunt Mary. She was a very special person. She died on October 28, 1995. I wrote this poem because I wanted everyone to know Aunt Mary, and how much I loved her! She was 36 yrs old.; [a.] Staten Island, NY

SORENSON, JULIE ANNE
[b.] September 24, 1958, Rochester, MN; [p.] Robert and Emma Richardson; [m.] Tim Sorenson, April 19, 1986; [ch.] Celinda Christine Sorenson; [ed.] Dover - Eyota H.S., Eyota, MN, Mankato St. University, Mankato, MN; [occ.] Lakeville Community Education; [hon.] Dean's List, Community Education Supervisor of the Year Award; [oth. writ.] Several non-published poems; [pers.] I strive to give God honor in my writing and have been influenced by him and the 12 step program.; [a.] Lakeville, MN

SOUZA, SALOME M.
[pen.] Sally LaValee; [b.] March 7, 1940, Hartland, ME; [p.] Evelyn and Raymond Thompson; [m.] Frederick J. Souza, June 30, 1995; [ed.] Coney High Augusta ME, U.M.A. 3 yrs Augusta ME; [occ.] Entertainer - most of my life was lived in New Jersey; [hon.] Guitar player - singer, song writer - Poet, was on TV, Radio - Worked night clubs and shows throughout United States and Canada; [oth. writ.] Have wrote many songs and poems. Most of my life has been in music - I now do blue grass music; [pers.] I believe God put the songs in my heart and the music in my soul. A world without music would be a sad place to be.; [a.] Dover Foxcroft, ME

SPARKS, TWANA L.
[b.] July 18, 1954; [m.] J. K. Williams, December 21, 1989; [ed.] B.S. Lubbock Christian College, M.D. University of New Mexico; [occ.] Physician; [oth. writ.] Diary of Hippocrate, published by Vantage Press, 1996; [pers.] Forget the bank. Break into a bookstore and read all night.; [a.] Silver City, NM

SPAULDING, VICKI M.
[b.] March 21, 1958, West Stewartstown, NH; [p.] Homer Palmer, Georgetta Palmer; [m.] John A.

Spaulding, January 30, 1988; [ch.] Megan E. Spaulding; [ed.] Stratford High, Las Pasitas College, New Hampshire College; [occ.] Visual Merchandiser, Yokosuka Japan Navy Exchange (Spouse is currently on active duty here); [oth. writ.] "The Final Voyage," "The Home Coming" compiled for USS Navy ships returning from deployments and decomissioning ships.; [pers.] I try to reflect the innermost feelings that a military spouse experiences. I was inspired by my own personal experiences and by observing and talking with other military wives.; [a.] Brunswick, VT

SPEARS, BRANDY LYNN
[b.] July 31, Seminole, OK; [p.] Keith and Melinda Spears; [m.] Single; [ed.] Just completed 7th grade at New Lima Public Schools; [occ.] Student; [memb.] Student Council Class Representative 1 year, 4-H Club Member 4 years; [hon.] Superintendent's Honor Roll 1995 and 1996, Presidential Honor Society 1995 and 1996, Various Class Awards and Various 4-H Awards; [oth. writ.] I have written a few poems that have been printed in our local school paper.; [pers.] I write to reflect love and kindness worldwide. My poem was written in hope that families everywhere will love and care for each other forever.; [a.] Seminole, OK

SPROAT, PEGGY L.
[pen.] Peggy O'Neill/Sproat; [b.] May 27, 1931, Grant County; [p.] Henry and Saraha O'Neill; [m.] James E. Sproat, August 20, 1948; [ch.] One, James Michael; [ed.] I received my G.E.D. diploma from Ball State University, I am self taught on word processor and computer, both mine; [occ.] Retired, time for poetry poetry poetry; [memb.] A.A.R.P. National Library of Poets, Earlham College Library (Lee County Genealogical Society Dixon IL) Police Alliance, Cops for Kids, Veterans Handicaped - Mattese Society; [hon.] I feed it an honor that Illinois and Indiana have gone beyond to help me find my family from Ireland, it is an honor (two of my poems were chosen for publication) by the National Library of Poetry and I was invited to their convention in August of 96; [oth. writ.] I have written poetry for twenty years, the reason for processor and computer. My son has the printer with his computer. Handy huh! My love is poetry my therapy, so much to write about.; [pers.] I thank "The National Library of Poetry" for making my dream come true, never did I hope or think my poetry was good enough for publication. I am so pleased you chose "My Dad Henry O'Neill".; [a.] Richmond, IN

SPROTT, PAMELA A.
[b.] June 18, 1950, Atlanta, GA; [p.] Melba and Guy Miles; [m.] Robert P. Sprott, July 11, 1992; [ch.] Jonathan Robert Sprott; [ed.] A. A. Santa Monica College, B.A. Loyola Marymont University; [occ.] Executive Litigation Specialist; [memb.] Palmdale Chambers of Commerce - Legislative Committee, SAG, AFTRA; [hon.] Worked on the making of numerous films - such as Burt Reynolds - Smoky and The Bandit, Cannonball Run, and others as well as John Frankenheimer's Black Sunday and numerous other films.; [oth. writ.] Children's stories Samme Sunny Bear, Raspberry Hallow, Thackerby Thicket Tales, The Kiss, Articles for various publications; [pers.] People have always told me that a child will forever change your life. Since I gave birth to Jonathan, I now understand the gravity of that statement. He has truly made me a more challenged individual.; [a.] Lancaster, CA

SRIDHAR, PRIYA
[b.] December 17, 1984, Boston; [p.] Bala Sridhar and Madhu Sridhar; [ed.] 5th Grade South Elementary

School Andover, MA; [occ.] Student; [hon.] Won 1994-1995 Massachusetts Science Poetry Contest - 3rd Place, Won Honorable Mention in the Spring poetry contest for lawrence eagle tribune - 1996; [a.] Andover, MA

ST. MICHELL, LORA L.
[b.] September 19, 1973, Plymouth, NH; [p.] William Greg and Dona Spangenberg; [m.] Robert F. St. Michell, August 6, 1994; [ed.] Capital High School (Boise, ID), Seattle Pacific University, George Fox College; [occ.] Teacher; [hon.] National Dean's List; [pers.] And whatever you do, whether in word or deed, do it all in the name of the Lord Jesus, giving thanks to God the Father through him. Colossians 3:17.; [a.] Bend, OR

STAATS, DOTTIE EGAN
[pen.] Dottie Egan; [b.] November 16, 1925, Middlesex, NJ; [p.] Helen and Patrick Egan; [m.] Divorced; [ch.] Kathellen M. Gargiulo, Maureen M. Roschell, grandson Sean Aziz; [ed.] Graduated Bound Book High School 1943, Night classes and Banking Courses; [occ.] Working on Retiree Basis in Florida's largest bank; [memb.] Distinguished member International Society of Poets Bound Brook High School Honor Society Editors Choice Award; [hon.] Honor Society, Awards in Banking for Sales; [oth. writ.] Courage Editor's choice award published in "Shadows and Light" God Bless my daddy published in "Where Dawn Lingers" My daughters to be published in "The Best Poems of the 90's".; [pers.] To all the volunteers all over the world you truly answered God's calling especially at holiday's.; [a.] Lighthouse Point, FL

STANTON, VIRGINIA LOUISE
[b.] September 20, 1982, Godsen, AL; [p.] Charles N. Stanton Jr., Terri Drinkard Stanton; [ed.] Brewbaker Jr. High, Booker T. Washington Magnet High School; [memb.] H.I.S. Kids Club Heroes in service National Geographic Society, honorary member of Montgomery Womens Citizen Club; [pers.] The things that are the most uncontrollable, are the things people want to control the most.; [a.] Montgomery, AL

STAPLES, RUTH
[b.] July 21, Alabama; [p.] Thomas and Savannah Baldwin; [m.] Deceased, December 7; [ch.] One; [ed.] High School; [occ.] Retired; [memb.] Laurenceville Church of God; [oth. writ.] Poems for friends for special occasions. Poems for family.; [pers.] I like writing poetry of encouragement, of people, pets, and about God, my inspiration Helen Steiver Rice.; [a.] Suwanee, GA

STATEN, LATONIA
[b.] February 16, 1966, Philadelphia, PA; [a.] Takoma Park, MD

STEFFENS, GAYLE C.
[pen.] Gayle C. Steffens; [b.] July 7, 1966, Pennsylvania; [p.] Ann Tara Meier; [m.] William Joseph Steffens, March 29, 1996; [ch.] Scott, Eric, Gage, Ashley, R.J.; [ed.] Penn Wood High School, Venus Beauty Academy; [occ.] Domestic Engineer; [hon.] Creative Writing Awards; [pers.] I wrote this poem for my husband. The man of my dreams. You always love but when you get love back, it is the most wonderful gift of all. For it is a different kind of love I have for my children.; [a.] Little Egg Harbor, NJ

STEMRICH-HOOVER, CRYSTAL
[pen.] Crystal Liberatore; [b.] November 14, 1952, Philadelphia; [p.] James and Ida De Marco; [m.] Dean Hoover, May 19, 1996; [ed.] Waterford High, Waterford, CT, Tidewater College, Florida Keys Community College;

[occ.] Housewife and Antique Collector; [memb.] National Wildlife Fund, S.P.C.A.; [oth. writ.] Short story published in local newspaper. Poems in school publications.; [pers.] Frost, Sandburg and Dickenson lit the flame in my youth, discovering haiku added fuel to the fire. My heart and spirit thrive on the natural world that surrounds us all.; [a.] Luzerne, PA

STEPHENS, LAURA M.
[b.] February 4, 1995, Oneida, TN; [p.] Carolyn M. Stephens, David Allen Stephens; [ed.] Oneida Baptist Institute, McCreary Central High School, Cumberland College (2 yrs.), Christ for the Nations Institute (Fall 950; [occ.] Secretary, Clerk at Gateway Counseling; [memb.] Victory Christina Fellowship Victory Young Adult/Singles Group; [hon.] Who's Who in American High Schools (2 yrs.); [oth. writ.] Approximately 50-60 other original poems/prose 2 short stories; [pers.] My talent and inspiration come from God the Father, the son, and the Holy Spirit alone. He is the true Author, I am His transcriptionist.; [a.] Strunk, KY

STEVENS, SUSAN AMBURGEY
[pen.] Susie Amburgey; [b.] October 9, 1968, Chillicothe, OH; [p.] Earl and Betty Amburgey; [m.] Kevin Stevens, July 17, 1993; [ch.] Wayne, David and Samantha Stevens; [ed.] Waverly High School, Waverly, OH 45690, Vern Riffe Joint Vocational School Piketon, OH 45661; [occ.] Income Maintenance Worker II at Pike County Department of Human Services; [memb.] Peta, AICR, Jackson Township activities committee, and a charter member of the Beaver community Church of Christ; [oth. writ.] Although I have written poems for many years, I have not attempted to have any of them published previously.; [pers.] I have written many poems on many subjects, but I feel I have to give credit to my husband, Kevin, who inspired the first poem I ever wrote, back in 1981. However my entire family has been very supportive and inspirational from the beginning.; [a.] Beaver, OH

STEVENSON, CYNTHIA
[pen.] Cindy Stevenson; [b.] June 18, 1950, Houston, TX; [p.] Edward and Verne Surovik; [m.] Junius Stevenson, December 26, 1986; [ed.] Jefferson Davis High Clark County Community College Pasadena City College Saddleback College; [occ.] Sr. Secretary; [memb.] Natl. Foundation for Cancer Research South Shores Church; [pers.] I wrote this poem after my husbands death. It was my way of dealing with my loss and focusing on the happiness and love we shared.; [a.] Laguna Niguel, CA

STEWART, GERLDENE
[b.] March 26, 1957, Childress, TX; [p.] Houston and Merle Love Elmore; [m.] Samuel Stewart, July 30, 1977; [ch.] Abby Jo; [ed.] Cooper High School; [hon.] National Honor Society; [pers.] I love putting words together, especially for my daughter, Abby Jo Stewart, who is the sunshine of my life.; [a.] Sulphur Springs, TX

STEWART, TRISHA
[b.] December 29, 1941, Oahu, HI; [p.] Charles Stewart, Ruth Stewart; [ch.] Stacey Rebecca, Deborah Shantih; [ed.] San Diego State University; [occ.] Assistant to the Chair, Department of Sociology, University of California, San Diego; [memb.] Storymakers, Women's Journal Community; [hon.] Dean's List; [oth. writ.] Humor column for Coast Dispatch (newspaper), Anthology of Women's Writings titled Life Sentences (published by the Wildflower Hotline) various newspaper articles, short stories two novels, various poems.; [pers.] I am fasci-

nated by the struggle of the human spirit and its power to resolve and triumph.; [a.] Del Mar, CA

STOLFI, ELIZABETH A.
[b.] April 25, 1950; [p.] Joseph Stolfi, Anne Del Grosso Stolfi; [ed.] Wilkes University B.A, University of Pennsylvania Cert. of Women's Studies, Rutgers University M.S.W.; [occ.] Therapist, Teacher; [hon.] Who's Who in America's Teachers, 1992; [oth. writ.] Poems will be published in anthology, women in spirit rising, due December '96.; [a.] Cranford, NJ

STONE, EILEEN GEARY
[b.] March 6, 1953, West Plains, MO

STONE, MICHAEL
[b.] October 11, 1910, Riga, Latvia; [p.] Both Deceased; [m.] Raquel, September 19, 1943; [ch.] Richard (Mar.) with 2 sons; [ed.] Grad. Real-Gymnasium, Berlin, Germany. Later, diploma by State of Saxony for graduation 3 semester Textile Institute in Chemnitz, Saxony.; [occ.] Author, after retiring as V.P. serving 35 years, Wall St. invest. firm; [memb.] AAMS (American Air Mail Society), APS (American Philatelic Society), APS Writer's Unit #30, The Metropolitan Air Post Society; [hon.] Specialty: Aero-Philatelic Exhibits, i.e. Historic First-Flight Airmail Covers, ex: "New York-London" of "Gold" received, the most valuable: 11/71 at National Show/Madison Square Garden (80 exhibitors) awarded "Blue Ribbon Best First"; [oth. writ.] Articles on pioneer aviation published Nationally. Letters to Editor published in The N.Y. Times, The Wall Street Journal, Daily News, The Miami Herald, The Long Island Press until ceased publication.; [pers.] Epitaph: In hope we live - In trust we love - In peace we leave...; [a.] Rego Park, NY

STONER, VELVA
[b.] September 6, 1923, Chambersburg, PA; [p.] Jacob C. and Ada C. Sprow; [m.] Ralph Stoner (Deceased), February 21, 1953; [ch.] One (Deceased); [ed.] 10th Grade; [occ.] Retired

STORY, ELVERA
[p.] Harriet Burroughs (Deceased); [ch.] Valerie, Audrey, Jennifer; [occ.] Retired; [memb.] Member of Tabernacle Missionary Baptist Church, Dr. Frederick G. Sampson, Pastor; [hon.] Editor's Choice Award, For poem presented by The National Library of Poetry 1996; [oth. writ.] Poem published in the Rainbow's end. Also, a poem published in Best of 90's poetry.; [pers.] My poem is dedicated to my daughters. Special dedication to Russell Montgomery, Erica, Derrick, Rodney Douglas story. Also to Ashley, Kevin, Melissa, Travis and Whitney. Each day I realize my many blessings, through my family and friends. Let us continue to pray for peace.; [a.] Detroit, MI

STRAND, CINDY
[pen.] Mrs. C. Lee White; [b.] May 12, 1953, Salt Lake City, UT; [p.] Mr. and Mrs. Albert Eric Strand; [m.] Mr. Richard Michael White (Divorced), October 13, 1973; [ed.] University of Utah 1971-1975, Bellevue Community College, Bellevue, WA, 1989; [occ.] Computer Information Systems; [memb.] Library of Congress "Civilizations", Sierra Club, Seattle Art Museums, Kappa Alpha Theta Sorority, Phi Theta Kappa Honor Fraternity; [hon.] Presidential Honor Roll, Bellevue Community College, International Society of Poets, 2000 Notable American Women by Biographical Institute, Inc.; [oth. writ.] Poems: "One Last Goodbye", "He Strengthens Us To Stand", "Froggies and Lillyponds", and "If I Were A Tree"; [pers.] To evoke a spiritual moment in

the reader is the poet's greatest reward. So it is with me.; [a.] Seattle, WA

STRUCH, RACHEL
[b.] December 19, 1984, San Diego, CA; [p.] Leonard and Marian Struch; [occ.] Student at Hughes Academy; [hon.] Lt. Governor's Writing Award, AA Honor Roll Student, PTA Reflections, President's Education Award; [oth. writ.] Red Ribbon Essay; [a.] Taylors, SC

STRUCK, HELEN
[pen.] Jay Bird; [b.] March 12, 1926, Indianapolis; [p.] Bernard and Marie Niehoff; [m.] Donald Harold Struck, June 12, 1948; [ch.] Grace Marie Worley, Donna Ann Andis, Christine Louise Struck, Martha Susan Struck, Kathryn Helen Struck, Ruth Elaine (Adrienne) Boyd, Daniel Bernard Struck, Thomas James Struck, Lois Antoniette Struck, Bonnie Jane Struck, Steven Harold Struck and Nancy Jean Struck; [ed.] High School Sacred Heart High School, Indpls., IN, Two years - I.U. Indiana University; [occ.] Day Care Teacher; [memb.] Indpls. Museum of Arts., Indpls. Zoo; [oth. writ.] Eighteen poems published in my church paper and one at Somerset Heights day care; [pers.] I found the best way I could express my emotions was thru poetry at an early age.; [a.] Indianapolis, IN

STRUCKMAN, PENNEE
[b.] October 8, 1949, St. Louis, MO; [ed.] Columbia College, BS Accounting Magna Cum Laude; [occ.] Controller; [memb.] AMA-American Mgnt. Assoc.; [pers.] Believe that Jesus is the center of all things and use my writing to bring Him glory.; [a.] Saint Louis, MO

STRUMAN, SCOTT
[b.] June 12, 1963, Los Angeles, CA; [ed.] Bachelor's Degree in Political Science of U.C. Berkeley; [occ.] Office Assistant; [oth. writ.] My poetry has appeared in Riverfalls, and Ojai, CA Poetry Journal, Poetry Motel and Golden Apple Press.; [a.] Camarillo, CA

STUART, VANESSA YVONNE
[pen.] Nessa; [b.] October 15, 1978, Astoria, NY; [p.] Vivian Y. Stuart and Thomas W. Stuart; [ed.] Forest Hills High School now attending Johnson C. Smith University in N.C.; [occ.] Student; [memb.] St. Albans Congregational Church, Inspirational Choir; [hon.] Highest Honors in vocal music, Leadership Award, from Forest Hills High School, $750 Academic Scholarship from St. Albans Congregational Church U.C.C.; [a.] Rosedale, NY

STULL, KURT
[b.] January 4, 1960, Pittsburgh; [p.] Charles Stull, Helen Stull; [ed.] Some college CMU; [occ.] Unemployed former truck driver/delivery boy; [oth. writ.] Letters to the editors of local newspapers concerning politics, taxes, economics, religion; [pers.] I am not a poet and I don't read poetry. "Dear Janice" is a true story, the words came from my heart, and her description is no exaggeration, words cannot do her Justice.; [a.] Pittsburgh, PA

SUCHLAND, JEANNE L.
[b.] January 21, 1949, St. Johns, MI; [p.] James and Mildred Tanner; [ch.] Heather N. White; [ed.] Ashley High, Goshen College (one year); [pers.] I enjoy talking with people and sharing life's experiences. At times, I am inspired to put to pen what I learned in conversation. We are all unique and so special, each in his/her own way.; [a.] Morrisville, NC

SUMMERS, BO
[b.] August 8, 1985, Norfolk, VA; [p.] Michelle Summers, Mark Summers (Divorced); [ed.] Currently a 6th

grader at JN Fries Middle School in Concord NC; [memb.] Boy Scouts of America, Martial Arts Training Institute of Harrisburg. Youth group at Rocky Ridge United Methodist Church

SUTTER, RODNEY
[b.] September 17, 1953, Buckeye, AZ; [p.] Carl Sutter and Merrell Sutter; [m.] Susan Sutter; [ch.] Debra Sue and Kyle Leland; [ed.] Paradise Valley High; [occ.] Restaurant Manager, The Barn Steak House; [oth. writ.] Many poems, this is my first time to send out publicly.; [pers.] I love to write poems and short stories, and love to send out feeling for everyone to feel.; [a.] Phoenix, AZ

SUTTON, JAMES O.
[b.] May 24, 1933, Hardesty, OK; [p.] Oda and Anna Sutton; [m.] Rachel B. Pederson Sutton, December 21, 1956; [ch.] Jim II, Jonathan and Jene; [ed.] B.S., M.A. and Ed. Sp. in Education; [occ.] Retired public school administrator; [memb.] National Society of Sons of American Revolution; [hon.] Too numerous to mention; [oth. writ.] Albee Township History, Sutton, Stump, et. all (family) Newspaper Series; [pers.] My life has been serving others as Christ serves His Church.; [a.] Broken Arrow, OK

SWANN, VERONICA L.
[b.] January 19, 1974, Raleigh, NC; [p.] Pearl E. Swann; [ed.] 3rd year at Campbell University - Education Major/Psychology Minor. Buies Creek, N Carolina; [occ.] Waitress - "Chowda House" Fuquay - Varina, N. Carolina; [hon.] Freshman Class Rep, Elected to Harrest 2 Consecutive years Member of College Democrats 93-94 and CU Student Government Assoc.; [oth. writ.] Writings published throughout High-School, always noted for touching the heart; [pers.] All of my poems, reflect me as a person. Throughout my writings other people find a common bond. This land transcends race, sex, and religion, and releases senses to the heart.; [a.] Buies Creek, NC

SWINNEY, ERIN
[b.] October 19, 1980, Memphis, TN; [p.] Edward Swinney, Marsha Swinney; [ed.] Junior in White Station High School; [occ.] Artist, Poet, Singer and Musician; [memb.] The Healing Center Full Gospel Baptist Church, Girlsn-the Hood Outreach Program; [oth. writ.] 180 degree turn, Mrs Smith, S.O.S., Psalms 23 Revised, Mrs. Gloria Watkins, Reaching Out To Getwell Gardens, Generation X, Letter to God from Erin, etc. (non published); [pers.] Keep God first, and trust Him with every area of your life. Stand, for what is right, but don't risk your life because of an insult. Don't break peace, but make peace.; [a.] Memphis, TN

SYLVESTRE, SARAH
[pen.] Sa; [b.] September 16, 1982, Bidd., ME; [p.] Raymond Sylvestre and Cathy Sylvestre; [occ.] Babysitting; [oth. writ.] I have done many other writing such as a book of poetry, a short childrens story and many other writings for school assignments, gifts, and just for fun.; [pers.] I think all poems express who you are and how you feel; [a.] Lyman, ME

TAIT, TONYA NICOLA
[b.] October 25, 1969, Pascagoula, MS; [p.] Thomas and Sara Tait; [ed.] B.S. Degree Communication from the University of Southern, MS, Hattlesburg, MS; [occ.] Unemployed; [a.] Pascagoula, MS

TALLANT, DAVID
[pen.] David Tallant; [b.] December 23, 1946, Des Moines, IA; [p.] William and Roslyn; [ch.] Scott and

Allison; [occ.] Sales; [oth. writ.] None published; [pers.] The poems I have written are inspired by a very special lady. She is my best friend, my soul mate, the love of my life, my beloved Kimberly.; [a.] West Des Moines, IA

TALLMAN, EVELYN
[b.] November 13, 1922, S. Westerlo, NY; [p.] Mrs. Hazel F. Mabie; [m.] Deceased, January 23, 1940; [ch.] One; [ed.] Greenville Central High School, National Baking School, 835 Diversey Parkway. Chicago, IL; [occ.] Retired and write poetry; [memb.] Social Service with Albany County Social Security Benefits; [oth. writ.] Golden Poetry gram world peace poem World of Poetry

TANKSLEY, KELLI KENNEDY
[pen.] Kelli Kennedy Tanksley; [b.] December 27, 1959, Mt. Pleasant, MI; [p.] Timothy John Kennedy and Jeannine Reynolds Kennedy; [m.] Stephan Ray Tanksley, August 19, 1995; [ch.] First child due December 1996; [ed.] Bachelor of Arts, English and Tesol Certificate, California State University, Stanislaus 1994; [occ.] Writer, Homamaker; [pers.] To be able to write well is a gift from God. I strive for excellence so as to point others toward Him. Solo Deo Gloria!; [a.] Brentwood, CA

TANNIS, TAMIKA
[b.] May 17, 1989, Brooklyn, NY; [p.] Albert Tannis, Gaylene Tannis; [ed.] P.S. 235, 525 Lenox Rd., Brooklyn NY 11203; [occ.] Student; [hon.] Student of the Month May 1996

TATUN, MIKE
[b.] January 12, 1943, Brooklyn, NY; [p.] John and Florence Tatun; [m.] Janet Lee Tatun, June 26, 1966; [ch.] William Michael, Jonathan Michael, Jill Jaye, Corey Michael; [ed.] Graduate 1960 North Babylon H.S.; [occ.] Retired Conductor, Long Island R.R.; [a.] Patchogue, NY

TAUB, LISA
[b.] April 23, 1982, Huntington, NY; [p.] Brigitte Taub, Edward Taub; [ed.] T.J.L. Elementary School, NY, Oldfield Middle School, NY; [occ.] Student (9th grade) Harborfields H.S.; [memb.] National Junior Honor Society, School Newspaper, Fieldhockey, and Gymnastics teams (school); [hon.] 8th Grade Major Service Award, 8th Grade German Award, 1st and 2nd places in Poetry Contest for School. Principal's Honor Roll all year (97 all-year average), School 1st, 2nd yrs in a row for our Sprachfest. (Long Island German competition). Place - Spelling (2nd), Culture Bowl (1st), Folk Dance (1st and 3rd), Scrabble (3rd), Fitness Award, President's Education Award - 4 Academic Achievement; [oth. writ.] Poems for school contests; [pers.] I'm only 14, how can I have a philosophical statement? I have an identical twin sister, Allison.; [a.] Greenlawn, NY

TAYLOR, GRACE M.
[b.] September 4, 1911, Eureka, IL; [p.] August and Catherine Larson; [m.] John V. Taylor (Deceased), August 1, 1936; [ch.] Two sons, Edard and John V. (Deceased); [ed.] A.A. and A.E. Williamwoods U., B.S. in Early Ed. - Mo. U., Col. Mo. Masters Studies; [occ.] Retired Elem. Teacher Retired Literary Volunteer; [memb.] Pi Alpha Gamma Phi Theta Kappa; [hon.] Honor Grad. from W.W.C. and Mo. U.; [oth. writ.] Women of the Bible, Miracles of the Bible, Parables of the Bible, Men of the Bible - Genesis; [pers.] My hope is that my life has made a differences to someone.; [a.] Fulton, MO

TAYLOR, JULIE
[b.] December 4, 1982, Portland, OR; [p.] Darlene Tay-

lor, Bob Taylor; [ed.] 8th grade; [occ.] Student; [a.] Beaverton, OR

TAYLOR, LEROY DOUGLAS
[pen.] Dough Taylor; [b.] June 19, 1945, NYC; [p.] LeRoy Taylor and Winifred Grant; [m.] Mina Halpren, May 11, 1992; [ch.] Michelle; [ed.] W.H. Taft H.S., Marymont College; [occ.] Clinical Psychotherapist; [memb.] International Society of Poets; [hon.] Poet of Merit Award from International Society of Poets 1996 and Editor's Choice Award from The National Library of Poetry 1996; [oth. writ.] Book titled "How to Quit Drugs Including Alcohol" in publication; [pers.] We suffer not so much for the want of things but from the wanting of them.; [a.] New York, NY

TEETER, PAUL J.
[b.] October 29, 1973, San Diego, CA; [p.] James and Mary Ellen Teeter; [ed.] B.S. Physics Santa Clara University, High School, St. Augustine's San Diego, 2nd year M.S. Physics student Creighton University; [occ.] Grad. student/teaching fellow Creighton University; [oth. writ.] One poem published in Santa Clara University Literary Review; [a.] Omaha, NE

TERRY, CHIRSTOPHER LEE
[b.] June 30, 1979, Lakeland, FL; [p.] Ed and Laura Terry; [ed.] Lakeland Christian; [occ.] Student/Work Part Time at Dad's Tropical Fish Farm; [memb.] West Lakeland Church of God, LCS Varsity Basketball, Cross Country Team Track Team; [hon.] Lettering in Basketball, Track and Cross Country; [oth. writ.] Personal collection of poetry unpublished.; [pers.] My poetry is written from the heart through personal glimpses and experiences.; [a.] Lakeland, FL

TERZIAN JR., CHARLES G.
[b.] June 14, 1957, Camden, NJ; [p.] Charles Terzian Sr. and Eleanor Terzian; [m.] Ginnine M. Terzian, November 2, 1991; [ch.] Demetrius A. Terzian; [ed.] Williamstown High School, Williamstown, New Jersey; [occ.] Owner/operator of South West Pest Control, Sarasota, Florida; [memb.] American Diabetes Assoc., USGA, Art Hall of Fame; [pers.] It's not how much you know, but how you apply the knowledge you've obtained.; [a.] Sarasota, FL

THIBEAULT, KAREN E.
[b.] April 21, 1977, Leominster; [p.] Brian and Marlene Thibeault; [ed.] 1995 Graduate of Leominster High School freshman at Mount Wachusett Community College in Gardner, MA; [occ.] Student; [hon.] 1994 Bay State Games Silver Medalist in figure Skating, also 1994 Bay State Games Bronze Medalist in Precision Skating; [pers.] Never sell yourself short of anything, for you may never know what your talents are.; [a.] Leominster, MA

THIGPEN, VIOLA P.
[pen.] Viola P. Thigpen; [b.] February 1, 1948, Philadelphia; [p.] Lydia J. Slater, Henry W. Dunn; [m.] Craig D. Thigpen, August 7, 1971; [ch.] 2 sons, 1 daughter; [ed.] 2nd year student LaSalle University, Sociology, English Minor; [occ.] Homemaker/Student; [memb.] St. Augustine Church of the Covenant Episcopal Church, Parent-Advisor for the Rhoer Club of Sigma Gamma Rho Sorority, Inc., Alpha Eta Sigma Chapter for High School girls; [hon.] Gimble's Young Artist Award, 1st Place '65, High School Honor Student; [oth. writ.] "Search For Financial Aid", Phila. Tribule Mag. 9/95, Narrative, "The Funeral", Poems: "Feeding The Hunger", "Love Is...", "Revelations Of Past Remembrances", "Portrait Of My Love" - all unpublished; [pers.] I find writing to be a powerful catharsis. Writing puts me in touch with

my subconscious thoughts, and emotions. Writing poetry is new for me. I enjoy it. I like to say that, now, Langston Hughes and I share more than our birthday.; [a.] Philadelphia, PA

THOMAS, RICHARD
[b.] July 22, 1963, Charlotte, NC; [p.] JoAnn and Garland Thomas; [ed.] Central Piedmont Community College, Charlotte, NC; [occ.] Manager - Inventory Control; [hon.] Nat'l Library of Poetry 96'; [oth. writ.] "Consenual Emotion Surviving the Mourning After", (unpublished/compilation, "The Nature of Things" (unpublished compilation); [pers.] A career path is your life's journey, follow your bliss.; [a.] Charlotte, NC

THOMAS, SARA D.
[b.] November 30, 1965, Birmingham, AL; [p.] Rexann Thomas; [occ.] Disabled; [memb.] Chess Club; [oth. writ.] True Love, The Hand, Dancing With a Lady, Short Friction - The Decision; [pers.] My tears, my terror, my rage they find their way on the page, for my poetry purges the bowels of my emotions.; [a.] Hot Springs, AR

THOMPSON, CHERI
[b.] September 15, 1972, Festus, MO; [p.] Paul and JoAnn Thompson; [ch.] Kayla and Kyle Thompson; [ed.] Crystal City High School; [occ.] Part-time Model; [pers.] This poem I dedicate to Ira, for who is so deeply embedded in my heart, I could never let go.; [a.] Festus, MO

THOMPSON, JOE
[b.] April 4, 1951, Scott AFB, IL; [p.] Duane S. Thompson, Jeane Thompson; [ed.] B.A. University of Colorado at Colorado Springs; [occ.] Owner, Colorado Downlink Satellite Television Specialists since 1980; [a.] Colorado Springs, CO

THOMPSON, KARI
[pen.] Kari; [b.] July 21, 1968, Beckley, WV; [p.] Clarence and Betty Hoag; [m.] Pat Thompson, February 20, 1988; [ch.] Dallas and Rebecca, step children: Melissa, Mandy, Samantha; [occ.] Community Living Instructor - Black Hills Workshop; [pers.] I write from my heart.; [a.] Rapid City, SD

THOMPSON, SHAINA J.
[b.] December 21, 1949, Vallejo, CA; [p.] Howard and William Barkhill; [m.] William W. Thompson Sr., December 7, 1973; [ch.] Joseph Aaron, Rebecca Anne, Wayne, David, Tammy; [ed.] Sonoma State University (B.A., credential: E.C.E.), Santa Rosa Junior College (A.A.), Master's candidate - San Francisco State, Piner High School; [occ.] Teacher - English as a second language, Master's Candidate - Education; [memb.] Title IX-Indian Ed. Jefferson School District, Daly City, CA, CSEA, ASA, SKINS; [hon.] Dean's List, award of merit, SHOFAR award (for work with youth), third place - Poetry, San Mateo Co. Fair, Second place - Art (Basket of Dreams), Third place art - Spirit Warrior (Mask), Hon. mention - Art (Spirit Window): County Fair; [oth. writ.] Various articles in newspaper, book of poetry: Shades of Blue (unpub.), Race: Reading Readiness Program (unpub.), Your Brother's Native American Curriculum Unit (unpub.), romance books (unpub.), poems published in high school and college papers; [pers.] I have a rich cultural background from which I draw on for my writings.

THOMPSON, WYNEMIA O.
[pen.] W. T.; [b.] July 28, 1957, Los Angeles, CA; [p.] Verneal McKnight; [m.] Billy E. Thompson Jr., January 7, 1978; [ch.] Terrance, Syreeta and Bobby Thompson; [pers.] I am a christian whose purpose in life is to inspire

and uplift each individuals inner sprit whenever deemed necessary, not only verbally but in my writing as well.; [a.] Lakewood, CA

THURSTON, WANDA
[b.] November 21, 1947, Louisa, KY; [p.] George P. Younce and Jewell Dixon; [m.] George Thurston; [ch.] Three with four granddaughters; [ed.] Graduated 1965 - from Walter E. Stebbins High School - Completed Computer and Accounting courses at New Mexico Jr College and Certificate of Graduation from National Tax Training School in New York; [occ.] Business Administrator, Business Services Message Communication Systems - owner; [memb.] Former Active Member of Credit Women International, International Traders Association and The Highlanders Club, also National Association of Female Executives (NAFE); [hon.] Recognition for poem "Long Ago" 1988. Teacher Recognition for Computer Learning Essay; [oth. writ.] Published 1988 - Great American Poetry Anthology "Long Ago". "Processing Accounts Payable" and "Hesperia Hoodlums" in progress "The Good Life" - to be published 1996 - in Morning Song and The Sound of Poetry.

TIDWELL, MELISSA
[b.] January 6, 1981, Hoopa, CA; [p.] Debbie and Jim Harrington, Mike and Phila Tidwell; [ed.] Sophmore at Tahoe Truckee High; [occ.] Lifeguard at North Star Ski Resort; [oth. writ.] Best Friend, Dream Life, Death For You, The Passing of Grandma, Not For Me and Summer. All yet to be published.; [pers.] This poem was written for Vito the first man I have ever loved. He knows I will always be his girl until he chooses otherwise. I love you always.

TIJERINA, LUIS LAZARO
[b.] December 29, 1945, Salina, KS; [p.] Luis and Rachel Tijerina; [ch.] Eli L. Tijerina Lyons; [ed.] Kansas State University Major, Western European Intellectual History/U.S. Army 1976-79 4th Infantry Division; [occ.] Free-lance TV Interviewer and Journalism, Art Critic, Soccer Coach; [oth. writ.] Several poems and articles published in small presses and newspapers, etc. Brattleboro Reformer, Stage And Studio, Arts Council of Windham County, VT; [a.] Brattleboro, VT

TOEDTER, CARYL ANDERSON
[b.] July 13, 1913, Beattie, KS; [p.] John G. Anderson, Alma Anderson; [m.] Wallace W. Toedter, August 24, 1941; [ed.] Beatlie High, BA University of Kansas, Nebraska V., Kansas State, Emporia State.; [occ.] Retired Marysville, KS High School Math Teacher; [memb.] Life Member: NEA, KSTA, Kualumni, Gold Medal Club, AAUW, Nat. Math Ass., Presbyterian Church, Order of Eastern Star, Marysville Study Club.; [hon.] Phi Beta Kappa Pi Lamda Theta, PSI Chi, Omocron NU at KU Delta Kappa Gamma Master Teacher-Marysville High 1974 Six National Science Foundation Scholarship Awards Modern Math. Highest grade ever in KS. Normal Training Teacher's Exams.; [oth. writ.] A personal book of poems covering many different subjects.; [pers.] Reading and writing poetry for me is an enjoyable, awarding experience I appreciate a rare blend of serious discussions and humor with a wide diversity of subject matter.; [a.] Marysville, KS

TOLSON, FRANCES E.
[b.] September 15, 1913, Licking, CO; [p.] H. H. and Mary Hoover; [m.] Melvin L. Tolson (Deceased January 18, 1994), November 8, 1953; [ch.] One stepdaughter - Deceased 4 grandchildren - 4 great-grandchildren; [ed.] Newark High School Bachelor's Ohio State Uni-

versity Masters Art Education - Kent State University; [occ.] Retired Art Teacher; [memb.] State Retired Teachers Carroll County Retired Teachers and Carroll County Commission for Advancement of the Arts; [hon.] Who's Who in American Education Who's Who in the Arts 1971-1972; [oth. writ.] Christian Life Letters The Lookout Free Press Standard World of Poetry Christian Evangelist; [pers.] I try to put feelings into words that paint a picture to the reader; [a.] Carrollton, OH

TOMECSEK, JANNA S.
[b.] February 1, 1977, Allentown, PA; [p.] John Jr., and Judith A. Tomecsek; [ed.] William Allen High School, currently at Delaware Valley College; [occ.] Student - studying Small Animal Science, Pre-Vet.; [hon.] Individual Media History Day Awards (6 years in a row); [oth. writ.] Several poems and short stories (unpublished); [a.] Allentown, PA

TORRES, PAUL
[pen.] The Quiet One; [b.] December 15, 1976, New York, NY; [p.] Anna Torres, Angel Torres; [ed.] Drake Business School (present), Pace University (last); [occ.] Student, Drake Business School; [memb.] Beach Channel Boat Squad; [hon.] Academic Honors at Taylor Business Institute; [oth. writ.] Several, but unpublished; [pers.] My poems reflect the feelings I have toward the relationships I've been through. I want to thank my Mom, Dad, Kay, Lisa, Omi, Opi, Jasmine Mihalics and Shawn Grant. I also want to thank Iris, Louis, Sherry, Deidre, Any and Silhouette.; [a.] Woodside, NY

TOVAR, ETHEL K.
[pen.] Jessica Smith; [b.] January 9, 1984, Chiapas, Mexico; [p.] Loyda and Luis Tovar; [ed.] Whittler Elementary, Bennion Elementary, West High School; [occ.] Student; [memb.] National Junior Honor Society; [hon.] Coloring Award, Principal's Award, 100% attendance award, good citizenship award, random acts of kindness award; [oth. writ.] Short stories; [pers.] I try to express the emotions of the subject I'm writing about. The topics I particularly enjoy writing about are the outdoors and nature.; [a.] Salt Lake City, UT

TRIM, DERRICK R.
[b.] December 8, 1973, Saint Croix, VI; [p.] Miriam Trimm and Joe Chang; [ed.] Senior at Centenary College in Hackettstown; [occ.] Student; [memb.] Centenary College Soccer Team; [hon.] S.E.E.N. Program Summer '95, selected to act as a Counselor Cetenary College National Small College Athletic Champion Fall '95; [oth. writ.] None at the moment; [pers.] "The bird of death", was originally written in the loving memories or Reggienal Rivera, who was kill from a shot to the heart. He was one of my best friend and I miss him very much. I want to dedicate this poem to Cherryse Rivera (sister) and the family of Reggie, love you always and forever, R.I.P.; [a.] Hackettstown, NJ

TRIMMER, PAUL THEODORE
[b.] November 23, 1977, Las Vegas; [p.] Dr. H. Theodore and Paula Sue; [ed.] Bonanza High School Entering Freshman year at University of Southern California (USC); [occ.] Student; [memb.] Green Athletic Club - ha!; [hon.] Dean's List; [oth. writ.] Write for the school newspaper the Eye of the Tiger; [a.] Las Vegas, NV

TROY, ADAM
[b.] December 26, 1979, Manchester, CT; [p.] Dianna and William Troy; [ed.] Woodstock Public School, Woodstock Academy; [occ.] Student Junior Year at Woodstock Academy, Woodstock, CT; [memb.] Student Council, Athletic Council, Varsity Basketball; [hon.]

High Honors - Honor Roll; [oth. writ.] Several poems published in local literary magazines: At The Plate, On The Baseline Calenture.; [pers.] I have been influenced by the great works of Shel Silverstein.; [a.] Woodstock, CT

TRUEBLOOD, ANGELA MARIE
[b.] July 23, 1983, Scotland County Hosp., Memphis, MO; [p.] Mr. and Mrs. Corl Trueblood; [ed.] I have just completed 6th grade. I'll be in my 1st year of Jr. high this fall.; [occ.] Student; [hon.] Honor roll student art award, music award, history award - district level, reading award - Life Certificate; [oth. writ.] Other poems; [pers.] This is the first poem that I have ever had published and I'm proud of that. But, on a sad note - I wrote this poem after a young man was killed in a car crash close to our home.; [a.] Memphis, MO

TUCKER, JO
[b.] September 28, 1941, Dallas, TX; [p.] Joseph and Robbye Doucet; [ch.] Timothy, Jesse, Cody; [ed.] Univ. of Texas at Arlington, Texas; [occ.] Admin. Assistant, Genesis Center, Inc. Manchester, CT; [memb.] AARP; [hon.] Ordained Minister; [oth. writ.] Several poems published by Nat'l Lib. of Poetry, also write music and fiction.; [a.] Manchester, CT

TUCKER, PEGGY
[pen.] Peggy Tucker; [b.] February 18, 1949, Walton County, GA; [p.] Mr. and Mrs. C. E. White; [ch.] Christy McCart, Stacey Biggers, Leslie Biggers; [ed.] Graduate - Loganville Elementary and High School; [occ.] Manager - Joe Ray Bonding Co.; [oth. writ.] First publication.; [pers.] Thoughts come to me and I have to put them on paper in the form of a poem.; [a.] Loganville, GA

TULLY, DEIRDRA
[b.] November 2, 1983, Secaucus, NJ; [p.] Robert Tully, Denise Tully; [ed.] 6th grade Union Avenue, Middle School, Hazlet NJ; [occ.] Student; [hon.] Enrichment Program, Honor Roll/High Honors, Odyssey of the Mind, State and Regional Tournaments - 3rd place and Ranatra Fusca Creativity Award; [oth. writ.] Two poems printed in prior school yearbooks.; [pers.] I enjoy writing poems and have been since 1st grade. I write about anything that comes to mind or that I think is interesting.; [a.] Hazlet, NJ

TURNBOW, DAWN D.
[b.] July 12, 1958, Utah; [p.] Bruce and Pilar Turnbow; [ch.] Troy Robert Pierson Jr.; [occ.] Certified Nurses Assistant; [oth. writ.] In fifth grade I lived in England and wrote a poem called "Butterfly" for my homework assignment and was accused of plagiarism because it was too good.; [pers.] My son is my inspiration, he's 4 yrs. old.; [a.] Olympia, WA

TURNER, BRITANY
[pen.] Britany L. Turner; [b.] July 7, 1983, Saint Louis County, MO; [p.] James Turner, Wanda Turner; [ed.] 8th grade student at Jennings High School; [memb.] Conflict Mediation Team; [hon.] Honor Roll Student since 1st grade, Award for Superior Achievement and Excellence of Performance in English Lit. Class. Numerous awards for Outstanding Citizenship.; [oth. writ.] I have written other poems I hope to get published.; [pers.] This is my first poem to be published. When I write my poems, I use my inner emotions and try to express in words what I see and feel, hoping to get across to the reader the picture and feelings I have in my mind.; [a.] Jennings, MO

TUZZEO, CAMILLE
[b.] January 29, 1934, Brooklyn, NY; [p.] William and Catherine Tuzzeo; [m.] October 14, 1951; [ch.] Three boys; [ed.] High School - Vocal Scholarship from Metropolitan Opera House Studios Studied under Srs. of St. Dominic to Assist in Teaching; [occ.] Retired; [oth. writ.] In capacity of teaching and music - I have written many Cantatas and respective librettos for same song words and music-directed choirs both adult and children's organ and piano; [pers.] Faith is the center of my life and has always been. I believe that all is only good. I look for only the best in others and totally accept the concept of self-healing. We are all one and each of us affects the whole.; [a.] Clearwater, FL

TWERSKY, DIANNE JURAN
[pen.] Dianne Juran Twersky; [ed.] B. A. Queens College Post grad. studies - Poetry and Writing Workshops, New York Univ., New School, NYC; [pers.] All the Arts have the same configuration - Music - Sculpture - Painting - Poetry.

TWETE, ANNIE LOIS
[b.] September 21, 1921, San Antonio, TX; [p.] William and Lois Housewright; [m.] Rudolph E. Twete, December 24, 1944; [ch.] Carol Anne DeBow and Judy Lea Powers; [ed.] Riverside High School, Ft. Worth, TX, A. and M. Junior College, Arlington, TX; [occ.] Legal Secretary and Housewife; [memb.] United Methodist Church, League of Women's Voters, National Christian Women's Club; [oth. writ.] "Adam and Eve", published by Sparrowgrass Poetry Forum; [pers.] I write to state my beliefs and love, of God and Brotherhood, and what I cannot otherwise express.; [a.] Austin, TX

TYLER, CYNTHIA M.
[pen.] G. M. Tyler; [b.] July 18, 1962, Chicago, IL; [p.] Wade Montgomery, Linda Montgomery; [m.] Arrick P. Tyler, July 22, 1989; [ch.] Antwoine Tyler, Arvier Tyler; [ed.] Manley High, Catherine College; [occ.] Homemaker; [hon.] Perfect Attendance, Honor Roll; [pers.] I am deeply honored to have this special poem, that was written for my first love, who is now my husband will be admired by others.; [a.] Schaumburg, IL

TYNES, MILDRED B.
[m.] Deceased; [ch.] Three-all educators; [ed.] B.S. Degree - Va. State College, Two summers further study on Master's Degree; [occ.] Retired, Teacher - thirty-five years; [memb.] St. Phillips Episcopal Church, National Cancer Soc. Nat. Retired Teacher's Assn. Richmond - Henrico Retired Trs. Assn. National and Richmond Chap. of American Assn. of Retired Persons; [hon.] 1992 Awarded a Certificate of Merit by the World of Poetry for first poem. 1993 same poem printed in Our World's Favorite Poems by The National Library of Poetry.; [oth. writ.] Quarterly write poems for AARP newsletter, article for Church Anniversary Bulletin; [pers.] Creating poems gives me a feeling of happiness nothing else can.; [a.] Richmond, VA

ULMER, FERN KEY
[b.] August 4, 1930, Colleton County, SC; [p.] Mary Clarkson Key and Corey P. Key; [m.] John Wesley Ulmer, October 20, 1950; [ch.] Corey, John William, Richard, Randall, Russell; [ed.] Graduate University of South Carolina College of Nursing; [occ.] Retired Registered Nurse - Farm Homemaker; [a.] Lodge, SC

ULMER, SIDNEY GALE
[pen.] Sidney G. Ulmer; [b.] January 10, 1937, Chicago, IL; [p.] Sidney D. Collisson; [m.] Dolly J. Collisson, March 9, 1973; [ch.] Five, ages 38, 36, 35, 13 and 12;

[ed.] BFA Corcoran School of Art D.C. Endicott College, Beverly Mas; [occ.] Professional Artist and Retail in Arts; [memb.] Wilmington Arts Association Unity Church - Studies for Pastoral Counselor Southport Art League; [hon.] Recognition for prose written for Unity Church Newsletter Regularly. Many Fine Arts Awards in D.C., VA MD and NC; [oth. writ.] Poetry read on WHQR Radio Design and write original prose and poetry with art for cards sold in NC and VA areas commercially one of writers for contemplative locally; [pers.] What I write comes through me as I journal and continue to record in response to living experiences Both in times of introspection and activity. I was an environmental art interpreter for 1 year with Nat. Pk Service in Accokeek Ind. 1972-1991. And cover artist for Hill Rag in Capt. Hill - artwork still used by then annually.; [a.] Wilmington, NC

UPCHURCH, DORIS
[b.] February 5, 1941, Colorado; [m.] Clarence O. Upchurch Jr., August 26, 1961; [ch.] Dorene, Larraine, Twila; [ed.] Two years college; [occ.] Day Care Professional, Mufon Investigator; [memb.] Mutual UFO Network, Texas Professional Home Day Care Association; [hon.] Editor's Choice Awards; [oth. writ.] "Freedom," "What Age Would You Be," "For Which I Search," "I Believe," "Journey North To Alaska," "Crystal University Method of Soul Sensitivity Tramming."; [pers.] To express deeply felt emotions in words.; [a.] Corpus Christi, TX

VALENTE, ANNA MARIA
[pen.] Anna Valente; [b.] May 13, 1973, Neptune, NJ; [p.] Mary Ann and Victor Valente; [ed.] Ridgewood High School Newport Richey, FL; [occ.] NJ Elementary School, Food Service,; [hon.] Graduated with Honor in 1992; [oth. writ.] "Creation of The Universe", "My Cousins Hobbies" published in school publication.; [pers.] My relatives inspire me to write about them.; [a.] New Port Richey, FL

VALENTIN, JENNIFER
[b.] February 9, 1982, Smithtown; [p.] Greg Valentin, Lorraine Celada; [ed.] Presently in the 9th grade; [pers.] I was influenced by my mother because these days a lot of kids can't talk to their mothers the way I can and I'm glad I have a mother like her.; [a.] Brentwood, NY

VAN HAVERBEKE, CRYSTAL
[b.] June 26, 1966, Ronan, MT; [p.] Maria Gress, Al Sloan; [m.] Terence McLure; [ch.] Thomas, Terence, Quinten; [occ.] Proof Operator, Washington Trust Bank; [oth. writ.] Several still awaiting in my personal text only my dearest ones have read.; [pers.] I have healed many hurts through my writing. In each poem I gain strength and spirit to be a better person; [a.] Spokane, WA

VAN HEMERT, KATHRYN C.
[pen.] Kathryn Christie; [b.] January 12, 1952, Greenwich, CT; [p.] John S. and Kathryn F. Edwards; [m.] Donald Van Hemert, November 25, 1976; [ch.] Sean Strong Van Hemert; [ed.] New Milford High School, St. Lawrence University; [occ.] Bookkeeper Robert Arthur Corporation; [memb.] Animal Welfare Society, Last Race Greyhounds, ReGap of CT, Peta; [hon.] Dean's List, Kappa Delta Sigma; [pers.] It is my hope that one day man will learn to treat animals with the respect they so deserve.; [a.] Bridgewater, CT

VAN ORMAN, ELVIRA
[b.] June 15, 1920, Camden, NJ; [p.] Charles and Anna (Zirs) Smith; [m.] Ellis Van Orman, April 24, 1943; [ch.] Paul, Esther, Philip, 5 Grandchildren; [ed.] Graduate,

Camden High School, 1938 AB Degree, Juniata College, 1942 French Institute, Penn State, Summer 1941 Harrisburg School of the Bible, courses, 1970's; [occ.] Homemaker; [memb.] East Shore Evangelical Free Church, Pennsylvania Pro-life Federation, International Society of poets 1994-1995; [hon.] Editor's Choice Award for "Parable" published in at Water's Edge; [oth. writ.] Letters of personal opinion to local newspaper, twice censored! Current events and prevailing attitudes are sources of ideas for my poetry. "A Timely Reminder" was prompted by President Clinton's public veto of the legislation banning partial birth abortions.; [pers.] Another poet has written: "Only one life, 'twill soon be past, only what's done for Christ will last".; [a.] Harrisburg, PA

VANDERVORT, MARCIA L.
[pen.] Angelica P. Emmons; [b.] June 5, 1951, Logansport, IN; [p.] William J. Andrews, Martha A. Andrews; [m.] Dennis E. Vandervort, June 28, 1969; [ch.] Alan E., Richard L. and Michael W.; [ed.] North White High School and LaSalle Institute; [occ.] Homemaker; [memb.] International Society of poets 1994-95; [hon.] Editor's Choice Awards 1993, 1994 and 1995; [oth. writ.] "I Have Someone" and "A Family Moment", published in Treasured Poems of America Fall 1993. "Summer Days' published in "Wind In The Night Sky" 1993 vol. "The Parting" published in "Outstanding Poets of 1994". "Thoughts To Ponder" published in Best Poems of 1995; [pers.] It's always amazing how close you can get to someone, just by talking to them.; [a.] Kokomo, IN

VARELA, JESSE M.
[pen.] James Willoby; [b.] December 31, 1958, Nuevo Casas Grandes, Mexico; [p.] Carlos and Maria T. Varela; [m.] Alicia Castillo, June 23, 1996; [ed.] San Pedro High School Class of 1976, Los Angeles Harbor College; [occ.] McDonnell Douglas Corporation - Electrical Assembly; [memb.] Calvary Chapel Costa Mesa, CA; [hon.] Dean's Honor List, Essay contest winner, Elementary school; [oth. writ.] The Big Yellow Bus, The Wind; [pers.] Life's course can so easily change. One moment, one word, one action. Then all things change, like the changes of the seasons, so subtle and yet bringing in the new and leaving behind the old.; [a.] Fountain Valley, CA

VARGAS, BRENDA LOU
[b.] November 10, 1969, Bronx, NY; [p.] Confessor Vargas, Sylvia Castro; [m.] John A. Finch, November 14, 1995; [ed.] Medgar Evers College; [oth. writ.] Various Other poems; [pers.] Thanks for believing in me John, "Para Siempre". My writing is influenced from life experience. Feel my life through my words.; [a.] Queens Village, NY

VAUGHAN, CAROL B.
[b.] March 16, 1952; [m.] Douglas B. Vaughan, August 24, 1974; [ch.] Brett and Kate; [occ.] Physician Assistant for a plastic and reconstructive surgeon; [oth. writ.] Five papers in plastic and reconstructive surgery journals, "Caribbean eyes," "tapestries", "Rainy day", "Blink", "Male Phallicy", "Sensitivity", "Trust"; [pers.] Growing older is not so bad, as long as one, realizes that "Growing" is the operative word.; [a.] North Olmsted, OH

VAUGHN, EDDIE
[pen.] L. C. Vaughn; [b.] October 9, 1969, Chicago, IL; [p.] Amy and L. C. Vaughn; [ed.] Eldorado High in Kansas, Arkansas State University in Jonesboro.; [occ.] Actor/Model; [memb.] Eastside Baptist Church, Trim Gym, Jaycees, Photo Club, GNC, Christian Coalition; [hon.] Certificate of Baptism, 1994 Freshman Writing Award,

Certificate for Criminal Law Education Program, Certificate for graduating John Casablancas Modeling and Career Center; [oth. writ.] 1994 ASU Freshman Writing Contest; [pers.] Don't take life too seriously or the joke will be on you, laugh, love live.; [a.] Jonesboro, AR

VENA, JASON
[b.] March 9, 1980, Islip, NY; [p.] Carolyn Vena and James Vena (Deceased); [ed.] Albany Ave School - New York, Lindenhurst Junior High - New York, Congress Middle School Florida, Atlantic High School - Florida; [oth. writ.] Several poems, a few horror stories, and a couple of dramas; [a.] Boynton Beach, FL

VERRET, EDITH ANNE
[pen.] Camilla Verret; [b.] July 25, 1936, Omaha, NE; [p.] George L. and Marguerite Verret; [ed.] Music, Religious Education; [memb.] Sisters of Mercy of the Americas Co-director: Women's Intercultural; [a.] Anthony, NM

VERTER, IRVING I.
[pen.] Irving I. Verter; [b.] March 5, 1913, New York City; [p.] Abraham and Minnie Verter; [m.] Tamara, February 24, 1995; [ch.] Sheila, Regina, Allan, Marcia; [ed.] Average Good Education; [occ.] Retired (Supervisor U.S. Post Office and Pharmacy Union-1199); [memb.] Knights of Pythias, City of Hope, National Association of Retired Employees, Salesiam Missions Delray Beach Mens Club, Many Charitable Organizations and Marriage Encounter; [hon.] Many Government Awards - But the letters from your office Re: My poetry. I am elated thank you; [oth. writ.] Many other poems - 20 lines, 30 and 40 lines. It would be a pleasure for some poetic ability to read and advise me it they are good or n.g. written or original scraps of paper.; [pers.] Quite some poetry was written 12 years ago before the last of my grandchildren were born. I look back and I love the poetry I wrote so long ago. My heart is in my writing - my greatest pleasure. Presently writing again.; [a.] Delray Beach, FL

VILLALBA, JOSE
[b.] September 17, 1959, Margarita, Venezuela; [p.] Victor Villalba, Elba Reenault De Villalba; [m.] Rita Ordaz De Villalba, November 10, 1984; [ed.] University of Eastern Venezuela (U.D.O.-Venezuela), Rensselaer Polytechnic Institute, Troy, NY (MSc.); [occ.] Chemical Engineer; [oth. writ.] Several poems and tales published in newspapers; [pers.] Author's poems are embedded in a lyrical atmosphere. They reflect both the necessity of the beloved woman and the presence of his native town.; [a.] Menands, NY

VILLARREAL, DENISE
[b.] June 3, 1983, Galveston, TX; [p.] Dr. and Mrs. J. A. Villarreal; [ed.] Calallen Middle School Calallen, Texas; [occ.] Student; [memb.] School Clubs: Fellowship of Christian Athletes, Science Club, University Interscholastic League (UIL) Spelling, Writing, Reading, Impromtu, and Math, National Junior Honor Society, National Piano Guild Auditions; [hon.] Dukes TIP program, TAAS Academic Recognition, A&B Honor Roll, Middle School Spelling Bee, 2nd place in piano theory, 3rd Music Memory, 2nd in "Reflections" contest, USS and Summer Swim Team.; [oth. writ.] Many others (for academic purposes).; [pers.] I write to express my feelings and moods. My poems are influenced by material I read.; [a.] Corpus Christi, TX

VILLINES, LETITIA VANIA
[b.] March 30, 1947, Sylvester, GA; [p.] Arthur and Ilene Clark; [m.] James Benjamin Villines Sr.; [ch.] Fabrienne, Sabian Nico, James Benjamin Jr.; [ed.] J. W. Holly High,

Dekalb Community College; [occ.] Housewife and mother taking care of her 6 yrs. old precious son; [memb.] AIG, The Tabernacle; [hon.] Dean's List; [oth. writ.] I have written 14 poems, mostly about love and religion, but haven't tried to have any published.; [pers.] I strive to express my own true feelings when I am writing, because I believe there are others. Who can sympathize with my thoughts.; [a.] Decatur, GA

VINCENT, STEPHANIE DENISE
[pen.] Tandy "S"; [b.] May 7, 1972, Washington, DC; [p.] Evelyn Brisbane; [ed.] Northern High School 12 yrs.; [occ.] I use to work at Minnesota Fabric Store; [hon.] I have made Honor Roll in High School 5 times. I received the Most Improved Math Student Certificate at Northern Middle School, I also received a French Certificate at Woodson Jr. High School.; [pers.] I would like to have respect for myself and to share my experience with others.; [a.] Huntingtown, MD

VINEYARD, JANE M.
[b.] May 24, 1941, Knoxville, TN; [p.] Ernest and Myrtle Weaver (Father Deceased); [m.] Jack E. Vineyard, September 4, 1965; [ch.] Amy Hubbard, Angie Vineyard, Dana Vineyard; [ed.] Graduate Fulton High School, Knoxville, TN 1959; [occ.] Secretary - Director of Employee Benefits - Baptist Home Mission Board - Atlanta, GA; [oth. writ.] "Gatlinburg — I Knew You When" published in Knoxville News Sentinel 1984. Full page publication. Various articles for local newspapers.; [pers.] Have always been interested in poetry and reading as a hobby. Very fond of Edna St. Vincent Milay and Elizabeth Barrett Browning.; [a.] Duluth, GA

VIVAS, CAROLYN T.
[b.] July 13, 1940, Rochester, NY; [p.] John Mastowski and Alberta Mastowski; [m.] Rene M. Vivas (Deceased); [ch.] John R. Lindsay, Sally R. Montoya, Cassandra Vivas (Martinez); [ed.] Graduate Benjamin Franklin High School, Rochester, NY (1958); [occ.] Secretary-Pediatrics Department Harbor/UCLA Medical Center, Torrance, CA; [memb.] Fraternal Order of Eagles #4001, American Legion Post #833, American Legion Auxiliary, St. Philomena Roman Catholic Church; [pers.] My work reflects my life with its trials and tribulations - and eventually an acceptable outcome and solution.; [a.] Wilmington, CA

VOCHATZER, GARY JOSEPH
[b.] March 9, 1940, CA; [p.] Mary and Ed Kuhn; [m.] Shirley, March 23, 1991; [ch.] Herb, Liz, Susan, Irma and 7 grandchildren; [ed.] High School; [occ.] Insurance Broker since 1962; [memb.] Stockton Life Under writers; [hon.] Racquet-ball Player - Team sponsor; [oth. writ.] Multiple writings - generally written for specific people, the newspaper, friends and family and church pastors.; [pers.] Believe in God - my family - my job and enjoy pursuing talents related to writing.; [a.] Stockton, CA

VYVLECKA, SHELBY A.
[b.] February 9, 1961, East Liverpool, OH; [p.] Ann and Orville Leaisure; [m.] Stanley G. Vyvlecka, August 7, 1982; [ch.] Dillon (son) - Rhiannon (daughter); [ed.] Oak Glen High School, Victoria College; [occ.] Interior Decorator; [oth. writ.] I have written and performed many of my songs for various night clubs; [pers.] I want my words to touch your heart and pull emotions out of you when you read them. I hope you enjoy my poems as much as I enjoyed writing them.; [a.] Victoria, TX

WADDELL, HEATHER MACKENZIE
[b.] December 28, 1968, Tucson, AZ; [p.] Bruce and Evelyn MacKenzie; [m.] Stephen Waddell, November

26, 1994; [ed.] BSFCS in Child and Family Development from University of GA, Education Degree from GA, College; [occ.] Elementary School Teacher, Southside Elementary School, Milledgeville, GA; [memb.] Kappa Delta Pi, International Honor Society; [hon.] Dean's List, Charter Member and Foundations representative for Kappa Delta Pi International Honor Society; [pers.] A smile can break any language barrier.; [a.] Greensboro, GA

WADDELL, REATHA HEATH
[pen.] Retha; [b.] February 28, 1953; [p.] Cecil and Selma Heath; [m.] Jerry Waddell, June 23, 1972; [ch.] Rodney, Brian, Clint and Heidi; [ed.] Hokes Bluff High; [occ.] Bostrom Seating; [oth. writ.] Little Girls, Rag Doll, Summer's Day, Tell Me A Story Little Fairy, Bobby's Toad, Silly Sally, What's Your Will O' Lord, Bended Knees, A Dove Same Down; [pers.] In life's struggles, writing helps put things in focus.; [a.] Piedmont, AL

WAKE, CHIHOKO
[b.] August 30, 1940, Japan; [ed.] Sacred Heart University, (BA) Hiroshima University, (MA) Ball State University (MA); [occ.] University Professor, teaching Japanese and Japanese literature; [memb.] Association of Asian Studies/Midwest Association for Japanese Literary Studies/American Council in the Teaching of Foreign Language; [hon.] Valedictorian, High School, Prefectural Governor's Award, Teaching Honors, Governor's Honors, Program of Georgia, Honor Student, Sacred Heart University; [oth. writ.] 1) About 50 Haiku published in several academic annual reports magazine of the Research Society of the Modern Literary Arts (Japan), 2) A paper on Asticulation (Bridging between high schools and universities in Japanese Education) at South Eastern Association of Teacher of Japanese.; [pers.] I started composing Haiku since 1983. It sharpens and deepens things around me people and nature, and the creator of these things.; [a.] Greenville, SC

WALFORD, JUANITA L.
[b.] October 23, Little Rock, AR; [p.] Aaron T. and Ida Mae Cole; [m.] George E. Walford, November 5, 1968; [ed.] Divall Elementary School, Vashon N: Homer G. Phillips School of Nursing St. Louis, MO, Boston University; [occ.] Retired R.N.; [memb.] Boston Univ. Alumni, Homer G. Phillips Nurses Alumni Inactive Member, Lambda Kappa Mu Sorority; [hon.] B.L.S. in Social Work Cum Laude; [oth. writ.] "Night Riders", a copy - right musical composition, class E. other poems, and one play; [pers.] Life's treasures are all about us, even within reach, through the eyes of the optimist!; [a.] Punta Gorda, FL

WALKER, ANTHONY L.
[pen.] Tony Walker; [b.] February 8, 1962, Lexington, KY; [p.] Joseph and Sophia Walker; [m.] Separated, August 15, 1988; [ed.] High School Graduate, Glenville High School; [occ.] Male Nurse; [memb.] Community Clubs; [pers.] I enjoy writing poetry in my spare time. It is one of the hobbys I enjoy most. Also I like playing my guitar.; [a.] Cleveland, OH

WALKER, ERIC MARCUS
[pen.] Heirmark B.C., Heirmark A.D.; [b.] June 10, 1971, Colorado Springs, CO; [p.] Florence Walker, Eddie Walker; [occ.] Concierge, Intercontinental Concierge Corp.; [memb.] Christ Our Shepherd Church, Washington, DC; [oth. writ.] Many poems including "Bird From Paradise", "The Apology", "Reflections", "The Storm" and "The Stand".; [pers.] For me, poetry writing is a journal for the accounts of my soul. It is a description of a personal pilgrimage where the destination has not yet been reached.; [a.] Upper Marlboro, MD

WALKER, JENNIFER ANN
[pen.] Jennifer Ann Walker; [b.] March 11, 1968, Wilmington, DE; [p.] Mr. and Mrs. Walter D. Faville; [m.] Michael Lee Walker, October 31, 1995; [ch.] Renee Doreen Faville; [ed.] Delaware Technical and Community College; [occ.] Performer; [memb.] American Heart Assoc.; [hon.] #1 place in "Young Authors Workshop" in 1978; [oth. writ.] Freelance poetry; [pers.] When I write I feel a mystical flow through my body. Thoughts almost like memories of medieval times engulf my senses; [a.] Dover, DE

WALKER, TOSHA
[b.] October 26, 1973, Miami, FL; [p.] Shirley Ellison and Arthur Walker; [ed.] Alabama State University, graduation date 5/97, BS - English Minor - Public Relations; [occ.] Student; [hon.] Honor Roll; [oth. writ.] Play - "Candices Misunderstanding", short story - "Is There Or Isn't There A Santa Claus", poems - "Life", "A Precious Jewel Lost"; [pers.] Always remember to pray because prayer change things.; [a.] Montgomery, AL

WALKER, ZACH
[b.] February 7, 1980, Lubbock, TX; [p.] Mike and Milynda Walker; [ed.] McKinney High School (2 years); [occ.] Student McKinney High School; [pers.] Judge me not by what I am, but by what I will become; [a.] McKinney, TX

WALLACE, SHERI LYNN
[pen.] Sheri Lynn, Sheri Carrell, Sylin Rhine; [b.] Missoula, MT; [p.] Harold and Nancy Wallace; [m.] Jeffery Carrell, January 1, 1988; [ed.] Hellgate High School, Missoula, MT, Edmonds CC - Edmonds, WA, USPTR Tennis University - Hilton Head, South Carolina; [occ.] Tennis Coach, Manager Claims Health Insurance; [memb.] USTA, USPTR, World Team Tennis; [hon.] Dean's List, State Champion Tennis Player, Poise and Appearance Jr Miss Pageant, Miss Personality Jr Miss, Employee of the Year; [oth. writ.] Currently working on: Poetry compilation, a children's book, a nonfiction novel; [pers.] Before I leave this earth I want to make a "positive" difference in at least one person's life.; [a.] Mesa, AZ

WALLACE, VICTOR S.
[b.] November 30, 1924, Harrisburg, IL; [p.] William F. and Verba P. Wallace; [m.] Ruby V. Wallace, February 3, 1964 - 2nd marriage; [ch.] David E. Wallace and Linda L. Bishop (1st marriage); [ed.] High school grad., Plus grad. as a Physical Therapist, Hydro. and Electro. - age 18, about 18 months in the front lines, Europe, 27 months overseas. World War II was a full Education.; [occ.] Writer of short stories, lyricist and songwriter, plus about 140 pieces of poetry; [memb.] American Legion - International Society of Poets. "Dial-A-Demo"; [hon.] U.S. Army - Good Conduct Medal, (5) Five Bronze Battle Stars, European Theater of Operations, French Medal of Appreciation-Africa, Italy, France, Germany, and Austria; [oth. writ.] Publishing a Hard-back book, 23 short stories, called "Action Galore" - Love, surprise, joy, mystery, adventure torture, murder, romance, rape, ghosts, sex, hope, surprise endings. Publisher Wayne County Press, Illinois. Over 400 pages. Will be out by Oct. 1996. Also Hard back book of poetry, (140) pieces of poetry called "Rhyme with Reason" about 120 pages, will be out by Dec. 1996. I have two (2) song contracts with "Big Wedge Music", Nashville, Tenn. for songs "The Upper Hand" and "On Hold to Hold Me Darling".

I have written about 35 songs. One published in Calif. called "Los Angeles". Another one published in Florida, called "Sanibel-Captiva", on a 20 minute video called "A Vacation to Remember". I have poems published. "Flowers" published in hard-back called, "Beyond the Stars", NLP. Another poem called "New Year", published in "Through the Hour Glass". Another called "Love at First Sight", published in "Best Poems of the '90's". Another called, "March Winds" published in "Of Sunshine and Daydreams". Another poem called "June Wedding" published in "Daybreak of the Land".; [pers.] Eat correctly and stay healthy. Breathe deeply!; [a.] Cape Coral, FL

WALLER, MILES E.
[b.] April 7, 1962, San Fernando, CA; [ch.] Miles E. Waller Jr.; [ed.] A.A. at a J.C.; [oth. writ.] I have a special request for a peach or peach tree somewhere around the poem. Thanks!

WALTON, PATRIK
[pen.] Walton; [b.] March 15, 1968, Hollywood, CA; [m.] Jeanette Walton, June 10, 1995; [ed.] Arcadia High School, Pasadena City College (P.C.C.); [occ.] Musician, Songwriter, Poet; [oth. writ.] Original music, songs, and lyrics. Currently a performer with my band, guitarist, and vocals.; [pers.] I fell from the nest at an early age. I hit the street, where life is a struggle. I never give up!; [a.] Temple City, CA

WAMPLER, TODD
[b.] March 8, 1973, Huntsville, AL; [p.] Lynn and Toni Wampler; [ed.] BS in Marketing from the University of Tennessee; [occ.] Marketer for the Knoxville Arts Council; [oth. writ.] Currently working on a novel; [pers.] Dedicated to Sonny Lee Padgett - A Soul Friend "To each a passing, we travel a Highway".; [a.] Knoxville, TN

WARD, BRAD
[b.] October 20, 1985, Jackson, MS; [p.] Robert E. Ward Jr. and Jo Ann Kemp Ward; [ed.] Currently enrolled in 5th grade at Madison Avenue Elementary, Madison, MS; [memb.] Project Advise (Gifted Program), First Baptist Church, Madison, MS; [hon.] Honor Roll

WARD, LOUISE
[pen.] Louise Ward; [b.] December 19, 1928, Bassett, VA; [p.] Jim Martin and Ida Martin; [m.] Clarence M. Ward, August 16, 1947; [ch.] Linda Kay and Sandra Fay; [occ.] Retired; [memb.] Member of the New Hope Church of The Bretheren; [oth. writ.] I have right many more poems I've written I also like to write children poems and stories.; [pers.] I enjoy waiting about God and things related to his love for all mankind. I also enjoy writing some numerous poems.; [a.] Stuart, VA

WARD, R. A. EUGENE G.
[pen.] Eugene G. Ward R.A.; [b.] September 15, 1917, Virginia, MO; [p.] George E. Ward and Agnes M. Ward Nelson; [m.] Mary M. Schwartz, September 5, 1953; [ch.] Timothy 40, and Therese 38 years old 1 granddaughter Gloria, and great-grand daughter Marrisa; [ed.] 8th grade; [occ.] Retired-Arc Welder Active Poet; [memb.] National Authors Registary Registered Author - Distinguished Member International Society of Poets; [hon.] 2 President Awards, 3 Editors Choice Awards, 3 Achievement Awards, 2 Honorable Awards and poem in 17 books; [oth. writ.] 24 short stories 4,800 poems; [pers.] I believe in prayer and know all of the words come from God for my poems - so why ask for more poets are the backbone of today.; [a.] Muskogee, OK

WARREN, ANNE
[b.] June 24, 1938, Muncie, IN; [p.] Ralph R. and Lula G. Warren; [ed.] Muncie Central H.S., Indiana University, BA Ball State Teachers Coll. MA Ball State; [occ.] Emergency Planning dir., SF Unified School District; [memb.] Alpha Kappa Alha Sorority; [hon.] Educator of the Year - Phi Delta Kappa, 1996; [oth. writ.] Featured columnist H.S. paper; [pers.] Reality is perceived as pregnant with promise.; [a.] San Francisco, CA

WARREN, LATILIA
[pen.] Latilia, Tilli, Ti, Latilia; [b.] January 16, 1970, Chicago, IL; [p.] Deceased; [ed.] John Farren Elem. Ann Arbor Huron H.S., Eastern Michigan University; [occ.] Student and Music Tech, part-time light industrial worker; [hon.] Finalist in the national his. Forensic contest in Michigan for an original play I've written, "Partners at all Time" and a finalist winner in my elementary school for a essay I've written; [pers.] I don't want to look back because I'm constantly looking forward maybe I'm not the best but I'm not what I use to be as long as I'm alive I can make a change in me. I believe human beings can do almost anything once they put their mind to it. Making a difference (positive) in someone's life is important to me. Strive, we strive to feel and be free.; [a.] Saint Paul, MN

WASHINGTON, CLARENCE
[b.] June 1, 1935, Boston; [p.] William and Martha Washington; [ch.] Dannielle and Meaghan; [ed.] B.S. Tufts - Univ. 61/Diploma Museum School - 62/Graduate Traveling Fellow, Museum Of Fine Arts - 63/MFA. Tufts Univ. 71; [occ.] Artist - Buston Public School Teacher; [memb.] MFA Alumnae, Tufts Alumnae; [hon.] Full bright to Africa - 72 citation, city of Boston for multicultural contributions - 1990 traveling fellowship, to Europe - Museum of Fine Arts Boston - 63; [pers.] My poetry is influenced by EE Cummings and such friendly mysticisms. I am also am aware of a degree of dadaism in my work.; [a.] Boston, MA

WASHINGTON, EUGENE L.
[pen.] Gene Washington; [b.] July 5, 1929, Youngstown, OH; [p.] James and Larue Washington; [m.] Ilene Patricia Washington, July 18, 1974; [ch.] Eight - 5 girls, 3 boys; [ed.] Rayen High School graduate, Youngstown State University Dropout; [occ.] Now retired on S.S.; [memb.] Centenary Methodist Church; [hon.] Honorably discharged from U.S. Navy, service from July 21, 1948, July 22, 1952 served in Korean conflict; [oth. writ.] "Birth to Music"; [pers.] Have a great love for all types of poetry.; [a.] Youngstown, OH

WASILEWSKI, ANNA
[b.] December 31, 1979, Chicago, IL; [p.] Janina and Stanislaw; [ed.] Currently a Junior at Ridgewood H.S.; [oth. writ.] Some poems published in the Ridgewood H.S. Literary Magazine "Creative Waves".; [pers.] In my writings I try to make the reader feel what I've gone through. In every poem I write, the words come from my mind, but the feelings come from my heart, and there is always a certain message in each of my that reflects the person I am.; [a.] Harwood Heights, IL

WATERMAN, JOHN
[b.] January 5, 1981, Ithaca, NY; [p.] Steven and Diane Waterman; [ed.] Wilton High School; [occ.] Student; [hon.] High School Honor Roll; [a.] Wilton, CT

WATSON-JONES, SYBILLE
[pen.] Sybille; [b.] April 29, 1946, Germany; [p.] Richard and Ruth Laib; [m.] Ernest Jones, May 6, 1978; [ch.] Christine M., Alfred W., Naomi R.; [ed.] Limestone High

School, the Institute of Children's Literature; [occ.] Home maker, Child Care Manager; [oth. writ.] Articles in local newspaper and in the "Poetry Digest"; [pers.] "I find that life is much like a drawing board. The only piece missing is an eraser".; [a.] Medford, OR

WATTS, JENNIFER
[b.] August 14, 1982, Price, UT; [p.] Randy and Paula Watts; [ed.] Freshman at Hoover High School, Alabama; [occ.] Student; [memb.] National Junior Honor Society; [pers.] My poetry tends to reflect the darker side of my personality, but also has something to do with nature and with human nature.; [a.] Hoover, AL

WAUGH, BETTY M.
[pen.] Betty M. Waugh; [b.] October 7, 1932, Forsyth County; [p.] William Franklin Myers, Ethel Lineback Myers; [m.] Cecil O. Waugh Sr., July 22, 1989; [ch.] Cecil 4, Betty 2 adopted; [ed.] Forsyth Tech. Community College ADN, LPN, Gardener Wolf College Lack 3 academic for BA degrees; [occ.] Registered Nurse (Neurosurgery) North Carolina Baptist Hospital and Bowman Gray School of Medicine; [memb.] Knitting Guild of America, Cultured Purls Knitting Club, First Assembly of God Church, Lifelong Evangelism; [hon.] The greatest award was a Big "Thank You" When my husband and I sent boxes of sweaters, and accessories to the homeless people clothing each year for persons who are in need; [oth. writ.] Autumn published in Tapestry of Thoughts; [pers.] Seek God's will incellency, compassion, and love as I endeavor to serve the sick and hurting in their greatest time of need both physically, and emotionally.; [a.] Winston Salem, NC

WEAVER, MADELINE F.
[b.] July 19, 1949, Detroit, MI; [p.] Herman Iott, Maureen Blaney Iott; [m.] Carl Ray Weaver, February 14, 1995; [ch.] Alexandria Walentowski, Jordan Weaver, Corey Weaver; [ed.] Wayne State Univ.; [memb.] Farm Bureau, VAW local 1892, YMCA; [hon.] Poem included in the Nat. Library of Poetry, "Frost At Midnight"; [oth. writ.] Seeking publisher for first volume of poems, "Angry Salad", illustrated by author.; [pers.] My poetry speaks for me.; [a.] Maumee, OH

WEBB, ELLEN KAYE
[pen.] Ellen Kaye Webb; [b.] March 19, 1941, Monticello, IL; [p.] Mrs. Ida Rogers; [m.] Rex Webb, February 14, 1993; [ch.] Julie Parker, Samuel Haight; [ed.] Registered Nurse; [occ.] Worker in Ducky Day Care Center - Infant room Monticello, IL; [memb.] First Christian Church Monticello, IL - International Society of Poets as of 1996; [oth. writ.] "Give Your Soul to God, Sam" A Tapestry of Thoughts - Anthology 1996 won Editors Choice Award. "Thanks be to God" Anthology entitled: "Famous Poems of the Twentieth Century" as well as lyrical heritage winter 1996; [pers.] I write about ones who have touched I have admired, ones whom I love, and who love me.; [a.] Deland, IL

WEBSTER, ROSE MARY
[pen.] Rose; [b.] November 4, 1952, Fremont, MI; [p.] Vera Jankowski and Clayton Parrott and Don and Julia Newenhouse; [m.] (Divorced April 16, 1993), March 21, 1970; [ch.] Tracy L. Rothley, Erick M. Webster, Tammy M. Webster, five grandchildren; [ed.] Wyoming Community Ed. of my GED 3-95 J and H, Oil Co. Mobil; [memb.] Wyoming Jaycee and Christian Motorcyclist's Association; [oth. writ.] This one was my first one to ever be publish. I have others and hope to have a book made of them someday.; [pers.] The biggest influence in my life and writing. Comes from my Lord and Savior

above. As well my 3 children and 5 grandchildren.; [a.] Jenison, MI

WEEKS JR., FRED
[b.] July 18, 1949, Mansfield, LA; [m.] Ruth; [ch.] Tanya, Love, Fred; [pers.] In memory of our son, Fred N. Weeks III.; [a.] Oklahoma City, OK

WEINER, ELIZABETH
[b.] May 8, 1976, Plymouth, MA; [p.] Richard Weiner, Janis Weiner; [ed.] Sandwich High School, Cape Cod Community College (currently attending); [occ.] Teacher's Aide, Sandwich, MA/Student; [memb.] The Companion Animal Program, The Shooting Stars, Cape Cod Women's Cancer Collective, Inc.; [hon.] Phi Theta Kappa, Dean's List, The National Dean's List; [oth. writ.] I was a staff writer for my high school's newspaper and I contributed to my high school's literary magazine; [pers.] My poetry is all very personal. Reading my poetry is like peering through a window into my soul. I am constantly influenced by the brilliant energy of the world around me.; [a.] Sandwich, MA

WELCH, JOHN CLIFFORD
[b.] November 25, 1946, Detroit, MI; [p.] Ruth and Harold Welch; [ed.] H.S., 2 years Junior College (High School); [occ.] Sales Clerk, 7-11 Store; [memb.] The Aetherius Society; [hon.] Member-Initiate Aetherius Society; [pers.] My greatest influence is the The Aetherius Society, an international meta-physical organization. God is omnipresent, omniscient, omnipotent.; [a.] Farmington Hills, MI

WELK, RICHARD A.
[pen.] R. A. W.; [b.] October 25, 1943, Harvey, ND; [p.] August and Doris Welk; [m.] RoAnn Fitzer (Divorced), July 31, 1963; [ch.] Dean, Lisa and Sara; [ed.] Ruby High School, attended classes at Dickinson State University, and North Dakota State School of Science; [occ.] Self-employed, Draftsman, and Estimator, Single and Multi-dwelling Designer; [memb.] Current member of Knights of Columbus, and St. Wenceslaus Church. Rough Rider Archery Past Pres. of the Dickinson JC's, Past-Pres of Dickinson Rough Rider Commission, Past-Co Chairperson of Dickinson Centennial Com. Past-Trinity Mardi Gras Chairman, Past-Board of Directors, United Way, Past-Board of Directors, Dickinson Builders Exchange, Past-Board of Directors, Rough Rider Archery; [hon.] Many awards in there fields; [oth. writ.] I have written poems, all are in a file. This first poem I have made public.; [pers.] All my poetry has been influenced, not by me alone, but the inspiration of the people around me, the places and things. It is to them I dedicate my poetry, a small effort to show my thanks, and appreciation, for sharing their lives with me. I enjoy classical music, the outdoors, and painting, oil water colors; [a.] Dickinson, ND

WELLS, JOYCE LAVON
[b.] August 25, 1962, Ann Arbor, MI; [p.] Albert Lee Elam, Corine Elam; [ch.] Paris Elijah Iman Addie (14), Steven Zaire Garner (13); [ed.] Ypsilanti High School, and went to Washtenaw Community College; [occ.] Currently working at the University of Michigan Hospital in Ann Arbor, MI; [oth. writ.] The First Time We Met, Free, Dreams of Love, Devotion, are just a few of my heart felt poetry; [pers.] This is one of the poems I wrote to my first love in "1980", I have always been a "Hopeless Romantic", with a love for writing. I was inspired by my loving brother, Larry Elam to summit my poem. My Heart and thoughts are a Design and a gift from God, to whom I give all my Thanks.; [a.] Ypsilanti, MI

WELLS, LISA LEE
[pen.] Lisa W.; [b.] March 10, 1961, Memphis, TN; [p.] Grant L. Wells, Thelma L. Wells; [ed.] Graduated Magna Cum Laude, 1982, Shelby State Community College, Cum Laude, 1985, Shelby State Community College in Memphis; [occ.] Scheduling Receptionist for Health First Medical Group - Memphis; [hon.] Consistently made the Dean's List - Shelby State Community College, National Honor Society, Member in High School, (1978) - Memphis Technical High - Memphis; [oth. writ.] Currently working on A Children's mystery and other poetry; [pers.] "Without dreams, life has no magic, no purpose for which to strive, continue to dream, and the door of infinite possibilities will swing open."; [a.] Memphis, TN

WELLS, WANDA
[b.] August 12, 1957, Greenwood, SC; [p.] Curtis and Carol Wells; [ed.] Ware Shoals High, Piedmont Tec.; [occ.] Secretary; [memb.] Harmony Methodist Church; [a.] Ware Shoals, SC

WENDT, KRISTINE
[pen.] Kristine, Kristine Cayman; [b.] January 5, 1966, Denver, CO; [p.] Marion and Shirley Wendt; [ed.] Elmwood Public High School, Elmwood, NE, Nebraska Wesleyan University, Lincoln, NE, University of Central Oklahoma, Edmond, OK, University of Oklahoma, Norman, OK; [occ.] Office Representative State Farm, Insurance, Oklahoma City, OK; [memb.] Alpha Gamma Delta, American Civil Liberties Union; [hon.] Valedictorian, performing John Rutter's Requiem at Carnegie Hall New York, NY, Kaleidoscope dancers company, performing at the Gazette Music awards, Oklahoma City, OK; [oth. writ.] Double Think Magazine; [pers.] In memory of Neill Frank Gilstrap, 2/24/73 - 7/1/96. His strength encouraged me to put my thoughts on paper.; [a.] Norman, OK

WESLEY, PATRICIA JABBEH
[b.] August 7, 1955, Liberia, West Africa; [p.] Moses Jabbeh and Mary Williams; [m.] Mlen-Too, December 19, 1980; [ch.] Besie Nyesuah, Mlen-Too II, Gee and Ade-Juah; [ed.] Msc. English Ed. Indiana University (1985), BA (Cum Laude) English University of Liberia (1980); [occ.] Instructor of English and Lit.; [memb.] Poetry Society of America, MI College Eng. Ass., Kalamazoo Council of Arts; [hon.] World Bank Fellowship for Graduates Studies (1983-1985), African Graduates Awards 1982; [oth. writ.] Articles - "Africans In America" (Essay published in Summer Issue of Bridges, Who Do You See (Bridges), Forthcoming - Poetry collection, Our Home Coming, 90 poems by Pat Wesley.; [pers.] I have been greatly influenced by my father, Moses C. Jabbeh, my 10th grade english teacher, S. Henry Cordor and the writings of Africans like Leopold Sedan Senghor.; [a.] Kalamazoo, MI

WESSEL, PATRICIA A.
[pen.] Patricia Fanning Avery Bawcum Wessel; [b.] May 11, 1942, Weehawken, NJ; [p.] James J. and Elizabeth C. Fanning Sr.; [m.] James R. Wessel, March 1989; [ch.] Deborah K. Avery O'Mara (Daughter), Jayson Keith Bawcum (Son); [ed.] St. Mary's High School Albuquerque, Attended The University of New Mexico, Albuquerque, NM; [occ.] Retired Administrative Secretary, Current Occupation Housewife; [memb.] The International Society of Authors and Artists, National Authors Registry, International Society of Poets, Songwriters Club of American; [hon.] 4th place Captured Moments thru Creative Arts and Sciences, Ent., Honorable Mention from several books Certificate of Merit, Editors Choice Awards National Library of Poetry. etc.; [oth. writ.] Numerous poems in various anthologies by Creative Arts and Sciences, Ent. Sparrowgrass Poetry Forum, Inc. World Art Publishing The Amherst Society Iliad Press Poets Guild, Best new poems of 1995 and of 1995 and Who's Who is New Poets of 1996, etc.; [pers.] When I write poetry song lyrics I try very hard to write about a subject matter that I feel will be of interest to the majority of readers of those who hear my songs. The majority of my writing tells a true story and is either about an experience I have had or an experience someone else had had. I write about my feelings, about issues within our society and my personal beliefs or someone else's beliefs. I write about life, both its happy and sad times in an effort to make the reader be able to identify with what I am saying. Any agreement with what I say is not necessary to me. To the exchange of feeling, beliefs and experiences, that is enjoyable and educational.

WEST, ALICE K.
[pen.] A. K. West; [b.] April 20, 1950, Johnson City, TN; [p.] Frances M. Fowler and George Robert Fowler Jr.; [m.] Billy S. West Jr., October 11, 1969, Divorced September 2, 1977; [ch.] Laura and Michael West; [ed.] Graduate of Happy Valley High in Elizabethton, TN took course at Voc Tech in Bradenton, FL; [occ.] Receptionist; [memb.] T.O.P.S. Club - Take off lbs. sensibly; [hon.] Employee of the month; [oth. writ.] None published, I write poetry when I am moved by a subject; [pers.] I express my feelings and opinions of my life's experiences through my poetry. Poetry can heal the heart when written with sincerity.; [a.] Palmetto, FL

WESTMORELAND, TAMEKA LYNETTE
[b.] May 29, 1979, Harbor City, CA; [p.] Conroy and Suzette Westmoreland; [ed.] George Washington Prep High School (Los, Angeles CA) 12th grade student; [memb.] Who's Who, Advance Drama, Church of Christ; [hon.] Honor Student, Scholastic Awards, Outstanding Achievement. Acting Roles in "Purle Victorious" Played the role (Missy) and fame role (Miss Sherman)" and Teacher Asst-Choir Director U.C.O.L. sings in new generations; [oth. writ.] "The Torch", "One Sunny Day", Dreams; [pers.] I hope my writings will touch the heart's of many, and the minds of the young to strive for their goals (long) or (short), and to have a vision.; [a.] Los Angeles, CA

WESTON, RANDAL M.
[b.] May 18, 1963, Richmond, IN; [p.] Marion and Barbara Weston; [ed.] Rushville Consolidated High School; [occ.] Factory Worker; [memb.] American Legion, V.F.W., Amvets; [hon.] Honorably discharged from United States Marine Corps (Sergeant); [oth. writ.] Letters published in local newspaper. 'Big Foot' published in frost at midnight.; [pers.] Live confidently and have a passion for life.; [a.] Connersville, IN

WHEELER, ANGELA P.
[b.] August 2, 1971, New Orleans, LA; [m.] Myles E. Wheeler, July 30, 1988; [ch.] Dylan Edward (4), Elizabeth Kay (6); [occ.] Franchisee, Steak-out Charbroiled Delivery; [memb.] Johnson City Chamber of Commerce, Kingsport Chamber of Commerce; [pers.] Thanks to my step father this it he only poem I have submitted to anyone. I have boxes full! There really is hope up there!; [a.] Gray, TN

WHITE, CHEVELLE
[b.] March 19, 1973, Baltimore, MD; [p.] Maggie White, Phillip I. White, Jr.; [ed.] Frederick Douglass High School Graduate, Baltimore City Community College; [occ.] College Student, Artist, Teachers Assistant; [memb.] Boy Scouts of America, National Rifle Association, Sharon Baptist Church Security Force, Fellowship of Lights, U.S. Army, Americorps National Service; [a.] Baltimore, MD

WHITE, ELDON
[b.] September 2, 1926, Wallins Creek, KY; [p.] Lewis White, Fannie White; [m.] Betty Jean White, May 6, 1950; [ch.] Roger, Dale, Patricia, Georgina; [ed.] B.S. degree, Eastern Kentucky State College; [occ.] Retired: General Supervisor, General Motors Corp.; [memb.] Bethany Baptist Church; [pers.] I was inspired to write "Sounds of Freedom" because of my love of God, country and those who protect our freedom.; [a.] Hamilton, OH

WHITE, JACINTA V.
[b.] June 23, 1972, North Carolina; [p.] Brenda Williams White, The Late Rev. Dr. William M. White Sr.; [ed.] BA Speech Communications/Public Relations at the University of North Carolina of Greensboro; [occ.] Freelance writer; [memb.] Public relations Society of America (PRASA), Blacks in Advertising Radio and Television (BART); [hon.] Public Speaking Awards; [oth. writ.] Currently compiling and editing the inspirational writings of the late Rev. Dr. William M. White, Sr. to be published 1997 titled "And He Walked With God."; [pers.] I hope that my writings will inspire, motivate and speak to others for others, that the falling I have when I stoke the paper with my pen will be felt by others.; [a.] Detroit, MI

WHITE, SANDRA S.
[b.] December 19, 1938, Gastonia, NC; [p.] Grafton and Edith Spargo; [m.] Kenneth B. White, July 25, 1980; [ch.] Johna, William G., Fred Murphy, Amy Barker; [ed.] Frank L. Ashley High, Brevard College, Stone Modeling School; [memb.] Treasurer New Voice Club Charlotte, NC Memberial; [oth. writ.] God's Plan - Through The Hourglass; [pers.] Since losing my voice to cancer, I enjoy writing poems about people and events in the news. My experiences with others have directed the content of my poems. The thoughts that they maybe of benefit to others, gives me great satisfaction and joy.; [a.] Gastonia, NC

WHITEHOUSE, GEORGE C.
[pen.] Carl Whitehouse; [b.] June 3, 1953, Marion County, KY; [p.] Virgil and Jeanette Whitehouse; [m.] Divorced; [ch.] Chafin and Marion May Whitehouse; [occ.] Electric Sign Fabracater and Artist; [oth. writ.] Winnen of Greensburg KY. Record and Herald, Most romantic poem, 1995.; [pers.] I see every day as a new challange.; [a.] Campbellsville, KY

WILDER, ROY W.
[b.] July 20, 1960, Covington, KY; [p.] Pauline Wilder; [ed.] BS - Accounting - Georgetown College, Georgetown, KY; [memb.] Lambda Chi Alpha Alumnus, Member of International Chemical Workers Union; [pers.] I try never to let fear stand in the way of my dreams. Dream it, believe it, achieve it! You are a success when you use your assets. You are happy when you accept your faults; [a.] Florence, KY

WILKINSON, TIFFENY
[b.] February 10, 1981, Niagara Falls, NY; [p.] Sue and Claudio Venditti; [ed.] LaSalle Senior High School; [occ.] Student; [pers.] I have been greatly influenced by a former English teacher by the name of Mr. Alessi.; [a.] Niagara Falls, NY

WILL, LINDA L.
[b.] January 3, 1949, Erie, PA; [p.] Wilmajean Osborne, Richard Will; [ed.] Watsburg High School graduate, Silver Mine School of Horsemanship New Canaan, CT; [occ.] Equestrian, trainer, horse breeder; [memb.] American Horse Show Association; [oth. writ.] Currently writing my Equestrian experiences through poetry, titled Reading, Riding and Rhythm; [pers.] I'm fascinated with the powers of the universe we call nature my life and writing is an attempt to share my feelings with others.; [a.] Milroy, PA

WILLIAMS, ALLENE
[b.] February 2, 1921, Sale Creek, TN; [p.] Carl and Sarah Francisco; [m.] Joseph Fred Williams, May 4, 1946; [ch.] Linda, Peggy, Karen, Anthony; [ed.] Sale Creek High School; [occ.] Retired from Kayser Roth, Quality Control OP; [memb.] New Providence Urited Methodist Church; [hon.] Best all-around student 1st and 2nd high school years. D.A.R. Representative 3rd year. Valedictorian of Senior Class.; [oth. writ.] An Auto-biographical book "Sense and Nonsense" for grandchildren, containing many events of my life, favorite recipes, and many other original poems of mine.; [pers.] I love life, I love people, most of all I love my Lord Jesus for all the blessing of life. To God be all glory for anything I might accomplish.; [a.] Sale Creek, TN

WILLIAMS, ANTHONY LANAR
[pen.] Spud; [b.] December 18, 1986, Detroit, MI; [p.] Mr. and Mrs. Qur'an and Lashaun Mustafaa; [ed.] Fourth Grader at Daniel J. Healy International Academy in Detroit Michigan; [memb.] Member of Daniel J. Healy Student Council; [hon.] Received a Certificate of Achievement for the Young Writers Program, and also received Certificate of Achievement from Reading Rainbow 2nd Annual Young Writers and Illustrations Awards Competition; [oth. writ.] Stock - Dancing - My Hero - The African American I most admire (my mom) - Thanksgiving - My Plan - Easter - Brotherhood, Sisterhood is the Key; [pers.] I strive to be the best that I can be at anything that I do or try. My goal is to one day write a book of short stories for children.; [a.] Detroit, MI

WILLIAMS, CATHEDRAL LORETTA
[b.] July 29, 1966, Albany, GA; [p.] Mr. Frank Williams, Mrs. Loretta and Nathaniel Nelson; [pers.] Poetry is emotions put into worlds... there is a poet in each of us.

WILLIAMS, COURT
[b.] March 16, 1963, Bellingham, WA; [ed.] North Salem High, Salem, OR Illinois Central College, Peora, IL; [occ.] Processing Analyst, Hewitt Associates; [hon.] Phi Beta Kappa, Deans List; [pers.] I try to convey a feeling or emotion with my poems. Frost and Poe are my favourite writers.; [a.] Lake Bluff, IL

WILLIAMS, DEBBIE ANN
[pen.] Annie; [b.] March 25, 1943, Evans County; [p.] Authur and Ruby Bacon; [m.] Willie Williams, June 22, 1961; [ch.] Connie, Tammie, Victor, Tracy, Terrance, Laura Maurice; [ed.] Evans County High, Savannah Vo-tech Childcare Diploma, Certified Nursing Assistant, Teacher of Holy Pray Temple; [occ.] Certified Nursing Assistant Chatham Nursing Home, Missionary; [memb.] Holy Pray Temple, Red Cross Association, Affliation of Chatham Nursing Home; [hon.] Graduate Honors, High School Dean List - Voc-tech (Savannah) First Prizes - Poetry and First prizes Essays Chatham Nursing Home local papers; [oth. writ.] Several poems published in local newspapers, several poems for Chatham Nursing Home, Readings for church, poem for Olympic. Read-

ing for Day Cares.; [pers.] I strive to get over to mankind that life has values in my writing and there's time for everything and changes for everyone. I have been influenced by teaching of bible (Psalmes) and changes of love in life by beautiful expression of David.; [a.] Savannah, GA

WILLIAMS, DONALD M.
[b.] June 27, 1959, Bainbridge, GA; [p.] Mary Johnson; [ch.] Myeasha L. Williams; [ed.] Robinson High School; [occ.] U.S. Navy; [oth. writ.] First poem to be published; [pers.] My writing reflect some of my life's experience and the pursuit of happiness that life brings.; [a.] Tampa, FL

WILLIAMS, MARY NELL
[pen.] Mary Williams; [b.] December 19, 1959, Caldwell County; [p.] David and Mattie Hollar; [m.] Word W. Williams, April 10, 1960; [ch.] Stuart Wesley and Cara Ann; [ed.] Hudson High 1958; [occ.] Housewife; [memb.] Setzer's Creek Baptist Church; [oth. writ.] Several songs and poems - none published, several puppet skits - not published; [pers.] I try to reflect God's love and goodness to all people. I have been influenced by what God has done for me.; [a.] Lenoir, NC

WILLIAMS, MAXWELL B.
[b.] April 12, 1915, Artie, WV; [p.] Alfred E. and Hattie P. Williams; [ed.] 2 yrs High School; [occ.] Retired; [pers.] Born and reared in artie, West Virginia, spent 6 years in the marines June 27, 1941- June 27, 1947 overseas duty, Okinawa a few months. I since a little and strum the guitar.; [a.] Hastings, MI

WILLIAMS JR., ALBERT T.
[b.] January 7, 1981, Ocean Springs, MS; [p.] Martha L. Williams and Albert T. Williams; [ed.] Leaksville Elementary, Leaksville Jr. High, Leaksville, MS; [occ.] Student; [a.] State Line, MS

WILLIAMSON, YVONNE C.
[b.] July 26, 1969, Binghamton, NY; [p.] Minnie and Troy Williamson; [m.] Fiancee, Dwayne Harris; [ch.] Nikita Chabris Williamson; [ed.] Trenton Central High School, Institute of Business Careers, Mercer County Community College; [occ.] Sales Associate at Dean Witter Reynolds, Inc.; [hon.] Academic All-American, Dean's List, Honorable Mention for my poem's 'Success', Golden poet Award 1989, 1990, 1991; [oth. writ.] 'Success', 'A Letter To Dr. Martin Luther King', 'The Love Of A Friend', 'Insane', 'Dawud (Beloved)'; [pers.] Many things have influenced me in my life. However, finding unconditional love has been the greatest influence, and I thank both my daughter, Nikita and my fiancee, Dwayne for their influence. A.P.D.T.A; [a.] Trenton, NJ

WILLMON, AARON
[b.] February 3, 1980, Ft. Payne, AL; [p.] Anthony and Donna Willmon; [ed.] Currently Junior at Plainview High School; [occ.] Bank Teller (summer job); [memb.] United States Achievement Academy, Beta, Club, Mu Alpha Theta; [hon.] United States Achiever at Academy Award, selected to attend leadership conferences at Birmingham Southern, University of South Alabama, and Troy State University; [oth. writ.] Will have a poem published in Iliad Press's Winter Anthology Meditations.; [pers.] Inspired deeply by music. The two writers I admire the most are William Shakespeare and Edgar Allen Poe.; [a.] Rainsville, AL

WILLOUGHBY, ANGELA
[pen.] Angela Kiel Willoughby; [b.] January 8, 1936,

Brussels, IL; [p.] William Charles Kiel, Dorothy Schmidt Kiel; [m.] Joseph Victor Willoughby, March 9, 1957; [ch.] Mary Kay Willoughby, Nancy Anne Tinsley, Andrea Lynne Donnally, Jeanne Marie Cory; [ed.] Graduate of Nursing Diploma Program Completed Studies - Real Estate Broker; [occ.] Labor and Delivery Nurse; [memb.] I have membership in environmental, animal, mammal and other humane causes.; [oth. writ.] My personal collection of writings include articles, letters, poems and tributes to family and friends.; [pers.] Born of soul wealth parents, I have awakened to the intrinsic, worth of every living soul, I am pro-active with love for human and animal kingdom; [a.] Burlingame, CA

WILSON, ANNA LOIS
[pen.] Lois Wilson; [b.] May 30, 1930, AL; [ed.] Life's experience, WCG College, Mich., Michigan State University.; [occ.] Disable House Keeper, Writer; [memb.] St. Francis, Mich., Elks #1283 Mich., Fezz Club #1283 Mich., Library of poetry MD.; [hon.] President R. Reagan, Whitehouse DC., Social Service Mich., Scholarship for family living - and education Mich., Extension Service Mich., Library of Poetry MD., Named sealed in a space capsule - Mich., WPAG Radio Mich. (Gill Theater Mich.); [oth. writ.] None Fiction, Nursery, Blues. Spirituals, Country - Western, Jazz; [pers.] Is reality for and so all mankind. That life is not all a game. It is a real "world" out here in my writings. I hope to help people all over the world to seek a peace of mind. Through reality.; [a.] Vallejo, CA

WILSON, DAVID L.
[pen.] D. L. Wilson; [b.] May 2, 1961, Salem, MA; [m.] Barbara A. Wilson, March 15, 1992; [ch.] Elizabeth and Carl Wilson; [ed.] B.S. in Business majoring in Accounting; [occ.] Accountant; [memb.] Phi Theta Kappa National Honor Society; [hon.] Graduated Magna Cum Laude, Phi Theta Kappa; [oth. writ.] I have over one hundred poems that I have written.; [pers.] My poetry has a wide range of subject, from life to death, from Christianity to atheism, all based on what I was going through in my life at the time it was written. My goal is to someday have all of my poetry published in one book.; [a.] Tempe, AZ

WILSON, EARIL
[b.] September 29, 1955, Brawdy, Wales; [p.] Anise and Jack Lysaght; [m.] George Allen, December 20, 1996; [ch.] Corwyn; [ed.] Bachelor Fine Arts, Ohio State University, Associate Fine Arts Thompkins Cortland Com. College; [occ.] Shamanic Therapist and Counselor; [oth. writ.] "Persephone's Exile" (Limited) edition book of Photographs Books in Progress "Swamp Mama's Karma Free Frozen Dinners."; [pers.] Each of us are on our own individual path of evolution, as well as that path we share as a race. Therefore any way in which I can help to further the efforts of every person on either path is my most joyous task; [a.] Meriden, CT

WILSON, ELSIE
[b.] November 30, 1930, Alabama; [p.] George Green, Leola Green; [m.] Oscar Wilson Jr.; [ch.] Robbie Wilson Welfare; [ed.] Knox Academy, Selma Alabama; [occ.] Nurse's Aide Nassau County, N.Y.; [memb.] Deaconess at Calvary Baptist Church, State Leader of NY Prayerathon Ministry; [pers.] I've been in teaching and ministry most of my life, so my deepest desire, is to shed some light on someone's dark path way.; [a.] Queens Village, NY

WILSON, HARMONY
[b.] August 21, 1981, Hanover, NH; [p.] Ernest Wilson

and Elizabeth Wilson; [ed.] Woodstock Elementary School, Woodstock Union Middle School, Entering High School; [occ.] Stable Hand at a Horse farm; [memb.] Fan Clubs, Stone Blossoms 4-H Club BMG Music Club; [oth. writ.] Poems, Stories, Autobiography; [pers.] "Poetry is an escape, to free my thoughts and let my emotions run wild".; [a.] Woodstock, VT

WILSON, REV. LINDA G.
[pen.] Rev. Linda G. Wilson; [b.] April 29, 1943, Jax., FL; [p.] Mr. and Mrs. James C. Mott; [m.] Mr. Glenn C. Wilson, October 20, 1980; [ch.] Lisa Joy Beasley, Tricia Rose Beasley, Bobby Lee; [ed.] 11th grade My Pastor is Hamilton; [occ.] Homemaker involved in Church Worm-First Christian Church Prayer Chain; [memb.] K-Frog Club - Treasurer long time ago, Church - Member I belong to C.W.F. at Church Class and Mary Magdalaine; [hon.] I won something in Science class and Art class - years ago - but ribbon's are gone.; [oth. writ.] "Women's Wright's and the Burning of the American Flag - "Jesus Is My Handy" I am trying to get titles to sermon's now.; [pers.] I want to say I give all the credit to my Heavenly Father who inspires me most of the time - through the Holy Ghost. If I be lifted up I will drow all man high to me.; [a.] Ontario, CA

WILSON, RICHARD S.
[pen.] Riki Stevens; [b.] July 3, 1956, Phila, PA; [p.] Rich and Terri Wilson; [m.] Debbie Wilson, February 12, 1988; [ch.] "Stefanee Dean"; [ed.] James Caldwell High School; [occ.] Piano Technician; [oth. writ.] Lyricist for local bands; [pers.] Treasures are found, but then they are forgotten.; [a.] Penn Lake, PA

WILSON, ROGER
[pen.] Duck; [b.] December 9, 1966, Fort Worth, TX; [p.] Elzie Wilson, Elizabeth Wilson; [m.] Ann Wilson; [ed.] Granbury High, US Army; [occ.] Dragline Tech.; [memb.] VFW; [hon.] 3 army achievement medals, 6 certificate of achievement awards, 3 good conduct awards, 3 overseas awards, 1 combat award; [oth. writ.] Fist one to be submitted for publication; [pers.] I see poetry as the best way to slow my emotions, with family, friends, and loves.; [a.] Granbury, TX

WILSON, TIFFANY
[b.] June 11, 1981, Orlando, FL; [p.] David and Joy Wilson; [ed.] River Valley High School; [hon.] Freshman Academic Letter, Merit Roll; [oth. writ.] A couple of poems published in a school paperback book; [pers.] I enjoy reading and writing poetry. When I write, I can express my feelings. When reading poetry, I can see a clear picture of what the writer is writing about.; [a.] Marion, OH

WINEGAR, ANTHONY C.
[b.] October 22, 1961, Jefferson City, MO; [p.] Dr. Alvon Winegar; [ed.] 1981 Graduate Helias High School, Jefferson City Missouri, 1995 took Creative Writing Lincoln University Jefferson City; [memb.] International Society of Poets 1996 Distinguished Member; [hon.] Editor's Choice Award for Dayton Winegar is Dead Nominated Poet of the year 1996; [oth. writ.] Dayton Winegar is Dead Pub. Spirit of the Age Upcoming Being Born Pub. Best Poems of the '90's Both published 1996.; [pers.] I strive for meaning in my poems; [a.] Jefferson City, MO

WINES, BRIDGETT
[b.] February 4, 1980, Monroe, LA; [p.] Joan Turner Green, Pha Green; [ed.] The High School for the Performing and Visual Arts in Houston, TX; [occ.] Student; [memb.] RPVA, The Chosen Generation, Windsor Vil-

lage UMC, school RPVA - Broadcasting and Sound Technical Group; [hon.] Honor Student, HSPVA, 4.0 GPA, Duke Talent Search Program, 1992, Louisiana Creative Scholars Program, 1992, Outstanding Freshman, 1995, BET Network Personal Best, February 13, 1993; [oth. writ.] Personal collection of poems and essays; [pers.] If you put your heart into the things you do, and you are sincere about it, then you've done your best.; [a.] Houston, TX

WINSTEAD, DAVID A.
[b.] December 30, 1949, Sanford, NC; [p.] Graham and Marguerite Winstead; [m.] Sharon L. Winstead, October 7, 1995; [ch.] Thomas, Richard, Jennifer, Robert and David II; [ed.] Altoona Area High, Altoona, PA; [memb.] Southwest Writer's Guild; [pers.] I believe a country can only succeed when backed by it's leaders with God behind them. My writing reflects what I believe it should be.; [a.] Albuquerque, NM

WINTERS, RUTH A. F.
[b.] August 9, 1933, Canton, OH; [p.] Rev. Dennis W. and Etta A. (Nee Boehm) Foreman; [m.] Dale O. Winters, July 12, 1951; [ch.] Bruce, Colleen, Mike and Heather; [ed.] Masters - Religious Educ. from United Theological Seminary, Dayton- Ohio - 1994, (no college), 12 years elem. and high school; [occ.] Minister of Congregational Cave at Middleton U.M.C. Middletown, KY, (Suburb of Louisville); [memb.] Middletown Unit. Methodist Church; [hon.] From UTS, Co-Recipient of Rummel Award for excellence Rel. Educ. in a rural setting, '1993'; [oth. writ.] (Photos and) articles as a stringer in following newspapers, Voice Jeffersonian - Lul. Ky's Oldham Era - La Grange, KY, Louisville Defender - Louisville, KY, about 25-30 years ago, article in church school magazine (a Unit math, publication), article in Sun. supplement (Mothers Day issue) of Lvl. Courier Journal and Times; [pers.] Although I've been writing a "little" for a long time, my poetry only began emerging recently. This poem helped me express my grief over the MVA death of our Son Mike Two days after christmas, '93, at age 29.; [a.] Crestwood, KY

WISE, DENA
[b.] September 28, 1982, Mission Viejo, CA; [p.] Scott Wise, Pam Wise; [ed.] Shorecliffs Middle School, Twin Peaks Middle School; [hon.] Two presidential academic achievement awards, National Science Merit award, honor student; [oth. writ.] Many poems, songs, and stories, none published yet; [pers.] I feel "It's better to regret something you did than something you didn't do".; [a.] San Clemente, CA

WISE, MYRA
[pen.] Em Eljay; [b.] November 16, 1960, Geneva, AL; [p.] James Wise, Esther Wise; [ed.] Florala High School, Lurleen B. Wallace State Junior Troy State University; [hon.] Phi Theta Kappa, Sigma Tau Delta, Dean's List; [oth. writ.] Several articles and poems published in local paper during high school. As a ghost writer, I contributed an article and photo of my niece, Lindsay, which appeared in "Happiness Magazine", vol. 28, no. 9 in 1945; [pers.] My writing reflects and explores the mysteries which are hidden in everyday existence. Children are blessed with a sense of wonder and discovery. I wrote this poem for my niece because she taught me to celebrate the wonders of life.; [a.] Florala, AL

WITZEL, RUBY FOSTER
[b.] March 16, 1921, Attalla, AL; [p.] Richard and Florence Foster; [m.] Paul B. Witzel, September 29, 1946; [occ.] Homemaker; [memb.] Church of Christ; [oth.

writ.] Other unpublished poems.; [pers.] I was a wave in WWII and stationed at the armed guard school Camp Shelton, VA and worked in the post office there.; [a.] Rossville, GA

WOJTOWICZ, JOHN
[pen.] "Wojo"; [b.] November 24, 1959, Chicago, IL; [p.] Constance Czajka, Jerry Wojtowicz; [m.] Laura Lee Wojtowicz, January 29, 1983; [ch.] Joshua Adam Wojtowicz, Jacob Aaron Wojtowicz; [occ.] USAF since 1982; [pers.] Poem written in 1973, it's alright to plan but don't plan the outcome.; [a.] Fort Walton Beach, FL

WOLT, JOHANNA KLUDT
[b.] November 28, 1905, Herreid, SD; [p.] Caroline Huether, Emanuel John Kludt; [m.] Emanuel R. Wolt, February 18, 1928; [ch.] 3 sons Myron, Charles, Dean; [ed.] Teachers Life Certificate 33 yrs. of Teaching in N.D. A Jr. High Elementary Teacher; [occ.] Retired; [memb.] N.D. Teacher's Association, Auxiliary Member of the Gidens. A member of the Evangelical Church of North America; [hon.] Recognition as an Amateur Poetess.; [oth. writ.] Poems - Raindrops, October Swirls, Crystal Springs Slumbered, The Fisherman, Tribute to My Husband Jackie Frost; [pers.] Learn all you can while your young it well always stay with you. Education is so important.; [a.] Tappen, ND

WOOD, LOIS
[b.] June 22, 1926, Shelbina, MO; [p.] Chester and Ruby Stewart; [m.] Leonard Wood, May 7, 1950; [ch.] Charles L. Wood; [ed.] High school and some college; [occ.] Homemaker; [memb.] Prairie View Baptist Church and Women's Missionary Union; [oth. writ.] I have written several poems that have not been published.; [pers.] My God and personal Saviour has inspired me to write the poetry I have written and without Him, I could not do it. He has given me the talent to do it I also have some musical ability. I give God all the credit.; [a.] Emden, MO

WOOD, SHANNON
[b.] June 12, 1967, Sierra Madre, CA; [ed.] Monrovia High, Citrus College; [pers.] I am influenced by Kahlil Gibran, Edgar Allen Poe, Hans Christian Anderson, Emily Dickinson, Rumi. I admire works of Geothe, Hyppolite Flandrin, Mozart's life/death, Italian vogue Michaelangelo and cultural diversions of the Indo-European man. Inspired by bleeding stains of life knowledge,I love so my Quicksilver and subtle rebellion amidst perfect Merlot. I desire to emphasis personal awareness gained as emotional recognition spills into release. I strive to quench, what I believe to be, the thirsting spirit in man.; [a.] Alta Loma, CA

WOODALL, NICOLE
[b.] June 7, 1983, Cincinnati, OH; [p.] Kim and Clint Woodall; [ed.] St. Ann's Elementary and St. Bartholomews Consolidated Elementary; [occ.] Student; [memb.] Girl Scout, Karate; [hon.] First Honors at School.; [oth. writ.] Short stories and poems yet none have been published.; [pers.] Life's unexpected so expect it. (Nicole has always written for enjoyment. We're very proud of her).; [a.] Cincinnati, OH

WOODBURN, KAREN LESLIE
[pen.] Karen Woodburn; [b.] October 13, 1978, Dearborn, MI; [p.] Bruce and Linda Woodburn; [ed.] Plymouth Salem High School, Central Michigan University; [occ.] Daycare teacher, Discovery Learning Center; [hon.] State of Michigan Competitive Scholarship award, nominated to be in the Who's Who of America Book for High School Students.; [oth. writ.] Other original poems, some short stories.; [a.] Canton, MI

WOODRING, PATRICIA
[pen.] Pat Hale; [b.] April 16, 1931, Trenton, NJ; [p.] Sara and Herman Hale; [ch.] Tracy Ann Schou; [ed.] Muhlenberg High School, American Academy of Dramatic Arts, Kutztown University - B.S. Ed. - A.O.S., Marywood College - M.S. Ed.; [occ.] Counselor/Vocational Specialist, Reading Area, Community College; [memb.] Alpha Gamma Delta, Mensa, Actors Equity Association; [hon.] Edna Geiss Award - (Outstanding English Student), Kutztown University, Magna Cum Laude - Kutztown University, Best Actress - Green Hills Theater, Reading, PA; [oth. writ.] Family Portraits, Sara's Shoes, Behind and Beyond the Wall of Words, What about John?, Patsy's Patchwork Quilt.; [pers.] I strive to reflect the human condition and the "Passages" in life in order to inspire strength and courage in others. I have been greatly influenced by 17th and 18th century English poets.; [a.] Reading, PA

WOODS, MICHELLE SHAVONNE
[pen.] Dotty Woods; [b.] August 8, 1981, Saginaw, TX; [p.] James Woods, Janette Woods; [ed.] Sims Elementary, Pearce Junior High, L.B.J. High School; [occ.] Student; [hon.] Certificate of Merit, passing all my classes (8th grade in 1994 and 1995), Award for passing TAAS practice and writing tests, Diploma signifying graduation for a Saturday of classes at the University of Texas, Certificate of Achievement for girl scouts; [pers.] I write poetry from my mind and heart, I write and read poetry cause it's beautiful.; [a.] Austin, TX

WOODWARD, NICOLLE
[b.] Springfield, VT; [p.] Frank and Sylvia Fleming; [m.] Dennis Woodward; [ch.] Cynthia, David and Denise; [pers.] Writing is an intensely personal endeavor. To share one's thoughts with others on the written page is to open the doors of privacy.; [a.] Bennington, VT

WOOLDRIDGE, SHAWN RAG
[b.] June 28, 1974, Garland, TX; [p.] Jim and Betlie Wooldridge; [ed.] 11th Grade; [oth. writ.] Shawn Rag Wooldridge, Born 6/28/1974, Deceased 8/7/94 age 20, as a present I hope this poem will touch other young reasons.; [pers.] Shawn was a young man with many problems related to fees pressures. he quit school 10th grade, to live life his way be experiences problems with the law, drugs, and alcohol. He was killed is a car week while driving too fast on 8/7/94. The wreck also took and friends life.

WORTHY, LUCILLE
[pen.] Lucille Light and Expressed Light; [b.] March 10, 1966, Chester, SC; [p.] Bemice Worthy and Earl Sanders; [ed.] Chester High School, University of South Carolina - Columbia; [occ.] Teacher, Chester Pack Elementary Chester SC; [pers.] I firmly believe that God is the giver of all good gifts and that He intends that I write and glorify Him. He is my greatest inspiration.; [a.] Chester, SC

WRIGHT, FAYE
[pen.] Precious; [b.] January 27, 1951, Queens, NY; [p.] Maria Wright, William Wright; [ch.] Andre Milton; [ed.] William H. Maxwell Vocational High School; [occ.] Certify Pharmacy Technician, V.A. Medical Center Brooklyn NY; [memb.] First Central Baptist Church, Basic Cardiac Life Support; [oth. writ.] This is my first try at writing. I wrote year ago. I always write my thoughts down on paper. I glad, I continued.; [pers.] My whole existence, I was told, to be still and know God. And he has not fail me once.; [a.] Staten Island, NY

WRIGHT, KRISTINA
[pen.] Tina Wright; [b.] January 2, 1981, Manteca, CA; [p.] Ken Wright, Chris Wright; [ed.] Student, Calaveras High School, San Andreas, CA; [memb.] School Site Council, California Scholarship Federation, Future Business Leaders of America, and American Field Society; [pers.] Expand your thoughts, and open your mind. Life has so many experiences to offer. There can be hope in our future.; [a.] West Point, CA

WRIGHT, LORI LYNN
[b.] January 6, 1965, Wisconsin; [p.] Donna Tobys, Wayne Le'Bonbard; [m.] Bill Wright, December 24, 1984; [ch.] Brandon 11, Dustin 8, Brittney 6; [ed.] Mountlake Terrace High School - one year of Community College, (Everett) graduating G.P.A. 4.0, Deca Student (Distributive Educ. Clubs of America) honor student, president and cheer squad; [occ.] Licensed Child Care Provider; [memb.] I am a member of the American Child Care Association, and I sit on the board, as treasurer of the P.T.A. at Olivia Park Elementary; [oth. writ.] I am a free-lance writer. I enjoy writing poems and short stories. I currently have no other published material but hopefully await the day that I will see more of my work to print.; [pers.] Through my writing I hope to motivate and inspire people. My goal is to find the hidden inner self that we all have, touch it ever so slightly to awaken and renew our love for life and our fellow man.; [a.] Everett, WA

WRIGHT, MELANIE ANN
[b.] January 30, 1983, Charleston, WV; [p.] Linda and Michael Wright; [ed.] Cross Lanes Elementary, Andrew Jackson Middle School; [memb.] Girl Scouts - 9 years, Majic'n Motion Dancers - 4 years, KCPL Teen Volunteer; [hon.] Kanawha County Social Studies - honorable mention (2 years) Highest G.P.A. in english at AJMS (1996); [pers.] My greatest loves are dancing, hiking, and animals.; [a.] Cross Lanes, WV

WRIGHT, NAN
[b.] May 7, 1934, Laing, WV; [p.] Samuel and Edna Wright; [ed.] Garnet High School, B.S. W. Va. State College M.A. The University of Chicago; [occ.] Retired Junior High School English Teacher; [memb.] Alpha Kappa Mu, Pi Lamdba Theta (Honor Societies) Sorority, N.A.A.C.P AAUW FIANS General Semantics; [hon.] Our Lady of Assumption R.C. Church Listed in Who's Who in American Women Who's Who in American Education; [pers.] I think that each person should all that help other do the same.; [a.] Amityville, NY

WRIGHT, REGINA
[b.] April 13, Los Angeles; [p.] Willie and Laura Wright; [m.] Ron Cole, May 15, 1993; [ch.] Poodle - Aja, Cats - Majik and Gizmo; [ed.] CSULA; [occ.] Actress, Buyer; [memb.] NAFE, NAACP, HSUS; [pers.] To write poetry, I bare my soul for all to see. I hope the readers feel the honesty, other influential poets Maya Angelou and Emily Dickinson; [a.] Los Angles, CA

WUGAN, ANN M.
[pen.] Ann Wugan; [b.] March 9, 1917, Evanston, IL; [p.] Carl Wugan, Maria Benedicta Wugan; [ed.] Jennings Seminary, Aurora, Ill. (High School) Univ. of Cincinnati, B Sin Ed. Univ. of Hawaii, U.C.L.A., California State University, Northridge - M.A., Reading Specialist Certificate; [occ.] Retired Primary Teacher, Reading Specialist; [memb.] California Retired Teachers Assoc., Women in Military Service for America (WIMSA) Volunteer Reading Instructor; [hon.] WAC 1st Lt. World War II American Campaign Medal, Asiatic Pacific Campaining Medal with two bronze stars; [oth. writ.] Won Univ. of Cincinnati Poetry Contest 2 years. Published book of poems (bittersweet); [a.] Hemet, CA

WUHRAIZER, ANDREW
[pen.] Josh Levi; [b.] May 8, 1961, Accra, Ghana; [p.] Joshua Wuhraizer; [ed.] University of Ghana, Puskin Institute, Mosclow Houghton College NY; [occ.] English/French teacher; [memb.] PAWA - Pan African Writers Ass. Christian Research; [hon.] Won a Gramota whilst a student in Russia for a poem entitled "Bambooshoots"; [oth. writ.] Published articles, writes short stories, working on a book of poems. Published: English French - A conversational approach.; [pers.] "Those who know cannot say, and those who say cannot know" Lao Tzu ancient Chinese philosopher.; [a.] Buffalo, NY

WYNN, WILLIAM H.
[b.] July 23, 1941, Selmer, TN; [p.] Dorothy Wynn; [m.] Jackie Patterson Wynn, May 27, 1994; [ed.] High School Graduate McClymonds High School, Calif; [occ.] Auto Assembler; [memb.] Black Men in Unions (University of Mich. Labor Studies Center); [oth. writ.] "The world is A Ghetto" twins I twins II, "Dumb is a Dumb does", "you can't win", "the Devil may care", "Images"; [pers.] I seek to educate or ghetto the knowledge of ghetto people through poetry, that they can relate, through their environmental experience.; [a.] Grandview, MO

WYSOCKI, JENNIE
[b.] March 5, 1976, Newark, NJ; [p.] Chester and Wanda Wysocki; [ed.] North Plainfield High School, Seton Hall University; [occ.] Asst. Manager Carlton Cards Bridgewater NJ; [memb.] Alpha Sigma Tau; [oth. writ.] The Music Box - NPHS literary magazine; [pers.] My greatest influence is life itself, practice does not make perfect - perfect practice does. "...we are the music makers, and we are the dreamers of dreams..." Roald Dahl/Willy Wonka; [a.] North Plainfield, NJ

YACENDA, JACKLYN
[b.] April 6, 1981, Chester, NJ; [p.] Bernice Yacenda; [ed.] Public Schools, and Villa Walsh Academy in Morristown, NJ; [occ.] Student at Villa Walsh Academy; [memb.] Red Cross, Sit up, and Church Groups; [hon.] Honor roll, Athletic Awards Forensics Awards, Martin Luther King Jr. Award; [oth. writ.] Other poems and stories for school purposes; [pers.] My poems reflect the inside soul of any hidden person that has a craving to release their feelings.; [a.] Chester, NJ

YAMAZAWA, WILFRED
[pen.] Yamazawa; [b.] May 31, 1949, Kona, HI; [m.] Jessica, November 26, 1976; [ch.] Jill 15, Samuel 7; [ed.] B.F.A. 1972 University of Hawaii, MFA 1925 University of Hawaii; [occ.] Artist, Glassblower, Kona Coffee Farmer; [memb.] American Craft Council, Corning Museum, others; [hon.] New Glass Review 17, Corning Museum, "The Spoiled Child 1995", Golden Fever, Perfume container, purchase award Hawaii, Craftman 1993, others; [oth. writ.] 405 unpublished manuscripts; [pers.] Living in the middle of an ocean is a great place to be. The isolation is tremendous, but it helps rather than hinders the creative process.; [a.] Holualoa, HI

YAN, MICHAEL
[b.] October 18, 1979, Los Angeles, CA; [p.] Kim Yan, Helen Yan; [ed.] Wilshire Crest Elementary, John Burroughs Junior High, LAUSD/USC Math, Science, and Technology Magnet High School; [occ.] Student, High School Senior; [memb.] Heart, History, English, and Art are Together - 1993; [hon.] Los Angeles Trade

Technical college Dean's List for Spring 1995, ECCLA 1st place Essay and Poetry 1994-1995, ECCLA 1st place Poetry and 2nd place Essay 1995-1996, Math Association of America High Recognition of 1996, Los Angeles City Honorable Mention in Essay of Cultural Diversity; [oth. writ.] Human Relations: "LA Making Our Living Mosaic Succeed," FCCLA 1994-1996 Essays and Poetry.; [pers.] One must know that in order to obtain success, one must seek it. By having that knowledge, one can do so.; [a.] Los Angeles, CA

YEAGER, GAYLE
[pen.] Rashanka Ake Latawna; [ch.] Two children; [occ.] Manager, Promotor, and Producer for almost 4 years now; [pers.] If you truly go within your own Heart and listen-all of your Dreams and Destiny will be fulfilled. Believe with all your Heart and nothing will stand in your way. Always love life and it will reward you tenfold.; [a.] Spokane, WA

YILMA, SELAMAWIT
[b.] Addis Ababa, Ethiopia; [p.] Yilma Teshame, Abebech Asiqid; [occ.] (Music) Producer, Writer, Lyricist, Singer and Poet; [oth. writ.] Have over sixty poems that I have written, and will soon submit a book form to different publishing companies.; [pers.] My hope and desire is that my writing fill your hearts with truth and give you hope, and to inspire you. Remember love is the key faith unlock, any door and prayer gives us the power to obtain our dream.; [a.] Atlanta, GA

YODER, DIANE MYERS
[b.] June 4, 1952, Cleveland, OH; [p.] Eugene and Eleanor Myers; [m.] Dale Yoder; [ch.] Derek, Camille, and Mason (twins); [ed.] Miami Norland Sr. High, Miami Dade Community College, Barry University, International College for Hypnosis Medical Ctr., Studies and Mount Sinai Hospital; [occ.] Ultrasound Tech.; [memb.] R.D.M.S., South Florida Professional Artist; [hon.] Who's Who Award in Jr. American College, Four Outstanding Academic Awards, Elected Member Barry University Alumni, and a Delta Epsilon Sigma Award; [pers.] May we strive for peace on earth and may we protect our most valuable resource our children. Thanks to some of the great teachers that have influenced my life.; [a.] Houston, TX

YONGUE, PAT
[b.] April 30, 1948, Monroe, CA; [p.] Mavis Nichols, J. D. Nichols; [m.] Divorced after 24 yrs. of marriage, September 9, 1967; [ch.] 2 daughters: Jana and Nikki; [ed.] BSEd Speech Language Pathology, MEd Education of Hearing Impaired, Partial Completion of PhD; [occ.] SS Disability; [memb.] St. Mary's Catholic Church, Rome, GA; [hon.] Summa Cum Laude Graduate, Zodiac Honor Society, Phi Kappa Phi, Who's Who Among Colleges, Jaycee Outstanding Young Educator; [oth. writ.] A few poems published in local newspapers, church bulletins, framed, sold and given as gifts, poems written/personalized for special occasions.; [pers.] My writings are very eclectic, ranging from free form to structured. My writings have served to vent emotions and as an outlet to trials and personal disasters.; [a.] Cedartown, GA

YOUNG, DWAVALON L.
[pen.] Avalon Rose; [b.] January 8, 1974, Houston, TX; [p.] Mildred D. Young; [ed.] High School for Law Enforcement and Criminal Justice Art Institute of Houston; [occ.] Graphic Designer; [hon.] Urban Art Mural Design for Slice Kra'z Flavors; [pers.] "A man can't ride your back when, you're standing up tall." Unknown.; [a.] Houston, TX

YOUNG, JARED E.
[b.] March 31, 1973, Ithaca, NY; [p.] Edgar Young, Celinda Young; [ed.] Randolph High School, NJ University of Pennsylvania; [hon.] Cum Laude, Dean's List; [pers.] Poetry will continue to expand if we use post writings not for imitation, but as inspiration.; [a.] Wilmington, DE

YOUNG, JEFFERY BRIAN
[b.] February 9, 1979, Portland, OR; [p.] Dan Reynolds, Judy Meisner; [ed.] Clarksville High School, currently a Junior; [occ.] Home Improvement; [memb.] Oakland Church of Christ (song leader); [oth. writ.] Several poems published in school newspapers/magazines.; [pers.] When I am writing a song or poem, I usually write dawn the first thing that comes to my head. God seems to be my main attraction.; [a.] Clarksville, TN

YOUNG, KIMBERLY PANDORA
[b.] March 27, 1963, Lawton, OK; [p.] Earlen Brown Judge/Sheffield Lorenzo Young II; [ch.] Anthony Louis Phillips Jr.; [ed.] Horace Mann High (Inch.), Henderson State University (AR.), Bachelor of Science Human Services, Bachelor of Art-Sociology, Minor-Psychology; [pers.] In loving memory of my parents William and Earlen Judge. Deepest thoughts of my son Anthony L. Phillips Jr. My ability to write was inspired by Markcus Ceivelle Fischler.; [a.] Gary, IN

YOUNG, REGINA M.
[b.] September 21, 1969, St. Louis; [p.] Billy and Lonnie Young; [ch.] Daniel A. Young; [occ.] Banking Equality Savings; [memb.] First Baptist Church of Lemay; [hon.] Who's Who Among American High School 85-86, 86-87; [oth. writ.] I write about various subjects, but mostly spiritual uplifting poems.; [pers.] If we pray to God He will direct our paths to which we should follow; [a.] Saint Louis, MO

YUHAS, JACQUELIN IVENE
[pen.] Jacquelin Ivene Yates; [b.] April 28, 1961, El Monte, CA; [p.] Loretta J. Ryan, Jack Ivan Yates; [ch.] Bruce Anthony and Kyle Victor Moore; [ed.] Nogales High - Valley Vocational; [pers.] This poem is dedicated to my one and only love "My Mother" Loretta Jean Ryan; [a.] Las Vegas, NV

ZANON, RENATA S.
[b.] October 17, 1961, Burlington, WI; [p.] Richard and Lois Zanon; [m.] Jonathan E. Zanon, June 19, 1981; [ch.] Matthew Alexander, Sarah Christine Nicole; [ed.] V.W. Platteville and Technical Colleges - there is so much to learn and so little time to absorb!; [occ.] Lands' End telephone operator; [memb.] R.A. Fox Society; [hon.] Grand Prize - Helen Meiers art contest - (Portrait), Musical and Theatrical awards through the years; [oth. writ.] Many unpublished poetry and children's books; [pers.] To write poetry is to find oneself. To look back on a piece of work is to measure personal growth.; [a.] Reedsburg, WI

ZARTNER, GEORGE A.
[pen.] George A. Zartner; [b.] October 2, 1933, Wauwatosa, WI; [p.] George and Rose; [m.] Deceased; [ed.] 2 year Pre-Law. Marquette Technical Schools Radio and T.V.; [occ.] Self employed publishing, Ads, Sales; [memb.] Vets St. Vincent Society Catholic Charities.; [hon.] Boxing Football, Basketball, Baseball Track.; [oth. writ.] Many poems, several screen plays, re-writes for others T.V. programs; [pers.] Take time for others. Visit them whether at home or in the hospital. "Communicate" "Care"; [a.] Los Angeles, CA

ZIAKIN, BETTE BRODHAGEN
[pen.] Alice Spring; [b.] September 19, 1930, Camas, WA; [p.] Chas and Ida H. Kuhnke; [m.] Peter S. Ziakin, January 14, 1969; [ch.] 4 Adults; [ed.] High school - Apprenticed 10 years to an eminent artist in old Master technique of Painting Commercial Courses in Art. Private writing classes. Owned Fine Art School; [occ.] Retired all time devoted to writing and painting; [memb.] Memorial Lutheran Church, Steven Ministries, Veteran of Foreign Wars, International Society of Poets, Prayer Warriors Group; [hon.] Presidents Gallery at Concordia College (Portland) Permenant Collect, on of Portraits Commissioner by College (by B. Ziakin) many Art Awards, ARticles Chosen for magazines and papers; [oth. writ.] I write for the missile (church paper) have written 4 books and a 150 poem book many poems and short stories am composing large look of misc writings from years back.; [pers.] I believe strongly in keeping a humble spirit within give God the credit for ones ability for we are but guests in His world.; [a.] Vancouver, WA

ZOGBY, EDWARD G.
[b.] December 11, 1934, Utica, NY; [p.] Gabriel J. Zogby, Deebe Francis; [ed.] Ph.D. in Religion and Literature at Syracuse University 1975; [occ.] Theological/Educational Consultant/Writer/Teacher; [hon.] Years of Teaching in Higher Education; [oth. writ.] Article on C. S. Lewis in longing for a form, Ed. by Peter Schakel - Kent State Press; [pers.] We are beings of love. Critiques of the way things are, are needed, they are more valuable of they can celebrate the possibilities of the world as well. I choose to be an agent of hope in that we are on an upward turn in human development and consciousness.; [a.] New York, NY

ZUPANCIC, LINDA L.
[pen.] Pookie Lee; [b.] July 5, 1961, Geneva, OH; [p.] Norm and Jean Smith; [m.] Robert Zupancic, February 21, 1992; [ch.] Kimberly Kangeter and David Kangeter; [ed.] 8th grade level, continuing adult education now.; [occ.] Sales Associate; [memb.] Unity Church Member; [hon.] Marine Corps Physical Fitness Award; [oth. writ.] Several other poems no yet published or submitted.; [a.] Port Richey, FL

Index

of

Poets

Index

Black, Tracey 154
Blackburn, Gary E. 233
Blackford, Samantha 55
Blackman, Herb 89
Blackman, Veronica 109
Blackmon, Tony 147
Blackwelder, Nathan J. 210
Blackwell, Nelda 464
Blailock, Mary B. 278
Blamire, Todd 355
Blankfard, G. Kathryn 544
Blann, Cindy L. 337
Blanton, Paul R. 323
Blazejewski, Ronald 263
Blechner, Janet C. 7
Bledsoe, Hershella B. 353
Bledsoe, Phillip D. 360
Bleecher, Vanessa 519
Bleich, April 385
Blessing, Jedda 384
Bletch, Mark R. 519
Blevin, Kandace 208
Blevins, Jerrye Cargill 272
Blevins, Shara 467
Blithe, Peggy S. 324
Blizzard, Diana 351
Bloch, Milton 400
Blodgett, Melissa K. 463
Blotkamp, Danielle 77
Blount, Tiffany 368
Blume, John D. 452
Blundin, Sara E. 3
Blyler, Donald Norman 464
Blyman, Sheena 352
Blyskal, Elena M. 340
Boben, Greg 250
Bobo Hennecy, Bobbie 543
Bocock, Monique 224
Bohlinger, Linda 526
Bohm, Josh A. 549
Bolander, Noralyn 530
Boldt, Christopher W. 317
Bolich, Susan 246
Bolstetter, Brianne 120
Bombace, Dominic 99
Bomenka, James A. Jr. 149
Bomgardner, Joel 523
Bondurant, Carolyn 287
Bone, Haley 207
Bonelli, Philip 479
Bonin, Kelly 152
Bonitto, Michael Christopher 504
Bonner, Julia O. 295
Bonnie Lou 331
Bono, Kenneth 44
Bonventre, Barbara 418
Book, E. A. 157
Boomer, Angela 221
Boon, Linda Grace 222
Boone, Chanda 266
Boothroyd, John 543
Borchers, Marie Brady 181
Borger, Geraldine 104
Borowski, Nikki 473
Borthwick, Jeanette 367
Bosen, Camille 393
Boss, George 424
Boswell, Rodney K. 500
Botts, Dorris M. 18
Boucher, Karen E. 196
Boudwin, Sara 348

Bounds, Keyon 144
Boundy, Brian 60
Boutin, Angela 515
Bow, Barbara 197
Bowers, James Alan 336
Bowers, Shirley 40
Boy, Robin 139
Boyce-Benson, Kenyon 424
Boydman, Kerrie 415
Boylan, Blanche L. 280
Boyle, Brian 39
Brabec, Laurie L. 445
Bradbury, Amy 213
Bradley, Mary Elizabeth 508
Bradshaw, C. Michael 60
Bradshaw, Dorothy 379
Brailford, Athalone H. 218
Brakefield, Gary R. 435
Braley, Jesse C. IV 109
Brannelly, Sandra 449
Branum, Heather 311
Braskie, Rita M. 552
Bratcher, Juanita 96
Bratt, Krista 291
Braun, Ernest A. 246
Bready, Mark 241
Breitenstein, Angela 322
Brennan, Helen 454
Brennick, Joan 544
Brewer, Jeanne 42
Brey, Kristi Marie 359
Brickley, Sean P. 396
Brigden, Kate 254
Briggs, Bonnie Allen 54
Brigham, Sharon O. 320
Bright, Heather 512
Bright, R. Joel 203
Brightwell, Charles W. 356
Brines, Sara 94
Brinson, Richard D. 380
Briscoe, Evelyn V. 74
Britt, Millie 266
Britton, Owen R. 27
Britton, Shannon 321
Brocato, Sarah 245
Brock, Donna M. 246
Brockington, Mitchell 106
Broderick, Jocelynne E. 137
Brogan, Allen E. 121
Bromley, Steven M. 292
Brooks, Christina 218
Brooks, Dianne 178
Brooks, Eric 337
Brooks, Janice 9
Brooks, Kiera 550
Brooks, Mary 74
Brooks, Thomas A. 241
Broski, Velma M. 320
Brosnan, Jo Anne B. 468
Broussard, Jill 382
Brower, Eric 383
Brown 450
Brown, Azel R. 34
Brown, Barbara J. 273
Brown, Bernice 387
Brown, Bobby 184
Brown, Carla 317
Brown, Carlos 401
Brown, Chris 66
Brown, Dianne 476
Brown, Elly Sparks 293

Brown, Eric 369
Brown, Geoffrey Scott 272
Brown, Helen M. 334
Brown, James C. 73
Brown, Jean E. 139
Brown, Jeremy 316
Brown, Judith C. 376
Brown, Keith 107
Brown, Krista 554
Brown, Liane 489
Brown, Melissa Jean 545
Brown, Neville 302
Brown, Paul 321
Brown, Quiana 87
Brown, Robin Dee 242
Brown, Shanequa 451
Brown, Stephanie V. 204
Brown, Sylvia 248
Brown, Tara Courtney 271
Brown, Teresa A. 288
Brown, Timothy T. 438
Browne, Elizabeth 361
Browning, Frances G. 47
Brownton, Laura Lee 443
Bruce, Letamae 437
Brueske, Margaret D. 18
Brumley, Jack 155
Bruner, Jermaine 302
Brunner, Morgan L. 272
Brunsink, Trevor 114
Bryan, Joyce 370
Bryan, Lindz 251
Bryan, Michelle 357
Bryant, Kim 478
Bryant, Stanford James 158
Bryte, Wynter 23
Buchanan, Gary 206
Buchanan, Irene 312
Buckles, Brian C. 283
Buckner, Angela 319
Bucko, Nancy 292
Buckrem, Dianna M. 192
Bucquoy-Brown, Caroline 221
Budd, Vicki 393
Buford, Janet 202
Buglione, Vera 300
Bunt, Grace A. 205
Buono, Dana 236
Buracker, Dave 391
Burdick, Stephen M. 406
Burfield, Emily 301
Burke, Charlotte 104
Burke, Suzanne M. 490
Burkett, James 304
Burleson, Angie Rinehart 480
Burnett, Bradley Scott 55
Burnett, Matia 429
Burns, Barbara L. 372
Burns, Eleanor A. 68
Burns, Jessica 319
Burns, Vennie L. 454
Burroughs, Sonja F. 300
Burton, Janet 11
Burton, Janice S. 239
Burton, Philip Arthur 49
Burwell, Michelle L. 183
Buscaino, Giacomo S. 359
Bushong, Nadine M. 16
Bussey, Jeannette 408
Butera, Maria 167
Butler, Debbie 155

Butler, Kevin 144
Butler, Roger J. Jr. 504
Buttler, Jennifer Ayn 511
Byard, Brandy M. 115
Bycholski, Aimee 318
Byers, Karen 303
Byrd, William R. 453

C

Cabak, Pam 530
Cacan, Alma 306
Cacy, Charlene 276
Cagle, Nell 261
Cahill, Cabrini 348
Cahill, Kathleen 425
Calce, Nunzio 148
Caldarone, Joey 391
Caldwell, Billy W. 263
Calfee, Janet 287
Calhoun, Jennifer 457
Calhoun, Robert 121
Calixto, Rosalyn 461
Callaghan, Sandra W. 72
Callaway, Linda H. 155
Calo, Diana 130
Calvano, Joni 150
Calvillo, Brooke 461
Calvillo, Ernest A. 437
Camargo, Clair 404
Camargo, Ollie Marie 537
Cameron, Elizabeth Victoria 503
Campbell, Barbara 51
Campbell, Danny E. 259
Campbell, Karen K. 213
Campbell, Robert 256
Campbell, Sue M. 402
Campitiello, Toni 421
Canada, Beverly J. 300
Canillas, Anna Maria 275
Cannavo, Stephen Jr. 452
Cannon, Bonnie 24
Cantalamessa, Joe 123
Cantrall, Kathleen 222
Cantrell, Debra 323
Cape, Shannon 551
Capelle, Becky 374
Capps, Joanna B. 308
Capuano, Melissa 449
Caraza, Danny 424
Carcieri, Albert R. 209
Card, Emily 82
Cardwell, J. D. Bryan 276
Cardwell, Rachel 497
Carey, Dianne Vaughan 401
Carfi, Jacqueline M. 167
Carino, Yolanda 549
Cario, John P. 520
Carloni, Irene 377
Carlson, Steven Elmer 483
Carmody, Robert Jr. 214
Carney, Racheal 138
Carnicle, Ann 215
Carpenter, Corey Andrew 514
Carpenter, Lisa 101
Carr, Holly 317
Carr, Jessi 318
Carr, Kari 370
Carrier, Brenda 361
Carrier, Debra M. 273
Carrigan, Angie 252
Carrillo, Sue 208

Essler, Susan 24
Estabrook, Sandra J. 318
Estes, Jessica Elaine 225
Estrup, Carole 432
Etessami, Soudabeh 288
Evans, Donna Tisdale 113
Evans, Rachel 505
Evans, Susan L. 385
Everman, Janet M. 397
Ewersen, Virginia Pease 29
Eyerman, Eugenia C. 131

F

Faber, Rebecca 334
Facey, Jennifer 550
Factor, Maxine 399
Fahey, Jack 316
Fahrenbruch, Gary Robert 470
Fahy, John E. 429
Fahy, Teresa 387
Faisy, Helen E. 322
Faitoute, Eric 439
Falber, Rachael 347
Famisaran, Trisha 100
Farah, Jeffrey J. 235
Farahay, M. L. 25
Farb, Jason Wade 135
Farmer, Danny 500
Farmer, Mary Ann 204
Farrant, David 541
Farrell, J. M. 502
Farrell, Susan Marie 128
Farrington, June E. 94
Farrow, Barbara 55
Faucher, Tracy 178
Fawcett, Roger 207
Fay, Cathy L. 449
Fealy, Paris Jason 172
Feekin, Donald R. 470
Feidt, Cory M. 462
Feigt, Alicia R. 248
Feiner, Andra 299
Fejerang, Joseph D. 466
Feldman, Elias 418
Feldman, Robert J. 258
Felix, Ronald R. 127
Fell, Dolores 395
Fellows, Samuel Chapin 515
Fenninger, Peter L. 310
Ferguson, Kelly M. 405
Fern, Azure 147
Fernandez, Miguel Angel 497
Ferrari, Rose 194
Ferrini, Jackie 315
Fielden, Jonathan 398
Fielder, Timothy 428
Fields, Ron 44
Fienhage, Lucinda K. 214
Figueroa, William 250
Finch, Henrietta 87
Fine, Saralee Gelman 482
Finkel, Joel H. 17
Firgau, Alice D. 102
Firth, Ashley 62
Fischer, Ashton John Jr. 28
Fish, Sandra M. 193
Fish, Duane 91
Fisher, Christy 320
Fisher, Matthew 549
Fisher, Roger F. 36

Fissel, Ryan 229
Fistes, Jacob 243
Fitchie, Katie 112
Fite, Bekah 367
Fitzgerald-Swanson, Patricia 535
Fitzpatrick, Robert J. 203
Fitzsimmons, Shawn 140
Flavin, Elizabeth 390
Fleming, Bill 100
Fletcher, Caitlin C. 524
Fletcher, Caleb Michael 529
Fletcher, Dorothea 406
Flick, Kathy P. D. 265
Floore, M. Barry 320
Flores, Daniel 393
Flournoy, Martha 211
Flowers, Paulette G. 35
Floyd, John L. 7
Floyd, Norma Jean 35
Fluker, Gloria J. 178
Foard, Merideth W. 173
Fontenot, Allison Nicole 18
Fontenot, Kathy 63
Foor, Iva L. 98
Ford, Carol Owens 214
Ford, Joyce 402
Ford, Mary Lou 291
Ford, Shalita 508
Ford, Venitia Malika 444
Forman, Donna 152
Formoso, Michele 384
Fortier, George Lawrence 455
Fortson, Andrew 504
Fortuna, Paula J. 547
Foscaldo, James 48
Foster, Charles M. 486
Foster, Christy 520
Foster, Jacquilyn Ann 438
Foster, Milton 371
Fourzan, Ray 388
Fouts, Jerry 265
Fouts, Paul D. 295
Fowler, Rhonda 465
Fox, Barbara L. 316
Fox, Frances L. 168
Fraise, Carrie 397
Fraley, Micheal 111
Fraley, Paula K. 396
Francis, Courtney A. 364
Franclemont, Dave 432
Frank, Aimee 69
Frank, Beverly 216
Franklin, Debra 139
Franklin, Virginia 463
Franks, Jennifer 71
Franz, Lili 289
Frasure, E. P. 37
Frazier, Doug 120
Free, Joshua L. 81
Freedman, Michael 382
Freeman, Devery W. 183
Freeman, Jovan Nicole 159
Freer, Candace 66
Freimuth, Kim 490
French, Brian Hugh 516
French, Joshua 436
French, Sandra 285
French, Walter E. 493
Frenkel, Marc Brandon 214
Fretwell, Julie 374
Frey, Diana L. 111

Fritz, Desiree' M. 456
Fritz, Steven E. 61
Fromme, Timothy L. 394
Fry, Margaret J. 214
Fugate-Hopper, Shirley 12
Fuller, Ananda 96
Fuller, Jenese 180
Fulp, Catherine D. 421
Funke, Sarahann Marie 9
Funkhouser, Lindsay 151
Furlong, Margaret 58
Furr, Pamela M. 536
Futterman, Robyn 115
Fyfe, Dorothy 85

G

Gabor, Kim Celeda 305
Gabriel, Matt 163
Gabusi, Donna 100
Gaier, Mary Lee 19
Gainer, Susan Cruit 515
Gaines, Karen 44
Galicinao, Josh 128
Gallagher, Lillian L. 135
Gallivan, Leo G. 374
Galvin, Stephanie 181
Gamet, Thomas 297
Ganem, Bruce 187
Gangwisch, Edna 514
Gantz, Keith N. 224
Garate, Diane 411
Garber, Jordan 507
Garcia, Ellen B. 198
Garcia, Karen 133
Garcia, Kiana Lynn 158
Garcia, Tina R. 512
Gard, Becky 192
Gardias, Sophia 109
Gardner, Aaron Lee 206
Gardner, Elbert Jr. 546
Gardner, Georgene 320
Gardner, Janet 278
Garland, Grace P. 405
Garrett, Cathy M. 458
Garroutte, Kimberly 70
Garrow, Celeste 13
Garver, Evan 354
Gasper, Heather 339
Gatchalian, John-Joseph A. 488
Gatchell, John Jr. 99
Gates, Stacie 283
Gatewood, Sheldon 125
Gatwood, James Leslie Jr. 453
Gaunt, David A. 377
Gawronski, Shannon 397
Gay, Nathan 424
Gaye, Donald Ravanne 450
Gayton, Laura Grace 345
Gearhart, Eunice Ann 29
Gebhardt, Ashleigh E. 451
Gebhart, Tammie 453
Geers, Brent 426
Geibel, Stacy 359
Geiger, Dennise 405
Geisler, Krista Marie 467
Geisz, Charles Jr. 329
Gelner, Annie 328
Gendreau, Margaret 514
Gentry, Tara 220
George, Rebecca L. 436

George, Scott 428
Geraci, Heather 377
Gero, Catherine 395
Gerst, Aaron 469
Gerth, Kristen 150
Gertz, Richard 422
Gheorghiu, Mandy 82
Ghose, Preshona 441
Giammarinaro, Nicholas J. 179
Gibbons, Corrie J. 404
Gibbons, Kathleen 485
Gibbons, Mary L. 371
Gibson, Glenn L. Jr. 338
Gibson, Joel 526
Gibson, Norman W. 327
Gibson, Wendy 51
Gierczynski, Marlo 418
Gilbert, Norma Florence 197
Gilbert, Robert 178
Gilbertson, Kyle 379
Giles, Evelyn 407
Gill, Angie 220
Gillard, Elizabeth 329
Gilles, Emily Christine 201
Gillespie, Shelley 376
Gillespie-Dipinto, Mark H. 45
Gillpatrick, Chris 499
Gilman, Jennifer 263
Gilman, Luci 292
Gilmore, Anna 477
Gilmour, Mae 69
Gilpin, Nicole 305
Gines, Signe 555
Gingles, Annette 232
Ginn, Scott 83
Ginsberg, Julie 48
Gipson, Nancy S. 222
Giuliani, Jannice 294
Given, Megan 153
Givens, Mary Ann 401
Glaser, David 98
Glenn, Anthony 223
Glenn, Mark 325
Glisson, Mariah J. 323
Glover, Robert W. 298
Glynn, Kevin 258
Glynn, Xi'an 303
Godwin, Nathan 233
Goeddertz, Jennifer 304
Gohl, Raymond A. 262
Goldberg, Susan 268
Golden, Brandi Leigh 219
Golden, Jon 215
Goldsmith, Lauren 258
Goldstein, Elise 343
Goldstein, Rita 553
Gomillion, Robin 305
Gomolinski, Adam 140
Gonski, John 14
Gonzalez, Kattie 110
Gonzalez, Peggy 4
Gonzalez, Tammy 173
Good, Karleen Wagner 406
Good, Linda Kay 85
Good, William 375
Goode, Nancy L. 93
Goodell, Amber 364
Gooden, Kimone 463
Goodenough, Diane 274
Goodman, Nikki 15
Goodrich, Bruce W. 84